Footprint Bri

Charlie Godfrey-Faussett, Alan Mu

1st edition

History is what holds Britain together, and history is what holds it back.

Tim Lott, *Rumours of a Hurricane*

Britain Highlights

See colour maps at back of book

1 Sandwood Bay
Pure white sands, turquoise seas and not another soul

2 Callanish
Scotland's answer to Stonehenge – minus the crowds

3 Glencoe
Hauntingly beautiful glen with a bloody history

4 Iona
Scotland's spiritual home is one of the most appealing of all the Hebridean islands

5 Corryvreckan
Take a white-knuckle ride across the second largest whirlpool in the world

6 Glasgow
One of the coolest and friendliest cities in Europe

7 Wastwater
The quietest and most secluded of the lovely lakes

8 Imperial War Museum of the North
Stunning new architecture modelled on a broken teapot

9 Conwy Castle
Medieval town topped by a wonderful castle

10 Pembrokeshire Coast
Spectacular coastline traversed by a 68-mile path

11 The Gower
Peninsula rightly famed for its great beaches

N

0 km 50
0 miles 50

⑫ Hay-on-Wye
This pretty little border town is the world capital of secondhand books

⑬ Quantocks
Ancient Somerset hills, ideal for mountain biking or horse trekking

⑭ Cotswolds
Honeystone towns dotted amongst ravishing green hills

⑮ Eden Project
Ground breaking transformation from claypit into biodome

⑯ Edinburgh
Home of the world's biggest arts festival

⑰ Newcastle/ Gateshead
Revitalized northeast stalwart winning all the architectural plaudits

⑱ Chatsworth House
Huge 16th century estate full of art treasures and adventure

⑲ Suffolk Coast
Eerie marshes, lost towns and delicious smoked fish

⑳ Oxford
Dreaming spires on the River Thames

㉑ London
Britain's sensational capital – irresistible and essential

Contents

East Anglia

The Midlands

Yorkshire

North of England

Northwest England

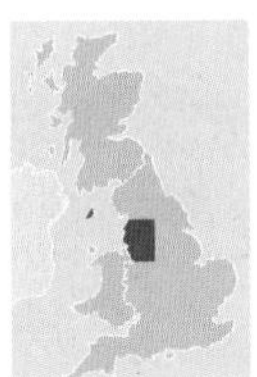

South Wales

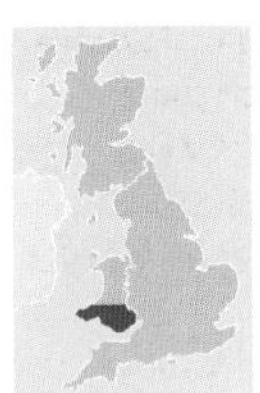

Mid Wales

North Wales

Edinburgh

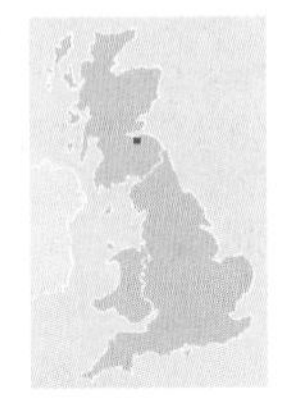

Southern Scotland

Glasgow

Argyll and Inner Hebrides

Northeast Scotland

The Highlands

Scotland's capital city has shrugged off its reputation for dourness and is buzzing with a new-found energy.

Skye and the Outer Hebrides

Orkney and Shetland

Background

Footnotes

Inside front cover

Bigger and better

The Great Court at the British Museum illuminates world cultures like never before with its latticework roof and 3312 unique panes of glass making it the largest covered square in Europe.

A foot in the door

Britain is an extraordinary place: fiercely independent, inclusive, stubborn and often bloody-minded, a melting pot of ideas and cultures. It is full of contradictions: inventive and backward, innovative and conservative, radical and patriotic – caught between the two stools of Europe and the US. It cannot seem to make up its mind what it wants to be. Indeed, one of the very few unifying features of the UK is an obsession with the notoriously fickle weather; that and the monarchy, property prices, a love of root vegetables and curry.

Britain is not one country but three rolled into one. Celts, Anglo-Saxons and Normans have jostled for position and influence over the centuries and learned to live together, often in less than peaceful co-existence. Factor in a long history of imperial expansion, which led to a postwar influx of immigrants from erstwhile colonies, and it's not surprising that Britain speaks with more than one voice. The resultant cultural cocktail is, however, one of Britain's greatest assets. Such a diversity of races, ideas, cuisines, views and influences have left it with a gloriously multi-cultural landscape, one which cannot be matched in Continental Europe.

The outsider's view of Britain is generally past its sell by date. Forget little old ladies sipping tea, warm beer and soggy veg and cricket on the village green. What the inquisitive visitor will find in Britain today is cutting-edge fashion, vibrant youth culture, a gastronomic revolution and a tsunami-like wave of interest in high-adrenaline sports such as surfing and snowboarding. Of course, there are some things that will never change. There is still a deep love of scatalogical jokes and, despite the recent bad press, the British still keep a place in their hearts for the monarchy. As Johnny Rotten himself once famously sneered: "We love our queen, god bless."

10 Union, Jack?

As Britain begins to get to grips with the noughties, the very notion of Britishness is being questioned. What is Britishness? It's more an attachment to an idea than to a place, associated with the Empire for good or ill, and an old-fashioned ideal of fair play and justice. It's an idea that has now been most strongly adopted by black and Asian UK citizens who aren't comfortable with calling themselves either English, Scottish or Welsh. It's often been suggested that England's confidence in itself was born out of its long dominion over Scotland and Wales. Not any more. One of the major features of the political and cultural landscape has been a burgeoining Celtic confidence, fuelled by devolved government in Edinburgh and Cardiff, and an explosion of artistic talent, particularly in music, film-making and literature. All the while poor England has been left to ponder the future of its own identity. With the Welsh and Scottish revelling in their new found – albeit limited – freedom, both are, crucially, less ambivalent than the English towards closer ties with Europe. Is London in danger of losing its influence over the far reaches of the kingdom? Even the English regions themselves, especially Cornwall, the Northeast and Northwest have all expressed a strong interest in self-government, viewing Westminster as remote and too wrapped up in the Southeast.

Northern exposure
Snowdonia's cloudy peaks dominate the northern part of Wales, a fitting backdrop to the castles and walled medieval towns that fringe its coast.

Town and country

"A working class hero is something to be", sang John Lennon. But the dead Beatle would not recognize the classless society which many believe we live in today. As one working class politician famously said, "We're all middle class now". Even the north-south divide appears to be a thing of the past. Witness the northern English renaissance. It's hard to exaggerate the importance of the rebirth of Manchester, Leeds, Liverpool and Newcastle as exciting, optimistic places to live after such a terrible 20th century: two wars, unemployment, neglect, deprivation and despair were the lot of millions of northerners for more than 100 years. In Scotland and Wales, too, Glasgow and Cardiff can also be added to the list of brave, new cities. This has only sharpened the biggest division in British society today – that between town and country. While urban dwellers prosper, the British farmer has had to cope with the adverse effects of BSE and foot and mouth disease. Not surprisingly, the suicide rate of farmers is at an all-time high. The countryside lobby, now one of the strongest political groupings in Britain, is up in arms at what it sees as a governing metropolitan elite showing disdain for everything rural. This has been crystalized in the attempts to ban fox hunting – ironically an issue which has united the land-owning gentry and the rural poor.

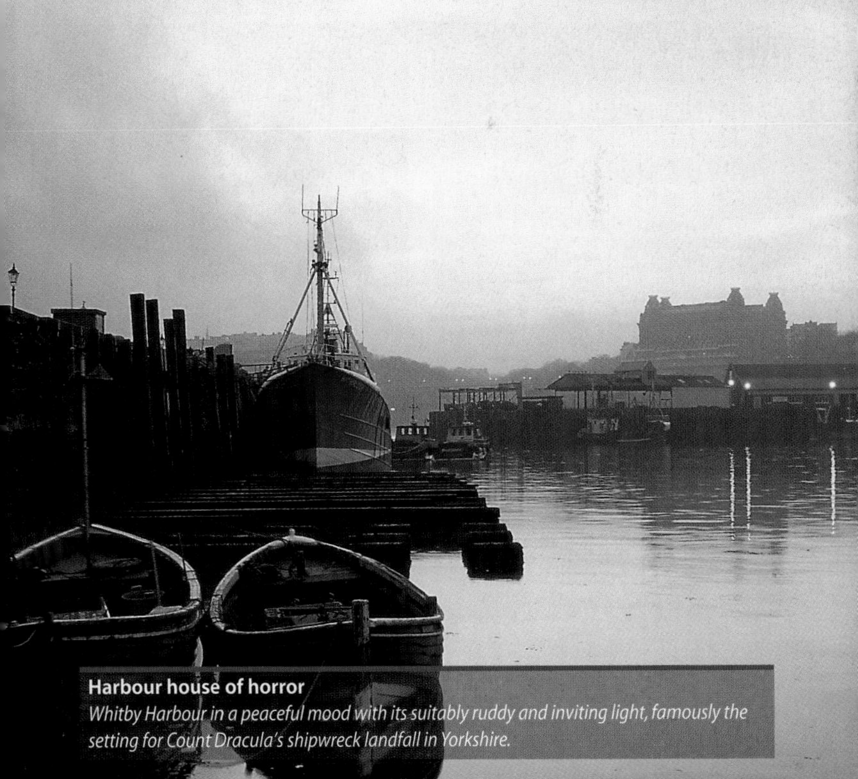

Harbour house of horror
Whitby Harbour in a peaceful mood with its suitably ruddy and inviting light, famously the setting for Count Dracula's shipwreck landfall in Yorkshire.

1
2
4
5
7
8
10
11

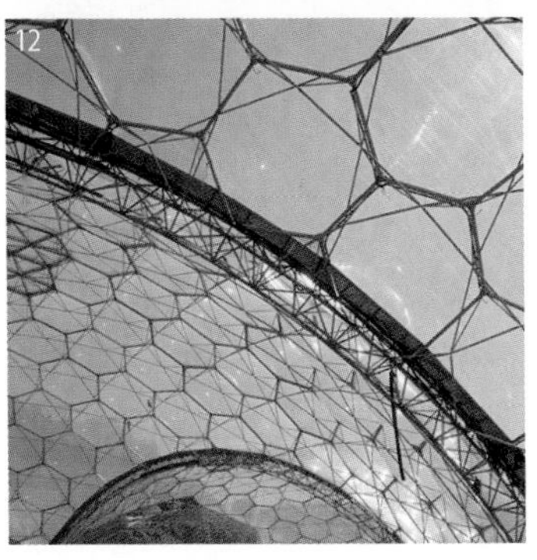

1 *Holy Island, Lindisfarne, where St Aidan fished for men in the seventh century.* ▶▶ *See page 482.*

2 *A carpet of late summer heather on the north Devon coast.* ▶▶ *See page 278.*

3 *The Angel of the North, Antony Gormley's giant gliderman sculpture, inspires traffic on the A1 into Newcastle Gateshead.* ▶▶ *See page 469.*

4 *Oxford does Venice with Hertford College's Bridge of Sighs.* ▶▶ *See page 157.*

5 *Rhossili Beach marks the western extremity of the glorious Gower Peninsula.* ▶▶ *See page 568.*

6 *The red pantile roofs of Robin Hood's Bay stack up on the precipitous Yorkshire coast.* ▶▶ *See page 418.*

7 *Welcome! The Sanctuary Knocker on the door of Durham Cathedral has been admitting all comers for centuries.* ▶▶ *See page 476.*

8 *Subtropical vegetation bursts into bloom on the Isles of Scilly thanks to the warming waters of the Gulf Stream.* ▶▶ *See page 295.*

9 *A restored drainage windpump is reflected in Horsey Mere, one of the wildfowl wonderlands of the Norfolk Broads.* ▶▶ *See page 313.*

10 *A Cotswold post box: something to write home about.* ▶▶ *See page 228.*

11 *Astonishing stones at Stonehenge, the centre of one of the most ancient civilizations on the planet.* ▶▶ *See page 191.*

12 *The cellular hexagons of the extraordinary Eden Project in Cornwall. Its 'biomes' nurture an amazing wealth of plantlife.* ▶▶ *See page 288.*

London's burning

The capital of the United Kingdom dominates southern England and is still a must-visit, even briefly, for its wealth of extraordinary museums and art galleries, markets, music, nightlife and general mayhem. There's no getting round it. Many features of London echo aspects of the regions but they do things bigger here: the British Museum, with its massive hoard of rare treasures from around the world; the Victoria and Albert Museum, stacked with astonishing treasures; and Tate Modern, with its vast variety of modern art. But London is much more than just the sum of its cultural attractions. For most visitors it's the excitement of spotting a landmark for the first time; rooting about in the canalside markets in Camden; eating in buzzy restaurants; getting into the latest clubs in the East End.

Provincial pride

Britain still likes to think of itself as a green and pleasant land but, for the vast majority of the population, packed firmly into its cities, that remains a rather nostalgic and unattainable dream. The provincial cities of Britain have rarely been so confident: from Liverpool with its contemporary art to Newcastle and Gateshead with its regenerated riverside, via Cardiff's café culture. What's more, these cities are only a few hours' drive from some of Britain's most traditional and beautifully conserved countryside: the Cotswold hills, the Peak District, Yorkshire Dales, Northumberland National Park, Brecon Beacons and Loch Lomond National Park. The British, it seems, are having their cake and eating it.

The 13th century feudal village of Lacock is a birthplace of photography, where William Fox Talbot discovered the principle of photographic negatives.

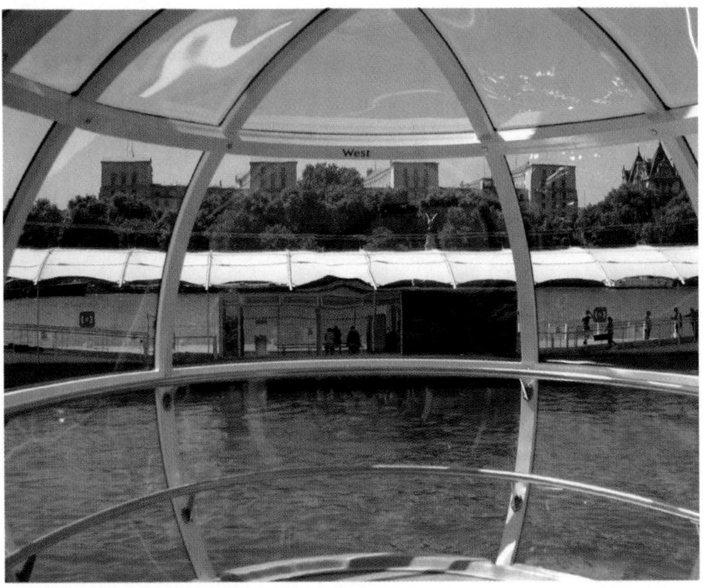

Look west! The start of a panoramic trip on the big wheel of the London Eye. Its high-tech capsules have been providing a bird's eye view of the capital since the Millennium.

Coastal votes

Not surprisingly, Britain's coastline is one of its prime natural assets. While north Norfolk, Northumberland and Yorkshire all have their charms, it's the southwest of the country that has long been most appreciated. The beaches of Devon and Cornwall call surfers, optimistic sunbathers and the bucket and spade brigade west every summer. Studded with tiny fishing villages beneath cliffs and headlands, the coast dips in and out of the Atlantic all the way to Land's End. The mild climate has been capitalized upon by the Eden Project, a vast high-tech greenhouse in an abandoned clay pit, while the quality of the light has drawn a generation of artists down to St Ives.

Celtic charms

Scotland is one of the least densely populated countries in Europe. Not much smaller than England, it has only one tenth of its population, mostly crammed into the narrow central belt, leaving two-thirds of the country unspoiled. The Highlands are one of Europe's last great wildernesses: one of the few places in this increasingly cluttered continent where you can really get away from it all. Wales, on the other hand, might be small but punches above its weight. If it's the great outdoors you're after, head for the mountains of Snowdonia, the hills of the Brecon Beacons, or the coast of Pembrokeshire. Those looking for some r'n'r might prefer urban honeypots like Cardiff or St David's, the tranquil little city on the sea.

Medieval moods

Rebel pebbles! The evocative ruins of John of Gaunt's 14th-century castle at Dunstanburgh above the Bays of Embleton and Beadnell in Lonely Northumberland.

Essentials

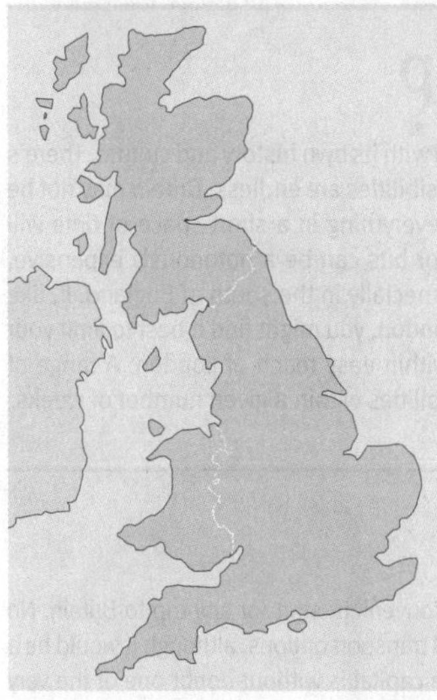

Planning your trip

Britain is three countries rolled into one, each with its own history and culture. There's an awful lot to see on this island and the possibilities are endless. Britain may not be a particularly large place, but trying to see everything in a short space of time will prove difficult. Getting around by car, train or bus can be a notoriously expensive, time-consuming and frustrating business, especially in the south of England. If, like the majority of visitors, your arrival point is London, you might find it best to limit your exploration of the country to destinations within easy reach of London. A range of options are listed below, outlining the possibilities within a given number of weeks.

Where to go

One week

London is the obvious and likely to be most convenient start for any trip to Britain. No other city has anything like the range of onward transport options, although it would be a shame to make use of them immediately. The capital is without doubt one of the very best things about the UK. However you choose to travel, several places within two hour's train ride are all a real treat: **Oxford**, **Brighton**, **Cambridge**, **Bath**, **Windsor**, **Stratford-upon-Avon** and **Canterbury** should be somewhere near the top of any list. Each are likely to appeal for different reasons and present a variety of options for exploring the regions around. With the advent of cheap flights north of the border, it's also possible to spend a few days in the Scottish capital, **Edinburgh**, one of the world's truly great cities.

Two weeks

With two weeks to spare, a trip northwards to **Yorkshire**, the **Peak District** or the **Lake District**; or westwards to **Devon** and **Cornwall** becomes an option. Northbound itineraries could include: **Cambridge** and the medieval cathedral cities of **Norwich**, **Lincoln** and **York**, even **Durham** too; **Oxford, Stratford-upon-Avon** and then either the **Peak District** or **Yorkshire Dales** for superb walking country; or **Stamford** for its Georgian townscape and extraordinary churches, followed by **Lincoln, York** and the **North York Moors.**

Alternatively, you could head west to the Welsh capital, **Cardiff**, another of Britain's revitalized provincial cities, or explore the beautiful **Gower Peninsula**, only a short drive from Cardiff. The real jewel in the Welsh crown, however, is the spectacular **Pembrokeshire coast**, an alternative to Devon and Cornwall. Scotland's other great city, **Glasgow**, is less than an hour from Edinburgh and could be added to a two-week itinerary. Though it lacks the capital's tourist credentials, it is worth a visit for its Victorian architecture. If you want to see some Highland scenery, you can head straight for the hills from Glasgow. A short distance north is **Loch Lomond,** gateway to the Western Highlands and a beautiful introduction to the spectacular sights which lie in wait farther north. From Loch Lomond you should head north through **Glencoe**, one of the main highlights of a visit to Scotland, to **Fort William**, the main tourist centre for the Western Highlands.

Three to four weeks

With three to four weeks at your disposal, England's your oyster. In fact if its oysters you're after, **Whitstable** or the Essex coast are the places to go. There's superb seafood too on the **Isles of Scilly,** an untouristy archipelago even further west than Cornwall. **Herefordshire** and **Shropshire,** on the border with Wales, are still just about off the beaten track, although the charms of **Ludlow** and Church Stretton have been drawing in hillwalkers for some time.

Statistically it actually rains least in the east of the country, although it's likely to be some time before the wetlands of the **Norfolk Broads** dry out. That news won't disappoint the small navy of boating enthusiasts that embarks here each summer. The Broads can easily be combined with a trip along the **North Norfolk coast**.

At the other end of the country, in the far north, Northumberland and its neighbour **Newcastle upon Tyne** could hardly be more different from each other: one furnishes mile upon mile of unspoilt beaches, ruined castles on headlands and **Hadrian's Wall**. Hardy, outdoor types should head for the mountains of **Snowdonia**, the hills of the **Brecon Beacons** – where the SAS do their training.

Three or four weeks would also allow for a more detailed exploration of the Highlands of Scotland. From Fort William there are two routes to another of Scotland's most popular attractions, the **Isle of Skye**. The quickest route is by road and bridge, via **Kyle of Lochalsh**, but by far the most romantic and scenic route is by **train** from Fort William to **Mallaig**, and by **ferry** from there to **Armadale**. You should then leave at least three days to explore the island, or more if you plan to do any hillwalking in the **Cuillins**, Britain's toughest mountain range.

To get away from it all, sail from Ullapool across to the wild and windswept **Outer Hebrides**, or take a flight from Glasgow and land on the islands' only airstrip – a cockleshell beach. Or you could include a trip to the **Orkney Islands**, with their Stone Age ruins, or the culturally-distinct **Shetland Isles**, which are closer to Norway than London and so far north of the mainland that they can only be included on maps as an inset.

When to go

The high season runs from April until October, when most attractions are open and summer festivities are organized in almost every town and village. **School holidays** (most of July and August) are even busier, when the most popular tourist destinations – the Lakes, Devon and Cornwall, the Scottish Highlands, Cotswolds and Pembroke Coast – are really best avoided altogether. The best accommodation anywhere in the countryside must be booked well in advance for the summer months.

London and the major cities don't really have a tourist season as such, which makes them an excellent alternative in the autumn and winter months (September-March). That said, many of Britain's seaside hotspots are also best appreciated once the weather's turned nasty or even in clear winter sunlight, if you're lucky.

Climate

The British temperate climate is notoriously unpredictable. Bright, sunny mornings can turn into a downpour in the time it takes to butter your toast. Predicting the weather is not an exact science and tables of statistics are most likely a waste of time. Very generally, the west side of the country receives more rain than the east, and the east coast gets more sunshine. The west is also milder in the winter because of the relatively warm waters of the Gulf Stream. Winters in the north can be pretty harsh, especially in the mountains, making hiking conditions treacherous. Generally speaking, May to September are the warmest months (in particular July and August), but you can expect rain at any time of the year, even in high summer. So, you'll need to come prepared, and remember the old hikers' adage that there's no such thing as bad weather, only inadequate clothing.

Tours and tour operators

There are many companies offering tours of Britain. Travel agents will have details, or you can check the small advertisements in the travel sections of newspapers, or contact the *British Tourist Authority* for a list of operators (see next page).

General sightseeing tours

Classique Tours, T0141-8894050, www.classiquetours .co.uk. Wonderfully quirky and a bit different, 5-day tours start at £275 and their 7-day Grand Hebridean Tour is £485.
Exodus Travels, T020-8772 3882, www.exodus.co.uk A London-based company offering a wide variety of specialist holidays.
Saga Holidays, Saga Building, Middelburg Square, Folkestone, Kent CT20 1AZ, T0800-300500, www.sagaholidays.com. A British company with tours aimed at the mature traveller. Also in the USA, at 222 Berkeley Street, Boston, MA 02116; and in Australia, at 10-14 Paul Street, Milsons Point, Sydney 2061.
www.uktrail.com A good resource for bus, walking, cycling and adventure tours, designed for budget and adventure travellers. The site also has information on accommodation.

In the USA

Abercrombie & Kent, T1-800-3237308, www.abercrombiekent.com
Cross-Culture, 52 High Point Dr, Amherst MA01002-1224, T800-4911148, www.crosscultureinc.com
Especially Britain, T1-800-8690538, www.expresspages.com/e/especiallybritain
Sterling Tours, T1-800 -7274359, www.sterlingtours.com

In Australia and New Zealand

Adventure Specialists, 69 Liverpool St, Sydney, T02-92612927, www.totaltravel.com.
Adventure Travel Company, 164 Parnell Rd, Parnell, East Auckland, T09-3799755. New Zealand agents for Peregrine Adventures.
Peregrine Adventures, 258 Lonsdale St, Melbourne, T03-96638611, www.peregrine.net.au; also branches in Brisbane, Sydney, Adelaide and Perth.

Backpackers and adventure tours

Haggis Backpackers, 11 Blackfriars Street, Edinburgh EH1 1NB, T0131-5579393, www.haggis-backpackers.com, run trips from London to Edinburgh, calling in at several tourist sights in England en route. These companies also run Highland tours, leaving from Edinburgh. Prices start at £75 for three days, up to around £139 for six days. Prices do not include accommodation or food.
Karibuni, T0118- 9618 577, www.karibuni.co.uk, offer weekend adventure tours including skiing, watersports, walking, climbing and lots more from around £50 to £175. They can also arrange custom tours for groups.
Road Trip, T0845-200 6791, www.roadtrip.co.uk, who have a variety of weekly tours from five to nine days for around £130.
Stray Travel, T020-7373 7737, www.straytravel.com, who offer hop-on, hop-off tours around the country from £34 for a day to £159 for six days.

British tourist authorities overseas

The BTA is an excellent source of information for visitors to England. More information can be obtained from their website (www.bta.org.uk), or from the offices listed below:
Australia Level 16, The Gateway, 1 Macquarie Pl, Circular Quay, Sydney NSW 2000, T02-93774400, F02-93774499. **Belgium and Luxembourg** 306 Av Louise, 1050 Brussels, T2-6463510, F2-6463986. **Canada** 111 Avenue Rd, Suite 450, Toronto, Ontario MR5 3J8, T416-9256326, F416-9612175.
Denmark Montergade 3, 1116 Copenhagen K, T33-339188, F33-140136. **France** Maison de la Grande-Bretagne, 19 Rue des Mathurins, 75009 Paris, T1-44515620, F1-44515621.
Germany, Austria and Switzerland Taunustrasse 52-60, 60329 Frankfurt, T69-2380711. **Ireland** 18/19 College Green, Dublin 2, T1-6708000, F1-6708244.
Italy Corso Vittorio Emanuele II No 337, 00186 Rome, T6-68806821, F6-6879095.
Netherlands Stadhouderskade 2 (5e), 1054 ES Amsterdam, T20-6855051, F20-6186868.
New Zealand 17th Floor, Fay Richwhite Building, 151 Queen St, Auckland 1, T09-3031446, F09-3776965. **South Africa** Lancaster Gate, Hyde Park Lane, Hyde Park 2196, Johannesburg, T011-3250342.
USA 7th Flr, 551 Fifth Av, New York, NY 10176-0799, T212-986-2200/ 1-800-GO-2-BRITAIN. 10880 Wilshire Blvd, Suite 570, Los Angeles, CA 90024, T310-4702782.

Finding out more

A good way to find out more before your trip is to contact the **British Tourist Authority** (BTA) in your home country, or write (or email) direct to the head office of the **English Tourist Board** (ETB). The BTA and ETB can provide a wealth of free literature and information such as maps, city guides, events calendars and accommodation brochures. Travellers with special needs should also contact their nearest BTA office. The **visitor information centre** in London's Leicester Square (T020-729 22 333, daily 0800-2300) provides information and a free hotel booking service.

Useful websites

Several websites give more information about Britain:
www.visitbritain.com
www.britainusa.com
www.aboutbritain.com
www.britannia.com
www.londontown.com
For a guide to what's on, try the excellent www.bbc.co.uk.

Language

The official language is English, which is spoken throughout the country (in a variety of accents). In parts of the largest cities, non-European languages such as Bengali, Urdu, Turkish and Arabic are also common. In Wales, especially the northern part, Welsh is widely spoken but in Scotland, Gaelic (pronounced 'gallic') is only spoken by a small percentage of the population and is restricted to a few Hebridean islands.

Disabled travellers

For travellers with disabilities visiting Britain independently can be a difficult business. While most theatres, cinemas and modern tourist attractions are accessible to wheelchairs, accommodation is more problematic. Many large, new hotels do have disabled suites, but will charge more, and most B&Bs, guesthouses and smaller hotels are not designed to cater for people with disabilities. Public transport‹Wo is just as bad, though newer buses have lower steps for easier access and some train services now accommodate wheelchair-users in comfort. Taxis, as opposed to minicabs, all carry wheelchair ramps, and if a driver says he or she can't take a wheelchair, it's because they're too lazy to fetch the ramp.

Wheelchair users, and blind or partially sighted people are automatically given 30-50% discount on train fares, and those with other disabilities are eligible for the **Disabled Person's Railcard**, which costs £14 per year and gives a third off most tickets. There are no reductions on buses, however.

Contacts

If you are disabled you should contact the travel officer of your national support organization. They can provide literature or put you in touch with travel agents specializing in tours for the disabled. The **Royal Association for Disability and Rehabilitation** (RADAR), Unit 12, City Forum, 250 City Road, London, EC1V 8AF, T020-7250 3222, www.radar.org.uk, is a good source of advice and information, and produces an annual guide on travelling in the UK (£7.50 including P&P).

The Holiday Care Service, 2nd floor, Imperial Building, Victoria Rd, Horley, Surrey RH6 7PZ, T01293-774535, provides free lists of accessible accommodation and travel in the UK. In London, tour operator **Can Be Done**, T020-8907 2400, www.canbedone.co.uk, will arrange holidays for disabled visitors in a range of accommodation to suit individual requirements. Another useful contact is **Artsline**, T020-7388 2227, www.dircon.co.uk/artsline, which has information on arts, attractions and entertainment for disabled people in London.

The Royal National Institute for the Blind, T020-7388 1266, publishes a *Hotel Guide Book* for blind and partially sighted people. They also have maps for the blind of London and other cities.

Gay and lesbian travellers

Homosexuality is still frowned upon, or worse, in some parts of the country. Gay couples are not guaranteed a warm reception in too many rural areas, especially the north. It's not all doom, gloom and prejudice though. Outside London, Brighton made a name for itself with its gay scene, as have Edinburgh and Manchester, which prides itself on its gay nightlife.

Contacts

For a good selection of gay events and venues, check out www.whatsonwhen.com, or the UK gay-scene index at www.queenscene.com, which has information on clubs, gay groups, accommodation, events, HIV/AIDS and cultural and ethical issues. Other good sites include www.gaybritain.co.uk www.gaytravel.co.uk www.rainbownetwork.com and www.gaypride.co.uk

Student travellers

There are various official youth/student ID cards available. The most useful is the **International Student ID Card** (ISIC). For a mere £6 the ISIC card gains you access to the exclusive world of student travel with a series of discounts, including most forms of local transport, up to 30% off international air fares, cheap or free admission to museums, theatres and other attractions, and cheap meals in some restaurants. There's also free or discounted internet access, and a website where you can check the latest student travel deals, www.usitworld.com. You'll also receive the ISIC handbook, which ensures you get the most out of services available. ISIC cards are available at student travel centres, such as **STA Travel**, 86 Old Brompton Road, London, SW7 3LH, T020-7361 6161, www.statravel.co.uk; and **Trailfinders**, 194 Kensington High Street, London, W8 6FT, T020-7938 3939, www.trailfinders.co.uk. US and Canadian citizens are also entitled to emergency medical coverage, and there's a 24-hour hotline to call in the event of medical, legal or financial emergencies.

If you're aged under 26 but not a student, you can apply for a Federation of International Youth Travel Organisations (FIYTO) card, or a **Euro 26 Card**, which give you much the same discounts. If you're 25 or younger you can qualify for a **Go-25 Card**, which gives you the same benefits as an ISIC card. These discount cards are also issued by student travel agencies and hostelling organizations.

Studying in Britain

If you want to study in Britain you must first prove you can support and accommodate yourself without working and without recourse to public support. Your studies should take up at least 15 hours a week for a minimum of six months. Once you are studying, you are allowed to do 20 hours of casual work per week in the term time and you can work full-time during the holidays. In **North America** full-time students can obtain temporary work or study permits through the **Council of International Education Exchange** (CIEE),

205 E 42nd Street, New York, NY 10017, T212-8222600, www.ciee.org. For more details, contact your nearest British embassy, consulate or high commission, or the **Foreign and Commonwealth Office in London,** T020-7270 1500.

Travel with children

Britain still lags some way behind southern Europe in its attitude towards young children and unlike their Mediterranean cousins, most British citizens are unlikely to feel better disposed towards foreign visitors travelling with kids in tow. There are, however, lots of attractions geared to children, so finding something to keep the ankle-biters amused while the rain tips down outside shouldn't be a problem. The most frustrating aspect of travelling with kids in Britain is eating out. Some establishments are happy to help with high chairs and kids' menus while too many are downright unhelpful. In major towns and cities Italian restaurants are often more child-friendly. In more remote areas, however, most people are helpful and friendly.

www.babygoes2.com is a very useful source of advice.

Women travellers

Travelling in Britain is neither easier nor more difficult for women than it is for men. Generally speaking, people are friendly and courteous and even lone women travellers should experience nothing unpleasant. In the main cities and larger towns, take the the usual precautions and avoid walking in quiet, unlit streets and parks at night.

Working in Britain

Citizens of **European Union** (EU) countries can live and work in Britain freely without a visa, but **non-EU residents** need a permit to work legally. This can be difficult to obtain without the backing of an established company or employer in the UK. Also, visitors from Commonwealth countries who are aged between 17 and 27 may apply for a working holiday-maker's visa which permits them to stay in the UK for up to two years and work on a casual basis (ie non-career orientated). These certificates are only available from British embassies and consulates abroad, and you must have proof of a valid return or onward ticket, as well as means of support during your stay. **Commonwealth** citizens with a parent or grandparent born in the UK can apply for a **Certificate of Entitlement to the Right of Abode** , allowing them to work in Britain.

British embassies abroad

Australia High Commission: Commonwealth Av, Yarralumla, Canberra, ACT 2600, T02-6270 6666, www.uk.emb.gov.au.
Canada High Commission: 80 Elgin St, Ottowa, K1P 5K7, T613-2371530, www.britain- in-canada.org.
France 9 Av Hoche, 8e, Paris, T01-42663810, www.amb-grandebretagne.fr
Germany Wilhelmstrasse 70-71, 10117 Berlin, T030-20457-0, www.britischebotschaft.de.
Ireland 29 Merrion Rd, Ballsbridge, Dublin 4, T01-2053700, www.britishembassy.ie.
Netherlands Koningslaan 44, 1075AE Amsterdam, T20-6764343, www.britain.nl.
New Zealand High Commission: 44 Hill St, Wellington, T04-4726049, www.britain.org.nz.
South Africa 91 Parliament St, Cape Town 8001, T21-4617220, www.britain.org.za.
USA 3100 Massachusetts Av NW, Washington DC 20008, T1-202-588 7800, www.britain-info.org, regional consulates in 12 other cities.

Before you travel

Visas

Visa regulations are subject to change, so check with your local British embassy, high commission or consulate before leaving. Everyone needs a passport to enter. Citizens of Australia, Canada, New Zealand, South Africa or the USA do not need a visa and can stay for up to six months, providing they have a return ticket and sufficient funds to cover their stay. Citizens of most European countries do not need a visa and can stay for three months. Citizens of Albania, Bosnia, Bulgaria, Macedonia, Romania, Slovakia, Yugoslavia, all former Soviet republics (other than the Baltic states) and most other countries need a visa from the commission or consular office in the country of application.

The **Foreign Office's** website (www.fco.gov.uk) provides details of British immigration and visa requirements. Also the **Immigration Advisory Service** (IAS) offers free and confidential advice to anyone applying for entry clearance into the UK: County House, 190 Great Dover Street, London SE1 4YB, T020-73576917, www.vois.org.uk

For **visa extensions** once in England, contact the **Home Office,** Immigration and Nationality Department, Lunar House, Wellesley Rd, Croydon, London CR9, T020-86860688, before your existing visa expires. Citizens of Australia, Canada, New Zealand, South Africa or the USA wishing to stay longer than six months will need an **Entry Clearance Certificate** from the British High Commission in their country. For more details, contact your nearest British embassy, consulate or high commission, or the **Foreign and Commonwealth Office** in London, T020-72701500.

Insurance

Insurance is crucial if things go seriously wrong. A good insurance policy should cover you in case of theft, loss of possessions or money (often including cash), the cost of any medical and dental treatment, cancellation of flights, delays in travel arrangements, accidents, missed departures, lost baggage, lost passport, and personal liability and legal expenses. There's nearly always small print: some policies exclude 'dangerous activities' such as scuba diving, skiing, horse riding or even trekking. Older travellers should note that some companies won't cover people over 65 years old, or may charge high premiums. Not all policies cover ambulance, helicopter rescue or emergency flights home. Find out if your policy pays medical expenses direct to the hospital or doctor, or if you have to pay and then claim the money back later. If the latter applies, make sure you keep all records. Whatever your policy, if you have something stolen, make sure you get a copy of the police report, as you will need this to substantiate your claim.

Before shopping around for prices, check whether your credit card and home insurance companies already offer overseas travel within your policy. If not, a good place to start is **STA Travel** at www.sta-travel.com. Travellers from North America can try **Travel Guard,** T1-800-8261300, www.noelgroup.com; **Access America,** T1-800- 2848300; **Travel Insurance Services** (1-800-9371387) and **Travel Assistance International,** T1-800-8212828. Travellers from Australia could also try www.travelinsurance.com.au.

Customs and duty free

There are various import restrictions, most of which should not affect the average tourist. It is difficult to bring pets into Britain, and tight quarantine restrictions apply (with some exemptions for dogs and cats travelling from Europe). For more information on bringing a pet, contact the **Department of Environment, Food and Rural Affairs**, Nobel House, 17 Smith Square, London SW1P 3JR, T020-72386000 or check their web site at www.defra.gov.uk/animalh/quarantine

Visitors from EU countries do not have to make a declaration to customs on entry into the UK. The limits for duty-paid goods from within the EU are 800 cigarettes, or 1kg of tobacco, 10 litres of spirits, 20 litres of fortified wine, 90 litres of wine and 110 litres of beer. There is no longer any duty-free shopping. Visitors from non-EU countries are allowed to import 200 cigarettes, or 250g of tobacco, two litres of wine, and two litres of fortified wine or one litre of spirits.

For more information on British import regulations, contact HM Customs and Excise, Dorset House, Stamford Street, London, SE1 9PJ, T020-79283344, www.hmce.gov.uk

What to take

Your main problem is going to be the weather, which is very unpredictable. You should pack layered clothing, therefore, and bring a lightweight waterproof jacket and warm sweater whatever the time of year. Light clothes are sufficient for the summer. You'll be able to find everything else you could possibly need in any British city, so you can pack light and buy stuff as you go along.

A sleeping bag is useful in hostels. A sleeping sheet with a pillow cover is needed for staying in **Youth Hostel Association** (YHA) hostels to save you the cost of having to hire one. A padlock can also be handy for locking your bag if it has to be stored in a hostel for any length of time. Other useful items include an alarm clock (for those early ferry departures) and an adapter plug for electrical appliances.

Money

The **British currency** is the pound sterling (**£**), divided into 100 pence (**p**). Coins come in denominations of 1p, 2p, 5p, 10p, 20p, 50p, £1 and £2. The main notes (bills) are £5, £10, £20 (£50 are not widely used and may be difficult to change). Scottish banks have the right to produce their own banknotes, in denominations of £5, £10, £20, £50 and £100. These are legal tender in the rest of Britain, though some shopkeepers south of the border may be reluctant to accept them.

Credit cards and ATMs

Most hotels, shops and restaurants accept the major credit cards Access/MasterCard, Visa and Amex), though some places may charge for using them. Some smaller establishments such as B&Bs may only accept cash. Visa card and Access/MasterCard holders can use all major High Street banks (**Barclays, HSBC, Lloyds TSB, NatWest, Royal Bank of Scotland** and **Bank of Scotland**). Amex card holders can use the **HSBC**, the **Royal Bank of Scotland** and any other bank or building society displaying the 'Link' symbol. The Cirrus symbol is accepted in most ATMs. Note that your bank may charge you for using a foreign ATM, and many card companies charge high interest rates for cash withdrawals.

Travellers' cheques

The safest way to carry money is in travellers' cheques. These are available for a small commission from all major banks. **American Express (Amex)**, **Visa** and **Thomas Cook** cheques are widely accepted and are the most commonly issued by banks. You'll normally have to pay commission again when you cash each cheque. This will usually be 1%, or a flat rate. No commission is payable on Amex cheques cashed at Amex offices. Make sure you keep a record of the cheque numbers and the cheques you've cashed separate from the cheques themselves, so that you can get a full refund of all uncashed cheques should you lose them. It's best to bring sterling cheques to avoid changing currencies twice. Also note that in Britain travellers' cheques are rarely accepted outside banks, so you'll need to cash them in advance and keep a good supply of ready cash.

No vaccinations are required to enter the UK. See the Health section, page 44.

Banks and bureaux de change

Branches of the main High Street banks are found throughout the country: **Barclays, HSBC, Lloyds TSB** and **NatWest** in England and Wales; **Royal Bank of Scotland** and **Bank of Scotland** in Scotland. Bank opening hours are Monday-Friday from 0930 to 1600 or 1700. Some larger branches may open later on Thursdays and on Saturday mornings. Banks tend to offer similar exchange rates and are usually the best places to change money and cheques. Outside banking hours you'll have to use a bureau de change, which can be easily found at the airports and train stations and in larger cities. **Thomas Cook** and other major travel agents also operate bureaux de change with reasonable rates. Avoid changing money or cheques in hotels, as the rates are usually poor. Main post offices and branches of **Marks and Spencer** will change cash without commission.

Money transfers

If you need money urgently, the quickest way to have it sent to you is to have it wired to the nearest agent via **Western Union** (T0800-833833) or **Moneygram** (T0800-89718971). Charges are on a sliding scale, and it will cost proportionately less to wire out more money. Money can also be wired by **Thomas Cook** or **American Express,** though this may take a day or two, or transferred via a bank draft, but this can take up to a week.

Cost of travelling

Britain can be an expensive place to visit, and London and the south in particular can eat heavily into your budget. The minimum daily budget if you're staying in hostels or cheap B&Bs, cooking your own meals and doing minimal travelling will be around £30 per person per day. Those staying in more upmarket B&Bs or guest houses, eating out at pubs or modest restaurants and visiting tourist attractions can expect to pay around £60 per person per day. Single travellers will have to pay more than half the cost of a double room in most places and should budget on spending around 60% of what a couple would spend. In order to enjoy your trip to the full then you'll need at least £70 per day.

Taxes

Most goods in Britain are subject to a **Value Added Tax** (VAT) of 17.5%, with the exception of books and food. VAT is usually included in the price of goods. Visitors from non-EU countries can save money through the Retail Export Scheme, which allows a refund of VAT on goods that will be taken out of the country. Note that not all shops participate in the scheme and that VAT cannot be reclaimed on hotel bills or other services.

Getting there

Air

The majority of visitors to Britain fly to London, which has five airports. The largest of these, Heathrow, is the busiest airport in the world with direct flights to most major cities on all continents. There are also good air links to all parts of the British Isles. More and more people are turning to budget airlines, which offer a variety of routes throughout Europe. Note, however, that the main hubs in London (Stansted and Luton) are not near the city itself and will require some extra overland travel. Direct flights from Europe also arrive at Birmingham, Bristol, Cardiff, Edinburgh, Glasgow, Leeds, Liverpool, Manchester, Newcastle, Newquay, Plymouth and Southampton airports.

Buying a ticket

There are a mind-boggling number of outlets for buying your plane ticket and finding the best deal can be a confusing business. **Fares** will depend on the season. Ticket prices are highest from around early June to mid-September, which is the tourist high season. Fares drop in the months either side of the peak season – mid-September to early November and mid-April to early June. They are cheapest in the low season, from November to April, although prices tend to rise sharply over Christmas and the New Year. It's also worth noting that flying at the weekend is normally more expensive.

One of the best ways of finding a good deal is to use the **internet**. There are a number of sites where you can check out prices and even book tickets. You can search in the travel sections of your web browser or try the sites of the discount travel companies and agents and the budget airlines listed in this section. Also worth trying are: **www.expedia.com, www.lastminute.com, www.e-bookers.com, www.cheapflights.co.uk, www.deckchair.com, www.flynowww.com, www.dialaflight.co.uk, www.opodo.com** and **www.travelocity.com.**

Those wishing to fly on to other parts of Britain should note that it may be cheaper if you use an Airpass or Europass bought in your own country. These are offered by British Airways and British Midland and are valid only with an international scheduled flight ticket. You can also try specialist agencies such as **STA** who offer Domestic Air Passes on **British Airways** and **British Midlands** flights to full-time students and travellers under 26 years old. These give substantial discounts on flights from Heathrow and Gatwick to specified destinations in England, Scotland, Northern Ireland and Jersey, in the Channel Islands. Flights work out at between £28 and £32 each, with a minimum of four flights per person. Alternatively, there is a growing number of low-cost airlines which offer cheap air tickets on the Internet and on back pages of weekend national newspapers.

Airport tax All tickets are subject to taxes (£10-20 depending on route), insurance charge (around £6) and passenger service charge, which varies according to airport. This adds up quickly – for economy-fare flights within the UK and from EU countries expect additions of £20-30. For inter-continental flights, this will rise to around £60-70.

Flights from North America

There are regular non-stop flights to London from many US and Canadian cities, including Atlanta, Boston, Calgary, Chicago, Dallas, Denver, Houston, Las Vegas, Los Angeles, Miami, Montreal, New York, Philadelphia, Phoenix, San Francisco, Seattle, Toronto, Vancouver and Washington DC, and many more connections to other cities. Non-stop flights are also available from New York, Chicago and Toronto to Glasgow and from New York to Manchester and Birmingham.

Discount flight agents in North America

Air Brokers International, 323 Geary St, Suite 411, San Francisco, CA94102, T1-800-8833273, www.airbrokers.com. Consolidator and specialist in RTW and Circle Pacific tickets.

Discount Airfares Worldwide On-Line, www.etn.nl/discount.htm. A hub of consolidator and discount agent links.

STA Travel, 5900 Wilshire Blvd, Suite 2110, Los Angeles, CA 90036, T1-800-7770112, www.sta-travel.com. Discount student/youth travel discount company with branches in New York, San Francisco, Boston, Miami, Chicago, Seattle and Washington DC.

Travel CUTS, 187 College St, Toronto, ON M5T 1P7, T1-800-6672887, www.travelcuts.com. Specialist in student discount fares, IDs and other travel services. Branches in other Canadian cities.28

For low-season Apex fares expect to pay US$200-450 from New York and other East Coast cities, and US$300-600 from the West Coast. Prices rise to around US$500-800 from New York and US$400-900 from the West Coast in the summer months. Low-season Apex fares from Toronto and Montreal cost around CAN$600-700, and from Vancouver around CAN$800-900, rising to $750-950 and $950-1150 during the summer.

Flights from Australia and New Zealand

The cheapest scheduled flights to London from Australia or New Zealand are via Asia with **Gulf Air, Royal Brunei** or **Thai Airways.** They charge A$1300-1500 in low season and up to A$1800 in high season, and involve a transfer en route. Flights via Africa start at around $2000 and are yet more expensive via North America. Flights to and from Perth via Africa or Asia are a few hundred dollars cheaper. The cheapest scheduled flights from New Zealand are with **Korean Air, Thai Airways** or **JAL,** all of whom fly via their home cities for around NZ$2000-2300. The most direct route is via North America with **United Airlines,** via Chicago or Los Angeles. Fares range from around NZ$2800 in low season to NZ$3200 in high season.

Connecting service from London to other British airports is available on a number of airlines, including **British Airways, Qantas** and many of the budget airlines. Emirates flies to Birmingham and Manchester from Sydney via Dubai, and Manchester is also served via Singapore on Singapore Airlines. Prices are slightly higher than flights to London.

Flights from Europe

In addition to regular flights operated by the major national carriers, the surge in **budget airline** routes means that you can fly from practically anywhere in Europe to anywhere in Britain at cheap rates. The budget airlines specialise in routes to provincial and smaller cities, and it's always worth checking what the onward transport arrangements are, since airports are often a long way from town. The flight consolidator www.opodo.com can often offer good rates, but it's worth noting that flight consolidators do not include budget airline fares – you'll have to search those out separately (see box). Fares for a return ticket can range from €15 to €300 on a scheduled flight. Budget airlines offer no frills: no meals, no reserved seating and baggage restrictions. However, you can sometimes travel for as little as €5. Check terms and airport location before booking: **www.ryanair.com, www.flybe.com, www.easyjet.com, www.flybmi.com, www.virginexpress.com**

Rail

Eurostar, T0990-186186, www.eurostar.com, operate high-speed trains to London Waterloo from Paris (three hours) and Brussels (two hours 40 minutes) via Lille (two hours).

Standard-class tickets to Paris and Brussels range from £70 for a weekend day return to £300 for a fully flexible mid-week return. There are substantial discounts for children (4-11 years) and for passengers who are under 26 years on the day of travel. It is worth keeping an eye open for special offers, especially in the low season. All other rail connections will involve some kind of ferry crossing (see below). For full details on rail services available, contact your national railway or **Rail Europe**, www.rail europe.com, for information on routes, timetables, fares and discount passes.

Road

If you're driving from continental Europe you can take the **Eurotunnel Shuttle Service**, T0800-969992, www.eurotunnel.com, a freight train which runs 24 hours a day, 365 days a year, and takes you and your car from Calais to Folkestone in 35-45 minutes. Fares are per carload, regardless of the number of passengers, and range from £135 one way to £270 return depending on the time of year or how far in advance you book. For bookings, call T08705-353535. Foot passengers cannot cross on the Shuttle.

Sea

Ferry

Ferries operate along 33 routes to England and Wales, arriving at Ramsgate, Dover, Newhaven, Portsmouth, Bournemouth and Plymouth, Harwich, Hull and Tynemouth (east coast) and Liverpool, Fishguard and Holyhead, as follows. Prices vary enormously according to season. You can check prices for specific dates on one of the many online booking agent websites: **www.cheapferry.com**, **www.ferry-to-france.co.uk**, **www.ferrycrossings-uk.co.uk** or **www.ferrysavers.com**, or by contacting major route operators direct: **P&O Stena Line**, T0870-6000600, www.posl.com (Spain, France, Irish Sea & North Sea routes), **Brittany Ferries**, T0990-360360, T(33)299-828080 in France, T(34)942-360611 in Spain, www.brittanyferries.com, (Spain and western France to south coast): **Fjord Line**, www.fjordline.com, (North Sea routes from Scandinavia). These also handle information on shipping.

The only direct route to Scotland from Europe is on the **Smyril Line** (Aberdeen T01224-572615; Faroe Islands T01-5900) service to **Lerwick** (Shetland) from Norway and Iceland. You then have to get to the Scottish mainland. **P&O Scottish Ferries** (T10224-572615) sail from Lerwick to Aberdeen. From Northern Ireland **Larne to Cairnryan**: P&O Irish Sea, T0870-2424777, www.poirishsea.com, has several crossings daily to Cairnryan. **Belfast to Stranraer**: **Stena Line**,T0870-707070, www.stenaline.co.uk, run numerous ferries and high-speed catamarans. **Belfast to Troon**: **Seacat Scotland** run daily services, T08705-523523, www.seacat.co.uk

Touching down

Airport information

Most visitors arrive in Britain via one of London's five airports: Heathrow, Gatwick, Stansted, City or Luton. Long-haul flights also land at Glasgow, Manchester and Birmingham. Other common points of entry include the ports of Dover and Holyhead (in Wales) and by car at Folkestone via *Le Shuttle*. Those arriving by budget airline at one of the other regional airports (Bristol, Cardiff, Edinburgh, Leeds, Liverpool,

 Inverness, Newcastle, Newquay, Plymouth or Southampton) should check arrival information via the airline's website. For information on all UK airports, visit www.baa.co.uk

London Heathrow Airport

London Heathrow Airport (LHR), Hounslow, Middlesex, TW6 1JH, T0870-0000123, is the world's busiest international airport and it has four terminals, so when leaving London, it's important to check which terminal to go to before setting out for the airport. Transport for London and British Rail have travel information points in Terminals 1, 2 and 4. Bus and coach sales/information desks are located in all four terminals. There are hotel reservations desks in the arrivals area of each terminal (a booking fee is charged). For general enquiries, passengers with special needs should contact the Call Centre, T0870-0000123. If further help or advice concerning travel arrangements is required call Heathrow Travel-care T020-8745 7495.

By train and tube The airport is on the **London Underground** Piccadilly Line, which runs trains every 5-9 minutes to the centre of London and beyond, with an approximate journey time of 50 minutes. There are two stations: one serving Terminals 1, 2, and 3; the other for Terminal 4. The first train from central London arrives at Terminal 4 at 0629 (0749 on Sun) and the last arrives at 0107 (0008 on Sun). Allow a further five minutes to reach the station for Terminals 1, 2 and 3. Details of timetables and fares are available on T020-7222 1234 (24 hours). **Heathrow Express**, T0845-6001515, W.heathrowexpress.co.uk, non-stop train to and from Paddington Station in central London. The journey takes 15 minutes to Terminals 1, 2 and 3, and 20 minutes to Terminal 4. Trains depart every 15 minutes between 0510 and 2340, 365 days a year. There is plenty of luggage space and wheelchairs and pushchairs are catered for. Some airlines have check-in facilities at Paddington. Tickets cost £12 (single), £22 (return). A £2 premium is charged for tickets purchased on board the train. Discounted fares are available and tickets purchased via the website are also cheaper. Children travel free when accompanied by an adult.

By bus An **Airlink**, T0990-747777, 'Hotel Hoppa' shuttle service serves most major hotels near the airport. **Airbus A2**, T020-8400 6655, runs every 30 minutes throughout the day to and from a number of stops in central London. During the night, the **N97** bus connects Heathrow with central London. **National Express**, T08705-808080, coaches run from Victoria Coach Station every 30 minutes. Airlinks also operates frequent coach services between Heathrow, Gatwick, Luton, Stansted and other airports.

By car/taxi Heathrow is 16 miles west of London at Junctions 3 and 4 on the M4 motorway. A taxi from Heathrow Airport to central London takes approximately one hour and should cost around £40. There are taxi desks in the Arrivals area of all four terminals (Terminal 1, T020-8745 7487; Terminal 2, T020-8745 5408; Terminal 3, T020-8745 4655; Terminal 4, T020-8745 7302).

London Gatwick Airport

London Gatwick Airport (LGW), Gatwick, West Sussex, RH6 0JH, T0870-0002468. London's second airport 28 miles south of the capital, has two terminals, North and South, with all the facilities including car hire, currency exchange, 24-hour banking, Flight Shops (T08000-747787), Hotel Reservations Desks (T01293-504549) and a Travel Shop in the South Terminal (T01293-506783). There are many help points for passengers with special needs and free wheelchair assistance or help with baggage to reach check-in.

By train All trains arrive at the South Terminal where there is a fast link to the North Terminal. A number of airlines offer check-in facilities at London's Victoria Station. The fastest service is the non-stop 30-minute **Gatwick Express**, T0990-301530, which runs to and from London Victoria every 15 minutes during the day, and hourly throughout the night. Standard tickets cost £10.50 single and £20 return; first-class and cheap-day returns are available. **Thameslink** rail services run from King's Cross, Farringdon, Blackfriars and London Bridge stations.

By bus **Airbus A5** operates hourly to/from Victoria Coach Station. For further information call the Airport Travel Line, T0990-747777.

By car Gatwick is at Crawley, off Junction 9 on the M23 motorway, about an hour's drive from central London. A taxi to central London for up to 4 people costs around £75.

London Luton Airport

London Luton Airport (LTN), Luton, Bedfordshire, LU2 9LU, T01582-405100. Luton airport, about 30 miles north of central London, deals particularly with flights operated by budget airlines. All the usual facilities are available plus fax, internet, a children's play area and an airport chapel. There is also a Skyline Travel Shop, T01582-726454.

By train Regular **Thameslink** trains leave from London Bridge, Blackfriars, Farringdon and King's Cross stations to Luton Airport Parkway station; a free shuttle bus service operates between the station and the airport terminal. The Thameslink station at King's Cross is about 100 yards east of the main station, along the Pentonville Road.

By bus **Green Line** coaches run to and from Victoria Coach Station, Hyde Park Corner, Marble Arch, George Street and Baker Street in central London.

By car The airport is southeast of Luton, 2 miles off the M1 at Junction 10. The 30-mile journey into London will take around 50 minutes, and costs around £55 by taxi. Two companies operate from outside the terminal.

Stansted Airport

Stansted Airport (STN), Stansted, CM24 1RW, T08700-000303, 35 miles northeast of London (near Cambridge), is another budget airline hub. Terminal facilities include car hire, ATMs, 24-hour currency exchange, shops, restaurants and bars. There's a *Book and Go* Travel Shop, T08700-102015, a hotel reservations desk, T01279-661220, and AAS Assistance, T01279-663213, for passengers with special needs and also for left luggage.

By train **Stansted Express**, T0845-8500150, runs trains every 15 minutes from London's Liverpool Street Station to the main terminal building. The journey takes 45 minutes and costs £13 single and £23 open return.

By bus **Airbus A6** runs every hour from Victoria Coach Station, Hyde Park Corner, Marble Arch and Baker Street. **Airbus A7** also runs an hourly service from Victoria Coach Station, Embankment and Aldgate. The journey takes around 1 hour 30 minutes. **Jetlink**, T08705-747777, operates a frequent service between London's four main airports.

By car The airport is north of London by Junction 8 of the M11. The 35-mile journey to/from central London takes around an hour to 1 hour 30 minutes depending on traffic.

Manchester Airport

Manchester International Airport (MAN), T0161-4893000, www.manchesterairport.co.uk The airport has three terminals with all the usual facilities, and is located south of the city centre, at Junction 5 of the M56.

By train, bus and car The airport is well-served by public transport, with trains to and from Manchester Piccadilly as well as direct and connecting services from all over the north of England. **National Express**, T08705-808080, runs from Terminals 1 and 2 on routes covering the whole of the UK. A taxi into the city centre should cost around £15.

Birmingham International Airport

Birmingham International Airport (BHX), T0121-7675511, www.bhx.co.uk Birmingham airport is 8 miles east of the city centre and has two terminals with standard facilities.

By trains, bus and car A taxi into the centre should cost around £12. Several trains per hour run the 10 minute journey into the city centre, and other connections across England and Wales can be made by rail or coach, with **National Express**, T08705-808080. There are no local bus services at night.

Glasgow Airport

Glasgow International Airport (GLA), T0141-8871111, is 8 miles west of the city, at junction 28 on the M8 and has two terminals with the usual facilities.

By trains, bus and car To get into town take a Glasgow Airport Link bus from outside Arrivals. They leave every 10-15 mins to Buchanan bus station, with drop-off points at Central and Queen St train stations; 25-30 mins, £3.30 single, £5 return. Buses to the airport leave from Buchanan St bus station and stop outside the main TIC. A taxi from the airport to the city centre costs around £16.50.

Tourist information

Most cities and towns that you're likely to visit in Britain have a local tourist information centre (TIC), which can give you information on local attractions, restaurants and accommodation (including handling bookings – for a small fee) and help with visitors' enquiries, such as where to find an internet café. Many sell books, local guides, maps and souvenirs, and some have free street plans and leaflets describing local walks. In general, tourist offices tend to cater to those interested in taking tours or day trips, and are less useful if you're on a tight budget, in which case youth hostels can provide much the same information. See individual town information sections for lists of local TICs.

Museums, art galleries and stately homes

Over 300 stately homes, gardens and countryside areas in England are cared for by the **National Trust** (NT), 36 Queen Anne's Gate, London SW1H 9AS, T0870-609 5380, www.national trust.org.uk. National Trust properties are indicated in this guide '(NT)', If you're going to be visiting several sights during your stay, then it's worth taking annual membership or investing in a *National Trust Touring Pass*. A similar organization is **English Heritage**, 23 Savile Row, London W1S 2ET, T020-79733000, www.english-heritage.org.uk, which manages hundreds of monuments and sights around England, including Stonehenge, and focuses on restoration and preservation. In Scotland over 100 of the country's most prestigious sights, and 185,000 acres of beautiful countryside, are cared for by the **National Trust for Scotland** (NTS), 26-31 Charlotte Square, Edinburgh EH2 4ET, T0131-2439300, www.nts.org.uk National Trust properties are indicated in this guide as 'NTS'. **Historic Scotland** (HS), Longmore House, Salisbury Place, Edinburgh EH9 1SH, T0131-6688800, www.historic- scotland.gov.uk, manages more than 330 of Scotland's most important castles (including Edinburgh and Stirling), monuments and other historic sites. Historic Scotland properties are indicated as 'HS'.

Local customs and laws

In general, customs and laws are the same as you would encounter in any other western country. Informal clothing is acceptable throughout Britain, except at special events that specify a dress code (such as Glyndebourne Opera). If you are planning to work in Britain, business clothes may be appropriate. Visitors may find the British to be reserved, and, as in most countries, politeness is appreciated.

Tipping

Tipping in Britain is at the customer's discretion. In a restaurant you should leave a tip of 10-15% if you are satisfied with the service. If the bill already includes a service charge, you needn't add a further tip. Tipping is not normal in pubs or bars. Taxi drivers expect a tip, usually of around 10%. As in most other countries, porters, bellboys and waiters in more upmarket hotels rely on tips to supplement their meagre wages.

Prohibitions

If you use mace or pepper spray for self defence at home, you should note that both are illegal in the UK, and if you are caught carrying or using them, you may be arrested. Marijuana is illegal, as are all the usual drugs. However, under a recently introduced law, police most cities can turn a blind eye to possession of small amounts of cannabis.

Responsible tourism

Sustainable or eco-tourism has been described as, "...ethical, considerate or informed tourism where visitors can enjoy the natural, historical and social heritage of an area without causing adverse environmental, socio-economic or cultural impacts that compromise the long-term ability of that area and its people to provide a recreational resource for future generations and an income for themselves..."

Many parts of Britain are areas of outstanding natural beauty, and home to both wildlife and people who make their living from the land. Please behave responsibly in the countryside, and around ancient monuments. For further information on what action is being taken throughout UK or across the world to control the negative aspects of tourism on the natural environment and traditional cultures, contact **Tourism Concern**, 277-281 Holloway Road, London, T020-77533330, www.tourismconcern.org.uk

Safety

Generally speaking, Britain is a safe place to visit. British cities have their fair share of crime, but much of it is drug-related and confined to the more deprived peripheral areas. You should take heed of the usual advice and avoid wandering alone around unlit city centre streets, parks and lonely railway stations. Trust your instincts, and if in doubt, pay for a taxi. (See Women travellers, page 23.) Your main problem is going to be remembering to look right, not left, when crossing the road.

Getting around

Compared to the rest of Western Europe, public transport in Britain is generally poor and can be expensive. Rail, in particular, can cost an arm and a leg, and is notoriously unreliable. Coach travel is cheaper but much slower, and is further hampered by serious traffic problems around London, Manchester and Birmingham. Some areas, such as the Highlands of Scotland, the Cotswolds, Peak or Lake District, are poorly served by public transport of any kind, and if you plan to spend much time in rural areas, it may be worth hiring a car, especially if you are travelling as a couple or group. A useful website for all national public transport information is www.pti.org.uk

See Ins and outs and Transport sections for further local details

Air

Britain is a relatively small country, and other than the far north of Scotland and the islands, air travel isn't strictly necessary to get around. However, with the railways in disarray and traffic a problem around the cities, some of the cheap fares offered by budget airlines (see page 28) may be very attractive. There are good connections between London and all the regional airports, although travel from region to region without coming through London is more difficult and expensive. Services between

 British cities are operated by many of these budget airlines and by **British Airways,** T08457-733377, www.british-airways.com. Bear in mind the time and money it will take you to get to the airport (including check in times) when deciding whether flying is really going to be a better deal.

Bus and coach

This is the generally the cheapest form of travel in the UK. Road links between major cities are excellent and a number of companies offer express coach services day and night. The main operator, **National Express,** T08705-808080, www.nationalexpress.com, has a nationwide network with over 1000 destinations. Tickets can be bought at bus stations or from a huge number of agents throughout the country. The two main operators between England and Scotland are **National Express,** and its sister company **Scottish Citylink,** T08705-505050, www.city.link.co.uk Fares from London to Glasgow and Edinburgh with **National Express** are between £30 and £40 for an economy advance return. Fares to Aberdeen and Inverness are a little higher. The London to Glasgow/Edinburgh journey takes around eight hours, while it takes around 11-12 hours for the trip to Aberdeen and Inverness.

Postbus services Many rural areas in Scotland, particularly in the Highlands and Islands, can only be reached by Royal Mail postbuses. A free booklet of routes and timetables is usually available from local Tourist Information Centres. For more information on postbuses call the **Royal Mail** in Edinburgh, T0131-2287407.

Car

Visitors from Continental Europe may be shocked by the levels of congestion on British roads. This is particularly heavy on the M25 which encircles London, the M6 around Birmingham and the M62 around Manchester. The M4 and M5 motorways to the West Country can also become choked at weekends and bank holidays and the roads around Cornwall often resemble a glorified car park during the summer. There are two main routes to Scotland from the south. In the east the A1 runs to Edinburgh and in the west the M6 and A74(M) runs to Glasgow. The journey north from London to either city takes around eight to 10 hours.

Petrol stations and garages in the Highlands and Islands are few and far between.

Rules and regulations To drive in the UK you must have a current driving licence. Although foreign nationals may use their own licence for one year, international driving permits, available from your country of origin, may be required for some rentals, especially if your own licence is not in English. Visitors importing their own vehicle should also have their vehicle registration or ownership document. Make sure you're adequately insured. In all of the UK you drive on the left. Speed limits are (unless otherwise indicated) 30 miles per hour (mph) in built-up areas, 70 mph on motorways and dual carriageways and 60 mph on most other roads. www.dvla.gov.uk has details on every aspect of driving in the UK.

Organizations Britain has two main motoring organizations, which can help with route planning, traffic advice, insurance and breakdown cover. These are the **Automobile Association** (*AA*), T0800-444999, www.theaa.co.uk, and the **Royal Automobile Club** (*RAC*), T0800-550550, www.rac.co.uk. One year's membership starts at £43 for the AA and £39 for the *RAC*, which will cover you for emergency assistance. They also provide many other services, including a reciprocal agreement for free assistance with many overseas motoring organizations – check to see if your organization is included. Their emergency numbers‹Wo are: *AA* T0800-887766; *RAC* T08000-828282. You can still call these numbers if you're not a member, but you'll have to a pay a large fee.

Discount travel cards

Full-time students or those aged under 25 or over 50, can buy a **Coach Card** for £9 which is valid for one year and gets you a 20-30% discount on all fares. Children normally travel for half price, but with a **Family Card** costing £15, two children travel free with two adults. The **Tourist Trail Pass** offers unlimited travel on all National Express services throughout Britain. Passes cost from £49 for two days' travel out of three up to £190 for 15 days' travel out of 30. They can be bought from major travel agents, at Gatwick and Heathrow airports, as well as from bus stations. In North America these passes are available from **British Travel International**, T1-800-3276097, W.britishtravel.com, or from **US National Express**, T502-2981395. There are a variety of **railcards** which give discounts on fares for certain groups. Cards are valid for one year and most are available from main stations. You need two passport photos and proof of age or status. **Young Person's Railcard**: for those aged 16-25 or full-time students in the UK. Costs £18 and gives 33% discount on most train tickets and some ferry services. Senior Citizen's Railcard: for those aged over 60. Same price and discount as above. **Disabled Person's Railcard**: costs £14 and gives 33% discount to a disabled person and one other. **Family Railcard**: costs £20 and gives 33% discount on most tickets (20% on others) for up to four adults travelling together, and 81% discount for up to four children.

Vehicle hire

Car hire is expensive in Britain and you may be better off making arrangements in your home country for a fly/drive deal through one of the main multi-national companies: The minimum you can expect to pay is around £150 per week for a small car. Always check and compare conditions, such as mileage limitations, excess payable in the case of an accident, etc. Small, local hire companies often offer better deals than the larger multi-nationals. Most companies prefer payment with a credit card otherwise you'll have to leave a large deposit (£100 or more). You need to have had a full driver's licence for at least one year and to be aged between 21 (25 for some companies) and 70. Motorcycle hire is very expensive, ranging from around £200 up to £350 per week. See individual town Transport sections for more information on local car hire companies.

Ferry

There are around 60 or so inhabited islands off the coast of Scotland, and nearly 50 of them can be reached by a scheduled ferry service. Most ferries carry vehicles and can be booked in advance. If you're travelling to the islands by car, it's a good idea to book ferries in advance whatever the time of year, particularly to the more popular islands. The majority of ferry services on the west coast are operated by **Caledonian MacBrayne** T01475-650100, www.calmac.co.uk, or **CalMac** as they're more commonly known. They sail from Oban, Mallaig and Ullapool to over 20 islands in the Inner and Outer Hebrides. Fares are expensive, especially with a car, but if you're planning on using ferries a lot, you can save a lot of money with an **Island Hopscotch** ticket, which offers reduced fares on 17 set routes. **P&O Scottish Ferries** run car ferries to Orkney and Shetland. Ferries depart from Aberdeen or from Scrabster, near Thurso (for Orkney only).The Orkney islands are linked by services run by **Orkney Ferries,** T01856-872044, while Shetland's inter-island ferries are run by **Shetland Islands Council,** T01806- 244234.

Rail

There are four main companies operating rail services between London and other towns and cities in England: **GNER**, T08457-225225, www.gner.co.uk, leave from London King's Cross and run up the east coast to the East Midlands, Yorkshire and northeast England; **Virgin Trains**, T08457-222333, www.virgin.com, operate a cross-country and a west coast service from London Euston to the Midlands, and the northwest. Trains to the west of England are run by **First Great Western**, T08457-000125, www.great-western-trains.co.uk, from Paddington Station in London. Local operators manage routes between cities in the north and Midlands. **Scotrail**, T08457-550033, www.scotrail.co.uk, operate services throughout Scotland.

The system of fare pricing is complex. To help you navigate the railways, enlist the help of **National Rail Enquiries**, T0845-7484950, www.nationalrail.co.uk, who will provide advice on routes, timetables, fares and connections. Better still, visit www.chester-le-track.co.uk. You can also book tickets and consult timetables online at www.qjump.com.

Maps

You'll find a good selection of maps of Britain in most book shops and at the main tourist offices. Road atlases can be bought at service stations. The best of these are the large-format ones produced by the **AA**, **Collins** and **Ordnance Survey**, which cover all of Britain at a scale of around three miles to one inch and include plans of the major towns and cities. The **Michelin** and **Bartholomew** fold-out maps are also excellent, as are the official regional tourist maps published by **Estate Publications**, which are ideal for driving and which are available from most tourist offices.

The best detailed maps for walking are the **Ordnance Survey** maps, which are unsurpassed for accuracy and clarity. These are available at different scales. The **Landranger** series at 1:50,000 (1¼ inches to a mile) covers the whole of Britain and is good for most walkers. The new **Explorer** and **Outdoor Leisure** series are 1:25,000 and offer better value for walkers and cyclists. An excellent source of maps is **Stanfords** at 12-14 Longacre, London WC2E 9LP.

Sleeping

Accommodation in Britain is plentiful, although unfortunately much of it is either expensive or shabby. Hotels range from world-class luxury, for which you can expect to pay at least £250 a night, to delapidated concerns with dodgy plumbing and threadbare carpets. For the privilege of staying at one of these places you can still expect to pay £50 a night for a double room. Most of the more salubrious hotels, the ones that can afford to pay the cleaner but may not offer full room service, are likely to cost between £80-£160 for a double room for a night. Generally it's still true to say that guests paying over £100 a night can expect a superior level of comfort and service: from well-sprung mattresses to fluffy bathtowels and flowers in the room.

See inside the front cover for a guide to the hotel price codes used in this book

Guesthouses occupy the middle ground between hotels and Bed & Breakfasts. The quality of accommodation in guesthouses varies wildly: some provide exceptional value for the money in houses of great character; others have seen much better days. They can usually charge anything from £50-£100 for the night, sometimes quoting initially for half-board (dinner, bed and breakfast). Most have a restaurant and bar, which may or may not be open to non-residents.

Bed & Breakfasts (B&Bs) are something of an British speciality. As their name suggests, they usually offer fairly staightforward accommodation in a private home, with a heart-stopping breakfast fry-up thrown in. Many are run by empty-nesters with beautiful period houses and gardens; elsewhere, the best of them tend to be on working farms. Again, their standards are extremely variable, but they're unlikely to cost much more than £60 for the room for the night, some as little as £40 – depending on their location as much as the quality they offer – and some hosts can really bring their area to life. Many hotels, guesthouses and B&Bs offer discounts for stays of more than one night, weekend deals, and high and low season prices. They can be booked through Tourist Information Centres (TICs). Some TICs charge a booking fee. Note that many B&Bs charge more than 50% of the room rate for single oocupancy, so check beforehand.

Budget accommodation is offered by basic **backpackers hostels** and **YMCAs** in the cities and tourist hotspots, campsites and youth hostels run by the **Youth Hostel Association**, Trevelyan House, Dimple Rd, Matlock, DE4 3YH, T01629-592600, or customer services T0870-870 8808, www.yha.org.uk, in most major cities, the national parks and other areas of outstanding beauty. A bed in a dormitory usually costs less than £15 a night. The Scottish Youth Hostel Association (SYHA) 7 Glebe Cres, Stirling FK8 2JA, T01786-451181, www.syha.org.uk, is separate from the YHA in England and Wales.

Some TICs and a large number of private organizations keep lists of **self-catering** options on their books. Two of the more interesting are **The Landmark Trust**, Shottisbrooke, Maidenhead, Berks, SL6 3SW, T01628-825925, www.landmarktrust.co.uk, who rent out renovated historic landmark buildings, at a price, and **The National Trust**, 36 Queen Anne's Gate, London, SW1H 9AS, T0870-6095380, brochure line T0870-4584411, www.nationaltrustcottages.co.uk, who provide a wide variety of different accommodation on their estates. A reputable agent for self-catering cottages around the country is **English Country Cottages**, Springmill, Earby, Barnoldswick, Lancs, BB94 0AA, T01282-841785, www.countrycottages.co.uk

Food and drink

Food

Only a decade or so ago, few would have thought to come to Britain for haute cuisine. Since the 1980s, though, the British have been determinedly shrugging off their reputation for over-boiled cabbage and watery beef. Now cookery shows are the most popular on TV after the Soaps, and thanks in part to the wave of celebrity chefs they have created, visitors can expect a generally high standard of competence in restaurant kitchens across the land. The sheer variety of different menus can be bewildering. Gourmets are particularly well-catered for, at around £80 a head, in London and the South. Slightly less fussy eaters won't be disappointed just about everywhere else, while towns like Ludlow, Padstow, and Whitstable have carved reputations for themselves almost solely on the strength of their cuisine. Beyond the south of England, gourmet cooking can be enjoyed at more reasonable prices, and in cities such as Edinburgh, Glasgow and Cardiff you can dine well on a fraction of what you'd pay in London.

See inside front cover for a guide to eating price categories

So what are you likely to eat in Britain? Some things seem to stay the same: the full English/Scottish/Welsh breakfast (fried egg, bacon, sausages, tomatoes, mushrooms, beans and black pudding) is still going strong. Other breakfast fortes are kippers (the best are from Scotland), scrambled eggs and boiled eggs with toasted soldiers.

For much of the working population, at lunchtime, the sandwich is King and comes in all shapes and sizes: from fashionable breads and prosciutto in the major cities to *Mother's Pride* white and reconstituted ham in pubs. That said, pub food has also been transformed in recent years, and now many so-called 'gastropubs' them offer ambitious lunchtime and supper menus. Watch out for extensive use of the microwave, though, especially in pubs that offer food all day. Most restaurants also offer something for lunch, usually a cheaper and lighter version of their supper menu. It may not be the healthiest time to eat, but the evening meal has become the main meal in Britain. In the north it's still known as 'tea', while in the south the same word refers to an institution on a par with breakfast. (Oddly enough most 'tearooms' are not open at 'teatime', which is generally around 1630.) The ceremony ranges from a cup of tea and a biscuit to platefuls of cucumber sandwiches, cakes and of course its tour de force, the cream tea. These achieve their apotheosis in Wales and the southwest of England, where the quality of the fresh clotted cream served up with warm scones and jam can be exceptional, although they're widely available throughout the countryside.

The evening meal has also experienced a revolution in the quality of its ingredients and preparation in recent years. Menus from all over the world are on offer in all the major cities (curry has been declared the new national dish) while in the countryside the freshest local produce, much of it organic, can create memorable dining experiences. Most parts of the country still boast regional specialities, from the dubious delights of Welsh laverballs to succulent Loch Fyne oysters. Seek out some of the finest beef, lamb, duck or game in the world, generally served with roast potatoes (or chips of course), broccoli, peas or carrots. Other British specialities are absolutely fresh seafood, especially oysters, scallops, langoustines, winkles, and crabs, as well as fish from the sea – often bass, mullet and sole, and from the farm – trout and salmon mainly. For a much cheaper supper, Fish'n'Chip shops can still be found in most small towns, especially in the north. They usually have restricted 'frying times' (lunch and supper again) and the fish served with fat chips tends to be battered and deep-fried cod, haddock, sole, plaice or rock. Approach with caution.

Eating out

For a cheap meal, you're best bet is a pub, hotel bar or café, where you can have a one-course meal for around £6-7 or less, though don't expect gourmet food. The best value is often at lunch time, when many restaurants offer three-course set lunches or business lunches for less than £10. You'll need a pretty huge appetite to feel like eating a three-course lunch after your gigantic cooked breakfast, however. Also good value are the pre-theatre dinners offered by many restaurants in the larger towns and cities (you don't need to have a theatre ticket to take advantage). These are usually available from around 1730-1800 till 1900-1930. The biggest problem with eating out in the UK is the ludicrously limited serving hours in most pubs and hotels. These places only serve food between 1230 and 1400 and 1700 and 1900, seemingly ignorant of the eating habits of foreign visitors, or those who would prefer a bit more flexibility during their holiday. In small places especially it can be difficult finding food outside these strictly enforced times.

Drink

Drinking is a national hobby and sometimes a dangerous one at that. Real ale – flat, brown beer known as bitter, made with hops – is the national drink, but now struggles to maintain its market share in the face of fierce competition from continental lagers and alcopops. Many small independent breweries are still up and running though, as well as microbreweries attached to individual pubs. Cider (fermented apple juice) is also experiencing a resurgence of interest as small producers perfect recipes that smack deliciously of the countryside. In Scotland, connoisseurs should sample one of the many excellent types of **heavy**, which is a thick, dark ale served at room temperature with a full, creamy head. Types of heavy are graded by the shilling, which indicates its strength; the higher the number the stronger the beer. The usual range is 60 to 80 shillings (written 80/-). No visit to Scotland would be complete without availing oneself of a 'wee dram' – but make sure it's a single malt. See pages 764 and 818

The pub is still the traditional place to enjoy a drink: the best are usually 'freehouses' (not tied to a brewery) and feature real log or coal fires in winter, flower-filled gardens for the summer (even in cities occasionally) and most importantly, thriving local custom. In the countryside, many also offer characterful accommodation, and hence may call themselves an 'inn'. Bars tend to be more contemporary in design, with lots of blonde wood and chrome, though in Scotland pubs are also called bars. Pubs and bars are usually open from 1100 till 2300 Monday-Saturday and Sunday from 1100-1200 till 2230. In towns and cities many pubs are open till 2400 or 0100 on Friday and Saturday nights, or even later in Edinburgh, which has more relaxed licensing laws.

Entertainment

Britain enjoys one of the most vibrant arts and entertainment scenes in Europe. London is often accused of soaking up all the talent in the performance arts, although a trip to Bristol, Birmingham, Cardiff, Edinburgh, Glasgow, Manchester, Newcastle or Leeds will quickly prove that the regions are alive and kicking. All these cities play host on a regular basis to world-class theatre, music and dance, and plenty of smaller towns and villages have also made a name for themselves with their festivals and events (see below). Again, it's the sheer variety of what's on offer that impresses most and much of it of a very high standard. See individual town Entertainment sections for local listings.

Nightlife in the regions is wide awake too, although thankfully still only in the major towns and cities. Every Thursday to Saturday most of the Midlands, Sheffield and Tyneside get mad, bad and dangerous to know, usually but not always very enjoyably so, with an astonishing array of restaurants, bars, pubs and nightclubs. Manchester, Leeds and Liverpool have practically turned their ailing fortunes around simply on the strengh of their music scene and party atmosphere alone and Glasgow remains one of the most up-for-it cities in Europe when it comes to having a good time.

Festivals and events

Festival time is when the normally repressed British shake off the yolk of inhibition and let rip. Summer in Britain is punctuated by an astonishing number of festivals – many of them centuries-old – ranging from the quaint to the dangerously eccentric. Every town, village and hamlet has its own tradition, some involving months of careful planning and preparation of costumes and choreography, others requiring simply a worrying desire to make a complete and utter fool of oneself. A particular feature of the British summer is the music festival. During the months of July and August the country moves to the beat of a thousand rock bands and dance DJs, proving that there's more to life than Glastonbury. In Scotland the most popular tourist events are the **Highland Games** (or Gatherings), a series of competitions involving lots of kilts, bagpipes and caber-tossing, which are held from June to September. See also individual town Festivals sections also visit www.whatsonwhen .com

Festival faves

January Up-Helly-Aa Re-enactment of the ancient Viking fire festival held on Shetland. **Burns Night** Burns suppers held on 25th all over Scotland to celebrate the poet's birthday. Lots of haggis, whisky and poetry recitals.
April **Boat Race**, first weekend in April. The 149-year-old race between Oxford and Cambridge Universities held on the Thames.
May May Day, 1 May. Celebrated up and down the land. Highlights include Morris Dancers strutting their stuff atop a huge, erect chalk penis at Cerne Abbas in Doset.
June **Glastonbury Festival**, last weekend in June, at Pilton, near Glastonbury. The UK's biggest and best music festival. **Wimbledon**, two weeks of tennis, tears and tantrums in southwest in London.
July **Henley Royal Regatta**, first week in July. Large gathering of hooray Henrys and Henriettas horsing around on the River Thames. T01491-572153.
August **Edinburgh Festival**, the greatest arts extravaganza on the planet, held over three weeks in August. **Notting Hill Carnival**, August Bank Holiday weekend. Largest street festival in Europe, T020-7229 3819.
November Guy Fawkes Night, 5 November. Bonfires are lit and fireworks set off in everywhere in the country (see also page 142).
December Hogmanay Old year's night, and the most important Scottish celebration. Edinburgh's huge street party is the largest such celebration in the northern hemisphere.

Public holidays

New Year's Day (1st January); Easter (March/April) Good Friday and Easter Monday; May Day Bank Holiday (1st Monday in May); Spring Bank Holiday (last Monday in May); August Bank Holiday (last Monday in August); Christmas Day (25th December); and Boxing Day (26th December).

Shopping

Shopping in Britain is expensive when compared with the rest of Europe and the US. Even so, the variety of different opportunities makes browsing a real treat, even in some of the smallest villages. Although the brand names of the big retail chains may come to seem depressingly familiar in town centres and High Streets up and down the country, independent retailers are still just about holding out in pockets around them, especially in the north of England and parts of Scotland and Wales. Shop hours are generally Monday to Saturday from 0900-1730 or 1800. In larger towns and cities, many shops also open on Sundays and late at night, usually on a Thursday and Friday. Large supermarkets and retail complexes found outside large towns are open till 2000 or later Monday-Saturday and till 1600 on Sunday. In more remote parts few shops are open on Sunday, most notably in the Outer Hebrides where nothing is open on a Sunday. Also note that in many rural areas there is an early-closing day when shops close at 1300. This varies from region to region, but the most common day is Wednesday.

Sport and activities

Climbing and hillwalking

Walking is popular in Britain and there's a wide variety of walking terrain, from the gentle, rolling downs of the south to the more rocky peaks of northern England, Scotland and Wales. Some of the most popular areas for walking in England are in the National Parks. The **Lake District** offers by far the toughest challenge, with proper mountains, but also the greatest rewards. Next in terms of popularity are the **Yorkshire Dales** and the **Peak District**, while Northumbria offers a couple of excellent routes in **Hadrian's Wall** and the **Coast Walk**. Walking in the south of England is altogether gentler, and the likelihood of good weather greater. The three main routes are the **South Downs Way**, **Cotswold Way** and the **South West Coast Path**, which at 630 miles travels around the entire Cornish peninsula and offers some amazing scenery.

There is a network of long-distance paths (LDPs) carefully prepared to provide ideal walking conditions together with sufficient places for accommodation and supplies en route. These walks can be attempted in full or sampled in part by less experienced walkers. Area tourist boards and local tourist offices can provide information and advice for their own particular sections. These include the 259-mile **Pennine Way**, from Edale to Kirk Yetholm (in Scotland) and the Coast to Coast Walk, from St Bees in the west to Robin Hood's Bay in the east.

The toughest, and most rewarding walking is to be found in Scotland and Wales. Here, there are plenty of opportunities to get off the beaten track and explore the wild countryside. The hugely popular **West Highland Way**, stretching from Milngavie near Glasgow to Fort William, is only one of a number of long-distance paths. One of the best known in Wales is the **Offa's Dyke Path**, a 178-mile journey running from the Severn Estuary in Chepstow to the northern coast near Prestatyn. Another recommended LDP is the **Pembrokeshire Coast Path** (186 miles of spectacular cliff-top scenery).

The best time for hiking in the mountains is from May to September, though in the more low-lying parts, April to October should be safe. Winter walking in the Highlands requires equipment such as ice axes and crampons as well as experience. July and August are the busiest times, though only the most popular routes, such as Ben Nevis, get really crowded. Another problem during these months are midges. May to mid-June is probably the most pleasant time, as the weather can often be fine and the midges have yet to appear. September is also a good time, though it can be colder.

Many of the hills are straightforward climbs, but many also entail a high level of fitness and experience, and all require proper clothing. Visitors should be aware of the need for caution and safety preparations when walking or climbing in the mountains, especially in the Scottish Highlands or Lake District. The nature of British weather is such that a sunny day can turn into driving rain or snow in minutes. A blizzard can be raging on the summit when the car park at the foot of the mountain is bathed in sunshine. It is essential to get an up-to-date weather forecast before setting off on any walk or climb.

The country is covered by the excellent series of maps published by Ordnance Survey (OS). The most detailed are the Outdoor Leisure series which covers areas such as national parks at a scale of 1:25,000, but the Landranger series (1:50,000) which covers the entire country, is detailed enough for most walks. OS maps can be found at tourist offices and also at outdoor shops.

Useful contacts There are a number of organizations that can help with suggested routes, maps or people to get in touch with. The biggest is the **Ramblers' Association**, T020-7339 8500, www.ramblers.org.uk, which has resources in different languages. Other good sources of information are www.walkingbritain.co.uk and the **British Tourist Authority**, www.visitbritain.com/walking

 Climbing The Cairngorms and Cuillins on Skye offer the most challenging climbing in Britain, as do Glencoe and Torridon. Visitors to Scotland, however, should be aware of the need for caution and safety preparations when walking or climbing in the mountains. **In the winter** extra warm clothing is needed, as well as an **ice axe** and **crampons** (and the ability to use them). The skills required for moving over ice or snow should be practised with an experienced and qualified mountain guide/instructor. For more detailed information, contact the Mountaineering Council of Scotland, 4a St Catherine's Road, Perth, T01738-638227.

Cycling and mountain biking

Britain is not particularly cycle-friendly. If you want to explore the country by bike it's best to stick to rural backroads, especially unclassified roads and country lanes, which are not numbered but are signposted and marked on OS maps. The only problem with more remote areas is the scarcity of spare parts should something go wrong with your machine. There are also forest trails and dedicated routes along canal towpaths and disused railway tracks. These are part of the expanding National Cycle Network which is covered by the *Official Guide to the National Network* (£9.99), published by the charity SUSTRANS. There is also a series of demanding long-distance routes. **Useful contacts Cyclists' Touring Club** (CTC), Cotterell House, 69 Meadrow, Godalming, Surrey, GU7 3HS, T01483-417217, www.ctc.org.uk The largest cycling organization in the UK, providing a wide range of services and information on transport, cycle hire and routes, from day rides to longer tours. **SUSTRANS**, T0117-9290888, www.sustrans.co.uk

You can cut down on the amount of pedalling you have to do by transporting your bike by train. Bikes can be taken free on most local rail services on a first come-first served basis, and only outside morning and evening rush hours (0730-0930 and 1600-1900). On long-distance routes you'll have to make a reservation at least 24 hours in advance and pay a small charge. Space is limited on trains so it's a good idea to book as far in advance as possible. Bus and coach companies will not carry bikes, unless they are dismantled and boxed. Details are available on the CTC website.

Bike rental is available at cycle shops in most large towns and cities and tourist centres. Expect to pay from around £10-20 per day, with discounts for longer periods, plus a refundable deposit. There are cycle shops in most large towns, and smaller towns and villages in popular tourist areas. Addresses and phone numbers are given under the transport sections of individual towns in this book. See individual town Directory sections for local cycle hire companies.

Diving

There are thousands of dive sites around Scotland's shores, with a rich variety of marine life and plenty of wrecks to explore. The **West Coast** offers the best diving, as the water is warmed by the effects of the Gulf Stream and is not cold, even without a dry suit. Among the best sites are the **west coast of Harris**, the **Summer Isles** and the remote island of **St Kilda**. There are lots of wrecks in the **Sound of Mull**, and the chance to find a Spanish Galleon off **Tobermory**. **Scapa Flow** in Orkney is world-renowned as the burial site of the German World War I fleet. On the **East Coast**, there is a great marine reserve off **St Abb's Head**, near Eyemouth, with some spectacular rock formations. Contact the **Scottish Sub Aqua Club**, 40 Bogmoor Place, Glasgow, G51 4TQ, T0141-4251021.

Golf

Scotland is the home of golf and has more courses per head of population than any other country in the world. One of the unique attractions of golf in Scotland is the accessibility of its famous venues. These include Carnoustie, St Andrews or Turnberry. **Green fees** for one of the top championship courses will cost from around £40 upwards. Many clubs offer a daily or weekly ticket. A **Golf Pass Scotland** costs between £46 and £70 for five days (Monday-Friday), depending on the area. *Golf in*

Scotland is a free brochure listing 400 courses and clubs with accommodation details. For a copy contact the *Scottish Tourist Board*. The *British Tourist Authority* (BTA) has a very useful *Golfing Holidays* booklet which provides details of golfing holidays and major golf tournaments in Britain. (BTA and STB address on page 20).

Skiing

Conditions in Scotland are not as good or reliable as anywhere in the Alps, but on a clear, sunny day, and with good snow, you can enjoy some decent skiing. However, at weekends, in conditions like these, expect the slopes to be very busy. Scotland offers both **alpine** (downhill) and **nordic** (cross-country) skiing, as well as the increasingly popular **snowboarding**. The high season is from January to April, but it is possible to ski from as early as November to as late as May. Ski packages are available, but it's easy to arrange everything yourself and there's plentiful accommodation and facilities in and around the ski centres. There are five ski centres in Scotland. The largest are **Glenshee** (see page 778), which has the most extensive network of lifts and selection of runs, as well as snow machines, and **Cairngorm** (see page 878), which has almost 30 runs spread over an extensive area. **Glencoe** (see page 848) is the oldest of the ski resorts, and the **Nevis Range**, at Aonach Mor near Fort William (see page 844), has the highest ski runs and only gondola in Scotland, as well as a dry slope. The **Lecht** (see page 816) is the most remote centre, and is good for beginners and families and for nordic skiing. Access to all five centres is easiest by car. Each resort has a ski patrol and facilities for snowboarding. For further general information contact the **Scottish Tourist Board** for its *Ski Scotland* brochure and accommodation list, or visit their website, www.ski.scotland.net, which is updated daily. Or you can contact the **Scottish National Ski Council**, T0131-3177280, www.snsc.demon.co.uk They produce a useful *Snowsport Scotland Handbook*.

Surfing

Britain may not be top of your list when you're thinking of that perfect break, but surfing is becoming increasingly popular across the UK, and there are some great waves to be found, especially in Cornwall and along the northeast coast, from Scarborough to Berwick-upon-Tweed. Wherever you surf, you'll need a wetsuit and, depending on how tough you are, boots, gloves and hat. Generally, the best surf is to be found in late summer/early Autumn. Most surf spots in England are beach breaks, and there are hundreds of remote and scenic beaches to choose from. The better-known ones are on Cornwall's north coast.

If you're planning a serious surf trip, you should also consider travelling to the far north of Scotland, where the waves are on a par with Hawaii, which unfortunately can't be said of the weather. Surfing in Scotland is strictly for the hardy, with water temperatures rarely above 15°C and often as low as 7°C. A good wet suit is therefore essential. The main season is September to December. The best beaches are to be found at the northern tip of the **Isle of Lewis** and at **Thurso**, especially at Dunnet Head to the east of town. Wales also has some stunning surf beaches. One of the favourites among aficionados is **Llangennith** on the Gower Peninsula. In Pembrokeshire, **Freshwater West** has an awesome reputation. To find a break and get information on facilities including board rental, accommodation, tide charts and surf reports, try www.surf-uk.org.uk.

Wildlife watching

Almost anywhere around the northern coasts of Scotland there is a chance to see dolphins and occasionally porpoises, seals and whales. The most popular place to see **dolphins** is in the Moray Firth area which has a resident population of about 150, most frequently seen in the summer months. **Seals** can be seen in abundance. They can often be observed lolling about on sandbanks when the tide is out, and there are plenty of seal-spotting boat trips on offer from spring to autumn. **Otters** are more elusive. They tend to live on undisturbed remote stretches of the seashore or quiet areas of a river. If you are determined to spot the creatures, for further information contact **Skye Environmental Centre** (home to the **International Otter Survival Fund**, T01471-822487. **Whales**, Minke and Orcas, inhabit the Atlantic, Pentland Firth and the Moray Firth. See under Gairloch and Tobermory.

Spectator sports

Football

Football is the king of British sport. The passion generated by the game is unmatched – not only in any other national sport but also in almost any other walk of life. Anyone with more than just a passing interest should certainly endeavour to catch a game while they're here. The football season runs from mid-August to early May. Most matches are played on Saturday, at 1500, and there are also midweek games (mostly on Wednesdays) and some games on Sunday afternoons and Monday evenings. Ticket prices range from £20 and upwards for top-class games, to £15 and less for the lower divisions.

Cricket

If one sport sums up the English mentality then it must be cricket. Two teams will battle it out for four of five days and then at the end, having had to spend most of the time watching from the pavilion as the rain pours down, settle for a draw. Tickets for internationals are very hard to come by. If you can't get a ticket, and don't fancy watching on TV, then you can witness the zen-like atmosphere of a county cricket match, which takes place over four days, from the comfort of a deckchair. There are also one-day competitions. Ticket prices for international Test matches range from £15 to £40 for one day. One-day international cost £20-50, while county games cost less than £10. For details of forthcoming Tests and county fixture, contact the **England and Wales Cricket Board** (ECB), Lord's Cricket Ground, St John's Wood, London NW8 8QN, T020-7432 1200.

Rugby

The 'hard game' is actually two distinct games: **Rugby Union** and **Rugby League**. While the latter (13-a-side) variety is of working-class origins and largely played in the northern towns and cities of England, the former (15-a-side) variety originates from the country's fee-paying public schools, hence the name – Rugby. Though 'rugger' lags behind football and cricket in terms of mass appeal it has, in recent years, been earning plenty of column inches in the sports pages, mainly thanks to England's World Cup success. England now dominate the annual Six Nations Championship (comprising England, Scotland, Wales, Ireland, France and Italy) which is held around February and March.

Tennis

The well-mannered suburb of southwest London is home to the **All England Lawn Tennis and Croquet Club**, which hosts the only 'Grand Slam' tennis tournament played on grass. For details of how to find a ticket for Wimbledon visit www.wimbledon.com.

Health

No vaccinations are required for entry into Britain. Citizens of EU countries are entitled to free medical treatment at National Health Service hospitals on production of an E111 form. Also, Australia, New Zealand and several other non-EU European countries have reciprocal health-care arrangements with Britain. Citizens of other countries will have to pay for all medical services, except accident and emergency care given at

Accident and Emergency (A&E) Units at most (but not all) National Health hospitals.
Health insurance is therefore strongly advised for citizens of non-EU countries.

Pharmacists can dispense only a limited range of drugs without a doctor's prescription. Most are open for normal shop hours, though some are open late. Local newspapers carry lists of which are open late. **Doctors' surgeries** are usually open from around 0830-0900 till 1730-1800. Outside surgery hours you can go to the casualty department of the local hospital for any complaint requiring urgent attention. For the address of the nearest hospital or doctors' surgery, T0800-665544.

Medical emergency: dial 999 or 112 (both free) for an ambulance. See individual town directory sections for hospital and medical services listings

Keeping in touch

Communications

Internet

Many hotels and hostels offer internet access to their guests, and cybercafés are springing up all over the place (these are listed in the directory sections of individual towns in the main travelling section of this book). Email works out much, much cheaper than phoning home, and is also useful for booking hotels and tours and for checking out information on the web. However, some internet cafés are expensive, and it may be worth enquiring whether they operate a discount card scheme. In the absence of any internet cafés listed under a particular town listing, try the public library for internet access or ask at the tourist office.

Post

Most **post offices** are open Monday-Friday 0900-1730 and Saturday 0900-1230 or 1300. Many smaller sub-post offices operate out of a shop. Some rural offices may close on Wednesday afternoon.

Telephone

Telephone operator, T100; International operator, T155; national directory enquiries, 118 500 (calls to this number cost £0.20); overseas directory enquiries, T153. Any number prefixed by 0800 or 0500 is free to the caller. Note that many cell phones from the USA/Canada/Latin America will not work in the UK.

Most payphones are operated by **British Telecom (BT)** and can be found evrywhere, BT payphones take either coins (20p, 50p, £1 and occasionally £2) or phonecards, which are available at newsagents, post offices and supermarkets displaying the BT logo. These cards come in denominations of £3, £5, £10 and £20. Some payphones also accept credit cards (Delta, Visa and Diners Club). For most countries (including Europe, USA and Canada) calls are cheapest between 1800 and 0800 Monday-Friday and all day Saturday and Sunday. For Australia and New Zealand it's cheapest to call from 1430 to 1930 and from midnight to 0700 every day. To call Britain from overseas, dial 011 from USA and Canada, 0011 from Australia and 00 from New Zealand, followed by 44, then the area code minus the first zero, then the number. To call overseas from Britain dial 00 followed by the country code and the number (minus the first zero). Country codes include: Australia 61; France 33; Ireland 353; New Zealand 64; South Africa 27; USA and Canada 1. Most phone boxes display a list of international dialling codes

Media

Newspapers

Newspapers are published nationally, with all the main daily and Sunday newspapers widely available throughout the UK. Some, (e.g. The Guardian and many tabloid newspapers) publish regional editions. There is a huge variety of national newspapers and competition between them is fierce. The national dailies are divided into two distinct camps; the tabloids, which are more downmarket; and the broadsheets, which are generally of a higher standard. Foreign visitors may find the broadsheets easier to understand as they tend to use less slang than the tabloids.

The broadsheets include *The Times* and *The Daily Telegraph*, which are politically conservative, and *The Guardian* and *The Independent*, which have more of a liberal/left-wing leaning. There's also the distinctively coloured and very serious *Financial Times*, which focuses on business and finance. The Saturday editions of these papers carry their own listings guides with useful reviews of movies, clubs, restaurants, theatre, etc. The broadsheets' Sunday versions are huge and would take most of your holiday to read thoroughly. They include the *Independent on Sunday*, *Sunday Times*, *Sunday Telegraph* and the *Observer* (a stablemate of *The Guardian*).

The list of tabloids (known also as redtops) comprises *The Sun* and *The Mirror* which are the most popular and provide celebrity gossip and extensive sports coverage, the *Daily Mail* and *Daily Express* which are right-wing and aimed directly at 'Middle England'. The tabloids have their own Sunday versions, which, are, if anything, even more salacious: these include the notorious *News of the World*; the *Sunday Mirror*, *Sunday People* and *Sunday Sport*.

Foreign newspapers and magazines, including the *Die Zeit, Le Monde, El Pais, USA Today* and *The New York Times* are widely available in larger city newsagents, at airports and in railway stations.

Television

There are five main television channels in the UK; the publicly funded BBC 1 and 2, and the independent commercial stations ITV, Channel 4 and Channel 5. The BBC and ITV both offer regional programming, some of which is aimed at local special interest.

The paucity of channels is more than made up for by the generally high standard of programming, especially in news, documentaries and drama. There are plenty of imported US shows, game shows and reality TV as well, but if you want to get a sense of what Britain is about, one evening watching TV during your trip is a good way of getting it. If, however, the terrestrial channels can't satisfy you, you can approach one of the various digital cable TV companies, such as **Sky Digital**, which currently has 170 channels, and **ONdigital**. Packages include movie channels such as **FilmFour, Sky Movies** and the **Movie Channel**, as well as sports-only channels like **Sky Sports,** which also show sports from around the world. Most upmarket hotels will have at least some of these channels on the TV in your room.

Radio

The BBC network also broadcasts several radio channels, most of which are based in London. These include: **Radio 1** aimed at a young audience; **Radio 2** targeting a more mature audience; **Radio 3** which plays mostly classical music; **Radio 4** which is talk-based and features arts, drama and current affairs; and **Radio 5 Live** which is a mix of sport and news. In addition, the BBC broadcasts on local and regional affairs, through a network of local radio stations. There are a large number commercial radio stations including **Jazz FM** (102.2), **Virgin FM** (1215AM, rock), **Classic FM** (99.9-101.9FM), and hundreds of local radio stations (try **XFM** on 104.9 FM in London), which can all be found at the touch of a dial.

London

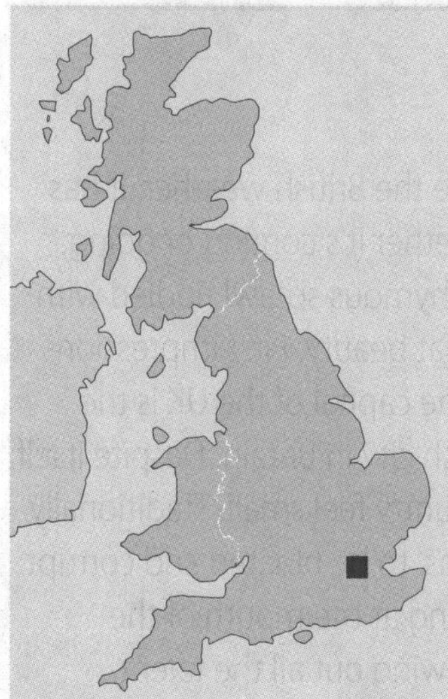

Introduction

London is a great big jumble. Like the British weather, it has difficulty making up its mind whether it's coming or going. The city is a hotch-potch, an anonymous sprawl riddled with diversity, character and often great beauty. First impressions are likely to be decidely mixed: the capital of the UK is the largest and apparently least British city in Britain. Despite itself, London makes the rest of the country feel small. Traditionally it's been perceived by 'the regions' to be bloated and corrupt, an overblown metropolis squatting at the mouth of the Thames, daily sucking in and spewing out all the talent, energy and traffic within a 50-mile radius. Not a pretty sight, you might think. And yet, and yet… Dilapidated and shambolic, the city wheezes into the 21st century freighted with some shiny new millennium projects – Tate Modern, the London Eye, the Millennium Bridge – and all the old problems: overcrowded accommodation, unreliable transport and alarming prices. The good news though is that finally there seems to be a determination to do something about it: all the major museums are free; the Channel Tunnel rail link to St Pancras is in development; and the city centre congestion charge is having a radical and very desirable effect. London still rejects any attempt to make it conform to expectations. With its ethnic mix, street markets and multinational business, its political pragmatism and creative chaos, London remains one of the most global, engaging and invigorating places on the planet.

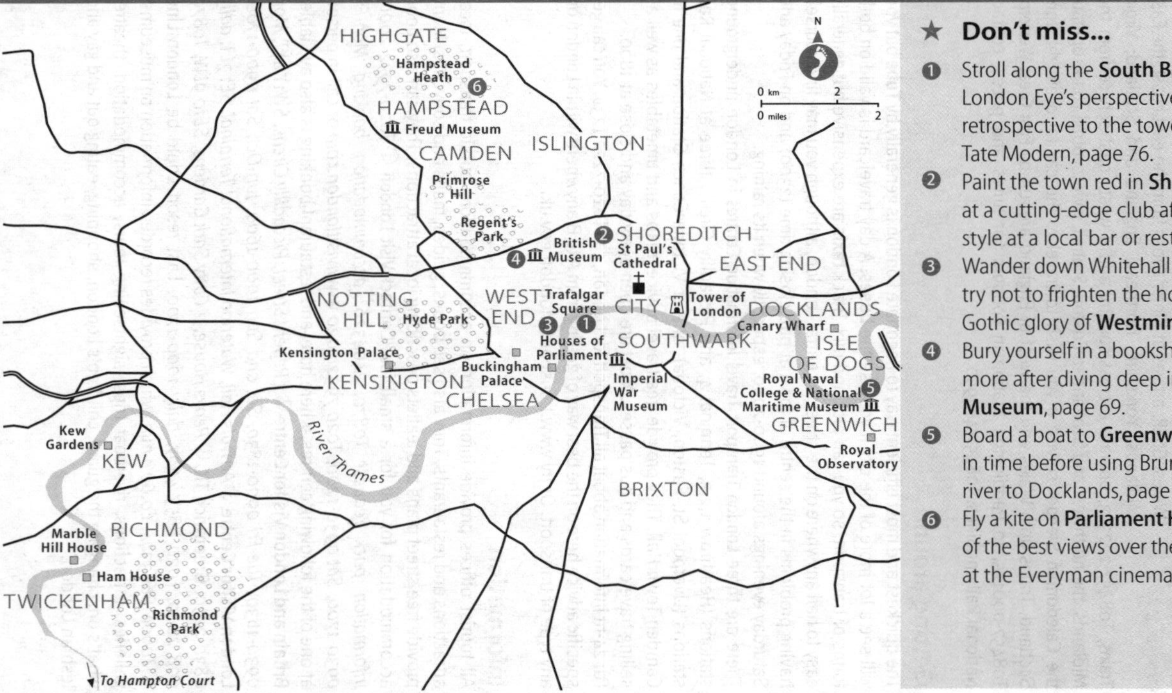

★ Don't miss...

1. Stroll along the **South Bank** of the river from the London Eye's perspective and a Saatchi Gallery retrospective to the towering talent on display at Tate Modern, page 76.
2. Paint the town red in **Shoreditch** or **Clerkenwell** at a cutting-edge club after drinking and dining in style at a local bar or restaurant, page 99.
3. Wander down Whitehall from Trafalgar Square and try not to frighten the horses before taking in the Gothic glory of **Westminster Abbey**, page 62.
4. Bury yourself in a bookshop in Bloomsbury to learn more after diving deep into the past at the **British Museum**, page 69.
5. Board a boat to **Greenwich** for a breezy ride back in time before using Brunel's foot tunnel under the river to Docklands, page 82.
6. Fly a kite on **Parliament Hill** in Hampstead for some of the best views over the city and then catch a film at the Everyman cinema, page 83.

Ins and outs

Getting there

The main **coach** operator, **National Express**, T08705-808080, www.gobycoach.com, operates out of Victoria Coach Station and has a nationwide network serving more than 1000 destinations. Tickets can be bought at bus stations or from a huge number of agents throughout the country. **Traveline**, T0870-6082608.There are four main companies operating frequent **rail** services between London and other towns and cities in England, Scotland and Wales: **GNER**, arrives at Kings' Cross from the east coast, the East Midlands, Yorkshire, Northeast England and Scotland; **Virgin Trains**, T08457-222333, operate a cross-country and a west coast service from the Midlands, the northwest and Scotland to Euston. **Scotrail**, www.scotrail.co.uk, operate the **Caledonian Sleeper** service if you wish to travel to the capital overnight from Scotland. Trains from Wales and the west of England are run by **First Great Western**, T08457-000125, to Paddington Station in London. For times and prices, contact National Rail enquiries: T08457-484950.

For information on getting to London from outside the UK, and from the city's airports, see page 27.

Getting around

The quickest and most efficient way to negotiate London is generally by **Tube** but you will see a lot more of the city if you use the **buses**. A day travelcard is valid on both forms of transport, so you can pick and mix. Black **taxis** are expensive but generally easy to hail anywhere on the street in central London, although you may find yourself having problems in the centre of town at pub closing time (2300) and on Friday and Saturday evenings around 1900-2000, especally when its raining.

There are three **London Transport Travel Information Centres** in London underground stations (Heathrow 1,2,3, Terminal 4, and Piccadilly Circus, three at National Rail stations (Liverpool St, Euston, Victoria), one at Victoria Coach Station and one in Camden Town Hall. They provide free travel advice, maps and timetables as well as selling travelcards and bus passes. Most are open every day and close at 1800.

For 24-hr information about all Transport for London, call T020-7222 1234. You can get specific advice here on the best way of getting from A to B anywhere within London on any type of transport. Or try www.transportforlondon.gov.uk.

Information

All tourist offices provide information on accommodation, public transport, local attractions and restaurants. They also sell books, guides, maps and souvenirs. Many provide free street plans and leaflets describing local attractions. They can also book accommodation for you for a small fee. Contact **Visit London** ⓘ *T020-7932 2000, information pack request T0870 2404326, accommodation booking Mon-Fri 0930-1700, Sat 0930-1200, T020 7932 2020 www.visitlondon.com* or call in person at one of the following centres, where hotel and restaurant booking is also available: **Britain and London Visitor Centre** ⓘ *1 Regent Street, Piccadilly Circus, SW1Y 4XT, Mon 0930-1830, Tue-Fri 0900-1830, Sat and Sun 1000-1600, Jun-Oct, Sat 0900-1700.* **London Visitor Centre** ⓘ *Arrivals Hall, Waterloo International Terminal, SE1 7LT, daily 0830-2230.* **Greenwich TIC** ⓘ *Pepys House, 2 Cutty Sark Gardens, SE10 9LW, T0870 608 2000, F020 8853 4607, daily 1000-1700.* Last resort could be **London Line** ⓘ *T0906-8663344, £0.60 a min*, which provides recorded information on museums, galleries, attractions, riverboat trips, sightseeing tours, accommodation, theatre, what's on, changing the guard, children's London, shopping, eating out and gay and lesbian London.

24 hours in London

Seeing much of London in a day is really only for the brave, although with sensible shoes and some stamina it can certainly be attempted. Try the following as a suggested tour. Start the day with a coffee from one of the outlets near the Embankment tube. Take a croissant into the **Victoria Gardens** and sit among the statuary. Stroll across Hungerford Footbridge (the right hand side of the railway is best for views of the London Eye and Houses of Parliament) and then turn left for a 20-min walk along the South Bank. Pass beneath Waterloo Bridge and the Royal National Theatre to be at **Tate Modern** on Bankside when it opens at 1000. Here you can see some modern and contemporary art in a converted power station and the morning sun catching the dome of St Paul's Cathedral across the river. After digesting as much of the artwork as you like, head for lunch in **Soho** by taking the tube from Southwark northwards on the Jubilee Line to Green Park and walking east down Piccadilly to the Circus. If you want to see the outside of **Buckingham Palace** make a detour across Green Park itself before heading down Piccadilly. After a leisurely lunch in Soho, somewhere like **Patisserie Valerie** perhaps, or a browse around the shops, walk east across Tottenham Court Road to the **British Museum** (about 20-mins again). Spend the afternoon wondering at some of the things in the finest museum in the country. Head out to **Clerkenwell** for supper, a well-deserved steak at Smith's perhaps, and then dance the night away at **Fabric** or another of the area's clubs. Stumble out again at daybreak and get yourself a hearty breakfast and pint of Guinness in the **Cock Tavern** in **Smithfield Market**, after which you should feel sufficiently restored to remember where your hotel is.

Central London

Trafalgar Square → *Tube: Charing Cross*

Trafalgar Square is the centre of London, avoided by Londoners if at all possible. It's the lynch pin of the West End's tourist triangle between Piccadilly Circus and Leicester Square. But it's the breadth of Whitehall approaching from Westminster and the south that explains the prominence of the square in London's geography. This is where the administrative offices of government meet the people, and the monarch comes too, with The Mall marching straight up from Buckingham Palace into the southwest corner through Admiralty Arch. The recently pedestrianised north side of the square in front of the National Gallery makes it a much more attractive space to hang out.

The square itself, hardly very beautiful, well-designed, or even square, does at least have a focal point in Nelson's Column. Admiral Horatio Nelson is just about the only military commander ever to have been truly taken to heart by the British people. Even so, it took 40 years after he was mortally wounded while defeating Napoleon's navy at Trafalgar in 1805 before his Column was finally erected. Around the base the bronze relief sculptures were cast from captured French cannons, celebrating his sea victories at Copenhagen, the Nile, and Cape St Vincent, as well as Trafalgar. The oldest and finest of the buildings surrounding the square is the **Church of St Martin-in-the-Fields** ⓘ *T020-7766 1100, Mon-Fri 0745-1800, Sat 0845-1800, Sun 0745-1930.* Like St Mary-le-Strand nearby, but on a larger scale, it's an impressive fusion of classical and Baroque by James Gibbs, dating from 1722-26. The interior includes a font from the original medieval church. Notables such as Joshua Reynolds, Hogarth, and Charles II's mistress Nell Gwynne are buried in the churchyard. Regular

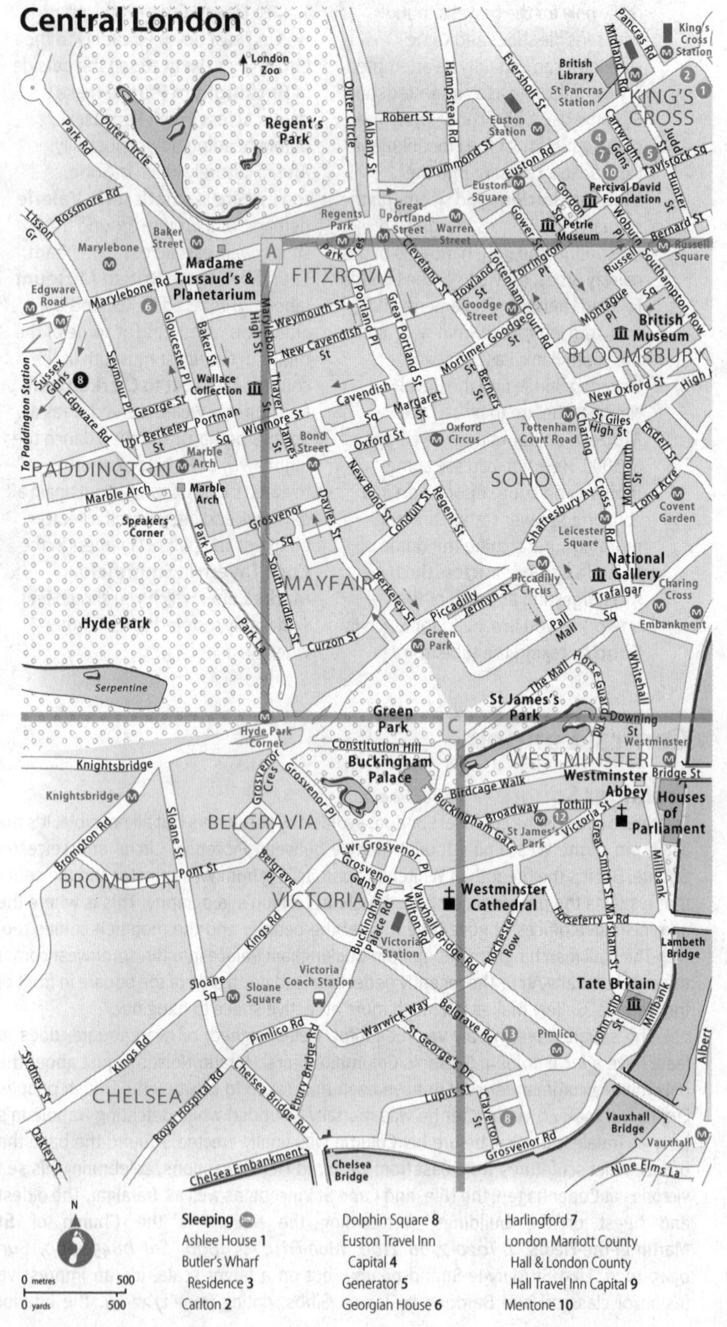

lunchtime and evening concerts are also given here and there's an excellent café in the crypt (see Eating section).

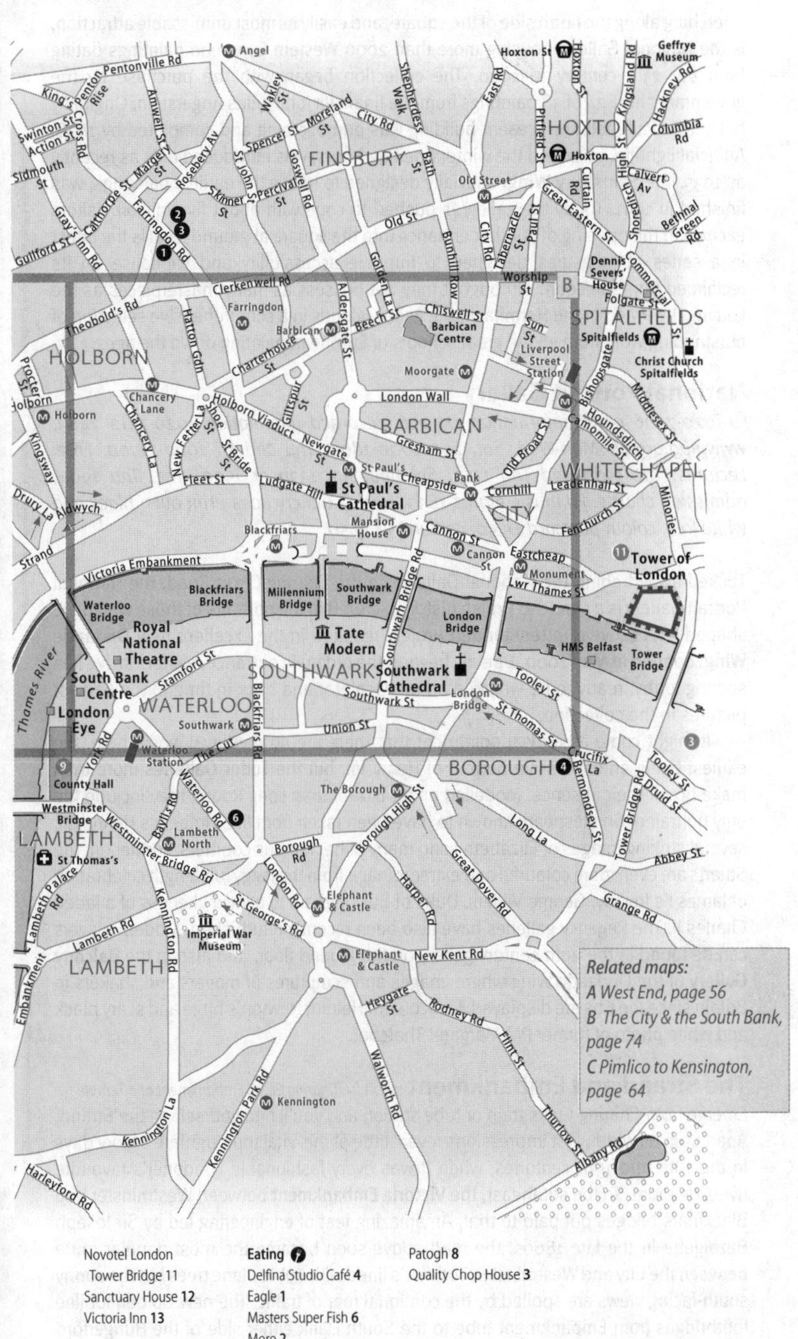

National Gallery

ⓘ *T020-7747 2885, www.nationalgallery.org.uk, daily 1000-1800, Wed 1000-2100. Free.*

Stretching along the north side of the square, and easily its most unmissable attraction, is the National Gallery, housing more than 2000 Western European paintings dating from the 13th century to 1900. The collection began with the purchase by the government in 1824 of 38 paintings from the financier John Julius Angerstein. Originally housed in Pall Mall, the present building was purpose built and completed by 1838. Artificial lighting, to extend the winter opening hours, was introduced only as recently as 1935. The **Sainsbury Wing**, specially designed to house the earliest paintings, was finished in 1991. Today the gallery is pushed to cope with about five million visitors each year: the opening of another entrance into the square at ground level is the latest in a series of measures designed to improve accessibility and capitalise on its reclaimed front forecourt. Although it may not possess as many masterpieces as the Louvre, the Prado or the Hermitage, the gallery glories in a comprehensive selection of outstanding work from all the great schools of European painting down the ages.

National Portrait Gallery

ⓘ *T020-7306 0055, information ext 216, recorded information T020-7312 2463, www.npg.org.uk Mon-Wed, Sat, Sun 1000-1800, Thu and Fri 1000- 2100. Free. Lectures: Tue 1500 and Thu 1310, Sat and Sun 1330 or 1500, free. Thu 1900, admission charge. Fri music nights 1830, free. IT Gallery does print outs; black and white free, colour postcard £5.50, colour A4 £17.50.*

Tucked away behind the National Gallery, up the Charing Cross Road, the National Portrait Gallery is a shrine to British history pictured in the portraits of those who have shaped it. A six-year lottery-funded project resulted in the excellent new **Ondaatje Wing**, opened in May 2000. Directly beyond the old main entrance, visitors arrive in a soaring lobby, ready to be whisked up an escalator and back in time to the earliest pictures in the collection.

It might come as a disappointment that there are no medieval works here, the earliest being an impressive portrait of Henry VII, but the **Tudor Galleries** more than make up for their absence. Modelled on an Elizabethan Long Room, they include the only portrait of Shakespeare known to have been taken from life, Holbein's Henry VIII, several striking images of Elizabeth I and many of her famous courtiers. Further on, the Stuarts are even more colourful and extraordinary: from the leggy full-length celebration of James I's toyboy, George Villiers, Duke of Buckingham to a vivid likeness of a jaded Charles II. The Regency galleries have also been recently refurbished. Modern players can be found in the 20th century gallery on the ground floor, and also in the **Balcony Gallery** of the Ondaatje Wing where images and sculptures of movers and shakers in Britain since the 60s are displayed. Look out for Helmut Newton's huge and scary black and white photo of former PM Margaret Thatcher.

The Strand and Embankment → *Tube: Charing Cross, Embankment and Temple*

Emerge from Charing Cross train or tube station and you'll find yourself on the Strand. Apart from its width, first impressions reveal little of this vital thoroughfare's glory days in the 18th and 19th centuries, when it was every fashionable Londoner's favourite riverside prom. To the southeast, the **Victoria Embankment** between Westminster and Blackfriars bridges put paid to that. An amazing feat of engineering led by Sir Joseph Bazalgette in the late 1860s, the road above soon became the most popular route between the City and Westminster. Today it's lined with noble plane trees but the sunny south-facing views are spoiled by the continual roar of traffic. The new Golden Jubilee footbridges from Embankment tube to the South Bank either side of the Hungerford railbridge now provide superb views of the riverbanks east and west.

Cleopatra's Needle is easily the oldest thing around here, and just about the oldest monument in London exposed to the weather. The pink granite obelisk is one of a pair that once stood in Heliopolis, around 1500 BC, long before the Egyptian queen with the famous nose, although the inscriptions on the stone apparently refer to her. It was given to George IV by the viceroy of Egypt in 1820 but only made it to the banks of the Thames over 50 years later.

Somerset House

Further east along the Strand, on the right, stands Somerset House, acclaimed as one of the most important 18th-century buildings in Europe. It was designed by Sir William Chambers in 1776 for George III's Naval office, with the wings on the Strand purpose-built for the fledgling Royal Academy of Arts (which was founded in 1768 but moved to Piccadilly in 1837), the Royal Society, and the Society of Antiquaries. Appropriately enough, since 1990, this northern wing has been occupied by the **Courtauld Institute and Gallery** ⓘ *T020-7848 2526, www.courtauld.ac.uk Daily 1000-1800 (last entry 1715), £5, under 18s free, concession £4. Joint ticket with Gilbert Collection or Hermitage Rooms £8, concession £7, or all three £12, concession £10, free on Mon 1000-1400 except bank holidays.* Ascending the wonderful winding stairway, the 11 rooms afford a delightful potted introduction to Western art; from early Dutch through the Renaissance in Italy and Northern Europe, via Rubens, to the Baroque, 18th-century British portraiture and the post-Impressionists.

As recently as 2000 the southern buildings were opened up to display Arthur Gilbert's collection in what ranks as London's newest museum of decorative art, providing access for the first time to the river frontage. Described as the single most generous gift ever made to the nation, the **Gilbert Collection** ⓘ *T020-7420 9400, daily 1000-1800 (last entry 1715), £5, students and under 18s free, OAPs £4, disabled and helpers £2 (joint ticket with Courtauld Gallery £7, OAPs £5)*, includes an astonishing hoard of gold and silverware, precious snuff boxes and peculiar Roman micromosaics. The most recent addition to the exotic collections at Somerset House are the contents of the **Hermitage Rooms** ⓘ *T020-7845 4630, daily 1000-1800 (last entry 1715), £6, concession £4, children free*, designed to exhibit changing selections of artefacts from the great St Petersburg museum. The five rooms have been decorated in the Imperial style of the Winter Palace, with replica chandeliers, gilded chairs and marquetry floors and include, amongst changing exhibitions, a live feed to St Petersburg, looking across Palace Square, and a 6-min video taking you on a tour of the Hermitage itself.

The great central courtyard of Somerset House has been rechristened the **Edmond J Safra Fountain Court** and blessed with a diverting but controversial computer-operated fountain. In December and January it becomes an open-air **ice rink** ⓘ *Book first, T0870 1660423, www.ticketmaster.co.uk, daily 1000-2200, £9.50, children £6 including skate hire per hr.*

Leicester Square and around → *Tube: Leicester Square or Piccadilly Circus*

Leicester Square always gets bad press, written off as a charmless tourist-trap rife with pickpockets, bagsnatchers and mediocre buskers. Since the little square's pedestrianization and then refurbishment in the early 90s it has provided a much-needed focal point for the entertainment scene in the West End. The two main draws are the cinemas, not only the blockbusting first-run multiscreens surrounding the square, but also places like the cult rep the Prince Charles, or the fashionable Curzon Soho, and the nightclubs, like the Wag, Sound and Limelight. Just north of the square lies **Chinatown**, not really the home of London's Chinese community, more like its market place, and only consisting of a couple of streets of restaurants, but still an area with one of the most distinctive cultural identities in the capital. It squeezes into a little niche between the square itself, **Shaftesbury Avenue**, the high street of 'Theatreland', and **Charing Cross Road**, the bookseller's favourite address.

West End

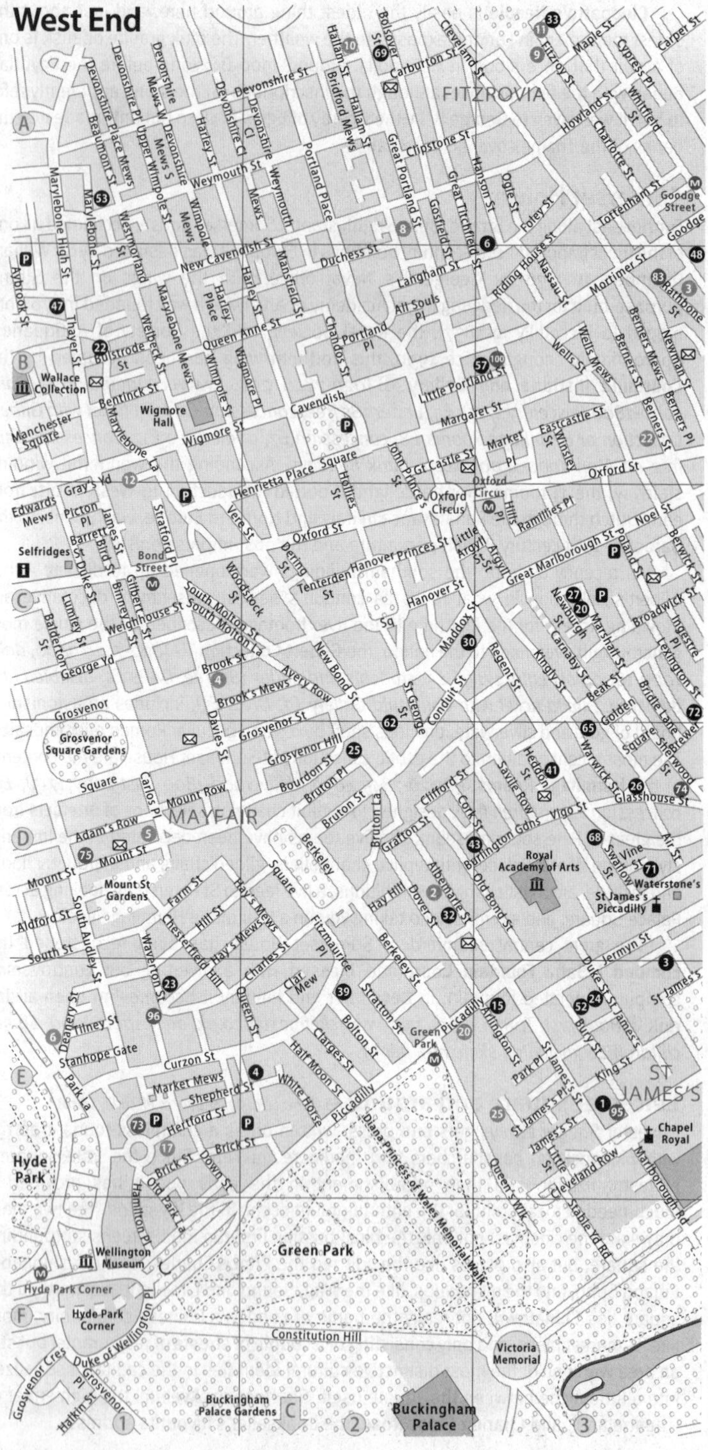
FITZROVIA
MAYFAIR
ST JAMES'S
Devonshire Pl
Devonshire Place Mews
Devonshire Mews W
Devonshire Mews S
Devonshire St
Devonshire Cl
Beaumont St
Upper Wimpole St
Harley St
Hallam St
Bridford Mews
Bolsover St
Carburton St
Cleveland St
Fitzroy St
Maple St
Cypress Pl
Carpenter St
Whitfield St
Howland St
Charlotte St
Marylebone High St
Marylebone St
Westmorland St
Weymouth St
Weymouth Mews
Wimpole Mews
Portland Place
Great Portland St
Clipstone St
Great Titchfield St
Hanson St
Ogle St
Foley St
Tottenham St
Goodge Street
Goodge
New Cavendish St
Mansfield St
Duchess St
Gosfield St
Riding House St
Nassau St
Mortimer St
Rathbone St
Aybrook St
Thayer St
Marylebone Mews
Harley Place
Queen Anne St
Chandos St
Langham St
All Souls Pl
Portland Pl
Bulstrode St
Welbeck St
Wimpole St
Wigmore Pl
Wells St
Wells Mews
Berners Mews
Berners St
Newman St
Berners Pl
Wallace Collection
Bentinck St
Marylebone La
Wigmore Hall
Wigmore St
Cavendish Square
Little Portland St
Margaret St
Eastcastle St
Manchester Square
John Prince's St
Gt Castle St
Market Pl
Winsley St
Oxford St
Gray's Yd
Henrietta Place
Hollies St
Oxford Circus
Edwards Mews
Picton Pl
James St
Barrett St
Stratford Pl
Vere St
Hills Pl
Ramillies Pl
Noel St
Berwick St
Selfridges
Bird St
Duke St
Bond Street
Dering St
Tenterden St
Hanover Sq
Princes St
Little Argyll St
Argyll St
Great Marlborough St
Poland St
Lumley St
Balderton St
Gilbert St
Binney St
Weighhouse St
South Molton St
South Molton La
Woodstock St
Hanover St
Maddox St
Newburgh St
Marshall St
Broadwick St
Ingestre Pl
George Yd
Brook St
Brook's Mews
Avery Row
New Bond St
St George St
Conduit St
Regent St
Carnaby St
Kingly St
Beak St
Lexington St
Bridle Lane
Grosvenor
Grosvenor Square Gardens
Square
Davies St
Grosvenor St
Grosvenor Hill
Bourdon St
Bruton Pl
Bruton St
Bruton La
Golden Square
Warwick St
Sherwood St
Brewer St
Heddon St
Savile Row
Glasshouse St
Carlos Pl
Mount Row
Clifford St
Cork St
Vigo St
Adam's Row
Mount St
Berkeley Square
Grafton St
Burlington Gdns
Royal Academy of Arts
Swallow St
Vine St
Air St
Waterstone's
St James's Piccadilly
Mount St Gardens
Farm St
Hill St
Hay's Mews
Hay Hill
Dover St
Albemarle St
Old Bond St
Alford St
South Audley St
Chesterfield Hill
Charles St
Fitzmaurice Pl
Berkeley St
Jermyn St
South St
Waverton St
Queen St
Clarges Mews
Stratton St
Piccadilly
Duke St St James's
St James's St
Deanery St
Tilney St
Bolton St
Arlington St
Bury St
Stanhope Gate
Curzon St
Half Moon St
Clarges St
Green Park
Park Pl
King St
Park La
Market Mews
Shepherd St
White Horse St
St James's Pl
Hertford St
Brick St
Down St
Little St James's St
Cleveland Row
Chapel Royal
Marlborough Rd
Hyde Park
Hamilton Pl
Old Park La
Diana Princess of Wales Memorial Walk
Queen's Wlk
Stable Yd Rd
Wellington Museum
Hyde Park Corner
Constitution Hill
Duke of Wellington Pl
Victoria Memorial
Grosvenor Cres
Grosvenor Pl
Halkin St
Buckingham Palace Gardens
Buckingham Palace

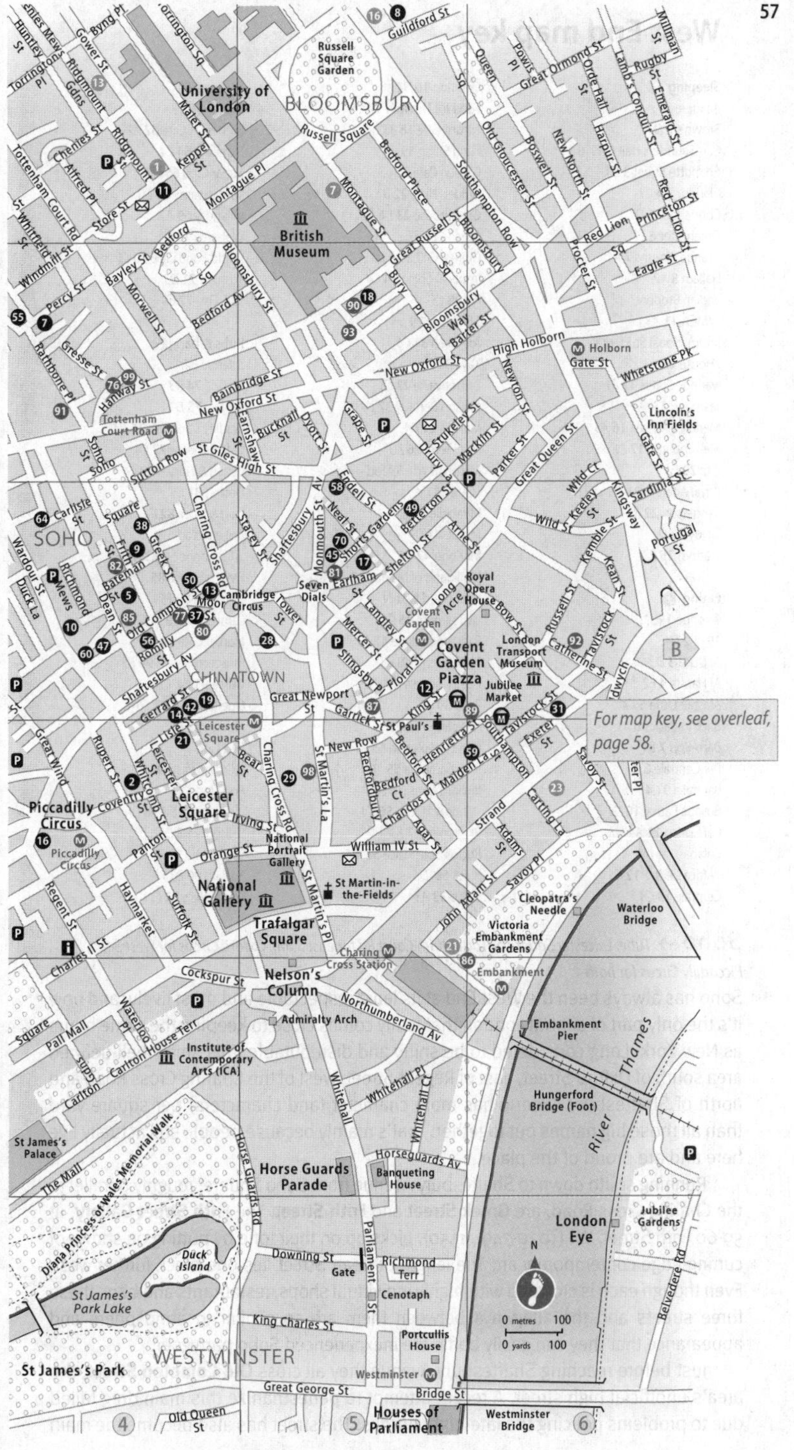

For map key, see overleaf, page 58.

West End map key

Sleeping
Academy **1** *A4*
Brown's **2** *D2*
Carr Saunders Hall **9** *A3*
Charlotte Street **3** *B3*
Claridge's **4** *C1*
Connaught **5** *D1*
Dorchester **6** *E1*
Grange Blooms **7** *A5*
Hallam **8** *A2*
Indian Student YMCA **11** *A3*
International Student's House **10** *A2*
Ivanhoe Suites **12** *B1*
Jesmond **13** *A4*
Meridien Russell **16** *A5*
Metropolitan **17** *E1*
Ritz **20** *E2*
Royal Adelphi **21** *D5*
Sanderson **22** *B3*
Savoy **23** *D6*
Stafford **25** *E3*

Eating
@venue **1** *E3*
1997 **2** *D4*
Al Duca **3** *D3*
Al Hamra **4** *E2*
Alastair Little **5** *C4*
Back to Basics **6** *A3*
Bam-Bou **7** *B4*
Bar Centrale **8** *A5*
Bar Italia **9** *C4*
Busaba Eathai **10** *C4*
Café Deco **11** *A4*
Calabash at the Africa Centre **12** *C5*
Centrale **13** *C4*
Criterion **16** *D4*
Food for Thought **17** *C5*
Forum Café **18** *B5*
Fung Shing **19** *C4*
Garden Café **20** *C3*
Golden Hind **22** *B1*
Greenhouse **23** *E1*
Greens **24** *E3*
Guinea Grill **25** *D2*
Imperial China **14** *C4*
Ivy **28** *C5*
J Sheekey **29** *D5*
Joe Allen **31** *C6*
Kaya **32** *D2*
La Trouvaille **27** *C3*
Maison Bertaux **37** *C4*
Manzi's **21** *D4*
Mar I Terra **26** *D3*
Mildred's Wholefood Café **38** *C4*
Mirabelle **39** *E2*
Momo **41** *D3*
Mr Kong **42** *C4*
Mulligan's of Mayfair **43** *D3*
Neal's Yard Bakery & Tearoom **45** *C5*
Patisserie Valerie **47** *C4 & B1*
Pied-à-Terre **48** *B3*
Poetry Society **49** *C5*
Pollo **50** *C4*
Quaglino's **52** *E3*
Quiet Revolution **53** *A1*
Rasa Samudra **55** *B4*
Richard Corrigan at Lindsay House **56** *C4*
RK Stanley **57** *B3*
Rock & Sole Plaice **58** *C5*
Rules **59** *D6*
Sardo **33** *A3*
Satsuma **60** *C4*
Sketch **30** *C2*
Sotheby's Café **62** *C2*
Star Café **64** *C4*
Sugar Club **65** *D3*
Veeraswamy **68** *D3*
Villandry **69** *A2*
Wolseley **15** *E3*
World Food Café **70** *C5*
Yoshino **71** *D3*
Zilli Fish **72** *C3*

Pubs & bars
Atlantic Bar & Grill **74** *D3*
Audley **75** *D1*
Bradley's Spanish **76** *B4*
Café Bohème **77** *C4*
Coach & Horses **80** *C4*
Detroit **81** *C5*
Dog & Duck **82** *C4*
Duke of York (Rathbone St) **83** *B3*
French House **85** *C4*
Gordon's **86** *E5*
Lamb & Flag **87** *C5*
Market Café **89** *C6*
Museum Tavern **90** *B5*
Office **91** *B4*
Opera Tavern **92** *C6*
Plough **93** *B5*
Red Lion (Crown Pass) **95** *E3*
Red Lion (Waverton St) **96** *E1*
Salisbury **98** *D5*
Sevilla Mia **99** *B4*
Social **100** *B3*
Trader Vic's **73** *E1*

Soho → *Tube: Leicester Square or Tottenham Court Rd for east Soho, Oxford Circus for west Soho, Piccadilly Circus for both*

Soho has always been the West End at its least respectable and most lively, and now it's the only part of central London that really comes close to keeping the same hours as New York. Long considered to be shifty and disreputable, this small well-defined area south of Oxford Street, east of Regent Street, west of the Charing Cross Road and north of Shaftesbury Avenue has more character (and characters) per square yard than all those big names put together. That's mainly because people still actually live here and are proud of the place.

Running south down to Shaftesbury Avenue from Soho Square, roughly parallel to the Charing Cross Road, are **Greek Street** and **Frith Street**. The **Frith Street Gallery**, at 59-60 Frith Street, W1 (T020-7494 1550), picks up on their tone by putting on shows of cutting-edge contemporary art. The length of **Dean Street** lies one block further west. Even though each is crowded with highly individual shops, restaurants and bars, these three streets and the alleyways between them are so similar in atmosphere and appearance that they can easily baffle the inexperienced Soho partygoer.

Just before reaching Shaftesbury Avenue they all cross **Old Compton Street**, the area's unofficial high street. A recent attempt to pedestrianize this main drag failed due to problems policing the late-night hordes. The street has also become the main

66 99 Soho has always been the West End at its least respectable and most lively, and now it's the only part of central London that really comes close to keeping the same hours as New York...

artery of the gay scene, while its junction with Greek Street and Moor Street must be one of the most characteristic and crowded spots in the area.

The west side of Soho is generally more money-grabbing than boho high Soho. Nearer Regent Street, around **Carnaby Street**, it also becomes even more fashion-conscious, especially along Newburgh Street. Carnaby Street itself, a by-word for anything groovy in the 60s, has begun to reclaim some of the cachet that it let slip in the 1980s after becoming a tacky tourist trap trading on its heyday.

Covent Garden → *Tube: Covent Garden*

Covent Garden has been attracting traders, entertainers, their customers and audiences for at least 300 years but it only became a respectable tourist hotspot about 30 years ago, a fairly successful transformation of one of the oldest meeting places in the West End into one of the youngest. Thankfully it's still largely free of the depressing tat peddled to visitors around Leicester Square.

Sandwiched between the Charing Cross Road, Bloomsbury, the Strand and Holborn, the area is almost as well defined as Soho. The focal point is still what was once London's largest and most famous fruit n' veg market before it moved out to Nine Elms in 1974. Now an impressive piazza, it still bears a faint flavour of those bustling times thanks to its converted Victorian covered market and the crowds that flock here day and night to shop, eat, drink and enjoy a pleasant place away from all the traffic. North of Long Acre, what were once narrow streets of warehouses and slums have experienced a boom in youth-orientated shops and bars, led by long-established crowd-pullers like the Donmar Warehouse theatre and Neals Yard wholefood hippy enclave.

To the east of the piazza, the **Royal Opera House** has reopened to great acclaim following great controversy after its multi-million pound redevelopment. Open to the general public throughout the day, it includes a terrace overlooking the piazza while the refurbished Floral Hall provides a soaring space to enjoy a coffee or light meal.

The west side is dominated by the classical portico of **St Paul's Church** ⓘ *T020-7836 5221. Mon-Fri 0900-1630. www.actorschurch.org,* a 17th-century box designed by Inigo Jones that has long been known as the actors' church thanks to the plaques inside commemorating bygone stars of the stage and screen. The portico on the piazza forms the backdrop to street theatre events of varying quality throughout the year.

On the south side, the **Jubilee Market** is another covered market with a much lower-rent selection of clothing and jewellery stalls as well as some reasonable snack stops. Things improve here on Mondays when an antiques market sets up shop and at weekends when craftworkers arrive with their wares.

Next door, in the old flower market in the southeast corner of the piazza, the **London Transport Museum** ⓘ *T020-7379 6344, www.ltmuseum.co.uk, Mon-Thu, Sat, Sun 1000- 1800, Fri 1100-1800 (last entry 1715), £5.95, concession £4.50, children free,* is an excellent place to take the kids for free. As well as a host of antique carriages, trams, buses and tube trains, many of which can be boarded and explored, the great glass-roofed hall contains a formidable battery of hands-on exhibits, push-button panels and a cunning labyrinth of aerial walkways.

Piccadilly Circus and around → *Tube: Piccadily Circus*

Piccadilly Circus, the heart of the West End, is usually so relentlessly busy that it's not a particularly pleasant place to linger, but thousands do, gathering around the endearing little monument representing the Angel of Christian Charity but persistently taken to be the God of Love, dubbed **'Eros'**. Erected in 1893 in memory of the stern philanthropist Lord Shaftesbury, who did much to help abolish child labour, the winged boy with his bow was so unpopular that the sculptor Sir Arthur Gilbert went into retirement. Nowadays it is dwarfed by the neon-lit logos of Macdonalds, Nescafé and Coca Cola on the north side. Opposite them is the grand façade of *The Criterion Restaurant*. Progressing westwards for about a mile to Hyde Park Corner, Piccadilly itself is a top-class and congested strip of extraordinary shops, world-class hotels, green space and fine architecture.

One of the most beautiful church interiors in London is on the left a few hundred yards down from Piccadilly Circus. **St James's Piccadilly** ⓘ *197 Piccadilly, T020-7734 4511, daily 0800-1900, café (T020-7437 9419), daily 0830-1900, antique market Tue 1000-1730, craft market (T020-7437 7688), Wed-Sat 1000-1730,* known as the 'visitors' church', was its architect Christopher Wren's personal favourite. Completed in 1684, the church sustained severe bomb damage in the Second World War and needed extensive restoration. The interior retains its delightful balance and poise, best appreciated in bright daylight, and includes a spectacular limewood altar-screen carved by Grinling Gibbons in the 17th century, who may also have been responsible for the font here in which William Blake was baptized.

Burlington House, on the opposite side of Piccadilly, has been the home since 1869 of the **Royal Academy of Arts** ⓘ *T020-7300 8000, Mon-Thu 1000-1800, Fri-Sun 1000-2200, admission to exhibitions varies*. Under the directorship of Norman Rosenthal, the Academy has determinedly cast off an increasingly fusty image by mounting popular attention-grabbing exhibitions of contemporary British art, with titles like 'Sensation' and 'Apocalypse'. Guided tours of the permanent collection, which includes works by Reynolds, Turner, Constable and Stanley Spencer, are given Tuesday-Friday at 1300 and are free (be there on time).

Mayfair and Regent Street → *Tube: Bond Street or Oxford Circus*

North of Piccadilly, and south of Oxford Street, Mayfair is the West End at its most swanky. Protected from the chaos of Soho to the east by the grand swathe of Regent Street, it still earns its place as the last and most expensive stop on the Monopoly board by boasting the capital's most luxurious hotels, the hautest couture and cuisine, and some of its wealthiest residents. Lavish and louche, Mayfair smells of money and the area's traditional exclusivity has ensured that there's little of the usual 'see and do' variety. At weekends the wide streets can be almost deserted. But recently Mayfair is supposed to have become less stuffy and more fashionable. Although superficially little seems to have changed, digging a bit deeper behind those imposing façades is likely to unearth some stylish and affordable surprises.

Hyde Park Corner → *Tube: Hyde Park Corner*

Piccadilly continues downhill to Hyde Park Corner, past the Inigo Jones-designed Devonshire Gates into Green Park. They were remov ed from Devonshire House, one of the grand houses that once lined the length of Piccadilly's north side. Hyde Park Corner itself terrifies drivers and pedestrians alike. The main reason to come here and not hurry through is a visit to **Apsley House** ⓘ *T020-7499 5676, www.apsley house.org.uk, Tue-Sun 1100-1700, £4.50, £3 concessions, children free, guided tours on request, £30 for groups of up to 25 people*, the house that Arthur Wellesley, the Duke of Wellington, bought off his brother after Waterloo. It stands on the north side of Hyde Park corner, by the entrance to Park Lane. Known as No 1 London, for being the first house in the West End on the road from Knightsbridge, it's now The

Harrods' Hall of Fame

Harrods is hard to miss: well signposted at Knightsbridge tube, its famous terracotta building, picked out like a fairground at night, has dominated the Brompton Road for almost a hundred years. Founded half a century earlier by Charles Harrod, his small perfume and cosmetics store became the largest general shop in the world, boasting the first escalator in London and employing thousands of staff. Its seven floors remain a sumptuous five-star shopping experience, featuring the marble chiller cabinets of the legendary Food Halls, acres of designerwear and an alarmingly tidy toy shop. Since the 1980s though it has become almost as famous for the notoriety of its current owner, Mohammed Al Fayed. A controversial character who loves the limelight, he has stamped his personality all over the store, sadly all the more so since the death of his son Dodi with Princess Diana. Whatever they may be looking to purchase upstairs, most visitors don't want to miss the Diana and Dodi Memorial in the basement at the foot of one of the Egyptian escalators. Portrait photos of the tragic pair are sentimentally enshrined on a sort of funereal ivy-bedecked wishing-well, a fairly second-rate exhibition of the window dresser's art sandwiched between the Harrods marketing shop and the lost property department. Its most macabre feature is an actual wine glass supposedly in use on that fateful night at the Paris Ritz. As everybody knows, the couple were killed in a car accident pursued by paparazzi, making it all the more ironic that this is the only part of the whole store where photography is permitted.

Wellington Museum, a dignified monument to the man and the post-Napoleonic era in Britain. It was restored in Louis XIV style, and refurbished throughout in its original colour scheme in 1995.

Green Park → *Tube: Green Park*

Laid out by Henry VIII, the 53-acre park's name is self-explanatory enough, kept free of formal flower beds out of respect for the lepers from the Hospital of St James's buried beneath. More fancifully, Charles II is supposed to have picked a flower here to give to the next beautiful woman he saw. Queen Katharine was so furious that she banned flowers from the park for good. Nowadays the plane trees, crocuses, daffodils and deck chairs make it a charming spot to wile away an afternoon in the spring.

St James's → *Tube: Piccadilly Circus or Green Park*

St James's is the land that time forgot, stuck in a fantasy of the English past, peddling classy airs and graces as though they had never lost influence. The layout of its streets little changed since the 17th century, it has preserved a more intimate scale than Mayfair, although the grandeur of its aspirations are forcefully expressed in **St James's Square** and along **Pall Mall**. Above all, this is the part of London that enshrines the idea of the English gentleman. Parallel to Piccadilly, off St James's Street to the left, **Jermyn Street** sets the tone for the shops that cater for the area's clubbable gents.

At the bottom of St James's Street, where it turns sharp left into Pall Mall, two fully armed redcoats in their bearskin busbies stand or stomp about like clockwork beneath the red-brick Tudor gatehouse of **St James's Palace**. Now used as offices for various Royals, the palace is closed to visitors, although the **Chapel Royal** inside is open for Sunday services from October until Good Friday.

The Mall is an imposing public space, lined with trees and flagstaffs, its pink tarmac matching the forecourt of Buckingham Palace, that comes into its own for ceremonies like Trooping the Colour. Just beyond, **St James's Park**, work of the indefatigable John Nash and the finest and most carefully laid out of the Royal parks, is the Palace's front garden. At the bottom of the steps on the left, the **Institute of Contemporary Arts (ICA)**, ⓘ *12 Carlton House Terr, To20-7930 3647, www.ica.org.uk, daily 1200-1930, galleries Mon-Fri £1.50, Sat and Sun £2.50, day membership Mon-Fri £1.50, Sat and Sun £2.50,* was founded in 1948 by the anarchist Herbert Read. Nash's stately Georgian terrace seems an incongruous setting for the radical film, theatre, dance and art shown here.

Buckingham Palace

ⓘ *To20-7930 4832, tickets in advance by credit card on To20-7321 2233, 7766 7300 or by post to The Visitor Office, Buckingham Palace, London, SW1A 1AA, www.royal.gov.uk 0930-1630 Aug and Sep. Ticket Office in Green Park near The Mall, for tickets on the day, 0900-1600. £12.50, concessions £10.50, child £6.50. Changing of the Guard at 1130 daily Apr 1 to the end of Jul; alternate days the rest of the year.*

In 1993 the Queen opened the doors of the palace for the first time to raise money for the restoration of the fire-damaged Windsor Castle. A maximum of 250 visitors are admitted every 15 mins, in a fairly successful attempt to avoid overcrowding (or perhaps for fear of a rebellion) on a one-way route around 14 state rooms, with the recent addition of the Ballroom, shepherded by 200 extra staff in navy blue and red uniforms who are generally friendly and well informed.

The **Queen's Gallery** ⓘ *Daily 1000-1630, £6.50, concessions £5, children £3,* is open all year, and houses the Queen's collection of Old Masters and portraiture, an extraordinary hoard founded by Charles II, which has recently been re-hung in purpose-built new galleries.

If you've still got a stomach for all things Royal, next door to the Palace are the **Royal Mews**, ⓘ *To20-7930 4832, Feb-Oct daily 1100-1515, Aug-Sept Mon-Thu 1000-1515, last admission 30 mins before closing, £5, concessions £4, children £2.50,* also open most of the year, where all the Queen's stately transport is kept, including her gilded State coach and her Windsor grey horses. If anything the array of splendid carriages gives a better value and more atmospheric insight into the pageant of British sovereignty than the Palace itself.

Westminster Abbey → *Tube: St James's*

ⓘ *Information and tours To20-7654 4834. Mon-Fri 0930-1645 (last admission 1545), Sat 0930-1445 (last admission 1345). £6, concessions £4, children £4, under-11's free with adult. Chapter House, Pyx Chamber and Museum: summer 1000-1700 daily. Main Cloister open same hours as Abbey. Free (from Dean's Yard). Little Cloister and College Garden: Tue-Thu summer 1030-1800, winter 1030-1600. Free. Buses 3, 11, 12, 24, 53, 77a, 88, 159 and 211 all pass Westminster Abbey.*

A surprisingly small church for one of such enormous significance in the Anglican faith and British state (especially for its monarchy), Westminster Abbey's charm lies in its age. It has also long been a well-managed tourist trap. That said, despite the milling crowds clutching the fairly patronizing audio guide and bossy 'free' floorplans, it remains a sacred building and anyone wishing to pray here (or join in a service on Sunday when the Abbey is closed to tourists) is allowed to do so free of charge. And there's also plenty worth seeing for the money.

The length and especially the height (over 100 ft) of the Nave are awe-inspiring. On the tourist route round from the north entrance, this impressive view is left until the end, the tour beginning in the oldest part of the main building, the central Crossing built in the 13th century. Visitors then turn sharp left to skirt the Sanctuary of the High Altar (where sovereigns are crowned) and the founder St Edward the Confessor's Chapel, past the tombs of Edward I and Henry III, to look at the **Coronation Chair**. Made to order for the 'Hammer of the Scots', Edward I, and used to crown every English monarch except three since 1308, the old wooden chair's most obvious feature now is the empty space below the seat purpose-built for the Stone of Destiny. (The sandstone coronation block of Scottish monarchs since the ninth century is now back home in its native land and on display in Edinburgh Castle.) Beyond is **Henry VII's Chapel** (or Lady Chapel), dating from the early 16th century, an extraordinary medieval pageant of flags, stalls, and tombs below a vaulted stone roof. On either side of this chapel are the hushed tombs of Elizabeth I and Mary Queen of Scots.

Heading back towards the Crossing, the tour passes **Poet's Corner**, decorated with sculptures and monuments to Shakespeare, Chaucer and other poets and actors, as well as scientists, architects, historians and other worthies.

Then it's out into the fresh air of the Cloisters of the 11th-century monastery, past the Chapter House, Pyx Chamber and Museum. In the octagonal **Chapter House**, where the House of Commons sat from the mid 14th-16th centuries, the medieval wall paintings of the Last Judgement and the Apocalypse, and remarkable tiled floor, decorated with griffins, lions, and mythical beasts, have a faded splendour. The dark little **Pyx Chamber** was the monastery's strong room and is the oldest building on site. And the **museum** in the monks' Common Room contains some weird Royal funeral effigies from the Middle Ages as well as a more recent and peculiar one of the Duke of Buckingham.

Houses of Parliament → *Tube: Charing Cross or Embankment for the top of Whitehall nearest Trafalgar Square. Westminsterfor Big Ben and Parliament Square*

Guided historical tours ⓘ *T0870-9063773 roughly every 15 mins from 0915-1630, £7, £5 concessions) of both houses are available (either book in advance or queue up outside). Commons Information Line T020-7219 4272; Lords Information Line T020-7219 3107; www.parliament.uk Parliament usually in session mid-Oct to Christmas, Jan to Easter, Jun and Jul: Mon 1430-2200, Tue-Thur 1130-1900, Thu until 1800 approximately.*

The **Palace of Westminster**, better known as the Houses of Parliament, has been the seat of the government of England since the reign of Edward III, when the King and his court of barons and bishops would meet in St Stephen's Chapel. The chapel and surrounding palace were almost completely razed to the ground by fire in 1834, resulting in the building of the golden Gothic glory in use today.

Its most famous feature is **Big Ben**, the clock tower overlooking Westminster Bridge. The clock strikes the hour on the 13-ton bell that gives the tower its name, and which can be heard up to 4 ½ miles away.

The oldest part of the building though is **Westminster Hall**, which survived the fire, behind the statue of the victor in the Civil War, Lord Protector Oliver Cromwell. The interior of the Hall with its great hammer-beam roof and the beautifully decorated **St Stephen's Crypt** can only be seen on a guided tour.

When Parliament is in session the public are admitted (after a thorough security check) to the 'Strangers' Galleries' of either House through St Stephen's Gate, just beyond Cromwell's statue. Generally it's easier and quicker gaining access to the **House of Lords**, a very grand and gilded debating chamber with its benches of red morocco. By contrast, the **House of Commons** seems very small and businesslike, its green leather benches looking quite tatty. The Government sit to the Speaker's right and the Opposition to his left with the front benches reserved for Cabinet Ministers and shadow-Ministers.

Apart from during Prime Minister's Question Time on Wednesdays at 1500, which can only be seen on application to your MP or embassy, both houses are often half-empty or half-asleep.

Pimlico to Kensington

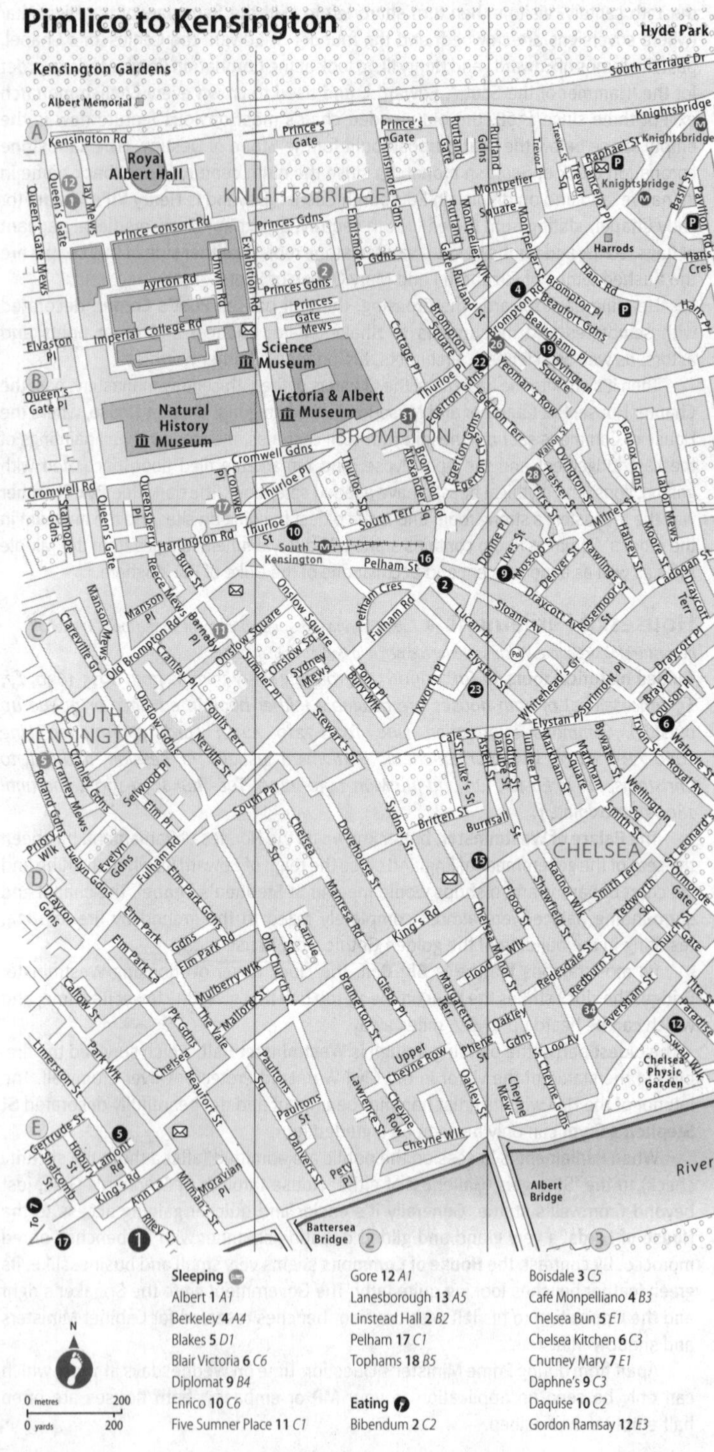

Sleeping
Albert **1** *A1*
Berkeley **4** *A4*
Blakes **5** *D1*
Blair Victoria **6** *C6*
Diplomat **9** *B4*
Enrico **10** *C6*
Five Sumner Place **11** *C1*
Gore **12** *A1*
Lanesborough **13** *A5*
Linstead Hall **2** *B2*
Pelham **17** *C1*
Tophams **18** *B5*

Eating
Bibendum **2** *C2*
Boisdale **3** *C5*
Café Monpelliano **4** *B3*
Chelsea Bun **5** *E1*
Chelsea Kitchen **6** *C3*
Chutney Mary **7** *E1*
Daphne's **9** *C3*
Daquise **10** *C2*
Gordon Ramsay **12** *E3*

0 metres 200
0 yards 200

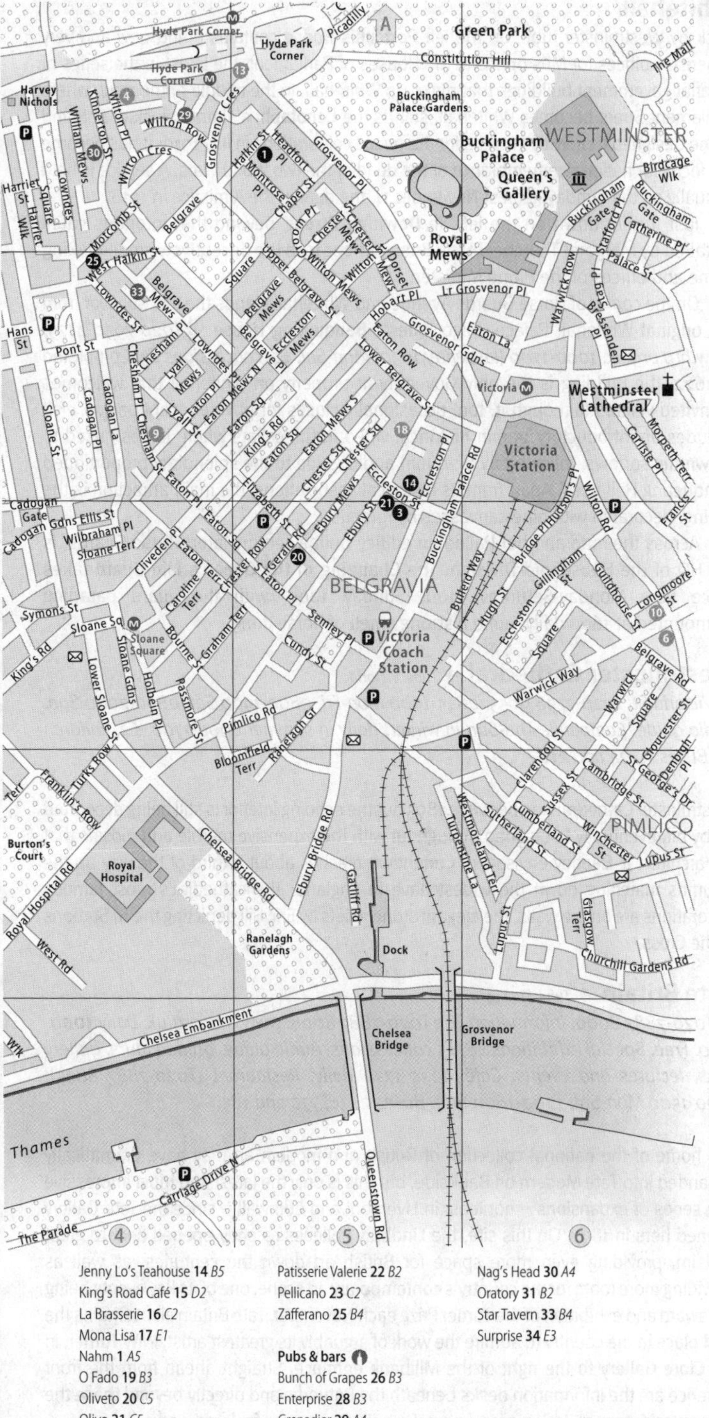

Jenny Lo's Teahouse **14** *B5*
King's Road Café **15** *D2*
La Brasserie **16** *C2*
Mona Lisa **17** *E1*
Nahm **1** *A5*
O Fado **19** *B3*
Oliveto **20** *C5*
Olivo **21** *C5*
Patisserie Valerie **22** *B2*
Pellicano **23** *C2*
Zafferano **25** *B4*

Pubs & bars

Bunch of Grapes **26** *B3*
Enterprise **28** *B3*
Grenadier **29** *A4*
Nag's Head **30** *A4*
Oratory **31** *B2*
Star Tavern **33** *B4*
Surprise **34** *E3*

Whitehall

Back by Westminster tube, on the left **Portcullis House** contains brand new and very expensive offices for MPs opposite the Houses of Parliament, the latest in the series of palatial government buildings that make up Whitehall. In the middle of the road, where Parliament Street becomes Whitehall, stands the **Cenotaph**, a simple block of Portland Stone designed rapidly by Lutyens for the peace celebrations in July 1919; it has become the focus for national remembrance of the dead of the two World Wars. A service is held annually on the Sunday nearest November 11, the date of the Armistice in 1918.

Just further down on the left, in **Downing Street**, beyond the notorious gates installed by Margaret Thatcher in the 80s, number 10 is the deceptively small-looking home and offices of the Prime Minister.

On the corner of Horse Guards Avenue and Whitehall stands the last survivor from the original Whitehall Palace, Inigo Jones's **Banqueting House** ⓘ *T020-7930 4179, www.hrp.org.uk, 1000-1700 (last entry 1630) Mon-Sat, £4, concessions £3*. Completed in 1622, the building is the only Government property on Whitehall that welcomes uninvited visitors (although it, too, occasionally closes for private receptions). A visit includes an introductory 15-min historical video in the cellars where James I used to drown his sorrows, followed by a 20-min audio guide to the splendidly proportioned Banqueting Hall itself. Apart from its historical associations, the main attraction is the ceiling, decorated with nine canvasses by Rubens.

Across the road another Palladian edifice built a century later, **Horse Guards**, is the HQ of the Household Division. The **Changing of the Queen's Life Guard** takes place here Monday-Saturday 1100, Sunday 1000, with the guard parading dismounted at 1600 daily, amid a strong smell of horse dung.

Westminster Cathedral → *Tube: Victoria*

ⓘ *Victoria St, T020-7798 9055. 0645-1900 Mon-Fri, 0800-1900 Sat, 0800-2000 Sun. Audio guide. Campanile Thu-Sun in winter, daily in summer 0900-1700. £2, children £1. Buses 11, 24 and 211.*

Westminster Cathedral was begun in 1895 but the echoing interior is still being decorated bit by bit, eventually to be lined throughout with the expensive marble and mosaic that the architect JF Bentley envisaged. Currently it reaches about a third of the way up the columns marching down the widest nave in England. The cathedral's most famous decorations are on the walls, the elegant stone reliefs by Eric Gill depicting the 14 Stations of the Cross.

Tate Britain → *Tube: Pimlico*

ⓘ *T020-7887 8000, information line T020-7887 8008, www.tate.org.uk. Daily 1000-1750. Free. Special exhibitions £8, £5 concessions. Audio guide, guided tours, gallery talks, lectures and events. Café: 1030-1730 daily. Restaurant (T020-7887 8825): 1200-1500 Mon-Sat, 1200-1600 Sun. Buses 2, 36, 77a and 185.*

The home of the national collection of British and modern art may have dramatically expanded into Tate Modern on Bankside, but this is only the latest and most impressive of a series of expansions – not least in Liverpool and Cornwall – since the Tate Gallery opened here in 1897. On this site, the Lindbury galleries recently opened here to great acclaim, providing even more space for British art down the centuries, as well as providing more room for the country's contemporary art scene, one of its key events being the award and exhibition of the Turner Prize each November. Tate Britain also remains the best place in the country to admire the work of arguably its greatest artist, JMW Turner, in the **Clore Gallery** to the right of the Millbank entrance. Straight ahead from the front entrance are the information desks beneath the Rotunda, and directly beyond these the **Duveen sculpture galleries**, monumental meditative spaces for large works.

How to act like a Londoner on the tube

After the incredibly annoying London Underground tannoy warning of 'Mind the Gap', which is repeated ad nauseum by equally annoying tourists, should be added, 'and do not, under any circumstances, talk to, or even look at, the natives'. Visitors please take note: that broadsheet newspaper is not for reading. It is the London tube traveller's shield against the outside world. London can be a tough place, full of highly undesirable and dangerous people, and those precious few millimetres of newsprint is all that stands between the London commuter and the excrutiating pain and social embarrassment of human interaction with a perfect stranger in a crowded place. So, please, dear visitor, be sensitive. Do not engage your neighbour in conversation – even if it's to tell them their hair's on fire – and do not attempt to read their newspaper. This can result in a severe bout of tut-tutting or, worse still, a filthy look. Just head straight for the nearest seat, open your copy of the *Financial Times*, and ignore everything and everyone around you – especially if it's someone asking if this tube stops at Buckingham Palace.

Hyde Park and Kensington Gardens → *Hyde Park Corner*

The wide open stretch of grass between **Park Lane** and the Serpentine often seems deserted, even in summer, except during the regular open-air concerts, demonstrations and Royal occasions. The Lido (T020-7298 2100), the more attractive of the two café-restaurants in the park, is a good place to hire a boat on the **Serpentine Lake**. The *Lido* can be reached across the bridge that divides the Serpentine from the Long Water and hence Hyde Park from Kensington Gardens. The path in Hyde Park along the north side of the Long Water, past the **Henry Moore Arch**, ends up among the fish ponds and fountains of the Italian Gardens at Lancaster Gate. Look out here for the classical arch known as **Queen Anne's Alcove**, designed by Wren.

Over the Long Bridge though, towards the *Lido*, is Kensington Gardens' prize asset, the **Serpentine Gallery** ⓘ *T020-7402 6075, www.serpentinegallery.org.uk, daily 1000-1800, free.* The quiet gallery was completely refurbished in 1998, confirming a reputation steadily acquired since its opening in 1970 for being one of London's most exciting small spaces for international contemporary art, charmingly at odds with its dinky situation.

Kensington Gardens spread out behind the gallery, criss-crossed with signposted paths leading to the Round Pond, the Peter Pan statue beside Long Water, and the Broad Walk in front of Kensington Palace. The latest suggested route is the seven-mile **Diana Princess of Wales Memorial Walk** ⓘ *for more information T020-7298 2000, or call into the Old Police House information centre,* through four of central London's Royal parks.

On the southern fringe of the park looms the Gothic spire and canopy of the **Albert Memorial**, designed by Sir George Gilbert Scott and finished in 1872. Much against his own wishes, Victoria's far-from-pompous consort is surrounded by an excess of ardently imperialist statuary and fancy stonework recently renovated at huge expense. Across the road is his much more fitting memorial, the great domed oval of the Royal Albert Hall. Next up on Exhibition Road, however, is the first of the area's main events in the form of the Science Museum and on the Cromwell Road next door to it the Natural History Museum.

Science Museum → *Tube: South Kensington*

ⓘ T020-7942 4455; booking and information T0870-8704868; www.sciencemuseum.org.uk. Daily 1000-1800. Free, charges for combinations of IMAX and Virtual Voyage (£2.50 extra). Screenings in IMAX Cinema (£6.95 including museum): at 1045 (Sat, Sun only), 1145, 1245, 1345, 1445, 1545, 1645 daily. Free 20-min guided tours on the hr every hr, as well as one 50-min tour of the whole museum usually at 1400. Buses 14, 70 and 74.

The Science Museum prides itself on being one of the most forward-thinking, interactive and accessible museums in the country, a claim that has been enhanced with the opening of the new Wellcome Wing: four floors dedicated to displaying cutting-edge science and technology incorporating an IMAX cinema and the first Virtual Voyage simulator in Europe. With origins similar to the V&A's (see below), the emphasis here has always been on education. One of the best things about the Science Museum is that guidebooks or guided tours are hardly necessary: most of the exhibits either speak for themselves or are thoroughly labelled. In the basement is Launch Pad, a very popular hands-on gallery of educational scientific games.

Natural History Museum → *Tube: South Kensington*

ⓘ T020-7942 5000, www.nhm.ac.uk Mon-Sat 1000-1750, Sun 1100-1750. Free. Buses 14, 70 and 74.

Behind the Science Museum, on Cromwell Road, stands the extraordinary old orange and blue terracotta building of the Natural History Museum. Until 1963 part of the British Museum, and since then also gobbling up the Geological Museum, this is a serious academic research institution that has become seriously fun-packed. Divided into Life Galleries and Earth Galleries, it tells the history of our animated planet with a not entirely successful combination of venerable artefacts and playschool attractions. Occasionally it feels as if the museum had been entrusted to an over-excited and over-budget biology teacher. Even so, it never disappoints children, and adults are sure to learn something about the natural world whether they want to or not.

Victoria and Albert Museum → *Tube: South Kensington*

ⓘ T020-7942 2000, information T020-7942 8090, www.vam.ac.uk Daily 1000-1745, last Wed and Fri of each month 1000-2200. Free. Buses 14, 70 & 74.

Also known as the V&A, the Victoria and Albert Museum is one of the world's greatest museums. Surprisingly, considering its grand façade on Cromwell Road, it wears that greatness lightly. Originally founded in 1857 with the intention of educating the populace in the appreciation of decorative art and design it exhibited superb examples of what could be achieved in that field. Never a narrowly nationalistic enterprise, its remarkable collection was gathered like the British Museum's from all corners of the globe. The overall impression it makes though is much more human and domestic. Many of the objects on display around its seven-miles-worth of galleries would once have decorated or been in everyday use in people's homes – very wealthy and powerful people's homes for the most part – as well as in magnificent places of worship. And most are nothing like as ancient and remote as the antiquities in the BM. On making first acquaintance with the V&A, instead of trying to see as much as possible with a limited amount of time, wander slowly around it in the certain knowledge that you'll find a rewarding number of amazing things.

Chelsea → *Tube: Sloane Square*

It's easy to see why Hillary and Bill Clinton named their daughter Chelsea: the name has a pleasant sound and a familiar ring in certain social circles. As far as London is concerned, it means a very comfortable part of town with an impeccable bohemian pedigree, occasionally displaying bursts of street cred. Its High Street, the **King's Road**, became one of the pivots of 'swinging London' in the 1960s and outraged middle England again a decade later by spawning the Sex Pistols, the shock troops of punk rock. Nowadays much quieter and more expensive, freighted with designer boutiques and the sleek Chelsea boys and babes they attract, the well-heeled King's Road treads its well-worn path between the Fulham Road and the river, threading its way through a district characterized by smart residential squares and quaint cobbled mews. The most interesting streets to explore lie on its south side, towards the river, along Royal Hospital Road and the Chelsea Embankment up to the Albert Bridge. Apart from the Royal Hospital itself, very grand almshouses from another era for retired soldiers, this pretty area conceals the peaceful delights of the **Chelsea Physic Garden** ⓘ *T020-7352 5646, www.chelseaphysicgarden.co.uk, Apr-Oct, 1200-1700 Wed, 1400-1800 Sun (as well as daily throughout the Chelsea Flower Show and Chelsea Festival), £5, children £3*. Further down the King's Road, around the World's End, Chelsea loosens up a little to become fertile browsing ground for offbeat fashions and better-value restaurants.

Oxford Street and Marble Arch

'Don't stop, shop!' could be Oxford Street's strapline, but then there's not much worth seeing here anyway. Emerging from Tottenham Court Road tube station at the east end of the street brings you out beneath the unmistakable honeycomb of the Centrepoint tower. Walking west you have to squeeze along the street's busiest, scruffiest and most second-rate stretch. **Hanway Street**, just up on the right, is a curious little alley of private drinking clubs, secondhand record shops and Spanish bars and restaurants. Apart from a few good shops there's nothing remarkable until the horrendously busy crossroad of **Oxford Circus**. Any of the roads off left lead into Soho; those to the right into Fitzrovia. Beyond Oxford Circus, Oxford Street begins to acquire the dignity the capital's High Street deserves.

Apart from the great early 20th-century Ionic block of **Selfridges**, a sight in itself, the only other real sight Oxford Street has to offer is **Marble Arch**. Designed by John Nash in 1827 to stand in front of Buckingham Palace, it wasn't quite grand enough and was moved to this site on the edge of Hyde Park 25 years later, eventually stranded in the middle of a hectic roundabout. Nearby, on Sundays, **Speaker's Corner** has been providing a spot for any budding orator to let off steam since the middle of the 19th century. Nowadays the soap boxes are dominated by religious extremists and speakers with more passion than eloquence, but some still draw surprisingly large and attentive crowds.

British Museum → *Tube: Tottenham Court Rd*

ⓘ *T020-7323 8000; information T020-7323 8299; disabled information T020- 7636 7384; minicom T020-7323 8920. Sat-Wed 1000-1730, Thu Fri 1000-2030 (late view of main floor galleries, Egypt and Ancient Near East galleries and special exhibitions only). Free (donations appreciated); prices of temporary exhibitions vary. Great Court Thu-Sat 0900-2300, Sun-Wed 0900-1800. Reading Room, T020-7323 8162, www.thebritishmuseum.ac.uk. Guided tours: Highlights tour (90 mins) £8, concessions £5, 1030, 1300, 1500 daily;Spotlight (1315, 20 mins) and EyeOpener Gallery tours daily (1100- 1530 on the hr and ½ hr), free.*

With its new slogan 'illuminating world cultures', the British Museum now comes closer to that ideal in spectacular style. Architect Norman Foster's redevelopment of the central Great Court replaced the roof with a latticework glass canopy, turning the museum's long-hidden central quadrangle into the largest covered square in Europe. From beneath the front portico on Great Russell Street little seems different. Through the tall front doors though, visitors pass straight into a vast creamy space to be confronted by the Reading Room, freshly clad in white stone like a huge post box in the middle of the indoor square. The overall impression of light and space the new design creates is generous and magnificent.

On entering the **Great Court** from the south, the information desk is on the left and the box office for special exhibitions and audio guides on the right, the places to pick up floorplans and get your bearings. Within the square itself there are two cafés, two shops and, up the wide staircases round the outside of the reading room, a temporary exhibition area and a restaurant. Twelve sculptures are set around the place at ground level making up the Great Court Concourse Gallery, introducing the museum's collections.

Straight ahead as you enter is the little door into the **Reading Room**. Designed by Robert Smirke in 1823, the Round Reading Room was first opened in 1857 and its original colour scheme of light blue, cream and gold leaf has now been restored. A host of famous thinkers, writers, politicians and idlers have studied, mused or snoozed beneath the lofty dome at one of the 35 long tables fanning out from the central enquiry desk.

The main part of the museum is on the ground floor in the **west wing**, through the left-hand wall of the Great Court after entering from the main southern entrance. The galleries stretching the length of this wing are devoted to Ancient Egyptian sculpture, the Ancient Near East (including art from the palaces of Nimrud and Nineveh, and Assyrian sculpture), and Ancient Greece (including the sculptures from the Parthenon, the Nereid Monument and the Mausoleum of Halikarnassos). These collections also spill downstairs onto the lower floors of this wing.

On the right-hand side of the Great Court is the **east wing**, once the wonderful old King's Library, now transformed into an exhibition space devoted to seven different aspects of the Renaissance.

Straight ahead past the Reading Room leads into the **north wing**, and the museum's other recent new addition, the Wellcome Trust Gallery. Some of the Department of Ethnography's extraordinary collection is displayed here on the theme of 'living and dieing', alongside rooms devoted to artefacts from China, Southeast Asia, India and the Americas, with the African collection housed below.

> *The sheer range and variety of exhibits on display often provokes the observation that there's not much that's British in this museum at all.*

On the **upper floors**, above the galleries in the west wing – best reached up the south stairs on the left just before entering the Great Court from the front entrance – are more objects from Ancient Greece and also from the Roman Empire. Straight ahead at the top of these stairs leads into the rooms in the east wing devoted to Europe from the Middle Ages to modern times. Beyond these, on the upper floors of the east wing, can be found Roman Britain, Prehistory, and more monuments and treasures from the Ancient Near East which continue round into the north wing, also home to the museum's extraordinary collection of early Egyptian funerary objects – including mummies – as well as the Korean and Japanese collections.

It would be quite impossible to see everything in one day: apart from the guided and audio tours, it's well worth finding out from the Information desk when and where the free 50-min 'EyeOpener' Gallery Talks are taking place (the first usually at about 1100 and the last at about 1500). Every day many of the museum's main areas are covered, with enthusiastic and well-informed volunteers describing the contents of a particular room in fascinating detail.

Around Bloomsbury

Bloomsbury is the academic heart of London, the home of the acronym, full of august institutions better known as SOAS, UCL, RADA and ULU than by their full names, most of them part of the sprawling University of London. North of High Holborn, south of the Euston Road and west of Judd Street, its long straight streets of Georgian and

Victorian brick can be gloomy in winter, but in bright sunshine the area's severe little squares with their flower- and tree-filled gardens are a delight. The monumental British Museum may be the reason most people visit Bloomsbury, but there are a couple of less obvious attractions.

The **Petrie Museum of Egyptian Archaeology** ⓘ *Malet Place, off Torrington St, T020-7679 2000 (Ext 2884), Tue-Fri 1300-1700, Sat 1000-1300, free (donations appreciated). www.petrie.ucl.ac.uk*, is a hidden gem, bound to delight anyone whose appetite for all things Ancient Egyptian has been whetted by the British Museum. Donated by Sir Flinders Petrie to University College London (UCL) in 1933, this old-fashioned academic museum is a glass-cased treasure trove of amulets, beads, ornaments, instruments and decorative art.

The **Percival David Foundation of Chinese Art** ⓘ *T020-7387 3909, Mon-Fri 1030-1700, free (donations appreciated), under-14s must be accompanied by an adult, www.pdfmuseum.org.uk*, is in the southeastern corner of Gordon Square (No 53), it consists of a series of quiet, serene rooms containing a large collection of exquisite Chinese ceramics from the 10th-18th centuries. Ming, Qing, Song and Tang vases, dishes, pots, incense burners and water droppers, many of the items were previously owned by Chinese emperors. The cumulative effect of such an absorbing wealth of fine detail is memorable.

Marylebone and Regent's Park → *Tube: Bond St or Baker St*

A discreet Georgian and Victorian backwater just to the north of the busiest street in the West End, Marylebone has recently, and surprisingly become almost fashionable. Marylebone's hidden treasure, the **Wallace Collection** ⓘ *T020-7935 0687, www.the-wallace-collection.org.uk, Mon-Sat 1000-1700, Sun 1200-1700, free (£3 donation requested), restaurant and bookshop, buses: 2, 13, 30, 74, 82, 113, 139, 189, 274*, of 18th-century French paintings in Hertford House, has had a centennial overhaul courtesy of the National Lottery Heritage Fund. Along with the Wigmore Hall, one of London's most endearing venues for chamber music and song, the Wallace Collection continues to conjure the ghost of 19th-century and Edwardian London.

Madame Tussaud's ⓘ *T0870-400 3000, www.madame-tussauds.com, Mon-Fri 0930-1730, Sat and Sun 0930-1800, 1000-1730 bookable in 30 min timeslots, admission to Tussaud's and Planetarium, £21.99 before 1400, £20.99 after 1400, £14 after 1700, children £16 before 1400, under-5s free*, has been a surefire hit with tourists since shortly after the French Revolution when the aristocratic French woman exhibited the waxwork portraits of some of her friends who had lost their heads. In those days it may have been understandable, when people had little chance to see what the rich and famous looked like. Nowadays it's more baffling.

Next door, the **Planetarium** ⓘ *T0870-400 3000, see above for combined entry tickets with Madame Tussaud's, 1030-1700 first show summer 1030 daily, winter weekends 1030, weekdays 1230, not bookable in advance, £3, concessions/children £2*, tells the story of space exploration. Movie music and projections onto the darkened roof of the dome whizz through the history of the cosmos in an attempt to explain astronomy. The refurbished exhibition has been made more interactive but even so, it's probably still only worth seeing if visiting the much more famous Madame Tussaud's next door.

Regent's Park, just to the north, is still the most delightful place in central London to escape the crush of the West End. Here also is the chance to get close to some of the protected wildlife in **London Zoo**, ⓘ *T020-7722 3333, www.londonzoo.co.uk, daily 1000-1730 summer, 1000-1630 winter (last admission 1hr before closing), £12, concessions £10.20, children £9, bus 274 from Camden Town or Baker St.*

British Library → *Tube: King's Cross*

By the neo-Gothic palace of **St Pancras Station** over Midland Road, at 96 Euston Rd, NW1, stands the British Library. Whatever people have made of the exterior, with its straight lines of plain red brick and dark green trim offset by its splendid Victorian neighbour, the interior has provoked few complaints. Cool acres of white stone and careful attention to details, such as the handrails, the spacing of the steps and the diffusion of light, all combine to make the building a joy to use. Anyone engaged in research can apply for free membership to gain access to the reading rooms and some 18 million volumes, while the two permanent exhibitions (that can be seen without a pass) are worth a visit.

The **Treasures Gallery** ⓘ *T020-7412 7332, www.bl.uk 0930-1800 Mon, Wed, Thu, Fri; 0930-2000 Tue, 0930-1700 Sat, 1100-1700 Sun, free,* is a beautiful and carefully explained display of precious books and manuscripts: the illuminated Lindisfarne Gospel from around 700AD; a copy of the Magna Carta of 1215; the Sherborne Missal – the only painted book in England to have survived the Reformation; Shakespeare's First Folio from 1623; and many other manuscripts of great authors.

Lincoln's Inn Fields → *Holborn or Chancery Lane*

At 12-14 Lincoln's Inn Fields, the largest square in London, is **Sir John Soane's Museum** ⓘ *T020-7405 2107, www.soane.org, Tue-Sat 1000-1700, first Tue of month also 1800-2100 by candlelight in winter, free, guided tour on Sat at 1430, £3, concessions free,* one of the city's most unusual museums, a remarkable memorial to the imagination of one of Georgian London's greatest architects. Most famous for designing the Bank of England, Sir John Soane left his treasured project of a lifetime to the nation on his death in 1837. The eight or so rooms in No 13 that can now be seen are a purpose-built showcase for his highly idiosyncratic and eclectic collection of antiquities, artworks and objets d'art. At its most atmospheric (although often also most crowded) during the late openings on the first Tuesday of every month (candlelit in winter), an hour spent here is usually enough to persuade most people that they need to come again with more time.

On the south side of Lincoln's Inn Fields, at 35-43, is the **Hunterian Museum of the Royal College of Surgeons** (call for details T020-7869 6560). In the 18th century John Hunter amassed a huge collection of pathological specimens, human and animal, in the course of his anatomical studies. With the addition of thousands more in the 19th century, the museum once held a world-beating variety of pickled parts and dissected exhibits. The museum is being given an overhaul due for completion in late 2004.

Smithfield Market

Clerkenwell is one of the more exciting parts of London to wander around, not simply because of the clutch of new shops, restaurants, clubs and bars that have opened up here in the last decade, but also because it's an old part of town still visibly in a state of fashionable flux. A good place to start is in the south of the area around Smithfield Market, London's meat distribution centre. Unlike the other wholesale fish and fruit and veg markets at Billingsgate and Covent Garden, the market has managed to cling on to its ancient site in the city centre. Especially late at night and at dawn, when the area round about is partying hard or fast asleep, the comings and goings of huge articulated and refrigerated lorries unloading endless fresh carcasses into its grand late 19th-century building can take on a surreal quality. Try a pint of Guinness and a fry-up breakfast in The **Cock Tavern** (T020-7248 2918), at 0600 to complete the Smithfield experience.

St Paul's Cathedral → *Tube: St Paul's*

ⓘ *T020-7236 4128, www.stpauls.co.uk, 0830-1600 Mon-Sat. £7 including Cathedral Crypt and Galleries, concessions £6, children £3, family £17. Guided tours 1100, 1130, 1330, 1400 Mon-Sat. Adult £2.50, £2 concessions and under-16s. Audio guide £3.50. Organ recitals 1700 Sun. Free. Buses 4, 11, 15, 17, 23, 26, 76, 100 & 172*

The City holds little of interest for the recreational visitor. After the money-makers have gone home for the week, the square mile becomes a gigantic modern ghost town sprinkled with empty little churches. The grand exception is St Paul's Cathedral, its great stone interior always echoing with sightseers or worshippers, its dome one of the most beautiful, symbolic landmarks in London and a spectacular view point. At least the fifth church on the site, St Paul's was started in 1675, took about 35 years to complete and was paid for with taxes raised on coal and wine coming into the Port of London. Hemmed in on all sides over the centuries, Wren's relatively colossal church still inspires awe and wonder.

During the summer, the crowds can be avoided by arriving first thing in the morning during the week.

The redevelopment of Paternoster Square has opened up new views of the place, reflecting its Portland stone in plate-glass office blocks, while the Millennium Bridge now provides a neat approach from the South Bank riverside and Tate Modern. Wren had originally hoped to build a church in the form of a Greek cross, but this plan, and his desire to top it with a dome rather than a steeple, were vetoed. Instead he settled on the more traditional Latin cross for the ground plan, and then carried on the building work in such secrecy that no one could complain before his vision, including the dome, was substantially in place. He could see the work in progress from his house across the river (still standing next to the modern Globe Theatre). The final result is a kind of mini version of St Peter's in Rome, much less flamboyantly decorated, and one of the most successful Classical interpretations of Gothic in the world.

Twenty-two wide steps lead up to the West Front, looking down Ludgate Hill, with its double portico containing a bas-relief depicting the conversion of the tax-collector Paul. At the apex stands St Paul himself, the patron saint of the City of London, with St Peter on his right and St James on his left. At the time of writing, the whole west front is receiving a thorough refurbishment. Behind is the Great Dome, invisibly supported with reinforced concrete and a chain of steel after it was discovered that Wren's builders had skimped on the use of solid stone for the supporting columns.

Inside, the massive nave of the Cathedral is wonderfully vast and bare. In fact most of the decoration was only added in the late 19th and early 20th centuries, and not very well at that. It's definitely well worth climbing up the long, wide wooden spiral staircase to the **Whispering Gallery**, around the base of the inner dome, decorated with statues of Early Church Fathers and painted scenes from the life of St Paul. People press their ears to the wall here hoping to catch what their friends are whispering on the other side. Unfortunately the hubbub from far below often drowns out the famous effect.

Several steep and narrow flights of stone steps with regular resting places then lead up to the **Stone Gallery** outside, where the views through the balustrade are quite spectacular. In order to look west from here though it's necessary to brave the extraordinary series of vertiginous cast-iron spiral stairways heading up to the **Golden Gallery**. The tremendous wrap-around open-air views from the cramped little balcony up here easily rival those from the London Eye.

Back in the main body of the Cathedral, sights include the **choir** gorgeously carved by Grinling Gibbons; **Henry Moore's sculpture** of Mother and Child in the north choir aisle; the copy of Holman Hunt's *The Light of the World* in the north transept; a display on the firewatch that saved the building during the Blitz; and the **American Memorial Chapel** at the very east end of the church in the apse, consecrated to the memory of over 28,000 US servicemen based in Britain who died in the Second World War.

The City & the South Bank

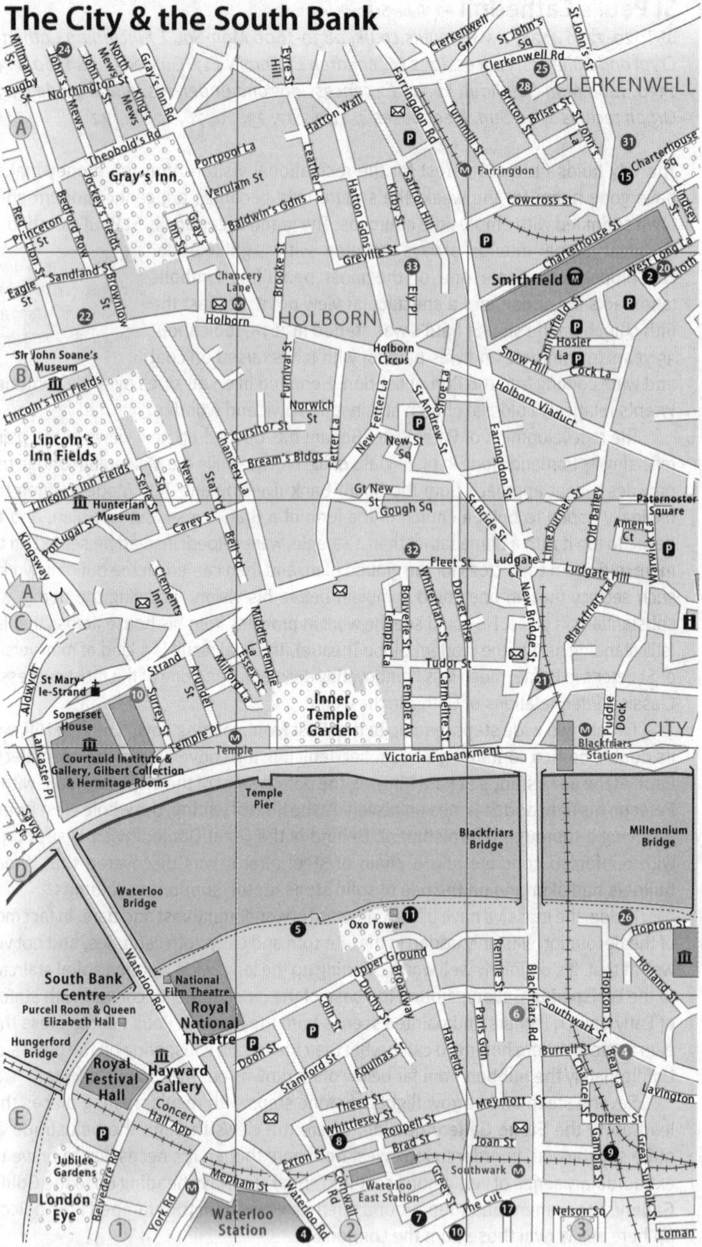

0 metres 100

0 yards 100

Sleeping

Bankside House **1** *E4*
Barbican YMCA **2** *A4*
Great Eastern **3** *B6*
Holiday Inn Express **4** *E3*
London City YMCA **5** *A5*
Mad Hatter **6** *E3*
St Christopher's Inn Backpackers Village **9** *E5*
Strand Continental **10** *C1*

Eating

Bespoke Bakery & Fine Food Shop **8** *E2*
Club Gascon **2** *B3*
De Gustibus **3** *E5*
Fire Station **4** *E2*
Gourmet Pizza Company **5** *D2*
Konditor & Cook **7** *E2* & *E5*

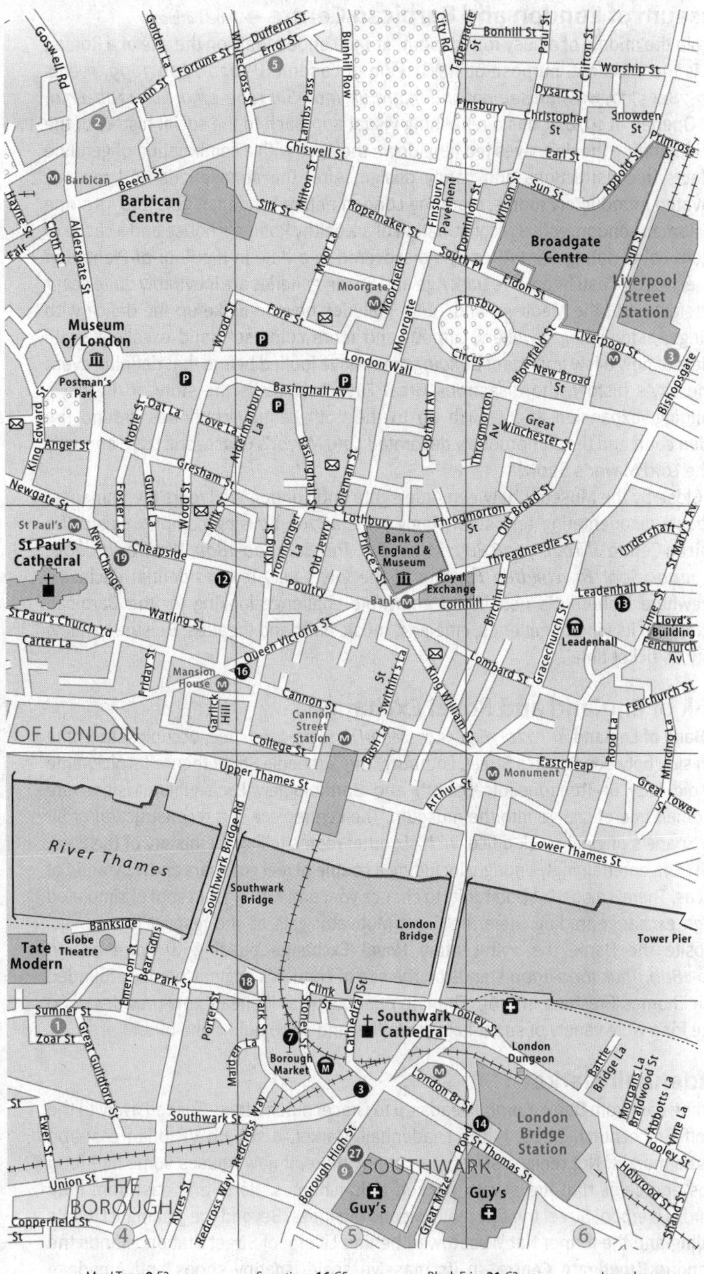

Mar I Terra **9** *E3*
Mesón Don Felipe **10** *E2*
Oxo Tower **11** *D2*
Place Below **12** *C4*
Prism **13** *C6*
Spiazzo Café **14** *E6*
St John **15** *A3*
Sweetings **16** *C5*
Tas **17** *E3*

Pubs & bars
Anchor Bankside **18** *D5*
Ball's Brothers **19** *C4*
Barley Mow **20** *B3*
Black Friar **21** *C3*
Cittie of York **22** *B1*
Duke of York (Roger St) **24** *A1*
Dust **25** *A3*
Founders Arms **26** *D3*
George Inn **27** *E5*
Jerusalem Tavern **28** *A3*
Vic Naylor's **31** *A3*
Ye Olde Cheshire Cheese **32** *C2*
Ye Olde Mitre Tavern **33** *B2*

Museum of London and Barbican Centre → *Tube: Barbican*

Bang in the middle of a busy roundabout, at 150 London Wall, on the site of a Roman fort, is the excellent, purpose-built Museum of London ⓘ *T020-7600 3699, events T020-7814 5777, www.museumoflondon.org.uk, Mon-Sat 1000-1750, Sun 1200-1750, free.* Opened in 1976, it has a refreshing visual approach to the social history of the city, illustrating the daily lives led here down the ages with a combination of genuine artefacts, reconstructions and canny design. After the atmospheric and recently renovated introductory rooms, featuring London before London, it gets into its stride with Roman London, with a reconstruction of a wealthy Roman's house and a cache of 43 gold coins dating from AD65-170 discovered in a hole in the floor of Plantation House, just off Eastcheap. The Dark Age and Saxon galleries are inevitably quite scant in artefacts, but the Medieval and Tudor galleries beyond make up the deficit with carvings, astonishing jewellery, armour and more coins set amid excellent scale models of how a few important buildings may have looked before that defining event in the city's history, the disastrous Great Fire. Downstairs the story of the city's rebuilding, expansion and growth up to the 20th century continues around the Garden court and the sumptuously decorated Lord Mayor's Coach, still used annually for the Lord Mayor's Show.

Close by the Museum between Aldersgate and London Wall rears the immense, famously disorientating and surprisingly popular 70s housing complex called the Barbican Centre ⓘ *T020-7638 8891, Mon, Tue, Thu-Sat 1000-1800, Wed 1000-2000, Sun 1200-1800, £7, children £4,* one of the City's very few residential enclaves. Somewhere in here it's usually an enjoyable challenge looking for the Barbican Centre, with its vibrant galleries, cinemas, music halls and theatres. Be sure to allow plenty of 'ticket time'.

Bank of England and Royal Exchange

The **Bank of England** ⓘ *T020-7601 5545, Mon-Fri, 1000-1700, free*, occupies the entire north side between Prince's Street, Lothbury, Threadneedle Street (hence its nickname 'the old lady of Threadneedle Street') and Bartholomew Lane where visitors are welcomed free of charge into the museum. The centrepiece is a reconstruction of Sir John Soane's original stock office, with six other rooms telling the history of the Bank since 1694 entertainingly enough, including a couple of real gold bars and a pyramid of replicas. There's also the opportunity to chance your arm with a 3 min spot of simulated foreign exchange trading. Here the Great Motivator gets all the respect it deserves. Opposite the Bank, the 19th-century **Royal Exchange** building ⓘ *Mon-Wed, Fri 1000-1800, Thur 1000-1900* stands on the site of London's original 'bourse', founded by Sir Thomas Gresham in 1565. The fine quadrangle at its heart now provides shop space for a wide variety of super-luxury retailers and a few quirky one-offs.

Leadenhall Market

Heading east from Bank, Cornhill leads up to Gracechurch Street. Tucked away to the left off Gracechurch Street is the Leadenhall Market, a superb Victorian cast-iron covered market. Not really a street market any more, it now houses some fine food shops and cafés that are always packed at lunchtimes. North and east from here towards Liverpool Street the City really means business. Beyond the gleaming **Lloyd's Building** and the former Nat West tower, behind Liverpool Street Station, stands the enormous **Broadgate Centre**. In its massive scale, snappy shops and American confidence it makes interesting comparison with the quaint old Leadenhall Market.

Tate Modern → *Tube: Southwark or Blackfriars*

ⓘ *T020-7887 8000; ticket bookings T020-7887 8888; information T020-7887 8008, www.tate.org.uk/modern. Sun-Thu 1000-1800; Fri and Sat 1000-2200. Free (charges for special exhibitions). Buses 45, 63, 100, 381.*

Over the last 10 years the south bank of the river between Blackfriars and Tower Bridge has been transformed. The conversion of the old Bankside Power Station into a world class modern art gallery at Tate Modern is the latest and most spectacular confirmation of the area's new-found success. Opened in May 2000, the converted Bankside Power Station now houses the Tate's collection of international modern art from 1900 to the present. An extraordinary great solid box of brick with a single free-standing square chimney front centre, the power station was designed by Sir Giles Gilbert Scott to be a striking landmark, responding architecturally to its position across the river from St Paul's Cathedral.

Opposite Tate Modern, the Millennium Bridge – a footbridge designed by architect Norman Foster with the sculptor Anthony Caro – arcs gracefully over the river to St Paul's.

In a much-publicized break with traditional historical and chronological hangings, the collection is permanently arranged around four themes suggested by the four genres of fine art laid down by the French Academy in the 17th century: Still Life, Landscape, the Nude and History. It contains examples of work by most of the big names of 20th-century art, from Duchamp, Matisse and Picasso through to Bacon and Warhol, whose pieces are likely to be found in striking juxtaposition to those of lesser-known or more contemporary artists.

From the main entrance a wide sloping ramp of brick leads down into the immense **Turbine Hall**, an astonishing space for artworks on a grand scale. In here, towering up through seven storeys on the north side of the building facing the river, linked by central escalators and stairways, are the galleries themselves, standing proud as illuminated boxes of light. On **level 3**, Still Life/Object/Real Life covers the contents of the 14 exhibition spaces on the east side of the building, while Landscape/Matter/Environment covers those on the west side. **Level 4** is taken up with temporary exhibitions (admission charged), while on **level 5**, the Nude/Action/Body galleries are on the east side, and History/Memory/Society on the west. Under these headings the galleries are devoted to selections from the collection that are changed every six months or so, arranged as monographs to single artists, such as Bruce Nauman, Joseph Beuys, or Stanley Spencer, or under themes like *The Intelligent Object*, *Inner Worlds* and *Transfiguration*.

From the Turbine Hall information desk and also on level 3, **hand-held audio tours** (£1) in several languages are available, including the **Collection Tour**, with illuminating commentaries by artists and curators explaining the galleries' themes (each room also has an explanatory panel), specific works and artists. Free audio points are also available in some of the rooms and **free guided tours** leave from level 2 at 1030, 1130, 1430, and 1530, from near the Starr Auditorium, which incorporates a cinema showing free films throughout the day and special seasons by art directors in the evenings. A visit to the website in the **Clore Study Room** on level 1 enables the location of specific works or of artists room by room.

Around Bankside and Southwark → *Tube: Southwark or Blackfriars*

A short walk downstream brings you to Bankside pier and Shakespeare's **Globe Theatre** ⓘ *T020-7902 1500, www.shakespeares-globe.org, May-Sep, 0900-1200 daily, Oct-Apr, 1000-1700 daily, guided tours £8, concession £6.50, children £5.50*. The brainchild of American actor and film-maker Sam Wanamaker, who sadly didn't live to see its completion, this sweet little open-air Elizabethan playhouse – Shakespeare's 'wooden O' – reconstructed using original techniques and materials, has been an enormous success: under the inspired directorship of Mark Rylance, its summer season of four productions played in rep, some in period dress, often sells out well in advance.

Nearby, in Montague Close, is **Southwark Cathedral** ⓘ *T020-7367 6700, www.dswark.org, daily 0900-1800 (closing times vary on religious holidays), three services each day throughout the week, free (donations appreciated)*, a beautiful place of worship dating back to the seventh century. It may be small in comparison to other cathedrals in the country, but its place in the heart of a crowded inner-city community makes it distinctive. Inside, notable monuments include the tomb of John Gower, a friend of Chaucer's and like him one of the fathers of English poetry; a monument to Shakespeare; and a rare wooden effigy of an unknown 13th-century knight.

Nestling beneath the cathedral, **Borough Market** is a wholesale fruit 'n' veg market that has probably been trading near this spot since the Middle Ages and certainly on this spot since the middle of the 18th century. Nowadays it shelters beneath a great cast-iron Victorian canopy but like other old buildings around here is under threat from the proposed widening of the railway viaduct above. The market itself caters mainly to the restaurant trade and other fruit 'n' veg stallholders, and is at its busiest at dawn, although there are some interesting one-offs. The retail food market (Friday 1200-1800 and Saturday 0900-1600) is famous for the superb variety of high-quality produce. This is the place to find some of the finest bread, meat, fish, fruit, nuts and veg in the capital. Saturday is busiest with epicurean picnickers. ▶▶ *See also Shopping, page 104.*

From the market, steps lead up onto **London Bridge**. Built 1967-72, this is the third stone bridge called London Bridge to have crossed the river near this point. The first, a little further downstream, stood for over 600 years, crowded with houses, a chapel in the middle, and almost damming the river with its 19 arches.

The second bridge, built 1823-31, was sold and rebuilt in Lake Havasu City, Arizona.

Not far away is the **London Dungeon** ⓘ *28-34 Tooley St, T020-7403 7221, www.thedungeons.com, Oct-Mar, 1030-1700 daily, Apr-Sep 1000-1930 daily, £12.95, children under 10 £8.95, children 10-14 £9.95, concession £11.25.* Waxwork animatronic models, reconstructed instruments of torture, and sensationalist light effects on a variety of 'dark rides' are intended to scare the living daylights out of visitors. Themes include the Jack the Ripper Experience, Judgement Day and most recently, the Great Plague of London. Children enjoy it, judging from the attraction's enduring popularity, but adults are likely to be less enthralled.

London Eye → *Tube: Westminster, Embankment or Waterloo*

ⓘ *T0870-5000 600, www.ba- londoneye.com, Jan-Apr, Oct-Dec daily 0930-2000, May, Sept Mon-Thu 0930-2000, Fri-Sun 0930-2100; Jun, Mon-Thu 0930-2100, Fri-Sun 0930-2200; Jul-Aug daily 0930-2200. £11, concessions £10, children £5.50, under-5s free (advance booking available on the web or on the phone, prices subject to change). The ticket hall for the Eye is in County Hall. Buses:12, 26, 53, 59, 68, 76, 159, 168, 176, 188, 211.*

The vast white spoked wheel of the London Eye beside Westminster Bridge has already become one of the most welcome additions to the London skyline in years. Well over 100 m in diameter, the largest structure of its kind in the world, it's visible from unexpected places all around the city. The half-hour 'flight' in one of its surprisingly roomy glass 'capsules', moving at a quarter-metre a second, provides superb 25-mile views over the city, and is neither vertiginous nor at all boring. On a clear day you can see all of London and beyond, including Guildford Cathedral, Windsor Castle and the river flowing out into the North Sea. If the weather is less fine, and there's no banking on it if you've been sensible and booked in advance (or even stood in the queue for an hour), you're at least guaranteed the sensation of looking down on the top of Big Ben and overlooking Nelson on his column. River cruises down to the Tower of London and back are also available.

County Hall

Built just before the First World War for the London County Council, the fate of this magisterial building, which became the seat of the left-wing Greater London Council (GLC), is one of London's odder ironies. Since the GLC's abolition by Margaret Thatcher in the mid-80s, London's town hall has been thrown open to the people by its Japanese owners as a hotch-potch leisure and tourist development. It now houses the London Aquarium, a Macdonald's, a Namco videogame arcade, a 24-hr health club, and a Chinese restaurant, as well as a five-star Marriot Hotel and a budget Travel Inn. The new kid in the block is the **Saatchi Gallery** ⓘ *T020-7823 2363, Sun-Thur 1000-1800, Fri, Sat 1000-2200, £8.50, children £6.50*, which houses advertising guru Charles Saatchi's contemporary art collection. Probably the single most famous exhibit is Damien Hirst's pickled shark, entitled 'The Physical Impossibility of Death in the Mind of Someone Living' but it's the sheer variety and accessibility of the sculptures (mainly) and also paintings that makes a visit here wonderfully provoking. Next door, appropriately enough, is the **Dali Universe at the County Hall Gallery** ⓘ *T020-7620 2720, daily 1000-1730, £8.50, concessions £7.50, children £4.95*, devoted to the famous 20th-century Spanish surrealist Salvador Dali, far from publicity-shy himself. The darkened rooms feature more than 500 works, including drawings and sculptures, and the opportunity to buy one to take home.

Underneath these galleries is the London Aquarium ⓘ *T020-7967 8000, www.londonaquarium.co.uk, daily 1000-1800 (last admission 1700), £8.75, children £5.25*, which consists of three darkened floors of aquaria designed around two huge tanks, Atlantic and Pacific, home to small sharks, stingrays and conger eels among others. The favourite attractions for children of all ages are the open-top 'touch pools' downstairs: a rock pool alive with crabs and anemones, and the beach pool full of thornback rays. On the way out, there's a display on the threat mankind's activities pose to the marine environment.

The South Bank Centre

Downstream from County Hall and Jubilee Gardens, just beyond the Hungerford railway and footbridge, stands the South Bank Centre (SBC). The largest arts complex of its kind in Europe, it grew up around the **Royal Festival Hall**, the centrepiece of the Festival of Britain. Apart from the main concert hall, the Grade I listed building also houses an exhibition space, a good bookshop, the Poetry Library, and the high-class *People's Palace* restaurant. Nearby, connected by concrete terraces overlooking the river, are more concert halls, the **Purcell Room** and **Queen Elizabeth Hall** (see page 102), as well as the cutting-edge **Hayward Gallery**, ⓘ *T020-7928 3144, www.sbc.org.uk, Mon, Thu-Sun 1000-1800, Tue, Wed 1000-2000, admission price varies according to exhibition, buses 26, 59, 68, 76, 168, 176, 188*. Opened in 1968 and one of the few remaining examples of 'brutalist' architecture in London, it has recently been reburfished and furnished with an airy glass entrance hall and café. This is the place to come for major state-subsidized temporary exhibitions of contemporary art.

Next door is the Royal National Theatre and National Film Theatre (T020-7928 3535), whose restaurant and bar have become one of London's favourite meeting places.

Imperial War Museum → *Tube: Lambeth North*

ⓘ *T020-74165320, www.iwm.org.uk, daily 1000-1800, free.*

Heading away from the river down Lambeth Road brings you to The Imperial War Museum, founded in 1917 to record the British Empire's involvement in the First World War. Since then it has dedicated itself to the history and consequences of all 20th-century warfare. The bronze cast of the Kalachakra Mandala, associated with world peace, is a good object of contemplation in juxtaposition with the grand entrance to the museum, guarded by a pair of the largest naval guns ever built.

On the ground floor you'll find an even more fearsome collection of military hardware, all quiet, cleaned up and cut away for easy viewing: tanks, mini-subs, aeroplanes and more peculiar equipment like the little observer's pod that was dangled beneath zeppelins hidden in the clouds. A reconstructed First World War trench, 'The Trench Experience', is genuinely unpleasant, although thankfully nothing like as awful as the original must have been. A large and relatively new exhibition on the Holocaust also puts the whole bloody business in perspective.

The Tower and around → *Tower Hill*

ⓘ *T0870 751 5177, www.tower-of-london.org.uk. Mar-Oct Mon-Sat 0900-1700, Sun 1000-1700; Nov-Feb Mon, Sun 1000-1600, Tue-Sat 0900-1600. £13.50, children £9 (various combined, group and family prices, phone for details). Free Yeoman Warder tours (1hr) every 30 mins from 0925, (Sun, Mon from 1000), last tour 1530. Tower Gateway DLR.*

Londoners traditionally dislike the **Tower of London** dismissing it as a tourist trap. In fact it's less a trap than a treat, making an enormous effort to elucidate its wealth of historical associations and bring the old buildings to life for their two and a half million or so visitors each year. Inevitably the gate pressure means that the castle and its grim story come across a bit like a sanitized medieval theme park, but the central place it occupies in the Royal heritage and history of Britain and its capital is impossible to deny. Outside Tower Hill tube a viewing platform overlooks The Tower of London, a classic photo-opportunity for an overall picture of the layout of the fortification and its many towers, with Tower Bridge and the river in the background. In the middle stands the original fortress, the White Tower, one of the first, largest and most complete Norman keeps in the country, surrounded at a respectful distance by smaller buildings erected over the last 900 years.

With some justification, the Tower claims to be several tourist attractions in one and for clarity's sake divides itself into seven colour-coded areas, each taking a suggested 20 or 30 mins to see: the Western Entrance and Water Lane, the Medieval Palace, the Wall Walk, the Crown Jewels, Tower Green, the White Tower and the Fusiliers' Museum.

East London → *Tube Old St for Hoxton and Shoreditch; Aldgate East for Whitechapel and Brick Lane.*

The **East End** has long been forced to make the best of a bad lot. North and east of the wealth in the City of London, there's little room here for complacency about cheery cockneys weathering the worst of it with their colourful rhyming slang and robust attitude to a fair deal. That said, the small area round Shoreditch, Hoxton Square, Spitalfields and Whitechapel has changed considerably in recent years, now attracting a large number of outsiders and boasting the most vibrant nightlife in the city beyond Soho. The spectacular boom in late-night clubs, bars and restaurants here has made the area one of the most exciting after-work destinations in town later in the week. In **Docklands,** where once the masts of tall ships dominated the skyline, the massive obelisk of Canary Wharf now towers over gleaming office blocks and swish apartments, winking across lots of landlocked riverwater. Even so, the peculiar history of the place makes it an intriguing destination and the views from Island Gardens are compensation enough for the architectural eyesores. Across the river, **Greenwich** rewards the journey east with a convenient cluster of top attractions, most especially the National Maritime Museum, but also the Royal Observatory, and the 18th-century grandeur of the Royal Naval College.

East End

Hoxton Square was the epicentre of Shoreditch's rebirth as the most happening place in the East End. The square itself is a gloomy little spot but then that adds to its offbeat appeal. By contrast **Hoxton Market** next door has had a thorough makeover, now a smart pedestrianized area, and not to be confused with **Hoxton Street Market** further up the eponymous street on Saturdays, one of the most welcoming and laid-back of London's local street markets. Halfway down is Hoxton Hall, the last surviving Victorian music hall, with a fashionable programming policy.

On Kingsland Road, the 18th-century almshouses of the Ironmongers' Company have housed the **Geffrye Museum** ⓘ *T020-7739 9893, www.geffrye-museum.org.uk, Tue-Sat 1000- 1700, Sun 1200-1700, free,* since 1913. A beautifully laid out history of furniture and interior design is told here, a series of period rooms along the front of the old building decorated as they might have been at various times between 1600 and the late Victorian age.

Southbound Shoreditch High Street heads into the City via Bishopsgate. Off to the left just before Liverpool Street Station stands the green cast-iron and brick spectacle of the old **Spitalfields Market**. The wholesale fruit 'n' veg market here was closed down in 1992, and since then the building has been the subject of local concern about its future, a campaign being rallied under the acronym SMUT. It now looks as if half will inevitably soon be replaced by a new development, while the Victorian eastern part will be preserved. Catch the ramshackle whole while you can, at its best during the Farmers' and Crafts Market on Sundays.

Behind Spitalfields Market, on Commercial Street, rears the huge Hawksmoor creation of **Christ Church Spitalfields** ⓘ *T020-7247 7202, Mon-Fri 1300-1500, 1030 for Sun services,* where the Spitalfields Festival of Music takes place every year in June and during the two weeks before Christmas (T020-7377 0287), with concerts of mainly Baroque music, as well as some by new composers. Beyond the church the mid-18th-century streets like Fournier and Princelet running towards Brick Lane are some of the most atmospheric and evocative in London. Still gaslit at night, the old brick terraces adapted for weavers have not yet been over-restored, while a few have been converted into galleries and shops.

Nearby, at 18 Folgate Street, is **Dennis Severs' House** ⓘ *T020-7247 4013, www.dennisseversshouse.co.uk, 'The Experience' on first and third Sun of month 1400-1700 (£8) and the Mon after 1200-1400 (£5), and 'Silent Night' by candlelight every Mon evening (£12) or by appointment.* Here, the desire to slip back into the past was taken to an artistic extreme by the late Dennis Severs, who ran an eccentric 'living museum'. His life's work, a painstaking recreation of period décor from the mid-18th century to early 20th can now be explored on 'The Experience', where visitors are encouraged to reassess their attitudes to their own thoughts and feelings about past, present and future in the mysterious light of Dennis Severs' obsessive attention to detail. Certainly one of the oddest visitor attractions in London, the current caretakers discourage anyone not prepared to enter into the spirit of their friend's vision.

Running roughly parallel to Commerical Street, **Brick Lane** is the main artery of 'Bangla Town', famous for its Bengali and Bangladeshi curry houses and warehouses, and also for the extraordinary market held at its top end every Sunday morning. Next to Bethnal Green tube station, the **Bethnal Green Museum of Childhood** ⓘ *T020-8983 5200, www.vam.ac.uk, Mon-Thu, Sat and Sun 1000-1745, free,* is a delightful offshoot of the V&A housing an extensive, superior and priceless collection of antique doll's houses, old puppets, model trains and just about anything else that has been manufactured in the last few centuries to keep nippers amused. Near Aldgate East tube station is the **Whitechapel Art Gallery** ⓘ *80-82 Whitechapel High St, E1, T020-7522 7888, Tue, Wed and Fri-Sun 1100-1800, Thu 1100-2100, free,* one of London's most innovative and exciting public spaces for contemporary art, opened in 1901. Its art nouveau façade belies the radical edge to many of its shows.

Docklands → *Shadwell (East London line) and Canary Wharf*

The Docklands are a pristine and ultimately bland extension of the teeming money-driven office life of the City of London. Arriving on the DLR at Canary Wharf, or emerging from Norman Foster's fairly awe-inspiring new station for the Jubilee line, it's impossible to miss the **Canary Wharf Tower**, 1 Canada Square, E14, the beacon at the heart of Docklands. A little to the north, the new **Museum in Docklands** ⓘ *Warehouse No 1, West India Quay, Hertsmere Rd, E14, T020-7001 9800, daily*

 1000-1800, £3, takes the themes of River, Port and People to tell the story of the area from salty seafarers via desolation to corporate hospitality. The full history of Docklands is covered in some depth at this outpost of the Museum of London, going some way towards recapturing some of the area's exciting past with Sailor Town, a recreation of a local 19th-century street.

Nearer the tip of the Isle of Dogs, the **Island History Trust** ⓘ *197 East Ferry Road, E14, T020-7987 6041, Tue, Wed 1330-1630, free*, hold at least 5000 photos depicting the Isle of Dogs in the 20th century. Along with the new museum, a visit here is a must to fully appreciate the changes, good and bad, the area has undergone in recent times. Nestling at the tip of the Isle of Dogs, **Island Gardens** is a small park that makes an ideal place to sit and admire the glorious view of maritime Greenwich and the Cutty Sark. Look over your shoulder, and you're back in the 21st century with a bang, Canary Wharf still oddly close though more than a mile away. From Island Gardens, the Greenwich foot tunnel, constructed in 1902 for the West India dockers, sneaks under the river and back in time.

Greenwich

As well as being the home of Greenwich Mean Time, the area's ancient Royal and naval associations made it seem an appropriate spot to wave goodbye to the lost Empire of the 20th century and welcome in the era of 'New Britain'. Unfortunately the future of the Millennium Dome still hangs in the balance. A fairly short river trip from Westminster past many of London's most famous sights, the town itself is also pleasant to explore, with a variety of salty sights. Appropriately enough, visitors to Greenwich arriving by boat land next to the **Cutty Sark** ⓘ *T020-8858 3445, www.cuttysark.org.uk, daily 1000-1700 (last admission 1630), £3.95, concession £2.95*, the only surviving tea clipper. Built in 1869 on the Clyde, and named after the skimpy nightie on a dancing witch in Robert Burns' poem, *Tam O'Shanter*, she made her last commercial voyage in 1922, and was dry-docked in Greenwich in 1954. Two decks can be explored, including the Captain's cabin, as well as a collection of figureheads from other tall ships.

The **Royal Naval College** ⓘ *T020-8269 4744, www.greenwichfoundation.org.uk, daily 1000-1700 (last admission 1615), free, guided tours £9, concessions £5*, represents English architecture at its grandest and most formal. Three of the most celebrated 18th-century British architects had a hand in the design – Wren, Hawksmoor and Vanbrugh – and its twin domes and columns still make a stunning picture when seen from Island Gardens, the river or from the hills of Greenwich Park. Now part of Greenwich University, visitors can wander its riverside quads and see the Painted Hall, beneath the southwestern cupola, an extraordinary room, busy with murals beneath a magnificent ceiling, all painted by Thornhill over a period of 19 years.

The **Queen's House** ⓘ *T020-8858 4422, daily 1000-1700 (last admission 1630), free*, was the first truly Renaissance house constructed in England, now standing bang in the middle of the National Maritime Museum. It contains a portrait gallery of old sea captains and other mariner types but nothing could diminish the beauty of the architecture: the Great Hall is a perfect cube, while the 'tulip staircase' named after the designs on its bannisters is beautiful too. Look out for **Canaletto**'s view of the Royal Hospital and Greenwich from the Isle of Dogs, little changed today. A covered colonnade connects Queen's House on either side to the large **National Maritime Museum** ⓘ *T020-8858 4422, www.nmm.ac.uk, daily 1000-1700, free*, with its three levels pretty much doing justice to their enthralling subject, the sea. In a bold move the museum was transformed in early 1999 by the completion of architect Rick Mather's extraordinary £21 million glass roof over the central Neptune Court, manufactured by the company that built the Eiffel Tower. A steep walk up the hill through the park behind the Museum leads to the **Royal Observatory** ⓘ *T020-8858 4422, daily 1000-1700 (last admission 1630), free*. Most prominent of the buildings is **Flamsteed House** which looks and sounds like something out of Harry Potter but is in fact the 17th-century home of the Astronomer Royal.

North London

North of Euston, St Pancras and King's Cross, **Camden** is the spigot around which north London spins. And a strange mixed-up place it is too, with its music, markets and self-aware media-savvy, its dirt, hard drinking and organic juice bars. The Chalk Farm Road carries Camden High Street on northwest past the genteel slopes of Primrose Hill, a chi-chi celebrity hideout overlooking Regent's Park, towards the heights of **Hampstead**, a London high point. An affluent town astride the hills to the north, it competes in both elevation, social status and antique authenticity with the neighbouring hilltop village of **Highgate**. Although no longer the liberal, bohemian enclaves they once were, both remain strongly associated with their literary and cultural heritage. They are also deservedly famous for the 800 or so acres of rolling grassland, meadows and woodland of Hampstead Heath that divides them. To the east, sitting on a low hilltop northwest of the City, **Islington** likes to think of itself – with some justification – as the left-wing Notting Hill of north London. Its transformation over the last 20 years into the fashionable stamping ground of the liberal middle classes has not always been entirely happy, but is now more confident than ever, credited with nurturing the politics of the current Labour government.

Camden → *Tube: Camden Town, although it becomes one-way into the area on Sat and Sun*

The **markets** are Camden Town's main attraction, the city's weekly street festival, and the reason most people come to Camden in the first place. The **market** (daily 0900-1730) has ballooned from lowly beginnings into a series of stalls occupying any vacant space on the High Street between Camden Town tube and Camden Lock every Saturday and Sunday. Camden Market and the Electric Ballroom and the High Street itself, with its outsize shop signs, are a pop kids' Mecca, awash with cheap leather jackets, brashly sloganed T-shirts and hectic drinking holes. In recent years though, **Camden Lock Market** (daily 1000-1800), just off Chalk Farm Road, with its array of more interesting clothes, jewellery, books and handicraft, and **Stables Market**, off Chalk Farm Road at the junction with Hartland Road, with its furniture and bric-a-brac, have provided satisfying browsing. The **Canal Market** runs off Chalk Farm Road, just over the bridge from the High Street on the right, with a mish-mash of stalls inside and out. If none of these tickles your fancy you can always plump for plain old fruit 'n' veg at the market on Inverness Street.

A few minutes walk from the High Street, or best reached directly over the railway bridge from Chalk Farm tube, the pretty village of Primrose Hill could hardly be more different from its raving eastern neighbour. The hill itself affords magnificent vistas over central London and Kent beyond. The London Eye in the distance makes a striking addition to one of the city's greatest views, much marred in the 60s by a series of thoughtless housing projects.

Hampstead and Highgate

There's a distinctive 'villagey' feel to Hampstead. Highgate is often seen as the poor relation, but its famous cemetery and village atmosphere make it a rewarding destination on the more attractive eastern side of the Heath. From Hampstead tube, Heath Street heads sharply uphill towards Hampstead Heath, an oasis of uncultivated land where it is easy to forget the urban mayhem as one wanders leafy avenues, open fields and shaded woods. Spectacular views of London can be found from the top of Parliament Hill, which is also a great place to fly kites.

At 20 Maresfield Gardens, NW3, is the **Freud Museum** ⓣ *T020-7435 2002, Wed-Sun 1200-1700, £5, concessions £2*, where the great psychoanalyst spent the last years of his life. The house has been preserved for posterity, now including a reconstruction of his study and consulting room, complete with the famous couch, and a number of classical antiquities testifying to Freud's passionate interest in the ancient world.

Highgate Cemetery ⓘ *T020-8340 1834, eastern cemetery Mon-Fri 1000-1600, Sat and Sun 1100-1600, western cemetery Oct-Feb Sat, Sun tours at 1100, 1200, 1300, 1400, 1500, Mar-Oct weekdays also at 1400, tours cost £4*, is most famous for being the burial place of Karl Marx, in the more modern eastern part of the cemetery. The western part, the most overgrown and one of London's most extraordinary and atmospheric burial grounds, is carefully protected by a society of friends who offer informative guided tours taking in the remarkable Egyptian catacombs, famous graves, monuments and an abundance of wild flowers. Both parts are sometimes closed to the public during funerals.

Islington

→ *Tube: Angel for the southern end of Upper St; Highbury and Islington for the northern end*

Islington rewards visitors not with its sights but with a welcoming attitude, a wide array of ethnic restaurants, old pubs and fashionable bars, a thriving theatre and music scene and two excellent small markets. The antique shops in **Camden Passage** have long been a major draw, while **Chapel Market** is a thriving local street market and increasingly hot nightspot. Friday and Saturday night excitement in Islington can be just as mad, bad and dangerous-to-know as anywhere in the West End – which is quite an achievement in itself.

Most of the action in Islington takes place on Upper St and the streets immediately around, including Chapel Market.

East of Upper Street lies Canonbury, best appreciated by a visit to the **Estorick Collection of Modern Italian Art** ⓘ *39 Canonbury Sq (entrance on Canonbury Rd), T020-7704 9522, www.estorickcollection.com, Wed-Sat 1100-1800, Sun 1200-1700, £3.50, concession £2.50*, not least for a good opportunity to take a look inside a fine Georgian house and enjoy some good food from the café indoors or out. The intriguing permanent collection of Italian art here, featuring an especially strong selection of Futurist work, is often complemented by eye-catching contemporary exhibitions.

South and West London

West of Hyde Park, **Notting Hill** basks in celebrity status, even if sometimes for all the wrong reasons. One of London's original and now more successful gentrified multicultural districts, its sloping terraces may not be the most attractive in town but the fashionable types patrolling its boutiques, galleries, cafés and bars probably are. Most famously, once a year at the **Carnival** on the last weekend of August these spectacularly cool media darlings give way to the biggest and most uninhibited street party in Europe. Just to the east, in the west end of Kensington Gardens, stands one explanation for the persistence of the area's cachet, **Kensington Palace,** former home of Princess Diana and still the second most important Royal residence in London after Buckingham Palace. Way out southwest, on the river, a visit to Kew or Richmond is likely to take up a whole day, but with fine weather the 2-hr riverboat or ½-hr train journey will be well rewarded. The varying seasonal delights of the **Royal Botanical Gardens** at Kew are world famous, while the town of **Richmond** with its tree-lined riverside walk, views from the hill and rolling deer park are the most 'rural' places within easy reach of the city. Further up river, **Hampton Court** is the most beautiful of the Royal palaces in London. It set the standard for grand houses along the river and is best seen at sunset, when its mellow red Tudor brick glows with warmth and the riverside gardens take on an other-worldly quality.

Notting Hill and High Street Kensington

Notting Hill Gate tube station straddles the street at the point where Kensington Church Street dips south to High Street Kensington and Pembridge Road heads north to the Portobello Road, Ladbroke Grove and Westbourne Grove. **Portobello Road**

Market continues to pull in the punters every Saturday for its antiques, groovy secondhand clothes and bric-a-brac. The Portobello Road gradually goes downmarket as it approaches the Westway flyover. This is the end to look for most of Notting Hill's more happening retailers and restaurants. Bear in mind that it's less of a walk from Ladbroke Grove tube. Sandwiched between the slopes of Holland Park and South Kensington, Kensington itself is a quieter, more residential and family-friendly continuation of Knightsbridge west of Museumland.

Kensington Palace ⓘ *T020-7937 9561, www.royal.gov.uk, Mar-Oct 1000-1800 (last admission 1700), Nov-Feb daily 1000-1600 (last admission 1500), £10.50, concession £8, children £7, under 5's free, price includes audio guide.* Queen Victoria's birthplace, is one of the most significant and evocative of the Royal palaces, unfortunately all the more so since the death of Princess Diana, who lived here after her separation from Prince Charles. The Palace itself has been open to the public for at least a century, the 20 or so rooms on the 1½ hr audio-guided tour including the antique-stuffed King's State Apartments, William Kent's *trompe l'oeil* ceilings and staircases, a considerable selection of old master paintings from the Royal Collection in the Long Gallery and some fine views over the lakes and gardens. Also on display is the Royal Ceremonial Dress Collection, which now rather ghoulishly contains some of the dresses that Diana wore on state occasions, as well as the gilded pageantry of the 19th century. As the Palace is keen to point out, everything that can be seen is the genuine article. What any of it really represents is more of a mystery.

Richmond and Kew → *Tube: Richmond and Kew*

Here in the buckle of Surrey's stockbroker belt, the English dream of house and garden – *rus in urbe* – reaches its most complete expression. As well as the more obvious attractions such as Kew Gardens, Richmond Hill and Hampton Court, many of the area's other old mansions are also worth travelling to find, especially the early 17th-century **Ham House**, just over the river by foot ferry from Marble Hill House.

Richmond Park, Europe's largest city park and a former Royal hunting ground dating from the 13th century, Richmond Park is a popular attraction due largely to its freely roaming deer and the historic attraction of the panorama over Surrey, the river and London (especially from **King Henry VIII's Mound**, the highest point in the park).

North of the river, on Richmond Road in Twickenham, a rare survivor of the string of grand villas which once lined the Thames, **Marble Hill House** ⓘ *T020-8892 5115, Apr-Oct, Wed-Sun 1000-1800, £3.50, reached most easily from St Margaret's train station*, was built in the 1720s for Henrietta Howard, mistress of George II. Regally decorated and perfectly proportioned, this handsome Palladian mansion, refreshing in its authenticity, also possesses examples of early Georgian painting and furniture.

Maybe because of its slightly disjointed position away from the rest of Richmond's box of delights, but easily reached by the foot ferry from the end of Orleans Road, **Ham House**, ⓘ *T020-8940 1950, Apr-Oct, Mon-Wed, Sat, Sun 1300-1700, £5* is often overlooked by visitors to the area. It's a shame really as it's also one of the most appealing of the local estates with original 17th-century artwork (including Van Dyck) and furniture, the ornate extravagance of the Great Staircase, and an enchanting garden with statutory tearoom.

Kew Gardens

ⓘ *T020-8940 1171, www.kew.org.uk.Feb-Oct Daily 0930-1800, last admission 1730, Nov-Jan 0930-1615, last admission 1545. £7.50, concessions £5.50, children free.*

In an area rich in parkland, gorgeous scenery, antique architecture and oodles of stereotypical English charm – somewhat disturbed by the airliners roaring overhead every 2 mins into Heathrow – the Royal Botanical Gardens (Kew Gardens for short) are the jewel in the crown, recently declared a UNESCO World Heritage Site. Originally founded as a pleasure garden in the grounds of what became Kew Palace by Prince Frederick, the ill-fated heir to George II, in 1731, Kew has evolved into a 300-acre site containing more than 33,000 species grown in plantations, borders and glasshouses and is a world-renowned centre for horticultural research.

Hampton Court Palace

ⓘ T020-8781 9500, advance booking T0870-753 7777 recorded information T0870-752 7777 switchboard T0870-751 5175 www.hrp.org.uk Oct 28-Mar 24 1015-1630 Mon, 0930-1630 Tue-Sun (last admission 1545), Mar 24-Oct 27 1015-1800 Mon, 0930-1800 Tue-Sun (last admission 1715). £11.50, concessions £8.50, children £7.50, under 5's free, Privy Garden only £2, £1.50 under-16s. Maze only £2.50, £1.50 under-16s. Self-service cafeteria in the grounds and coffee shop in the Palace.

Like the Tower of London, Hampton Court Palace is run by Historic Royal Palaces and bears some of that company's hallmarks: lively costumed tours, clarity in the signposting, and division into different themed areas of interest. Unlike the Tower though, the history of the Palace and its presentation to the public focuses mainly on two particular reigns: Henry VIII (1509-1547) and his many wives, and William and Mary (1689-1702) who until Mary's death in 1694 were unique in sharing the monarchy. What particularly marks it out as a visitor attraction is the variety of this history on display, from the late-medieval architecture of Henry VIII's court to the Georgian splendour of the Cumberland Suite.

Six different routes around the interior take in Henry VIII's State Apartments, the Tudor Kitchens, the Wolsey Rooms and Renaissance Picture Gallery, the King's Apartments (William's), the Queen's State Apartments (Mary's) and the Georgian Rooms (decorated by George II – 1727-1760 – the last monarch to use the Palace).

Sleeping

Accommodation in central London has always been expensive. That said, fierce competition has meant that even the smartest hotels have been forced to do deals in recent years, especially during the quieter months (January to March, October and November). London's grandest hotels are almost all in Mayfair, Knightsbridge and Belgravia, with a sprinkling east towards the City. The most central areas with the largest selection of less expensive rooms are on the fringes of these districts, in Victoria, Earls Court, Bayswater and Bloomsbury. Many are cheaper at weekends and most mid-range hotels include breakfast in the price, although it's worth checking. Be sure to book well ahead, especially for the Youth Hostels and other budget options.

Central London

The Strand and Embankment *p54, map p52*

L **The Savoy**, Strand, WC2, T020-7836 4343, F7240 6040, www.savoy-group.co.uk. Opened by Richard D'Oyly Carte in 1889, it retains a reputation for the understated and traditional British comfort of its 263 rooms, with superb views over the river from the 4th floor and above. Art deco luxury on the top floor and new cuisine in the old-fashioned Savoy Grill.

B **Royal Adelphi**, 21 Villiers St, WC2, T020-7930 8764, F7930 8735, www.royaladephi.co.uk. Very central, small hotel with 47 rooms, not much changed since the 60s, though clean and friendly with a 24-hr bar.

C **Strand Continental**, 142 Strand, WC2, T020-7836 4880. Pretty basic, cash-only Indian hotel with running hot and cold water in 24 bedrooms. Shared bathrooms. Above the *India Club* restaurant.

Soho *p58, map p56*

L **Hazlitt's**, 6 Frith St, W1, T020-7434 1771, F7439 1524, www.hazlittshotel.com. 23 period rooms of fine character, in memory of the great essayist, many people's favourite London hotel. No restaurant or bar as yet but plenty round about.

L **Sanderson**, 50 Berners St, W1, T020-7300 9500, F7300 1400, www.ianschrager hotels.com. 150 rooms. The latest in the ultra-modern Philippe Starck-designed chain that includes the **St Martin's Lane Hotel**. Ultra-chic **Spoon Plus** restaurant, **Purple Bar** for residents only, and **Lobby Bar** open to the public until 0100 nightly.

Mayfair and Regent Street *p60, map p56*

L **Claridge's**, Brook St, W1, T020-7629 8860, F7499 1200, www.savoy-group. com. Mayfair's most cosmopolitan hotel, restored to its 1920s glamour. The bar designed by David Collins has won awards.

L **The Connaught**, Carlos Pl, W1, T020-7499 7070, www.savoy-group.com. The famous restaurant has recently been refurbished and is run by Angela Hartnett with mediterranean flair. A quiet country-house atmosphere prevails elsewhere.

L **The Dorchester**, 54 Park Lane, W1, T020-7629 8888, F7409 0114, www.dorchesterhotel.com. One of the city's most famous hotels, refurbished in dazzling style and now a strong contender for the title of London's finest. The mirrors in the bar are a sight to behold.

L **The Metropolitan**, Old Park Lane, W1, T020-7447 1000, F7447 1100 www.metropolitan.co.uk. Probably still the most fashionable 5-star hotel in London. Not for wallflowers, although you could always do like J-Lo who booked the whole top floor for her privacy. **Nobu** restaurant and Met bar complete the star-studded scene.

Piccadilly and St James's *p60, map p56*

L **The Ritz**, 150 Piccadilly, W1J, T020-7493 8181, F7493 2687. www.theritzlondon.com 133 rooms. One of the world's most famous hotels. Take tea in the Palm Court for £32 and dine en plein air on the Terrace overlooking Green Park in the summer.

L **The Stafford**, St James's Pl, SW1, T020-7493 0111, F7493 7121, www.the staffordhotel.co.uk Converted Carriage House apartments. Expensive restaurant with classic English menu, American bar festooned with hats and baseball helmets, a convivial spot.

Oxford Street and Marble Arch *p69, map p56*

C **The Ivanhoe Suites**, 1b St Christopher's Pl, W1, T020-7935 1047, F7722 0435. 7 rooms, clean, must book about a week in advance.

Westminster and Whitehall *p62, map p52*

A **Sanctuary House Hotel**, 33 Tothill St, SW1, T020-7799 4044, F7799 3657. www.sanctuaryhousehotel.com 34 clean rooms above a Fuller's Ale and Pie House, cheaper at weekends. Breakfast not included.

Victoria, Belgravia and Pimlico *p66, map p64*

L **The Berkeley Hotel**, Wilton Pl, SW1, T020-7235 6000, F7235 4330 www.savoy-group.co.uk. 168 rooms. Home of the design classics **Boxwood Café** (T020-7235 1010) and **Blue Bar** amid one of the last words in swish jet-set accommodation.

L **Dolphin Square Hotel**, Chichester St, SW1 T020-7834 3800, www.dolphinsquarehotel. co.uk. At the lower end of this bracket, a large, comfortable and relatively informal hideaway near the river with its own gardens, swimming pool and fine-dining restaurant Allium.

L **The Lanesborough**, Hyde Park Corner, SW1, T020-7259 5599, F7259 5606. www.lanesborough.com 95 rooms. Once the St George's Hospital although you'd never know it, now done up in restrained Regency style incorporating the discreet pleasures of the **Library Bar** presided over by celebrity barman Salvatore Calabresi.

A **Tophams**, 28 Ebury St, SW1, T020-7730 8147, F7823 5966. www.tophams.co.uk Charming small country-house style hotel, family-run with friendly service.

C **The Blair Victoria Hotel**, 78-84 Warwick Way, SW1, T020-7828 8603, F7976 6536, sales@blairvictoria 50 rooms. A good example of the area's countless small hotels, rated for its warm welcome and efficient service.

C **The Victoria Inn**, 65-67 Belgrave Rd, SW1, T020-7834 6721, F07931 0201, www.victoriainn.co.uk. 43 rooms. No-nonsense place on the busy Belgrave Rd.

D **Enrico Hotel**, 79 Warwick Way, SW1, T020-7834 9538, F7233 9995, www.enricohotel.com 25 rooms. Tiny and basic but still very good value.

Knightsbridge, South Kensington and Hyde Park *p67, map p64*

L **Blakes**, 33 Roland Gdns, SW7, T020-7370 6701, F7373 0442, www.blakeshotels.com. 47 rooms. Another Anoushka Hempel concern and a celebrity and honeymooner favourite without self-consiousness, a place to be pampered. Private, recherché and cramped. Each room is different.

L **The Gore**, 189 Queen's Gate, SW7, T020-7584 6601, F7589 8127 www.gorehotel.com. 53 rooms. Wood-panelled, and with that certain something for special occasions, family-run by the same people as Hazlitt's in Soho. Now with the added attraction of the Bistro 190 bar and restaurant.

L **Pelham Hotel**, 15 Cromwell Pl, SW7, T020-7589 8288, F7584 8444 www.firmdale.com. 50 rooms. Genuinely warm and effortlessly gracious staff, a decent rival to **Blakes** with untrendy but delicately tasteful rooms, 2 lobbies and nestling spots just for visitors. In the same group as the Charlotte Street and Covent Garden hotels, and also Number 16.

A **Diplomat**, 2 Chesham St, SW1, T020-7235 1544, F7259 6153 www.btinternet.com/~diplomat.hotel 26 rooms. Beautiful staircase, old building, near **Harrods**. The quietest rooms are at the front.

A **Five Sumner Place**, 5 Sumner Pl, SW7, T020-7584 7586, F7823 9962 www.sumnerplace.com. Another cosy, chintzy and award-winning hideaway.

D **Linstead Hall** Imperial College Campus (Accommodation Link), Watts Way, Prince's Gdns, SW7, T020-7594 9507, www.imperialcollege-accommodationlink.co.uk– Student hall of residence in pole position for museum visits.

E **Albert Hotel**, 191 Queen's Gate, SW7, T020-7584 3019 www.thealberthotel.uk.com. Student halls let in the summer holiday, 70 beds, 10-bed dorms £15 a night, all including breakfast. Book well ahead.

Marylebone and Regent's Park *p71, map p56*

L **Landmark Hotel**, 222 Marylebone Rd, NW1 T020-7631 8000 F7631 8033 www.landmarklondon.co.uk , 299 rooms, about 100 years old, refurbished, individually furnished rooms.

B **Georgian House Hotel**, 87 Gloucester Pl, W1, T020-7935 2211/7486 3151, F7486 7535 www.londoncentralhotel.com. 20 largish rooms with bathrooms in an nice townhouse.

C **Hallam Hotel**, 12 Hallam St, Portland Pl, W1, T020-7580 1166, F7323 4527. Another small townhouse with 25 rooms.

D **Carr Saunders Hall**, 18 Fitzroy St, W1, T020-7580 6338, www.lse.ac.uk/vacations, LSE hall of residence just beneath Telecom Tower. 10 twin rooms available during Easter and summer holidays. Book as early as possible.

D **Indian Student YMCA**, 41 Fitzroy St, WC1, T020-7387 0411 www.indianymca.org. Anyone can stay. 109 rooms, dinner and breakfast included in an Indian canteen.

D **International Students House**, 229 Great Portland St, W1, T020-7631 8300, F7631 8315, www.ish.org.uk. Not necessary to be a student, 275 rooms, open to public throughout, but very full at all other times. Restaurant with international food in the basement, refurbished bar open late to residents. Laundry, cyber-café, microwave.

Euston, St Pancras and King's Cross *p72, map p52*

C **The Carlton Hotel**, Birkenhead St, WC1, T020-7916 9697, www.smoothound.co.uk/hotels/Carlton5. 32 clean rooms in what was once a NatWest bank.

C **Euston Travel Inn Capital**, 1 Duke's Rd, WC1, T0870-2383301, www.travelinn.co.uk. 220 rooms. Clean, safe, modern and impersonal.

D-E **Ashlee House**, 261-265 Gray's Inn Rd, WC1, T020-7833 9400. Clean, secure and bright designer budget backpackers hostel. Twin room £50, 8-10 bed dormitory £15.

D-E **The Generator**, 37 Tavistock Pl, WC1, T020-7388 7666. 217 funky cell-like twin bunk rooms £23 per person, 8-bed dormitories £14 a night, 4-bed dorms £16 a night, including breakfast, busy bar in an old police station.

Bloomsbury and Fitzrovia *p69, map p56*

A **Academy**, 21 Gower St, WC1, T020-7631 4115, www.theetoncollection.com Georgian townhouse, library and conservatory, charming staff, with breakfast, and bar open to non-residents. By the same people as the new Glasshouse hotel in Edinburgh.

L **Charlotte Street Hotel**, 15-17 Charlotte St, W1, T020-7907 4000, F7806 2002. www.firmdale.com Super-fashionable, with

52 rooms, restaurant and buzzy bar Oscar. Popular with film people.

A **Grange Blooms**, 7 Montague St, WC1, T020-7323 1717, F7636 6498 www.grangehotels.com. Behind the British Museum, 18th-century house and furniture to match, and a walled garden.

A **Hotel Meridien Russell**, Russell Sq, WC1, T020-7837 6470, 7837 2357, www.principalhotels.co.uk 336 rooms, not including breakfast. Extraordinary Edwardian bar.

B **Harlingford**, 61-63 Cartwright Gdns, WC1, T020-7387 1551, www.harlingfordhotel.com. 43-room B&B in a refurbished old house.

C **The Jesmond**, 63 Gower St, WC1, T020-7636 3199, F7323 4373, www.jesmondhotel.org.uk, 16 rooms. Excellent value small hotel, with a garden and quieter rooms at the back away from thundering Gower St.

C **Mentone Hotel**, 54-56 Cartwright Gdns, WC1, T020-7387 3927, F7388 4671. En suite bathrooms, tastefully decorated, family-run B&B that's good value.

The City *p73, map p74*

L **Great Eastern Hotel**, Liverpool St, EC2, T020-7618 5000, F7618 5001, www.great-eastern-hotel.co.uk. 267 rooms. Sir Terence Conran's first hotel, right on top of Liverpool St Station, with several excellent restaurants (Terminus brasserie, Aurora fine dining, Fishmarket and Miyabi) and bars.

D **Barbican YMCA**, 2 Fann St, EC2, Admin@barbican.ymca.org.uk, T020-7628 0697, F7638 2420. Single and double rooms for 240 people, £52 including breakfast.

D **London City YMCA**, 8 Errol St, EC1, T020-7628 8832, F7628 4080. Breakfast included. 4 twin rooms only. 101 capacity.

Bankside and Southwark *p76, map p74*

B **Holiday Inn Express**, 103-109 Southwark St, SE1, T020-7401 2525, F020-7401 3322 www.hiexpress.com/lon-southwark. Continental breakfast included. 88 rooms all en suite, internet access, bar, book well in advance.

C **Bankside House**, 24 Sumner St, SE1, T020-7633 9877, bankside-reservation@lse.ac.uk. LSE hall of residence behind Tate Modern, beds in 4-bed rooms for £55 double including breakfast, own shower, 30 Jun-21 Sep only, book as early as possible.

F **St Christopher's Inn Backpackers Village**, 161-163, 121 and 57 Borough High St, SE1, T020-7407 1856 www.stchristophers.co.uk. 160 beds; £15 beds in four 12-bed dorms, internet access, laundry, sauna £1 a day, no kitchen, book a week in advance for weekends. Sweaty discos downstairs on Fri and Sat, about £5.

South Bank and Waterloo *p78, map p74*

L **London Marriot County Hall Hotel**, T020-7928 5200, F7400 7300. 5-star, 200 rooms, majority with river views, from £245 excluding VAT, up to £750 for the Westminster suite. **County Hall Restaurant**, cocktail area, **Leader's Bar**, open to the public.

A **Novotel London Tower Bridge**, 10 Pepys St, EC3, T020-7265 6000, F7265 6060. Fairly new, 203 rooms, *Pepys Bar*, garden brasserie and fitness centre.

B **The Mad Hatter**, 3-7 Stamford St, SE1, T020-7401 9222, Madhatter@fullers.demon.co.uk. Bright new rooms above a Fuller's pub, largish, double-glazed against noise from the busy road junction outside.

C **London County Hall Travel Inn Capital**, Belvedere Rd, SE1, T0870-2383300, www.travelinn.com, 313 surprisingly large rooms, basic, secure and very central.

D **Butler's Wharf Residence**, Gainsford St, SE1, T020-7407 7164. For self-catering flats next to Design Museum, another LSE property, approx £22.50 per person per night, each flat for 6/7 people, own room, not right on the river, needs booking well in advance.

East London

East End *p80*

B **Holiday Inn Express London-City**, 275 Old St, EC1, T020-7300 4300, www.hiexpress.com Over 200 rooms. Functional and efficient branch of the hotel chain.

F **Lea Valley Campsite**, Sewardstone Rd, E4, T020-8529 5689. Apr-Oct only. £6 per person per night, £2.50 for electricity.

Docklands *p81*

L **The Four Season's Hotel, Canary Wharf**, 46 Westferry Circus, E14, T020-7510 1999, F7510 1998. Giant space-age structure for the wheeler-dealers of Canary Wharf. In-room facilities include multiline telephones and CD players, in-house hydrotherapy centre and fitness suite. Doubles range from £260 to £310.

A **The International Hotel**, Brittania Group, 163 Marsh Wall, E14, T020-7515 1551. Clean and modern with superb views of the tower and waterfront. 3 restaurants and in-house gym and swimming pool.

C **Ibis, Isle of Dogs**, Prestons Rd, E14, T0207-517 1100. Standard chain fare. Near Canary Wharf and shopping complex.

D **Urban Learning Foundation**, 56 East India Dock Rd, E14, T020-7987 0033. Single beds only in shared self-catering flats. £30 per person per night, £25 per night for two nights or more. Bargain for the area.

South and West London

Notting Hill and High Street Kensington *p84*

L **Miller's Residence**, 111a Westbourne Grove, W2 T020-7243 1024 F7243 1064 www.millersuk.com Popular with the likes of Hugh Grant and very English country house in style, with antique candle holders and log fires, and just eight individually furnished rooms, from £170-250 including a free cocktail bar.

L **The Royal Garden Hotel**, 2-24 Kensington High St, W8, T020-7937 8000. This modern monstrosity next to Diana's old Kensington Palace is a popular stopover with all the usual business facilities, as well as spectacular views from the bar on the 10th floor.

A **The Abbey Court Hotel**, 20 Pembridge Gdns, W11, T020-7221 7518, F7792 0858, www.abbeycourthotel.co.uk. The cleanest and most luxurious of this street packed with modest hotels. The breakfast is served ad lib in the conservatory in its quiet garden. Breakfast included in price.

A **K-West**, Richmond Way, W14 F7674 1050, www.k-west.co.uk 224 rooms, four-star. £158 a standard room. Refurbished hotel near Shepherd's Bush. Spa, sauna and gym.

A **Portobello Hotel**, 22 Stanley Gdns, W11, T020-7727 2777, F020-7792 9641 www.portobello-hotel.co.uk Internationally trendy hotel to the stars. Johnny Depp and Kate Moss allegedly bathed in champagne here.

C **London Visitors Hotel**, 42-44 Holland Rd, W14, T020-7602 1282, F7602 0736. Big double-fronted, cheap hotel. Round corner from Olympia and nearby Holland Park.

Earl's Court

There is nothing worth seeing in Earl's Court but it is a good area for finding cheaper accommodation.

B **Albany Hotel**, 4-12 Barkston Gdns, SW5, T020-7370 6116, albany@realco.co.uk. Rooms for 1-4 people.

B **Barkston Gardens Hotel**, 34-44 Barkston Gdns, SW5, T020-7373 7851. Less fancy, and more businesslike, offers conference facilities. Breakfast extra.

B **The Burns Hotel**, 18-26 Barkston Gdns, SW5, T020-7373 3151. Price excludes breakfast (English £8.75 per person/ mContinental £5.75 per person). The biggest and briskest of the row.

C **Henley House Hotel**, 30 Barkston Gdns, SW5, T020-7370 4111, henleyhse@aol.com. With bookshelves and tartan sofas, this hotel appeals to the olde-worlde visitor. More individual and charming than the rest.

C **Maranton House Hotel**, 14 Barkston Gdns, SW5, T020-7373 5782, F7244 9543. Single, double and triple rooms available. Breakfast included.

D **The Court Hotel**, 194-196 Earl's Court Rd, SW5, T020-7373 0027, F7912 8500. Right beside the tube station above the newsagents. Frequented by Ozzie backpackers, offering 15 rooms with TV, a kitchen and a microwave to share.

Bayswater, Paddington and Little Venice

Again, there is little in the way of traditional attractions for the visitor in these parts of London, but Baywater in particular is full of hotels and restaurants.

L **The Colonnade**, 2 Wellington Crescent, Little Venice, W9, T020-7286 1052, F7286 1057, www.theetoncollection.com. 43 rooms. Bar and restaurant.

L **The Hempel**, 31-35 Craven Hill Gdns, W2, T020-7298 9000, www.the-hempel.co.uk. 41 rooms, 6 apartments. The smartest hotel in the area designed by the Queen Bee of designer hotels – former model Anouska Hempel aka Lady Weinberger.

L **Royal Lancaster Hotel**, Lancaster Terrace, W2 T020-7262 6737 F7724 3191, www.royallancaster.com, Nipa Thai restaurant with authentic. 416 rooms at the lower end of this bracket, as well as the famous Nipa restaurant, doing immaculate

Thai cuisine in authentic surroundings.
B **Columbia Hotel**, 95-99 Lancaster Gate, W2 T020-7402 0021, F7706 4691, www.columbiahotel.co.uk. Grand-looking hotel just off the Bayswater Rd, popular with visiting rockers and musos and hence often a very lively post-gig late bar. £83 a double including VAT and breakfast.
C **Lancaster Hall Hotel**, 35 Craven Terr, W2, T020-7723 9276, www.lancaster-hotel.co.uk. 103 rooms. Tucked away, this large, concrete block is surprisingly quiet in the heart of Bayswater backstreets, between the hub of Queensway and Paddington, only a stone's throw from Lancester Gate entrance to the park. Very pleasant despite its 60s concrete exterior and being a corporate favourite.
D-E **Dean Court Hotel**, 57 Inverness Terr, W2, T020-7229 2961, F7727 1190. Australian-managed. 3-4 to a room, £15 a night, £75 a week, including breakfast. Double £45. Dorm room only bookable 2 nights.

Eating

Leicester Square and Chinatown *p55, map p56*
£££ **J Sheekey**, 28-32 St Martin's Court, WC2, T020-7240 2565. A name that has long been associated with fish, and has been given an overhaul by the people responsible for **The Ivy** and **Le Caprice**. Now it's the most stylish place in the area for seafood.
££ **Fung Shing**, 15 Lisle St, WC2, T020-7437 1539. Has also long had a good reputation for its seafood and Cantonese cooking. It was one of the first restaurants in London to serve up Chinese haute cuisine and standards reportedly remain high.
££ **Manzi's** 1/2 Leicester St, WC2, T020-7734 0224. Has been around for over 70 years, drawing in a generally sedate crowd of regulars, often an elder statesman or two, who come for its old-fashioned Italian service and traditional ways with fish.
£ **1997**, 19 Wardour St, W1, T020-7734 2868. Named after the year of Hong Kong's handover, is open 24 hrs for consistently good-value Cantonese cooking.
£ **Imperial China**, White Bear Yard, 25a Lisle St, WC2, T020-7734 3388. Another large restaurant, hidden away in the tranquility of its own courtyard off Lisle St and recently thoroughly re-decorated, does very good dim sum until 1700 as well as a wide range of good value Cantonese dishes.
£ **Mr Kong**, 21 Lisle St, WC2, T020-7437 7923. Does some excellent Cantonese dishes and is open until 0300.

Soho *p58, map p56*
£££ **Alastair Little**, 49 Frith St, W1, T020-7734 5183. The eponymous trailblazer of Anglo-Italian cooking no longer runs the kitchen here but it continues to come up with the freshest of well-prepared recipes, majoring on fish, served up in an intimate setting.
£££ **Richard Corrigan at Lindsay House**, 21 Romilly St, W1, T020-7439 0450. Makes waves with his modern Anglo-Irish menu. The great man himself is still very much in charge while the 18th-century atmosphere of his Soho townhouse creates an appreciative mood.
£££ **The Sugar Club**, 21 Warwick St, W1, T020-7437 7776. Still the most fun and one of the most fashionable smart eateries in Soho. A dressed-up crowd flock here for New Zealand-Asian fusion food in a see-and-be-seen setting. Downstairs is a bit quieter, away from the buzzy bar upstairs.
££ **Busaba Eathai**, 106-110 Wardour St, W1, T020-7255 8686. A busy newish 'Thai casual dining room' with large windows onto Wardour St, open 1200-2330.
££ **Centrale**, 16 Moor St, W1, T020- 7437 5513. Last orders at 2130. A slower-paced joint serving up great bowlfuls of Italian dishes.
££ **La Trouvaille**, 12a Newburgh St, W1 T020 7287 8488. Does a terrific set lunch at £20 for three courses, a supremely competent small restaurant bursting with Gallic flair.
££ **Mar I Terra**, 17 Air St, W1 T020-7734 1992. Dinky new branch of the Waterloo Spanish restaurant, its toothsome menu served up in a bright little place close to Piccadilly Circus.
££ **Masala Zone**, 9 Marshall St, W1 T020-7287 9966. Busy and bustling Indian restaurant specialising in street food from Mumbai and recipes from south-west India, serving food all day.
££ **Mildred's Wholefood Café**, 58 Greek St, W1, T020-7494 1634. Licensed, clean and

non-smoking vegetarian.

££ Pollo, 20 Old Compton St, W1, T020-7734 5917. Last orders at 2330. A large and popular late-night pasta joint where you'll end up making new friends with the people shoe-horned in beside you.

££ Satsuma, 56 Wardour St, W1, T020-7437 8338 is a well-established Japanese doing fine ramen soups and good value bento boxes.

££ Zilli Fish, 36-40 Brewer St, W1, T020-7734 8649. The original part of the expanding empire of the far-from-retiring Aldo Zilli. Slightly formal.

Cafés and sandwich bars

This pair of French fancies are among the best for good, old fashioned cakes: **Maison Bertaux**, 28 Greek St, W1; and **Patisserie Valerie**, 44 Old Compton St.

Bar Italia, 22 Frith St, T020-7437 4520. Open 24 hrs daily (except Mon) and still as hip and football and coffee crazy as ever.

Star Café, 22 Great Chapel St, W1, T020-7437 8778. Its check tablecloths presided over by the same family since 1933 (open for lunch Mon-Fri 1200-1500).

The Garden Café, 4 Newburgh St, W1, T020-7494 0044. On the other side of Soho is a sweet little place that comes into its own when the sun shines, with its quirky little back garden.

Covent Garden *p59, map p56*

£££ The Ivy, 1 West St, WC2, T020-7836 4751. Wood panelling, stained glass, modern art, superb service and Italianate brasserie food have made the tables here the most sought after in London. Long popular with thespians and wealthy families treating themselves, the well-deserved hype has ensured that booking weeks in advance is often the only way of enjoying a meal here in the evenings. Lunchtimes are often booked solid too, but it's well worth having a go.

£££ Rules, 35 Maiden Lane, WC2, T020-7836 5314. One of the oldest English restaurants in Britain and now something of a tourist trap, but nonetheless a highly atmospheric Victorian venue for some classic recipes majoring on game.

££ Café Pacifico, 5 Langley St, Covent Garden T020-7379 7728. Busy and cheerful Mexican restaurant tucked away on Langley St, with great Marguerìtas at the bar while you wait for your table.

££ Calabash at the Africa Centre, 38 King St, WC2, T020-7836 1976. Probably one of the best African restaurants in London, in a cosy basement which also hosts excellent African live music in a laid-back atmosphere that's not too expensive either.

££ Joe Allen, 13 Exeter St, WC2, T020-7836 0651. Hard to find but worth the effort. The American menu served up in this traditional basement diner never fails to please a host of theatre-going regulars as well as tourists in the know and it's open late throughout the week.

£ The Rock and Sole Plaice, 47 Endell St, WC2, T020-7836 3785. Does famously good fish and chips, in the restaurant or to take away.

£ Food For Thought, 31 Neal St, WC2, T020-7836 0239. Is a very good-value vegetarian old timer. Bring your own wine.

Cafés and sandwich bars

Neal's Yard Bakery and Tearoom, 6 Neal's Yard, WC2, T020-7836 5199. Busy vegetarian.

Poetry Society, 22 Betterton St, WC2, T020-7420 9880. An endearing little bar and vegetarian wholefood café run by reliable poem-promoters.

World Food Café, Neals Yard Dining Room, 1st floor, 14 Neal's Yard, WC2, T020-7379 0298. With a self-explanatory name and basic décor, vegetarian and non-smoking.

Mayfair and Regent Street *p60, map p56*

£££ Al Hamra, 31-33 Shepherd Market, W1, T020-7493 1954. Serves good Lebanese food in an attractive room and there are tables outside for those who want to observe the street life of this strange little corner of London. £20 minimum charge.

£££ Le Gavroche, 43 Upper Brook St, W1 T020-7408 0881. A subterranean gourmet's lair that usually needs booking well in advance for some superbly accomplished French haute cuisine. A great place to treat yourself.

£££ The Greenhouse, 27a Hay's Mews, W1, T020-7499 3331. Does a very good-value (and very busy) set lunch at £23 for two courses Mon to Fri. Evenings in the comfortable basement are more expensive but the modern British cuisine is worth it.

£££ Kaya, 42 Albemarle St, W1, T020-7499 0622. The finest Korean restaurant in London. It specializes in table-barbecues and traditional dishes from the region of Seoul. Set menus £40 and £45 per person.

£££ The Mirabelle, 56 Curzon St, W1, T020-7499 4636. Marco Pierre White re-opened this classic Mayfair restaurant in the 90s to rave reviews. Everything here justifies the average £90 tab for two, from the impeccable service to the presentation of top-notch Frenchified food.

£££ Momo, 25 Heddon St, W1, T020-7434 4040. North African dining experience with a distinctly metropolitan approach to taking reservations. The glamorous members-only Kemia Bar in the basement can be visited before diners begin their alloted sitting. **Mô**, is a much cheaper Moroccan snack bar nest door run by the same people.

£££ Sketch, 9 Conduit St 0870 777 4488. Run by the same people as Momo (see above) must be one of the most hyped and theatrical new restaurants to open in the city in a while, a heaving complex of bars and restaurants (which certainly need to be booked).

££ Chisou, 4 Princes St, T020-7629 3931. One of the best Japanese restaurants in the West End, just off Regent's St. Check out the presentation of their humble spinach salad for an idea of the care in the kitchen, served up in a cheerful and efficient atmosphere.

££ The Guinea Grill, 30 Bruton Place, W1, T020- 7499 1210. Tucked away behind the Young's pub of the same name and is famous for its steak and kidney pies. Cordial service, good food and a pleasant ambience have been keeping a wide cross-section of diners coming back for more since the 1950s.

££ Mulligan's of Mayfair, 13 Cork St, T020-7409 1370. Traditional place offering interesting dishes with an Irish twist in a woody, masculine basement that gets lively in the evenings. Last orders at 2130.

££ Veeraswamy, Victory House, 99 Regent St (entrance on Swallow St), T020-7734 1401, www.realindianfood .com. Claims to be the first Indian restaurant in London and the quality of the food certainly demonstrates their years of experience.

££ Yoshino, 3 Piccadilly Place, W1, T020-7287 6622. Tucked away in a corner off Piccadilly and designed by cult architect Rick Mather, the restaurant used only to print its menu in Japanese. Now there's an English translation but the food (much of it fish) and service are still as genuine as ever.

Cafés and sandwich bars

Sotheby's Café, 34-35 New Bond St, W1, T020-7293 5077. A fairly expensive but very English and genteel establishment for the taking of tea in the old auction house. Last orders are at 1645 and it's closed at weekends.

Piccadilly and St James's *p60, map p56*

£££ The Criterion, 224 Piccadilly, W1, T020-7930 0488. Grand and beautiful setting for some typically assured Marco Pierre White recipes. The interior of this old dance hall is a symphony in wood and gold, the prices are surprisingly reasonable and the atmosphere quite laid back considering the sumptuousness of the surroundings.

£££ Greens, 36 Duke St, SW1, T020-7930 4566. Has long been one of the English gent's favourite haunts, serving up fish and traditional British food in a congenial atmosphere.

£££ Quaglino's, 16 Bury St, SW1, T020-7930 6767. Has proved to be one of Terence Conran's most successful and reasonably priced brasserie-style ventures. Even a drink or light meal at the bar has a sense of occasion thanks to the efficient staff, late opening hrs (until 0100) and the glamour of the dramatically lit subterranean interior.

£££ Shumi, 23 St James's St, SW1, T020-7747 9380. Swish, minimalist place that's caused quite a stir with its Italian-Japanese menu.

£££ @venue, 7/9 St James's St, SW1, T020-7321 2111. The huge glass frontage and spacious minimalist design easily soaks up the buzz of bankers young and old.

£££ The Wolseley,160 Piccadilly, W1, T020-7499 6996. In the splendid setting of the old Barclays bank on the corner of Piccadilly and Arlington St, this is a newish restaurant run by the same people as **The Ivy**. Smart dining in the shadow of the Ritz that needs to be booked well ahead.

££ Al Duca, 4-5 Duke of York St, SW1, T020-7839 3090. Trendy hangout where Milan meets New York in the glass and wood décor and the modern Italian menu.

££ Red Room, on the lower ground floor of Waterstone's bookshop, 203 Piccadilly, T020-7851 2464. An attractive restaurant run by Searcey's, who are also responsible for the brasseries at the Barbican, the new National Portrait Gallery restaurant, and the catering at the Royal Opera House.

£ The ICA Café, The Mall, SW1, T020-7930 8619 (£1.50 day membership required).

Offers imaginative meals, several vegetarian, that are good value at about £4.50-£7 each.

Victoria *p66, map p64*

£££ Boisdale, 15 Eccleston St, SW1, T020-7730 6922. One of London's very few specifically Scottish restaurants (although with a French twist). Its old-school whisky and cigar room at the back beyond the courtyard is a treat. Recently it has also opened up another small bar, christened the **Macdonald Bar**, open Mon-Sat until 0100, at the back of the main green, red and tartan restaurant. The whole creaking complex can become impossibly busy with shirt-sleeved bonhommie but then again it is a cheerful place.

£££ Nahm, in the Halkin Hotel, 5 Halkin St, SW1, T020 7333 1234. Probably the most sophisticated Vietnamese restaurant in the capital, a Michelin-starred dining experience in the super-chic Halkin Hotel.

£££ Olivo, 21 Eccleston St, SW1, T020-7730 2505. Closed for lunch at weekends. For a wider variety of Sardinian dishes, the more grown-up (and expensive) sibling of **Oliveto** (see below).

££ Oliveto, 49 Elizabeth St, SW1, T020-7730 0074. A swish spot in Belgravia for some reasonably priced pizzas and pasta.

£ Jenny Lo's Teahouse, 14 Eccleston St, SW1, T020-7823 6331. An excellent Chinese noodle bar (eat in or takeaway) run by the daughter of celebrity chef Ken Lo. Marginally more expensive than some elsewhere that have followed in its wake, the quality of the ingredients and fine vegetarian options keep it a cut above.

Knightsbridge *p67, map p64*

£££ Bibendum, 81 Fulham Rd, SW3, T020-7581 5817. Conran's great big gastrodome above a stylish oyster and champagne bar, on the first floor of the old Michelin building.

£££ Zafferano, 15 Lowndes St, SW1, T020-7235 5800. Easily the best value (at lunchtimes it only just scrapes into this bracket), not at all intimidating and worth every penny. It's often fully booked though.

££ La Brasserie, 272 Brompton Rd, SW3, T020-7581 3089. A proper Parisian all-day nosherie that shows up some of its chain competitors, best for an evening rendezvous at the bar or a sit down with your shopping for a late brunch or high tea.

££ Daquise, 20 Thurloe St, SW7, T020-7589 6117. Perennially fading but stubborn survivor, a Polish restaurant that sums up the spirit of old South Ken.

££ O Fado, 45-50 Beauchamp Pl, SW3, T020-7589 3002. Old Portuguese restaurant with bags of character, never afraid to let the joint start jumping to live music and usually open until late (around 0100).

Cafés and sandwich bars

Café Monpelliano, 144 Brompton Rd, SW3, T020-7225 2926. Busy, bustling Knightsbridge Italian institution.

Fifth Floor Café, Harvey Nichols, Knightsbridge, T020-7235 5000. Not cheap but then that's not the point.

Patisserie Valerie, 215 Brompton Rd, SW3, T020-7823 9971. Another fine branch of this delicious and sophisticated eatery.

Chelsea *p68, map p273*

£££ Daphne's, 112 Draycott Avenue, SW3, T020-7584 6883. Run by the same team as the **Ivy** and **J Sheekey's**. Glamourpusses, jet-setters and flashy businessmen have long enjoyed basking in the brisk Italian atmosphere here.

£££ Gordon Ramsay, 68 Royal Hospital Rd, SW3, T020-7352 4441. Run by the famously bad-tempered celebrity chef and named after himself. This is the most celebrated gourmet and Michelin-starred restaurant in Chelsea.

££ Chutney Mary, 535 King's Rd, SW10, T020-7351 3113. Top-quality Indian restaurant in grand surroundings, just off Lots Rd.

££ Pellicano, 19 Elystan St, SW3, T020-7589 3718. A minimalist place to enjoy some good modern Italian food with a Sardinian accent.

£ Chelsea Bun, 9a Limerston St, SW10, T020-7352 3635. Another Chelsea institution, almost but not quite as popular as its 19th-century namesake, offering over 200 different straightforward meals like pasta or filled baked potatoes.

£ The Chelsea Kitchen, 98 King's Rd, SW3, T020-7589 1330. Once a branch of the Stockpot chain and still doing basic meals at rock-bottom prices for this part of London.

£ King's Road Café, 208 King's Rd, T020-7351 6645. Open 1000-1730 daily, in the branch of Habitat, where the ingredients of the mainly Italian dishes are usually absolutely fresh.

Cafés and sandwich bars

Mona Lisa, 417 King's Rd, SW1, T020-7376 5447. Very friendly one-off, run by Italians (surprise, surprise) doing good-value hot meals and snacks.

Marylebone *p71, map p56*

£££ Defune 34 George St, W1 T020-7935 8311. A wonderfully lit and cavernous basement and some very good softshell crab. One of the better Japanese restaurants in the area.
£££ Locanda Locatelli, 8 Seymour St, W1 T020-7935 9088. Designed by the same team as the bar at Claridges, with superb fish dishes a forte. Booking ahead is advisable.
£££ The Providores, 109 Marylebone High St, W1 T020-7935 6175. Busy, cheerful little tapas bar on the ground floor and some very fine Iberian-New Zealand recipes and excellent wines served upstairs with a smile.
£££ Villandry 170 Great Portland St, W1, T020-7631 3131. Top-notch French cuisine served in minimalist premises, with amazing continental comestibles on sale out front.
££ The Golden Hind, 73 Marylebone Lane, W1, T020-7486 3644. Old-school eat-in or takeaway fish and chip shop done up in a timeless style but perhaps more expensive than you might expect.
£ Patogh, 8 Crawford Place, W1, T020-7262 4015. Unlicensed (BYOB), Persian food.

Cafés and sandwich bars

Patisserie Valerie, 105 Marylebone High St, T020-7935 6240. An excellent outpost of the patisserie française, less arty but more sophisticated than the one in Soho.
Quiet Revolution, 62 Weymouth St, W1, T020-7487 5683. Specialize in 100% organic soups and delicious stews for about £5 to eat in or take away.

Bloomsbury and Fitzrovia *p69, map p56*

£££ Hakkasan, 8 Hanway Place, W1 T020-7907 1888. Must be the funkiest basement Chinese in the capital, with its blue-lit stylish décor and a Michelin star for the food. Expensive but worth it.
£££ Bam-Bou, 1 Percy St, W1, T020-7323 9130. Another local favourite, a modern Southeast Asian restaurant with an airy wooden interior and high-style quotient.
£££ Pied-à-terre, 34 Charlotte St, W1, T020-7636 1178. Closed Sun. Two Michelin-starred French restaurant expert at nouvelle cuisine. More traditional in atmosphere.
£££ Back To Basics, 21a Foley St, W1, T020-7436 2181. Closed Sat and Sun. Another very good destination for seafood, a cheerful little restaurant at the lower end of this bracket.
££ Rasa Samudra, 5 Charlotte St, W1, T020-7637 0222. Closed Sun. The most laid-back branch of the excellent and expanding Rasa chain, distinguished from the others by doing seafood alongside the famously fragrant vegetarian south Indian dishes and also having a smoking section.
£ RK Stanley, 6 Little Portland St, Fitzrovia, W1, T020-7462 0099. Open until 2400 Mon-Sat. Very good purveyors of fine sausages and real ale in a stylish modern British take on American diner-style eating and drinking.
£ Eagle Bar Diner, 3-5 Rathbone Place, W1 T020-7637 1418. Fairly pricey but pretty cool cod-American diner doing big burgers and chips by day and excellent cocktails by night.
£ Sardo, 45 Grafton Way, W1 T020-7387 2521. Reasonably priced and very popular little Sardinian restaurant.

Cafés and sandwich bars

Bar Centrale, 4 Bernard St, WC1, T020-7278 5249. A very popular 70s-style Italian café/sandwich shop, with a restaurant next door, doing a wide range of fillings and breads.
Cafe Deco 43 Store St, WC1, T020-7323 4501. Has an interesting range of Italian sandwiches and home-made pasta.
Forum Café, 62 Great Russell St, WC1, T020-7404 1878. Is right opposite the British Museum, doing a wide variety of high-quality sandwiches, salads and hot snacks.

Holborn and Clerkenwell *p72, map p74*

£££ Club Gascon, 57 West Smithfield, EC1, T020-7796 0600. Specializes in the regional produce of Gascony, foie gras of course, exquisite (and expensive) gastronomic delights served plate by plate in a gentle, slightly fey and appreciative atmosphere.

£££ **Moro**, 34-36 Exmouth Market, EC1, T020-7833 8336, is a large modern Spanish restaurant that has been wowing the area's hipsters, shakers and movers for some time with its artful way with super fresh ingredients. It's been so successful that one of its main suppliers, **Brindisa Spanish Food Importers**, have even opened up a deli next door.

£££ **St John**, 26 St John St, T020-7251 0848, where offal-based recipes as well as fresh fish and freshly baked bread are served up in a stark whitewashed old smokery celebrating 'nose to tail' eating.

££ **The Eagle**, 159 Farringdon Rd, T020-7837 1353, was one of the first pubs to go gastro, cooking up excellent modern European food right behind the bar.

££ **The Quality Chop House**, 92-94 Farringdon Rd, T020-7837 5093. Long-standing cod-working-class diner doing very good (but fairly expensive) basic British fare, including fish and chips.

£ **Little Bay**, 171 Faringdon Rd, EC1, T020-7278 1234. Very good value little place with a no-nonsense approach to good European food all day every day, main courses about £5 before 1900 and not much more than that until 2300.

City *p73, map p74*

£££ **Aurora**, T020-7618 7000, on the ground floor of the **Great Eastern Hotel** at Liverpool St Station. A reliable Conran option similar in its prices and modern European cooking to the **Orrery** in Marylebone.

£££ **Prism**, 147 Leadenhall St, EC3, T020-7256 3888. Harvey Nichol's venture in the City, where accomplished brasserie-style food can be enjoyed in chic designer surroundings.

£ **The Place Below**, St Mary-le-Bow, Cheapside, EC2, T020-7329 0789. Bargain vegetarian breakfasts and lunches in the crypt of the church on Cheapside.

£ **Sweetings**, 39 Queen Victoria St, T020-7248 3062. A City institution, a very traditional and down-to-earth fresh fish restaurant.

Bankside *p76, map p74*

££ **Tate Cafés** on levels 2 and 7 of the Tate Modern, T020-7401 5020. Open throughout the week for lunch (expect to queue) and in the evenings on Fri and Sat, last orders at 2130 but open until 2300, both offering excellent brasserie-style modern European food, sandwiches and snacks. Tables cannot be reserved, so it's best to arrive not much later than 1830 to guarantee a window seat in the evenings. The one on level 7 has the extraordinary views and a full wine list, while the one on level 2 is bigger, has more buzz and a smoking area. Both are at the lower end of this price bracket.

££ **Delfina Studio Café**, 50 Bermondsey St, SE1, T020-7357 0244. Open for lunch only, closed weekends. Away from the river, and much more gastronomically ambitious (and also more expensive). The name belies the quality of the food but declares the place's affiliation to one of the first of the wave of fashionable galleries still opening up in Bermondsey. Booking is advisable for some imaginative modern British dishes using top-quality ingredients.

££ **Mar i Terra**, Gambia St, T020-7928 7628. Open 1200-2330, closed Sun. Very good authentic Catalan tapas bar and restaurant. The food is great value and prepared from the finest ingredients direct from Spain, served up in a very jolly atmosphere.

Cafés and sandwich bars

De Gustibus, on Borough High St, T020-7407 3625. Opposite London Bridge tube, this is the place to go for high-quality sandwiches, featuring a choice of 19 varieties of bread, also hot food and soups.

Konditor and Cook, 10 Stoney St, SE1, T020-7407 5100. Next to Borough Market. The local branch of the exceptional Waterloo outfit, the home of luxury cakes, sandwiches, biscuits, teas and top-notch natural ingredients.

Spiazzo Café, Unit 3, 21/27 St Thomas St, SE1, T020-7403 6996. Reliable Italian café/sandwich bar, with home-made pasta and fresh baguettes, popular with workers at Guy's Hospital opposite.

South Bank *p78, map p74*

£££ **Oxo Tower Restaurant**, 8th Floor, Oxo Tower Wharf, Barge House St, SE1, T020-7803 3888. It's a busy, costly but friendly place run by Harvey Nichol's Fifth-Floor team doing excellent modern European food with the best views on the river from just beneath the Oxo Tower.

£££ The People's Palace, Level 3, Royal Festival Hall, SE1, T020-7928 9999, F7928 2355. Also has superb views onto the river through the huge plate-glass windows of the Festival Hall. Solicitous staff serve upmarket French food in the spacious Soviet-style dining room.
££ The Fire Station, 150 Waterloo Rd, SE1, T020-7620 2226. Service can be erratic, and the large bar area at the front sometimes gets very loud, but the reliable food is excellent value. More casual, but with a varied and interesting global menu.
££ Four Regions, County Hall, SE1, T020-7928 0988. Relatively expensive but unusually grand Chinese restaurant with tremendous views of floodlit Big Ben.
££ Mesón Don Felipe, The Cut, T020-7928 3237. For some high-quality tapas in a very lively atmosphere complete with live Spanish guitar. Tables are bookable before 0830, it's always packed after that.
£ Gourmet Pizza Company, Gabriel's Wharf, 56 Upper Ground, SE1, T020-7928 3188. Right on the river and rated by some as the best pizza in the capital.
£ Masters Super Fish, 191 Waterloo Rd, T020-7928 6924. Closed Mon lunchtime. For fish and chips, possibly the best in London.
£ Tas, 33 The Cut, SE1, T020-7928 1444. For good value this Turkish restaurant is probably your best option. Fixed-price mezes, decent main courses, friendly staff and cheerful, modern décor set it apart.

Cafés and sandwich bars
Bespoke Bakery and Fine Food Shop, at 22 Cornwall Rd, SE1, T020-7261 0456. Make some of London's most superb pastries and cakes as well as sandwiches and soup.
Casse Croute, 19 Lower Marsh, T020-7928 4700. Another gourmet sandwich bar.
Konditor and Cook, next to the Young Vic Theatre on The Cut. Stylish place for patisserie and people-watching.

Pubs, bars and clubs

Strand *p54, map p52*
Gordon's, 47 Villiers St, WC2, T020-7930 1408. Subterranean wine-bar at the bottom of Villiers St. Exceptional wines can be enjoyed in the candlelit gloom of its convivial vaults. It also does fairly expensive salad bar-style food.

Leicester Square *p55, map p56*
The Salisbury, 90 St Martin's Lane, WC2, T020-7836 5863. Classic West End boozer, its gleaming Victorian interior fully renovated and as popular as ever (sometimes too popular), especially with tourists, theatregoers and thesps, darling.
Salvador & Amanda, 8 Great Newport St, WC2, T020-7240 1551. A subterranean designer tapas bar with a good range of cocktails.

Soho *p58, map p56*
Atlantic Bar and Grill, 20 Glasshouse St, W1, T020-7734 4888. Book a table at the restaurant if you want guaranteed entry, although it's often not that fussy. The louche comfort of **Dick's Bar** (members only Thur-Sat) remains the main attraction.
Café Bohème, 13-17 Old Compton St, W1, T020-7734 0623. Admission £3 after 2200, £4 after 2300 Fri, Sat (last orders for alcohol 0230 daily). This was one of the bars that led the way for late-night Soho, a relaxed, continental-style brasserie on a busy corner with a top-notch restaurant attached. Expect to queue if arriving late. Booking advisable.
The Coach and Horses, 29 Greek St, W1, T020-7437 5920. Has long established itself as the archetypal Soho boozer, thanks to its famously rude landlord and alcoholic regulars like the late Jeffrey Bernard. It's still a refreshingly unpretentious place for a plain pint and a very old-style ham sandwich.
Dog and Duck, 18 Bateman St, W1, T020-7494 0697. A busy little corner pub on two floors pumping very good beer. The film industry's favourite old-fashioned pub.
French House, 49 Dean St, W1, T020-7437 2799. Famous haunt of Soho's boho boozers such as Francis Bacon and George Melly, where the wine is very good and beer served in halves only.

Covent Garden *p59*

Bünker, 41 Earlham St, WC2, T020-7240 0606. Underground venue, more airily done out in stainless steel and pale wood where beer is brewed on the premises and there's a separate dining area for food at reasonable prices.

Detroit, 35 Earlham St, WC2, T020-7240 2662. Open until 2400 Mon-Sat. Has lots of character, a subterranean warren of alcoves, excellent cocktails and decent food.

Lamb and Flag, 33 Rose Street, WC2, T020-7497 9504. Best approached down a tiny covered alley off Floral St, but its warm and woody interior and front courtyard can become impossibly busy.

Market Café, 21 The Piazza, WC2, T020-7836 2137. Open until 0200 Thur-Sat (£5 admission after 2100 Fri, Sat). In the Piazza itself, this is the best bar for its views, value, hours and avoiding the crush. In the southwest corner with a small terrace overlooking the courtyard in front of St Paul's.

Opera Tavern, 23 Catherine St, WC2, T020-7379 9832. With its grand Victorian interior, pays respect to the Royal Opera House.

Mayfair and Regent Street *p60, map p56*

Audley 41-43 Mount St, W1, T020-7499 1843. Many of the old pubs, like this one hark back to Mayfair's grand old days and indulge tourist expectations. Its historic and palatial dark red and dark wood décor is reminiscent of a rather run-down gentleman's club.

The Red Lion, tucked away at 1 Waverton St, W1, T020-7499 1307. Famously feels more like a country pub than many pubs in the country, with its snug set of panelled rooms and high-backed wooden benches. No music and an expensive but high-quality restaurant in the back room.

Trader Vic's at the Hilton Hotel, Park Lane, W1, T020-7493 8000. With its South Island Beach bar theme and glamorous waitresses, is an old-timer that still delivers a kick with its famous hot rum cocktails served in shiver-me-timbers skull mugs. Good Chinese oven-roast food too and live music on Sun evenings.

Piccadilly and St James's *p60, map p56*

The ICA Bar, The Mall, SW1. £1.50 day membership required, open Mon until 2300, Tue-Sat until 0100, Sun until 2230. Is a lively late-night hang-out for the arts brigade.

The Red Lion, 23 Crown Passage, SW1, T020-7930 4141, is a bog-standard British boozer that seems to have landed in St James's from some remote provincial outpost a long time ago, and the area would be much poorer without its reassuring cosiness, as welcoming to dogs and old men as suits and bohos. Closed Sun.

Oxford Street *p69, map p56*

Bradley's Spanish Bar, 42-44 Hanway St, W1, T020-7636 0359. Open daily until 2300, is a tiny place, a long-standing media boho favourite, with a basement dive bar and excellent jukebox on the ground floor.

Victoria *p66, map p64*

Star Tavern, 6 Belgrave Mews West, SW1, T020-7235 3019, is a rewarding find, a cosy wood-panelled place for some reasonable food, through an arch in its own little mews.

The Grenadier, 18 Wilton Row, SW1, T020-7235 3074, is similar but with honest-to-goodness old-soldiering associations and often understandably overcrowded.

The Nag's Head, 53 Kinnerton St, SW1, T020-7235 1135. Freehouse with excellent beers, the largest and most rambling of the three pubs in this area.

Knightsbridge *p67, map p64*

Bunch of Grapes, 207 Brompton Rd, SW3, T020-7589 4944. Has a certain Victorian cosiness about it.

The Enterprise, 35 Walton St, SW3, T020-7584 3148. Has been turned into a swanky but still quite cosy gastrobar with a considerable reputation for the quality of its food.

Oratory, 232 Brompton Rd, SW3, T020-7584 3493. An unpretentious wine bar in an old building with seats outside and amazing toilets located in the bowels of the Brompton Oratory itself, very convenient for the V&A.

Chelsea *p68, map p64*

The Surprise, 6 Christchurch Terr, T020-7349 1821. A roomy local place with bare floorboards, large tables and pleasant atmosphere. Good for Sun lunches.

Bloomsbury and Fitzrovia *p69, map p56*

Duke of York, 47 Rathbone St, W1, T020-7636 7065. Cosy little Greene King pub on the corner of the chi-chi shopping mews of Charlotte Place.

Museum Tavern,Museum St. It has a refurbished Victorian interior and serves reasonable food throughout the day to hordes of tourists.
Office, 3-5 Rathbone Place, Fitrovia, W1, T020-7636 1598, is another large basement bar, funkily lit and always jumping late in the week.
Plough, 27 Museum St, WC1, T020-7636 7964. Large and often less packed than other pubs. Convenient for the British Museum.
Sevilla Mia, 22 Hanway St, W1, T020-7637 3756. Scruffy, cosy little basement tapas bar that often has live Spanish guitar music.
The Social, 5 Little Portland St, W1, T020-7636 4992. An industrialized music bar serving food upstairs, hardcore sounds and demon cocktails in the basement, popular with twenty-somethings on pre-club warm-ups.

Holborn and Clerkenwell *p72, map p74*

Cittie of York, 22 High Holborn, WC1, T020-7242 7670. With its extra long bar, cubby holes for lawyers and crude wallpaintings of famous tipplers.
Duke of York, 7 Roger St, WC1, T020-7242 7230. Near the Dickens' House Museum, it does good real ales, has tables outside and serves up scrummy but expensive food.
Dust, 27 Clerkenwell Rd, EC1, T020-7490 5120. Open until 0200 Fri, Sat, 2400 on Thu. Fairly typical of Clerkenwell bars. A music bar with bare wooden floorboards, basic furnishings, loud music and hip drinks.
Jerusalem Tavern, 55 Britton St, T0200-7490 4281. The sole London outlet for St Peter's Ale from Bungay in Suffolk.
Vic Naylor's, 38-40 St John St, EC1, T020-7608 2181. Open until midnight Mon-Thu, till 0100 Fri and Sat, was used as the location for Sting's bar in Guy Ritchie's hit movie *Lock, Stock and Two Smoking Barrels*. More old-style, the restaurant and bar is loud and cheerful
Ye Olde Cheshire Cheese, 145 Fleet St, EC4, T020-7353 6170. Featuring a warren of historic wooden rooms.
Ye Olde Mitre Tavern, Ely Court, Ely Place, EC1, T020-7405 4751. The last word in cosy and quaint, tucked away up a tiny alleyway.

City *p73, map p74*

Ball's Brothers, 6-8 Cheapside, EC2, T020-7248 2708. Open 1130-2130 Mon-Fri. Fine wines and a genteel atmosphere as well as outside seating with views of St Paul's are among the strong points.
The Barley Mow, 50 Long Lane, EC1, T020-7606 6591. Open 1100-2300 Mon-Fri. A surprisingly laid-back Hogshead pub pulling some good real ales.
Black Friar, 74 Queen Victoria St, EC4, T020-7236 5474. Open Sat 1200-1500. Famous for its extraordinary carved interior and outdoor drinking area near Blackfriars Bridge.
Prism, 147 Leadenhall St, EC3, T020-7256 3888. Open 1200-2300 Mon-Fri. The basement bar has expensive bottled beers and is a sophisticated place to enjoy some top-quality bar snacks.

Bankside *p76, map p74*

Anchor Bankside, 34 Park St, SE1, T020-7407 1577. Is almost too famous for its own good, a much older, very busy warren of rooms, very touristy but also with a riverside terrace tucked beneath the railway line into Cannon St.
Founders Arms, 52 Hopton St, SE1, T020-7928 1899, is an excellent Young's pub that must be laughing all the way to the bank since the opening of Tate Modern. That said, its combination of large riverside terrace with outside seating and efficient, friendly service of decent food all day and everyday deserves to be a success.
George Inn, 77 Borough High St, SE1, T020-7407 2056. London's last remaining coaching inn, its galleried design the inspiration for Elizabethan theatres, and now a convivial low-ceilinged series of rooms much enjoyed by both local office workers and tourists.

Clubs

Time Out magazine rounds up a pretty comprehensive weekly list of nightlife events and flyers for one-offs litter fashionable stamping grounds like Exmouth Market and Hoxton Square. Clubs aren't the only places to hear good dance music and DJs. Bars have become increasingly popular since London relaxed its entertainment licensing laws. Across London there are dozens of bars which now open until 0100 or 0200 and feature DJs and club music. Without a doubt the best place to experience this thriving bar culture is in Shoreditch, just east of central London.

333, 333 Old St, EC1, T020-7739 5949. Fri 2200-0500 , Sat 2200-0500, Sun £5 before 2300, £10 after. This is perhaps the quintessential Old Street clubbing experience.

Bagley's Studios, King's Cross Goods Yard, off York Way, N1, T020-7278 2777. One of the most popular and long-running clubs around.

Cargo, Rivington St, EC2, T020-7739 3440, www.cargo-london.co.uk. Poplular club based in the Old Street area.

The Cross, The Arches, 27-131 King's Cross Goods Yard, off York Way, N1, T020-7837 0828, www.the-cross.co.uk. House garage.

Electricity Show Room, 39a Hoxton Sq, N1, T020-7739 6934. Small fashionable bar 5 mins from Old Street tube station.

The End, 18 West Central St, WC2, T020-7419 9199. One of the best designed and run clubs in the capital for all your Garage needs.

Fabric, 77a Charterhouse Street, T020-7336 8898. London's most fashionable super club is without a doubt this purpose-built venue in the cool Clerkenwell area of East London.

Fridge, Town Hall Parade, Brixton Hill, SW2, T020-77326 5100. Banging trance and techno is the staple of Brixton's largest club, though it also hosts several popular gay nights. Admission is generally between £8 and £12.

Ministry of Sound in Elephant and Castle, at 103 Gaunt St, SE1, T020-7378 6528. One of London's biggest and most famous nightclubs is just south of the river Thames in London's Elephant and Castle district. The Ministry was Britain's first ever purpose-built 'super club' and has built itself into a multinational business and the biggest dance brand name in the world. The club itself remains as popular as ever.

Woody's, 41-43 Woodfield Rd, W9, T020-7266 3030, www.woodysclub.com. Features young mixed crowds and a hip hop and R'n'B party atmosphere.

Entertainment

Cinema

Expect to pay £6-10 for screenings in the West End; less before 1700. It's a good idea to book by credit card for the first weekend of a film's release. There's often a small handling fee when booking by phone. Like Londoners themselves, cinemas come in every conceivable shape and size. There are small, sweaty booths at the back of seedy bookshops, and seats for nearly 2000 at the Odeon Leicester Square. Leicester Square satisfies all visitors needs. Seats are pricier here than at local cinemas but the rumbling special effects look, sound, and feel better simply because of the scale and sophistication of the equipment. **Odeon Cinemas** (T0870-5050007), the **Warner Village West End** (T020-7437 3484) and the **Empire** (T020-7437 1234) showcase the crop of current releases. More challenging experiences are to be found in London's excellent network of repertory cinemas which specialize in themes, seasons, festivals, and retrospectives. They aren't grouped in one nicely accessible square, but then they aren't miles away either.

Repertory cinemas

Barbican Centre, T020- 7638 8891, www.barbican.org.uk

British Film Institute IMAX cinema/theatre is quite tricky to reach, marooned in the middle of a busy roundabout. It's best approached from Belvedere Rd through a tunnel studded with blue stars.

Coronet, Notting Hill Gate, W11, T020-7727 6705.

Curzon Mayfair, 38 Curzon St, W1, T020-7465 8865, is probably the most comfortable cinema in London and not as expensive as you might expect for such cosseting. It generally shows middle to highbrow mainstream movies on its 1 screen.

Electric Cinema, Portobello Rd, T020-7229 8688. The lovely old art deco cinema on the Portobello Rd has been fully restored once again, redesigned by the team responsible for hip restaurant

Everyman Hampstead, 1 Hollybush Vale, Hampstead, NW3, T020-7431 1777. Famous independent local cinema repeatedly saved from extinction by passionate local support. Offers a mix of mainstream and repertory films in a recently refurbished beautifully luxurious space. Standard, deluxe and 'love seats' available. Bar for drinks. Sat morning kids' club.

ICA Cinema, Nash House, The Mall, SW1, T020-7930 6393 for recorded information, T020-7930 3647 for credit card bookings, www.ica.org.uk, is the place for very rare or independent films.

The National Film Theatre (NFT), South Bank, T020-7928 3535, will eventually be moving to the BFI complex under development in Jubilee Gardens. Until then it continues to fulfull its role as London's flagship repertory cinema, showing a truly international selection of rare, first-run and classic films on its 3 screens. Every Nov it forms the focal point of the increasingly prestigious **London Film Festival**.

Renoir, Brunswick Centre, Brunswick Square, WC1, T020-7837 8402. Usually foreign films, 4 screenings a day on 2 screens, excellent café and bar.

Ritzy's, Brixton Oval, Coldharbour Lane, SW2, information T020-7737 2121; booking: T020-7733 2229. 5-screen cinema offering the best of both arthouse and mainstream and something of a Brixton institution.

Screen on Baker St, 96 Baker St, NW1, T020-7935 2772. Two screens showing runs from the artier side of the spectrum.

Music

Rock, jazz, and folk

If London really is the most cosmopolitan city in Europe, it shows clearly in the bewildering array of live music it has to offer. Central London presents rich pickings for the discerning live music fanatic.

The 12 Bar Club, Denmark Pl, Denmark St, WC2, T020-7916 6989, tickets T020-7209 2248. Presents a fusion of country, folk and funk in intimate and friendly surroundings, and a bar extension and new restaurant out front can only enhance a club whose reputation has soared in recent years making it one of London's finest.

The 100 Club, 100 Oxford St, W1, T020-7636 0933, www. the100club.co.uk. Open Mon-Thu 1930-2400, Fri 1200-1500, 2030-0200, Sat 1930-100, Sun 1930-2330. Admission £7-10. Free lunchtime jazz 1130-1500 in summer. This venue has a healthy record in the music annals having staged the birth of British punk in 1976.

The Africa Centre, 38 King St, WC2, T020-7836 1973, 2130-0300, Fri-Sat, £6-8. On first entry this venue resembles an ill-equipped youth club, though the bona fide African bands who can be found here most Fridays are absolutely top notch.

Astoria, 157 Charing Cross Road, T020 7344 0044, on the outskirts of Soho is arguably the most eminent and varied venue, despite the lack of aesthetic value.

Borderline, 16 Manette St, W1D 4JB, T0207-7342095, is a club of the more intimate variety, and the bands are generally new and unheard of.

Brixton Academy, 211 Stockwell Rd, SW9. Box Office: T020-7771 2000. The Academy is an old Victorian hall has a capacity which attracts the biggest of artists while not appearing over-large, and in any case it is invariably full.

Cecil Sharp House 2 Regent's Park Rd, NW1, T020-7485 2206, open at 1900, nights vary, £3-6. This is one for the Folk fans, undiluted and traditional, it is a leader in an otherwise under-represented field and involves nigh-on mandatory audience participation.

Jazz Café, 3 Parkway, NW1, T020-7916 6060. Here you'll find an eclectic mix of world, funk and folk music, as well as its jazz staple, and the acts are always of a decent standard. It often pulls in the big names and the atmosphere is relaxed and enjoyable.

Kentish Town Forum, 9-17 Highgate Rd, NW5, T020-7344 0044. Undoubtedly one of the best venues in London.

Ronnie Scott's, 47 Frith St, W1, T020-7439 0747, opens at 2030, admission Mon-Thu £15, Fri and Sat £20, still smokin' like a train and often needs to be booked at least a fortnight in advance. The Mecca of the central jazz scene and still boasting some of the finest jazz in the metropolis. A night out here isn't cheap, though the quality of the music remains strong and no visiting jazz enthusiast can seriously miss paying the place a visit.

Shepherd's Bush Empire, Shepherd's Bush Green, W12, T020-7771 2000, box office open Mon-Fri 1000-1800, Sat 1200-1800. Admission £5-20. Bearing a strong similarity to the Brixton Academy and the Forum not only in terms of exterior and decor but also in the strength and range of what's on.

Underworld, 174 Camden High St, NW1, T020-74821932. A wide selection of mainstream and more underground rock sounds, it is one of the (comparatively) larger Camden venues, and its appearance fits its name.

University of London Union, (ULU for short) University of London Union, Manning Hall, Malet St, WC1, T020-7664 2000. Open 2030-2300, nights vary. Admission £5-10. Offers quality indie stock to a predominantly student audience. As the name suggests its primary role is as a student bar. The soulless, expensive and unatmospheric Wembley Arena apart, the live north London scene is largely centred around three areas – Camden Town, Kentish Town and Highbury and Islington. The Camden scene was especially potent throughout the early 80s and 90s when it gained its reputation as the hang-out of the likes of Madness and then a decade later as the creative centre of the Britpop explosion. Camden has retained its reputation and is still a hotbed of fresh and undiscovered talent, though still mainly of the Indie variety.

Vibe Bar, Truman's Brewery, Brick Lane, E1, T020-7377 2899, an East End venue for occasional live bands, and regular sound system sessions.

Classical and opera

One of the best places in Europe to hear classical music, London boasts at least four world class orchestras and numerous notable ensembles. The **London Symphony Orchestra**, based at the notoriously difficult-to-find Barbican Centre (the Barbican Hall, T020-7638 8891, www.barbican.org.uk) is arguably the pick of the bunch, though it is closely followed by the **Philharmonia** and the **London Philharmonic Orchestra** (both resident at the South Bank Centre), as well as the itinerant and slightly weaker **Royal Philharmonic Orchestra**. In addition, there are a number of venues, large and small, which hold regular concerts by internationally renowned musicians, local artists and students.

South Bank Centre, T020-7960 4242, is really three venues in one. The positively huge **Royal Festival Hall** holds large-scale symphonic orchestral and choral concerts, whilst the smaller **Queen Elizabeth Hall** and smaller still **Purcell Room** stick to chamber music, though the QEH can also stage opera.

Royal Albert Hall, Kensington Gore, SW7, T020-7589 8212, is home to the world-famous Sir Henry Wood Promenade Concerts (Proms for short), the annual classical feast running from July to September with music ranging from the well-loved to the new and cutting-edge. Seats can be booked in advance, but to truly sample the essence of the season try slumming it with one of the dirt-cheap Arena standing tickets. But it is a grand setting for just about any and every type of entertainment spectacular from high to lowbrow.

Wigmore Hall, 36 Wigmore St, W1, T020-7935 2141, www. wigmore-hall.org.uk, one of London's premier small concert halls, purpose-built in 1901 by the piano-maker Bechstein, stages a huge variety of world-class performances of chamber music and song, lunchtimes at 1300 and evenings at 1930 Mon-Sat, 1600 and 1900 Sun, and popular hour-long coffee concerts at 1130 on Sun, tickets £8-30.

Opera is best served in London by the **Royal Opera House**, Bow St, WC2, T020-7240 1200, box office/information T020-7304 4000, www.royalopera house.org, and the English National Opera at the **London Coliseum**, St Martin's Lane, T020-7632 8300, www.eno.org. Despite the Royal Opera House's rather stuffy and conservative reputation, the old place appears to have loosened up a touch since its long-awaited refurbishment. Prices remain exorbitant (up to £115), though there are seats available in the gods for under £20. There is also a restaurant and bar in which to while away the day, and tours are available for the curious. The Coliseum, on the other hand, likes to think of itself (without necessarily being so) as the antithesis of the ROH. Housing the English National Opera, its programme tends to be more ambitious, tickets are cheaper and the music is sung in English.

Theatre

The best place to discover the latest on what's just opened where are the reviews and listings is *Time Out*, available weekly in central London on Tue. The phenomenal vitality of the theatre in London continues to amaze Londoners and visitors alike. From record-breaking blockbusting musicals to the tiniest two-handers in the back rooms of pubs, almost every day of the year except Sundays the city gears up for an astonishing variety of stage performances on a scale unmatched anywhere else on the planet. The heart of all this activity is still very much the West End, where about 40 venerable old theatres put on a surprisingly diverse range of shows. Long criticized for pandering to the bottom denominator with a numbing array of tacky musicals, the competition for audiences has become so fierce that producers are now often much more adventurous. Many of the smaller theatres and production houses categorized by *Time Out* as 'Off West End' are the places to take the pulse of current theatre practice, generally staging more challenging work. A very small selection of the city's major players are listed below. The official half-price ticket booth is on the south side of Leicester Square. Run by the Society of London Theatre (SOLT), T020-7557 6700, it offers discounted tickets, first-come-first-served.

Donmar Warehouse, 41 Earlham St, WC2, T020-7369 1732. The most innovative, fashionable and exciting small-scale theatre in the West End, where Sam *American Beauty* Mendes still directs occasional productions, as well as welcoming top-class touring companies. Seats are usually at a premium and need to be booked well in advance.

Garrick Theatre, Charing Cross Rd, WC2, T020-7494 5085. Also built in 1889, famous for a long run of *No Sex Please We're British*, and more recently of Stephen Daldry's striking production of JB Priestley's *An Inspector Calls*.

Gielgud Theatre, T020-7494 5065. Built in 1906, now usually shows straight plays, (was called *The Globe*). **Globe Theatre**, see page 77.

Haymarket Theatre Royal, Haymarket, SW1, T020-7930 8800. There's been a theatre on this site since 1720, famous for staging Oscar Wilde's *Ideal Husband* and in 1914 the first London production of Ibsen's *Ghosts*.

London Palladium, Argyll St, W1, T020-7494 5400. An entertainment house since 1910 that now specializes in musical spectaculars.

Lyric Shaftesbury, T020-7494 5045. Built in 1888, famous in the 50s for staging plays by TS Eliot and later Alan Bennett, now tends towards West End dramas and star vehicles.

Old Vic, The Cut, SE1, T020-7928 7616. Built in 1817 as Royal Coburg Theatre, and later known as the 'Bucket of Blood' because of the cheap melodramas staged here, the *Old Victoria* theatre was taken over for 25 years from 1912 by Lilian Baylis, the founder of Sadler's Wells. In 1962, it became the birthplace of the National Theatre Company under the directorship of Laurence Olivier. More recently, following sympathetic restoration by Canadian Ed Mirvish, the theatre was home to Sir Peter Hall's own company, unfortunately a short-lived experiment. It narrowly avoided being turned into a lap-dancing venue and is now run by a board of affectionate trustees headed up by Kevin Spacey.

Palace Theatre, T020-7434 0909. Built as an opera house in 1888, staged the *Sound of Music* in the 60s, *Jesus Christ Superstar* in the 70s, and, since 1985, *Les Miserables*.

Queen's Theatre, T020-7494 5040. Built as twin to *The Globe*, now stages a wide mix of classics, musicals and new plays.

Royal Court Theatre, Sloane Square, SW1, T020-7565 5000, most famous for starting the 'kitchen sink' school of drama under George Devine in the 50s with plays like Osborne's *Look Back in Anger* (although it had already carved out a reputation for radicalism by staging the first productions of many of GB Shaw's plays). It has recently been fully refurbished and still pursues an adventurous policy of commissioning new writing. The refurbishment includes an atmospheric and happening restaurant and bar in the basement (T020-7565 5061). The **Royal Court Theatre Upstairs** stages experimental small-scale work (same box office as main theatre).

Royal National Theatre, South Bank, T020-7452 3000. The foundation stone was laid in 1951, but Denys Lasdun's terraced concrete ziggurat only opened in 1976, the new home for the National Theatre Company under the directorship of Peter Hall. It has 3 stages: the *Olivier*, the largest, with an open stage, steeply raked auditorium, and massive revolve. For some productions, the theatre has been brilliantly converted into a vast theatre in the round. The *Lyttelton*, slightly smaller, is the most traditional, with the option of a proscenium arch. The *Cottesloe*, round the side, is a much more intimate studio theatre for experimental productions.

Sadler's Wells, Rosebery Av, EC1, T020-7863 8000, and **Lilian Baylis Theatre** (nearest tube Angel Islington). Superb state-of-the-art new North London base for large scale dance and opera, and a smaller studio space for adventurous new work, both sadly struggling financially.
Soho Theatre and Writer's Centre, 21 Dean St, W1, T020-7478 0100, is an excellent brand new base for new playwriting in the West End.
Theatre Royal Drury Lane, Catherine St, WC2, T020-7494 5000. One of London's oldest theatres, founded in 1663, managed by David Garrick in the 18th century, and rebuilt in the early 19th century after 2 disastrous fires. Now usually stages large-scale musicals. Enjoyable backstage tours, which involve actors encouraging audience participation, tell the history of the theatre. Taking about 1 hr, they are at 1230, 1415, 1645 on Mon, Tue, Thu and Fri, and at 1100 and 1300 on Wed, Sat matinee days. £7.50 per person, bookable on box office number.
Young Vic, 66 The Cut, SE1, T020-7928 6363. The best middle-scale experimental theatre in the country.

Shopping

If you can't buy it in London, you can't buy it anywhere. The difficulty is knowing where to begin… A very broad summary of shopping areas in London might look something like this: Oxford St for department stores and high street names; **Tottenham Court Rd** for computers and electronics; **Charing Cross Rd** and **Bloomsbury** for books new and secondhand; **Covent Garden** for clothes, specialist foods and gifts; **Bond St** for high fashion and expensive jewellery; Knightsbridge for more high fashion and **Harrods**; and **Chelsea** or **Notting Hill** for one-offs and independents.

Activities and tours

Bus, boat or taxi tours

Big Bus Company, 48 Buckingham Palace Rd, T020-7233 9533, www.bigbus.co.uk. Daily sightseeing tours from hop-on, hop-off, open-top double- decker buses. Tickets include a free river cruise and a choice of walking tours. The commentary is live, or else digitally recorded in 12 languages. £15 adults, £6 children.
Black Taxi tours of London, T020-7289 4371, www. blacktaxitours.co.uk Sightseeing tours in licensed taxi cabs. Commentary from trained London 'cabbies'. 2-hr day and night tours. Pick-up and return to hotel. Costs £70 for up to 5 people.
Evans Evans Tours, T020-7950 1777, www.evansevans.co.uk. Half- and full-day coach tours of London with stop-offs at key sights. Prices start at £17 for adults (£14.50 for children between 3 and 16). Sightseeing trips to major tourist destinations outside London also available, as are tours in Japanese and Spanish.
London Frog Tours, T020-7928 3132, www.frog tours. com Starting at County Hall, these 'road and river' tours of London last 80 mins in yellow amphibious vehicles. The Frogs 'splash down' into the Thames at Lacks Dock Vauxhall and the river part of the tour lasts about 30 mins. Tours cost £12 for adults and £9 for children; family tickets are also available. Driver-guides operating general and special-interest tours for individuals and small groups in and around London are another option.
Driver-Guides Association (DGA), T020-8874 2745, www.driver-guides. org.uk, can provide details of professional blue-badge driver-guides throughout the country.

Walking tours

Walking is an excellent way to get to know London whether it be on your own with a map or book or as part of a group on an organized tour. More and more companies are running these tours, either pre-booked or regular, turn-up-and-go walks that leave from the same place at a fixed time every week. There are walks in the morning, afternoon or evening, seasonal walks, and dozens of special-interest walks, from Dickens and Jack the Ripper, to Bohemians and Bluestockings, to Bishops,

Brothels and the Bard. Most walks last between 1½ hrs and 2 hrs and cost about £5. **The Original London Walks**, T020-7624 3978, F7625 1932, www.london.walks.com, have over 40 walks to choose from. Other enjoyable walks, if the weather is good, are around London's many parks, gardens and cemeteries. One of these is the circular **Diana Princess of Wales Memorial Walk**, a 7-mile route through St James's Park, Green Park, Hyde Park and Kensington Gardens. For more information: T020-7298 2000. Also try www.london.walks.com

 Transport

Bus

There's generally a bus route near you wherever you are in the city and buses are a great way to get to know London, especially from the top deck. Traffic congestion is a serious problem though and bus journeys often take longer than the tube. Daytime buses, like the London Underground, run until about 0030. After that, an extensive system of night buses takes over. Most areas of Greater London are within easy reach of at least one night bus service. All night bus route numbers start with the letter 'N'. Most of the central London night buses pass through Trafalgar Square. The standard single Zone 1 day and night bus fare is £1 and in central London must be bought at the bus-stop ticket machines before boarding. If you're only making two or three trips a day, then another option to travelcards are the Bus Saver tickets that can be bought in books of six at newsagents and underground stations.

Boat

Daily services operate from most central London piers. Riverboats travel to and from Greenwich and the Thames Barrier in the east, and as far as Hampton Court in the west. There are over 20 piers along this stretch of the Thames and apart from Hampton Court Palace and the sights at Greenwich, the river gives access to Kew Gardens, Richmond Park and many of the central London attractions. Tickets for most trips can be bought at the pier or, in some cases, on the boat.

Car

If you are only planning to spend a short time in London, don't bother hiring a car, it's not worth it. Traffic-clogged central London is still a nightmare to drive in, despite the newly introduced congestion charges of £5 per day (congestion charging area marked out with a white 'C' on a red background on the road and on signs) Mon-Fri 0700 and 1830. Indeed, Londoners themselves tend to use public transport during the day, saving their cars for night and weekends. Apart from the heavy traffic and complicated web of one-way streets, parking is hard to find and exorbitantly expensive. The charge can be paid on the day at any one of 300 Paypoint-equipped shops, petrol stations or car parks until 2200. Failure to pay before 2400 incurs another £5 penalty fee, after which time the driver owes Transport for London £80. Call T0845-9001234 for more details, or look up www.cclondon.com. Beware of parking illegally too, as you are very likely to get a ticket or else be clamped or towed away and impounded (in which case you should call T020-7747 4747). This can set you back anywhere between £60 and £205.

Cycling

Cycle lanes are still not the norm in London and, compared with some European or Scandinavian cities, London is not an easy ride for cyclists. Make sure you always wear a helmet and never leave your bike unlocked. A 1000-mile cycle network is planned for the city and several organizations and direct action groups are continually pressing for improvements and to convince the Greater London Authority of the importance of making London more bicycle friendly. The best known is the **London Cycling Campaign**, T020-7928 7220 (Mon-Fri, 1400-1700 only), F020-7928 2318, www.lcc.org.uk. Their magazine *London Cyclist*, publishes a diary of rides and related events for all London. They also publish the *Brand New Central London Map* (£4.95), a cycling map with traffic-free routes, safe cycle crossings and bike shops. Cycling.uk.com is a cycling information station with over 200 links to other useful sites.

Taxi

The famous London black cabs are almost as much of an institution as the old, double-decker buses. Licensed cabs can be hailed in the street when the yellow 'For Hire' sign is displayed; they all have meters which start ticking as soon as you get in, and fares increase by the minute thereafter. Surcharges are added late at night and for luggage or extra passengers. Most 'cabbies' will expect a tip of 10-15%. Any comments or complaints should be made to the Public Carriage Office, T020-7230 1631, whilst lost property should be reported to T020-7833 0996 (make a note of your taxi's licence number and the driver's badge number). 24-hr **Radio Taxis**, T020-7272 0272. As well as black cabs there are also regular taxis, which are known as minicabs. It is advisable to book these directly from the cab office, as there are many unlicensed cab drivers operating in Central London. Minicabs can be more economical, especially during busy times, as they charge a flat fee for the journey instead of using a meter, but you will need to know the going rate for a particular journey in order to avoid being ripped off. A journey from central London to somewhere in the tube's Zone 2 area will cost from around £15-20 in the evening.

Tube

The London Underground, or tube, is the fastest way of getting around town (although that's not saying much) and most Londoners use it. The 12 lines are colour coded, the map is easy to follow and the system is relatively straightforward to use. However, it is worth avoiding during rush hour (0800-0930 and 1700-1830) if at all possible. Services run from 0530 until just after midnight. Fewer trains run on Sundays and public holidays. The underground is divided into six fare zones, with Zone 1 covering central London. Travel between two stations in Zone 1 costs £2 (child £0.60); a journey crossing into Zone 2 will cost £2.20 (child £0.80). Anyone planning to make more than two journeys in one day will save money by buying a Day Travelcard £4.20, Weekend Travelcard £6.40, or Family Travelcard (Zones 1 and 2) £2.80 per adult and £0.80 per child for one day's travel.

Directory

Embassies

Australia, T020-7379 4334. **Canada**, T020-7258 6600. **Denmark**, T020-7235 1255. **France**, T020-7073 1400. **Germany**, T020-7824 1300. **Italy**, T020-7312 2200. **Japan**, T020-7465 6500. **Netherlands**, T020-7590 3200. **New Zealand**, T020-79308422. **South Africa**, T020-74517299. **Spain**, T020-7589 8989. **Sweden**, T020-7917 6400. **Switzerland**, T020-7616 6000. **USA**, T020-7499 9000.

Hospitals

Charing Cross Hospital, Fulham Palace Rd, T020-8846 1234. **Chelsea Royal Hospital**, Royal Hospital Rd, T020-7730 0161. **Guy's Hospital**, St Thomas St, T020-7955 5000. **St Thomas's Hospital**, Lambeth Palace Rd, T020-7928 9292.

Internet

There are internet cafés all over London where you can acces the internet and pick up your email. **easyEverything**, probably the biggest and cheapest option (access from £1), has five locations in central London: 9-16 Tottenham Court Rd (Oxford St end); 7 Strand (Trafalgar Sq end); 358 Oxford St (opposite Bond St tube station); 9-13 Wilton Rd, Victoria (opposite main line station); 160-166 Kensington High St. For other options, www.queenscene.com, has a directory of about 70 cybercafés in different areas of the capital listed by area, postcode or nearest tube station. Local libraries often provide cheap or free internet access.

Language schools

English in Britain website, www.englishinbritain.co.uk, lists the accredited schools and colleges in London and the rest of the UK. From the website you'll be able to search the database, contact the schools and colleges, visit their websites, and book a course.

Southeast England

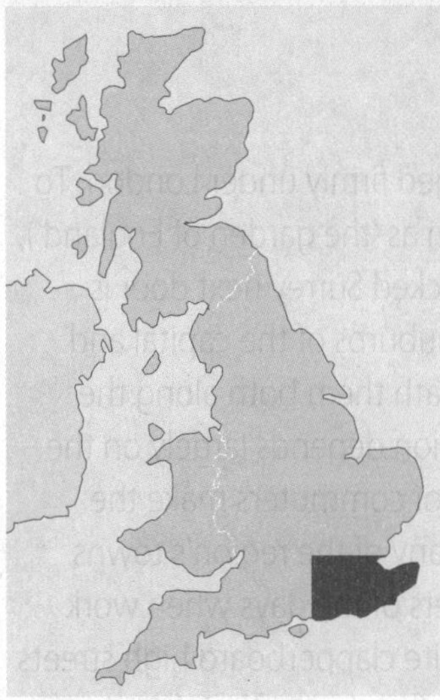

Introduction

The southeast of England is wedged firmly under London. To the east, Kent (traditionally known as 'the garden of England'), stretches out to the coast. Landlocked Surrey next door is taken up with the southwestern suburbs of the capital and beyond. Sussex is squashed beneath them both along the south coast. And much of the region depends largely on the big city for its livelihood. Millions of commuters make the return trip every day, although many of the region's towns and villages cherish fond reminders of the days when work was closer to home. From the white clapperboard high streets of the Weald with its tile-hung Kentish farms, their hop gardens and converted oast houses, to the fishermen's huts in Hastings or Whitstable and the grand guesthouses on the seafront at Brighton, relics of local industry still litter the landscape. Now mainly of archaeological and tourist interest, the traditional industries of the southeast could never have created the prosperity that most of the area enjoys today. This can best be appreciated with a stay at one of the many genteel farmhouse B&Bs nestling in gorgeous countryside, while metropolitan tastes (and expense accounts) mean that in these parts you're never that far from good coffee or a top-notch restaurant kitchen.

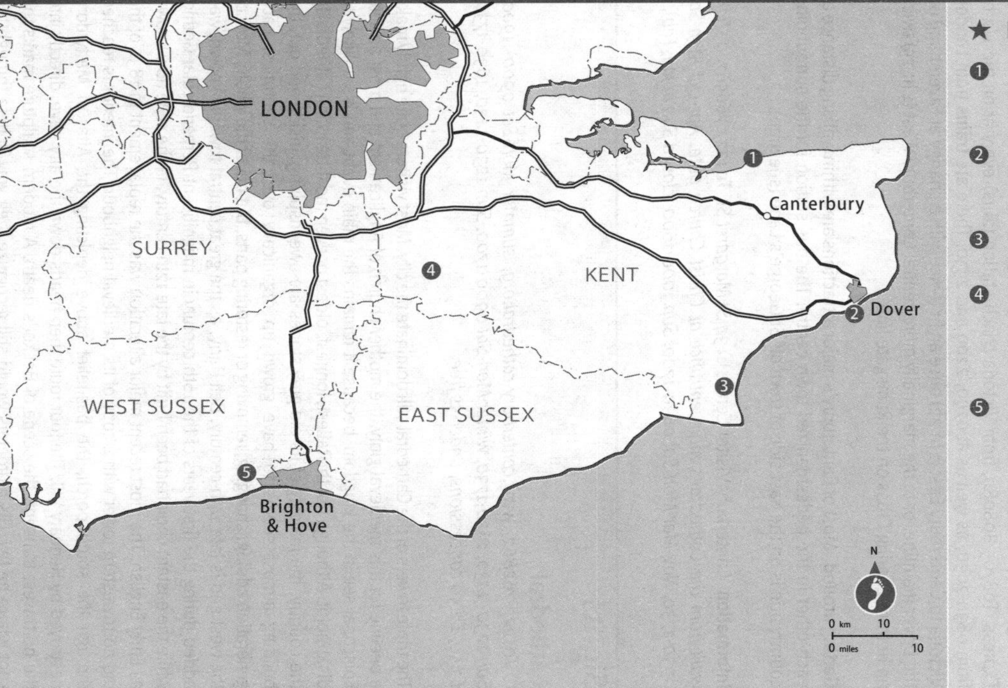

★ Don't miss...

1. Suck down a plate of oysters in **Whitstable** and watch the sun set over Southend from Peter Cushing's favourite beach, page 116.
2. Dive beneath **Dover Castle** to explore the entrails of the White Cliffs, from where the army was rescued from Dunkirk, page 119
3. Ride the miniature **Romney, Hythe and Dymchurch railway**, page 121
4. Sink your teeth into Elizabethan history at **Penshurst Place** before enjoying a pub supper in the Tudor village of Chiddingstone, page 128.
5. Work up a thirst walking along the **South Downs Way** enjoying superb views of the Channel and then dance all night in **Brighton**, page 130

Canterbury

→Colour map 2

Canterbury is probably the single most popular tourist destination in the southeast. Not surprisingly it can become very congested, but the city also does an excellent job of combining its medieval roots with mass tourism on a charming and manageable scale. Although parts of the centre of town were bombed flat in the Second World War, they have been fairly sympathetically rebuilt and enough of the old timber-framed buildings and narrow streets remain to maintain the antique tone. The pedestrianized heart of the city, within the medieval walls, is an enjoyable place to explore, despite the crowds, and thanks to its cathedral and university Canterbury has more style and energy than anywhere else in east Kent. » For Sleeping, Eating and other listings, see pages 113-114

Ins and outs

Getting there Take the M2/A2 from London (about 1 hr 45 mins) to Dover. National Express, T08705-808080, from Victoria coach station (2hrs) every hr on the 1/2 hr from 0830-2030, as well as at 0700, 2200 and 2330. There are **trains** from London Victoria to Canterbury East (1 hr 22) once an hr (twice with a change at Faversham) on the Dover mainline, or to the marginally more central Canterbury West (1 hr 25) twice an hr from Charing Cross on the Ramsgate line.

Getting around Most of Canterbury's major attractions are within walking distance of each other in the pedestrianized town centre. The bus station for the surrounding countryside is on the east side of town off St George's Lane (see map).

Information Canterbury Visitor Centre ⓘ *34 St Margaret St, T01227-766567, a short walk from the Cathedral's main entrance at Christ Church gate. Apr-Oct Mon-Sat 0930-1730, Nov-Mar Mon-Sat 0630-1700, Sun 1000-1600 (closed Sun in Jan, Feb).*

Sights

Cathedral

ⓘ *T01227-762862, www.canterbury-cathedral.org, summer Mon-Sat 0900- 1900, Sun 1230- 1430, 1630-1730, winter Mon-Sat 0900-1700, Sun 1230-1430, 1630-1730, £3.50, £2.50 concessions, under-5s free.*

The triple towers of the Cathedral still dominate the city. Most visitors quite rightly make a beeline for this medieval glory, the mother church of Anglicanism and most ancient Episcopal see in the kingdom, because it remains the main event and it's unlikely to disappoint. Although not the tallest, longest, oldest or even most beautiful cathedral in the country, the majesty of its old grey stones are awe-inspiring. Inside and out, the building almost seems to have grown up organically over the centuries, each generation adding, changing, removing or restoring parts, but never the whole. Most of the west end is late 14th-century. Bell Harry, as the great central tower is known, was added during the first years of the 16th century in magnificent Perpendicular Gothic, while the eastern choir had been built by the late 12th century, in the style now known as Early English. The most recent major alteration was the replacement in 1834 of the old northwestern tower with a copy of its medieval neighbour. The interior is reached through the south porch, the bas-relief above depicting the Altar of Martyrdom destroyed by Heneary VIII. The tour route then heads down the airy nave, directly into the northwest transept, the scene of Becket's death. A modern sculpture marks the spot where he fell. His murderers would still recognize their way in here through the doorway from the cloisters. Steps then lead down into the Crypt, the earliest and most atmospheric part of the building. It's the finest Norman undercroft in the country, with remarkable stone-carving on pillars and capitals, especially on St Gabriel's chapel in the southeast corner which also features a 13th-century painted ceiling. Back on ground level, the tourist route enters the long Quire, with its Grinling Gibbons stalls at the west end, before heading round to the famous Royal tombs (Heneary IV and the Black Prince) in the Trinity Chapel behind the High Altar.

Central Canterbury

The visitors' entrance to the Cathedral precincts is through the ornate 16th-century Christ Church gate on the **Butter Market**. Best approached from Mercery Lane, this is the centre of tourist Canterbury and often impossibly busy with schools of bored-looking French and Italian teenagers milling around the war memorial.

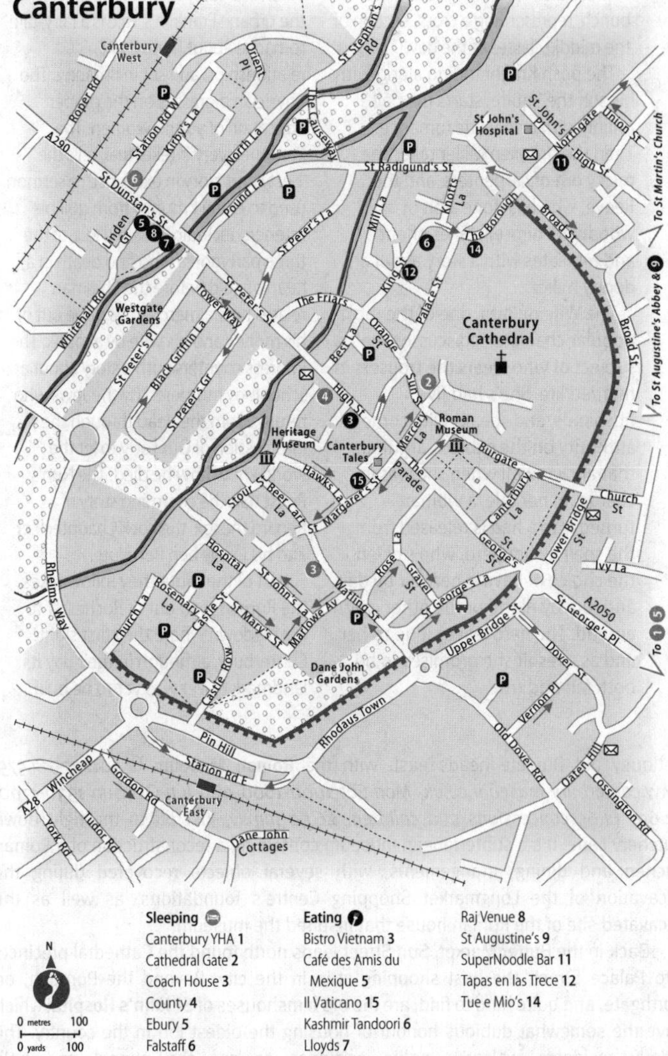

The Canterbury Tales

The poet Geoffrey Chaucer is generally accepted as the father of English literature, and his late 14th-century Canterbury Tales his most famous work. "Whan that Aprill with shoures soote/ The droghte of March hath perced to the roote… Thanne longen folk to goon on pilgrimages" it begins, as 30 pilgrims set out from Southwark for Canterbury on April 17, telling tales in prose and verse. They're a mixed bunch, representing a cross- section of the middle classes of the day.

The posh Knight, riding along with his son the Squire, starts the ball rolling with a chivalric romance. Then the drunken Miller takes the micky out of carpenters, and the Reeve, who has done a bit of woodwork himself, takes offence, and retaliates with a story about a dodgy miller.

The Wife of Bath, one of the most popular characters, discusses the subject of who wears the trousers in married life. She's had five husbands, and speaks with some authority on the subject, arguing that all was well when she was in charge. In her tale, a woman turned into a hag is released from the spell by her hero, who's given the choice of having her 'fair by day and foul by night' or the other way around. The hero leaves it up to her and as a result she promises to be both fair and true.

The Friar and Summoner then mock each other before the Clerk relates the patience of Griselda in putting up with her husband's absurd demands. The Merchant, unhappily married himself, tells a tale of old man January who suffers from the wicked wiles of his wife May.

The Squire's romantic interlude involves a sadly abandoned lady, while the urbane Franklin's Tale is a fairy-tale romance about honesty in relationships, and set in Britanny. The Physician digresses on the proper education of young women. The Pardoner, very intellectual, tells the 'best short story in existence': a sermon used to extract money from gullible listeners, including the old tale of the three partygoers who find death in a heap of gold before the Shipman relates how a merchant is done out of his money and his wife by a monk. The Prioress counters with a story about a schoolboy murdered by the Jews who returns from the dead through the intercession of Our Lady to let the world know how he died. The Nun's Priest tells the charming story of Renard the fox, the cock Chauntecleer and his lovely hen Pertelote.

Part of the route they follow takes the Roman road out of Rochester to Harbledown where they first sight Canterbury, although in their day its landmark tower was yet to be built.

Antiquey old Burgate heads east, with the **Roman Museum** ⓘ *T01227-785575, www.canterbury-museum.co.uk, Mon-Sat 1000-1600 also Jun-Oct Sun 1330-1700, £2.60, £1.65 concessions and children, £6.50 family,* just off to the right down Butchery Lane. It's a subterranean museum containing a reconstruction of a Roman kitchen and dining arrangements, with several objects recovered during the excavation of the Longmarket Shopping Centre's foundations, as well as the excavated site of the Roman house that inspired the museum.

Back in the Butter Market, Sun Street leads north round the Cathedral precincts into Palace Street, the best shopping strip in the city. Beyond the Borough, on Northgate, and quite hard to find, are the old almshouses of **St John's Hospital** which have the somewhat dubious honour of housing the oldest loo in the country. The elderly residents welcome polite enquiries to see the chapel and hall.

ⓘ *T01227-451621.* Mercery Lane heads across the High St into St Margaret's Street, where you'll find the **Visitor Centre** and also the **Canterbury Tales** ⓘ *St Margaret's St, T01227-479227, Nov-Feb 18th 1000-1630, 19th Feb-May and Sep-Oct 1000-1700, Jul-Aug 0930-1730, £6.75, £5.75 concessions, £5.25 children, £25 family,* a reasonably entertaining 'visitor attraction' based on the stories told by Chaucer's pilgrims on their way from London to Canterbury. The animatronics now look badly dated but the humour of the tales comes across well.

St Augustine's Abbey and around

East down Burgate, beyond the old medieval walls, **St Augustine's Abbey** ⓘ *T01227-767345, Apr-Sep daily 1000-1800, Oct 1000-1700, Nov-Mar 1000-1600, £3, £2.30 concessions, £1.50 children*, is the birthplace of the Roman Catholic Church in England. There's not much left of the buildings themselves now except a few old walls and foundations, but this is where St Augustine and his convert King Ethelbert are buried. The English Heritage visitor centre and audio tour try hard to bring the grassy emptiness back to life, and also detail the Abbey's use as a palace by Elizabeth I, Charles I and Charles II after Heneary VIII's split from Rome.

Another short walk northeast from here brings you to **St Martin's Church**, in North Holmes Rd, the oldest church in continuous use in England, where Queen Bertha apparently worshipped before St Augustine's arrival. Now it's best visited for its position in one of the city's more pleasant districts beyond the city walls, for a look at the Norman font supposedly also comprising part of the Saxon font in which King Ethelbert was baptized, and perhaps to pay hommage at the grave of local hero Mary Tourtel, the creator of the yellow-check trousered cartoon hero Rupert the Bear in the *Daily Express*.

Sleeping

Unfortunately Canterbury is not blessed with many outstanding hotels. It makes up in quantity what it generally lacks in quality though, especially when it comes to affordable B&Bs and guesthouses. The TIC or web is the best place to track down these, but the stretch of straightforward places on the New Dover Rd is a good place to start looking on spec.

A-B **Falstaff Hotel**, 8-10 St Dunstan's St, T01227-462138, www.corushotels.com/thefalstaff For an antique hotel just outside the city walls this is hard-to-beat Part of its building dates from the early 15th century, but the new building within and around blends in sympathetically enough. It's part of the *Corus* chain and perfectly comfortable, with all the facilities you'd expect for the price. Three more expensive rooms with 4-poster beds.

C **Ebury Hotel**, 65-67 New Dover Rd, 10 mins on foot out of town, T01227-768433. Fifteen rooms, breakfast included. One 4-poster, 2 family rooms.

D **County Hotel**, High St, T01227-766266, F784324. A small, neat and very central Victorian townhouse.

D-E **Cathedral Gate Hotel**, 36 Burgate, T01227-464381, F462800. Right next to Christ Church Gate and a creaking warren of rooms of all shapes and sizes, some quite basic. The views of the cathedral – beautifully floodlit at night – from the back rooms make it quite romantic and the best value place in the centre.

D **Coach House**, 34 Watling St, T01227-784324. Six individual family rooms in a 3-storey Georgian townhouse, with a courtyard garden, breakfast included.

F **Canterbury YHA**, Ellerslie, 54 New Dover Rd, T01227-462911. Three-quarters of a mile from Canterbury East station, fully equipped (85 beds).

Eating

£££ **Lloyds**, 89-90 St Dunstan's St, T01227-768222. One of the more recent openings and one of the more ambitious doing a sophisticated modern British and traditional French menu in a cunningly converted bank.

£££ **St Augustine's Restaurant**, 1 and 2 Longport, T01227-453063, Not central, but with an enviable long-standing reputation, this is the place for some thoroughly civilized and well-prepared European dishes in a restrained atmosphere.

£££ Tue e Mio's, 16 The Borough, T01227-761471. Generally agreed to be the smartest Italian in town: quite a formal but welcoming place for some traditional Italian food with Arabic and Sicilian influences.

££ Tapas en las Trece, 13 Palace St, T01227-762639. Does a reasonably priced Spanish menu in a laid-back atmosphere.

££ Kashmir Tandoori, Palace St, specializes in tandooris from Kashmir, although the Tudorbethan dining room is unusual.

££ Il Vaticano, 35 St Margaret's St, T01227-765333. A very lively Italian restaurant, reasonably priced, bang in the middle of town.

££ Bistro Vietnam, White Horse La, T01227-760022. Comes highly recommended for its fish recipes from Saigon.

£ Café des Amis du Mexique, 95 St Dunstan's St, T01227-464390. Combines Mediterranean and Mexican cuisine in a bright, busy atmosphere, very popular with students.

£ Raj Venue, 92 St Dunstan's St, T01227-462653. Colourful Bangladeshi restaurant and take away.

£ SuperNoodle Bar, 87-88 Northgate St, T01227-457888. A good bet for some very tasty, fast and inexpensive Chinese noodles. Bright and cheerful restaurant and takeaway.

Activities and tours

Canterbury City Official Guide (tickets are available from the TIC). Walking tours lasting about 1 hr 30 mins and leaving from the centre at 1400 daily Apr-Nov, and also at 1100 daily from Jun-Aug.

Dr Thomson's Tours of Historic Canterbury, 37 The Crescent, T01227-455922. A private operator with considerable experience.

Transport

Bike hire

Downland Cycle Hire, Canterbury West Railway Station, T01227-479643.

Car hire

Drive Easy, Halletts, Station Rd West, T01227-451155. Victoria Hire, 22 St Dunstans St, T01227-455001. S & B Car Hire Kent Ltd, Canterbury East Railway Station, T01227-781180.

Taxis

Cabwise Taxi Services, 112 Sweechgate Broad Oak, T01227-712929. City Cars, Unit 26, Roper Cl, T01227-454445. Lynx Taxis Ltd, Unit 6, Dane John Works, Gordon Rd, T01227-464232.

Directory

Hospitals The Chaucer Hospital, Nackington Rd, T01227-455466. Kent & Canterbury Hospital, Ethelbert Rd, T01227-766877. **Language schools** Canterbury Language Training, 73-75 Castle St, T01227-760000. Carl Duisberg Language Centre Canterbury, 26 Oaten Hill, T01227-764123. **Police** Canterbury Police Station,Old Dover Rd, T01227-762055. **Post office** 29 High St, T0845-7223344.

North Kent Coast

→Colour map 2

Although so close to London, the southern shores of the Thames estuary are not an obvious destination for visitors. Bypassed by the M2 en route to Canterbury and Folkestone, and overshadowed by the North Downs, the riverside and coastal towns along here are surprisingly isolated. Rochester, Chatham and the Medway Towns may not be the most prepossessing places, but all have several attractions of more than passing interest. The biggest draw in these parts is undoubtedly Whitstable which has fairly recently achieved considerable cachet with the capital's weekenders, not only for its famous oyster restaurants but also for its working harbour and thriving nightlife. ▸▸ *For Sleeping, Eating and other listings, see pages 117-118*

Ins and outs

Getting there Rochester is on the A2/M2, about 50 mins from London, unless travelling at peak times, which can add 40 mins to the journey. There are infrequent daily Greenline, T0870-6087261, and North Kent Express, T01474-330330, bus services from London Victoria to both Rochester and Chatham which take around 2 hrs. Rochester is easily reached from London by **train**, either from Charing Cross (1 hr) or more quickly from Victoria (40 mins) 2-3 times an hr on the mainline to Ramsgate. **Whitstable** is the first properly coastal, as opposed to estuarine, town on the North Kent coast, easily reached off the A299 from the end of the M2 (junction 7) about 1 hr 30 mins' drive from London, or by train direct from London Victoria (1 hr 15 mins) twice an hr. **Broadstairs** lies between Margate and Ramsgate, about 2 hrs 30 mins from London. **National Express**, T08705-808080, coaches run 5 times a day from London Victoria to both Margate and Ramsgate, taking about 2 hrs 30 mins. Broadstairs can be reached from either London Victoria via Rochester, Chatham and Whitstable in about 1 hr 50 mins on one of the few direct trains, on a good day. More regular services require a change at Faversham, adding 20 mins to the journey time. From London Charing Cross it's necessary to change at Rochester.

Information Rochester Visitor Centre ⓘ *95 High St, T01634-843666, www.medway.gov.uk, Mon-Sat 1000-1700, Sun 1030-1700.* **Whitstable Visitor Centre** ⓘ *7 Oxford St, T01227-275482, www.whitstable.org.* **Broadstairs TIC** ⓘ *on the seafront near Peter's Fish Shop, 6b High St, T01843-865650.*

Rochester

Rochester has occupied its dominant position overlooking the mouth of the River Medway since long before the Romans arrived, and boasts the second oldest cathedral in the country and one of the most impressive Norman keeps. It's also the heart of Dickens country and won't let you forget it. Either bone up on your Pickwick before visiting or track down a copy in one of the town's many second-hand bookshops.

Rochester **Cathedral's** ⓘ *T01634-401301, daily 0800-1800, free, £2 donation requested.* Saxon foundations were laid by King Ethelbert of Kent on his conversion in 604, although the small but perfectly formed Norman cathedral of today was founded a little to the east in 1080 by Gundulf, also responsible for the Tower of London's White Tower. The rounded arches of the nave remain one of the finest examples of Norman cathedral architecture in the country.

Over the road from the Cathedral's west front, the great ruined keep of the Norman **castle** ⓘ *T01634-402276, Apr-Sep daily 1000-1800, Oct-Mar 1000-1600,* overlooks the river above civic gardens incorporating fragments of the town's Roman walls. A stairway winds up the hollow shell of the old castle to the top battlements, from where the wide valley of the Medway can be seen meandering into the distance, bridged by the M2 and the new Channel Tunnel rail link.

A few steps nearer Chatham, the **Charles Dickens Centre** ⓘ *T01634-844176, Apr-Sep daily 1000-1800, Oct-Mar 1000- 1600, £3.90, concessions £2.80*, is a tourist attraction on the author's life and works, with a few mildly distracting audio-visual reconstructions from his works and one of his actual desks. The star attraction is probably his gaudily painted writing chalet from Gads Hill (see below), which can be seen in the garden of the Centre even when the Centre is closed.

Chatham

Next door to Rochester, Chatham in its heyday had one of Britain's most important naval dockyards, now skilfully converted into an entertaining visitor attraction. The **Historic Dockyard** ⓘ *T01634-823800, www.worldnavalbase.org.uk, Apr-Oct daily 1000-1800 (last entry 1600), Nov, Feb and Mar Wed, Sat, Sun 1000-1600 (last entry 1500), £9.50, £7 concessions, £6 children, £25 family, take any of several buses marked Chatham Maritime/Historic Dockyard from the train station or High St.* (or World Naval Base as it now likes to be known) is about a mile and a half from the ugly town centre. The dockyard itself is a must for all seadogs, especially the large Royal National Lifeboat

Exhibition, with its well-presented array of life-saving boats, as well as the extraordinary Ropery, 'the longest room in England' at nearly quarter of a mile, and continually in use since the early 19th century. The ropemakers, who can be seen working on Wednesday to Saturday, recently made the ropes for the opening of Buckingham Palace's Garden to the public. Elsewhere around the huge site, the destroyer **HMS Cavalier** and inshore patrol submarine **Ocelot** can be looked over on guided visits. The latter feels like the ocean-going equivalent of a tank: very cramped and very dangerous. Elsewhere on the huge site, **Wooden Walls** is a fairly successful attempt to describe how the navy that defeated Napoleon at Trafalgar was built, as seen through the eyes of a young apprentice of the time.

Whitstable

Whitstable has long been associated with oysters. Those succulent molluscs have been happily breeding in the warm salty inshore waters here since Roman times. The town now depends on them for its popularity, if not for its livelihood, as it did a century ago when a dozen slithery mouthfuls were a staple meal for poor people across the land.

The relatively high cost of oysters today, along with the mildly decadent frisson that eating them can arouse, accounts for much of the town's current success with weekending Londoners. Also, unlike most of the towns on the coast to the east, Whitstable remains a working town, its hatchery in the harbour one of the largest in Europe. Never developed as a seaside resort, the High Street casually turns its back on the sea, only a pebble's throw away. It's certainly not a quaint or even particularly attractive place, but the shingle beach (sandy at either end) affords beautiful sunsets looking across to the Isle of Sheppey and Southend beyond, the harbour is still quite busy, and the rows of oyster huts (not all as yet converted into holiday homes) were once sketched by Turner. The history of the place can be explored next door to the TIC at the **Whitstable Museum and Gallery**, *5a Oxford St, T01227-276998, Mon-Sat 1000-1600 winter, summer also Sun 1300-1600, free.*through a diverting collection of local memorabilia, exhibitions on oysters and divers, as well as natural history (especially the local birdlife) and maritime history. In 1830, Whitstable also became famous as the terminus of the first passenger railway in the world, designed by George Stephenson to take steamboat passengers from London onward to Canterbury. The sea-going part of the trip can still be experienced twice each summer on the last ocean-going paddle steamer in the UK, the **PS Waverley** ⓘ *T01227-275482*, although the railway is now defunct.

Broadstairs

Northeast of Canterbury and once cut off from the mainland by the Wantsum channel, the Isle of Thanet is a wide-open stretch of flat country fringed by coastal resorts of variable quality. Pick of the bunch is Broadstairs, the kind of resort that the Victorians liked to call a 'watering-place', altogether more dignified and refined.

Dickens was a great admirer, taking regular working holidays here and describing it as "one of the freest and freshest little places in the world". He wrote *Barnaby Rudge* in a house in Harbour St and other places associated with his writing and visits have been turned into quirky old museums (see Sights below). Everything looks a little tired these days as the town slopes steeply down to its little sandy beach in Viking Bay with the small port alongside. More self-contained than either Margate or Ramsgate, Broadstairs is a good base from which to explore the area. Quiet and old-fashioned– witness the survival since 1913 of the little single-screen Windsor Cinema on Harbour St (see Entertainment below) under the York Gate inscribed 1510– it has a good selection of comfortable places to stay and several reasonable restaurants.

Whitstable's most famous resident, Peter Cushing, had his own bench looking out to sea and even a carpark named in his honour.

High on the cliffs overlooking the bay, in a prominent position way above the beach, **Bleak House** ⓘ *Fort Rd, T01843-862224, Mar-Nov daily 1000-1800, Jul and Aug 1000-2100, £3, £2.80 OAPs, £2.50 concessions, £2.20 children*, is named after the novel that Dickens planned there and where he wrote David Copperfield. His study with its glorious sea view has been recreated, along with his bedroom and dining room. Downstairs there's an interesting exhibition on the wreckers of the Goodwin sands during the golden age of smuggling when the town apparently did very well for itself.

The other main Dickens attraction is down on the seafront, the **Dickens House Museum**, in the former home of Mary Strong ⓘ *Victoria Pde, T01843-864353, daily 1400-1700, £2, children £0.50*, the inspiration for the character of Betsey Trotwood in *David Copperfield*. The little house is neatly laid out with Victoriana and memorabilia associated with the great author. About a mile north of Viking Bay, set back some distance from the sea, is the **North Foreland Lighthouse** ⓘ *North Foreland Rd, T01843-861869, www.ekmt.fsnet.co.uk, Easter-Sep weekends (summer school holidays Tue-Sun) 1100-1700, £2, £1.50 OAPs, £1 children, £5 family*. Constructed in 1732, this stubby little beacon was the last in the country to be automated, in 1998. The views from the top stretch from Margate to Ramsgate and beyond.

Sleeping

Rochester *p115*

B **Newington Manor Hotel**, Callaways La, Newington, out of town on the road to Sittingbourne, T01795-842053. More expensive and comfortable than either of the above, this is a small old manor house with a large garden on the edge of the village, with 3 rooms in the old house (4-poster bed £98, others £78) in stable block and annexe, 12 rooms in all. Restaurant closed at weekends.
D Royal Victoria and Bull Hotel, 16 High St, T01634-846266, www.rvandb.co.uk. If an overnight stop is necessary this is the traditional option.

Whitstable *p116*

Accommodation in Whitstable can be very difficult to find on Fri and Sat nights, so it's best to book well ahead, even during the week.
C **Hotel Continental**, 29 Beach Walk, T01227-280280, www.oysterfishery.co.uk. The most stylish place to stay in Whitstable, with its fine Art Deco frontage and renovated rooms, some with balconies looking out to sea west of the harbour. It's owned by the Whitstable Oyster Fishery Company, who also run the top-notch restaurant the **Royal Native Oyster Stores** (see Eating below), so the restaurant does all manner of absolutely fresh fish very well. The same company also manages a group of self-catering converted beach huts for £125 a night, each sleeping 4, that always need to be booked months in advance.
D-E **Barnsfield**, 5 miles out of town, south towards Canterbury, near the village of Hernhill, T01795-536514. A pleasant B&B in a 16th-century house.
D-E **Copeland House**, 4 Island Wall, T01227-266207. A cosy B&B very close to the beach.

Broadstairs *p116*

C **Royal Albion Hotel**, Albion St, T01843-868071. Right on the seafront with wonderful views over Viking Bay. Sea-facing rooms including breakfast marginally more expensive.
D **Hanson Hotel**, 41 Belvedere Rd, T01843-868936. Not in quite such a special position, but less expensive, this is a cosy little place in an old Georgian house where some of the decor seems to be stuck in the 70s but all the better for it. Good budget options in the area are the 2 youth hostels:
F **Broadstairs YHA**, Thistle Lodge, 3 Osborne Rd, T01843-604121. A clean, comfortable hostel especially popular with families.

For an explanation of the sleeping and eating price codes used in this guide, see the inside front cover. Other relevant information is provided in the Essentials chapter, page 36.

Eating

Rochester *p115*

££ **Barnacles Seafood**, 86 High St. Has a small back garden and some reasonably priced fish dishes.

££ **Casa-Lina Restaurant**, 146 High St, T01634-844993. A good bet for pizza and pasta in a jolly atmosphere (closed Sun and Mon).

£ **Eon Internet Café**, 32 High St. The place to log on with a coffee and cheap sandwich.

Whitstable *p116*

Oysters can be had all year round, although the best homegrown varieties are only available in season (when there's an 'r' in the name of the month).

£££ **Royal Native Oyster Stores**, on the beachfront, T01227-276856. The town's most upmarket (and expensive) option in the old warehouse that was once packed full of the little blighters.

££ **Crab & Winkle**, South Quay, T01227-779377. Above the fish market with a balcony that seats 20. Friendlier than its famous rival (see above) and cheaper. Cod and chips costs under £10.

££ **The Sportsman**, Faversham Rd, Seasalter, T01227-273370. The uninspiring exterior gives no hint of the delights on offer inside. Sublime cooking of the strictly non-poncey variety. Kids welcome. Tue-Sat for lunch and dinner, Sun lunch. Booking advised.

££ **Wheeler's Oyster Bar**, 8 High St, T01227-273311, open till 2100 Mon-Thu and Sun, 2130 Fri, 2200 Sat (closed Wed). The oldest and still the pick of the bunch. Out front there's an old-fashioned and unpretentious counter serving a wide variety of fresh seafood and sometimes very good ginger ice cream. It's BYOB (available from *Thresher's* over the road) which makes a meal here very good value, even if dining in the cosy parlour round the back.

Broadstairs *p116*

££ **Marchesi's**, 16-18 Albion St, T01843-862481, is more expensive, a traditional Anglo-French restaurant specializing in rich sauces.

££ **Tartar Frigate**, Harbour St, T01843-862013. The best fresh fish restaurant in town, although a little twee.

Entertainment

Whitstable *p116*

Imperial Oyster Cinema, T01227-770829. In the same beachfront building as the Royal Native Oyster Stores, showing an interesting mix of mainstream and more offbeat movies several times daily.

Broadstairs *p116*

Windsor Cinema, Harbour St, T01843-865726, is a tiny little one-screen cinema showing new releases in its old purpose-built picture house.

Pavilion Theatre, Broadstairs, T01843-600999, is the town's home-from-home for touring shows.

Festivals and events

Rochester *p115*

Dickens Festival in the first week of **Jun** sees Rochester jump to the great novelist's tune with even more alacrity than usual, including a Victorian pageant, music and readings from the novels all round the area.

Whitstable *p116*

Whitstable Oyster Festival (details from TIC) usually takes place towards the end of **Jul**, involving a sea-going regatta of antique yawls, as well as maritime morris dances and general fairly drunken celebrations of the first small haul of the season (which actually runs Sep-May).

Broadstairs *p116*

Broadstairs Dickens Festival takes place in the middle weeks of **Jun** with parades, Victorian cricket matches, and other celebrations of the town's local hero.

Broadstairs Folk Week, T01843-604080, in the second week of **Aug**, is a well-respected folk music festival that takes over various venues all over town.

East Kent Coast →*Colour map 2*

Kent's eastern seaboard south of Thanet is a strange and contradictory affair. To the south, the widest expanse of shingle in Europe juts into the Channel at Dungeness which is blessed with a weird assortment of attractions, from a nuclear power station to the UK's longest miniature railway, running between Romney, Hythe and Dymchurch. Inland, the mysterious atmosphere of Romney Marsh can best be appreciated at a handful of lonely fog-bound churches surrounded by quietly grazing sheep and unusual birdlife. To the east is Dover, with its impressive castle and busy ferry terminals, still many visitors' first impression of England and not always a happy one. ▸▸ *For Sleeping, Eating and other listings, see pages 123-125*

Ins and outs

Getting there **Dover** is 71 miles southeast of London and can usually be reached in under 2 hrs on either the M20 via Ashford or the M2/A2 via Canterbury. **National Express,** T08705-808080, run coaches from Victoria Coach Station to Dover town centre and ferry port every hr between 0700 and 2330 taking around 2 hrs 30 mins.Trains from London Charing Cross (1 hr 40 mins) and from London Victoria (1 hr 50 mins) pull into Dover Priory, close to the town centre. A free bus service runs from the station down to the docks. **Rye** lies on the South Coast trunk route (A259), between Brighton, Lewes and Hastings and Dover. Local buses link Hastings and Rye rail stations hourly (1 hr). Longer distance coaches run hourly to Dover (2 hrs, £4.20), and Brighton via Lewes with a change at Eastbourne (3 hrs, £7.30). **Stagecoach East Kent,** T08702-433711. A delightfully knackered diesel train links Rye to Hastings (20 mins) and Ashford (25 mins). From Hastings you can pick up connections to London Charing Cross (2 hrs); Lewes (1 hr 30 mins) and Brighton (1 hr 45 mins). From Ashford you can make connections to Dover (1 hr), and Canterbury (1 hr 15 mins). To visit Winchelsea from Rye, there are hourly train services (5 mins, £1.90), or there are various local buses (10 mins). Camber Sands can be reached by the No11 bus (15 mins).

Information **Dover TIC** ⓘ Townwall St, T01304-205108, daily 0900-1800. **Folkestone TIC** ⓘ *Harbour St, T01303-258594.* **New Romney TIC** ⓘ *Magpie, Church Approach, T01797-364044.* **Rye TIC** ⓘ *Strand Quay, T01797-226696, daily Jun-Aug 0900-1730, Sep-May 1000-1600.* You can pick up a map and guide here, but if you're planning a quick trip, it might be best to opt for the Rye town walk (£1) guided tour, or an audio-tour £2/£1.

Dover

Sitting in the mouth of the River Dour at the southern end of the North Downs, Dover and its famous white cliffs have long been an important landing-place. The Roman Dubris (one of its guiding lighthouses still stands in the grounds of the castle) was the starting point for Watling Street, the main road up to London via Canterbury. During the Dark Ages, the Saxons fortified its position, but it's thanks to Henry II that there's something really worth seeing in the town today. In the late 12th century he ordered the construction of the great stone castle on the cliffs that has since become known as the 'key to England'. As the closest town to mainland Europe (17 miles away at Cap Griz Nez), a procession of historically significant characters have stepped its streets. Unfortunately, however, for a place with such an important place in history, modern Dover is a disappointment, hemmed in by huge roads and some seriously ugly post-war developments.

Without doubt the highlight of any visit to Dover is the remarkably well-preserved medieval **castle** ⓘ *(EH), T01304-211067, Apr-Sep daily 1000-1800, Oct 1000-1700, Nov-Mar 1000-1600, £8, £6 concessions, £4 children, £20 family.* It dominates the town, a steep climb directly above the port. (In fact it is better to approach it by car from Deal and the east.) Henry II's stern square keep (1168-80s) looms proud on the hilltop, surrounded by a series of concentric walls with fortified towers. These are a familiar feature of most medieval castles but they first appeared in western Europe here, thanks to Crusaders who had got wise attacking the Moslems' fortifications. Although the castle occupies the site of an Iron Age fort, the oldest visible testament to the importance of its position is the hexagonal base of the Roman lighthouse. In the 15th century, this was heightened to become the belltower of the Saxon church next door. Inside the keep, the chapel dedicated to Thomas à Becket has some fine Romanesque carving, while the views from its battlements are superb. Most people's favourite part of a visit, though, are the secret wartime tunnels that burrow through the cliffs. Begun after the French had successfully undermined one of the northern gate towers in the siege of 1216, only to be driven back in hand-to-hand combat, the tunnels were expanded 600 years later during the Napoleonic Wars, providing barracks for up to 2000 troops ready to repel invaders below the clifftops. During the Second World War, further underground space was created from which to mastermind the retreat from Dunkirk. During the summer the castle gets busy with re-enactments of its eventful history and throughout the year there's enough to see and do to occupy most of the day.

In the centre of the town itself, there's sadly not much to linger over, except for the award-winning local history **museum** ⓘ *T01304-201066, www.dovermuseum.co.uk, summer daily 1000-1800, winter daily 1000-1730, £1.70, £0.90 concessions*, in Market Square which includes the new interactive Bronze Age Boat Gallery. Archaeological finds in the area are on the ground floor, from Roman times as well as from the important Buckland Anglo-Saxon cemetery. On the first floor there are regular special exhibitions. The Bronze Age Boat Gallery is on the second floor, dedicated to the remains of the world's oldest known sea-going boat, about 3500 years old and discovered as recently as 1992.

Round the corner from the museum, in New Street, is the **Roman Painted House** ⓘ *T01304-203279, Apr-Sep Tue-Sun (Jul and Aug also Mon) 1000-1700, £2, £0.80 concessions*, the fairly impressive remains of a Roman 'Mansio', or official hotel, including its wall paintings and hypocaust.

Folkestone

Despite or perhaps because of the Channel Tunnel, Folkestone is a shadow of its former self. Even so, with its transport links and faded Edwardian splendour, it remains the most obvious place to start an exploration of one of the oddest corners of Kent. Folkestone hardly merits an overnight stay, although anyone with time to kill and an interest in Cold War technology can look over the **Russian** Submarine ⓘ *T01303-240400*, moored at South Quay, a Soviet-era hunter killer and one of only four in the world. Or take a stroll along **The Leas**, an Edwardian clifftop boardwalk reached via a water-balanced chairlift. Otherwise the town's uneasy mix of old and new makes it a faintly depressing place to linger.

Romney and Walland Marshes

Between Hythe in the east and Rye in the west, the once sea-swamped Romney and Walland marshes, known locally as 'the marsh', is a miniature fenland. The marshes are dotted with more than 20 small churches, built in the later 13th century by the wool-rich locals on man-made mounds. Along with the sheep, the loneliness and the eerie quiet – despite the encroaching bungalows – the atmosphere around these old places make the marsh a strange and special area to explore. On the coast the marsh juts into the channel at Dungeness, a remarkably desolate shingle spit dotted with a weird array of attractions. Actually, Rye (see below) is probably the best base from which to explore the marsh.

Appledore is a lovely little town on the **Royal Military canal**. Constructed to fend off Bonaparte, with a kink every few 100 yards for a cannon, the banks of the canal are still lined with pillboxes from 1940. Overlooking the marsh from the church, it's easy to picture the marsh under water all those years ago. Many of the local churches, with their heavy angled buttresses, look a little like upturned boats.

At **St Mary in the Marsh**, apart from the grave of E Nesbit, the author of *The Railway Children*, the church has little more than a solitary pub, the *Star Inn*, for company. Apart from New Romney, **Lydd** is the largest settlement in the area, with a faintly dilapidated air. Its church is proportionately larger than most of the others, known as 'the cathedral of the marsh', but was bombed almost flat in the Second World War. Reconstructed, it remains the focal point of this low-lying town with most major facilities.

Nearby at **Old Romney**, the church has some fine 18th-century box pews and a minstrel's gallery, as well as a beautifully carved Purbeck marble medieval font. The most unusual of all the marshes churches is at **Brookland**, with its triple-coned wood-shingle belltower in a Norwegian style, detached from the main body of the early Gothic church. Inside there's a wall painting of the murder of Thomas à Becket and a remarkable 12th-century font decorated with the signs of the zodiac and the pastoral activities with which they're associated. **Fairfield** is the most lonely of the churches, a 13th-century timber- framed building bricked over in the 18th century and restored in the 20th. It can only be reached along a raised dyke off the road in the middle of nowhere.

Hythe, New Romney and Dungeness

On the eastern seaboard of the marsh, Hythe and Romney were two of the original Cinque Ports. **Hythe** suffered extensive damage during the war, leaving little of note to look at now, but thankfully its magnificent **church** survived in the older part of town. In its crypt, beneath an impressive early Gothic chancel, higher than its nave, and reminiscent of Canterbury Cathedral's but on a much smaller scale, is a gruesome array of thigh bones and skulls (from an estimated 4000 people), all neatly stacked up. Nobody minds if you handle them. Near Hythe, are the Norman ruins of **Lympne Castle** with breathtaking views over the marshes.

New Romney is the main town of the marsh, not much to look at, although the **Museum of the Romney Hythe and Dymchurch Railway** is worth checking out. ⓘ *T01797-362353, www.rhr.demon.co.uk, Easter-Sep daily, Mar, Oct weekends only. £9.20 return Hythe-Dungeness, with many other tickets available, phone for details.* Constructed by the millionaire racing driver Captain Howey in 1927, the Romney Hythe and Dymchurch Railway runs for 13 miles along the coast from Hythe to Dungeness, calling at Dymchurch, St Mary's Bay, New Romney and Romney Sands. The whole thing, track, engines and carriages, is one-third full size: adorable coaches are pulled along by hard-working little replica steam and diesel engines. The journey from Hythe to Dungeness takes just over an hour and is easily the most charming way of reaching the strange and desolate tip of the shingle spit at Dungeness.

Without doubt one of the weirdest places on the south coast, **Dungeness** is not only the end of the line for the little railway, it's also home to a nuclear power station, two lighthouses, and a string of beach huts popular with recluses. Occasionally, the quiet is broken by a massive roar, like a low-flying jet, as the power station lets off steam. The **Dungeness A Power Station Visitor Centre** reassures the public that they are quite safe. ⓘ *T01797-321815, Mar-Oct daily, Nov-Feb by appointment, booking required, free (no under-5s)*. The best place to appreciate the outlandish position and the peculiar light

The church at Appledore, now at least 10 miles from the sea, was built on the site of a fort established by Danish berserkers storming ashore from their longships in the Dark Ages. Hence the English word 'berserk'.

reflecting off the sea all around is from the top of the **Old Lighthouse** ⓘ *T01797-321300, May-Sep daily 1030-1700, Mar, Apr and Oct weekends only, £2.40, £1.40 concessions, £6.20 family*. After climbing 169 steps, you can enjoy the scale problems caused by the miniature railway steaming across the flat lands- cape, for all the world like the Santa Fe express heading into the desert. The fourth lighthouse on the site, built in 1901, it also contains a few displays on the local history. When the power station blocked the light, it was replaced by the award- winning modern one in 1961. Birdwatchers and nightfishers flock to the **Dungeness RSPB Nature** Reserve ⓘ *T01797-320588*, to see the local colonies of rare seabirds and catch unlikely fish enjoying the warm waters of the power station's outfall.

Rye

Rye is a sleepy market town perched on a hill overlooking Romney Marsh and the English Channel. Its maze of cobbled streets, towers and half-timber buildings make it a serious contender for prettiest town in England. This picturesque idyll belies the town's past– the centre was once encircled by water and her winding streets, secluded inns and cubby-holes made the place a safe haven for smugglers and brigands. But from the 18th century, Rye cleaned up its act, becoming a magnet for artists and writers. The modern town's carefully planned tourist industry feeds on both elements of her past, with all manner of 'contraband' alongside the tributes to Henry James, former resident. Despite its understandable appeal as a day-trip venue, Rye is more than just a vacuum-packed fillet of England's past. There are some quality hotels and estimable restaurants here, many in quaint tumbledown premises, which make it worth forking out a few extra pounds to prolong your stay. Despite the crowds in high season, the legacy of a history this colourful and a setting this idyllic is hard to resist.

The Story of Rye at the TIC ⓘ *Strand Quay, T01797-226696, daily Jun-Aug 0900-1730, Sep-May 1000-1600*, is an audio-visual presentation, set within the Rye town model, which offers a glimpse of Rye's turbulent past. Continue up Wish Ward, and you'll come to Mermaid Street and **The Mermaid Inn**. The street is one that regularly features on patriotic postcards, and with its timber-framed 15th-century houses, and cobbles, it's easy to see why. The notorious Hawkhurst gang of smugglers used the Inn for riotous nights on the tiles after successful raids. These days it's a very genteel hotel and restaurant with more cocoa than contraband. A right turn at the top of Mermaid Street takes you to **Lamb House** ⓘ *West St, T01797-227709, Wed and Sat 1400-1800 Apr-Oct, £2.60, £1.30 child*. This lovely 18th-century house has been home to Henry James, and EF Benson, and there's a small exhibition inside containing some of the former's possessions.

At the end of West Street is the gorgeous Church Square. The **Church of St Mary the Virgin**, is a 15th-century rebuild of an earlier church, and the clock in the tower (the oldest to use a pendulum in England) features two golden cherubs who emerge on each quarter hour. You can climb the tower for a splendid view over the rooftops (£2). Leading off one corner, is **Watchbell Street**, containing yet more attractive timber-framed houses, there is a viewing-point on the little promontory over Strand Quay, affording a wide vista of the river valley.

Another corner of Church Square leads to the **Ypres Tower** (1249). Part of anti-French fortifications, the tower is now home to one half of the **Rye Castle Museum** ⓘ *T01797-226728, Apr-Oct 1000-1300 and 1400-1700 Mon-Fri and Sun, 1030-1300 and 1400-1700 Sat-Sun, only the Ypres section is open in winter 1030-1530 Sat, £6, child £1.60*, and contains smuggling memorabilia, medieval pottery, and an exhibit on the unique Romney Marsh sheep! The other half of the museum is in East St, and features locally made toys and pottery. Heading down East Cliff, you'll come to **The Landgate**.Part of Edward III's 1329 town fortifications, the gate pays testimony to Rye's watery past: it used to be the only way in at High Tide.

Sleeping

Dover *p119*
B-C **Churchill Hotel**, Waterfront, T01304-203633, F216320. A straightforward and fairly smart Best Western chain hotel.
C **Loddington House**, East Cliff, Marine Pde, T/F01304-201947. Also reasonable, if noisy, being on the main road from the ferry terminal. Breakfast included. Convenient for the ferries.
F **YHA Dover**, 306 London Rd, T01304-201314, F202236. About half a mile from Dover Priory station, a mile or so from the Docks, with 132 beds in 2 separate townhouses, open all year.

Folkestone *p120*
D **Chandos Guest House**, 77 Cheriton Rd, T01303-851202. A reliable B&B option.
D **Kentmere Guest House**, 76 Cheriton Rd, T01303-259661. A little further afield, but nearer the Channel Tunnel, a comfortable 18th-century farmhouse,

Hythe, New Romney and Dungeness *p121*
C **Romney Bay House**, Coast Rd, Littlestone, New Romney, T01797-364747, F367156. Designed in the 1920s by Sir Clough Williams-Ellis, the creator of the Italianate coastal town of Portmeirion in Wales, for a wealthy American divorcee. Currently looking for a buyer, so catch it while you can, it's pretty much the only top-notch hotel in the area.
E **Martinfield Manor**, Lydd Rd, New Romney, T01797-363802. Has 5 comfortable en-suite rooms overlooking the marsh.

Rye *p122*
A **The Mermaid Inn**, Mermaid St, T01797-225069. Rye is such a captivating place that it's worth parting with a few quid for a weekend here in one of the finest hotels and one of England's oldest and prettiest hostelries.
C **Rye Lodge Hotel**, Hilder's Cliff, T01797-223838, in the centre of town with stunning views across the estuary, luxury suites and a decent dining room.
C **White Vine House**, High St, T01797-224748. Another upmarket floral gem on the High St with some luxurious rooms.
D **The Little Orchard House**, West St, T01797-223831. In a quiet cobbled street and does excellent breakfasts.
D **The Old Vicarage**, 66 Church Sq, T01797-222119. In the thick of it, opposite the church tower, a very twee, pink Georgian affair surrounded by roses.
D-E **The Durrant House Hotel**, 2 Market St, T01797-226639. A family-run Georgian townhouse hotel.
D-E **Jeake's House**, Mermaid St, T01797-222623. A stylishly restored townhouse with a book-lined bar.
D-E **The Old Borough Arms**, The Strand, T01797-222128. A family-run, 300-year-old former sailor's inn.
E **Windmill Guesthouse**, off Ferry Rd, T01797-224027. Comfortable and good value.

Self-catering
Camber Sands Holiday Park, T01797-225555. Offers self-catering cabins along the beach.

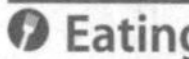

Eating

Romney and Walland Marshes *p120*
££ **Bayleaves**, 33-35 The Street, Appledore, T01233-758208, (closed Mon, daytime only). Do an excellent variety of home-made light meals, including several vegetarian options, in a cheerful atmosphere.
££ **The Woolpack**, Brookland, T01797-344321, is a delightful marsh pub with an above-average menu.

Rye *p122*
There are restaurants to cater for all tastes and budgets in Rye. Look out for locally caught seafood, game, and Romney Lamb.
£££ **The Landgate Bistro**, 5 Landgate, T01797-222829, has been the top gourmet destination for some time and definitely needs to be booked.
£££ **The Copper Kettle**, The Mint, T01797-222012, also offers local specialities such as rabbit and pheasant pâté, and Whitstable oysters.
££ **The Flushing Inn**, 4 Market St, T01797-223292, provides some wonderful-looking local produce, including 'the Flushing Inn agglomeration of crustaceans and molluscs'.
££ **Union Inn**, East St, T01797-222334, is a bog-standard alehouse, with a curious penchant for outlandish food– a nicely grilled crocodile steak for example.

£ **The Bell Inn**, The Mint, T01797-222232, is a pleasant pub with a flowery beer garden. A good bet for a cheap feed, with something and chips starting at around £4.

£ **The Mermaid Inn**, Mermaid St, T01797-223065, has a bar/bistro in the pub serving drinks and bar snacks, as well as more substantial fare like Fisherman's Pie.

£ **Mermaid Street Coffee House**, West St/Mermaid St, T01797-224858, has some very naughty cakes for around £2.

£ **Rye Fish Shop**, The Mint. Your best bet for a greasy takeaway. You can also eat-in, but the place has a uniquely English aura of conversational repression amongst cheap cutlery.

£ **Simon the Pieman**, Market St, offers some interesting sweet and savoury snacks. The fudge is delicious.

£ **Ypres Castle Inn**, Gungarden, T01797-227460, is a lovely place for a pint beneath the tower.

Entertainment

Rye *p122*

Understandably, as a quaint old town, there is not much in the way of nightlife in Rye. Local bands do grace the town's pubs from time to time, so keep an eye out in local papers.

Rye Art Gallery, Ockman Lane, off Market St, has occasional exhibitions by local painters, tending toward twee oil colours of local vistas.

Festivals and events

Rye *p122*

Medieval Weekend, each Aug locals dressed as Lords and Ladies, serving wenches, and jongleurs parade through the streets to a 2-day fair at the Town Salts, and there's a medieval street market on the High St. Fans of small-scale civic nostalgia will adore it, others may find it infuriating.

Rye Festival, music, film, drama, literature, visual arts and lectures in a number of venues across the town each Sep.

Rye Bonfire Weekend, Rye's Nov 5th celebrations are not on the same scale as Lewes's, but societies from all over the county parade the streets in mild anti-papal solidarity.

Activities and tours

Rye *p122*

Swimming at Camber Sands is excellent, if usually chilly. Sea fishing, with local fishermen can be arranged through the TIC, T01797-226696. Hire of windsurfing equipment is available at Camber Sands, Winchelsea Beach, and Northpoint Water, T01797-225238.

Transport

Dover *p119*

Boat

P&O Stena Line, T08706-000600, www.posl.com, run about 32 ships a day to Calais from Dover Eastern Docks, (1 hr 15 min). Also from the Eastern Docks, **Seafrance**, T0870-5711711, make the trip 15 times a day, (15 mins longer but marginally cheaper). **Hoverspeed**, T08705-240241, from Hoverport Western Docks, 8 times day to Calais (just under an hr), or Ostend 2 times a day at 1100 and 1845 (2 hr).

Bus

Stagecoach East Kent, T08702-433711, run buses from Dover to the North Downs, east coast, and countryside inland.

Car hire

Practical Car & Van Rental, 17 Elms Vale T01303-279603; **Winchelsea Car Hire**, Unit 3 The Chalk Pit, Winchelsea Works,Winchelsea Rd, T01304-226633; **Sixt Kenning Rent-a-car**, Ferry Approach Filling Station, Maison Dieu Rd, T01304-240340.

Taxis

Central Taxis, 21 Pencester Rd, T01304-204040. **Dover Taxis**, 53 Castle St, T01304-201915. **Star Taxis**, 321 London Rd, T01304-202027.

Train

From Dover Priory the mainline runs east up the coast via **Walmer**, **Deal** and **Sandwich** to **Ramsgate**, west via **Folkestone** to **Ashford** and **London Victoria** and also northwest via **Canterbury**, **Faversham** and **Chatham** to London.

Folkestone *p120*

Boat

Hoverspeed, T08705-240241, run regular services to Boulogne taking just under an hr.

Bus

National Express, T08705-808080, run coaches to Folkestone every 2 hrs between 0900 and 2330 (2 hrs 30 mins).

Train

Folkestone is on the mainline from London Charing Cross via Ashford (1 hr 40 mins). Le Shuttle, T01303-271100, run the hourly car-on-the-train service to **France** from just north of Folkestone, time about 30 mins.

Rye *p122*

Bus

Buses pull up in front of Rye rail station. Rambler Coaches, T01424-752505 and Coastal Coaches, T01825-723024 provide local buses to Hastings, Camber and Winchelsea. Stagecoach, T08702-433711, serves Brighton via Eastbourne and Hastings, and Dover.

Cycle hire

Rye Hire, T01797-223033. £10 per day.

Taxis

Rye Motors, T01797-223176.

Train

Rye station is just off Cinque Ports St, and very close to the town centre. For train times, Connex South Central, T08706-030405.

Directory

Dover *p119*

Internet Cafe En-Route 66, 8 Bench St, T01304-206633. **Medical services** Buckland Hospital, Coombe Valley Rd, T01304-201624. **Police** Dover Police Station, Ladywell, T01304-240055. **Post office** 68 Pencester Rd, T01304-241747.

Rye *p122*

Internet Rye Library, Lion St, T01797-223355. **Medical services** Local doctor with an emergency surgery at Posten Gate, Cinque Ports St, T01797-224924. Hastings Conquest Hospital, The Ridge, Hastings, T01424-755255. **Post office** Cinque Ports St. **Police** Rye has no police station, but you can call Sussex Police (non-emergency), T08456-070999.

North Downs and The Weald

→*Colour map 2*

The North Downs stretch in an almost unbroken line all the way from Farnham in Surrey to the white cliffs of Dover. Their geology may be similar to the South Downs, but they hardly compare very favourably, lacking their sea air and being too close to all the main roads to France for comfort. That said, these rolling hills conceal a few attractions well worth seeking out and the North Downs Way is a surprisingly bracing long-distance ridgeway. Near Maidstone, lake-bound Leeds Castle draws the crowds in the summer while further east, tucked into the folds of the hills, small villages like Chilham are highly picturesque.

Southwest of the North Downs, and north of the South Downs, the Weald is a rich bowl of clay soil, unique to England and once entirely wooded. Nowadays it's affluent commuter country. The Restoration spa town of Royal Tunbridge Wells at its heart still bears traces of its 17th-century heyday, in the colonnaded Pantiles and church of King Charles the Martyr. Within easy reach are some of the most memorable old houses in southern Britain: Knole Park in Sevenoaks, Penshurst Place the ancestral home of Sir Philip Sydney and Hever Castle, millionaire newspaper proprietor William Waldorf Astor's medieval castle condo. Near Westerham, Winston Churchill's relatively modest home at Chartwell is one of the most-visited and most evocative of the National Trust's properties. To the south, Ashdown Forest is all that remains of the great Wealden wood. ▸▸ *For Sleeping, Eating and other listings, see pages 129-130*

Ins and outs

Getting there Unfortunately, accessing the North Downs by road is all too easy. The A2/M2 roars along their northern side to Canterbury and Dover, while the M20 slices through them just above Eynsford, squeezes past Maidstone and hurtles along their southern slopes all the way via Ashford to Folkestone. Even so, barring the stretch around Rochester and Maidstone, the distance between these 2 big roads is just great enough to allow pockets of the Downs to remain fairly remote and secluded. A network of local buses operates out of Maidstone, Sittingbourne, Faversham, Canterbury and Ashford, but the Downs themselves are not very well served. Two particularly useful routes are the No 667 run by Poynters Coaches T01223-812002 between Canterbury and Charing via Chartham, Old Wives Lees, Chilham and Challock 4 times a day; and for Leeds Castle and the North Downs Way, the No 10 Stagecoach East Kent, T08702-433711, service is hourly between Maidstone and Folkestone via Bearsted, Harrietsham, Lenham, Charing and Ashford. The Channel tunnel rail link roughly follows the line of the M20 to the south. This being commuter country, there are plenty of small stations served by stopping **trains** on the main Charing Cross to Folkestone line, as well as Victoria to Ashford and Folkestone. Stations with bus connections to surrounding attractions include Hollingbourne, Harrietsham, Lenham, Charing.

Information **Maidstone TIC** ⓘ *The Gatehouse, Palace Gardens, Mill St, T01622-602169.*

Around Maidstone

Maidstone, the county town of Kent, is really best avoided. Apart from a traffic-choked old riverbank on the Medway and a moderately diverting local museum, the town is an eyesore. Best push on past on the M20 to junction 8 to find **Leeds Castle** ⓘ *T01622-765400, Mar-Oct daily 1000-1700, Nov-Feb 1000-1500, £11, concessions £9.50, children £7.50, family £32.*. Proudly billing itself as the 'loveliest castle in the world', it is indeed as pretty as a picture, sitting on a pair of small islands in a large lake surrounded by wooded hills and parkland. It's also quite expensive, an undeniably successful commercial enterprise, with regular special events, ballooning, a maze, underground grotto, an aviary and series of gardens. The interior was restored in the early 20th century and features rooms from a variety of different periods. The oldest part of the castle is the Gloriette, rising straight out of the water, containing the former owner's collection of Impressionist paintings. More interesting perhaps is the unusual collection of antique dog collars in the Gatehouse, although the highlight of a visit here is likely to remain the memorable views of the lakeside. Take a picnic, but leave the dog at home.

A mile west of Leeds Castle, a much less well-known medieval treasure albeit on a much smaller scale is **Stoneacre** ⓘ *(NT), Stoneacre, Otham, Near Maidstone, T01622-862871, Apr-Oct Wed, Sat 1400-1800 (last entry 1700), £2.60, concessions £1.30*, a hall-house restored in the 1920s by the keen antiquarian, Morrisite and Fabian, Aymer Vallance. Tucked away in its own wooded valley, the great oak front door gives on to the little beamed hall, beautifully restored to its former glory. A lovely little garden includes a rare gingko tree, a herb garden, and tiny back courtyard with a path leading to a summerhouse giving views over the surrounding orchards. A few miles northeast, on the way to Canterbury, **Chilham** is a picture-postcard hilltop village with its very own Jacobean castle (closed to the public), antique-stuffed main square and attractive old church.

Royal Tunbridge Wells and around

Shakespeare would never have heard of Tunbridge Wells, because in his day it hadn't been invented. It was only in 1606, when Dudley Lord North recovered from his 'consumptive disorder' after drinking water from a hole in the ground on the Earl of Abergavenny's estate that fashionable society began to flock down from London. As well as sampling the iron-rich (chalybeate) spring, they brought with them the prosperity that is still much in evidence today. By the time Charles II visited after the Restoration, giving the place its Royal title, it had become what Brighton was to be to the Regency court 150 years later, somewhere to see and be seen. Surprisingly enough, judging from some of the local names like Mount Ephraim and Mount Sion, the town liked to project a pious puritanical image, possibly because the waters were notoriously foul. They still are, and can be sampled by the brave in their original pump room in the Pantiles. Today, Tunbridge Wells is a typical Home Counties commuter town: prosperous, polite and smug in equal measure.

Ins and outs

Getting there Tunbridge Wells is just off the A21, about an hr from central London and is on the mainline from London Charing Cross and Waterloo East as well as London Victoria, 2 trains an hr (1hr).

Getting around Tunbridge Wells is small and pleasant enough to explore on foot, although some of its steeper hills can be surprisingly exhausting. The countryside around is best reached on buses run by Arriva Kent and Sussex, T01634-281100. There's also the Tunbridge Wells Heritage Hopper, T08457-696996, May 5-Sep 16 Sat, Sun and bank holidays. Departs Tunbridge Wells War Memorial at 1005, 1305, 1505 via Bayham Abbey, Scotney Castle, Bewl Water, Bedgebury Pinetum, Goudhurst, and Finchcocks round trips back at 1134, 1434, 1634. Also Scotney Castle to Tunbridge Wells at 1750 back at 1854. £2.50, £1.50 concessions.

Information Tourist Information Centre ① *Old Fish Market, The Pantiles, T01892-515675, www.heartofkent.org.uk.*

Sights

The **Pantiles** are the place to get some idea of how the town may have looked in its heyday. A dinky 18th-century colonnade stretches away from the Chalybeate Spring (pronounced Kalibiyet) and Bath house (*open Easter- Sep*) at one end, with its modern and much less appealing equivalent at the other. Next to the pump house is the splendid Restoration church of **King Charles the Martyr**. A small alleyway leads up from here into the High Street, lined with boutiques and fashion labels, past the station and up hill to the Town Hall. **A Day at the Wells** ① *T01892-546545, Apr-Oct daily 1000-1700, Nov-Mar 1000-1600, £5.50, concessions and children £4.50, family £17.50.* is the inevitable see-hear-and-smell show, run by the same people as the Canterbury Tales, taking visitors through a day in the life of the 18th-century town in about half an hour. It's housed in the old Corn Exchange.

At the top of the hill, the **Tunbridge Wells Museum and Art Gallery** ① *T01892-554171, www.tunbridgewells.gov.uk/museum, Mon-Sat 0930-1700, free*, in the Town Hall, is an impressive example of its kind, not only for its 'Tunbridge ware', a world-beating collection of the local talent for marquetry, but also for its antique toys, dolls and natural history displays, as well as a thorough display on the history of the town and its various claims to fame.

Just west of town, the **High Rocks** ⓘ *T01892-515532, take the A264 towards East Grinstead, just over a mile out of Tunbridge Wells is a signpost for the rocks, £2 (ticket obtainable from High Rocks Hotel by the car park)*, are very strange looking sandstone rock outcrops which are worth a clamber around. This was once a Neolithic settlement and is now a Site of Special Scientific Interest, so be careful where you trample.

Sevenoaks

Sevenoaks is a reasonably attractive dormitory town on the mainline to London but the only reason to visit is the extraordinary Elizabethan pile of **Knole House** ⓘ *(NT), T01732-450608, Apr-Oct Wed-Sat 1200-1600, Sun, bank holidays 1100-1700, gardens May-Sep first Wed of the month, £5.50, children £2.75*, a long walk uphill from the station. This is where the writer, gardener, and lover of Virginia Woolf, Vita Sackville-West grew up, at the largest private house in the country, with a room for each day of the year, and an impressive art collection. The gardens and deer park surrounding the house are as enjoyable as the house itself.

A mile to the east, and accessible across the park from Knole House, **Ightham Mote** ⓘ *(NT) T01732-811145, Apr-Oct Mon, Wed-Fri, Sun 1100-1730, £6, concessions £3*, is one of the most endearing (and popular) moated manor houses in the country. Also National Trust, its little rooms can become impossibly busy, but it's worth going with the flow to see some of the most sensitive restoration work ever undertaken. At dusk, when the coach parties have departed, the house's position in a quiet valley is quite magical.

Penshurst

Seven miles west of Tunbridge Wells, off the A26 on the B2176, Penshurst is a charming village at the confluence of the rivers Eden and Medway. Its main claim to fame is **Penshurst Place** and **Gardens** ⓘ *T01892-870307, www.penshurstplace.com Apr-Oct daily 1200-1730, gardens 1030-1800; Mar weekends only, £6.50, children £4.50, concessions £6, family £18.*, seat of the Sidney family since 1522. A more modest and much more charming version of Knole, the Barons Hall at the heart of the house was built in 1341, kept very much as it would have looked in the Middle Ages. Outside, the Elizabethan gardens and 11-acre walled garden are delightful, and there's also the Woodland Trail, adventure playground and walks in the surrounding parkland.

Hever Castle

ⓘ *T01732-865224, www.hevercastle.co.uk Apr-Oct daily 1100-1800 (last admission 1700), Mar-Nov 1100-1600, £8.40, £7.10 concessions, under-14s £4.60, family £21.40, gardens only £6.70, £5.70, £4.40, £17.80.* A few miles to the west, the moated little castle at Hever (since 1270) was where Anne 'of a Thousand Days' Boleyn was brought up before catching the eye of King Henry VIII and eventually losing her head on 19th May 1536. Inside the place is more country house than castle, with 16th- and 17th-century portraits and a collection of model houses showing how castles were turned into these elegant homes between 1086 and 1901. Outside is better, with excellent topiary, yew maze and water maze for the kids (open Apr-Oct only) as well as beautiful Italian gardens with ancient Roman sculpture laid out by Waldorf Astor, the millionaire newspaper proprietor, in the early 1900s. There's also a peaceful lake with piazza and waterfowl.

Chartwell

ⓘ *(NT), T01732-868381. Information: 01732 866368, Apr-Jun, Sep, Oct Wed-Sun (Jul, Aug also Tue) 1100-1700 (last admission 1615), £6.50, concessions £3.25.* Near the idyllic little hilltop village of **Ide Hill**, and 4 miles north off the B269, Chartwell is one of the National Trust's most popular houses, formerly the home of Winston Churchill. Not a particularly attractive house in itself, its position overlooking the Weald and preservation as the great man left it make it somewhere really special. Inside, apart from his study, dining room and bedroom, the gift room includes valuable donations from grateful well-wishers as well such as his badge of membership for the Hastings Winkle Club. The grounds are just as evocative, the rose garden's wall inscribed, "The greater part of this wall was built between the years 1925 and 1932 by Winston with his bare hands" and including Marycot, the little summerhouse he built for his youngest daughter, complete with carpet sweeper and broom.

Sleeping

Around Maidstone *p126*

A **Eastwell Manor**, Eastwell Park, Boughton Lees, T01233-219955/213000. A very deluxe Tudor country house hotel and health spa in 3000 acres of its own land. Also have self-contained mews cottages ideal for families.
B-C **Harrow Hill Hotel**, Warren St, near Lenham, T01622-858727. A reasonable no-frills place on the Pilgrim's Way, on the top of the downs near the A20.
D-E **Barnfield**, Charing, near Ashford, T01233-712421. A smart non-smoking B&B that represents good value for money despite being relatively expensive.
D-E **Woolpack Inn**, High St, Chilham, T01227-730351, F731053. The local Shepherd Neame establishment, with comfortable reasonably priced rooms above a busy pub with good food.

Royal Tunbridge Wells and around *p127*

B **The Old Parsonage**, Church La, Frant, T01892-750773. A superior B&B.
C **Hotel du Vin & Bistro**, Crescent Rd, T01892-526455. A Georgian townhouse, this is probably the most stylish place to stay, with a well-respected restaurant (the Bistro bit means that a meal here can be affordable).
C **Jordan's**, Sheet Hill, Plaxtol, T01732-810379. A tile-hung farmhouse and non-smoking B&B deep in the countryside.
C **Spa Hotel** Mount Ephraim, T01892-520331, F510575. Overlooking the common with a stately dining room. From another era, and altogether very grand.
D **Ephraim Lodge**, The Common, T01892-523053, a superior guesthouse in a quiet position near the common.
D **Hoath House**, Chiddingston Hoath, Near Edenbridge, T01342-850362. The rambling Tudor and Edwardian home of one of the oldest families in the area, the Streatfeilds.
D-E **Blundeston**, Eden Rd, T01892-540255, a very central upmarket B&B.
D-E **The Crown Inn**, Groombridge, T01892-864742, has rooms above a lovely old pub doing decent food on the village green.
D-E **Egypt Farm**, Hamptons, Near Tonbridge, T01732-810584. The large garden, swimming pool and tennis court complement an antique-filled oast houses and barn conversion.
D-E **Leicester Arms**, Penshurst, T01892-870551. Seven rooms above an attractive 17th-century inn, including a couple with 4-posters, done up in a chintzy style but nonetheless good value.

Eating

Around Maidstone *p126*

££ **The Plough Inn**, at Eynsford, has seats outside by the river and a more ambitious menu than many.
££ **The Rose and Crown**, Perry Wood, Selling, Near Faversham, T01227-752214, has cosy well-kept gardens including a 'bat and trap' pitch on the top of Crown Hill with woodland walks, great views all around from the surrounding hills. Real ales, log fires and reasonable food (not Sun, Mon).
££ **Pepperbox Inn**, Fairbourne Heath, near Ulcombe, T01622- 842558, is perched up on Windmill Hill, also doing some adventurous food which can be enjoyed at tables outside with good views over the Downs.

Royal Tunbridge Wells and around *p127*

£££ **The Hare**, Langton Rd, Langton Green, T01892-862419. A short hop out of town is this attractive pub with an original menu that won't disappoint foodies served in the restaurant at the back.
£££ **Thackeray's**, 85 London Rd, T01892-511921, recently revamped and serving up accomplished modern British and French food in fairly swish surroundings for a price (around £50 a head).
££ **Honours Mill**, 87 High St, Edenbridge, T01732-866757. An expensive but atmospheric small Anglo-French restaurant

in the pretty little town of Edenbridge.

££ **Spotted Dog**, Smarts Hill, Penshurst, T01892-870253, is a hilltop pub doing very good food with a garden outside giving views over the surrounding countryside.

££ **Zapata Mexican Restaurant**, 1-3 Union Sq, T01892-513950, is a lively place in the modern part of the Pantiles for some fiery food from south of the border.

Activities and tours

The **Darent Valley Path** goes past Lullingstone between Dartford and Otford. The North Downs Way is the long-distance footpath between Farnham and Folkestone, including a branch off to the north to Canterbury. In the west near Sevenoaks and Maidstone it runs along the course of the old Pilgrim's Way. The **Stour Valley Walk** runs from Sandwich via Canterbury and Ashford to Lenham.

Transport

Royal Tunbridge Wells and around *p127*

Chartwell Explorer, weekends and bank holidays 26 May-2 Sep, Wed-Sun and bank holidays Jul, Aug from Sevenoaks station. T08457-696996 £3.50. **Bewl Bike Hire**, T01323-870310.

Brighton and Hove →*Colour map 2,*

From the good-time girls and gangsters of Graham Greene's Brighton Rock via the mods and rockers of the cult film Quadrophenia to its current status as clubbing capital of the country, Brighton has always had that air of dangerous cool. This is Bohemia British style. Once the Prince Regent's coastal retreat, Brighton is now home to avant-garde artists and musicians, an exuberant gay and lesbian community, thousands of students and a few blue-rinse bungalow-dwellers who must be wondering where it all went wrong. The town has an atmosphere somewhere between hippy trail and Mediterranean sleaze-pit. In summer the streets around North Laine and the Prince's bizarre oriental Pavilion are a throng of trendy stalls and cafés, the pebbly beach awash with vocal youngsters and the clubs bursting at the seams seven nights a week. Throw in an arts festival second only to Edinburgh and the best eating in England outside of London and you have a city which takes culture seriously. Surely all this enjoyment can't last forever. One day Brighton is going to have to grow up and get a job, indeed many fear this may already have happened. House prices have rocketed, and grotty old dives have become post-modern enormodromes with overpriced cocktails. Bohemia, it seems, has been bought. This said, Brighton remains a highlight of any trip to the south coast. If you can't find fun here, you're unlikely to do so almost anywhere. ▸▸ *For Sleeping, Eating and other listings, see pages 134-139*

Ins and outs

Getting there Brighton is notoriously difficult and expensive to park in, so if you must come by car use the Park and Ride Scheme at the Withdean Stadium (clearly signposted from all main roads). From London take the A23, once you've got as far as the M25, it's about a 1 hr drive to Brighton. The A27 is the south coast trunk route and connects Brighton to Chichester, Portsmouth and Southampton to the west, and Lewes, Hastings, and Dover to the East. Getting to Brighton by **bus** is trouble-free, if slow, and considerably cheaper than the train. Brighton is excellently served by **rail**. There are 2 fast trains each hr from London Victoria (50 mins), and 2 from London King's Cross, London Blackfriars and London Bridge (1 hr). There are numerous trains to Gatwick Airport (25 mins), and Luton Airport (1 hr 45). A coastal line leads west to Chichester (40 mins), Portsmouth (1 hr 20), Southampton (1 hr 30) and Winchester (2 hrs). To the east, you can reach Lewes (15 mins) and Hastings (1 hr). There are also less frequent through trains from Edinburgh via Manchester, Birmingham and Oxford, and from Cardiff via Bristol and Bath. ▸▸ *See Transport, page 130, for more details.*

Prinney

A statue of the man responsible for Brighton's transformation into the most happening and fashionable place on the south coast stands largely ignored outside the North Gate of the Royal Pavilion. But then even many of those around at the time would be pushed to recognize that man in the stately statue of George IV, because it was as young Prinney, the flamboyant Prince of Wales, that the son of George III had captured their imaginations and drawn high society down from London. Prinney was introduced to Brighton by his wicked uncle the Duke of Cumberland in the 1780s, visiting several times to go to the races and take the sea cure for his swollen glands. Soon he was cavorting at extravagant parties here on a regular basis and had secretly married Maria Fitzherbert, an ardent Catholic, much to the concern of the establishment. He put her up in a house in Marlborough Row: North Gate House, which stood at the end of the Row, can still be seen. Ten years later, saddled with massive debts, he was forced by his father to part with Maria and marry the Protestant Princess Caroline of Brunswick, mother of the Princess Charlotte whose room can be seen in the pavilion. A few years on, much to the locals' delight, Prinney got back together with Maria, who settled in Steine House (now the YMCA), and the party went on. He became Prince Regent in 1811, thanks to his father's illness, and built the Royal Pavilion that stands today as an appropriate monument and backdrop to their romance. On his coronation as George IV in 1821, the slighted Princess Caroline caused a famously ugly scene by forcing her way into the celebrations. The King remained loyal to Maria though. A happy pensioner, she died peacefully in Brighton in 1841, the year the railway opened spelling the end of the town's royal heyday, the young Queen Victoria soon finding the place far too crowded and popular for her liking.

Getting around Brighton is a relatively small city, much of which can be reached by foot. If your feet are swollen, however, there's an extensive network of local buses which ply the city's streets (1 day pass, £2.80), many continue to nearby places of interest mentioned in this chapter: Lewes (Nos 28, 28X, 729 from Churchill square or Old Steine, 30 mins); Rottingdean (No 22A, 30 mins from Churchill Sq); Devil's Dyke (No 77 from Brighton Pier, 30 mins) and Stanmer Park (No 25 from Churchill Sq, 25 mins), many of these buses continue from Churchill Sq into Hove. For travel at night there are night buses to most parts of town, departing from North St, until about 0300; miss these and it's a walk or queues by the taxi ranks that give Russian soup kitchens a bad name.

Information The main **TICs** are at ⓘ *10 Bartholomew Sq and Hove Town Hall, T09067-112255, Jun-Aug 0900-1700 Mon-Fri, 1000-1700 Sat, and 1000-1600 Sun, Sep-May 0900-1700 Mon-Sat.*

Sights

Around The Lanes and the Seafront

Only Brighton could boast, as its most important piece of architecture, an Indo-Chinese royal palace inspired by an obsessive and mildly decadent half-German prince. Fresh from a thoroughly sensitive £10 million renovation programme, at the **Royal Pavilion**

ⓘ Church St, T01273-290900, Jun- Sep 1000-1800 daily, Oct-May 1000-1700 daily, £5.80, child £3.40, concesssions £4, family £15. You can now enjoy John Nash's 1815-23 masterpiece, with its dragon-shaped chandeliers and lotus-shaped lanterns, in its full glory. Nearby, is the splendid **Brighton Museum and Art Gallery** ⓘ *Church St, T01273-290900, Tue 1000-1900, Wed-Sat 1000-1700, Sun 1400-1700, closed Mon, free*, which has just undergone renovation. Two new galleries, entitled the 'Body' and 'Performance' spaces promise 'a celebration of modern humanity'. In many other cities this might involve a set of exhibits by the local Save the Whale group, but is the kind of thing Brighton normally manages to pull off, dignity intact. There are also two local history galleries– one depicting life and work in Brighton – and one devoted to the seaside resort, double-entendre ridden postcards et al.

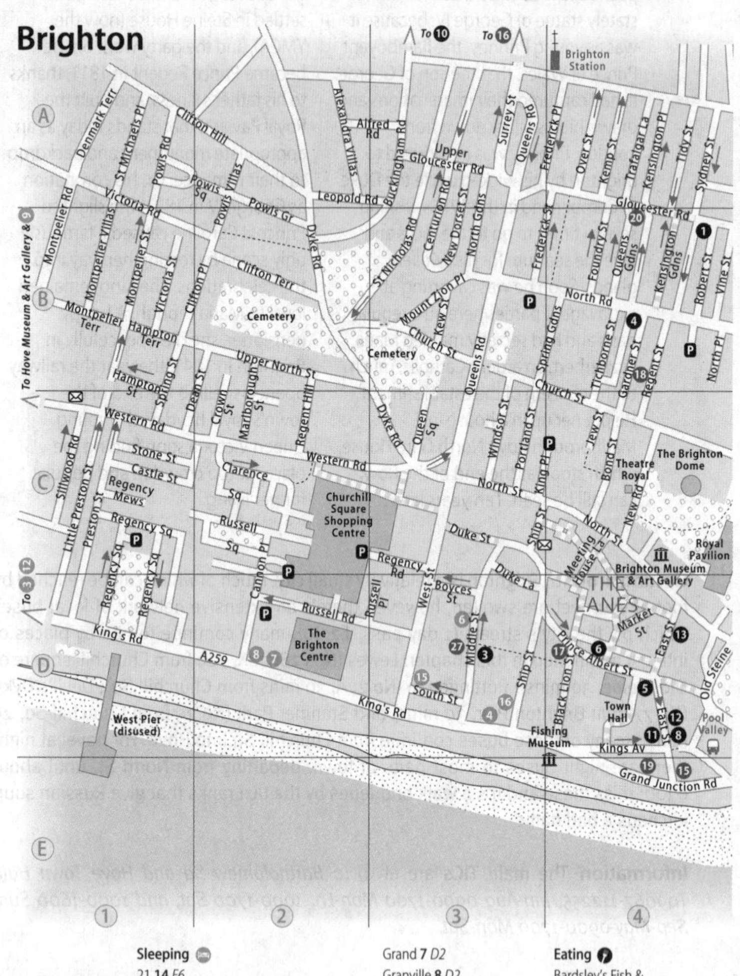

Sleeping
21 **14** *E6*
Amalfi **1** *D6*
Aquarium **2** *D5*
Baggies Backpackers **3** *D1*
Brighton Backpackers **4** *D3*
Brighton YHA **5** *A5*
Du Vin **16** *D3*
Friese Green Backpacker's Rest **6** *D3*
Grand **7** *D2*
Granville **8** *D2*
Lichfield House **9** *B1*
Nineteen **10** *D5*
Oriental **12** *D1*
Penny Lanes **13** *D6*
Walkabout Backpackers **15** *D3*

Eating
Bardsley's Fish & Chip Shop **1** *B4*
Blanch House Bar **2** *E6*
Coach House **3** *D3*
Dorset **4** *B4*
English's Oyster Bar **5** *D4*
Food for Friends **6** *D4*
George **7** *A5*

N
0 metres 100
0 yards 100

The area between West Street and the Steine was, until the 18th century, a small fishing village named Brighthelmstone. These days **The Lanes** are a maze of passageways containing antique and jewellery emporia of varying quality, and a host of cafés, restaurants and pubs. Few original features remain, but **English's Oyster Bar** occupies a former fisherman's cottage.

Brighton's **beach** is not exactly Copacabana, but a pebbly spot for a cheap ice cream, a pint in a plastic glass or, weather permitting, even a swim in the cold, green (and surprisingly clean) English water. In summer, come nightfall, the beach is awash with the local youth, drinking beer, lighting barbecues, patting bongos, smoking joints, fondling one another, falling in the sea, and generally making the place their own. There are also events like open-air cinema, fireworks, and live music. Perhaps the place's most captivating sight is the flocks of swallows that zig-zag around the ruined West Pier at dusk.

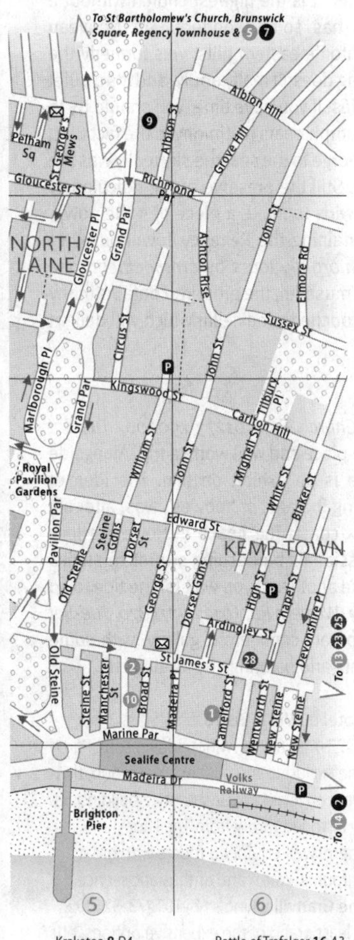

Krakatoa **8** *D4*
Rock Street Café **9** *A5*
Seven Dials **10** *A3*
Strand **11** *D4*
Terre à Terre **12** *D4*
Tootsie's Chargrill **13** *D4*

Pubs & bars
Alicats **15** *E4*
Battle of Trafalgar **16** *A3*
Cricketer's **17** *D4*
Curve at Komedia **18** *B4*
Dr Brighton's **19** *E4*
Heart & Hand **20** *B4*
Pressure Point **23** *D6*
Sidewinder **25** *D6*
Sumo **27** *D3*
Tin Drum **28** *D6*

The tiny electric **Volks Railway** ⓘ *283 Madeira Dr, T01273-292718, Easter-Sept daily 1145-1700, £1.50, family £5.20*, clicks its way along the eastern seafront. It's not exactly the bullet train but, pushing 120 years of age, it is the world's oldest electric railway, and that you can't knock. Meanwhile, sharks, stingrays and all manner of piscine delights are on display at the **Sealife Centre** ⓘ *Marine Pde, T01273-604234, 1000-1700 daily, £7.95, child £4.95, family £24.95*, one of the country's finest aquariums.

Much to the indignation of the locals, the 'Palace Pier' was renamed **Brighton Pier** to celebrate Brighton's recent entry in the great big A-Z in the sky under the section marked 'cities.' Corporate re-branding aside, it's still the unselfconsciously kitsch amalgam of fairground rides, money-swallowing machines and calorific cuisine that it always was. You can buy Brighton rock (the local sickly, minty sweet with the name running through it) by the yard here, and only the staunchest cultural snob wouldn't. After all, even Fatboy Slim has been known to frequent the Hog Roast here. *Madeira Dr, T01273-609361. Open dawn-dusk, daily.*

West of the Palace Pier is one of the city's most understated gems, the **Fishing Museum** ⓘ *201 King's Rd Arches, T01273-723064, 1000-1700 daily*. Exhibits and film chart the history of Brighton's seafood trade in more prolific times. Further West on King's Road you reach the **West Pier**, the country's only grade I-listed pier, once a magnificent piece of architecture which featured some of the most demure restaurants and theatres in the realm. Having been in a state of woeful disrepair for some time, it finally fell prey to winter storms in 2002, much of it claimed by the sea. Remarkably the regeneration campaigns continue, watch this space.

North Laine, Kemp Town and Brunswick Square

North Laine, a raggle taggle of trendy and secondhand shops, delis, cafés and pubs between Trafalgar Street and Church Street, is the womb from which Brighton's current DJ-chic youth emerged. The denizens here are ridiculously fashion conscious, in a scruffy kind of way, and it's a great place to people-watch and pick up a few souvenirs. **St Bartholomew's Church** ⓘ *Ann St, T01273-620491*, from the exterior looks like an outsize railway shed. For trivia fans, it is the highest church without a tower in the country, is grade I listed, and has some wonderful Art Nouveau furnishings. **Kemp Town,** which occupies Brighton's eastern hills, was formerly the town's gay centre. These days such pigeon-holing doesn't really apply, and it's a quiet area full of B&Bs and some quiet shops and cafés. If you have time, you should try to get out to **Lewes Crescent**. This vast Regency triumph bears testimony to the fact that, as London's hypochondriacs followed Prince George to the sea, the sky really was the limit when it came to real estate development. Still the preserve of the ridiculously rich, mere mortals are left dreaming of lottery wins to make a piece of it their own. **Brunswick Square** is an elegant structure containing the Regency Townhouse, **13 Brunswick Square** ⓘ *T01273-206306, www.rth.org.uk, tours by arrangement, one open day per month, both £3*. Eventually to be a museum, the property contains many original features, the basement housing an untouched wine cellar which will delight any nostalgic dipsomaniacs.

Hove

The **Hove Museum and Art Gallery** ⓘ *New Church Rd, T01273-290200, Tue-Sat 1000-1700, Sun 1400-1700*, is a fascinating little place and well worth a trip. Alongside local artefacts dating to the Stone Age, there is an exhibit on film. The idea of sequencing still photographic images into moving footage, or 'movies', was, after all, conceived in this genteel haven on the Sussex coast. The **beach** in Hove is a less cluttered, litter-strewn affair; think young professionals barbecuing swordfish steaks rather than lusty youths clinging drunkenly to one another. If you wait for the tide to go out you'll even see some sand. The **White Gallery** *Western Rd, T01273-774870, Tue-Sat 1000-1800, Sun 1100-1600, free.*, is a contemporary commercial gallery, with some appealing jewellery and ceramics alongside prints and paintings by local artists.

Sleeping

There are myriad B&Bs (where you ought to be able to get a bed for around £20-£30 a night), in Kemp Town, and out towards Hove. They are all much the same, so it's probably best to ask the accommodation service at the TIC to make enquiries for you.

Around The Lanes and the Seafront *p131, map p132*

L-A **The Grand**, King's Rd, T01273-321188. Saunas, jacuzzis, swimming pools, deferent room-service, good enough for conferencing PMs and IRA bombers. Don't argue about the price, just cough up, it's the best in town.

A **Hotel du Vin & Bistro**, Ship St, T01273-718588, www.hotelduvin.com. Part of the exclusive and chi-chi hotel group, this clever conversion of Gothic-style buildings is only a stone's throw from The Lanes. Modern, well-equipped rooms with great bathrooms. Warm and enthusiatic service.

C **The Granville**, King's Rd, T01273-326302. The least grand of the expensive options, but you can't knock the sea view and you're unlikely to stumble upon a fringe meeting of the Young Conservatives at their annual party conferences.

D **Penny Lanes**, 11 Charlotte St, T01273 603197. Good-sized rooms with bathrooms in a quiet street near the beach, breakfast included.

D 21 Hotel, 21 Charlotte St, T01273-686450. Clean and moderately trendy B&B.
E The Amalfi Hotel, 44 Marine Pde, T01273-607956. Reasonably priced and on the seafront, even if a little grotty out front.
E Aquarium Hotel, 13 Madeira Pl, T01273-605761. Clean, friendly, and close to the Pier.
E Lichfield House, 30 Waterloo St, Hove, T01273-777740. Excellent value hostel-cum-hotel.
F Brighton Backpackers, 75-6 Middle St, T01273-777717, stay@brightonbackpackers.com £11/12 dorms. One of the first independent globe-trottery places in town, and consequently full of 'creative' wall-paintings by former residents, and anecdotes about smoking too much in Malawi.
F Brighton YHA, Patcham Pl, London Rd, T01273-556196. £10 dorms. All the usual hostel facilities, but a little out of the way (20-30 mins on the bus to the city centre).
F Friese Green Backpacker's Rest, 20 Middle St, T01273-747551. £10 dorms. A small, friendly hostel for people whose Bible is *The Beach*.
F Walkabout Backpackers, 79-81 West St, T01273-770232. £12 dorms. Right next to the *Walkabout Bar*, scooner-quaffing antipodeans aplenty.

North Laine, Kemp Town and Brunswick Square *p134, map p132*

A Nineteen, 19 Broad St, T01273-675529, F675531. Hip Kemp Town small hotel, one of the most stylish places in the city.

Hove *p134*

D Oriental Hotel, 9 Oriental Pl, T01273-205050. A lovely small hotel which is getting something of a reputation among weekending Londoners of the chattery, world cuisine-loving Islingtonian variety. Book early, or not at all if you want to avoid overhearing conversations about how well Josh's play is going.
F Baggies Backpackers, 33 Oriental Pl, T01273-733740. £11 dorms. Better situated than the other budget options, *Baggies* is in a quiet area of Hove and near the burgers, kebabs, and noodle bars of Preston St.

Eating

Around The Lanes and the Seafront *p131, map p132*

£££ Blanch House Bar, 17 Atlingworth St, T01273-603505. Technically a hotel, you can enjoy a classic French meal, and a cocktail in the retro bar, if you book. Uber-cool and rather expensive, the place is run by a former Groucho club bar manager, so you get the picture.
£££ English's Oyster Bar, 29-31 East St, T01273 327980. A Brighton institution: Crustaceans, molluscs, flatfish – if it swims, it's here – usually on large plates with chips garnished with salad. A tad pricey, the place is redeemed by a pleasant outside dining area and its status in local legend.
££ The Coach House, Middle St, T01273-719000. Mediterranean style cantina, with excellent value moules (£6/£8) and a small secluded terrace.
££ Krakatoa, 7 Pool Valley, T01273-719009. You sit on the floor Indonesian-style here, but the food is best described as oriental fusion (carnivores beware, seafood and vegetarian only). Book early as the place is attracting a national reputation.
££ The Strand, 6 Little East St, T01273-747096. Tiny, but popular restaurant offering adventurous modern-European recipes. Mains around £13. Bookings essential.
££ Terre à Terre, 7 East St, T01273-729051. Regarded by many as Brighton's finest restaurant, the vegetarian and organic menu here is mind-bogglingly innovative. Mains start at around £10, and you'd be hard put to find a finer diner in its field.
££ Tootsies Chargrill Restaurant, 16-18 Meeting House La, T01273-726777. Not for dieters or hardcore veggies, Tootsies serves up some of the best simple meat dishes in town to those of a hunter-gathering dietary disposition. Efficient service and a pleasant heated terrace.
£ Food for Friends, Prince Albert St, T01273-202310. An early-starter on the vegetarian scene, this self-service restaurant has been serving consistently excellent lunches, dinners and cakes over the years.

North Laine, Kemp Town and Brunswick Square *p134, map p132*

££ The Dorset, 28 North Rd, T01273-605423. Half pub, half quality eaterie, this joint is bustling with beautiful but jovial punters most hours of the day. A fine example of Brighton's most prominent citizens – professional loafers – in their cig-smoking, pose-striking element.

£ **The George**, 5 Trafalgar St, T01273-681055. When vegetarians were regarded as laughable eccentrics with dogs on strings, they could pop in here for a quality quorn burger in a dingy old boozer. These days the punters and the décor are equally modern and streamlined, and the food is some of the best (and best value) vegetarian in town. They even do vegetarian beer.

££ **Seven Dials**, 1-3 Buckingham Pl, T01273-885555. New kid on the block and wowing the locals and visiting Londoners alike, this place has a fresh approach to British fusion cuisine without being too pretentious or stuffy despite to media darlings who seem to be its main source of income.

£ **Bardsley's Fish and Chip Shop**, 106 Gloucester Rd, T01273- 681601. The best examples of the national dish are to be found away from the soggy batter and staggering Scousers of the seafront, in this little shop at the end of Kensington Gardens.

£ **The Rock St Café**, Rock St. Superior local caff, with mouth-watering cakes. Probably one of the most tempting places in town to while away a rainy day.

Hove *p134*

££ **The Black Chapati**, 12 Circus Pde, New England Rd, T01273-699011. Forget your Chicken Madras and Nan with the lads at chucking out time, this Indian restaurant is about as ambitiously authentic as you get in the UK. It's been there for donkey's years, and featured in virtually every discerning critic's national highlights along the way. Well worth the trip off the beaten track.

££ **Harry's English Restaurant**, 41 Church Rd, Hove, T01273-727410. A welcome reminder that the English can cook as long as they keep away from saturated fats and microwave dinners. Bangers and mash have never tasted this good. Mains start around £8.

££ **Oki-Nami**, 208 Church Rd, Hove, T01273-773777. Brilliant Sushi and the like in a very Japanese minimalist space. Mixed meal £8.50.

££ **Sole Mio**, 64 Western Rd, Hove, T01273-729898. Despite a glut of pizza/pasta joints in the city centre, it's well worth the trip out to Hove for the genuine article in a gorgeous, high-vaulted building. Pasta dishes from £6.

Pubs, bars and clubs

Brighton's club scene is regarded as one of the best in England outside London. Aside from the big hitters and perennial favourites listed below, there is an ever-changing local scene: good places go bad and vice versa, and there are invariably some very good nights in some very bad clubs. The best way to keep up to date is to check local listings (*The Insight* and *City News* are good bets, available free from the tourist office), or ask around in city centre pubs and bars.

Around The Lanes and the Seafront *p131, map p132*

Alicats, Brills Lane 80 East St, T01273-220902. After negotiating the bins and other less salubrious street smells, this underground bar is a great place to sup on a cheap brew and take in an arty film on the big screen in the corner.

The Beach, 171-181 Kings Rd Arches, T01273-722272. Despite its big, brash mainstream appearance, *The Beach* still packs in an alternative crowd most nights of the week, with a mixture of drum and bass and hard house. Curiously for a club where music is taken seriously, the bar is slap bang in the middle of things.

Concorde 2, Madeira Dr, T01273-207241. Never mind its association with the stars (DJ Fatboy Slim is on the sacred decks twice each month), the club is a laid-back, unpretentious venue (trainers positively encouraged), in which virtually everybody is in a chemically good mood.

The Cricketer's, Black Lion St, T01273-329472. This pub, with its wonderfully camp pink frilly décor, is a reminder of Brighton's more traditional seaside resort roots. Refreshingly, there's not a spiky hair cut or a pair of skate pants to be seen, and the gaff is heaving with hearty locals at weekends.

Dr Brighton's, 16 King's Rd, T01273-328765. One of the city's longest established gay drinking spots. The place is popular with gay men and women, and has a cheerful pre-club buzz about it most nights of the week.

Honeyclub II, 214 Kings Rd Arches, T07000-446639. Host to some seriously big-time DJs over the past few years, the *Honeyclub* is back, hopefully bigger and better.
Jazz Place, 10 Ship St, T01273-328439. Think along the lines of stylishly clad young things strutting and smoking Gauloise, rather than dubiously bearded middle-aged gentlemen tapping their feet and smoking cigars, for this is the cutting edge of jazz.
The Joint, 37 West St, T01273-321692. Trends come and go, but *The Joint* seems to have weathered them all and maintained its cool.
Paradox, 78 West St, T01273-321628. Although primarily a large sweaty pit for a night of alco-pop abuse and ill-directed thrusting, the 'Dox offers big name DJs, and the famous 'Wild Fruit' gay night, about once a month.
Revenge, Old Steine, T01273-606064. The city's biggest specifically gay club, boasting cabaret nights and strippers.
Sumo, 9-12 Middle St, T01273-823344. One of the few late night bars in town, and rather self-consciously cool, best to get here early and dress like a diva.
Pressure Point, Richmond Pl, T01273-235082. A pleasant pub with live music and club nights upstairs.
Sidewinder, 65 Upper St James St, T01273-679927. Sofas, couches, candles, this sloth-like bar raises lethargy to new heights.
Tin Drum, St James St, T01273-624777. Fine Gastro-pub, with Polish vodka-centric undertones, home to London's 30-something chattering class refugees.
Volks Tavern, 3 The Collonade, Madeira Dr, T01273-682828. Before Brighton's club explosion, dancing in the city often revolved around gaunt and 'ironically' dressed Jarvis Cocker types posing camply to cheesy tunes in basement venues. The *Volks*, under the arches on the Eastern seafront, is a survivor of these more innocent times.
Zap Club, King's Rd Arches, T01273-202407. Despite many years at the centre of the clubbing scene, the twin arches of the Zap still burst with youthful enthusiasm across musical genres ranging from cheese to hard house.

North Laine, Kemp Town and Brunswick Square *p134, map p132*

Battle Of Trafalgar, 34-35 Trafalgar St, T01273-882276. Just up the hill from the station, this no-nonsense boozer is one of few left in the centre to have survived the onslaught of garishly painted walls and zebra-print sofas. Pull up a pew by the fire and sup on a pint of Harvey's (brewed down the road in Lewes), in traditional environs.
Curve Café/Bar at the Komedia Theatre, Gardner St, T01273-603031. Cocktails, overpriced wines, bottled beers and Fine Modern European Cuisine in pristine surroundings. Beware, however, as the watering hole of preference of Brighton's theatre folk and mediaocracy, **Curve** may be artier than thou.
The Heart and Hand, Upper Gardner St, T01273-624799. This tiny old pub used to be a pre-club haunt for the town's indie and mod glitterati. You'll still see the odd skinny guitar type in here (Bobby Gillespie of Primal Scream is rumoured to frequent), and it's less pretentious than many other alehouses.

Hove *p134*

Cooper's Cask, 3 Farm Rd, Hove, T01273-737026. Extremely cosy alehouse with cheap, filling food options.
Freemasons, 39 Western Rd, T01273-732043. This easy-going boozer is full most nights of the week and has an above-average dining room upstairs.
Nan Tuck's Tavern, 63 Western Rd, T01273-736436. Despite the unnecessary and naff ghoulish motif, this is one of the area's better pubs.

Entertainment

Cinemas

Duke of York, Preston Circus, T01273-602503. Top draw independent arthouse cinema, a little out of the way.
Gardner Arts Centre, University of Sussex, Falmer, T01273-685861. This modern arts venue at the University offers occasional screenings, usually of small, independent films.

Theatres, live music and comedy

BNI, 5 Preston St, T01273-232161. Away from the centre, and at the end of an unpromising basement staircase, this venue has a reputation for kick-starting young careers.
The Brighton Centre, King's Rd, T0870-9009100. Multi-purpose venue that stages a good few gigs. Radiohead, Oasis and the like have all graced the stage here.

The Brighton Dome, 29 New Rd, T01273-709709. Three venues under one roof – the Dome Auditorium, Pavilion Theatre and Corn Exchange offer both mainstream crowd-pullers and smaller productions.
The Event II (see above), occasionally plays host to bands of national significance.
Gardner Arts Centre, University of Sussex, Falmer, T01273-685861. This medium-sized auditorium has hosted everything from student productions, to touring companies and comedians.
Komedia, 44-47 Gardner St, T01273-647100. Now installed in a plush new home in North Laine, cabaret and comedy downstairs, theatre upstairs, both of them first-rate.
Marlborough Theatre, 4 Princes St, T01273-570028. Small but loved and respected theatre above a city centre pub.
Theatre Royal, New Rd, T01273-328488. A lovely old theatre specializing in touring companies and pre-west end productions.

Festivals and events

Brighton Festival, T01273-700747. England's largest arts festival takes place each **May**, and comprises over 800 events ranging from street performers to serious theatre. There's a good range of live music, comedy, dance, film screenings, and a fringe which is emerging as a showcase of young talent on a par with Edinburgh. If you're in Brighton in May, there'll be something to suit all but the most boorish cultural cretin, in one of the festival's many venues.
Pride, Madeira Drive and Preston Park. Each **Aug** the city celebrates 'gay and trans-gendered' culture, in a British interpretation of Sydney's Mardi Gras. There's a huge parade on the seafront before participants head for a free party in Preston Park.

Transport

Bus

Intercity buses arrive at Pool Valley, near Old Steine, T01273-383744. **National Express**, T0870-5808080, for London Victoria (2 hrs) and long-distance. **Stagecoach**, T01903-237661, for Hastings (2 hrs), Dover (5 hrs), Portsmouth (2 hrs), Southampton (2 hrs), and Lewes (30 mins). **Jetlink**, T0870-5757747, for Gatwick (1 hr) and Heathrow (2 hrs), Luton (3 hrs) and Stansted (3 hrs 30 mins) airports. Brighton and Hove buses, T01273-886200, have an extensive local network in the Brighton, Hove and Lewes areas. **Guide Friday**, T01273-746205, for open-top tours.

Car hire

Avis, 6a Marina Village Brighton Marina, T01273-673738. **Beetle Hire**, 4 Parkmoor Terr, T01273-279926. **Europcar**, Cannon Pl, T01273-329332.

Cycle hire

Brighton is well served by cycle paths, but you do sometimes have to plough through some chaotic traffic. You can hire a bike for a day from **Sunrise Cycle Hire**, T01273-748881 at the West Pier, or **Freedom Bikes**, 45 George St, T01273-6816980.

Train

The main railway station is on Queen's Rd, a little North from the centre. There are local stations at London Rd (on the line to Lewes and Hastings), and Preston Park (served by stopping trains to London and the North). Hove Railway Station is on Goldstone Villas, a 10-min walk from central Hove, and is served by trains to Portsmouth. **Connex South Central**, T08706-030405. For London Victoria (1 hr), Lewes (15 mins), Hastings (1 hr 15 mins) and Portsmouth (1 hr 30 mins). **Thameslink Trans**, T08457-484950, for London King's Cross (1 hr 20 mins), London Blackfriars (1 hr 10 mins), London Bridge (1 hr), Luton Airport (1 hr 50 mins) and Gatwick Airport (30 mins). **South West Trains**, T02380-213600, for Chichester (50 mins) and Winchester (1 hr 50 mins). **Wales and West**, T08709-000766, for Cardiff, Bristol, Bath and Southampton. **Virgin Trains**, T08457-222333, for Edinburgh, Manchester, Birmingham and Oxford.

Taxi

Metered cabs congregate at various points around the centre – the main ranks are on West St (outside the Kingswest Complex), East St (opposite the Pavilion gardens), and at the Station. Otherwise: **Brighton Streamline Taxi-cab Ltd**, T01273 -747474; **24 Hour Cabs**, T01273 414141; and **B&H Radio Cars**, T01273-204060.

Directory

Internet Pursuit Internet, 22 Preston St is a good bet. **Terraces Bar & Grill**, Unit 8, Madeira Dr, T01273-570526, www.the-terraces.co.uk. Brighton's first free wireless broadband internet access with seating for 100, meals and drinks. Open Mon-Sat 1100-2300, Sun 1200-2230.

Medical services Royal Sussex County Hospital, Eastern Rd, T01273-696955. Has an accident and emergency department. **Police** Brighton Police are at John St, Hove at Holland Rd, T0845 60708999. **Post office** Brighton has post offices at 51 Ship St, and 142 Western Rd, Hove at 120 Church Rd. T08457-223344.

The South Downs →Colour map 2

The far end of the South Downs Way, between Eastbourne and Brighton, contains many of the route's most attractive features. Over the centuries, the English Channel has carved its way into the chalk hills as they meet the sea, leaving a spectacular series of cliffs. Beachy Head and The Seven Sisters remain a symbol of England as an island nation – pure white cliffs, a natural fortress against invaders. Inland too, smooth grassy hills, and toy-town settlements provide enduring examples of 'quintessential England'. The villages of Alfriston, Ditchling and Firle, with their flint and half-timber cottages and ancient churches nestling at the feet of the hills, are the stuff of wartime postcards, reminding British troops of the idyll they were fighting for. Despite being more populated than other stretches of the South Downs Way, there's still a rural feel to this part of Southern England, with some gorgeous ramshackle farmhouses and barns dotting the countryside.

From the eerily named but extremely scenic Devil's Dyke, just behind Brighton, to Arundel in the west, the Downs move further inland. The flat coastal plain to their south is largely built-up but contains some interesting architecture at Lancing and Shoreham. To the north lie traditional villages and towns along the spring-line, like Poynings, Fulking, Bramber and Steyning and the utterly twee Amberley. There are also a number of sites of archaeological import – for example the Iron Age Settlement at Chanctonbury Ring and the Roman villa at Bignor. This stretch of downland has a more rural, wild feel to it than the rolling hills around Eastbourne and Lewes, and the area's relatively isolated nature means that access and accommodation are not as plentiful as to the east. That said, this is still southeast England, and you're never more than a few miles from a pub or a B&B. In summer, it may be best to head to these parts for a quieter and more authentic, if less spectacular, taste of the South Downs .

▸▸ *For Sleeping, Eating and other listings, see pages 146-149.*

Ins and outs

Getting there The A27 runs along the South Coast from Dover to Southampton and passes by Lewes, Eastbourne (where the A22 leads to London) and Brighton (where the A27 heads for Gatwick and London). **Stagecoach South Coast** buses run infrequent services along the A27 road from Hastings to Brighton via Eastbourne and Lewes. From Brighton you can pick up connections to London. The A22 from London meets the A27 just north of Brighton and this stretches west along the coastal plain a few miles south of the Downs. **Stagecoach Coastline**, T01903-237661, buses run along the A27 from Arundel to Brighton where you can pick up connections to London. To the North of the Downs, there are infrequent local buses connecting the towns and villages to Arundel, Chichester, Shoreham and Brighton. The slow but frequent South Coast **rail** line links the area to Hastings and Ashford in the west, Chichester, Portsmouth and Southampton in the east. Direct trains to London Victoria run from Eastbourne via Lewes and from Brighton. West of

Brighton, in Shoreham-by-Sea, you can pick up connections to Brighton (20 mins) and Chichester (25 mins). You can pick up trains to London from Arundel and Brighton and there is a local service from Brighton to Chichester which stops frequently along the built-up coastal plain. Shoreham is about 5 miles from the Downs.

Getting around Access to the South Downs Way itself is relatively easy but you will obviously have to expect to walk. If you're arriving by train, your best bet is Eastbourne, where the start of the route is about 3 miles from the station. Alternatively, you can join the path halfway between Eastbourne and Brighton by taking a train from Lewes to Southease. The tiny station is on the South Downs Way as it crosses the River Ouse. You can also access the Downs at Devil's Dyke, a short bus ride from Brighton, or at Arundel. Both are connected by rail to London. In terms of exploring the countryside and villages away from the main pathway, you'll need patience and initiative if you're not prepared to walk and don't have a car. That said, many of the major sights in the section can, with patience, be accessed by buses, which run along the A27 on the inland side of the Downs and along the A259 coastal road. Seven Sisters, Alfriston and Beachy Head all have services to Seaford and Eastbourne. There are also infrequent local buses to Arundel, Chichester, Shoreham and Brighton. If you're feeling adventurous, you can also get up to the Downs from Shoreham; the station is about 5 miles from the top of the hills and Truleigh Hill Youth Hostel. If you have a car, the country lanes along the spring-line to the north of the hills are a pleasant drive but the hills themselves are best explored on foot.

Information **Eastbourne TIC** ⓘ *Cornfield Rd, T01323-411400.* **Lewes TIC** ⓘ *School Hill, 187 High St, T01273-483448, Mon-Fri 0900-1700, Sat 1000-1700, Sun 1000-1400.* **Arundel** TIC ⓘ *High St, T01903-882268. Apr-Sep 1000-1800, Nov-Mar 1000-1500.* **Chichester TIC** ⓘ *29a South St, T01243-775888. 0915-1700 Mon-Sat.*

Eastbourne, Beachy Head and inland

If you're taking the South Downs Way seriously, you'll end up in Eastbourne sooner or later. If you arrive with aching limbs after a trek from the west you'll not be alone in putting your feet up here. The place's reputation for retired middle-class pensioners waiting for God by the sea has earned it the moniker 'Costa Geriactrica'. If you want the fast living and tacky glamour of the English seaside, you're better off staying in Brighton. That said, Eastbourne has its advantages: it's clean, has a beautifully maintained seafront with some elegant hotels and some lovely sandy beaches when the tide is out. The town centre is pleasant if uninspiring and has a few places worth popping into. The **Lifeboat Museum** ⓘ *T01323-730717*, on King Edward Parade, is an informative homage to seaborne heroics. The **Towner Gallery** and **Local History Museum** ⓘ *Manor Gdns, T01323-411688* includes some impressive art exhibitions. The **Eastbourne Heritage Centre** ⓘ *Carlisle Rd, T01323-411189* is an illuminating history of the town.

If you take the coastal stretch of the South Downs Way out of Eastbourne, or travel along the A259, you feel like you're right on the edge of England. And you are: the white cliffs here put the more famous ones at Dover to shame. The views of the English Channel and Eastbourne's little bay just to the west of the town are breathtaking. From here you can reach the granddaddy of all south coast sea cliffs. It's awesome yet precipitous beauty has made **Beachy Head** at once an icon of fortitude and the nation's premier suicide spot, and at 162 m of sheer chalk leading directly to a rocky shelf and the lighthouse like a little toy below, you can see why on both counts. The **Beachy Head Countryside Centre** ⓘ *Beachy Head Rd, Eastbourne, T01323-737273,* tells the tale of the surrounding coastline and features interactive exhibits. If you fancy a scramble, it's worth heading west along Eastbourne's seafront, which eventually becomes a rocky path leading to the beach at the cliff's foot. The area around Eastbourne is as famous as the Isle of Wight for having the best weather in England (despite the temptation to mock, summer here genuinely features long sunny days) and on this little path you'll see a microclimate which allows plants to grow which otherwise only exist by the Mediterranean. From here you'll get a good view of the sheer height of the cliff, and the famous little red and white striped **lighthouse** at its foot – it's a captivating place to be at low tide. Back atop the cliff, head a couple of miles further west along the coast from Beachy Head and you'll come to **Belle Toute Lighthouse**, originally built in the 1830s. A fine example of the English triumphing over often foul natural elements, the building was recently uprooted and moved 220 yards inland as the cliff-edge threatened to recede. A little further along is **Birling Gap**, a tiny former coastguard's settlement whose terraced houses look certain not to evade the fate from which Belle Toute escaped. It's a good place to stop for a drink in the ramshackle and rather grotty hotel and, as it's a gap in the cliffs, you can clamber down onto the pebble beach.

The **Seven Sisters**, the name given to the eight (typically English that) white cliffs between Seaford and Beachy Head, are one of rural Britain's most photographed sights. A path leads from the Country Park entrance the half mile or so down to Cuckmere Haven, where the white wonders span out in all their glory. Beware, however, the place is a tourist blackspot and in summer the prevalence of day trippers means it can feel a bit like wandering around a rock festival. If you come in the evening much of the throng will have dispersed and you may even catch a sunset turning the cliffs a mellow and alluring orange. An even better view of the cliffs can be had from **Hope Gap**, a short drive (or an hour's walk) along a track leading off Seaford's eastern seafront. It's also worth a wander around the inland country park. From **Exceat Hill**, there's a wonderful view of the winding meanders of the Cuckmere and it's ox-bow lakes, leading down to Cuckmere Haven, while **Friston Forest** *Seven Sisters Country Park and Friston Forest, T01323-870280.* is a leafy reminder of what the South Downs must have been like when covered in woodland.

A tourist trap, but one it would be a shame to miss, **Alfriston** is an impossibly pretty little village 3 miles up the River Cuckmere from the Seven Sisters Country Park. The main street is a mish mash of half-timbered buildings in which smugglers once stashed their ill-gotten gains. The **Tye**, meanwhile, is an ancient grassy patch by the river, on which stands Alfriston's magnificent **Parish Church of Saint Andrews**, known modestly as the 'Cathedral of the Downs'. The National Trust's first ever property, **Alfriston Clergy House** ⓘ *T01323-870001, Mar-Nov Sat-Mon, Wed and Thu 1000-1700, £2.80, child £1.40*, stands on the edge of the Tye and is a charming 14th-century thatched affair which contains some enlightening material on life in rural Sussex. A wander along the river bank in either direction is a worthwhile journey into gorgeous countryside.

To the south of the A27, between Lewes and Eastbourne lies an enigmatic hill carving, the **Long Man of Wilmington**. Suggestions as to its origin vary wildly: some have it as an Iron Age fertility symbol, others as a Roman landmark. Thinking has recently been hijacked by sane and rational killjoys, who insist it was merely the hobby of a local farmer in the last couple of centuries. Above the Village of Firle (and accessible from it by a road leading from the western end of the village) **Firle Beacon** is the highest point in this stretch of downland. From here you can get an excellent idea of the geography of the area. To the south, the Downs descend slowly to the sea at Seaford, to the east you can see them jutting into the Seven Sisters, to the west they swing inland towards Brighton, Chichester and Winchester. Look north and you'll see the whole of Sussex spanning before you. The foot of the hill is where the chalk Downs hit the Sandstone Weald, an area of rolling lowland which spans north to Surrey.

Bonfires of the insanities

Lewes remembers the 5th November like nowhere else. The town's Protestants were always situated towards the hellfire end of the religious thermometer, and were driven into a fervour by Guy Fawkes's attempt to blow up Parliament in 1605. Over the years, the town's more boisterous citizens insisted on torching effigies of the Pope, and throwing blazing tar barrels at one another, in a violent reminder that the Fifth must never be forgot. By the 19th century, religion had less to do with it and things were just getting gratuitously nasty, people started dying and the Riot Act was read. These days the event is properly policed, devoid of any sectarian feeling, and the town's 'Bonfire Boys' organized into five societies, each with its own traditions and identity. On the 5th November, the narrow streets still play host to the world's largest torch-lit procession. After this curtain raiser, up to 50,000 onlookers follow their society of choice to fire-sites, where fireworks are thrown at society members dressed as Cardinals. Effigies of the Pope, Fawkes and 'enemies of Bonfire' (Thatcher, Blair, Clinton, Delors and most recently Osama Bin Laden have all suffered) are then unceremoniously blown sky high. It's an anarchic, politically incorrect experience. At one recent celebration, after scurrilous suggestions that Cliffe and Commercial Sq societies were about to merge, the Cliffe chief reassured his masses that he would 'never surrender' to 'the poofters from Commercial Square.' The Bonfire Boys, it seems, haven't lost the rock.

Lewes

If Brighton is the scruffy, hedonistic, yet ultimately sensible and successful offspring, then Lewes (pronounced Loo-is) is its concerned but mildly nostalgic parent. Ostensibly, Lewes is your average pretty country town – built up a hill in a gap in the Ouse Valley, it is East Sussex's administrative centre, complete with Norman castle, a number of buildings of historical importance and a family-run brewery. Yet the town is also the guardian of a radical history. Simon de Montfort was an early starter, leading the rebellion which captured the King at the Battle of Lewes in 1264, Thomas Paine (of *The Rights of Man* fame) was a Lewes man and the town's uniquely raucous and extensive 5 November celebrations have their roots in a particularly virulent Puritanical strain. These days, locals spend their time supping on the brewery's syrupy outpourings, playing bowls on the Castle's ancient tilting green or at the Rotary club. The closest you'll get to radicals is an influx of middle-aged liberal intellectuals seeking respite either from the staff rooms of Sussex University and London's media offices or a misspent youth in Brighton. The town is surrounded by beautiful rolling downland.

The **Norman castle** ⓘ *Lewes Castle and Barbican House Museum, High St, T01273-486290, 1000-1730 Mon-Sat, 1100-1730 Sun and bank holidays, £4.20, child £2.10, family £11.40*, was erected by William de Warrenne, shortly after the Battle of Hastings, and is one of only two in the country to boast two Mottes. The Keep, sections of the fortifications, and a 14th-century Barbican remain. Climb to the top of these and you'll see why William chose the spot, the panoramic views over the Ouse valley allow any invaders to be spotted a mile off. These days, invasions are confined to local amateur dramatics societies putting on summer productions in the grounds, and groups of local old codgers playing bowls in the castle Bailey. The **museum** has local artefacts dating from prehistoric times, and there's a scale town model of Lewes in the 1870s.

Turn right along High Street from the castle, and you'll come to **Bull House**, where famous son Tom Paine resided from 1768 and 1774 as an excise officer. Over the road is **St Michael's Church**, which has a 12th-century round flint tower, a 14th-century arcade, and a Georgian façade. Just past this on your left is **Keere Street**, Lewes's entry for the most cosily English cobbled-street-on-a-hill award. Supposedly, George IV, Prince Regent, forced his coach and horses at breakneck speed down the vertiginous route for a dare.

Brighton to Arundel

Head west beyond Hove and the city turns into a green but uninspiring sprawl of suburbs, head north just a couple of miles, and you're in the breathtaking downland scenery of **Devil's Dyke**. This steep, sharp valley was actually carved by a stream, rather than forces from behind the fiery gates, and is a lovely spot for some fresh air at sunset. Just west of the Dyke, the South Downs Way passes over **Poynings** and **Fulking**. These two pretty villages lie along the spring-line (where the chalk downs spill their excess water onto the lowlands). The church of the **Holy Trinity** at Poynings is a classic flint Sussex Church and its village a pleasant place to wander or sample some local ale. The main street at the unfortunately named Fulking, meanwhile, features an area where yokels used to dam the spring to create a sheepdip. Doing this every week in freezing cold flowing water is rumoured to have crippled much of the town's male population until the early 20th century saw more civilized agricultural practices introduced. The **Fulking Escarpment** behind the village is a Site of Special Scientific Interest, containing some fine downland flora and fauna including some rare orchids.

Bramber is a sleepy little place about half way between Brighton and Arundel, and a good watering hole if you get tired of walking. The main sites of interest are the Parish Church of **St Nicholas**, a tiny Norman affair dating to 1073. Of the same era is the largely ruined **Bramber castle**, constructed by Norman baron William de Braose, again in 1073, to protect his fiefdom. Only the gatehouse remains in any quantity, but you can walk around the leafy ruins of the motte and bailey.

South of the Downs

To the south of the Downs, the main spots of interest are **Lancing College** ⓘ *T01273-452213, Mon-Sat 1000-1600, Sun 1200-1600, free* and **Shoreham.** Lancing College is a fairly upmarket public school featuring a gorgeous Gothic Chapel (1868), which dominates the plain to the south. Shoreham is a straggly town on the coast, but is worth visiting for remnants of its Norman heritage. Dominated by the large Norman church of St Mary, the town is also home to the **Marlipins Museum** ⓘ *T01273-462994, High St, Tue-Sat 1030-1630*, which documents local and maritime history in an attractive Norman customs house.

North of the Downs

Steyning, to the North of the hills is an attractive place for a pit-stop. This little country town was once a port and features a number of unusually intact medieval streets, especially Church Street which has some wonderfully ramshackle old houses, and a sizeable Norman Church. A little further west along the South Downs Way, **Chanctonbury Ring** is the area's best vantage point with magnificent views over the inland countryside. Once swathed in a ring of beech trees (which fell foul of a nasty storm in the late 1980s) extensive remains of Roman and Iron Age settlements have been found.

Amberley

Amberley Village is a couple of minutes on the train from Arundel, and is perhaps even more of an English idyll. All cutesy architectural styles seem to be represented from thatch, through flint to half-timber. It's the kind of place they used to put on First World War recruitment posters to highlight to future cannon-fodder what they were fighting to preserve. Pleasingly, it doesn't suffer from the bus loads of tourists which have blighted the likes of Alfriston (see page 141) and is a lovely spot to wander for a couple of hours. The castle is now an exclusive country hotel but it's worth popping into **St Michael's church**, a Norman effort just outside the castle walls, and **Amberley Museum** ⓘ *T01798-831370*, which, given its situation in gentrified Sussex countryside, features a rather incongruous collection of industrial memorabilia.

Arundel and around

Travelling up the Arun valley, the casual observer could be forgiven for thinking they were arriving at Windsor, the cynical, at EuroDisney. Completely dominating this little town perched up on the Western hillside is its expansive motte and double bailey castle. There has been some kind of fortification here since well before the Norman Conquest and successive Earls of Arundel have added to it over the centuries, accounting for both its size (it is the country's biggest) and contrived appearance. Like Rye, Arundel was once a port and its history is dominated by seafaring and smuggling. The current town is a cutesy place with ubiquitous antique shops, frilly tea rooms and conservative hotels. Although you can easily see it in a day, it's worth holing up here for a bit longer as a base to explore the countryside and villages of the Arun Valley – some of the area's most beautiful.

Ins and outs

Getting there Arundel lies just off the A27 Portsmouth to Brighton trunk road and is about an hour's drive from both, and just 20 mins from Chichester. Coming from London, you'll need to take the A29 and turn off at Houghton, the drive can take anything from 1-3 hrs. Direct Stagecoach, T08702 433711, services operate along the A27 from Brighton (2 hrs) and Chichester (1 hr). Arundel is on the main line from Chichester (20 mins) to London Victoria (1 hr 25 mins) via Gatwick airport (45 mins). From Chichester you can pick up connections east to Brighton and west to Portsmouth, Southampton and Winchester. Connex South Central, T08706-030405.

Getting around Arundel is a very small town and you should be able to reach it all on foot. For Amberley village it's a single stop on the train (5 mins) and trains run hourly.

Sights

Museum and Heritage Centre ⓘ *High St, T01903-882268. 1030-1700 Mon-Sat, 1400-1700 Sun. £1.* is right next to the TIC, and gives you the lowdown on the town's history. **Arundel Castle**, *T01903-883136, 1200-1700 Sun-Fri, Apr-Oct, £9, child £5.50, concessions £7, family £24.50*, was built by Roger de Montgomery, Earl of Arundel, in the 11th century, and has been the seat of the Dukes of Norfolk for over 500 years. It has been rebuilt on numerous occasions since, most thoroughly in the 19th century, and now has a fairly-tale quality, with a maze of towers and turrets perched on the hill over the Arun valley. On view inside are some personal possessions of Mary, Queen of Scots, some 16th-century tapestries and clocks, and portraits by Van Dyke and Gainsborough. If you are here during the summer months, you should try and catch a game of cricket in the castle's very own ground (T01903-882462); Sussex County Cricket club play the odd fixture here, and touring international teams play an MCC team each summer.

Outside the castle entrance on London Road is the Parish church of **St Nicholas**. Built in the perpendicular style in 1380, it is one of history's anomalies – during the Reformation, the western part of the chapel converted to the Church of England, the eastern portion, however, as part of the jurisdiction of the catholic Duke of Norfolk, was forced to stay loyal to Rome. A little further along the crest of the hill is **Arundel Cathedral** ⓘ *T01903-882297*. Despite its 15th-century style, it was actually built between 1869 and 1873 to plans drawn up by one JA Hansom, he of the Hansom cab.

A 1km walk to the North of Arundel, along Mill Road, brings you to **Swanbourne Lake and Arundel Park** ⓘ *T01903-883355, daily 0930-1730, £5.50, child £3.50*. A former millpond, it's now home to many species of wildlife. The park itself is 1100 acres of untampered downland, and ideal for strolling in this idyllic grassy landscape. A little further along Mill Road, is the **Waterfowl Park**, ideal for those with an eye for the birds.

Chichester

This elegant little city has been a major centre across several eras of English history and has an extraordinarily rich architectural heritage from the Roman walls of Noviomagnus and the Villa at Fishbourne, to some fine 18th and 19th century townhouses. Dominating the skyline and incorporating virtually all aspects of the city's history is the cathedral – one of the country's finest. The modern city is a bustling if rather staid place perhaps accounted for by a rather geriatric population. Yet the architecture of the place should make it a stopping point on anybody's tour of the region and come in July and you'll be treated to regional theatre second only to Stratford-upon-Avon at the Chichester Festivities.

Ins and outs

Getting there The A285 or the A29 wind their way up to London, and this can take anything from 1 1/2 – 3 hrs, depending on traffic. Portsmouth and Brighton are both about an hr away on the A27. Chichester is well served with regular direct trains to Brighton, Portsmouth and London Victoria via Gatwick airport.

Getting around Chichester itself is easily covered on foot. For the outlying places mentioned in this section you'll need to head for the bus station: Bosham (15 mins), Fishbourne (10 mins), Goodwood (15 mins).

Sights

The **Market Cross**, is the logical place to start a walk around the city centre. Donated to the town's poor by Bishop Storey in 1501, so that they might trade 'without let or hindrance,' these days it's still the city's centrifuge and all classes meet there for a rest and a chat during a haul around the shops. Along West Street, is the city's magnificent **Cathedral** ⓘ *T01243-782595, 0730-1900, guided tours are available at 1100 and 1415, Mon-Sat, Easter-Oct, (and there is a 'roving' guide at all times), and are well worth it for a deeper appreciation of the cathedral's many treasures.* There has been a building on this spot since Roman times, and a fragment of an intricate second-century mosaic can be found to the right of the current retrochoir. Today's building began taking shape in 1076, and was ready for the consecration of Bishop Luffa in 1108. Much has been added since then – the sacristry, retrochoir and clerestory (under Bishop Seffrid II – 1180-1204), are of the Early English Gothic style; the Lady Chapel (early 14th-century), with its gorgeous Lambert Barnard ceiling, is in the Decorated style; the bell tower, cloisters and independent belfry (15th-century) were built in the Perpendicular style – but the building conveys much more of the integrity of the original than many of its English counterparts. The cathedral contains paintings, sculpture and masoneary from over a millennium as a centre of worship and pilgrimage, and you should take your time over it.

Outside the Cathedral, the unique, free-standing **Bell Tower**, has a peal of eight bells, with one surviving from 1583. St Richard's walk, is a pretty walled-alleyway leading from the Cathedral down to Canon Lane, whilst **Vicar's Close** is a terrace of 15th-century houses, once occupied by the vicar's choral and their refectory. At the end of the lane, you can see the Palace Gateway, the Tudor red-brick entrance to the **Bishop's Palace**. Cut through and you'll come to the Bishop's Palace Gardens, a beautifully manicured public space, which is an ideal spot to sit down in and enjoy the view over the Cathedral and her precincts.

Pallant House, is an elegant historic house and art gallery, built in 1812, now host to an estimable collection of British art, and regular talks and events. Up on thronging North Street is the Saxon church of **St Olave's** ⓘ *9 North Pallant, T01243-774557, 1000-1700 Tue-Sat, 1230-1700 Sun and bank holidays, £4.00, child £3.00*, built in 1050, possibly by roving Scandinavian merchants; it contains remains of an earlier Roman foundation.

Just off Priory Road is the venerable **Greyfriars building**, a chancel built in the 13th century, it is now all that remains of the former monastery of the Greyfriars. Genteel sacrilege now surrounds it in the form of a nicely groomed cricket pitch surrounded by the city walls. For a good overview of the city's saga it's worth popping into **Chichester District Museum** ⓘ *29 Little London, T01234-784683, 1000-1730 Tue-Sat, free*. The former cornstore contains, amongst other local delights, an array of the militaria of the Royal Sussex Regiment.

Around Chichester

Fishbourne Roman Palace, *Salt Hill Rd, Fishbourne, T01243-539266, Mar-Jul 1000-1700, Aug 1000-1800, Sep-Dec 1000-1600, Jan Sat and Sun 1000-1600, £5, child £4.10*, is Britain's largest Roman residence. Built for King Tiberius Claudius Togidubnus it is a fine example of Latinate luxury dating from the first century AD. Surviving hypocausts and mosaics suggest the king was something of a bon viveur, and the gardens have been lovingly re-replanted to original plans. Alas, the decline in residential planning over the subsequent two millennia has resulted in many of the remains being housed in a building that looks like your average ring-road garden centre.

'Glorious Goodwood,' is a phrase uttered in reverence of a quasi-fictional summer upper class idyll. Normally by *Daily Mail* readers from the Rotary Clubs of Surrey. It's fair to say, **Goodwood Racecourse,** T01243-75502, is a venue of some grandeur, situated as it is in some breathtaking downland scenery. If you can bear the mild air of social aspiration and some ridiculous head attire its summer programme is a grand excuse to go and stick a few bets on the gee-gees. Distinctly less frenetic is **Goodwood House** ⓘ *T01243-755048, Sun and Mon afternoons Apr-Oct, £7, concessions £6, teenagers and students £3, under-12s free*, home to the celebrated Duchess of Richmond, who organized the Franco-foxing ball on the eve of the Battle of Waterloo.

Sleeping

Eastbourne, Beachy Head and inland *p140*

L **Grand Hotel**, King Edward's Pde, Eastbourne, T01323-412345. Indeed very grand, restored to its 19th century glory at huge expense, with 2 pools (outdoors and indoors) and 2 restaurants, one of which is The Mirabelle (see Eating).

C **Deans Place Hotel**, Alfriston, T01323-870248. An elegant establishment.

D **Crossways Hotel**, Wilmington, T01323-482455. Clean and friendly, although a little close to the A27 main road.

D **Tudor Manor Hotel**, Eastbourne Rd, Seaford, T01323-896006. More elegant than the Avondale and has en-suite doubles for £35 including breakfast but is, alas, still in Seaford.

E **Avondale Hotel**, Avondale Rd, Seaford, T01323-890000. Has clean doubles with baths.

E **Lindau Lodge**, 71 Royal Pde, Eastbourne, T01323-640792, is a no-frills seaside B&B for around £20.

E-F **YHA** have hostels at Frog Firle, Alfriston, T01323-870423 and Bank Cottages, Telscombe, T01323-301357.

Lewes *p142*

L **Shelley's**, High St, T01273-472361. The real deal, a 16th-century house with plush lounges and bar, and an excellent restaurant. The place was rumoured to be curiously full when New Labour held their Party conference in nearby Brighton last year, provoking local outrage and accusations of champagne socialism.

A **The White Hart**, 55 High St, T01273-476694. Does its best to look classy, but adding Holiday Inn type swimming facilities, and a rear restaurant that looks like a Travelodge to an otherwise attractive townhouse hotel, barely justifies the expense.

C **Berkeley House Hotel**, 2 Albion St, T01273-476057, is an attractive Georgian townhouse with an alcohol licence.

D-E **Black Horse**, Western Rd, T01273-473653. Cosy traditional boozers with well-maintained rooms up top.

D-E **Pump Cottage**, 6 St Nicholas La, T01273-473765. A small (1/2 bedroom) B&B.

E **The Crown Inn**, 191 High St, T01273-480760, is a curiously appealing small town hotel of the kind most towns have consigned to history.

F **YHA Hostel** at Telscombe, Bank Cottages, Telscombe, T01274-304357, £10 dorms, but by the time you've got up and trekked into Lewes it'll be dusk.

Brighton to Arundel *p143*

C-D **Woodstock House Hotel and Restaurant**, Charlton, Near Chichester, T01243-811666. A country-lodge style place with doubles ranging £35-£80.

D **Old Tollgate Restaurant and Hotel**, The Street, Bramber, Steyning, T01903-879494. Has a chain feel about it, but is clean and reasonably priced.

D **Springwells**, 9 High St, Steyning, T01903-812446. A clean, modern B&B with outdoor heated swimming pool.

D **Tottington Manor Hotel**, Edburton, T01903-815757. Good value rooms in a 16th-century manor house.

E **Poynings Manor Farm**, T01273-857371. Has 3 rooms on a working farm.

F **YHA** Hostel at Truleigh Hill, Shoreham, T01903-813419, right on the South Downs Way overlooking Shoreham and the coast.

Camping

At the **Bridge Public House**, Amberley, T01798-831619, next to a pub which serves simple, but excellent, food.

Arundel and around *p144*

B **Norfolk Arms Hotel**, High St, T01903-884275. A charming 18th-century coaching inn in the shadow of the castle. The poshest in town, it's worth splashing out for a night or two.

B **The Old Railway Station**, Petworth, north of Arundel on the A272, T01798-342346. Six bedrooms in converted Pullman carriages with en suite bathrooms, brass beds and breakfast on the old platform (if the weather's fine). This is 'rail' luxury.

C **Burpham Country House Hotel and Restaurant**, Burpham, north of Arundel, T01903-882160. An upmarket B&B.

D **The Swan Hotel**, High St, T01903-882314. B&B in a pleasant Victorian hotel next to the river, the in-house restaurant makes the most of local seafood and game.

E **Arundel House**, 11 High St, T01903-882136. A 16th-century licensed restaurant with 6 characterful rooms.

E **Dukes of Arundel**, 65 High St, T01903-883847. A prince amongst B&Bs with 400-year-old interior architecture.

F **Warningcamp Youth Hostel**, Sefton Pl, Warningcamp, T01903-882204. Dorms £8, camping £3.90. The local budget option and is clean and friendly, if a little out of the way.

Chichester *p145*

C **Ship Hotel**, North St, T01243-778000. A classic 18th-century townhouse hotel, perhaps a little overpriced, though.

D **Suffolk House Hotel**, 3 East Row, T01243-778899. Respectable classic Georgian affair.

D-E **Encore**, 11 Clydesdale Av, T01243-52827. A reliable B&B, a stone's throw from the centre.

E **University College Chichester**, Bishop Otter Campus, College Lane, T01243-816070. Lets out its student rooms for £23 per night from Jun to Aug. Ignore the evidence of student occupation (blu-tack on walls etc), and you won't come to much harm.

Eating

Eastbourne, Beachy Head and inland *p140*

£££ **Hungry Monk**, Jevington Village, T01323-482178, is housed in a couple of old flint cottages. This venerable restaurant has built up a fine local reputation over the years. The gamey food and decent continental wine list make it an ideal venue for a night out.
£££ **The Mirabelle**, Grand Hotel, Royal Marine Pde, Eastbourne, T01323-435066. Now in the hands of top German chef, Gerald Röser, offering dishes such as pike soufflé and salad of smoked salmon, avocado and foie gras.
££ **George Inn**, High St, Alfriston, T01323-870319. With its oak beams and fireplace, this place is almost too quaint, but it does decent English food at the bar and à la carte.
££ **Rose Cottage**, Alciston. You might want to descend from the Downs halfway between Alfriston and Southease for a pint and a bite here. The food is genuinely English.
£ **The Sussex Ox**, Milton St, Near Alfriston, T01323-870840. On the South Downs Way just to the east of Alfriston is this country boozer.
£ **The White Horse**, Ditchling, is a homely boozer at the foot of the downs, worth a bash for the giant sized portions of fresh fish and chips and a good range of real ales.

Lewes *p142*

£££ **Shelley's Hotel**, High St, T01273-472361, is Lewes's only 'posh' restaurant. There's an estimable wine list, and the food is rich and gamey.
££ **Snowdrop Inn**, South St, T01273-471018. If you're in town for the evening, it's worth the trek to this eccentric little pub. With an excellent vegetarian and seafood menu.
£ **Patio Pizzeria**, Market St, T01273-479539, is Lewes's best budget option, serving up excellent and simple Sardinian cuisine at wallet-friendly prices.

Brighton to Arundel *p143*

££ **Chequer Inn**, High St, Steyning, T01903-814437, is a small town place with a traditional restaurant.
££ **The Shepherd and Dog**, Fulking, T01273-857382, is an old alehouse with a decent menu and a beer garden looking up into Devil's Dyke.

Arundel and around *p144*

£££ **Norfolk Arms**, High St, T01903-882101, does cream teas in a quaint old room; there's also a meaty, gamey English restaurant, but it has a little too much impact on the wallet for the quality.
££ **The Eagle**, Tarrant St, is a quiet pub, with some excellent cold lunches à la Parma ham and melon, and Greek salad.
££ **Tudor Rose Restaurant**, 49 High St, T01903-883813, is a safe bet for English meals.
££ **Xavier's**, Castle Mews, Tarrant St, T01903-883477, is a wine-bar type affair with delicious crêpes.
£ **Belinda's Tea Shop**, 13 Tarrant St, T01903-882 977, has teas, coffees, light meals, and plenty of cakes.

Chichester *p145*

££ **Chichester Inn**, 40 West St, is a no-nonsense boozer with garden, wholesome stodge, bar snacks and, well, beer.
££ **Little London Indian Restaurant**, 38 Little London, T01243-537550, does exactly what it says on the tin to a better standard than most.
££ **Pizza Express**, South St, T01243-786648. If imagination deserts you, head for the superior end of the High St chain.
£ **Cathedral Refectory**, Chichester Cathedral, West St, T01243-782595, in the Cathedral vaults and offers decent light lunchs in ecclesiastical environs.

Entertainment

Eastbourne, Beachy Head and inland

The Curzon Cinema, T01323-731441, has all the latest from Hollywood.
Congress Theatre, on Carlisle Rd and **Devonshire Park Theatre**, Compton St can both be reached on T01323-412000 and attract some surprisingly high-quality productions and touring companies.

Festivals and events

Lewes *p142*

Lewes Festival, takes place each **Jul**, and comprises some surprisingly good classical concerts in the town's many old churches. Call TIC for details, T01273-483448. For details of the town's (in)famous **Bonfire Night Celebrations**, see p142.

Transport

Eastbourne, Beachy Head and inland *p140*

Bus
Eastbourne bus station is on Terminus Rd. National Express, T0870 580 8080, run 2 buses to **London Victoria** coach station per day (3 hrs). The hourly Stagecoach, T01903-237661, bus from **Dover** (4 hrs) to **Brighton** (1 hr 30 mins) also calls by. County Busline, T01273-474747, or Bus Enquiries, T01256-464501.

Cycle hire
Cuckmere Cycle Co Ltd, The Granary Barn, Seven Sisters Country Park, Exceat, Seaford, T01323-870310.

Taxi
Eastbourne & Country Taxis, T01323-720720. **Eastbourne Station Taxis**, T01323-725511.

Train
Eastbourne Station is on Ashford Rd, trains run every 30 mins to London Victoria (1 hr 35 mins) and 2-3 times an hr to Brighton via Lewes (45 mins) and Hastings (30 mins). Seaford Station is right in the centre and has services 3 times an hr to Brighton via Lewes (30 mins). There are also stations at Southease on the line from Seaford to Lewes for access to the South Downs Way, and at Glynde, on the line from Eastbourne to Lewes and Brighton.

Directory

Eastbourne
Internet At the Public Library, Grove Rd, T01323-434206. **Post office** Oklynge Rd, T01323-731277. **Hospitals Eastbourne District General Hospital**, King's Dr, T01323-417400. **Police** Terminus Rd, T01323-412999.

Surrey

→*Colour map 2*

Surrey usually gets a bad press, written off as a polite suburban extension of southwest London, the city's stockbroker belt. Even so, once beyond the M25, the combination of affluent homeowners and strict planning regulations has promoted an attractive mix of town and country. Between Guildford and Dorking, the North Downs roll up to the highest point in the southeast at Leith Hill. Just to the north an even more popular viewpoint is Box Hill, close to the Edwardian splendours of Polsden Lacey. To the south, rolling wooded countryside and heathland dotted with little commuter villages stretches down to the border with Sussex. ▸▸ *For Sleeping and Eating listings, see page 150.*

Ins and outs

Getting there Guildford is on the A3, about 1 hr's drive from central London. National Express, T08705-808080, coaches leave Victoria at 0900, 1300, 1500, 1700, and 1900, taking about 1 hr.Fast trains run from London Waterloo via Woking twice an hr taking 35 mins.

Guildford

The county town of Guildford is not the most attractive place in Surrey but it's certainly one of the busiest. Dominated by its stark modern cathedral, there have unfortunately been other much less impressive developments in the second half of the 20th century. That said, the old High Street hidden away among the multistorey car parks and office blocks remains much as it would have looked before the cathedral was built, and the banks of the Wey have recently received some much needed attention.

Guildford's cobbled High St slopes uphill lined with all the usual big names in retail. Its most famous feature is the ancient gilded clock jutting out from the old Guildhall. A pleasant retreat from the crowds, the stubby stone keep of Guildford's **Norman castle** is tucked away behind the High Street in flower-filled gardens. Some distance from the town centre stands the **Cathedral**. Construction on this highly contemporary interpretation of Gothic magnificence started in 1936. The completed fabric, designed by Edward Maufe, was consecrated in 1964. Three miles northeast of Guildford, off the A25, **Clandon Park** ⓘ *(NT), T01483-222482. Apr-Nov Tue-Thu, Sun 1100-1700, gardens only all year Tue-Thu, Sun 1100-1700, £6, family £15.*, near West Clandon, is a very fine and stately Palladian mansion stuffed with valuable furniture, pictures and porcelain collected early in the 20th century.

A similar distance northeast of Guildford are the **Royal Horticultural Society's garden** ⓘ *Wisley, T01483-224234, www.rhs.org.uk, all year Mon-Fri 1000-1800 or dusk, weekends 0900-1800 or dusk, £6, £2 children.*, 240 acres of expertly tended gardens, including a 16-acre fruit field bursting with an astonishing variety of apples, as well as herbaceous borders, ornamental walks, greenhouses, and the inevitable shop, restaurant and café.

Dorking and around

More attractive but also more of a 'dormitory' town than Guildford, Dorking's only real attraction is **Box Hill** ⓘ *NT Warden, T01306-885502*, popular with weekenders looking for some fresh air and geography field trips exploring the peculiarities of the River Mole's course through the Downs. Just to the north of the town, it's a good 4-hr trek over stepping-stones across the river. It can also be reached off the A24. Long walks can be taken along the ridge via Pebble Combe to Reigate, or along Mickleham Down to Leatherhead. A mile west of Box Hill, **Polesden Lacey** ⓘ *(NT), T01372- 452048, Apr-Sep Wed-Sun, bank holidays 1100-1700, £7, grounds only all year daily 1100-1800 or dusk £4 gardens only..*, with its superb Edwardian rose gardens and grounds, was the lavish party home of Mrs Greville, where she entertained Edward VII and babysat the Queen Mother. Five miles south, **Leith Hill** ⓘ *T01306-711777, tower Nov-Mar weekends and bank holidays 1000-1500, Apr-Oct Wed, weekends 1000-1630, £1.50*, is the highest point in the southeast, from where on a very clear day, St Paul's and Canary Wharf can be seen, as well as the sea at Shoreham on the south coast.

Sleeping

Guildford *p149*

A-B **Jarvis Guildford Hotel**, Upper High St, T01483-564511, F531160. A very central chain hotel in a fine old Georgian building.

C-D **Hampton**, 38 Poltimore Rd, T01483-572012, vgmorris@aol.com A Tudor-style detached house in a quiet cul-de-sac with views over the town.

Dorking and around *p150*

L **Nutfield Priory**, Nutfield, Redhill, T01737-824400. One of the most luxurious and expensive options in a former Gothic folly surrounded by acres of parkland, with views, a health club and everything you'd expect from a smart country house hotel, including award-winning restaurant.

E **Bulmer Farm**, Holmbury St Mary, Near Dorking, T01306-730210, is an attractive old house, convenient for exploring Leith Hill, with self-contained accommodation available in an annexe.

D-E **Herons Head Farm**, Mynthurst, Leigh, T01293-862475. A Jacobean farmhouse with jacuzzis, outdoor swimming pool and a lake.

Eating

Dorking and around *p150*

£££ **La Barbe**, 71 Bell St, Reigate, T01737-241966. Classic French food in a busy atmosphere.

£££ **The Dining Room**, 59a High St, Reigate, T01737-226650. A treat for foodies with Mediterranean and British cuisine.

£££ **Mulberry Restaurant** at Langshott Manor, Langshott, Near Horley, T01293-786680. Needs to be booked, surprisingly low-key given its smart hotel location.

££ **White Horse**, in Shere, T01483-202518, 'the prettiest village in Surrey', is a rickety old place with decent food.

South of England

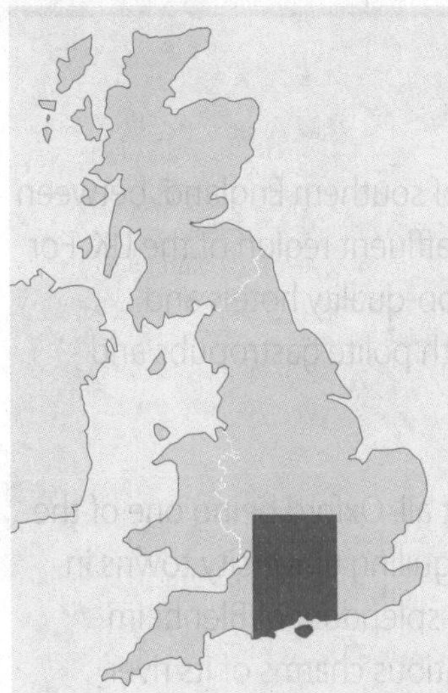

Introduction

Five counties make up the core of southern England: between them they're probably the most affluent region of the UK. For the visitor this means plenty of top-quality hotels and restaurants, well-kept villages with polite gastropubs and acres of attractive parkland.

Oxfordshire's name almost says it all, Oxford being one of the most polyglot, venerable and beguiling university towns in the world. Nearby is the Baroque splendour of Blenheim Palace, as well as the less ostentatious charms of its river valleys – the Cherwell, Windrush and Thames – winding between the Cotswold, the Chiltern and the White Horse hills. South and east, the River Thames flows on towards London past ancient Dorchester and into Berks and Bucks: through the high-tech light industry of Reading, beneath Georgian-looking Henley, literary Marlow and Conservative Cookham, to Royal Windsor, with Eton at its feet. To the north of the river stretch the rolling chalk hills of the Chilterns up to the hilltop cathedral city of St Albans. To the south, West Berkshire and Wiltshire are all about racehorses, sweeping downlands and monuments of neolithic civilization – Avebury, Stonehenge and Silbury Hill – with the extraordinary spire of Salisbury cathedral poking up out of the Middle Ages. Winchester, the county town of Hampshire next door, was the medieval capital of England, with a beautiful cathedral, school and the St Cross Hospital still to show for it.

On the south coast, the New Forest was the kings' playground, and is now peaceful heathland grazed by quiet ponies. Offshore, the Isle of Wight totters into the 21st century freighted with an ageing population, crowded prisons and some beautiful scenery – not unlike England itself.

★ Don't miss...

1. Tickle your fancy with a few totemic charms at the **Pitt Rivers Museum** in Oxford, before swanning downstream in a punt, page 157.
2. Dredge the wellsprings of your imagination with a trip to **Stonehenge**: imagine if there were no car park, or just go to Avebury, pages 191 and 188.
3. Wander through the watermeadows around the medieval monastery of **St Cross Hospital**, Winchester, page 195.
4. Jump on a ferry from the New Forest to Yarmouth on the **Isle of Wight**, page 207.

Oxford

→Colour map 2

Very much the capital of its county, although England's oldest and most famous university town was dubbed "the home of lost causes" by the poet Matthew Arnold, it rarely disappoints. He also noted that seen from a distance the city's spires, turrets and domes seem to be dreaming. Broader and more spread out, it is just as beautiful as Cambridge, its equally celebrated sister in the east and walking around the old stone colleges or through their surrounding meads and gardens, it's impossible not to be aware of the weight of centuries of scholarship, culture and learning. Thankfully, though, the streets are as alive today as they've ever been, and Oxford continues to be one of the most remarkable, least isolated and most intellectually engaging of modern European cities. First-time visitors can hardly fail to be impressed by the sheer number of beautiful old colleges that make up this pinnacle of British academe. And it comes as some surprise at the start of the 21st century that these mellow stone buildings, with their beamed halls, chapels, quads and spires, continue to be used pretty much for their original purpose. Christ Church is the grandest, Merton the oldest, New College the most authentic in its groundplan and Magdalen the most lovely, but all the colleges in the centre of the city are worth looking around. There's much else in the city to enjoy. Views over the 'dreaming spires' can be had from several church towers in the middle of town. Along with two of the most extraordinary museums in the country, the Ashmolean and the Pitt Rivers, the Botanical Gardens are a delightful retreat on the riverside, next to flowering watermeadows and meads just beyond the old city walls. And then there's punting on the river, almost a mandatory activity in summer for students and visitors alike. If all the boats are booked up, simply taking a stroll in the green acres so close to the city centre makes for an exceedingly pleasant afternoon. »» *For Sleeping, Eating and other listings, see pages 160-163.*

Ins and outs

Getting there Thames Trains run twice-hourly express services from London Paddington via Reading to Oxford, usually at 18 and 48 mins past the hr, taking just under an hr. Stopping services (via Didcot Parkway and stations along the Thames valley) take 1hr 30mins. Oxford's one-way **road** system has reduced motorists to tears, and parking is almost impossible in the middle of the city. Unfortunately, the pedestrianization of the city centre also means that traffic even clogs up the Park & Ride buses. The Botley Rd Park and Ride, to the west, is the closest to the centre, but takes almost as long as the others because of the bottleneck at the railway bridge. If you must arrive on 4 wheels, you'll find Oxford just off the M40, about an hr from London, ½ hr from the M25. Oxford is very well served by coach companies. »» *For further details, see also Transport, page 163.*

Getting around Walking or cycling around central Oxford is one of life's real pleasures. For some of the slightly further-flung parts of the city, taxis are relatively cheap and the bus network from Gloucester Green along the High St and around Carfax is regular and reliable.

Information TIC ⓘ *15-16 Broad St, T01865-726871, www.visitoxford.org Mon-Sat 0930-1700, Sun 1000-1530*. Accommodation booking service (including fee). Official guided tours leave from the TIC, where there are also some good self-guiding leaflets available on walks along the river or canal and around the town.

Sights

The centre of the city of Oxford is Carfax, the crossroads at the top of the High Street coming in from the east over Magdalen Bridge. Pedestrianized Cornmarket heads north towards wide St Giles, and eventually Woodstock and Banbury. Queen Street continues the High Street west, down past the Norman Castle and prison towards the train station. St Aldate's slopes downhill south, past Christ Church college with its prominent Tom Tower, crossing the Thames at Folly Bridge and continuing out of town as the Abingdon Road.

West of Carfax

A right turn eastward at the meeting of Worcester Street and Walton Street leads on to Beaumont Street. Here stands the Oxford Playhouse, opposite the Ashmolean, the oldest museum open to the public in the country. It was opened early in the 17th century by Elias Ashmole, one of Charles I's tax-men. Today it ranks as one of the most extraordinary collections under one roof outside London. The grand classical façade of the **Ashmolean Museum** ⓘ *Beaumont St, T01865-278000, www.ashmol.ox.ac.uk, Tue-Sat 1000-1700 (also Jun, Aug on Thu until 1900), Sun 1400-1700. Free. (Cast Gallery, Pusey La, off St John St, Tue-Fri 1000-1600, Sat 1000-1300)* hides more than 50 rooms, some very beautiful, others not, all with stories to tell and on a very manageable scale. A wide staircase to the right of the front entrance leads up to the Founder's Collection, a right turn at the top of the stairs, displaying a few of gardener John Tradescant's 'curiosities', later purchased by Elias Ashmole. These include Powhatan's Mantle, 'perhaps the most important North American Indian relic to survive anywhere' – four deerskins stitched together and decorated with shells. Sadly it's now thought unlikely that it was in fact worn by Pocahontas' dad. Other items on display, that Tradescant was either given or collected while out plant-hunting for his boss King Charles I, are Henry VIII's hawking gear, Guy Fawke's Lantern, a Chinese rhinoceros-horn cup and an African drum and trumpet. In a room next door surrounded by other rare musical instruments sits one of the most precious violins in the world, *Le Messie*, made by Antonio Stradivari at Cremona in 1716. Straight ahead at the top of the stairs leads on to many people's favourite part of the museum, the Department of Western Art.

With the **Randolph Hotel** on the corner, Beaumont Street meets the wide tree-lined north-south thoroughfare of St Giles at the spikey **Martyrs Memorial**. It was put up in 1841 in memory of the Protestant bishops Cranmer, Ridley and Latimer who were burned at the stake during the counter-Reformation of 'Bloody Mary' in the mid-16th century. A cross marks the exact spot where their ashes were found outside Balliol College on the Broad (see below). Over the way is **St John's College**, consistently one of the highest academic achievers, with one of the most beautiful gardens in Oxford, fronted by a striking combination of Gothic and neoclassical architecture.

East of Carfax

The block of old streets and colleges formed by the Cornmarket, the Broad, Catte Street and the High Street is pretty much the heart of the university, embracing the University Church of St Mary the Virgin, the Radcliffe Camera, the Bodleian Library and Sheldonian Theatre, as well as Jesus, Exeter, and Brasenose colleges.

At the top of the Cornmarket, the **tower of St Michael's** ⓘ *Apr-Oct daily 1000-1700, Nov-Mar 1000-1600, £1.50, concessions £1, children £0.80. Café for rolls and tea,*at the North Gate, on the corner of Ship Street, was built in about 1040, allowing it to be dubbed the 'oldest building in Oxford', although the rest of the church is 13th-century. The view from the top, reached via displays on the history of the church and some large bells, is definitely worth the climb.

A right turn at the end of Cornmarket heads into the Broad, perhaps the archetypical University street. On the corner, the city's inevitable see-hear-smell tourist trap, the **Oxford Story** ⓘ *6 Broad St, T01865-790055, www.oxfordstory.co.uk, Jan-Jun, Sep-Dec 1000-1630, Jul, Aug 0930-1700, Nov-Mar Mon-Sat 1000-1630, Sun 1100-1630. £6.75, concessions £5*, whisks customers through the university's story in an hour as they sit at mobile desks. Opposite is **Balliol College**, not much to look at but one of the university's more radical powerhouses. Next door **Trinity** has a cottage for a porter's lodge instead of a grand gatehouse, but the college's beauties include a late-17th-century chapel with carved limewood and juniper screen by Grinling Gibbons and Wren's lovely Garden Quad, the first neoclassical building in the university.

Opposite Trinity, in the splendid late-17th-century building that once housed the Ashmolean, becoming the first public museum building in the land, the **Museum of the History of Science** ⓘ *Broad St, T01865-277280, www.mhs.ox.ac.uk, Tue-Sat 1200-1600, free*, displays a fascinating and old-fashioned collection of scientific landmarks: early chemical stills, chronometers, the original apparatus for manufacturing penicillin and even Einstein's blackboard.

Next door, the **Sheldonian Theatre** ⓘ *Broad St, T01865-277299, www.sheldon .ox.ac.uk, Apr-Oct daily 1000-1230, 1400-1630; Nov-Mar 1000-1230, 1400-1530 (subject to variations). £1.50, children £1* is the university's hall of ceremonies, also designed by Wren, who studied astronomy nearby at All Souls, its ceiling painted with the triumph of Truth, allied with Arts and Sciences, over Ignorance. An octagonal rooftop cupola above provides sheltered wraparound views of that famous skyline come wind or rain.

Its neighbour, the **Clarendon Building**, was constructed by Wren's pupil Hawksmoor, to the plans of Vanbrugh, architect of Blenheim Palace, as a printing house. Now it makes a grand front door for the **Bodleian Library**, ⓘ *Broad St, T01865-277000, www.bodley.ox.ac.uk, tours lasting 45 mins Apr-Oct Mon-Sat 1030, 1130, 1400, 1500, Nov-Mar Mon-Fri 1400, 1500, Sat 1030, 1130, 1400, 1500, £3.50 (no under-14s allowed). Divinity School and shop, usually an exhibition, donations requested, Apr-Dec Mon-Fri 1000-1600, Sat 1000-1230*, the university's chief academic resource and one of the greatest, certainly the oldest public libraries in the world. Its extraordinary Gothic Jacobean central courtyard has to be seen to be believed. Through the glass doors on the right, the 15th-century Divinity School is the oldest part of the building, with a magnificent vaulted stone ceiling. The library itself, one of the wonders of the western world, including its most ancient room, the mysterious and magical Duke Humphrey's, can be seen on guided tours that need to be booked in the summer.

The library makes up the north side of Radcliffe Square, effectively the centre of the university with 18th-century Scottish architect James Gibbs's majestic domed **Radcliffe Camera** plonked unceremoniously in the middle. Originally intended as a medical library, it now houses the English literature section of the Bodleian library, closed to the public. On the south side of the square, the **University Church of St Mary** ⓘ *0900-1700 (Jul, Aug 0900-1900, last admission 50 mins before closing), £1.60, children £0.80*, seals the university off from the High Street behind. The church itself did the job that the Sheldonian Theatre took over, and has a long history of ecclesiastical wrangling, but most visitors come for the climb up the tower to overlook the Radcliffe Camera, probably the best viewpoint (and the highest) in the centre of the city. Round on the High Street side, the barleysugar columns and broken pediment of the original church porch were possibly inspired by a Raphael cartoon in the collection of Charles I.

Nathaniel Hawthorne described the High Street as the "noblest old street in England", an impression confirmed now that it's virtually traffic-free apart from buses. It curves round to the south, with the postgraduate college **All Souls** (the 15th-century stained glass and oak roof of its chapel can be inspected on request) on the left, facing **University College**, not the oldest but certainly one of the most academic colleges. Next door, over Logic Lane, are the Victorian Examination

Schools, still in use, opposite **Queen's College** which occupies flamboyant Baroque buildings. A left turn beyond up narrow Queens Lane runs past the medieval **St Edmund Hall** into New College Lane, which is lined with famous gargoyles and twists around beneath the mock **'Bridge of Sighs'** back to the Broad. **New College** is most famous for its chapel, hall and cloisters, and its beautiful gardens dominated by the old city wall and a viewing mound supposedly marking the site of a plague pit.

Back on the High Street, continuing south, the **Botanic Gardens** ⓘ *T01865-286690, Apr-Sep daily 0900-1700, Oct-Mar daily 0900-1630 (last admission 1615), Apr-Aug £2, under-12s free, donation requested at other times*, are on the right beyond Rose Lane, sheltering behind high walls and ornate Jacobean stone gates. The oldest of their kind in Britain (dating from 1621), they evolved from an apothecary's herb garden into this well-labelled horticultural wonderland, a new bog garden, tropical glasshouses and charming riverside walks. Rose Lane leads into **Christ Church meadow**, Oxford's answer to Cambridge's 'backs'.

Over the road, next to its bridge and beneath its unmistakable Perpendicular tower, stands **Magdalen** (pronounced *Maudlin*) **College**, the most spread-out and gloriously sited of all the old colleges. The medieval chapel, hall and cloisters should be seen, but the highlight is the so-called New Building of 1733, an elegant neoclassical edifice standing in its very own deer park close by the confluence of the Rivers Thames (or 'Isis' as it's called in Oxford) and Cherwell (pronounced *Char-wool*).

University Parks and museums

The wide green expanse of the **University Parks** to the north are the destination of many a leisurely punt up from Magdalen Bridge or down from the Cherwell Boathouse. The parks also border on a couple of unmissable museums. The **University Museum of Natural History** ⓘ *Parks Rd, T01865-272950, www.oum.ox.ac.uk, daily 1200-1700, free,* is housed in a striking neo-Gothic fancy of a building. Inside, the Victorian stone carvers went wild with nature, turning just about every stone surface in sight into a vegetable shape. Beneath its great glass roof, supported on graceful columns of wrought iron replete with more fecundity, the museum features many wonders from the natural world, including an observation beehive, a skeletal T-Rex, and some dodos.

Just behind, the **Pitt Rivers Museum** ⓘ *Parks Rd, T01865-270927, www.prm.ox.ac.uk, Mon-Sat 1300-1630, Sun 1400-1630, free* displays the university's anthropological and ethnographic collections in a famously fusty Victorian way: slide open draws to discover African charms, Inuit ornaments, and peer through glass cases at shrunken heads and Native American Indian scalps. Children love it. Over the road from the museums, another Victorian marvel is the stripey red-brick and stone **Keble College**, where Holman Hunt's *Light of the World* in the chapel is the main attraction.

South of Carfax

Carfax Tower on the south side of the crossroads is all that remains of St Martin's Church, once the parish church of the city. The name Carfax derives from the Latin *quadri furcus* (four-forked), and indeed it was the church's position on such a busy crossroads that necessitated its demolition in 1896. The view south from **Carfax Tower** ⓘ *Apr-Oct 1000-1715, Nov-Mar 1000-1530, £1.20, concessions £0.60* is dominated by Wren's imposing gatehouse for Christ Church College, topped by Tom Tower.

Christ Church ⓘ *College T01865-286573, www.chch.ox.ac.uk, Mon-Sat 0930-1730, Sun 1200-1530, £4. Christ Church Cathedral Mon-Sat 0900-1645, Sun 1300-1630. Chapter House Apr-Sep Mon-Sat 0930-1730, Sun 1300-1730; Oct-Mar Mon-Sat 0930-1700, Sun 1300-1700. Hall Mon-Fri 0930-1145, daily 1400-1730. Picture Gallery Apr-Sep Mon-Sat 1030-1300, 1400-1730, Sun 1400-1730; Oct-Mar Mon-Sat 1030-1300, 1400-1630, Sun 1400-1630 (£2 additional fee)*, largest, most spectacular and most commercialized of the colleges, was founded by Cardinal Wolsey, (hence 'Cardinal College' in Hardy's *Jude the Obscure*) and re-founded by Henry VIII after his break with Rome who saved some money by making its chapel the city's cathedral. The college is the university's largest and in Tom Quad you know it. Used by Royalists in the Civil War as a cattlepen, during the 18th century it became famous for the antics of its equally bovine aristocratic undergraduates or 'junior members' as they're known at 'the house'. Tom Quad, the cathedral and the picture gallery are well worth a look round. The cathedral is the country's smallest, and

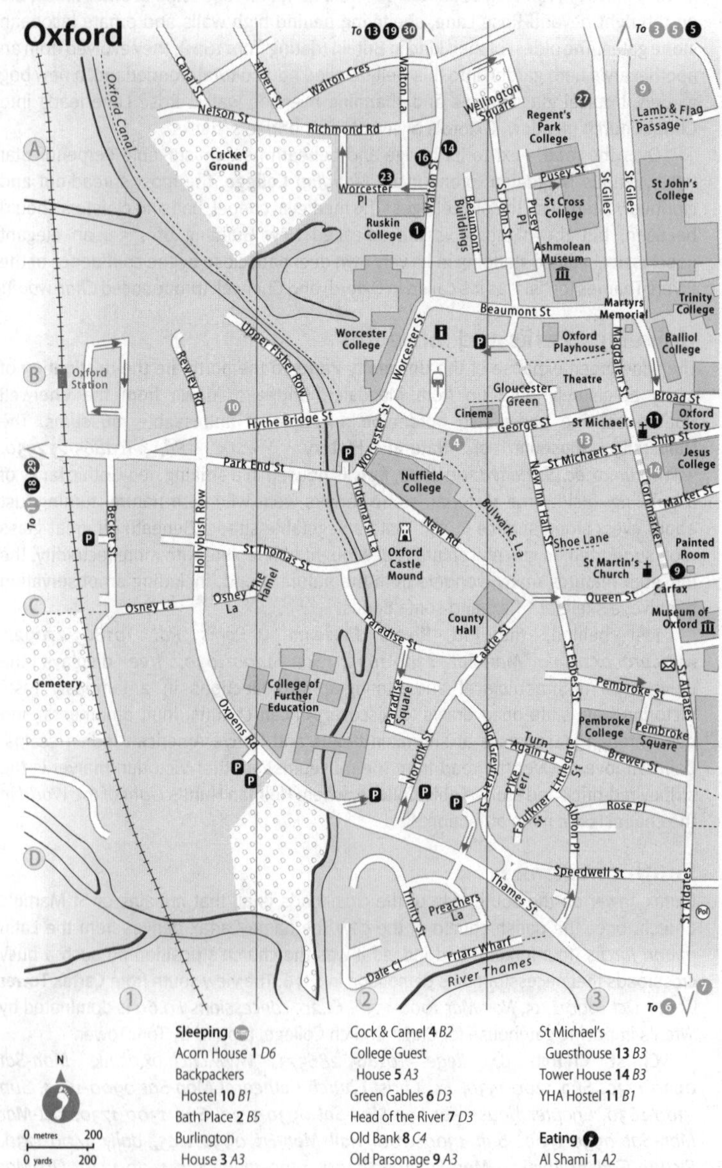

contains the recently restored shrine of the city's patron saint St Frideswide, as well as some beautiful pre-Reformation stained glass, including an unusual depiction of the murder of St Thomas à Becket which survived because the martyr's head was replaced with plain glass. His face is still missing. Look out too for the illustration in the south transept of Osney Abbey, long since vanished. The picture gallery, housed in a purpose-built modernist block sunk next to the library, is particularly famous for its collection of Old Master drawings. As well as 13 future prime ministers, the Elizabethan soldier, courtier and poet Sir Philip Sydney, Robert Burton, author of *The*

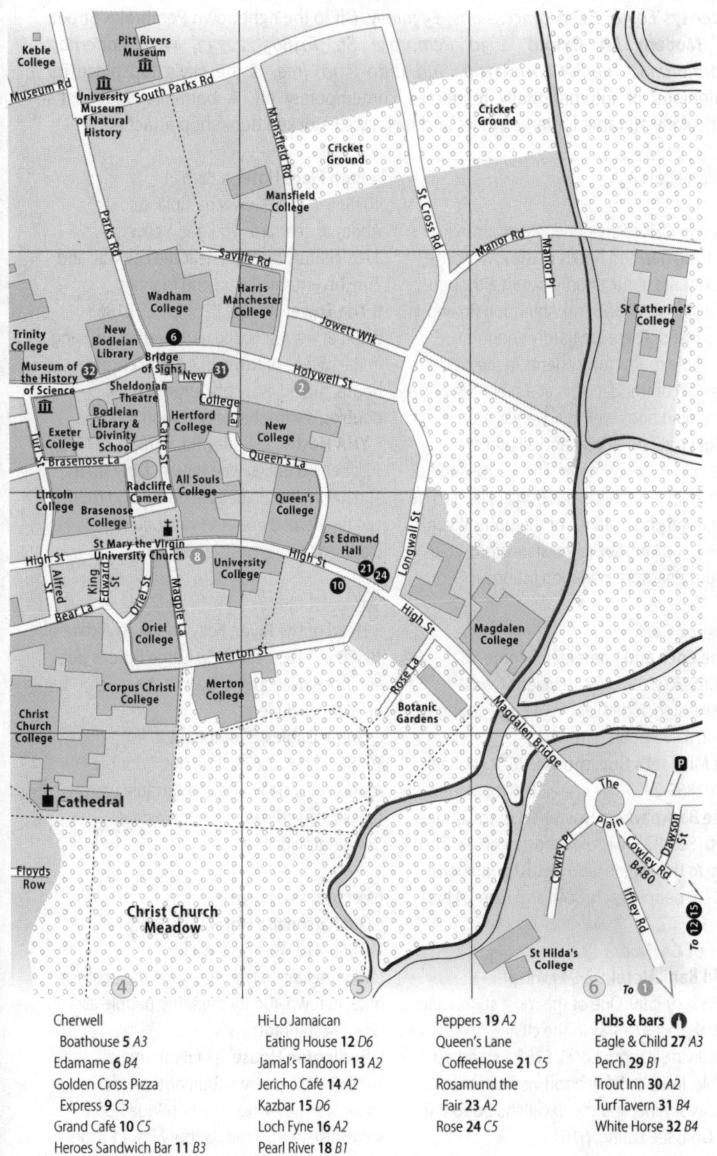

 Anatomy of Melancholy, the poet and playwright Ben Jonson, art historian John Ruskin and archeologist William Buckland, probably the college's most famous alumnus is Charles Lutteridge Dodgson, aka Lewis Carroll, the author of *Alice in Wonderland*. The garden gate behind the cathedral that supposedly inspired the mathematician's story has become something of a shrine.

Just up the hill from Christ Church on St Aldate's, next to the Town Hall, the **Museum of Oxford** gives the full low-down on the history of the city with the help of some well laid-out artefacts and some entertaining wall texts. ⓘ *Museum of Oxford, St Aldate's, 01865-252761 Tue-Fri 1000-1600, Sat 1000-1700, Sun 1200-1600. £2, under-17s £0.50, £1.50 concessions, £5 family.* Off to the right down Pembroke Street, the **Modern Art Oxford** ⓘ *30 Pembroke St, T01865-722733, www.modernartoxford.org.uk, Tue-Sat 1000-1700, Sun 1200-1500, free*, is the city's top place for exhibitions of internationally respected contemporary art. A barn-like space, it's particularly suitable for large works and has a well-stocked bookshop attached.

Sleeping

Hotels in Oxford are generally expensive for what you get, and hotels in the lower price brackets are almost non-existent although there are lots of B&Bs on Abingdon Rd and Banbury Rd. There are hardly enough affordable rooms for students in the city, so visitor accommodation is at a premium and you should book well in advance, for the budget options all year and all others especially in the summer. The TIC runs the usual booking service, but don't expect to be within walking distance of the sights if you leave it too late. See www.stayoxford. co.uk for further accommodation listings.

West of Carfax *p 155*

B **The Cock and Camel**, 24 George St, T01865-203705, F792130. Eight rooms (breakfast included) above a huge Young's pub in a lively part of town.

D **St Michael's Guesthouse**, 26 St Michael St, T01865-242101. Central, £50 for a double.

F **The Backpackers Hostel**, 9a Hythe Bridge St, T01865-721761, www.hostels.co.uk. Also close to the station, and has 10 bunkrooms for 4-10 people each. Both are open 24 hrs.

East of Carfax *p155*

A **Old Bank Hotel**, 92-94 High St, T01865-799599. One of the most stylish and central places to stay in the city, 42-individual room hotel, £155 a standard double, likely to have good views of the famous skyline, and the excellent **Quod Bar and Grill**, see Eating, p161.

A **Bath Place Hotel**, 4 Bath Pl, T01865-791812, www.bathplace.co.uk About as central as you get, a cosy 17th-century building near the city wall and **Turf Tavern**, family run and friendly.

B **The Tower House**, 15 Ship St, T01865-246828, www.scoot.co.uk/towerhouse. Bang in the middle of town, in a 17th-century house, tucked away off Cornmarket, 4 doubles, 3 with shared bathrooms.

F **YHA Hostel**, 2a Botley Rd, T01865-727275. Just behind the railway station, fairly smart and new with 180 beds in dorms and rooms, can be reached from the westbound platform through a little alleyway.

South of Carfax *p157*

B **Head of the River**, Folly Bridge, St Aldate's, T01865-721600, F726158. Large Fuller's pub and hotel overlooking river to the south. Breakfast included.

C **Green Gables**, 326 Abingdon Rd, T01865-725870, F723115. Has 7 double rooms, fairly clean and comfortable with breakfasts, some way out town near Donnington Bridge.

North of the centre

L **Old Parsonage Hotel**, 1 Banbury Rd, T01865-310210. Oscar Wilde's undergraduate digs, since 1989 the poshest hotel in town, run by the same people as **Gee's Restaurant**.

B **Burlington House**, 374 Banbury Rd, T01865-513513, www.burlington-house.co.uk. Non-smoking little boutique hotel some distance up the Banbury Rd, 11 rooms, with a very good breakfast.

C-D **College Guest House**, 103-105 Woodstock Rd, T01865-552579, r.pal@ukonline.co.uk, 10 mins walk from centre. South of the centre

C **Acorn House**, 260 Iffley Rd, T/F01865-247998. Four comfortable non-smoking double rooms, a 20-min walk into town. Both the above are similar in price and style to many of the B&Bs strung out along the main road into town from the south and east.

Oxford Camping International, on the ring-road south of Oxford, 1.5 miles from centre. T01865-244088. All year, 129 sites.

Eating

East of Carfax *p155*

££££ **Quod Bar and Grill**, in the Old Bank Hotel (see Sleeping), a stylish brasserie-type place with some abysmal artwork on the walls but a zinc-topped bar and outdoor drinking deck in summer (£8-£12 for some accomplished pasta, pizza and main courses like slow-roast lamb shank with pumpkin and mint pesto).

££ **Edamame**, 15 Holywell St, T01865-246916. One of the few excellent restaurants right in the middle of Oxford. Lunches Tue-Sun (£5-7), sushi on Thu night, a Japanese tapas bar at lunchtimes, very good value dinners (£12-14), no bookings taken, popular with students who queue up some nights.

££ **Golden Cross Pizza Express** in the old Golden Cross Inn off the Cornmarket, heavily restored in 1988. A fall-back option if the others are booked, often packed.

Cafés

Grand Café, 84 High St, T01865-204463. Claims to be the oldest coffee house in England, completely refurbished of course.

Queen's Lane Coffee House, 40 High St, T01865-240082. Considerably more authentic these days and very popular with students, for some sensibly priced espresso (£1), cakes and a legendary BLT. Further down on the left towards Magdalen Bridge, **The Rose**, 51 High St, T01865-244429, is a bright little café with an imaginative menu – buckwheat pancakes with smoked salmon, capers and crème fraiche – main courses about £6 and also meals on summer evenings.

Heroes Sandwich Bar and Takeaway, 8 Ship St, T01865-723459, has a good array of innovative fillings. Open until 2100 Mon-Fri.

North of the centre

There are several restaurants well worth making tracks for just north of the centre. Some within walking distance are grouped around Little Clarendon St and Walton St.

£££ **The Cherwell Boathouse**, Bardwell Rd, T01865-552746, is the place to have a fine 'modern European' feast (about £30 a head for lunch) in a clapperboard hut, then hire a punt perhaps, or a more expensive and leisurely supper on the waterside.

£££ **Loch Fyne**, Walton St, opposite Jericho Café, T01865-292510. Fish bistro chain doing some very fresh seafood from north of the border for about £30 a head.

££ **Al Shami**, 25 Walton Cres, T01865-310066, around £15 a head will buy you some superior Lebanese cuisine, with a particularly good array of mezes.

££ Branca Bar Kitchen, 111 Walton St, T01865-556111, is a newish Italian peasant favourite, with contemporary art on the walls, the kitchen upstairs on the balcony, above the snazzy low-lit dining room.

££ **Jamal's Tandoori**, 108 Walton St, T01865-310102, is an excellent and locally popular Indian where you can take in your own alcohol.

££ **Rosamund the Fair**, Cardigan St, T01865-553370, is a charming restaurant boat based in Castlemill Boatyard.

£ **Jericho Café** on Walton St, next door to Branca Bar Kitchen. Good for egg and chips.

£ **Peppers**, 84 Walton St, their pure beefburgers a hit with students, some say it's the best takeaway burger in Oxford. The bar is stacked with flyers for clubnights.

South of the centre

£££ **Hi-Lo Jamaican Eating House**, 70 Cowley Rd, T01865-725984. Caribbean institution, for fresh red snappers in a laid-back though occasionally riotous West Indian atmosphere.

££ **Kazbar**, 25-27 Cowley Rd, T01865-202920. Spanish and North African restaurant owned by the same people as the **Grand Café** on the High St. Fairly expensive (£10 main course), but worth the walk. Down by the station, on the other side of town, beyond the railway bridge,

£ **Pearl River**, Botley Rd, is a takeaway Chinese understandably popular with students and local backpackers.

Pubs, bars and clubs

The other option for food as well as booze is one of the pubs. The city, however, is surprisingly short on good nightclubs, many of which clubs come and go very quickly. Oxford doesn't lack excitement, but much of it is student-generated. The invaluable broadsheet posted in most college lodges and some bars and restaurants, daily during termtime, weekly at other times, is *Daily Information*, T01865-554444.

Pubs

Bookbinder, 17-18 Victor St, T01865-553549, is hidden away behind the canal. An eccentric collection of bizarre decor, trick toilet doors, parrots and very friendly locals.

Eagle and Child, St Giles, known as the Bird and Baby, is another in a similar mould, once the favourite haunt of JRR Tolkien and CS Lewis.

The Perch, well out of town in Binsey but a pleasant walk away across Port Meadow, with its tree-shaded riverside garden. Open lunch and evenings only.

The Trout Inn, Lower Wolvercote, T01865-302071, also out of town, beside an old bridge and weir, but worth the walk. Diners usually need to book.

Turf Tavern, beyond Bath Pl off Holywell Lane, does a truly staggering array of real ales (and an award-winning Scrumpy) under low ceilings, with reasonably priced pub grub served up all day (cash only), outside to heaving crowds beneath the old city wall of New College and inside in the snug low-ceilinged bars.

The White Horse, 52 Broad St, T01865-728318, is a donnish, cosy little place and another of TV detective Inspector Morse's favourite haunts.

Bars and clubs

Backroom at the Bully, 162 Cowley Rd, T01865-244516. Crams the punters in for more of the same at the **Bullingdon Arms**. In Jericho **Bar Risa**, 3-5 Hythe Bridge St, have popular cheesy dance nights.

Cellar Bar, Frewin Ct, T01865-244761, is studenty, for techno, drum'n'bass, and house nights Wed-Sat until 0200.

Freuds, 119 Walton St, T01865-311171, usually have live music, jazz and blues mainly, in their old Palladian church on Fri or Sat (charging after 2200).

Love Bar, 3 King Edward St, T01865-200011, is one of the latest offerings, complete with unisex loos and a glass ceiling between the ground floor and the dancefloor in the basement below. Open till 0200.

Park End Club, 37-39 Park End St, near the train station, T01865-250181, open Thu-Sat 2130-0200. With 3 floors of house, R'n'B and party sounds, this is the people's choice, the biggest and brashest in Oxford, smart casuals (no trainers), £7.50 after 1000.

PoNaNa Bar, 13-15 Magdalen St, T01865-249171. In the middle of town.

Thirst Bar, 7/8 Park End St, T01865-242044, until 0100, is very loud, lively and late, and free.

Zodiac, Cowley Rd, T01865-420042. A student hang-out and a popular stage for indie bands during the week. Indie club on Sat nights and cheesy listening on a Thu.

Entertainment

Cinemas

Odeon ABC, Magdalen St and George St, T0870-5050007, are the mainstream screens in the centre of town.

The Phoenix, Walton St, T01865-512526, is the local arthouse cinema.

The Ultimate Picture Palace, T01865-245288, the mainstream and independent rep.

Theatre and comedy venues

Apollo, George St, T0870-6073500. Large-scale touring productions, musicals, operas and pantomimes.

Burton Taylor Theatre, Gloucester St, T01865-798600. Makes up the triumverate of good Oxford fringe theatres.

Jongleurs, 3-5 Hythe Bridge St, T01865-722437, T0870-7870707, is a regular comedy club chain, runs Thu-Sat.

Old Fire Station, George St, T01865-297170, for short-run fringe theatre, student and small-scale touring productions.

Oxford Playhouse, Beaumont St, T01865-305305, www.oxfordplayhouse.com, is tThe main theatre for drama and middle-scale touring productions by the likes of the National Theatre and Almeida Theatre Company.

Pegasus Theatre, Magdalen Rd, T01865-722851. Another good fringe theatre.

Activities and tours

Boating

Punts can be hired at **Magdalen Bridge Punt Hire**, T01865-761586 (the busiest), or the **Cherwell Boathouse**, T01865-515978 (the most rural), or the **Head of the River**, Folly Bridge, T01865-721600 (the one on the Thames). Boat trips on the Thames are run by **Salter Brothers**, Folly Bridge, T01865-243421, www.salterbros.co.uk.

College Cruisers, Combe Rd Wharf, Combe Rd, T01865-554343, www.collegecruisers.com, hire out cruising boats on the river by the week.

Walking

Oxford Guild of Guides, T01865-250551, for walking tours of the city. The Oxford Canal walk runs all the way up to Coventry, on level ground, through picturesque countryside. The Thames Path can also be joined here.

Transport

Bus

The intercity and local bus terminus is at Gloucester Green, very close to the city centre. **National Express**, T08705-808080, for London Victoria and long distance. Also **City Link Oxford Express**, T01865-785400, **Oxford Tube**, T01865-772250 (24 hr London-Oxford Express, every 12 mins. Most local buses are run by **Stagecoach Oxford**, T01865-772250. **Jetlink** for airport buses T08705-757747, **Guide Friday**, T01865-790522, for open-top tours.

Car

Car hire: **Midlands Vehicle Rental Ltd**, Salle Suit, Wolvercote Mill, Wolvercote, T01865-311180. **Oxford Hatchback Hire**, Longcot, Shotover Kilns, Old Rd, Headington, T01865-763615. **Thrifty**, Osney Mead, T01865-250252. **Car parks**: Central car parks (many of which have hefty overnight charges) include Gloucester Green, Westgate, Worcester St, Abbey Pl and Oxpens Rd. Park and Ride is run by **Oxford Bus Co**, T01865-785400. Day return bus fare £1.50.

Cycling

Oxford is brilliant for bicyclists as it's the students' favourite mode of transport. You can hire a bike for a day/week/or month from **Bike Zone**, at the back of the Covered Market on Market St, T01865-728877 for £10 a day, £60 a week.

Taxi

These are relatively cheap in Oxford, and it's not usually a problem finding one on the street. Otherwise, try **City Taxis**, T01865-201201, **Eurocabs**, T01865-43043, or 24-hr minicabs from **001 Taxis**, T01865-24000.

Train

National Rail Enquiries, T08457-484950. The main railway station is in the west of the city, where the Botley Rd meets Hythe Bridge street, a 15-min walk into the centre. Trains are run by **Thames Trains**, T0118-9083678 (recorded train info T08457-300700) www.thamestrains.co.uk, and **Virgin Trains**, T0870-7891234 (recorded train info T08457-222333) www.virgin.com/trains and **First Great Western**, T01793-499400 (booking T0845-7000125) www.firstgreatwestern.co.uk. Trains from Oxford to **London Paddington**, **Birmingham** via Banbury, **Leamington Spa**, **Bicester**, **Buckingham** and **Milton Keynes**, and to **Hereford** and **Worcester** via the Cotswolds.

Directory

Internet Mices.com, 118 High St, T01865-726363, open daily 0900-1100 (Sun from 1000), £1 for 30 mins. **Internet Exchange**, 8-12 George St, T01865-241601. **Language schools** EF Language Travel Ltd, 3rd floor, Cherwell House, London Pl, T01865-200720. **Oxford Brookes University**, Gipsy La, Headington, T01865-483692. **Libraries** Central Library, Westgate, T01865-815509. See under Sights for other University libraries. **Medical facilities** John **Radcliffe Hospital**, Woodstock Rd, T01865-311188, is the nearest casualty department.

For an explanation of the sleeping and eating price codes used in this guide, see the inside front cover. Other relevant information is provided in the Essentials chapter, page 36.

North of Oxford

→Colour map 2

North of Oxford, the river Cherwell and the Oxford Canal twist alongside each other across wide open countryside, sneaking through a gap in the Cotswolds up to Banbury. The river may have been responsible for Oxford's strategic importance in the early Middle Ages, but it was the cutting of the canal in the late 18th century that opened the city up to the industrial heartland of the country in the Midlands. Now the Oxford Canal is one of the most popular pleasure boat routes, despite the proximity of the M40 that follows much of its route up to Banbury. Woodstock, a few miles west of the canal, is very famous, almost too famous for its own good, because of Blenheim Palace on its doorstep. Banbury may not be much of a destination any more, but Tooley's boatyard on the canal has become the centrepiece of a brand new museum, in the gleaming Castle Quay shopping centre. The town is surrounded by less well-known places of interest, like Edgehill, site of a bloody Civil War battle, and Broughton Castle. ▸▸ *For Sleeping, Eating and other listings, see pages166-166.*

Ins and outs

Getting there The main roads north out of Oxford are: the A44 dual carriageway via Woodstock to Chipping Norton and the Cotswolds beyond; the A34 dual carriageway up to Bicester and the M40, the fastest route to Banbury and Stratford; and also the smaller A4260 through Kidlington and Deddington to Banbury. Even the big roads can be very slow at rush hour. The X59 **Stagecoach**, **bus** service (T01788-535555) shuttles Mon-Sat hourly between Banbury, Bodicote, Adderbury, Deddington, Steeple Aston, Tackley, Kidlington and Oxford (1 hr 10 mins). Buses 25, 27, 28 and 29 run out to Bicester on a variety of different routes. From Banbury bus station, the 488 (also Stagecoach) runs Mon-Sat every 2 hrs to Chipping Norton via Hook Norton and Bloxham. Two stopping **trains** an hr, run by **Thames Trains**, head north of Oxford from London and Reading or Didcot Parkway to Banbury via Tackley, Heyford, and Kings Sutton, taking about 1/2 hr. They carry on to Stratford-upon-Avon, while faster trains run straight through to Birmingham via Banbury and Coventry. Trains to Bicester Town (23 mins) from Oxford and Reading also call at Islip. ▸▸ *For further details, see Transport, page 166.*

For the area of Oxfordshire south of Oxford and the Vale of the White Horse to the southwest, see the River Thames section on page 170.

Information **The Oxfordshire Museum** ⓘ *Woodstock, T01993-813276. Mar-Oct Mon-Sat 0930-1730, Sun 1300-1700; Nov-Feb Mon-Sat 1000-1630, Sun 1300-1700.* **Bicester TIC** ⓘ *Unit 6a, Bicester Village, Pingle Dr, T01869-369055. Daily 1000-1800.* **Cherwell Valley TIC** ⓘ *Junction 10 M40 Services, Ardley, Nr Bicester, T01869-345888. Apr-Oct daily 0930-1645; Nov-Mar 1000-1545.* **Banbury TIC** ⓘ *Castle Quay Shopping Centre, T01295-265464/259855. Mon-Fri 0930-1700, Sat 0930-1700, Sun 1030-1630.*

Blenheim Palace

ⓘ *T01993-811091, palace and park: mid-Mar to Oct daily 1030-1730 (last admission 1645), £11.50, under-17s £8, 5-15s £5, park only also Nov-Mar daily 0900-1645, £7.50 with car, £2.50 pedestrians.*

Woodstock, 6 miles northwest of the A40's junction with the A34 on the ring road north of Oxford, on the A44, is an attractive stone-built market town, sadly a little spoiled by the busy road and also by the hordes of visitors that come for its star attraction, Blenheim Palace. A gift to the Duke of Marlborough for winning the Battle of Blenheim in 1704, Sir John Vanbrugh's immense Baroque building certainly deserves to be called a palace, the only one in the country in fact that isn't inhabited by royalty. Winston Churchill was born here, but the building's chief glories now are outside rather than in. Much of the artwork in the sumptuous interior has been moved elsewhere over the years. Even so, the Long Gallery and Churchill exhibitions are worth a look, while the formal gardens and grounds have plenty to keep the masses amused: a miniature railway, butterfly house and boating lake for example. The park, hundreds of acres landscaped by Capability Brown around a large lake and a wonderful half-flooded bridge (also by Vanbrugh) means that there's plenty of room here to escape the crowds if you're prepared to walk a little.

Woodstock

Woodstock itself has long entertained royalty, most especially the Plantagenet kings. Sadly nothing remains of their medieval palace except a memorial after the Duchess of Marlborough had it removed for being an eyesore, despite protests from her husband. Apart from several top-quality eateries, the town boasts a predictable number of tourist-orientated boutiques. Worth seeking out, though, is the **Oxfordshire Museum** ⓘ *Fletcher's House, Park St, T01993-811456, Tue-Sat 1000-1700, Sun 1400-1700 (last admission 1645), £2.50, concessions £1, children £0.50, family £4.50*. This recently revamped county museum contains illuminating displays on local history, archaeology, agriculture and wildlife, right in the middle of the town.

Banbury and around

Banbury itself is not the most charismatic of towns, but makes a reasonable workaday base within easy reach of both Oxford and Stratford. The 'Historic Town Trail' takes in the Victorian cross marking the spot of the one immortalized in the nursery rhyme: "Ride a cock-horse to Banbury Cross/ To see a fine lady on a white horse,/ With rings on her fingers and bells on her toes,/ She shall have music wherever she goes." before taking in various merchants' houses, churches and pubs that have also suffered the ravages of time with their dignity scarcely intact. Part of the new Castle Quay shopping centre development, the new Banbury Museum incorporates the canalside, with interactive displays on local history, the Broughton Castle coin hoard and costumes from the 17th century as well as the fully refurbished **Tooley's Boatyard**, a rare survival from the first industrial revolution, before the coming of the railways.

Three miles west of Banbury off the B4035 for Shipston-on-Stour, **Broughton Castle** ⓘ *T01295-276070. Late May-mid Sep Wed, Sun (and Thu in Jul, Aug) 1400-1700, £4.50, under-15s £2, concessions £4. The park is open throughout the year* is a beautiful moated medieval manor house, the family home of Lord and Lady Saye and Sele, still more of a home than a visitor attraction. Three miles or so further on the same road, **Swalcliffe Great Barn** ⓘ *T01295-788278, Easter-Oct Sun 1400-1700, free*is one of the dozen best-preserved and restored medieval tithe barns in England, similar in date to Broughton Castle and built of the same ironstone. Constructed to house the produce of the farms owned by New College Oxford, the 15th-century great-beamed barn now keeps an antique agricultural implement collection dry.

Seven miles northwest of Banbury on the A422 to Stratford-upon-Avon, **Edgehill** was the site of the first major (and indecisive) battle of the Civil War. The steep hill can best be approached from Tysoe village along the ridge overlooking **Upton House** ⓘ *(NT), T01295-670266*, with its famous terraced garden descending from a Restoration house containing paintings by Stubbs, El Greco and Hogarth among others.

Seven miles northeast of Banbury off the B4525, the village of **Sulgrave** is notable for **Sulgrave Manor** ⓘ *T01295-760205, Apr-Oct Mon, Tue, Thu-Sun 1030- 1730, Nov, Dec and Mar weekends only 1030-1300, 1400-1630, guided tours £4, children £2, family £12.*, George Washington's ancestors' sweet little pad, a stone-built manor house erected in 1539 and restored meticulously to look as it might have done in the Elizabethan era, where patriotic Statesiders are made most welcome.

Sleeping

Woodstock *p165*

L **Feathers Hotel**, Market St, T01993-81299, F813158. The most expensive option, a very grand public house, but the food is worth every penny, booking essential, especially for the courtyard garden.

A **The Bear**, Park St, T0870-4008202, www.heritage-hotels.com. Another hotel in the same mould, more of a pub but very comfortable with all the facilities you'd expect for the price.

B **King's Arms Hotel**, 19 Market St, T01993-813636, F813737. An 18th-century townhouse that makes no concessions to its antiquity in its décor or with its stylish Mediterranean-style restaurant. Not quaint at all.

Banbury and around *p165*

A **Whately Hall**, Banbury Cross, Banbury T0870-4008104, F271736. A smart 17th-century building in the middle of the town, although some good B&Bs near the town (see below) may be a better bet.

C **Mill House**, Shenington, near Banbury, T01295-670642. Distinctly superior, a large south-facing house with a snooker table.

C **The Castle Inn**, Edgehill, near Banbury T01295-670255, F670521. Offers the unusual opportunity to stay in a folly tower on the top of Edgehill, above a reasonable pub with a big garden, on the site that Charles I mustered his army before the battle.

D **Wemyss Farm**, Sulgrave, Banbury, T01295-760323. A working farm with one double room.

Eating

Woodstock *p165*

££ **The King's Head**, Chapel Hill, Wootton, near Woodstock, T01993-811340, is a gourmet's haven serving up an imaginative menu either in the traditional pub or non-smoking restaurant, in a village that has consistently won the 'best-kept' award.

££ **The Swan Inn**, Lower St, Islip, near Kidlington, T01865-372590. Excellent home-made meals (except on Sun) near the spot where Edward the Confessor was born. The village station makes it a convenient walking base too.

Banbury and around *p165*

££ **The Bell**, High St, Adderbury, 3 miles south of Banbury off the A4260, T01295-810338, is a charming folksy pub in a little village, doing fresh food in the restaurant and a good range of bar snacks.

££ **Stag's Head**, Swalcliffe, does food with a high reputation, handy for visitors to the Swalcliffe Great Barn.

££ **The Star Inn**, Manor Rd, Sulgrave, T01295-760389. Anyone visiting Sulgrave Manor can find a very good spot for lunch here, in a pretty garden or inside in the 17th-century interior.

££ **Thai Orchid**, 56 North Bar St, Banbury, T01295-270833. Highly rated for its authentic menu.

Entertainment

Banbury and around *p165*

The Mill Theatre, Spiceball Park, Banbury, T01295-279002. Hosts small-scale fringe touring productions, some of a very high standard.

Transport

Banbury and around *p165*

Car hire Budget, Unit 6, Thorpe Way Industrial Estate, Banbury, T01280-704433.

Taxi Cherwell Cars, 53 George St, Banbury, T01295-255555. **Castle Cars**, Banbury Railway Station, T01295-270011.

For an explanation of the sleeping and eating price codes used in this guide, see the inside front cover. Other relevant information is provided in the Essentials chapter, page 36.

West of Oxford

→See colour map 2, see also Thames Valley section, p170

Although the Thames actually enters Oxford from the north, its broad valley dominates the area west of the city. The largest town, the old market centre of Witney, in fact straddles the River Windrush, one of the most charming of the Thames' tributaries. Descending from the Cotswold hills, it passes through the beautiful honey-coloured town of Burford, famously the 'gateway to the Cotswolds'. Then it winds through peaceful villages like Asthall, passing the romantic ruined manor house at Minster Lovell. Further up the Thames, the 16th-century manor house at Kelmscott was the delightful summer retreat of William Morris in late Victorian times. ▸▸ *For Sleeping, Eating and other listings, see page 169.*

Ins and outs

Getting there The A40 heads west from north Oxford via Witney (10 miles) and Burford (17 miles) to Cheltenham and Gloucester. Major roads run north-south at both Witney and Burford. Stagecoach, T01865-772250, run the hourly X3 bus between Oxford and Milton-under-Wychwood via Eynsham, Witney, Minster Lovell, and Burford, also the 11 and 100 between Oxford and Witney. From Witney the No 7 bus runs to Lechlade and Swindon, the No 45 to Stanton Harcourt and South Leigh, the 102 and 103 to Minster Lovell, the 19 to Bampton, and the 42 to Woodstock.

Information **Witney TIC** ⓘ *51a Market Sq, T01993-775802, Easter-Oct Mon-Sat 0930-1730; Nov-Easter 1000-1630.* **Burford TIC** ⓘ *The Brewery, Sheep St, T01993-823558. Easter-Oct Mon-Sat 0930-1730, Sun 1000-1500; Nov-Easter Mon-Sat 1000-1630.*

Witney and around

Bypassed by the A40, the old market town of Witney has an attractive centre and splendid church but was until recently the fastest growing town in England, with predictably hit-and-miss results. Just to its north, off the A4095, the **Coggos Manor Farm Museum** ⓘ *Church La, Witney, T01993-772602. Mid-Mar to Oct Tue-Fri 1030-1730, weekends 1200-1730, £4.20, £2.10 children, £2.65 concessions* is worth the short detour. George Orwell must have been thinking of a place like this when he wrote *Animal Farm*. In fact, it's a charming reconstruction of a working farm from around 1900, with heavy workhorses, sheep, chickens, and thankfully only one pig, so there may be hope for it yet.

Three miles west of Witney, **Minster Lovell Hall and Dovecote** ⓘ *(EH) open any reasonable time, free.* is a picturesque ruined 15th-century manor house in a pleasant spot on the banks of the river Windrush, alongside an ancient dovecote.

Six miles west of Tadpole, **Kelmscott Manor** ⓘ *T01367-252486, Apr-Sep Wed 1100-1300, 1400-1700; third Sat in Apr, May, Jun and Sep 1400-1700; first and third Sat in Jul, Aug 1400-1700 (last admissions 30 mins before closing), £7, concessions £3.50* is a very fine 16th-century house hidden behind high walls in a quiet out-of-the-way village, where the great Socialist William Morris summered from 1871 until his death in 1896. He shared it with the pre-Raphaelite poet Gabriel Dante Rossetti and the place has been restored and preserved by the Society of Antiquaries as a home for a considerable collection of Morris's works – furniture, textiles and ceramics – in his highly influential, flowery (and usually poorly imitated) neo-medievalist style. Overall, a visit here confirms what Morris believed – that a great opportunity was lost during the industrial revolution to beautify the world with mass-production rather than cheapen it.

Alive and kicking?

Should you arrive in an English village to find the locals waving hankies and clashing sticks to the accompaniment of a squeezebox, do not be unduly alarmed. What you are witnessing is Morris Dancing. Once the quintessence of English heritage, Morris Dancing may, however, be a dying tradition. In a recent poll only 24% of young Britons saw it as a key part of the country's heritage and it ranked just below the Rolling Stones in terms of popularity. Indeed, today's Morris Dancers are seen as practically a secret society, confined to the margins of modern life. A sad state of affairs for a 200-year-old tradition that began in the village of Bampton, in Oxfordshire. Some people, though, argue that, far from being on its last bell-clad legs, Morris Dancing is in rude health. There are now more than 1,000 teams across the UK, North America and the Antipodes. Champion Morris dancer, Simon Pipe insists that bell ringing and stick waving still has a place in modern society and states: "There's something basically all right about any country in which men, women and children can leap about in public with bells and other improbable adornments attached to their bodies."

Lechlade and around

Three miles northwest of Buscot, Lechlade on Thames (actually in a little pocket of Gloucestershire) is the highest navigable point on the river, and consequently a Mecca for pleasure cruisers. Best seen from the old St John's Bridge, next to yet another Trout Inn (see below), the spire of **St Lawrence's church** rises above the trees while the river snakes lazily across the meadows. The mainly 16th-century church inspired Shelley's *Stanzas in a Summer Evening Churchyard* on his boating trip up to Lechlade in 1815. The town itself comes as a bit of a disappointment, with its slightly desperate antique shops and poky little cafés, but nonetheless has a welcoming and friendly attitude, well-accustomed as it is to a stream of strangers messing about on the river.

Three miles further up the road to Burford, the **Cotswold Wildlife Park** ⓘ *T01993-823006, www.cotswoldwildlifepark.co.uk, Mar-Sep daily 1000-1700, Oct daily 1000-1600, Nov-Feb daily 1000-1530, £6.50, concessions and children £4* is set in acres of fine parkland around a Victorian manor house, a hugely popular local attraction where zebras and rhinos can be seen roaming their generous enclosures from the picnic lawns, while a miniature steam railway chugs around in the summer months. As well as caring for some endangered red pandas, the zoo also takes its gardening seriously, with a tropical house, 'hot bed', and walled garden.

Burford

Since its decline as an important medieval wool town, Burford has long billed itself as the 'Gateway to the Cotswolds' and strikingly lovely and stone-built it is too. That's no secret though, which means that during the summer months the gate pressure can be intense: the long broad High Street, sloping down to the old bridge over the little river Windrush, becomes impossibly busy. Even so, the crush in the antique shops, pubs, and tearooms can easily be avoided on the smaller side streets. One such, at the lower end of the High Street, leads to Burford's **church of St John**, the most outstanding parish church in the county. Its Norman tower has survived, later topped with a spire, easy to miss from the town if not from the river, but the medieval warren of arches, chapels, nooks and crannies inside should definitely not be missed. Apart from some intriguing monuments, including one to Heneary VIII's hairdresser, featuring the first known depiction of a Red Indian in England, and a possible likeness of a fertility goddess from the second century, the font bears the scratched name of one of the mutinous Levellers imprisoned here by Oliver Cromwell for three nights in 1649.

The town itself has retained, virtually unaltered, its medieval street plan. Originally the main road ran east-west past the 16th-century market hall, called the **Tolsey** (now housing a local history museum), and around this crossroads with the High Street there are still several houses that bear traces of the Middle Ages.

Sleeping

Witney and around *p167*

C **The Ferryman Inn**, Bablock Hythe, Northmoor, a couple of miles from Stanton Harcourt, has a foot ferry across the river, T01865-880028. A famous waterside freehouse with pub grub, right on the water.

C **The Old Vicarage**, Minster Lovell, T01993-775630. A beautiful old house beside the Windrush, £350 per week in the summer for the self-catering garden house, sleeping 6.

C **Rectory Farm**, Northmoor, near Witney, T01865-300207 (no single Sat in summer). A fine early 17th-century stone farmhouse that once belonged to St John's College, Oxford.

Burford *p168*

L **Bay Tree Hotel** Sheep St, T01993-822791, www.cotswold-inns-hotels.co.uk. Wysteria-clad on the outside, chintzy within, country townhouse hotel, very comfortable with a reputable restaurant.

L **Burford House Hotel**, 99 High St, T01993-823151, www.burfordhouse.co.uk. Non-smoking family-run hotel with plenty of friendly touches and pleasant atmosphere.

A **The Lamb**, Sheep St, T01993-823155. Log fires, flagstone floors and formerly the home of Sir Lawrence Tanfield, Lord Chief Baron of the Exchequer in the reign of Queen Elizabeth I around 1580. Real ales and a fairly expensive restaurant doing top-notch food (about £30 a head), as well as well-filled sandwiches at the bar. Most famously 'good pub' in Burford.

B **Jonathan at the Angel**, Witney St,, T01993-822714, is a very highly rated non-smoking old pub-restaurant (about £12 a main course) with 3 attractive double rooms. Recommended.

C **The Fox Inn**, Great Barrington, near Burford, T01451-844385. Pulls a very good pint in a charming riverside pub with a garden, and also manages some very decent English country cooking 7 days a week. Three rooms with bathroom en suite. Recommended.

Eating

Witney and around *p167*

££ **The Royal Oak**, Ramsden, near Witney, T01993-868213, is a freehouse that does good food, and outside tables opposite the war memorial in a village on Akeman St, the Roman road that connected Bicester and Cirencester.

Lechlade and around *p168*

££ **The Trout Inn**, St John's Bridge, Lechlade, T01367-252313, www.the-trout-inn.sagenet.co.uk, does good food, is a busy waterside oasis and also the base for Cotswold Boat Hire (see below).

Burford *p168*

££ **Mermaid Inn**, High St, Burford, T01993-822193, is in a very old building, with decent enough pub grub.

£ **Priory Tearoom**, High St, Burford, does good breakfasts.

Pubs, bars and clubs

The Bell, Ducklington, near Witney, T01993-702514, is a thatched pub that has extraordinary flowers outside, live folk music and real ales inside.

White Hart Inn, Wytham, near Oxford, T01865-244372, is near the River Thames, nestling in the shade of the A34. Heated barn for winter, on a quiet backroad.

Activities and tours

Boating

Cotswold Boat Hire, T01793-700241, same-day enquiries T07946-655730 (mob). Six-seater rowing boats £6 per hr, £30 full day. Electric boats £12 per hr, £30 for 3 hrs, £55 full day, all from St John's Bridge on the river next to *The Trout Inn*. Rowing boats can also be hired in Lechlade itself, at **Riverside (Lechlade) Ltd**, Park End Wharf, Lechlade, T01367-252229, www.riverside-lechlade.co.uk

Vale of the White Horse to Goring Gap

→Colour map 2

Below Oxford, about 70 miles from its source in Gloucestershire, the country's most venerable waterway winds through the pages of history. Above Dorchester the river is also known as the Isis, but here it's joined by the river Thame and becomes the Thames proper, at a place that has been continuously settled for more than 3000 years. The ancient riverside town of Abingdon is the adminstrative centre of the Vale of the White Horse. It claims to be the oldest town in the land and though it's lost much of its antique appeal over the last 30 years, the town hall, bridge and old churches still make it memorable. It's not surprising that most visitors prefer to escape the traffic chaos and head west into the Vale instead. This broad watery valley, named after the old hill figure at Uffington, is overlooked by the Ridgeway, the prehistoric east-west line of communication across the country. The views afforded from here over Oxfordshire and the upper Thames Valley are some of the finest in the south. As the river flows on to Dorchester, an old abbey and substantial evidence of pre-Roman settlement testify to the area's Celtic and early Christian significance. ▸▸ *For Sleeping, Eating and other listings, see pages 173-174.*

Ins and outs

Getting there M40 Junction 7 to Abingdon, Junction 6 to Wallingford. Vale of White Horse most easily reached via Jct 13 on the M4, following A34 dual carriageway up to Didcot. Didcot Parkway is on the main railline from London and Reading to Oxford, Bicester, and Birmingham. **Trains** to Bicester and/or Oxford also usually stop at Goring & Streatley, Cholsey, Radley and Appleford. Connecting **bus** services X3 from Oxford and 32 from Didcot Parkway run to Abingdon. Wantage can also be reached by bus from Didcot Parkway.

Getting around Although Abingdon and several other Thames-side towns can be reached by train, really the only way to explore the Vale of the White Horse is by car or bike or on foot along the Ridgeway. One useful bus is the 47a, which links up the villages strung along the line of springs in the valley, and the **Ridgeway Explorer Bus** which runs Apr-Oct on Sun only T01865-810224. The local bus networks are run by **Stagecoach**, T01865-77250, **Oxford Bus Company**, T01865-785400, **Thames Travel**, T01491-837988 and **Whites** (Oxfordshire County Council transport line T01865-815683).

Information Abingdon TIC ⓘ *25 Bridge St, T01235-522711, Apr-Oct Mon-Sat 1000-1700, Sun 1330-1615, Nov-Mar Mon-Fri 1000-1600, Sat 0930-1430*. Helpful with details of local transport and accommodation. **Wallingford TIC** ⓘ *Town Hall, Market Pl, T01491-826972, Mon-Sat 0930-1700*. **Faringdon TIC** ⓘ *7a Market Pl, T01367-242191, Apr-Oct Mon-Fri 1000-1700, Sat 1000-1300, Nov-Mar Mon-Sat 1000-1300*. **Wantage TIC** ⓘ *Vale and Downland Museum, 19 Church St, Wantage, T01235-760176.*

Abingdon and around

Abingdon, once Berkshire's county town, was subsumed into Oxfordshire in 1974 and since then has almost trebled in size, now ringed with high-tech industrial complexes that cause traffic chaos every rush hour. It's also famously the 'oldest inhabited town in England'. Best seen from the river or from the bridge (medieval but reconstructed in 1927) little now remains of the **Benedictine abbey** ⓘ *Apr-Oct Tue-Sun 1400-1600, £0.60* founded in the seventh century that once dominated the site. Its scale can still be appreciated though, near the 15th-century Gateway and Long Gallery. A little upstream from here, **Abingdon Lock** and **Andersley Island** are celebrated for their population of greedy mute swans.

Two sights in the town are worth a look though. Hard to miss is the 'Wrenaissance' magnificence of the **County Hall**, one of the grandest in the country, now the Town Hall and home to the **Abingdon Museum** ⓘ *T01235-523703, Apr-Oct 1100-1700, Nov-Mar 1100-1600, free. Roof viewpoint open Apr-Sep Sat only, £1, children £0.50.*. The museum tells the history of the town 'from the Stone Age to the MG' (the cars were built here for 50 years and regular vintage rallies occur in the summer, for details T01235-555552), although the highlight has to be the view from the roof. East St Helen Street heads down to the river from here, where no 26A is a late-15th-century **merchant's hall house** ⓘ *T01865-242918, open by appointment*, complete with remarkable wall paintings, an oak ceiling and traceried windows.

Pleasant riverside walks downeariver from Abingdon along the **Thames Path** reach **Sutton Courtenay** (2 miles), an attractive village with a late 12th-century manor house, church and the grave of one Eric Arthur Blair – better known as George Orwell – in the churchyard. A mile further south of Sutton Courtenay, although a little too close to the A34 for comfort, **Milton Manor** ⓘ *T01235-862321, daily for first 2 weeks of May and Aug 1400-1700, also bank holiday weekends, tours at 1400, 1500, 1600, £4, children £2, grounds only £2.50, children £1* is a pretty little brick-built doll's house supposed to have been designed by Inigo Jones in the 17th century, still well lived in. Pony rides are given from the stables in the summer.

Vale of the White Horse

Named after the 3000-year-old chalk hill figure above Uffington, the watery Vale of the White Horse now has Abingdon as its administrative headquarters. The broad flat floodplains of the River Thames and its little brother the Ock spread west from the town, overlooked by soft undulating downlands topped by the **Ridgeway**, a national trail and prehistoric east-west line of communication. Small brick-built villages like Woolstone and Kingston Lisle are strung along the spring-line of the downs, delightful places to drop down into for refreshment after tramping the grassy heights. The Ridgeway itself runs for 85 miles from Avebury in Wiltshire to Tring in the Chilterns, but this is its most historic (and most popular) stretch.

The birthplace of Alfred the Great in 848, **Wantage** is the old market town at the heart of the region. Narrowly bypassed in the 19th century by the Great Western Railway between Didcot and Swindon, it missed out on the Industrial Revolution and became severely depressed, earning the nickname 'Black Wantage'. Colonel Loyd Lindsay, the inheritor of a banking fortune, came to its rescue, reviving the ironworks and linking the town to the railway with the first steam tram (now defunct) in the country. The **Vale and Downland Museum** ⓘ *Church St, Wantage, T01235-771447, www.wantage.com/museum, Mon-Sat 1000-1630, Sun 1430-1700, £1.50, children £1, family £4*, tells the full story, an accomplished local history museum, with a few interactive displays, including a push-button illuminated landscape of the Vale, a Victorian kitchen, a video narrated by David Attenborough, as well as contemporary PR from local concerns like *Crown Technologies*, the designers of the Coke bottles, and Damon Hill's Williams team Formula-one racing car.

Most visitors head west of Wantage though, along the B4507, to explore the villages nestling beneath the hills. **Uffington** is the largest, its church of St Mary almost perfect early English, dating from the 13th century, although its spire was lost in a storm and the octagonal tower raised a storey in the 18th century. The porch is flanked by modern sculptures of King Alfred and St George, and inside there's a memorial to Thomas Hughes, author of *Tom Brown's Schooldays*. The 20th century's most popular poet laureate, John Betjeman, was a church warden here. Nearby, is **Tom Brown's School Museum** ⓘ *Broad St, T01367- 820259,* www.uffington.net/museum, Easter-Oct weekends, bank holidays 1400- 1700 or by appointment, £0.60, children £0.30 with information on recent archaeological discoveries on White Horse hill, as well as mementoes of both Thomas Hughes and John Betjeman.

The **White Horse** itself is best seen from the turning off the B4507 to Woolstone, another achingly pretty little village, with a good pub/restaurant. Up on the downs is a favourite place for kite-flying, hang-gliding and all kinds of other outdoor activities along the Ridgeway. The delicate curves of the White Horse hill figure itself gallop along the top of the ridge above a natural amphitheatre, a dry valley called **The Manger**. The sweeping white pattern is not in fact a cut-turf figure but metre-deep trenches filled in with chalk, one of the oldest hill figures in Britain, possibly created as some sort of tribal logo about 3,000 years ago. Legend has it that on at least one night a year the ghostly white horse descends the Giants Steps into the Manger for a feed, always back in place on the hill by dawn. To one side, the odd little knoll known as **Dragon Hill** may or may not be man-made and has caused as much speculation about its origin and purpose as the horse. Was this where St George slew the dragon, hence the bald chalk patch on top where its poisonous blood was spilled? Or was it raised up as a sacrificial site? Probably neither, but the almost abstract design of the horse looks good from the summit. Above the horse, an Iron-Age hill fort, **Uffington Castle**, commands wide-reaching views over the Upper Thames Valley towards the Cotswolds in the distance. A mile to the west, **Wayland's Smithy** is one of the finest and most mysterious neolithic chambered long barrows in the country, much older than the horse, dating from around 2500BC. Archaeologists think it may once have been covered in white chalk as one of a series of shining monuments along the ridge marking a processional route for neolithic funerals. Set in a grove of peaceful trees, it too has spawned many legends, including that of the mythical blacksmith Wayland's apprentice, Flibbertygibbet. He dawdled on an errand, got hit on the heel by a boulder thrown by his impatient boss, and can apparently still be heard nearby at Snivelling Corner.

Dorchester

Back beside the Thames below Abingdon, Dorchester was once the vital fortified meeting point of three tribes of ancient Britons at the confluence of the rivers Thames and Thame. Then it became a small Roman town on the river. Now it's more of a large and rather dignified village. As well as the extensive Iron Age and Roman earthworks nearby, the main attraction is **Dorchester Abbey** ⓘ *T01865-340703, May-Sep (also Easter, weekends in Apr, early Oct) Tue-Sat 1100-1700, Sun and bank holidays 1400-1700, free*, originally founded as a cathedral in the seventh century by St Birinus. With another Decorated Jesse window, similar to the one in Abingdon, and the medieval tomb of Sir John Holcombe – drawing his sword in an unusually dramatic manner – and some of the oldest stained glass in England, the Abbey was eventually superseded by Winchester in the 15th century. A museum tells the story in the Old Monastery Guest House, a 14th-century building itself.

In Long Wittenham, the **Pendon Museum of Landscape and Transport in Miniature** ⓘ *T01865-407365, www.pendonmuseum.com, all year weekends 1400-1700, also on Wed in Jul, Aug, £4, children £3.50, concessions £3* reproduces the Vale of the White Horse in the 1930s in miniature detail (cottages 4 ins high) on a 70-ft model landscape, next door to the Madder Valley Model Railway. Engineered in the 1930s, both are craftworks of astonishing patience and detail.

Sleeping

Abingdon and around p170

A **The Upper Reaches Hotel**, Thames St, Abingdon, T0870-4008101, www.heritage-hotels.co.uk. In a converted mill, with smart chintzy rooms but you're paying for the 'heritage' location right on the river.

C **22 East St Helen St B&B**, Abingdon, T01235-550979, F533278. Bang in the middle of town, in an old house full of character close to the river, with an eminently capable family atmosphere, 1 double room, 1 single and 1 twin.

D **Helensbourne**, 34 East St Helen St, Abingdon, T01235-530200, F201573. B&B also right in the centre of town, and competitively priced, 1 double and 1 family room.

D **Hollies Guest House**, 8 New Rd, Radley, near Abingdon, T01235-529552, F529552. Very friendly, well connected by bus to Abingdon 31/2 miles away, also on the mainline to Oxford, 2 double rooms.

Vale of the White Horse p171

C **Old Bull's Head**, in Ardington, a pub with rooms in the old estate village.

C **White Horse Inn**, Woolstone, T01367-820726 does superior food and cosy accommodation.

C **The Craven**, Fernham Rd, Uffington, T01367-820449, has a family atmosphere in a thatched cottage freshly done up.

C **Lamb Inn**, Buckland, T01367-870484, is a pub grub restaurant with rooms above (about £50 a night) in a secluded estate village.

F **The YHA Ridgeway Centre**, Court Hill, Wantage, T01235- 760253, F768865. Converted barns close to the long distance path, above Letcombe Regis Ridgeway Centre, one of a series of barns rescued by Dick Squires, founder of the Vale and Downland Museum. Open Dec-Mar Fri, Sats only, Sep-Nov not Sun, Mon.

Camping Eco-friendly camping (without facilities, leave the pitch as you found it) is acceptable in many places along the Ridgeway.

Dorchester and Wallingford p172

L **Beetle and Wedge Hotel**, Ferry La, Moulsford, T01491-651381, F651376. Small riverside lawns, 2 expensive restaurants with good reputations, on the stretch of river where the *Wind in the Willows* was set, where the old ferry crossed to South Stoke.

A **Crazy Bear Hotel**, Bear La, Stadhampton (north of Dorchester), T01865-890714, www.crazybearhotel.co.uk. Highly idiosyncratic place with wacky furnishings.

B **The White Hart Hotel**, Dorchester, T01865-430074, www.oxford-restaurants-hotels.co.uk standard doubles £80.

B **The George Hotel**, Dorchester, T01865-340404, F341620. Marginally more expensive, and more spruce, less character but pleasant enough.

C **Fords Farm**, Ewelme, Wallingford, T01491-839272. Sheep farm B&B in a pretty little village right opposite the Chaucer church, with its heraldic shields.

D **North Farm B&B**, Shillingford Hill, Wallingford, T01865-858406. A welcoming working farm. The bugdet option is

F **YHA Streatley-on-Thames**, Reading Rd, Streatley, T01491-872278, F873056. Not open all year. Call for opening times.

Eating

Abingdon and around p170

£££ **Le Manoir aux Quat'Saisons**, Church Rd, Great Milton, T01844-278881, is a 2-Michelin starred restaurant with very plush (and equally expensive) rooms above. Book many months ahead.

££ **The Plough Inn**, Abingdon Rd, Clifton Hampden, T01865-407811, is an old pub with a good reputation for its food, entirely non-smoking and also with rooms (£82.50 a double), within walking distance of Abingdon along the river.

££ **Old Anchor**, St Helen's Wharf, where the river Ock meet the Thames, is a characterful old pub also doing decent food.

££ **White Hart**, a little further afield in Fyfield, T01865-390585, does excellent real ales, a medieval pub with reasonably priced modern pub grub.

Vale of the White Horse p171

££ **Coach and Horses**, Uffington, is an unprepossessing place that is considerably more friendly than it looks from the outside and sells excellent ales and is a good place to view the Horse from.

Dorchester and Wallingford *p172*

£££ **The Goose**, Britwell Salome, T01491-612304, is a successful gastropub established by Prince Charles's former chef, dinner about £26 for 3 modern British courses.

££ **The Bell Inn**, Aldworth, T01635-578272, a virtually unspoilt 14th-century inn, with geese in the back yard, patriotic family-owned and doing very popular lunches and ales. Worth a special trip.

££ **Red Lion**, Chalgrove, T01865-890625, is an attractive pub with highly-rated food.

££ **Leatherne Bottle**, Goring-on-Thames, T01491-872667, does rooms, and an exotic, popular menu in cramped surroundings. It's often very busy, so booking is advisable.

££ **Queen's Head**, Crowmarsh, near Wallingford, an offbeat hybrid of a Thai Orchid restaurant in an old Fuller's pub.

£ **John Barleycorn** pub in Goring serves one of the best pints of Brakspear's Special you'll get outside Henley – worth sampling over a game of bar billiards.

Activities and tours

Abingdon and around *p170*

Boating Boat day-hire in Abingdon from **Redline**, Wilsham Rd, T01235-521562, or from the **Abingdon Boat Centre**, The Bridge, Nag's Head Island, T01235-521125. For longer trips, contact the **Thames Hire Cruiser Association**, Secretary Mr P Allen, T0208-9791997. River trips to Oxford from Nags Head island in Abingdon run from May-Sep, by **Salter Bros**, T01865-243421.

Dorchester and Wallingford *p172*

Boating Benson Waterfront, near Wallingford, T01491-838304. **Upper Thames Passenger Boat Association**, T0870-2415016, for wine and dine, a disco dance, commentaries and steamboats on the river.

Reading to Maidenhead

→Colour map 2

Reading, the largest town on the river between London and Oxford, is hardly a beauty. But then that's not the point. Berkshire's administrative headquarters, the transport hub of the south and one of its most thriving business centres, it pulls in the punters with its special events and late night clublife. Henley-on-Thames, on the other hand, just downstream, seems to be stuck in a dream of England past, one that becomes a strange spectacle every July at its historic regatta. Marlow is less pompous and has long been culturally more interesting, while Cookham is a riverside spot popular with weekending Londoners. *» For Sleeping, Eating and other listings, see pages 177-178.*

Ins and outs

Getting there Reading is a major national transport interchange, on the mainline to Bristol and the west country down to Penzance (and also Birmingham and the north) from London Paddington, and hence very well-served by rail: frequent medium-fast Thames Trains (stopping at Twyford and Maidenhead for Henley and Marlow) take about 45 mins; express trains, run by First Great Western, about 25 mins. From London Waterloo, South West Trains run a stopping service to Reading via the western suburbs of London, with interconnecting services to Windsor, taking about 1hr 20mins. For Henley, one stopping train an hr (more at peak times) runs on the branch line from Twyford (10 mins), via Wargrave and Shiplake. Reading is on the M4, 30 mins from central London. Henley is a few mins closer, most easily reached using the A404(M) Maidenhead bypass at Junction 8/9 on the M4. National Express, T08705-808080, run coaches to Reading-Calcot, Savacentre, M4 Junction 12 from London Victoria, once an hr between 0745 and 2330, taking 1hr 15 mins (£8 one-way).

Getting around Reading's small town centre is relatively pedestrian-friendly and there are reliable bus services to most parts of town and outlying areas. Traveline, T0870-6082608. Buses between Reading and Henley are run by Arriva.

Information Reading Visitor Centre ⓘ *Church House, Change St, T0118-9566226. Mon-Fri 0930-1700 Sat 0930-1600.* **TIC Henley** ⓘ *The Barn (beside the Town Hall), Kings Rd, T01491-578034. Daily 0900-1700.* **TIC Marlow** ⓘ *31 High St, T01628-483597. Mon-Fri 0900-1700, Sat 0930-1700 (until 1600 Nov-Mar).*

Reading

Reading, at the confluence of the rivers Kennet and Thames, is Berkshire's capital city and the largest town on the congested 'M4 corridor' between London and Bristol: the buckle of England's affluent southern belt. Surrounded by thousands of acres of light industry, hi-tech office complexes and business parks, most of its ancient riverside character has long been buried beneath the consequences of this 21st-century prosperity. Today, with its massive brand new shopping and entertainment mall, The Oracle, its rock and world music festivals, a thriving university and intriguing museum, Reading has more than enough going for itself.

The centre of town, pedestrianized Broad Street and parallel Friar Street, is cut off from the river Thames by the railway. Five minutes' walk from the station, on the Market Place, the **Museum of Reading** ⓘ *Town Hall, T0118-9399800, www.readingmuseum.org.uk, Tue-Sat 1000-1600 (Thu until 1900), Sun 1100-1600, free* is well worth a look for its archaeological finds. Here are most of the Roman artefacts dug up at nearby Silchester, including a British brooch uncannily similar in design to the White Horse, and the little 'Silchester Eagle' that inspired Rosamund Sutcliffe to write her best-selling historical novel for children, *The Eagle of the Ninth*. The painstaking copy of the Bayeux Tapestry, embroidered in 1835 by over 35 industrious hands, is housed in its own purpose-built gallery, allowing this medieval comic strip celebration of the battle of Hastings to be seen in full light, unlike the original in France. The **John Madejski Art Gallery**, in the same complex as the museum and named after the billionaire owner of the local football club, mounts changing exhibitions of the city's extensive art collection in a refurbished Victorian space, next door to galleries featuring Epstein's *Rebecca* and a display of local biscuit-makers *Huntley and Palmers'* decorated biscuit tins, including one that was given to Captain Scott for his ill-fated expedition to the South Pole.

Apart from taking a stroll beside the river Thames (best undertaken along the Thames Path west of Caversham Bridge) there's not much else in the way of sightseeing in Reading. A 10-min walk east of the station, through a 13th-century gatehouse, the extensive **Abbey** ruins are where the embalmed left hand of St James was found in a casket in the 19th century (now in Marlow's church of St Peter). They stand next to **Reading Gaol**, still very much in use, a Victorian prison famous for accommodating Oscar Wilde as he wrote *De Profundis* in 1897, on being betrayed by his lover Alfred Lord Douglas – his *Ballad of Reading Gaol* was written in Paris after his release.

Henley-on-Thames and around

Henley-on-Thames, 8 miles downeariver from Reading, is a very well-to-do riverside town, not much changed at its heart since the early 19th century. Most famous for its summer regatta, held since 1839, when it becomes very busy indeed, it's also a popular launch pad for walks in the Chiltern hills and along the Thames Path. East of the station, the town itself perches neatly on the north bank of the river, Hart Street running up from the bridge to the Market Place and grand Town Hall. Most of the boating action in July takes place downstream of the bridge on the south bank, much of it enclosed for members only. All year this proper little town place boasts a healthy array of independent retailers and good quality restaurants.

West of the station, the revamped **River and Rowing Museum** ⓘ *Mill Meadows, T01491-415600, www.rrm.co.uk, May-Aug daily 1000-1730, Sep-Apr 1000-1700, £4.95, children £3.75, family £13.95* tells the story of the town's obsession with paddling with oars on the river as fast or as elegantly as possible, from old tubs and beautiful launches to super-sleek Olympic eights. Apart from the permanent displays of boats ancient and modern, the temporary exhibitions are often well worth a look, on subjects as diverse as the town's 18th-century gentility and the reasons for the Thames' flooding.

Marlow, Cookham and Bray

About 8 miles downeariver from Henley, **Marlow** is another old river town, exceptional for its clutch of unusual former residents and beautiful situation. Mary Shelley wrote *Frankenstein* here, in Albion House on West Street, where she lived with Byron's illegitimate daughter Allegra, the girl's mother, and her new husband Percy Bysshe Shelley. He visited all the local places of interest within a day's walk and was considered by most of the local gentry to be mad. The novelist and poet Thomas Love Peacock also lived in the town, and over a century later, Jerome K Jerome's comic classic *Three men in a Boat* was inspired by his experiences living on the waterside here. TS Eliot too had a house in Marlow, next door to Sir William Borlase's school. The impressive old Georgian house on the High Street called Remnantz, close to the town centre, was the birthplace of the Royal Military Academy now at Sandhurst. Today, despite being a London commuter dormitory, the town remains a dignified but unassuming little place, immediately more friendly than Henley and a pleasure to go poking around.

Cookham, 3 miles east of Marlow, is a small, smart riverside village, pretty in a self-conscious kind of way, most famous for its **Stanley Spencer Gallery** ⓘ *T01628-471885, Easter-Oct daily 1030-1730, Nov-Easter weekends, bank holidays 1100-1700*, accommodating the tortured religious artist Sir Stanley Spencer. This memorial gallery dedicated to his extraordinary paintings was opened in 1962 in the old Methodist chapel in the middle of town. Occasional temporary exhibitions by other artists are also shown here. Nearby, the town centre is marked by the **Tarry Stone**, once used as a racing mark for games on the village green on the Feast of the Assumption and believed by some locals to be a meteorite. **Cookham Lock** is one of the most beautiful on the river, although the first to be mechanized in the 1950s. **Boulter's Lock** nearer Maidenhead still tends to draw the summer crowds, which makes Cookham's all the more attractive.

Between Cookham Lock and Maidenhead, along one of its most beautiful stretches, the river runs quietly beneath the majestic beech woods surrounding **Cliveden** ⓘ *(NT), T01628-605069, information T01494-7555562, garden mid-Mar to Dec daily 1100-1800, Nov and Dec 1100-1600, £6, children £3, family £12.50; house and Octagon Temple Apr-Oct Thu, Sun 1500-1730 (entry by timed ticket, £1 extra on cost of garden admission)*, perched high up on the north bank with spectacular views. An Italianate villa designed in the middle of the 19th century by Sir Charles Barry for the Duke of Sutherland it was bought by the American newspaper millionaire William Waldorf Astor in 1893. A house purpose-built for lavish entertainment has stood on this extraordinary site since 1666 when the Duke of Buckingham chose it for "pleasure, frolic and extravagant diversion". The south-facing brick terrace he had built still survives, now complemented by the Astors' extravagant formal gardens and their recently renovated secret garden, as well as the Octagon Temple with its amazing mosaics. In the last century, Cliveden achieved notoriety for entertaining Nancy Astor's political 'set' of Hitler appeasers and later the protagonists of the **Profumo** scandal in the 60s. Appropriately enough, it's now a super-luxury hotel (see Sleeping below), although still in the care of the National Trust.

Sleeping

Reading *p175*
A **The French Horn**, Sonning-on-Thames, downstream of Reading, T0118-9692204, F9442210. Small smart riverside hotel, complete with restaurant, as well as some luxury riverside cottages for hire.

Henley and around *p175*
A **White Hart Hotel**, Nettlebed, T01491-641245. Individually designed rooms in an immaculate modern pub conversion, with the superior clean-cut **Nettlebed Restaurant** and **White Hart** pub below.
C **Appletree Cottage**, Backsideans, Wargrave, on the A321 between Reading and Henley, T0118-9404306. A small and secluded cottage tucked away behind the High St of an attractive town 3 miles upriver towards Reading from Henley.
C **Avalon** 36 Queen St, Henley, T01491-577829. A very central B&B in a Victorian house in Henley.
C **Stag and Huntsman**, Little Hambleden, north of Henley, T01491-571227. Victorian flint and brick pub with highly rated food and accommodation in a charming old village.
D **Flowerpot Hotel**, Ferry La, Aston, near Henley, T01491-574721. A large old Victorian pub which has a prepossessing fishing theme, real wood fires, very reasonably priced grub and big garden. There are big riverside campsites at Hurley and Swiss Farm in Henley (contact TIC for details).

Marlow, Cookham and Bray *p176*
L **Cliveden** Taplow, T01628-668561, F661837, www.clivedenhouse.co.uk. One of the most luxurious hotels in the country, offering the chance to stay in Nancy Astor's bedroom (about £30,000 for the run of the whole place for 24 hrs, £1200 for the riverside cottage per night including champagne, £900 for most expensive rooms per night, £400 standard) with its oak-panelled hall, library with tremendous views. Restaurants include the French Dining Room with panelling imported by Waldorf from Madame de Pompadour's chateau outside Paris. Set menu £60 for 3 courses in Waldo's, £20 for 2 courses on Terrace, chef from the *Waterside Inn* at Bray.
L **The Compleat Angler**, Marlow Bridge, T0870-4008100, www.heritage-hotels.co.uk. Riverside rooms in a beautifully situated hotel, from over £200 per night.
C **Acorn Lodge**, 79 Marlow Bottom, Marlow, T01628-472197, small and welcoming B&B run by the Acorn Natural Therapy Centre.

Eating

Reading *p175*
££ **The Greyhound**, Gallowstree Rd, Rotherfield, Peppard, T0118-9722227 Very good value, attractive garden and fishpond.

Henley and around *p175*
££ **Loch Fyne Restaurant**, 20 Market Pl, T01491-845780, is a particularly good branch of the fish-friendly chain, with cool tiles in the oyster bar out front and a barn-like restaurant beyond a cosy bar area.

Marlow, Cookham and Bray *p176*
£££ **Compleat Angler**, Marlow (see Sleeping above), the riverside restaurant here is the top-end option, its 3-course set lunch costing £23.50. Wonderful wraparound views of the river and weir.
£££ **Fat Duck**, High St, Bray T01628-580333, is a little less expensive than the **Waterside Inn** (see below) and almost as sensational with exotic and unusual combinations conjured up by celebrity chef Heston Blumenthal.
£££ **Waterside Inn**, Ferry Rd, Bray, T01628-620691, has 3 Michelin stars, the only place to win them in Britain – a gourmand's treat by Albert Roux for about £100 a head.
££ **Alfonso's**, 19 Station Pde, Cookham, T01628-525775, is an innovative Italian
££ **Bel and the Dragon**, High St, Cookham, T01628-521263, is overpriced but does do very good modern European food.
££ **Belgian Arms**, Holyport, near Bray, T01628-634468, a friendly old pub overlooking the village green, with no-nonsense pub grub and real ales.
££ **The Fish at Bray**, Old Mill La, Bray, T01628-781111, an old pub with a very good fish menu, decent wine list and real ales.
££ **Malik's**, High St, Cookham, T01628-520085, is the best Indian restaurant in town, in the old *Royal Exchange* pub, run by renegade Bangladeshi staff from the **Cookham Tandoori** down the road.

Bars, pubs and clubs

Reading *p175*

The Crooked Billet, Stoke Row, near Reading, T01491-681048. Very good food (especially fish) in a serious wine-lovers' country pub.
Dew Drop Inn, hidden away up the tiny road to Burchetts Green opposite Hurley off the A4130, with good walks in the woods and views over the valley.
After Dark, 112 London St, T0118-9576847. Grungy indie club with some reasonable live bands every now and then.
Eldon Arms, Eldon St, near the university, is a good old friendly place serving up a decent pint and some reasonable live music.
The Matrix, 75 London St, Reading, T0118-9590687. On Thu this is a happy combination of 'old, new and future funkin' disco' and very cheap (£1 a drink) booze. Also a platform for UK Garage and hard house artistes.
Sweeney and Todd, 10 Castle St, Reading, T0118-9586466, is a highly individual and inexpensive home-made pie shop and pub with very good real ales.

Henley and around *p175*

The Anchor on Friday St and the **Three Tuns** in the Market Pl are 2 good pubs of the many in Henley.

Marlow, Cookham and Bray *p176*

Clayton Arms, Oxford Rd, Marlow, T01628-478620, is a pigeon-fanciers' and anglers' pub in an old chair-bodgers stopover.
Jolly Farmer, Cookham Dean, T01628-482905, is a typical 18th-century country pub, not too woefully refurbished.

Entertainment

Reading *p175*

Hexagon, Queen's Walk, Reading, T0118-9606060. A democratic selection of everything from 'An Evening with Keith Harris and Orville' to English Touring Opera productions.

Henley and around *p175*

Kenton Theatre, New St, Henley, T01491-575698. Amateur theatricals and professional touring productions.
Nettlebed Folk Club, T01628-636620, W.nettlebed.freeserve.co.uk. Mon, Wed 2000. Bluegrass and other American acoustic sounds, folk on Mon.
Regal Cinema, Bell St, Henley, T01491-414160, www.regalcinema-henley.co.uk. Single screen upper-crust mainstream releases.

Festivals and events

Reading *p175*

The country's largest festival of world music, **WOMAD**, takes place in Reading in late **Jul**, T01225-744494, www.womad.org The **Reading Festival** is organized by the Mean Fiddler group, T020-88961549, over the **Aug bank holiday**, a thumping great feast of indie rock.

Henley and around *p175*

Henley Royal Regatta, T01491-572153, takes place in the first week of **Jul** (finishes on the first Sun).

Marlow, Cookham and Bray *p176*

Marlow Regatta, third Sat in **Jun**, a 1-day event. **Cookham Regatta** on the 1st Sat in Sep. **Swan-upping** in the 3rd week of **Jul** along the river from Cookham to Windsor.

Activities and tours

Marlow, Cookham and Bray *p176*

Boating Bray Boats, Maidenhead, T01628-637880. **IPG Marine**, Marlow, T01895- 235347, both run passenger services on the river, and also motor boats for hire at Higginson Park, Marlow.

For an explanation of the sleeping and eating price codes used in this guide, see the inside front cover. Other relevant information is provided in the Essentials chapter, page 36.

Windsor and Eton

→Colour map 2

Everyone who loves anything Royal loves Windsor. English Kings and Queens have lived in the impressive castle that glowers over the town since the 15th century and it remains the monarch's preferred residence. During the First World War it gave a good name to the current royal family (the Saxe-Coburg-Gothas), after a precedent established by Edward III in the 14th century. Easily accessed from London, tourists descend on the place in thousands during the summer and are generally not disappointed. Apart from the castle itself, the town centre is an attractive place to explore and the crowds can easily be escaped in the Great Park or along the river. Over the old bridge, visitors clog up Eton's quirky little High Street on their way to see the world-famous school, one of the oldest in the country. ▸▸ *For Sleeping, Eating and other listings, see pages 181-182.*

Ins and outs

Getting there South West Trains operate a twice-hourly service from London Waterloo to Windsor and Eton Riverside, taking about 50 mins. From London Paddington, Thames Trains, T0800-3583567, run regular connecting services from Slough (on the mainline from London to Reading) taking 6 mins. Windsor is just south of the M4, 26 miles from London at Junction 6, a journey from central London that can take 30 mins-1 hr, depending on the traffic. Green Line, T0870-6087261, operate bus services to Windsor from London. ▸▸ *For further details, see Transport, page 182.*

Getting around The Long Walk stretches dead straight for several miles from the castle gates into the Great Park, but Windsor town centre and the castle are easily small enough to walk around. Eton College is a 15-min walk from the castle over the river.

Information Royal Windsor TIC ⓘ *24 High St, T01753-743900 (accommodation booking T01753- 743907), www.windsor.gov.uk, Mon-Fri, Sun 1000-1600, Sat 1000-1700. Also small free exhibition upstairs on 'Town and Crown'.*

Windsor Castle

ⓘ *T020 7321 2233, www.the-royal-collection.org.uk (24-hr information T01753-831118), Mar-Oct daily 0945-1715 (last admission 1600), Nov-Feb daily 0945-1615 (last admission 1500). Semi-State Rooms also open Oct-Mar only. State Rooms usually closed for one week mid- to late-Jun and occasionally at other times. £11.50 (£6 when State Rooms closed), over-60s £9.50 (£5), under-17s £6 (£3.20), under-5s free. Guided tours of the restored areas not on the main public route including the medieval Undercroft and Great Kitchen. One tour each morning and afternoon on Tue and Wed Oct-Mar only.*

Windsor Castle is hard to miss. Walk uphill anywhere in the town and you'll find yourself beneath its walls. It was built as part of a circle of Norman control around London. Unlike the other castles – Rochester, Tonbridge, Reigate, Berkhampstead, Ongar, Hertford and Guildford, all roughly equidistant from the Tower of London – it has survived intact and been much extended over the centuries. Today, the Royal control extends to banning dogs, radios, mobile phones, bicycles or alcohol from the castle precincts. Founded on a strategic sight affording far-reaching views by William the Conqueror within a day's march of the Tower of London, it ensured the dominance of the invading monarch over the western approaches to the city. The Queen still lives here most of the year. The public are admitted throughout the year (except on state occasions, phone first), to the **State Apartments**, including Charles II's apartments and the Waterloo Chamber, decorated with paintings from the Royal Collection by

Van Dyck, Holbein, Rubens and Rembrandt and some very fine furniture; the castles' precincts and Heneary VIII's gorgeous Gothic **St George's Chapel**, where 10 sovereigns are buried (and where Edward and Sophie tied the knot). The highlight of the State Apartments is **St George's Hall**, fully restored after the fire in 1992, where the Queen holds banquets and receptions.

From April to June, the **Changing of the Guard** occurs here at 1100 Monday-Saturday. From July to March, the ceremony takes place on alternate days. The best vantage points are the Lower Ward of the Castle or outside on Windsor High Street. During summer, the Semi-State rooms are also open, featuring some of the Castle's most splendid interiors. One very popular curiosity is Queen Mary's Dolls' House, the most famous of its kind in the world, a complete palace built to a scale of 1 in 12 by at least 1,000 master craftsmen in the 1920s. All the little palace's fixtures and fittings are in full working order, including the bathrooms, lifts and electricity supply.

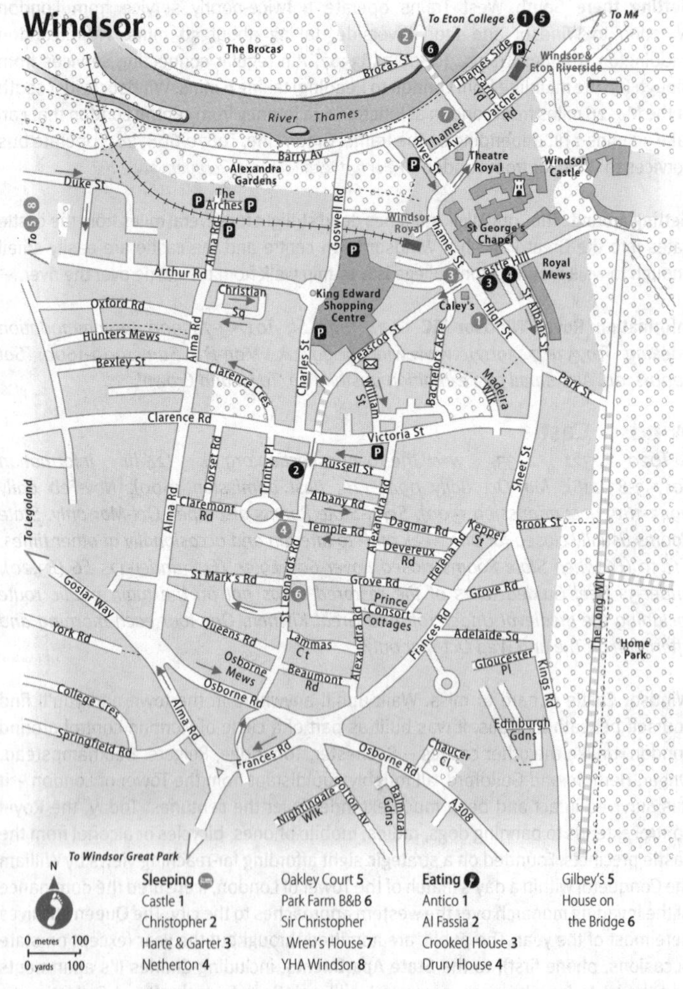

Around the castle

South of the Castle stretches the wide expanse of the **Great Park**, most easily reached from town via the fine Georgian street Park Street. Look out for the large and noisy flock of incongruous green parrots at the top of the Long Walk, which runs dead straight south for 3 miles towards a distant statue of George III on horseback. There are very fine views of the castle and Thames Valley from this giant statue, which by car is closest to the Bishop's Gate entrance to the Great Park.

Back in the town, **Castle Hill** runs down from the visitors' entrance past Henry VIII's gate into Peascod Street, the main shopping drag. The High Street comes up from the south, past the grand Guildhall designed by Wren. The TIC is just opposite, next to the department store *Caleys*. Continuing north, Thames Street runs along the foot of the castle walls down to the river bridge. On the corner of River Street is the birthplace of Robert Keayne 1595-1656, a founder of Harvard University and also of the oldest military organization in America the Honourable and Ancient Artillery Company of Massachusetts in 1638.

Over the bridge, Eton High Street begins, running north for a few hundred yards before fetching up outside **Eton College** ⓘ *(Includes the Museum of Eton Life) T01753-671177, Mar-Oct daily termtime 1400-1630, school holidays 1030-1630, £4.50, concession £3.50, guided tours at 1415 and 1515.*. The guided tours illuminate the history of this the most exclusive boys school in the country, its high fees once described by 'old boy' George Orwell as "a tax the middle classes must pay to join the system".

A left turn over the bridge leads to The Brocas, a pleasant riverside park popular with picnickers.

Around Windsor

Well-signposted from Windsor and the M4, expensive but generally hugely enjoyable, **Legoland** ⓘ *Winkfield Rd, Windsor, T08705-040404, www.legoland.co.uk, daily mid-Mar to Oct 1000-1800 (until 1900 in late Jul and Aug, until 1700 various days Mar-Jun, Sep-Oct, phone for details), £19, under-15s £16, OAPs £13*, is a fairly large theme park adored by under 12s, with lots of mini rides – castles, rollercoasters, speedboats and waterslides – as well as models using more than 20 million of the plastic bricks with knobs on.

Sleeping

L **The Castle Hotel**, High St, Windsor, T0870-4008300, F01753-621540. Heritage hotel, as central as it gets, front rooms with views of the castle and changing of the guard.

L **Oakley Court Hotel**, Windsor Rd, Water Oakley, T01753-609988. Famous film location and now top-end moat house hotel with lawns sloping down to the river.

L **Sir Christopher Wren's House Hotel**, Thames St, Windsor, T01753-861354, F442490. Individually designed rooms in Sir Christopher's old house which he designed himself down by the river bridge, as well as a top-notch restaurant.

A **Christopher Hotel**, 110 High St, Eton T01753-852359, www.christopher-hotel.co.uk. Best Western hotel in an old coaching inn with *Renata's* restaurant.

A **Harte and Garter Hotel**, High St, Windsor, T01753-863426, F830527. Beneath the Castle walls although a little shabby for the price.

B **Netherton Hotel**, 98-98 St Leonard's Rd, Windsor, T01753-855508, F621267. Family-run hotel within walking distance of the Castle.

C **Park Farm B&B**, St Leonard's Rd, Windsor, T01753-866823, F850869. Smart and fairly central guesthouse.

F **YHA Windsor**, Edgeworth House, Mill Lane, Windsor, T01753-861710, F832100. In a big old house on the outskirts of town.

Eating

Fine dining has really yet to arrive in Windsor, marginalized perhaps by the establishments upstream at Bray, see p178

£££ **Al Fassia**, 27 St Leonard's Rd, Windsor, T01753-855370, has a good reputation for its North African food, friendly atmosphere.

££££ **The House on the Bridge**, Windsor Bridge, Eton, T01753-860941, does accomplished French cooking for about £40 a head, £30 set menus.

££ **Antico**, 42 High St, Eton, T01753-863977, is a long-established Italian very popular with the locals.

££ **Gilbey's Bar and Restaurant**, 82 High St, Eton, T01753-854921, is also usually busy, a wine bar with a fairly expensive menu.

£ **Drury House**, 'Windsor's oldest teashop', at 4 Church St, right opposite King Henry VIII gate, an archetypal examples of the genre.

£ **Crooked House**, Queen Charlotte St (apparently the shortest street in Britain), is a funny little non-smoking tearoom doing real clotted Cornish cream teas next to the impressive Guildhall.

Entertainment

Theatre Royal, T01753-853888. The local repertory theatre for touring and amateur productions.

Windsor Arts Centre, St Leonard's Rd, T01753-859336, www.windsorartscentre.org Small independent repertory cinema, theatre, gallery, dance and music venue with an innovative and often exciting programme of events.

Activities and tours

French Brothers Ltd, Clewer Boathouse, Clewer Court Rd, Windsor T01753-851900 Easter-Oct 1100-1700, boat trips.

Orchard Poyle Carriage Hire, T01784-435983, T07836-766027 (mob). 30 min £19, 1 hr £38. Victorian Hackney carriage pulled by 2 bay horses. Walking along the Thames Path, contact National Trails Office T01865-810224.

Transport

Car

Car hire D.J.B Self Drive Hire, Homelands, North St, Winkfield, T01344-890608. Baldocks, 43-44 The Arches, Alma Rd, Windsor, T01753-868870.

Cycling

Cycle hire Windsor Cycle Hire, Alexander Gardens, Windsor, T01753-830220.

Taxi

Windsor Radio Cars, 59b St. Leonards Rd, T01753-677677.

Chilterns and St Albans

→Colour map 2

The Chiltern hills stretch from near Henley-on-Thames in the south to just beyond Tring in the north, almost as far as the Midlands. These rolling chalky hills are often overlooked by visitors heading for Oxfordshire or stopping at Windsor, even though they offer some superb open and wooded walking country, as well as a handful of the prettiest villages in the south. The M40 motorway slices through the middle of the region, choked every morning and evening, although thanks to some sensitive landscaping, it leaves much of the surrounding countryside undisturbed. The model village at Beaconsfield enshrines the kind of dream village many of the cars would like to come from and that can still be found nestling nearby. To the north, with its hilltop cathedral, St Albans is the most historically interesting town within 20 miles of London, where even a fleeting visit provides an insight into the developing course of English settlements since the Iron Age. ▸▸ *For Sleeping, Eating and other listings, see pages 185-186*

Chiltern Hundreds

From proper old Beaconsfield with its model of Little England in the east, to the Goring gap on the river in the west, the southern end of the Chiltern hills is the most well-to-do and the most accessible region of these chalky woodlands. Their low ridges are capped with magnificent beech trees and their dry valleys shelter well-ordered commuter villages with cosy pubs, providing fine walking country within easy reach of London. They're also blessed with a surprising profusion of flora and fauna, including rare orchids and red kites. To the north, West Wycombe is a peculiar survival: a village bought by the Royal Society of Arts in the 1920s, now in the hands of the National Trust. Its single old street is complemented by the strange follies at West Wycombe Park and the caves where its owner Sir Francis Dashwood held his Hellfire Club revels in the 18th century.

Ins and outs

Getting there The southern Chilterns can be reached most easily on the M40, which slices through the hills between junctions 5 and 6, about 30 mins' drive from central London. High Wycombe and Beaconsfield are served by Chiltern Railways, T08705-165165, from London Marylebone, on the line to Birmingham via Bicester, Banbury and Leamington Spa. Journey times to Beaconsfield about 30 mins, to High Wycombe about 35 mins. There's also another line from London via Aylesbury which goes to Great Missenden and Princes Risborough. ▸▸ *For further details, see Transport, page 186.*

Getting around A car is unfortunately the only really practical way of exploring the Chilterns. Local buses to the more attractive villages and walking areas are few and far between. Traveline, T0870-6082608.

Information **High Wycombe TIC** ⓘ *Pauls Row, T01494-421892, Mon-Sat, 0930-1700.* **Thame TIC** ⓘ *Market House, North St, T01844-212834, www.thame.net, Mon-Fri, 0930-1700, Sat and Sun, 1000-1600.*

Beaconsfield

The star attraction in Beaconsfield is well-signposted off the M40. A five-minute walk from the station, the 'model village' called **Bekonscot** ⓘ *Warwick Rd, Beaconsfield, T01494-672919, www.bekonscot.org.uk, Feb-Oct daily 1000-1700, £4.50, under-15s £2.75, concessions £3.50, family £12.50,* was started in 1929 by Roland Callingham as a hobby and now claims to be the oldest of its type in the world. About 11/2 acres of little paths and waterways are dotted with 2-ft tall model houses served by the most extensive gauge 1 model railway in the country. Billing itself as "a little piece of history that is forever England", it certainly preserves a typically 1930s vision of little England: cricket on the green, windmills and even a fishing fleet. Children are thrilled by the small scale of everything and spotting what's going on around the place.

Milton's Cottage

ⓘ *Deanway, Chalfont St Giles, T01494-872313, Mar-Oct Tue-Sun 1000- 1300, 1400-1800, £2.50, under-15s £1.* Three miles northeast of Beaconsfield, beyond Jordans (where William Penn, his two wives and five of his children are buried next to the atmospheric old Quaker Meeting House) in Chalfont St Giles, Milton's Cottage is one of the few memorials to England's greatest epic poet. Fleeing the plague in London, Milton stayed in this 'pretty box' for 11 months finishing *Paradise Lost.* A fine collection of his works can be seen, the sweet garden enjoyed, and the curator is happy to share his enthusiasm for the great blind poet and his works.

West Wycombe and around

A couple of miles west of High Wycombe, **West Wycombe** is a single street of 16th-18th-century houses preserved by the National Trust, along with reminders of some of the area's traditional livelihoods, like the chair bodgers that once knocked up a wooden chair a minute. Far from being too nicely pickled or over-restored, West Wycombe remains quite dilapidated, struggling to cope with the traffic along the A40.

Overlooking the village behind long walls is **West Wycombe Park and House** ⓘ *(NT), T01494-513569, grounds only Apr-May Mon-Thu, Sun 1400-1800, house and grounds Jun-Aug Mon-Thu, Sat 1400-1800 (last admission to time with tours 1715), house and grounds £5, child £2.50, family £12.60, grounds only £2.60*, the home of the Dashwood family since the 18th century. Most extraordinary is the Rococo landscape garden surrounding the striking Italianate house. Various classical temples and follies are artfully dotted about the lakes and artificial vistas. The interior of the house is famous for its Palmyrene ceilings.

Overlooking West Wycombe House to the north are the **church, mausoleum and caves** ⓘ *T01494-533739, Mar-Oct daily 1100-1730, Nov-Feb weekends 1100-1730, £3.50, concessions £2.50*, built in the 1750s by the first Sir Francis Dashwood on the site of an old quarry. The surprisingly extensive caves have been turned into a visitor attraction, complete with ridiculous mannequins in 18th-century costume representing Dashwood's famous friends: the likes of Benjamin Franklin, Lord Sandwich and radical MP John Wilkes, some of them members of the scandalous Hellfire Club. In some ways the church, standing in an Iron Age hill fort, with its interior copied from the Sun Temple at Palmyra in Syria and offering superb views from its tower, as well as the hexagonal roofless mausoleum next door, combine to make more of an impression than the tacky caves beneath.

St Albans

Hertfordshire is oddly hidden away, usually dismissed by Londoners as an expensive suburb, but much of it is rural enough, away from all the main roads thundering north. With the possible exception of Windsor in the west, St Albans is the most tourist-orientated and certainly the most tourist-friendly town within easy reach of London. A modern commuter town as well, it provides the opportunity to appreciate at a glance the development of a small English city over the last 2000 years. Buried beneath municipal football pitches in Verulamium Park, the Roman fortified town is overlooked by the great Norman abbey church, its tower built using Roman bricks. From the park itself the whole monastic complex seems to float above the trees beside the lake. A continuously prosperous northern satellite of London, at the very least St Albans makes for a very pleasant day trip from the capital.

Ins and outs

Getting there St Albans is on the King's Cross Thameslink line from Luton via London to Brighton, about 4 trains an hr, journey time usually about 20 mins. St Albans is 20 miles from London, just off the M25 at Junction 21a, near M1 junction 6. Journey time from central London is usually about 45 mins. Green Line buses run services from west London to St Albans, also connected by bus to Luton. » *For further details, see also Transport, page 186.*

Getting around St Albans' small town centre is perfectly manageable on foot and also surprisingly easy to park a car in or near.

Information St Albans TIC ⓘ *Town Hall, T01727-864511, www.stalbans.gov.uk, Easter-Oct Mon-Sat 0930-1730 (Jul-mid-Sep also Sun 1030-1600), Nov-Easter Mon-Sat 1000-1600.*

Sights

Although by no means the most beautiful **cathedral** ⓘ *Sumpter Yard, T01727-860780, daily 0900-1745 (guided tours T01727-890200)* in the country, St Albans is one of the most dramatically situated (along with Lincoln) and also has the longest nave. The central crossing remains much as it was when built by the first Norman abbot, Paul of Caen, and completed in 1116. The nave achieved its claim to fame by 1235 and the east end of the church was also remodelled from that date until the early 14th century. Sir George Gilbert Scott began restoration in 1856 but the west front was badly mucked around a little later by Lord Grimthorpe, a fanatical ecclesiastical and architectural controversialist. Highlights of the interior include the 13th-century wall paintings, including one of the Crucifixion by Walter of Colchester, and St Albans chapel with a monument to the brother of Henry V, Humphrey, Duke of Gloucester decorated with the only surviving pre-Reformation statues of English kings.

The centre of the town is the **Clock Tower** ⓘ *Market Pl, Easter-Oct weekends 1030-1700*, put up by the townsfolk in the early years of the 15th century as a statement of their independence from the all-powerful abbey, overlooking the city and the only surviving medieval belfry in the country. Its bell, cast in 1355, is known as Gabriel. The views from the top are well worth the very small admission fee.

The market place runs north from the tower as St Peter's St to the **Museum of St Albans** ⓘ *Hatfield Rd, T01727-819340, Mon-Sat 1000-1700, Sun 1400-1700, free*, on the right just before the church of St Peter. The museum holds the Salaman collection of trade tools, and mounts interesting exhibitions, as well as telling the story of the city after the Romans had gone.

South of the Clock Tower, **French Row** is a narrow old street lined with small shops leading down towards the cathedral and site of the old abbey. A five-minute walk down Abbeymill Lane reaches the edge of **Verulamium Park** where the Roman town once stood. Quite substantial sections of wall remain, along with a badly vandalized hypocaust, but the star attraction is at the western edge of the park. The **Verulamium Museum** ⓘ *T01727-751810, Mon-Sat 1000-1730 (last admission 1700), Sun 1400-1730 (last admission 1700), £3.50, concessions £2.50*, does a pretty good job of illuminating everyday life in Roman Britain with the help of cemetery finds, including Roman pottery, coffins complete with occupants from AD 200, and some impressive mosaics of a lion holding a stag's head in its mouth.

A 5-minute walk west of the museum, past the still operational **Kingsbury Watermill** ⓘ *T01727-853502, Tue-Sat 1100-1800 (1700 in winter), Sun 1200-1800 (1700 in winter), £1.20. Roman Theatre: Bluehouse Hill, T01727-835035, daily 1000-1700 (1600 in winter), free*, are the impressive remains of a **Roman amphitheatre**, as well as the foundations of a contemporary townhouse, a sacred shrine and a Roman shop.

Sleeping

Chiltern Hundreds *p183*

B **Chequers Inn Hotel**, Kiln La, Wooburn Common, T01628-529575, www.chequers-inn.com, a 17th-century tavern done up in a typically country commuter belt style with a popular and delicious restaurant.

C **George and Dragon**, High St, West Wycombe, T01494-464414, www.george-and-dragon.co.uk. An ancient coaching inn, a couple of old rooms with 4-poster beds.

C **Little Parmoor Farm B&B**, Frieth, T01494-88160. R&F Emmett, brick and flint farm up on the downs.

D **Swan Inn**, High St, West Wycombe, T01494-527031. Has bags of character, does just passable food but in an environment seemingly unchanged since the 50s or early 60s. Extraordinary.

F **Bradenham YHA** Bradenham, High Wycombe, T01895-673188, T01494-562929. Within walking distance of Saunderton train station, a small hostel in an old schoolhouse in the National Trust village of Bradenham, a good launchpad for walks into the Chilterns.

F **Jordans Youth Hostel**, Welders La, Jordans, near Beaconsfield, T01494-873135, F875907. Apr-Dec, small wooden lodge in 2 acres of grounds with 22 beds in dormitories and family rooms.

St Albans *p184*

L **St Michael's Manor**, Fishpool St, T01727-864444, www.stmichaelsmanor.com. A very peaceful place for a full pampering with a garden and top-notch restaurant.

C **Lower Red Lion**, 34 Fishpool St, T01727-855669, is one of the city's many real ale pubs (also does rooms) in a 17th-century coaching inn.

C **Park House**, 30 The Park, T01727-832054. Three double rooms in a comfortable, fairly central B&B.

C **Wren Lodge**, 24 Beaconsfield Rd, T01727-855540. A comfortable ETB recommended B&B with 4 double rooms.

Eating

Chiltern Hundreds *p183*

££ **Bull and Butcher**, Turville, good value food, including Brunswick Stew, apparently made with squirrel. Jolly and welcoming landlord a fount of local knowledge.

££ **The Chequers**, Fingest, Breakspear's with huge garden opposite its bell-gabled church.

££ **The Crown Inn**, Pishill, a 15th-century brick-built food pub with real fires.

££ **Yew Tree**, Frieth, T01494-882330. Very 70s menu, country pub and restaurant.

St Albans *p184*

£££ **The Conservatory**, St Michael's Manor, Fishpool St, T01727-864444. The closest St Albans comes to a gourmet modern British restaurant, in a pleasant greenhouse affair with lawns and lake, about £40 a head for dinner.

££ **Claude's Creperie**, 15 Holywell Hill, T01727-846424, as it says on the label, and for some reliable Italian staples,

££ **Sukiyaki**, 6 Spencer St, T01727-865009. Excellent Japanese restaurant doing good value set lunches for around £10.

££ **Thai Rack**, 13 George St, T01727-850055, is very popular for its Royal Thai cuisine in a theatrical setting.

£ **Courtyard Café**, 9 George St, T01727-844233, has a little secret garden.

£ **WT Harrington and Co**, 3 Market Pl, T01727-853039, is the place to pick up sandwiches or pies in the centre of town.

£ **Inn on the Park**, near the Verulamium Museum, good coffee and snacks (no alcohol) indoors or out, open daily.

Entertainment

St Albans *p184*

Maltings Arts Theatre, T01727-844222, and **Abbey Theatre** T01727-857861, for small to mid-scale touring productions.

The Alban Arena, T01727-844488, www.alban-arena.co.uk, for the big-name acts.

Activities and tours

St Albans *p184*

Free guided tours, T01727-833001, leave the Clock Tower on Sun at 1115 and 1500, and from Verulamium Museum at 1415 and during summer also on Wed from the Clock Tower at 1500.

Transport

St Albans *p184*

Bus

Sovereign Bus, T01727-854732, runs the regular direct Intalink services to **Luton** (45 mins) and **Cambridge** (2 hrs 20 mins) at 0939 changing at **Luton**. **National Express**, T08705-808080, runs the hourly direct service to **London Victoria** (1 hr 10 mins). The regular service to **Stansted airport** (1 hr 40 mins) changing at **University of Herts** is run by **University Buses**, T01707-255764, and **Cambridge Coach Services**, T08705-757747.

Train

City Station, Station Way, (off the Hatfield Rd) for **London King's Cross**, **Brighton**, **Gatwick airport**, **Luton**, **Bedford** and connections to the **East Midlands**. Abbey Station, St Stephens Hill, for **Watford** and connections to the **West Midlands**, **North West** and **Scotland**. (Buses from St Peter's St).

Directory

St Albans *p184*

Post office 14 St. Peter's St, T0845-7223344. **Medical services** St Albans City Hospital minor injuries only T01727-866122. Hemel Hempstead General, T01442 213141. A&E. **Libraries** Central Library, The Maltings, T01438-737333. **Police** Victoria St, T01727-796000.

Wiltshire

→Colour map 1-2

Wiltshire was apparently the homeland of the earliest human inhabitants of the British Isles and they made an impression on the landscape that has survived to this day. Southwest of Reading, Marlborough is an attractive destination, with beautiful downs to the north and the extraordinary prehistoric remains at Avebury just to the west. On Salisbury Plain, Stonehenge is the pièce de résistance of course, although just one of a wealth of longbarrows, stone circles, tumuli and other earthworks dotted about the region. Seven miles to the south, the use of stone in the Middle Ages achieved one of its most dramatic expressions in the spire of Salisbury Cathedral, pointing skyward above a lively and beautiful market city surrounded by watermeadows and quiet little river valleys. ▸▸ *For Sleeping, Eating and other listings, see pages 192-194*

Marlborough and around

Marlborough is a rewarding destination. During summer, its wide Georgian high street throngs with visitors exploring the surrounding downland and making for Avebury, possibly the centre of the most developed neolithic culture in England. Unlike Stonehenge, you can get close to the stones here and in many lights their brooding presence around their ancient earthwork can be quite magical. To the south, Pewsey lies at the foot of a peaceful valley threaded by the Kennet and Avon Canal. To the west, Devizes is another solid Georgian market town, home to the acclaimed Wiltshire Heritage Museum.

Ins and outs

Getting there and around Trains from London Paddington serve Pewsey (1 hr) on the line to the southwest and Exeter. Marlborough is about 9 miles south of junction 15 on the M4, reachable in under 2 hrs from London. Pewsey is a 15-min drive south, Devizes about 30 mins west of here. Local buses are run by the **Wiltshire Bus Line**, T08457-090899.

Information **Marlborough TIC** ⓘ *George Lane car park, T01672-513989. Apr-Oct Mon-Sat 1000-1700; Nov-Mar Mon-Sat 1000-1630.* **Avebury TIC** ⓘ *United Reform Chapel, T01672-539425, Tue-Sun 1000-1700.* **Devizes TIC** ⓘ *Cromwell House, Market Pl, T01380- 729408, Apr-Oct Mon-Sat 0930-1700, Nov-Mar Mon-Sat 0930-1630.*

Marlborough

Marlborough itself is a quiet and attractive place, once an important market town and staging post on the old London to Bath and Bristol coach road, now more of a tourist-pleasing stopover for visitors to Avebury and Stonehenge. Its colonnaded high street is one of the widest in Europe, topped by a Victorian town hall and church with a Norman arch in the west front. Many of the solid stone-built Georgian buildings along its length were erected after the town was almost completely destroyed by a disastrous fire in 1653, prompting thatch to be banned by order of Parliament. One of the finest, No 132 High Street, was built in 1656 for a wealthy silk merchant and is in the process of being restored to open to the public, featuring the Great Panelled Chamber with original floor-to-ceiling oak panelling. At the west end of town, **Marlborough College** is a famous public school, founded in 1843 for the sons of the clergy. The grounds contain a mound said to be Merlin's tomb, known as Merle Barrow. Some consider this to be the origin of the town's name, although it's more likely to derive from the local chalk 'marl'.

Avebury and around

Anyone remotely interested in British prehistory eventually makes a pilgrimage to the UNESCO World Heritage Site of Avebury. In some ways more impressive and certainly more atmospheric than Stonehenge, the broken monoliths here make up for what they lack in architectural accomplishment with sheer quantity and the extent of their original plan, which appears to include a large number of other monuments close by. **Fyfield Down** and **Lockeridge**, 3 miles west of Marlborough, are also neolithic sites of great significance, dry valleys littered with sarsens, including a particularly fine group called the **Grey Wethers** and a capped dolmen called the **Devil's Den**. They both make a good introduction to the wealth of neolithic remains in and around Avebury itself. Much of the village is surrounded by the stone circle, ditch and bank, and was built in part using old sarsen stones. The ditch and stone circle were probably in place about 4,500 years ago, the latter now consisting of about 27 standing stones out of an estimated original total of 250. Their story is thoroughly explored, questioned and intriguingly not fully explained at the **Alexander Keiller Museum**. ⓘ *T01672-539250, Apr-Oct 1000-1800, Nov-Mar 1000-1600, £4, concessions £2, family £10*. Named in honour of the champion golfer and archaeologist who found and relocated many of the stones in the 1930s, the museum is adjacent to the **Barn Gallery** (NT), a 17th-century thatched barn housing an interactive exhibition entitled 'Avebury 6000 Years of Mystery', included in the museum entrance fee. Nearby, complete with a beautiful walled garden, **Avebury Manor and Garden** ⓘ *(NT), T01672-539250, Apr-Oct Tue, Wed, Sun, bank holidays 1400-1730, £3.70, child £1.90, garden only £2.80/£1.40*, is also worth a look in wet weather for its Queen Anne interior and Edwardian renovations.

A mile south of the village, via the West Kennet Avenue of standing stones alongside the B4003, **Silbury Hill** is an even more spectacular and strange survivor from prehistory, the largest Bronze Age man-made mound in Europe. Clambering up the grassy slopes is forbidden but its looming 130-ft bulk has an impressive presence at dusk despite the A4 rushing past its foot. About half a mile beyond, south of the A4 from here, **West Kennet Long Barrow** is an unusually large chambered tomb dating from around 3700BC. The West Kennet Avenue in fact heads east from Avebury to The Sanctuary, possibly an even older stone circle, now consisting of two concentric rings of stone and six that were wooden, their position now marked by concrete posts.

Pewsey and Devizes

Seven miles south of Marlborough, Pewsey is a quaint little town at the head of the Vale of Pewsey, one of the most lovely stretches of the Kennet and Avon Canal. Another White Horse overlooks the town from Pewsey Hill. At the other end of the valley to the west, beyond a string of little villages with beguiling names like Honey Street and Etchilhampton, sits Devizes, the major market town in north Wiltshire. Devizes's market place is the largest in England, and is still surrounded by grand old Georgian houses and two Norman churches. An hour's walk west from the centre of Devizes, the Cain Hill flight of 29 locks on the Kennet and Avon Canal is an inspiring feat of Victorian engineering. In Long Street, the accomplished **Wiltshire Heritage Museum** ⓘ *41 Long St, T01380-727369. Mon-Sat 1000-1700. £3, concession £2, free on Mon* contains galleries of artefacts on Natural History, Stone Age, Bronze Age, Iron Age, Roman, Saxon, Medieval and recent history. It's especially rich in its prehistoric finds. The art gallery, with its John Piper stained-glass window, puts on temporary exhibitions by local artists.

Salisbury

Salisbury wins out in the league of beautiful cities of the south mainly because it has been lucky enough to keep out the way of big new road-building programmes. Which comes as some surprise given that nine major old roads meet here near the confluence of four rivers on the banks of the River Avon. The Market Square is the centre of things, alive and busy every Tuesday and Saturday, while the Close and its Cathedral remain very peaceful and serene behind their old walls a few hundred yards away. The Cathedral, with its magnificent spire, is still the main event, although Salisbury is large enough to boast some thriving nightlife, characterful pubs and one of the best theatres in the south.

Ins and outs

Getting there Salisbury is about 7 miles south off the main A303 between London and Exeter, and about 14 miles north of the main A31 between London and Bournemouth. A major road junction itself, it's easy to reach by car, taking about an 1 hr 30 mins from the M25 London Orbital. **National Express**, T08705-808080, run 3 direct services from London Victoria daily (3 hrs). **Southwest Trains** run hourly services to Salisbury from London Waterloo, taking 1hr 30mins. ▸▸ *For further details, see Transport, page 194.*

Getting around Salisbury City Centre is small and charming enough to make walking around it a pleasure. Destinations out of town can be reached on **Wilts and Dorset Buses**, T01722-336855.

Information Salisbury TIC ⓘ *Fish Row, T01722-334956, May-Sep Mon-Sat 0930-1700 (Jun- Aug until 1800), Sun 1030-1630 (Jul and Aug until 1700), Oct-Apr Mon-Sat 0930-1700, free accommodation booking service.*

Sights

Although most visitors are inevitably drawn towards the Cathedral's towering spire, the city centre is also worth exploring. Unlike the twisting Saxon layout of Canterbury, the regular grid of old medieval streets around Market Square can reasonably claim to be one of the earliest examples of new town planning in Europe. Clearly Salisbury's Norman founders had learned a thing or two from the Romans. Dominated by the **Guildhall**, the square still lives up to its name on Tuesdays and Saturdays, at other times doing service as a fairly grand car park.

North of Market Square, Castle Street runs alongside the Avon. To the east, Blue Boar Row leads into Winchester Street, one of the city's more intriguing shopping strips for antiques and other one-offs. Just to the west, **St Thomas's Church**, consecrated to Canterbury's Thomas à Becket, was founded in the 13th century, at the same time as the Cathedral, but rebuilt in the 15th. Inside, the chancel arch is decorated with a superb Doom painting, and there are medieval murals depicting the Annunciation, Visitation and Nativity as well as some fine pre-Reformation stained glass.

From St Thomas's Square, the High Street leads south to the **Close**, although St John Street provides the most satisfying approach to the Cathedral. Pretty much undisturbed by the passing of time, the Close seems to be in a world of its own, its gates locked at night, protecting the seclusion of residents such as former Conservative prime minister Edward Heath. The High Street entrance leads into Choristers Green, where stands **Mompesson House** ⓘ *(NT), The Close, T01722-335659, Apr-Oct Mon-Wed, Sat, Sun 1200-1730 (last admission 1700), £3.90, children £1.95, garden only £0.80*, a stately Queen Anne building with a remarkable interior featuring some very fine plasterwork and oak staircase, as well as an 18th-century collection of drinking glasses, antique furniture and a walled garden. It featured as Mrs Jennings' home in Ang Lee's film adaptation of Jane Austen's *Sense and Sensibility*.

The **West Walk**, backing onto the watermeadows of Queen Elizabeth Gardens, is home to three engaging attractions that can satiate the most anoraky thirst for local history. The first is the most specialized and often the least overwhelmed: **The Wardrobe** ⓘ *58 The Close, T01722-414536, www.thewardrobe.org.uk, Apr-Oct daily 1000-1700, Feb, Mar, Nov, Dec Tue-Sun 1000-1700, £2.50, concessions £1.90, children £0.50*, is the Royal Gloucestershire, Berkshire and Wiltshire Regiment's museum with beautiful gardens leading down to the river and watermeadows. A few doors down, 'The Secrets of Salisbury' in the **Medieval Hall** ⓘ *10 Shady Bower, T01722-412472, Apr-Sep 1100-1700, £1.50, under-18s £1*, the old 13th-century dining hall of the Deanery, one of the oldest domestic buildings in the close, offers a 40-min presentation shown continuously from 1100. Next door, the **Salisbury Museum** ⓘ *The King's House, 65 The Close, T01722-332151, Mon-Sat 1000-1700 (also Jul and Aug Sun 1400-1700), £3, concessions £2, children £0.75* is an excellent example of its type, complete with Stonehenge and Early Man Gallery, the Pitt Rivers Gallery full of intriguing anthropological finds, the Brixie Jarvis Wedgwood Collection of almost 600 pieces of fine china and an award-winning costume gallery called 'Stitches in Time'.

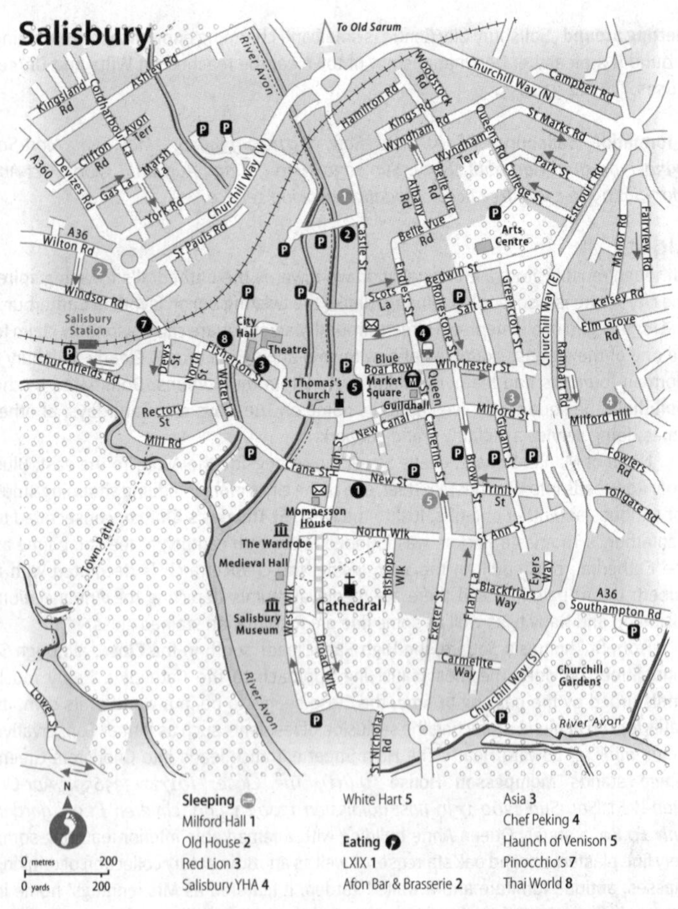

Opposite stands the perfection of the west from of the **Cathedral** ⓘ *Information T01722-555113, www.salisburycathedral.org.uk, daily 0730-1815 (Jun-Aug Mon-Sat until 2015), suggested donation £3.50, concessions £2.50, under-17s £2, family £8.* Along with St Paul's Cathedral in London and Truro in Cornwall, Salisbury is remarkable in representing the church-building achievement of a single generation. Sitting in probably the most beautiful and certainly the largest cathedral close in the country, it was built at miraculous speed between 1220 and 1258, in the style now known as Early English Gothic and almost too much of a piece for some tastes. Half a century or so later this great medieval palace of worship was blessed with a soaring 400-ft spire that has beautified distant views of Salisbury ever since. Famously portrayed by the painter John Constable as the centrepiece of a quintessentially English landscape, the story of its construction also inspired novelist William Golding's dark tale simply entitled *The Spire*. The main entrance is to the right of the West Front through a small door via the lovely old Cloisters, the largest in England, surprisingly enough given that they were never part of an abbey, and built at the same time as the main body of the cathedral. The recommended tourist route then leads into the nave, past probably the oldest working clock in the world, put together in about 1386 and designed without a face just to strike the hours. The nave itself is tall, narrow, and bare, lined with columns of Purbeck marble which were never going to be strong enough to support the spire and required the addition of flying buttresses and strainer arches. The rest of the interior is not as special as some other cathedrals, but highlights include the effigies of William Longespee, half-brother and advisor to King John and the first to be buried in the church, and of the great knight Sir John Cheney, Henry VII's bodyguard who helped defeat Richard III at Bosworth, as well as the base of the shrine of St Osmund complete with holes for the healing of the sick.

The remarkable octagonal **Chapter House** ⓘ *Daily 0930-1730, Jun-Aug Mon-Sat until 1945* off the main cloisters was also built in the mid-13th century, with beautiful 'Geometric' windows, richly carved Purbeck marble columns bursting with flora and fauna and an extraordinary medieval frieze depicting Genesis and Exodus. Also on show is one of the four surviving original copies of the Magna Carta, the foundation stone of the rule of law in the country during the despotic reign of King John.

Almost a mile north of the city centre, **Old Sarum** ⓘ *(EH), Castle Rd, T01722-335398, Apr-Jun, Sep daily 1000-1800, Jul and Aug 0900-1800; Oct 1000-1700, Nov-Mar 1000-1600, £2, £1.50 concessions, £1 children*, is a beautifully situated hill fort. Constructed in the Iron Age, it was continuously inhabited until the Middle Ages when the church moved its cathedral into the valley below. Good views from the walks around the walls and the foundations of the original Norman cathedral can still be seen, where William the Conqueror made all the landowners in the country swear allegiance to him.

Around Salisbury

Salisbury's appeal doesn't end at its magnificent cathedral. Only 7 miles north on the A303 London-Exeter road, stands Britain's most famous and most visited prehistoric monument, Stonehenge.

Stonehenge

ⓘ *T01980-624715, www.stonehengemasterplan.org, Jun-Aug daily 0900-1900, Mar 16-May and Sep-Oct 15 daily 0930-1800, Oct 16-Oct 23 daily 0930-1700, Oct 24-Mar 15 daily 0930-1600 (closed 25, 26 Dec, Jan 1), £5 including free audio tour, £3.80 concessions, £2.50 children. Personalized out-of-hours tours, T01980-626267.*

First impressions of Stonehenge may be disappointing: big roads rush very close by; the whole place is often mobbed with visitors; walking among the stones is forbidden;

 and if you've only seen photographs, the standing stone doorways may seem unimpressively small. That said, the informative and entertaining audio guide quickly provokes a sense of wonder at humankind's achievement here during the Bronze Age. The main features of the monument are a circular ditch and bank (a henge), the ancient Heel Stone just outside it (the only naturally shaped stone on site), and in the middle the ruins of a circle of sarsens capped with lintels, a circle of bluestones, a horseshoe of trilithons and the fallen Altar Stone. Speculation continues as to the true purpose of the thing, broadly agreed to have been erected over the period 3000 BC to 1500 BC. It's sobering to think that it was probably in use for at least 3,000 years, the hub of one of the earliest cultures on the planet. Whether a temple to the sun, an astronomical clock, or gruesome site of ritual sacrifice, its importance can be judged from the fact that many of its stones were somehow transported all the way from the mountains of Wales. Others, including the distinctive 30-ton sarsens and their capping stones, were dragged off the Marlborough Downs some 20 miles to the north. At present, the car park, ticket queues and gift shop keep visitors firmly in the present until they pass through a tunnel under the road to emerge the other side of the fence. Big plans for the future include burying the roads, creating a visitor centre further from the stones in a 4,000-acre Prehistoric Millennium Park, and hence restoring the monument to its magnificent isolation. Sadly it's hard to see how they're ever going to be able let people wander among the stones ever again though.

South and west of Salisbury

Down the Avon valley on the A338, just north of the New Forest and Fordingbridge, at **Breamore**, there's a beautiful Elizabethan manor house still lived in by descendants of its early 18th-century purchaser Sir Edward Hulse, physician to Queen Anne and the first two Georges. The interior contains paintings from the 17th- and 18th-century Dutch schools, a unique set of Mexican ethnological paintings and a rare Jacobean carpet. The **Countryside Museum** ⓘ *Breamore House, T01725-512233, Aug daily; May-Jul and Sep Tue-Thu, Sat, Sun; Apr Tue, Wed, Sun 1400-1730*, next door illustrates the lives led in the surrounding 17th-century village and boasts a very unusual Bavarian four-train turret clock from 1575. The village church, detached from the main cluster of buildings, is one of the finest examples of pre-Conquest Saxon architecture in the south.

A mile or so west of Salisbury up the Nadder valley, **Wilton House** ⓘ *T01722-746729, www.wiltonhouse.com, Apr-Oct daily 1030-1730 (last admission 1630), £7.25, concessions £6.25, under-15s £4.50. Grounds only £3.75, under-15s £2.75* is quite a commercialized stately home, owned by the Earl of Pembroke, but very special inside, with a visitor centre in the Old Riding School, featuring a Victorian laundry and Tudor kitchen. Its most famous room is the Double Cube Room, by Inigo Jones, hung with paintings by Van Dyck and Joshua Reynolds. There's an adventure playground and 21 acres of romantic gardens and the strange Italianate church in town is also worth a look.

Sleeping

Marlborough and around *p187*

B **Castle and Ball Hotel**, High St, Marlborough, T01672-515201, with rated 'Taste of the West' restaurant.

B **Ivy House**, Marlborough, T01672-515333, is another decent option on the High St.

C **Red Lion**, High St, Avebury, T01672-539266. 4 rooms, needs booking well in advance, in the middle of the village (and the circle).

C **Castle Hotel**, New Park St, Devizes, T01380-729300, www.castledevizes.com. Welcoming and cheerful family-run establishment where nothing seems too much bother.

Salisbury *p189, map p190*

A **Red Lion**, 4 Milford St, T01722-323334, www.the-redlion.co.uk. Founded in the 13th century, courtyard hotel in the middle of the city with a reliable restaurant.

A **White Hart**, St John St, T0870-4008125, www.heritage-hotels.com. Very comfortable refurbishment of an old townhouse, with real fires, clean rooms and friendly service.

A **Milford Hall**, 206 Castle St, T01722-417411, F419444. Close to the centre, family-run in an extended Georgian mansion.

C **Old House**, 161 Wilton Rd, T01722-333433. Beamed rooms and friendly family home with charming garden, within walking distance of the city centre.

F **Salisbury YHA**, Milford Hill, Salisbury, T01722-327572, F330446. Has 70 beds in one single, one double, 7 4-bedded and dormitory rooms, walking distance of the Cathedral.

Around Salisbury *p191*

A **Howard's House Hotel**, Teffont Evias, near Salisbury, T01722-716392, www.howardshousehotel.com. Small and very comfortable country hotel in an idyllic setting with a sweet little garden and boasting a high-quality restaurant that draws in diners from Salisbury and further afield (£30 a head without wine). Recommended.

C **The Bell Inn**, High St, Wylye, T01985-248338. In the shadows of the A303 and A36 but a lovely old pub with comfortable rooms and good local ingredients in its accomplished restaurant.

D **Pembroke Arms**, Fovant, T01722-714201. Creeper-clad coaching inn on the A30 with a hearty local atmosphere and displays on the First World War camp on the downs that created the Fovant Badges.

Eating

Marlborough and around *p187*

£££ **George and Dragon**, High St, Rowde (just north west of Devizes), T01380-723053. Very fresh fish from Cornwall deep inland, served in a bog-standard boozer.

£££ **Harrow Inn**, Little Bedwyn, T01672-870871. Cosy gourmet restaurant in a converted pub, about £50 a head for some accomplished 'modern European' food.

££ **Bell Inn**, Ramsbury, T01672-520230. Another village local with reputable food.

££ **Coles**, Kingsbury St, Marlborough, T01672-515004. Do a modern European menu confidently enough, large starters available at lunchtimes.

££ **Red Lion**, Axford, T01672-520271. Pub on the river with highly rated food and a favourite with the locals.

££ **Royal Oak**, Wootton Rivers, T01672-810322. Half-timbered and thatched, fairly expensive food but very welcoming atmosphere, jolly in summer when the canal is busy with passing punters.

££ **Taste of Bengal**, 58 New Park St, Devizes, T01380-725649. Excellent Indian cuisine.

£ **Circle Restaurant**, High St, Avebury, T01672-539514. Vegetarian and organic restaurant catering expertly to the new agers visiting the stones.

£ **The Polly Tearooms**, High St, Marlborough T01672-512146. The most famous tearooms in Marlborough, always buzzing with tea-drinkers wondering whether to have one more tempting piece of patisserie.

£ **Tudor Tearooms**, 115 High St, Marlborough, T01672-52853. Less expensive than the Polly with less sophisticated home-made cakes for £3.50, sometimes less crowded too.

£ **Truffles Bakery**, 7 Little Brittox, Devizes, T01380-720049, can provide delicious ingredients for a picnic.

Salisbury *p189, map p190*

£££ **Haunch of Venison**, 1/5 Minster St, T01722-322024. A famous old pub with a very decent menu of pub grub in the restaurant upstairs.

£££ **LXIX**, 67-69 New St, T01722-34000. The most stylish restaurant in the city, if not the whole of Wiltshire (and it knows it), booking essential for £30 a head modern British cuisine in sleek designer surroundings.

££ **Afon Bar and Brasserie**, Millstream Approach, off Castle St, T01722-552366. A vaguely Australian-style, reasonable value menu in a pleasant enough spot beside a confined stretch of the Avon stream where boats and punts can be hired.

££ **Asia**, 90 Fisherton St, T01722-327628. A reliable but quite pricey Indian restaurant.

££ **Chef Peking**, Fisherton St, T01722-326063. A very tasty and popular Chinese with a lively atmosphere.

££ **Pinocchio's**, near the station, T01722-413069. A busy and cosy Italian.

££ **Thai World**, off Fisherton St, T01722-333870, is a good Thai alternative.

Around Salisbury *p191*

££ **The Cartwheel**, Whitsbury, T01725-518362. A proper country pub with a pool table, garden, pub grub and well-kept beers.

££ **Crown Inn**, Alvediston, is a charming thatched 15th-century pub.
££ **Radnor Arms**, Nunton, T01722-329722. Do an interesting modern European menu backed up with some real ales.

Festivals and events

Salisbury *p189, map p190*
Salisbury Festival, usually last week of May and first of Jun, T01722-332977, box office T01722-320333, www.salisburyfestival.co.uk A formidable multi-arts festival with fireworks, outdoor classical concerts, theatre and street shows.

Transport

Salisbury *p189, map p190*
Car hire Europcar, Fisherton Yard, Fisherton St, T01722-335625. **Thrifty**, Brunel Rd, Churchfields Ind Est, T01722-411919.
Cycle Hire Hayball Cycle Centre, Black Horse Chequer, 26-30 Winchester St, Salisbury T01722-411378.
Taxi City Cabs Salisbury Ltd, T01722-334477.

Hampshire
→*Colour map 2*

Hampshire is a county of chalk downlands above winding valleys of the swift little Itchen, Test and Meon streams and the open heathland and woods of the New Forest in the south (see page 204). In the middle sits Winchester, a bit mauled by the M3 motorway, but still boasting one of the noblest cathedrals and most beautiful old schools in the country. » *For Sleeping, Eating and other listings, see pages 201-203.*

Winchester

Former capital of the country under King Alfred the Great, Winchester lost out to London some time in the late Middle Ages. Its Royal glory days may be over but it remains a very prosperous city with a distinctive ecclesiastical air. The great cathedral's interior is one of the most inspiring in the land and William of Wykeham's public school for boys provided the model for most others. In fact the cathedral with its close, the college and its grounds taken together make up one of the most beautiful medieval complexes in the country, capped by the peace of St Cross Hospital, still standing quietly close to lovely water-meadows a mile or so to the south, and probably the best-preserved medieval sight in England, where Keats was inspired to write his *Ode to Autumn*. That said, the city centre itself is only recovering from some urban planning; and the destruction of Twyford Down by the M3 caused widespread protest as areas of outstanding natural beauty and sites of scientific interest surrounding the city were destroyed.

Ins and outs

Getting there Winchester is just off the M3 at junctions 9-11, about 1 hr's drive from London. **National Express,** T08705-808080, have 9 services a day to Winchester from London Victoria (2 hrs). Twice hourly direct trains from London Waterloo take about 1 hr, run by **South West Trains,** T023-80213650. » *For further details, see Transport, page 203.*

Getting around Winchester, the cathedral close, town and college, is small enough to walk around, although the walk from train station to the city would take an hour. The network of local buses are run by **Wilts and Dorset Buses,** T01722-336855 (to the southwest, Salisbury, Romsey etc) and **Solent Blue Line,** T023-80618233 (to Southampton, Eastleigh). The council also subsidizes some local buses T01962-846924.

Information Winchester TIC ⓘ *Guildhall, The Broadway, T01962-840500, www.winchester.gov.uk Jun-mid to Sep Mon-Sat 1000-1800, Sun 1100-1400; mid-Sep to May Mon-Sat 1000-1700. Accommodation booking service (£3 per booking, online booking £5.)*

Sights

From the railway station in the northwest of the town, a 5-min walk brings you to the old medieval **Westgate** ⓘ *T01962- 848269, Apr-Oct Mon-Sat 1000- 1700, Sun 1200-1700, Feb and Mar Tue-Sat 1000-1600, Sun 1200-1600, £0.30, concessions £0.20*, at the top of the High Street. Inside there's a brass rubbing centre, and some debtor's graffiti testifying to its use as a prison for more than a century. Better perhaps to hurry on next door to the **Great Hall** ⓘ *T01962-846476, Apr- Oct 1000-1700, Nov-Mar 1000- 1600, free*, the last remnant of Winchester Castle, impressive nonetheless, where the city's famous Round Table has hung on the wall for more than 500 years. Long associated with King Arthur, he is depicted at its centre in the Tudor costume of the time when it was repainted. Big enough to seat all 24 of his knights, it probably actually originates from sometime in the 13th century. Heneary VIII took the Emperor Charles V to see it in 1522. Queen Eleanor's pretty little medieval garden has been reconstructed outside.

Continuing down the High Street, the **Buttercross** is the local youth hang-out, kids sitting vacantly around the heavily restored 15th-century market cross. A passage through the old shops on the right leads into the Square, site of the **City Museum** ⓘ *T01962-848269, www.winchester.gov.uk/heritage, Apr-Oct Mon-Sat 1000-1700, Sun 1200-1700, Nov-Mar Tue-Sat 1000-1600, Sun 1200-1600, free* and a good approach to the west front of the cathedral. The recently revamped local museum tells the story of the city's former national importance entertainingly enough and also includes some of the latest archaeological finds from the site of King Alfred's grave.

Even a passing visitor to the city should not fail to look inside **Winchester Cathedral** ⓘ *T01962-857200, www.winchester-cathedral.org.uk, daily 0830-1700. Suggested donation £3.50, concessions £2.50, family £7. Visitor Centre, T01962-857258, open daily 0930-1700, free*. On low ground beside the river Itchen – so low in fact that it began to sink into the marshy ground and was only saved by a brave diver called William Walker pumping concrete into its rotten wooden foundations in the 1920s – the stubby tower may make first impressions disappointing. Approaching the west front from the Square though, the building's scale and grandeur gradually make themselves felt. Inside, the longest medieval nave in Europe never fails to stir the spirit, soaring up to a magnificent vaulted ceiling supported by a splendid march of perpendicular columns. Work was begun on the building 13 years after the Battle of Hastings and completed 14 years later in 1093. Almost two centuries later, the West Front (and main entrance) was remodelled and the nave transformed by Bishop William of Wykeham, founder of St Mary's College (see below) and New College, Oxford. Things to look out for inside include fine statues of Kings James I and Charles I, the grave of Jane Austen, the 12th-century black marble font, extraordinary ancient choir stalls and the marble tomb of William Rufus. Shortly after Rufus – who was possibly assassinated in the New Forest – was buried in the central crossing, the Norman tower collapsed on his grave, many thought as a consequence of his misrule. The east end of the building boasts some of the earliest pure Gothic architecture in the country. Beneath, the crypt – which is still prone to flooding – has become an atmospheric setting for modern sculptor Anthony Gormley's *Sound II*. The Winchester Bible, on display in the library, is a beautiful illuminated 12th-century manuscript, gorgeously gilded and decorated with lapis lazuli from Afghanistan. Guided tours of the cathedral include a trip up the tower, or round the library, triforium (above the nave) and treasury.

To the right of the cathedral's main entrance in the west front a passageway leads beneath flying buttresses into the **Deanery Close**, a very peaceful place near the remains of the old monastery. Dean Garnier's Garden is a reconstructed Victorian garden beneath the cathedral walls. At the other end of the close is **Cheyney Court**, a much-photographed half-timbered house where the Bishops once held court, next door to **Pilgrim's Hall**, an early 14th-century room with a well-preserved hammer-beam roof. Through the old wall, the city's other surviving medieval gateway, the Kingsgate separates the cathedral from the college.

College Street, where Jane Austen lived out the last years of her life, leads off to the left and the impressive main gate of St Mary's College, better known as **Winchester College**. One of the oldest (founded 1382), most exclusive and most beautiful schools in the country, guided tours include the dinky little Chamber Court

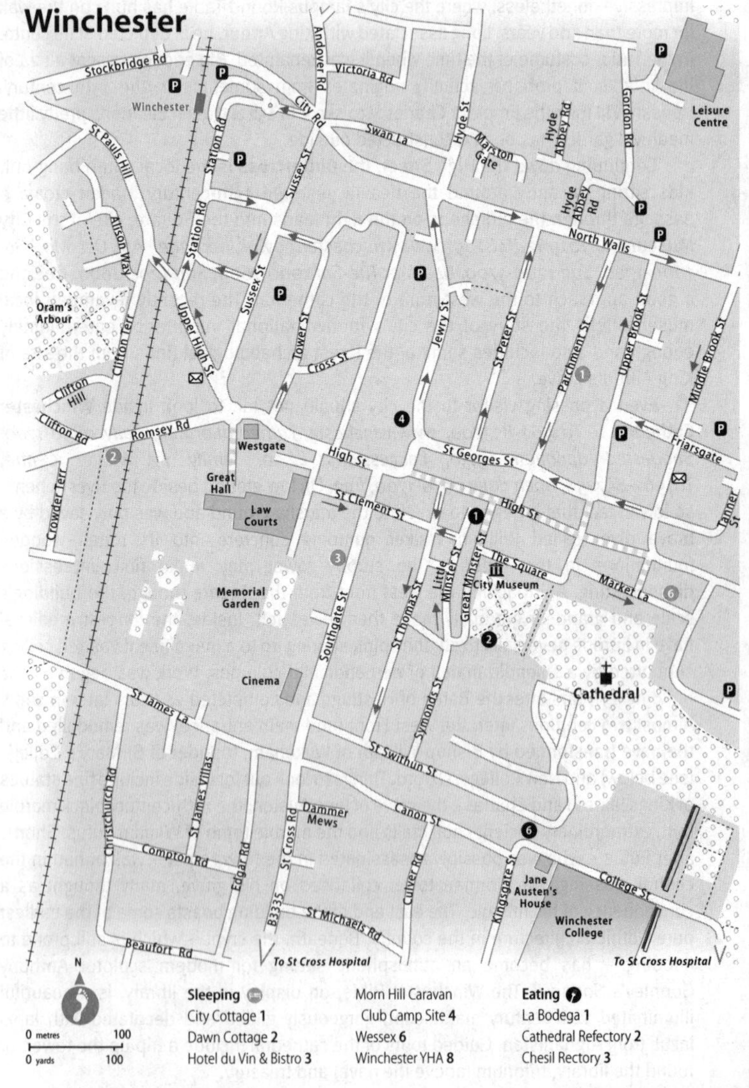

– a sort of mini Oxbridge college quad for kids – the chapel, quiet cloisters and old dining hall, as well as School, a very correctly proportioned building attributed to Wren, and a funny old picture of the Trusty Servant, a hybrid creature embodying the school's motto: 'Manners maketh man'. ⓘ *T01962-621209, www.wincoll.ac.uk, guided tours Mon-Sat 1045, 1200, also 1415, 1530 (not Tue, Thu), Sun 1415, 1530, £2.50, concessions £2.*

On the other side of College Street are the ruins of the **Old Bishop's Palace** (Wolvesey Castle), once one of the most important medieval buildings in Europe, where Raleigh was tried and condemned to death, although there's not a huge amount left to see now. Atmospheric nonetheless. ⓘ *(EH), T01962-854766, Apr-Sep daily 1000-1800, Oct daily 1000-1700, £1.80, concesssions £1.40, children £0.90.*

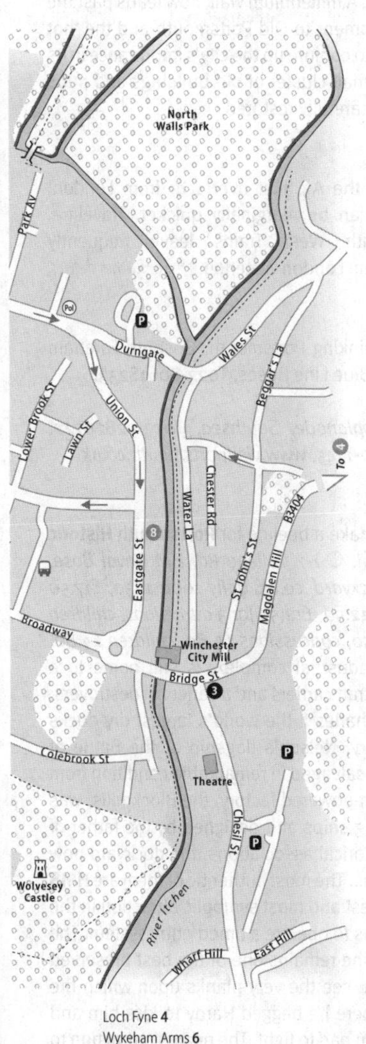

At the end of College Street, a very pleasant walk leads straight on through 'the weirs' of the Itchen to **Winchester City Mill** ⓘ *(NT) Bridge St, T01962-870057, www.winchestercitymill.co.uk, Apr-Sep Wed-Sun (daily Jul and Aug) 1100-1645, £2, child £1*, a working watermill almost back in the middle of town with an impressive rushing water race and island garden. It's also a youth hostel (see below). A right turn at the end of College Street heads towards the **watermeadows**, a delightful tract of reedbeds and tiny waterways burgeoning with wildlife. A good mile's walk between these meadows and the school's playing fields along the riverbank finally reaches the other unmissable highlight of a visit to Winchester, **St Cross Hospital** ⓘ *T01962-851375, Apr-Sep Mon-Sat 0930-1700, Oct-Mar Mon-Sat 1030-1530, £2, £1.50 concessions, guided tours bookable in advance in writing*. Founded in 1136, these beautiful old almshouses (the oldest in England) and their wonderful Norman abbey on the riverbank survived the dissolution of the monasteries thanks to being for lay brothers rather than the clergy. Today it must be one of the most perfectly unspoiled medieval places in the country. The current occupants still hand out the Wayfarer's Dole – a little bit of bread and beer – to visitors or pilgrims during visiting hours and show people around their little adorable church with its chunky round Norman pillars, wealth of zigzag stonework and adjoining Tudor courtyards.

Portsmouth

Portsmouth usually hits the news for all the wrong reasons, like when a mob here attacked a paediatrician they had mistaken for a paedophile. Since the millennium regeneration of the harbourfront, though, the city's future has been looking up. That said, it still bears the scars of the ill-conceived regeneration of its extensive Second World War bomb damage during the 60s and first impressions are likely to be uninspiring. The Historic Dockyard remains most visitors' favourite destination, and quite a sight it is too, still just about a working naval base and also a series of very popular old ships in dry dock, including HMS Victory and the Tudor warship Mary Rose. From the dockyard's main entrance, The Hard stretches along the harbourfront, recently the subject of a much-needed facelift. A millennium walk now leads past the new Gun Quay leisure and shopping development to Old Portsmouth and the 'hot walls'. These old stone defences still manage to conjure up the city's importance in its seafaring heyday, a good introduction to a small cluster of old buildings and pubs that either survived the bombs or have been carefully restored.

Ins and outs

Getting there Portsmouth is at the end of the A3, just over 1 hr from London, although at peak times the M3 and M27 can be marginally quicker. Traveline, T0870-6082608, www.traveline.org.uk South West Trains leave frequently throughout the day for Portsmouth Harbour from London Waterloo. ▶▶ *For further details, see also Transport, page203*

Getting around South Downs Explorer Bus linking Portsmouth, Gosport, Fareham with Petersfield and the Meon Valley. Solent Blue Line Buses, T023-80618233.

Information Portsmouth TIC ⓘ *Clarence Esplanade, Southsea, T023-92826722, daily 0930-1745. Also on The Hard, daily 0930-1745, www.visitportsmouth.co.uk*

Sights

Most visitors to Portsmouth with time to kill make a beeline for **Portsmouth Historic Dockyard**, a 10-min walk west of the station. ⓘ *1-7 College Rd, HM Naval Base, Portsmouth, T023-92861512, www.historicdockyard .co.uk, daily 1000-1630, £17.50 all attractions, concessions £15.50, children £12.50, £12.50 for 3 attractions, children £9.30, concessions £11, single attraction £6.50, concessions £5.80, children £4.80.* **HM Naval Base**, once the world's largest industrial complex, is still home to a significant part of the fleet, including three aircraft carriers and a variety of destroyers, frigates and minesweepers. In the reign of Charles II the world's largest dry docks were built here, now harbouring HMS *Victory*, Nelson's flagship at the Battle of Trafalgar, and the *Mary Rose*, a Tudor warship salvaged in remarkable condition from the Solent silt. In 1802, the world's first steam-powered factory, the Blockmills, was built here, turning out pulley blocks for sailing ships and designed by the father of Isambard Kingdom Brunel. Apart from its historical associations, the dockyard now draws in the punters to its five visitor attractions. The most authentic of them are **HMS Victory** and HMS *Warrior*. The *Victory*, the oldest and most symbolic attraction in the yard, is enormously popular and frequently has to operate a timed-entry system. The measures are not that surprising, given that she remains one of the best preserved and most rewarding ships in the yard to visit: see the very planks upon which the one-eyed Admiral fell in 1805, the cockpit where he begged Hardy to kiss him and marvel at the cramped conditions in which men had to fight. The nearest attraction to the main entrance, **HMS Warrior**, is also a treat, the first iron-clad steam-powered battleship, which thanks to successfully avoiding any action remains in pristine condition, as good as when she first steamed into the Channel in 1860. The latest and predictably most gimmicky attraction is Action Stations, 'showcasing the modern Royal Navy' with a multimedia exhibition that tries to let you in on the glamour of life in the navy using a huge screen showing a film called *Command Approved*, a simulator ride and some pretty effective Naval PR. All in all it's a marked improvement on the press gang as a method of recruitment. Opposite HMS *Victory*, the **Royal Naval Museum** features *Trafalgar*!, a multimedia portrait of the decisive sea battle, as well as displays on the history of the sailing navy and the life of Nelson. The salvaged remains of the **Mary Rose**, not particularly impressive in themselves, can be found a short walk away. This Tudor warship was built in 1511 and capsized within sight of port in 1545. The televised and tricky salvage operation has ensured the vessel's continuing celebrity even though its original performance hardly seems to justify it. That said, the exhibition does a good job of illuminating life at sea in the very early days of the great age of sail. Finally, Warships by Water offers water-borne 40-min tours of the modern dockyard in summer for £3.50.

Portsmouth Harbour was transformed for the millennium, with the creation of a new harbourside walkway. The new **Gun Quays** development (T023-92836700) features all the usual suspects of noisy mass-market retailing, with cinemas, discount fashion outlets, a bowling alley and chainstores aplenty, but it has also reinvigorated a tired and run-down stretch of the harbour between the naval base and Old Portsmouth. More controversial (because of its impact on the old harbour's skyline) has been the 500 m **Spinaker Tower**, opened in 2003 and destined to be a very prominent landmark and observation tower dominating the waterfront. Beyond, the 'hot walls' stretch around Old Portsmouth, a 20-min walk south from the Historic Dockyard.

Around Portsmouth

Over the waters of Portsmouth Harbour lies Gosport, not much of a destination except for submarine buffs heading for the **Royal Navy Submarine Museum** ⓘ *Haslar Jetty Rd, Gosport, T023-92529217, www.rnsubmus.co.uk, Apr-Oct daily 1000-1730; Nov-Mar daily 1000-1630, £4, concessions and children £2.75, family £11*, which offers guided tours of HMS *Alliance* and displays the navy's first submarine *Holland I*. Further up Gosport's Millennium promenade, **Explosion!** ⓘ *T023-92505600, Apr-Oct daily 1000-1730, Nov-Mar 1000-1630, £5, child/concessions £3*, is the Museum of Naval Firepower at Priddy's Har and a surefire hit with kids for its celebration of big bangs at sea set in the Grand Magazine.

At the top of the harbour, on a prime defensive site for the last 2000 years, **Portchester Castle** ⓘ *(EH), near Fareham, T023- 92378291, Apr-Sep daily 1000-1800, Oct daily 1000-1700, Nov-Mar daily 1000-1600, £3.50, concessions £2.60, child £1.80*, has the most complete Roman walls in Europe still standing, as well as a squat Norman keep, the remains of Richard II's palace and the prison where thousands of French prisoners were 'sardined' during the Napoleonic wars. Great views over the Solent.

Nearby, the Victorian fort on Portsdown Hill is home to the **Royal Armouries Museum** ⓘ *Fort Nelson, Down End Rd, Fareham, T01329-233734, www.armouries.org.uk, Apr-Oct daily 1000-1700, Nov-Mar Thu-Sun 1030-1600, free*, with underground magazines, tunnels and pieces of the Iraqi supergun and displays on artillery in action.

Southampton

Like Portsmouth, Southampton's position on a peninsula jutting into the deep-water estuary of the rivers Itchen and Test has ensured its maritime importance since the Middle Ages. The Mayflower sailed from here, as did the Queen Mary and the Titanic. Nowadays it's still a thriving commercial port, with supertankers noseing their way deep inland. No surprise then that it was virtually flattened by the Luftwaffe and fairly unattractively redeveloped after the war. A few older parts of town have survived to give the town centre some character, especially the Old Bargate at the top of the High Street, but apart from a quick look around the city's museums or art galleries, and a stroll along the harbour front around Town Quay, there's not a huge amount to keep visitors long as they pass through to the New Forest, the Isle of Wight or France and beyond.

Ins and outs

Getting there Southampton is well connected by road, to London via the M27 and M3 (about an hr away), and to Birmingham via the M40 and A34 (about 21/2 hrs). Junction 3 on the M27 accesses the city centre quickest via the M271. Direct **train** services link Southampton with many parts of the UK. **South West Trains** operates a 15 min interval daytime fast service between London Waterloo and Southampton Central. South West Trains, Wales and West, South Central Trains and Virgin Trains operate regular services along the south coast. Traveline, T0870-6082608. ▸▸ *For more details, see Transport, page 203*

Getting around The centre of Southampton is clustered around the railway station and stretches down to the harbour (a 20-min walk) along Above Bar St. Stagecoach, T01256-464501, run frequent bus services throughout the city and surrounding area, including Eastleigh, Hedge End, Fareham, Portsmouth and Southsea, Chandlers Ford, Romsey, Totton, and the New Forest. Other buses around town and beyond are run by Solent Blue Line, T023-80618233, Wilts and Dorset, T01590o-672382, and First Southampton, T023-8022 4854. Blue Funnel Cruises T023-80223278 operate tours of Southampton Water.

Information Southampton TIC ⓘ *Civic Centre Rd, T023-80833333, www.southampton.gov.uk/cityinfo, Mon-Sat 0830-1730*. Accommodation booking service (no fee, 10% deposit). Guided Walk of Old Southampton free tour every day at 1030 and 1430 Jun-Sep, Sun at 1030 all year, bank holidays at 1030, T023-80221106.

Sights

Most visitors head south on arrival at the train station, towards Town Quay and the boats for Hythe and the Isle of Wight. However, there are two art galleries worth looking into on the way. The **Southampton City Art Gallery** ⓘ*Guildhall, Commerical Rd, T023-80832277, Tue-Sat 1000-1700, Sun 1300-1600, free*, boasts a fine permanent collection of mid-20th-century artists and others, as well as temporary exhibitions. Beyond the Civic Centre with its prominent clock tower and the East Park is the **Millais Gallery** ⓘ *T023-80319916, www.millais.solent.ac.uk, Mon-Wed, Fri 1000- 1700, Thu 1000-1900, Sat 1200-1600*, an innovative space for contemporary art with regularly changing exhibitions.

The route south past the TIC leads past the **Tudor House Museum and Garden** ⓘ *Bugle St, T023-80635904, Tue-Fri 1000-1700, Sat1000-1600, Sun 1400-1700, free.*. The house was built for Sir John Dawtry and his family in 1495, and has been reconstructed to illustrate life in Tudor, Georgian and Victorian times. There's also a Tudor Knot Garden with fountains, bee skeps and appropriate 16th-century herbs. A short distance away is **Medieval Merchants House** ⓘ *French St, T023-80221503, daily Apr-Nov 1000-1800, £2.30 including audio tour.*, which illustrates the history of the house decorated as it would have been in the 14th century, as shop, office, and home to a wealthy merchant of the time.

The **Southampton Maritime Museum** ⓘ *Town Quay, T023-80635904, Tue-Fri 1000-1700, Sat 1000-1600, Sun1400-1700, free*, has displays on the history of the port and a model of how it might have looked in the 1930s on the ground floor, while upstairs there's the Cunard town display, a 22-ft model of the *Queen Mary* and the story of the *Titanic*.

The Shipping Forecast

Broadcast four times a day on BBC Radio 4 Long Wave, shortly before 0500, 1200, 1800 and midnight, the shipping forecast has become almost as sacred an English institution as Trooping the Colour and cream teas. Heard for the first time in 1924, it uses a strange set of seemingly totemic names and mysterious coded shorthand to warn mariners of the weather conditions over the next 24 hours. The names pinpoint 30 sea areas. Some, such as Dover, Plymouth, Irish Sea and Hebrides, are self-explanatory and provide handy summaries of what it's likely to be like beside the seaside. The sound of others – Dogger, Bailey, Rockall, Sole, and Forties – brings the smack of the cold and briny open sea into cosy homes across the land. After the gale warnings and general synopsis, the forecast begins in the northeast with Viking, North and South Utsire, near Norway, and moves clockwise around the British Isles, through Tyne, Humber, Thames, Dover, Wight, Portland, Plymouth, and Lundy, and back up to the Faeroes, Fair Isle and southeast Iceland in the north again. Each sea area is followed by a three-part forecast describing the wind direction and strength on the Beaufort Scale, the weather expected, and the visibility: 'Cromarty, southwesterly backing southerly 4, increasing 5 or 6, occasionally 7. Rain spreading northeastwards. Moderate, becoming poor.' Controversy has recently surrounded the proposed replacement of the lullaby tune, Sailing By, that has introduced the midnight forecasts since 1965. Originally commissioned by the BBC to accompany an epic hot-air balloon ride over the Alps, its twee and lilting harmony would apparently be sorely missed by grizzled seafarers and snug landlubbers alike.

Sleeping

Winchester *p194, map p196*

L **Wessex Hotel**, Paternoster Row, T0870-4008126, www.wessexhotel.co.uk. Long- time the smart option (if a touch impersonal) in an excellent position on the close, many rooms with cathedral views, only scrapes into this price bracket (superior rooms £170 per night).

A **Hotel du Vin and Bistro**, 14 Southgate St, T01962-841414, www.hotelduvin.com. Stylish and comfortable hotel with pleasantly informal service and top-notch brasserie. Great views of the Cathedral's west front and over Winchester from the top rooms.

A **Royal Hotel**, St Peter St, T01962-840840, W.the-royal.com. Renovated old hotel of great character with beautiful garden and famous conservatory dining room.

B **Westgate Hotel**, 2 Romsey Rd, T01962-820222. Fairly recently refurbished family-run hotel close to the top of the High St with good bar and fresh, interesting ingredients on the menu in the restaurant.

B **Wykeham Arms**, 75 Kingsgate St, T01962-853834, F854411. Comfortable rooms in one of the best pubs in the city, right by the College and Cathedral Close.

C **St John's Croft**, St John's St, T01962-859976. Period house B&B on St Giles Hill with high ceilings, 10-min walk from the cathedral.

C **Dawn Cottage**, Romsey Rd, T01962-869956. Professional non-smoking B&B a mile from the centre with views over town.

D **City Cottage**, 51 Parchment St, T01962-863971. Sweet little B&B in small old terraced street tucked behind the main shopping drag.

D **Mrs Fetherston-Dilke**, 85 Christchurch Rd, T01962-868661. Large Victorian house some way out of city centre but close to St Cross.

F **Winchester YHA**, 1 Water La, T01962-853723, F855524. Worth booking well in advance for pole position in National Trust City Mill on the Itchen, at the foot of the High St and Broadway. 31 beds in 1-, 4-, 9- and 18-bedded rooms.

Camping

F **Morn Hill Cararvan Club Site**, Morn Hill, 3 miles east of the city centre, off the A31, T01962-869877. Open Apr-Oct.

Portsmouth *p198*

A **Portsmouth Marriott Hotel**, Southampton Rd, T023-92383151, F92388701. 24-hr room service with conference facilities available accommodating up to 400 delegates. A corporate favourite but also one of the most comfortable options for holidaymakers.

B **Old House Hotel**, The Square, Wickham, T01329-833049, F833672. Acclaimed restaurant in a pleasant old-style hotel with walled garden and period features.

C **The Sally Port**, 57-58 High St, Old Portsmouth, T023-92823045. A 16th-century pub with comfortable rooms, opposite the Cathedral, 2-min walk along the 'hot walls'.

D **Langdale Guest House**, 13 St Edwards Rd, Southsea, T023-92822146, F9235-3303. Friendly, family guesthouse.

D **Sailmaker's Loft**, 5 Bath Sq, Old Portsmouth, T023-92823045. 3 double rooms, 2 with views over the water, in the old town.

D **Woodville Hotel**, 6 Florence Rd, Southsea T023-92823409, F92346089. Family-run hotel, 2 mins from the sea and centrally located close to all of Southsea's entertainments.

F **Portsmouth and Southsea Backpackers**, 4 Florence Rd, Southsea, T023-92823045, www.portsmouthbackpackers.co.uk. £10 per night, 2 double rooms £22 per night.

F **YHA Portsmouth**, Old Wymering Lane, Cosham, T023-92375661, F92214177. Tudor manor house in the north of the city, some way from the seafront.

Southampton *p199*

L **De Vere Grand Harbour**, West Quay Rd, T023-80633033, F023-80633066. The most expensive hotel in Southampton, smart corporate feel, with haute cuisine in **Allerton's** restaurant (£50 a head without wine).

B **Novotel**, 1 West Quay Rd, T023-80330550, F80222158. Clean and efficient mid-range chain option, with swimming pool, restaurant and bar.

C **The Star**, 26 High St, T023-80339939. Top end of this bracket, bang in the middle of town in an old building that survived the bombs.

Eating

Winchester *p194, map p196*

£££ **Chesil Rectory**, Chesil St, T01962-851555. Smart modern food, Michelin-starred, in one of the oldest buildings in the city.

££ **The Bistro** in the *Hotel du Vin* (see above) has become easily one of the best dining options in the city, and needn't break the bank with its liberal attitude to combining choices from the simple Frenchified menu (anything from £15 to £40 a head).

££ **Wykeham Arms**, 75 Kingsgate St, T01962-853834. Very popular top-quality old pub with wholesome traditional food and welcoming scholarly atmosphere. Reliable cooking for about £15 a head. Recommended.

££ **Cathedral Refectory**, Inner Close, T01962-857258. Reasonably priced fresh local ingredients confidently put together in the shadow of the cathedral with tables outside.

££ **William Walker's** in the **Wessex Hotel** (see above) has good value 'carvery' deals and views of the cathedral's south transept.

££ **Loch Fyne**, 18 Jewry St, T01962-872930. One of the fresh fish chain from Scotland in a renovated 16th-century building.

££ **La Bodega**, 9 Great Minster St, T01962-864004. Tapas bar downstairs, proper Italian upstairs (main course of home-made pasta £7, kilo of ribeye £15).

Portsmouth *p198*

££ **Still and West**, Bath Sq, Old Portsmouth, T023-92821567. Right on the seafront with a good range of seafood dishes and a real ales.

££ **Sur La Mer**, 69 Palmerston Rd, Southsea, T023-92876678. Reliable little French restaurant with a variety of good deals on its set menus and fish dishes.

Entertainment

Winchester *p194, map p196*

The Screen at Winchester, Southgate St, T01962-877007/recorded information T01962-856009, www.screencinemas.co.uk. Two cinema screens with luxurious auditoria showing middle-to-high-brow new releases.

Theatre Royal, Jury St, T01962-840440, W.theatre-royal-winchester.co.uk. Touring middle-scale dramas of a high standard.

Festivals and events

Winchester *p194, map p196*
Winchester Hat Fair, 5a Jewry St, T01962-849841, www.hatfair.co.uk. Usually in early **Jul**, is the longest running festival of street theatre in Britain. Over 40 companies from all over the world take part in the festival.

Transport

Winchester *p194, map p196*
Car hire
Enterprise Rent-a-Car, Winchester Train Station,T01962-844022. **Hendy Hire**, Easton La, T01962-891891.

Taxi
A1 Alpha Cars, 15 West Hayes,Sarum Rd, T01962-820416. **Winchester Airport Link**, 171 Stanmore La, T01962-843057.

Portsmouth *p198*
Boat
Ferries from Portsmouth for France and Spain with P&O, T0870-2424999, to **Cherbourg**, **Le Havre** and **Bilbao** or Britanny Ferries, T08705 360360, to **Caen** and **St Malo**. For the **Isle of Wight** Wightlink, T0870-5827744, runs services over 3 routes to and from the island. Portsmouth to **Ryde** (High Speed Passenger Service) £12 standard return, taking 15 mins, every 1/2 hr. Portsmouth to **Fishbourne** (Car and Passenger Service) £67 standard return car and driver, £9.80 each additional passenger, taking 40 mins, every 1/2 hr. £39 night service for car and driver valid for a month so long as you travel both ways between 2300 and 0400.

Bus
National Express, T08705-808080, run the local services from Portsmouth, The Hard Interchange, direct every 2 hrs to London Victoria (2 hrs 30 mins), direct twice hourly to Brighton, Pool Valley (3 hrs 40 mins), direct at 1040 to Bournemouth Travel Interchange (1 hr 40 mins) and also 8 times per day direct to Southampton Harbour Parade (50 mins).

Train
South West Trains, T08456-000650, run the frequent direct service from Portsmouth Harbour to **London Waterloo** (1 hr 45 mins). Wessex Trains, T08709-002320, runs the regular direct service to **Southampton Central** (45 mins) and the frequent service to **Bournemouth** (1 hr 30 mins), changing at **Southampton**. South Central Trains, T08708-306000, run the hourly direct service to Brighton (1 hr 30 mins).

Southampton *p199*
Air
Southampton Airport has its own train station, Southampton Airport Parkway. Fast trains 3 times an hr from **London Waterloo** directly to the airport station. From Southampton Airport, business and leisure passengers can reach 22 destinations, with over 200 long haul worldwide destinations via 6 key hubs including Amsterdam, Brussels, Paris, Frankfurt, Manchester and Dublin.

Boat
Red Funnel, T023-80334010, run passenger/vehicle services to East Cowes from Southampton (55 mins, £67 standard return, plus £9.40 per passenger) every 50 mins. **Red Jet Hi-Speed** service to and from West Cowes (£13.50, 22 mins) every 30 mins.

Bus
National Express, T08705-808080, run the direct service to Bournemouth (50 mins) 7 times per day and 9 times to Portsmouth Hard Interchange (50 mins). There is also an hourly direct service to London Victoria (2 hrs 35 mins) and a direct service to Salisbury (40 mins) at 1000, 1330 and 2125.

Train
South Central Trains, T08708-306000, run the regular direct service from Southampton Central to **Bournemouth** (40 mins). **Wessex Trains**, T08709-002320, run a regular direct service to Salisbury (35 mins) and 3 direct morning services to Portsmouth Harbour (50 mins). **South West Trains**, T08456-000650, run the direct service to London Waterloo (1 hr 25 mins) every 15 mins.

Directory

Winchester *p194, map p196*
Internet The Byte, 10 Parchment St, T01962-863235. **Medical services** Royal Hampshire County Hospital, Romsey Rd, T01962-863535.

New Forest

→Colour map 2

Neither new, nor really a forest, the New Forest remains without doubt one of the most individual stretches of countryside in the south of England. Ever since William the Conqueror made it his personal hunting ground almost a thousand years ago, the forest has been a playground for Londoners. Much of the area could now more aptly be described as open heathland, one of the most ecologically important sites in lowland Britain, although the wooded parts do contain a notable variety of trees. The Norman king's son and successor, William Rufus, was shot by an arrow in mysterious circumstances while out hunting – and the Rufus Stone, an unremarkable 18th-century boulder near Fordingbridge, marks the spot. Deer do still abound, but their stocky little four-legged cousins, the New Forest ponies, are much more high profile around here. Amiable enough when not with foal, these peaceable free-range grazers give the area its special character. The historic towns and villages dotted about heave with visitors during summer, but it's always possible to get away from them all by taking a walk in the woods. ▸▸ *For Sleeping, Eating and other listings, see pages 205-207.*

Ins and outs

Getting there The New Forest stretches away to the coast south of the M3/M27/A31 between Southampton and Ringwood, most of it accessible in about 2 hrs from London. A fairly comprehensive network of local buses is run by **Wilts and Dorset,** T01202-673555. Trains to Ashurst from Waterloo every 2 hrs take about 1hr 20mins. **Southwest Trains, Connex South Central** and **Virgin Cross Country** trains to Brockenhurst leave Waterloo about 3 times an hr, taking 1 hr 30 mins. Change at Brockenhurst for Lymington. Beaulieu Road is a station in the middle of nowhere between Lyndhurst and Beaulieu, a good starting point for walks. ▸▸ *For further details, see Transport, page 207.*

Getting around The New Forest is best explored on foot, pony or by bike. Local buses require some patience but connect the main towns and villages during the main part of the day, except on Sun. ▸▸ *For details of walking and riding tours, see p206. For cycle hire, see p207.*

Information New Forest TIC ⓘ *Lyndhurst, T023-80282269, www.thenewforest.co.uk, Apr-Oct daily 0900-1700, Nov-Mar daily 1000-1600.* Efficient information centre with accommodation booking service. **Lymington TIC** ⓘ *New St, T01590-689000, Apr-Oct Mon-Sat 1000-1700, Nov-Feb Mon-Sat 1000-1600.* **Forestry Commission** ⓘ *T023-80283141.* Details of guided walks and camping facilities within the Forest.

Lyndhurst

Lyndhurst, 5 miles south of Junction 1 of the M27, is the capital of the New Forest, a quaint and surprisingly unspoiled little town with a single main street. The church contains some good pre-Raphaelite stained glass. Close by, the old **Queen's House** and **Verderer's Hall** are the antique setting for the Verderer's Court, which sits on the third Monday of every month except August and December. This occasionally lively anachronism settles disputes over the forest dwellers' rights to peculiarities like turbary (cutting firewood), marl (digging for lime) and pannage (letting their pigs out to graze). In the main car park of the town, the place to find out about the area's special status and much more is the New Forest Visitor and Information Centre, where there's also a mildly diverting exhibition on the local history.

Beaulieu and around

From Lyndhurst, three roads fan out across the forest. The most attractive (and often a slow-moving traffic jam in high season) is the B3056 to **Beaulieu** past Beaulieu Road station. Beaulieu is indeed a 'beautiful place', its ancient Abbey brooding at the head of the river estuary across the water from the peaceful old estate village. Most of the cars are quite likely to be heading for Lord Montagu's **National Motor Museum** ⓘ *T01590-612345, www.beaulieu.co.uk, May-Sep daily 1000-1800, Oct-Apr 1000-1700, £11.95, concessions £9.95, children £6.95, family £33.95.*in the grounds of his family's old house, once the gatehouse of the Abbey. The Museum was started to indulge Montagu's own interests, and now there are over 250 vehicles to see, including the recordbreaker Bluebird. Almost as much a theme park as museum, you can also take a stroll down a 1930s street and race through time in a space-age pod. In the house itself are Victorian costumed guides and there's an exhibition on monastic life at the Domus of Beaulieu Abbey, dating from 1204. Or try a ride on the monorail. The high price of admission is usually justified, especially during one of the regular motoring club events at weekends.

From Beaulieu a narrow road winds for 3 miles down the estuary to **Buckler's Hard** ⓘ *T01590-616203, www.bucklershard.co.uk, Apr-Sep daily 1030-1700, Oct-Mar daily 1100- 1630, £3, concessions £2, child £1.50*, built from scratch in the 18th century by Montagus as a speculative sugar harbour and then used as a Naval dockyard for the construction of several of Nelson's ships of the line. The single grassy street slopes down to the riverside, often very crowded in summer but well worth an overnight stay to enjoy the tranquility of the place once all the trippers have gone home. Now it's also a popular yachting centre with a couple of museums on the living quarters and activity in the shipyard during its heyday.

Lymington and around

From Buckler's Hard the long-distance footpath the **Solent Way** heads along one of the few undeveloped stretches of forest coastline, passing the impressive ruins of one of the largest medieval tithe barns in England at St Leonard's Grange, to Lymington, 7 miles west. A yachting centre to rival Cowes further up the Solent, Lymington is the leaping off point for Yarmouth on the Isle of Wight and scarcely preserves its dignity under the onslaught of braying boaties and their flashy fibreglass toys. The little harbour area throngs with holidaymakers looking over the tackle and cramming into dinky alleyways lined with gift shops, tearooms and nautical nick-nacks. Sloping uphill, the town's Georgian High Street is also worth a look. The **St Barbe Museum and Art Gallery** ⓘ *New St, Lymington, T01590-676969, www.stbarbe-museum.org.uk, Mon-Sat 1000-1600, Jul and Aug also Sun 1400-1700, £3, concessions £2, family £6* puts on temporary exhibitions of contemporary artists, and is also a small permanent local history museum.

Sleeping

Beaulieu and around *p205*

L **Master Builder's House Hotel**, Buckler's Hard, Beaulieu, T01590-616253, www.themasterbuilders.co.uk. Done up in that slightly characterless but ever-so tasteful style beloved by smart hotels in the country. Its location on the banks of the Beaulieu river, at the end of the single grassy street that is Buckler's Hard, makes the Master Builder somewhere quite special.

Lymington and around *p205*

L **Chewton Glen**, New Milton, T01425-275341, www.chewtonglen.com, voted top hotel in the south, at £370 per night you expect a lot. The old house and grounds are elegant but the facilities are no less than one would expect and the pervading feel is slightly corporate.

A **Westover Hall Hotel**, Park La, Milford-on-Sea, T01590-643044. Charming informal atmosphere in a Victorian millionaire's seaside villa, with individual rooms of great character, many with sea views as well as a beautiful restaurant, bar and garden.

B **Gordleton Mill**, Silver St, near Lymington, T01590-682219, F683073. Attractive pub and restaurant hotel with twee water gardens and rated restaurant.

D **Carrington Farmhouse**, 22 Keyhaven Rd, Milford-on-Sea, T01590-642966. A 16th-century cottage B&B close to Keyhaven ferry.

Ringwood and Fordingbridge

C **Compasses Inn**, Damerham, near Fordingbridge, T01725-518231. Pleasant rooms in an attractive pub doing reasonable grub on the western fringe of the forest.

C **Alderholt Mill**, Sandelheath Rd, Fordingbridge, T01425-653130, W.alderholtmill.co.uk. A working watermill doing B&B with a lovely back garden. Very good value. Recommended.

F **Burley YHA**, Cott Lane, Burley, near Ringwood, T/F01425-403233. Former family house with 36 beds in 1-, 4-, 6- and 10-bedded rooms, next to the **White Buck Inn**. Quite hard to reach without a car.

Eating

Lymington and around *p205*

£££ **Westover Hall Hotel**, Park La, Milford-on-Sea, T01590-643044. Has a beautiful little dining room, overlooking Christchurch Bay with views of the Needles in the distance, doing an excellent dinner menu which should be booked in advance.

££ **Bistro on the Bridge**, 3 Bridge St, Christchurch, T01202-482522. Simple fresh ingredients well-presented at this offshoot of Bournemouth's famous **Bistro on the Beach**.

££ **East End Arms**, Lymington Rd, East End, T01590-626223. New Forest gastropub run by the same people as the **Master Builder's House Hotel**.

££ **Egan's Restaurant**, 24 Gosport St, Lymington, T01590-676165. Cheerfully decorated fresh fish restaurant just off the High St in Lymington. Good value £10 3-course lunch.

Bars, pubs and clubs

Lyndhurst *p204*

New Forest Inn, Emery Down, T023-80282329. Large back garden (and B&B) in a picturesque village at the heart of the forest with standard pub food.

Lymington and around *p205*

Red Lion, Ropehill, Boldre, T01590-673177. Old boozer on the edge of the forest with beamed rooms and decent bar food.

Gun Inn, Keyhaven, T01590-642391. Basic inexpensive food and good beer in a cheery old local boozer near the ferry to Hurst Castle and Isle of Wight.

The Chequers Inn, Lower Woodside, Lymington, T01590-673415, www.chequersinn.com. Country pub with barbecue, very popular with the hearty boating community.

Ringwood and Fordingbridge

Royal Oak, North Gorley, T01425-652244. A country pub in picturesque surroundings on the western edge of the Forest, where you can sit and watch the ducks on the pond while supping your pint from the local Ringwood Brewery. Good value pub grub too.

Activities and tours

Calshot Activities Centre, Calshot Spit, Fawley, T023-80892077, www.hants.gov.uk/calshot One of the largest in Britain: 3 ski slopes, climbing wall, indoor velodrome, watersports, in an extraordinary position next to Calshot Castle on the spit.

New Forest Waterpark, Ringwood Rd, North Gorley, T01425-656868. Water-skiing, jet-skiing, inflatable banana boats. Jun-Sep daily 1000-2100, Apr and Oct weekends only, May Wed-Sun. Water-skiing from £15; aquarides £6; jet-skiing £30. Advisable to book.

Boating

Puffin Cruises from Lymington Town Quay to Yarmouth, Isle of Wight, T0850-947618.

Sea fishing trips from Keyhaven, 8-6 hr deep sea trips, 3 hr mackerel trips Ray Pitt T01425-612896.

Riding

New Forest Riding Centre, The Old Barn, Dale Farm, Manor Rd, Applemore, T023-80843180. Tue-Sun 0900-1500 30 mins horse rides, 1 hr rides (£15), swimming on horseback and residential holidays.

New Park Manor Stables, New Park, Lyndhurst Rd, Brockenhurst, T01590-623919. Another reputable residential riding school and stables, marginally less expensive than most.

Burley Villa School of Riding, near New Milton, T01425-610278, www.burleyvilla.co.uk. Riding Western style.

Walking
Solent Way Milford-on-Sea to Emsworth (60 miles), a long-distance coastal footpath.

Transport

Cycle hire
AA Bike Hire, Lyndhurst, Fernglen, T023-80283349, www.aabikehire newforest.co.uk;
Adventure Cycles, 97 Station Rd, New Milton, T01425-615960;
Burley Bike Hire, Burley, T01425-403584;
Beaulieu, T01590-611029;
Cyclexperience, Island Shop, 2-4 Brookley Rd, Brockenhurst, T01590-624204, www.cycleX.co.uk;
Perkins, 7 Provost St, Fordingbridge, T01425-653475 Inexpensive tourers for £5 a day.

Taxi
Marchwood Motorways Taxi service
T0800-5250521.

Isle of Wight

→Colour map 2

Like many of its fairly half-baked attractions, the Isle of Wight charges an entrance fee. If you're taking the car, it's likely to cost you more than a trip to France. That said, this 23-mile wide, 13-mile deep 'sunshine isle' does have a quirky charm. It's often observed that it represents the south of England in miniature. Geologically speaking that's certainly accurate, the heavy clay in the north giving away to a pair of downland chalk ridges, one of them breaking up in quite spectacular style in the sea to the west at the Needles. And there's more than a touch of little England about the place as a whole, with its old Norman castle, high-security prisons and social problems besetting the capital Newport in the middle, busy harbours in the north and tidy manor house villages snuggled up in the rolling hills inland. The east coast is where the majority of trippers fetch up, in the retirement and seaside entertainment resorts of Sandown, Shanklin and Ventnor. The south has a beautiful coastline, while the north can boast one of the epicentres of world yachting at Cowes. ▸▸ *For Sleeping, Eating and other listings, see pages 213-216.*

Ins and outs

Getting there **Car ferries** leave the mainland from Southampton (at the end of the M3, 77 miles from London (1½ hrs' drive), Portsmouth (about 10 miles from the M3, down the M27 eastwards and M275), and Lymington (about 22 miles beyond Southampton via the M27 westwards and the A337 across the New Forest, at least a 2 hr drive). **Mainline rail services** to Southampton run from London Waterloo about twice hourly taking 1 hr 30 mins, to Portsmouth more often, also from London Waterloo, taking about 1 hr 45mins. Lymington is on the mainline to Weymouth. ▸▸ *For further details, see Transport, page 215*

Getting around The east coast resorts of Ryde, Sandown, Shanklin and Ventnor are well served by public transport, by the **Island Line**, Isle of Wight Steam Railway, T01983-884343, and by buses run by **Southern Vectis**, T01983-522456. Buses also serve the west end of the island (including Southern Vectis' useful Island Explorer) but much less regularly. A car or bicycle are the best ways of reaching some of the island's beauty spots. Bicycling is a joy out of season on the smaller roads that criss-cross the southwest of the island around Godshill, Wroxall and Brading, or from Yarmouth to the south coast. During the summer traffic usually finds its way into the remotest corners of the island.

Information **Isle of Wight Tourism** ⓘ *Westridge Centre, Brading Rd, Ryde, T01983-813800, www.islandbreaks.co.uk.*

Northwest Wight

The old harbour town of Yarmouth is the most attractive port of entry on the island. The pubs, restaurants and hotels gathered around its small town square can become impossibly busy in the summer, but out of season they can make a very enjoyable day trip from the New Forest. A few miles east the marshland around the pretty little estuarine village of Newtown throngs with visiting birdlife. Almost bang in the middle of the island, Carisbrooke Castle on its little hill looks suitably noble and battered given its long history as a Royal prison and Norman powerhouse. Directly due north, at the mouth of the Medina, Cowes has become synonymous with international yachting and all that that very expensive sport entails.

Ins and outs

Getting there and around Services 1/1A: Cowes, Newport, Ryde, Tesco, Bembridge. 7/7A: Ryde, Sandown, Shanklin, Ventnor, West Wight, Ryde, Binstead, Wootton, Newport, West Wight and Ryde, Newport, Brighstone, Brook, Totland. 33/34: Ryde, Havenstreet, Newport, Gurnard, Cowes and Ryde, Haylands, Swanmore, Ryde. All hourly during the main part of the day. Two open top buses serve the area. 42: Yarmouth, Alum Bay, Needles Battery and 43: Newport, Yarmouth.

Information **Yarmouth TIC** ⓘ *The Quay, T01983-760015, Mon-Sat 0930-1630 Sun 1000-1600.* **Cowes TIC** ⓘ *Fountain Quay, T01983-291914, Tue-Sat 0930-1630.* **Newport TIC** ⓘ *The Guildhall, High St, T01983-823366, Mon-Sat 0900-1730 Sun 1000-1600.*

Yarmouth

Yarmouth is one of the most attractive towns on the island, its old harbour and town square yet to be overwhelmed by tourist tat, although it gets very crowded in the summer.

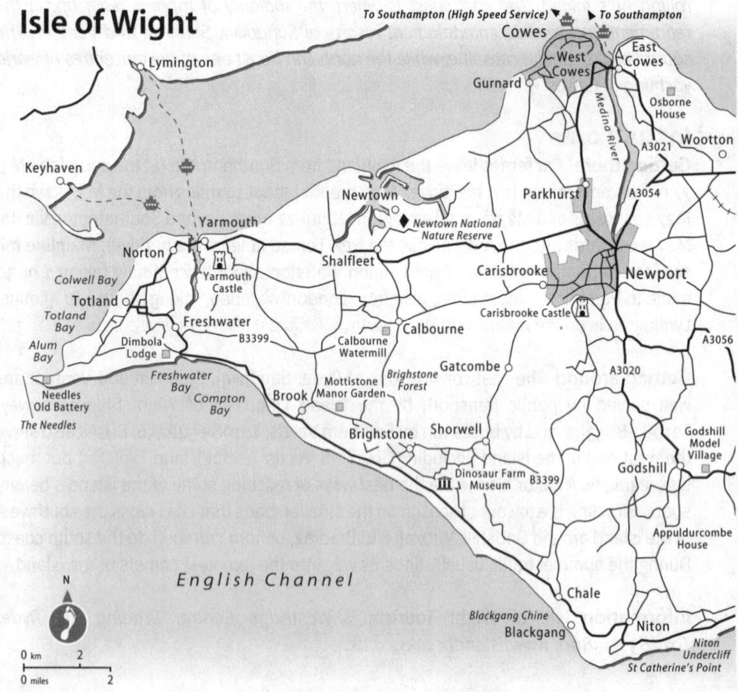

Overlooking the harbour, **Yarmouth Castle** ⓘ *(EH), T01983-760678, Apr-Sep daily 1000-1800, Oct daily 1000-1700, £2.50, concessions £1.90, child £1.30*, was Henry VIII's final coastal fortification, completed in the mid-16th century to protect the town from the French, now a building housing exhibitions of local painting and photos of old Yarmouth, with battlements affording fine views over the Solent, good for picnics.

Newtown

About 5 miles east of Yarmouth, north of the main road to Newport, the tranquil little village of Newtown often wins the 'best-kept' award on the island, its cottage gardens a feast for the eyes in spring and summer. The strangely isolated little 17th-century brick and stone **Old Town Hall** ⓘ *(NT) T01983-531785, Apr-Oct Mon, Wed, Sun 1400-1700, Jul and Aug Mon-Thu, Sun 1400-1700, £1.60, child £0.80* is evidence that this was an important town in the Middle Ages, and one that became an infamous 'rotten borough', hugely over-represented in Parliament and done away with by the Reform Acts of the 1820s. Birdwatching and excellent coastal and marsh walks can be enjoyed in the **Newtown National Nature Reserve.**

Carisbrooke Castle

ⓘ *(EH), T01983-522107, Apr-Sep daily 1000-1800, Oct daily 1000-1700, Nov-Mar daily 1000-1600, £5, concessions £3.80, children £2.50, family £11.50.*

The island's most important castle, at Carisbrooke, 5 miles further east on the A3054, commands tremendous panoramic views from its wallwalk and remains surprisingly complete, its great stone walls and gatehouse standing proud at the top of a small hill. It started life as a Saxon camp, parts of which can still be seen below the Norman keep. The Redvers family ran the island from here until the death of Countess Isabella in 1293, when the castle was bought by Edward I, his son adding the great gatehouse. King Charles I was imprisoned here during the Civil War before his execution. The working donkey wheel deep well in the wethouse is the star attraction inside, along with engaging museum displays on island and castle life down the ages.

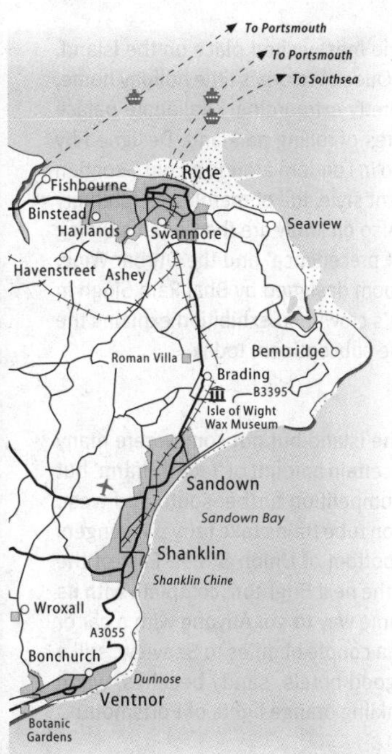

Cowes

Back on the coast, Cowes is the most renowned town on the island thanks to its global yachting associations. The home of the Royal Yacht Squadron, during Cowes Week (early Aug), and at boating events throughout the summer, the narrow old streets of Cowes are awash with yellow wellies, hearty boatowners, old seadogs and very focused professional yachties. The snob value of Cowes Week in the social calendar was confirmed when sailing became a Royal hobby in the 19th century and shows no sign of diminishing, although the whole event has become significantly less amateurish. At any other time, the old town of West Cowes is an attractive and genteel place to poke around, connected to the more workaday East Cowes by the floating chain bridge.

Northeast Wight

Queen Victoria's favourite summer retreat at Osborne House now draws in hordes of curious visitors. The opulence of its interior is unlikely to disappoint. Further west, Ryde is the other main ferry port, a Victorian town that has never quite achieved its grand aspirations. The more unassuming and quietly well-to-do seaside village of Seaview just along the coast is more of a magnet. Bembridge is another major yachting centre at the mouth of the River Yar. At Brading the downs rise up to the south and the island's holiday spirit gets into gear.

Ins and outs

Getting there and around Ryde is the main ferry port on the eastern side of the island. The **Island Line** electric railway links Ryde with Smallbrook Junction, Brading, Sandown, Lake and Shanklin. The **Isle of Wight Steam Railway** runs from Smallbrook (£9 Island Liner ticket allows unlimited all-day travel on both). **Island Explorer** runs bus services 7/7a; service 8 Tesco, Oakfield, Ryde, Seaview/Nettlestone; services 33/34, and an hourly service round the island in both directions. **Southern Vectis**, T01983-532373, services 1/1A, services 4/5 Ryde, Binstead, Wootton, East Cowes, Newport, Osborne, East Cowes.

Information **TIC Ryde** ⓘ *Western Esplanade, T01983-562905, Mon-Sat 0900-1630 Sun1000-1600.*

Osbourne House

Osborne House ⓘ *(EH), East Cowes, T01983-200022, Apr-Sep daily 1000-1800 (last admission 1600, house closes at 1700), £8, concessions £60, child £4, family £20, grounds only £4.50/£3.40/£2.30.*

A mile or so east of East Cowes, this is the single most visited place on the island, especially since featuring in the film *Mrs Brown*. Queen Victoria's little holiday home, where she grieved for her beloved Albert, is a pretty extraordinary Italianate palace looking down on wide-terraced gardens and acres of rolling parkland. Designed by Thomas Cubitt (responsible for the look of Pimlico in London) around an old Georgian house in 1846, the inside is finished in an opulent style, full of marble, gilt, statuary and portraits of 19th-century European royalty. Also on show are the Queen's Dining Room, with place settings showing the 'order of precedence' and the Durbar Wing, where her daughter Beatrice lived, including a room designed by Bhai Ram Singh in the 1890s to show off India, the jewel in Victoria's crown. An exhibition explains the lavish furnishings' contemporary relevance to the subcontinent today.

Ryde and Seaview

Ryde is the main ferry terminal on the east of the island but not somewhere many people would otherwise choose to visit. It has a certain amount of 'faded charm' but even in that department can't really beat the competition further south and west. Getting into the holiday spirit, though, old London tube trains take ferry passengers inland along the pier, depositing them at the bottom of Union Street. East of the Hoverport, the Esplanade might like to become the next Brighton, complete with its miniature oriental pavilion, but it clearly has some way to go. Anyone with a car or bike is likely to do much better heading east for a couple of miles to Seaview, still a quiet little seaside village with a selection of good hotels, sandy beaches, warm breezes and views across the Solent of the twinkling orange lights of Portsmouth.

Brading

From Bembridge a quite spectacular road heads over Culver Downs. Here is the well-sited but bog-standard pub, the **Culverhaven Inn**, as well as various gun emplacements, and good views overlooking Sandown and Shanklin. After 3 miles or so the road arrives in Brading, which provides a foretaste of the full-on appeal to the tourist purse made further along the coast. As well as the **Isle of Wight Wax Museum** ⓘ *T01983-407286, daily 1000-1700, £5, under-14s £3.40*, with its inevitable Chamber of Horrors, there's **Morton Manor**, ⓘ *T01983-406168, Apr-Oct Mon-Fri, Sun 1000-1730, £4*, a 13th-century manor house surrounded by an ancient 6-acre garden – a sight for sore eyes in spring – as well as a maze and vineyard. The remarkably good value **Lilliput Antique Doll and Toy Museum** ⓘ *T01983-407231, www.lilliputmuseum.com, daily 1000-1700, £1.95, children £1*, is typical of the island in many ways: the museum's really impressive collection of old playthings is presented in a charming and amateurish way. Equally, the privately run **Roman Villa** ⓘ*T01983-406223, Apr-Oct daily 0930-1700, £2.75, children £1.35*, with its well-preserved hypocaust, intriguing and beautiful floor mosaics in a Roman room with a view crying out for a new roof, is much more accessible and enjoyable than many an overtended English Heritage site.

Southeast Wight

The island's reputation for seaside holiday heaven (or hell) emanates from the resorts of Sandown and Shanklin, amusement arcade wonderlands with a tacky style all their own – love 'em or loathe 'em. Round the corner, Bonchurch is quietly superior to their boisterous charms, tucked into the peculiar geological landslip bursting with exotic vegetation known as the Undercliff. Next door, Ventnor is a solidly picturesque seaside town tumbling down to a little sandy bay. A short hop inland, Godshill draws in the crowds to wonder at its picture-postcard setting, model village and remarkable church.

Ins and outs

Getting there and around Route Rouge services 2/3/3A/3B, Cowes-Newport-Shanklin-Sandown-Ryde; Cowes, Newport, Godshill, Ventnor; and Cowes, Newport, Robin Hill, Sandown. **Island Explorer Services** services 7/7A. Service 47, Sandown-Shanklin (Old Village-Town-Esplanade).

Information Sandown TIC ⓘ *8 High St, T01983-403886, Mon-Sat 0930-1730*. **Shanklin TIC** ⓘ *67 High St, T01983-862942, Mon-Sat 0930-1630, Sun1000-1600.* **Ventnor TIC** ⓘ *T01983-853625, Apr-Oct only.*

Sandown and Shanklin

Two miles south of Brading, the wide sweep of Sandown Bay is almost entirely taken up with the resorts of Sandown and Shanklin. These two fulfill most people's image of the 'holiday island', with their esplanades, sandy beaches, crumbling hotels and tacky amusements. Sandown is marginally more geriatric, while Shanklin boasts the thatched, illuminated (May-Sep) and twee **Shanklin Chine** ⓘ *T01983-866432, www.shanklin chine.co.uk, Apr-Oct daily 1000-dusk*, a ravine running down the cliff full of rare plants and used as a training ground for Commandos during the war. Henry 'Hiawatha' Long- fellow visited it in 1868, leaving some verses on the fountain near the top of the chine.

Bonchurch and Ventnor

Round the corner beyond Dunnose, 3 miles along the pretty Undercliff, the closest the Isle of Wight comes to a corniche road, Bonchurch and Ventnor are a much more solidly attractive south-facing mix of seaside amusements, good restaurants and reasonable accommodation. All of which contributes effectively to a happy holiday mood, nestling below St Boniface Down.

Three miles north of the Botanic Gardens along the B3327, a narrow track leads off to the left and a striking ruined stately home set in Capability Brown-landscaped gardens. **Appledurcombe House** ⓘ *Wroxall, T01983-852484, www.appuldurcombe.co.uk, May-Sep daily 1000-1700, Oct-Apr daily 1000-1600, £2, children £1.50, concessions £2.25*, was once the grandest on the island but fell prey to some strange adulterous shenanigans amongst its owners, an amusing story told on information boards in the empty shell. Now its austere Palladian architecture stands lonely and elegant in its gardens, crying out to be sketched. The grounds are a beautiful spot for a picnic and there's a falconeary centre next door.

As if the Chine were not enough, Godshill, 5 miles west of Shanklin on the A3020, must rank as one of the most quaint little villages in England. Its double-naved church claims to be among the top 10 'most visited' in the country, perhaps to see the Lily Crucifix mural from 1440 – painted over during the Reformation and uncovered in the 19th century – but also no doubt to ask forgiveness for the huge cream teas taken in the village. Almost inevitably, in the gardens of the old vicarage, there's a **model village** ⓘ *T01983-840270, Mar-Sep 1000-1700 (Jul and Aug until 1800), £2.75, children £1.25, concessions £2.50*, a good example of its type, with tiny people enjoying a hearty variety of outdoor activities dotted about between 1/10-scale stone houses with miniaturized gardens and a 1/20-scale model railway. The other attraction, the Shell Museum, a collection of fossils, shells and minerals, is almost overwhelmed by its gift shop.

South and West Wight

The least over-developed and most scenic part of the island, the southern coast path around St Catherine's Point, St Catherine's Hill and the downs above Brighstone provide the best walking country. Along with a few less busy old villages like Shorwell and Calbourne, the southwest is also home to several good quality visitor attractions like the gardens at Mottistone Manor, the Dinosaur Farm Musem, the working watermill at Calbourne and Dimbola Lodge, the former home of pioneer portrait photographer Julia Cameron. To the west, the island peters out beyond Freshwater in dramatic style with the sea-swept chalk stacks of the Needles.

Ins and outs

Getting around Island Explorer services 7/7A and 42 Yarmouth, Alum Bay, Needles Battery (open-top bus).

St Catherine's Point

Six miles west along the coastal A3055 from Ventnor, St Catherine's Point is the most southerly headland on the island, a lovely cliffside spot with a little lighthouse overlooked by St Catherine's Hill, the highest point on the island (by 1 m over St Boniface Down to the east). On the summit, a medieval **lighthouse** known as the Pepperpot, officially St Catherine's Oratory, stands next to the **Saltcellar**, an abortive 19th-century attempt at a lighthouse (because of the frequent fog), used as a gun emplacement during the Second World War. On the road at the foot of the hill, close to the rather desperate **Blackgang Chine Amusement Park** (partly because it's gradually falling into the sea), there's a strange little **temple to Shakespeare**, a shrine quoting verses from the *Two Gentlemen of Verona* put up by Thomas Letts of diary fame.

The A3055 runs northwest along the coast, a military road constructed to repel French invaders, after six miles passing the **Dinosaur Farm Museum** ⓘ *T01983-740401, www.wightonline.co.uk/dinosaurfarm, £2, concessions £1.50, children £1.* Established following the discovery of a well-preserved brachiosaurus in 1992, it's where fossils found on hunts can be identified and rare specimens can be seen in the process of conservation by experts.

Shorwell and Brighstone

At Chale, the B3399 heads north inland to the picturesque village of Shorwell, an excellent base for walks on the central downland. **Limerstone Down,** 2 miles west of the village, provides particularly wide-reaching views of almost the entire sea-girt little island. At the foot of the hill is another sweet village, Brighstone, with an interesting Village Museum in a row of cute thatched cottages with a National Trust shop. The Trust's most impressive property on the island is 2 miles west of Brighstone, at **Mottistone Manor** ⓘ *(NT), T01983-741302, garden open Apr-Oct Tue, Wed 1100-1730, Sun and bank holidays 1400-1730, £2.80, concessions £1.30,* the place to take in sea views, teas and some colourful herbaceous borders in a 16th-century manor house garden.

Freshwater Bay and The Needles

Back on the south coast, at Freshwater Bay, five miles west of Mottistone, the large seaside house called **Dimbola Lodge** ⓘ *Terrace La, Freshwater Bay, T01983-756814, www.dimbola.co.uk, Tue-Sun 1000-1700, £3, children free,* where the pioneer photographer Julia Cameron lived and worked has been preserved, with a permanent exhibition of her Victorian portraits 'Famous Men and Fair Women' and also changing shows on contemporary photographers, an excellent vegetarian restaurant with sea views as well as workshops and other events.

The walk from Brighstone continues west along Compton Down affording magnificent sea views southwards. To the south below is **Compton Bay**, famous for its very clean beaches. The chalk ridge continues along **Tennyson Down** and **High Down,** ending up at The Needles in the west. It's worth arriving in time to check out the **Needles Old Battery** ⓘ *(NT), West Highdown, Totland, T01983-754772, Apr-Jun, Sep, Oct Mon-Thu, Sun 1030-1700, Jul and Aug daily 1030-1700, £3.50, family £7.50,* built into the cliffs here, alongside a strange rocket testing site. The fort was built in 1862 to protect against the threat of French invasion, with a 200-ft tunnel leading to spectacular views of the Hampshire and Dorset coast. Its gun barrels are still in place, and the searchlight position accessible up winding spiral staircase. The 1940s tearoom is a treat.

Sleeping

Northwest Wight *p208*

The standard of accommodation in Cowes is generally poor. Also expect the whole town to be booked solid in the summer.

A **The George Hotel**, Yarmouth, T01983-760331. One of the best hotels on the island, run by the same people as the **Master Builder's House Hotel** in Buckler's Hard, New Forest, see page 205. Good brasserie with outdoor seating next door to a smart restaurant.

C **Fountain Arms** High St, Cowes, T01983-292397. A central pub with comfortable rooms, if not that quiet.

C **Duke of York**, Mill Hill Rd, Cowes, T01983-295171. A very lively and friendly old pub just up from the floating bridge.

D **Jireh House**, St James Sq, Yarmouth, T01983-760513, is a B&B well worth trying.

D **Wavell's,** T01983-760738, above their own deli, with a clean, comfortable guest annexe.

Northeast Wight *p210*

A **Priory Bay Hotel**, Priory Dr, Seaview, T01983-613146, www.priorybay.co.uk. Probably the classiest hotel on the island, on the site of an old priory with converted barns, gardens and a highly rated restaurant.

A **Biskra Beach Hotel**, 17 St Thomas's St, Ryde, T01983-567913, www.biskrahotel.com. The other contender in the style stakes, right on the beach with an Italian restaurant.
B **Seaview Hotel**, High St, Seaview, T01983-612711, www.seaviewhotel.co.uk. Popular award-winning restaurant and hotel in the centre of the village, both acclaimed by the national press, something of a haven for the more affluent Seaviewers.
B **Northbank Hotel**, Seaview, T01983-612227. Pleasant 18-room family-run Victorian hotel right on the beach in the middle of the village boasting an Aga-cooked menu.
B **Springvale Hotel**, Seaview, T01983-612533. Beautifully positioned Edwardian house overlooking the Solent makes an eccentric alternative to staying in the village.
C **Crab and Lobster Inn**, 32 Foreland Fields Rd, Bembridge, T01983-872244. Busy pub with rooms in a fine position on the most eastern tip of the island. Local seafood is a speciality, but parking in summer can be next to impossible.
C **Newham Farm**, Binstead, Ryde, T01983-882423, www.newhamfarm.co.uk. 17th century working farm built on the site of an abbey. Easy-going, friendly atmosphere, impeccable service and magnificent breakfasts. A real find..

Southeast Wight *p211*

A **Royal Hotel**, Belgrave Rd, Ventnor, T01983-852186, www.royalhoteliow.co.uk. The grandest hotel in Ventnor, recently refurbished in a restrained and airy way, with heated outdoor pool and sea views.
A **Windcliffe Manor**, Sandrock Rd, Undercliffe T01983-730215. Another option near Ventnor.
B **Shanklin Manor House Hotel**, Manor Rd, Old Village, Shanklin, T01983-862777. Welcoming and friendly old house with pool indoor, outdoor and in the games room, close to thatched old Shanklin.
C **Kerne Farm**, Alverstone, Sandown, T01983-403721. Old farmhouse B&B full of rustic charm, with self-catering cottages, conservatory and large garden.
D **Hillside Hotel**, Mitchell Av, Ventnor, T01983-852271. Small family-run thatch-roofed hotel overlooking Ventnor from the foot of Boniface Down. Good value vegetarian menu.
D **Spyglass Inn**, Esplanade, Ventnor, T01983-855338, F855220. Small rooms with sea views above a very convivial pub (see below).
F **Sandown YHA**, The Firs, Fitzroy St, T01983-402651, F403565. A 47-bed hostel in a converted townhouse 300 yds from the Esplanade.

South and West Wight *p212*

A **Swainston Manor Hotel**, Calbourne, T01983-521121. Grand old country house in a beautiful garden with old-fashioned, slightly run-down furnishings.
B **Sandpipers**, Coastguard Lane, Freshwater Bay, T01983-758500 with **Fat Cat on the Bay** restaurant.
C **North Court**, Shorwell, T01983-740415. Jacobean mansion, snooker table in the library, set in 14 acres of carefully tended gardens, croquet and lawn tennis. No smoking.
C **Rockstone Cottage**, Colwell Chine Rd, T01983-753723. B&B with attractive garden, near Totland.
D **Westcourt Farm**, Shorwell, T01983-740233. Charming old Elizabethan manor house with beautiful views and cosy rooms. No smoking.
F **Totland Bay YHA**, Hurst Hill, Totland Bay, T01983-752165, F756443. The best budget option near the Needles.

Eating

Northwest Wight *p208*

£££ **Salty's**, Quay St, Yarmouth, T01983-761550, is a harbourside restaurant patronized by the locals who come for the fish and busy downstairs bar, one of the most highly rated places on the island.
££ **Café Mozart**, 48 High St, Cowes, T01983-293681, do some Frenchified light meals, main courses about £10.

For an explanation of the sleeping and eating price codes used in this guide, see the inside front cover. Other relevant information is provided in the Essentials chapter, page 36.

££ Murray's, 106 High St, Cowes, T01983-296233, has a long-standing reputation for its fresh fish and seafood.
££ New Inn, Mill Rd, Shalfleet, T01983-531314, is a pub with riverside garden doing food to a high standard and a reputation for excellent fish dishes.
££ Valentino's, 93 High St, Carisbrooke, T01983-522458, is a mid-range Italian restaurant popular with the locals.
£ Primefood, 62 High St, Cowes, T01983-291111, is a superior deli, a good place to pick up provisions for your boat or put together a picnic.
£ Yorkies Fish and Chips, 55 High St, Cowes, T01983-291713, is a famous old-fashioned chippy.

Northeast Wight *p210*
£££ Seaview Hotel (see above) is well worth booking.
££ Ivar Cottage, Hillway, Bembridge, T01983-874758. Sweet little cottage garden on the B3395 4 miles west of Bembridge, where absolutely fresh crab and lobster can be enjoyed or taken away for a picnic.
££ Net, Sherbourne St, Bembridge, T01983-875800, is a newish style restaurant that's a winner with the sailing fraternity with a brasserie menu and regularly changing fusion food dinner menu.
££ The Old Fort, Esplanade, Seaview, T01983-612363, a strange combination of diner and bar, a social hub right on the seafront doing competent cuisine.

Southeast Wight *p211*
££ Bonchurch Inn, The Shute, Bonchurch, T01983-852611. Italian food and English staples in a curio-crammed olde-worlde pub in a very pretty village.
££ Spyglass Inn, Esplanade, Ventnor, T01983-855338. South-facing and right beside the sea, very popular with families (also does rooms) and doing reasonably good food that can be enjoyed outside braving the gulls and spume at high tide.

South and West Wight *p212*
££ Bay View Restaurant, Totland, T01983-756969. Great position on the beach, with stunning sunset views, unfortunately only complemented by adequate and expensive cuisine and a noisy bar area.
££ Blacksmiths Arms, Calbourne Rd, near Newport, T01983-529263. A surprising find perched high in the middle of the island, a fully equipped German beerkeller in an old pub with great views north to the mainland. German dining room and live music nightly.
££ The Red Lion, Church Pl, Freshwater, T01983-754925. Quiet but very popular pub doing an above-average menu prepared from fresh ingredients, in one of the more attractive corners of Freshwater, up by the old church. Recommended.
£ The Buddle Inn, St Catherine's Rd, Niton Undercliff, T01983-730243. Attractive old pub with a large garden and model of Carisbrooke Castle out front, near the south coast path, doing reliable and reasonably priced pub grub (cod and chips £5.25).
£ Gatcombe Tearooms, Little Gatcombe Farm, Newbarn Lane, Gatcombe, T01983-721580. Sidney the peacock patrols outside this modern farmhouse where good home- made teas can be taken just beneath the downs in the middle of the island (also a B&B).
£ The Oasis, Castlehaven Caravan Site, Niton, T01983-730461, winter T01983-855556. Do basic snacks in a funny little hut near St Catherine's Lighthouse, good for coast pathers.

Transport

Boat
Wightlink, T0870-5827744, runs ferry services over 3 routes to and from the island. Portsmouth to Rydge (high speed passenger service) £12 standard return, taking 15 mins, every 30 mins. Portsmouth to Fishbourne (car and passenger service) £67 standard return car and driver, £9.80 each additional passenger, taking 40 mins, every 30 mins. £39 night service for car and driver valid for a month so long as you travel both ways between 2300 and 0400. Lymington to Yarmouth (car and passenger service) £67 standard return car and driver, £9.80 each additional passenger, taking 30 mins, every 30 mins. **Red Funnel**, T023-80334010, run passenger/vehicle services to East Cowes from Southampton (55 mins, £67 standard return, plus £9.40 per passenger) every 50 mins. **Red Jet Hi-Speed** service to and from West Cowes and Southampton (£13.50, 22

mins) every 30 mins. **Hovertravel**, T01983-811000, run passenger services between Ryde Esplanade and Southsea in under 10 mins (£11.30 return). They have a frequent service running 7 days a week. For day tripping foot passengers, the cheapest and most charming option late May-Sep is the tiny **Keyhaven to Yarmouth Ferry**, T01590-642500, which takes about 40 mins leaving Keyhaven at 0915, 1030, 1230, 1630 and returning from Yarmouth at 1000, 1130, 1330, 1530, 1715. £7 day return.

Car

Bartletts Service Station, 5 Langbridge, Newchurch, Sandown, T01983-865338. **Ford Rental**, River Way, Newport, T01983-523441. **Hillstone Self Drive Car Hire**, Osborne Rd, Shanklin, T01983-864263. **Solent Self Drive Ltd**, 32 High St, Cowes, T01983-282050. **Volkswagen Rental**, George St, Ryde, T01983-562322.

Cycle

Battersby Cycles, Ryde, T01983-562039. **Bikemech**, Freshwater, T01983-756787. **Bikestore**, Ryde, T01983-812989. **GP Rentals**, Bembridge, T0800-9173494. **Island Cycle Hire**, Sandown, T07712-363134. **Isle of Bikes**, Brading, T01983-406306. **Isle Cycle Hire**, Yarmouth, T01983- 760219. **Offshore Sports**, Cowes, T01983-290514 and Shanklin, T01983-8662. **Wight Mountain**, Newport, T01983-533445.

Southwest England

Introduction

The Southwest is a consistently delightful region of England and one of the most popular with visitors. Relatively warm and wet, here's the place that homesick Englishmen are supposed to see in dreams: the honeystone villages of the Cotswold hills in Gloucestershire; the golden flagon of cider from Somerset's apple orchards; the winding green lanes and clotted cream of Dorset; the foaming breakers on Devon's rocky coast; and the mystical light bathing Cornwall. Surprisingly enough it does still exist, but you'll need to escape the traffic, overpriced food and shabby accommodation to really live the dream. A refreshing place to wake up might be its unofficial capital, Bristol, an earthier and more businesslike kind of Brighton.

Next door, Bath isn't slumbering either, as it makes the most of its Roman spa town heritage and elegant 18th-century architecture. Gloucestershire is one of the most aristocratic of counties, its rolling Cotswolds hardly a guarded secret though, with a glorious cathedral in Gloucester and another 18th-century spa town at Cheltenham.

Further west, in Devon, the natural wildernesses of Dartmoor and Exmoor are sandwiched between a high wooded coastline to the north and the reddish rocks of the Jurassic Coast in the south. Even further west, Cornwall entices visitors with some brilliant beaches, headlands and harbour towns before England finally peters out with the subtropical granite rocks that are the Isles of Scilly. Cornwall is also home to the magnificent new climate-controlled biospheres in a disused clay pit called the Eden Project, a millennium project that sums up something about the Southwest as a whole: it's all about the sea, stone and whatever can be done with what's in between.

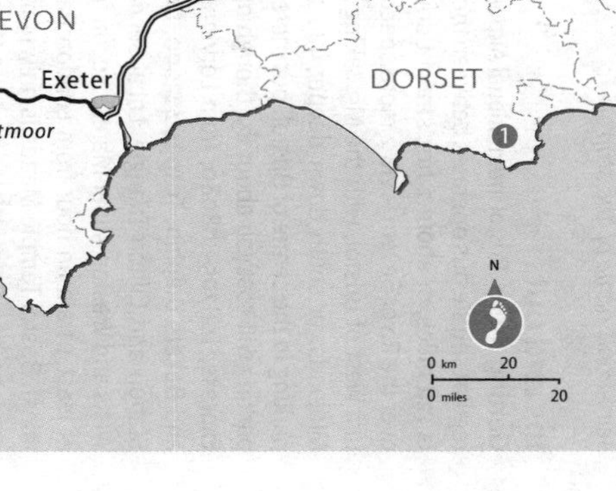

★ Don't miss...

1. Wonder at the spectacular position of **Corfe Castle** at the entrance to the Isle of Purbeck, page 258.
2. Pause for thought or drink cider on the top of **Glastonbury Tor** before losing your religion, page 248.
3. Look for point break with a surfboard at **Croyde Bay** near Ilfracombe before watching working sheepdogs at Mortehoe (summer only), page 279.
4. Take a boat, plane or chopper ride out to the **Scilly Isles** to spot puffins, seals and rare flora on the foreshore, page 295.

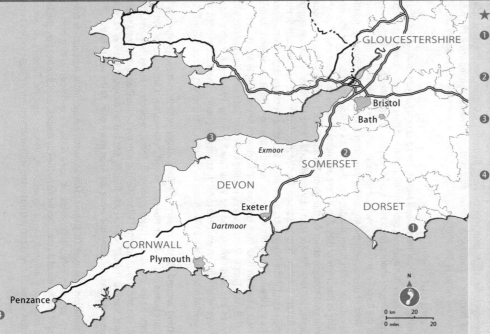

Bristol

→Colour map 1

Bristol's busy history continues to defy complacent preconceptions, either about its role in the slave trade or its contribution to the music industry and the arts. It was not until the early 1990s that the rest of the country began to associate Bristol with anything more than crumbling Georgian terraces and headbanging cider drinkers. At that point, a triumvirate of triphop bands – Tricky, Massive Attack and Portishead – determinedly mining a deep vein of alienation and despair, nonetheless linked the city in the popular imagination with a certain kind of urban cool. By the time of the millennium, the prosperity of a booming local economy and of herds of predominantly middle-class students was really beginning to make itself felt. Most obviously, the area around the floating harbour was opened up and turned into a vast Euro-style visitor attraction, featuring a funky modern bridge, and incorporating two previously established arts centres, open-plan eateries, an IMAX cinema and two state-of-the-art multimedia '@Bristol' exhibits. Heading uphill, the hitherto rather staid Park Street now boasts a riot of trendy clothes shops and coffee bars and, further on, a section of sedate Whiteladies Road became a continuous line of bars and restaurants, earning itself the new, semi-ironic name of 'the strip'. » *For Sleeping, Eating and other listings, see pages 224-227.*

Ins and outs

Getting there **Bristol International Airport**, T0870-1212747, is just south of the city. A regular shuttle bus operates between the airport and the city centre. London to Bristol is 122 miles, or about 2 hrs, straight down the M4. The M4 then heads further west over the River Severn – via 2 more spectacular bridges – into Wales. It also links up, just west of Bristol, with the M5, taking you either north up to Birmingham and the Midlands, or south down deeper into the West Country. There is hardly any free parking in the centre of Bristol, but there are plenty of car parks where a whole day's parking will cost you about £5, though on Sat and Sun it's often only £1.50. **National Express**, T08705-808080, from London Victoria to the Marlborough St bus station and **Bakers Dolphin**, T01934-413000, from Marble Arch to the Marlborough St Bus Station and Clifton Triangle. Local services, including buses to Bath, Glastonbury, Wells and Weston-super-Mare, also run from the Marlborough St bus station. There is at least 1 train an hour from London Paddington to Bristol Temple Meads (1 hr 45 mins). Bristol Temple Meads is only 15 mins away from Bath and also connects with services into South Wales and the West Country. Bristol Parkway, the city's other railway station – unless you need to catch a train going north – should be avoided, as it is several miles out of the city centre. » *For further details, see also Transport, page 227.*

Getting around Bristol is becoming increasingly pedestrian-friendly, which is a definite bonus for the visitor. However, to walk between, say, Clifton and the Old City is quite a hike, even if one is going downhill. There are plenty of buses, however. The 8, 9, 180 and 500 all link the Clifton Triangle with the Centre Promenade and Temple Meads Station. The city is also cycle-friendly and has an extensive network of cycle lanes and paths, including one along the Avon which goes all the way to Bath.

Information The main **TIC** ⓘ *next to the @ Bristol exhibits in the harbourside area, T0117- 9260767, www.visitbristol.co.uk, open daily.* It's well worth getting hold of a copy of the excellent A3 map produced by the city council, available free from the TIC and from many different shops. In addition, *Venue* magazine, Bristol's answer to London's *Time Out*, will keep you up to date with what's on in the city, as well as being a lively read in itself.

Sights

Bristol divides itself into a number of different pockets, each with its own distinctive atmosphere. Of these, four are of particular interest to the visitor: the harbourside; the Old City and the pedestrian area around the Old Vic Theatre; a two-mile stretch of road linking the Anglican cathedral, just above the harbour, up Park Street, past the university and museum at the top of the hill and on to the Clifton Triangle of shops and restaurants, finally veering right up into Whiteladies Road; and Clifton Village, elegant if slightly precious, with its desirable Georgian properties, chi-chi boutiques and beauty parlours, set below the famous Clifton Suspension Bridge. In addition, Montpelier, the bohemian quarter of town, boasts at least one great restaurant and one great pub.

Harbourside

A good way of taking it all in is on a **ferry ride** around the harbour from Bordeaux Quay. There are four companies plying for your trade, all at much the same price ⓘ *£3.50/£2 for a 40-min tour or £1.20/£0.80 for a one-way trip.* Glimpse the SS Great Britain and the Clifton Suspension Bridge, or stop off at the **Bristol Industrial Museum** ⓘ *T0117-9251470, Apr-Oct Sat-Wed 1000-1700, Nov-Mar weekends only, free*, to learn a little about the history of this port, including its murky role in the slave trade of the 18th century. Bristol's involvement in the slave trade has recently become a bit of a local hot potato and the TIC will even provide you with a 'slave trade trail' leaflet. More details are also available at the **British Empire and Commonwealth Museum** ⓘ *next to Bristol Temple Meads railway station, 1000-1700 daily, £4.95, concessions £4.35, child £2.45.*

The **SS Great Britain** ⓘ *T0117-926 0680, Apr-Oct 1000-1730, Nov-Mar 1000-1630, £6.25, children £3.75*, the world's first luxury ocean liner resides in the dock where she was first built in 1843 alongside the Clifton Suspension Bridge, one of Brunel's great Bristolian triumphs. The ship's passengers included 15,000 emigrants to Australia, and the first England cricket team going on tour down-under. In 1886, she was caught in a storm off Cape Horn and abandoned in the Falkland Islands. Your visit to the dock, accessible also by foot or the harbour railway (£1 return) beside the Industrial Museum, includes a ticket to a maritime heritage centre and a replica of the *Matthew*, John Cabot's three-masted caravel, which, in 1997, re-enacted Cabot's voyage across the Atlantic.

On **Millennium Square** are two vast, glass-fronted structures of hidden promise, which can each take up several hours of your time. **At Bristol** ⓘ *T0845-3451235, £8.95/£7 for each of the attractions, with special deals for multiple tickets* consists of **Explore**, an interactive science museum, with additional planetarium and simulator ride, and **Wildwalk**, a three-dimensional meditation on mankind's relationship to nature – featuring a walk-through rainforest. Wildwalk is also home to the IMAX cinema, showing an increasingly varied selection of films on its big screen.

Over Pero's Bridge, you will see a bronze statue of a man looking intently towards the west. This is **John Cabot**, one of Bristol's favourite adopted sons (formerly Giovanni Caboto of Genoa and Venice), who, hitching a ride with Bristolians, sailed from here to Newfoundland in 1497, five years after Christopher Columbus had stepped ashore in the Bahamas. You will also see that the **Arnolfini Arts Centre** is situated here, but unfortunately you will have to wait until 2006 for its free exhibitons of modern art, modern cinema screening and dramatic performances.

Old City

Behind the Arnolfini, near Queen Square, is the site of the 18th-century **Old Vic** ⓘ *T0117-9877877, most Fri and Sat mornings, except Jul and Aug*, the oldest working theatre in the country and a real treat for theatregoers. Walk north up Welsh Back, with Bristol Bridge on your right at the top, and cross over Baldwin Street into St Nicholas Street and the Old City area. Here you will find a couple of indoor markets – the **St**

Nicholas Market and the **Exchange Market** in the old Corn Exchange – and the bustle of Bristol's professional quarter, including the law courts. Things to look out for include, at 36 Horsefair, **John Wesley's Chapel** ⓘ*T0117-9264740, Mon-Sat 1000-1800, free*, the oldest Methodist building in the world built by Wesley himself in 1793 and, at 37 Broad Street, a rare and very striking example of **William Morris's English Art Nouveau architecture**, now the offices of NatWest Insurance Services.

Back at the Centre Promenade, head up Park Street, past the statue of Queen Victoria, to College Green, where the gargantuan red-brick council offices to the north succeed only in dwarfing the Anglican **cathedral** ⓘ *0800-1800 daily*, to the south. The cathedral was extensively rebuilt in the 19th century, but contains many features from

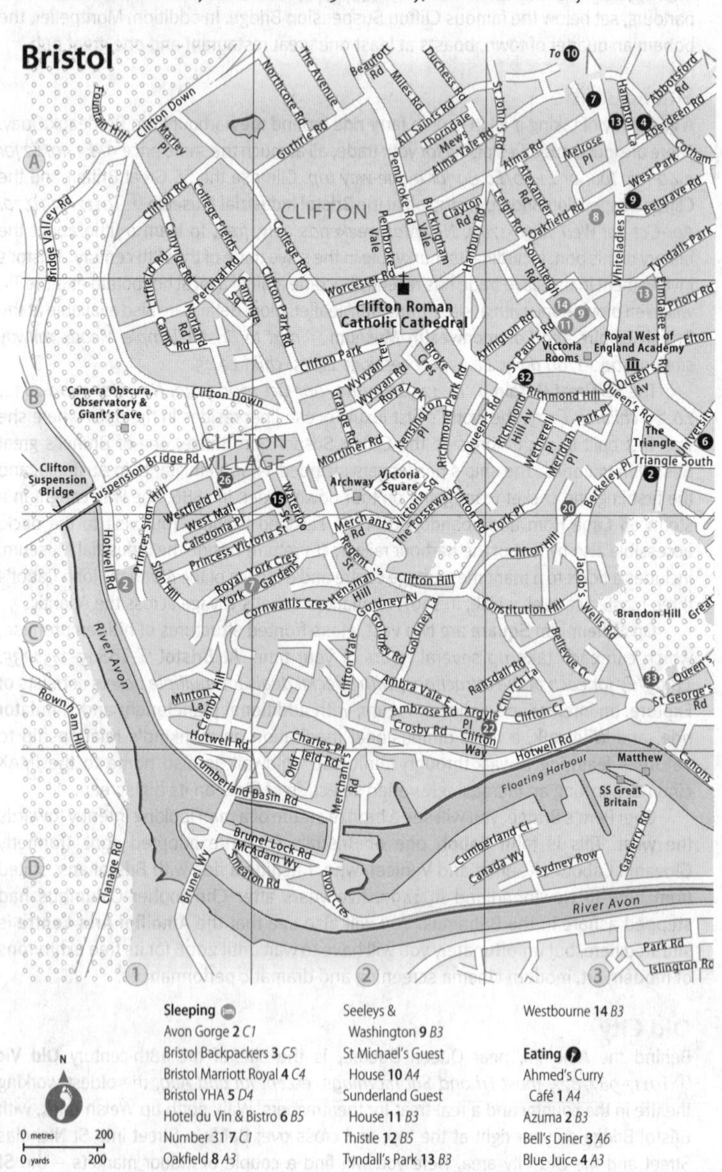

Sleeping
Avon Gorge 2 *C1*
Bristol Backpackers 3 *C5*
Bristol Marriott Royal 4 *C4*
Bristol YHA 5 *D4*
Hotel du Vin & Bistro 6 *B5*
Number 31 7 *C1*
Oakfield 8 *A3*
Seeleys & Washington 9 *B3*
St Michael's Guest House 10 *A4*
Sunderland Guest House 11 *B3*
Thistle 12 *B5*
Tyndall's Park 13 *B3*
Westbourne 14 *B3*

Eating
Ahmed's Curry Café 1 *A4*
Azuma 2 *B3*
Bell's Diner 3 *A6*
Blue Juice 4 *A3*

earlier times, including a Norman Chapter House and an early English Lady Chapel. Halfway up the hill on the left, in Great George Street, is **St George's Church** ⓘ *T0117-9230359*, with its impressive classical portico and excellent acoustics, it's now a music venue presenting a diverse programme of classical, jazz and world music. At No 7 is the **Georgian House** ⓘ *T0117-9211362, Apr-Oct 1000-1700, free*, a homage to all things Georgian, including a recreation of the dwelling of John Pinney, a slave trading merchant who lived here then. In addition, the **Red Lodge** ⓘ *T0117-9211360, 1000-1700 Apr-Oct, free*, a few minutes away on Park Row on the other side of Park St, is an odd, but engaging mixture of the Georgian and Elizabethan periods, including a 16th-century portrait of Elizabeth I.

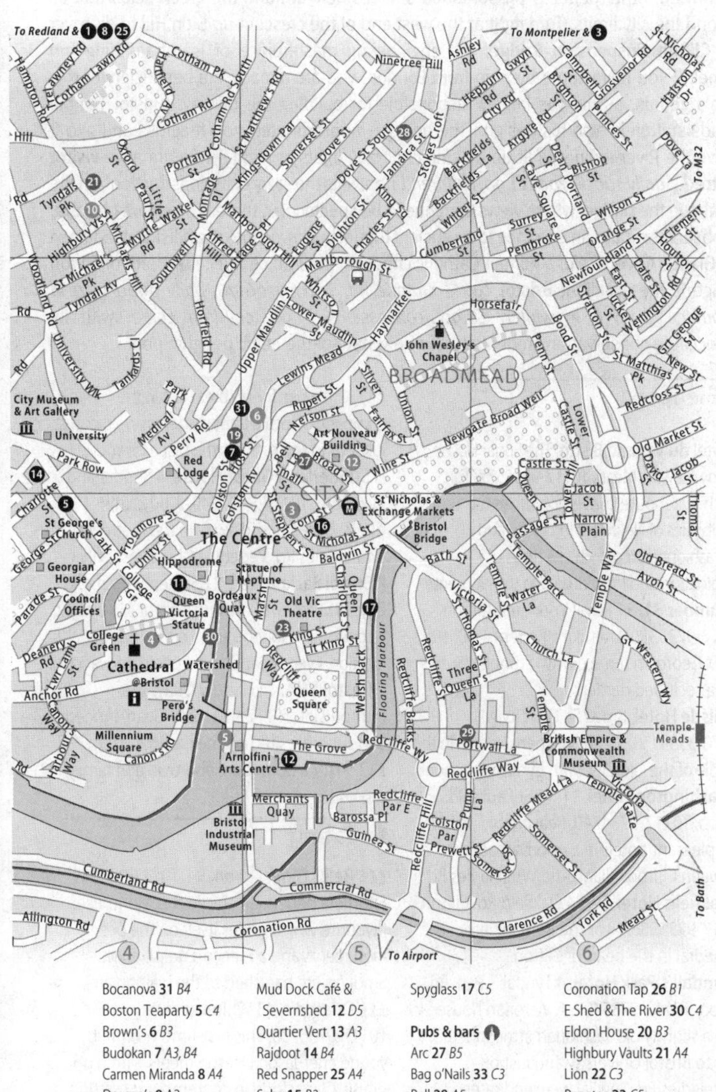

Bocanova **31** *B4*
Boston Teaparty **5** *C4*
Brown's **6** *B3*
Budokan **7** *A3, B4*
Carmen Miranda **8** *A4*
Deason's **9** A3
Fish Works **10** *A3*
Harveys **11** *C4*
Mud Dock Café & Severnshed **12** *D5*
Quartier Vert **13** *A3*
Rajdoot **14** *B4*
Red Snapper **25** *A4*
Saha **15** *B2*
San Carlo **16** *C5*
Sands **32** *B3*
Spyglass **17** *C5*

Pubs & bars

Arc **27** *B5*
Bag o'Nails **33** *C3*
Bell **28** *A5*
Brewery Tap **19** *B4*
Byzantium **29** *D5*
Coronation Tap **26** *B1*
E Shed & The River **30** *C4*
Eldon House **20** *B3*
Highbury Vaults **21** *A4*
Lion **22** *C3*
Renatos **23** *C5*

At the top of Park Street, just beyond the 1920s tower of Bristol University, lies the **City Museum and Art Gallery** ⓘ *T0117-9223571, daily 1000-1700, free*. Highlights here are a selection of Egyptian mummies, a 19th-century gypsy caravan, some wonderful pre-Raphaelite paintings and the world-class Schiller Collection of Chinese Ceramics; as well as travelling exhibitions.

Clifton

From the top of Park Street follow Queen's Road as it leads past the monstrous students' union building, across Victoria Square and under an archway into **Clifton Village**. Walk along Royal York Crescent to experience the grandeur of the Georgian architectural vision, the rows of other perfectly proportioned terraces beneath and the green fields that lie beyond the city limits. Turn right at the west end of the crescent up Sion Hill to discover the **Clifton Suspension Bridge**, the engineering masterpiece of Isambard Kingdom Brunel. If you have come by train from London, you are already the beneficiary of this man's genius, as he was largely responsible for building the railway. (Bristol Temple Meads station is also his design.) The bridge – approximately 700 ft across and 250 ft above the River Avon – is lit up by strings of fairy lights at night. An informative **visitor centre** ⓘ *daily 1000-1700, £1.90, children £1.70*, tells the story of its construction. On the hill above the bridge, where views continue to be spectacular, there is a **camera obscura**, an observatory and an entrance to an ancient tunnel burrowed into the hillside, leading to the **Giant's Cave,** site of a Roman Catholic chapel in the 15th century. Just north of Clifton Village is the excellent **Bristol Zoo** ⓘ *Guthrie Rd, T0117-9706176, daily 0900-1730 in summer, till 1630 in winter, £8.90, consessions £7.90, children £5.20*, with its impeccable conservation credentials and new state-of-the-arctic penguin pool.

Sleeping

L **Hotel du Vin and Bistro**, The Sugar House, Narrow Lewins Mead, T0117-9255577. This stylish warehouse conversion mixes the sensibilities of New York loft living and old-fashioned French chic. A hotel of imagination and individuality in the city centre.

C **Number 31**, 31 Royal York Cres, Clifton, T0117-9735330. Live like a Regent, in Bristol's finest Georgian terrace, with stunning views and a secluded garden.

C **Thistle Hotel**, Broad St, Old City, T0870-3339130. Smart, inexpensive and in the middle of the Old City, with gym/indoor pool.

C **Washington Hotel**, 11-15 St Paul's Rd, Clifton, T0117-9734740. Reasonably priced and pleasant hotels in a good situation between Clifton Village and Whiteladies Rd.

D **Oakfield Hotel**, 52-54 Oakfield Rd, Clifton, T0117-9735556. Near the Roman Catholic Cathedral in the heart of Clifton.

D **Tyndall's Park Hotel**, 4 Tyndall's Park Rd, Clifton, T0117-9735407. A Victorian house with a slightly old-fashioned atmosphere near to Bristol University and just off Whiteladies Rd. Special weekend rates.

D **St Michael's Guest House**, 145 St Michael's Hill, T0117-9077820. If you fancy starting the day with a big, fry-up breakfast in the company of recalcitrant students and the best jukebox in town, this is the place for you.

D **Sunderland Guest House**, 4 Sunderland Pl, Clifton, T0117-9737249. A tidy, little guesthouse, tucked away in a side street off Whiteladies Rd. Vegetarian breakfast only.

F **Bristol Backpackers**, 17 St Stephen's St, Old City, T0117-9257900. Dorm beds at £13 a night, a comfortable lounge and a bar in this central location. Even cheaper if you book in advance.

F **Bristol YHA**, 14 Narrow Quay, Harbourside,T0117-9221659. Clean, modern and superbly sited on the harbour. From £12.50 for a dorm bed, also twin and family rooms.

Eating

£££ **Bell's Diner**, 1 York Rd, T0117-9240357. Effortless bohemian chic in this Montpelier favourite which prides itself on the best ingredients and a French-English style. Smokers are banished to the waiting area.

£££ **Deason's**, 43 Whiteladies Rd, T0117-9736230. This first-time venture by young chef Jason Deason meets with high praise. Classy food in contemporary setting. No-smoking dining room. Starters about £7, main courses about £15.

£££ Fishworks, 128 Whiteladies Rd, T0117-9744433. One of the new breed of sleek, classy fish brasseries – all stainless steel and chunky wood – that also doubles as a fishmonger, an offshoot of the one in Bath.
£££ Quartier Vert, 85 Whiteladies Rd, T0117-9734482. Humming tapas bar in the middle of 'the strip' with à la carte Mediterranean dining at the back.
££ Ahmed's Curry Café, Chandos Rd, Redland, T0117-9466466. A bit of Bradford comes to Bristol in this basic, reasonably priced, formica-top, candlelit eating den serving curry in a haandi.
££ Azuma, 4 Byron Pl, Clifton Triangle, T0117-9276864. Sushi chef Yuji recently moved to this central location after 15 years at his old, Redland restaurant. Simple, authentic, personal, slightly quirky and delicious – without being particularly pricey for Japanese food.
££ Brown's, 38 Queens Rd, Clifton, T0117-9304777. The winning Brown's formula rides again, in Bristol University's old refectory. Open plan dining, great cocktails, attractive waitresses and a terrace and steps from which to survey life from on high.
££ Budokan, Colston St and Whiteladies Rd, T0117-9141488. Two Asian fuelling stations in traditional Japanese canteen setting, serving inexpensive Thai, Japanese and Indonesian food.
££ Red Snapper, 1 Chandos Rd, Redland, T0117-9737999. A seasonal fish restaurant with fresh red and yellow décor. Still the best fish place in Bristol.
££ San Carlo, 44 Corn St, T0117-9226586. Bristol's answer to London's **La Caprice**. Glitzy Italian bistro, also serving shellfish and oysters.
££ Sands, 95 Queen's Rd, Clifton, T0117-9739734. An atmospheric Lebanese restaurant serving reasonably priced good food in a cavern-like interior, or outdoors on the terrace (with heaters). They also have shishas to smoke or share. Apple is the most popular flavour.

Cafés

Blue Juice, 39 Cotham Hill. Restorative fruit/veg juices and herbal shots just behind Whiteladies Rd. The 'flu fighter' hits the spot. Medium/large juices £1.80/2.35.
The Boston Teaparty, 75 Park St, T0117-9298601. Comfy, old sofas upstairs and mellow terrace-garden at the back in this popular unlicensed café. Open all week.
Carmen Miranda, Chandos Rd, Redland. Relaxed verging on the chaotic. Licensed café, serving lunch and teas, a box or 2 of second-hand books, some vegetables and a few plants for sale, with a basement chill-out zone for the evenings.
Mud Dock Café, 40 The Grove, T0117-9349734. Popular harbourside spot for Sat/Sun brunch, with a bicycle shop underneath. Licensed, with DJs, for evening dining. About £8 for a main course.
Saha, 12-13 Waterloo St, Clifton Village, T0117-3179696. Leave Clifton for Marrakech, in this cool, unlicensed Moroccan café that also doubles as a gallery. Closes 1800.

Pubs, bars and clubs

Club nights in Bristol change regularly, so check *Venue* or the free *Synergy* magazine for the latest listings. There's also a busy music scene – pop and classical – in the city. Alongside the larger venues, such as Colston Hall, the Bristol Academy, the Victoria Rooms and St George's, there are plenty of other smaller places.
Arc Bar, Broad St, T0117-9226456. An arty space where regulars might well be dedicated to the destruction of global capitalism.
Bag o'Nails, St George's Rd, Hotwells, T0117-9406776. Very fine ales in a small wood-panelled pub that can get impossibly busy.
The Bell, 18 Hillgrove St, off Jamaica St, T0117-9096612. One of the city's original music pubs, DJ-driven and decent food.
The Brewery Tap, Colston St, T0117-9213668. The modern wooden interior and chequer tile floor creates the perfect, unpretentious setting to savour the Smiles beers brewed on site. Contains a no-smoking room and will also arrange tours of the brewery.
Byzantium, Portwall Lane, Redcliffe, T0117-9221883. Swish, stylish pleasuredome with deep sofas and Eastern notes. Also a decent place for a quality bite to eat.
Coronation Tap, Sion Pl, T0117-9739617. This pub usually has four or five brews of West Country cider to choose from, advisedly sold in halfs. Clifton based students and serious cider heads.
Cosies, 34 Portland Sq, St Pauls, T0117-9424110. A place to get seriously chilled.
Eldon House, 6 Lower Clifton Hill, T0117-9264964. Friendly, no-nonsense boozer with a snug, back parlour. Live music.

E Shed, Canon's Rd, T0117-9074287. Waterside place that has been described by its designer as possessing "high-class New York hooker-chic".
Elbow Room, Park St, T0117-9300242, where you can dance and shoot pool.
Fuchsia, Nelson House, Nelson Street, T0117-945 0505, www.fuchsia-bristol.com. Combining a sleek Chinese restaurant with a sassy club.
Highbury Vaults, St Michael's Hill, T0117-9733203. Popular student pub near the university, dark and cosy inside with a terrace at the back for alfresco drinking.
The Lion, Church Lane, Clifton Wood, T0117-9268492. Bristol at its laid-back best. Tucked away amongst steep, multicoloured terraces, serving good food – including a wild boar roast on Sun. DJs at the weekend.
Nocturne, 1 Unity St, T0117-9292555. Probably the most cutting-edge drinking den in town, formerly owned by Massive Attack, decorated with Brit-art, atmospheric and underground. Non-members should look smart and get in early.
The Palace Hotel, 1-2 West St, Old Market, T0117-9557095. Revamped old hotel bar celebrating the city's revved up music scene.
Pam-Pam, 3 Beacon House, Queens Avenue, Clifton, 0117-973 1249. Burly bouncers and a red rope keep out the hoi-polloi from this style-conscious bar. Dress to impress.
The Park, 38 Triangle West, Clifton, Bristol , 0117-940 6101, www.theparkbristol.com. Bristolians endure the tight squeeze to enjoy the tunes and vodka specials at this hip bar.
Renatos, 33 King St, T0117-929 7712. A fairly standard Italian trattoria by day, site of frenzied thespian revelry by night for after-show drinkers from the Old Vic.
Severnshed, The Grove, T0117-9251212. Large and airy waterside Victorian warehouse designed by Brunel (girders and all) with good organic food.
The Thekla, a boat moored at Phoenix Wharf in the harbour, one of the best clubs and live music venues in town.
The White Lion Inn, Avon Gorge Hotel, Sion Hill, T0117-973 8955. Fabulous sun terrace, with unrivalled views of the Clifton Suspension Bridge and barbecue in the summer.
Then find out what's playing at **The Fez Club**, 26-28 St Nicholas St, T0117-9259200, **The Old Firestation** in Silver St, **Blue Mountain** in Stokes Croft or **Creation**, in Baldwin St.

Entertainment

Cinema

The harbourside is home to Bristol's 2 art cinemas **Arnolfini**, T0117-9299191 (closed for renovations until further notice), and **Watershed**, T0117-9253845. There's an **Odeon** in Broadmead, T0870-5050007, and **Orpheus** in Northumbria Dr, T0117-9621644, and a multiplex **Showcase** on the outskirts of town towards Bath, T0117-9723800.

Theatre

The **Old Vic**, King St, T0117-9877877, is a great theatre and well worth visiting. **The Hippodrome**, on the other side of the Central Promenade, T0870-6078500, has a much bigger auditorium and tends to stage blockbuster musicals – and occasionally opera. The **QEH** on Jacob's Wells Rd, T0117-9250551, and **The Redgrave**, in Percival Rd, Clifton, T0117-3157600, are the largest of the fringe theatres. **The Tobacco Factory**, Raleigh Rd, Southville, T0117-9020344. Shows excellent theatre regularly. It also boasts views of the massive 19th-century tobacco depositories that dominate the skyline. Also with a very cool bar-restaurant and events centre.

Festivals and events

Bristol Community Festival, a kind of mini-Glastonbury, is held over the course of one weekend in **Jul** on the Ashton Court Estate, just the other side of the Clifton Suspension Bridge, T0117-9042275.
St Paul's Carnival, a celebration of West Indian culture, is held at about the same time in the St Paul's part of town, T0117-9444176.
Bristol Balloon Fiesta & Nightglow in **Aug**, T0117-9535844, Ashton Court. Watching brightly coloured balloons floating gently overhead is one of Bristol's happiest sights.

Activities and tours

For an unusual and fascinating tour of mercantile medieval Bristol, ask at the main tourist office, T0117-9260767, about the possibility of a tour of Redcliffe caves, a network of about 8 miles of caves and cellars stretching under the city centre, where merchants hoarded their valuables and slaves piled Bristol's wealth into vast caverns. Usually available at 2 days notice from a local guide. Wellies and torches essential. For personal balloon trips try **Bristol Balloons**, T0117-9637858, or **Bailey Balloons**, T01275-375300.

Transport

Air

Bristol International Airport, T0870-1212747, offers direct flights to 27 UK and European destinations, including low cost flights with EasyJet and Ryanair.

Bus

National Express, T08705-808080, run services at least hourly to **London Victoria** (2 hrs 30 mins) and to many other towns throughout England, eg **Exeter** (2 hrs), **Birmingham** (2 hrs).

Taxi

Apex, 433 Gloucester Rd, T0117-9232626. Bristol Taxi Co, 204a Cheltenham Rd, T0117-9428080. Dads Cabs, 138 Grosvenor Rd, T0117-9350044.

Train

First Great Western serve Bristol Temple Meads station from **London Paddington** (1 hr 45 mins). Other stations on this line are **Reading** (1 hr 15 mins), **Swindon** (45 mins), **Chippenham** (30 mins) and **Bath Spa** (15 mins).

Directory

Car hire National, Bristol International Airport, Lulsgate, T01275-474821 and 248 Muller Rd, Horfield, T0117-9525414. **Sixt Kenning**, 59 Hartcliffe Way, T0117-9662296. **Thrifty**, 127 Queen Anne Rd, Barton Hill, T0117-9711133. **Cycle hire** Black Boy Hill Cycles, 180 Whiteladies Rd, T0117-9731420. For bicycle repairs go to the **Bristol Bicycle Workshop**, 84 Colston St, T0117-9268961. **Hospitals** Bristol Royal Infirmary, Maudlin St, T0117-9230000. **Internet** The Netgates Café, 51 Broad St, T0117-9074040. Oncoffee.net, 11 Christmas Steps, T0117-9251100. **Police** Avon and Somerset Constabulary PO Box 37, Valley Rd, T01275-818181. **Post office** Prince St, T0845-7223344.

Gloucestershire

→*Colour map 1*

Gloucestershire, like Norfolk, was fabulously wealthy in the Middle Ages. Unlike Norfolk, the county has also largely escaped the ravages of 20th century agribusiness. Along with the Stroud Valley cloth mills, the first industrial revolution in the 17th century only adds to the charms of the county today. They're no secret though. The limestone Cotswolds are overwhelmed with admirers every summer and many of their genteel honey-coloured villages pander unashamedly to a nostalgic vision of England past. That said, their immaculate state of preservation and the apparently organic way they seem to have grown up from the soil makes them truly irresistible. Gloucester is the county town, with one of the most wonderfully well-preserved cathedrals in the country. Its very different neighbour is the elegant Regency spa town of Cheltenham. Both sit on the western edge of the Cotswolds overlooking the Severn Valley. In the south of the county, hearty Cirencester is the regional capital, an ancient Roman town surrounded by beautiful river valleys. ▸▸ *For Sleeping, Eating and other listings, see pages 234-236.*

Ins and outs

Getting there and around Many areas of Gloucestershire's countryside are accessible by **bus**, new rural bus services make The Cotswolds, the Forest of Dean (see page 361) and the Severn Vale all accessible by public transport. Buses run from the main towns such as Cirencester, Cheltenham, Gloucester and Stroud, or from the rural railhead stations at Kemble, Lydney and Moreton- in-Marsh. There are weekday and Sun services. There are **railway stations** at Gloucester, Cheltenham, Kemble,

 Stroud, Stonehouse, Moreton-in-Marsh and Lydney. The **Message Link Information Line,** T01452- 425543, is a telephone service for bus and rail timetable information (available Monday-Friday 0745-2000, Saturday 0800-1700, Sunday 0900-1400, and bank holidays 0800- 1700). ▸▸ *For further details, see also Transport, page 236.*

North Cotswolds → *Colour map 1*

Beyond Burford, north of the A40, the heartland of the Cotswolds is so popular that the roads in summer often become choked with coaches and cars. The scenery is almost as stunning in winter though. If anything the warm yellowy-grey limestone-built villages, becoming more and more honey-coloured in the north, look even prettier in clear winter sunshine. The trio of Bourton-on-the-Water, Stow-on-the-Wold and Moreton-in-Marsh are the top destinations, but many of the smaller villages also suffer from serious congestion. And it's not hard to see why: the combination of rolling little hills, sparkling streams and tidy old villages is hard to resist. They're also sprinkled with a variety of rewarding and carefully maintained attractions, especially gardens and great houses. The Indian dream of Sezincote is one of the most extraordinary, although even more eccentric is the collection of antique crafts and handiwork on display at delightful Snowshill Manor. To the northeast is Chipping Campden, one of the most distinctive and fiercely protected of Cotswold towns. To the west, the countryside becomes impossibly picturesque, especially around Stanway and Broadway.

Ins and outs

Getting there From London the M40/A44 is the most direct route, although the A44 is a notoriously slow road. Even so, Moreton-in-Marsh can usually be reached in 2 hours. Moreton-in-Marsh is on London Paddington-Worcester line. ▸▸ *See also Ins and outs for Gloucestershire above.*

Information **Cotswold TIC** ⓘ *Hollis House, Market Sq, Stow-on-the-Wold T01451-831082, www.cotswold.gov.uk/tourism, Apr-Oct daily 0930 Sun 1030-1600; Nov-Mar Mon-Sat 0930-1700. £2.50 accommodation booking fee.* **Bourton-on-the-Water Village Information Centre** ⓘ *Victoria St, T01451-820211, Apr-Oct Mon-Sat 0930-1700, Sun 1000- 1600, Nov-Mar Mon-Sat 0930-1630, Sun 1000-1300.* **Chipping Norton TIC** ⓘ *T01608-644379, www.oxfordshirecotswolds.org, Mar-Oct Mon-Sat 0930-1730, Nov-Feb Mon-Sat 1000-1500.* **Chipping Campden TIC** ⓘ *The Old Police Station, High St, T01386-841206, www.chippingcampden.co.uk, Apr-Oct daily 1000-1730, Oct-Mar daily 1000-1700.* **Winchcombe TIC** ⓘ *Town Hall, High St, T01242-602925, www.visitcotswoldsandsevernvale.gov.uk, Apr-Oct daily 1000-1700, Nov-Mar Sat, Sun 1000-1600.*

Bourton-on-the-Water

Bourton-on-the-Water is one of the most typical and also the most touristy of Cotswolds villages and worth a look for all that. It has been making the most of its charms since it made its name by reducing itself to a ninth of its size in 1937, using the same stone and water as the village, similar small scale trees and shrubs, and a model of the model at the **Model Village.**ⓘ *T01451-820467, www.theoldnewinn.co.uk, £2.75, concessions £2.25, children £2.* **The Cotswold Motoring Museum** ⓘ *The Old Mill, T01451-821255, Feb-Nov daily 1000-1800, £2.50, children £1.75*, is popular with kids, being the home of Brum from the TV series, as well as a variety of other (full scale) vintage vehicles. Another kids' favourite is the **Model Railway** ⓘ *Box Bush, High St, T01451-820686, www.bourtonmodelrailway.co.uk, Apr-Sep daily 1100-1730, Oct-Mar Sat, Sun 1100-1730, £1.90, children £1.50*, with 400 sq ft of displays.

Stow-on-the-Wold and around

Some of Bourton's tourist hordes spill over in high season into the **Slaughters**, Upper and Lower, a pair of impossibly twee little stone villages. Three more miles up the A429, **Stow-on-the-Wold** is the capital of the Cotswolds, where most roads meet before heading off across the hills. Its market place and walled sidestreet sheep-runs become crammed in summer with crowds browsing the antique shops and admiring the village's quaint proportions. Even so, along with **Moreton-in-Marsh**, 5 miles north, Stow has a marginally more businesslike and workaday air than many Cotswold settlements, and both are surrounded by some of the region's most enticing destinations for a day out. Moreton's famous **Tuesday market** is still a sight to behold and the town benefits from being on the main London-Worcester railway.

Six miles east of Moreton, near the utterly idyllic village of Great Tew, the **Rollright Stones** are an eerie collection of standing stones. The King's Men and the Whispering Knights, as the two main groups are known, are shrouded in legends of their supernatural powers. Close by, beneath Bourton-on-the-Hill, **Sezincote House** ⓘ *May-Jul, Sep Thu, Fri 1430-1800, gardens Jan-Nov Thu, Fri 1400-1800, house and garden £5, gardens only £3.50, children £1* is an even rarer wonder. The inspiration for the Brighton Pavilion, this extraordinary onion-domed affair was designed by SP Cockerell surrounded by an Oriental water garden.

Snowshill and Stanway

Stranger still is the collection of things gathered together at **Snowshill Manor** ⓘ *(NT), T01386-852410, Mar-Nov Wed-Sun 1200-1700, garden 1130-1730, £6.40, children £3,20*. From the early 1920s the eccentric architect and craftsman Charles Wade amassed an array of ordinary domestic antiques, musical instruments, suits of armour, Japanese masks, tapestries, reliquaries and furniture among other things, the emphasis being on anything and everything individually hand crafted. Wade gave the property to the National Trust on his death in 1956. Both house and gardens are endlessly surprising.

A couple of miles away from Snowshill as the crow flies, **Stanton** and **Stanway** are a pair of delightful honey-coloured villages. At the latter, **Stanway House** ⓘ *T01386- 584469, Jul, Aug Tue, Thu 1400-1700, £3.50, children £1*, where Lord Neidpath has lovingly and imaginatively restored the garden, stands out. The pyramid folly overlooks a 185-yd long waterfall as it cascades gently down from the canal. Fountains and dreamy gardens to wander through. Lord Neidpath is most accommodating if you wish to arrange a visit on out of season days.

Broadway and Chipping Campden

Broadway is yet another serious contender for most beautiful village in the Cotswolds, true to its name with its roomy High Street it also has a wonderful peal of church bells. A few miles north, Chipping Campden is not as commercialized as many parts of the Cotswolds, fiercely protective of the architectural legacy of the woollen boom and its sedate atmosphere. The gently curving and really quite grand High Street is a delight, surrounded by various styles of well-preserved terraced housing. Chipping Campden is also the start of the **Cotswold Way** ⓘ *www.cotswold-way.co.uk, the 102-mile long-distance footpath to Bath. The walk can be completed in a week or less depending on your fitness. There is plenty of accommodation along the way, but it gets booked up quickly, especially during the summer months so make sure you plan well ahead.*

Winchcombe

Heading southwest again on the beautiful B4632 towards Cheltenham from Broadway, Winchcombe was the ancient capital of the Anglo-Saxon kingdom of Mercia, with very old squat stone buildings and a prosperous air. Close by is 15th-century **Sudeley Castle** ⓘ *T01242-602308, Apr-Oct daily 1100-1700, £6.70, concessions £5.70, children £3.70, family £17.50*, which despite being a hot tourist destination deserves its accolades. It boasts fantastic shrub roses in the Queen's garden, sculptured yews and pools in the grounds. The venerable and rambling home of the Dent-Brocklehursts has a long history and inside a slightly less absorbing display of Victoriana and old master paintings.

Cheltenham and Gloucester

Two very different towns of similar size lie within 6 miles of each other either side of the M5 Bristol-Birmingham motorway. To the east Cheltenham is a very polite and conservative Regency spa town set in a bowl of the western Cotswolds. Famous for its hunting and horse-racing events, which draw huge crowds, it also bills itself as a year-round festival town building on the strengths of its famous music and literature festivals. It also has a surprisingly young population thanks to the variety of different colleges and schools based here. Gloucester could hardly be more different: an ancient county town, its magnificently preserved cathedral is the main draw, visible from afar, as well as a tiny Beatrix Potter museum. Its Victorian docks have been redeveloped into a visitor attraction, featuring the National Waterways Museum and an absorbing military museum. Otherwise Gloucester is not a particularly pretty sight, but the whole workaday city provides a refreshing counterbalance to ever-so slightly ever-so Cheltenham.

Ins and outs

Getting there From London take the M4 for approx 110 miles, then join the northbound M5 until junction 12 followed by the A38 which enters Gloucester from the south, alternatively you can exit the M5 at the new junction 11a to the west of the city. Approximate driving time: 2 hrs 20 mins; distance: 140 miles. The M40/A40 is the main route to Cheltenham, about 2 hrs from London. By **bus** from Victoria coach station the journey is between 3 hrs and 3 hrs 45 mins. Buses generally leave hourly throughout the day. There are frequent **trains** from London Paddington (2 hrs) to both towns. **First Great Western** have some direct services, otherwise change at Swindon, other operators include **Virgin** and **Central Trains**. Bristol and the West Country have direct rail services to Gloucester, as does Wales and the Midlands. ▸▸ *For further details, see also Transport, page 236*

Getting around Both Cheltenham and Gloucester are small enough to walk around. In Cheltenham especially it's easily the best way to enjoy the town. A network of buses to the **Cotswolds** and outlying villages is run by **Stagecoach**, T01452-527516. There are now 6 bus routes from Gloucester to Cheltenham. For a fast journey, try service X94 along the Golden Valley bypass. If you want to avoid Gloucester City Centre, the new 90 goes direct from the estates. From **Hucclecote** and **Brockworth**, service 10 now runs every 20 mins into Cheltenham. Service 94 provides a frequent service all day, every day and late bus N94 runs until 0200 on Friday and Saturday nights. And the 97 and 98 continue to provide a convenient service for **Innsworth** and **Churchdown** villages.

Information Cheltenham TIC ⓘ *77 Promenade, T01242-522878, www.visitcheltenham.gov.uk, Mon-Wed, Fri, Sat 0930-1715, Thu 1000-1715.* Produces a good mini-guide to the town and is generally very helpful. **Gloucester TIC** ⓘ *28 Southgate St, T01452-421188, www.gloucester.gov.uk/tourism, Mon-Sat 1000-1700 (also Jul, Aug Sun 1100-1500).* Free accommodation booking service.

Cheltenham

Cheltenham is a really very pretty town and it knows it. The elegant Tunbridge Wells of the west, the medicinal properties of its waters were 'discovered' in the early 18th century, encouraging George III to spend more than a month in town sampling them for his health. Competing spas were developed in the early 19th century at Pittville (where the Pump Room remains, still dispensing waters to the brave) and Montpellier, which is now the town's exclusive shopping strip. Cheltenham Ladies College was founded in 1841 for the education of young society girls and became one of the most exclusive girls schools in the country. Cheltenham, with its stucco and limestone, shady tree-filled squares and crescents, delicate ironwork verandas and balconies, on a small scale still presents one of the most complete Regency townscapes in Britain, on a par with Bath and Edinburgh. The wide and partly pedestrianized Promenade is the main drag, with the TIC and bus station tucked behind in front of Royal Crescent, a fine little half-moon of a terrace built in 1805. A few steps north, on Clarence St, a world-beating collection of furniture, ceramics and jewellery from the Arts and Crafts movement as well as displays on the town's 18th-century development and social life can be seen at the **Cheltenham Art Gallery and Museum** ⓘ *T01242-237431, www.cheltenhammuseum.org.uk Mon-Sat 1000-1720, Sun 1400-1620, free.* Next to the museum's late-Victorian building stands Cheltenham's oldest survivor, the **church of St Mary's** with its severe stone spire. Five minutes' walk north up North Street, **Holst's Birthplace** ⓘ *4 Clarence Rd, Pittville, T01242-524846, www.holstmuseum.org.uk, Tue-Sat 1000-1600, £2.50, children £1.25*, preserve the composer's memory and his piano, as well as giving a glimpse inside a Regency terraced townhouse, with its cosy Victorian drawing room, nursery and working kitchen.

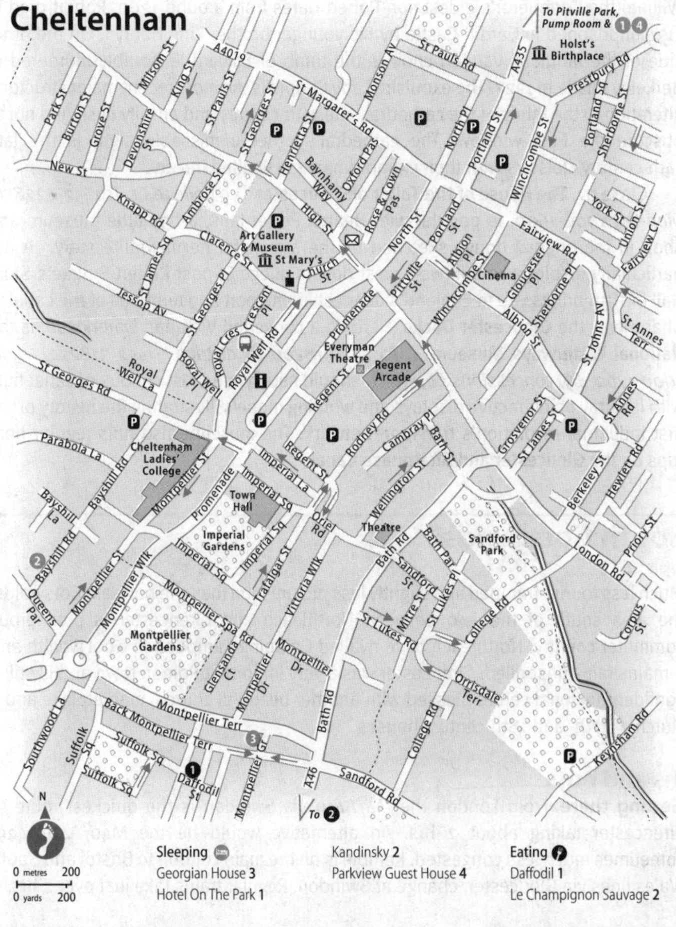

Sleeping
Georgian House 3
Hotel On The Park 1
Kandinsky 2
Parkview Guest House 4

Eating
Daffodil 1
Le Champignon Sauvage 2

Continuing north along West Drive, past two dignified Georgian squares, Clarence and Wellington, a 20-min walk brings you to the green acres of **Pittville Park**, a bit spoiled by all the traffic on Evesham Road. The **Pump Room** ⓘ *T01242-523852, Mon, Wed-Sun 1100-1600*, has been refurbished on the ground floor to what it may have looked like when built in the 1820s, the centrepiece of Joseph Pitt's ambitious and ultimately failed development of Cheltenham's spa capacity. The waters can still be tasted though.

Gloucester

Cheltenham's workaday brother, the capital of Gloucestershire, may not be much to look at, either at its centre or on its outskirts, but the distant views of the **cathedral** ⓘ *T01452-528095, www.gloucestercathedral.co.uk, Mon-Fri 0730-1800, Sat 0730-1700, Sun 0730-1600*, which has found new fans after featuring in the Harry Potter film *The Philosopher's Stone*, are compensation enough. Close up, beneath its glorious Painswick-stone tower, the church turns out to be very well preserved. Standing proud on College Green, this is English Perpendicular architecture at its very best. Built over the course of a century with funds raised from pilgrims to the shrine of Edward II, the astonishing embellishment of the original Norman church began in the 1330s. Highlights of the interior are the huge Norman columns of the nave, and the way that the 14th-century vaulting leaps around them, as well as the East window of the same date, the largest in Britain. Beyond the south transept the wooden effigy of William the Conqueror's eldest son Robert dates from around 1260. Robert died in 1134 imprisoned in Cardiff Castle by his younger brother King Henry I. On the other side of the fabulous vaulted choir is the tomb of Edward II, horribly murdered in Berkeley Castle in 1327. The exquisite Lady Chapel is the most recent major structural alteration to the fabric of the cathedral, late 15th-century and artfully designed not to obscure the East window. The cathedral's other unmissable sight is the late 14th-century cloisters with their extraordinary fan vaulted tracery.

Close by, **The House of the Tailor of Gloucester** ⓘ *9 College Ct, T01452-422856, Mon-Sat 1000-1600*, is popular with Beatrix Potter fans, a tiny little museum and shop in the original house sketched by the author for her favourite story. A not particularly inspiring 10-min walk west down College St past Robert Smirke's Shire Hall of 1816 brings you to England's deepest inland port and terminus of the canal to Sharpness, the **Gloucester Docks**. Here, in a converted Victorian warehouse, is the **National Waterways Museum** ⓘ *T01452-318200 (boat trips 01452 318222), daily 1000-1700, £5, concessions £4*, which should satisfy the most curious of canal fans with its array of interactive displays and working models illustrating the history of the first industrial revolution's transport network. The museum also runs regular boat trips on the **Gloucester and Sharpness Canal**.

South Cotswolds

Much less tourist-tramped and slightly less picturesque than the northern Cotswolds, the area south of the A40 between Northleach and Cirencester is prosperous commuter country. Northleach once rivalled Chipping Campden in wool wealth and remains fairly unspoiled. Cirencester was a very important Roman town and is still a confident regional centre blessed with another beautiful church, marketplace and a clutch of 17th- and 18th-century houses.

Ins and outs

Getting there From London the M4/A419 via Swindon is the quickest route to Cirencester taking about 2 hrs. An alternative would be the M40/A40/A429, sometimes much less congested. Kemble is on the main London to Bristol and South Wales lines via Gloucester, change at Swindon. Regular trains take just over 2 hrs.

Information **Cirencester TIC** ⓘ *Corn Hall, Market Pl, T01285-654180.* **Malmesbury TIC** ⓘ *The Town Hall, Cross Hayes, T01666-823748, Easter-Sep Mon-Thu 0900-1630, Fri 0900-1620, Sat 1000-1600, Oct-Easter Mon-Thu 0900-1630, Fri 0900-1620.* **Northleach TIC** ⓘ *Cotswold Heritage Centre, Fosse Way, T01451-860715, Easter-Oct Mon-Sep 1030-1700, Sun 1200-1700.* **Stroud TIC** ⓘ *Kendrick St, T01453-760960.*

Northleach

Beyond Burford in Oxfordshire, the 'gateway to the Cotswolds' (see page 168), the A40 heads into Gloucestershire up the Windrush valley. After 9 miles it bypasses **Northleach**, in the Middle Ages the most prosperous of the Cotswold wool towns. Now it's much less commercialized than many and its magnificent **church of St Peter and St Paul** survives as a reminder of its glory days. The town's other unmissable attraction is the **World of Mechanical Music** ⓘ *The Oak House, High St, T01451-860181, www.mechanicalmusic.co.uk, daily 1000-1800, £5, concessions £4, children £2.50*, a hymn to self-playing musical instruments, from tiny singing birds in snuff boxes to grand pianolas.

Three miles south of Northleach, in a wooded valley near Yanworth is the **Chedworth Roman Villa** ⓘ *(NT) T01242-890256, Mar, Oct Tue-Sun 1100-1600, Apr-Oct Tue-Sun 1000-1700, £3.90, children £2, family £9.80*, one of the best in the country, the surprisingly extensive remains of a rich Roman's house, complete with floor mosaics, two bathhouses and a hypocaust. There's also a small museum of finds from the site, which as a whole is a kind of museum of Victorian archaeology in itself.

Bibury and Barnsley

Bibury, about 5 miles southeast of Chedworth, is another of the Cotswolds' picture-postcard villages, a peaceful string of stone-built cottages nestling beside the little river Coln. Arlington Row, a terrace of cottages purpose-built for weavers in the 17th century, must be some of the most photographed in the county. There's also a mill museum, several teashops and some good pubs. Heading towards Cirencester from Bibury on the pretty B4425 fetches up after 3 miles in Barnsley. Less to see as far as the village is concerned, although the pub has a formidable reputation for its food (see Eating, page 235), the big draw (and deservedly so) is **Barnsley House** ⓘ *T01285-740561, daily 1000-1730 Apr-Oct, £3.* Pioneering TV gardener Rosemary Verey's well-publicized garden and darling box-hedged potager has changed little since her death in 1999. Everything is on a delightful scale, each area with a different mood, and very well tended by her son, who carries on the daily grind.

Cirencester and around

Cirencester is the most important town in the southern Cotswolds, an ancient meeting of the roads and still a thriving, good-looking market town with a hearty complement of agriculture students. The Romans called it Corinium, second only to Colchester and London in importance, and retired their legionaries here, since when it's never really looked back. The grassy remains of their amphitheatre can still be seen west of the town. The **Corinium Museum** ⓘ *Park St, T01285-655611, Mon-Sat 1000-1700, Sun 1400-1700, £2.50, concessions £2, students £1, children £0.80,* offers a quite exceptional insight into their way of life, easily comprehensible to kids, as well as displaying the famous Hunting Dogs and Four Seasons mosaics, along with other less spectacular finds from the area.

Further down the A433 past Tetbury, **Westonbirt Arboretum** ⓘ *5 miles southwest of Tetbury on A433, T01666-880220, daily 1000-dusk or 2000, Jan-Mar £5, Apr-May and Sep-Dec £6, Jun-Sep £7.50, children £1*, covers 600 acres of landscaped grounds, where 17 miles of paths run through a collection of over 18,000 trees. Westonbirt is magnificent at any time of year but is at its dizzying best in autumn when the leafy sunlit glades become a thousand luminous hues, from lustrous gold to flaming scarlet and blazing orange. Try to avoid weekends, however, when half the country seems to be visiting.

Sleeping

North Cotswolds *p228*

L **Cotswold House Hotel**, Chipping Campden, near Moreton-in-Marsh, T01386-840330, www.cotswoldhouse.com. This Edwardian manor house has been recently refurbished in a mixture of contemporary and antique styles. Special rates on weekdays.

L-A **The Royalist Hotel**, Digbeth St, Stow-on-the-Wold, T01451-830670, www.theroyalisthotel.co.uk. Supposedly the oldest inn in the country. Owned by the Knights of St John in AD 947 and used then as an almshouse. Beams, fireplaces, nooks and crannies abound.

A **Lords of the Manor Hotel**, Upper Slaughter, near Cheltenham and Stow-on-the-Wold, T01451-820243, F01451-820696. This former rectory was built in 1650 and is set in one of the prettiest villages in the Cotswolds. Meticulously manicured gardens. Riding, tennis, and croquet on offer.

A **Lower Slaughter Manor**, Lower Slaughter, T01451-820456, F822150. This manor house was built in 1651 on the site of a 1068 Domesday manor. A lavish fine dining award-winning restaurant (approx £50 a head) and 16 well-appointed rooms with home-made biscuits and English toffee in each.

A **Old Bakery**, Blockley, near Chipping Campden, T01386-700408. Better than most country-house hotels, a stay here is a sheer delight, not to say a privilege. Superb cooking from the kitchen to complement the deliciously-decorated rooms.

A **The Malt House**, Broad Campden, near Chipping Campden, T01386-840295, F841334. Welcoming and comfortable former 18th-century malt house now a family-run hotel with an eye on detail. Roaring fires and hosts that oversee meals made from their own garden vegetables.

B-C **Westward**, Westward Sudeley Lodge, Winchcombe, T01242-604372, www.westward-sudeley.co.uk. Looking over Sudeley Castle, this Georgian manor house has grand formal gardens and perfect lawns.

B-C **King's Head**, The Green, Bledington, near Stow-on-the-Wold, T01608-658365, F658902. A 16th-century inn in an idyllic setting. Burbling brooks and quacking ducks surround this stone inn with its exposed beams, benches and fireplaces. The bedrooms are comfortable in the annexe off the courtyard.

C **Rectory Farm**, Rectory Farm, Salford, near Chipping Norton, T01608-643209. This 18th-century farmhouse is set in an uninhabited 450-acre valley. Well-stocked trout fishing lakes on their property.

C **Guiting Guest House**, Post Office Lane, Guiting Power, T01451-850470, www.guitingguesthouse.com. Formerly an Elizabethan pub, this has been tastefully transformed into a home using local stone and timber.

Cheltenham *p230, map p231*

A **Hotel On The Park**, Evesham Rd, Cheltenham, T01242-518898, www.hotelonthepark.co.uk. A stylish Regency townhouse, 6 mins' walk from the centre of Cheltenham. The 12 rooms are beautifully decorated with fine linens and antiques. The *Bacchanalian* restaurant also has a good reputation.

B **Hotel Kandinsky**, Bayshill Rd, Cheltenham, T01242-527788, www.hotelkandinsky.com. Five mins' walk from the town centre, a Regency townhouse with a cheerful atmosphere and clean, comfortable rooms. There's a retro nightclub in the basement.

C **Moorend Park Hotel**, 11 Moorend Park Road, Cheltenham, T01242-224441, F572413. Family-run refurbished Victorian mansion about 15 mins' walk from the town centre with ample private parking.

C **Georgian House**, 77 Montpellier Terr, Cheltenham, T01242-515577, F545929. Across the park from fashionable Montpellier, with individually designed bedrooms in a house that lives up to its name.

D **Orion Guest House**, 220 London Rd, Cheltenham, T01242-233309. Small, family-run guesthouse with an environmentally friendly attitude, about a mile from the town centre.

D **Parkview Guest House**, 4 Pittville Cres, Cheltenham, T01242-575567. A fine Regency house 5 mins' walk from the centre of Cheltenham in Pittville Park close to the Regency Pump Room thus providing a peaceful place to stay.

South Cotswolds *p232*

L **Calcot Manor**, near Tetbury, T01666-890391, F890394. Sixteenth-century manor house with extensions in the heart of the Cotswolds. Converted 16th-century barn and courtyard. Top restaurant and attentive service, particularly for familes.

L **Lucknam Park**, Colerne, near Chippenham, T01225-742777, www.lucknampark.co.uk. Famous spa and country house hotel, approached through a mile-long avenue of beech trees, with haute cuisine in its restaurant and a family atmosphere.

A **Bibury Court Hotel**, Bibury, T01285-740337, www.biburycourt.co.uk. A lovely place, a Tudor mansion with a venerable history, the river running through its fine back garden, a gate into the churchyard from the orchards and river walks into Bibury and up to Coln St Aldwyns. The rooms are comfortable and the restaurant has a good reputation.

A **Hatton Court**, Upton Hill, Upton St, Leonard's, near Painswick, T01452-617412, F612945. Overlooking the Severn Valley, this 17th-century manor house has peerless views. Have drinks or tea on the terrace overlooking the woodlands below.

B **The New Inn at Coln**, Coln-St-Aldwyns, T01285-750651, www.newinn.co.uk. This old coaching inn has 14 rooms and a restaurant that serves old English recipes from ancient cookbooks. Family-run with courteous staff and beamed ceilings in rooms.

C **Winstone Glebe**, Winstone Glebe, Winstone, near Cirencester, T01285-821451, www.winstoneglebe.com. A former Georgian rectory set in 5 acres of garden and fertile grazing land. The proprietor is also a professional chef.

C **1 Cove House**, 1 Cove House, Ashton Keynes, south of Cirencester, actually in Wilts, T01285-861226. Expect a hearty greeting at this 16th-century manor house, with 5 beautiful bedrooms, all en suite and lovely gardens and lawns.

C **Hampton Fields**, Hampton Fields, Meysey Hampton, east of Cirencester, T01285-850070. A renovated 19th-century barn with a sunken garden, orchard and fields with horses grazing. Gorgeous views abound.

Eating

North Cotswolds *p228*

£££ **Lygon Arms Hotel**, High St, Broadway, T01386-852255. Try the splendid oak-panelled **Great Hall** restaurant for dinner or **Oliver's** for cheaper brasserie style lunches at this renowned member of the Savoy group.

££ **Baker's Arms**, Broad Campden, T01386-840515. Good value bar food in a pretty village.

££ **The Craven Arms**, Brockhampton, T01242-820410. Real ale destination pub with a garden and restaurant which needs to be booked at weekends.

££**Churchhill Arms**, Paxford, near Chipping Campden, T01386- 594000. This village pub pulls in the crowds for lunch and dinner.

Cheltenham *p230, map 231*

£££ **Le Champignon Sauvage**, Suffolk Rd, T01242-573449, Ambitious French cuisine is on offer at this Michelin-starred establishment, book 3 weeks in advance for a Sat night.

££ **Belgian Monk**, 47 Clarence St, T01242-511717, does good-value £5 lunches of moules and frites with the usual strong lagers.

££ **Choirs**, 5 Well Walk, T01242-235578, do a good job of French country cooking at reasonable prices (dinner about £18 for 3 courses, less at lunchtime).

££ **Daffodil**, 18 Suffolk Parade, T01242-7000055, is one of the city's more lively venues, in an airy converted Art Deco cinema with straightforward English and fusion food done well. £10 two-course lunches.

South Cotswolds *p232*

££ **The Bear Inn**, George St, Bisley, near Stroud, T01452-770265. Excellent home-made food in this cosy village pub. Book well ahead. Recommended.

££ **The Village Pub**, Barnsley, near Cirencester, T01285-740421. Handsome boozer not much like your average local. Down-to-earth top-quality food. Also Comfortable rooms (**C**).

Pubs, bars and clubs

North Cotswolds *p228*

Eagle and Child, Digbeth St, Stow-on-the-Wold, T01451-830670. Outshines *The Royalist* next door, also claims to be England's oldest inn.

Eight Bells Inn, Church St, Chipping Campden, T01386-840371. Fresh pub food in an old stonemasons' lodgings with good real ales.

South Cotswolds *p232*

££ **Daneway Inn**, Sapperton, T01285-760297. A delightful old pub near the western end of the Sapperton tunnel.

££ **Woolpack Inn**, Slad, T01452-813429. Where Laurie Lee drank his cider with Rosie, a very good freehouse famous for its pies.

Festivals and events

North Cotswolds p228

Chipping Campden Cheese Festival on the last weekend of Sep, T01452-425673, www.thecheeseweb.com. Over 750 different varieties of the humble fermented curd can be sampled at venues around town.

Cheltenham p230, map 231

Cheltenham National Hunt Festival in Mar with the Cheltenham Gold Cup is the nation's most prestigious steeplechase.
The **Festival of Music** in Jul, started in 1945 like the Edinburgh Festival. Mainly classical.
The **Festival of Literature** in Oct, one of the longest-running in the world.
Also **Jazz** in May, **Science** in Jun, and **Folk** in Feb, all using a variety of venues around the town, including the Pump Room, Town Hall, Everyman Theatre and various restaurants, pubs and bars. Festivals line: T01242-237377, www.cheltenhamfestival.co.uk

Activities and tours

Walking

Walking is certainly one of the best ways to see the surrounding countryside and there are a number of long-distance footpaths to choose from. **The Cotswold Way**, is 100 miles from Chipping Camden to Bath via the outskirts of Cheltenham. The Gloucestershire Way, travels 100 miles from Tewkesbury to Chepstow via Winchcombe and the Forest of Dean. The Warden's Way and Windrush Way are circular routes that link Winchcombe and Bourton-on- the-Water, 26 miles in all. The North Cotswold Diamond is a 60-mile circular route around Stow-on-the-Wold taking in Chipping Camden, Moreton-in-Marsh and Northleach. The Cheltenham Circular Footpath circles the town of Cheltenham.
Compass Holidays, T01242-250642, organize luggage transfers and accommodation along the Cotswold Way.
Cotswold Walking Holidays, 10 Royal Parade, Bayshill Rd, Cheltenham, T01242-254353, www.cotswold walks.com, specialise in self-guided and guided walks.

Transport

North Cotswolds p228

Taxis

David Prout, Herons Gate, Rissington Rd, Bourton-on-the-Water, T01451-821478.
Cotswold Private Hire, see above.

Gloucester p227

Bus

National Express, T08705-808080, run regular direct services from Gloucester to **London Victoria** (3 hrs 30 mins), 3 direct services daily to **Birmingham Digbeth** (1 hr 45 mins) and 4 to **Bristol** (55 mins). There is also a service to **Bristol airport** (1 hr 55 mins) 4 times per day, changing at Bristol and services to **Bath** (2 hrs 5 mins) at 1405 and 1435, also changing at Bristol. There is no direct service to Cardiff.

Train

Wessex Trains, T08709-002320, www.wessex trains.co.uk. run the regular services direct from Gloucester to **Bristol Temple Meads** (45 mins) and to **Bath Spa** (1 hr 15 mins) changing at Bristol Temple Meads. There is also a regular service to **London Paddington** (2 hrs 20 mins) changing at Bristol Parkway. **Virgin Trains**, T08707-891234, www.virgintrains.co.uk, run the regular direct service to **Cardiff Central** (1 hr) and **Birmingham New Street** (1 hr).

Directory

North Cotswolds p228

Car hire Cotswold Private Hire, 3 Wolds End Close, Chipping Campden, T01386- 840500. Also a taxi service. **Cycle hire** Cotswold Country Cycles, Longlands Cottage Mickleton, Chipping Campden, T01386-438706. **Country** Lanes Cycle Centre, Station Rd, Moreton-In-Marsh, T01608-650065.

Cheltenham p230, map 231

Car hire Avis Rent a Car, Unit 7, Chancel Close Trading Estate, T01452-380356. **Thrifty** Car Rental, 153a, Bristol Rd, T01452-383866. Sixt Kenning Rent-a-Car, Hempsted Bridge Filling Station 271, T01452-310511. **Jackies Self** Drive Hire, The Old Airfield More- ton Valence, T01452-720666. **National Car Rental**, 207-211 Westgate St, T01452-421133. **Cycle hire** Compass Holidays, Queens Rd, T01242- 250642. Forest Adventure, Coleford, T01594-834661.

Bath and around

→Colour map 1

Quite a serious contender for top prize in the beautiful cities of Britain pageant, Bath attracts crowds in thousands during the summer. If arriving by rail, first impressions may be a little disappointing, although it only takes a five-minute walk north to begin to appreciate what the fuss is about. Better perhaps to approach the city from north or south by bike, when it suddenly reveals itself spread out below in all its honey-stoned glory nestling in a wooded loop of the Avon Valley, cradled by seven hills. Eighteenth-century fashionable society's mania for the place is what makes it a sight to behold, the highlights of their architectural legacy being the neoclassical Palladian splendours of the Circus, the Royal Crescent and Pulteney Bridge with its famous weir. Most visitors, though, still come to see the thing that's got everyone going for at least the last 2,000 years – the only hot springs in the British Isles. After seeping through the Mendip limestone for some 10,000 years, warmed in the bowels of the earth, like few others the waters have been worshipped, channelled, contained, drained and splashed about in. The Roman Baths remain the main event, one of the country's most popular and intriguing archaeological sites, and have now been joined – at last – by the accident-prone Thermae Bath Spa, a 21st century take on the art of taking the waters. Although famously soporific, Bath boasts a wealth of distinctive hotels, shops, restaurants and small businesses, and remains resolutely independent of its much bigger brother Bristol, 10 miles downriver. ▸▸ *For Sleeping, Eating and other listings, see pages 242-244.*

Ins and outs

Getting there Estimated time from London by car is about 2 hrs. Total distance: 116 miles. From London take the M4 west (about 100 miles) exit at junction 18, head south on A46, and follow signs to town centre. From London, Victoria coach station, to Bath Spa, bus station, Manvers Street, the coach takes between 2 hrs 30 mins-3 hrs 50 mins. **First Great Western** serve Bath Spa from London Paddington every 30 mins, direct services taking about 1 hr 30 mins. ▸▸ *For further details, see also Transport, page 244.*

Getting around Bath is best walked around at a leisurely pace, although its hills can prove surprisingly wearing on the legs. Local buses are infrequent and unnecessary to take in the town centre. It's worth taking one of the double-decker tour buses for insight into the city's history and convenience. Taxi ranks are found outside the train station and the Abbey. Bradford-on-Avon is 8 miles east of Bath on the A363. Buses from Bath (X5, X6 on the Bath-Salisbury route). There are also regular trains to and from Bath.

Information Bath TIC ⓘ *Abbey Chambers, T01225-477101, www.visitbath.co.uk, May-Sep Mon-Sat 0930-1800, Sun 1000-1600, Oct-Apr Mon-Sat 0930-1700, Sun 1000-1600.* Accommodation booking, T0906-7112000 (premium rate £0.50), 10% deposit on first night's accommodation and £5 booking fee.

Sights

Roman Baths and Pump Room

ⓘ *T01225-477785, www.romanbaths.co.uk, daily Mar-Jun, Sep-Oct 0900-1800, Jul-Aug 0900-2200, Nov-Feb 0930-1730, last entry 1 hr before closing, after 1800 daily torchlit evenings in Aug with last admission 2100, until 2200), £8.50, concessions £7.50, unemployed/children £4.80, family £22. (Combined ticket with Museum of Costume for £11). Free guided tours on the hour every hour. Free audio handset tours.*

 To this day the centre of Bath remains its hot springs and Roman Baths, now one of the most popular fee-paying visitor attractions in the country. Expect to have to queue (although it's generally quieter before 1000, and after 1800 in August) although they're well worth the wait. All in all, they provide one of the best insights in northwestern Europe into the Romans' achievement and their comfortable and sophisticated way of life. The Roman remains only began to be excavated in the late 19th century and first impressions today are still of the fine 18th-century neoclassical buildings erected on the site at the height of the hot springs fashionable heyday. After looking down into the open-air Great Bath from the Victorian gallery terrace, visitors descend to the water level. The bases of the columns that once supported the Roman roof and the paving stones around the edge of the steaming green tank are the first original features on display, along with the steps descending into the murky depths. If you want to take the free guided tour, it's worth arriving half an hour early to have a look around the museum and Temple Precinct first. As well as the altar, objects on display include the gilded head of the goddess Sulis Minerva, dug up in Stall St in 1727, some floor mosaics, a model of the Roman buildings' full extent and the Gorgon's Head pediment from the original temple. The handset audio guide then takes you round the Great Bath, the newly restored and illuminated East Baths, on to the circular Cold Bath, from where you can look out into the smaller open-air Sacred Spring or King's Bath, the bubbling source of the whole complex. The variety of objects on display mean that a visit could easily last up to 3 hrs, although two would be enough.

Next door to the entrance to the Roman Baths, the Pump Room ⓘ *T01225-444477. 0900-1600, reservations Mon-Fri, first come at the weekends*, is a beautifully proportioned late-18th-century hall overlooking the open-air King's where you can enjoy a candlelit supper or a cream tea.

Abbey

ⓘ *T01225-422462 (Mon-Fri 0830-1530), daily 1000-1600 (last admission 1530), £2, £1 children.* Architecturally of just as much interest as the Baths, is Bath Abbey, next door. Building began in 1499 at the instigation of Bishop Oliver King. He had had a dream, depicted in stone on the west front, of angels climbing up and down a ladder reaching to heaven. The highlight of the church's interior are its windows and the Tudor fan-vaulting designed by Henry VII's master mason William Vertue, reminiscent of his work in Westminster Abbey. The vaulting in the chancel and choir is original, while the nave's was well restored by Sir George Gilbert Scott in the 1860s. Altogether the Abbey adds up to one of the finest examples of a purely Perpendicular church in the country, the last to be built in England before the Reformation. The Heritage Vaults beneath tell the history of the site.

Thermae Bath Spa

ⓘ *Hot Bath St, T01225-780308, T01225-477051, www.thermaebathspa.com, daily 0900- 2200, packages range from £45 - £65. At the time of going to press the Spa had not yet opened – please check website for further details.*

A few hundred yards in the opposite direction, across Stall Street, colonnaded Bath Street leads down to five more listed historical buildings that have been seriously redeveloped into the city's latest visitor attraction and centre of interest. Thermae Bath Spa promises to reinvigorate not only its clients but also spa culture across the land. The 18th-century **Royal and Hot Bath** and sweet little **Cross Bath** are the centrepiece of the development, with a new building designed by Nicholas Grimshaw behind the Hot Bath, which will house the centre's medical facilities, as well as a Turkish bath, beauty treatment salons, restaurant and bar. The Cross Bath itself lies close to the original Sacred Cross spring, and has been remodelled to feature a small open-air thermal pool.

William Herschel Museum

ⓘ *19 New King St, T01225-311342, www.bath-preservation-trust.org.uk, Feb-Nov daily 1400-1700 except Wed, £3.50, children £2, family £7.50. Weekends 1100-1700.*

A five-minute walk west of the Cross Bath, the William Herschel Museum preserves the home of a prominent figure in 18th-century Bath society. William Herschel was an organist, composer and amateur astronomer. In 1781, from the garden of his home here, using a telescope of his own design, he discovered Uranus. The museum is a great find for keen astronomers.

The Circus, the Royal Crescent and the Jane Austen Centre

A stiff climb up Gay Street passes the **Jane Austen Centre** ⓘ *40 Gay St, T01225-443000, www.janeausten.co.uk, Mon-Sat 1000-1700, Sun 1000-1730, £4.45, concessions £3.65, children £2.45, family £11.95*, which aims to show how the city influenced her works, especially *Northanger Abbey* and *Persuasion*, both set in the city, and 'find out why Jane Austen's TV adaptations are so popular'.

At the top of Gay Street, **The Circus** was the first of its type in the country and represents Georgian architecture at its most ladylike, with its little balconies (originally painted not black, but dark red and green), and delicate columns beneath arcane decorative symbols and stone acorns. Based on the dimensions of Stonehenge, its three graceful crescents surround five majestic plane trees planted in 1804. From The Circus, unassuming Brock Street leads to **The Royal Crescent**, the third and most spectacular of the Wood developments. The Royal Crescent sweeps round to the right, facing south over **Royal Victoria Park** and the river valley with views right over to Beechen Cliff beyond. Completed by John Wood the Younger once the Circus was finished, over a period of seven years, its positioning, its rhythm, scale and scope, still give just as lively an impression of fashionable 18th-century life as any Jane Austen adaptation. And if it's period detail you're after, at **Number 1** ⓘ *T01225-428126, Feb-Nov Tue-Sun 1030-1700 (last admission 1630) and first 2 weekends of Dec, £4, concessions £3.50, family £10*, the interior of the very grand end house was painstakingly returned to its Georgian condition in the late 1960s.

Museum of East Asian Art and Assembly Rooms

Back in the Circus, Bennett Street leads northeast past the **Museum of East Asian Art** ⓘ *12 Bennett St, T01225-464640, Mon-Sat 1000-1700, Sun 1200-1700, £3.50, concessions £2.50*, which devotes three floors to treasures from East and Southeast Asia, dating from 5000BC to the present day, with an extensive collection of Chinese jade and ceramics, as well as gourds, sculpture, including ivory and bamboo carvings.

The Assembly Rooms, once the social hub the city, are now owned by the National Trust. The Ball Room, Octagon, Tea Room and Card Room are the public rooms designed by John Wood the Younger in 1769 that have recently been restored, including the nine great chandeliers. The **Museum of Costume** ⓘ *Bennett St, T01225-477789, www.museumofcostume.co.uk, daily 1000-1700 (last admission 1630), £5, concessions £4, children £3.50, family £14*, in the basement is an exhibition of fashion wear from the 16th century to the present day, featuring over 150 dressed-up life-size dolls (and a few action-men).

Pulteney Bridge and Holburne Museum

Pulteney Bridge, designed by Robert Adam in the early 1770s, is another unmissable piece of 18th-century architecture in the city. The bridge is unique in the country for still being lined with its original booths for shopkeepers. Along with the famous horseshoe weir on the Avon, it provides one of the most popular images of Bath. The bridge is best seen from North Parade, but a walk across it is mandatory in order to appreciate the splendour of Great Pulteney Street. The widest in Europe when it was built, wide enough for a horse and carriage to turn without having to back up, it provided the inspiration for the dimensions of the Champs Elysées. Up to the right are the dignified old pleasure gardens of Henearietta Park, a good spot for a picnic.

In a commanding position at the end of Great Pulteney Street, the **Holburne Museum** ⓘ *T01225-466669, www.bath.ac.uk/holburne, Mid-Feb-Nov Tue-Sat 1000-1700, Sun 1430-1730. £3.50, concessions £3, children £1.50*, in a former 18th-century hotel is the appropriately elegant setting for the fine art collection of 19th-century collector Sir William Holburne. It features a number of Old Masters, as well as silver, porcelain, furniture and portrait miniatures , alongside a strong showing from great English landscape and portrait painters like Turner and Gainsborough.

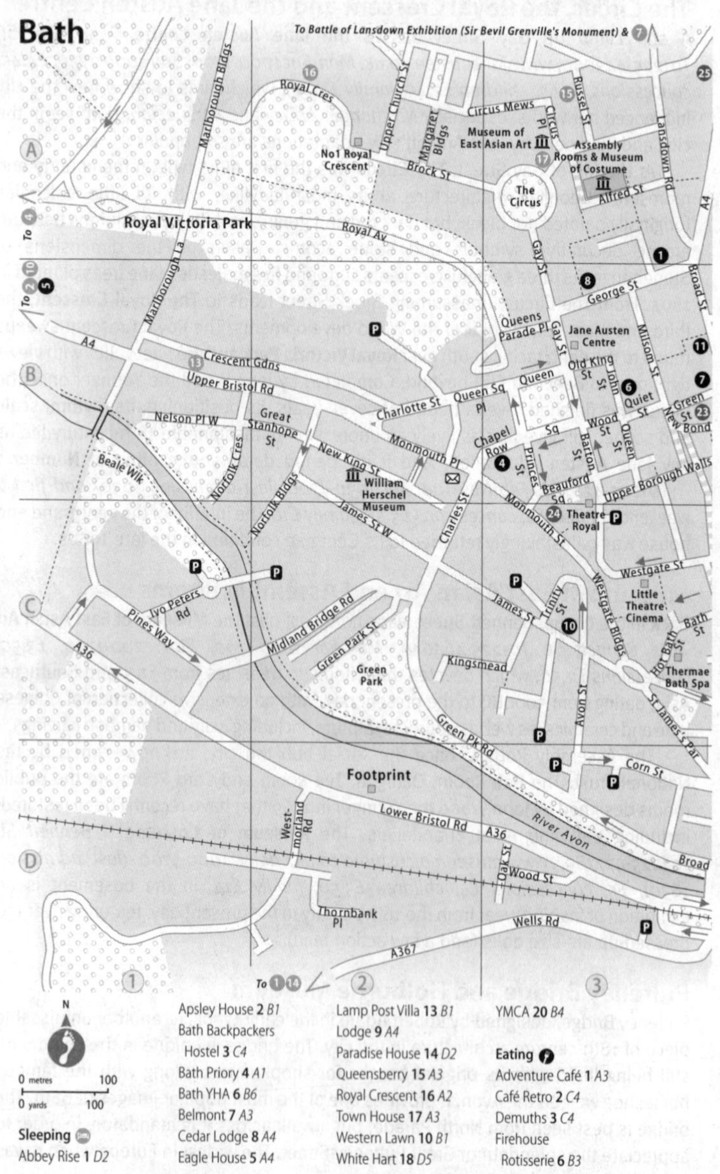

Around Bath

A few miles upstream of Bath, just inside Wiltshire, is the lovely old woollen mill town of **Bradford-on-Avon**. The birthplace of the British rubber industry and for centuries a rich woollen mill centre, the old town snuggles up to the Avon, its old stone bridge still supporting a little 17th-century shrine which was later used as a lock-up. A short walk from the bridge via the Shambles, a dinky little shopping strip, and Dutch Barton, the area made prosperous by Huguenot weavers, the architectural highlight of the town is the Saxon Church of **St Laurence**. It was only discovered in 1856, having been a school, warehouse and private house, and is believed to have been rebuilt in the 11th century after being founded by St Aldhelm in the late 700s. Now it stands surrounded by later

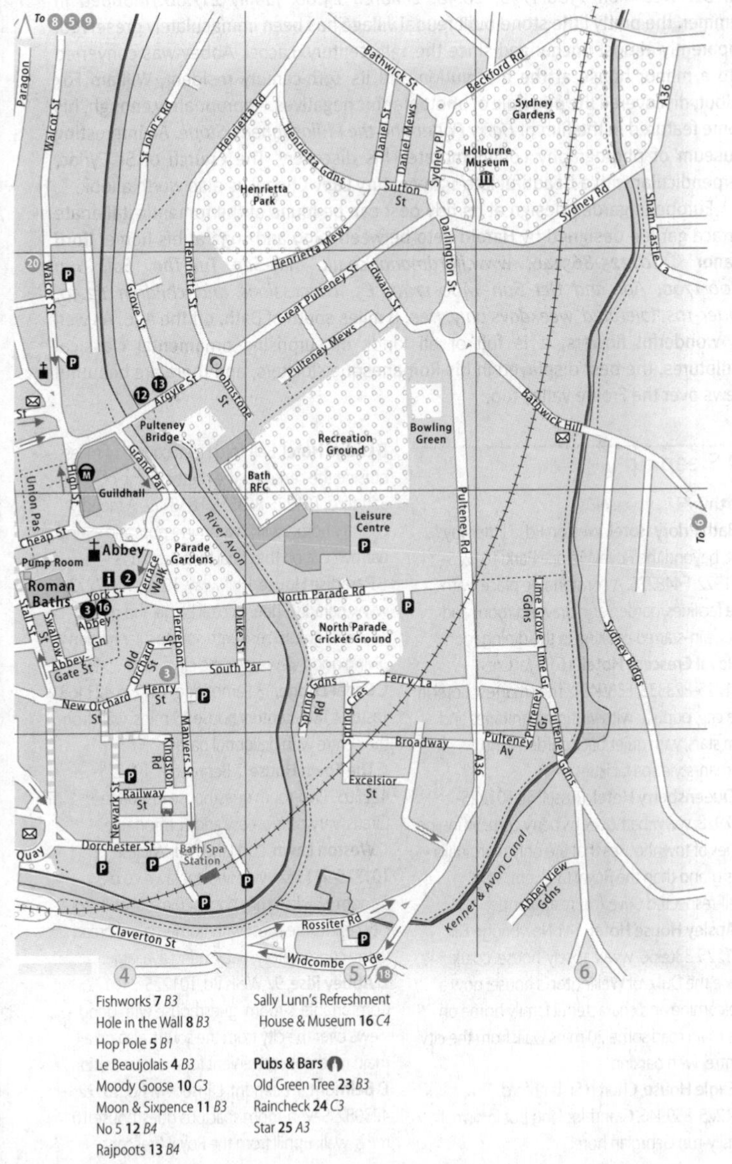

housing, an empty and atmospheric old place. A half-mile walk away along a footpath across the river is another, the **Tithe Barn** ⓘ *Daily 1030-1600, free*. This medieval great barn once belonged to Great Barton Farm, an outlyer of Shaftesbury Abbey, a Benedictine nunnery of considerable wealth. It was built in the mid-14th century and used primarily for farm produce although parish tithes (a 10th of each serf's produce) would also have been stored here. Also very atmospheric, with its cathedral-like cross window in the west wall and old oak-beamed roof, it's surrounded by old farm buildings that have been turned into tearooms, antiques and gift shops.

Another 8 miles upriver from Bradford lies the National Trust village of **Lacock** ⓘ *Abbey, museum, cloisters and garden (NT), Mar-Oct daily 1100-1730 (abbey Apr-Oct Wed-Mon 1300-1730, £6.50, children £3.60, family £17.60*. Mobbed in summer, the pretty little stone-built feudal village has been immaculately preserved, apparently almost unchanged since the 13th century. Lacock Abbey was converted into a manor house at the dissolution and its 19th-century resident, William Fox Talbot, discovered the principle of photographic negatives. Appropriately enough, his home featured in the film of *Harry Potter and the Philosopher's Stone*. An interesting museum of photography commemorates his discovery. The Church of St Cyriac, Perpendicular with a beautiful late-15th-century Lady Chapel, is also worth a look.

European garden design at its tidy best can be found at the romantic Italianate terrace garden designed by Harold Peto between 1899 and 1933 at his home, **Iford Manor** ⓘ *T01225-863146, www.ifordmanor.co.uk, May-Sep Tue-Thu, Sat, Sun 1400-1700, Apr and Oct Sun 1400-1700, £3, concessions and children £2.50, under-10s 'tolerated' weekdays only, free*, 8 miles south of Bath, off the A36. As well as wonderful flowers, it is full of all kinds of surprising ornamental classical sculptures, the best displayed in his Romanesque cloisters, and there are beautiful views over the Frome valley too.

Sleeping

Bath *p237, map p240*

L **Bath Priory Hotel**, Weston Rd, a little way out, beyond the Royal Victoria Park, T01225-331922, F448276. A comfortable place, with spa facilities, garden and drawing room and Michelin-starred cooking in the dining room.

L **Royal Crescent Hotel**, 16 Royal Cres, T01225-823333, F339401. The smartest hotel in the city, popular with visiting dignitaries and film stars, with quiet back gardens and Roman-style spa facilities.

A **Queensberry Hotel**, Russell St, T01225-447928, www.bathqueens berry.com. Stunning series of townhouses that are only marginally less grand than the Royal Crescent, very well-respected *Olive Tree* restaurant.

B **Apsley House Hotel**, 141 Newbridge Hill, T01225-336966, www.apsely-house. co.uk. Once the Duke of Wellington's house, now a welcoming and characterful family home on the main road some 20 mins walk from the city centre, with parking.

B **Eagle House**, Church St, Bathford, T01225-859946. Grand-looking but informal family-run Georgian hotel.

B **Lodge Hotel**, Bathford Hill, a couple of miles outside the centre, in the pretty village of Bathford, T01225-858575, F858172. A friendly country home, with swimming pool and even a narrowboat on the canal for guests use.

B **Paradise House**, Holloway, T01225-317723, www.paradise-house.co.uk Large and grand 11-room guesthouse with spectacular garden giving good views over the city.

C **Cedar Lodge**, 13 Lambridge, T01225 423468. Tasteful 18th-century house 15 mins' walk from the centre with delightful garden.

C **The Town House**, 7 Bennett St, T01225-422505. Two-room guesthouse just off the Circus, very central cosy and comfortable.

C **Weston Lawn**, Lucklands Rd, Weston, T01225-421362, www.westonlawn.co.uk. 3-room B&B in family home 20 mins' walk from city centre. Breakfast with home-baked bread in the conservatory. Babysitting available.

D **Abbey Rise**, 97 Wells Rd, T01225-316177. Comfortable 3-room guesthouse with good views over the city from the south, also on a main road but convenient for the train station.

D **Belmont**, 7 Belmont, Lansdown Rd, T01225-423082. Seven-room spacious guesthouse 10 mins' walk uphill from the Royal Crescent.

D **Lamp Post Villa**, 3 Crescent Gardens, Upper Bristol Rd, T01225-331221. Popular little 4-bedroom B&B at the bottom of Victoria Park, on the main road but quiet nonetheless.
E **YMCA**, International House, Broad St, T01225-460471, www.bath.org/ymca. Very central basic accommodation in dorms (£12), singles and doubles (£32), including breakfast. Best budget option in town. Recommended.
F **Bath Backpackers Hostel**, 13 Pierrepont St, T01225 446787, www.hostels.co.uk No frills, 50 beds close to the station. No breakfasts.
F **Bath YHA**, Bathwick Rd, T01225-465674, F482947. 124 beds a little over a mile uphill from the station (take Badgerline No 18).
F **White Hart**, Claverton St, Widcombe, T01225-313985, www.whitehartbath.co.uk. Provides some of the best value beds in town, from backpacker dorms at £12.50 per person to en-suite and family rooms. Self-catering kitchen, licensed café/bar, enclosed garden at back. Recommended, booking advisable.

Around Bath *p241*
L **Babington House**, Kilmersdon, near Radstock, T01373-812266, www.babington house.co.uk. Swimming pool and spa facilities at this country house offshoot of the trendy London members club, Soho House.
L **Woolley Grange**, Bradford-on-Avon, Wilts T01225-864705. Family-friendly hotel with excellent restaurant using orgnanic produce.
B **Priory Steps**, Newtown, Bradford-on-Avon, T01225-862230. Family-run Wolsey Lodge in a row of old cottages on the edge of town with good views and cosy dining room.
D **The Hermitage**, Bath Rd, Box, Corsham, Wilts, T01225-744187. Small country house with fine heated outdoor swimming pool.

Eating

Bath *p237, map p240*
££ **Moody Goose**, 7a Kingsmead Sq, T01225-466688. Top-notch modern British seafood and game with distinct French and Italian influences in an inviting subterranean restaurant and cosy vaulted dining room. Two Michelin stars for chef Stephen Shore.
£££ **Olive Tree** at the **Queensberry Hotel** (see above). The other serious foodie option in Bath, a great place to pamper those taste buds.
£££ **Fishworks**, 6 Green St, T01225-448707. Quite expensive but wholesome and fresh.
££ **Le Beaujolais**, 5 Chapel Row, just of Queen Sq, T01225-423417, is a French bistro-style restaurant, with plenty of ambience but rather small portions. Good value lunch menu.
££ **Demuths**, 2 North Parade, off Abbey Green, T01225-446059.A long-standing, straightforwardbut versatile veggie restaurant.
££ **Firehouse Rotisserie**, 2 John St, T01225-482070. Delicious brick oven fired pizzas at this stylish restaurant. Generous portions and attentive service.
££ **Hole in the Wall**, 16 George St, T01225-425242. Another enduringly popular vaulted brasserie, serving Michelin award-winning modern British cuisine. Good-value set menus during the week.
££ **Hop Pole**, 7 Albion Buildings, Upper Bristol Rd, T01225-425410. Opposite Victoria Park, this 'gastropub' has a growing local support for its fine selection of ales and superior grub.
££ **Moon and Sixpence**, 6a Broad St, T01225-460962. Intimate candlelit bistro, in the middle of town. Eclectic dishes, including corn-fed chicken with spicy Thai risotto.
££ **No 5**, 5 Argyle St, almost on Pulteney Bridge, T01225-444499. Laid-back local favourite, good value despite being in pole position for tourists, doing very competent French cuisine.
££ **Rajpoot**, 4 Argyle St, T01225-466833. Superior curry house, the decor and atmosphere may be OTT but the food is impeccable.

Cafés
Adventure Café, 5 Prince's Buildings, George St, T462038. Extremely popular with locals and tourists alike. Also good smoothies, cakes, sandwiches and panini.
Café Retro, 18 York St, T01225-339347. Just behind the abbey. Café downstairs is a good place to hang out for a leisurely brunch while upstairs in the evenings the menu is Anglo-French and a little more formal.
Sally Lunn's Refreshment House and Museum, 4 North Parade Passage, T01225-461634. Sample the buns perfected by French mrefugee Sally Lunn in the 1680s.

Pubs, bars and clubs

Bath *p237, map p240*
Moles, 14 George St, T01225-404445. Bath's best-loved and oldest music venue has seen the likes of Radiohead and Oasis play. Offers a variety of themed nights.

Old Green Tree, 12 Green St. Popular pub with good real ales, wood-panelled rooms (one non-smoking) and cheery chatter.
Raincheck, 34 Monmouth St, T01225-444770. Tiny Eighties-style wine bar with banquette seating and table service. Gets very busy at weekends.
The Star, 23 Vineyards, on the Paragon. Snug and wood-panelled and unchanged since Beau Nash was in nappies.

Entertainment

Bath *p237, map p240*

Cinema

Little Theatre, St Michael's Pl, T01225-466822. The city's arthouse refuge, complete with quirky booking system and commissionaire.

Comedy

The Porter, 15 George St, T01225-424104. Sun night sets. See also listings in *Venue*.

Theatre

Theatre Royal, T01225-448844, www.theatreroyal.org.uk West End previews, touring opera, dramas and comedies in the Georgian main house, and more experimental work in the smaller Ustinov studio. £3 tours on the first Wed and Sat of each month, 1100 and 1200.

Festivals and events

Bath *p237, map p240*

Bath Festival (box office, T01225-463362, www.bathmusicfest.org.uk) is a very prestigious music festival, spanning world, jazz and classical geneares in **late-May and** early Jun. **Mozart Festival** in Nov, and **Literature Festival** in early-Mar.

Activities and tours

Boating

Bath Boating Station, Forester Rd, T01225-466407, has skiff and punt hire for river expeditions upstream from Pultney Bridge to Bathampton.
Cleopatra Boat Trips, T01225-480541. From the riverside next to the Rugby Football Ground, the only tour boat that cruises downstream of the weir. £5.95, concessions £4.95, children £3.95 for 55 mins.

Walking

Bizarre Bath, T01225-335124. Comedy walk that leaves the Huntsman Inn every evening at 2000 Apr-Sep.
The Mayor's Corps of Honorary Guides, T01225-477411. Entertaining and free 2-hr walking tours leaving from outside the Pump Room throughout the year, Mon-Fri, Sun at 1030 and 1400, Sat 1030 only, and also May-Sept Tue, Fri and Sat at 1900.

Transport

Bus

First Bus, run the frequent direct X39 service to **Bristol** (40 mins). **National Express**, T08705-808080, run the direct service at 1225 to **Cardiff** (2 hrs 35 mins), 10 direct services per day to **London Victoria** (3 hrs 20 mins) and a regular service to **Bristol airport** (2 hrs), changing at Bristol bus station.

Taxi

Abbey Radio Taxis, South Parade, T01225-444444. Bath Taxis, Cheltenham St, T01225-447777. **Widcombe Cars**, 21 Greenacres, T01225-422610.

Train

First Great Western, T08457-000125, run the frequent direct service from Bath Spa to **Bristol Temple Meads** (15 mins) and twice hourly direct to **London Paddington** (1 hr 30 mins). Wessex Trains, T08709-002320, run the direct hourly service to **Cardiff Central** (1 hr 5 mins).

Directory

Car hire Avis, Unit 4b Bath Riverside Business Park, T01225-446680. **A1 Self Drive** Hire, 376 Wellsway, T01225-830630. **Ford** Rental, Kingsmead Motor Co Ltd, 5-10, James St West, T01225-402234. **Hertz**, Bath Spa Rail Station, Dorchester St, T01225-442911. **Cycle hire** Avon Valley Cyclery, Bath Spa Railway Station, Dorchester St, T01225-442442. **Hospitals** Royal United Hospital, Combe Park, T01225-428331. **Internet** Click Internet Café, 13 Manvers St, near the station, T01225-481008.

Somerset

→Colour map 1

Somerset is often portrayed as a place of insular, cider-guzzling farming communities and New Age freaks, but this is one of the most ancient and sacred parts of the country, evidenced by the miniature cathedral-city at Wells and confirmed at nearby Glastonbury. Here all the myths come together – not just of Arthur, Wessex, and Joseph of Arimathea, but also of every type of alternative philosophy. To the west, the county town of Taunton sits beneath the Quantocks, a charming little range of sandstone hills, where acres of wild oaks and heather give glimpses of the sea. ▸▸ *For Sleeping, Eating and other listings, see pages 250-251.*

Ins and outs

Getting there Buses to **Wells** go almost every hr from Bristol and Bath. If you are making a round, day trip to Wells and Glastonbury, ask for an Explorer ticket, which enables you to hop on and off whenever and wherever you want. There are regular, hourly buses from Bristol and Bath, via Wells, to **Glastonbury**. There is also a daily **National Express** service between Glastonbury and Dorchester, leaving Dorchester at 0955 and returning from Glastonbury at 1655. The nearest railway station is 10 miles away at Castle Cary (from London Paddington, 2 hrs direct or 2 hrs 30 mins if you change at Bath). However, there is only 1 bus a week (Tue at 1000) that goes direct from Castle Cary to Glastonbury. Otherwise, a spasmodic Mon-Sat service goes – very slowly – as far as Street, from where there are regular buses to Glastonbury. A taxi from Castle Cary might cost you anything up to £30. It is probably easier to go by train to Bath or Bristol Temple Meads and catch the hourly bus which stops outside the railway station to Glastonbury. Trains to **Exeter** from London Paddington (2 hrs) via Reading (1 hr 30 mins) passes through Taunton. Also from Bristol (30 mins) and the West Midlands. A fairly comprehensive network of local buses are run by **First National**, T01823-272033.

Information **Wells TIC** ⓘ *Town Hall, Market Pl, T01749-672552, wells.tic@uk online.co.uk, daily from Mar to Nov.* **Glastonbury TIC** ⓘ *At the bottom end of the High St, in The Tribunal, T01458-832954, www.glastonburytic.co.uk Apr-Sep 1000-1700 Sun-Thu, 1000-1730 Fri and Sat, 1000-1630 Oct-Mar.* **Taunton TIC** ⓘ In the Library on Paul St, T01823-336344, Jun-Sep Mon-Thu 0930-1730, Fri 0930-1900, Sat 0930-1700.

Longleat and Stourhead

Longleat House and Safari Park ⓘ *T01985-844400, www.longleat.co.uk, house open Easter-Sep daily 1000-1730, Oct-Dec by guided tours 1100-1500, £9, concessions and under-14s £6, safari park mid to Mar-Oct Mon-Fri 1000-1600, Sat, Sun, bank holidays (and school holidays) 1000-1700, £9, concessions and children £6, passport to all attractions £15, concessions and children £11.* The first stately home to open its doors to the public on a regular basis, Longleat is a strange place. The grand Elizabethan house is approached along a 2-mile drive through beautiful ornamental woodland, overlooking the star attraction that first made the estate a household name, the safari park. Deer, giraffe and rhino can be seen grazing in the distance, matchbox-sized cars crawling around among them, getting close to the famous lions, as well as hippos, seals and zebra. Otherwise there's plenty else for all ages to enjoy at this highly commercialized entertainment complex, including the gaudy interior of the old house itself, featuring the current Lord Bath's erotic murals and a display of Nazi memorabilia in the Life & Times of Lord Henry Bath exhibition.

Some 6 miles south of Longleat, at Stourton, is **Stourhead** ⓘ *T01747-841152 (NT), garden daily 0900-1900 (or dusk if earlier), house Apr-Oct Fri-Tue 1100-1700, King Alfred's Tower Apr-Oct daily 1200-1700, house and garden £8.90, children*

 £4.30, family £21.20, garden or house only £5.10, children £2.90, one of the most beautiful English landscape gardens. Designed by the amateur landscape gardener and banker Heneary Hoare between 1741 and 1780, it embraces a large lake with woodland walks revealing surprising views of neoclassical monuments and follies all the way round, right up to the original Bristol city market cross. The house itself has a remarkable library and contains a variety of Old Master paintings and interesting sculpture. A 2-mile walk across the estate leads to King Alfred's tower, a brick folly with fabulous views over the surrounding countryside.

Wells

Perhaps because of its close proximity to Glastonbury, Wells – the smallest cathedral city in England – feels eminently sensible and well-behaved in comparison to the bohemian unruliness and mystical excess of its crazy cousin. Its awe-inspiring medieval cathedral, which many consider to be the loveliest in the country, might today as easily serve a vast urban sprawl. Though possibly not grand enough to count as a destination in its own right, Wells certainly makes a highly satisfactory stopover, the evening floodlighting of its historic buildings adding extra atmosphere to an overnight stay.

The **cathedral** ⓘ *Daily, voluntary donations welcome, evensong 1700 Mon-Sat and 1500 on Sun*, towers over the town centre. Its vast 13th century west front contains the largest gallery of medieval sculpture in the world – a veritable panoply of bishops, kings, saints and apostles with the figure of Christ, at its apex, a modern piece installed in 1985. Once inside, your eye is immediately drawn to the unique 'scissor arches' at the east end, a superbly elegant design of deceptively modern appearance, which was, in fact, a 14th-century solution to the problem of redistributing the weight of a building threatening to sink into its foundations. Look out for the ancient astronomical clock in the north transept, whose jousting knights revolve in ceaseless tournament, before climbing the worn stone steps up to the octagonal Chapter House, where ecclesiastical business was traditionally conducted. Undoubtedly the best way to experience the great beauty of the cathedral is to sit through choral **evensong**. If your visit is at lunchtime, however, the cloisters – with its 15th-century library – also includes a shop and restaurant (main courses about £5, with an impressive array of cakes made by the ladies of the diocese).

On the north side, the quiet precincts of the cathedral include the **Vicar's Close**, said to be the oldest continuously inhabited street in Europe, and, with its miniature Gothic architecture, cobbles and extraordinary chimneys, almost a work of art in its own right. The **Wells Museum** ⓘ *T01749-673477, daily Easter-Oct, Wed-Mon, Nov-Easter, £2.50*, the pinkish building looking onto the green, contains a display of local history and archaeology, including the macabre remains and belongings of the legendary witch of the Wookey Hole caves. On the south side is the **Bishop's Palace** ⓘ *1030-1700 Tue-Fri and 1200-1700 Sun, Apr-Oct and most days in Aug, £3.50*, some of whose rooms are open to the public. The grounds contain some unusual trees and, at the back, a pool produced by the 40 gallons of water supplied per second by the natural springs seen bubbling up at its base.

The Mendips

Just north of Wells are the large caves called **Wookey Hole** ⓘ *T01749-672243, www.wookey.co.uk, Apr-Oct daily 1000-1700, Nov-Mar 1030-1630, £8.80, children £5.50*, hollowed out of the Mendips by the river Axe over thousands of years, have been turned into a full-blown tourist attraction. Admission includes a 40-min tour of the illuminated cave system, with observations of the stalactites, stalagmites ('mites go up and tites go down') and rock formations with silly names, including the 'Witch of Wookey', as well as a Victorian papermill, still in production, old-fashioned penny arcade, mirror maze and the Caves Museum, which explains their geological and local history. Allow a couple of hours to do the whole lot.

Druids: Bronze Age to New Age

When Julius Caesar invaded Britain in the first century BC he already knew from his experiences conquering Gaul that the Druids would give him trouble. Recent research suggests that these warrior priests presided over a settled and sophisticated agrarian Celtic community, probably undertaking most of the roles occupied by the professional classes today. They were doctors, lawyers and chartered surveyors all rolled into one. Indeed the Romans only finally crushed their resistance more than a century later at a bloody battle on Anglesey Island in Wales.

Archaeologists have suggested that the siting of burial mounds and stone circles over former domiciles indicates that the Druids practised a religion that believed in an underworld peopled by their tribal ancestors. These monuments were taken to be the gateway to the land of the dead. Sadly the historical evidence is at odds with the popular image of the priesthood epitomised by Getafix in the Asterix cartoons. Rather than wandering affably around in search of mistletoe with their golden sickles, they're more likely to have been found ritually garotting young men – the probable fate of Lindow Man, now preserved in the British Museum – and instilling their followers with a casual lack of concern for personal safety, something that bothered the Roman legionaries. Modern Druids espouse a more limited faith – in the sanctity of the seasons and respect for mother nature, in the animistic spirits of wood and stream and in flowing facial hair. Its these gentle although not entirely unprofessional souls that have earned the right to celebrate their faith at Stonehenge on the summer solstice each year and thankfully not their reincarnated Bronze Age brethren.

A few miles northwest of Wookey Hole, **Cheddar Gorge** ⓘ *T01934-742343, www.cheddarcaves.co.uk, Apr-Oct daily 1000-1700, Nov-Mar 1000-1630, £8.90, children £5.90*, may have given its name to the world's most famous cheese (thanks to Victorian local man Joseph Harding and his wife who invented its scientific manufacture), but visitors today are more likely to come for its caves. Wookey's main rival charges for parking, although it has the added attraction of the gorge (its lower and more spectacular end spoilt by the traffic) and boasts two slightly smaller caves, Gough's and Cox's, as well as a Crystal Quest, Jacob's Ladder (a long flight of steps leading up to a viewpoint), and an open-top tour bus.

Glastonbury

There is nowhere more imbued with the mythical – even mystical – idea of England than Glastonbury. The romantic ruins of the town's ancient abbey, a sacred well, a thorn tree from the holy land and the tor – a kind of miniature magic mountain – have variously become part of the warp and woof of two of this country's greatest stories. Glastonbury has been identified both as the Isle of Avalon, the site of King Arthur's final resting place and, also, as the birthplace of English Christianity, where Joseph of Arimathea – who made the arrangements for Jesus' burial – is said to have brought the holy grail, the vessel used by Christ at the Last Supper. Somewhat more prosaically, the first thing the visitor to Glastonbury is likely to be struck by is the cornucopia of shops selling all the paraphernalia of the modern spiritual bazaar – crystals, incense, buddhas, beads and the like. The town is home to so many healers and seekers of different shapes and sizes that, without the solid centre that the abbey must once have provided, the whole thing can occasionally feel like rather a dispiriting, amorphous mess.

Glastonbury Abbey ⓘ *T01458-832267, daily 0930-1800, or dusk if earlier, 0900 Jun-Aug, and 1000 Dec-Feb, £3.50, children 1.50,* is a stone's throw away from the Market Place and the main bus stop. This once-great building, now all but a ruined shell, was demolished during the Reformation by Henry VIII and subsequently used as a stone quarry. This was where the Christian gospel was believed to have first taken root on English soil – graphically illustrated by the Syrian thorn tree grown out of the staff that Joseph of Arimathea is said to have struck into the earth at Glastonbury. The thorn tree in the abbey – just to the left as you enter the grounds – is an offshoot of an older tree and is said to flower at Christmas and Easter time.

The only complete building to survive Henry's onslaught is the abbot's kitchen, a structure dating from about 1340. Still vaguely intact is the Lady Chapel, of Norman style, which is believed to have been built over the site of a much earlier church – some say Joseph's own. The ruins of the nave contain the grave of King Arthur and his queen Guinevere which was discovered in 1191. The relics were then placed in a marble tomb before the high altar: the debate still rages on as to whether or not this was an elaborate fake, a piece of monkish mummery invented to capitalize on this royal cult. There is also a museum attached to the abbey, included in the entry fee.

Glastonbury Tor ⓘ *24 hrs daily, free, 20-30 min walk from the town centre, a Tor Bus operates a round trip from St Dunstan's car park beside the abbey, via the well and the Rural Life Museum, to the foot of the tor about every 30 mins, 0930-1700, £1/£0.50).* Rising some 164 yards above sea level, this natural feature of the landscape is – depending on who you talk to – a meeting point of ley lines (channels of energy that run through the earth), a temple dedicated to the great Goddess, or a secret entrance to the underworld. The distinctive patterns of its terraced slopes, generally understood to be the result of a medieval field system called strip lynching, have also been interpreted as the remains of an esoteric labyrinth. Whatever is truly the case, the summit of the tor is an indisputably exhilarating place to sit – take a picnic with you – due in no small part to the wonderful sense of place and space and the 360 degree view of the Somerset countryside, extending as far as the Bristol Channel. From the tor, one can appreciate how Glastonbury really was once an ancient isle, rising out of marshy land that was often flooded in the winter. Like St Michael's Mount in Cornwall and the Mont St Michel in Normandy, the tor is dedicated to St Michael, the destroyer of demons. The tower on the tor is all that remains of a medieval church – built to replace an earlier building destroyed by earthquake – and archaeologists have unearthed material from the sixth century and what seem to be 10th-century monastic cells.

Somerset Levels and the Quantocks

South and west of Glastonbury stretch the drained flatlands of the Somerset Levels, famous for their cider farms and with views of the Quantocks. The geology of these sandstone hills introduces the characteristic look of Exmoor and much of north Cornwall. As well as being fine walking country, the Quantocks have a literary reputation disproportionate to their size thanks to the Romantic poets Wordsworth and more especially Coleridge, and writers like Evelyn Waugh. Nether Stowey nestles on their northern flank, within reach of the sea, and the site of Coleridge's Cottage, one of the earliest of literary shrines, now preserved by the National Trust.
The ancient history of the Somerset Levels can be explored 5 miles west of Glastonbury at **Westhay**, where the council's **Peat Moors Centre** ⓘ *Shapwick Rd, Westhay, T01458-860697, Apr-Oct 1000-1630, £2.50, concessions and children £1.95, family £8* demonstrates how neolithic man lived in these marshes, with entertaining mock-up huts and a reconstruction of the extraordinary pre-fab wooden track they used to get about on.

The Cheddar Man exhibition displays the remains of someone buried here about 9000 years ago, whose DNA was matched in 1997 with that of local teacher Adrian Target.

All the fun of the fayre

The summer music festival is an intrinsic part of British life, and the most famous of all, Glastonbury, is as much a part of the cultural calendar as Last Night of the Proms or the panto season. From humble origins when it was known as Glastonbury Fayre, 'Glasto' has grown into a musical behemoth and, according to many, largely lost its radical kudos, as well as having gained a nasty reputation for crime. It was very different back in September 1970 (on the day after Jimi Hendrix died), when local farmer, Michael Eavis, allowed the first festival to take place on his land, charging the princely sum of £1 (which included free milk from his cows) and 1500 turned up to hear Marc Bolan and Al Stewart amongst others. Now well over 100,000 are charged over £100 a head for the privilege of attending. But at least the purists don't moan about changes to the dubious on-site sanitation and greater security measures put in place in 2002 seem to have given rise to a happier vibe, if making it harder to jump the fence.

Eight miles southwest of Glastonbury, **Muchelney Abbey** ⓘ *(EH), T01458-250664, Apr-Sep daily 1000-1800, Oct daily 1000-1700, £2.50, concessions £1.90*, is a little visited treasure: the remains of a monastery founded in the seventh century and re-founded in 950. The Abbot's lodging still looks much as it would have done when handed over to Henry VIII in 1539. **Muchelney Pottery**, T01458-250324, is worth a visit for the work of John Leach.

Montacute House ⓘ *(NT) T01935-823289, Apr-Oct Mon, Wed-Sun 1100-1700, £6.50, children £3*, 12 miles south of Glastonbury, is one of the finest late Tudor mansions in the country containing a series of Elizabethan and Jacobean portraits, surrounded by a formal garden with enormous yew hedges, a lake and gazebo. The place became famous after featuring in the film adaptation of Jane Austen's *Sense and Sensibility*.

Quantocks

The Quantocks roll for 12 miles or so northwest of Taunton towards the sea. The name apparently derives from the celtic word for 'rim'. With their wooded valleys, winding roads, high hedges and glimpses of the sea, they are a delightful place to explore. Their official visitor centre and the headquarters of the Somerset Wildlife Trust is a couple of miles north at **Fyne Court** ⓘ *T01823-451587, daily 0900-1800 (or sunset if earlier)*, in the old pleasure gardens of the home of pioneer electrician Andrew Crosse, now demolished. Maps, walking trails and general information on the area are provided here, as well as a teahouse and ruined folly being turned into a haven for bats.

Walking and cycling are the best way to get around the Quantocks. TIC offices below can provide a set of leaflets on local walks.

After 6 miles along the same road, the Quantocks suddenly dip down into **Nether Stowey**. **Coleridge's Cottage** ⓘ *T01278-732662, Apr-Sep Tue, Wed, Thu, Sun 1400-1700, £3, children £1.50*, is a sweet little place with three rooms on show, as well as a good bookshop on the Romantics and an exhibition room including manuscripts. Although much altered, having been a pub for a while, the little house gives you a good idea of how the great man lived during his most creative period (at the age of 23), when he was writing the *Rime of the Ancient Mariner* and *Kubla Khan*, disturbed by a man on business from Porlock.

The road over to Crowcombe from Nether Stowey heads through wonderful wild oak woodland up onto the top of the heather-clad, bracken-infested hills, laced with footpaths, and dotted with large white puffballs in Autumn. Peaceful **Crowcombe** has an excellent pub (see page 251) and in the church amazing carved bench ends alive with

Green Men. A few miles further down the west side of the hills, the main A358 passes **Combe Florey**, where Evelyn Waugh and then his son Auberon lived in the manor house. The **West Somerset Railway**, *T01643-704996*, *www.west-somerset-railway.co.uk*, runs steam engines in summer up this side of the hills, from **Bishop's Lydeard** 20 miles to **Minehead**, popular with hikers, birdwatchers and families.

Sleeping

Wells and the Mendips *p246 & p246*

L **Ston Easton Park**, Ston Easton, near Midsomer Norton, T01761-241631. Handsome Palladian country house set in Repton parkland, with wonderfully comfortable bedrooms and elegant public rooms.

B **Swan Hotel**, 11 Sadler St, Wells T01749-836300. One of several traditional coaching inns on this street. Log fires, 4-poster beds and English food, with a door leading straight onto the cathedral green.

C **The Crown**, Market Pl, Wells, T01749-673457. A large 15th-century inn at the heart of Wells, with lively bar, a French bistro and spacious courtyard. Four-poster beds available.

D **The Old Poor House**, 7A St Andrew St, Wells T01749-675052. A secluded 14th-century cottage away from all traffic in the cathedral precincts.

Glastonbury *p247*

B **No. 3 Hotel**, 3 Magdalene St, T01458-832129. An elegant Georgian house adjoining the abbey grounds. Classy accommodation, all en-suite bathrooms, with secure parking.

C **King William Inn**, 19 Market Pl, T01458-831473. Three rooms above this centrally located, no-nonsense hostelry.

C **Shambhala Health & Healing Retreat**, Coursing Batch, T01458-831797. Peaceful garden, Egyptian, Chinese and Tibetan-style rooms, massage and other therapies available, just out of town next to the Tor.

D **Hawthornes Hotel**, 8-12 Northload St, T01458-831255. The best value hotel in Glastonbury, just off the High St. Not a trace of the New Age in its tasteful, contemporary decor, with a restaurant, bar and lounge.

D **Tordown**, 5 Ashwell Lane, T01458-832287. Healing and 'higher self' sessions available at this B&B. Shared bathroom.

E **Little St Michael's**, Chilkwell St, T01458-831154. A delightful retreat house that is part of the Chalice Well gardens with rooms from £20 a night for anyone paying an additional £18 to become a 'companion to the well' (cheaper rates for couples and senior citizens). Vegetarian.

F **Glastonbury Backpackers**, 4 Market Pl, T01458-833353. Dorm beds at £10 a night and rooms at £25/30 a night in this converted 16th-century coaching inn right in the centre of things. Communal kitchen and living room upstairs, with bar and café downstairs.

Somerset levels, Taunton and the Quantocks *p248*

C **Frog Street Farm**, Beercrocombe, near Taunton, T01823-480430. An old farmhouse tucked into the Somerset countryside, with exposed beams and good cooking. Evening meal optional at £18 a head.

E **Quantock Hills YHA**, Sevenacres, Holford, near Nether Stowey. A country house with 28 beds (4 6-bedded and 2 4-bedded) in a fine position on the northern Quantocks.

Eating

Wells and the Mendips *p246 & p246*

££ **The Good Earth**, Broad St, T01749-678600. A well-scrubbed organic and vegetarian restaurant in a country cottage setting, doubling as a health food shop and potager. Open from 0900-1700.

Glastonbury *p247*

££ **Hawthornes Hotel**, 8-12 Northload St, T01458-831255. Smart, attractive lentil-free zone in this unpretentious hotel brasserie, specializing in fish, with a garden courtyard.

£ **Blue Note Café**, 4 High St, T01458-832907. Vegetarian eating with outside tables in a little courtyard tucked away off the High St.

£ **Café Galatea**, 5a The High St, T01458-834284. Vegetarian food in this lively café, with internet access, which also serves as a gallery for local arts and crafts. Closed Tue.

£ **Knights Fish Restaurant**, 5 Northload St, T01458-831882. Sit down for your fish supper in one of England's oldest chippie's, established in 1909.

£ **Spiral Gate Organic Café**, 24 High St, T01458-834633. Friendly atmosphere in a relaxed setting. Live music and juice bar. Open fires in winter, courtyard seating in summer.

Somerset levels, Taunton and the Quantocks *p248*

£££ **The Castle at Taunton**, Castle Bow, Taunton, T01823-272671, www.the-castle-hotel.com. Very high standards in this restaurant which has launched the careers of TV chefs such as Gary Rhodes. The **Brazz** brassrie offers a more informal and less expensive alternative.

££ **Carew Arms**, Crowcombe, near Taunton, T01984- 618631. Cheerful old pub with a roaring fire and locally grown food well prepared in the kitchen.

Festivals and events

Glastonbury *p247*

For information on the famous annual **Glastonbury music festival** – which actually takes place on a farm at the neighbouring village of Pilton – look up www.glastonburyfestivals.co.uk

Exmoor

→*Colour map 1*

Around 267 square miles of windswept, rainlashed sandstone upland, Exmoor is one of the most romantic of England's national parks. Wordsworth, Coleridge, Hazlitt and Co. didn't do quite such a thorough job on it as the Lake District, though, despite all three staying nearby in their twenties and Shelley honeymooning on the coast. RD Blackmore sealed its Victorian reputation for bodice-ripping adventure with his novel Lorna Doone. Wooded valleys, tidy farmland and winding roads in its eastern and northern parts give way to bare tracts of bleak moorland in the west. If the sun does shine, the rolling acres of heather, bracken and bog can seem quite tame. ▸▸ *For Sleeping and Eating, see page 254.*

Ins and outs

Getting there The A39 from Bridgewater (about 2 hrs 30 mins from London down the M4/5) is a notoriously slow road in the holiday season. Bridgewater to Lynton, some 35 miles as the crow flies, 44 miles by road, can sometimes take anything up to 2 hrs to cover. The southern edge of Exmoor is much more easily reached along the A361 from Tiverton, junction 27 on the M5 (almost 3 hrs from London). Tiverton to Dulverton usually takes about 45 mins. There are regular **buses** between Barnstaple and Lynton. Local travel information, T01823-251151. No trains go into Exmoor itself, but the **West Somerset Railway**, T01643-704996 (24-hr talking timetable T01643-707650), runs a summer steam service (and some weekends in winter) from Bishops Lydeard (4 miles west of Taunton) via Williton, Watchet, Cleeve Abbey, Blue Anchor and Dunster to Minehead on the moor's northeastern corner (see Somerset section).

Getting around Car, bike or horse are really the only alternatives to footwork on Exmoor, although there is a network of local buses, contact **Devon Busline,** T01392-382800. **First Southern National,** T01823-272033 (0830-1730), run the No 300 bus service shuttle along the A39 daily in summer, at weekends in winter, between Ilfracombe and Taunton via Porlock and Minehead. Distances can be deceptive, so it's well worth being equipped with a good map, plenty of wet-weather gear and a compass.

Information National Park Authority Information Centres, www.exmoor-nationalpark.gov.uk, at: **Dulverton** ⓘ *Fore St, T01398-323841, Apr-Oct daily 1000-1700, Nov-Mar daily 1030-1530*; **Dunster** ⓘ *The Steep, T01643-821835, Apr-Oct daily 1000-1700, Nov-Mar Sat, Sun 1100- 1500*; **Lynmouth** ⓘ *on the Esplanade, T01598-752509, Apr-Oct daily 1000-1700, Nov-Mar Sat, Sun 1100-1500*; **Combe**

 Martin ⓘ *Cross St, T01271-338819, Apr-Oct daily 1000-1700*; **County Gate** ⓘ *on the A39 at Countysbury, T01598-741321, Apr-Oct daily 1000-1700*; **Porlock Visitor Centre** ⓘ *West End, High St, T01643-863150, www.porlock.co.uk*

Exmoor National Park

All the moorland of interest falls within the boundaries of the National Park, but the essence of Exmoor is the almost treeless expanse of Exmoor Forest around Simonsbath. To the east the landscape becomes increasingly enclosed, farmed and also beautifully wooded. Tough little **Exmoor ponies** wander freely around many parts of the National Park, especially off the B3223 north of Simonsbath, around Withypool in the valley of the Barle and on Winsford Hill. If you're very lucky you might also spot some of the largest herd of red deer in England, buzzards, bats and badgers, and even perhaps an otter.

Dulverton is the main centre on Exmoor for organizing activities like walking and fishing on the moor, very busy with holidaymakers in summer. A minor road off to the left leads down to the **Tarr Steps**, an ancient and quite impressive clapper bridge over the Barle, about 170 ft long, washed away in the floods of 1952 and since restored. **Winsford**, off the B3223 to the right, is another important huntin', shootin', and fishin' centre and also a confusing minor-road junction. Picturesquely placed at the coming together of several streams, including the river Exe, with thatched cottages and old stone bridges, it makes a good base for walks, especially up to the heights of **Winsford Hill**.

The other major settlement in this generally more gentle, farmed and well-wooded part of Exmoor is **Exford**, upstream of Winsford on the Exe. Not quite as pretty, it boasts a petrol station and various teashops, pubs and hotels of middling quality. To its northeast, **Dunkery Beacon** (519 m), the highest point on Exmoor and reachable by road from Cloutsham, provides spectacular views over the **Holnicote Estate** (see below), a large swathe of farmland, woodland and moorland stretching from Wheddon Cross to the sea between Minehead and Porlock. **Simonsbath** is the most isolated settlement on the moor, surrounded by the former Royal Forest of Exmoor. To the southeast of the village, **Birch Cleave** is an unusually high stretch of beech woodland.

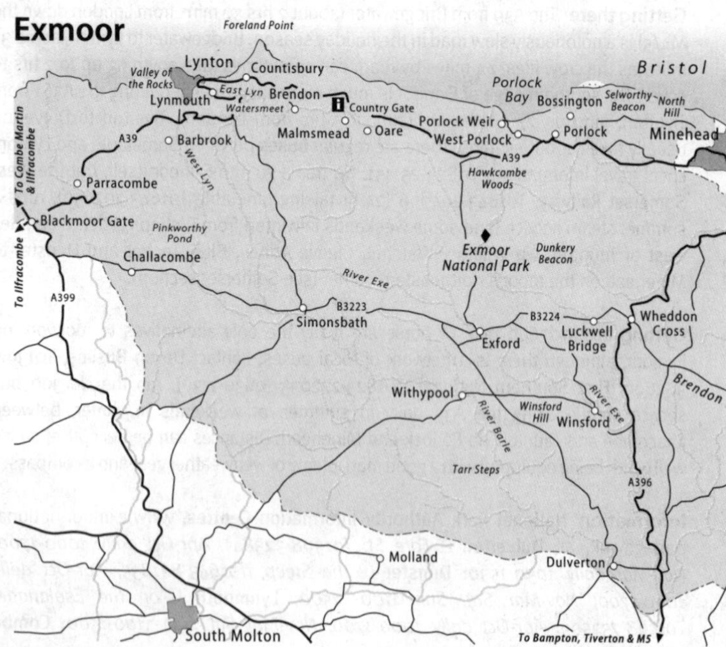

Exmoor Coast: Dunster to Lynton

Just under a mile from the coast, on the northeastern edge of Exmoor, Dunster is a little medieval village in the adorable valley of the River Avill. Frequently overrun with tourists, it's not hard to see why. With its steam train and marshy beach, its higgledy-piggledy roofscape and funny little 17th-century octagonal yarn market, all overlooked by a picturesque castle and curious folly tower looming out of the trees above on each side, it adds up to a picture-postcard treat. Once an important port, rich in Exmoor wool, it now manages quite nicely thanks to its olde-worlde charm. Apart from its antique shops and tearooms, the main visitor attraction is **Dunster Castle** ⓘ *(NT), T01643-821314, Apr-Oct Mon-Wed, Sat, Sun 1100-1700 (till 1600 in Oct), garden and park Apr-Sep daily 1000-1700, Oct-Mar daily 1100-1600, £6.40, children £3.20, family £16.* Built in the Middle Ages but completely remodelled in the 19th century, in a deliberately scenic manner, it now belongs to the National Trust. The 18th-century folly tower on Conygar Hill is a remarkable eyecatcher. The little packhorse Gallox bridge is also worth a look and the views from Grabbist hill over the village are memorable too.

Two miles west of Dunster on the A39, **Minehead** is this coast's main seaside resort, with all the usual entertainments and also once famous for its massive Butlin's holiday camp. A minor road winds west out of town up North Hill, overlooking the minehead Bluff and on to the quite spectacular viewpoint at **Selworthy Beacon**, with views of Porlock.

Porlock is the next tourist hotspot on the coast road, famous for its hill, which also contributes to its magnificent position in a natural amphitheatre looking out over Porlock Bay. Its thatched cottages and stone streets heave with visitors in summer. Cars choose to climb out of the place westwards either on the very steep A39 or on the lovely twisting toll roads (£2 cars, £5 caravans). The coast road leads down to charming little **Porlock Weir**, the old harbour, from where the **South West Coast Path** wanders along just inland past the woodland church at **Culbone**, supposedly the smallest in the country.

At Countisbury the A39 begins the steep descent into **Lynmouth**, a delightful little harbourside village nestling in a wooded valley that within living memory was the scene of destruction on a biblical scale. On the main street is a mark of the mud level set on 15 August 1952, when 20,000 cu ft of water swept through the village, killing 34 people and destroying 62 buildings. The tide of visitors ebbing and flowing through the village is the chief concern today, although nothing can detract from the superb location. The village's main tourist attraction is the **Glenn Lynn Gorge** ⓘ *T01598-753207, Easter-Oct daily 1000-1700, £3, concessions £1.50*, where visitors are encouraged to "Experience the awesome power of nature in this place of mystery, tragedy and extreme beauty". The ravine contains an informative 'Power of Water' exhibition, various water pumps and jets, and the largest privately owned hydro-electric scheme in England. Water is also put to good use by the water-powered **Lynton and Lynmouth Cliff Railway** ⓘ *T01598-753486, Mid-Feb to mid Nov daily 1000-1900 (or dusk if earlier), £2.20 return, £1.20 single*, a quaint feat of Victorian engineering that takes passengers up 500 ft to the clifftop resort of **Lynton**.

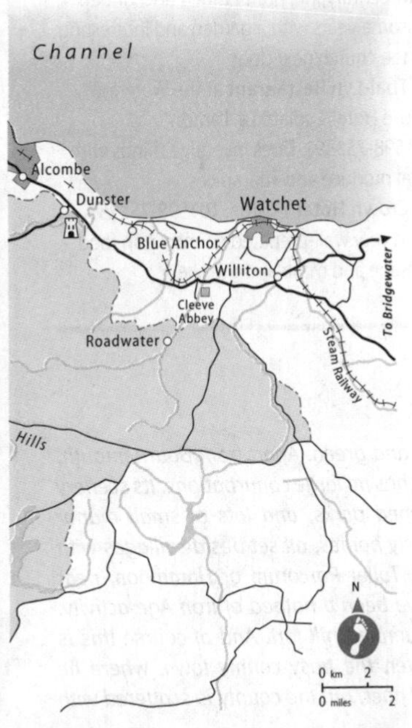

Sleeping

Exmoor National Park

C **Little Quarme**, Wheddon Cross, near Luckwell Bridge, T01643-841249, www.littlequarme.co.uk. Superior farmhouse accommodation.
D **Twitchen Farm**, Challacombe, near Simonsbath, T01598-763568. Courtyard farmhouse with wonderful views and good home cooking.
D **Larcombe Foot**, near Winsford, T01643-851306. Comfortable farmhouse with fine south-facing views.
D **Little Brendon Hill Farm**, Wheddon Cross, T01643-841556, www.exmoorheaven.co.uk. Non-smoking professionally run farmhouse accommodation with en-suite rooms;
F **Exford YHA**, Exe Mead, Exford, T01643-831288, F831650. With 51 beds in 2 2-bedded, the rest 4-6 bedded rooms, in a Victorian house close to the river Exe.

Camping

Camping barns, T01200-420102, at Woodadvent, near Roadwater, and at Northcombe.

Exmoor Coast

A **Porlock Vale House**, Porlock Weir, T01643-862338, www.porlockvale.co.uk. Price includes dinner. Former hunting lodge set in wooded coutnryside with magnificent views over the Bristol Channel. Specialise in equestrian holidays.
B **Rising Sun Hotel**, Harbourside, Lynmouth, T01598-753223. The best upmarket option and probably the place where Shelley actually stayed, it's a thatched pub and top-notch (fairly expensive) restaurant with quirky little rooms up the tiny staircase.
C **Andrews on the Weir**, Porlock Weir, T01643-863300. Also a highly rated restaurant, serving up local produce innovatively and well, with rooms overlooking the little harbour, £19 3-course set dinner and boasting one of the best cheeseboards in the West Country.
C **Bales Mead**, West Porlock, T01643-862565. A well-known B&B in an Edwardian country house with a few extra frills.
C **Shelley's Hotel**, Lynmouth, T01598-753219, www.shelleyshotel.co.uk. Comfortable and has rooms that have some amazing views.
F **Lynton YHA**, Lynbridge, Lynton, T01598-753237, F753305. With 36 beds in 2 2, 2 4- and 4 6-bedded rooms.

Eating

Exmoor Coast

See also **Andrews on the Weir** and the **Rising Sun** in Sleeping.
£££ **The Restaurant in the High St**, 3 High St, Dunster, T01643-821304. Award-winning local fare, especially game and seafood, in a typically Dunster-ish ambience.
££ **The London Inn**, Molland, near South Molton, T01796-550269. A thatched 15th-century inn, pretty much unchanged for some years with a garden and interesting village church next door.
££ **Thai-Lyn Restaurant** at the Waterloo House Hotel, Lydiate La, Lynton, T01598-753391. Does inventive things with local produce and Thai spices.
££ **Crown Hotel**, Lynton, T01598-752253. Does very well-prepared country pub food – sausage and mash and the like.

Dorset

→*Colour map 1/2*

Dorset is little England at its most rural, cosy, and green. Apart from Bournemouth, which was always traditionally in Hampshire, it has no large conurbations. Its scenery embraces acres of rolling farmland, landscaped parks, and lots of small manor houses and castles, rather than a few big stately homes, all set beside villages with impossibly quaint names like Purse Caundle, Toller Porcorum or Hammoon, near Fiddleford. Like Wiltshire, it also seems to have been a hotbed of Iron Age activity. Every other hillock has been carved into a crumpled hill fort. And of course this is Thomas Hardy country. Its centre is Dorchester, the busy county town, where he became a fatalistic old curmudgeon and great poet, but the county is scattered with

scenes memorably described in his novels. Warm-stoned Sherborne with its astonishing Abbey is a medieval market town in the north. Bournemouth needs little introduction, a coastal boomtown on the site of the Victorians' favourite watering place, its hillside villas change hands for rocketing prices almost as quickly as polite Poole's next door. Across Poole Harbour, the Isle of Purbeck is the stonemason and quarryman's heartland, a strange and until relatively recently all but forgotten corner of the south coast. Now it's been designated a World Natural Heritage Site. On the freshly branded 'Jurassic Coast', the most popular spots are still the rock arches at Durdle Door and the beach at Lulworth Cove, but it's the natural wonder of Chesil Beach and the little resort of Lyme Regis and its surrounding cliffs that have really earned the attentions of UNESCO. ➤➤ *For Sleeping, Eating and other listings, see pages 261-263.*

Sherborne and Dorchester

Mellow-stoned Sherborne sits on one side of the Blackmore Vale, boasting a spectacular old Abbey, and no less than two castles, one of them very old. Easily reached on the A303 from London, the town makes the best base in north Dorset from which to explore the surrounding countryside. Dorchester, meanwhile, is a prosperous but not entirely prepossessing market town, milking the tourist dollar for all it's worth. Nearby, the carved hill figure wielding a club above his proud phallus draws the crowds to the little village of Cerne Abbas.

Ins and outs

Getting there **Sherborne** is about 2½ hrs from London down the M3 and A303. **National Express** serve Sherboune by coach direct from London Victoria (3 hrs 30 mins-4 hrs) but there is usually only 1 service a day. About 1 slow train an hr leaves London Waterloo for Sherborne, taking around 2½ hrs. **Dorchester** can be reached by **National Express** bus in 1 hr from Bournemouth. Dorchester South is on the **Southwest Trains** mainline to Weymouth from London Waterloo (2 hrs 30 mins) but not many trains stop there. **Wessex Trains** from Bath and Bristol (2 hrs) to Weymouth call at Dorchester West. ➤➤ *For further details, see also Transport, page 263.*

Getting around A fairly good network of local buses is run by the **Wilts and Dorset Bus Company,** T01202-673555, but a car or bicycle are easily the most convenient ways of exploring the Blackmore Vale.

Information **Sherborne TIC** *ⓘT01935-815341, www.westdorset.com, Apr-Oct Mon-Sat 0900-1700, Nov-Mar Mon-Sat 1000-1500.* Free accommoation booking service. **Dorchester TIC** *ⓘUnit 11, Antelope Walk, T01305-267992, May-Sep Mon-Sat 0900-1700, Sun 1000-1500, Oct-Apr Mon-Sat 0900-1600.*

Sherborne

The jewel in Dorset's crown, Sherborne is set in a thickly wooded valley amid beautiful countryside immortally associated with the name of Digby. The pièce de résistance is its rusty-red old stone abbey. **Sherborne Abbey** was a cathedral until 1075 and displays a continuous procession of confident church-building up to the 15th century and the Reformation. Its Perpendicular fan vaulting is the astonishing highlight of the interior, as well as a variety of monuments (such as a full-length statue of the late-17th-century local squire John Digby) and the air of ancient peace. Sherborne town surrounds but does not hustle its abbey, fended off by some impeccably polite medieval almshouses. An interesting antiques and flea **market** (T01963-250108) takes place on the fourth Saturday of each month in the Digby Church Hall up Digby Road opposite the Abbey. Built by Sir Walter Raleigh in 1594,

 Sherborne Castle ⓘ *T01935-813182, Easter-Sep Thu, Sat, Sun, bank holidays 1230-1700* is the Digby family seat but it's not really a castle at all, more of a big old house beside a lake. The real thing is half a mile east of town, the ruins of the 12th-century **Sherborne Old Castle** ⓘ *T01935-812730, Apr-Sep daily 1000-1800, Oct daily 1000-1300, 1400- 1700, Nov-Mar Wed-Sun 1000-1300, 1400-1600, £1.80, concessions £1.40, children £0.90*, also inhabited by Raleigh, which once took Cromwell over a fortnight to capture during the Civil War.

Dorchester

Hardy's Casterbridge and Dorset's county town is an old market town with attitude, wooing tourists with a shameless variety of attractions, the strangest of all being run by *World Heritage Ltd*, some more successful than others. On its outskirts it has also provided the site of Prince Charles's surreal experiment in town-planning at **Poundsbury**. The Prince no doubt regrets that the town's single main street will be almost unrecognizable to readers of *The Mayor of Casterbridge* but Hardy fans can find plenty of solace elsewhere. **Max Gate** ⓘ *(NT), T01305-262538, www.thomas-hardy .connectfree.co.uk, Apr-Sep Mon, Wed, Sun 1400-1700, £2.40, children £1.30*, was the house that he designed himself and lived in from 1885 until his death in 1928. The dining and drawing rooms can be seen, with some of his furniture. Better still, the **Dorset County Museum** ⓘ *T01305-262735, May-Oct daily 1000-1700, Nov-Apr Mon-Sat 1000-1700, £3.50, children £1.70, family £8.70*, recreates his study, tells the story of Maiden Castle and the local geology, flora and fauna in its wonderful old Victorian exhibition hall. The setting for Victorian and Georgian justice can be seen nearby at **The Old Crown Court and Cells** ⓘ *High West St, T01305-252241, www.westdorset .com, court room Mon-Fri 1000-1200, 1400-1600, free, cells Aug Tue, Thu, Fri 1415-1615, Wed 1015-1215*, where the Tolpuddle Martyrs (see below) were tried and transported.

Over the road, Dorchester's other attractions are harder to explain: the latest is the **Terracotta Warriors Museum** ⓘ *High East St, T01305-266040, daily 1000-1730, £4.75, children £2.95*, with eight full-size Chinese-made replicas of the figures unearthed in 1976 in Xian. They've joined the recreation of **Tutankhamun's tomb and treasures** ⓘ *High West St, T01305-269571, www.world-heritage.org.uk*, the **Dinosaur Museum** ⓘ *Icen Way, T01305-269741*, and **Teddy Bear House** ⓘ *Antelope Walk, T01305-263200.*

Views over the town can be had from the extensive **Keep Military Museum,** ⓘ *T01305-264066, www.keepmilitary museum.org, Mon-Sat 0930-1700 (also Sun 1000-1600 in Jul, Aug)*in the mighty mock-medieval Victorian castle gate: medals, machine guns and interactive displays.

Escaping from Dorchester itself, a variety of less carefully stage-managed attractions may prove more rewarding. A mile to the south, **Maiden Castle** is the mother of all hill forts, the largest in Europe and astonishing proof of our early ancestors' ability to shape the landscape to their own ends. Apparently it would have been home to about 200 families, quite possibly fiercely resistant to the Roman invasion of AD 43 but incapable in their isolation of joining up with other tribes to be effective in the struggle. The evidence of their colonization is the site of a Roman temple within the earth ramparts.

Seven miles north of Dorchester on the road to Sherborne, the delightful little village of **Cerne Abbas** is regularly overwhelmed in summer with visitors, the site of the country's most famous hill figure, the priapic Cerne Abbas giant. Three miles northeast of Dorchester is **Thomas Hardy's birthplace** ⓘ *T01305-262366, Apr-Oct Mon-Thu, Sun 1100-1700. £2.80*, a small cottage in Higher Bockhampton, little altered since being built by his great grandfather. Four miles east, on the edge of the Isle of Purbeck and the remains of Hardy's wild Egdon Heath at Affpuddle, the Elizabethan manor house at **Athelhampton** ⓘ *T01305-848363, www.athel hampton.co.uk, Mar-Oct Mon-Fri, Sun 1030- 1700, Nov-Feb Sun 1100-dusk*, is still a family home with spectacular Victorian gardens.

Bournemouth and Poole

Bournemouth, the grand dame of the South Coast, is enjoying a second honeymoon. Miles of long golden sands and safe waters continue to lure holidaymakers from far away to its sturdy cliffside seaside attractions as they have done since it first drew the steam-railway crowds in 1870. Recently recast as a more upmarket sunshine resort, Bournemouth's clean-cut and rather staid image has suddenly caught on. Since horticultural fashions have become all the televised rage, Bournemouth's generous array of immaculate Victorian gardens makes it a year-round choice for big firms and pre-retirement types. Villa-lined valleys slope towards the sea boasting house prices that would make even Londoners think again. Youth culture has also arrived with the new prosperity and looks all set to give Brighton a run for its money.

Ins and outs

Getting there Bournemouth is very well connected to London via the M3 then M27, from London takes under 2 hrs. Poole maybe half an hour more. **National Express** run coaches 16 times a day between Bournemouth, Poole and London. With connecting services to Wareham, Corfe Castle, and Swanage or Wareham, Dorchester and Weymouth. **First**, T01305-766393, runs services between London and Weymouth and Dorchester. Regular trains run by **South West Trains**, T0845-6000650, on the mainline to Weymouth from London Waterloo taking around 2 hrs, also calling at Southampton.

Getting around Bournemouth is a relatively small city, much of which can be reached by foot, bus or taxi. The **Guide Friday** buses operate here for a guided tour of the city, T01789-294466. Or explore the whole seafront by train and Cliff Lift (T01202-451781). Local bus routes are run by **Yellow Buses**, Bournemouth T01202-636060 and **Wiltshire & Dorset Buses**, T01202-673555.

Information **Bournemouth TIC** ⓘ *Westover Rd, T0906-8020234, www.bournemouth.co.uk, Mon-Sat 0930-1730, 0930-1900 and also Sun, mid Jul-Aug.* **Poole TIC** ⓘ *4 High St, T01202- 253253, www.pooletourism.com*

Sights

The centre of Bournemouth is a curious mix of concrete and heavy-handed modern architecture, side by side with swathes of abundant lush greenery and tailored Victorian arcades. The beachfront starts at the grand old **Bournemouth Pier** ⓘ *0900-2100, £0.40, children £0.20*, an old-fashioned iron pier, with theatre and mini funfare at the end. It's the place to book local trips on eg Grand Firework Cruise, Scenic Tour to Sand Banks, Poole Harbour or 'Old Harry' Rocks and Swanage. Prices and times vary. The view from the pier is unfortunately blighted by a spanking new Waterside development boasting a vast 3-D IMAX cinema, but the fun and excitement of the seaside remains undiminished. The walk from the sea is cut up by the toughest of one-way systems, but the hordes can clamber up through the pleasantly cooling **Lower Gardens** to a mosaic-paved 'Square' and central Camera Obscura café which kick off the pleasant central pedestrian precinct. In Lower Gardens, wraparound views are also available from the **Bournemouth Eye** ⓘ *T01202-314539, Apr-Sep 0730-2300, Oct-Mar 0900-dusk, £10, concessions £7.50, children £6*, a tethered hot-air balloon which lifts up to 28 passengers 500 ft above sea level, giving panoramic views across town from Poole to the Isle of Wight. Back on ground level, the **Russell-Cotes Art Gallery & Museum** ⓘ *East Cliff, T01202-451800, Tue-Sun 1000-1700, free.*, is an awarding-winning museum, newly restored with Heritage Lottery funding, displaying a wealth of famous Victoriana, as well as Japanese artefacts and contemporary art exhibitions. The seafront itself teems with all the usual attractions. The **Oceanarium** ⓘ *T01202-311993, www.oceanarium.co.uk, daily 1000-1800, £6.25, concessions £4.95, children 3-15 £3.95, family £18-21*, boasts over 10,000 sea creatures and also a charming 'turtle beach café'. Watch sharks, turtles and rays being fed daily. The best **beaches**, although always crowded in summer, are Sandbanks, Branksome Chine, Flaghead and Alun Chines. Rowing boats, canoes, deckchairs, windbreaks, parasols, sunbeds and beach huts can all be hired.

Poole

A polite harbour extension of Bournemouth, Poole lives up to its name thanks to Sandbanks and the Isle of Purbeck creating tranquil Poole Harbour, with lovely **Brownsea Island** ⓘ*(NT), T01202-707744, Apr-Sep daily 1000-1700, Jul and Aug 1000-1800, Oct-Mar 1000-1600, £3.70, children £1.70, family £9*, in the middle, the last refuge of the red squirrel. **Brownsea Island Ferries** ⓘ*T01929-462383, www.brownseaislandferries.com, £5, children £3*, sail from Poole Quay and Sandbanks several times daily. In the town itself, the **Poole Aquarium and Serpentarium** ⓘ *Hennings Wharf, The Quay, T01202-686712, daily 1000-1730, Jul and Aug 0900-2100, £6.50, concessions £5.*, is a cut above the average fishtank exhibition, including a variety of scary reptiles. The **Study Gallery** ⓘ *The college, North Rd, Parkstone, T01202-205200*, is home to Bournemouth and Poole College's important mid-20th century Art collection, with works by Henry Moore, Barbara Hepworth and Bridget Riley. Poole is also the official start of the **South West Coast Path**, the longest and one of the most attractive National Trails in the UK, see page 259.

Isle of Purbeck

Not strictly an island, the Isle of Purbeck is a delightful stretch of chalky upland that drops into the sea in the east beside the funny old seaside town of Swanage. This is quarry country, the coast bearing witness to centuries of stone extraction and recently blessed with the grand designation of World Natural Heritage Site, the first of its kind in the country. Branded the Jurassic Coast, the ancient rock formations between Durlston Head and Weymouth have been pulling in the crowds for some time, to the limestone sea arch at Durdle Door and crescent bay of Lulworth Cove especially although the whole coastline is well worth exploring.

Ins and outs

Getting there **Wareham** is about 20 mins west of Poole on the A351. **Swanage** would take at least another 30 mins to reach, possibly more in high season when Purbeck's roads can become congested. Wareham is on the main line to Weymouth from London via Bournemouth and Poole. A regular and very good value steam train service runs from Norden, 3 miles south of Wareham, via Corfe Castle to Swanage.

Information **Swanage TIC** ⓘ *Shore Rd, T0870-4420680, www.swanage.gov.uk, Easter-Oct daily 1000-1700, Nov-Easter Mon-Fri 0900-1700.* **Wareham TIC** ⓘ *South St, T01929-552740, www.purbeck-dc.gov.uk, Easter-Oct daily 0930-1700, Nov-Easter Mon-Sat 1000-1500.* Accommodation booking service free.

Wareham to Swanage

The main town at the entrance to the Isle of Purbeck, **Wareham** is a solid, well-to-do market town with a prosperous air on the banks of the rivers Piddle and Frome. Boats can be hired from its old bridge, and beautiful walks across the floodplain of the Frome head towards its mouth in Poole Harbour. In the distance rise the Purbeck Hills, with the dramatic ruins of **Corfe Castle** ⓘ *(NT), T01929-481294, Apr-Oct daily 1000-1800, Nov-Feb daily 1000-1600, Mar daily 1000-1700, £4.40, children £2.25,* *family £11*, sitting on a small mound in their central gap. A Norman and early English castle which once commanded the entire island, it was destroyed in the Civil War. Now one of the most popular and extraordinarily situated ruins in the country, it's often overrun with visitors in season playing hide and seek and scrambling up and down its steep grassy flanks.

Just north of Corfe Castle on the Wareham Road, Norden is the jumping off point for the superb **Swanage Steam Railway** ⓣ *T01929-425800, Mid-Mar to Oct daily, Nov-Dec at weekends, £6 return*, from Norden Park and Ride, via Corfe Castle, Harmonds Cross, and Herston, to Swanage. Steam trains run down to Swanage with wonderful views of Nine Barrows Down on the left, good for great breezy ridge walks (four miles) back to Corfe Castle across the neolithic burial mounds.

Swanage and Durlston Head

Swanage is one of England's most endearing seaside towns, just out of the way enough not to be competely ruined by the hordes. It does all the usual seaside things in a mini way, with regular visits from the steam paddleship *Waverley* in the summer. The town hall boasts a Baroque façade originally from the Mercer's Hall in Cheapside, and various other bits of old London were collected and brought down here by the indefatigable George Burt in the 19th century. The most rewarding of his eccentric collection can be found after the stiff walk up out of town to the south, on Durlston Head, a great big globe of Portland Stone. Durlston Head is the most easterly point of the World Heritage Site now branded the **Jurassic Coast** as far as Exmouth. The first natural World Heritage Site in Britain, it celebrates the variety of rocks Triassic (200-250 million years old), Jurassic (140-200 million years old) and Cretaceous (65-140 million years old) and the unique forms, fossils, flora and fauna they have created and supported. The most spectacular of its geological features are the sea arches and rock stacks at **Durdle Door** and the extraordinary shingle bank of **Chesil Beach** (see page 260). Less obvious features include ripple marks on the rocks around Osmington that suggest Dorset once enjoyed a Bahaman climate and the fossil forest just east of Lulworth Cove.

St Aldhelm's Head to Lulworth Cove

From Durlston Head, a superb 5-mile stretch of the **South West Coast Path** runs along to St Aldhelm's Head. A couple of miles along, at Dancing Ledge, there's a swimming pool blasted out of the spectacular rocks by quarrymen. All along here, the quarries have left their mark, the stone being loaded at great risk into boats beside vertical walls of rock. Swimming in the sea along here is still only for the brave. **Seacombe** has a good rocky beach, and so does **Winspit**, just before steps lead up onto the wild and lonely St Aldhelm's or St Alban's Head itself. An atmospheric Norman chapel, a coastguard's lookout and cottages brave the south-westerlies in this desolate spot, although quiet valleys filled with gorse and blackberry bushes run inland to the little village of **Worth Matravers**.

Continuing along the coast path, beyond the eerie quiet of **Chapman's Pool**, a seaweed filled bay, you arrive after 4 miles in **Kimmeridge**, a popular spot with surfers. The Clavel Tower on the headland was built in 1820. The path on from here is at the discretion of the MOD, who use this beautiful 6-mile shoreline for target practice. The walks are usually open at weekends and during school holidays, but it's worth contacting the Lulworth Range Information Officer, T01929-404819, to check. He should also be able to provide information as to the accessibility of **Tyneham**, the village requisitioned by the army at the start of the Second World War and never given back. As well as the tumbledown old cottages, schoolroom and manor houses, there are impressive walks out onto the headland and beach at **Worbarrow Tout** from here. Overlooking the ranges on the tiny road between East Creech and Lulworth, the **Franklin Viewpoint** commands a tremendous coastal panorama.

Lulworth Cove itself, 3 miles west of Tyneham, is a picturesque semicircle of sandy beach beneath the cliffs that can become impossibly crowded in summer. Almost as popular is **Durdle Door,** with its famous sea arch and beaches beneath Chaldon Down with views of Weymouth and the Isle of Portland.

Weymouth to Lyme Regis

The Jurassic Coast continues west of Weymouth, a jolly seaside resort in summer, pretty sad in winter, past Portland Bill on to Chesil Beach, a remarkable shingle strand braving the breakers beneath superb downland scenery. It's well worth heading inland around these parts to enjoy the countryside: tucked away down tiny lanes are hidden gems like Mapperton Gardens, or Eggardon hill fort.

Ins and outs

Getting there Weymouth is about 30 mins beyond Dorchester down the A354. A car or bike is really the only way to explore the coast. The terminus for regular trains via Bournemouth and Poole (50 mins) from London Waterloo (2 hrs 40 mins), Weymouth also has direct services to Bath (2 hrs), Bristol (2 hrs 20 mins) and Wales.

Weymouth and Chesil beach

Weymouth has an attractive old Georgian seafront and not much else to recommend it. It's a family holiday place that looks good from a distance. Weymouth's best feature, **Portland Bill**, can be found on the Isle of Portland, another mock island which is, in fact, a strange outcrop of rock that has long provided the stone for many of Britain's grandest buildings, as well as sanctuary for squadrons of seabirds, including the only puffins between the Scilly Isles and the Humber. Some of Portland's old quarries have been turned into visitor centres, the best of which is the **Lighthouse Visitor Centre** ⓘ *T01305-861233, Apr-Sep Mon-Fri, Sun 1100-1700 (last tour 1630),* on its most southerly point. It's well worth the trek out here, for the views of **Chesil Beach**, a long dead-straight 7-mile strip of pebbles sheltering a lagoon rich in wildlife called The Fleet. The beach is not at all safe for swimming but very good for endless calf- stretching walks.

The best views of Chesil's extent can be had from the top of the **Hardy Monument** ⓘ *T01202-882493, Apr-Sep Sat, Sun 1100-1700, £1,* on Black Down. A memorial to Nelson's flag-captain on HMS *Victory* at Trafalgar, Sir Thomas Masterman Hardy.

West to Lyme Regis

The **coast road** from Abbotsbury to Bridport is glorious, rolling through wild gorse and heather with the sea shining bright down below. The coastal settlements themselves are a little disappointing, although Bridport's seaside village at **West Bay** has a couple of good restaurants (see Eating, page 262) and a little harbour. Best to press on to Lyme Regis or head inland to visit **Eggardon Hill**, a spectacular Iron Age hill fort, or **Mapperton Gardens** ⓘ *T01308-862645, Mar-Oct daily 1400-1800 (from 1300 Wed, Thu, Sat)*, near Beaminster for their ornamental lakes and terraces in a spellbinding valley beneath a crumbling old manor house, little church and tearoom barn.

Lyme Regis

Lyme Regis may not quite live up to being twinned with St George's, Bermuda, but it's undeniably very pretty. Approached through rolling woodland on the coast road, this little fishing village was the setting for John Fowles' *French Lieutenant's Woman* and has a sandy dog-free beach at low tide. Its Marine Parade was the first public prom created in England, in 1771, its lower part being a cart road. More interestingly, Mary Anning 'the Fossil Woman' discovered the Icthyosaurus in the fossil encrusted cliffs, lower Jurassic topped by younger rocks, created by continual landslips. Today, people enjoy strolling along the prom and up the town's impossibly quaint little streets and looking out over the **Cob,** the medieval harbour wall. At its tip, the **Marine Aquarium** ⓘ *T01297-443678, Easter-Oct daily 1000-1700, £1.40,* is a display of sealife, as well as wreckage, fishing gear and old photographs. There are great views out to Portland along Chesil Beach and it's possible to take a trip out to see the Jurassic Coast by boat (Phone a Boat, T07765-501539). For anyone with kids, it's well worth checking with the TIC when the Lifeboat station will be showing off its extraordinary sea-tractor.

Sleeping

Sherborne and Dorchester *p255*

L **Summer Lodge**, Evershot, near Dorchester, T01935-83424, F83005. A charming 18th-century lodge with swimming pool. Expertly prepared local seafood, beef, pheasant, rabbit and game are on the menu.

A **Plumber Manor**, Sturminster Newton, T01258-472507/472507, F473370. Homely family-run hotel B&B with a good traditional restaurant in a Jacobean manor house with garden crossed by the Devilish stream. Rooms in the main house and in the converted stables.

B **Fox Inn**, Corscombe, Dorchester, T01935-891330. Rose-covered thatch from 1620 and 3 bedrooms, very good food.

B **Yalbury Cottage**, Lower Bockhampton, near Dorchester, T01305- 262382, www.smoothhound.co.uk/hotels/yalsbury Two 350-year-old thatched cottages. The restaurant also specializes in local produce and makes its own bread and ice cream.

C **Cromwell House**, Long St, Sherborne, T01935-813352. Three bedrooms in a Georgian townhouse B&B bang in the middle of town.

D **Quiet Corner Farm**, Oak Vale La, Henstridge, halfway between Shaftesbury and Sherborne, T01963-363045. An 18th-century farmhouse with a glorious garden and Shetland ponies.

Bournemouth and Poole *p257*

A **Beechleas Hotel & Restaurant**, 17 Poole Rd, Wimborne Minster, near Bournemouth, T01202-841684, www.beachleas.com. A Georgian hotel a few mins' walk from Wimborne Minster with 9 smart rooms.

A **The Mansion House Hotel**, Thames St, Poole, T01202-685666, www.themansionhouse.co.uk. This 32-room hotel boasts the top restaurant in Poole. All rooms are modernized and have Edwardian antique furnishings.

B **Langtry Manor**, Derby Rd, Bournemouth, T01202-553887, F290115. This Edwardian manor house was built by the Prince of Wales (King Edward VII) as a hideaway for his paramour, Lillie Langtry. All rooms have individual themes and are spacious. A beautiful dining hall with stained-glass windows and a gallery.

B **Menzies East Cliff Court**, Bournemouth, T01332-513330. Set in an endless row of hotels overlooking the sea, this peppermint green one stands out with its newly refurbished cool summer stucco front, stylish rooms, 4-star rating, private pool and waft of cocktails from the terrace.

C **The Antelope Inn**, Old High St, Poole, T01202-672029. 21 rooms, 1 with 4-poster. This old coaching inn boasts a carvery, cask-conditioned bitters and a fireplace dating from 1465, a lively place, once serving as a molasses store, a 19th-century Judges Court and a base for commando operations in the Second World War.

C **The Studland Drive**, Studland Dr, Bournemouth, T01202-765445. A corner hotel on West Cliffe, high on the promontory, with a Thai 'Pacific bar and Restaurant' included.

Isle of Purbeck *p258*

A **Priory Hotel**, Church Green, Wareham, T01929-551666, F554519. Set on the banks of the river Frome, this 16th-century priory is peaceful and quiet. The owners have converted the former boathouse into 2 luxury suites. Rooms in the priory look onto the Purbeck Hills. The restaurant has moorings for diners arriving by boat (about £50 a head).

D **Scott Arms**, Kingston, T01929-480270. Pub with tremendous views over Corfe Castle in the distance from its garden, decent food and 2 double rooms, breakfast included.

D **Bradle Farmhouse**, Bradle, near Church Knowle, T01929-480712, www.bradlefarmhouse.co.uk. Some comfortable rooms with en suite bathrooms in a delightful location near Corfe Castle.

Weymouth to Lyme Regis *p260*
A **Manor Hotel**, West Bexington, near Bridport, T01308-897785, F897035. With flagstone floors, intricately carved panelling, a low ceiling cellar bar, stone walls and oak, this 16th-century stone building is an olde worlde kind of place. Rooms with sea views.
B **Bay View Hotel**, Marine Parade, Lyme Regis, T01297-442059. Right on the seafront, with a hip 50s feel to it, and a very fresh fish restaurant doing 2 courses for £19.50.
B **Thatch Lodge Hotel**, The Street, Charmouth, near Lyme Regis, T01297- 560407, F560407. Thatch Lodge was built in 1320 as a resting place for monks. The rooms are all unique and the cooking is based on fresh local produce.
D **Old Monmouth Hotel**, Bridge St, Lyme Regis, T01297-442456, www.lyme-regis-hotel .co.uk. Good option just across from the TIC.

Eating

Sherborne and Dorchester *p255*
££ **The Acorn Inn**, Evershot, near Dorchester, T01935-83228. Comfortable village pub with good food.
££ **Benett Arms**, Semley, near Shaftesbury, T01747-830221, www.benettarms.co.uk. Does English favourites in a friendly 3-storey pub on the green, with local ingredients: Wiltshire ham and good ploughman's lunches.
££ **The Crown**, Fontwell Magna, near Shaftsbury, T01747-812222. Good selection of well-crafted meat, fish and vegetarian dishes.
££ **Frampton Arms**, Moreton, T01305-852253. Conveniently close to the station, in the village where TE Lawrence is buried, with wide menu of home-made food.
££ **Rose and Crown**, Trent, near Sherborne, T01935-850776. Another good local pub with a large garden, and slightly fancy menu, open fires and flagstone floors beneath the thatch.
££ **White Horse**, Hinton St Mary, Sturminster Newton, T01258-472723. Home-made traditional English food on the menu for lunch and supper and a flower-filled garden. Book for the weekends.

Bournemouth and Poole *p257*
££ **Alcatraz Brasserie**, 127 Old Christchurch Rd, Bournemouth, T01202-553650. Offers modern Italian dining in an elegant dining room with open-air patio.
££ **Coriander**, 22 Richmond Hill, Bournemouth, T01202-552202. Mexican eaterie with a friendly local buzz, that beats the constant diet of seaside fish bars or big pick-up joints.
££ **Hardy's Restaurant**, 14 High St, Poole, T01202-660864. Family-owned bistro offering baked snapper in a friendly more authentic atmosphere.
££ **John B's**, 20 High St, Old Town, Poole, T01202-672440. French double-fronted dining offering snails and all the usual gourmand treats in a formal manner.
££ **West Beach**, Pier Approach, Bournemouth, T01202-587785. Fish and seafood restaurant that's a real summer find. Right on the beach it overlooks the pier and nestles under the cliff. The main restaurant offers mussels and fresh catch of the day in some Cote d'Azur style.

Isle of Purbeck *p258*
£££ **Nomad**, 12a North St, Wareham, T01929-555275. Do superb suppers for about £30 a head Wed-Sat.
££ **Fox Inn**, West St, Corfe Castle, T01929-480449. Has log fires, views of the castle and daily specials on the menu. The best of the pubs in the village.

Weymouth to Lyme Regis *p260*
£££ **Perry's**, 4 Trinity Rd, The Old Harbour, Weymouth, T01305-785799. Do simple fresh fish dishes in a cosy spot on the harbourfront.
£££ **Riverside Restaurant**, West Bay, T01308-422011. Freshly prepared seafood restaurant. Booking advisable.
££ **Three Horseshoes**, Powerstock, T01308-485328. Excellent local produce and seafood with spacious gardens and panelled dining room in a working village.
££ **Spyway Inn**, Askerswell, near Bridport T01308-485250. Close to the impressive hill fort at Eggardon, good home-cooked food and superb views from the garden.
££ **The Bridport Arms Hotel**, West Bay, T01308-422994. A thatched hotel beside the beach, with daily fish specials.

Pubs, bars and clubs

Bournemouth and Poole *p257*
Casa, 4-15 Bourne Av, Bournemouth, T01202-780154. Vast wooden and highly modern bar and sofa home. During all day

dining, the students and designer wearer can munch and chatter before the DJ kicks in for the dating crowd at night.

Consortium, The Square, Bournemouth. Another music bar directly opposite *Casa*, offering the same vibe. Free entry till 2230, £5 afterwards. Tue in for a £1.

Daisy O'Briens, 77 Old Christchurch Rd, Bournemouth, T01202-290002. This old one-off Irish pub in the heart of the high-street shopping district offers a much-needed break from the chainstore stranglehold.

Oyster Quay, Port Saint James, the Quay, Poole, T01202-668669. There's high summer fun with weekend DJs at this waterfront bar and grill, sporting live tropical fish behind the bar and biweekly firework displays. Bournemouth's club scene is hotting up. **Wave FM** on 105.2 seems to plug the local scene and most bars offer DJs in the evening and cater to the student crowd during term time. **The Brasshouse**, 8-9 Westover Rd, T01202-589681, is a vast cavernous pub in the day, with request DJs and grooves every night. Also recommended are **Elements**, Circo and the **Opera House** nightclubs.

Isle of Purbeck *p258*

Square and Compasses, Worth Matravers, T01929-439229. An old boozer with basic snacks and regular live music of sorts, pretty much the heart of the headland. The landlord may find room for your tent if you ask nicely.

Festivals and events

Sherborne and Dorchester *p255*

Sherborne Town and Abbey Festival in early May, concerts on Sat nights in the Abbey.

Great Dorset Steam Fair, Tarrant Hinton, near Blandford at the **end of Aug, early Sep**, www.steam-fair co.uk. One of the largest gathering of steam buffs in Europe.

Transport

Bournemouth and Poole *p257*

Taxi

Central Taxis, 13 The Triangle, Bournemouth, T01202-394455. **Bournemouth Taxi Ranks**, Central Station, Bournemouth, T01202-556166. **Star Cars**, Christchurch Rd, Boscombe, T01202-391919.

Directory

Bournemouth *p257*

Car hire Avis, 33-39 Southcote Rd, T01202-296942. **Europcar**, Station Approach, Ashley Rd, T01202-293357. **Cycle hire** Rent a Bike, 88 Charminster Rd, T01202-315855. Action Bike, Dolphin Centre, Poole, T01202-680123. **Hospitals** Bournemouth Nuffield Hospital, 67-71 Lansdowne Rd, Bournemouth, T01202-291866.

Devon

→ Colour map 1

Devon, England's biggest and arguably most beautiful county is huntin', fishin', shootin' and farmin' country. The russet-red south Devon coast became fashionable in the early 19th century, especially around the polite Regency resort of Sidmouth, while Exeter remains the adminstrative heart of the county. Slightly bewildered perhaps, the atmosphere of this ancient cathedral city can best be summed up as the living embodiment of the generation gap. On the coast to the south, the seaside resorts of Torbay have no such doubts. The prosperous land south of the river Dart, known as South Hams, contains the epicentre of free-thinking in the Southwest at Totnes as well as the Royal Naval College at Dartmouth and the boating middle-classes' favourite seaside rendezvous at Salcombe. The Navy crops up again in a big way at Plymouth, the biggest city in the county and one with an undeniable sense of its place in the history of the world. In its heyday it sent its prisoners of war north, to Dartmoor, still one of the most eerie swathes of moorland in England. The north Devon coast is the most romantic wooded shoreline in the British Isles and birthplace of British surfing. It finally peters out in the west with the rocks and wilds of Hartland.

Exeter and around

→Colour map 1

Exeter, at the mouth of the River Exe, is a city with a very visible generation gap. The regional capital of the Southwest, it has only fairly recently begun to cotton on to the various different ways in which today's twenty- or thirty-somethings like to divest themselves of their cash. There is an old-fashioned decency about the place, a pride in its central role in county affairs and in its civic status, which – though not without a certain charm – can sometimes make it seem a bit stodgy. There is more to life, after all, than a medieval cathedral (however beautiful) and a worthy provincial museum. Now attracting a youngish crowd that increasingly regards the city as a lively base from which to explore the various outdoor attractions of Devon and Cornwall, Exeter's teashops are just waking up to the fact that the shop next door is now just as likely to be selling skateboards and Pacific-style surfwear, as it is sensible shoes and tweed caps. At the forefront of this revolution, the Quay development down on the river is in the process of carving out the kind of space familiar to many European cities: a stretch of water to perambulate, a whiff of culture, and a selection of bars, cafés, restaurants and nightclubs. East of Exeter, the World Heritage Coast runs from Exmouth to the Dorset border. There's a wonderful beach walk from the Regency resort of Sidmouth all the way to Beer, via lovely Branscombe. ▸▸ *For Sleeping, Eating and other listings, see pages 267-268.*

Ins and outs

Getting there **Exeter International Airport** is 6 miles out of the city. A regular shuttle bus, T01392-367433, serves the centre. **National Express** operate **coaches** to Exeter from most parts of the country (9 coaches a day from London). Exeter is well served by **rail**. From London trains depart about once an hr from both Paddington (2 hrs 20 mins) and Waterloo (3 hrs 20 mins). The Waterloo trains, though a lot slower, have the advantage of depositing you at Exeter Central, right in the middle of the city, while the Paddington trains go to Exeter St Davids, a 15-min walk, or a short taxi (about £3.50) or bus ride (take the H or N) into town. By **car**, from London, the safe bet is to stick to the M4 and M5 motorways (about 3 hrs). The M3/A303/A30 route is more direct and more interesting, but it is by no means dual-carriageway all the way, so you can find yourself stuck behind a lorry or a caravan, especially at peak holiday times. There are plenty of car parks in the centre of Exeter. ▸▸ *For further details, see also Transport, page 268.*

Getting around Exmouth and Budleigh Salterton are both easily reached by bus from Exeter. Honiton is the closest mainline station to Sidmouth, connected by bus service 340. Regular buses connect Lyme Regis with Seaton, Sidmouth, Budleigh Salterton and Exmouth. **Axe Valley Mini Travel,** 26 Harbour Rd, Seaton, T01297-625959, run a coastal service from Seaton via Beer and Branscombe to Sidmouth.

Information **Exeter TIC** ⓘ *Paris St, opposite the coach and bus station, T01392-265700, www.exeter .gov.uk, Mon-Sat 0900 1700 and Sun in summer only.* Pick up a copy of The List, Exeter's free listings magazine to find out what's on. **Seaton TIC** ⓘ *The Underfleet, T01297-21660.* **Sidmouth TIC** ⓘ *Ham La, T01395- 516441.* **Budleigh Salterton TIC** ⓘ *Fore St, T01395-445275.* **Exmouth TIC** ⓘ *Manor Gdns, Alexandra Terr, T01395-222299.* The centre of Exeter is compact enough to negotiate on foot.

City centre

A good place to begin a tour of the city is outside the *Royal Clarence Hotel* looking out onto the Cathedral Green. On your left are *Mol's Coffee Shop* – now selling maps – allegedly an old Tudor haunt of Sir Francis Drake and St Martin's Church, and an interesting little red sandstone church dedicated in 1065. The whole scene is dominated by **St Peter's Cathedral**. St Peter, who stands naked with a fishing net in his hands at the apex of the building, is a recent, 1980s addition to the other statues of the 14th/15th century image screen. Once inside the impressive, vaulted nave, look out for the minstrels' gallery on the north side, with its 14 musical angels, and the 15th-century astronomical clock in the north transept. Wander past the gigantic oak Bishop's Throne, dated 1312, near the altar and explore the series of intimate chapels that surround the north end of the chancel. The Exeter Rondels, the tapestry cushions that line both sides of the nave, form a fascinating record in pictures and text of Exeter's history from Roman times right up to 1983, having taken 65 local ladies 4 years and 14 million stitches to complete.

Retrace your steps past the *Royal Clarence Hotel* up St Martin's Lane, a narrow alleyway leading onto the High Street. A few yards to the left is the **Guildhall** ⓘ *T01392-265500, limited opening times, free*, quite possibly the oldest municipal building in the country, whose Tudor portico is a late addition to a 14th-century structure. Straight ahead of you, a short walk down Queen Street, is the **Royal Albert Memorial Museum** ⓘ *T01392-665858, Mon-Sat 1000-1700, free*, whose ground floor hotchpotch of natural and local history is surmounted by a genuinely interesting 'world cultures' exhibit on the first floor. Tucked away to the right and parallel to Queen Street is the cobbled Gandy Street, home to some quirky boutiques and cafés. Further to the right up the High Street, a left turn up Castle Street will take you to the Regency gardens of **Rougemont House**, which contain some of the original walls of William I's castle and a memorial to the last four witches to be tried and hanged in Devon in 1685. In Romangate Passage, next to *Boots*, you have the opportunity to descend into the **Underground Passages** ⓘ *T01392-665887, Mon-Sat 1000-1700 summertime, 1200-1700 at other*

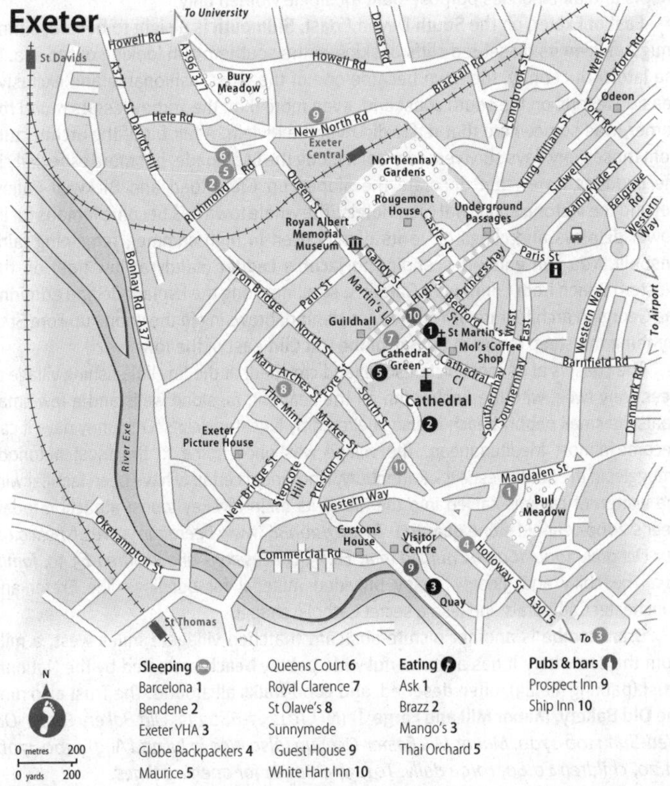

 times of year, £3.75, children £2.75, a network of 14th-century tunnels used to bring fresh water into the city – unusual, if nothing else.

Heading back along the High Street, continue over the brow of the hill into Fore Street down towards the Quay. There, amongst the bars and cafés, you will find a handsome 17th-century **Customs House** – recently restored and open sporadically – and a Visitor Centre, containing a display about the history of the Quay and an audio-visual story of Exeter, both a little bit past their sell-by date. ⓘ *T01392-265213, daily 1000-1700 Apr-Oct, weekends only 1100-1600 Nov-Mar, free.* The Quay is also the place to hire a bicycle or canoe to head out into the waterways and countryside of the Exe estuary, see Activities and tours, page 268.

Around Exeter

Due south of the city, **Exmouth's** broad sweep of sandy beach fronts a faintly neglected esplanade, nonetheless popular for family-holiday fun, with fish and chips aplenty and donkey rides on the beach in summer. Boat trips run across the mouth of the river Exe to **Powderham Castle** and the even larger beach at **Dawlish Warren**.

Just outside Exmouth off the Exeter road is the world-famous folly house, **A La Ronde** ⓘ *(NT) Summer La, Exmouth, T01395-265514, Apr-Nov Sun-Thu 1100-1730, £3.80, children £1.90*, built with 16 sides to the designs of the Parminter spinsters, Jane and Mary, apparently inspired by the church of San Vitale in Ravenna. Completed in 1798, it still displays the fruits of their 18th-century Grand Tour of Europe and their curious taste in interior design: a shell-decorated gallery (only viewable via CCTV), and a feather frieze. Only once owned by a man, the house can be compared with the Parminters' other pet project, up the road, called 'Point of View', a chapel and almshouses purpose-built for single women only.

East of Exeter, on the South Devon Coast, **Sidmouth** is a sight to behold, sitting snug between its russet-red cliffs basking in the southern sun looking out to sea. In the late 18th century, the town became one of the most fashionable and exclusive seaside resorts on the south coast and, even more than the Torbay resorts round the corner, was somewhere that really did rival the Riviera. A fair bit of the architecture from those glory days survives, some of it along the Esplanade, but more especially in the *cottages ornés* that decorate the slopes up Glen Road and Bickwell Valley, beyond the Victoria and Royal Glen Hotels. The whole town has become famous for its flower displays and clings on to its dignity even in high summer, remaining fairly unspoilt. You can enjoy descending to **Jacob's Ladder** (sandy at low tide) on the Western Beach from Connaught Gardens, strolling along the Esplanade and admiring the Georgian architecture of York Terrace behind, browsing in the shops up Fore St or climbing the steep footpath up **Salcombe Hill Cliff** east of the town.

The coast is at its most picturesque (and crowded) at the tiny little fishing village of **Beer**. Very twee, with the **Anchor Inn** on the seafront, ragstone walls and a few small boats, its small pebbly beach is also sheltered by limestone cliffs. On sunny days it can become almost Mediterranean. The village was once home to the most notorious smuggler in the Southwest, Jack Rattenbury, who would certainly have been familiar with the warren of **caverns** carved into the hill at its main low-key tourist attraction today, Beer's 2000-year-old stone **quarry** ⓘ *T01297-20986, www.beerquarrycaves.fsnet.co.uk, Apr-Oct daily 1000-1600 by guided tour, £4.75, concessions and children £3.50, family £15*. The chilly and gloomy quarry provided material for buildings like Exeter and Winchester Cathedrals and also a secret Catholic chapel.

Branscombe is another picture-postcard thatched village 2 miles west, a mile from the sea where it has a wonderful wide pebbly **beach** protected by the National Trust (parking fee £3), often deserted, and good walks all around. The Trust also runs the **Old Bakery, Manor Mill and Forge** ⓘ *(NT) T01297-680333, Old Bakery Easter-Oct Wed-Sun 1100-1700, Manor Mill Easter-Oct Sun (also Wed in Jul and Aug) 1400-1700, £1.20, children £0.60, Forge daily, T01297-680481 for opening times.*

Sleeping

Exeter *p264, map p265*

A **Royal Clarence Hotel**, Cathedral Yard, T01392-319955. The first English inn to use the French term 'hotel', its regal site at the very heart of the city injects a sense of history and occasion.

A **St Olave's**, Mary Arches St, T01392-217736. Intimate, characterful hotel in an elegant Georgian merchant's house with its own walled garden.

B **Hotel Barcelona**, Magdalen St, T01392-281000. Exeter's biggest surprise. A funky, Gaudi-inspired designer fantasy, in what used to be the West of England Eye Infirmary.

B **White Hart Inn**, 66 South St, T01392-279897. The genuine article. A real 14th-century coaching inn, all beams, flagged floors and dark panelled rooms.

C **Bendene Hotel**, 15-16 Richmond Rd, T01392-213526. A 5-min walk to the cathedral. Good value, with outdoor pool.

C **Queens Court Hotel**, 6/8 Bystock Terr, T01392-272709. Recently refurbished family-run hotel, in central location, with French-style restaurant.

D **Hotel Maurice**, 5 Bystock Terr, T01392-213079. Non-smoking, family-run hotel in a quiet Georgian square.

D **Sunnymede Guest House**, 24 New North Rd, T01392-273844. Small, non-smoking guesthouse in a Grade II listed building a short walk from the centre.

F **Exeter YHA**, Mount Wear House, 47 Countess Wear Rd, Countess Wear, T01392-873329. Exeter's youth hostel is 4 miles out of the city on the way to the pretty estuary town of Topsham. Dorm beds for £11.25, rooms from £29.

F **Globe Backpackers**, 71 Holloway St, T01392-215521. Centrally located hostel, with communal TV lounge, dining area and kitchen. Dorm beds for £11.

Around Exeter *p266*

A **Combe House Hotel**, at Gittisham, near Honiton, T01404-540400. An Elizabethan manor house hotel with an exceptional restaurant and lovely quiet grounds.

A **Hotel Riviera**, The Esplanade, Sidmouth, T01395-515201, www.hotelriviera.co.uk. The grandest of the town's Regency hotels.

B **Masons Arms**, Main St, Branscombe, T01297-680300. A large pub and hotel with reasonable food in the middle of the village, thatched roof.

C **Royal York and Faulkner Hotel**, Sidmouth, T0800-220714. Considerably less expensive than the *Hotel Riviera*, but also in a good position on the Esplanade.

D **Glendevon Hotel**, Cotmaton Rd, Sidmouth, T01395-514028, www.glendevon-hotel.co.uk. Another good option, tucked up Glen Rd.

D **Lower Pinn Farm B&B**, Peak Hill, Sidmouth, T01395-513733, www.lowerpinnfarm.co.uk In an excellent position on the coast road beyond Peak Hill to the west. Friendly and comfortable farmhouse accommodation.

D **Ryton Guest House**, 52-54 Winslade Rd, Sidmouth, T01395-513981. A comfortable B&B in the middle of town.

F **Beer YHA**, Bovey Combe, Beer, T01297-20296. At the top of the town, above the Pecorama gardens, 40 beds in a country house.

Eating

Exeter *p264, map p265*

£££ **Michael Caines**, Royal Clarence Hotel, Cathedral Yard, T01392-310031. Part of the growing empire of the eponymous award-winning chef, the poshest venue in town's fine French menu is worth splashing out on.

£££ **Thai Orchard**, The Three Gables, Cathedral Yard, T01392-214215. Welcoming Thai eaterie with a good reputation, looking onto the cathedral. Five set menus from £20.50-£26 per person, or à la carte main dishes about £8. Also cheaper set lunch menu.

££ **Brazz**, 10-12 Palace Gate, T01392-252525. A large tropical fish tank dominates the pleasing modern interior of this stylish brasserie-bar-café. Cheaper express menu at lunchtime.

££ **Café Paradiso**, Hotel Barcelona, Magdalen St, T01392-281010. A stunning contemporary space – a kind of organic, circus tent – serving a genuine Mediterranean menu. Pizzas from the wood-burning oven about £6.

£ **Ask**, 5 Cathedral Cl, T01392-427127. Its setting within the elegant, panelled rooms of an ancient, ecclesiastical building right next door to the cathedral gives this dependable pizza joint a real touch of class.

£ **Mango's**, King's Wharf, The Quay, T01392-438538 (closes at 1700). Colourful café serving sandwiches, salads, tortilla wraps, cakes, teas and breakfasts at reasonable prices.

Around Exeter *p266*

£££ **The Galley**, 41 Fore St, Topsham, south of Exeter, T01392-876078. Very good fish restaurant looking out to sea downriver.

££ **Fountain Inn**, Street, just up from Branscombe, T01297-680359. Seafood and own-brew beers in a cosy little place.

££ **The Dolphin**, Beer, does huge portions of fish and chips and has a little garden.

££ **The Bridge Inn**, Bridge Hill, Topsham, T01392-873862. Excellent sandwiches, tables by the creek and rambling old rooms inside, very friendly landlord and superb real ales.

Pubs, clubs and bars

Exeter *p264, map p265*

The Cavern, 83 Queen St, T01392-495370. At the forefront of live music in Exeter, with a particular emphasis on punk, indie and hard rock. Also drum'n'bass DJs.

Double Locks, Canal Banks, T01392-256947. Hire a canoe or a cycle and head down to this riverside pub, serving food, a mile and a half away from the Quay, with the option of cruising further down to the *Turf Hotel*.

Havana, The Quay, T01392-498181. Live music, comedy and salsa, also features a tented dining area serving French-style food. Cuban/Mexican flavour to the main club area.

The Prospect Inn, The Quay, T01392-273152. Lots of different levels, nooks, crannies and fireplaces. The best place for a pint down on the Quay.

The Ship Inn, St Martin's La, T01392-272040. Reputedly a watering-hole of Francis Drake and Walter Raleigh is this busy, low-ceilinged pub just off Cathedral Yard.

Festivals and events

Exeter *p264, map p265*

Bishopstock Blues Festival, in Aug, is the biggest blues festival in the country. For more details, T01392-875220, www.bishopstock.co.uk.

Around Exeter *p266*

On the Fri before the first Mon in Aug, for a week, is Sidmouth's **Folk Festival**, T01629-760123, drawing in people worldwide, with events selling out.

Activities and tours

Around Exeter *p266*

Exe Cruises, depart at 1215 and 1445 from Ferry Steps in Exmouth, T01395-279693.

Transport

Exeter *p264, map p265*

Air

Exeter International Airport runs flights to **Dublin**, **Belfast**, **Guernsey**, the **Channel Islands**, **Toronto**, and a wide variety of Mediterranean destinations, but no flights within England or Scotland.

Bus

Stagecoach, runs the 56 service hourly to Exeter Airport (30 mins). National Express, T08705-808080, runs 4 times daily to **Plymouth** (1hr 5 mins), 4 times to **Bristol** (1 hr 50 mins), 8 times to **Paddington** (4½ hrs) and to **Bournemouth** (3 hrs 35 mins) at 1135.

Train

Virgin Trains, T08707-891234, run the services twice hourly direct to **Plymouth** (1 hr 5 mins) and regularly direct to **Bristol Temple Meads** (1 hr 15 mins). First Great Western, T08457-000125, run the hourly direct service to **London Paddington** (2 hrs 20 mins to 3 hrs). There is no direct service to Bournemouth or Exeter Airport. Exeter St Davids also connects with trains north to **Birmingham**, south into **Cornwall** and operates the Dawlish Donkey steam service to **Paignton** in the summer.

Taxi

A1 Cars, 54 Queen St, T01392-218888.

Castle Cars, 81 Victoria St, T01392-436363.

Directory

Exeter *p264, map p265*

Car hire Avis, 29 Marsh Green Rd, East Marsh Barton Trading Estate, T01392-259713. **Thrifty**, Grace Rd South Marsh Barton Trading Estate, T01392-204460. **Hospitals** Royal Devon and Exeter Hospital, Gladstone Rd, T01392-411611. **Internet** Hyperactive, 1b Central Station Buildings, Queen St, T01392-201544.

Torbay and South Hams

→Colour map 1

The sheltered east-facing coastline that runs south from the mouth of the River Exe here has long been dubbed the 'English Riviera'. Although finding any similarities to the Cote d'Azur can test the imagination, its situation, temperate climate and cabbage palms probably come as close as England gets. Torquay, the capital of the region, is certainly stacked up on Hope's Nose, a headland faintly reminiscent of St Tropez, if you like, overlooking the sweep of Tor Bay to the south. It even boasts a tiny corniche road twisting down to Babbacombe Bay in the north. Down beside the seaside, Paignton is its more family-orientated neighbour, with the busiest sandy beaches, while the fishing town of Brixham nestles further south on Berry Head. This distinctive threesome adds up to the south Devon coast at its most marketed, most visited and often most congested. West and south of Torbay, South Hams has become one of the most expensive and desirable places to live in Devon. Totnes is the capital, centre for all thinkers-with-a-difference, at the head of the wonderfully winding Dart estuary, but it's the rhomboid of pretty farmland between Dartmouth, Start Point, Salcombe and Ivybridge that has given the area its reputation for haute-cuisine and fine living. Dartmouth, across the foot ferry from Kingswear, is a naval yachting port of impeccable pedigree with a laid-back atmosphere. Salcombe is the tidiest and most picturesque of all south Devon holiday resorts. Marginally less well-known and frequented coastal treats include Bantham and Bigbury-on-Sea. ▸▸ *For Sleeping and Eating, see page 271.*

Ins and outs

Getting there **Stagecoach Devon**, T01392-427711, run the No 85 bus from Exeter every 30 mins to Dawlish Warren, Teignmouth, Shaldon and Torquay. Bus No 12 links Torquay with Paignton and Brixham. Totnes is most easily reached on the A38 from Exeter to Buckfastleigh, and then taking the A384. The rest of South Hams lies south of Totnes off the A381. Salcombe, the end of that road, is about 30 mins from Totnes. Dartmouth, on the A3122, slightly less. Regular bus services from Newton Abbot to Totnes. **Tally Ho!**, T01548-853081, run service 164 7 times a day between Totnes and Kingsbridge. The main **rail** line from London Paddington to Plymouth via Exeter usually calls at Newton Abbot. Otherwise, regular services from Exeter St Davids run to Exeter St Thomas, Dawlish, Teignmouth, Newton Abbot, Torre, Torquay and Paignton. Regular service connect Totnes with Exeter and direct trains also run through to Birmingham and the Midlands.

Getting around Regular local **bus** services make it easy to hop around this stretch of coast, although these too can get caught up in holiday traffic. A bicycle would be the best bet, although the rolling roads can be punishing on Shanks's pony. The **Dawlish Donkey** is a hop-on, hop-off steam train that runs from Exeter to Paignton in Aug during the week, T0871-8714119, departing Exeter at 0935 and 1440, arriving at Paignton (calling at Dawlish Warren, Dawlish and Torquay) at 1050 and 1545. Unfortunately a car is the most efficient way of exploring South Hams, and if there weren't as many of those, then a bike would be much more fun.

Information **Torquay TIC** ⓘ *Vaughan Parade, T01803-297428, www.theenglishriviera.co.uk* **Paignton TIC** ⓘ *The Esplanade, T01803-55383.* **Brixham TIC** ⓘ *The Old Market House, The Quay, T01803-852861.* **Totnes TIC** ⓘ *The Town Mill, Coronation Rd, T01803-863168. Open all year.*

Torquay

Torquay is the epitome of suburbia-on-sea, immortally lampooned by John Cleese's bitter, bigoted, and frustrated hotelier in one of TV's best sitcoms *Fawlty Towers*, but still providing holidays to remember for thousands each year. Cleese no doubt drew inspiration from the town's most famous resident, Agatha Christie, who died in 1976 and lived at Ashfield House. Today the resort boasts lots of language schools, and all the usual seaside amusements, with that added frisson of class. On a warm summer evening, the twinkling lights and cafés around the harbour are just about Riviera enough. Apart from the exceptionally clean beaches, the town's other attractions include **Torre Abbey** ⓘ *T01803-293593, www. torreabbey.co.uk, Apr-Oct daily 0930-1800 (last admission 1730), Nov- Mar Mon-Fri by appointment, £3.50, children £1.70*, with its 20 historic rooms, stunning paintings and Victorian tearooms and monastic remains, small Agatha Christie room with some of her personal belongings including her typewriter, and nightgown. Real Agatha Christie fans won't want to miss the **Torquay Museum** ⓘ *T01803-293975, www.devonmuseums.net/torquay, Mon-Sat 1000-1700 Apr-Oct also Sun 1330-1700, £3, concessions £2*, with much more information (although less genuine artefacts than at Torre Abbey), in the Agatha Christie gallery, and from Kent's Cavern the oldest remains (31,000 years old to be precise) of modern humans in Britain.

Paignton and Brixham

Just down the road from Torquay, Paignton is the jolly one, with candy floss, toffee apples and crazy golf, and also very clean beaches. Brixham, beyond the caravan parks at Goodrington, is still a working fishing port, though a very polite one, with seafood restaurants galore and a busy yachting marina. This is where Napoleon was expected to arrive after his defeat at Waterloo, off Berry Head. Four miles to the south, **Coleton Fishacre** was designed in 1925 for the D'Oyly Cartes, the impressarios responsible for Gilbert and Sullivan. The house is a good example of the Arts and Crafts style, but is most famous for its luxuriant 25-acre exotic gardens. They include a formal pool garden, and wild flower walks winding down to the sea. Delicate plants flourish in the microclimate here. ⓘ *T01803-752466 (NT), Mar Sat, Sun 1100-1700, Apr- Oct Wed-Sun 1030-1730, £5, children £2.50, family £12.50.*

South Hams

Totnes, 5 miles west of Paignton, is the centre of New Age and alternative thinking in the Southwest. A pretty town, overlooked by its redbrick church and old castle sitting on the top of the hill, its steep High Street has a formidable history. Next to a shop called **Forever England** is the **Brutus Stone**, commemorating the landing of King Brute, descendant of Aeneas, here in 1170 BC according to Geoffrey of Monmouth. A right turn just beyond leads onto the Ramparts Walk, and good views round the Castle. The *Riverside Café* near the ferry port on Steamer Quay is always busy during the summer with people enjoying the river trip down to Dartmouth, and riverside walks opposite the famous Baltic Boatyards run downeariver into open countryside. On the other side of the river, a little ferry (£0.75) leaves from the **Steampacket Inn**, taking you up to the steam railway, one of the most popular in England: **The South Devon Railway** (T0845-3451420) runs from mid-March to October from Totnes to Buckfastleigh, on the edge of Dartmoor, calling at Staverton on its way along the banks of the Dart.

A mile from Staverton, **Dartington Hall** has beautiful terraced gardens dotted with sculpture, and has been a centre for the arts since 1925 when it was bought by the Elmhirsts. They also set up the scandal-rocked liberal public school where people like Bertrand Russell, Barbara Hepworth, Ben Nicholson, Jacob Epstein and the Freuds sent their kids. **High Cross House,** an inspiring piece of Bauhaus architecture, designed in 1936 by William Lescaze, now mounts exhibitions from the Elmhirst's art collection.

Nine miles by riverboat, 16 by road from Totnes, **Dartmouth** is a photogenic yachting centre, with quaint eateries and B&Bs in abundance, and it's also the home of the prestigious **Royal Naval College**. Designed by Aston Webb, also responsible for Admiralty Arch on Trafalgar Square and the front of Buckingham Palace, the College looks down on the little harbour from a commanding position on the hill above. The **Butterwalk** is a Caroline half-timbered building that now houses the local history museum. Higher Street is also very picturesque, leading up to Ridge Hill and **Newcomen Lodge**, where the town's most famous son, Thomas Newcomen, developed an atmospheric steam engine in 1712.

Salcombe, 17 miles south of Totnes on the A381, is a very desirable and well-established little resort, on a picturesque estuary, with cafés overlooking the water, and even a Park and Ride. Three miles west inland, Buckland is a sweet little thatched village tucked away down narrow lanes, near Bantham on the sea. From here an estuary walk skirts the Avon for 9 miles, a way of crossing the river when the ferry is out of action (mid-April to October). **Bantham** itself is a string of whitewashed and dark green thatched cottages leading up the main street, to the estimable **Sloop Inn** (see Sleeping below).

Sleeping

Torquay *p269*

L **The Imperial Hotel**, Torquay, T01803-294 301. Top of the range in Torquay and worth the expense for the superior ambience.

B **Gabriel Court Hotel**, a couple of miles from Paignton, T01803-782206. Perfect seclusion with a garden near Stoke Gabriel on the river Dart, 4 miles or so from Totnes and Brixham.

B **Nonsuch House**, Church Hill, Kingswear, T01803-752829. Overlooks the mouth of the Dart, with balconies and en-suite bathrooms.

C **Mulberry House**, 1 Scarborough Rd, Torquay, T01803-213639. Rooms above an excellent dinner restaurant.

D **Belmont** 66 Belgrave Rd, Torquay, T01803-295028. Good value overlooking the Torre Abbey gardens.

D **The Garlieston Hotel**, Bridge Rd, Torquay, T01803-294050. Friendly, family-run guesthouse with 5 en-suite rooms, 10 mins walk from the sea behind Torre Abbey.

D **Leicester House** 2 Winterbourne Rd, Teignmouth, T01626-773043. A reliable B&B in a tall Victorian house overlooking the sea.

South Hams *p269*

L **Burgh Island Hotel**, Bigbury-on-Sea, T01548-810514. Restored in the 1980s by fashionistas, it's now a somewhat expensive trip down memory lane at £260 per night including dinner (1930s black tie requested). It's worth stopping for a cocktail in the bar though.

B **The Sloop Inn**, Bantham, T01548-560489. Does excellent bar meals and also has rooms that need to be booked well in advance during high season.

C **The Dolphin Inn**, Kingston, near Bigbury, T01548-810314. Has 3 small rooms above a flowery pub in a pretty flowery village.

C **Gara Rock Hotel**, T01548-842342. Isolated on the southern tip of South Hams, not far from upmarket Salcombe. Great for families.

C **Tally Ho!**, Littlehempston, near Totnes, T01803-862316. Antiques and low beams, very good Brixham fisherman's pie and 4 en-suite bedrooms, open all year.

F **YHA Salcombe**, Sharpitor, Salcombe, T01548-842856 On the NTproperty with gardens and views, 51 beds, busy in summer.

Eating

Torquay *p269*

££ **The Crown and Sceptre**, 2 Petitor Rd, St Marychurch, Torquay, T01803-328290. A good real ale pub that does fresh pub grub high up above Petitor beach.

££ **Nobody Inn**, Doddiscombsleigh, T01647-252394. A popular pub in the middle of nowhere with famous food and wines.

££ **Remy's**, 3 Croft Rd, Torquay, T01803-292359. 3 courses of good French food for £18.75, just up the hill off Belgrave Rd.

South Hams *p269*

£££ **The Carved Angel**, 2 South Embankment, Dartmouth, T01803-832465. Has one of the most rated menus in South Hams served up overlooking the estuary (about £40 a head).

£££ **Clare's**, 55 Fore St, Salcombe, T01548-842646. Absolutely fresh fish in cheerful surroundings.

£££ **The Galley**, 5 Fore St, Salcombe, T01548-842828. More very fresh local fish in a very straightforward seafront café.

££ **Church House**, Rattery, South Brent, T01364-642220. Claims to be the oldest pub in the country, apparently connected to the church by a tunnel, with real ales and woods all around.

££ **Church House Inn**, Harberton, near Totnes, T01803-863707. Another very ancient old pub, oak-panelled and serving up fresh local food.

££ **The George Inn**, Main St, Blackawton, T01803-712342. A friendly village pub with exceptionally good beer.

££ **Maltsters Arms**, Tuckenhay, near Totnes, T01803-732350. Another waterside pub on a tributary of the River Dart, also with Brixham fish on the menu.

££ **Oyster Shack**, Millburn Orchard Farm, Stake Hill, near Bigbury-on-Sea, T01548-810876. Simple seafood restaurant, only open for lunch, with fabulous views towards Burgh Island. BYOB.

Plymouth

→ *Colour map 1*

Devon's biggest city, in a strategic setting overlooking Plymouth Sound, is even more dramatically bound up with the navy, the sea and seafaring than Portsmouth, its great naval rival on England's south coast. Epic arrivals and departures from the Sound characterize its long history, and like mercantile Liverpool, it was the launchpad of the British Empire. It too was heavily bombed during the Second World War but its subsequent redevelopment has been marginally happier than the others'. The city centre is divided by a long wide strip of lawn running south up to the Hoe which is top of most visitors' list of places to visit, for its superb views and memorable sense of place. A 10-min walk to the east, beneath the Royal Citadel, the Barbican is the oldest part of the city and site of most of its tourist attractions, including the Mayflower steps and the excellent National Marine Aquarium on Coxside. ▸▸ *For Sleeping, Eating and other listings, see page 274.*

Ins and outs

Getting there **Plymouth Airport** is about 4 miles north of the city centre on the Tavistock road. T0345-222111. Plymouth is about 3 hrs 30 mins-4 hrs (240 miles) from London down the M4 to junction 20 and M5 to Exeter and then the A38. This route is usually at least half an hr quicker than the M3/A303 route which only saves you around 15 miles in distance although it is a lot more picturesque. **National Express**, T08705-808080, run a Rapide luxury coach service taking about 4 hrs 30 mins. Other services take 4 hrs 40 mins- 6 hrs 25 mins. Most go via Heathrow Airport. Regular direct **trains** from London Paddington take around 3 hrs 30 mins. There are also direct services to South Wales, the Midlands, the North and Scotland. The train station is about half a mile north of the city centre, at the top of Armada Way, a mile from the Hoe and Barbican. ▸▸ *For further details, see also Transport, page 274.*

Getting around The Hoe and city centre are fairly compact and can be explored on foot. Local buses are run by **Plymouth Citybus**, T01752-662271, and **First Western National**, T01752-402060. No 25 bus service runs a circular route from Plymouth railway station, along Royal Parade, through The Barbican, over The Hoe and past Plymouth Pavilions. There are many car parks in the city centre but, owing to limited parking available in the Barbican area, it's a good idea to leave your vehicle in the multi-storey car park at Coxside and walk across the lock gates.

Information **Plymouth TIC** ⓘ *Island House, The Barbican, T01752-304849, www.plymouth.gov.uk, Mon-Sat 0900-1700, Apr-Oct also Sun1000-1600.*

Sights

The Hoe, a stirring place to contemplate the death of Empire, is where Drake insisted on finishing his game of bowls as the Armada sailed up the channel. His statue stands here still, hand jauntily on hip, surrounded by a host of other naval greats and less-than greats. More dramatic is the former Eddystone lighthouse, **Smeaton's**

Light, with its revamped interactive exhibition on the history of the Hoe inside. Next door is the **Plymouth Dome** ⓘ *T01752-600608, daily 0900-1700*, which tells the city's history in a gimmicky, interactive way.

Otherwise, the main attractions are clustered around the **Barbican**, from where the Pilgrim Fathers set sail in 1620, commemorated by a dinky little Greek arch, erected in 1934. Here skippers tout for trade like market criers for boat trips round the Sound. The latest visitor attraction to arrive on the Barbican is the **Plymouth Mayflower** ⓘ *T01752-306330, Apr-Oct 1000-1800 (last admission 1730), Nov-Mar 1000-1700 (last admission 1630), £3.50, children £1.50, joint ticket with Aquarium £10, children £5*, a fairly lavishly illustrated account of the city's history on three floors, with excellent views over the old harbour from the top. A short film, model ships, a treasure chest, Jacobean pottery and interactive graphic panels are among the things on display.

On Coxside, across a swing bridge (access possible daily 0730-2000) and lock gate from the Barbican, in a large glass-front building, is the city's lottery-funded asset, one of the best and certainly the biggest, aquariums in the country. The **National Marine Aquarium** ⓘ *T01752-600301, information line T01752-220084, www.national-aquarium.co.uk, 1000-1800 (last entry 1700), £8, concessions £6.50, children £4.50, family £22, joint tickets including admission to the Plymouth Mayflower Exhibition are also available (see above)*, boasts Europe's deepest fish tank, holding two and a half million litres of water, and home to an enormous number of fish, including sharks and seahorses. Various other water-based habitats are also displayed, from the Dartmoor stream to offshore reefs, and at feeding time the excitement is palpable.

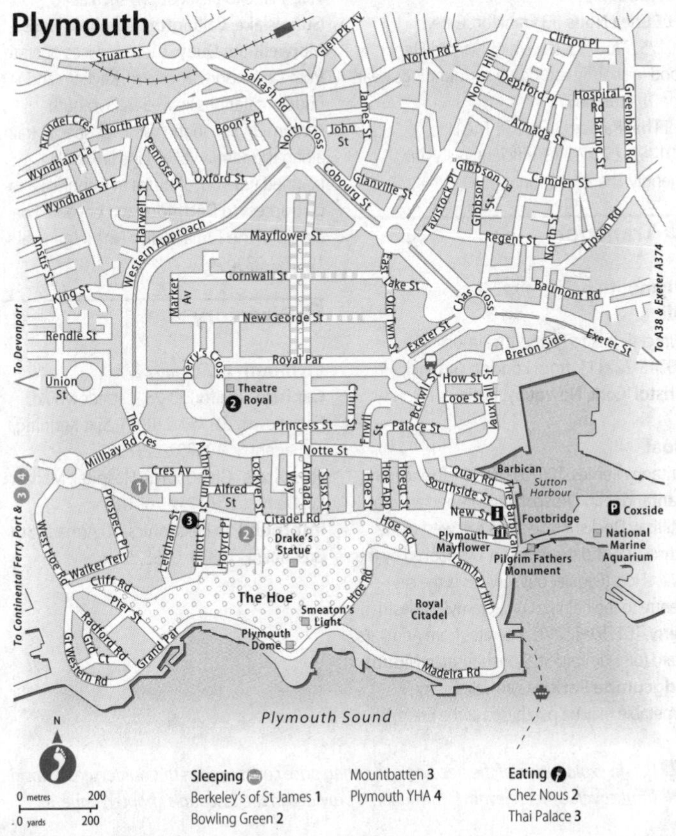

Sleeping

Plymouth *p272, map p273*

C **Bowling Green Hotel**, 9-10 Osborne Pl, Lockyer St, The Hoe, T01752-209090. A friendly, family-run hotel with comfortably furnished rooms looking over the Hoe.

D **Berkeley's of St James**, 4 St James Pl East, The Hoe, T01752-221654. A Victorian non-smoking guesthouse with plush en-suite rooms.

D **Mountbatten Hotel**, 52 Exmouth Rd, Stoke, T01752-563843. A little way out of town toward the Tor ferry, a quiet family-run Victorian guesthouse near Devonport station.

F **Plymouth YHA**, Belmont House, Belmont Pl, Stoke, T01752-562189, F605360. On the western fringe of the city, near Devonport station, with 62 beds, mainly 4-bed rooms.

Eating

Plymouth *p272, map p273*

£££ **Chez Nous**, 13 Frankfort Gate, T01752-266793. Does highly rated French food in slightly run-down surroundings near the Theatre Royal.

££ **Thai Palace**, 3 Eliot St, The Hoe, T01752-255770. An efficient, tasty and friendly Thai restaurant.

Transport

Plymouth *p272, map p273*

Air

Direct flights to Plymouth airport, T0345-222111, from **London Gatwick**, **Bristol**, **Cork**, **Newquay**, **Paris**.

Boat

Britanny Ferries, T08705-360360, to and from **Santander** and **Roscoff** embark and arrive at **Millbay Docks**, a mile and a half west of the city centre and the Barbican, overlooked by the West Hoe. (Regular bus service via the city centre to the train station.) Cremyll Pedestrian Ferry, T01752-822105, operates from Admiral's Hard (off Durnford St, Stonehouse) to **Mount Edgcumbe Park** in Cornwall. A ferry timetable may be purchased at the Cremyll Tollgate. Plymouth Boat Cruises, T01752-822797, operate boat trips from Plymouth Barbican, also linking with the Tamar Valley Line trains. The **Torpoint Ferry**,T01752-812233, is a regular and frequent car and pedestrian ferry service operating between Torpoint and **Devonport**.

Taxi

Tower Cabs 138, North Rd East, T01752-252525. Central Taxis, Wolseley Rd, T01752-363636.

Train

Plymouth railway station is on the main London-Penzance railway line. **First Great Western** provide a frequent service throughout the day and an overnight sleeper to **London Paddington** while **Virgin Trains** operate cross-country services to major cities in the **Midlands**, the **North of England** and **Scotland**. Wessex Trains operate the Tamar Valley Line to destinations such as **Gunnislake**, **Callington**, **Cotehele House**, **Morwellham Quay**. These services operate from Devonport, Dockyard, Keyham and St Budeaux stations as well as Plymouth station. On Sun in the summer, special trains along the Tamar Valley Line link with a planned network of buses at Gunnislake to give access to **Dartmoor** and beyond. For details of the Tamar Valley Line in general T01752-233094.

Directory

Plymouth *p272, map p273*

Car hire Thrifty, 20-28, Cattedown Rd, Cattedown, T01752-210021. Sixt Kenning, 11 Regent St, T01752-221860.
Hospitals Glenbourne Hospital, Morlaix Rd, Derriford, T01752-763103.
Internet Fab Electronics, 50 Armada St, Greenbank, T0870- 0756256.

For an explanation of the sleeping and eating price codes used in this guide, see the inside front cover. Other relevant information is provided in the Essentials chapter, page 36.

Dartmoor

→Colour map 1

The last wilderness in England, a mineral-rich moorland 1500 ft above sea level, the largest expanse of granite upland in the country, the biggest open space in the south of England, Dartmoor is difficult to define: 200 bleak and lonely square miles somewhere between Plymouth and Exeter, the source of the Dart, the Tavy, the Taw, the Plym and the Teign rivers. This chilling landscape is surrounded by sweet little villages nestling in green valleys, very different though from Exmoor, its little neighbour to the north. Dartmoor's most famous characteristic – along with Her Majesty's prison, the ghosts, bogs and 'letterboxes' – are its distinctive Tors, stumpy granite towers left behind during the last Ice Age. ▸▸ For Sleeping, Eating and other listings, see pages 277-278.

Ins and outs

Getting there The most attractive drive is the B3212 via Dunsford and Moreton-hampstead from Exeter. South Dartmoor is easily reached along the A38 from Exeter, Buckfastleigh being about 30 mins from the end of the M5. **National Express,** T08705-808080, run coaches from London to Plymouth and Exeter, both well connected to Dartmoor by bus. Plymouth, Exeter and Newton Abbot are the closest mainline stations to the Park. **Wessex Trains** to Crediton on the Tarka Line from Exeter to Barnstaple.

Getting around For walkers, a surprising amount of Dartmoor is accessible by bus. **Traveline,** T0870-6082608, or Devon County Council publish annually an excellent 'Discovery Guide to Dartmoor by Bus and Train', available from most National Park and Tourist Information Centres. **DevonBus,** T01392-382800. OS Outdoor Leisure map 28 covers the entire area.

Information The main National Park headquarters is at **High Moorland Visitor Centre** ⓘ *Old Duchy Hotel, Princetown, Yelverton, T01822-890414, www.dartmoor-npa.gov.uk, Apr-Oct daily 1000-1700, Nov-Mar 1000-1600.* Other information centres: **Newbridge** ⓘ*T01364-631303, Easter-end Oct 1000-1700, and winter weekends 1000-1600*; **Postbridge** ⓘ *T01822-880272, Easter-end Oct 1000-1700*; **Haytor** ⓘ *T01364-661520, Easter-end Oct 1000-1700.* A good range of leaflets on walks in the entire surrounding area is available at these offices and the TICs listed below.

South Dartmoor TIC ⓘ *Leonards Rd, Ivybridge, T01752-897035.* **Okehampton TIC** ⓘ *Museum Courtyard 3, West St, T01837-53020.* **Tavistock TIC,** *Town Hall, Bedford Sq, T01822-612938.* All are open all year round but have reduced opening times in winter. There are Community Information Points in the smaller towns around the moor: **Moreton hampstead CIP** ⓘ *11 The Square, T01647-440043.* **Ashburton CIP** ⓘ *Town Hall, T01364-652142.* **Buckfastleigh CIP** ⓘ *The Valiant Soldier, 80 Fore St, T01364-644522. Easter-Oct.* **Dartmoor Military Firing Range** ⓘ *T0800-4584868, www.dartmoor -ranges.co.uk.* **Forestry Commission** ⓘ *Bullers Hill, Kennford, Exeter, T01392-832262.*

Northeast Dartmoor

Okehampton is an army town, with a large base on the edge of the Okehampton Common, servicing the **Ministry of Defence firing ranges** that occupy most of northeastern Dartmoor. These desolate restricted areas provide some of the very best yomping country. They are always accessible in the summer and in fact very rarely closed for live firing (contact the free information line above to check). **Yes Tor,** the highest point in the National Park, is one of the most popular destinations for a serious ramble. Not far away is the **source of the Dart** and several other rivers, **Cranmere Pool,** a notorious bog in one of the most remote and inaccessible stretches of the moor. This was also where the first 'letterbox' was placed by James Perrott of Chagford in 1854.

The rolling half-wooded hills east of here, strung with stone walls and beech hedges, could hardly be a greater contrast to the open moor. Just to the south, an Edwardian cornershop baron, Julius Drew, founder of Home and Colonial Stores, discovered his ancestral roots. **Castle Drogo** ⓘ *Drewsteington, T01647-433306 (NT), Apr-Oct Mon-Thu, Sat, Sun 1100-1730, garden open daily all year 1030-dusk, £5.90, children £2.90, garden and grounds only £3, children £1.50,* was the result, designed by Lutyens and disappointingly small because unfinished when building work stopped in 1930, it is, nevertheless remarkable for being an early-20th-century mock-medieval castle of solid granite with an extremely comfortable fully electrified country house inside. Outside there are great views over the surrounding woodland.

Moretonhampstead, 3 miles southeast, is an attractive stone-built village, the 'Gateway to the High Moor' and indeed easily the most scenic approach to the National Park from the east and Exeter on the B3212. Along with the slightly more-out-of-the-way **Chagford**, its neighbour 3 miles to the northwest, these two large unspoiled villages are the last outposts of refined civilization before the moor begins.

The Moor

From Moretonhampstead the B3212 continues its lonely way southwest on to the moor itself. A tin rush occurred in the middle of the 12th century along this road, which is famously haunted by the 'hairy hands'. They suddenly grab motorbike handlebars and car steering wheels, so it's best not to exceed the 40 mph speed limit. Two miles past the **Miniature Pony Centre**, a haven for the diminutive Dartmoor breed, a small road on the left leads to **Grimspound**, one of the finest remains of a Bronze Age settlement in the country. The places where 24 huts would have stood can be seen, in a 4-acre enclosure surrounded by a low stone wall. The site can be compared with the gravemounds near Chagford at Shoveldown and especially the other Bronze Age settlement at Merrivale (see below), which also has some standing stones.

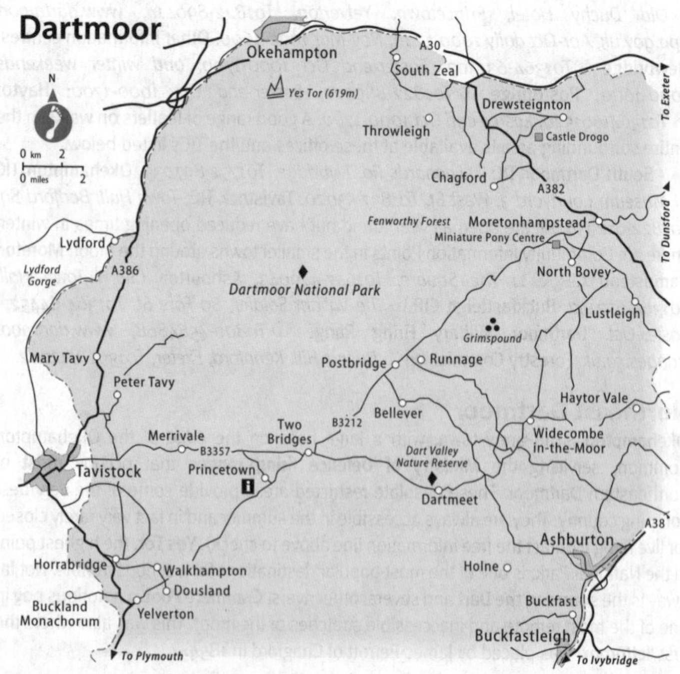

The tree-clad settlement of **Two Bridges** is the crossroads at the heart of the High Moor on the West Dart. Not much to look at, although the smart **Two Bridges Hotel** provides congenial refreshments. A left turn onto the B3357 runs the 4 miles into **Dartmeet**, a delightful but very popular spot where the East and West Dart rivers come together, surrounded by the extensive **Dart Valley Nature Reserve**. **Widecombe-in-the-Moor**, immortalized in Devon's anthem, *Tom Pearce*, is, not surprisingly, the most popular village in Dartmoor. A green and very picturesque oasis, its beautiful Perpendicular church tower is a reassuring landmark seen across the eastern moor. Back on the B3212 at Two Bridges, the road continues for a mile and a half into **Princetown**, the grey, hard-bitten and gloomy capital of the moor, where the main National Park Information Centre is based, before carrying on to **Yelverton**. The atmosphere in Princetown emanates entirely from the **prison** and its situation, constructed in 1809 by French prisoners of war, out of solid granite, and used as an overflow for the prison hulks in Plymouth Sound during the war with America. It became a convict prison in the mid-19th century, and still houses about 700 low-risk criminals.

Sleeping

Dartmoor *p275, map p276*

L **Gidleigh Park**, Chagford, T01647-432367, www.gidleigh.com. Internationally renowned mock-Tudor country house boutique hotel, with 15 luxurious rooms and celebrity West Country chef Michael Caines' menu in the restaurant (about £60 a head, needs booking in advance).

A **The Horn of Plenty**, Gulworthy, Tavistock, T01822-832528. Great views over the Tamar valley and inventive food.

A **Holne Chase Hotel**, Two Bridges Rd, Ashburton, T01364-631471. Country house hotel with 16 rooms in a former hunting lodge, 5 or 6 miles outside Ashburton. Accomplished restaurant about £45 a head.

B **Lydgate House**, Postbridge, T01822-880209, www.lydgatehouse.co.uk. In a superb location beside the East Dart River, a small award-winning non-smoking country house hotel with 7 rooms (bathroom en suite).

C **Cherry Brook Hotel**, Two Bridges, T01822-880260, www.cherrybrook-hotel.co.uk. Right in the middle of the moor, between Two Bridges and Postbridge, also with 7 cosy bedrooms (bathroom en suite).

C **Church House Inn**, Holne, near Ashburton, T01364-631208. Organic food on the menu and views over the moor from a good pub in the middle of a village. Comfortable rooms.

D **Little Meadow B&B**, T01364-621236, Widecombe-in-the-Moor. Attractive clapperboard house, good B&B option, book well ahead for high season.

F **Okehampton YHA**, Klondyke Rd, T01837-53916, F53965. With 102 beds.

F **Steps Bridge YHA**, near Dunsford, near Exeter, T01629-592707 (for bookings more than a week in advance), T01647-252435, F252984. With 24 beds in a chalet in the Teign Valley on the edge of East Dartmoor.

F **Bellever YHA**, near Postbridge, T01822-880227, F880302. Right in the middle of the moor, with 38 beds.

Camping

F **YHA Camping Barns** (which need to be booked on T01200-420102) at Runnage (2, on a farm near Bellever Forest and the River Dart), at Houndtor (near Manator, and Widecombe, with 2 sleeping galleries), at the Fox and Hounds (near Lydford, with a pub next door), at Lopwell (on the banks of the Tavy), and at Watercombe (with bunk beds, close to Cornwood on the southern tip of the moor).

Eating

Dartmoor *p275, map p276*

££ **Mountain Inn**, Old Church La, Lutton, near Cornwood, Ivybridge, T01752-837247. Fish and chips and good pub grub in a cosy village pub with some good beers.

££ **Rugglestone Inn**, Widecombe-in-the-Moor, T01364-621327. Sweet little place with a garden, fire and stone floors as well as decent home-cooked food and lots of dogs.

'Letterboxing' has become a popular pastime and involves finding a hidden box containing a stamp and notebook which you then fill in to prove you've found it. There are over 21,000 such 'letterboxes'. See page 278.

Pubs, bars and clubs

Dartmoor *p275, map p276*

Drew Arms, Drewstignton. Very fine old pub where they still pass beers through the hatch.

Peter Tavy Inn, T01822-810348, near Tavistock. Good for walks up onto the moor.

The Rock, Haytor Vale, T01364-661305. Has 2 log fires and is a friendly local with good beers and a pretty garden that gets busy in summer.

Warren House Inn, Postbridge, T01822-880208. Has had a fire burning continually for 129 years. It's the third highest pub in England, 1425 ft above sea level, close to the King's Oven prehistoric entrance grave.

Activities and tours

Dartmoor *p275, map p276*

Climbing

Shilstone Rock Stud, near Widecombe-in-the-Moor, T01362-621281.

Cycling

The Granite Way on an old railway line runs from Okehampton to Lydford, part of the Devon Coast to Coast Cycleway. Cycles can be hired from **Tavistock Cycles**, Paddons Row, Brook St, Tavistock, T01822-617630 and **Okehampton Cycle Hire**, Bostock Garden Centre, Okehampton, T01837-53248.

Letterboxing

Letterbox 100 Club, 1 Dryfield, Exminster, Exeter, T01392-832768. Membership available after collecting 100 stamps.

Riding

British Horse Society, Dartmoor Representative is Mrs Radford, T01364-631287.

Swimming

Open-air swimming Pool, Chagford, T01647-432929. May-Sep daily 1400-1900.

Walking

Rambler's Association (Devon), Mrs EM Linfoot, 14 Blaydon Cottages, Blackborough, Cullompton, www.ramblers.org.uk.

North Devon coast →Colour map 1

Apart from the tourist hotspots at the seaside resort of Ilfracombe and pickled cliffside fishing village of Clovelly, the North Devon coast just about continues to remain amazingly unspoiled although hardly undiscovered. It's a wonderland of sweeping sands, crumbling cliffs, tiny roads and wild rocky headlands. Ilfracombe gives a good taste of what's in store with its crazy coastal scenery, while Woolacombe and Croyde are the original English surfers' beaches. Barnstaple, the staid and slightly bewildered market town at the heart of the region, wonders how to keep up with arty Bideford and its little neighbour Appledore. From both Bideford and Ilfracombe boats run out to Lundy Island, famous for its very occasional glimpses of puffins but also a delightful day trip for a bracing walk. Boats also go to Lundy from Clovelly, but most visitors are content to struggle up and down its impossibly photogenic main street, awestruck by how quaint a singularly sited fishing village in private hands can be. Beyond, the Hartland peninsula is one of the best places in Britain to get lost in. Head any way towards the setting sun and you'll end up on a dramatic nub of granite butting into the Atlantic. ▸▸ *For Sleeping, Eating and other listings, see page 281.*

Ins and outs

Getting there The quickest way of reaching Barnstaple, Bideford and the north coast between Lynton and Ilfracombe is via junction 27 on the M5 to Tiverton and then the A361. The A39 is a beautiful but congested route from Bridgewater (junction 24 on the M5). Barnstaple is about 4 hrs from London by car by the former route, about 5 by the latter. The Tarka Line, run by **Wessex Trains**, T08456-000880, reservations on T0870- 9000773, covers 39 exceptionally scenic miles between Exeter and

Barnstaple, every couple of hrs or so, taking just over an hr, and passing through Crediton and small villages like Umberleigh, Eggesford, Morchard Road, Copplestone and Newton St Cyres en route.

Getting around Barnstaple is the hub of the bus network in the area, with regular services to Ilfracombe and Bideford, fewer out to Hartland. Many of the buses are run by **First** in Devon, T01271-376524. Good bus maps and guides can be obtained from **Devon Bus**, T01392- 382800. Cycling is a very good option round the coast and in Hartland. ▸▸ *For details of transport to Lundy Island, see page 281.*

Information **Barnstaple TIC** ⓘ *36 Boutport St, T01271-375000*. **Bideford TIC** ⓘ *The Quay, Kingsley Rd, T01237-477676*. **Ilfracombe TIC** ⓘ *The Seafront, T01271-883319*. **Lynton TIC** ⓘ *The Town Hall, Lee Rd, T01598-752225*. **Woolacombe TIC** ⓘ *The Esplanade, T01271-870553*. **Lundy Shore Office** ⓘ *The Quay, Bideford, T01237-470422. Lundy Island T01237-470074, www.lundyisland.co.uk*

Ilfracombe and around

Ilfracombe is the largest resort on the north Devon coast, yet still more innocent than the seaside resorts in south Devon. A Victorian and Edwardian resort of considerable note, the town spreads itself out over a confusion of low cliffs, beaches and bays looking out to sea. A walk up bald **Capstone Hill** on the seafront beyond the pepperpot cones of the Landmark Arts Centre and TIC will clear the head and give uninterrupted views of the town's peculiar layout behind its old Promenade, little harbour and the sea. Old-timers looking to escape the crush for more tranquility head for the old Quay and boat trips round the bay or out to Lundy island (see below) on **MS Oldenburg** (tickets from TIC or the office on Ilfracombe pier T01271-863636), while families make for the rockpools on the **Tunnel Beaches**. **Ilfracombe Museum** ⓘ *T01271-863541, Apr-Oct daily 1000-1730, Nov-Mar Mon-Fri 1000-1230, £1.50, concessions £1, children £0.50*, close to the Landmark Arts Centre, is a collector's paradise, an extraordinary array of odds and ends from days gone by in an old laundry house.

Woolacombe

Round the promontory of Bull Point and Rockham Bay, Woolacombe's sandy beach stretches for almost 3 miles south. Very popular with surfers as well – the first full-time surf hut in England was established here in the 60s – who head for the Putsborough end of the beach, it never seems that crowded even though surrounded by holiday homes and camping parks spread around the **Bay Hotel**. Woolacombe Beach Huts can be hired, each with a table, four chairs and a windbreak, bookable in advance, T01271-870234. Round the promontory of Baggy Point to the south, little **Croyde Bay** is the place the surfers go when Woolacombe won't deliver.

Barnstaple

Nine miles east of Croyde, past the 4-mile wide expanse of Saunton Sands, Barnstaple is the region's market town, a pleasant enough place spoiled by too much traffic, at the head of the Taw Estuary. The impressive remains of its role as a marketplace can be seen in the centre of town at the **Pannier Market** and along Butcher's Row, although the shops and markets themselves are a bit tired. There's not much to keep visitors here long, most using the town as a convenient base for exploring the area inland and along the coast.

Lundy Island

A flattened granite outcrop 3 miles long and half a mile wide, 10 miles north of the Devon coast, windswept Lundy Island sits in the middle of the Bristol Channel like a giant petrified whale. Boats run out to it regularly in summer from Ilfracombe,

 Bideford, and Clovelly. Inhabited by about 30 people, as well as lots of seabirds, rabbits, Soay sheep and a herd of Sika deer, it's owned by the National Trust and run by the Landmark Trust, who maintain and let the small amount of delightful but quite pricey self-catering and B&B accommodation. The island's own ship, **MS Oldenburg**, carrying its capacity of 267 passengers in the summer, makes regular day trips most months of the year. On arrival at the jetty on the very southern tip of the island, a fairly steep climb up past the lighthouse arrives at the main settlement, gathered around the **Marisco Tavern** (see below). Day trippers usually have about 5 or 6 hrs to spend on the island: admiring the strange rocks on the coastline, looking hard for puffins (only a good idea in June when these colourful burrowing birds breed on the west coast) and just enjoying the fresh air. The island has a long history of piracy and later, comfortable respectability, which it pretty much still maintains thanks to the restrictions on access. No dogs allowed either. Short stays are available on the island in March-June and September-December through the **Landmark Trust** ⓘ *Shottesbrooke, Maidenhead, Berks, T01628-825925, www.landmarktrust.co.uk*

Bideford to Hartland

Seven miles southwest of Barnstaple is its great maritime rival, Bideford. Marginally more picturesque, and smaller, it was described by local novelist Charles 'Water Babies' Kingsley as the "the little white town". It once owed its prosperity to its 27-arch medieval bridge over the River Torridge. Trips to Lundy (see above) can be taken aboard **MS Oldenburg**, while next door to Victoria Park is the **Burton Art Gallery** ⓘ *Kingsley Rd, T01237-471455, www.burtonartgallery.co.uk, Apr-Oct Tue-Sat 1000-1700, Sun 1400-1700, Nov-Mar Tue-Sat 1000-1600, Sun 1400-1600*, an interesting space for temporary exhibitions, with the local history museum on the first floor.

Further upriver, the little fishing village of **Appledore** is a surprising delight: a kind of mini St Ives in north Devon, with an arty but unpretentious atmosphere, its pretty little harbour feeding small boats into the mouth of the Torridge where it meets the Taw. On the opposite bank, near Instow, **Tapeley Park Gardens** ⓘ *T01271-860528, Easter-Oct Mon-Fri, Sun 1000-1700, £4, concessions £3.50, children £2.50*, are an Italian garden created by the architect Sir John Belcher in the 19th century, with a walled vegetable garden, curious shell grotto, ornamental terraces lined with lavender and fuschia, a variety of other gardens and a lake surrounded by ancient evergreens.

Clovelly ⓘ *T01237-431781, www.clovelly.co.uk, daily 0930-1730, £4, children £2.75*, 12 miles west of Bideford on the A39, must be one of the most photographed villages in Britain. A privately owned and immaculately preserved fishing village that tumbles down a steep gorge on a wooded hill to a tiny harbour, it's really only for the sweet-toothed, but nonetheless has to be seen to be believed. And thousands do want to do just that, despite the entry fee charged at the The Clovelly Visitor Centre, at the top of the hill.

West of Clovelly, some of England's most beautiful and rugged coastal and inland scenery stretches out towards **Hartland Point**. The town of Hartland itself seems to be pretty much stuck in another era, a peaceful enclave of whitewashed houses with lead roofs. A mile to the west, in a beautiful sheltered valley about a mile from the rugged Atlantic coast, **Hartland Abbey** ⓘ *T01237-441264, www.hartlandabbey.com, Apr-Sep Wed, Thu, Sun, bank holidays (also Tue in Jul and Aug) 1400-1730, gardens only Apr-Oct Mon-Fri, Sun 1400-1730*, is an unexpected oasis of ordered calm. The mock-medieval house stands on the site of an Augustinian priory founded in the mid-12th century and the last to be dissolved, given by Henry VIII to his wine keeper. A lovely mile-long wooded walk leads down to the sea.

Sleeping

Ilfracombe and around *p279*
C **Greyven House**, 4 St James Pl, Ilfracombe, T01271-862505. Cosy place close to the harbour and TIC.
C **Lyncott House**, 56 St Brannock's Rd, Ilfracombe, T01271-862425. Comfortable non-smoking Victorian guesthouse close to Bicclescombe gardens.
F **Ocean Backpackers**, 29 St James Pl, Ilfracombe, T01271-867835. One double room (£30) with 38 beds, £10 a night, and a cheap restaurant and a late bar.

Barnstaple *p279*
A **Saunton Sands Hotel**, near Braunton, T01271-890212. Lively hotel with smallish rooms but 4-star facilities, including a heated outdoor pool, health club and babysitting, and a private path to the beach, with magnificent views over the sands from its terrace.
C **Broomhill Art Hotel**, Muddiford, near Barnstaple, T01271-850262, www.broomhillart. co.uk. Small country house hotel with a heated swimming pool, in a wooded valley with a sculpture park. Dog friendly.
C **Huxtable Farm**, West Buckland, near Barnstaple, T01598-760254, www.huxtable farm.co.uk. 16th-century farmhouse 5 miles east of Barnstaple, with local produce.
D **Bradiford Cottage**, Halls Mill La, Bradiford, near Barnstaple, T01271-345039, www.humesfarm.co.uk. Little old cottage in a quiet out-of-the-way village, just outside Barnstaple towards Braunton.

Woolacombe *p279*
C **Headlands Hotel**, Beach Rd, Woolacombe, T01271-870320, www.headlands-woolacombe.com. Beautiful situation overlooking the beach and coast.

Bideford to Hartland *p280*
C **Golden Park**, Hartland, near Bideford, T01237-441254. Seventeenth-century farmhouse with sea views and walled garden, 3 bedrooms with en suite bathrooms.
C **Hartland Quay Hotel**, Hartland, T01237-441218. Sweet family-run hotel in a spectacular position overlooking the spume-ridden waves.
C **Red Lion**, Clovelly, T01237-431781, www.clovelly.co.uk. Comfortable accommodation by the harbour, with good food.

Eating

Barnstaple *p279*
££ **Corner House**, 108 Boutport St, Barnstaple, T01271-343528. Popular working-men's local with decent bar snacks and unspoilt interior.
££ **Pyne Arms**, East Down, near Barnstaple, T01271-850207. Flower-filled tubs in the garden and good food on the table in a low-ceilinged pub.

Lundy Island *p279*
££ **Marisco Tavern**, T01237-431831. The only pub on the island, and luckily it's a good one, with a garden and traditional filling pub grub, ideal after a bracing day hunting puffins. Booking office for Lundy Island: T01237-470074.

Festivals and events

Ilfracombe and around *p279*
Victorian Celebrations in the middle of Jun, when the whole town goes mad for old times, dressing up in crinolines and bonnets

Transport

Lundy Island *p279*
Departures on **MS Oldenburg** Mar-Dec various days, T01271-863636, from Bideford usually between 0800 and 1000, from Ilfracombe usually 1000 or 1030, arriving back at either between 1800 and 2100. Sailing time just under 2 hrs. £25 day return, £12.50 children, £4 under-4s, family £60. Period return £40, children £21. Also the **Jessica Hettie** sails Apr-Oct Wed, Thu from Clovelly £22.50 return, T01237 431042 www.clovelly-charters.ukf.net

For an explanation of the sleeping and eating price codes used in this guide, see the inside front cover. Other relevant information is provided in the Essentials chapter, page 36.

Cornwall

England's far southwestern corner, Cornwall is as Celtic as Britanny. A sainted, holy place, it was Christian long before the rest of England, buzzing with missionaries from Ireland and Wales, and today still possesses a proudly independent spirit, a significant and surprisingly serious separatist movement mustering under its black and white banner and nurturing the Cornish language. But it also has the lowest income per capita in the country, and in parts remains severely depressed. Quite apart from the instability of the tourist trade generally, the popularity of certain areas of the peninsula with visitors, especially in July and August, threatens to rob them of any magic. The north Cornish coast has the busiest beachlife and harbours: the Arthurian mysteries of Tintagel, the gourmet's haven at Padstow on the Camel estuary, and Newquay, the full-on surf capital of the UK. In the middle of the county squat the bare granite wastes of Bodmin Moor, sliced in half by the A30, surrounded by amazingly luxuriant gardens. Now easily the most famous of them is the Eden Project, an extraordinary 21st-century redevelopment of a disused clay pit into a spectacular greenhouse. The south coast nearby is worth exploring for its more traditional gardens and tiny little harbour villages. Further west, Falmouth and the Lizard repay a visit for their mild climate and coastal scenery. Arty St Ives sets the tone for the Penwith Peninsula, which peters out at Land's End with a notorious visitor attraction hailing the 'Relentless Sea'. Some 30 miles beyond, the Isles of Scilly are a delightful little subtropical archipelago where our Bronze Age ancestors went to bury their dead in the path of the setting sun.

North Cornish coast →*Colour map 1*

The continuation of the superb North Devon coast to the south and west into Cornwall is one of the most spectacular stretches of the South West Coast Path. Sure it's had its fair share of ill-advised developments, bungalows and fixed caravan parks, but the cliffs and beaches between Bude and Newquay keep hikers and surfboarders happy throughout the long season. Bude is the typical north Cornish seaside resort, flanked by wonderful surfing beaches at Sandy Mouth and Widemouth, both better for beginners on the board than overcrowded Newquay to the south. Boscastle is the most picturesque fishing village on the coast, owned by the National Trust like much of the treasured coastline along here, and very busy in summer. Crowds and coaches also make for Tintagel, legendary birthplace of King Arthur, but out of season the dramatic situation of this ruined coastal castle should satisfy the most demanding romantic. On the Camel Estuary, the only large river to meet the sea in north Cornwall, the medieval harbour town of Padstow has been given a new lease of life by TV chef Rick Stein, whose restaurants draw people down from London. And the arrival of low-cost airfares to Newquay looks set to boost that resort's already booming reputation for being up for it – surf culture and Ibizan nightlife that is. *⏩ For Sleeping, Eating and other listings, see pages 285-286.*

Ins and outs

Getting there Ryanair fly daily to Newquay from Stansted, T0871-2460000, www.ryanair.com Newquay Airport, T01637-860600, is about 15 mins from town with regular buses run by **Summercourt Travel,** T01726-861108. **Bus National Express,** T08705-808080, run daily services to Bude from London Victoria, via Exeter (7 hrs) and to Newquay (7 hrs) direct once a day. Hartland Point and the north Cornish coast remain one of the most remote and inaccessible destinations in the southwest. The only express routes by **road** involve either the A361 via Barnstaple from the Tiverton exit on the M5, or the A30 and A3079 via Holsworthy, joining the A39 at Bude. Either way will take a good 5 hours from London. Padstow is about 15 miles from the main M5/A30 route, 4 hours from London on a very good day, Newquay a little further on the same route. Barnstaple is the closest **train** station, on the Tamar Valley line from Exeter. Padstow can easily be reached by bus from Bodmin Parkway (4 hours from London Paddington), on the main line to Penzance, and a branch line runs out to Newquay (5-6 hours). » *For further details, see also Transport, page 286.*

Getting around **First Western** run a good network of **buses** around the North Coast to places like Tintagel and Bude from Truro, Bodmin, Okehampton, Plymouth, and Exeter, but covering any distances will require patience.

Information **Tintagel Visitors' Centre** ⓘ *T01840-779084, Apr-Oct 1000-1700, Nov-Mar 1030-1600 daily.* **Padstow TIC** ⓘ *The Red Brick Building, North Quay, Padstow, T01841-533449, www.padstow.co.uk, Apr-Oct 0930-1700, Nov-Mar Mon-Fri 0930-1700.* Accommodation booking service £3. **Newquay TIC** ⓘ *Marcus Hill, T01637-854020, www. Newquay.co.uk* Accommodation booking service £3.50. There's also a state-of- the-surf information line, T09068-360360 (£0.60 a min).

Bude and Boscastle

Cornwall's Atlantic coast provides one of the country's finest walks along a particularly inspiring stretch of the **South West Coast Path**. **Sandy Mouth** beach (NT) gets the ball rolling, a 3-mile long surfer's delight, where the Atlantic rages higher and harder than anywhere else in Cornwall. At its southern end sits Bude, quite a sweet Regency seaside resort, developed but not ruined, with donkey rides on the prom and peace and quiet only a short walk away. The town straddles a little estuary, flanked by superb cliffs, looking out over miles of sand at low tide.

Even more popular with surfers is Widemouth (pronounced 'widdymuth') Bay, 3 miles to the south, with a good mile of steady breakers. Widemouth is fairly heavily commercialized though, so those looking for a less rowdy spot press on for 5 miles or so round Dizzard Point to **Crackington Haven** (NT). With a teashop, a few pubs and a little sandy beach (also with reliable surf) tucked behind the Cambeak headland, the place has also long been a favourite with crusties, campers and alternative types. Even more seclusion can be found just south at the **Strangles**, a lovely beach with no facilities and quite tricky to reach down a 500-ft drop from the clifftop but worth the effort to find weird rock formations and sea arches. About five miles south, **Boscastle** is a National Trust village that was once a delightful little harbour town and the main point of embarkation for Delabole slate. A bit overwhelmed by tourism these days, nothing can detract from its extraordinary position wedged into the valley of the Valency like a miniature Norwegian fjord. It's worth walking out beyond the pretty thatched riverfront and stone harbour onto the sea slates for the impressive views of the coastline north and south.

Tintagel and around

The 4-mile **clifftop walk** from Boscastle to Tintagel has often been described as one of the finest in England. Arthur is the name of the game here and Tintagel's single street takes the commercialization of the legendary King to the heights of tack. The spectacular ruins of the 14th-century **Tintagel Castle** ⓘ *(EH), T01840-770328, late Mar to mid-Jul and Oct daily 1000-1800, mid-Jul to Aug daily 1000-1900, Nov-Mar daily 1000-1600, £3.20, concessions £2.40, children £1.60,* and thin neck of land leading out to the 'island' rock are the main event and would be worth a trip even if they weren't believed to be the birthplace of King Arthur. A crumbling battlemented

Cornwall for the Cornish...

'After you've rinsed the glus-dyns out of your mouth with dowr, you might feel like taking a tollgar down to the treth through fields full of woolly davas' . Apologies to Mebyon Kernow – the Cornish separatist party – for the attempt at Cornglish, but then they're likely anyway to have more important matters in hand than cleaning their teeth for a taxi ride to the beach through the sheep fields. The Cornish language, closely related to Breton, belongs to the family of Celtic tongues of which Irish Gaelic remains the most robust member. Like Scottish Gallic, it flourished until the 17th century, when a combination of official repression and local snobbery contributed to its decline. Unlike the Gallic, by the late 19th century it had died out completely as a native tongue, although the scholastic efforts around that time of one Henry Jenner ensured its survival. What is now called Standard Cornish was developed in the last century under the guidance of Morton Nance. More information on learning the language and contributing to its revival can be found at www.clas.demon.co.uk

Meanwhile, Cornish separatists are gaining growing support for their vision of a self-governing county, a backlash against perceived ignorance of the area's economic plight in Westminster. The possibility of a devolved assembly for the region is in fact being discussed, in English.

wall runs up the sheer 300-ft headland and on the other side of the chasm, the mystical spot itself, perched on a rock battered by the sea. This is where his father Uther Pendragon is supposed to have seduced Queen Igraine, with help of the magic of Merlin, whose **cave** roars in the waves down below.

Also very busy in summer, but this time with surfers and their sport, is the seaside resort of **Polzeath** just round the spectacular lonely headland of Pentire Point. A charming coast path leads round to **Trebetherick**, where the pet poet of Middle England John Betjeman is buried in the graveyard of the old church of St Enodoc, half-buried itself in the sand. **Daymer Bay** here is another good spot for surfing. A mile further, strung along the Camel estuary looking across to Padstow, connected by foot ferry, the village of **Rock** has become known as 'Fulham-on-Sea' thanks to the influx of second-homers from London.

Bodmin Moor

Inland, east of Tintagel, the wide tract of bleak granite upland that most people rush across on the A30 on their way to the Eden Project, Bodmin Moor is surrounded by surprisingly beautiful gardens. At **Pencarrow House** ⓘ *Washaway, T01208-841369, Apr-Oct Sun-Thu, £6*, there are 50 acres of woodland around this little stately home with a world-renowned parkland of specimen conifers. Formal gardens designed by Sir William Molesworth boast many varieties of rhododendrons and camellias. Much better known, **Lanhydrock** ⓘ *(NT) Near Bodmin T01208-73320, £7, garden and grounds only £3.90*, the grandest house in Cornwall with exceptional gardens. A house and gardens visit could make for a lovely afternoon combined with a stop at the **Duchy of Cornwall Nursery** which is only a couple of miles away for shrubs, trees and perennials. Nearby, towards Lostwithiel in the valley of the River Fowey, **Restormel Castle** ⓘ *T01208-872687 (EH), Apr-Sep daily 1000-1800, Oct daily 1000-1700, £2, children £1*, is a remarkable Norman castle, much of its extraordinary circular keep still standing and in very good condition.

Padstow and around

Back on the crowded coast, across the Camel Estuary from Rock, Padstow is a busy fishing and holiday harbour town, made famous and apparently almost single-handedly kept in business by TV-chef Rick Stein. People still travel for miles to eat in one of his several fish restaurants here. Others are happy just to wander around the old streets sloping down to the harbourside or pick up some fresh shellfish when the boats come in. The **National Lobster Hatchery** ⓘ *T01841-533877, May-Aug daily 1000-1800, Sep-Apr 1000-1600, £1.50, children £1*, on the quayside opens its doors to visitors interested in the farming and life-cycle of the delicious things with tasty pincers. Named after St Petrock, who came over from Ireland in a coracle, Padstow provided sanctuary for criminals before the Reformation and was once packed with shrines to saviour saints. **St Petrock's**, the town church on the hill, is the only one to survive, its 15th-century tower resting on a 13th-century base.

Newquay and around

South along the coast road from Padstow, the 3-mile stretch of sand at Watergate Bay is a good place to learn to surf and introduces the capital of surf culture in the UK at Newquay. Although it does have a tiny harbour, Newquay has been pretty much taken over by the sport and its enthusiasts and has the biggest and busiest beaches in Cornwall. Once a fairly quiet family holiday resort, it now imitates Ibiza-style nightlife, can easily be reached on a cheap flight with **Ryanair**, and milks youth culture for all its worth. **Watergate** and **Fistral Bays** are the most popular beaches for the sport, at either end of the scale in difficulty, Fistral particularly unpredictable in the challenges it throws up. Special surfing areas operate here from mid-May to September, 1000-1800. Best of the beaches is **Lusty Glaze**, a naturally sheltered privately run cove, with exceptionally high water quality and headquarters of the National Lifeguard Training Centre.

Sleeping

Bude and Boscastle *p283*

C **Manor Farm**, Crackington Haven, Bude, T01840-230304. A sketch of romantic English life offering a spare kind of luxury in this 11th-century manor house a mile inland from the sea. Rolling hills and oil paintings, tastefully decorated rooms. Prearranged dinners where guests meet in the drawing room for drinks and proceed together for their meal (£25 per person). Dress smart.

C **St Gennys House**, St Gennys, Bude, T01840-230384. Tucked in a spring-fed woodland, a long driveway leads to this former 16th-century vicarage with Georgian additions. Views straight onto the sea and sandy beaches. Secluded, comfortable and idyllic.

C **Slipway Hotel**, Port Isaac, T01208-880264, www.portisaac.com. Young, friendly seaview hotel on the harbour front with rated seafood and a bit of a buzz about it.

C **Trevigue**, Crackington Haven, near Bude, T01840-230418, F230418. The Crocker family farm is lovingly worked on in the old school way – small plots of worked land produce eggs from heaven, and their own bacon and sausages. The stone house is a stone's throw from the sea. Period features surrounded by a cobbled courtyard and lush verdant foliage.

Tintagel and around *p283*

B **The Mill House Inn** Trebarwith Strand, near Tintagel, T01840-770200. Stone building with 9 rooms that are understated but luxurious. Irish linen sheets and lovely amenities. Big baths to pamper yourself in. Close to the quay where locals jump into the blue clear water. The old mill itself is surrounded by fully mature pines. Walks in their quiet solitude are restorative. The restaurant food is good and modern, the bar a bit trendy.

D **The Old Mill**, Tintagel, T01840-770234. Fresh breakfast and a helpful hostess in this old stone mill. Idyllic countryside and good value.

Padstow and around *p285*

D **Khandalla** Sarah's La, T01841-532961. A popular B&B with views over the Camel Estuary. For more Sleeping options, see Eating below.

Newquay and around *p285*

D-E **Aqua Shack Surf Lodge**, 30-32 Island Cres, just behind the bus station, T01637-879611, www.aquashacksurflodge.com. Dorm accommodation with restaurant, café-bar and rooftop BBQ and drinks terrace. Surfboard storage and lessons also arranged. Broadband internet access.

D-E **Base Surf Lodge**, Tower Rd, T01637-874852, www.base surflodge.co.uk. The town's newest surf lodge and has double and twin rooms as well as dorms.

D-E **Home Surf Lodge**, 18 Tower Rd, T01637-873387. Close to surf central, Fistral Beach, and the town centre, this has the benefits of a monster TV and a bar open till 0400 most nights. Dorm-style rooms with sea views. Price includes cooked breakfast served till 1000. Free tea and coffee.

Eating

Padstow and around *p285*

£££ **The Old Custom House**, South Quay, T01841-532359, F533372. Right on the harbour, this estimable fish restaurant also has rooms (**A**).

£££ **The Seafood Restaurant**, Riverside, T01841-532700. Top of the range, Rick Stein's restaurant with rooms (**A**), overlooks the estuary and harbour from a converted granary.

££ **Rick Stein's Café**, 10 Middle St, T01841-532359. For those who can't get a table at The Seafood Restaurant, this is the youthful economy version.

Activities and tours

Fishing

Blue Fox Fishing Charters, with Phil Britts, Padstow, T01841-533293. £200 a day for 6, £75 late run.

Surfing

British Surfing Association, T01736-360250. For a list of surf schools in the area.

Extreme Academy, Watergate Bay, Newquay, T01637-860840. Has won a reputation for reliable instruction in way-out ways to enjoy the beaches, from kite-surfing to mountainboarding to land-yachting.

Walking

Kernow Trek, T01637- 881752, www.walkingincornwall.co.uk. Organizes reputable walking holidays.

Transport

Padstow and around *p285*

Padstow Private Hire Taxi Service, T01208-813383.

Newquay and around *p285*

Bluebird Taxis, 8 Station Pde, T01637-852222.

Directory

Padstow and around *p285*

Cycle hire Padstow Cycle Hire Ltd, South Quay, T01841-533533.

Newquay and around *p285*

Hospitals Newquay Hospital, St Thomas Rd, T01637- 893600.

South Cornish coast

→ *Colour map 1*

The big noise in South Cornwall since the end of the 20th century has been the Eden Project, near St Austell. This astonishing conversion of a disused clay pit still causes controversy in the local area, but visitors to its two enormous 'biomes' are generally not disappointed (once they manage to get in) by the stunning array of international plantlife inside, even though still in its infancy, and the Project's upbeat, colourful and urgent ecological message. Sailing perilously close to becoming a victim of its own success, it's not the only attraction that this part of the county has to offer, although it has to be admitted that gorgeous gardens are something of a theme. To the north of

Plymouth, the Tamar Valley is a wooded riverside wonderland, best reached by rail to Calstock from Plymouth. Back on the coast, Fowey is a still fairly unspoiled harbour fishing town, popular with tourists but not overwhelmed, a fate that others like Looe, Mevagissey and Polperro have not managed to avoid. ▸▸ *For Sleeping, Eating and other listings, see page 288.*

Ins and outs

Getting there From Plymouth the A38 runs up to Liskeard, from where the A390 forks off to St Austell. Plymouth to the Eden Project should take about 45 mins. **National Express** run regular coaches from London Victoria to St Austell (7 hrs). From Plymouth the lovely Tamar Valley line runs up to Gunnislake. Regular buses link Bodmin Parkway, a beautiful station on the main London to Penzance line, with Padstow.

Getting around Truronian Buses, T01872-273453. **Calstock Ferry and Motor Launch Co,** Calstock, T01822-833331. Buses to the Eden Project go from Newquay and St Austell.

Information **St Austell TIC** ⓘ *Southbourne Rd, T01726-879500.* **Tamar Valley Tourism Association** ⓘ *6 Fore St, Calstock, T01822-835874, www.tamarvalleytourism.co.uk.*

Tamar Valley

North of Plymouth, Cornwall's border with Devon runs up the picturesque Tamar Valley, passing close to Tavistock, on the edge of Dartmoor, and up beyond Launceston. Trains run the 14 miles from Plymouth to Gunnislake via Bere Ferrers, Bere Alston and Calstock on the scenic **Tamar Valley Line** throughout the year, crossing the Tavy and Tamar on a series of great viaducts. **Boat cruises** (see page 289) also head upriver to **Calstock**, the unoffical capital of the region, described by John Betjeman as the "least known and most uninterruptedly Cornish town". Just downstream is the estate of **Cotehele** ⓘ *T01579-351346 (NT), Apr-Oct Mon-Thu, Sat, Sun 1100-1700 (-1630 in Oct), garden open all year daily 1030-dusk (last admission 30 mins before closing), £6.60, family £16.50, garden and mill only £3.80/£9.50*, the ancient seat of the Edgcumbe family. A wonderful medieval house built between 1485 and 1627, without electric light, it's surrounded by beautiful woodland, as well as being close to a restored watermill, and the old Quay on the river houses an outstation of the National Maritime Museum, and the industrial heritage of the Danescombe Valley. A walk through the woods leads to a 15th-century chapel on a bluff overlooking the river, built by Sir Richard Edgcumbe.

Looe to Fowey

Back on the coast, Looe is a typically touristy south Cornish seaside town, still with a few boats working out of its harbour. A walk west round Hannafore Point, though, arrives at a naturalist's dream: a series of gullies and tidepools with an abundant variety of sea flora. Since 1964, the seaside woods around Looe have been set aside for a **Monkey Sanctuary** ⓘ *T01503-262532, Easter-Sep Mon-Thu, Sun 1100-1630*, where a colony of woolly monkeys from the Brazilian rainforest swing through high beech trees, apparently enjoying life in south Cornwall. Round the corner at Talland Bay, the quaint appeal of the old fishing village of **Polperro** draws thousands to its single valley street of tacky souvenir shops. That said, the old harbour is undeniably picturesque, immortalized by the artist Oskar Kokoshka, and despite being a shadow of its former self as a storm-battered fishing boat haven, the village does well as a happy holiday spot in the summer.

Next stop along the coast, **Fowey** is a dear little harbour town, closely associated with the novelist Daphne du Maurier. A deep-water working port, it is also popular with tourists, who drop into the **Du Maurier Literary Centre** in narrow Fore Street running parallel with the waterfront. The **Hallwalk** is a memorable 2-mile circular walk with wonderful views across the river to Fowey and down the estuary mouth to Polruan. Catch the ferry across to **Bodinnick**, where there's a wide choice of places to eat. The walk continues to **St Catherine's Point** and the ruins of **St Catherine's Castle**, built by Henry VIII, guarding the entrance to the harbour. Across the river the boat building centre of **Polruan**, with its narrow streets clinging to the hillside leading down to the old waterfront and quay, is less touristy than Fowey and well worth the foot ferry trip.

Eden Project

ⓘ *Bodelva, T01726-811911, www.edenproject.com. Apr-Oct daily 0930-1800, Nov-Feb daily 1000-1630, £10, concessions £5, children £4, OAPs £7.50, family £25. Buses from St Austell and Newquay rail stations, T01872-273453.*

North of St Austell is the main event in south Cornwall, sometimes with queues 10 miles away from the site, and signs saying 'Eden Full'. Architecturally stunning and educationally stimulating, the Eden Project is an extraordinary enterprise: a 'Living Theatre of Plants and People', its highlights are the high-tech greenhouses: the **Humid Tropics Biome** for rainforest plantlife is the largest and most spectacular. Slightly smaller, the **Warm Temperate Biome** contains thousands of plants from South Africa and California. The **Roofless Biome** is outdoors (note the Roofless bit), planted with hemp, sunflowers and tea. Allow three hours to see the whole thing.

St Austell to St Mawes

Another, very different, old-fashioned garden in the area is also worth seeking out. **Tregehan** ⓘ *T01726-814389, £3.50*, at Par, near St Austell has an imposing 1846 glasshouse (making useful comparison with the Eden Project's biomes) and formal walled garden, these 20 delightful acres have belonged to the Carlyon family since 1565. A series of tiny villages are sprinkled along the rocky coast. **Portloe** is one of the most attractive, with its minuscule landing slip, cliffwalks and jolly tearooms. Further west, dinky little **St Mawes** looks across to Falmouth across Carrick Roads.

A few miles from St Austell, on the B3273 to Mevagissey, is the sign for the magical **Lost Gardens of Heligan** ⓘ *Pentewan, St Austell, T01726-845100, www.heligan.com, daily 1000-1800 (last admission 1630), 1000-1700 in winter, £7.50, concessions £7, children £4, family £20.* This remarkable Victorian garden, with its giant Himlayan rhododendrons, palm trees and glasshouses, was in a terrible state of neglect until it was rescued by the same Tim Smit whose vision helped create the nearby Eden Project. Rated as the best gardens in the country, they are also the most visited and you'll need at least half a day to do them justice.

Sleeping

Tamar Valley *p287*

C **Cotehele Holiday Cottages**, run by the National Trust in the wooded Tamar Valley, T01579-351346.

Looe to Fowey *p287*

A **The Cormorant Hotel**, Golant, near Fowey, T01726-833426, F833026. (£150 double occupancy including breakfast and 5-course dinner). On a high cliff with a spellbinding view of the River Fowey. This hotel is well managed with many amenities. Glorious views from most rooms. A heated pool and numerous walks into the countryside.

C **Botelet**, Herodsfoot, Liskeard, T01503-220225. If you like animals this is the place for you. Charolais bulls, ducks and a goat. Pretty drive and country setting. Reflexology and aromatherapy treatments available. Good breakfasts and fresh fish, home-made biscuits and tea.

St Austell to St Mawes *p288*

L **The Lugger**, Portloe, Truro, T01872-501322, F501691. Fantastic – this lovely and well-staffed and cared for hotel is a treasure. Perched atop the tiny harbour, it is meticulously clean and fresh. A small and romantic hotel, with an excellent fish restaurant.

B **Crugsillick Manor**, Ruan High Lanes, near St Mawes, T01872-501214, barstow_crugsillick@csi.com. This Queen Anne manor house is a perfect stopover for the pillage and plunder tour of Cornwall. A winding smugglers' path takes you down to the sea from the house.

B **Nanscawen House**, Prideaux Rd, Luxulyan, near St Austell, T01726-814488, keithmartin@compuserve.com. Set in the heart of a woodland this 16th-century manor house has an abundance of charm. Lovely light in the rooms and panoramic views.

C **Creed House and Gardens**, Creed, Grampound, Truro, T01872-530372. This listed house with outstanding gardens is notable for its gracious hospitality.

D **Woodlands Guest House**, Trewollock, Gorran Haven, near Mevagissey, T01726-843821. South facing bungalow with sea views, close to the South West Coast Path.

D **Piggy's Pantry**, The Willows, Gorran Haven, T01726-843545. Bungalow accommodation within walking distance of the sea.

Eating

Looe to Fowey *p287*

£££ **Food for Thought**, Fowey, T01726-832221. A small cottage on the harbourside. There are choices for those of you who don't fancy seafood but this is what people have been coming back for, for over 25 years. Fixed 3 course menu £19.95 Mon-Fri. Sat à la carte. 90 bottles on wine list, £10-£50.

St Austell to St Mawes *p288*

£££ **The Rosevine Hotel**, Rosevine, Portscatho, T01872-580206. Enjoy a seafood platter in the lovely garden that leads down to the cliff's edge.

£££ **Sharksfin Hotel**, The Quay, Mevagissey, T01726-843241. The Sharksfin is set right on the harbour of this pretty little fishing village. The restaurant is renowned for fresh seafood, all bought straight from the local fishermen. Lobster, mussels, shellfish, plaice, sea bass are standards on the daily menu. With a dozen rooms, all are comfortable with sea views (£59.50 per person includes B&B and supper).

Activities and tours

Boat trips

Tamar Cruising, T01752-822105, and Plymouth Boat Cruises, T01752-822797, head upriver to Calstock

Directory

St Austell to St Mawes *p288*

Cycle hire Pentewan Valley Cycle Hire, 1 West End Pentewan, St Austell, T01726-844242.

Falmouth and The Lizard

→Colour map 1

Resist the temptation to speed through Falmouth and The Lizard on your way to the far west and you will be richly rewarded. Falmouth's naval legacy and lively contemporary art scene are worth lingering for, while outside the towns and villages the natural beauty of the area is as stunning as it is varied. The Lizard peninsula stretches 12 miles south from Helston and the secluded charms of the Helford Estuary to the spectacular crags and crashing waves of Britain's most southerly point. Delightful subtropical gardens, secluded fishing villages, rocky coves and miles of unspoilt coastal paths draw considerable crowds in the summer. Deep green visitors might object to the dishes of Goonhilly Satellite Earth Station and the grey contours of the naval base but technophiles will be delighted by the peninsula's role in radio history and find plenty to interest them here on a rainy day. ►► For Sleeping, Eating and other listings, see page 291.

Ins and outs

Getting there The nautically inclined can take a boat in the summer from Truro (bus to Malpas at low tide). The trip takes 1 hr and costs £2.50. **Bus National Express** run numerous buses from Falmouth to destinations including twice daily to London, (7 hrs 30 mins), Bristol (6 hrs), and twice daily to Penzance (1 hr). Change at Truro for Newquay and St. Ives. **The Truronian** run 4 buses from Truro to Lizard Village daily (not Sun) via Falmouth and Helston taking 1hr 30 mins (£2.75). Connecting service to Coverack and St Keverne. **Car** The A39 takes you 20 mins southwest to Falmouth from Truro traffic depending (double road journey times in high season) and the A393 will bring you over from the north coast via Redruth in about the same time. Helston is about 30 mins southwest on A394. The A3083 takes you 40 mins south, down the spine of the peninsula to the Lizard Point, with smaller roads to Mullion on the west and St Keverne and Coverack in the east. Falmouth is on a branch line 20 mins from Truro, trains run every 1 hr 30 mins or so. Change at Truro for mainline services to Penzance in the west or Exeter (2 hrs) and London (7-8 hrs) in the east.

Information **Falmouth TIC** ⓘ *T01326-312300, www.falmouth-sw-cornwall.co.uk.* **Helston TIC** ⓘ *Meneage St, T01326-565 431.* See also www.lizard-peninsula.co.uk

Falmouth

Though one of Cornwall's largest towns, Falmouth is perhaps the least dominated by tourists. There is a large art student community and the world's second deepest natural harbour has so far dissuaded the Navy from embarking. There are three reasonably clean **beaches** within easy reach – Gyllyngvase, Swanpool and Maenporth. The new **Maritime Museum** ⓘ *T01326- 313388, www.nmmc.co.uk, Easter-Oct daily 1000-1700, Oct-Mar Mon-Sat 1000-1500, £2.20,* has an impressive collection of boats old and new as well as contemporary projects such as fine landscape photographs of Cornish seascapes. **Pendennis Castle** ⓘ *T01326-316594 (EH), Apr-Sep daily 1000-1800 (1600 in winter), £4.20, concessions £3.20, children £2.10,* is Cornwall's oldest and offers splendid views though never had quite the range that Henry VIII was looking for: it was still possible to sail up the river out of range of both Pendennis and St Mawes opposite.

Around the Lizard peninsula

The **Helford Estuary** would quell arguments even on the most demanding of family holidays. Nature lovers are spoiled with the **National Seal Sanctuary** ⓘ *T01326-221361, Apr-Sep daily 0900-1700 (call for times in winter), £7.50, children £5.50,* numerous walks along the estuary's wooded creeks and fine gardens, such as those at **Glendurgan** ⓘ *T01326-250906 (NT), Feb-Oct Tue-Sat 1030-1730, £4, family £10.* At the eastern end of the river this is one of the great subtropical gardens of the Southwest. Exotic trees and shrubs flourish amidst open glades carpeted with wild flowers in season.

In the west, follow the coastal path south through rocky **Porthkerris** to warm-hearted **St Keverne** a mile inland. **Coverack**, once a notorious smuggling haunt, retains its charm as a fishing village as does **Cadgwith** with its thatched cottages spilling down into the sea. For a day at the beach, head to the expanse of **Kennack Sands** or the stunning low-tide perfection of **Kynance Cove** on the east coast. The **Lizard** village itself is expanding rapidly preferring quantity to quality but the coves at **Housel Bay** and **Mullion** retain their charm.

Radioheads should follow their antennae to **Marconi's Museum** at Lizard Point or if it's size you're after, **Goonhilly Earth Station** (T0800-679593, www.goonhilly.bt.com) is the largest satellite station in the world, with a purpose-built multimedia Visitors Centre. Naval and helicopter enthusiasts can call **RNAS Culdrose** to arrange a guided tour (T01326-565085).

Sleeping

Around the peninsula *p290*

B **Nansloe Manor**, near Helston, T01326-574691. A Grade II listed building, parts of which date back to the 1600s. Set in 4 acres, the property is further surrounded by National Trust and privately owned woodland and farmland.

C **The Housel Bay Hotel**, at the southernmost tip, T01326-290417. A number of high Victorian hotels dot the area, the best of which is this place, with piano bar, eclectic photograph collection and warm welcome.

There are many B&Bs, but they do get booked up quickly. D Meaver Farm, Mullion Cove, T01326-240128, E Trevinock, St Keverne, T01326-280498, and E The Grange Fruit Farm, Gweek, T01326-221718, are all good.

Camping

Camping is also widely available try Little Trevothan, Coverack, T01326-280260, or Kennack Sands, T01326-290631, for starters.

Self-catering

For longer visits is highly recommended with cottages around Helford (B-C) from the National Trust at one end of the scale, T01225-791133, D Helford River Cottages, T01326-231666, in the middle to D-F Criggan Mill Timber Lodges, Mullion, T01326-240496, www.crigganmill.co.uk.

Eating

Falmouth *p290*

£££ **The Penmere Manor Hotel**, T01326-211411. Splash out with finest local fish and meat.

Around the peninsula *p290*

£££ **The White Hart**, St Keverne, T01326-280325. Locally reared and gathered fare for evening meal or a quick lunch (£5).

££ **The Beach Café**, Swanpool. Offers fine food in a lovely location.

££ **Cadgwith Cove Inn**, Cadgwith, T01326-290513. Delightful but crowded, has crab sandwiches (£5), jacket potatoes (£4.50) and ploughman's (£5.50) for lunch that give way to more substantial fish dishes in the evening (£10-15 for a main), afternoon teas also available.

££ **The Sticky Prawn**, Flushing, T01326-373734. Reasonably priced fish and meat sourced locally and served on the quayside.

££ **Trengilly Wartha Inn**, Constantine near the Helford River, T01326-340332. Bar food at lunchtime in a lovely setting, the Full Monty at dinner (book ahead and stay for the night).

Pubs, bars and clubs

Falmouth *p290*

The Pirate, Grove Pl. Bands play most nights and a 0100 licence keeps things busy.

The Star and Garter, Old High St. Mon jazz nights are worth attending.

Activities and tours

Watersports

Boats are available on the river whatever your experience: from dinghies (£10.50 for 2 hrs) to diesel pilots (£19.50 per hr). Hire is available at St Anthony and Helford village, T01326-231357. Diving at all levels can be arranged at T01326-221446, www.lizardiver.co.uk.

Windsurfing

Windsport, Mylor Harbour, Falmouth, T01326-376191. Daily 0900-2000 (summer) 1000-1600 (winter). Also for other watersports and land yachts.

Riding

Nanfan Farm, Church Rd, Cury, Helston, T01326-240591. Daily 0900-1800 (summer), 0900-1500 (winter), £8.00 per hr.

Walking

The South West Coast Path is a magnificent treat for walkers of all levels. Pick up the invaluable National Trust leaflets at NT car parks and TICs.

Directory

Cycle hire Bike Services, 13 Meneage Rd, Helston, T01326-564564.

Penwith Peninsula →Colour map 1

Miles of incomparable coastline offer swathes of golden sand, crystal waters and clifftops strewn with wild flowers, though in less benign mood nature's pounding surf, fierce squalls and treacherous reefs require all the vigilance the area's ubiquitous lighthouses and coastguards can muster. Just as extreme are the contrasts between the impossibly crowded town centres and the romantic splendour and unspoilt grandeur of the countryside in between. The delights of exploring a small, well-chosen area on foot keep smitten fans returning year after year. Packing it all in on a whistle stop tour could well ensure a rapid U-turn for the road bound. Where given the opportunity, the taste guardians of the National Trust have achieved the practically impossible, and maintain a delicate balance between the insatiable demands of holidaymakers and the wonderful natural surroundings that draw them. ▸▸ *For Sleeping, Eating and other listings, see pages 294-295.*

Ins and outs

Getting there National Express, T08705-808080, have 7 **buses** a day to London from Penzance (9 hrs) or St Ives (8½ hrs). Service takes 25 mins to St Ives every other hr. Newlyn, Mousehole, Land's End, and Zennor are all served. Penzance is the last major stop on the A30 30 mins from Redruth, with Land's End another 9 miles. Turn off 5 miles before Penzance for St Ives and the north coast. The southern coast road takes in Mousehole, Lamorna and Porthcurno on the way, going on through St Just to St Ives. **First Great Western** have 5 **trains** a day from London Paddington to Penzance (6 hrs), with service to St Ives every other hr (5½ hrs) and a local connecting service taking 20 mins.

Information Penzance TIC ⓘ *near the train and bus stations, T01736-362207, Mon-Fri 0900-1700, Sat 0900-1600, Sun 1000-1300.* **St Ives TIC** ⓘ *T01736-796297, Mon-Fri 0900-1700, Sat 0900-1600, Sun 1000-1300.*

Penzance

Sheltered in the western end of fertile Mount's Bay, this bustling town gets first prize for sticking its head in the sand and getting on with the unglamorous business of being a transport hub. Hard-working Newlyn is one of the busiest fishing ports in the Southwest though the plaintive 'Save our Fish' sign above the market paints a bleak picture for the future. The new marina will no doubt draw a different catch as a drink with the sun setting behind you lighting up the clouds as you look east to The Lizard will keep the shore densely packed even when all the fish are long gone.

Now owned by The Landmark Trust, The **Egyptian House,** in Chapel Street, T01628-825925, was built in 1836 by John Lavin, a Penzance mineralogist, to house a geological museum. It now houses self-catering apartments which are bookable by the week. The former home of a wealthy miller and merchant, **Penlee House** ⓘ *T01736-363625, Oct-Apr Mon-Sat 1030-1630, last admission 1600, May-Sep Mon-Sat 1000-1700, last admission 1630, £2, under-18s free* in Morrab Road offers a modern gallery concentrating on the Newlyn School of Artists (1880-1930) as well as a fine Natural History and Antiquarian museum covering 6000 years of Cornish history.

St Michael's Mount

ⓘ *T01736-710265, Mar-Oct Mon-Fri 1030-1730, last admission 1645, most weekends during the season also include admission to the private garden, call to check times, £4.80, children £2.40. Boats run regularly at high tide, £1 each way, £0.50 for children.*

The archangel is said to have appeared in shining form at the top of this spectacular rock, rising sharply from the sea at the eastern end of Mount's Bay, thereby ensuring that monks, pilgrims, soldiers and aristocrats would conspire to create one of the most picturesque and charming of monuments in the country. A causeway takes you across the sands at low tide, where you may then stroll along the delightful quay before climbing **The Pilgrim's Steps** amidst towering pine trees, and cascading subtropical gardens to the castle and chapel of St Michael perched above.

Originally a monastery affiliated with the Benedictines of Mont St Michel in France, it was used as a stronghold and during the Reformation – it was here that the Armada was first sighted – before being converted after the Civil War by the fortunate Col St Aubyn into a family seat of unique distinction. The labyrinth of rooms reflect the Mount's rich history with styles ranging from stark Medieval to playful Rococo. Helpful and welcoming guides are a mine of information while views from the upper levels – whatever the weather – give a powerful yet comforting sensation of being at sea.

Land's End

Nature has been generous to a fault at Land's End, man unfortunately less so. While tourists used to come and enjoy the simple pleasures of taking photos and totting up the miles they'd travelled to get here, the barren splendour of the promontory is now dominated by a monument to the unfulfilling greed of the 1980s. Perhaps the best thing is the promotional fanfare of billboards that bids you farewell, alerting you to other 'highlights' nearby. Hopefully the **Relentless Sea** will, in time, sweep the peninsula clear with a one-way 'Return to the Last Labyrinth' for the whole ill-advised eyesore. ⓘ *T01736-871501. 0930-1700 every day, £12.50, children £4.95.* A short walk will take you on to the coastal path and **Whitesands Beach** in Sennen Cove.

St Ives

The light that drew the eponymous St Ia to embark from her native Ireland on a magic leaf to this beautiful bay 1,500 years ago has inspired artists, writers, surfers and sun worshippers to follow in her footsteps ever since. The inspirational Tate makes as much of a show of the beach and sea through its wide windows and thoughtful design as it does to the illustrious artists the town has inspired. Ben Nicholson, Barbara Hepworth and Bernard Leach are the much celebrated early-20th-century trio while the legacy lives on in the work of Terry Frost and Willy Barnes-Graham not to mention architect Richard Gilbert, who built the now-revered slate fronted council houses next to the Tate.

Tate ⓘ *T01736-796226, Tue-Sat 1030-1730, daily in Jul and Aug, £3.95, £6.50 including the Barbara Hepworth Museum.* The empty building of the Tate would be worth a visit in its own right but as it masterfully complements the small but extremely inspiring collection of local talent and the well-considered temporary exhibitions, to visit it is to see modern art in a constant state of self-creation, inspiration, artist and viewer all contributing to the whole. An impressive array of work from one of the greatest sculptors of the last century is beautifully arranged at the **Barbara Hepworth Museum**, T01736-796226, in the house, workshop and garden where she lived from 1949 until 1975. The ceramics of **Bernard Leach** can be appreciated at his **pottery** ⓘ *T01736-796398, Mon-Fri 1000-1700, Sat in summer,* on the Zennor road. Visitors will see why he occupies such a pre-eminent and influential position as a ceramicist and will be struck by how contemporary his work appears nearly 100 years later.

Around the Peninsula

The 25-mile stretch of coastline from Penzance to St Ives has some of the most spectacular scenery of the whole **South West Coast Path** and is well worth exploring. The clifftops are strewn with wild flowers and the mild climate ensures a colourful and botanically diverse display pretty much all year round. The route has it all: sensational coves, towering cliffs, good surf and long clean beaches. Beyond the small but crowded village of Mousehole (pronounced *Mowsle*), the traffic thins out a little but go by foot and you'll find some space for yourself at any time of the year.

 Lamorna Cove and **Loggan Rock** a few miles further on are beauty spots well worth the name while the beach at **Creen** is charming. If you are in need of intrigue, try the **Museum of Submarine Telegraphy** ⓘ *Porthcurno, T01736-810966, Mar-Oct Sun-Fri, daily Jul and Aug*. Both sides of Land's End are extremely impressive and walking there ensures not getting caught up in the 'Experience'. Sennen Cove will clear your head if you do. **St Just-in-Penwith** is a good base from which to explore the extreme west and the surrounding country is starkly desolate, dotted with prehistoric monuments such as **Lanyon Quoit,** the **Mên-an-Tol** and **Chysauster Iron Age Village.**

Sleeping

See www.go-cornwall.com, for a huge selection of holiday lets.

Penzance *p292*

B **The Abbey Hotel**, T01736-366906. Penzance's finest and worth it if you really do want to stay in town.

St Ives

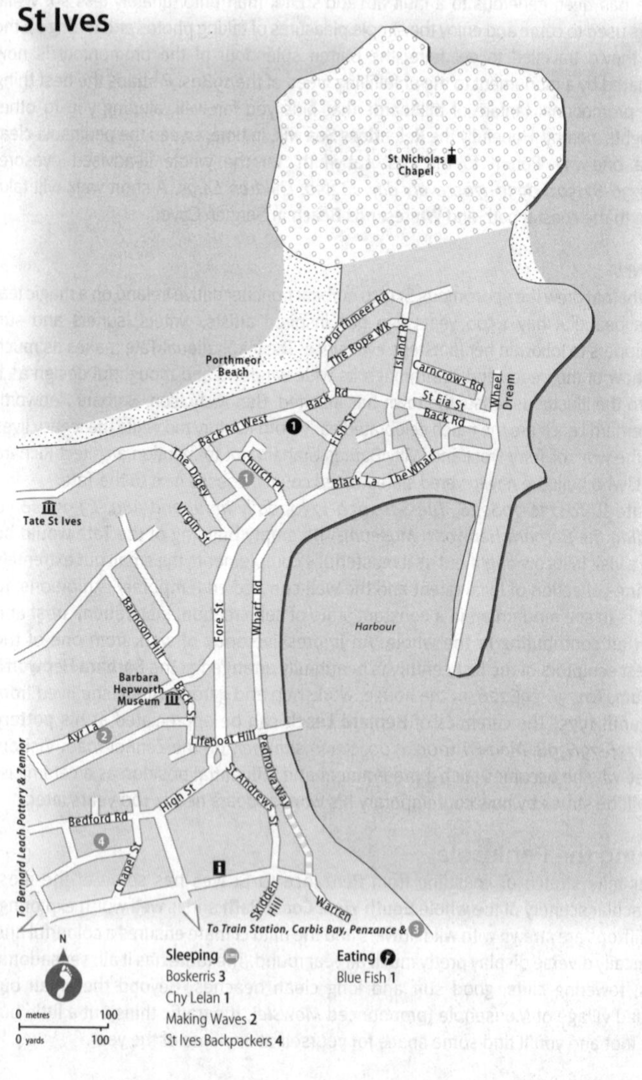

C **The Summer House**, T01736-363744, www.summerhouse-cornwall.com. Bright and stylishly bohemian with good food.
D **Chymorvah**, Marazion, T01736-710497. Overlooking St Michael's Mount, family run.

St Ives *p293, map p294*
C **The Boskerris**, in Carbis Bay, T01736-795295, www.boskerrishotel.co.uk. Fine views.
D **Chy Lelan**, T01736-797560. A charming 17th-century cottage guesthouse.
E **Making Waves**, T01736-793895. For the organically minded, welcoming and simple.
F **St Ives Backpackers**, The Stennack, T01736-799444. Basic and informal.

Around the peninsula *p290*
C **The Gurnard's Head**, T01736-796298. In a wonderful location high on a cliff top between St Ives and Land's End.
D **Kerris Farm**, 4 miles west of Penzance beyond Mousehole, T01736-731309. B&B.
D **Tregurnow Farmhouse**, above Lamorna Cove, T01736-810255. A handsome and welcoming farmhouse.
F **The Old Chapel Backpackers Hostel**, Zennor, T01736-798307. Cheap and peaceful.

Eating

Penzance *p292*
£££ **The Abbey**, Abbey St, T01736-330680, www.theabbeyonline.com. Superb food, especially seafood, will sweep you off your feet. Best in town, if you can afford it.
£££ **Chapel Street Bistro**, Chapel St, T01736-332555. More informal than The Abbey, with a bohemian atmosphere.
££ **The Hungry Horse**, in Newlyn, T01736-363446. Has some of the best local fish on offer.

St Ives *p293, map p294*
£££ **Blue Fish**, Norway La, above The Craft Market, T01736-794204. Has a lovely terrace with rooftop views of the sea, delicious fish, several dishes with a Mediterranean twist.
£££ **The Porthminster Beach Café**, overlooking Porthminster beach, T01736-795352. Best place for local fish and seafood.
££ **The Restaurant in The Tate**, suitably cool yet unpretentious and has unbeatable views.

Activities and tours

Harry Safari, T01736-711427. Offers history on horseback on the moors above Penzance to beginners and more experienced riders.

Directory

Penzance *p292*
Car hire Europcar, Station Yard, T01736-360356.

Isles of Scilly

→Colour map 1

The most southern and westerly outpost of England, the Isles of Scilly are a granite archipelago about 30 miles west-south-west of Land's End. Of around 150 of the low lumps of rock, only five are inhabited, although many more also support vigorous and varied wildlife and flora. The comparatively balmy climate, crystal clear blue water and white sand beaches make this England's best go at a subtropical paradise and a surprisingly good one it is too. The administrative hub of the islands' life is Hugh Town, on St Mary's, the largest of the five although only just over two square miles. Tresco is the pretty, glamorous, and exclusive one, with its famous gardens and timeshare cottages. St Martin's sheltered, quieter and hard-working, is a naturalist's heaven with amazing beaches. Bryher is the most rugged and storm-battered and self-contained little St Agnes, the furthest south. ▸▸ *For Sleeping, Eating and other listings, see pages 297-298.*

Ins and outs

Getting there Skybus from Bristol (£240 return), Exeter (£190 return), Newquay (£102 return, £75 day return), Land's End (£95 return, £60 day return). No flights on Sun. Short break returns available. Out by sea, back by air also cheaper. Flight time:

15 mins from Land's End. By helicopter, **British International Helicopter Travel Centre**, T01736-36871, www.scillyhelicopter.co.uk. From Penzance to St Mary's or Tresco (£100 return, £72 day return). Flight time 20 mins. **Scillonian III ferry** from Penzance to St Mary's about £72 return, short break £55, day return £35. Sailing time approx 2 hrs 40 mins. First Class from London with **First Great Western**, T0845-6010573, via helicopter, booked at least a week in advance, about £190 return.

Getting around **Bryher Boat Services**, T01720-422886, run boats between Bryher and Tresco, not so much St Mary's, but the best option for trips and private hires. On Sun there are circular trips, eg Round Island lighthouse, Samson, St Martin's, St Agnes. Boats cost about £3-£4 one-way between the islands. About £10 for a trip out to Bishops Rock. ▸▸ *For further details, see also Transport, page 298.*

Information **Hugh Town TIC** ⓘ *Old Wesleyan Chapel, St Mary's, T01720-422536, Easter-Oct Mon-Thu 0830-1730, Fri, Sat 0830-1700 (early Jun-Sep also Sun 1000-1200), Nov-Jan Mon-Fri 0830-1700; Jan-Easter Mon-Fri 0830-1700, Sat 0830-1300. Www.simplyscilly.co.uk.*

St Mary's

The largest of the islands, a little over two square miles in area, St Mary's is also the most 'normal' of them, although still far from ordinary. Hugh Town, the capital of the archipelago, sits on a sandy isthmus between Town Beach and Porthcressa below the Garrison headland. On Church Street, the antiquated **Isles of Scilly** Museum ⓘ *T01720-422337, www.iosmuseum.org, Easter-Oct daily 1000-1200, 1330-1630 (also Whitsun-Sep 1930-2100), Nov-Easter Wed 1400-1600, video evenings on Scilly past and present are given on Wed from Jun-Sep at 2015*, tells the story of Scilly with much shipwrecked gear. The **Garrison Walk** around the headland to the southwest takes about an hour and gives tremendous views of the other islands and an historical insight into the islands' strategic significance at the entrance to the Bristol and English Channels. On the top of the low hill, approached through an impressive stone gateway, near the 18th-century Rocket House, which holds an exhibition on the Garrison's history, the granite bulk of **Star Castle** (now a hotel) was built for Elizabeth I in 1593, a pointed defence against the Spanish after the defeat of the Armada. Continuously fortified until the 20th century, the Garrison Walls and Civil War fortifications remain largely intact.

Tresco

Considerably smaller than St Mary's, 20 mins across 'The Road' by boat, Tresco is the most prettified and most famous of the Isles, thanks to its extraordinary subtropical Abbey Gardens laid out by Augustus Smith on south-facing terraces around his well-wooded Victorian manor house. The whole private island has a strange and slightly unreal atmosphere, being entirely dedicated to plant propagation and mild, polite holidaymaking. All the accommodation (including a good selection of self-catering cottages) on the island needs to be booked through the estate office. That said, the northern part of the island is as wild, rugged and lonely as anywhere in the Southwest, its heather and gorse dotted with barrows and chambered cairns.

At low tide, boats are forced to use the landing quay at Carn Near on the very southern tip, near Appletree Bay, a delightful beach of fine white sand. Beyond the Heliport is the main entrance to **Tresco Abbey Garden**. Windbreaks, terracing and careful horticulture allow an exotic and wonderfully varied range of plants, trees and shrubs to flourish here, natives of Mexico, South Africa and Australasia in particular abound. The 12-acre gardens are full of surprises, not least the large collection of ships' figureheads rescued from wrecks in a stone cabin called Valhalla near the entrance. There's also a wholesome café. A stunning coast road with views of Bryher over Appletree Bay runs along the west coast of the island to **New Grimsby**, Tresco's main harbour and settlement. On the coast to the north, Cromwell's and King Charles's ruined castles guard the channel between the two islands. At the harbour the road turns east over the back of Tresco, past the New Inn, the island's one and only pub, to the delightful **Island Hotel**, in a superb position perched on the northeastern nub of civilization.

Bryher and Samson

Just west of Tresco, separated by a tidal channel, Bryher is very different, the least domesticated of the inhabited islands, facing the full force of the Atlantic from the west. The island's one settlement, called simply **The Town**, straggles along the eastern, Tresco side of **Watch Hill**, which true to its name gives glorious wraparound views across the entire archipelago. As well as its wild and broken west coast, Bryher has beautiful beaches on its southern shores, at Rushy Bay below Samson Hill, from where there are also extraordinary views in all directions. **Samson** itself, immediately due south, is the largest of the uninhabited islands. Its last 10 impoverished occupants underwent enforced evacuation by Augustus Smith in the mid-19th century, the remains of their village and industry still visible today on South Hill. Both North and South Hills, separated by a low sandy isthmus, are also topped with chambered cairns.

St Martin's

Many visitors' favourite island, but still unlikely to be crowded, St Martin's lies north of St Mary's beyond Crow Sound, in the comparative shelter afforded by Tresco, Bryher and Samson to its west. A ridge of granite, the northern coast is rugged, with the exception of **Great Bay**'s sandy beach, one of the widest and most remote in Scilly. Beyond Great Bay, a tidal causeway links the northwest of the island with **White Island**. The southern side has more superb beaches, especially **Par**, **Perpitch** and **Lower Town**, and is lined with flower farms along the mile-long road between Lower Town and Higher Town, where the boats come in. As well as its beach, Lower Town also boasts a hotel to rival Tresco's and the island's one and only pub, the **Seven Stones**.

St Agnes

The smallest, most southerly and most independent of the inhabited islands, separated from the others by the deep water channel of St Mary's Sound. A little white lighthouse, one of the oldest in the country, stands proudly in the middle, surrounded by a wonderful array of places to explore: sandy beaches, coves, tidal islands, high-hedged little flower farms, an ancient stone maze, a mysterious well, and strange rock formations among other things. Boats land at Porth Conger, in the north of the island, near the only pub, **The Turks' Head**. A single track road then climbs up to the hill to the lighthouse (disused), passing a small turning on the left leading to the tidal sand bar connecting St Agnes to Gugh, with its megalithic remains and weather-beaten castles of rock. **Beady Pool** on the Wingletang Peninsula gets its name from Spanish glass balls still occasionally found here over 200 years after the ship carrying them went down just offshore.

Sleeping

St Mary's *p296*

A **Tregarthens**, close to the quay, T01720-422540. The island's oldest hotel , which has recently undergone refurbishment.

B **Carnwethers Country House**, Pelistry Bay, T01720-422415. A mile and a half from Hugh Town on the other side of the island.

B **Star Castle Hotel**, The Garrison, St Mary's, T01720-422317, F422343. Quite expensive and chintzy but with superb views from some rooms.

Tresco *p296*

A **Island Hotel**, Tresco, T01720-422883, www.tresco.co.uk. Closed Nov 4th-first week Mar. Top of the range and the smartest hotel on the Scilly Isles, it's in a gorgeous position with a very accomplished restaurant and unfussy rooms that are very comfortable. Most have sea views and many their own sun terraces. The swimming pool is warm if you don't dare brave the waves.

St Martin's *p297*

A **St Martin's on the Isle**, T01720-422090, www.stmartinshotel.co.uk. Gives the *Island Hotel* (above) a run for its money in the comfort stakes, converted out of a terrace of fishing cottages in Lower Town.

C **Ashvale**, Ley-Greaves, Lower Town, T01720-422544, (closed Dec only). An old farmer's cottage on the top of the hill with superb sea views, where guests have their own shared living room. Very good value at the lower end of this bracket.

C **Polreath**, T01720-422046. 4 bedrooms in a cottage near the quay, it's the most famous B&B on the island and also runs the tearooms.

Bryher *p297*

A **Hell Bay Hotel**, T01720-422947, F423004. Owned by the Dorien-Smiths, not quite on the Bay but all the more restful for that.

St Agnes *p297*

C **Covean Cottage**, T01720-422620, with *Garden Café* with homemade cakes.

Eating

St Mary's *p296*

£££ **Juliet's Garden**, Seaways Flower Farm, Porthloo, T01720-422228. Mar-Oct daily 1000 and in the evenings Tue-Sun high season. The best restaurant on St Mary's. A 20-min walk from Hugh Town, with superb views from its rockery garden.

£££ **Mermaid Inn**, overlooking the harbour in Hugh Town. Evening meals feature fresh fish.

Tresco *p296*

££ **The New Inn**, New Grimsby, T01720-422883. The island's pub: the restaurant section a bit characterless but the bar area usually lively, open all year. Cottage rental on T01720-422566. Open all year.

St Martin's *p297*

££ **Seven Stones**, Lower Town, T01720-423560. The island's pleasant pub, open 1000-1630 and 1830-1100, less regularly in the winter. Sun lunches a speciality and can be booked.

St Agnes *p297*

££ **Turk's Head Pub**, T01720-422434. Famous Island pasties, crab sandwiches and very good real ale. Also B&B with views across St Mary's Sound and towards Gugh.

Festivals and events

Gig racing is when locals compete to row their old pilot boats from Nut Point to St Mary's as quickly as possible, a reminder of the days when first on won the contract, sometimes to take ships as far as Liverpool. **World Pilot Gig Championships** take place in the first May Day Bank Holiday. Wed nights the women race, Fri the men.

Activities and tours

Boat trips

Pettifox, T01720-422511. Trips on a 36ft gaff cutter, a registered tall ship, with Scillonian skipper Alfie Hicks. St Martin's Boating Association, T01720-422814. St Agnes Boating, T01720-422704, www.st-agnes-boating.co.uk. St Mary's Boating, T01720-422541.

Bus tours

Open Top Vintage Bus Tour, T01720-422901. Tour round St Mary's with enlightening commentary. Leaves daily from the park in Hugh Town.

Diving and snorkelling

Mark Groves, 'Nowhere', Old Town, St Mary's, T01720-422732, T07747-615732 (mob). Snorkelling with grey atlantic seals (£34), equipment provided. Also diving safaris, 3-hr instruction £40. 0900 or 1400 and sea safaris.

St Martin's Diving Services, Highertown, St Martin's, T01720-422848. Dive school and canoeing instruction.

Directory

Banks There are 2 banks on Scilly, both on Hugh St, St Mary's. The **Co-op** store in Hugh St offers a 'cashback' facility, accepting Switch and Delta. **Cycle hire** Buccabu Bike Hire, Porthcressa, St Mary's, T01720-422289. Mon-Sat with erratic opening hrs. Bike hire on Tresco T01720-422849. **Pharmacies** R Douglas at The Bank, Hugh Town, St Mary's, T01720-422403. The only chemist on the islands. **Post office** There are post offices on St Mary's, St Agnes, Bryher, Tresco, St Martin's. Mon-Fri (0815-1630) and Sat (0815-1215).

East Anglia

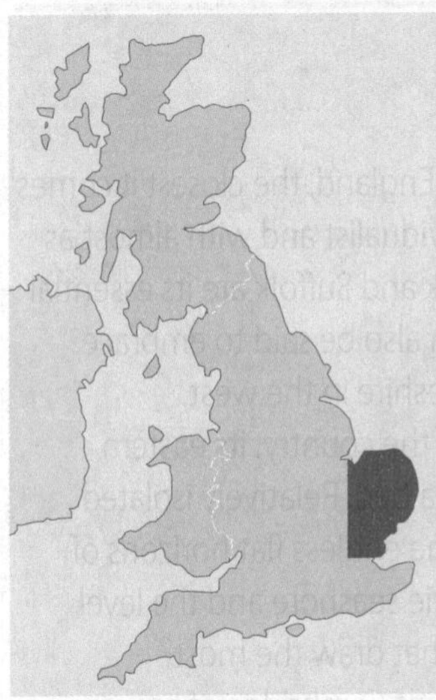

Introduction

East Anglia is a peculiar corner of England, the closest it comes to Holland, both offbeat and individualist and with almost as settled and civilized an air. Norfolk and Suffolk are its essential counties, although the region can also be said to embrace Essex in the south and Cambridgeshire in the west. Geologically the youngest part of the country, its eastern seaboard practically shares the sea bed. Relatively isolated from the rest of the country, it's the endless flat horizons of Norfolk's north coast, Suffolk's eerie seashore and the level watery marshland of the Broads that draw the most discerning visitors. Unless you count Cambridge of course, the most dinky of ancient university towns, legendary for its science faculties, collegiate architecture, Soviet sympathizers and V-neck sleeveless sweaters. During the Middle Ages, the wool trade made East Anglia fabulously wealthy: witness the number of extraordinary old Suffolk towns and churches – at Lavenham, Long Melford and Bury St Edmunds – and antique Norwich's atmosphere of ancient peace beneath its castle and cathedral. But that was all some time ago now. Today Cambridge is a hotbed of cutting-edge technological and intellectual activity; Norwich is the home of the flourishing University of East Anglia (UEA) and the world-class Sainsbury Centre of Visual Arts; Suffolk has received a shot in the arm from emigrant Londoners, the towns on its unearthly coastline Southwold, Dunwich, Aldeburgh, Orford – all awash with metropolitan gossip; and Essex, well it's one of the most mixed-up, in-yer-face counties within spitting distance of London.

★ Don't miss...

1. Discover more about the Anglo-Saxons at **Sutton Hoo** near Woodbridge and see how they liked to bury their dead, page 325.
2. Wonder at the art in the **Sainsbury Centre**, Norwich, after looking around one of the finest medieval cities in the country, page 312.
3. Find the horizon at **Holkham beach** after looking around the palatial neo-classical pile of Holkham Hall, page 319.
4. Go punting along 'the backs' of the colleges in **Cambridge**, page 302.

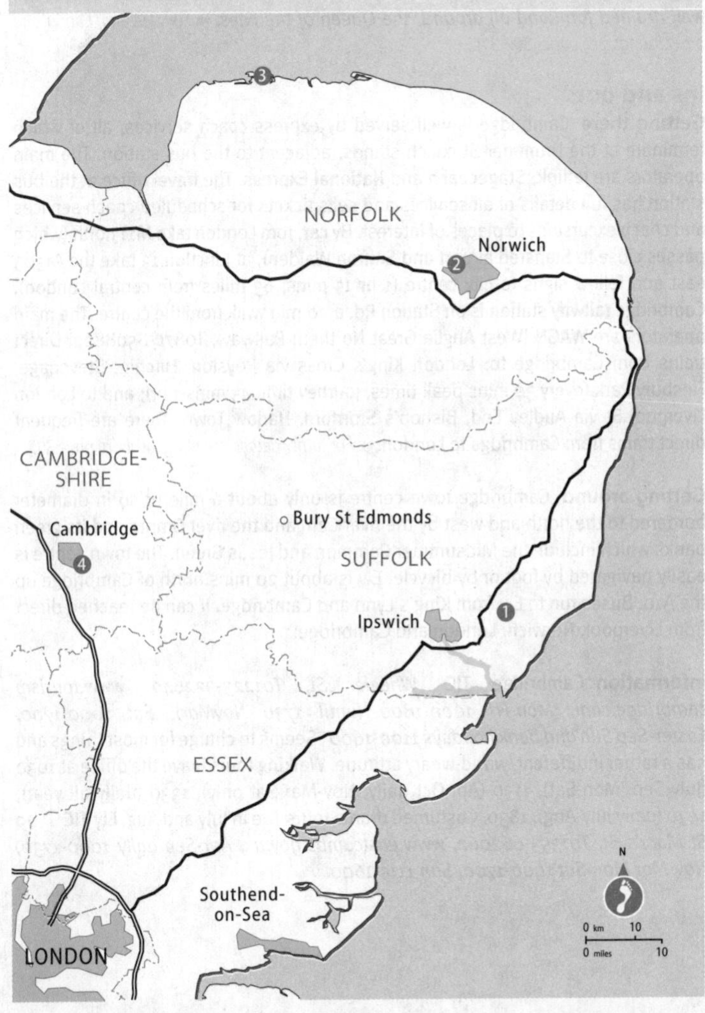

Cambridge and around →*Colour map 2*

More than anything else, Cambridge is its university. For the last 700 years or so, academia has made its mark in this little place more impressively than just about anywhere else in the world. If it's old colleges you want to see, with their medieval and Renaissance chapels, libraries, halls, gardens and courts, Cambridge is the place to come – and you won't be alone. Partly because of the tourist pressure, the whole town has a slightly unreal, self-conscious atmosphere, an impression compounded by the type of twee flannels-and-blazers pastoral idyll once promoted by the cult surrounding local poet Rupert Brooke. With enough time, in summer, a punt along the river here is still a must for a full appreciation of the place. The river winds out to Grantchester, the village immortalized by the poet Rupert Brooke. To the south of the city, off the M11, is the Imperial War Museum's vast museum of militarized flight at Duxford, just before the unexpected prominence of the mystical Gog Magog Hills. To the north, Ely Cathedral sails majestically above the well-drained farmland all around, the Queen of the Fens. ▸▸ *For Sleeping, Eating and other listings, see pages 307-310.*

Ins and outs

Getting there Cambridge is well served by express **coach** services, all of which terminate at the Drummer St coach stands, adjacent to the bus station. The main operators are **Jetlink, Stagecoach** and **National Express**. The travel office at the bus station has full details of all services and sells tickets for scheduled coach services and coach excursions to places of interest. By **car**, rom London take M11 north (which passes close to Stansted airport and Saffron Walden), at Junction 13 take the A1303 east and follow signs to city centre (1 hr 15 mins, 63 miles from central London). Cambridge **railway** station is on Station Rd, a 20-min walk from the centre. The main operators are **WAGN** (West Anglia Great Northern Railway), T0870-8508822. Direct trains from Cambridge to: London King's Cross via Royston, Hitchin, Stevenage, Finsbury Park (every 30 mins peak times, journey time 45 mins-1 hr); and to London Liverpool St via Audley End, Bishop's Stortford, Harlow Town. There are frequent direct trains from Cambridge to London. ▸▸ *For futher details, see also Transport, page 309.*

Getting around Cambridge town centre is only about a mile or so in diameter bordered to the north and west by the river Cam and the river Granta and its green banks which include the Midsummer Common and Jesus Green. The town centre is easily navigated by foot or by bicycle. Ely is about 20 mins north of Cambridge up the A10. Buses run to Ely from King's Lynn and Cambridge. It can be reached direct from Liverpool, Norwich, London and Cambridge.

Information Cambridge TIC ⓘ *Wheeler St, T01223-322640, www.tourismcambridge.com, Mon-Fri 1000-1800 (until 1730 NovMar), Sat 1000-1700, Easter-Sep Sun and bank holidays 1100-1600* Seems to charge for most things and has a rather indifferent/world-weary attitude. Walking tours leave the office at 1030 (July-Sep, Mon-Sat), 1130 (Apr-Oct daily, Nov-Mar Sat only), 1330 (daily all year), 1430 (daily July-Aug), 1830. Costumed drama tours Tue in July and Aug. **Ely TIC** ⓘ *29 St Mary's St, T01353-662062, www.eastcambs.gov.uk, Apr-Sep daily 1000-1730, Nov-Mar Mon-Sat 1000-1700, Sun 1115-1600.*

Sights

Market Hill, a square where a general market of sorts still takes place Monday to Saturday, is the centre of Cambridge, with the Guildhall on its south side, and the TIC round the corner in the Old Library on Wheeler Street. Most of the colleges of particular interest to a visitor are lined up along Trinity Street a few steps to the west down St Mary's Street past the church of St Mary the Great. Top of most visitors' places to visit, for the spectacular chapel on the north side of its Great Court, is **King's College** ⓘ *King's Pde, T01223-331250, www.kings.cam.ac.uk, during term-time Mon-Sat 0930-1530, choral evensong 1730, Sun 1315-1415, choral evensong 1030, 1530, vacations Mon-Sat 0930-1630, Sun 1000-1700 (no services), £3.50, concessions £2.50, under-12s free.* The simple elegance of the chapel's plan and exterior belie the wonders within: slender fan-vaulting soars overhead – surely one of the most impressive feats of ceiling-making in the western world – seeming to sprout organically from the walls, the whole space illuminated by a brilliant array of 16th-century windows, thankfully spared by the 17th-century iconoclasts. Construction on the chapel began in 1446 at the instigation of Henry VI, the centrepiece of his grand project for the University, and was completed by Henry VIII. The altarpiece at the east end of the simple rectangular plan is Rubens' *Adoration of the Magi*. The chapel's other pride and joy is its world-famous boys' choir, which can be heard in action at choral evensong most afternoons during term-time, as well as at the internationally popular Christmas carol service.

Back on Trumpington Street, the continuation of King's Parade, on the left is **Pembroke College**, with a fine classical chapel designed by Wren – his first major church project no less. The college has a long list of famous alumni, including Pitt the Younger – Prime Minister at the age of 23 – the poets Edmund Spenser and Ted Hughes, and comedian Peter Cook. Opposite Pembroke is **Peterhouse**, the smallest and oldest college in the University, founded by the Bishop of Ely in 1281. The college hall remains much as it was when built, while its well-kept garden and pretty octagonal courtyard are also worth a peek.

The museums

Thanks to the University, for a market town Cambridge is blessed with an unusually large and well-endowed collection of museums, at least 10 in total. Next door to Peterhouse stands their flagship, the grand neoclassical façade of the **Fitzwilliam Museum** ⓘ *Trumpington St, T01223-332900, www.fitzmuseum.cam.ac.uk, Tue-Sat 1000-1700, Sun 1415-1700, free*, without doubt one of the best reasons to visit the city in the first place. Founded in 1816, it houses a host of antiquities from Ancient Egypt, Greece and Rome, as well as applied arts from sculpture and furniture to clocks and rugs, alongside precious manuscripts and an outstanding collection of Old Master paintings, drawings and prints. Be sure to look up as you pass beneath its grand portico to enjoy its extraordinary gem-like Victorian coffered ceiling. Undergoing a comprehensive redevelopment of its main galleries at the time of writing, highlights of the collection on display in the magnificent Founder's Building include paintings by Titian, Vernonese, Rubens, Canaletto, Hogarth, Reynolds, Stubbs, Modigliani, Renoir, Cezanne and Picasso.

Close by in Downing Street, is the **University Museum of Zoology** ⓘ *T01223-336650, www.zoo.cam.ac.uk, Mon-Fri 1000-1300, 1400-1645, free*, displaying a wide array of recent and fossilized skeletal animals, including a huge whale, and an almost comprehensive display of stuffed British birds. Some of these specimens were collected by Darwin on his travels.

Next door is the **Sedgwick Museum of Earth Sciences**, the oldest museum in the University, where you are greeted by a full-size (18ft) model of an iguanodon. Highlights include the colourful mineral collection, and also some 250 million-year-old fossilized lightning, looking like a miniature volcano (about two or three inches across) from prehistoric beaches on the isle of Arran. It is the third biggest geology museum in Britain, with no restrictions on photography and new displays on interplanetary travel. ⓘ *T01223-333456, www.sedgwick.esc.cam.ac.uk, Mon-Fri 0900-1300, 1400-1700, Sat 1000-1300, free.*

A right turn south at the end of Downing Street, onto St Andrews Street, and a half-mile walk arrives at the **Scott Polar Research Institute**, founded in 1920 in memory of Captain Scott's ill-fated expedition to the South Pole. The small museum, dividing into Arctic and Antarctic galleries, includes maps, journals, photographs and equipment related to polar exploration past and present. ⓘ *Lensfield Rd, T01223-336540, www.spri.cam.ac.uk, Mon-Fri 1430-1600, free.*

The Backs

As the location of Peterhouse suggests, the University was founded between the High Street (now Trinity Street, King's Parade and Trumpington Street) and what was once called Milne Street (now only surviving as Trinity Lane and Queen's Lane) which ran alongside the river. Until the 18th century, 'the backs' of colleges like King's, Clare, Trinity and St John's overlooked busy coal and corn wharves. Now the view could hardly be more different. The Backs are one of the city's most celebrated assets, beautiful green lawns, playing fields and meadows, ablaze with flowers in the spring, strung together with charming old stone bridges crossing the Cam into college gardens. Their leafy extent can easily be viewed by cars or bikes crawling along the congested Queen's Road, but can only be fully appreciated by walkers and especially by punters. **Punting** could almost have been invented for the purpose of idling away a few hours here floating past some of the most beautiful old buildings in England. That's no secret though, which can mean that the footpaths are sometimes less crowded than the water. Private footpaths across the Backs head straight over the bridges into the colleges, open whenever the colleges are. Punts can be hired from Silver Street, Granta Place, Garret Hostel Lane or Magdalene Bridge (see Activities and tours). Granta Place on Mill Lane is the most popular, because here you have the choice of either heading upriver towards Grantchester, or downriver through the Backs. What the Grantchester way lacks in architectural wonder it makes up for in delightful pastoral stretches – cows ruminating on Coe Fen and entirely non-urban.

North of Market Hill

Back in the centre of town in the market square, a right turn on **Trinity** Street leads past the street's eponymous college, the University's largest (with over 600 undergraduates) and most grand. In fact it's a union of two old colleges, Michaelhouse and King's Hall, amalgamated by Henry VIII. At about two acres, its Great Court is also the most spacious of all Oxbridge quads, made famous in the film *Chariots of Fire* for the Great Court Run. A traditional wacky race in which undergraduates in full evening dress after a heavy supper try to complete a circuit of the court in the time it takes for the clock to strike midnight. It's only been successfully achieved once, by Lord Burghley in the early 1920s, an ancestor of Queen Elizabeth I's chancellor. During her reign, the oldest part of the Court was built using stones from the old Grey Friars monastery which stood where Sidney Sussex now stands. The college's other highlight is its magnificent Wren library, along the west side of Nevile's Court. Two decades or so before it was built, Isaac Newton was up at Trinity, in 1661. (He published *Principia Mathematica* in 1687 after being made Professor of Mathematics and allegedly hit on the head by an apple.)

Celebrated Trinity alumni include Lord Byron, who famously kept a bear in his rooms, Wittgenstein, Nabokov, the spies Philby, Burgess and Blunt, and Prince Charles.

Beyond Trinity is **St John's College**, the second largest in the University, founded by Bishop Fisher, who was martyred in the same year as Sir Thomas More under Henry VIII. Along with its fine Tudor gateway, the college has some of the most extraordinary buildings in the city, including its hammer-beamed hall, beautiful Tudor Second Court, and Combination Room, with a spectacular pannelled gallery and ornate plaster ceiling. The College also has some of the most beautiful and imaculately-kept gardens. The neo-Venetian **Bridge of Sighs** makes a picturesque river crossing from the college.

St John Street, as Trinity Street has become, ends at the junction of Bridge Street and Sydney Street, where stands the **Round Church of the Holy Sepulchre** ⓘ *Bridge St, T01223-311602, Mon-Sat 1000-1700, Sun 1300-1700*. As its name suggests, this unusual round church was based on the one in Jerusalem, and now houses a Christian visitor centre offering guided college tours, services on Wednesdays and a video on Cambridge history. It's one of only four round churches in England, founded by the Knights Templar.

A left turn onto Bridge Street leads down to the river and **Magdalene Bridge** and **Quayside**, a pleasant pedestrianized riverside spot for a drink outdoors. A boardwalk runs to the right along the river from here to Jesus Green, passing the old monastic buildings of Magdalene College. The river here is always busy with punts and chauffeur-punt touts in high season. Over the river on the left-hand side, the **Cambridge and County Folk Museum** ⓘ *Castle St, T01223-355159, www.folkmuseum.org.uk, Mon-Sat 1030-1700, Sun 1400-1700 (closed Mon, Oct-Mar), £2.50, concessions £1.50,* is housed in an old pub with eight different displays on various facets of local history, including domestic crafts, fens and folklore, and also the University and the City. A few yards up the road is another slightly more sophisticated local operation, **Kettle's Yard** ⓘ *T01223-352124, www.kettlesyard.co.uk, house Apr-Sep Tue-Sun 1330-1630, Oct-Mar Tue-Sun 1400-1600, gallery Tue-Sun 1130-1700, free*. Founded in 1957, the house contains artworks by the likes of Ben Nicholson, Barbara Hepworth, Brancusi and the St Ives School, and also holds chamber music concerts. The gallery puts on changing exhibitions of contemporary art.

Heading down to the river, Mill Lane is the most popular place in the city to hire a punt, near the Garden House Hotel.

Outside the city

A couple of miles southwest of the city centre, best reached by a leisurely stroll or punt along the Cam, is **Grantchester**, the epicentre of the Rupert Brooke cult that contributed so much to Cambridge's image between the wars. The Old Vicarage, where the poet stayed while at the university, is now the home of disgraced ex-Tory party chairman Jeffrey Archer. The church clock doesn't still stand at 10 to three although there could well be honey for tea, or a refreshing pint in one of the three pubs in the village. Six miles south of Trumpington, near Junction 10 of the M11, the **Duxford Imperial War Museum** ⓘ *T01223-835000, www.iwm.org.uk, Mid-Mar to Oct 1000-1800, Nov to mid-Mar 1000-1600, £8.50, concessions £6.50, children free*has one of the finest collections of antique and modern military aircraft in the world, with about 150 of the things in five vast hangars with an American Air Museum SR71 Blackbird spy-plane, the B24 bomber, Spitfires, Lancaster bombers, a flight simulator and also a land warfare museum.

Ely and The Fens

The Fens stretch out north of Cambridge and west of Breckland – a completely flat, oddly depressing area of rich farmland divided up by drainage ditches and dykes. One of the earliest entirely man-made and hence industrialized landscapes in Europe, the area was once a mysterious and inaccessible tract of marshland dotted with gravelly little islands. These provided safe havens in the east from Neolithic times right up to the 17th century and the accomplishment of the first serious drainage scheme. Down the ages they attracted a variety of colourful characters, from monks, monarchs and hermits to outlaws, traitors and poets. The most striking survivor from those times is Ely, best approached through fenland mists, when its extraordinary cathedral and octagonal lantern loom ahead, floating on a rise in the ground in the distance. The Isle of Ely, named after all the delicious eels that once squirmed round its shores, still boasts very little other than its beautiful cathedral, marooned in modern East Anglia as surely as it was once in marshland. **Ely cathedral** ⓘ *Chapter House, The College, T01353-667735, Apr-Oct daily 0700-1900, Nov-Mar Mon-Sat 0730-1800, Sun 0730-1700, £4, concessions £3.50*, one of the most beautiful in the country, was re-built by the Normans. In the 14th century it was

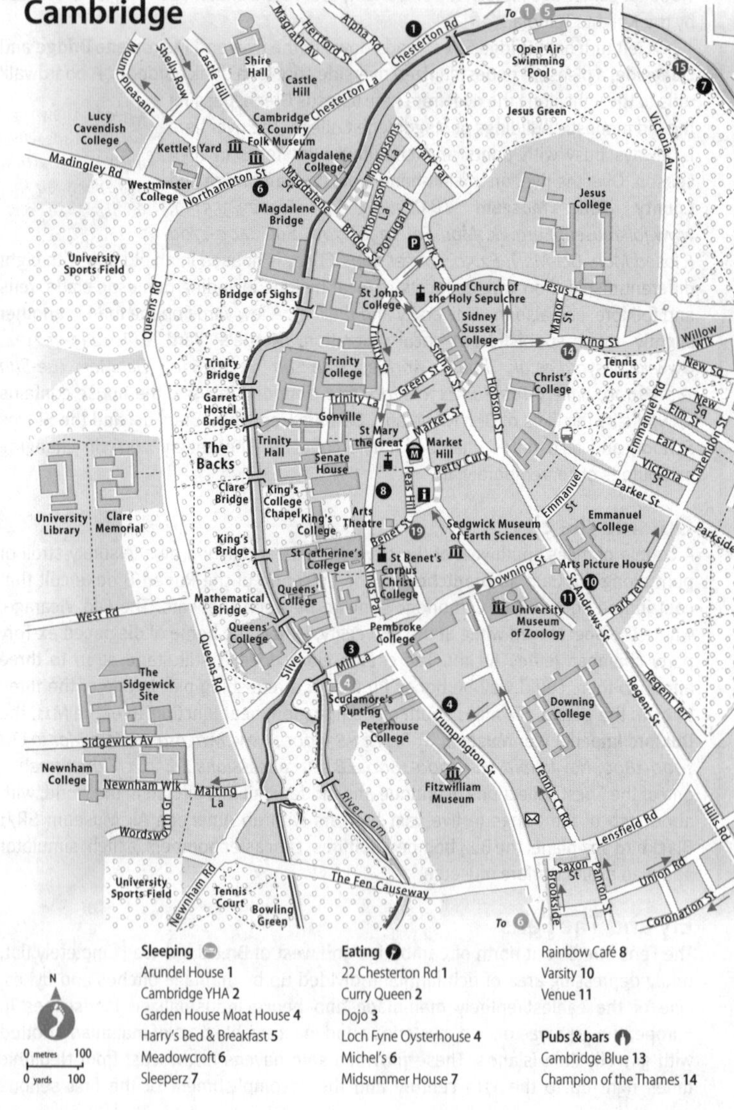

embellished with the inspiring octagonal tower that can be seen for many miles around on a clear day. This beautiful Gothic structure was designed and built by one of the greatest of medieval architects, local monk Alan de Walsingham. In Febuary 1322, as the brothers were retiring to bed, the old Norman tower collapsed. Alan rushed out to survey the ruins, and swore with God's help to 'set his hand to work'. The Lady Chapel has the broadest medieval vaulted ceiling in the country. In the Treforium, the **Stained Glass Museum** ⓘ *T01353-660347, www.stainedglassmuseum.org, Apr-Oct Mon-Sat 1030-1700, Sun 1200-1800; Nov-Mar Mon-Sat 1030-1700, Sun 1200-1630, £3.50, children £2.50, family £7,* contains over a hundred examples of coloured glass and courses on making it.

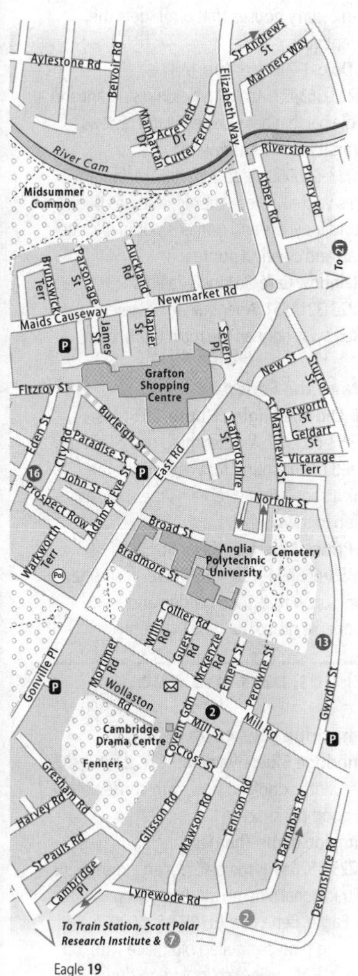

Eagle **19**
Fort St George of England **15**
Free Press **16**
Wrestler's Pub **21**

Sleeping

Cambridge *p302, map p306*

Accommodation in central Cambridge is expensive. There are plenty of B&Bs on the outskirts, some of the best along Milton Rd, and also in Chesterton Rd. Given that the nightlife is hardly jumping, it might be as good to go for better value rooms in one of the villages just outside town, many with regular and reliable bus services to and from the city.

L **Garden House Moat House Hotel**, Granta Pl, Mill La, T01223-259988, www.moathousehotel.com. The smartest hotel in the city, with a lovely terrace bar and brasserie backing onto the punt-crammed Cam, as well as spacious, comfortable rooms with river views.

A **Meadowcroft Hotel**, 16 Trumpington Rd, T01223-346120, www.meadowcroft.co.uk. A small, slightly chi-chi hotel with fine gardens and tasteful individually designed bedrooms.

B **Arundel House Hotel**, 53 Chesterton Rd, T01223-367701, www.arundelhousehotels.co.uk. Privately owned Victorian hotel overlooking the river Cam at the top end of this bracket with reasonably priced restaurant.

C **Suffolk House**, 69 Milton Rd, T01223-352016, F566816. Family-run, clean non-smoking guesthouse in a quiet area about 20 mins walk from the centre.

D **Harry's Bed and Breakfast**, 39 Milton Rd, T01223-503866. Small B&B in an Edwardian house about 20 mins from the city centre.

D **Sleeperz Hotel**, Station Rd, T01223-304050, www.sleeperz.com. Clean and comfortable budget option in a converted granary close to the station.

F **Cambridge YHA**, 97 Tenison Rd, T01223-354601, F312780. Close to the station, a Victorian townhouse about 15 mins' walk from the centre with 100 beds in 2-8 bedded rooms. Booking well in advance advisable.

Outside the city *p305*

B **The Grange Manor House**, Lolworth, T01954-781298, www.hotels.uk.com/thegrange. Has 7 gardens and a swimming pool set around a large non-smoking Victorian manor house off the A14.

C **Church Farm**, Gransden Rd, Caxton, near Cambridge, T01954-719543. A high-class B&B in an old farmhouse with beautiful gardens.

D **Springfield House**, 16 Horn La, Linton, T01223-891383, www.smoothhound.co.uk/hotels/springf2. Two-room B&B in a converted schoolhouse with bus service into Cambridge.

Ely and the Fens *p305*

B **Cathedral House**, 17 St Mary's St, Ely, T01353-662124, www.cathedralhouse.co.uk. Large rooms, a walled garden and very close to the cathedral. Worth splashing out on.

C **Old Egremont House**, 31 Egremont St, Ely, T01353-663118. Highly rated small B&B with cathedral views.

Eating

Cambridge *p302, map p306*

There are many mediocre restaurants in Cambridge doling out comfort food to careless students and tourists. Finding good-quality cooking is quite a challenge. See also pubs for cheap places to eat

£££ **Midsummer House**, Midsummer Common, T01223-369299. Universally acknowledged to be the best (and most expensive – about £50 a head for dinner, considerably less for lunch) but it deserves all the praise. Innovative and delicious gourmet cuisine is served up with unfailing attention to detail in a delightful conservatory and garden, with a balcony area overlooking the Cam. Booking essential.

£££ **22 Chesterton Rd**, 22 Chesterton Rd, T01223-351880. Also fairly expensive (set 4-course dinners for about £25), it's another classy joint that also needs to be booked. Quite staid but with a surprisingly innovative menu served up in an Edwardian dining room.

£££ **Loch Fyne Oysterhouse**, 37 Trumpington St, T01223-362433. In the middle of town, this is a fine example of the reliable national seafood chain doing very fresh fish in cheerful and easy-going surroundings (about £30 a head).

£££ **Venue**, 66 Regent St, T01223-367333. Another central option, also about £30 a head for supper, a sleek modern British restaurant not quite as swish as it likes to think it is but decent enough nonetheless. Booking advisable.

££ **Michel's**, 21 Northampton St, T01223-353110. A modern Italian restaurant just over Magdalene Bridge, doing fairly good-value £9 three-course lunches.

££ **Curry Queen**, 106 Mill Rd, T01223-351027. One of the city's more reliable curry houses that often gets the student vote.

££ **Dojo**, 1-2 Millers Yard, Mill La, T01223-363471. An Asian fusion restaurant and noodle bar that has received warm reviews.

£ **Varsity**, 35 St Andrew's St, T01223-356060. A 'continental' restaurant with a vaguely Greek theme, that has been around for years and remains popular for its cheap and cheerful approach.

£ **Rainbow Café**, 9a King's Parade, T01223-3211551. A vegetarian basement place tucked away right on the main tourist drag.

Ely and the Fens *p305*

£££ **Old Fire Engine House**, 25 St Mary's, T01353-662582. A welcoming place that has indeed been around for years and some think it shows, but it remains the smartest option in town.

££ **Prince Albert**, 62 Silver St, Ely T01353-663494. Very jolly flower-festooned town pub with a good garden and reasonable grub. The best in the city.

Pubs, bars and clubs

Cambridge *p302, map p306*

Cambridge Blue, Gwydir St, T01223-361382. An eccentric drinking hole with conservatory and good bar snacks.

Champion of the Thames, King St, T01223-352043. Is the place for an atmospheric and traditional pint (no food) in a snug.

The Eagle, Bene't St, T01223-505020. A rambling pine-pannelled old place with famous 'RAF ceiling' scribbled on during the Second World War by locally based British and American airmen.

Fort St George of England, next to Midsummer House (see Eating above). Good in summer, with outside seating on the river beside the boathouses.

Free Press, Prospect Row, T01223-368337. Sporty non-smoking Greene King pub in an old terraced house with attractive little garden.

Wrestler's Pub, 337 Newmarket Rd, T01223-566553. Does highly praised Thai food in a basic and busy boozer.

Entertainment

Cambridge *p302, map p306*

Film, theatre and music

Arts Picture House, St Andrews St, T01223-504444, www.picturehouse-cinemas.co.uk. Three-screen general release arthouse films.

Arts Theatre, St Edward's Passage, T01223-503333. Local rep playhouse with a high reputation as well as the reputable **Roof Garden Restaurant**, T01223-578930.

Corn Exchange, Wheeler St, T01223-357851. The city's front-rank venue for larger touring productions, including opera, dance and live music.

Kettle's Yard (see North of Market Hill above). For intimate classical and folk concerts.

Cambridge Drama Centre, Covent Garden, T01223-511511. Fringe drama and small-scale touring productions.

The Junction, Clifton Rd, T01223-511511, www.junction.co.uk. Club nights, comedy and live music.

Festivals and events

Cambridge *p302, map p306*

mid-Mar Cambridge Science Week, from , with lectures and other science-related events.

May Cambridge Beer Festival on Jesus Green, www.camra.co.uk.

Middle of Jun May Week, student japes and general hilarity to celebrate the end of exams.

End of Jul Cambridge Folk Festival, T01223-457245, www.cam-folkfest.co.uk. Booking essential for one of the world's first and most prestigious 4-day folk music festivals.

Jul Cambridge Film Festival, T01223-504444.

Jul Cambridge Shakespeare Festival, in the college gardens, T01223-357851.

Sun in early-mid Jun Strawberry Fair, . Full-on hippy trippy festival on Midsummer Common.

Activities and tours

Cambridge *p302, map p306*

Punting

Scudamore's Punting Company, Granta Pl, Mill La, T01223-359750, www.scudamores.com. Mar-Oct 0900-dusk, Nov-Feb Sat, Sun only 1000-dusk. £12 an hr. In high season, expect to queue if you want a punt any time after 1300. Choose either an upriver boat, for Coe Fen and the 3-hr round-trip to Grantchester or a downriver boat for the Backs and the 2-hr, 2-mile round-trip to Jesus Green Lock. The upriver boats and the stretches of river they ply are generally less busy and more rural than the downriver ones.

Transport

Cambridge *p302, map p306*

Bus

Stagecoach runs the service to **Norwich** (2 hrs 30 mins) every 2 hrs, changing at **Newmarket**. The direct service to **Ipswich** (1 hr 55 mins) is run by **National Express**, and departs from Drummer Rd coach stop at 1650. They also run the direct hourly service to **London Victoria** (2 hrs 20 mins), the regular direct service to **Stansted airport** (50 mins) and the direct service to **Luton** (1 hr 10 mins) every 2 hrs.

Taxi

Ranks on Drummer St, Emmanuel St, St Andrews St and at the Train Station. Local minicab firms include: **A1 Taxis**, T01223-525555; **Camtax**, T01223-313131; and **Regency Taxis**, T01223-311388.

Train

The twice hourly direct service to Norwich (1 hr 15 mins) is run by **Anglia Railways**, T08700-409090, as is the direct line to **Ipswich** (1 hr 20), which departs at 1009. The direct service to **London King's Cross** (50 mins) is run every 15 mins by **WAGN**, T08708-508822. **Central Trains**, T0121-6541200, run the direct hourly service to **Stansted airport** (30 mins), also **Peterborough** (1 hr), **Leicester** (1hr 50 mins) and **Birmingham** (3 hrs). There is no direct service to Luton.

Directory

Cambridge *p302, map p306*
Bike hire Cycle King, 195 Mill Rd, T01223-212222. Geoff's Bike Hire, 65 Devonshire Rd, T01223-365629. Ben Hayward & Son, 69 Trumpington St, T01223-352294. N.K. Bike Hire, Cherry Hinton Rd, T01223-505485. University Cycles, 9 Victoria Av, T01223-355517. **Car hire** Avis, 245 Mill Rd, T01223-212551. Budget Rent-a-Car, 303 Newmarket Rd, T01223-323838. Cambridge Car Hire, Coldhams La Garage, T01223-515151. Europcar, 22 Cambridge Rd, Impington, T01223-233644. Hertz, 264 Barnwell Rd, T01223-416634. **Hospitals** Addenbrooke's NHS Trust, Hills Rd, T01223-245151. **Brookfields Hospital**, Mill Rd, T01223-723000. **Internet** CB1, 32 Mill Rd, T01223-576306. CB2, 5-7 Norfolk St, T01223-508503. La Pronto Internet Café, 2 Emmanuel St, T01223-312700. The Internet Exchange, 2 St Mary's Passage, T01223-327600. **Language Schools** Language Studies International, 41 Tenison Rd, T01223-361783. Aspect International Language Academies, 75 Barton Rd, T01223-357702. **Police** Parkside Police Station, Parkside, T01223-358966. **Post office** 9-11 St Andrews St, T0845-7223344.

Norwich and the Broads

→Colour map 2

Never loud or brash, Norwich is quietly confident of itself. Stranded in the middle of the flatlands of East Anglia, it is, as its inhabitants are fond of saying, a "fine city", a typically understated boast that is nonetheless born out by the way in which the place manages to combine so many different layers of English history within the bustle of a busy provincial capital, set off by some bold forays into cutting-edge modernism. As recent excavations have shown, this bend in the River Wensum was used as a place of settlement in Bronze Age times and was subsequently occupied by successive waves of invading forces, from the Vikings and the Romans to – most significantly – the Normans, whose spectacular castle and cathedral still stand at the heart of the city. It is, though, entirely possible to tire of medieval churches – of which Norwich has a surfeit – the natural antidote to which is the Sainsbury Centre of Visual Arts, a latter-day temple to the new religion of modern art and a truly world-class museum. Between Norwich and the sea lie The Broads, Norfolk's most popular tourist destination and also one of Europe's most important wetland habitats. ▸▸ *For Sleeping, Eating and other listings, see pages 315-317.*

Ins and outs

Getting there Stansted International Airport, 85 miles away by road, is linked to Norwich by a Jetlink coach service, T08705-757747, www.gobycoach.com. Norwich also has its own airport, T01603-411923, www.norwichinternational.co.uk, a few miles to the north of the city, operating daily 40-min flights to Amsterdam and other worldwide connecting flights via Manchester and Paris. **National Express** operates daily **coach** services to Norwich from most cities in England. London to Norwich, 3 hrs. The **car** journey to Norwich from London, just over 100 miles, is likely to take you about 3 hrs. Take the M11 as far as Cambridge and turn off onto the A11. The city contains a number of multi-storey and pay-and-display car parks, as well as a limited number of short-term parking spaces in the centre of town. **Anglia Railways,** T08700-409090, operate a half-hourly service direct from London Liverpool St (1 hr 50 mins) as well as services from other local towns and villages. For trains to or from the Midlands, the North or Scotland, change at Peterborough. **Central Trains,** T08700-006060, operate local services. ▸▸ *For further details, see also Transport, page 317.*

The main road access points to the **Broads** are at Norwich, Loddon, and Lowestoft (for the southern section) and at Great Yarmouth, Wroxham, Horning, Stalham and Potter Heigham (for the northern section). Broadland villages that give some idea of the area's charm and can be reached by car include Rockland St Mary in the south, and Ranworth, Horsey and Woodbastwick in the north. Local **bus** services (few and far between) are run by **First Eastern Counties,** T08456-020121. The Broads can be reached by fairly regular **rail** services within an hour from Norwich, with stations at Reedham, Wroxham and Acle and also to Berney Arms which has no road.

Getting around Norwich city centre is compact enough to make most places accessible by foot. The 25 bus links the centre with the train station and the 21 or 22 take you to B&B land to the west of the city. For the Sainsbury Centre, a few miles away on the University of East Anglia campus, take the 25, 26 or 27 from the city centre. The most obvious way to get around The Broads is by boat, although they can also be very enjoyably explored on foot and by bike. One of the best boatyards on the Broads is **Martham Boats,** in Martham on the outer-reaches of the northern broads, T01493-740249, www.marthamboats.com. They have a variety of traditional wooden sailing and also wooden motor boats which they build themselves, also available for day hire. **Hoseason's,** Lowestoft, T01502-516900, www.hoseasons.co.uk. The big commercial operators in the area. **Moore and Co,** Staitheway Rd, Wroxham, T01603-783311, www.boatingholidays.co.uk. Another very popular option.

Information The main tourist office in Norwich is on the ground floor of **The Forum,** the vast, hi-tech library and visitor centre on the southwest corner of the marketplace. T01603-727927 Apr-Oct 1000-1800 Mon-Sat, 1030-1630 Sun; Nov-Mar 1000-1730 Mon-Sat. Walking tours with a Blue Badge Guide, lasting approx 1 hr 30 mins depart from the tourist centre. Apr-Oct.

Hoveton TIC ⓘ *Station Rd, T01603-782281.* **Ranworth TIC** ⓘ *The Staithe, T01603-270453.* **Loddon TIC** ⓘ *The Old Town Hall, 1 Bridge St, T01508-521028.* **Broads Authority Information Line** ⓘ *T01603-610734, www.broads-authority.gov.uk* **Broads Authority Information Centres**: Beccles, Great Yarmouth, Hoveton, Loddon, Ludham, Potter Heigham and Ranworth.

Sights

Begin your tour where the city began, inappropriately enough at a place called Tombland, the original heart of Norwich. The **Erpingham Gate,** given to the city by the eponymous gent who led the English archers at Agincourt in 1420 and whose statue stands above the archway, acts as an entrance to the cathedral grounds. **Norwich Cathedral** ⓘ *T01603-218321, vis&profficer@cathedral.org.uk, Mid-May to mid-Sep daily 0730-1900, mid-Sep to mid-May daily 0730-1800, visitors' centre open all year Mon-Sat 1000-1600, shop open all year Mon-Sat 0915-1700, services daily, free,* was begun in 1096 and finally completed in 1278, though the roof and spire (315 ft) date from the later medieval period, following a fire in 1463. A series of 255 painted bosses set high in the nave vaulting depict the entire Bible story, while other treasures include the exquisite carving around the prior's doorway leading onto the cloisters and the medieval paintings in St Luke's Chapel.

Perched high up on its grassy mound, **Norwich Castle** ⓘ *T01603-493636, Mon-Sat 1030-1700, Sun 1400-1700 and slightly longer during school holidays, café and shop, £4.70 for the whole castle, £2.25 for the exhibits only,* looks surprisingly modern for a Norman building, explained in part by the fact that it was resurfaced in the 19th century. Originally built as a royal palace, it subsequently became a prison, before its present incarnation as Norfolk's principal museum, refurbished in 2001 at a cost of £11.8 million. For that money, you get a high-quality minestrone of history, archaeology, natural history and fine art, both old and new. Move freely between the Twinings Teapot Gallery, the Norwich School of Painters and a celebration of Boudicca, the flame-haired local harridan who led the resistance against the Romans, featuring the world's only virtual chariot ride.

From the castle, stroll west down into Gentleman's Walk, leading onto the main market place, filled by an eyecatching patchwork of multicoloured awnings, where you can buy anything from jellied eels to a new dog lead. On the left of the square is **St Peter Mancroft**, the largest of the city's 31 medieval churches and a particular favourite of the 18th-century Methodist preacher and hymnist John Wesley. Soaring evermore heavenward, in the left-hand corner, is **The Forum**. Norwich's other modern giant, designed by Michael Hopkins and opened in 2001, is first and foremost the city's main public library, including an important archive dedicated to the American servicemen stationed in the area during the Second World War. The glass-fronted central atrium also has coffee bars and pizza restaurants, the tourist information centre and **Origins** ⓘ *T01603-727920, £4.95, child £3.50*, a multimedia interactive journey through 2000 years of Norwich and Norfolk.

Sainsbury Centre for Visual Arts ⓘ *T01603-456060, Tue-Sun 1100-1700 (1100-2000 on Wed), closed Mon, Christmas Eve and New Year's Day, £2, concessions £1, including special exhibitions*, part of the University of East Anglia, is in Norman Foster's vast 1970s aircraft hangar and contains top-notch modern art, provocatively displayed alongside a wondrous hoard of objects gleaned from all parts of the space-time continuum, including Africa, America, ancient Egypt, the Pacific and medieval Europe. The contemporary collection is justly famous for works by Francis Bacon, Alberto Giacometti, Henry Moore, John Davies and Lucy Rie.

The Broads

The Broads are made up of about 127 miles-worth of shallow but navigable waterways twisting through reedbeds and marshland, the flat landscape dotted with ruined windmills, occasionally opening out into wider lakes – the 'broads' themselves. The whole area is the main place that the British love to mess about in boats. Five rivers provide the water as they make their way east across the county to the sea at Great Yarmouth: the Waveney is the most southerly, creating the county's border with Suffolk as it flows in via Bungay and Beccles; the Yare comes in from Norwich; the Bure from Aylsham, joined by the Ant and Thurne near Ranworth. Clearly this strange and usually peaceful landscape can only really be appreciated and explored by boat.

The area divides neatly into northern and southern navigations: the former, based on the Bure, Ant and Thurne being the more popular and the most scenic (all the rivers are more attractive in their upper reaches) and with more of the broads themselves. These reed-fringed lagoons were created by peat-cuttings started in the 13th century which have slowly flooded over the years. They vary in size from small pools to the largest expanse at **Hickling Broad**. There are about 50 of them altogether, mostly in the northern area. Thirteen are open for free-range boating, as well as the navigable channels on **Martham** and **Sutton Broads**, and **Womack Water**. Two more, **Black Horse Broad** and **Horsey Mere**, are open during the holiday season.

Southern Broads

Breydon Water is a 2000-acre tidal lake next to Great Yarmouth, with glistening mudflats at low tide, fed by the rivers Yare and Waveney. Four miles up the Yare, **Berney Arms Windmill** ⓘ *(EH), T01493- 700605, Apr-Oct daily 0900-1300, 1400-1700, £2, concessions £1.50, children £1*, is the tallest drainage windmill in the UK with views over Breydon Water and the surrounding marshland from the top. It stopped pumping water as recently as 1951. The largest stretch of open water in the Yare valley is at **Rockland**

Nun the wiser

Rather than counselling or therapy, the world weary citizens of medieval Norwich were more likely to have sought the wit and wisdom of an anchorite monk or nun. At the end of the 14th century, there were about 50 of these professional Christian contemplatives in the city, each attached to a church, where they were often walled into a single room after undergoing the rites of their own funeral service. A window onto the altar inside meant they were still able to receive Holy Communion, while a window onto the street outside allowed them to dispense solace and advice to the troubled souls beyond. Julian of Norwich – the most famous of all these mystics – spent the last forty odd years of her life like this in a cell connected to St Julian's Church (from which, rather confusingly, Julian gets her name), situated along a grassy track between Rouen Road and King Street, a five-minute walk south from Norwich Castle. Julian is also generally regarded as the first Englishwoman to write a book in English, the diary of all her extraordinary visions and "showings", *Revelations of Divine Love*. The church and its accompanying guest house – run by nuns – attract visitors from all over the world, inspired perhaps by that most positive of all Julian's spiritual insights: "You shall see for yourself that all manner of things shall be well." For information on St Julian's Church and All Hallows House, telephone 01603 624738.

Broad, where day boats can be hired and there's a decent pub in Rockland St Mary. **Surlingham Broad**, at Brundall, has a Swallows-and-Amazons style maze of little channels connecting its two lakes. Seven miles or so further upstream stands Norwich, the centre of which can be reached along the river Wensum. Following the river Waveney upstream from Breydon Water passes **Burgh Castle** (open any reasonable time) where the impressive remains of a walled third-century Roman fort overlook the river. Five miles further the river is bridged at **St Olave's**, a small single-street 17th-century village named after the patron saint of Norway. The ruins of its 13th-century Augustinian priory stand too close to the busy A143 for comfort.

Northern Broads

The Bure enters Great Yarmouth from the north after an unattractive and congested three-mile stretch of the river below Stokesby. Five miles further upstream, the Bure comes into its own as it's joined by the Thurne, which has run south for three miles from **Potter Heigham**. A boat hire centre second only to Wroxham, Potter Heigham has an entertainingly difficult medieval bridge to navigate, where larger boats are required to take on a pilot to shoot the central arch at full speed. Southwest of the town, near Ludham, is **Toad Hole Cottage** ⓘ *How Hill, T01692-678763, Apr-Oct daily 1000-1800, free, boat trips Apr-Oct 1000-1700 Apr, May, Oct weekends only 1100-1500, £4, concessions £3, family £8*, an old eel catcher's cottage that conjures the atmosphere of Victorian country living and also runs quiet boat trips through fen and reedswamp on the river Ant aboard the *Electric Eel*.

Further up the Thurne, the sea feels very close. **Hickling Broad**, the largest of the Broads, is owned by the Norfolk Wildlife Trust, and comes closest to most people's idea of a typical broadland scene. Boats can be hired from the *Pleasure Boat Inn*, from where nature trails also head round the lake on boardwalks and dry land. A channel leads into **Horsey Mere**, another secluded lake, owned by the National Trust and overlooked by their **Horsey Windpump** ⓘ *(NT), Horsey T01493-393904, Apr-Sep daily 1100-1700 (last admission 1630), £2, children £1*, restored following lightning damage in 1943.

Back on the Bure at the mouth of the Thurne stands a well-preserved white **windmill** (T01603-222705 for the key), from where a beautiful two-mile walk leads up to the picturesque ruins of **St Benet's Abbey**. These are the remains of the only religious house in Norfolk founded before the Norman conquest, by King Canute, enclosed with a wall and battlements in 1327. It was also reputed to be the only

Norwich

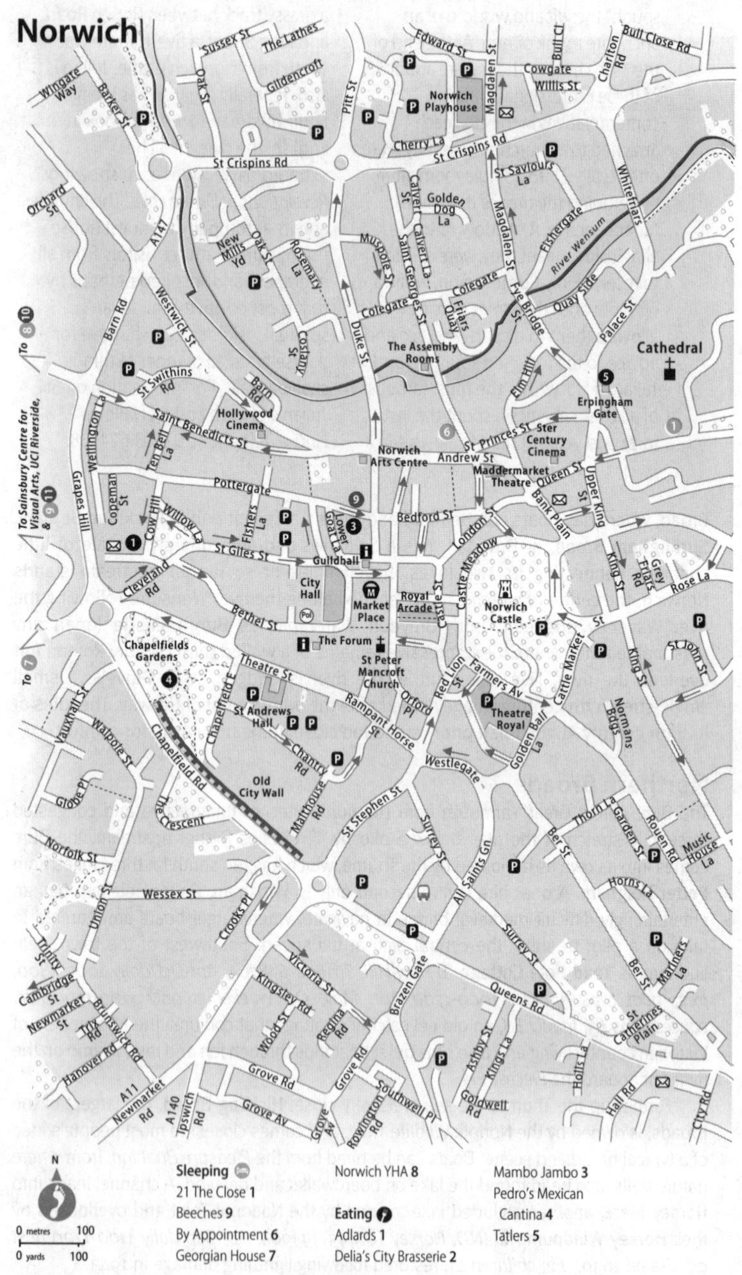

religious house in England not actually dissolved by Henry VIII, and the Bishops of Norwich have remained Abbots to the present day. The best way to reach the Abbey is by hiring a boat at **Horning**, beyond the mouth of the river Ant. The route passes the entrance to **Ranworth Broad**, where the delightful broad-side village of **Ranworth** (which can also be reached by car) is blessed with a church dating from 1370, containing an outstanding medieval painted screen. There are superb views over broadland from the top of its tower.

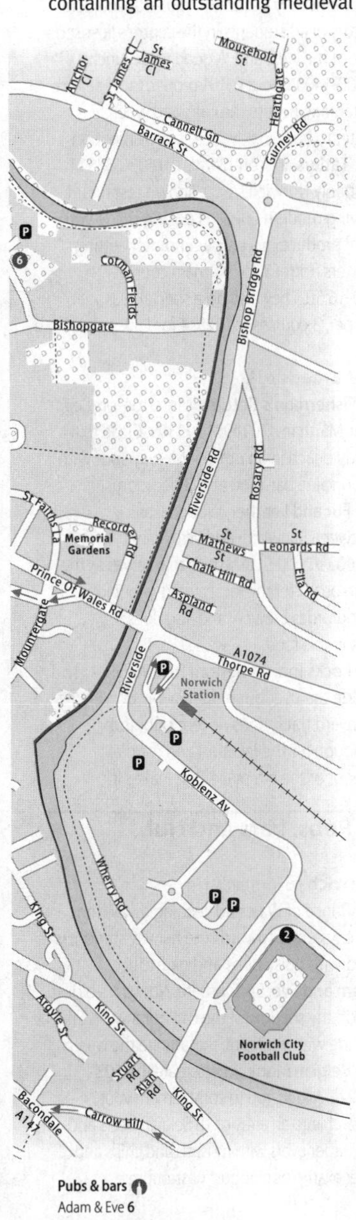

Pubs & bars
Adam & Eve **6**
Belgian Monk **9**
Fat Cat **10**
Garden House **11**

Five miles northwest of Ranworth, further up the Bure, **Wroxham** is the capital of the Broads sitting next to its 112-acre lake. The town is almost completely overrun with boaties, tourists and geese during summer, and the broad itself crammed with sailing dinghies. It's a reasonably good value place to hire a boat for the day though and also pick up picnic provisions. The **Bure Valley Railway** ⓘ *Norwich Rd, Aylsham, T01263-733858, May-Sep*, a narrow-gauge railway, built in 1990, runs the 9-mile, 45-min trip from Wroxham to Aylsham via Coltishall, Buxton and Brampton.

Sleeping

Norwich *p310, map p314*

Accommodation is hard to come by bang in the middle of town and the majority of visitors to Norwich find themselves booking into a B&B – for around £25-30 per person – in the area just west of the city centre down the Dereham and Earlham Rd.

A **The Beeches**, T01603-621167. Three converted Victorian houses grouped around the Roman Catholic Cathedral, offer 3-star accommodation within acres of gardens within walking distance of the city centre.

B **The Georgian House Hotel**, 32 Unthank Rd, T01603-615655. Also opposite the Roman Catholic Cathedral, this is a family-run hotel within easy reach of the centre.

B **By Appointment**, 25-29 St George's St, T01603-630730. For something a little theatrical, this is a 15th-century merchant's house in the middle of the city centre, which includes a well-respected restaurant.

E **21 The Close**, T01603-662562. A friendly one-room B&B at a desirable address right next to the cathedral.

F **Norwich YHA**, 112 Turner Rd, a 20-min walk west of the city centre, T01603-627647. A dorm bed is £10.25 (£7 for under-18s).

The Broads *p312*

A **The Norfolk Mead Hotel**, Coltishall, T01603-737531, www.norfolkmead.co.uk. A Georgian manor house that has become a discreet and sophisticated country house hotel, with individually furnished rooms and attractive grounds sloping down to the river Bure.

C **Le Grys Barn**, Wacton Common, near Long Stratton, T01508-531576, F01508- 532124. A newly converted barn decorated in a way that reflects its owner's African travels.

D **Hall Green Farm**, Norton Rd, Loddon, T01508-522039, www.geocities.com/hallgreenfarm A 10-min walk outside the village of Loddon, a Georgian farmhouse with 2 double rooms, both with en suite bathrooms.

D **Lower Farm B&B**, Horsford, T01603- 891291, www.norfolkbroads.com/lowerfarm Attractive old 17th-century farmhouse with 2 double rooms with en suite bathrooms.

D **The Old Chapel**, Horsey, T01493-393498. An interesting converted church B&B.

Eating

Norwich *p310*

£££ **Adlards**, 79 Upper St Giles St, T01603-633522. A British restaurant with a strong French influence, in an elegant, contemporary dining room. Norwich's only Michelin star, yet not outrageously expensive.

£££ **Delia's City Brasserie**, Norwich City Football Club, T01603-218705. Here you can combine an afternoon watching the beautiful game and an evening of the recipes of television chef Delia Smith, a director and majority shareholder of Norwich's first division football team, aka 'the Canaries'. The restaurant, inside one of the football ground's stands, is only open on Saturday nights and offers a 3-course menu for £25.

££ **39 Steps**, 17 St Benedicts St, T01603-619040. Live jazz every night and dining on 3 floors. A la carte menu and a special deal offering a glass of wine and main course for £8.

££ **Mambo Jambo**, 14 Lower Goat Lane, T01603-66802. Offers good-value southern cooking – Creole, Cajun, Mexican – with an upbeat ambience.

££ **Pedro's Mexican Cantina**, Chapelfields Gardens, T01603-614725. Large plates of nachos and enchiladas with a salsa backing track ensure a loyal student following at this fun old favourite.

££ **Sainsbury Centre**, T01603-456060. Join history of art students in the centre's licensed café at the west end. A good value lunch (1200-1400, about £3). A proper, table-service restaurant, next to the café, and where it is better to book in advance, is also an option.

££ **Tatlers**, 21 Tombland, T01603-633511. Probably Norwich's best-known restaurant, serving modern English cooking made with local produce in a chic yet homely setting. Starters from £3.75-10, main courses £10-16.50. They also do a special seasonal supper, 3 courses for £25, 4 for £30.

The Broads *p312*

££ **Fisherman's Return**, Winterton-on-Sea, near Martham, T01493- 393305. Close to a sandy beach in an out-of-the-way spot with good value bar-food and 3 bedrooms.

££ **Fur and Feather**, Woodbastwick (between Ranworth and Wroxham), T01603-720003. Large pub that serves as the main outlet for the local award-winning Woodfordes brewery and also does reasonable food.

££ **Locks Inn**, Geldeston, T01508-518414. Beside the river but hidden away down a farmyard track, does decent pub grub, although it's the location and candlelit interior of the old place that makes it.

Pubs, bars and clubs

Norwich *p310, map p314*

The Prince of Wales Rd, leading away from the city centre towards the railway station, is lined with noisy pubs and nightclubs.

Adam and Eve, Bishopsgate. Norwich's oldest pub in the shadow of the cathedral walls. Sit outside with your pint and admire the ivy.

The Belgian Monk, 7 Pottergate, T01603-767222. Allows you to complement your research into an array of 18 Belgian beers and 12 fruit Jenevers with mussels and chips and other examples of robust gastronomie.

For an explanation of the sleeping and eating price codes used in this guide, see the inside front cover. Other relevant information is provided in the Essentials chapter, page 36.

The Fat Cat, 49 West End St, off Dereham Rd. Beloved of real ale drinkers, stocking an impressive range of barrelled beers and a good stock of the Belgian bottled variety too. **The Garden House**, Pembroke Rd, off Earlham Rd. Like the above, another pub in the so-called 'Golden Triangle' of student living. Very popular, with a pool table, pinball table, huge garden and occasional DJs.

Entertainment

Norwich *p310, map p314*

Cinema

Hollywood Cinema in Anglia Sq, T01603-621903, **Ster Century** in the Castle Mall shopping centre, T01603-221900 and **UCI Riverside** in the new Riverside development, T0870-0102030; and one art house cinema, **Cinema City**, St Andrews St, T01603-622047.

Theatre and music

Norwich Playhouse in St George's St, T01603-598598, the **Theatre Royal** in Theatre St, T01603- 630000, and the more alternative **Maddermarket Theatre**, in St John's Alley, T01603-620917. Classical concerts are held in **The Assembly Rooms**, Theatre St, T01603-626402 and also in **St Andrew's and Blackfriars' Halls**, T01603-628477. There might also be something happening at the friendly **Norwich Arts Centre**, in St Benedicts St, T01603-660352 – Nirvana played there on their first UK tour to an audience of 87 people.

Festivals and events

Norwich *p310, map p314*

Visiting Writers' Festival is held from the **end Jan-mid Mar** at the University of East Anglia, where the creative writing course under Malcolm Bradbury and Andrew Motion has produced such luminaries as Ian McEwan, Timothy Mo, Graham Swift and Kazuo Ishiguro. **Norwich Beer Festival** in the **last week of Oct**. East Coast Jazz Festival in the **1st 2 weeks of Nov**.

Transport

Norwich *p310, map p314*

Bus

National Express run regular direct services from Norwich Bus Station to and from **London Victoria** (3 hrs) and every 2 hrs direct to **Stansted airport** (1 hr 45 mins). Services to **Cambridge** (2 hrs 30 mins), changing at **Newmarket**, are run by Stagecoach at 0915 and 1115.

Train

Anglia Railways, T08700-409090, www.angliarailways.co.uk, runs the main service to and from Norwich. Trains are twice hourly to **London Liverpool Street** (1 hr 45 mins), twice hourly direct to **Cambridge** (1 hr 15 mins) and twice hourly direct to **Ipswich** (40 mins). Central Trains, T0121-6541200, www.centraltrains.co.uk, run the regular service to **Stansted airport** (1 hr 50 mins), changing at **Ely**.

Taxis

City Hall Taxis, 41 Hurricane Way, T01603-789333. **Five Star Taxis**, 43a Prince of Wales Rd, T01603-455555.

Directory

Norwich *p310, map p314*

Bike hire Streetlife, 54 West End St, T01603- 626660. **Broadland Cycle Hire**, The Rhond, Hoverton, T01603-783096. **Car hire** Avis, Norwich Airport, T01603-416719. Thrifty, 1 Paddock St, T01603-666300. **Hospitals** Norfolk & Norwich University Hospital NHS Trust, Colney Lane, Colney, T01603-286286. **Internet** Flying Classrooms Internet Café, 14 Bank St, T01603-619091. **Norwich Market Internet** Café, 40-41 Provision Market, T01603-760808. **Police** Norfolk Police Norwich Division, Bethel St, T01603-768769. **Post office** 84/85 Castle Meadow Walk, Castle Mall, T0845- 7223344.

Norfolk Coast

→Colour map 4

The jewel in Norfolk's holiday box of tricks is undoubtedly its north coast. From Blakeney to Brancaster, the seemingly limitless sandy beaches, salt marshes, tidal inlets and quiet fishing villages have won the hearts of regular epicurean re-visitors. Beyond Cromer, the crumbling clifftop seaside resort in Norfolk's northeast corner, a really superb coast road wends west towards King's Lynn. It travels through a strange but no longer undiscovered seashore, half land and half sea, made up of shifting sands, shallow tidal inlets and wide stretches of salt marsh alive with waders, seabirds and geese. On the way, it takes in precious, little, one-time ports like Cley-next-the-Sea and Blakeney and the dilapidated dignity of Wells-next-the-Sea, its beach now more than a mile away. Holkham beach nearby must be one of the most beautiful in England, where the Household Cavalry sends its thoroughbreds for rest cures and partially owned by the very grand estate of the Earls of Leicester at Holkham Hall. A little inland, Felbrigg is another extraordinary country house, much more homely, while the Queen's modest retreat at Sandringham also draws in punters during the summer. ➤ *For Sleeping, Eating and other listings, see pages 320-321.*

Ins and outs

Getting there The A149 is the main coast road, about 3 hrs from London at either end. Local buses are run by **First Eastern Counties**, T08456-020121, who operate the Coastliner, T0845-3006116, which runs almost all the way along the A149. Although the Coastliner bus and rail to Cromer make this coast perfectly accessible without a car, many of the more surprising and secluded sights inland can only really be reached with your own transport. Cromer and Sheringham are on a branch line run by **Anglia Railways**, T08700-409090, from Norwich called The Bittern Line. Great Yarmouth is connected to Norwich (30 mins away) by regular stopping trains.

Information Broads Authority Information Centre ⓘ *The Quay, Fen Lane, Beccles, Suffolk T01502-713196, www.broadsauthority.gov.uk, Apr-Oct daily 0900-1700.* **Bungay TIC** ⓘ*T01986-896156.* **Wells TIC** ⓘ*Staithe St, T01328-710885, Mid-Mar to Oct Mon-Sat 1000-1700, Sun 1000-1600.* **Walsingham TIC** ⓘ*Common Pl, T01328- 820510, www.northnorfolk.co.uk, Easter-Oct daily 1000-1630.* **Great Yarmouth TIC** ⓘ *Marine Pde, T01493-842195, www.great-yarmouth.co.uk, also Town Hall T01493- 846345.*

Cromer and around

The first town of any size, more than 30 miles from Great Yarmouth, is faded, sunbleached Cromer. Standing on an impressive cliff, overlooking its long pleasure pier braving the steady ranks of breakers, the place was once quite grand. Dominated by a church with the tallest tower in the county, large Edwardian buildings line the clifftop promenade, but the prevailing atmosphere is forlorn and unloved. The **Cromer Museum** ⓘ *T01263-513543, Mon-Sat 1000-1700, Sun 1400-1700*, in a former fisherman's cottage next to the church has been converted into a sweet little local history museum. A mile or so inland to the south, **Felbrigg Hall** ⓘ *(NT), T01263-837444, Apr-Oct Sat-Wed 1100-1700 (house open from 1300), £6, children £3*, is the well-preserved seat of a Norfolk country gentleman that has been left as it was when given to the National Trust in 1969. Four generations of the Windham family's furniture, books and pictures fill the comfortable rooms almost as if it were still lived in, but its chief glory is architectural. The walled garden has recently been restored, with a thousand doves in the dovecote, and there's a pretty little church some distance away across the park.

The north Norfolk coast road

The A149 coast road from Sheringham to Hunstanton, another 30 miles or so, ranks as one of the most delightful coastal routes in England. The North Sea is never more than a couple of miles away to the north, occasionally visible across gleaming mudflats or glistening salt marsh, sometimes hidden completely behind woods and sand hills, as the road rolls through a string of places called 'next-the-sea' that have long been left high and dry. Cley-next-the-Sea (pronounced *Cly*) is the first, an adorable little town and another that was once an important medieval port. Its church now looks over a meadow instead of a harbour. Potteries, cafés and restaurants line its old High Street and this is also the jumping off point for the long (5 miles) and lovely walk out to **Blakeney Point Nature Reserve**. An easier option is to catch one of the grey seal-spotting boats that leave from Blakeney and Morston quaysides a few miles down the road.

One mile on from Cley, its medieval rival Blakeney also has an interesting **church**, belittling the harbour below, with an extra tower that was once believed to be a lighthouse. Another of the town's sights is the 14th-century brick-arched cellar of a merchant's house called the **Blakeney Guildhall**. The village itself has the calm and unhurried air of a place dependent on the tides and several good overnight stops. Not surprisingly very popular (especially with birdwatchers) is the section of the **Norfolk Coast Path** leading through the salt marshes from here to Wells-next-the-Sea.

Four miles down the road is the old town of **Wells-next-the-Sea**, not next the sea at all now, but nonetheless a fairly dignified, slightly down-at-heel seaside resort with a dinky little harbour, a cluster of rock shops and a sandy beach that's a mile's walk or **narrow-gauge steam train** ride from the quay. ⓘ *Train runs mid-Jul to mid-Sep, then weekends only to end of Sep, daily 1030-2310, every 40 mins to the Pinewoods campsite.* The town itself is not a bad place to poke around for a while, browsing in its small shops on Staithe Street or picking up some chips on the quayside.

Two miles west of Wells stands one of the most stately homes in England, the imposing neo-Palladian bulk of **Holkham Hall** *T01328-710227, www.holkham.co.uk, late-May to Sep Mon-Thu, Sun 1300-1700, £5, children £2.50*. This ponderous yellow brick-built palace, solidly Roman in inspiration, took over 30 years to complete, designed by William Kent who started work in 1734 for Thomas Coke. It's still inhabited today by his descendant the Earl of Leicester and both inside and out remains remarkably little altered since the 1770s, housing a great collection of old masters by the likes of Claude, Poussin and Rubens, powerfully evocative of the tastes of the time. There's also a Bygones Museum, famous pottery shop and a History of Farming exhibition in honour of the family's great mid-19th-century agriculturalist and pioneer of seed improvement, Coke of Norfolk.

A mile's walk towards the sea from one of Holkham Hall's many gates leads through pine woods and sand dunes to **Holkham Beach**, a serious contender for the title of most spectacular beach in England and up there with the best in the world. At low tide, mile upon mile of shining sand stretches towards the horizon, the sea seeming to have vanished from view. It returns faster than a man can run, rolling in to lap or break on the wide expanse of tussocky dunes.

Eight miles south is **Sandringham** ⓘ *T01553-772675, www.sandringham estate.co.uk, Apr-Jul, Aug-Oct daily 1100-1645, £6, concessions £4.50, children £3.50*, the Queen's country house. Edward VII had the place built in 1870 when he was Prince of Wales as a very grand shooting lodge. It still comes across more like a very comfortable late-Victorian home than a royal palace. As well as tours of the house and gardens, there's a museum housing some Royal possessions, ranging from a 1900 Daimler to a half-scale Aston Martin used by Princes Harry and William. Five miles east, 10 miles west of Fakenham, **Houghton Hall** ⓘ *T01485-528569, Mid-Apr to Sep Thu, Sun, bank holidays 1300-1730, £6, children £3*, is a much more grand and beautiful affair, an 18th-century Palladian mansion designed by James Gibbs for Sir Robert Walpole, the first prime minister of Britain from 1721-42. He was the father of Horace, the novelist and Strawberry

Hill arbiter of 18th-century taste, who apparently hated the place but is buried in the church. The church was stripped of its village to make way for the park, the inhabitants being relocated in cottages a short distance away. The estate was later inherited by the first Marquess of Cholmondeley whose descendants still live here.

Great Yarmouth

Great Yarmouth was one of the wealthiest towns in East Anglia during the Middle Ages thanks to its control of the seaport for the inland waterway system leading to Norwich. Substantial sections of its old town walls, built between 1261 and 1400, have been carefully preserved and restored, although like its southern neighbour, much of the rest of the town was flattened by bombing in 1942. It sits on a long sandy promontory south of the harbourside train station that proved vital to the town's prosperity during the Victorian herring boom. This situation is what gives the place its dubious charm, a combination of quiet old riverside quays and full-on seaside resort. Nowadays the town does just well enough for itself thanks to the North Sea oil industry and tourism, drawing in crowds of fun-seekers during the summer.

The crowds usually make straight for **Marine Parade** and the beach. Along its seafront in high season, Great Yarmouth makes a tremendously tacky neon-lit spectacle of itself: horse-drawn carriages ply the prom, fairground rides pump up the volume and its two piers, Britannia and Wellington, buzz with arcade amusements and slot-machine activity. Even in winter, this scene doesn't quite let up entirely.

The calmer 'inland' face of the town is South Quay, with its famous **'rows'**, little alleyways running like a ladder down from the impressive **Church of St Nicholas** with its wide west front and nave, the largest of any parish church in England. Gutted by fire during the war, it was restored in Victorian style in 1962. Three 17th-century houses in **Row 111** ⓘ *Apr-Oct daily, by guided tour only at 1000, 1200, 1400 and 1600, £3, concessions £2, children £1.50*, have been restored by English Heritage, with plasterwork ceilings and oak pannelling. South of the Market Place, where stands the cute little **Fisherman's Hospital**, built as almhouses for old seadogs in 1702, surrounded now by the town's main shopping area, the redundant **quayside** has recently been redeveloped as a heritage attraction, including a new **Nelson Museum** ⓘ *T01493-850698, Apr-Sep Mon-Fri 1000-1700, Sat, Sun 1400-1700, £2, concessions £1.50*, on 26 South Quay, featuring the Ben Burgess Nelson Memorabilia Collection of paintings and things connected to the one-armed and one-eyed naval hero. At no 4 South Quay, the **Elizabethan House** ⓘ *T01493-855746, Apr-Oct Mon-Fri 1000-1700, Sat and Sun 1315-1700, £2.60, concessions £2, family £6,* has been restored to give some idea of life in Tudor times as well as the Conspiracy Room, where the downfall of Charles I was supposedly plotted, and some Victorian kitchens. Tucked behind South Quay is **The Tolhouse Museum** ⓘ *Tolhouse St, T01493-858900, Apr-Oct Mon-Fri 1000-1700, Sat, Sun 1315-1700, £2.50*, one of the oldest civic buildings in the country with medieval cells beneath and displays on crime and punishment down the ages.

Sleeping

The north Norfolk coast road *p319*

L **Morston Hall**, Holt, T01263-741041, www.morstonhall.com. Small manor house with attractive rooms, a well-tended garden and really top-quality restaurant.

A **Blakeney Hotel**, Blakeney, near Holt, T01263-740797, www.blakeney-hotel.co.uk. Straightforward and comfortable modern 3-star hotel overlooking the marshes with friendly and efficient staff.

B **Hoste Arms**, The Green, Burnham Market, T01328-738257. In the middle of Burnham Market, this place thinks a lot of its kitchen and charges accordingly. Fresh local ingredients on the extensive modern British menu. The service tends towards the supercilious but the rooms are spacious and quiet.

B **The White Horse Hotel and Restaurant**, 4 High St, Blakeney, near Holt, T01263-740574, F741303. Ten cosy rooms, some overlooking the harbour, in an old coaching inn, with a highly rated restaurant below in the old stables.

C **Cley Mill**, Cley-next-the-Sea, T01263-740209. A remarkable converted windmill with wonderful marshland views and good food.
C **The King's Arms**, Westgate St, Blakeney, T01263-740341. Snug low-ceilinged old pub in 3 fishermen's cottages with cosy good-value little rooms and tempting fare on offer.
C **Whalebone House of Cley** High St, Cley-next-the-Sea, T01263-740336. Available by advance booking for stays of 2 nights or more. Homespun philosophy, contemporary vegan, vegetarian and organic, small and exclusive.
C **Buckinghamshire Arms**, Blickling, T01263-732133. Comfortable rooms in Blickling Hall's old stable block. Decent bar food too.
C **Saracen's Head**, Wolterton, near Erpingham, T01263-768909. Hard to find but worth the effort, for its food (booking advisable), real ales and cosy rooms with en suite bathrooms.
D **The Hill House**, Happisburgh, T01692-650004. Largish rooms above a characterful freehouse pub (once one of Arthur Conan Doyle's favourite haunts), in a quiet coastal village with great views over the Broads and out to sea.
D **Cambridge Guest House B&B**, East Cliff, Cromer, T01263-512085. Right on the seafront, with comfortable rooms and sea views.

Eating

The north Norfolk coast road *p319*
££££ **The Crown Hotel**, Buttlands, Wells-next-the-Sea, T01553-771483. Does modern British cooking of a high standard and high price in an old converted cottage.
£££ **Fishes**, Market Pl, Burnham Market, T01328- 738588. Know how to prepare their namesake with panache.
£££ **Jolly Sailors**, Brancaster Staithe, T01485-210314. Accomplished restaurant serving local seafood and very good ales in a quiet (although popular) creek-side village. Booking advisable.
£££ **Yetman's**, 37 Norwich Rd, Holt, T01263-713320. Smart restaurant (about £50 a head) serving top-quality local produce backed up by an excellent wine list.
£££ **Seafood Restaurant**, 85 North Quay, Great Yarmouth, T01493-856009. Quite expensive but the only really good seafood restaurant in the town.
££ **Lifeboat Inn**, Ship Lane, Thornham, T01485-512236. Does very good things with local produce at reasonable rates in a rambling 16th-century inn.
££ **Three Horseshoes**, Bridge St, Warham All Saints T01328-710547. Imaginative recipes for local produce at this atmospheric pub.
££ **The Red Lion**, Stiffkey, T01328-830552. Very good fresh local seafood in a hearty and unpretentious atmosphere.
££ **St Peter's Brewery and St Peter's Hall**, St Peter South Elmham, near Bungay, T01986-782322, www.stpetersbrewery.co.uk. Do good local-recipe lunch and dinners on Fri and Sat and lunches on Sun 1100-1800.
£ **Cliff Top Café**, Cliff Rd, Overstrand, T01263-579319. Steve and Les's delightfully eccentric café overlooking the sea and offering wholesome inexpensive food and afternoon cream teas. Open Jun-Sep 0800-1600.

Suffolk

→*Colour map 2*

Suffolk is an odd county. Famously known for being 'sleepy', the arrival in recent years of large numbers of commuters fleeing London house prices has livened up the area considerably. And yet the good people of Suffolk cling fiercely to their rural roots, carefully preserving their wonderful old medieval wool towns and well-ordered little villages. To the south, one of the area's most popular tourist destinations is provided by the wool-enriched splendours of Lavenham, Long Melford and also Clare. The coast though is really the county's pride and joy and an unmissable treat. From Woodbridge, high up the estuary of the river Deben, all the way to the seaside entertainments at Lowestoft, the A12 runs just inland of some of England's most peculiar and memorable coastal towns, villages and scenery. Orford, with its Norman castle, smokehouses and eerie shingle Ness, is the first stop. Next up is Aldeburgh, famous for its classical music festival. Then Southwold, even more classy, coupled with its arty little neighbour Walberswick. ▸▸ *For Sleeping, Eating and other listings, see pages 326-328.*

Ins and outs

Getting there and around **National Express** runs an irregular direct service from Ipswich to London Victoria (2-3 hrs). Travel to Norwich (3 hrs) involves changing at least once and can be arranged through **Traveline,** T08706- 082608. The only direct service to Cambridge (1 hr 40 mins) leaves at 0950. There is no direct service to Stansted airport. **Eastern Counties Buses,** T01473-253734, serve most towns and villages in Essex, Suffolk, Norfolk. **National Express** run services (3 hrs 25 mins) from London Victoria to Bury St Edmunds bus and coach station. Fewer direct services (2 hrs 10 mins). **Anglia Railways,** T08700-409090, www.angliarailways.co.uk, runs the local rail service, with journeys direct from London Liverpool Street (1 hr 15 mins) to Ipswich several times per hour. Travel to Norwich (40 mins) is twice hourly direct and to Cambridge direct (1 hr 15 mins) is every 2 hrs. The local Anglia stopping service runs from Ipswich to Woodbridge, Wickham Market, Saxmunham, Halesworth, Beccles and on to Lowestoft (1 hr 30 mins). There is no direct service to Stansted airport. London Liverpool St to Bury St Edmunds (1 hr 45 mins) with **Anglia Railways.** » *For further details, see also Transport, page 328.*

Information **Bury St Edmunds TIC** ⓘ *Angel Hill, T01284-764667, Easter-Oct Mon-Sat 0930-1730, Sun 1000-1500, Nov-Easter Mon-Fri 1000-1600, Sat 1000-1300.* **Lavenham TIC** ⓘ *Lady St, T01787-248207, Easter-Oct 1000-1645.* **Aldeburgh TIC** ⓘ *152 High St, T01728-453637, Easter-Oct daily 0900-1715.* **Southwold TIC** ⓘ *69 High St, T01502-724729, Easter-Oct daily 1000-1730.* **Woodbridge TIC** ⓘ *Station Buildings, T01394-382240, Easter-Oct Mon-Fri 0900-1730, Sat 0930-1700, Sun 0930-1700, Oct-Easter Mon-Fri 0900-1730, Sat 1000-1700, Sun 1000-1300.*

Bury St Edmunds

Famous for its brewery, sugar beet and medieval abbey, Bury St Edmunds has the happy atmosphere of a town completely at ease with itself. 'Bury' to the locals, it's long been the pride of Suffolk, billing itself as the 'Shrine of a King, Cradle of the Law', reminders of the pilgrim's wealth that the medieval monastery accrued and the hospitality it offered to the barons forcing bad King John's hand to make a gesture towards democracy. Today the town is the focus of the local farming community, pretty much slap bang in the middle of East Anglia.

For visitors, the centre of Bury St Edmunds is **Angel Hill**, an attractive square overlooked by the imposing old abbey gatehouse. Abbeygate Street heads uphill a short distance to the **Buttermarket** and a trio of19th-century buildings. The neoclassical Corn Exchange stands at the top of Abbeygate, inscribed with the motto 'The Earth is the Lord's and the Fulness thereof'. Turning right, into Cornhill, another square with a South African War Memorial in the middle, the third of the town centre's trio of buildings is now the **Bury St Edmund's Art Gallery** ⓘ *T01284-762081, www.burystedmundsartgallery.org, Tue-Sat 1030-1700, £1, concessions £0.50*, the Market Cross, which stages a series of exhibitions by contemporary artists and has a shop selling craftworks and jewellery. On the opposite side of the square is the **Moyse's Hall Museum** ⓘ *T01284-706183. Mon-Fri 1030-1630, Sat and Sun 1100-1600*, a renovated local history museum featuring the Suffolk Regiment gallery in an 800-year-old building.

Back at the top of Abbeygate Street, turning left instead of right, Guildhall Street heads south lined with attractive 17th- and 18th-century houses flanking the Guildhall itself with its 15th-century porch. Just beyond, another left turn leads back downhill along Churchgate Street, originally lined up with the Norman church's high altar. At the foot of the street stands the particularly fine Norman tower, all that remains of the church. Next to it is **St Edmundsbury Cathedral,** T01284-748726, its Gothic tower due for completion in 2004, to look like Bell Harry at Canterbury, and since the completion of Liverpool, the last unfinished cathedral in the country. Its nave was constructed in 1503, as part of the abbey of St Edmund, but ran out of funds. It was added to in the 1950s and again today.

A right turn at the bottom of Churchgate Street leads into Crown Street, past **St Mary's Church** which has a spectacular nave and rare hammer-beam roof, as well as being the last resting place of 'Bloody' Mary Tudor. A left turn beyond the church down Honey Hill leads to the **Manor House Museum** ⓘ *T01284-757072, Wed-Sun 1100-1600*, a Georgian house overlooking the Abbey Gardens behind the town's two most important churches, with a strange collection of antique costumes and all kinds of clocks.

Carrying straight on along Crown Street ends up at the **Greene King Brewery** ⓘ *Westgate St, T01284-714297. Mon-Fri 1300-1600, Sat and Sun 1100-1600, £2, children £1, tours (2 hrs 30 mins) Mon-Fri 1000, 1400, 1900, and on Sat 1100, 1400, £5*, where beer has been brewed continuously since 1799 and where the company runs a small and quite accomplished promotion of its product. Beyond the Brewery, at the end of Westgate, the **Theatre Royal** ⓘ *T01284-769505, www.theatreroyal.org, May-Sep Tue, Thu 1100-1300, 1400-1600, free, guided tours Tue, Thu 1130, 1430, Sat 1130, £2 for members*, is a rare example and one of the best-preserved Georgian playhouses in the country (built in 1819), now owned jointly by Greene King and the National Trust, and still stages some good quality touring productions.

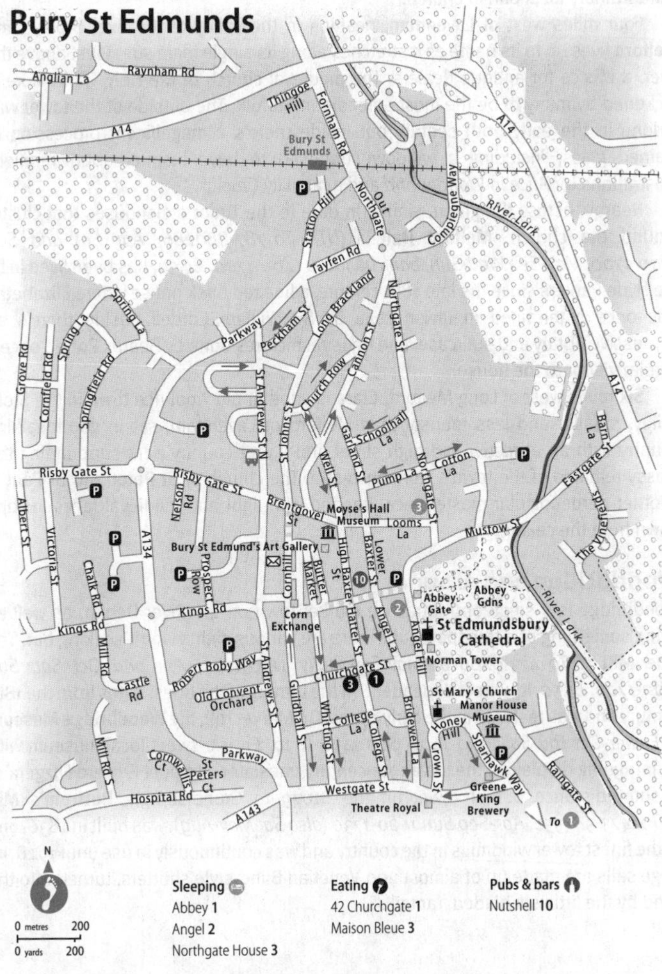

Lavenham, Long Melford and Clare

Ten miles southeast of Bury via the A134 and A1141 is Lavenham, the most visited and picturesque old inland town of Suffolk. Along with Long Melford and Clare, a short distance west in the Stour valley, these three small towns still most perfectly express the wool-rich elegance of the 16th and 17th centuries. Lavenham is the most tourist-orientated, even going so far as to boast a £3 headphone tour of the town available from the local pharmacy as punters wonder at the galleries of local contemporay art, the Al Paca studio, antiques shops and impressive array of half-timbered, plastered and pargeted houses. But the **Market Place** on top of the hill is the real highlight of the town, along with its mini-cathedral of a church, a 20-min walk south. The **Guildhall** ⓘ *(NT), T01787-247646, Mar and Nov Sat and Sun 1100-1600, Apr and Oct Wed-Sun 1100-1700, May-Sep daily 1100-1700, £3*, is a 16th-century timber-framed building on the Market Place with a small local history museum, walled garden and displays on the wool trade including a working loom. **Lavenham church** was built in the 15th century to rival Long Melford's, by the De Veres of Hedingham Castle and the clothiers called Spring. Restrained and serene, the length of the nave, the height of the tower and beautiful chancel arch make it quite an extraordinary local parish church.

Four miles west of Lavenham, nestling in the valley of the river Stour, **Long Melford** lives up to its name as it stretches along its single main street just above the river, a Mecca for antique dealers. The medieval church of the Holy Trinity here is reckoned by many to be the most splendid in Suffolk. The outside of the tower was redone in the early 20th century but inside there's a magnificent procession of stained glass, including a window supposed to have inspired John Tenniel's illustrations for *Alice in Wonderland* and a rare Lily Crucifix.

Nearby, across the green, similar in date to the Tudor almshouses that cluster around the church, **Melford Hall** ⓘ *(NT), T01787-880286, Apr Sat and Sun 1400-1700, May-Sep Wed-Sun, bank holidays 1400-1700, £4.50*, has been lived in by the Hyde Parkers since the late 18th century, a fine red brick house where Elizabeth I was once entertained in lavish style by Sir William Cordell. Inside there's an impressive library and staircase, and unusual pictures done by Beatrix Potter, once a regular visitor to the house.

Six miles west of Long Melford, **Clare** is another old wool-rich town in the Stour valley, smaller and less touristy than Melford or Lavenham, set in good walking country with an attractive old high street and sweet country park surrounding the grassy remains of the town's **Norman castle**. The church of **St Peter and St Paul** is another perpendicular masterpiece, flooded with light and medieval faces looking down from the ceiling.

Woodbridge and around

Woodbridge is a small and attractive market town on the River Deben, as well as being something of a transport hub. There are various sights worth seeking out. The **Tide Mill** ⓘ *T01473-626618, May-Sep daily 1100-1700, Apr and Oct Sat, Sun 1100-1700, £1.50*, its wheel dependent on the turning of the tides, dates from the 18th century and was restored in the early 1970s. On Market Hill, the **Woodbridge Museum** ⓘ *Easter-Oct Thu-Sat 1000-1600, Sun 1430-1630, £1*, is a sweet local museum with an intriguing display on the local 19th-century translator and poet Edward Fitzgerald. A short distance out of town, on the B1079 to Grundisburgh, **Buttrum's Mill** ⓘ *T01473-583352, Apr-Sep Sun 1400-1730 (also Sat May-Aug)*, was built in 1836, one of the finest tower windmills in the country and was continuously in use until 1928. Its huge sails are made up of almost 200 Venetian Blind-style shutters, turned into the wind by the little six-bladed 'fantail'.

However, the best reason for a visit to Woodbridge is to see the extraordinary Anglo-Saxon burial site, 2 miles to the east, on the B1083, at **Sutton Hoo** ⓘ *(NT) T01394-389700, Mid Mar-May and Oct Wed-Sun 1000-1700, Jun-Sep daily 1000-1700, Nov-Feb Sat, Sun 1000-1600, £4, children £2*. The new National Trust visitor centre features a full-scale reconstruction of the famous Anglo-Saxon ship burial c AD 625 with grave treasures on loan from the British Museum, next door to the site of the discovery in 1939. There's a sincere attempt to illuminate the Dark Ages and a little room of finds, although the reconstruction of a grave is a bit spurious.

Aldeburgh

Aldeburgh is a tidy, tranquil little town stretched along the coast with only one main street. Not entirely successfully developed for tourism in the late 19th century, its fortunes later declined with its fishing fleet (remnants of which survive, hauled up onto the shingle beach by winches). Things took a turn for the better thanks to classical music with the success of the **Aldeburgh Festival**, founded by Benjamin Britten in 1948 (now relocated to Snape Maltings nearby). Increasingly, houses in the town and on the seafront are being converted into holiday homes for the rich, and the town's prosperity has become more and more reliant on the tourist industry. The **marina** provides entertainment for yachty types but the place still has a genteel and faintly literary air.

Apart from strolling along the long pebbly beach (safe for swimming), enjoying top-notch fish and chips, or watching the sun rise out of the North Sea at dawn, there's not a whole lot to see or do in Aldeburgh itself, although it serves as an ideal base for explorations of the coast. The new lifeboat station is worth a look, as is **The Moot Hall** ⓘ *Apr-May Sat, Sun 1430-1700, Jun, Sep and Oct daily 1430-1700, Jul and Aug daily 1030-1230, 1430-1700, £0.80*, the timber-framed Tudor building that was once the town hall and stood in the middle of town and is now a museum only a stone's throw from the breakers. It contains some interesting old maps of the area in the council chamber, where Peter Grimes was tried in Britten's opera, and objects downstairs from the Snape Ship Burial, older by some years than Sutton Hoo, as well as other seafaring relics.

Five miles inland from the town, **Snape Maltings** concert halls stand on the beautiful reed-filled marshes on the River Alde. The main **Aldeburgh Music Festival**, T01728-453543, www.aldeburgh.co.uk, is in June, but there are also the Proms in August, and an Early Music festival usually in October, as well as regular concerts throughout the year. The interesting maltings buildings are also busy commercial enterprises, including house and garden shops and a brand new pub, as well as Hepworth sculptures and the Britton-Pears School of Music.

Orford and along the River Ore

Five miles south of Aldeburgh as the crow flies, although 12 by road, Orford is an attractive little red-brick Georgian town, nestling on the banks of the river Alde behind the strange shingle spit of Orford Ness and dominated by the 12th-century keep of **Orford Castle** ⓘ *(EH) T01394-450472, Apr-Sep daily 1000-1800, Oct daily 1000-1700, Nov-Mar Wed-Sun 1000-1600, £4, concessions £3, children £2, family £10*. There are fabulous views over the marshes, river and town to the sea from the top of the castle. The town itself can become very crowded during summer, with Orford Quay a busy little boatyard. From here there are beautiful walks along the River Ore although if you want to see the sea you'll have to cross to **Orford Ness** ⓘ *(NT), T01394-450900, Mar-Jun and Oct Sat only, Jul-Sep Tue-Sat ferries from 1000-1400, last return from the Ness at 1700, £5.70, children £2.85*, on the National Trust ferry. The largest vegetated shingle spit in Europe, it's littered with bizarre structures erected by the Ministry of Defence while it was a secret weapons research establishment from 1913 until the 1970s. Given to the National Trust in 1993, the windswept desolation now provides a unique habitat for numerous rare flowers, mosses and lichens.

North of Aldeburgh

A few miles north of Aldeburgh, along the attractive coastline, is the unmistakable presence of the **Sizewell B nuclear power station**, T01728-653890, www.british-energy.com. The vibrating floor in the turbine hall has to be felt to be believed, which it can be on the 1100 and 1300 tours that are often fully booked. A couple of miles further north is **Dunwich**, the Suffolk coast's famous lost town. In the Middle Ages it was one of the country's busiest seaports and boasted 14 churches, a 70-vessel fishing fleet and a population half as large as the City of London's. The story of its gradual collapse into the hungry sea is enthusiastically told at the **Dunwich Museum** ⓘ *St James St, T01728-648796, Apr-Sep daily 1130-1630, Mar Sat and Sun 1430-1630, Oct daily 1200-1600, free.* It includes a scale model of the town in its heyday as well as references to the many writers and artists – Henry James, Jerome K Jerome, Algernon Swinburne, WG Sebald and William Turner – who were inspired by its peculiar fate. All that can be seen today in the tiny village are the ruins of Greyfriars, a sweet little beach café and some crumbling cliffs. **Dunwich Heath**, a mile south of the village, is a wonderful heather-clad stretch of National Trust coastline (T01728-648505) also with a tearoom and visitor centre.

Southwold and around

Twelve miles north up the coast from Aldeburgh, Southwold is an older, more sedate and picturesque seaside town, its Georgian townscape set back from the sea, perched up on the cliffs and grouped around several spacious greens laid out as firebreaks after a devastating conflagration in the 17th century. The home town of George Orwell, who despaired of its precious gentility, Southwold remains a very dignified resort. Down beside the beach and the row of brightly painted beach huts, the 623-ft pier recently reopened to great acclaim: its telescopes, tearoom and family amusements are just about the town's only concession to seaside tack. Back in town, a charming 20-min walk over the common and across the old iron footbridge brings you to **Walberswick**, even quieter and more rarified, the sort of place favoured by Sunday afternoon watercolourists. This is a very popular spot for crabbing and also a small yacht haven. Its one pub, The Bell, can become impossibly busy on sunny summer afternoons, while in winter the little creekside village has a cosy and somnolent air.

Sleeping

Bury St Edmunds *p322, map p323*

A **Angel Hotel**, Angel Hill, T01284-753926, F714001. Old ivy-clad coaching inn opposite the Abbey gate, done up in a comfortable way, the most central address in Bury, where Dickens wrote some of *The Pickwick Papers*.

B **Northgate House**, 8 Northgate St, T01284-760469, F724008. Smart B&B in the restored Georgian splendour of novelist Norah Loft's old house.

C **Abbey Hotel**, 35 Southgate St, T01284-762020, www.abbeyhotel.co.uk. Reasonable option with spacious accommodation in outbuildings although fairly cramped rooms upstairs.

Lavenham, Long Melford and Clare *p324*

B **Angel Hotel**, Market Pl, Lavenham, T01787-247388, www.lavenham.co.uk/angel. Angel Hotel is the more laid-back option, with its rooms above a loud, cheerful pub on the market place. Tables outside in the square, reasonable food.

C **Brighthouse Farm**, Melford Rd, Lawshall, T01284-830385. Roberta Truin offers a warm welcome at her 18th-century farmhouse B&B with 3-acre garden.

D **Church Farm**, Bradfield Combust, T01284-386333. Good value B&B in an 18th-century house on a working fruit farm.

D **Gannocks House**, Old Rectory Lane, Shimpling, T01284-830499. Good views of the countryside from pleasant B&B on the outskirts of a small village.

Woodbridge and around *p324*

C **Old Rectory**, Campsea Ashe, T01728-746524. Wolsey Lodge with rated restaurant in a Georgian rectory.

C **Melton Hall**, Melton, near Woodbridge, T01394-388138. Lovely B&B in a Georgian house in its own fine grounds.

Aldeburgh *p325*

A **Wentworth Hotel**, at the northern end of the prom in Aldeburgh, T01728-452312, www.wentworth-aldeburgh.com. Has been top of the range for traditional teas and ocean view chintzy rooms since 1920.

A **White Lion Hotel**, Market Cross Pl, Seafront, T01728-452720, www.whitelion.co.uk. Not quite as grand, but has a pleasant oak-panelled restaurant and comfortable rooms, some overlooking the Moot Hall and the beach, at a price.

B **The Brudenell**, The Parade, Aldeburgh, T01728-452071, www.brudenellhotel.co.uk. The town's third high-class hotel is on the southern tip of the town, with a fine terrace for cocktails overlooking the sea and modern, comfortable rooms.

B **Crown and Castle**, Orford, T01394-450205 www.crownandcastlehotel.co.uk. The top place to stay in Orford, a renovated pub with rooms and the award-winning *Trinity* restaurant (with a Michelin 'Bib' gourmand) below and good deals on weekend breaks for 2.

C **Butley Priory Gatehouse**, T01394-450 482. For somewhere really quite special try this secluded and charming B&B in the remains of a medieval priory and run by Frances Cavendish.

C **Ocean House**, 25 Crag Path, Aldeburgh, T01728-452094. Good B&B option right on the beach with pleasant non-smoking family atmosphere. Deservedly immensely popular, so booking well ahead essential, preferably for the seaview room on the first floor.

Self-catering

B **Martello Tower** right at the southern tip of the town, the round Napoleonic fort guarding the approach to Orford Ness with 2 twin rooms, can be booked (well in advance) through the Landmark Trust, T01628-825925.

C **Crabbe Cottage**, Crabbe St, Aldeburgh T01359-270444. Self-catering in a quiet street close to the beach, not for dogs or children but cosy and recently refurbished.

Southwold and around *p326*

A **Swan Hotel**, Market Pl, Southwold, T01502-722186. The local brewers Adnams pretty much have the local hotel accommodation sewn up, and this is their flagship. Quite stuffy but great for a traditional tea.

B **Crown Hotel**, 90 High St, Southwold, T01502-722275. The less expensive or formal Adnams option with a very good brasserie restaurant and bar.

C **Acton Lodge**, 18 South Green, Southwold, T01502-723217. Antiques abound in a solid Victorian B&B overlooking one of the town's attractive greens.

Eating

Bury St Edmunds *p322, map p323*

£££ **42 Churchgate**, 42 Churchgate T01284-764179. £25 a head, 3 course £22 lunch and dinner, in a quaint provincial setting with a good variety of vegetarian options.

£££ **Maison Bleue**, 30 Churchgate St, T01284-760623 (closed Mon and Sun). Some very well-prepared fish dishes in a rustic setting, easily one of the best restaurants in town.

Lavenham, Long Melford & Clare *p324*

£££ **The Great House**, Market Pl, Lavenham, T01787-247431, www.greathouse.co.uk. Does cosy rooms and very good French food in an attractive old house with dining outside in the inner courtyard.

££ **The Beehive**, Horringer, near Ickworth, T01284-753260. Pretty pub on the fringe of Ickworth park with a good menu of ambitious pub grub.

££ **The Star Inn**, Lidgate, T01638-500275. Pub-cum-restaurant that does an innovative Spanish menu that draws people in from quite far afield.

Woodbridge and around *p324*

££ **Captain's Table**, 3 Quay St, Woodbridge, T01394-383145, is a pleasant little local seafood restaurant with tables outside, about £15 a head.

££ **Spice Bar Restaurant and Café**, 17 The Thoroughfare, T01394-382557. Malaysian restaurant with a good reputation.

££ **King's Head**, Gorman's Lane, Laxfield, T01986-798395. Thatched pub doing very good real ales and a hearty homemade menu for lunch and supper.

Aldeburgh *p325*
££ **152**, 152 High St, T01728-454152. A rated Mediterranean menu served up in a mellow environment that's been around some time.
££ **The Lighthouse**, 77 High St, T01728-453377. Another old-timer, a breezy café during the day, serving an accomplished modern British prix fixe menu (3 courses about £17) in the evenings. Booking advisable.
££ **Regatta**, 171 High St, T01728-452011. Another with a seafaring theme, slightly less expensive with very good value 'early bird' deals (£10 for 3 courses) and tasty seafood.

Orford and along the River Ore *p325*
££ **Butley Orford Oysterage**, Market Hill, Orford, T01394-450277. Serves very fresh seafood in simple surroundings, excellent value and often very busy. Lunch only in low season Mon-Thu, Sun)

Southwold and around *p326*
££ **The Anchor Inn**, Walberswick, T01502-722112. Uses fresh local ingredients in a traditional pub as well as freshly cut sandwiches and rolls.
££ **De Cressey's of Walberswick**, Manor House, Main St, Walberswick, T01502-723243. Small country restaurant using local produce, open all day but closed 1700-1900 when the fuller evening menu makes its appearance.
££ **Lord Nelson**, East St, Southwold, T01502-722079. Cosy pub close to the cliffside seafront, with real fires and fresh traditional food.

Pubs, bars and clubs

Bury St Edmunds *p322, map p323*
Nutshell, The Traverse, at the top of Abbeygate St, T01284-764867. Stands out for being the smallest pub in England, with a bar that can only accommodate about 8 people.

Entertainment

Bury St Edmunds *p322, map p323*
Theatre Royal, Westgate St, T01284-769505 www.theatreroyal.org. Guided tours May-Sep, exceptional Georgian theatre hosting some good quality touring productions.

Transport

Taxis

The main taxi rank in Bury St Edmunds is on Cornhill, and there is another at the Railway Station. **A to B Private Hire**, 31 Kingfisher Cres, Reydon, Southwold, T01502-722111. **M&R Cars**, Woodbridge Railway Station, T01394-386661. **B Dobson**, 29 Linden Cl, Aldeburgh, T01728-454116.

Train

There are at least 5 train services daily between Bury St Edmunds and **Ipswich** and **Cambridge** (both 45 mins). **Anglia Railways** have an Anglia Plus One Day Pass. Unlimited travel within the Anglia Plus area for £9 per adult, and up to 4 accompanied children can travel for just £2 each with this fare. You can use One Day Passes at any time at weekends and bank holidays or after 0845 Mon-Fri. You can also take your bicycle on board for a £1 supplement.

Directory

Car hire Europcar in *The Bird In The Hand Motel* Beck Rd, Mildenhall, Bury St Edmunds, T01638- 714747. **Thrifty**, Ames Rover, Dettingen Way, Bury St Edmunds, T01284 700222.

For an explanation of the sleeping and eating price codes used in this guide, see the inside front cover. Other relevant information is provided in the Essentials chapter, page 36.

Essex

→Colour map 2

Essex is the English county that has famously become the butt of many bad jokes, full of 'wannabe' girls and boys ridiculed for their easy virtue, flash consumerism and one-time worship of Margaret Thatcher. To the east of the county, Uttlesford embraces prosperous market like Saffron Walden and Thaxted. In the west, Colchester is a strange mixed-up kind of place on the site of one of the oldest towns in England and close to the countryside on the river Stour that the painter John Constable memorably committed to canvas in the 19th century. Along the coast, Southend-on-Sea has long been many Eastenders' favourite seaside resort, competing with Clacton-on-Sea further north. Nearby, Frinton-on-Sea is famous for being irredeemably middle class, perhaps in reaction to its neighbours. ▸▸ *For Sleeping and Eating, see page 332.*

Ins and outs

Getting there **National Express,** have **bus** services to Great Dunmow but not Saffron Walden. **Traveline** have further information on T0870-6082608. Saffron Walden is about 10 miles south of Cambridge, just east of Junction 9 on the M11, about an hr from London. National Express, T08705-808080, have services from London Victoria coach station to Colchester bus station, via Stansted Airport (3½ hrs). Direct services are less frequent (2½ hrs). **National Express,** T08705-808080, run regular coaches to Southend, Colchester and Harwich from London. By **car,** leave London from the east on the A12. Continue northeast on the A12 through Chelmsford, exit A12 at Beacon End on the outskirts of Colchester (1½ hrs, 60 miles). Southend is about 1 hr's drive from central London down the A13. Other parts of the coast are more easily reached along the A12. Maldon is about 1½ hrs from London, Harwich more like 2 hrs. By **rail,** Saffron Walden is a mile and a half east of Audley End station on the line to Cambridge from London Liverpool St. Hourly trains from London Liverpool St to Colchester Town Station (1 hr). Southend can be reached by train from London Fenchurch St in less than 1 hr. Trains for Burnham-on-Crouch leave from Liverpool St and also take about 1 hr. Clacton-on-Sea and Frinton-on-Sea are on a tiny branch line from Colchester.

Getting around All the towns and villages of Uttlesford are quite tricky to reach by public transport. A car is the most convenient way of getting about beyond them, despite all the slow minor roads and over-congested main routes. To the northeast Colchester links with Ipswich on the A12 and the A14 route to Birmingham and via the M1/M6 to the Midlands and the North of England. It is 45 mins from Stansted Airport and 30 mins from the East Coast ports of Harwich and Felixstowe. Tendring Peninsula is minutes away from Colchester by car, bus or train. Or can be cycled via the Wivenhoe Riverside Path. **Arriva Colchester,** 38 Magdalen St, T01206-764029 is the local bus service.

Information **Saffron Walden TIC** ⓘ *Market Pl, T01799-510444, Apr-Oct Mon-Sat 0930-1730, Nov-Mar Mon-Sat 1000-1700.* **Thaxted Community Information Centre** ⓘ *Clarance House, Watling St, T01371-831641, Apr-Oct Thu-Sun 1100-1600.* **Colchester TIC** ⓘ *1 Queen St, T01206-282920 and Flatford Lane, Flatford, East Bergholt T01206-299460.* **Southend TIC** ⓘ *19 High St, T01702-215120, www.southend.gov.uk, Mon-Sat 0930-1700, Jul and Aug also Sun 1000-1600.* **Clacton TIC** ⓘ *23 Pier Av, T01255-423400, www.essex-sunshine-coast.org.uk, Mid-May-mid-Sep daily 1000-1730, rest of the year: Mon-Sat 1000-1700,*

Saffron Walden, Thaxted and around

Saffron Walden is the prettiest and most lively town in northwest Essex. Originally called Chipping Walden, it became wealthy by growing and trading in saffron crocuses for dyes, medicines and flavouring from the 15th to 18th centuries. The dinky little **Market Square** remains the centre of town, its neoclassical old **Corn Exchange** (now a small library open Sunday only) overlooking market stalls on Tuesday and Saturday and a congested car park the rest of the week. A few steps north of the square, the graceful spire of **St Mary's** (the largest church in Essex) is a useful landmark and Church Street a good place to begin an exploration of the town's warren of gabled, half-timbered streets. On Castle Street is the **Fry Art Gallery** ⓘ *T01799- 513779, www.fryart gallery.org, Easter-Oct Tue, Sat, Sun, bank holidays 1400-1700, free, donations suggested*, with its interesting permanent collection of work by eminent local artists, especially the mid-20th century painters and engravers from Great Bardfield, like John Aldridge, Edward Bawden and Eric Ravilious, as well as Marianne Straub and Tom Deakins. At the top end of the street is the **Saffron Walden Museum** ⓘ *Museum St T01799-510333, Mar-Oct Mon-Sat 1000-1700, Sun and bank holidays 1400-1700, Nov-Feb Mon-Sat 1000-1630, Sun 1400-1630, £1, concessions £0.50, children free*, with the ruins of the town's Norman castle in its grounds. The museum's highlights include a Viking necklace, antique porcelain and the history of saffron as well as plenty to entertain the kids. A five minute walk east, on the Common, is the most extensive ancient **turf maze** in Europe – not much to look at but tricky to complete.

Half a mile or so west of Saffron Walden, **Audley End House** ⓘ *T01799-522399, Apr-Sep Wed-Sun, grounds 1100-1800, house 1200-1700 (last entries 1 hr before closing), Oct Wed-Fri 1100-1600, Sat and Sun 1100-1000, £6.95, concessions £5.95, children £3, grounds only £4, concessions £3, miniature railway, T01799-541354, www.audley-end-railway.co.uk, mainly weekends and Aug*, is a remarkable Jacobean palace set in lovely landscaped grounds and all the more remarkable because a substantial part of the original house was demolished in the early 18th century. It was built in the early 17th century for the Earl of Suffolk, Lord Treasurer to the indigent James I. Charles II later bought it as a convenient base from which to enjoy the Sport of Kings – going to the races at Newmarket. Highlights of the interior are a magnificent carved oak screen in the great hall, an early 18th-century Gothic private chapel, and a string of rooms sumptuously decorated in the 1820s (hung with paintings by Canaletto and Holbein among others). Best of all though is the delicate, painted beauty of the Robert Adam-designed apartments on the ground floor. Friendly well-informed guides are at hand to elucidate each of the rooms' finer points. Also at Audley End, great for the kids, is Lord Braybrooke's **miniature railway** chugging through the woods alongside and over the river Cam for a mile and a half.

Thaxted is another picturesque town but much quieter than Saffron, with its fine crumbly medieval Guildhall at the top of the High Street, a cobbled walkway below its flying-buttressed **church** on the hilltop where Holst was organist. Inside, a chapel commemorates John Ball, one of the leaders of the Peasant's Revolt in 1381, and there's lots of medieval stone carving and a beautiful 15th-century stained-glass window of Adam and Eve. The other prominent landmark is the early 19th-century brick-built **windmill**, T01371-830285. Another five miles to the east, **Finchingfield** is a pretty little village with a duck pond surrounded by teashops and old pubs, also overlooked by a much smaller church at the top of its hill.

Colchester and Constable Country

Colchester is and always was an army town. It confidently lays claim to being 'the oldest town in Britain', thanks to a mention by Pliny in AD 77. First known as Camulodunum, meaning 'fortress of the war god Camulos', in pre-Roman days, it is now the base for battalions of the Parachute Regiment, aka the 'Paras', the shock troops of the British Army. No change there then. Possibly also named after Old King Cole, the merry old soul, Colchester is a strange mix of ancient heritage and urban deprivation. The modern High Street follows the dead straight east-west line of the Roman town laid down over the hill in the first century AD. At its western end, the

Balkerne Gate was the Romans' entrance from the west, and its remains can still be seen. It looks like a bit of old subway, a short clammy tunnel with a curved brick roof giving onto the A134 rushing past just beneath, but it can claim to be the only surviving Roman gateway in Britain. That fact, along with its age and its setting – in the shadow of the striking bulk of the brick-built Victorian watertower, a hilltop landmark affectionately known as Jumbo, and next to the *Hole in the Wall* pub (aptly named) and Mercury Theatre – make the gate quite a strange and unusual sight.

The substantial remains of the **Norman castle**, built on the site of Claudius's temple, using bricks from the Roman town, stand at the top of East Hill, a few hundred yards above the old east gate (long vanished). Inside, the **museum** ⓘ *T01206-282939, Mon-Sat 1000-1700, Sun 1100-1700 (last admission 30 mins before closing), £4, concessions/children £2.70* is particularly strong on Roman finds, and medieval life in the town. Guided tours explore the foundations of Claudius's temple and take in the views from the roof.

Northeast of Colchester, the undeniable charms of Constable Country are milked for all they're worth round Dedham. Several other villages close by, including the painter's birthplace at East Bergholt, are usually appreciably less mobbed than the famous Flatford Mill. Northeast of Colchester, the river Stour (usually pronounced 'store') divides Essex from Suffolk and more famously inspired John Constable, one of Britain's greatest landscape painters. Remarkably enough many of the scenes that he made famous, brooded over by his magnificent skies, are still perfectly recognizable today. Dedham is the centre of 'Constable Country', although his birthplace **East Bergholt** and the charming village of **Stoke-by-Nayland** are in some ways more rewarding places to seek out the picturesque rural idyll of his paintings. The mills of Stratford St Mary also inspired the painter, although today the village is a bit spoiled by the A12. All are in the **Dedham Vale**, a protected AONB ('Area of Outstanding Natural Beauty').

Flatford Mill, the most celebrated of Constable's subjects, featured in several pictures, is reached by road through East Bergholt where the church bells are kept in a spooky old wooden cage in the churchyard, apparently because the devil stole the bell tower. Down by the river, the complex of attractions includes a John Constable Exhibition in thatched **Bridge Cottage** ⓘ *T01206-298260, May-Oct daily 1000-1730, Mar-Apr Wed-Sun 1100-1730, Nov- Feb Wed-Sun 1100-1530 (not Wed-Fri in Jan and Feb), free*. There's also the **Museum of Rural Bygones** in the old Granary, and the **Flatford Visitor Information Centre** ⓘ *T01206-299460, Mar Sat, Sun 1000-1700, Apr-Sep daily 1000-1700, Oct Mon-Fri 1000-1600*. The latter provides details on Dedham Vale and walks in the surrounding countryside. The **Stour Trust** ⓘ *T01206 393680, Wed during summer holidays, and every Sun Easter-Oct 1100-1700, every 30 mins, £2.50*, run silent electric launch river trips.

Southend, Southminster peninsula and Mersea Island

Southend, the closest seaside resort to the capital, has long been London's East End-on-Sea. Considerably more cheerful than some of its competitors on the opposite bank of the Thames estuary, the 7-mile long beach is surprisingly clean and fronts a south-facing esplanade that still retains some of its Regency splendour if none of its dignity, dominated as it is by loud pubs, fast-food joints and noisy amusement arcades. The resort's most famous feature, its more-than- mile-long **pier** ⓘ *Western Esplanade, T01702-215622, Apr-Sep Mon-Fri 0815-2100, Sat and Sun 0815-2200, Oct, Nov, Feb, Mar Mon-Fri 0815-1800, Sat, Sun 0815-2000, Dec and Jan Mon- Fri 0815-1600, Sat and Sun 0815-1800*, is definitely worth the train ride or walk along it right out into the estuary, even if the Pavilion and viewpoints at the end are not the most inspiring destination.

Seven miles north of Southend as the crow flies (considerably longer by road), **Burnham-on-Crouch** is a yachting centre, and makes a good day trip by train from London. Famous for its oysters, it's on the south side of the Southminster peninsula. At the foot of the peninsula is the port of **Maldon** on the river Blackwater, with its triangular-towered church and Washington window: the town was home to the captain of the *Mayflower*. A tidal causeway leads out to **Northey Island** ⓘ *(NT) Northey Cottage, Maldon, T01621-853142, open by appointment with the warden with 24 hrs notice, £1.50*, a top birdwatching site. On the north side of the Blackwater estuary, about 10 miles east of Maldon, Mersea Island is reached over a low causeway liable to flooding at peak tides. The *Company Shed* is a good place to eat them (see Eating and drinking below), looking south across the estuary.

Stour Estuary

Further north, **Wrabness Nature Reserve** provides another wetland habitat worth exploring, near the old estuary villages of Mistley and Manningtree on the river Stour. Mistley Towers were designed by Robert Adam, now standing oddly on the ground bereft of their church in an enclosure beside the main road. At the mouth of the Stour, **Harwich** is an international ferry port with boats to Holland and Germany. A mile east of the main terminals, the Old Town is well worth a look around, sensitively restored since the war. Easily reached from the Main Road railway station, the **Electric Palace Cinema** on King's Quay Street was purpose-built in 1911 and still shows films.

Sleeping

Saffron Walden, Thaxted and around *p329*

A **The Starr**, Market Pl, Great Dunmow, T01371-874321, www.the-starr.co.uk. Restaurant with rooms where TV-chef Jamie Oliver started. The 8 rooms are well furnished.

C **The Plough Inn**, Sampford Rd, Radwinter, 5 miles east of Saffron Walden, T01799-599222. Great local with fairly basic rooms (from £25 per person) and very good home-made pub food, real ales and some unusual wines.

Colchester and Constable Country *p330*

B-C **George Hotel**, High St, Colchester, T01206-578494, F761732. If an overnight stop in Colchester is necessary this is an honest-to-goodness revamped coaching inn on the High St with a lively bar.

Southend, Southminster peninsula and Mersea Island *p331*

C **Olde White Harte**, The Quay, Burnham-on-Crouch, T01621-782106. Very busy in Burnham Week when the world's yachties turn up to drink beside their boats, but otherwise a pleasant spot right on the water.

C **Cap and Feathers**, 8 South St, Tillingham, near Southminster, T01621-779212. Attractive and cosy clapperboard pub with its own smokehouse, a no-smoking room, and some very good real ales. Three double rooms upstairs.

Eating

Saffron Walden, Thaxted and around *p329*

£££ **The Pink Geranium**, Station Rd, Melbourn, near Royston, T01763-260215. Once Prince Charles' favourite restaurant, doing upmarket accomplished French-influence food.

£££ **The Restaurant**, 2 Church St, Saffron Walden, T01799-526444. Organic dining in the evenings – possibly the best in Saffron.

Colchester and Constable Country *p330*

£££ **Baumann's Brasserie**, Coggeshall, 4-6 Stoneham St, T01376-561453. Expensive and ambitious (£40 a head at least) but distinctly a cut above most of the competition.

£££ **Le Talbooth**, Dedham, T01206-323150. A posh option in a low, beamed room next to the river but within earshot of the A12.

££ **Lemon Tree**, 48 St John's St, Colchester, T01206-767337. A modern British restaurant with atmosphere thanks to some Roman walls.

Southend, Southminster peninsula and Mersea Island *p331*

£££ **Pipe of Port**, 84 High St, Southend, T01702-614606. Straightforward bistro food and probably the best on offer.

£££ **Blue Strawberry**, Hatfield Peverel, T01245-381333. About £35 a head for a sophisticated menu in a cosy cottage setting.

££ **Company Shed**, West Mersea, open shop hrs (not Mon) 0900-1700, Sun 1000-1700, bring your own bread and wine, last orders for eating taken at 1600.

The Midlands

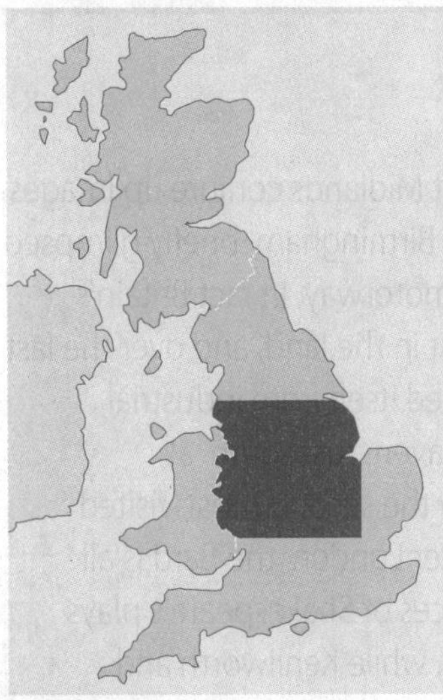

Introduction

For many British people the West Midlands conjure up images of an anonymous sprawl around Birmingham, briefly glimpsed to little advantage from the M6 motorway. In fact Britain's second city is one of the greenest in the land, and over the last couple of decades has transformed itself from industrial wasteland into a consumerist heaven. Just south, at Stratford-upon-Avon, apparently the second most-visited tourist destination in England after London, the Bard is all around but theatrical performances of Shakespeare's plays really do reach new heights here, while Kenilworth and Warwick close by, are both dominated by their castles. To the west, Worcestershire nestles on the banks of the river Severn, embracing the picture-postcard Malvern Hills. Herefordshire welcomes in the river Wye from Wales, arguably the most beautiful river in the country, passing through delightful countryside from the old books' home at Hay-on-Wye, dainty little Ross-on-Wye and the spooky Forest of Dean on its way to the Severn Estuary and the Bristol Channel. To the north, Shrewsbury is Shropshire's county town, the first in a string of attractive towns – Church Stretton, Ludlow, Bishops Castle – along the high border with Wales.

The East Midlands don't have much of a reputation. Stretching from Leicester in the west to Lincoln in the east, they suffer in comparison to their neighbours. Here there's none of the kudos of Cambridge, the northern pride of Yorkshire, or even the sheer balls of the West Midlands with their Brummies and Herefordshire bulls. Instead, unassuming and overlooked, the East Midlands reward visitors with a few world-class sights, some vibrant forward-looking towns and an old-fashioned attitude in the countryside.

★ Don't miss...

1. Check out a gem of a fine art collection at the **Barber Institute** in Birmingham before heading into the Gas Street Basin for a cocktail, page 340.
2. Taste some of the finest cuisine this side of the Welsh border in **Ludlow** after looking around its old castle, page 367.
3. Ask yourself in **Stratford-upon-Avon** whether Shakespeare knew he was going to be a household name in four hundred years' time, and then see what all the fuss has been about, page 345.
4. Explore the stratosphere at the **National Space Centre** outside Leicester and come down to earth for a curry on the Golden Mile, page 377.
5. Walk through the **Exchequer Gate** in Lincoln and experience a sight that's been stopping people in their tracks for centuries: the west front of the cathedral, page 393.

Birmingham

→ Colour map 2

Perhaps because for too many years Birmingham has been the butt of many a comedian's joke about smoking chimneys and heavy metal music, people are surprised to learn that it is Britain's second city. It's easy to be snobbish about Birmingham – it's easy to be a Birmophobe or sniffy about where it gets the money to maintain such splendid facilities as Birmingham City Museum and Art Gallery and the Barber Institute, and many people are. But ironically, heavy metal in the form of iron, steel and gold and silver has played a very important part in the town's development and still does. Birmingham, or Brummagem as it is known, is a world-famous jewellery quarter and as for the smoking chimneys, it's worth remembering that Birmingham has more trees than people, over a million. It's also probably Britain's most racially integrated city, with Chinese, Sikh, Moslem, Hindu, Irish, Jewish and Afro-Caribbean communities. Since the 1970s when the mighty Spaghetti Junction made Brum synonymous with pollution, the city has really cleaned up its act, in more ways than one. ➡ *For Sleeping, Eating and other listings, see pages 341-344.*

Ins and outs

Getting there Birmingham **airport** is the second busiest airport in the UK outside London with many of the low-cost airlines including it on their itinerary. It's handy for the NEC and Birmingham International Train Station where you can catch a train every 30 mins for the centre of town and New St Station. Long-term parking is available at the airport. Birmingham New Street station has a strong claim to be the most central **train** station in the country. Intercity trains run from London Euston every 30 mins everyday, as well as slower, cheaper and more picturesque services. Being partly famous as the meeting point of 3 **motorways**, it's no surprise that you can get to Birmingham by car very easily. From the south take either the M40 from London via Oxford or the M5 from Bristol. From the north take the M6. From the West take the M54 past Wolverhampton where it joins the M6 at Junction 10a. Birmingham city centre is well served with around 20 long-stay multi-storey **car parks**. Street parking is relatively easy and after 1800 free in many spots. ➡ *For further details, see Transport, page 344.*

Getting around Buses are one of the best ways to see and get around Birmingham, with day savers available for £2.50 which allow unlimited travel on all **Travel West Midlands** buses or £4 for 4 people and unlimited travel. The 50 bus is particularly good: it starts behind one of the main shopping areas, Corporation Street, will take you through a cool nightclub area (Digbeth), then on to Balsall Heath where you will find some of the best curries in the country, through Moseley with its fantastic hippy pubs and Tolkein connections and eventually to the Maypole, which is in spitting distance of the Lickey Hills. For more details there's a good website at www.travelwm.co.uk or call traveline on T0870-6082608. There's also the Travel Shop in the Pavilions Shopping Arcade (opening Mon-Sat 0830 –1700). Meanwhile, **CENTRO**, T0121-200 2700, operate a good train service from New Street for the north of the City, for trips to the Black Country and the wonderful Walsall Art Gallery, while **Chiltern Railways**, run from the city centre's other station, Snow Hill, to Stratford, Warwick, and Leamington.

Information There are 4 large **tourist offices**, all managed by **Marketing Birmingham** ⓘ *Level 2 Millennium Point, Curzon St, Birmingham, B4 7XG, T0121 202 5115. 0930-1730 Mon-Sat.* There is also the **Ticket Shop and Tourism Centre** ⓘ *City Arcade, T0121-643 2514, Mon-Sat 9.30-5.30*; the **International Conference Centre Office** ⓘ *Centenary Sq, off Broad St, T0121-780 4321, 0930-1730 Mon-Sat, 24 hour automated phone for accomodation information*; and the **Colmore Row Travel Centre** ⓘ *130 Colmore Row, T0121-693 6300, 0930-1730, Mon-Sat.*

Sights

Victoria Square and around

For a fresh-out-of New Street introduction to the city and all it has to offer walk up recently pedestrianized New Street to Victoria Square, where there is a tourist office and one of the largest fountains in Europe featuring a rampant naked lady and about 3000 gallons of water. Nicknamed **'The Floozie in the Jacuzzi'**, all Brummies know where this is and the square affords great views of **The Council House** (guided tours on T0121-303 2759), a fine building which features a proud mural of Britannia rewarding the manufacturers of Birmingham. On the other side of the square stands **The Town Hall**, a magnificent replica of the Temple of Castor and Pollux in Rome. It's a building rich in musical heritage, having played host to musos as diverse as Elgar and The Beatles.

Round the corner from The Council House is **Birmingham Museum and Art Gallery**. With one of the world's finest collections of Pre-Raphaelite art, the roomy but gloomy galleries allow you to relive DG Rossetti's obsession with the opium-addled Miss Siddall, the foremost Pre-Raphaelite model. Other Pre-Raphaelite highlights include Edward Burne-Jones' mighty *Star of Bethlehem*, one of the largest paintings you will see anywhere and his tapestry collaborations with Arts and Crafts head honcho William Morris.

True to the city's manufacturing heritage, there's also a terrific **Applied Arts Collection** featuring a treasure trove of enough ornamental gold and silver to fuel a dozen heist movies. Other unexpected delights include Jacob Epstein's brilliant sculpture *Lucifer* presiding magisterially over the Museum Shop and the Edwardian Tearoom. The **Waterhall Gallery** ⓘ *Chamberlain Sq, T0121-303 2834, www.bmag.co.uk, Mon-Thu, 1000- 1700, Fri 1030-1700, Sat 1000-1700, Sun 1230-1700, free, contributions welcomed*, contains the modern art collection.

Passing through Chamberlain Square with the **Central Library** on the right (a monstrosity likened by some to a bus shelter) and crossing the inappropriately named Paradise Circus you come to **Centenary Square** with the **International Conference Centre** (T0121-200 2000, www.necgroup.co.uk) and **Symphony Hall** (see Entertainment section) adjoining the top end of **Broad Street**.

While the City of Birmingham Symphony Orchestra (CBSO), transformed by Simon Rattle into one of the top 10 orchestras in the world and housed in Symphony Hall, offers supremely civilized entertainment, Broad St marks the beginning of around a mile of bars, clubs and night spots which have the reputation for being the most drunken and disorderly in the city.

Brindleyplace

Passing swiftly through the ICC atrium, avoiding the guided tour of what after all is just a very big conference centre, you emerge into an area known as **Wharfside** which is the entrance to one of the city's smartest new canalside developments. Brindleyplace even has its own visitor centre (T0121-6436866, www.brindleyplace.com) and though primarily a destination for Brum's glitterati, there's also the Norman Foster-designed **National SeaLife Centre** ⓘ *The Waters Edge, Brindleyplace, T0121-6436777, www.sealife.co.uk, daily from 1000-1600 Mon-Thu, 1000-1500 Fri and Sat.* This is the kind of place kids love, especially the 360 degree tank where sharks appear to surround you.

For more grown-up tastes, across the square from SeaLife is **The Ikon Gallery** ⓘ *1 Oozell's Sq, T0121-2480708, Tue-Sun 1100-1800, free*, which has long enjoyed – some say without justification – the reputation as a leading European contemporary art gallery. What isn't disputed is that it's one of the best restorations of a 19th-century school building in the country, with a great tapas bar and really wonderful exhibition space. It's just a pity they can't find any good art to put in it, in stark contrast to the amazing Walsall Art Gallery).

Gas Street Basin and the Canals

Brindleyplace has sensitively restored an area that had been synonymous with industrial grime for hundreds of years – it was the 19th-century equivalent of the spaghetti junction, whereby coal from the mines in the Black Country was transported to and through Birmingham. The hub of Brum's canal world is the superbly preserved

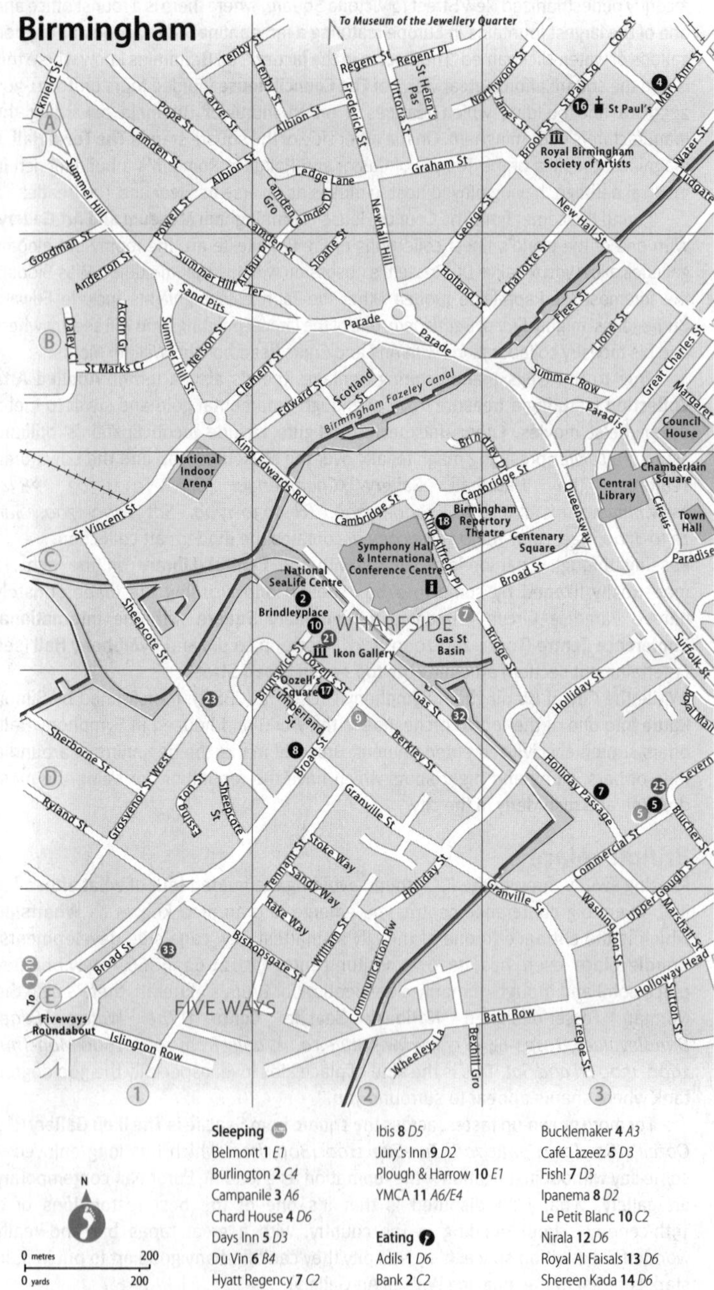

Gas Street Basin, a kind of living museum a few minutes' walk from Brindleyplace by the side of the canal where you can get a taste of what life was like on the waterways. If you're a real barge-spotter the actual **museum** or **visitors' centre** is operated by British Waterways. ⓘ *42a Gas St Basin, T0121-6326845, www.britishwaterways.co.uk. Wed-Sun 1000-1800.*

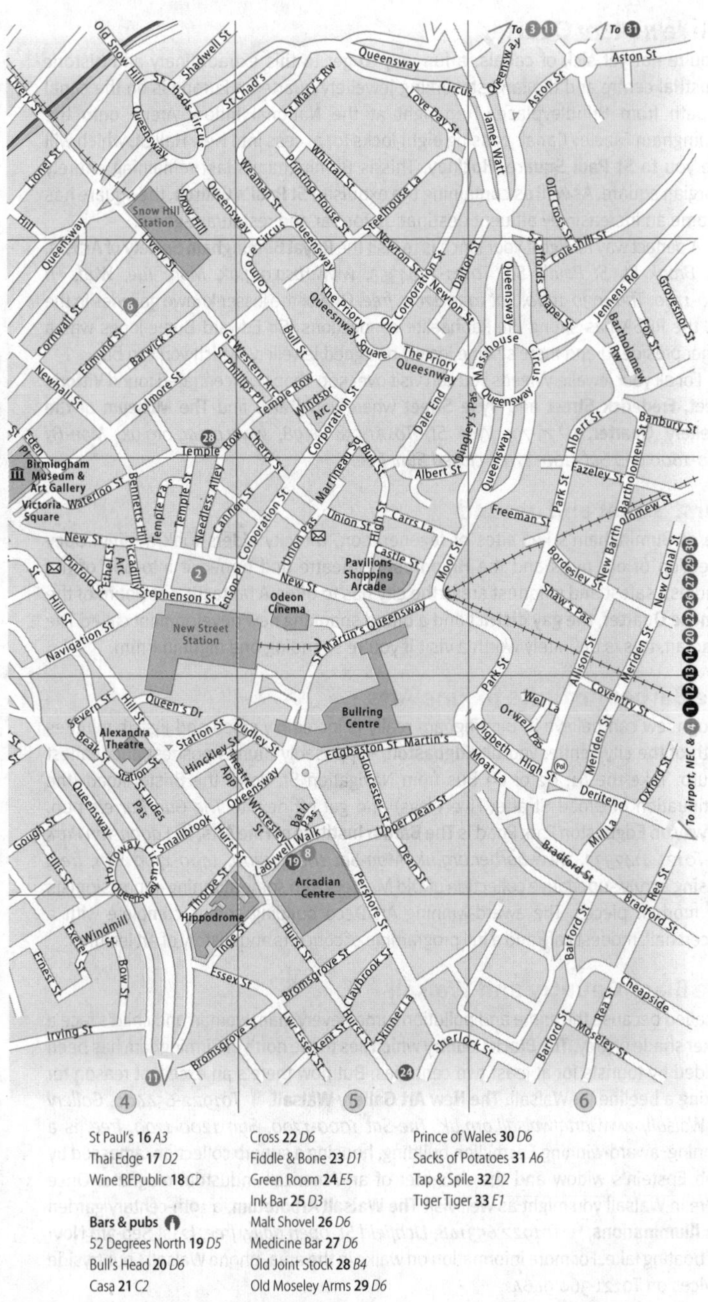

St Paul's **16** *A3*
Thai Edge **17** *D2*
Wine REPublic **18** *C2*

Bars & pubs
52 Degrees North **19** *D5*
Bull's Head **20** *D6*
Casa **21** *C2*
Cross **22** *D6*
Fiddle & Bone **23** *D1*
Green Room **24** *E5*
Ink Bar **25** *D3*
Malt Shovel **26** *D6*
Medicine Bar **27** *D6*
Old Joint Stock **28** *B4*
Old Moseley Arms **29** *D6*
Prince of Wales **30** *D6*
Sacks of Potatoes **31** *A6*
Tap & Spile **32** *D2*
Tiger Tiger **33** *E1*

Also worth a visit is **The Canal Shop** which provides cheap canal tours through **Second City Canal Cruises Limited**, ⓘ *T0121-2369811/6437700. 0800-2000 daily and 24hr answerphone. Tours 1hr £3.00, 30 mins £2.00, OAP/concessions/children 1hr £2.00, 30 mins £1.50.* For posher boats with bars on them you could try **Sherborne Wharf Heritage Narrowboats.** ⓘ *Sherborne St, T0121-4555153. 0900-1730.*

The Jewellery Quarter

If you're not yet sick of canals, a fun way to get to this extraordinary and historic industrial centre and the largest working jewellery quarter in Europe is on the canal towpath from Brindleyplace. Turn right at the National Indoor Arena onto the Birmingham Fazeley Canal, passing eight locks for access into New Hall St, which will take you to **St Paul Square, Hockley**. This is Birmingham's last remaining entirely Georgian square. As well as containing the exquisite **St Paul's Church**, the square has become an increasingly affluent destination for bar and restaurant-goers.

A perfect way to digest your lunch is to visit the **Royal Birmingham Society of Artists**, ⓘ *4 Brook St, St Paul's Sq, T0121-2364353, www.rbsa.org.uk, Mon, Tue, Wed, Fri 1030-1730, Thu 1030-1900, Sat 1030-1700, free.* One of the lesser-known galleries in the city, the RBSA has strong Pre-Raphaelite connections (Sir Edward Burne-Jones was a former president) and there's some locally designed jewellery, which you can buy.

For all your jewellery needs you can visit over 500 shops concentrated round **Vittoria Street, Frederick Street** and **Vyse Street** where you'll also find **The Museum of the Jewellery Quarter**, ⓘ *75-79, Vyse St, T0121-554 3598, www.bmag.org.uk, Mon-Fri 1000-1600 and Sat 1100- 1700, closed Sun, free.*

Hurst Street and around

One of Birmingham's key sites of regeneration, the city elders took a fairly ropey collection of old pubs and the Hippodrome theatre and turned it into one of the trendiest, safest and smartest areas the city has to offer. A fantastic pot-pourri of the **Chinese Quarter, the gay district** and a brand spanking new development called The Arcadian, this is definitely worth a visit if you're spending one night in Brum.

The Barber Institute of Fine Arts

Though few can believe it, Birmingham really is incredibly green and just 15 minutes south of the city centre, you hit **Edgbaston**, supposedly Brum's poshest and leafiest suburb. Take the 61, 62 or 63 Bus from Navigation St. down the Bristol Road (the continuation of Broad St after Five Ways) and get off next to *The Gun Barrels* pub. Halfway up Edgbaston Park Road is **The Barber Institute of Fine Arts**, ⓘ *Edgbaston Park Rd, T0121-4147333, www.barber.org.uk, Mon-Sat 1000- 1700, 1400-1700 Sun, free,* housing a truly superlative collection of Old Masters with some stunning impressionists and modern pieces. The award-winning Art Deco building comes complete with a concert hall, modest café and a full programme of concerts and History of Art lectures.

The Black Country and Walsall

So called because the grime and pollution turned every man, woman and child's face a darker shade of grey, **The Black Country** which lies to the north of Birmingham has been avoided by tourists for at least two centuries. But now there's an excellent reason for making a beeline for Walsall. **The New Art Gallery Walsall**, ⓘ *T01922-654400, Gallery Sq, Walsall, www.artatwalsall.org.uk, Tue-Sat 1000-1700, Sun 1200-1700, free,* is a stunning, award-winning £21million building, housing a superb collection, amassed by Jacob Epstein's widow and the daughter of an American industrial magnate. Once you're in Walsall you might as well visit **The Walsall Arboretum**, a 19th-century garden with **Illuminations**, ⓘ *T01922 653148, Lichfield St, open daily, free,* (21st Sep-3rd Nov) and boating lake. For more information on walks in the area, phone Walsall Countryside Services on T0121-360 9464.

Sleeping

Birmingham *p336, map p338*
Hagley Rd beyond Five Ways is awash with cheap and not-so-cheap hotels and B&Bs. The Birmingham Convention Bureau offers a free hotel booking service on T0121-7804321

L-A **The Hyatt Regency**, 2 Bridge St, T0121-6431234. The flashest hotel right next to the ICC, so it's popular with conference delegates. It's also got a sauna, steam room, gym and swimming pool.

A **The Burlington Hotel**, 6 Burlington Arcade, 126 New St, T0121-6439191. A consummately posh experience with fine dining in the Berlioz bar and restaurant: perhaps Brum's top hotel.

A **Hotel Du Vin**, Church St, T0121-2360559. A fantastic conversion of the old eye hospital, this place is one of the city's finest hotels. The wine cellar is unmatched by anywhere else in the region and the brasserie is wonderful. It's not as pretentious as the *The Burlington* and it looks superb both on the outside and inside.

A **Plough and Harrow**, 135 Hagley Rd, T0121-4544111. The poshest pub you're ever likely to spend the night in, without things like swimming pools or saunas, but a beautiful, peaceful garden instead.

B-C **Days Inn**, 160 Wharfside St, The Mailbox, T0121-6439344. A perfectly serviceable if somewhat utilitarian place, ideally situated for expensive shopping sprees in The Mailbox or a night out on Broad St.

C **Ibis**, Ladywell Walk, T0121-6226010. Like other Ibis hotels it's short on décor but long on convenience, especially if you want to gorge yourself on Chinese food; it's in the heart of Brum's Chinatown.

C **The Campanile**, Chester St, Aston, T0121-3593330. A bit too close to the Aston Expressway, this is nevertheless a very con- veniently located hotel with views of the canal.

C **Jury's Inn**, Broad St, T0121-6069000. A huge tower-block-like structure, right round the corner from the thriving melee of Broad St.

D **Belmont Hotel**, 419 Hagley Rd, T0121-4291663. A presentable bed and breakfast.

D-E **Chard House**, 289 Mackadown Lane, T0121-7852145. A friendly, clean guesthouse, with a family atmosphere but also very quiet for those who need a bit of peace to recover from the hustle and bustle of Brum's nightlife.

E **YMCA**, 200 Bumbury Rd, Northfield, T0121-4756218. There's a gym, squash courts and sauna which you have to pay for separately.

F **YMCA**, 300 Reservoir Rd, Erdington, T0121-3731937. Despite being in a fairly unsalubrious area this YMCA is clean and simple. It's also the closest you're likely to get to central Brum for this price.

Eating

Birmingham *p336, map p338*
£££ **Bank**, 4 Brindleyplace, T0121-633 7001. 'Liberated French cuisine', according to the menu, with a great view of the canals and an altogether upmarket dining experience.

£££ **Le Petit Blanc**, 9 Brindleyplace, T0121-6337333. Raymond Blanc's Brummie Brasserie, it's raised the stakes for French cuisine in the city.

££ **The Bucklemaker**, 30 Mary Ann St, St Paul's Sq, T0121-2002515. A bizarre mixture of tapas and traditional English cuisine in a truly atmospheric converted silversmith's cellar.

££ **Café Lazeez**, 116 Wharfside St, The Mailbox, T0121-6437979. Although another chain, it has a truly original twist on Indian food – quite an achievement in Balti city, though don't expect it to be as cheap.

££ **Fish!**, Wharfside St, The Mailbox, T0121-6321212. If you don't yet know this superior chain, then this is a great introduction. An elegant, airy, slimline interior, the staff are good and the food better.

££ **Ipanema**, 60 Broad St, T0121-6435577. Novel Brazilian restaurant and bar, with crazy dancing, another welcome change from the tack-fest that is Broad St.

For an explanation of the sleeping and eating price codes used in this guide, see the inside front cover. Other relevant information is provided in the Essentials chapter, page 36.

££ Leftbank, 79 Broad St, T0121- 6434464. A posh English cuisine restaurant on Broad St – wonders will never cease.
££ St Paul's, St Paul's Sq, T0121-6051001. It's chic, bijou and rivals *Bank* as Brum's smartest restaurant with a menu of the ubiquitous 'modern English cuisine'.
££ Thai Edge, 7 Oozell's Sq, Brindleyplace, T0121-6433993. An excellent Thai restaurant with stunning décor and reasonably priced.
££ Wine REPublic, Centenary Sq, T0121-6446464. The Rep Theatre's in-house bar, the wine selection's not bad and the food's unsurprising but alright, especially if you're planning a night at the theatre.

The Balti Triangle

The large Pakistani and Kashmiri communities in Birmingham invented this dish in the mid 70s and there are still many of the café-style restaurants with glass-topped tables that appeal to Balti purists dotted around this slightly down-at-heel but still perfectly safe area. The easiest way to get to the Balti Triangle is to go down The Moseley Rd (A435) or The Stratford Rd (A34). Both will take you to Sparkbrook and Balsall Heath where the best Balti houses are to be found, many of them on Ladypool Rd dubbed 'the corridor of curry'.
££ Adils, 148 Stoney Lane, T0121-4490335. Allegedly this is where it all started – it's one of the oldest balti houses and possibly the best. Beware of the green chilli bhaji starter – not for the faint-hearted.
£ Nirala, 530 Moseley Rd, T0121-4407600. Don't be put off by the flock wallpaper and smoky windows – if you're a connoisseur of balti, this is quite unbeatable for flavour.
£ Royal Al Faisals, 136-140 Stoney Lane, T0121-4495695. Another early arrival on the balti scene, it made its name by pioneering the 'family' naan which in one instance (the 747) could almost accommodate an entire family. Now it's famed for its Balti Buffet where you can eat as much as you like for £6.95.
£ Shereen Kada, 543 Moseley Rd, T0121-4404641. If you're into sugar overloads then this is the place for you, as its reputation as an Indian sweet centre is unparalleled. The baltis are pretty good too, and prepared in front of you.

Pubs, bars and clubs

Birmingham *p336, map p338*
52 Degrees North, The Arcadian Centre, T0121-6225250. There's a permanent hubbub around that you'd expect of a trend-setting bar which is the undisputed market-leader round these parts. Louche décor, glam types and pricey drinks all come as standard.
The Bull's Head, St Mary's Row, Moseley, T0121-7020931. An offshoot of the *Medicine Bar* in Digbeth and in keeping with the laid-back atmosphere established there, lots of banging tunes and cool punters.
Casa, Brindleyplace, T0121-6333049. It may be part of a chain, but compared to other bars in Brindleyplace it's cooler and looks better.
The Cross, Alcester Rd, T0121-4494445. Moseley's movers and shakers flock to what is a stylish addition to the Moseley pub scene, with a great space out front for that boulevardier feeling.
Fiddle and Bone, 4 Sheepcote St, T0121-2002233. A good canal pub with lots of live music.
The Green Room, Hurst St, T0121-6054343. It's opposite the Hippodrome Theatre (hence the name), is very camp and a good starting off point (though not too full-on) for sampling Brum's gay scene.
Ink Bar, 117 Wharfside St, T0121-6321321. Probably the trendiest bar the Mailbox has to offer, with an interior like a sci-fi set and a 'salon privé' for special events.
The Malt Shovel, 20 Brighton Rd, T0121-4422561. The former local of the band UB40 – they still pop in from time to time.
Medicine Bar, The Custard Factory, Gibb St, T0121-6936333. Along with *52 Degrees North* this place has a claim to be the trendiest bar in town, but it's more grunge than glam.

The origins of Balti are swathed in mystery – but what is known is that Balti simply means 'bucket' and refers to the flat-bottomed wok-like dish in which this distinctive recipe is cooked over an enormous flame

The Old Joint Stock, 4 Temple Rd West, T0121-2001892. You can tell from the spectacular interior that this place used to be something very grand – in fact it was the Birmingham Stock Exchange. Worth a visit, if only to see the domed ceiling.
The Old Moseley Arms, 53 Tindall St, T0121-440 1954. Despite being a down-home traditional boozer with excellent beer, this place is becoming a trendy young thing hang-out.
The Prince of Wales, 118 Alcester Rd, Moseley, T0121-4494198. Trendy bars come and go, but the *PoW* has remained unchanged for decades and is one of the least pretentious pubs you're likely to find anywhere. Highly recommended.
The Sacks of Potatoes, 10 Gosta Green, Aston Triangle, T0121-5035811. Though the surrounding area's a bit grim, this is definitely one of the highlights with a peerless pint and friendly landlord.
The Tap and Spile, Gas St, T0121-6325602. A real old-fashioned boozer with an older crowd, but a superlative pint.
Tiger Tiger, Broad St, T0121- 6439722. It's a restaurant, a boozer and a nightclub that manages to lift itself above the norm by attracting a more discriminating crowd.

Clubs

See also Live music, below
The Birmingham Academy, Dale End, T0121-2623000.This place used to be home to Brum's early rappers and toasters when it was the *Hummingbird*. Now it's more indie as well as being one of the best live music venues in the city, with more character than the National Indoor Arena or National Exhibition Centre.
Code, Heath Mill Lane, Digbeth, T0121-6932633. The closest Brum gets to a super-club with all the young raveaholics that you'd expect. God's Kitchen on Fridays is the night to go for.
DV8, 16 Kent St, T0121-6666366. The talk of the town, as it's the newest and trendiest gay club in a quarter packed with camp.
Liberty's, 184 Hagley Rd, Edgbaston, T0121-4544444. With ultra-glam and gang-star Moneypenny's a regular weekly feature on a Saturday night, there's an air of dangerous cool and sophistication about this place.
Moseley Dance Centre, 572-574 Alcester Rd, Moseley, T0121-4490779. A delightful throwback to the days of the school disco but without the annoying music. They do have regular 70s nights, though.

Entertainment

Birmingham *p336, map p338*

Live music

The Barber Institute, Edgbaston Park Rd, T0121-4147333. It has a fantastic gallery, and concert hall which specializes in chamber music and small ensembles.
Birmingham Academy, Dale End, T0121-2623000. A whole lot cooler than either the NIA or NEC, the Academy is smaller but with bags of musical heritage, it manages to attract some excellent acts.
The Jam House, 3 St Paul's Sq, T0121-2003030, has rhythm and blues acts mainly throughout the week with the don himself – Jools Holland – who co-owns the joint making the odd appearance.
NEC, M42, Junction 6, T0121-7673888. For those who prefer their rock large, loud and epic, here's one of the original stadia for which the term stadium rock was invented. Not surprisingly, it's a personality-free zone.
NIA, King Edward Rd, T0121-6446011. It's owned by the same people who own the NEC, so it's got the same sort of character (ie none), but you can catch the B list acts there.
Symphony Hall, Broad St, T0121-2002000. Does what it says on the tin – one of the best, most acoustically perfect, purpose-built venues in the country, the regular home of the CBSO and almost worth a visit even without live music. But the real thing is an incomparable experience.

Cinemas

IMAX Theatre, Millennium Point, Curzon St Bookings, T0121-2022222. Attached to the new Science Museum – 'the Thinktank', this enormous screen is more novelty than genuine contribution to the cinema scene in Brum.
Mac (Midlands Arts Centre), Cannon Hill Park, T0121-4403838. An intelligently programmed *and* cheap independent cinema.
Odeon, New St, T0121-6436103.

UGC, Arcadian Centre, Hurst St, Ladywell Walk, T08701-555177; also at FiveWays Leisure Park, Broad St, T0121-6430631, T0870-9070723.
Warner Village Cinemas, StarCity, 100 Watson Rd, Nechells T0870-2406020.

Theatres

Alexandra Theatre, Station St, T0870-6077544. West End hits as well as local fare.
Birmingham Repertory Theatre, Centenary Sq, Broad St, T0121- 2364455, www.birmingham-rep.co.uk A good programme of ancient and modern, this place offers the best, most thought-provoking theatre outside Stratford.
The Hippodrome, Hurst St, T0870-7305555. The beneficiary of a million pound refurbish- ment, hosts the Birmingham Royal Ballet and the Welsh National Opera when they're on tour. It's also got the facilities to stage the really big West End hits when they come to town.
Mac (Midlands Arts Centre), Cannon Hill Park, T0121-4403838. An eclectic mix of slightly more avant-garde theatre pieces with a world-renouned children's puppet theatre.

Festivals

Birmingham *p336, map p338*
Jul **Birmingham Jazz Festival** in the second week. Guaranteed to be more fun than the TV festival (see below), with dozens of live venues round Birmingham. Gas St Basin used to be full of jazz dives and even though poor Ronnie Scott's club has departed, there's jazz to suit all tastes at this superb week-long jamboree.
Sep **Artsfest** in the first week. Though this has a slightly worthy feel (on account of being arranged and paid for by Birmingham City Council), it is chock full of free events which include live performances by some of the city's Bhangra combos, Asian dub or house. There's also performance art and all the best other art the region has to offer.
Nov **Ramadan and Diwali**. The city has a vocal and active Asian community and they celebrate their festivals in style, often with fireworks, big park parties and delicious food.

Transport

Birmingham *p336, map p338*
Air
Birmingham Airport Flight Enquiries, T0121-7675511, www.bhx.co.uk. For long-term parking at the airport, T0800-0137477.

Train
Virgin Trains have Intercity trains from **London Euston** every 30 mins for at least 16 hrs of the day, every day. There's also a slower, more picturesque and cheaper **Silverlink** service (2 hrs 15 mins) running from **Euston** every hr throughout the week and at weekends. If you want to go to Birmingham by an even more rural and more leisurely route catch a train from the spectacular **Marylebone Station, London**, operated by **Chiltern Railways**, T020-73333190, travel enquiries T08705-165165. This is also an excellent way to explore the surrounding countryside including **Stratford**, **Warwick** and **Royal Leamington Spa**.

Directory

Birmingham *p336, map p338*
Bureaux de changes AmEx, Bank House, 8 Cherry St, T0121-6445533. **Thomas Cook**, 130, New St (inside HSBC), T0121-6435057.
Hospitals Birmingham Children's Hospital, Steelhouse Lane, T0121-3339999. Birmingham Heartland's Hospital, Bordesley Green East, T0121-4242000. **City Hospital**, Dudley Rd, T0121-5543801. Has A&E. **University Hospital**, Raddlebarn Rd, Selly Oak, T0121-6271627.
Internet Trulyeverything.co.uk, Pavilions Shopping Centre, T0121-6326156. £1 for 30 mins. Mon-Wed, Fri and Sat 0900-1800, Thu 0900-1900, Sun 1100-1700. **Medical centres** NHS Medical Centre at Boots, 66 High St, T0121-6266000. **Post office** 1 Pinfold St, and 19 Union Passage, T08457-223344. **Police** City Centre, T0121-6265000. Digbeth Police Station, 113 Digbeth, T0121-6266000. Also houses lost property office.

Stratford-upon-Avon and around

➔*Colour map 2*

As the world centre of an ever-expanding Shakespeare industry, and Britain's second most visited tourist destination after London, you would naturally expect there to be a preponderance of bard-related attractions in and around Stratford, but the place has nevertheless still managed to hold onto its authentic small market town atmosphere. The Royal Shakespeare Company is one of the artistic triumphs of the United Kingdom and no visit to Stratford is really complete without seeing some of Shakespeare's drama – the play really is the thing in comparison with the Birthplace Trust Shakespeare trail. But if you haven't got enough time, and you still want to do the 'Willgrimage', you might drop in on Shakespeare's birthplace which has a tolerable exhibition, or see where Shakespeare was buried in Holy Trinity Church. As for the locals, they live in peace with the bard's sometimes troublesome legacy. A hospitable crowd, they know which side their tourist bread is buttered. ▸▸ *For Sleeping, Eating and other listings, see pages 349-352.*

Ins and outs

Getting there As far as **trains** are concerned, there's an embarrassment of riches including Britain's fastest steamtrain service. For those not so enamoured of the age of steam, **Chiltern Railways** go from London and Birmingham twice an hr and even offer brilliant discounts for unlimited travel in the region over 1 and 3 days. Since the 1980s the mighty M40 has provided a speedy route for those coming from the north or south by **car**. Simply take exit 15 onto the A46, where Stratford is clearly signposted. If you prefer a more picturesque route coming up from the south, there's the A3400 from Oxford which will take you straight into Stratford town centre via some delightful Cotswolds towns like Shipston on Stour. From the southwest and the M5, take exit 9 at Tewekesbury and take the A46 to Evesham, then follow the signposts to Stratford. There's also a great deal of **parking** space in Stratford. ▸▸ *For further details, see Transport, page 351.*

Information There are 2 tourist offices for Stratford. The first is the **official TIC** ⓘ *corner of Bridgefoot and Broadway, Apr-Oct Mon-Sat 0900-1800, Sun 1100-1700; Nov-Mar Mon-Sat 0900-1700, Sun 1100-1600, T01789-293127, www.shakespeare-country.co.uk* Handily, it's also right next to the bus station which is on Bridgeway. You can book accommodation from here or by calling the main number. The other tourist office is provided by **Guide Friday** ⓘ *14 Rother St, adjoining the old Market Sq, T01789-299866*, and while it's well equipped, beware of its tendency to recommend its own tours of the town, Warwick Castle and the Cotswolds.

Stratford-upon-Avon

From the tourist office and Art Gallery see above, it's very easy to get to Stratford's main raison d'être: **The Royal Shakespeare Theatre,** ⓘ *24 hrs ticket availability T01789-403404, box office bookings T01789-403403, for the theatre tour pre-booking is essential, T01789-403405, theatretours@rsc.org.uk*, towering over the landscape like an Art Deco power station. In fact it's quite a complex set of buildings, carefully designed to serve the great god Thespus with a varied platter. Also nestling within the arms of this great beast is a more delicate flower, **The Swan Theatre**, which specializes in performing works by Shakespeare's contemporaries, like the bloodthirsty John Webster who loved his grand guignol. They also perform standard and not-so-standard pieces such as Chekhov and *Cosi Fan Tutte*.

Purists will warn you off what rightfully should be your next port of call: **Shakespeare's Birthplace**, the jewel in the crown of the Shakespeare Properties. Even if there are a few gaps in our knowledge of the truth of Will's life (just who was the Dark Lady?), the Birthplace Trust are determined to do Will proud. There is clearly quite a formidable team of Shakespeare scholars working with the Birthplace Trust and if you really want to do what they offer justice, you need to vist **The Shakespeare Centre and Library Birthplace** ① *Henley St, T01789-204016, The Shakespeare Centre Library, Mon-Fri 1000-1700, Sat 0930-1230 except at bank holidays, Shakespeare's*

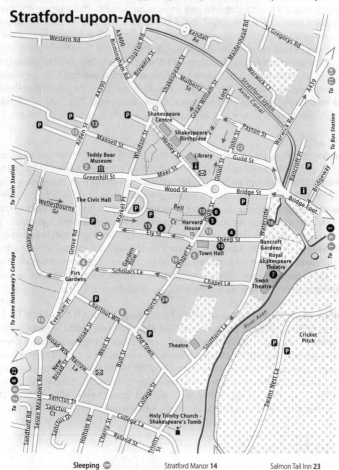

Stratford-upon-Avon

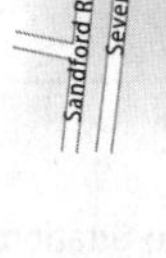

Sleeping
Alveston Manor 1
Avon Caravan Park 11
Backpacker's 3
Eversley's Bears 4
Falcon 5
Greenhaven Guest House 6
Marlin 8
Moat House 9
Nandos 10
Payton 12
Shakespeare 13
Stratford Manor 14
Stratford Racecourse Campsite 2
Stratford Victoria 15
Stratheden 16
White Swan 18

Eating
Alladin's 1
Lamb's Bistro 4
Marlowe's 5
Mayflower 6
Royal Shakespeare Theatre 7
Salmon Tail Inn 23
Santa Lucia 8
Sorrento 9
Thespians 10

Pubs & bars
Bar M (formerly The Frog & Elbow) 13
Cross Keys 15
Dirty Duck 16
Garrick Inn 19
Windmill Inn 24

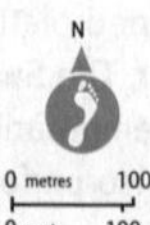

Birthplace, 1 Nov-24 Mar, Mon-Sat 1000-1600, Sun 1030-1600, 25 Mar-31 May and 1 Sep-31 Oct Mon-Sat 1000-1700, Sun 1030-1700, 1 Jun-31 Aug Mon-Sat 0900-1700, Sun 0930-1700, £6.50, children £2.50, family £15, which may not be the most picturesque of the properties, but is easily the most informative. With academics coming from round the world to look at this unique collection of first editions, history and scholarship, the centre can genuinely claim to be a site of world heritage.

In complete contrast, there's **The Falstaff Experience**, ⓘ *40 Sheep St, T01789-298070, www.falstaffexperience.co.uk, Mon-Sat 1030-1730, Sun 1100-1700, £3.50, child £1.50, concessions £2.50, family £10*, which tries to bring Shakespeare's world to life by the power of animatronics and weird smells. It's probably a bit more immediate and tangible for the kids than a 5-hour session in the theatre, but one can't help feeling these operations somehow cheapen history.

For those who want a break from the bard and are perhaps American, **Harvard House** is well worth a visit. This was the same Harvard who founded the free world's leading seat of learning, the mighty Harvard University but it's good to know that the guy who started it all off over 300 years ago was also a spoilt Brit. Sentimental, well-educated Americans will be overcome with awe here. ⓘ *High St, T01789-204016, www.shakespeare.org.uk*

Rejoining the Shakespeare Trail should now be your top priority and the **Holy Trinity Church** ⓘ *Old Town Stratford, T01789-266316, www.stratford-upon-avon.org, Mar-Oct, Mon-Sat 0830-1800, Sun 1400-1700, Nov-Feb Mon-Sat 0900-1600, Sun 1400-1700, Shakespeare's Grave £1, child £0.50,* is well worth the small entrance fee. Seeing Shakespeare's tomb and monument isn't the only reason for visiting. The church is right next to the river Avon and its setting and distinguished architecture give it a justifiable claim to be one of England's loveliest parish churches.

Anne Hathaway's Cottage, ⓘ *Shottery, 2 miles west of Stratford, T01789-292100, 1 Nov-24 Mar, Mon-Sat 1000-1600, Sun 1030-1600, 25 Mar-31 May and 1 Sep-31 Oct Mon-Sat 1000-1700, Sun 1030-1700; 1 Jun-31 Aug Mon-Sat 0930-1700, Sun 1000-1700, £5, children £2, family £12*, is the second most visited of the Shakespeare Properties and really is exquisitely maintained with one of the most beautiful gardens you will ever see.

On the way back you can visit **The Teddy Bear Museum** ⓘ *19 Greenhill St, T01789-293160, www.theteddybearmuseum.com, daily 0930-1730, £2.50, children £1.50, family £7.50*, which while rather eerie is bound to delight children. Better still is **The Ragdoll Shop**, ⓘ *11 Chapel St, T01789-404111*, the origin point for the Teletubbies. The creator is a local, Anne Wood, who cut her teeth making the hugely successful Rosie and Jim on the local canals. Now thanks to Messrs. Tinky-Winky et al she's a multi-millionairess many times over.

Warwick and Kenilworth

Warwick and its environs is really a tale of two castles. One is a romantic ruin and the other is a ruined opportunity. Between them, Kenilworth and Warwick Castles dominate this part of the world and have done for centuries. From medieval pageants to pitched battles, the castles are a fantastic double act. As always, it's the powerful elite who really grab our interest in the history of this little and fairly quiet town, the county capital of Warwickshire. Throughout history, royals couldn't keep away from the place, so it's not surprising that the local population have developed a habit of turning a blind eye to the more outlandish excesses of visitors. Since Warwick Castle still employs many local people – just as it used to when it needed an army of servants to satisfy the whims of its pampered weekenders – the locals have learnt the value of discretion, unlike some royal butlers. This all leads to a very pleasant atmosphere – intensely peaceful, although some might find it a mite too stately for their tastes.

Ins and outs

Getting there Warwick **station** is 10 minutes' walk from the town centre and castle. Regular trains run from Birmingham on the Chiltern Line which can be picked up in London from Marylebone Station or Paddington for other services. Use Leamington Spa for connections to Banbury, Coventry and Oxford. The best way to approach Warwick by **road** from the north is either via the M1, taking the M69 and A46, or M6 taking the M42 to M40 junction 15, then A429 to Warwick. From London also use the M40 to junction 15 then A429 to Warwick.

Information Warwick Castle has its own impressive visitors' centre and PR operation (see below), but Warwick's main **TIC** ⓘ *Jury St, T01926-492212, www.warwick-uk.com*, is within easy striking distance of the castle and most other attractions.

Warwick Castle

ⓘ *T0870-442 2000 (24 hr), T01926-406600, www.warwick-castle.co.uk (also for information on all events held at the castle). Daily except Christmas Apr-Sep 1000-1800; Oct-Mar 1000-1700. £11.25, concessions £7.35, student £7.80, children £6.95, family £34 (all prices less in winter).*

Admittedly Warwick Castle seems to be a classic tourist trap. It's full of live archers, waxwork tableaux and living exhibits which are all the trademarks of the 'heritage industry' – in this case Tussaud's, its most successful beneficiary and the owners since 1978. Actually Tussaud's have done a rather good job and spent over £20 milion restoring the castle from a fairly parlous state.

Warwick Castle is now a major site of historic interest with close to a million visitors a year. It's not only an incredible structure – a proper medieval fort – but it has also been an icon of taste and style for the upper classes of the past four centuries. Canaletto immortalized several famous prospects and even JMW Turner couldn't resist its perfect lines and fairy-tale romanticism. The real money shots, however, are to be found above the castle – where you can see the outlines of the original earthworks which Aethelwade built to defend herself over 1000 years ago.

Tussaud's come into their own, though, once you enter the castle through the magnificent **Gatehouse** and **Barbican**. The main precinct enclosed by the east and south walls is in tip-top condition with an immaculate lawn sometimes used for torchlit feasts. Immediately, you are surrounded by the walls and battlements of an honest-to-goodness fairy-tale castle. Assuming you're going to leave a stroll around the **towers and ramparts** for later, a good place to start your tour is at **The Kingmaker Experience**, commemorating the almost total power one Earl of Warwick, Richard Neville, enjoyed over the kingdom. Just around the corner from Kingmaker, there's the **Chapel, Great Hall and State Rooms**, where you'll find the Warwicks' fairly large collection of antiques, gorgeous furniture and slightly boring portraits. But the magic of waxworks really comes into its own in the adjacent rooms to the chapel and state rooms which are occupied by **The Royal Weekend Party** a faithful reconstruction of a house party held in 1898 at which two future kings were present as guests. But the holy of holies in this sequence is undoubtedly **The Kenilworth Bedroom**, a room set aside permanently for the Prince of Wales because he was such a frequent visitor.

Take a balloon tour of the region – Warwick Castle is an incredible sight from 3000 ft.

As you'd expect the grounds are immaculate and absolutely litter free; showing off some spectacular features like the **Victorian Rose Garden** and the **Pageant Field** as well as the **Peacock Garden** designed by 19th-century landscapist Robert Warnock. There's also a truly fabulous **Conservatory** designed in 1786 to house the famous **Warwick Vase** an enormous piece of Roman pottery gifted to an 18th-century Earl in recognition of his diplomatic skills.

Kenilworth Castle

ⓘ (EH) T01926-852078, www.english-heritage.org.uk 1 Apr-31 Oct daily 1000-1800 (1700 in Oct); 1 Nov-31 Mar daily, 1000-1600. £4.50, concessions £3.40, children £2.30, family £11.30. By car – at M6 junction (M42 Junction 7) take A452 south into Kenilworth. From Coventry and Warwick, Kenilworth is off the A46 on the A452 and the castle is signposted from the town centre. By train: Coventry Station is 8 miles. By bus: Stagecoach company – Leamington Spa from bridge outside Coventry Railway Station: X 18 stops near Castle, X16 stops nearby Clock in town.

In many ways, Kenilworth Castle has more history to offer than Warwick as its bloody story has witnessed savagery, skulduggery and at one point it even played its part in regicide. But unlike Warwick Castle it's an honest-to-goodness ruin, a fact not lost on its most famous chronicler, Sir Walter Scott, whose novel of 1821 describing the spectacular culmination of an alleged love-affair between Elizabeth I and Robert Dudley, Earl of Leicester, really put Kenilworth on the tourist map and helped to draw crowds wanting to experience the romance of an ancient ruin first-hand. Dickens used to pay frequent visits and more recently, the Castle has helped inspire modern fabulists obsessed by the medieval and spooky – JRR Tolkein and JK Rowling to name but two.

The current structure was begun in around 1120 by Geoffrey De Clinton, a counter-jumping Chamberlain to Henry I. De Clinton's formidable grasp of warcraft can be seen in the mighty Norman stone keep called **Caesar's Tower,** built in the style of a Roman fort – very high and very square, with walls that are over 20 ft thick. The castle passed ultimately to John of Gaunt, a medieval 'Godfather' figure who as son of Edward III became de facto king on the accession of Richard II who was only twelve at the time. His influence can be seen everywhere, but particularly in the remains of **The Great Hall** to the left of the **Keep.** But the beautification of Kenilworth reached its apotheosis under Robert Dudley, Earl of Leicester who wanted to impress his royal patron (and possibly mistress) with the most incredible reception and party which lasted nineteen days in 1575. He even built a special tower **The Leicester Building** for the Queen and her retinue as well as a new triumphal entrance to the castle, **Leicester's Gatehouse.**

Sleeping

Stratford-upon-Avon *p345, map p346*

L **Alveston Manor**, Clopton Bridge, on the way out of the town on the Oxford Rd, T0870-4008181. The best hotel in Stratford, it enjoys a spectacular view of the river and is within walking distance of the theatre. Pleasant Art Deco(ish) structure.

A **The Shakespeare**, Chapel St, T0870-4008182. Central, historic building, a cosy atmosphere that promises luxurious accommodation close to the attractions.

A **The Moat House Hotel**, Bridgefoot, T01789-279988. Originally built as a Hilton, you'd expect high standards, except when it comes to the building. Despite being 1960s, it manages to retain some character though and is next to the leisure centre.

B **The Stratford Victoria**, Arden St, T01789-271000. A handsome Victorian townhouse. This is very superior accomodation at a more affordable price.

C **The Falcon Hotel**, Chapel St, T01789-279953. A very comfortable, pleasant and informal hotel with a great bar and lounge.

C **Stratford Manor**, Warwick Rd, T01789-731173. Has a great indoor swimming pool and all mod cons. A very tidy modern building.

C **The White Swan**, Rother St, T01789-297022. A cosy inn-type hotel, with oak beams and open fires. Highly recommended.

D **The Payton**, 6 John St, T01789-266442. Perfectly respectable guesthouse.

D **Stratheden**, 5 Chapel St, T01789-297119. Another of Stratford's many B&Bs which offers consistently good service and hospitality.

E **Eversley's Bears**, 37 Grove Rd, T01789-292334. Another budget rooming house.

E **Greenhaven Guest House**, 217 Evesham Rd, T01789-294874. Dog-lovers and smoking-haters are more than welcome here.

E **The Marlin Hotel**, 3 Chestnut Walk, T01789-293752. A really good value establishment that takes dogs and lets you smoke.

E **Nandos**, 18-19 Evesham Pl, T01789-204907. There's a smoking lounge, dogs are welcome and there is ample parking for this very cheap B&B.
E-F **Backpacker's Hotel**, 33 Greehill St, T01789-263838. It's in the middle of town, does weekly rates and gets hideously booked up in season so be sure to book early.

Caravans and camping
Avon Caravan Park, Warwick Rd, T01789-293438. A beautiful location on the banks of the river with touring pitches and also static caravans. Toilets and showers on site.
Stratford Racecourse, T01789-267949. Caravan pitches and tents Easter to Sep for all those gypsies out there and those who fancy a flutter.

Warwick and Kenilworth *p347*
A-B **The Rose and Crown**, 30 Market Pl, Warwick, T01926-411117. A very smart newly opened hotel. Lots of bright colours, a cool bar and a somewhat trendy clientele.
C **Charter House**, 87-91 West St, Warwick, T01926-496965. A really old building and benefits from a great deal of privacy and a lovely garden. There's even a grand piano for the 'serious musician' and a strict no-smoking policy.
D **The Seven Stars**, Friar's St, Warwick, T01926-492658. Jolly inn-style establishment, enjoys the patronage of locals and is highly recommended.
E **Austin House Guest House**, 96 Emscote Rd, Warwick, T01926-493583. Perfectly acceptable guesthouse in the guesthouse ghetto of Warwick.

Eating

Stratford-upon-Avon *p345, map p346*
Stratford restaurants are an amiable mix of beautiful country pubs some of which have had the 'gastro' makeover, and smart, if a little old-school, silver service-type establishments. And of course, this being the Midlands, there are plenty of curry houses.
$$$ **Marlowe's Restaurant**, 18 High St, T01789-204999. A stunning late 16th-century building, this is one of the best restaurants in Stratford, though it is rather formal and prides itself on silver service waitering.
$$$ **Royal Shakespeare Theatre**, T01789-403414. The complex has 2 restaurants – a bistro-style affair which is always overflowing with punters, and a classier, and of course more expensive, restaurant serving a variety of modern English and French cuisine. Both have spectacular views of the river.
$$ **Alladin's**, Tiddington Main St, Tiddington Rd. Friendly curry house reasonably priced, recommended by locals.
$$ **Lamb's Bistro**, Sheep St, T01789-2922554. Fine dining, one of Stratford's best, but extremely busy, so book ahead.
$$ **Salmon Tail Inn**, Evesham Rd, T01789-551913. Traditional English pub between the town centre and the racecourse with excellent restaurant.
$$ **Santa Lucia**, 37 Shottery, T01789-414629. More family-orientated restaurant, boasting live music most weekends and some fairly over the top murals, but it's a fun place nevertheless.
$$ **Sorrento**, 8 Ely St, T01789-297999. Friendly Italian trattoria, simply but elegantly decorated with a pleasant easy-going atmosphere.
$ **Mayflower**, 22 High St, T01789-297161. One of Stratford's best Chinese restaurants it also does a roaring takeaway trade.
$ **Thespians**, 26 Sheep St, T01789-267187. An army of smiling, extremely courteous staff in this place which, despite its name specializes in north Indian cuisine, including Baltis. Caters for pre- and after-theatre dining.

Warwick and Kenilworth *p347*
££ **Cellar Restaurant**, 5/6 The Knibbs Smith St, Warwick, T01926-400809. This is one of the best restaurants in Warwick with an eerie atmosphere, located as it is in the eponymous cellar.
££ **Fanshawe's Restaurant**, 22 Market Pl, Warwick, T01926-410590. Not nearly as posh as some, it's a modest affair with an informal feel to it and more affordable, less fancy fare.
££ **Findons Restaurant**, 7 Old Sq, Warwick, T01926-411755. This place has a claim to being the best restaurant in Warwick. They do take themselves a bit seriously, though. Specialities include Seared Scottish King Scallops and Roast Leg of English Lamb.
££ **Giovanni's Restaurant**, 15 Smith St, Warwick, T01926 494904. A friendly and unsurprising Italian restaurant, though try to avoid the large parties of office workers out for an upmarket works do.

£**Hermans**, 11 Old Sq, Warwick, T07974-951257. This is a small friendly coffee shop with a distinctly cosmopolitan flavour, though the prices are very reasonable. Sandwiches, snacks, cakes, all day breakfast £2.60.

Pubs, bars and clubs

Stratford-upon-Avon *p345, map p346*

Bar Humbug, Guild St, T01789-292109. This ever-expanding chain is actually quite good news for the trendier type of punter. Beer garden and acceptable restaurant.

Bar M (formerly *The Frog and Elbow*), Arden St, T01789-297641. This is about the only place for a late night drink in Stratford, it also features live music every now and again, but there's quite a draconian door policy.

The Cross Keys , Ely St, T01789-293909. A great night out for younger types, this is one of the premier youth pubs in the area and is the assignation point for lots of foreign language students on the pull.

Dirty Duck, Waterside, T01789-297312. The ultimate luvvies pub in Stratford, frequented by members of the RSC and the multitude of hangers-on the theatre world has always attracted. Beware of the somewhat arrogant publicans; the smell of greasepaint seems to have gone to their heads.

Garrick Inn, High St, T01789-292186. This is the place to come if you like your pubs seriously beautiful and like a movie set from Olde Englande. The beer's not bad, either.

The Windmill Inn, Church St, T01789-297687. Another youth hang-out but extremely friendly with a network of cosy, really picturesque rooms that are begging to be occupied for at least an entire day of supping the local ale, Flowers.

Entertainment

Stratford-upon-Avon *p345, map p346*

Live music venues

The Civic Hall, 14 Rother St, box office T01789-414513, www.civichall.co.uk. The venue for variety shows, classical music, concerts, big band, pantomime and dance nights. Licensed bar.

The Bandstand on the Recreation Ground has bands on some Sunday afternoons during the summer.

Festivals and events

Stratford-upon-Avon *p345, map p346*

Apr **Shakespeare's Birthday Celebrations**, from the 24th-27th includes street entertainers, the ceremony of the unfurling of the flags, the floral procession of international dignitaries between the Birthplace and Holy Trinity Church, dancing by local children and much more.

Jun **Stratford Regatta**, held on the 3rd Sat, on the River Avon.

Jul-Aug **Stratford-upon-Avon International Flute Festival**, T01789-261561, stratflute@aol.com. 30 chamber music concerts, from 19th Jul-2nd Aug.

Oct **Stratford-upon-Avon English Music Festival**, T01926-496277, www.warwickarts.org.uk. Runs from 10th-19th.

Oct **Stratford Mop Fair**, over the 10th and 11th the central streets of Stratford are closed to traffic for this annual traditional street fair with fairground rides and stalls, and the roasting of a whole ox. It is one of the biggest mop fairs in the country.

Oct **Runaway Mop**. A smaller version of the Stratford Mop Fair on the 25th.

Activities and tours

Stratford-upon-Avon *p345, map p346*

Bus tours

Guide Friday run an opened top double decker tour of the town and of the surrounding areas. Details from *Guide Friday*, Stratford Civic Hall, 14 Rother St, T01789-294466.

Transport

Stratford-upon-Avon *p345, map p346*

Bicycle

Spencer-Clarke's Cycles, Guild St, T01789-450788. For cycle hire.

Bus

Long distance National Express, T08705-808080, run 3 direct services per day from **London Victoria** (3 hrs) at 0830, 1330 and 1830, **Birmingham** (1 hr).

Car

Marbella Car Hire, 1 Central Chambers, Henley St, T01789-268002. **Hertz Rent-a-car**, Rail Station, Station Rd, T01789-298827.

Taxi
Ranks are situated in Wood St, Rother St and Briedge St, Bridgefoot and the Railway station. **Shakespeare Taxis**, 17 Greenhill St, T01789-266100; **Stratford Taxis**, 27a Windsor St, T0800-243061.

Train
Stratford Railway Station is off the Alcester Rd. For timetable details call **Warwickshire Council's Traveline**, T01926-414140. There are 3 direct **Virgin Trains** services from **London Paddington** daily (2 hrs 30 mins) as well as many other slower services from Paddington, **Euston** or **Marylebone** stations. Hourly trains to and from Birmingham New Street (1 hr). The **Shakespeare Express**, T0121-7074696, which runs 2 return journeys a day on a steam train from **Birmingham's Snow Hill** station.

Directory

Stratford-upon-Avon *p345, map p346*
Hospitals Stratford Hospital, Arden St, T01789-292209. Minor injuries unit 0900-1700 daily. **Warwick Hospital**, Lakin Rd, Warwick, T01926-495321. 24 hr A&E. **Arden Medical Centre**, Albany Rd, T01789-414942. **Internet** The Cyber Junction, 28 Greenhill St, T01789-263400. **Library** Public library on Henley St, T01789-292209. **Police** Rother St, T01789-414111. **Post office** Henley St, T0845-7740740.

Worcester, the Malverns and the Vale of Evesham

→Colour map 1-2

Worcester is a perfect gem of a city nestling on the banks of the Severn river to the south of the Malvern Hills, some of the best countryside the West Midlands has to offer. The city is full of great history, quirky shops and beautiful medieval streets. Sir Edward Elgar, its most famous son, is commemorated admirably both in the Cathedral (a magnificent structure). And once you start exploring the town, you realize that Worcester has a lot going for it, especially if you like superb bars, pubs, restaurants and some really stylish shopping opportunities. To the southeast, the town of Evesham is swaddled in delightful and highly productive countryside best-known for its market-gardening and spring blossom. ▸▸ *For Sleeping, Eating and other listings, see pages 355-357.*

Ins and outs

Getting there There are regular **trains** from London Paddington to Shrub Hill Station Worcester, the journey takes around 2 hrs 15 mins. There are also twice hourly trains at peak times from Birmingham New Street to Foregate, which is more convenient for the centre. The M5 is an excellent nearby **motorway** and by exiting at Junction 7, you'll get to Worcester very quickly. This serves travellers from Birmingham in the north and as far southwest as Exeter. Coming from London the M4 joins the M5 just outside Bristol or if you prefer a more historical route passing through Oxford, you can take the M40 to Birmingham and then the M42 will connect you with the M5. The City stands on the banks of the River Severn and the Worcester & Birmingham Canal so there are plenty of opportunities to get a **boat** either from Bristol and Cardiff, or a canal barge from Birmingham. ▸▸ *For further details, see Transport, page 357.*

Getting around Making your way round Worcester centre can be fraught with frustration because of one major 2-lane road that divides most of the town from the wonderful Cathedral Precinct. Once you're away from this road, however, much of the centre is pedestrianized, including the approach to the tourist centre, in The Guildhall on the High St, ⓘ *T01905-726311, www.cityofworcester.gov.uk Daily 0930-1730.*

Worcester

On a purely visual level, Worcester does have an extraordinary range of spectacular street architecture from imposing Georgian Churches converted into smart bars to perfect examples of early Tudor buildings which have been pubs for over 300 years. There's an old saying that Worcester has a different pub for every day of the year and it's true that Friar Street – the superlatively preserved mainly Elizabethan and Tudor pedestrianized walkway – is a cornucopia of great restaurants, pubs and even smarter shops than those on the High Street.

The Guildhall (phone and address as tourist office) is as good a place as any to start your trip round Worcester and even though it's a walk from Foregate Station where most of the trains from London and Birmingham arrive, you'll get a taste of how smart Worcester is. Designed by a local, Thomas White, the building looks like an 18th-century palace from the outside with its amazing wrought iron gate and Italianate façade. The real glories, however, are reserved for the inside and the **Pump Room** which is like a beautiful highly decorated ball room, but now full of the worthy burghers of Worcester wolfing down roast dinners – the place is also a self-serve restaurant and tea room.

The Worcester History Centre and Archives, ⓘ *Trinity St, T01905-765922, www.worcestershire.gov.uk/records, free opening Mon 0930-1900, Tue-Thu 0930-1730, Fri 0930-1900, Sat 0930-1600*, is full of the inevitable genealogy buffs but also has some fascinating stuff on the history of Worcester. Although it's really only for hardcore lovers of history, at the time of writing half of **Worcester Museum and Art Gallery's** ⓘ *Foregate St, T01905-25371, www.worcestercitymuseums.org.uk, Mon-Fri 0930-1730, Sat 0930-1700 closed Sun, free*, collection was languishing in a basement under the building beyond Foregate Station, so the History Centre, The Museum of Local Life on Friar Street (see below) and The Commandery (see below) are the best places to go to find out about historic Worcester.

Once you do make it into the grounds of what has been called 'the most beautiful cathedral in Britain' you begin to realize what all the fuss is about. It's not as majestic as Salisbury, as weird as Exeter or as imposing as Durham. But if you want a church where you can really feel the mystery of history and the kind of awe that people must have felt a thousand years ago when they saw the majesty of this holy place, then **Worcester Cathedral** ⓘ *Chapter Office, 10a College Green, T01905-28854, www.cofe-worcester.org.uk*, is for you. Not that the Cathedral was above burying the odd unholy man, like King John whose body lies in a tomb near the main altar. In a codicil to his will he asked to be buried in Worcester Cathedral and being 'the faithful city', they obliged with a handsome tomb closer to the most sanctified part of the building than anyone else. Apart, that is, from **Prince Arthur's Chantry** which was built to house the remains of Henry VIII's elder brother. There's also a **Norman Crypt** – the oldest in the country – some really lovely Victorian stained glass which rivals Notre Dame and Canterbury, and an intriguing Georgian outbuilding called **The Guesten House** which may only be available for corporate events, but apparently does occasionally entertain tourists with talks which may also have to be pre-arranged with the Tourist Officer.

> ❢ *Visiting the Cathedral without hearing a sung service is like going to Stratford and not seeing any theatre. Choral Evensong is sung pretty much every day at 1730.*

The Cathedral Precinct consists also of **The King's School** and the world-renouned **Choir School**. Every year the Cathedral Choirs of Worcester, Hereford and Gloucester get down and strut their funky stuff in competition with each other. **The Three Choirs Festival** (see page 357) takes place in Worcester once every three years.

Leaving the Cathedral square by **The Edgar Gate** which looks as if it could be the inspiration for Worcester's Coat of Arms you enter a little network of streets but have to cross the dreadful Sidbury road to get to **The Commandery** ⓘ *Sidbury, T01905-361821, www.worcestercitymuseums.or.uk, Mon-Sat 1000-1700, Sun*

 1330-1700, £4, children £2.50, which started life around the time of St Wulfstan, founder of the current Cathedral in the 11th century. The place was originally a hospital where the sick were tended to by monks, but it really came into its own when a local wealthy clothier called Wylde put what was now his family home at the disposal of **Charles II** and his Royalist Army prior to the Battle of Worcester in 1651. It manages to score with a really thorough presentation on the history of this turbulent time, complete with a tableaux of the sentencing of Charles I to death by beheading.

Just across the road from the Commandery **The Royal Worcester Visitor** Centre ⓘ *Royal Porcelain Works, Severn St, T01905-23221, www.royal-worcester.co.uk, Mon-Sat 0900-1730, Sun 1100-1700*, is the perfect contrast to the blood, guts and diseases of the Commandery. With guided tours of the factory, a great little museum which shows you how the elite have coped with changing trends in place-settings over the last 300 years and a fabulous shop showcasing the work of the oldest continuous porcelain manufacturer in the country, this is one of the top places to visit in the city.

There is a wonderful new attraction a little way out of Worcester, the **Elgar Birthplace and Museum,** ⓘ *Crown East Lane, Lower Broadheath, Worcester, T01905-333224, www.elgar.org Museum open daily, 1100-1700 last admission 1615, exclusive evening visits by prior booking, longer hours 1000-1730, in Aug for Three Choirs Festival, just about accessible by public transport, but you need to call the County Busline for details T0345-125436.* Here you'll find all manner of Elgar treasures with regular concerts of his work and rare manuscripts to help you unlock the secret of the man who wrote 'Land of Hope and Glory', as well as a brilliant cello concerto. You'll also be in striking distance of the beautiful Malvern Hills (see below) where Elgar probably came up with that famous piece of patriotism.

There's a delightful canal walk from beside the Commandery which will take you to Birmingham along the Worcester & Birmingham Canal.

The Malvern Hills

For some, England has no more beautiful countryside to offer than the Malvern Hills, an ancient and mysterious eruption of 650-million-year-old granite and crystalline rock. Pushing their way upwards relatively dramatically from the surrounding flat landscape, the hills lie a few miles southwest of Worcester and divide the counties of Herefordshire and Worcestershire. The aptly named 'Land of Hope and Glory' may well have been inspired by the composer Elgar's frequent visits to this extraordinary and serene geographical anomaly, and he certainly first conceived the original tune upon which the *Enigma Variations* were based while walking here. William Langland, a 14th-century Christian radical mystic, was also so moved by the incomparable countryside that he was struck by a vision which became the basis for the epic poem *Piers Plowman*.

Great Malvern

The logical place to start, whether you're a walking fan or a water fan attracted to the famous English rivers Severn, Avon and Teme, is really the town of Malvern, which actually consists of seven different 'Malverns' spread around the slopes of the hills, from **West Malvern** via **Great Malvern** to **Little Malvern** in the south. Great Malvern is really the centre, with fantastic views to the west over the town as well as being the best starting point for the obligatory walk on the hills. It's also the oldest part of Malvern and because of its remoteness was chosen by the Norman Benedictine Monks for the location of the Great Priory Church (see below), built in 1085. Malvern continued as a relatively sleepy location until the 19th century when ailing city types and sophisticates were drawn by the famous Malvern 'water-cure', now transformed into a thriving bottled spring water business. Consequently, this Victorian blooming led to the architectural flavour of much of the town, best exemplified by Bellevue Terrace a sort of faux Georgian front which runs at right angles to Church Street, the main drag of Great Malvern. **Tourist information Centre** ⓘ *21 Church St, Great Malvern, T01684-892289, www.malvernhills.gov.uk Daily 1000-1700.*

The magnificent 11th-century **Priory Church** ⓘ *Parish Office, T01684-561020, www.greatmalvernpriory.org.uk*, has a rich heritage going back over 900 years. The building itself is a combination of Norman and Perpendicular Gothic and has some extraordinary stained glass depicting a rare example of the *arma Christi* – the wounds of Christ – which miraculously survived the English Reformation. The **gatehouse** ⓘ *Abbey Gateway, T01684-567811, Easter-Oct 1030-1700*, originally housed visitors to the Abbey, dates back to around 1400 and is an extraordinarily ornate structure which now is the location of **Malvern Town Museum**. There's a fascinating exhibit on the water-cure doctors and their hydropathic establishments, and the bottling of water since 1622.

The TIC will supply you with a plethora of walking guides to the Hills, but the best way to get to them is via the **North Hill** and **Worcesterhire Beacon**, at the north end of the range. The reward for reaching the top is a truly amazing view – one of the best in England and from which it is said you can see six counties. Luckily there's somewhere you can fortify yourself before attempting this climb: **St Ann's Well**, a lovely little building dating back to 1815, which became very popular for those taking the water-cure as there's a fresh-water spring on site. An elaborately carved font is one of the main attractions and you can still 'take the waters' there, (although a highly conscientious note from the council suggests that you boil it first). For those not wishing to take a risk, there's a more recently built octagonal extension to St Ann's Well which houses a superb **café** ⓘ *T01684-560285, reached from right next to the TIC via a leafy path and 99 steps*, with a wide range of health drinks and some wonderful cake.

Sleeping

Worcester *p353*

B **Fownes Hotel**, City Walls Rd, T01905-613151. This converted glove factory is a little bit outside the city centre but is extremely tasteful, has an à la carte restaurant and is a really comfortable base from which to enjoy Worcester in style.

B **The Star Hotel**, Foregate St, T01905-24308. An extremely comfortable billet right next to the hustle and bustle of Foregate and the station, very convenient if you've arrived by train and suitable levels of luxury.

C **The Diglis House Hotel**, Severn St, T01905- 353518. The nicest thing about this hotel is its location nestling right on the river bank in a beautifully preserved old part of Worcester. For lovers of history and convenient locations.

D **Burgage House**, 4 College Precincts, T01905-25396. Slap bang next to the Cathedral, this handsome Georgian guesthouse is very good value with tolerable levels of comfort and a great garden for strolling in, taking in views of the Cathedral.

E **Mrs V A Rogers**, Little Lightwood Farm, Lightwood Lane, Cotheridge, T01905-333236. It's a fair way out of Worcester, but you'll be hard put to to find anywhere cheaper or friendlier. Take the A44 out of Worcester in the direction of Broadwas, after about 4 miles you'll find a turning to the right into Lightwood Lane (direction Lower Broadheath). The farm is about half a mile up the road.

The Malvern Hills *p354*

C **Bredon House Hotel**, 34 Worcester Rd, Great Malvern, T01684-566990. A fairly small but impeccably respectable establishment enjoying spectacular views from the vantage point of the main Worcester Rd and also very near to the middle of Great Malvern.

C **Brook Farm**, Hanley Swan, T01684-310796, www.brookfarm.org.uk A lovely converted farmhouse with ample accommodation and fantastic walking country all around. It's a little way out of Malvern – take the A449 to Powick and then head south on the B4424 towards Upton. This road turns into the B4211 and then turn right on to the B4209 which will take you into the delightful village of Hanley Swan.

D **The Firs**, 243 West Malvern Rd, Nr Malvern, T01684-564016. Small, quiet and cheap this benefits from being actually on the hills and is ideal for the serious walker.

E **Como House**, Como Rd, Great Malvern, T01684-561486, kevin@como-house.freeserve.co.uk. A lovely 1850s Malvern stone house this is a good value, comfortable hotel within easy walking distance of Malvern town centre. They're also most obliging about lifts to the station and good vantage points for walks.

Eating

Worcester *p353*

In Worcester, well-heeled citizens take their fine dining seriously and you can have a substantial gastronomic odyssey.

$$$ **Glasshouse**, Church St, T01905-611120. Tucked away behind Church St, this place has superb interior décor, with plenty of stained glass. And the food's pretty good, too.

$$$ **Il Pescatore**, 34 Sidbury, T01905-21444. This is a proper Italian restaurant with outstanding fish and meat dishes.

$$$ **The Little Sauce Factory**, 55 London Rd, T01905-350159. Benefiting from having a master chef on the premises, this mixture of international cuisine does know what it's about, even if the interior feels a little cramped.

$$ **Azure**, 33-35 Broad St, T01905-25832. If you want Med eclectic, this place claims to be influenced by cuisine from Provence, Andalucía, Cyprus and Morocco. It's pretty laid back and has some great brunch treats.

$$ **Little Venice**, 1 St Nicholas St, T01905-726126. A simple, modern trattoria that resembles Pizza Express, but it's a good family place and pretty reasonable value for money.

$$ **Pasha Indian Cuisine**, 56 St John's, T01905-426327. An innovative approach to the food of the subcontinent.

$$ **Royal Balti Restaurant**, 50 The Tything, T01905-25694. Worth the few extra pennies for the quality.

$$ **Souvlaki Taverna**, 50 Friar St, T01905-22972. Don't expect too much plate-throwing, it's an altogether more sedate Greek dining experience, but the menu is very authentic and you'll have a really great evening here.

$$ **The Vauxhall Inn**, Abbey Rd, Evesham, T01386-446333. A great big place that proudly boasts over 20 different varieties of pie and of course lots of great big thick chunky pieces of steak. Also pretty conveniently situated right next to the Almonry Heritage Centre.

$ **Drucker's Vienna Patisserie**, 27 Chapel Walk, Worcester, T01905-616870. Though it specializes in creamy and cakey things you will also find some delicious savoury items here, too and although you shouldn't expect a full meal, it's a good place to fortify yourself at affordable prices.

$ **Olive Tree Pizza and Coffee Shop**, 80 Barnards Green Rd, Great Malvern, T01684-577446. A slightly fey pizza house, but a nice atmosphere and with the average pizza costing around £6 you can't go wrong.

Pubs, bars and clubs

Worcester *p353*

The Courtyard, St Nicholas St, T01905-23050. A far cry from the poncey *Conservatory Bar* on Friar St, this place is riotous at weekends with some good music events in an extremely historic setting. Very popular with the trendy and rather outré youth of Worcester, it's well worth a visit if you like your evenings hot and sweaty.

Don Pedro's, The Cellar Bar/90 Worcester Rd, Malvern, T01684-577666. Slightly more upmarket clientele with a great wine list and decidedly superior bar snacks.

Farmers Arms, Birts St, Birtsmorton, Malvern, T01684-833308. A bit more sleepy than some of the other Malvern pubs, it nevertheless is worth a visit for its cosy ambience and family atmosphere.

The Fleece, The Cross, Bretforton, Nr Evesham, T01386-831173. This place is a definite must for fans of ale and history. It's a 15th-century National Trust property, kept in its original condition with three open fires and beamed ceilings. Among the delights it offers are 15 different types of fruit beer and a large orchard to drink in. Really idyllic.

Horn and Trumpet, 12 Angel St, T01905-29593. Very popular with the locals, this place isn't your typical inner city pub.

Oliver's Cafe Bar, 36 Bellevue Terr, Great Malvern, T01684-562272. Friendly local bar really more for young people who want to get funky with the odd live DJ.

The Pheasant Inn, 25 New St, T01905-29635. Probably the oldest building

you'll ever have a drink in, this is a stunning 15th-century structure which used to be famous for cock-fighting.
RSVP, The Cross, T01905-729211. A tasteful conversion of a lovely Georgian church, serves food and has a big screen.

Festivals

Worcester *p353*
Aug The Three Choirs Festival is probably one of the most prestigious musical festivals in the world and even though Worcester shares it with Hereford and Gloucester, it's definitely worth catching it. Festival Administrator, 6 Edgar St, T01905-616200.
Nov-Dec Worcester City Christmas Fayre, an extremely successful Victorian themed street market from 28 Nov-1st Dec and attracts thousands. Stallholders get all dressed up in Victorian costume and there's plenty to distract the kids while you hunt down some Victorian bargains.

Transport

Worcester *p353*
Bus
Long distance National Express coaches, T08705-808080, stop on the edge of the city with links to scheduled city bus services.
Cambridge Coach Services go direct to Crown Gate Bus Station. Enquiries T0870-6082608.

Directory

Worcester *p353*
Hospital Worcestershire Royal Hospital, Charles Hastings Way, T01905- 763333. Newtown Hospital and Eye Unit, Newtown Rd, T01905-763333. **Library** Foregate St, T01905-765312. Worcestershire Library and History Centre, Trinity St, T01905-765922. **Post office** 8-10 Foregate St, T0845-722 3344. **Police** Castle St, T08457-444888.

Hereford and around

→*Colour map 1*

Hereford is a dignified, solidly built place on the banks of the Wye that has recently reinvented itself as a 'City of Living Crafts' thanks to the growing reputation of its technical college. Craft shops and cottage industries are doing well here, part of an increasingly diversified rural economy. Approached from the east across the broad floodplain of the Lug, unmissable sights in the city include the diminutive cathedral and its most prized possession: the Mappa Mundi. This extraordinary survival from the Middle Ages, a parchment atlas of the world, is on display in a purpose-built annexe that also provides room for the largest chained library in the world. The Cathedral also plays host to The Three Choirs Festival every three years, the oldest event of its type in Europe. The meanderings of the Wye run past rolling hills until they meet the Welsh border at Hay-on-Wye, secondhand book centre of the free world. To the north, the 'Black and White' village trail leads up through half-timbered settlements clustered around ancient churches towards charming old Leominster with its impressive Priory church, flourishing bric-a-brac shops and market produce. ▸▸ *For Sleeping, Eating and other listings, see page 360.*

Ins and outs

Getting there There are a few direct **trains** a day from London Paddington to Ledbury, Hereford and Leominster taking around 2 hrs 40 mins-3 hrs, but generally you will have to change either at Newport in Wales or Worcester. It's also at least a 2-hr journey to the area from Birmingham via Worcester. By **car** Hereford is 20 miles west of Junction 2 of the M50 , bypassing Ledbury on the A417 and the A438, about 3 hrs' drive from London. **National Express,** run 2 **coaches** a day to Hereford from London Victoria, taking about 4 hrs. ▸▸ *For further details, see Transport, page 360.*

Getting around Local **bus** services (patience needed to reach the outlying villages) are available. All the towns in the area are easily walked around.

Information **Hereford TIC,** ⓘ *1 King St, T01432-268430, www.visitorlinks.com. Daily 0900-1700, Sun 1000-1600.* **Ledbury TIC** ⓘ *3 The Homend, T01531-636147.* **Leominster TIC** ⓘ *1 Corn Sq, T01568-616460.*

Hereford

Hereford is a red-brick, Victorian-looking town on the banks of the river Wye, very much the heart of its county. The centre of the town today is **St Peter's Square**, a triangular road junction dominated by the imposing neoclassical Shire Hall. A few strides west lead into High Town past the Old House. Dating from 1621, the Old House is now a faintly forlorn-looking survival at one end of a broad pedestrianized open space lined with all the big brand names in retail. The ancient Jacobean half-timbered building contains the **Old House Museum** ⓘ *, High Town, T01432-260694, Apr-Sep Tue-Sun, bank holidays, Oct-Nov Tue-Sat*, reconstructing a few period rooms. Look out especially for the bargeboard carving of a cow being tugged at from both ends by two farmers, a lawyer milking their argument in the middle.

South of St Peter's Square, **Castle Green** is an early Georgian prom overlooking Castle Pool, still very pretty and a delightful place to picnic near the river. The park was laid out on the site of the city's Norman castle, hence the name. From here Castle St provides the most attractive approach to Hereford's idiosyncratic **Cathedral,** ⓘ *T01432-374200, www.herefordcathedral.co.uk 0800-2100 daily, tower Jul, Aug Mon-Sat, services Sun 0800, 1000, 1130, 1530, Mon-Sat 0730, 0800, Choral evensong (except Wed) 1730.* Dedicated to St Ethelbert, it's an endearingly small-scale affair, much of its well-weathered knobbly old pink stone covered in

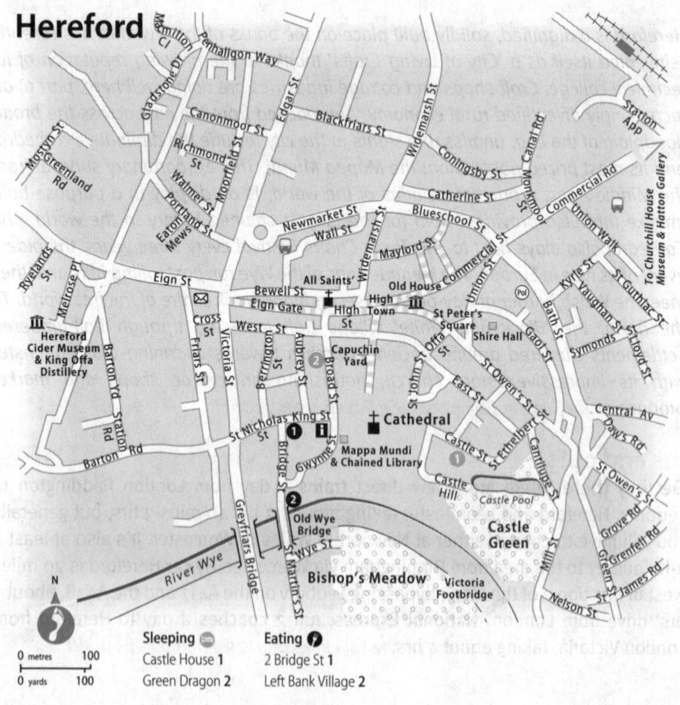

green lichens, situated in an atmospheric little close just north of the river. The building demonstrates just about the entire gamut of English cathedral architecture: the great round pillars of the Nave with their carved capitals stepping the unexpectedly short distance down to the carved 14th-century choir; beyond the High Altar, the Lady Chapel is one of the finest examples of the 13th-century Early English style in the country and has been undergoing urgent restoration; the tower and eastern transept are good examples of 14th-century Decorated. Other highlights of the interior include the early 16th-century Chantry of Bishop Audley and the Early English crypt, the most recent (13th century) of its kind in the country.

Next to the Cathedral, in a modern purpose-built cloister-style library building funded by Sir Paul Getty, the church's ancient **chained library** (the largest of its type in the world) has been restored and reconstructed. It makes an appropriate setting for the extraordinary **Mappa Mundi and Chained Library** ⓘ *Apr-Sep Mon-Sat 1000-1615, Sun 1100-1515, Oct-Nov Mon-Sat 1100-1515, £4.50, concessions £3.50, family £10*, a medieval world atlas that puts the Holy Land firmly at the centre of things. The Mediterranean Sea divided the known world into three parts: Asia, Europe and Africa. Britain is drawn much larger than it should be and is marked up with a variety of cathedral towns. Elsewhere there be dragons and depictions of various scenes from the Old Testament.

Two other sights worth seeking out on a rainy day are the reconstructed farm cider house and working distillery producing cider brandy at the **Hereford Cider Museum and King Offa Distillery**, ⓘ *21 Ryleands St, Hereford T01432-354207, Apr-Oct daily 1000-1730, Nov-Dec 1100-1500, Jan-Mar Tue-Sun 1100-1500, £2.60, £2.10 concessions*, and the quirky local **Churchill House Museum and Hatton Gallery** ⓘ *Venns Lane, Aylestone Hill, T01432-260693, Apr-Sep Wed-Fri 1400-1700*, displaying costume and furniture in a period house with gardens giving views over the city.

Around Hereford

The Weir, ⓘ *(NT) , 5 miles west of Hereford on the A438, T01981-590509, mid-Feb to Oct Wed-Sun, bank holidays 1100-1800, mid-Jan to mid-Feb Sat, Sun 1100-1600, £3.20, children £1.60*, is a beautiful riverside garden designed by Repton, well worth a look in spring for its bluebells and snowdrops, with commanding views over the Wye and into the Black Mountains beyond.

From Dorstone, the B4348 runs down the beautiful **Golden Valley** alongside the river Dore. Nestling in the green acres here, the remains of the Cisterician monastery at **Abbey Dore** ⓘ *T01981-240419, Abbey open dawn to dusk, free, gardens open Mar-Sep Tue, Thur, Sat, Sun, £3*, are a remarkable survival, thanks in part to the attentions of the Scudamore family in the 17th century, who perhaps felt remorseful about their ill-gotten gains after the Dissolution.

The **Black and White village trail** is the star attraction north of Hereford. **Weobley** is the quintessential example, with the *Red Lion* hotel, nestling in a village of black timber-frame and white brick. *The Olde Salutation* Inn ensconced behind topiary hedges could hardly be more typical of the area. The *Studio* gallery tearoom with its 'watercolour of the week' also tips its hat at passing trade. **Eardisland** is also typical of the area, while the *New Inn* at **Pembridge** is the local gathering place of the county's Sloane Rangers.

The town of **Leominster** can repay a visit thanks to its market square and quiet air of unhurried calm. School Lane is an alleyway of interesting independent shops, with the Old Merchant's House tearoom. Just north of Leominster, **Berrington Hall** ⓘ *T01568-615721, Apr-Oct Mon-Wed, Sun, Sat 1300-1700 (-1630 Oct, Nov) £4.40, grounds only £3, the costume collection can be seen by pre-arranged appointment only, contact the Costume Curator T01568-613720*, is the home of an astonishing costume collection, which Colonel Wade used to surprise guests like Graham Greene, Virginia Woolf, JB Priestley and John Betjeman at Snowshill Manor, his home in the Cotswolds. Berrington Hall itself is an austere neoclassical pile overlooking Capability Brown-landscaped gardens and the Brecon Beacons, with a delicate and elegant interior.

Sleeping

Hereford *p357, map p358*

A **Castle House**, Castle St, Hereford, T01432-356321. The most up-to-date in the city, in the most picturesque part of town and with beautifully appointed rooms.

B **Green Dragon Hotel**, Broad St, Hereford, T01432-272506, F352139. Genuinely ancient, fully refurbished Heritage hotel in the middle of the city, close to the cathedral, somehow more impressive outside than in but unbeatably convenient.

Around Hereford

C **The Green Man**, Fownhope, about 5 miles southeast of Hereford on the B4224, T01432-860243, www.smoothhound.co.uk/ hotels/greenman Pretty gardens not far from the River Wye and plenty of historical associations stretching back centuries at this welcoming family-run hotel. Also has leisure facilities close by, such as tennis, swimming and gym.

C **Grove House**, Bromsberrow Heath, near Ledbury, T01531-650584. A very superior B&B, the core of the house dates from the 14th century, with a large garden and large pond, and there are also recently refurbished rooms in the old dairy and summerhouse.

C **The Stagg**, Titley, T01544-230221, has a couple of bedrooms above a destination food pub in delightful border village about 12 miles west of Leominster. Near the Black Mountains and Golden Valley.

D **Mrs Ev Lloyd**, T01873-890263 and C **Diana Palmer**, T01873-890675, with her rare breeds farm, are both close to Abbey Dore.

F **The Pandy Inn**, on the main road in the bordertown of Pandy, about 20 miles southwest of Hereford on the A465, T01873-890208. Does B&B with bunkhouse accommodation. Useful for the Golden Valley and Black Mountains.

Eating

Hereford *p357, map p358*

There's not yet a huge variety of choice in the town. The **Left Bank Village** is the latest development, with good views of the river and the old Wye bridge, but it's also a rather characterless all-in restaurant bar complex. Reasonable food though.

£ The **Café in All Saints' Church**, High St, T01432-370415, is a good stop for a vegetarian lunch inside the Church.

£ **2 Bridge St**, T01432-279714, is a charming old-fashioned little coffeeshop on the corner of Bridge St.

Around Hereford

£ **Carpenter's Arms**, Walterstone, T01873-890353, is a cosy cottage pub close to the Welsh border and the Black Mountains with reasonable pub grub.

£ **Crown and Anchor**, Lugwardine, a couple of miles east of Hereford on the road to Ledbury, T01432-851303, is another beamed pub but with an accomplished menu.

£ **New Inn**, Pembridge, T01544-388427, does well-prepared local produce, with a fine array of ales, and it's the pub of choice of the young horsey set in the area.

£ **Salutation Inn**, Weobley, T01544-318443, is a superb village local in an ancient black and white building with a smartish restaurant attached.

£ **The Pandy**, Dorstone, T01981-550273, is a dinky old free house (apparently the oldest in Herefordshire) with a reasonable menu of bar meals in the wonderful Golden Valley east of Hay.

Transport

Hereford *p357, map p358*

Bus

Long distance National Express,T08705-808080, run 2 coaches a day to **Hereford** from **London Victoria**, taking about 4 hours. **Stagecoach**, T01633-485118, head into South Wales.

Local First, T01905-763888, and **Lug Valley Primrose Travel**, T01568-612759, out of Leominster.

The Wye Valley and Forest of Dean

→*Colour map 1*

Below Ross-on-Wye, and the famous viewpoint at Symonds Yat, the river Wye is worked almost as hard by canoeists and fishermen as it once was by barges taking the Forest of Dean's iron ore down to Bristol. The Wye Valley is treasured today – but still officially unprotected – for the ecological value of its broadleaf woodlands which step down the steep sides of its gorge, its early industrial archaeological remains, and its picturesque viewpoints. Sandwiched between the valleys of the Severn and the Wye, the Forest of Dean has long been a strange and isolated backwater. A wooded, hilly little landscape that is said to have inspired Tolkein's vision of Middle Earth in The Lord of the Rings, it's the mini-Appalachians of the West Midlands. ▸▸ *For Sleeping, Eating and other listings, see page 363.*

Ins and outs

Getting there The nearest **train** station to Ross-on Wye is at Gloucester, about 30 mins' bus ride away. The Forest of Dean can also be accessed from Lydney on the north bank of the Severn river. Ross-on-Wye is at the end of the M50, an arm of the M5 Birmingham-Exeter **motorway**. From London, though, it's most easily reached via the M4 and Severn Road Bridge (toll £4.40) to Chepstow (in Wales), then up the beautiful but often congested A466 to Monmouth and then the A40. Journey time approx 3 hrs. This is also the quickest route to the Forest of Dean from London. ▸▸ *For further details, see Transport, page 363.*

A steam train runs from Lydney (for network trains) to Norchard (for cars) from Easter-Oct T01485-541599.

Getting around There is a network of buses operating in the area but otherwise a car or bike are the best options for exploring the area. The **Wye Valley Wanderer** is a useful Sunday bus service linking Worcester, Malvern, Hereford, Ross-on-Wye and Symonds Yat. It runs May-September on Sun and also on bank holidays.

Information **Ross-on-Wye TIC** ⓘ *T01989-562768, www.visitorlinks.com, Easter-Sep Mon-Sat 0930- 1715, Oct-Easter Mon-Sat 0930-1630, mid-Jul to mid-Sep also Sun 1000-1600*. **Coleford TIC** ⓘ *T01594-812388, www.forestofdean.gov.uk, Nov-Mar Mon-Fri 1000-1600, Sat 1000-1400, Apr-Oct Mon-Sat 1000-1700, also Sun 1000-1400.*

Forest of Dean

The Forest of Dean covers about 35 square miles, much of it maintained by the Forestry Commission. Surprisingly for one of the first 'national forests' in the country, the Forest of Dean is not designated officially with any legal protection. On its edge, **Cinderford** is the most easterly town, its mining life long gone but it's still struggling gamely on. A couple of miles south, in between Upper and Lower Soudley, the **Dean Heritage Centre** ⓘ *T01594-822170, Apr-Oct daily 1000-1700, Nov-Feb 1000-1600, £4, concessions £3.50*, fills an old mill with four well-presented displays (recently refurbished courtesy of the Heritage Lottery Fund) on the history and working life of the area. Nearby, the **Blaize Bailey** viewpoint gives stunning views eastwards over the Severn's wide horseshoe bend. Four miles further east from Cinderford, on the A48 to Gloucester, **Westbury Court Gardens** ⓘ *(NT), T01452-760461, Mar-Jun, Sep and Oct Wed-Sun 1000-1700, Jul and Aug daily 1000-1700, £3*, are a very fine late 17th-century ordered Dutch water garden, restored in the early 1970s and planted with period trees quietly reflected in beautiful canals.

 From Cinderford the B4226 makes its 5-mile way west towards Coleford, the capital of the Forest. Almost half way along, the **Speech House** is the heart of the area. Now a hotel, it was built as the meeting place of the Court of the Verderers, which dates back to the reign of King Canute and had the power to order trespassers skinned alive and their hide nailed to the Speech House door. Nowadays all the woods around are free-range and most of the Forest's points of interest within easy reach along well-signposted paths. To the south, the **New Fancy Viewpoint** is one of the best of its type.

St Briavels ranks as one of the most delightful of the Forest's traditional villages, with its imposing old castle (now a spectacular youth hostel), views over the river, decent pub and a common beneath with an amazing patchwork of fields and ancient commoner's rights. Heading north the B4228 back towards Coleford passes the **Clearwell Caves** ⓘ *Near Coleford, T01594-832535, www.clearwellcaves.com, Mar-Oct, Dec daily 1000-1700*, a popular visitor attraction featuring go-as-you-please iron-ore mines, a few 'freeminers'. Nine caverns or 'churns' at a constant temperature of 10°C are lit up, dank, with safety walls. Ochres are still mined here.

To the south of St Briavels, **Brockweir**, just upstream from Tintern Abbey across the river in Wales, is another beautiful village with a good pub and canoes for hire on the river.

Ross-on-Wye and around

The place where appreciation of the Wye's scenic qualities first became a fashionable activity, Ross-on-Wye stands on a bluff overlooking a wide horseshoe bend in the river. A pretty neatly proportioned little place, it's still dominated by the spire of **St Mary's Church** which stands next to the Prospect. The spire was heightened and the Prospect laid out by John Kyrle 'The Man of Ross' in the early 18th century, capitalizing on the town's picturesque position. Kyrle's name is still remembered in the town for his philanthropy, and his hedgehog crest adopted as the town's unofficial logo. Nowadays a visit is unlikely to take up more than half a day, looking around the antique shops, admiring the view from the Prospect and look over the Church. The **Farmer's Market** on the first Friday of the month, 1000-1400, boasts a particularly impressive range of local produce and the general market on Thurs and Sat is also worth a look. The mid 17th-century **market house** ⓘ *Market Pl, T01432-260675, Apr-Oct Mon-Sat 1000-1700, Sun 1030-1600, Nov-Mar Mon-Sat 1030-1600*, has been quite entertainingly converted into a local history **museum** and heritage centre.

Below Ross, the Wye winds through increasingly sheer drops to the water. The next point of interest, **Goodrich Castle** ⓘ *(EH), T01600-890538, Apr-Sep daily 1000-1800, Oct daily 1000-1700, Nov-Mar Wed-Sun 1000-1300, 1400-1600, £3.70, concessions £2.80, children £1.90*, is best seen from the river in a canoe from Ross. Five miles downstream of the town, sitting on a red sandstone outcrop, Goodrich Castle has dominated this stretch of river since the Stone Age. Within its massive medieval outer walls nestles a perfect little Norman keep, possibly built by Godric (hence the name) in the 12th century. The formidable Gate Tower contains sluices designed for molten lead and boiling oil. Besieged for four months by the Parliamentarians in the Civil War, the castle was rendered useless on their victory but remains the most impressive in Herefordshire. Charming footpaths lead down to the river.

A couple more miles downstream, one of the most popular viewpoints on the Wye is at **Symonds Yat**, an old hill fort on the east side of the river. Very busy in high season, complete with toposcope, some of the crowds can be escaped by climbing up to **Yat Rock**, a limestone outcrop 160 yards above the water, a steep walk up from the *Forest View Hotel*. In summer the **Birds of Prey Centre** ⓘ *T0870-9901992*, in Newent put on spectacular displays from the rock. Further downstream, **Doward Wood** is a particularly lovely wood managed by the Woodland Trust, not driveable into, with **King Arthur's Cave** tucked away inside, a natural cave of passing interest, as well as another hill fort. The **Devil's Pulpit** is another superb viewpoint on the Offa's Dyke national trail along the border, near St Briavels and overlooking the remains of Tintern Abbey.

Sleeping

Forest of Dean *p361*

B **Speech House Hotel**, Coleford, Forest of Dean, T01594-822607, F823658. Chintz and pleated valances in one of the most historic houses in the forest, a 17th-century hunting lodge where the Verderer's Court was held.

Ross-on-Wye and around *p362*

B **Royal Hotel**, Palace Pound, Ross-on-Wye, T01989-565105, www.oldenglishinns .co.uk A fully refurbished Greene King hotel about 2 mins' walk from Market Sq. Dickens stayed here when planning his American tour. Breakfast included.

B **Wyndham Arms Hotel**, Clearwell, T01594-833666, www. thewyndham hotel.co.uk. A venerable old beamed and family-run establishment on the edge of the forest. Comfortable rooms (price includes breakfast) and oodles of traditional charm. Also serves straightforward and delicious home-cooked food.

C **Glewstone Court Hotel**, Glewstone, Nr Ross, T01989-770367, www.glewstone court.com. Good value this: a country house hotel with 8 rooms, the front rooms have beautiful views over the surrounding countryside, as well as a decent restaurant and bar.

C **The George**, St Briavels, next to the castle, T01594-530228, www.thegeorgeinn.com. Two doubles and a twin, is a convivial freehouse with a garden and passable pub grub.

F **YHA St Briavels Castle**, T01594- 530272, F530849. One 4-bedded, 3 6-bedded, 2 8-bedded and 3 dorms in this moated Norman castle, once King John's hunting lodge.

Camping Doward Park Camp Site, Great Doward, Symonds Yat West, Nr Ross, T01600-890438. Easter-Oct. £5-£8 per pitch per night. A small family-run campsite surrounded by woods.

Eating

Ross-on-Wye and around *p362*

$$ **Canio's**, Cantalupe Rd, Ross, T01989-567155, is a popular local Italian close to the public library, about £15 a head.

$$ **China Boy Jo's**, 27 Gloucester Rd, Ross, T01989-563533, is a superior Chinese restaurant: expect to pay about £20 a head, but it's worth it.

$$ **Cloisters**, High St, Ross, T01989-567717, is the locals' favourite bistro-type restaurant, with an emphasis on fish.

$$ **The Hostelry**, Goodrich, T01600-890241, has won plaudits for its food.

$$ The **Lough Pool**, Sellack, T01989-730236, also draws people in from afar to enjoy its ambitious and reasonably priced menu.

$$ **The Pheasant**, 52 Edde Cross, Ross, T01989-565751 has a good reputation doing modern British food at about £25 a head.

$ **Boat Inn**, Long Lane, Penallt, T01600-712615. A proper pub popular with walkers and canoeists, accessed via a footbridge over the river Wye. Reasonable grub (all day on Sat) and a precipitous garden overlooking the water.

Activities and tours

Ross-on-Wye and around *p362*

For walks around the area the Ordnance Survey Outdoor Leisure 14 map is ideal.

Paddles and Pedals, T01497-820604. Canoe hire at Symonds Yat West.

Pedalbikeaway, The Colliery New Road, Cannop, Forest of Dean, T01549-860065. For bike hire.

The Saracens Head, Symonds Yat East, T01600-890435, and

Ye Old Ferrie Inn, Symonds Yat West, T01600-890232.

Kingfisher Cruises, Symonds Yat East, 30-minute cruise trips up and down the river.

Tregoyd Mountain Riders, T01497-847351. Horse riding and pony trekking.

Wye Dean Canoe Centre, Symonds Yat East, T01600-890129. Have a public launch site at Kerne Bridge.

Wye Valley Canoe Centre, The Boat House, Glasbury-on-Wye, T01497-847213, www.wyevalleycanoes.co.uk. Hire out single kayak or Canadian canoes.

Transport

Ross-on-Wye and around *p362*

Bus

Long distance Stagecoach, T01452-523928, Red and White service 34 from **Gloucester** to **Monmouth**.

Local Stagecoach, T01452-523928, and H&H, T01989-566444, run most of the network of buses in the area,

Shropshire

→Colour map 3

Shropshire remains one of England's proud-to-be-undiscovered corners. Like Herefordshire, its relatively low population density and commitment to traditional farming have resulted in one of the least spoiled of England's rural landscapes. Shrewsbury is its county town, either pronounced 'Shrozebury' or 'Shroosbury', a well-to-do castellated market town in a lovely position on the River Severn. A string of very attractive little towns run south parallel to the border with Wales on the A49 south of Shrewsbury: Church Stretton for hillwalkers, Ludlow for antique collectors and gourmands, and on into Leominster and Hereford. The Severn Valley from Shrewsbury embraces the unassuming delights of Much Wenlock and then the well-packaged tourist attractions at Ironbridge, 'birthplace of the Industrial Revolution', before heading on to Worcester and Gloucester. Quiet old towns, hillwalking, nature reserves and industrial heritage are the county's forte as far as visitors are concerned. In fact whatever Shropshire does, whether it's food, farming or family fun, it still does it well, beautifully backward and happily isolated from the rest of the UK. ⏩ *For Sleeping, Eating and other listings, see pages 368-370.*

Shrewsbury

The county town of Shropshire, Shrewsbury makes up for the lack of a medieval cathedral with a variety of smaller examples of ecclesiastical architecture, quite an impressive old castle and a picturesque situation. Almost an island in a loop of the Severn river, this market town has been a fortified site since at least the fifth century. Visitors arriving by train still have to make their way beneath the castle walls up into the centre. Ignored by the Luftwaffe in the Second World War, many of the Tudor half-timbered buildings still survive. One of the best examples, Rowley's House, is now an excellent local history museum full of remarkable Roman finds. It's the unhurried pace and quiet atmosphere of this famously unpronounceable place that make it such a good base for exploring one of England's most lovely lost corners.

Ins and outs

Getting there There are hourly **trains** from London Euston, changing either at Crewe or Wolverhampton, taking around 3 hrs depending on the connection. Shrewsbury is also linked by rail to the north and Birmingham. By **car**, Shrewsbury is most easily reached from the south on the M54 from Junction 11 on the M6. It's about 3 ½ hrs from London. Regular **National Express** coach services run from London, Birmingham, Liverpool and elsewhere, arriving at the bus station a few hundred yards from the train station. ⏩ *For further details, see Transport, page 370.*

Getting around The town itself is easily negotiated on foot. The surrounding countryside really needs a car, although many local buses to places like Much Wenlock are available.

Information **Shrewsbury TIC** ⓘ *The Music Hall, The Square, T01743-281200, www.shrewsburytourism.co.uk Oct-Apr Mon-Sat 1000-1700, May-Sept Mon-Sat 0930-1730, Sun 1000-1600. Accommodation booking £1 fee.*

Sights

From the station, a few steps away the steep **Castle Gate** heads up into the heart of the town. The Castle itself dates largely from the 14th century, with a few 18th-century alterations, and contains the **Shropshire Regimental Museum** ⓘ *Castle St, T01743-358516, www.shrewsbury-museums.com, Mid-Feb to Mar Wed-Sat 1000-1600; Apr-May Tue-Sat 1000-1700, Jun-Aug daily 1000-1600, £2*. One of the largest of its kind in the country, the museum contains the usual collection of military memorabilia, weapons, uniforms, china and medals, but on an impressive scale, while the Norman motte is worth climbing for views over the town.

A couple of hundred yards beyond the castle, off Castle St on the left, the soaring 200-ft spire of **St Mary's Church** ⓘ *T01743-357006, Mon-Fri 1000-1700, Sat 1000-1600, Apr-Oct also Sun*, dominates the old part of town. The closest the town comes to a cathedral, set in a pretty little close, the church displays a satisfying mix of Norman and Gothic architectural styles and contains a remarkable Tree of Jesse in the beautiful east window, imported from old St Chad's. Much of the other glass is also very fine, including a variety of French medieval craftsmanship.

A hundred yards north of the Square, down Barker St, the **Shrewsbury Museum and Art Gallery**, ⓘ *T01743-361196, http://shrewsburymuseums.com, Apr-Oct Tue-Sat 1000-1700, Mon and Sun 1000-1600, Nov-Mar Tue-Sat 1000-1600, free*, in Rowley's House is well worth seeking out. Originally a warehouse for wool, built in the late Elizabethan era, the next door building was the first in the town to be made of brick. As well as many Roman finds from Wroxeter (see below) – including a mirror and the inscription over the town gate – and a medieval section, there's a highly rated Art Gallery with regular temporary exhibitions on local themes.

A similar distance west of the Square, up Claremont Hill, **St Chad's** is a very fine Georgian round church in a spectacular position overlooking the river with a prominent spire and elegant neoclassical portico. Apparently the building of it caused riots in protest at the demolition of part of the old town walls. Beyond the church, a spacious public park slopes down to the riverbank. From St Chad's, a charming walk down Murivance and Town Walls circles the town following the course of the river downstream to **English Bridge**, a venerable old stone structure and good viewpoint. Over the bridge, a hundred yards up Abbey Foregate, the **Abbey of the Holy Cross** ⓘ *T01743-232723, Apr-Oct daily 1000-1730, Nov-Mar 1030-1500*, is a masterful Victorian improvement on a Norman

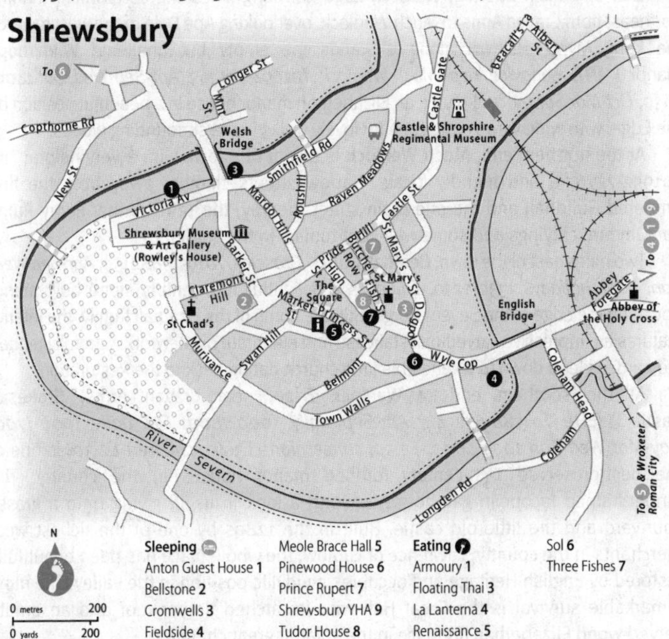

foundation. Founded in 1083, the Abbey survived the dissolution thanks to its use by the laity as their local place of worship. Its greatest claim to fame these days is as the real-life home of Ellis Peter's fictional 'Brother Cadfael'.

An interesting day trip can be made to **Wroxeter Roman City** ⓘ *T01743-761330, 29 Mar-30 Sep daily 1000-1800, 1-31 Oct daily 1000-1700, 1 Nov-31 Mar daily 1000-1600*. On the evidence still standing today, 'City' seems a bit of an exaggeration, but 5 miles southeast of Shrewsbury, there are some fairly impressive remains of a place called Viroconium that once housed some 6000 souls, the fourth largest town in Roman Britain and part of Emperor Hadrian's fortification of his empire. The site of the baths and a large dividing wall can be seen, as well as a small museum of finds, although the best are in Rowley's House (see above). There's also a working **vineyard** ⓘ *Wroxeter, T01743-761888*, which you can look round.

Church Stretton, The Long Mynd and Wenlock Edge

South of Shrewsbury, the best walking country in Shropshire can be found around the small Victorian resort town of Church Stretton, easily reached on the train. The Long Mynd is a 7-mile ridge of rounded hills just to the west of Church Stretton. Lonely walks lead up to heights of 1700 feet through bracken, heather and gorse, the most famous of which is the **Burway**. The **Port Way** runs along the top of the ridge, providing fantastic views into Wales and inland England almost as far as Birmingham. Deep secret valleys run down the Long Mynd's eastern slopes, accessible from villages like Little Stretton, Minton Batch and Priors Holt. Worth seeking out are the 20 or so acres of mixed deciduous woodland at **Old Rectory Wood**, just outside Church Stretton to the west. Details of all walks are available from Church Stretton **tourist information** (T01694-723133, Easter-October).

The Wenlock Olympian games were started in 1850 and are said to have inspired the modern Olympics.

East of Church Stretton, **Wenlock Edge** is a long limestone escarpment running northeast from Craven Arms to Much Wenlock, overlooking Ape Dale to the west towards the Long Mynd. Halfway along it stands the empty but unaltered **Wilderhope** Manor ⓘ *(NT), Longville, near Much Wenlock, T01694-771363, Apr-Sep Wed, Sat 1400-1630, Oct-Mar Sat 1400-1630, £1*, an Elizabethan manor house in a beautiful position on the Edge, with wide views and scope for lovely walks in the surrounding woods.

At the northern end, **Much Wenlock** is a gem of a town with a very helpful TIC, T01952-727679, and friendly locals. Narrow streets clamber away from the fine timbered Guildhall and the one main street. Nearby, the 12th-century Priory Ruins contain rare carvings and some well-kept topiary in the gardens.

Two miles east of the town, **Benthall Hall** ⓘ *Broseley, T01952-882159, Apr-Sep Wed, Sun, bank holidays 1330-1730, £3.60*, is a delightful 16th-century stone built manor house on the edge of the Severn Gorge. Still the home of the Benthall family, the interior features an impressive carved-oak staircase and elaborate plasterwork. Carefully tended old gardens lead down to a venerable little church dating back to the Restoration.

At the southern end of Wenlock Edge, near Craven Arms, **Stokesay** Castle ⓘ *(EH), T01588-672544, Apr-Sep daily 1000-1800, Oct daily 1000-1700, Nov-Mar Wed-Sun 1000-1600, £4.50, concessions £3.40, children £2.30*, is one of the best-preserved 13th-century fortified manor houses in the country. The timber-framed Jacobean gatehouse is worth a look in itself, giving onto a grassy courtyard and the little old castle. Built in the 1280s by one of the richest wool merchants in the country, Lawrence of Ludlow, the whole place has been beautifully restored by English Heritage and occupies an idyllic position in the valley. The most remarkable survival is the Great Hall with its arched timber roof and an ornate carved-wood Elizabethan fireplace in the solar or great chamber.

Severn Gorge and Ironbridge

East of Much Wenlock, the Severn Gorge plunges down from a glut of museums at the World Heritage Site at Ironbridge to the gorge-side town of Bridgnorth. In Ironbridge, the first iron bridge in the world is still well worth a look after all these years. The result of three generations' worth of the Darby family's expertise in iron-smelting, it was erected in 1779. Now a well-preserved footbridge crossing the steep-sided gorge from the Victorian high street of the town, it forms the centrepiece of a pretty comprehensive celebration of the Industrial Revolution in Britain. An exhibition on the history of the bridge is housed in the original Tollhouse on the south side, over the bridge from the main drag of Ironbridge itself. It's the first of no less than ten different museums of the period in the vicinity. The **Museum of the Gorge** ⓘ *T01952-432166, www.ironbridge.ws, daily 1000-1700, passport tickets to all 10 museums £12.95, under-16s and concessions £8.25, family £40*,a short walk west on the north bank, traces the history of the whole gorge in an 1830s warehouse, a highlight being the 40-ft scale model of the landscape in 1796. Up the road north from here in Coalbrookdale is the **Museum of Iron and Darby Houses**, on the site of Abraham Darby I's original blast furnace of 1709, with which he succeeded in smelting iron with coke rather than charcoal. The **Museum of Iron** offers a glimpse of the Great Exhibition of 1851 and also 'Enginuity', the new Coalbrookdale Interactive Technology Centre where visitors are encouraged to try out the principles of engineering for themselves.

Ludlow

The jewel in Shropshire's crown, Ludlow is a very picturesque hill town perched on the banks of the river Teme. Heavily fortified by the Normans under Roger Montgomery, the castle is still the main event, although just wandering around the town is also a joy. Ludlow **tourist information** ⓘ *Castle St, T01584-875053, www.ludlow.org.uk, daily 1000-1700 (-1600 on Sat), closed Sun in Jan-Mar.*

The **castle** ⓘ *Ludlow Castle, T01584-873355, www.lc.com Apr-Sep 1000-1700 (-1900 in Aug), Oct-Mar 1000-1600, £3.50, concessions £3, children £1, free Audio Guide*, was slighted by Parliamentarians during the Civil War, but not as badly as many others. The superb views from the top of the Norman keep, the Great Hall, where Milton's *Comus* was first performed, and an unusual round royal chapel are some of the highlights of a visit. The castle has a long and troubled history at the centre of centuries of border clashes. Eventually it became the HQ of the Marcher barons, the seat of the Council of Marches established in 1475 to govern Wales. Many unfortunate Princes of Wales were associated with the place, including Arthur, elder brother of Henry VIII – married aged 14 to Catherine of Aragon but dead in his bed here soon after – and Edward, briefly Edward V before being deposed and possibly murdered by his uncle Richard III. Regular events are now staged within the castle walls, the best during the Ludlow festival in June and July.

A few hundred yards from the fateful castle gates, across Castle Square (scene of lively markets most days of the week), the neoclassical **Butter Cross** is the centre of town. Behind it, the **Church of St Lawrence** well deserves its status as 'Cathedral of the Marches'. Evidence of the prosperity brought to the town by the wool trade, it contains a wealth of wonderful medieval glass, ancient tombs and royal misericords. From the Butter Cross, **Broad Street** slopes down to the river, surely one of the most delightful streetscapes in the country. Before reaching the river at Ludford Bridge, with its lovely views of the river, it passes through the **Broad Gate**, the sole survivor of the town's seven medieval gates.

Sleeping

Shrewsbury *p364, map p365*

B **Prince Rupert**, Butcher Row, T01743-499955, F357306. The smartest hotel in the centre of town, in a cunningly refurbished old house on the corner of Butcher Row and Pride Hill.

C **Meole Brace Hall**, Meole Brace, Shrewsbury, T01743-235566, www.meolebracehall.co.uk. ETC Silver Award, AGA Cook of the Year. About a 20-min walk, on the outskirts.

C **Tudor House**, 2 Fish St, T01743-351735. A good and central B&B.

D **Anton Guest House**, 1 Canon St, Monkmoor, Shrewsbury, T01743-359275, www.antonhouse.supernet.com. Another reasonable budget option near the centre.

D **The Bellstone**, Bellstone, Shrewsbury, T01743-242100. Good value budget hotel in the centre of town with a brasserie attached.

D **Cromwells Hotel**, 11 Dogpole, T01743-361440, www.cromwellsinn.co.uk. Opposite the Guildhall, reasonably priced and interesting food, and about to undergo substantial refurbishment.

D **Fieldside**, 38 London Rd, T01743-353143, F354687. Further out, but also very comfortable.

D **Pinewood House**, Shelton Park, The Mount, T01743-364200. A mile or so northwest of town, a 20-min walk, this is a sweet little B&B in a converted Victorian coach house.

F **Shrewsbury YHA**, the Woodlands, Abbey Foregate, T01743-360179. Has 54 beds in a Victorian ironmaster's house about a mile east of the train station.

Outside Shrewsbury

A-B **Soulton Hall**, Nr Wem, T01939-232786, F234097. Grand Elizabethan house with a family atmosphere, 4 rooms in the house, 23 in coachhouse. £107 for 4-poster bed in the Cedar Lodge at the side of the walled garden.

C **Upper Brompton Farm**, Cross Houses, 4 miles south of Shrewsbury, T01743-761629, www.upperbromptonfarm.com. Highly rated B&B on a working farm.

D **Burlton Inn**, Burlton, T01939-270284. Does good home-cooked food on the road to Ellesmere.

Church Stretton, Long Mynd and Wenlock Edge *p366*

B **Stretton Hall Hotel**, All Stretton, T01694-723224, www.strettonhall.co.uk £90 a double in a fine country manor house a short distance from Church Stretton.

C **Belvedere Guest House**, Burway Rd, Church Stretton, T01694-722232. One of the better guesthouses in Church Stretton (which has more than enough to go round), standing in its own gardens and handy for walks on the Long Mynd.

C **Three Tuns**, Salop St, Bishop's Castle, T01588-638797. Self-catering rooms (minimum 3-night stays) in an annexe of the town's oldest pub.

C **Wenlock Edge Inn**, Hill Top, Nr Much Wenlock, T01746-785678, www.wenlockedgeinn.co.uk Two doubles and a twin, £70 for the 3-bed room. Superbly positioned pub with acclaimed grub and comfortable rooms.

C **Willowfield Country Guesthouse**, Lower Wood, All Stretton, Nr Church Stretton, T01694-751471. A peaceful, dignified place with candlelit dinners in the Elizabethan dining room and its own gardens.

D **Brook House Farm**, T01694-771308. Wall under Heywood, 5 miles east of Church Stretton beneath Wenlock Edge, is a stone-built non-smoking farmhouse B&B with great views and gardens, as well as self-catering cottages.

D **The Talbot Inn**, High St, Much Wenlock, T01952-727077. Fine pub grub in a beamed and welcoming village-style pub.

F **Stokes Barn Bunkhouse**, Much Wenlock, T01952-727293. Superb views, windy camping and cosy bunk-ups.

F **YHA Wilderhope Manor**, Longville in the Dale, T01694-771363. Has 4 dormitories, one 6-bed room and one 4-bed in the National Trust's untouched Elizabethan manor house on Wenlock Edge.

Severn Gorge and Ironbridge *p367*

C **Thorpe House**, Coalport, T01952-586789. Offers 4 rooms in a Victorian house near the river, a little over a mile east of the bridge itself.

D **Woodlands Farm Guest House**, Beech Rd, Ironbridge, T01952-432741. Even closer to the bridge, a farm house on the edge of the gorge in 4 acres of its own grounds.

F **Ironbridge Gorge YHA**, High St, Coalport, T01952-588755. Has 160 beds in mainly 2-6 bedded rooms, spread over 2 sites at the Coalport China Museum.

Ludlow *p367*

A **Dinham Hall**, Dinham, T01584-876464, www.dinhamhall.co.uk A grand 18th-century hotel beneath the castle walls with a good reputation for its food.

A **Overton Grange**, Hereford Rd, Nr Ludlow, T01584-873524. Another top-end option, a bit stuffy but also with an ambitious and accomplished menu, a short distance out of town towards Hereford on the B4361.

B **Mr Underhill's at Dinham Weir**, Dinham Bridge, T01584-874431. A charming restaurant with rooms on the river, a Michelin star for the food and a short bracing walk up into town.

B **Number Twenty Eight**, 28 Lower Broad St, T0800-0815000, www.no28.co.uk Six period townhouses below the Broad Gate, close to the river. A distinctly superior B&B.

C **Eight Dinham** 8 Dinham, T01584-875661. Refined B&B in an elegant period house close to the castle.

C **The Charlton Arms**, Ludford Bridge, T01584-872813. Family-run pub overlooking the Teme rapids, close to the old town bridge.

C **Seifton Court**, Culmington, Nr Ludlow, T01584-861214. A very comfortable 16th-century farmhouse nestling in Corvedale, 6 miles north up the B4365.

D **Church Inn**, Buttercross, T01584-872174, www.thechurchinn.com A cheerful freehouse, tucked away behind the Buttermarket bang in the middle of town, which has reasonable rooms and does very filling, moderately priced meals in a jolly congenial atmosphere.

D **The Wheatsheaf Inn**, Lower Broad St, T01584-872980. At the bottom of Broad St, a family-run pub with clean, comfortable rooms.

Eating

Shrewsbury *p364, map p365*

£££ **Sol**, 82 Wyle Cop, T01743-340560. Local produce expertly but rather too expensively prepared. Widely regarded as the best restaurant in Shrewsbury.

£££ **Renaissance**, 29a Princess St, T01743-354289. Occupies grand Georgian dining rooms and uses fresh local produce.

££ **The Armoury**, Victoria Quay, Victoria Av, T01743-340525, does modern British food in a converted warehouse restaurant-bar overlooking the river. Book at the weekend.

££ **Floating Thai Restaurant**, Welsh Bridge, T01743-243123. As its name suggests, exotic food in watery surroundings, evenings only.

££ **La Lanterna**, The Old Vestry, St Julians, T01743-233552. A popular Italian trattoria.

££ **The Riverside Inn**, some 6 miles out of town to the southeast, beside the river on the road to Cressage, T01952-510900, does rooms (C) and some good British food on an attractive stretch of the river Severn.

£ **Three Fishes**, Fish St, T01743-344793, is worth seeking out for its excellent real ales in a fine Tudor building in the middle of town, as well as reasonably priced bar meals.

Ludlow *p367*

Ludlow has developed a reputation for its cuisine, attracting no less than 3 coveted Michelin stars at 3 of its establishments (including Mr Underhill's). For pub grub, *The Charlton Arms*, *Church Inn* and *The Wheatsheaf Inn* in Sleeping above, have plenty to offer.

£££ **Merchant House**, Lower Corve St, T01584-875438. The original and best, about £40 a head for some top-notch tucker, because of its Jacobean surroundings. Be sure to book.

£££ **Hibiscus**, 17 Corve St, T01584-872325, is another, also highly rated for its kitchen. Needs to be booked.

££ **Roebuck**, T01584-711230, in Brimfield, 4 miles south of Ludlow, also has a formidable reputation for its food.

££ **Koo**, 127 Old St, T01584-878462, is a small, reasonably priced (about £20 a head) Japanese restaurant that has won the hearts of the locals.

£ **Aragon's Restaurant**, 5 Church St, T01584-873282, is a café-restaurant that does filling sandwiches, soups, pastas and pizzas all day.

£ **Ego Café Bar**, Quality Sq, T01584 878000, is a wine bar with decent enough food and a friendly atmosphere.

£ **The Unicorn**, Corve St, T01584-873555, does above-average pub food in a cosy, beamed old place.

Pubs, bars and clubs

Church Stretton, Long Mynd and Wenlock Edge *p366*

Horseshoe Inn, Bridges, Nr Ratlinghope, T01588-650260. With self-catering accommodation and good food.

Royal Oak, Cardington, Nr Church Stretton, T01694-771266. Tables outside and wholesome meals for lunch and supper, close to Cardingmill Valley (NT).

Three Tuns, Salop St, Bishop's Castle, T01588-638797. Very old pub with its own brewery (granted a licence in the mid 17th century, none of yer fancy modern microbrews here) with quiet self-catering rooms available in an annexe.

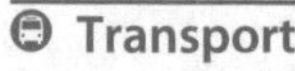

Transport

Long distance

Regular **National Express**, T08705-808080, services run from **London**, **Birmingham**, **Liverpool**.

Local

Arriva Midlands North, T0845-6012491, and several other companies (NB no buses to Ironbridge on Sun).

The Potteries

→*Colour map 3*

As their name suggests, the Potteries – aka Stoke-on-Trent – are best known for being a world centre of ceramics, and home to Royal Doulton, Spode and Wedgwood. These businesses still dominate the daily life of Stoke-on-Trent, the city of six towns. Dickens described it as 'opulent', Arnold Bennett immortalized it as 'Knype' in his 'Five Towns' books such as Clayhanger and more recently Robbie Williams and Anthea Turner both spent their early lives imbibing the cultural mix and flourishing nightlife of the city, which no doubt helped at least one of them on their way to international stardom. The manufacture of pottery in this area goes back to Roman times, but it wasn't until the coming of the Trent-Mersey Canal and the development of local coal-fields in the 18th and early 19th centuries, that the place really took off, with the names listed above as well as quite a few others setting up factories which were soon generating handsome profits. An early exemplar of the truism 'where there's muck, there's brass', Stoke paid the price for this prosperity with legendary levels of pollution and some of the worst working conditions to be found in the country – a fact commemorated in one of the contemporary museums by a special 'child labour exhibit'. These days the urban landscape isn't quite so grimy and the famous bottle-kilns associated with Stoke – many of which are still standing – don't belch filthy smoke 24/7. Meanwhile kids aren't pressed into labour before they reach their teens, but are more likely to be found pressing their parents into taking them to Alton Towers, the nation's favourite theme park which lies a few miles east of Stoke. » *For Sleeping, Eating and other listings, see page 372.*

Ins and outs

Getting there With **Virgin** Trains, T08457-222333, operating one of their main routes from London to Manchester via Crewe and Stafford, you can be assured of **trains** every 30 mins for most of the day. **Central Trains,** T08700-006060, run a local service from Birmingham and the West Midlands on a very regular basis. Handily situated just off the M6, Stoke-on-Trent is more or less slap bang in the middle of the country, so is easily accessible by **road** from all directions. From London take the M1 to Leicester and then the A50 takes you right into Stoke. Also the M40 from London will take you to Birmingham and you can get onto the M6 via the M42 and M5. Just after Newcastle-under-Lyme you turn right on to the A50 approaching Stoke from the west. From the southwest the M5 connects with the M6 outside Birmingham. From the north the M6 or the A1 will connect with the A50 for a fairly trouble-free journey.

Getting around With plenty of parking and a far from pedestrianized centre Stoke-on-Trent and its surroundings are ideal for those with cars. The centre of the city is Hanley, even though there's also an area called Stoke. The town museum is situated in this area, though there are visitors' centres and factory shops attached to most of the functioning Pottery concerns. Stoke-on-Trent does, however, benefit from having an excellent bus service. **First**, T01782-207999, have a Fareday ticket, priced £3 for an adult and £5 for a family (2 adults and 3 children), which you can buy on any PMT bus, and is valid for 1 day's unlimited travel on the local First network. For further bus information and a handy journey planner visit www.ukbus.co.uk.

Information Stoke-on-Trent TIC ⓘ *Quadrant Rd, Hanley, Stoke-on-Trent, T01782-236000, F01782-236005. Mon-Sat 0915-1715.* **Stafford TIC** ⓘ *Market St, Stafford, T01785-619619. Mon-Fri 0930-1700, Sat 1000-1700.*

Stoke-on-Trent

Most visitors to Stoke-on-Trent will want to head straight for its 'cultural quarter' and **The Potteries Museum and Art Gallery**, ⓘ *Bethesda St, Hanley, T01782-232323, Nov-Feb Mon-Sat 1000-1600, Sun 1300-1600, Mar-Oct Mon-Sat 1000-1700, Sun 1400-1700, book tours in advance via Visitor Desk, available during opening hours only. free*. Pick of the bunch, museum-wise, with the largest collection of pottery in the world, as well as an original Spitfire fighter plane from the Second World War, which was designed by local lad Reginald Mitchell. Commemorating local lads of a different industrial background, there's also the Coal Sculpture which is a memorial to the two local colliers who died on picket duty during the 1984 miner's strike. While there's an excellent narrative of the town's association with pottery in the town museum, an even better one can be found in the **Gladstone Pottery** Museum ⓘ *Uttoxeter Rd, Longton, T01782-319232,d aily 1000-1700, except Christmas to New Year, £4.95, children £3.50, concessions £3.95, family £14*, which is the only authentic reproduction of a Victorian pottery factory in the world and comes complete with cobbled yard, bottle-shaped oven-kilns and the chance to create your own pot. As befits a town that plays host to Royal Doulton, there's even a new exhibit at the Gladstone Museum waggishly called 'Flushed with Pride' which charts the history of the toilet. There's also an excellent Chintz tearoom and gift shop. For lovers of industrial history the **Etruria Industrial Museum** ⓘ *Lower Bedford St, Etruria, T01782-233144, car park is on Kiln Down Rd, off Etruria Vale Rd, Sat-Wed 1200-1630, except Christmas to New Year, closed weekends Jan-Mar, £1.50 children/concessions £1*, is Britain's sole surviving steam-powered potter's mill. Built in 1857 to grind materials for the pottery industry it's a great hands-on exhibit offering a superb insight into how it all worked back in the days when there were many others like it.

Around Stoke-on-Trent

Twenty miles east of Stoke-on-Trent, **Alton Towers** ⓘ *T08705-204060, daily from 16 Mar-3rd Nov, daily 0930-2000 or dusk if earlier www.altontowers.com*, is the UK's most famous theme park. Thrill rides galore on Europe's big flying rollercoaster. Also Nemesis and Oblivion – real screamers. Don't miss the ice illusion show.

Near Stafford, the county town that has suffered drastically thanks to the M6, the **Shugborough Estate**ⓘ *(NT) Milford, T01889-881388, Apr-Sep daily 1100-1700*, is the 900-acre ancestral home of Lord Lichfield. Nearby, the **National Forest**, T01283-551211, is a 200-square mile forest that impinges on three counties, with lovely woodland and walks. **Stafford**, the county town, is an undistinguished market town most closely associated with Sir Izaak Walton, the *Compleat Angler*. Its main attraction is the **Ancient High House** ⓘ *Greengate St, Stafford, T01785-619619, Mon-Sat 1000-1700*, the tallest timber framed townhouse in England. Built in 1595 and refurbished with Elizabethan period rooms.

Sleeping

Around Stoke-on-Trent *p371*

B **Garth Hotel**, Wolverhampton Rd, Stafford, T01785-256124, www.corushotels.co.uk, is a hotel that grew out of an old pub and now has 60 rooms.

B **The Little Barrow Hotel**, Beacon St, Lichfield, T01543-414500, www.tlbh.co.uk Five-minutes walk uphill from the cathedral, a small (24 beds) family-run hotel that was once a sweet shop.

C **Manor House**, near Denstone, Uttoxeter, T01889-590415. Three miles away from Alton Towers is this ancient Tudor manor house B&B, very welcoming with 3 double rooms (en-suite bathrooms), each with 4-poster beds.

D **Slab Bridge Cottage**, Little Onn, Church Eaton, T01785-840220. A Victorian cottage on the Shropshire Union Canal, with 2 bedrooms with en-suite bathroom and offering boat trips too.

Eating

Around Stoke-on-Trent *p371*

$$$ **Julians**, 21 High St, Stafford, T01785-851200, do acceptable bistro fare for lunch and supper in the middle of the county town (about £25 a head).

$$ **The Olive Tree**, 34 Tamworth St, Lichfield, T01543-263363, off the High St, does a Mediterranean menu in a buzzy and friendly atmosphere (about £12 a head).

$$ **The Queen's Head**, Lichfield, T01543-410932, does a huge variety of different cheeses to go with its very fine real ales.

Bedfordshire and Northamptonshire

→Colour map 2

Both these Midland counties are usually overlooked by visitors, not without some reason, although Northamptonshire embraces some beautiful countryside dotted with old stone-built villages, grand stately homes and innumerable church spires. Bedfordshire's defining character derives from the broad floodplain of the River Ouse, its clay soil traditionally used for bricks. The greensand ridge in the middle of the county is its most attractive feature though, with the much-publicized safari park and stately home at Woburn Abbey at its western end, and quaint Victorian estate villages like Old Warden at its eastern. Bedford itself is chiefly famous for bricks, hats, and being the place of imprisonment of John Bunyan. Northamptonshire boasts some very grand houses indeed, most impressively the Duke of Buccleuch's pad at Boughton and most popularly Althorp, last resting place of Diana, Princess of Wales. ▸▸ *For Sleeping, Eating and other listings, see pages 375-376.*

Bedfordshire

Apart from the extraordinary collection of art in the Cecil Higgins Gallery, anyone interested in the history of the Christian church or dissenters in general will want to look in on the John Bunyan museum in Bedford itself. Otherwise, the county's top visitor attractions are Woburn Abbey and Safari Park, a less colourful but just as well publicized version of Longleat in Wiltshire, and at Whipsnade the countryside outstation of the Zoological Society of London (aka London Zoo).

Ins and outs

Getting there Via **rail**, Bedford is connected via **Thameslink** to London King's Cross (1 hr). Midland Mainline goes from St Pancras to Bedford (30 mins) and then on to Leicester (40 mins from Bedford), Nottingham (1 hr 10 mins from Bedford) and

Sheffield (1 hr 40 mins from Bedford). Bedford can be reached easily by **road** from London on either the A1 or M1 in around an hr. **National Express**, T08705-808080, run a coach a day from London Victoria to Bedford.

Information Bedford TIC ⓘ *10 St Paul's Sq, T01234-215226, www.bedford.gov.uk/tourism. Daily Mon-Sat 0930-1700, May-Aug also Sun 1100-1500. Mid-Bedfordshire TIC, 5 Shannon Ct, High St, Sandy, T01767-682728. Apr-Oct Mon-Sat 1000-1630, Sat, Sun 1000-1500; Nov-Mar Mon-Fri 1000-1600, Sat 1000-1500.*

Bedford

The county town of Bedford, famous for once making quantities of bricks and hats, is now a pleasant enough large town on the banks of the river Great Ouse. The river is crossed at the southern end of the High Street, from where the Embankment runs along the waterside. Not much remains of the Norman castle except a mound in the park near Castle Lane and **Bedford Museum** ⓘ *T01234-353323, Tue-Sat 1100-1700, Sun 1400-1700, £2.10, concessions and under-18s free (also with Cecil Higgins)*, the local history museum with displays on local burial sites but mainly geared up to deal with schools. Next door is the highlight of a visit to the town, the **Cecil Higgins Art Gallery** ⓘ *Castle Lane, T01234-211222, www.cecilhigginsartgallery.org, Tue-Sat 1100-1645, Sun 1100-1645*, a reconstructed Victorian mansion and modern art gallery with an exceptional collection of watercolours, as well as sculpture, furniture, glass, ceramics and metalwork by internationally famous artists. The watercolour collection includes works by the likes of Turner, Constable, Blake, Landseer, Sickert, Lowry, Hepworth, Nicholson, and Henry Moore among others. The gallery also contains a room dedicated to the eccentric Victorian architect and designer William Burges, a leading exponent of the Gothic Revival. Interesting temporary exhibitions from the collection are also mounted.

Behind the museum, in Mill Street, the bronze doors of the **Bunyan Meeting Free Church** ⓘ *The Church Office, Bunyan Meeting Free Church, Mill St, T01234-213722, Mar-Oct Tue-Sat 1100-1600*, were donated by the Duke of Bedford in 1876, with 10 panels depicting scenes from *The Pilgrim's Progress*. Written by the preacher and Parliamentarian John Bunyan while he was imprisoned in Bedford jail for 12 years under Charles II's religious laws, it still ranks as one of the most influential pieces of Christian literature of all time. Bunyan bought a barn and orchard on his release from prison, which in 1707 was replaced by a Meeting House, and in 1850 by the church that stands here today. Next door, the **John Bunyan Museum** was opened in 1998, displaying exhibits and artefacts associated with his life and an illustrated display on *The Pilgrim's Progress*.

Around Bedfordshire

Set in a 3000-acre deer park, **Woburn Abbey** ⓘ *T01525-290666, daily Apr-Sep 1100-1600, Sat and Sun Jan-Mar, Oct 1100-1600, £8.50, concessions £7.50, children £4, take exit 13 off the M1 motorway, or leave the A5 at Hockliffe for the A4012, the Abbey is well signed from here, Safari Park £13, children £9.50*, is the home of the Marquess and Marchioness of Tavistock and their family. It houses one of the most important private art collections in the world, including paintings by Van Dyck, Gainsborough, Reynolds, and Canaletto as well as 18th-century French and English furniture, silver, gold and porcelain. Visitors can also enjoy the renowned antiques centre, coffee shop, gift shops, pottery and beautiful grounds including the famous Safari Park.

Opened in 1931 as the first open zoo in Europe, **Whipsnade** ⓘ *Dunstable, just west of Luton, T01582-872171, www.whipsnade.co.uk, Mar-Sep 1000-1800, Oct-Feb 1000-1600, £12.50, children £9.50, signposted from the M1 (junctions 9 and 12) and all major roads*, is the country base of London Zoo, with over 200 different species in about 600 acres of Chiltern downland. Larger animals, such as elephants, have been gradually moved here from the city.

Northampton and around

The county of 'squires, spires and mires' attracts fewer visitors than it deserves, perhaps because it's generally perceived to be in the middle of nowhere. The M1 slices through the southeastern part on its way north. Northampton itself sits right beside the motorway, ruined by recent developments but concealing some extraordinary churches and an unusual collection of footwear. Shoemaking once made this part of the country famous, although its wealth has always come from manufacturing industry and agriculture, both currently down on their luck. Large estates cover most of its northern part, the most spectacular and pompous being Boughton House, the most popular, for mawkish reasons, being Althorp, childhood home of Princess Diana.

Ins and outs

Getting there Northampton is on the main London-Birmingham line, with regular **rail** services running into London Euston (1 hour). By **car**, Northampton is just off the M1, easily reached in 1 hr 30 mins from London. **National Express**, T08705-808080, run coaches to Northampton 4 times a day, taking about 2 hours from London Victoria.

Getting around Town buses are run by **First Northampton**, T0870-6082608, and the network of local buses to outlying villages by **Stagecoach**, T01604-676060. Northampton itself can easily be walked around, but exploring beyond the town really requires a car.

Information **Northampton TIC** ⓘ *Northampton Museum and Art Gallery, Guildhall Rd, T01604-622677, www.northampton.gov.uk/tourism. Mon-Sat 1000-1700, Sun 1400-1700.* **Oundle TIC** ⓘ *14 West St, T01832-274333, Mon-Sat 0900-1700.*

Northampton

Northampton was once synonymous with shoemaking. As recently as the 1930s, almost half the town's population were cobblers of one sort or another. Today it's a fairly unprepossessing modern market town with little to suggest its ancient roots except a handful of fine churches. Charles II destroyed the Norman castle on his restoration but the **Church of the Holy Sepulchre** survives, one of the four round churches still standing in England. Like the castle, it was built by the Norman knight Simon de Senlis, inspired by his crusading experiences and looking more like the one in Jerusalem than the others. Its heavy rounded columns in a ring are original, topped with late-14th-century arches.

A few steps southeast from the church down Sheep Street is the **Market Square**, the centre of modern Northampton and still used for a market of sorts most days of the week. Just to the south again, **All Saints church** is a wonderful late-17th-century building, a vivid essay in Baroque enlivening the town centre. Its echoing interior is covered with a dome, a kind of mini-St Pauls. The poet John Clare used to worship here.

Further south, towards the train station, St Giles Square contains the Victorian neo-Gothic **Guildhall** and opposite, the **Northampton Museum and Art** Gallery ⓘ *Guildhall Rd, T01604-238548, Mon-Sat 1000-1700, Sun 1600-1700, free.* This local museum contains an extensive boot and shoe collection. The Followers of Fashion Gallery displays Manolo Blaniks down the ages, as it were, while the Life and Sole Gallery charts the history of the shoe. The most popular exhibits are the DMs worn in 'Tommy', and a shoe made for an elephant.

Around Northampton

Five miles northwest of Northampton is the county's most popular visitor attraction, for the saddest of reasons. **Althorp** ⓘ *T01604-770107 (advance booking on T0870-1679000) www.althorp.com, July-Sep daily 1000-1700 (last admission 1600),*

£11.50, concessions £9.50, children £5.50, off A428 to Rugby, has been the stately seat of the Spencer family for the last few hundred years but is now much more famous for being the childhood home and last resting place of Diana, Princess of Wales. Her grave lies on an island in the middle of a lake overlooked by a classical temple restored in her memory. As well as an exhibition of some of her personal effects, the house also contains an internationally renowned collection of paintings by Gainsborough, Reynolds, Van Dyck and others.

Four miles northeast of Kettering stands the palatial Northamptonshire home of the Duke of Buccleuch, **Boughton House** ⓘ *T01536-515731, www.boughtonhouse.org, Aug daily 1400-1630, grounds open May-Sep daily 1300-1700, £6, concessions £5, grounds only £1.50, concessions £1*, which has been compared to Versailles. The grounds include acres of parkland, lakes and long tree-lined avenues. The house itself took on its current imposing French appearance in the late 17th century and contains a sumptuous array of Old Masters and fine furniture.

Seven miles south of Northampton, **Stoke Bruerne** is England's most famous canal village, approached by a flight of seven locks from the River Tove. The canal forms the main road, and there's a museum of barge life. Just up the way is the **Blisworth Tunnel**. Boats can be hired from *Blisworth Tunnel Boats*, Mill Wharf, Gayton Rd, Blisworth, T01604-858868, to explore the 3000-yd long Blisworth Tunnel. It has no towpath so all boats once had to be 'legged' through the watery darkness.

Sleeping

Bedfordshire *p372*

A **Swan Hotel** The Embankment, Bedford, T01234-346565. This elegant hotel is in the heart of Bedford, built in 1794 for the Duke of Bedford. The staircase now in use here originally came from Houghton House in Ampthill, reputedly the inspiration for 'House Beautiful' in *The Pilgrim's Progress*.

B **De Pary's Hotel**, 41-45 De Pary's Av, Bedford, T01234-352121. Elegant Victorian hotel, secluded gardens with play area.

B **The Embankment Hotel**, The Embankment, Bedford, T01234-261332. Impressive black and white building overlooking the River Great Ouse.

D **Bedford Park House**, 59 De Pary's Av, Bedford, T01234-215100. Lovely Victorian House in avenue, close to town centre.

E **Saxby**, 38 Chaucer Rd, Bedford, T01234-301718. Three-storey family house, close to railway station.

E **Tithe Farm**, Renhold, T01234-771364. Farmhouse (16th-century) with secure parking, 5 miles from Bedford.

Northampton and around *p374*

B **Lime Trees Hotel**, 8 Langham Pl, Barrack Rd, Northampton, T01604-632188, www.limetreeshotel.co.uk. Half a mile north of the centre, the only 3-star hotel in the town, with about 20 rooms.

C **Coach House Hotel**, 8-10 East Park Pde, Kettering Rd, Northampton, T01604-250981, www.coach-house-hotel.com. 10 mins east of the centre, with 11 double rooms with en suite bathrooms and a welcoming atmosphere.

C **Wold Farm**, Old, Nr Northampton (8 miles north), T01604-781258. Charming 18th-century house with glorious gardens, a billiard table, and good breakfasts.

D **The Elms**, Kislingbury, near Northampton (4 miles west), T01604-830326. Comfortable rooms on a working farm. Very good value.

D **The King's Head**, Church St, Wadenhoe, near Oundle, T01832-720024. In a conservation village, the *King's Head* on the River Nene is a popular focal point for the area, with a variety of different bars, good food and a couple of bedrooms.

D **Wendy Cox**, Stoke Bruerne, T01604-863865. Does cosy cottage B&B.

Eating

Bedfordshire

££ **Carpenter's Arms**, Slapton, near Leighton Buzzard, T01525-220563. Rambling old 16th-century village pub with an above-average menu, well-kept real ales and a long stone's throw from the Grand Union Canal.

££ **Pizzeria Santaniello**, 9-11 Newnham St, Bedford T01234-353742. Original family-run pizza and pasta restaurant. Traditional family fare and atmosphere.

££ **Three Horeshoes**, 42 Top End, Renhold, T01234-870218. Welcoming pub with open fires on the road from Bedford to St Neots.

Northamptonshire

££ **Bruerne's Lock**, 5 The Canalside, Stoke Bruerne, T01604-863654. Serves up an ambitious menu in a picturesque setting by the canal.

££ **The Shuckburgh Arms**, Stoke Doyle, near Oundle, T01832-272339, is a cosy stone-built pub a couple of miles west of Oundle with a log fire.

Leicestershire and Rutland

→ *Colour map 4*

Leicestershire is a quiet, comfortable and undramatic sort of county. Undemonstrative in landscape or manner, it's considerably enlivened by the multicultural and reinvigorated city at its heart. Leicester itself rewards a visit not with its architecture or streetscape, but with its upbeat attitude and a clutch of innovative sights. Most prominent of these now is the National Space Centre, a lottery-funded Millennium project that looks set to last. With its 'Golden Mile' of curry houses and thriving arts scene, Leicester has little reason to be nostalgic for the days when it was dominated by light and heavy industry. Until the launch, in 2001, of the National Space Centre, voyagers to these regions have generally plotted a wide, circumnavigatory course around Leicester. The popularity, though, of this imaginative and inspiring attraction is drawing large numbers of visitors into the city's orbit and establishing a new place for the city on the tourist map. Next door, and defiantly not in Leicestershire at all, is Rutland, England's tiniest county and most fiercely independent. ▸▸ *For Sleeping, Eating and other listings, see pages 380-382.*

Ins and outs

Getting there **East Midlands Airport**, T01332-852852, and **Birmingham International Airport**, T0121-7675511, are, respectively, 30 and 45 mins away by car. There are several **trains** every hr on the **Midland Mailine** service from London St Pancras (1hr and 10 mins by the fast service). Leicester is 100 miles, or 2 hrs, from London by **car**, straight up the M1. The M1 is also linked, at junction 21, with the M69 west to Coventry, which is itself linked to the M6 for destinations in the West Midlands and the Northwest. For the city centre, turn off the M1 at junction 21 onto the A5460 Narborough Rd, before turning right onto St Augustine Rd, immediately crossing the river to the car park at St Nicholas Circle, where 24 hrs parking costs £6. **National Express**, T08705-808080, offers services throughout the country from St Margaret's Bus Station, just north of the city centre. ▸▸ *For further details, see Transport, page 382.*

Getting around The centre of Leicester is encompassed, unprepossessingly, by the busy A594 ring road. Inside this circle, the city is small enough to negotiate on foot. However, a trip out to the Belgrave Rd area or the National Space Centre will definitely require the use of a bus for at least one stretch of the journey.

Information **Leicester TIC** ⓘ *7-9 Every St, T0906-2941113, www.discoverleicester.com. Mon-Sat 0900-1730, opens 1000 Thu, closes 1700 Sat.* Its detailed website is well-worth checking out before your visit

Leicester and around

National Space Centre, ⓘ *T0116-2582111, www.spacecentre.co.uk, Tue-Sun and bank holidays from 0930-1800, last entry 1630, and on Mon during school holidays 1200-1800. £8.95, child £6.95 with concessions for families and groups. 2 miles north of the city centre, by car, brown signs give directions from the M1 via junctions 21a and 22, and, by public transport, the 54 bus departs regularly from outside the railway station via the main shopping area of town.* From a distance, the rocket tower of theenveloped in a hi-tech, silver sheath, looks like an enormous sci-fi maggot. Once inside, the museum is divided into five different zones exploring different aspects of space travel and the universe, all of which revolve around the Space Theatre, a huge, wraparound cinema screening a 20-minute film that is included in the ticket price. Highlights include a replica of the Columbus space station, showing how astronauts eat, sleep and go to the loo in space, and a Soyuz T space capsule used to ferry astronauts to the Mir space station. Expect to spend an absorbing three or four hours.

Coming back down to earth, the history of the terrestrial loo is laid out in all its glory at the **Abbey Pumping Station** ⓘ *T0116-2995111, 1000-1700 Mon-Sat, Sun,1300-1700, closes 1600 Oct- Mar, free*, next door, a Victorian sewage works reinvented as an engaging and slightly eccentric museum recording various aspects of transport and domestic life from the first half of the last century. From there, take the 54 bus back into town or walk down the River Soar and then left onto Abbey Park Road to arrive at the bottom of Belgrave Road.

The **'Golden Mile'** is actually best seen in the evening, when it turns into a neon-lit promenade, a place to window shop and meet friends, before diving into one of the many different eateries for a bite or a full-blown meal. See Eating and Shopping below.

Returning by 22 or 37 bus to the Haymarket, turn half-right at the clock tower along the High Street and left down Loseby Lane to find the diminutive **Cathedral** ⓘ *T0116-2625294, daily, free*, an essentially Victorian structure built over the remains of a much older church. The chancel contains the floor memorial to Richard III – with his hunched back, the inspiration for the Humpty Dumpty nursery rhyme – and the engravings on the modern glass doors illustrate the Escape from Egypt. The **Guildhall** ⓘ *T0116-2532569, Mon-Sat, 1000- 1700, Sun 1300-1700, closes 1600 Oct-Mar, free*, right beside the cathedral, is a beautifully preserved 14th-century half- timbered structure, the venue for many of the most significant events in Leicester's history and still in use for some civic functions to this day. Continue back along the High Street and over the A594 to find the **Jewry Wall** Museum ⓘ *T0116-2473021, Mon-Sat 1000-1700, Sun 1400-1730, free*, site of the moderately exciting remains of the Roman baths and display of local archaeology, that includes two genuinely impressive Roman mosaics.

From here, head a few steps further north to the **Guru Nanak Sikh Museum** ⓘ *T0116-2628606, Thu only, 1300-1600, or by appointment, free*, a working Sikh Gurdwara open daily for worship and free food, with a museum of Sikh history upstairs. A short walk south takes you to the castle gardens, containing the mound of the Norman castle and the **Newarke Houses Museum** ⓘ *T0116-2473222, Mon-Sat 1000-1700, Sun 1300-1700, closes 1600 Oct-Mar, free*, home to an eclectic collection of such things as clocks, toys and Indian embroidery, including the portrait and various possessions of Daniel Lambert, an enormously overweight 19th-century gentleman, who tipped the scales at 52 stone 11 lbs.

Around Leicester

North of Melton, the A607 heads up towards Grantham. Any turn left westwards leads up into undiscovered villages in the wolds, a surprising area of rolling hills overlooking the Vale of Belvoir (pronounced *Beaver*) and giving beautiful views over Leicestershire.

 Belvoir Castle ⓘ *T01476-870262, www.belvoircastle.com, May-Sep daily 1100-1700, Oct Sun 1100-1700, £7.25, concessions £6.75, under-16s £4.75*, the home of the Duke of Rutland, is an imposing exercise in Regency romantic medievalism, full of remarkable paintings and once the scene of very grand house parties.

Fifteen miles southeast of Leicester, Market Harborough is another even less assuming Midlands market town. The attractive old part of town, including a grammar school founded in the reign of James I, clusters beneath the impressive broach spire of St Dionysius. Nine miles east of the town, **Rockingham Castle** ⓘ *T01536-770240, www.rockinghamcastle.com, Easter-Sep Sun, bank holidays 1300-1700 (also Tue, Thu in Jul, Aug), £7, concessions £6, children £4.50, family £18.50*, is an impressive Tudor house built within the walls of a Norman castle. Charles Dickens was inspired to model Chesney Wold in *Bleak House* on the place and today the interiors and wild gardens (including a 400-year-old elephant hedge) and their superb views are still worth a look.

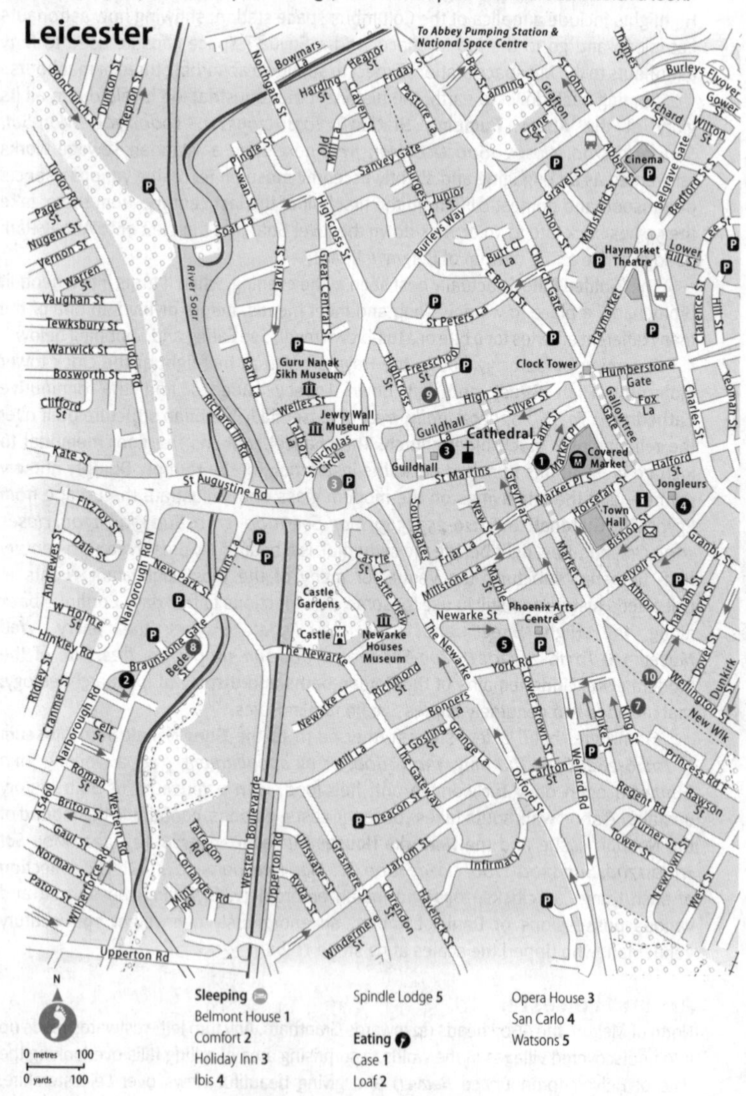

Rutland

About 17 miles long and 17 wide, tiny Rutland still retains an old-fashioned, decidedly genteel atmosphere. Old stone buildings, ancient villages and countless sheep dot its verdant landscape. At its centre, Oakham is the county town, the epicentre of resistance to the county boundary changes introduced in the 1970s and the fight to retain its Mercian roots. Rutland Water is a vast reservoir that draws in watersport enthusiasts, fishermen and ramblers from miles around.

Ins and outs

Getting there Oakham **train** station is a 10 min walk west of the town centre, with trains running to Birmingham and Norwich, regular connections with the main North-South lines via Peterborough and Leicester. By **road** Rutland is about 100 miles north of London, easily reached in 2 hrs on the A1. Rutland is best explored by car or bike, although Oakham is easily negotiated on foot and there's a reasonable network of local buses. Contact **Busline** on T0116-2511411.

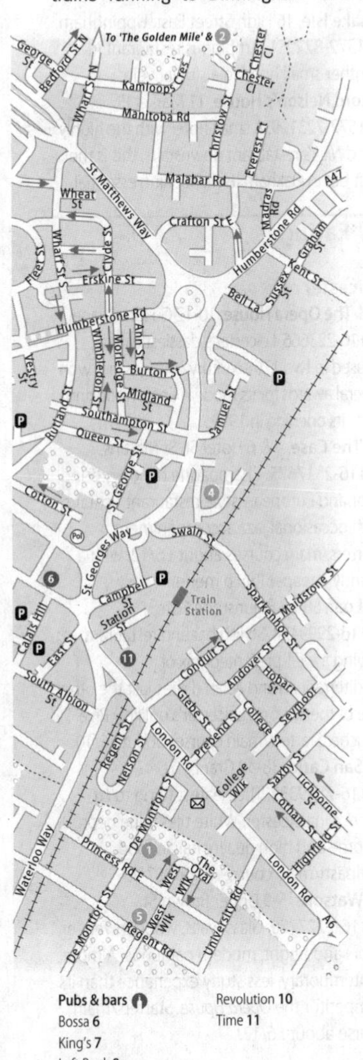

Information Rutland TIC ⓘ *Oakham, T01572-724329*. **Rutland Water** TIC ⓘ *T01572-653026*.

Oakham

Oakham is the miniature capital of Rutland, a prosperous town famous for being mad about horses and fox-hunting. First impressions may be a little grim, but the Market Place is attractive enough, next to **Oakham Castle** ⓘ *T01572-758440, Apr-Oct Mon-Sat 1000-1300, 1330-1700 (Nov-Mar-1600), Sun 1300-1700 (Nov-Mar-1600), free*. Although not much of a castle, being more of a defensive moated townhouse, its Norman Great Hall still stands and repays a visit to look at its medieval sculptures and strange collection of horeshoes. Probably the most unusual array of Royal memorabilia in the country, it was built up thanks to the forfeit paid by the reigning monarch passing through the town since the 15th century. A 5-minute walk down Catmose Street arrives at **Rutland County Museum** ⓘ *Catmose St, T01572-758440, www.rutland.gov.uk, Mon-Sat 1000-1700, Sun 1400-1700*. Housed in the old stables of the Rutland Fencibles, a volunteer cavalry force raised by a local landowner in 1794, the museum gives a good picture of the history of this strange little corner of the country and also holds the 13th-century Brooke Reliquary, a rare enamelled casket.

Rutland Water looks like an outsize waterhazard on a golf course, a very large (5-mile-long) reservoir created in the mid 1970s by flooding the valley of the Gwash. The main settlements on its 24-mile perimeter are Empingham, Whitwell and Barnsdale. Near Empingham there's a visitor centre, and the **Butterfly Farm and Aquatic Centre** ⓘ *Sykes Lane, T01780-460515, Easter-Aug daily 1030-1700, Oct 1030-1630*. **Rutland Water Nature Reserve,** ⓘ *Egleton, T01572-770651, www.ospreys.org.uk*, run by *Anglian Water*, offers the chance to see ospreys fishing from April through August. On the southern shore, the church at **Normanton** ⓘ *T01572-653026*, was rescued from the rising waters and now includes a museum on the construction of the reservoir.

Sleeping

Leicester *p376, map p378*

A **Holiday Inn**, 129 St Nicholas Circle, T0116-2531161. Next door to the remains of the Roman baths, this modern hotel is built on the site of a Roman temple to the Persian god Mithras. Conveniently located for the motorway and the city centre, facilities include an excellent gym and indoor pool.

C **Belmont House Hotel**, de Montfort St, T0116-2544773. This country house hotel is just 5 mins' walk from the city centre along the tree-lined New Walk, an old Roman road.

C **Spindle Lodge Hotel**, 2 West Walk, T0116-2338801. Victorian townhouse still with many of its original features, in a quiet location close to the city centre.

D **Comfort Hotel**, 23-25 Loughborough Rd, T0116-2682626. At the north end of the 'Golden Mile', this well-appointed hotel features the amazingly kitsch *Kabalou* restaurant, serving Indian food in an interior of mock Gothic-Indian-Egyptian-Greek design.

D **Ibis Hotel**, St George's Way, T0116-2487200. Right next door to the railway station, this functional, barn of a building offers Leicester's best-value accommodation.

Rutland *p379*

L **Hambleton Hall Hotel**, Hambleton, T01572-756991. Top of the range – a Victorian house on a peninsula in the middle of the reservoir with an expensive gourmet restaurant and wonderful views.

B **Barnsdale Lodge Hotel**, The Avenue, Rutland Water, T01572-724678. Partly a converted farmhouse hotel with views over the reservoir, well-placed for visiting attractions around about.

C **Lake Isle**, 16 High Street East, Uppingham, T01572-822951. Ambitious restaurant in another small hotel in a similar vein.

C **Lord Nelson's House**, 11 Market Pl, T01572-723199. A small hotel with the highly rated *Nick's* restaurant downstairs, this is the best bet in Oakham itself. Booking essential.

Eating

Leicester *p376, map p378*

$$$ **The Opera House**, 10-12 Guildhall Lane, T0116-223666. Leicester's classiest eaterie, housed in two 17th-century cottages, has won several awards for its modern English cooking since its opening in 1999..

$$ **The Case**, 4 & 6 Hotel St, St Martins, T0116-2517675. Champagne bar on ground floor and European-style restaurant upstairs, with occasional jazz accompaniment. Starters/main courses about £6/12, with a slightly cheaper lunch menu.

$$ **Loaf**, 58-62 Braunstone Gate, T0116-2999424. Stylish bar and restaurant, serving a well-presented mix of Mediterranean and Asian dishes just the other side of the Soar, on Leicester's unlikely Rive Gauche. Starters/main courses about £6/10.

$$ **San Carlo**, 38-40 Granby St, T0116-2519332. The nearest thing to *La Caprice* in Leicester. White tiles, blue neon, chrome and high quality Italian food. Antipasti/main courses about £7/12.

$$ **Watsons**, 5-9 Upper Brown St, T0116-2227770. Glass walls, wooden veneer floors and bright, modern paintings. A more contemporary, less stuffy experience than its competitor the *Opera House*. Starters/main course about £6/12.

$ **Bobbies** opposite, 154 Belgrave Rd, T0116-2662448, (closed Mon). Sell sweets and vegetarian savoury takeaways in the shop, and serve thalis and dosas in the restaurant.
$ **Chaat House**, 108 Belgrave Rd, T0116-2660513, (closed Tue). A little different, an intimate den serving many different versions of the eponymous North Indian snack.
$ **The Curry Fever**, 139 Belgrave Rd, T0116-2662941, (closed Mon). The menu here contains few surprises, but is highly regarded.
$ **Sharmilee**, 71 Belgrave Rd, T0116-2668471, (closed Mon), shop and restaurants serving up both sweet and savoury delights.

Rutland *p379*
£ **Olive Branch**, Main St, Clipsham, T01780-410355, is an upbeat and charming village pub with better than average food, in a village with a remarkable topiary yew hedge.

Pubs, bars and clubs

Leicester *p376, map p378*
Bossa, 110 Granby St, T0116-2334544. You might be in a small town in Italy, stepping inside this civilized little bar with its rack of weird spirits, coffee machine and glass case of ciabata sandwiches.
The King's, 36 King St, T0116-2551477. Leicester's most relaxed boozer. Soothing green benches, big wooden tables and newspapers, a selection of ales and decent food for a very mixed, laid-back clientele.
Left Bank, 26 Braunstone Gate, T0116-2552422. One of the first trendy bars to spring up in this popular little nightlife enclave west of the river. Also serves excellent fresh food.
The Orange Tree, 99 High St, T0116-2235256. Mellow wooden floors and wooden tables, an easy-going crowd, a wide range of cocktails and happy hours throughout the week.
Revolution, New Walk, T0116-2559633. Big, retro-style vodka bar, with high ceilings and groovy 70s décor, on this very pleasant, leafy pedestrian thoroughfare.
Time, 48a London Rd, T0116-2619301. A vast, warehouse-style establishment next to the railway station, with a concrete floor and miles of chrome barspace that gets very busy at weekends.

Entertainment

Leicester *p376, map p378*
Comedy, cinema and theatre
Phoenix Arts Centre, Newarke St, T0116-2554854, which also runs a programme of theatre, dance and other performance.
Haymarket Theatre, Belgrave Gate, T0116-2539797. Often used as a test bed for shows heading for London's West End.
Jongleurs, Granby St, T0870-7870707. The place to catch some stand-up comedy.

Festivals

Leicester *p376, map p378*
Feb Leicester Comedy Festival, T0116-2257770, is held over 10 days in the middle of the month, featuring established stars alongside brand new talent.
May and Jun Early Music Festival, T0116- 2709984, music lovers descend on Leicester in late May and early Jun for the held in museums, churches, the cathedral and Castle Park.
Jun Leicester International Music Festival, T0116-2473043, a mid month occurrence specializing in chamber music but also featuring jazz and world music.
Aug The city's big **carnival**, at the beginning of the month, is a celebration of the Caribbean community in the city. T0116-2257770.
Nov Leicester stages the biggest **Diwali** celebrations outside India. Marking the start of the Hindu New Year, this festival of light is held at the beginning of Nov, when the 'Golden Mile' is illuminated in spectacular style, the road is closed to traffic and a stage put up at the flyover end for music and dancing, with a firework display as a grand finale. T0116-2998888.

Activities and tours

Rutland *p379*
Rutland Water Cycling, Whitwell Car Park, on Rutland Water, T01780-460705, (also on the south shore at Normanton, T01780-720888).

Rutland Watersports, Whitwell Car Park, T01780-460154, www.rutlandwater.net
Rutland Sailing Club and School, Gibbet Lane, Edith Weston, T01780-720292.
Rutland Water Cruises on the *Rutland Belle* from Whitwell, leaving at 1300, 1400, 1500, calling at Normanton Church on the south shore. Daily May-Sep.
Rutland Water Trout Fishery, Normanton Car Park, T01780-686441.

Transport

Leicester *p376, map p378*

Bus
National Express, T08705-808080, run regularly direct to **Nottingham Broad Marsh** (45 mins) and direct every 2 hrs to **London Victoria**. They also run direct services 6 times per day to **Birmingham Digbeth** (1-1 hr 30 mins) and 7 times per day to **Derby** (1 hr).

Car
Avis, 1 Samuel St, T0116-2626523. Thrifty, Garden St, T0116-2620444.

Taxi
A1 Airport Taxis, 146 Belgrave Gate, T0116-2513188. Swift Taxis, 77a Church Gate, T0116-2531138.

Train
Midland Mainline, T08457-125678, run the regular direct services to **Nottingham** (35 mins), **Derby** (30 mins) and **London St Pancras** (1 hr 20 mins). Central Trains, T0121-6541200, run the regular direct service to **Birmingham** (1 hr).

Directory

Leicester *p376, map p378*

Hospital Leicester Royal Infirmary, Infirmary Sq, T0116-2541414.

Nottingham

→*Colour map 4*

Like Newcastle, Nottingham is visibly in a state of fashionable flux. Massive new building projects are underway right across the city centre as this once-drab Midlands manufacturing centre reinvents itself as a modern European cityscape. Paul Smith designerwear, Nottingham Forest Football Club and a thriving dance music scene have become the booming exports of a place that was once synonymous with hosiery and lace. Only bits of the old industrial city survive, much of it thankfully submerged beneath gloomy but marginally more liveable in housing projects and road junctions of the 60s. These bits are still likely to be of most interest to the visitor though: the area around the Lace Market and St Mary's church, neighbouring Hockley, and Nottingham castle. ▸▸ *For Sleeping, Eating and other listings, see pages 386-387.*

Ins and outs

Getting there East Midlands airport, T01332-852852, and **Birmingham International airport**, T0121-7675511, are, respectively, 20 and 30 mins away by car. There are several **trains** every hour from London St Pancras (1hr and 20mins by the fast service). Nottingham is 122 miles, or about 2 hours, from London by **car**, straight up the M1, 1 hr 30 mins from Leeds further up the M1. At Junction 24, the A42 becomes the M42 on its way to Birmingham, about 30 mins away. National **Express**, T08705-808080, offers **coach** services throughout the country from Broadmarsh Bus Station, just south of the city centre. ▸▸ *For further details, see Transport, page 387.*

Getting around The centre of Nottingham, within a busy ring road, is easily small enough to negotiate on foot. Victoria Centre Bus Station, Nos 737, 747 and 757 for Newstead Abbey.

Information **Nottingham City Information Centre** ⓘ *Council House, Smithy Row, off Market Sq, T0115-915 5330, www.visitnottingham.com, Mon-Fri 0930-1730, Sat 0900-1700 (and Sun 1000-1600 in Aug). Accommodation service £2.50.* ⓘ **Nottinghamshire County Information Centre** ⓘ *County Hall, West Bridgford, T0115-977 3558 (open same hrs).*

Sights

Market Square is the centre of Nottingham, about 600 yds almost directly north of the train station over the canal. The areas of the city of most interest to visitors fall either side of this north-south line passing through the Broadmarsh shopping centre. Beneath the shopping centre, though, **The Caves of Nottingham** are quite an unusual visitor attraction, large caves laid out to show how they have been used down the ages, up to their use as an air-raid shelter during the war. The self-guided audio tour is entertaining enough too. ⓘ *Broadmarsh Centre, T0115- 9520555, Mon-Sat 1000-1700 (last admission 1615), Sun 1000-1700 (last admission 1600), £4, concessions £3.*

Before Market Square, to the east, clustered around the church of St Mary's, the **Lace Market** area covers the site of Saxon Nottingham. **St Mary's Church**, High Pavement, is home to the Nottingham Bach Choir, who rehearse on Tuesday evenings, and is worth a look in itself, especially the door in the south porch which frames a bronze Art Nouveau relief of Christ with the Virgin.

Just before the church is the **Lace Market Heritage Point** at the Shire Hall, where you can take a half-mile audio tour round the area, voiced by Joanna Lumley, called *The Lace Market Unveiled*. The tour capitalizes on some of the few old buildings left standing by the urban planners in the 60s: red brick warehouses now converted into fashionable bars and shops. In the old **Shire Hall** n *High Pavement, Lace Market, T0115-9520555, www.galleriesofjustice.org.uk, Apr-Oct Tue-Sun 1000- 1700, Nov-Mar Tue-Sun 1000-1600*, dating from the mid-18th century, the Galleries of Justice is an interactive see-hear-and-smell show on the theme of crime and punishment, lent some authenticity by the original Victorian courtrooms and the old cells, where you're encouraged to "feel the atmosphere of 300 years of suffering seeping through the walls, bars and chains..." Not for delicate sensibilities then, but most kids seem to love it.

Opposite the *Pitcher and Piano* (see Pubs and bars, below) in the old Lace Hall, the **Lace Market Centre** ⓘ *3/5 High Pavement, Lace Market, T0115-9881849*, are two shops dedicated to local lace and silk, where you can see lace being handmade most days except Mondays. North of St Mary's, St Mary's Gate and Stoney Street lead up into **Hockley**, another area of reclaimed and renovated old buildings that make for rewarding browsing. Heading 100 yards west out of Hockley brings you back to Market Square, dominated by the Baroque **Council House** on pedestrianized Smithy Row.

Anyone interested in the history of the city should head west from the Broadmarsh centre towards Nottingham Castle, home to an impressive municipal art gallery. On the way, the old buildings by the castle gate contain the **Costume Museum** ⓘ *Castle Gate, T0115-9153500, www.nottinghamcity.gov.uk, Wed-Sun 1000-1600, free*. Six period room settings from 1790-1950s are inhabited by period costume-wearing dummies in faintly realistic action poses, as well as a textile exhibition and a history of lace room. Look out too for the cushion-cover possibly embroidered by Elizabeth I, the Map tapestries of the city embroidered in 1632, and from a similar date, the oldest pair of boys' stockings in the UK, in fine knitted silk. **Nottingham Castle** ⓘ *Off Maid Marian Way, T0115-9153700, daily 1000-1700 (last admission 1630), free Mon-Fri, £2, concessions £1 on Sat, Sun and bank holidays*, itself is well worth a look for its very fine collection of medievel alabaster carvings, a skill in which the city once excelled, as well

Nottingham

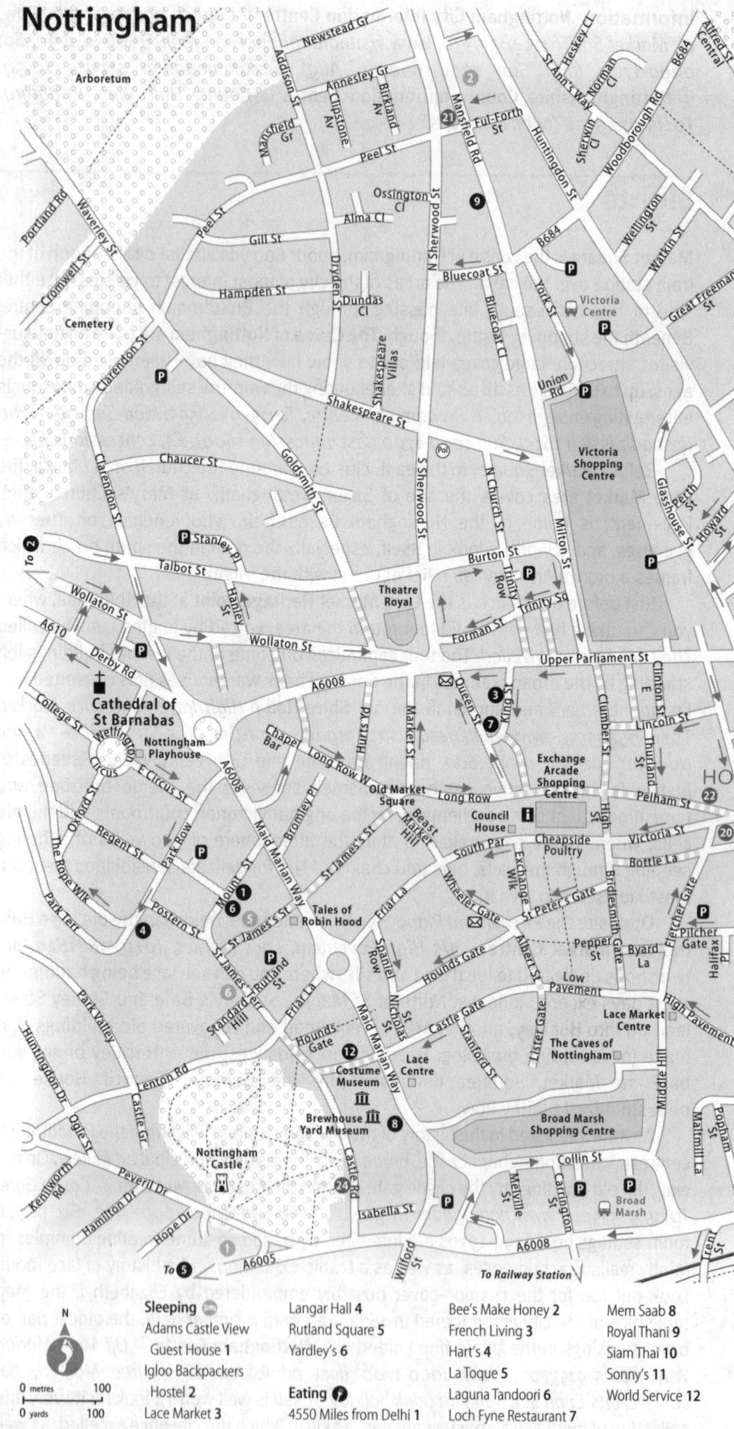

Sleeping
Adams Castle View Guest House 1
Igloo Backpackers Hostel 2
Lace Market 3
Langar Hall 4
Rutland Square 5
Yardley's 6

Eating
4550 Miles from Delhi 1
Bee's Make Honey 2
French Living 3
Hart's 4
La Toque 5
Laguna Tandoori 6
Loch Fyne Restaurant 7
Mem Saab 8
Royal Thani 9
Siam Thai 10
Sonny's 11
World Service 12

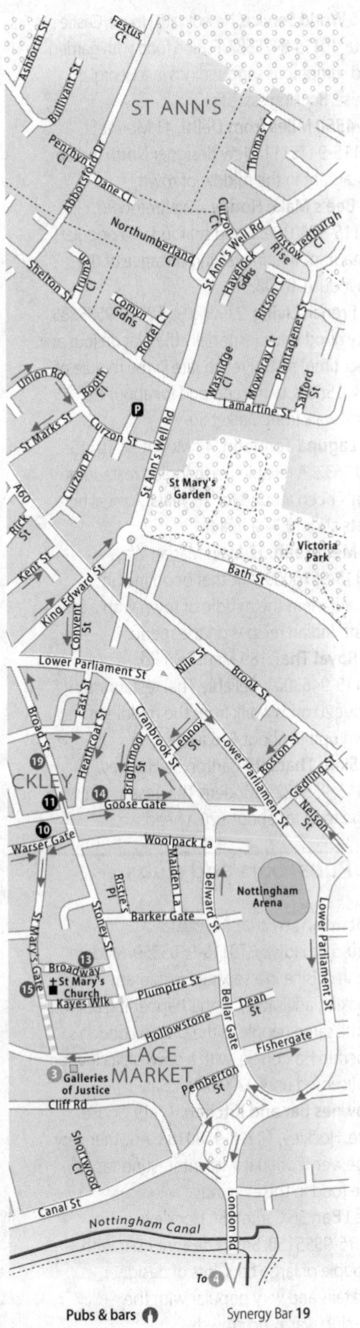

Pubs & bars
Bluu **13**
Brownes Bar & Kitchen **14**
Lizzard Lounge **15**
Synergy Bar **19**
The I Bar **20**
Loft **21**
Social **22**
Ye Olde Trip to Jerusalem **24**

as an intriguing array of Victorian paintings in a wonderful old gallery. There's also a Nottingham history room, 'The Story of Nottingham', which illustrates the city's past with the help of the latest interactive technology.

Next door to the Museum is theYe Olde Trip to Jerusalem Inn (see Pubs and bars below).

A stone's throw away, the **Brewhouse Yard Museum of Nottingham Life** ⓘ *Castle Boulevard, T0115-9153600, daily 1000-1630 (last admission 1600) Mon-Fri free, Sat, Sun, bank holidays £1.50, concessions £0.80*, covers the social history of the city rather than its manufacturing pride, with mock-ups of shopfronts and a period living room and kitchen.

Just by the junction of Maid Marian Way with Friar Lane, the **Tales of Robin Hood** ⓘ *T0115-9483284, www.robinhood.uk.com, Apr-Sep 1000-1800, Oct-Nov 1000-1730, £6.50, concessions £5.25, children £4.50*, is the inevitable dark ride exploiting the legend of Robin Hood and his dubious association with the city. That said, it's one of the more effective and educational of the genre, with falconry in the castle grounds and archery practice in addition to the usual manequins, sound effects and tacky light shows, as well as live actors.

Twelve miles north of Nottingham on the A60 (follow signs for Sherwood Forest from Junction 27 of the M1) is **Newstead Abbey** ⓘ *Ravenshead, T01623- 455900, www.newstead abbey.org.uk, House Apr-Sep daily 1200-1700 (last entry 1600), grounds daily 0900-dusk.* Lord Byron lived here between 1808 and 1814, before selling his ancestral home (since 1540 and the dissolution of the monastery on the site) in 1818. Medieval cloisters, Great Hall, Byron's favourite clothes for you to try on, and a mock-up of his quarters are all decent enough diversions. The Gardens are the main event, though – over 300 acres of extraordinary parkland, with a variety of different gardens from around the world established on the lakeside.

Sleeping

Nottingham *p382, map p384*

A **Lace Market Hotel**, 29 High Pavement, T0115-8523232, www.lacemarkethotel.co.uk. Boutique hotel with snazzy contemporary design and restaurant called *Merchants* to match.

A **Langar Hall**, Langar, T01949-860559, F861045 Regency house with bags of character in a beautiful village setting and acres of parkland, some way southeast of the city.

C **Rutland Square Hotel**, St James St, T0115-9411114, www.zoffanyhotels.co.uk Clean and comfortable chain hotel close to the castle.

C **Yardley's**, 11 St James Terr, T0115-9411997. Small hotel close to the castle with reasonable food in a recently refurbished restaurant and quiet, comfortable rooms.

D **Adams Castle View Guest House**, 85 Castle Boulevard, T0115-9500022. Victorian house with comfortable rooms, close to the city centre.

F **Igloo Backpackers Hostel**, 110 Mansfield Rd, T0115-9475250, www.igloohostel.co.uk. 36 beds in 4 rooms, £11 per person not including breakfast. See also National Water Sports Centre, in Sport below for camping and bunkhouse options.

Eating

Nottingham *p382, map p384*

$$$ **Hart's**, Standard St, Park Row, T0115-9110666. Generally considered to be the city's finest dining experience, a sophisticated ambience, professional service and superior modern European cuisine can be enjoyed here for about £35 a head with wine.

$$$ **Sonny's**, 3 Carlton St, T0115-9473041. Brasserie with a good reputation behind the Lace Market, about £30 a head, reliable seafood and meat dishes.

$$$ **La Toque**, 61 Wollaton Rd, T0115-9222268. About £40 a head for superior and elaborate French cuisine in a small bistro setting some way out on the road to Beeston. Booking advisable, essential on Sat.

$$$ **World Service**, Newdigate House, Castle Gate, T0115-8475587. Fusion food with garden and sumptuous surroundings in a Georgian house. Booking essential.

$$ **4550 Miles from Delhi**, 41 Mount St, T0115-9475111. New designer North Indian restaurant in the middle of town.

$$ **Bee's Make Honey**, 12 Alfreton Rd, T0115-9780109. Good seafood in a popular restaurant within walking distance of the Playhouse. BYOB.

$$ **French Living**, 27 King St, T0115-9585885. Very good value (especially the plat du jour at lunchtime) rustic French fare in the middle of town. Snails, game and pud for about £20, 5 mins' walk from Market Sq.

$$ **Laguna Tandoori**, 43 Mount St, T0115-9411632. A reliable north Indian restaurant that's been around for 26 years. A meal here costs about £17 a head.

$$ **Mem Saab**, 12 Maid Marian Way, T0115-9570009. Another good Indian restaurant in the middle of town with a few south Indian recipes on the menu.

$$ **Royal Thai**, 189 Mansfield Rd, T0115-9483001. Reliable Thai restaurant about 20 mins' walk from the middle of town uphill. About £16 a head.

$$ **Siam Thani**, 16 Carlton St, Hockley, T0115-9582222. Modern Thai restaurant with good food for about £20 a head.

Pubs, bars and clubs

Nottingham *p382, map p384*

Bluu, 5 Broadway, T0115-9505359. Modern British cuisine in a separate restaurant (booking advisable), at this happening bar run by the same people as the club in London's superhip Hoxton Sq, with a downstairs lounge bar licensed until 0200 on Fri, Sat.

Brownes Bar and Kitchen, 17-19 Goose Gate, Hockley, T0115-9580188. Another very large, very cool bar with interesting tapas type food in the evenings.

The I Bar, 36 Carlton St, Hockley, T0115-9555150. Smart designer bar with a couple of large bars, lots of designer cocktails and very popular with the pre-club warm-up crowd.

Lizzard Lounge, 41-43 St Mary's Gate, Lace Market, T0115-9523264. Still a very 'trendy' spot, a 3-floor bar with Thai restaurant attached and relatively laid-back, assorted crowd. It's late license means it gets busy mid-evening and entry is charged at weekends.

The Loft, 217 Mansfield Rd, T0115-9240213. Back-to-basics décor that pulls in the city's ambitious musos who appreciate its designer touches: innovative lighting and muted colour scheme. Burgers and chips, Thai and Indian platters and specials of the day.

The Social, 23 Pelham St, T0115-9505078. Relative newcomer to the latenight music scene, this offshoot of London's Portland St outfit is a harder-drinking DJ-driven club-bar with a late licence and bags of attitude.

Synergy Bar, Broad St, Hockley, T0115-9241555. Ignore the name and enjoy one of the city's more sophisticated operations, with decidedly superior cocktails (served to your table in the lounge upstairs at weekends).

Ye Olde Trip to Jerusalem, Castle Rd, T0115-9473171. Reputedly the oldest pub in Britain, where the Crusaders gathered before setting off to bash up the infidels. Today it's a quiet, interesting place, gouged out of the rock beneath the castle.

Entertainment

Nottingham *p382, map p384*

Cinema

Broadway Cinema, 14-18 Broad St, T0115-9526611, www.broadway.org.uk Mainstream arthouse releases.

Screen Room 'The World's Smallest Cinema', 25b Broad St, Hockley, T0115-9241133, www.screenroom.co.uk. On corner of Old Lenton St, opposite Lord Robert's pub. Arthouse mainstream releases and classics.

Live music

The Old Vic, Fletchergate, T0115-9509833. The place to hear Nottingham's up and coming indie bands.

Nottingham Arena, National Ice Centre, Lower Parliament St T0870-1210123. Venue for big names on tour.

Theatre

Nottingham Playhouse T0115-9153591. Contemporary drama and dance.

Sandfield Theatre, T0115-9526611, for experimental work.

Theatre Royal, T0115-5895555, for West End musicals, ballet and classical concerts.

Transport

Nottingham *p382, map p384*

Bus

Trent Buses, T01773-712265, run the regular direct service to **Derby** (35 mins) from Victoria bus station. **National Express**, T08705-808080, run a direct service from Broad Marsh bus station 5 times per day direct to **Birmingham Digbeth** (1 hr 15 mins to 2 hrs 15 mins) and 7 times to **London Victoria** (3 hrs 25 mins). There is also a regular direct service to **Leicester** (45 mins) and a direct service to **Manchester** central coach station (3 hrs 10 mins) at 1115 and 1535.

Car

Chegwidden Brothers, 28 Abbey Road West, Bridgford, T0845-6032901. **Jaeban UK Ltd**, 50 Lower Parliament St, T0800-212636. **Pacer Vehicle Rental**, 601 Woodborough Rd, T0115-9693166.

Taxi

Phonacar, 22a Lower Parliament St, T0115-9112211. **Streamline Taxis**, 63 Derby Rd, T0115-9242499. **Yellow Cars**, 8 Pavillion Building, Pavillion Rd, T0115-9818181.

Train

Central Trains, T0121-6541200, run the regular direct services to **Birmingham New Street** (1 hr 20 mins), **Derby** (25 mins) and the direct hourly service to **Manchester Oxford Road** (2 hrs). **Midland Mainline**, T08457-125678, run the frequent direct service to **Leicester** (35 mins) and the direct hourly service to **London St Pancras** (1 hr 45 mins).

Directory

Nottingham *p382, map p384*

Bike hire Bunneys Bikes, 97 Carrington St, T0115-9472713. **Hospitals** Nottingham City Hospital, Hucknall Rd, T0115-9691169. **Internet** Chill Out, 33 Heathcoat St, T0115-9476323. **Police** Nottingham Police HQ, Sherwood Lodge Arnold, T0115-9670999. **Post office** Nottingham Branch Office, Queen St, T0845-7223344.

Derby and around

→Colour map 4

Fifteen miles west of Nottingham, Derby is usually seen as that city's poor relation. In fact it's a very different kind of place, making up for its perceived lack of cool with some solid industrial heritage, mild-mannered local pride, very fine beer and an endearing cathedral. Not much to look at, except along the Georgian street called Friar Gate, home to the Pickford Museum and Old Derby Gaol, Derby has suffered as much as most other Midland towns at the hands of 60s redevelopers. That said, the pedestrianized area west and south of the cathedral can make for a pleasant enough wander around of an afternoon. A quarter of a mile to the north is the Derby Industrial Museum, housed in the first factory in the country, and the start of a mile-long riverside walk to Darley Abbey, both part of a UNESCO World Heritage Site. Nearby are the neo classical splendours of Kedleston Hall. To the northeast, the Amber Valley skirts abandoned mining country up to Hardwick Hall and Bolsover Castle. Northwest of the city, dignified old Ashbourne proudly proclaims itself the 'Gateway to Dovedale' and hence the Peak District as a whole. » *For Sleeping, Eating and other listings, see page 390.*

Ins and outs

Getting there Regular trains connect Derby with Nottingham (25 mins), Leicester (35 mins) and on to London (2 hrs). Derby is about 130 miles from London, reachable in 2 hours by **car**, straight up the M1. It's also about 1 hr 30 mins from Leeds further up the M1. The big A38 heads straight into Birmingham, no more than 30 mins away. **National Express**, T08705-808080, run six **coaches** a day to Derby from London Victoria, taking 3 hrs 30 mins).

Getting around Derby is a surprisingly large city.The centre is Market Place, about a mile and a half west of the train station (catch a bus, the walk's no fun) and a stone's throw from the grotty bus station in Morledge. But most of the sights worth seeing are within easy walking distance of each other.

Information **Derby TIC** ⓘ *Assembly Rooms, Market Pl, T01332-255802. Mar-Oct Mon-Sat 0930-1700, Nov-Feb Mon-Sat 1000-1600.* **Ashbourne TIC** ⓘ *13 Market Pl, T01335-343666, Mar-Oct Mon-Sat 0930-1700 (also Sun in Jul and Aug), Nov-Feb Mon-Sat 1000-1600.* **Amber Valley TIC** ⓘ *Town Hall, Market Pl, Ripley, T01773-841488, www.ambervalley.gov.uk.*

Derby

By car, Derby shows itself to its best advantage when approached from Ashbourne and the west down the red-brick Georgian street called Friar Gate, the opposite side of the city from the station. On Friar Gate itself, the **Derby Gaol** ⓘ *50 Friar Gate, T01332-299321*, reveals what lay in store for the offenders during the city's industrial heyday. A few doors down, the **Georgian townhouse** ⓘ *Pickford's House Museum, 41 Friar Gate, T01332-255363, Mon 1100-1700, Tue-Sat 1000-1700, Sun 1400-1700, free*, home of the architect Joseph Pickford has been restored to its 18th-century appearance. Some rooms have been furnished as they might have been when the Pickford family lived in the house. Others contain displays of costume and textiles and also the Frank Bradley collection of toy theatres.

At the end of Friar Gate, where it meets The Wardwick, a left turn down Curzon Street arrives at the Strand and the **Derby Museum and Art Gallery** ⓘ *T01332-716659, Mon 1100-1700, Tue-Sat 1000-1700, Sun 1400-1700, free*. This holds a fine collection of Joseph Wright of Derby's paintings, as well as a refurbished interactive ceramics gallery, and displays on the local archaeology, history, wildlife and geology.

A few steps down St James Street from here leads into Market Place, from where it's a short walk up Iron Gate to the cathedral. With its airy 18th-century neo classical nave, designed by Gibb and restored by Comper, and a medieval tower over the entrance porch, **Derby Cathedral** ⓘ *T01332-341201, www.derbycathedral.org, daily 0830-1800*, is delightful but only just deserves the name. In fact until fairly recently it was a parish church. Inside, highlights include the monument to the formidable Bess of Hardwick (1607) and Robert Bakewell's elegant early 18th-century ironwork.

A three-minute walk from the cathedral down Sowter Road arrives at the **Derby Industrial Museum**. This UNESCO World Heritage Site on the banks of the Derwent is an 18th-century Silk Mill. It now houses a museum dedicated to Derby's role in the birth of manufacturing industry, including Rolls Royce aero engines – Frank Whittle's prototype jet engine for example – displays on lead mining, silk weaving (illustrated by a loom that worked at the Ashbourne narrow fabrics factory until the early 1970s) and wrought iron work. The silk mill itself remains the main event, built between 1717 and 1721 for the Lombe brothers, it was hard-hit in the 19th century by overseas competition but only ceased production in 1908. ⓘ *Silk Mill Lane, off Full St, T01332-255308, Mon 1100-1700, Tue-Sat 1000-1700, Sun 1400-1700, free.*

A mile away by footpath along the river, the **Darley Abbey and Park** is also part of the World Heritage Site, the remains (much altered and redeveloped) of a late-18th-century factory village developed by Thomas Evans.

Seven miles north of Alfreton, just east of Junctions 28 and 29 on the M1, **Hardwick Old Hall** ⓘ *(EH), T01246-850431, Apr-Sep Mon, Wed, Thu, Sat, Sun 1000-1800, Oct Mon, Wed, Thu, Sat, Sun 1000-1700, £3.10, children £1.60, concessions £2.40*, is the ruin of Bess of Hardwick's Elizabethan family home, the **New Hall** ⓘ *Hardwick New Hall (NT), T01246-850430, Apr-Oct Wed, Thu, Sat, Sun 1230-1700, £6.60, children £3.30, family £16.50*, with spectacular views from the roof. Next door to the Hardwick Old Hall is the palatial Elizabethan residence that Bess built for herself in the 1590s. Highlights of its interior are the wealth of 16th-century furniture, tapestries and needlework. Outside, the glorious gardens stretching over to the Old Hall give superb views over the M1 and surrounding countryside.

Also visible from the M1, and particularly spectacular when floodlit at night, **Bolsover Castle** ⓘ *(EH), T01246-822844, Apr-Sep daily 1000-1800, Oct daily 1000-1700, Nov-Mar Wed-Sun 1000-1600, £6.20, concessions £4.60, children £3.10, off junctions 29 or 30 on the M1, in Bolsover 6 miles east of Chesterfield*, was built in the 17th century as a romantic lovenest on the site of a medieval castle. It was constructed by Sir Charles Cavendish as a retreat from the world, where he could indulge his fondness for all things chivalric and medieval. The Venus Fountain in the grounds, featuring cherubs relieving themselves into the water below, is typical of the playful tone Sir Charles wanted his guests to appreciate.

Around Derby

Eleven miles northwest of Derby up the A52, **Ashbourne** is a quaint red-brick town, proudly proclaiming itself the 'Gateway to Dovedale'. Its preserved medieval street pattern and Georgian rebuilding give the place its peculiar charm. St John Street is the most interesting architecturally, with its gallows cross still standing. Ashbourne was dubbed 'Oakbourne' by George Eliot in her novel *Adam Bede*. She also described St Oswald's Church with its beautiful spire as the "finest mere parish church in the kingdom". The interior is full of surprises, including carvings, and fine stained glass, and the Cockayne chapel commemorating two centuries-worth of local bigwigs. With its cobbled market place and old pubs, Ashbourne does make a good base from which to set off into the Peak District.

To the south of Derby, a couple of very grand houses are worth seeking out. **Kedleston Hall** ⓘ *(NT), T01332-842191, Apr-Oct Mon-Wed, Sat, Sun 1200-1630, £5.50, under-16s £3.20, family £13.20* is a beautiful neoclassical mansion built in the mid-18th century for the Curzons, its interiors designed by Robert Adam. Also an Eastern Museum displaying the loot acquired by Lord Curzon as Viceroy of India at the turn of the last century. More elegant Adam buildings dotted around the sweeping parkland.

Sleeping

Around Derby *p389*

A **Callow Hall**, Mappleton Rd, Ashbourne, T01335-300900, www.callowhall.co.uk. The smart option, an independent hotel about a mile west of the town in a large Victorian house. Good English food in the restaurant.

C **Beresford Arms Hotel**, Station Rd, Ashbourne, T01335-300035, www.beresford-arms.co.uk. Quite a large hotel in a Victorian house in the middle of town.

D **Beechenhill Farm**, Ilam, T01335-310274. Two double rooms and a self-catering cottage with superb views and colourful garden.

Eating

Derby *p388*

£££ **Darley's on the River**, Darley Abbey Mill, Derby, T01332-364987, www.darleys.com. Probably the smartest restaurant in Derby, with an ambitious but accomplished Frenchified menu at about £30 a head for lunch and supper. A 20-min walk along the river.

Around Derby *p389*

£ **Ye Olde Vaults**, 21 Market Pl, Ashbourne, T01335-346127. Another rambling, popular old pub right at the bottom of the market square with good value square meals.

Pubs, bars and clubs

Derby *p388*

The Flower Pot, 25 King St, Derby, T01332-204955. Just round the corner of the cathedral, with a small beer garden, lots of books and some very fine ales.

The Smithfield, Meadow Rd, Derby, T01332-370429. On the banks of the Derwent, next to the old cattle market, another pub with about 10 different real ales on offer.

The Brunswick, 1 Railway Terr, Derby, T01332-290677. One of the city's most popular real ale pubs, with an exceptional variety in barrels and on the pumps, very close to the railway station.

Ye Olde Dolphin, 6 Queen St, Derby, T01332-267711. A beamed 16th-century pub within walking distance of the cathedral, serving reasonable pub grub.

Lincolnshire

→Colour map 4

Lincolnshire is a large and not very densely populated county which advertises itself as the 'drier side of Britain'. There's some truth in that strapline, as regards both the prevailing weather and sense of humour. Biting winds whipping in from the North Sea can make even the sunniest days a trial in the east of the county. Lincoln itself sits on an escarpment in the west, its cathedral one of the most stunning examples of Gothic architecture in the land. Otherwise, like much of its county, this ancient city's atmosphere is reserved, old-fashioned even, some might say quietly desperate. To the east, the Lincolnshire Wolds are a surprising belt of chalky downland concealing a variety of little villages and dropping down to a gem of a market town at Louth. Along with Lincoln, Louth deserves to be much better known, for its neat Georgian town centre and fabulous church spire, but is quite content to slumber on in obscurity. The stone-built town of Stamford in the south of the county is no stranger to celebrity though, regularly featuring in period dramas thanks to being the most complete surviving Georgian townscape in the country. ▸▸ For Sleeping, Eating and other listings, see pages 396-398.

Ins and outs

Getting there Lincoln is well connected by **train**, with at least 1 **GNER** train an hour departing London King's Cross (2-3 hrs depending on connection) with a change at Peterborough or Newark. By **car**, Lincoln is about 20 miles east of the A1, which is easily the most direct approach from the North or London, some 200 miles away and taking approx 3 hrs 30 mins to reach. **National Express** run an afternoon (1600) **coach** a day to Lincoln from London Victoria, and a morning (0755) return one, each taking just over 4 hrs. By **car** Stamford is just off the A1, about 100 miles from London, a journey that usually takes about an 1 hour 30 minutes. **National Express**, T08705-808080, runs an evening bus to Stamford from London Victoria (3 hrs). A network of local buses serve the outlying villages. The council also publishes a useful bus timetable, available from the TIC. Market Rasen, 20 mins by **train** from Lincoln, is probably your best bet for Louth. Sleaford is useful for accessing the southern edge of the Wolds, on both the Nottingham-Skegness line as well as Lincoln-Peterborough-London. Otherwise the area is not well served by trains. Well removed from the major north-south routes, the Wolds can most easily be reached off the A158 Lincoln to Skegness **road. Stagecoach** run services that connect Louth with Lincoln, Grimsby and Skegness. ➡ *For further details, see Transport, page 397.*

Getting around Lincoln train station is in the southwest of town, 200 yds from the St Martin's High St. Most of the centre of Lincoln is pedestrianized. Local bus services, run by County Council, T0870-6082608. Apart from Shanks's pony, a car or bike are really the only convenient ways of exploring the Wolds. **TransLinc Services**, call T0870 6082608

Information **Lincoln TIC**, *9 Castle Hill, T01522-873213, also at Cornhill, T01522-873256. £4 accommodation booking fee. Also arrange walking tours of the up hill area of town for £2.50.* **Louth TIC** ⓘ *New Market Hall, off Cornmarket T01507-609289, www.poachercountry.co.uk.* **Woodhall Spa TIC** ⓘ *T01526-353775.*

Lincoln

Lincoln deserves to be seen, rising up out of the surrounding flatlands, its medieval cathedral and castle sitting high above the masses huddled down below. Even today the most polite parts of town remain 'up hill', comfortably close to those imposing Gothic and Norman edifices, while the majority of recognizable retail brands and their target populace sprawl around 'down hill'. Anyone arriving by public transport faces a stiff 20-minute climb up the well-named Steep Hill to reach the main event, which is undoubtedly the cathedral. It rewards the effort with its superb west front and thoroughly awe-inspiring interior. A stone's throw away on the top of the same hill, the castle is now much less impressive than it must have been once but does command wide, sweeping views. Between the two nestles a rambling array of half-timbered and stonebuilt 16th- and 17th-century houses, along with a few stately Georgian houses.

Sights

On the High Street, the **Stonebow** is the very fine 15th-century town gate, still in use as the Guildhall and the centre of the 'down hill' part of Lincoln. A right turn here leads down Saltergate to the **Greyfriars Exhibition Centre** ⓘ *Broadgate, T01522-530401, Tue-Sat 1000-1300, 1400-1600, free.* A variety of themed exhibitions culled from the county's archaeological and historical archives are mounted here in a 13th-century building, the oldest Franciscan church in the country. A left turn northwards up Broadgate arrives after a couple of hundred yards outside the **Usher** Gallery ⓘ *Lindum Rd, T01522- 527980, Tue-Sat 1000-1730, Sun 1430-1700, £2,* *concessions/children £0.50*, the home of the county's impressive art collection, which includes several paintings by local Victorian stars William Logsdail and Frank Bramley amongst other, and of the city and surroundings by the likes of Turner, Lowry and Piper. Pride of place goes to Peter de Wint's remarkable watercolours.

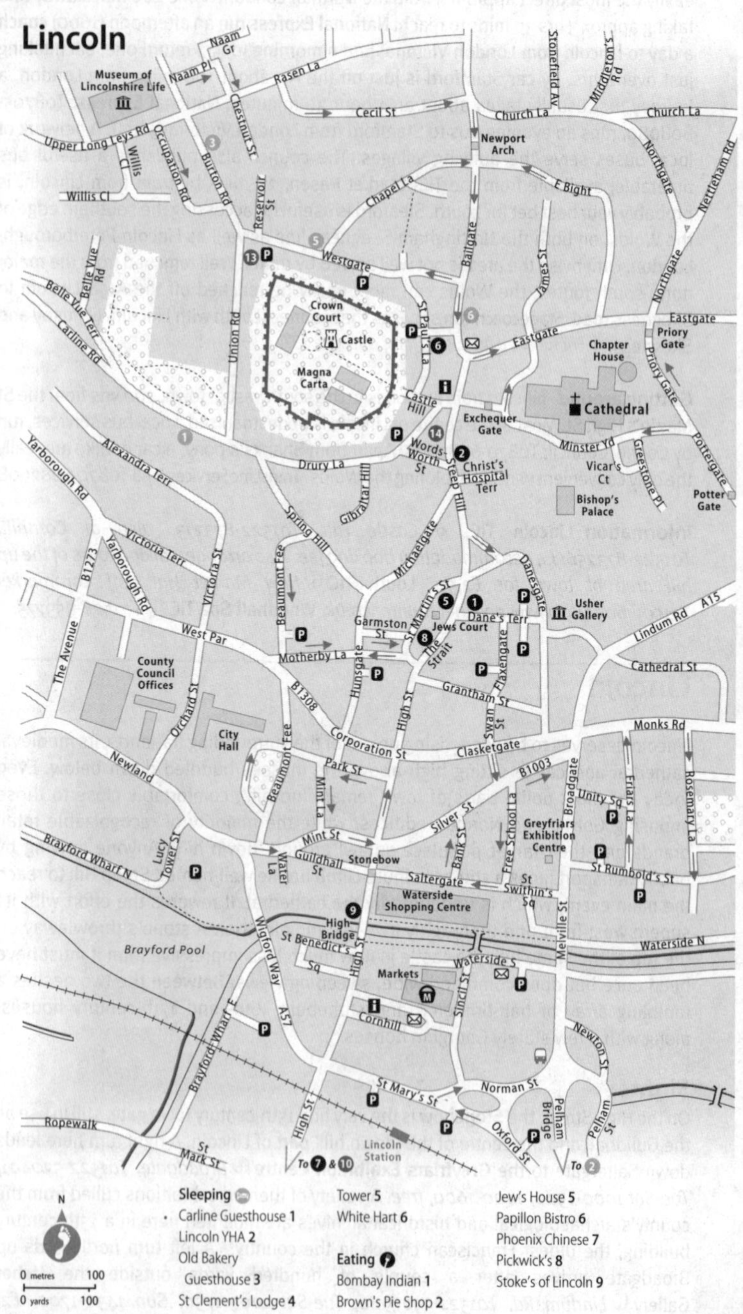

Back at the Stonebow, the High Street continues uphill, narrowing through the Strait where it becomes Steep Hill and the going gets tougher. On the left **Jews Court** is a medieval merchant's house now home to the Lincolnshire History and Archaeology Society, with an intriguing bookshop specializing in the county's topography and a smart restaurant in the **Jews House** next door, a building which dates from the late 12th century. From here it's a couple of hundred yards up past interesting small shops, pubs and restaurants to Castle Hill. A right turn heads through the 14th-century **Exchequer Gate** to the cathedral, a left turn leads to the castle.

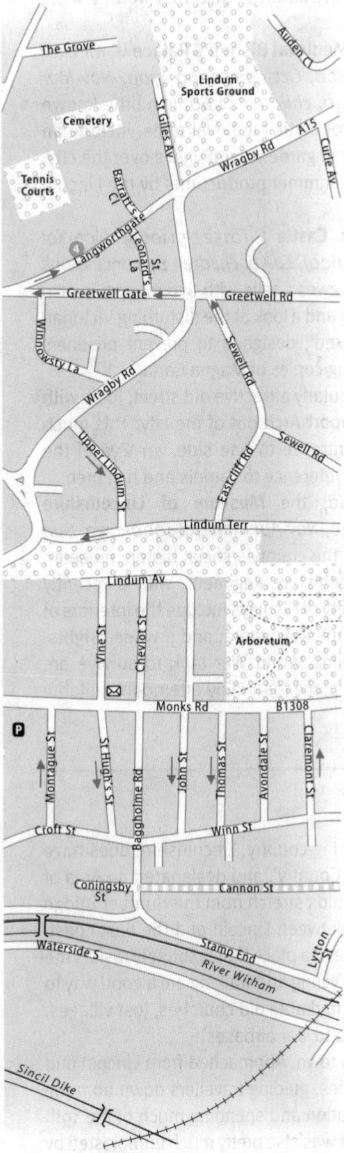

Walking through the Exchequer Gate to be confronted by the massive West Front of the **cathedral** ⓘ *T01522-544544, www.lincolncathedral.com, Apr-Oct daily 0800-2000, Nov-Mar daily 0800- 1800, £3.50, concessions £3,* is Lincoln's most impressive coup de théâtre. An earthquake in 1185 destroyed much of the church begun in 1072 but its rounded Romanesque arches remain here, incorporated into the mighty west front dramatically redeveloped in the 13th-century Early English style. The recently restored frieze, inspired by the cathedral at Modena, depicts scenes from the Old Testament on the south side and the New Testament on the north. The magnificent open nave and choirs behind demand at least an hour to explore thoroughly, soaking up the spirit of 900 years of worship. First stop on the tourist trail is the sturdy late-Norman **font**, made from black Tournai marble in the 12th century, on the south side of the broad nave with its carved columns of local limestone and Purbeck marble. On reaching the crossing, or Great Transept, beneath the central tower and its five-ton bell, 'Great Tom', the **Dean's Eye** is on the left and the **Bishop's Eye** on the right. These two beautiful stained-glass rose windows are another glorious effort, the former Early English (about 1230) and the latter Decorated (about a century younger). Straight ahead is the most ancient part of the Gothic cathedral, **St Hugh's Choir**, with its canopied choir stalls. Beyond this is the cathedral's pièce de résistance and its most holy place, the

Pubs & bars
City Vaults Wine Bar 10
Victoria 13
Wig & Mitre 14

 Angel Choir. An exquisitely carved angelic host looks down on the shrine of St Hugh, the Bishop responsible for the Early English reconstruction of the cathedral. Everyone looks for the **Lincoln Imp** here, a Puckish figure on the north side that was adopted as the city's logo in the late 19th century. To the north of the choirs, the peaceful cloisters lead into the 10-sided **Chapter House**, scene of one of the first English parliaments, called by Edward I in 1301. Above the cloister, the library is also well worth a look, remodelled by Wren in 1647.

Just to the south, by English Heritage, the **Medieval Bishop's Palace** ⓘ *Minster Yard, T01522- 527468, Apr-Sep daily 1000-1800, Oct daily 1000-1700, Nov-Mar Wed-Sun 1000-1600, £3.20, concessions £2.40, children £1.60*, is a little-known treasure in the shadow of the cathedral. The romantic medieval ruins, include an impressive vaulted undercroft and kitchen, set in gardens with views over the city. Various special events are held here including summer productions by the Lincoln Shakespeare Company.

Across Castle Hill, past the TIC, **Lincoln Castle** ⓘ *T01522-511068, Mon-Sat 0930-1730, Sun 1100-1730 (Nov-Mar daily until 1600), £2.50, children £1, concessions £1.50, family £6.50*, unusually constructed like Lewes Castle with two mottes, is also worth exploring, especially for its views over town and a look at the disturbing Victorian prison chapel, with pews that are literally 'boxed', designed to prevent prisoners fraternizing. Also on display is one of the surviving copies of Magna Carta.

East of the Westgate, the **Bailgate** is a particularly attractive old street, lined with independent shops and leading up to the **Newport Arch** out of the city. This much restored Roman gateway features a smaller entrance to one side, an 'Eye of the Needle' of the type mentioned in the Bible with reference to camels and rich men.

West of the Bailgate, on Burton Road, the **Museum of Lincolnshire Life** ⓘ *T01522-528448, May-Sep daily 1000-1730, Nov-Apr Mon-Sat 1000-1730, Sun 1400-1730, £2, children £0.60, family £4.50*, is the county's social history museum housed in the old barracks of the Royal Lincolnshire Regiment, with a recently refurbished museum on the subject. A wide variety of displays include the interiors of Victorian shops and workshops, chemists, co-operative store, and a wheelwrights. Also tractors, steam engines and the oldest First World War tank to survive are displayed, with occasional steam days. A great place for a rainy afternoon, suitable for all ages. Gift shop, tearoom, toilets.

The Wolds and around

Despite its reputation for being flat, boring farming country, Lincolnshire does have some pretty countryside. Marketed as 'Poacher Country', and designated an Area of Outstanding Natural Beauty, the Lincolnshire Wolds stretch from the Humber Bridge to Spilsby, a low rolling ridge of chalk upland between Lincoln and the east coast. Louth is the unofficial capital of the area, a picture of a place that resolutely resists the blandishments of 21st-century commercialism. Cycling and walking are a good way to enjoy this stretch of the country, seeking out remarkable old churches, lost villages, unreconstructed pubs or even former second world war airbases.

Louth is a delightful little red-brick Georgian town. Approached from Lincoln and the west, the spire of St James's is visible for miles, guiding travellers down from the Wolds. Almost bypassed by the Industrial Revolution and spending much of the 19th century in the grip of the agricultural depression, it was also pretty much unmolested by the Second World War. In fact it was only after the war that the population count rose again to its 1820s level. Famous sons of Louth include Captain John Smith (the founder of Virginia rescued by Pocahontas), the Arctic explorer Sir John Franklin and the Victorian's favourite Poet Laureate, Lord Tennyson. In 1969 Jeffrey Archer was returned as Conservative MP for the town, becoming the youngest member in the house.

Louth's most prominent landmark, **St James's Church** ⓘ *Apr-Dec Mon-Sat 1030-1600, Sun afternoons in Aug*, dominates the approach from the west. It dates from the 12th century but was substantially altered in the 1240s and the 1440s. The 295-ft spire (the tallest of any parish church) was added in the early 1500s. The interior is more modest, although the 'starburst' lantern beneath the tower is spectacular. It hovers over a serviceable little café.

The best way to enjoy the town is simply to take a stroll around, browsing around the unusually large number of small independent stores. The **Market Place** is the centre of town, about 100 yds east of St James's along Upgate. Unlike most English towns, the centre has yet to be pedestrianized beyond recognition. There's usually so little traffic that it hardly seems necessary. The helpful TIC is off Cornmarket, just west of the Market Place. A few steps to the north, Louth's local history **museum** ⓘ *4 Broadbank, T01507-601211, Apr-Oct Wed 1000-1600, Fri, Sat 1400-1600 (Mon-Sat 1000-1600 in Aug) £1, concessions £0.50, (times and prices may change after refurbishment*, is a little gem, and undergoing major extension and refurbishment designed to capitalize on the presentation of the *Louth Panorama*, a replica of an extraordinary early 19th-century painting by William Brown capturing a bird's eye perspective of a day in the life of the town during the 1840s.

West of Louth, nearer Lincoln, small villages like Tealby, Donington-on-Bain and especially Nettleton are worth seeking out for walks in the hills around. Dry valleys, glacial tills (large 'erratic boulders' that may have been carried from as far away as Norway by the last Ice Age), and fossils are some of the things to look out for. Many of the most attractive parts of the Wolds can most easily be explored along the **Viking Way**, a long-distance footpath that runs for 116 miles from the Humber Bridge to Oakham, in Rutland. From Donington, with its mill, weir and ruined manor, and Nettleton, with its relatively dramatic scenery, and also Belchford, are particularly good starting points. Belchford lies near the **Bluestone Heath Road**, a prehistoric ridgeway, with fine views from **Nab Hill** nearby. Near Donington, **Red Hill** also gives superb views over Lincolnshire. Further south, Somersby was the childhood home of Tennyson: his father was the vicar at Bag Enderby and the terraces of Harrington Hall (private) are supposed to have inspired his lines "Come into the garden, Maud". The area around Somersby also makes for rewarding exploratory rambles, with its shaded lanes and crumbling churches.

Stamford

Stamford is a very fine but atypical introduction to southern Lincolnshire. A prosperous honey-coloured limestone-built market town just off the A1, although it looks like it belongs in the Cotswolds, it ranks as one of the best-preserved Georgian towns in England. Once a major coaching stop on the great north road, straddling the river Welland, its chief glories today are its 200-year-old streetscape and at least four remarkable churches, especially St Mary's. One of the first designated Conservation Areas in England, the town was used extensively by the BBC for the filming of George Eliot's Middlemarch as well as a variety of other period dramas.

Stamford is best approached from the south, up St Martin's High Street, a street still recognizable as the one painted by JMW Turner in the 19th century. On the right, before the old stone bridge over the Welland, **St Martin's church** contains some fine late-medieval stained glass and the tomb of Queen Elizabeth's Treasurer, Cecil. Daniel Lambert (see below), the 53-stone man who died in 1809, takes up his fair share of space in the graveyard. Up the hill and over the bridge stands St Mary's, its magnificent early Gothic tower and broach spire one of the town's most prominent landmarks. Inside, all is Perpendicular: look out for the embossed roof of the north chapel, and wonder at the High Church Arts and Crafts woodwork.

A right turn at the top of the hill by St Mary's leads past the TIC in the Arts Centre into **St George's Square**, an atmospheric quiet old square that was used as the scene of the hustings in *Middlemarch*. **St George's church**, at its eastern end, contains heraldic stained glass depicting the arms and mottoes of the 200 original Knights of the Garter, a collection granted in a bequest of Sir William de Bruges in 1449.

From here Maiden Lane heads another hundred yards north to the parquet-paved pedestrianized High Street, emerging opposite the grand neo classical portico of the Public Library. Behind is **Stamford Museum** ⓘ *Broad St, T01780-766317, Mon-Sat 1000-1700 (also Sun 1400-1700 Apr-Sep)*, once lived in by Daniel Lambert, so hugely overweight they needed to knock the house down to get him out when he died. The small museum, accessed from Broad Street, contains a life-size replica of the man, displays on the history of the town and a collection of Stamford Ware, locally thrown pottery.

Sleeping

Lincoln *p391, map p393*

A **The White Hart**, Bailgate, T0870-4008117, F531798. Pretty much top of the range in Lincoln, a perfectly acceptable offering from the Macdonald chain of hotels in the thick of things on the Bailgate. The feature rooms are worth the extra spend, but service is rumoured to be a bit slack.

C **Carline Guesthouse**, 1-3 Carline Rd, T01522-530422. Well-respected B&B just at the bottom of the hill, clean, comfortable and quiet.

C **The Tower Hotel**, 38 Westgate, T01522-529999, F560596. Close to the castle walls, the *Tower Hotel* has been recently refurbished with quiet, comfortable but plain rooms.

D **Old Bakery Guesthouse**, 26-28 Burton Rd, T01522-576057. Has comfortable bedrooms close to the castle.

D **St Clement's Lodge**, 21 Langworth Gate, T01522-521532. Close to the cathedral, a B&B with a pleasant family atmosphere.

F **Lincoln YHA**, 77 South Park, T01522-522076. On the outskirts of town to the south of the train station.

The Wolds and around *p394*

A **Kenwick Park**, near Louth, T01507-608806, www.kenwick-park.co.uk. Part of the Classic British Hotels chain, and the high-end option in the area, with a golf course and oddly corporate atmosphere for such a charming setting.

B **The Beaumont**, 66 Victoria Rd, T01507-605005, F607768. A better bet, on the edge of Louth itself, a hotel 'with an Italian twist', comfortable rooms and friendly staff.

A **Petwood Hotel**, Stixwould Rd, Woodhall Spa, T01526-352411, www.petwood.co.uk. A fairly smart hotel (3-star) in what was once the Officer's Mess of the Dambusters squadron.

D **The Grange**, Torrington Lane, East Barkwith, near Market Rasen, T01673-858670. A Georgian farmhouse B&B, very warm and welcoming with large rooms and a lawn tennis court.

D **Mason's Arms**, Cornmarket, Louth, T01507-609525. A couple of reasonable double rooms bang in the middle of town, and a jolly pub doing decent enough food downstairs.

F **YHA Woody's Top**, Ruckland, Nr Louth, T0870-7706098. Extended and modernized former farm buildings with 20 beds in 2,4, or 6-bedded rooms, 6 miles south of Louth.

Stamford *p395*

A **George Hotel**, 71 St. Martins High St, T01780-750750 www.georgehotel ofstamford.com. In a very grand old building, a former coaching inn, with a monastic garden and widely acclaimed restaurant and brasserie serving English and Italian food in comfortable, elegant surroundings. The good service and friendly atmosphere make this a popular choice.

For an explanation of the sleeping and eating price codes used in this guide, see the inside front cover. Other relevant information is provided in the Essentials chapter, page 36.

B **Garden House Hotel**, St Martin's High St, T01780-763359, www. gardenhouse hotel.com. An 18th-century townhouse, true to its name with an attractive garden and about 100 yds up from St Martin's church, with 20 rooms with en suite bath.
C **Stamford Lodge Guesthouse**, 24 Scotgate, T01780-482932, www. stamfordlodge.co.uk. A fairly small, quiet but also very central guesthouse with 7 double rooms en suite.
D **The Willoughby Arms**, Station Rd, Little Bytham, near Stamford, T01780-410276, www.willoughbyarms.co.uk. Has its own microbrewery and a variety of guest ales as well as small but comfortable rooms.

Eating

Lincoln *p391, map p393*

$$$ **Jew's House Restaurant**, 15 The Strait, T01522-524851. A smart modern European restaurant in a 12th-century building: white tablecloths, high-backed chairs, competent cuisine.
$$ **Papillon Bistro**, St Paul's Lane , off Westgate, T01522-511284. A friendly informal bistro serving a wide-ranging French menu (on blackboards) including lots of fish and vegetarian options, super wine list. Nearly always busy.
$$ **Phoenix Chinese Restaurant**, Newark Rd end of High St, T01522- 527682. Large popular Chinese restaurant in downhill Lincoln. Large menu, set meals are good value, buzzing atmosphere.
$$ **Pickwick's**, 14 The Strait, T01522-545991. A splendidly old-fashioned sort of restaurant, unashamedly serving up platefuls of liver and bacon at remakarbly low prices.
$ **Bombay Indian Restaurant**, 6 The Strait, T01522-523264. Classic dishes in this recently redecorated restaurant, speedy service, usually quiet until 2200. Very tasty food.
$ **Brown's Pie Shop**, 33 Steep Hill, T01522-527330. An informal restaurant with rugged wooden furniture serving a wide range of dishes as well as its famous pies. Large portions, cheap wine and friendly service. Good value Sunday lunches.
$ **Garmstons**, 262 High St. Appealing café with wide range of wholesome food and tempting cakes. Sandwiches made to order, jacket potatoes, soup, salads and daily specials. Order and pay at counter before finding a table. Popular with locals.
$ **Stoke's of Lincoln**, High Gate, T01522-512534. A 2-course lunch for £3.50 and a commendable array of teas and coffees to boot in a wonderful old place at the bottom of the hill.

The Wolds and around *p394*

£ **The King's Head**, Tealby, T01673-838347. A thatched pub in a pretty setting beside the river in this attractive Wolds village, with reasonable food.

Stamford *p395*

££ **Loch Fyne Seafood Restaurant**, All Saints Pl, T01780-761370. For the finest fishy dishes.
££ **The Warehouse Restaurant**, 9a North St, T01780-762868, specializes in Spanish and Mexican food.

Pubs, bars and clubs

Lincoln *p391, map p393*

City Vaults Wine Bar, High St, T01522-521035. Lots of wines by the glass as well as the usual beers, etc. Friendly, useful stopping off point on the way into town from the south.
The Victoria, Union Rd. Real ale pub with wide range of guest beers and ciders. Very small and very popular.
Wig and Mitre, 30/32 Steep Hill. A famous and comfortable old pub with a well-rated menu.

The Wolds and around *p394*

The Wheatsheaf, off Westgate, T01507-603159, with real fires and a well-kept ales is worth checking out.

Transport

Lincoln *p391, map p393*

Bus

National Express, T08705-808080, run a direct service to **London King's Cross** (4 hrs 45 mins) at 0735.

Car

Avis, Ermine Filling Station, Riseholme Rd, T01522-511200; **Thrifty**, Chieftain Way,Tritton Rd, T01522-568777.

Taxi

County Cars, 381b High St, T01522-567878; Handsome Cabs, 10 Clasketgate, T01522-545352.

Train

Central Trains, T0121-6541200, run the regular direct service to **Nottingham** (1 hr) and the regular services to **York** (1 hr 40 mins) changing at **Doncaster** (50 mins) and to **London King's Cross** (2 hrs 30 mins) changing at Newark. Arriva Trains Northern, T08706-023322, run the regular service to **Manchester Piccadilly** or **Manchester Oxford Road** (2 hrs 40 mins) changing at **Sheffield** (1 hr 20 mins).

Yorkshire

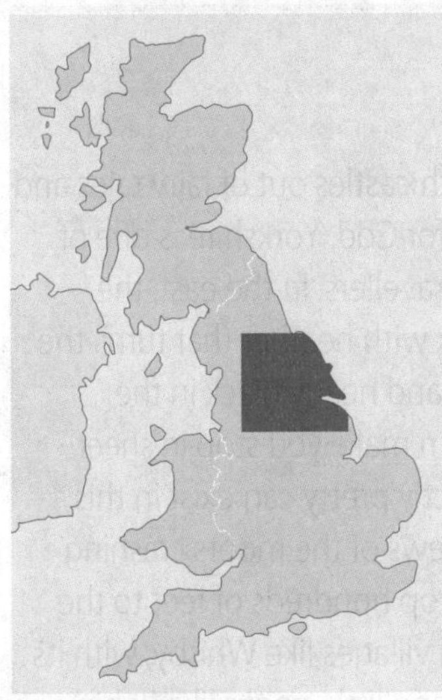

Introduction

Ruggedly beautiful, and filled with castles out of fairy tales and monuments to man's reverence for God, Yorkshire is one of the richest regions of Britain for travellers. In the east, the rolling hills of the moors are thick with heather that turns the horizon pink in the summertime and nearly black in the winter. Here, villages like Lealholm make you stop in sheer wonder that something so perfectly pretty can exist in this modern age. The breathtaking views of the moors crashing into the sea on sheer cliffs that drop hundreds of feet to the icy waters is broken up by fishing villages like Whitby, with its gothic edge and homely centre, and little nooks like Robin Hood's Bay, with its smugglers history and tiny cottages. In the west, the craggy rocks of the dales seem to defy anything to grow upon their sharp edges, and yet the heather persists, against the odds. Here walkers follow trails to picturesque waterfalls, and then retreat to soak their feet in the fabled waters of gorgeous Harrogate. At the centre of it all the soaring towers of York's historic cathedral is juxtaposed by the busy modern nightlife in Leeds and Sheffield, where the beat never stops.

★ Don't miss...

1. Walk the walls of **York** and wonder how much the view of the cathedral has changed in half a millennium, page 403.
2. See the cliffs giving up their dead in the crumbling churchyard at **Whitby**, where Bram Stoker had Dracula arrive in England, page 416.
3. Drop into Leeds for some serious student nightlife after an evening of top-class theatre at the **West Yorkshire Playhouse**, page 432.
4. Follow in the tempestuous footsteps of Heathcliff and Cathy from Wuthering Heights on the moors around **Haworth**, page 433.
5. Work up an appetite by walking in **Wensleydale** and stop off in Hawes at the Wensleydale Creamery for a cheese tasting, page 442.

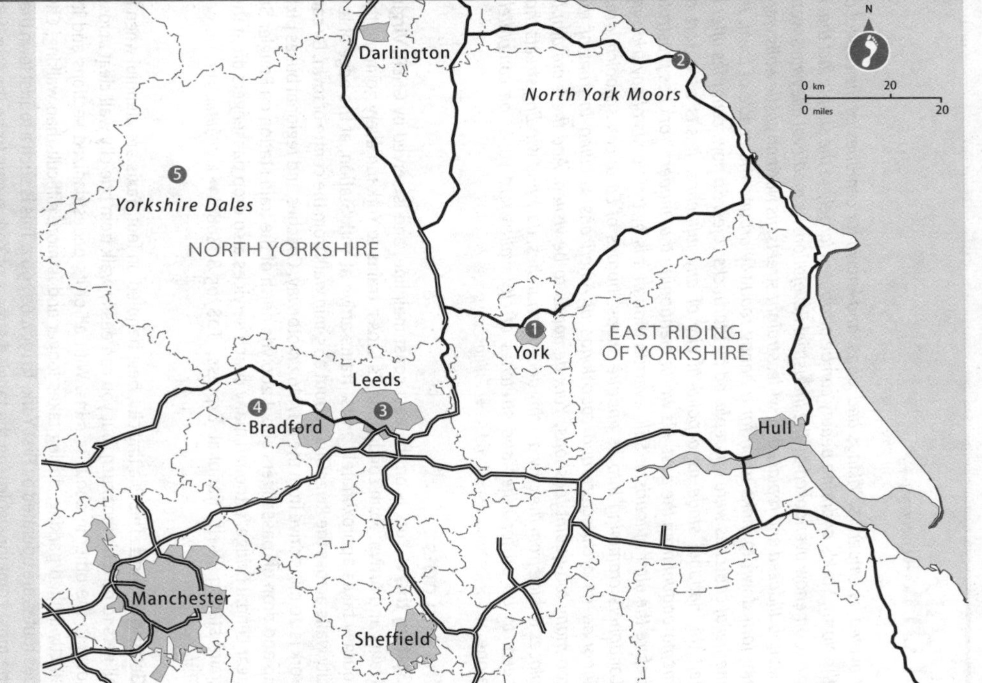

York →*Colour map 4*

Coveted by emperors, Vikings and kings, and known for centuries as the capital of the North, York's enduring beauty can be attributed largely to the simple fact that it was somehow overlooked by the Industrial Revolution. Its medieval alleyways were never bulldozed and replaced by wide, straight streets. Its Norman castle walls were not torn down to make room for a handy roadway around the centre of town. Its medieval churches were not replaced by Starbucks cafés. So now, centuries after it left the national stage as a political city of any influence, it sits as a sort of memorandum from the past. It's worth mentioning that modern York lies prostrate before the altar of tourism. Still, overrun though it is by trainloads of day-tripping Londoners cramming into its antique shops, hordes of European schoolchildren ignoring its architecture and coachloads of Americans queuing in front of the too-many too-quaint teashops, York demands to be visited. And there are ample places to hide from the crowds: tiny ancient churches, dark and winding streets that seem to go on for miles and stretches of city wall where you'll be completely alone. »» *For Sleeping, Eating and other listings, see pages 407-409.*

Ins and outs

Getting there York is on the east coast mainline, and is served by **GNER, Virgin Trains** and **Arriva.** From London King's Cross, **trains** to York run every 30 mins; the journey takes approximately 2 hrs. Trains arrive at York Station, at the edge of the city walls across the River Ouse about a 15-min walk from the centre of town. By **car,** York is 20 mins drive from the M1/M62 motorway. Coaches and regional buses pick up and drop off passengers about 200 yds north of the train station on Rougier St, near Lendal Bridge, although many coach services also drop passengers off at the train station itself. **National Express,** T08705-808080. »» *For further details, see Transport, page 409.*

Getting around This is a tiny city, best handled on foot. **Taxis** are plentiful when it all gets to be a bit too much, but you can easily walk from one city wall clear across town to the other in about 15 mins. With all of its pedestrianized sections and its strictly limited parking, driving takes longer and is more difficult than walking. City bus routes are operated by **First York,** T01904-622992. This is such a tourist town that the most common vehicle on the tangled streets of York seems to be the tour bus. There are dozens to choose from, and you can find brochures for most of them in the tourist office if you fancy adding to the road congestion. On the other hand, there are equally as many guided walks about, and these are often more interesting and hands-on. Some of the best are led by the **York Association of Voluntary Guides,** T01904-640780, www.york.touristguides. btinternet.co.uk, which generally meet daily in Exhibition Square.

Information All of Yorkshire is covered by the Yorkshire Tourist Board, T01904-707070, which has offices in York and Thirsk. Its website, www.yorkshirevisitor.com, features good background information on the region and ideas for walks. Another good walking guide is AA's 50 Walks in North Yorkshire. York's tourist offices are the biggest and best in Yorkshire. **TIC** ⓘ *Exhibition Square in front of Bootham Gate. Apr-Jun, Sep, Oct Mon-Sat 0900-1800, Sun 0930-1800; Jul-Aug daily 0900-1900; Nov-Mar Mon-Sat 0900-1700, Sun 0930-1500.* There's also a convenient branch located in York Station, ⓘ *T01904-621756. Apr-Oct Mon-Sat 0900-1700, Sun 1000-1700; Nov-Feb Mon-Sat 1900-1700, Sun 1000-1600; Mar Mon-Sat 0930-1730, Sun 1000-1700.*

Sights

Bootham Bar

A good place to start any walk through town is at Bootham Bar, the oldest of the four city gateways, dating, in part, from the 11th century, although most of it was built over the subsequent two centuries. It offers entrance to the city via High Petergate. This is the only of the four gates that sits on the site of one of the original entrances to the old Roman fortress. It bears the Stuart coat of arms, and still has its original wooden portcullis.

Just adjacent to the bar is the city's main tourist office in the De Grey rooms, while across the busy intersection from the gate is **Exhibition Square**, with its unimpressive fountain and a chunk of the old walls. This is where you'll find the **City Art Gallery**, and its small but varied collection of continental works incl- uding pieces by Bacchiacca (*Agony in the Garden*), Domenichino (*Monsignor Agucchi*) and Bellotto (*View in Lucca*). ⓘ *Daily 1000-1700, £2.*

Next to the gallery is the **King's Manor**, which once formed part of the abbot's lodging of **St Mary's Abbey**, which lies in ruins not far away. Sections of the manor date from 1270, although most of it is was built in the late 1400s. After the Dissolution it was taken over by the Lord President of the Council of the North, after which it was used as a royal headquarters in Yorkshire. During its time the manor was visited by James I, Charles I and Henry VIII. It's now used by the University of York and only its courtyard and a few rooms are open to the public.

Museum Gardens

Just a short distance down St Leonard's Place from the Manor, past the endless queues waiting for tour buses, is the lovely green space of the Museum Gardens, where a cluster of ruins sit in various stages of decay. To the right of the entrance are the remains of **St Leonard's Hospital**, which was founded in the 12th century. Nearby stands the **Multangular Tower**, which has a fourth-century Roman base and a medieval top; inside is a collection of Roman coffins unearthed in and around York. The gardens lead up to the **Yorkshire Museum** ⓘ *daily 1000-1700. £4.50*, with its extensive display of artefacts collected in the region. Included in the collection are pieces of the old Roman gateway to the city, Viking artefacts and the Middleham Jewel, believed to be one of the finest examples of medieval jewellery found in Britain. The museum's basement includes the original fireplace and walls of **St Mary's Abbey**, which was founded in 1080. The rest of the craggy abbey ruins are nearby, but there's not much left of them – just a few sections of the old walls and a row of apses.

The Minster

ⓘ *T01904-557216, www.yorkminster.org. Opening times vary each month and for different areas of the building. You can pick up a helpful diagram of the building at the front desk, where you can also make a donation to the building's maintenance and repair. Be warned, though, that if you plan on visiting the entire building, fees are charged to enter the crypt, the Chapter House and the central tower. You can easily spend £10 without ever leaving the building.*

If you walk into town through Bootham Bar down High Petergate, you're essentially following in Roman footsteps on a route they called Via Principalis. The street curves a short distance past restaurants, pubs and shops and leads directly to where the extraordinary **York Minster** soars above low-slung York. The single most important historic building in all of Yorkshire, and the largest medieval cathedral in Britain, its pale towers are 200 ft tall and can be seen from miles away. It stands on the site of the old Roman military headquarters, and impressive remains from Roman and Norman times have been found in its foundations. One of the most significant of the Roman finds stands to the right of the Minster in the form of the incongruously simple Roman column, which was unearthed in the Minster's basement and re-erected nearby in 1971, on the city's 1900th birthday. Historians believe the column was part of a huge Roman hall (the *Principia*) that once stood where the Minster is now.

The crowning glory of York Minster is its glass. The most beautiful example is the heart-shaped **West Window,** which was created in 1338. The oldest glass is to be found in the second bay window in the northern aisle of the nave. Created in 1155, it contains the oldest stained glass in the country. While in the nave, take note of the ceiling which, while made of wood (it was built in 1840 to replace the previous roof destroyed by fire), has been painted to resemble stone. Throughout the rest of the Minster, the roof is actual stone.

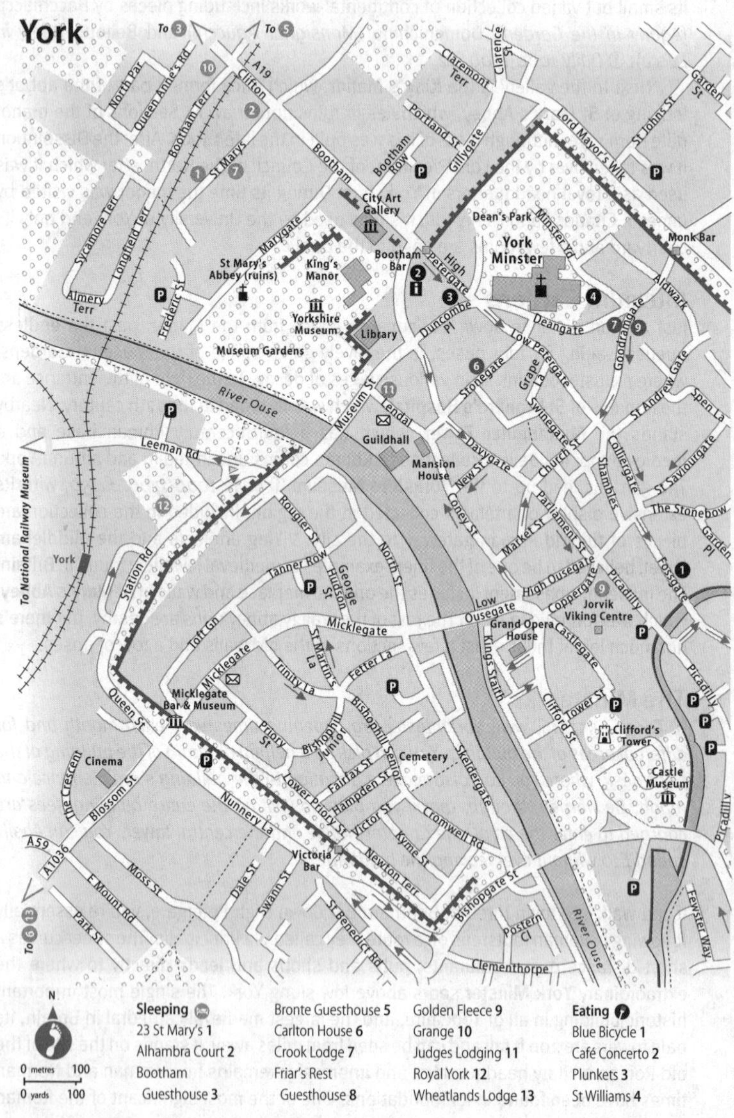

Back in the Cathedral, the window directly opposite the Five Sisters is the elaborate **Rose Window**, which was built to mark the marriage of Henry VII and Elizabeth of York in 1486. Also in the crossing is de Grey's own austere tomb, sadly dusty and lightly draped in cobwebs.

In the centre of the crossing, the **Choir** is separated from the **Nave** by a fascinating stone rood screen. Dating to the late 15th century, it features life-size statues of all the English kings (up to that date) except for Henry VI. At the end of the east aisle is the most impressive window in the Minster: the remarkable and awe-inspiring **East Window**, which, at 78 ft by 31 ft, is recognized as the world's largest medieval stained-glass window. Created around 1405 by John Thornton, its themes are varied, and include the beginning and the end of the world, with the upper panels telling the story of the Old Testament, and the lower panels the grim predictions of Revelations. Unfortunately, if understandably, visitors are kept so far from the window that, without binoculars, it's virtually impossible to make those scenes out. It's all a lovely, massive blur.

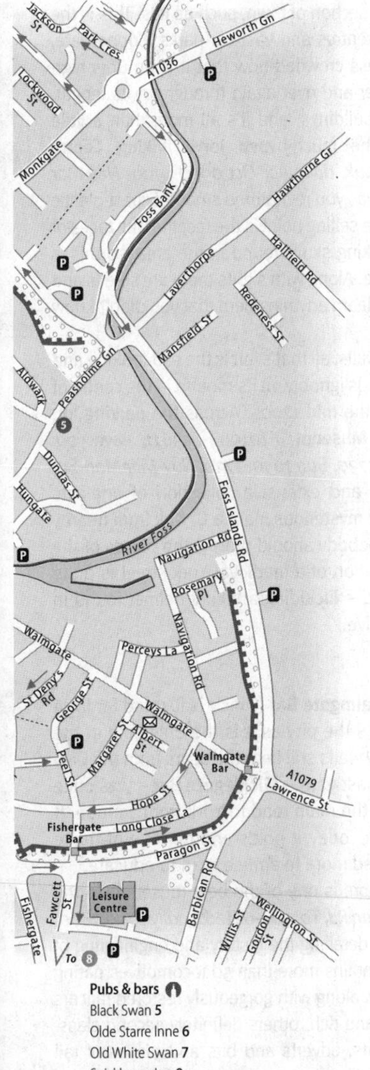

Pubs & bars
Black Swan 5
Olde Starre Inne 6
Old White Swan 7
Snickleway Inn 9

Stonegate

The streets around the Minster are sprawling shopping lanes, filled with tourist boutiques, tourist restaurants and tourist pubs. The most impressive of these streets is Stonegate, surely the most photographed street in all of York. This medieval lane made of the same stone as the Minster traces its history back to Roman times when it was called Via Praetoria. Today it is lined with antique jewellery shops and boutiques selling sweaters made of Yorkshire wool, alongside the usual suspects like *Crabtree & Evelyn*. Day and night it is packed with tourists, not least because it makes a handy cut-through from the Minster area down to Lendal Street along the river. Despite the constant throngs, it is still charming in its medieval completeness. This is also the street where Guy Fawkes' parents lived (look for the plaque). Sneaking down the little medieval pedestrian alleys – called snickleways or ginnels – that lead off of it can be rewarding. One ginnel leads to a fragment of a Norman house, while others lead to pubs and teashops. Look for the little red devil that squats on the wall outside No 33. Little figures like this one, high on the walls, once served as adverts or signs for the shops underneath them. This is one of the most unusual in York, and is believed to have served as a sign for a printworks once located here – printer's assistants were once called 'printers' devils'.

The Shambles

If you aren't lost by the time you stumble onto the Shambles, just at the edge of King's Square at the southern end of Goodramgate, you will be shortly. The narrow, crowded shopping lanes that run off of this street are generally overrated in terms of the shops they hold, but absolutely unmatchable in sheer historic charm. So old is this section of town, that it is the only street in York mentioned by name in the *Domesday Book* of 1086, which also lists the half-brother of William the Conquerer as owning a stall on the Shambles. While most of the stores today are the sadly predictable hocus-pocus magick shoppes or tepid stationery stores or sellers of Scottish/Irish/Yorkshire woollens, the streets are lined with wonderfully photogenic ancient timber-framed buildings. Near the Shambles is York's most whimsically named street – **Whip-ma-Whap-ma-Gate**.

Around the castle

The Shambles are a short stroll from the castle section of town, such as it is. This is the more modern section of York, with shopping centres and vast car parks. **Coppergate**, once the busiest street in Viking York, is no less crowded now that it is an über-high street. It tries to part you from your money over and over again throughout its length. Buskers sing sad songs outside unattractive buildings, and it's all more than a little depressing. At the end of the street is the much-hyped **Jorvik Viking Centre** ⓘ *T01904-543403, www.jorvik-viking-centre.co.uk, daily Apr-Oct 0900-1900, Nov-Mar 0900- 1730, £6.50*. You sit in a ferris wheel seat as you're motored smoothly past plastic blacksmiths and marketers of the Viking era. The selling point is the fact that the faces of the 'people' in the museum were based on Viking skulls found in the area, so this is probably what the early inhabitants did look like. Along with sights there are smells and sounds as well, but, all-in-all, you're unlikely to learn anything here that you didn't know already.

As for the **Castle** itself, aside from the city walls, all that's left is the sad-looking and sparse keep called **Clifford's Tower**, which stands ignobly on its mound in the centre of a modern car park. This version was built in the mid-1200s. Across the parking lot, though, is the wonderfully eccentric **Castle Museum** ⓘ *T01904-653611, www.yorkcastlemuseum.org.uk, Apr-Oct Mon-Sat 0930-1730, Sun 1030- 1730, Nov-Mar Mon-Sat 0930-1600, Sun 1030-1600*, with its bizarre and extensive collection of artefacts through the ages. These were amassed by one mysterious man, a Dr Kirk from nearby Pickering, who decided 80 years ago that somebody should protect the pieces of the area's heritage or all would be lost. His recreation of a medieval York street is quite magnificent, and some of the pieces he found – including a Viking helmet found in excavations on Coppergate – are truly impressive.

Elsewhere in York

One of the least visited of the city's bars is **Walmgate Bar** (which is located far from the action at the end of Fossgate), and more's the pity as it is the only gate in the country to retain its barbican. The 14th-century walls still bear the scars from the Civil War battles that took place here in 1644. The last gate – **Micklegate Bar** – was once the most important of the four, as it oversaw the main road to York from London. It also once served as a prison for the wealthy. Today it holds another one of those pointless museums-without-artefacts, designed more to amuse than to educate.

Past Micklegate Bar and the York rail station, is one of the best museums in the country. The **National Railway Museum** ⓘ *Leeman Rd, T01904-621261, daily 1000-1800, free*, is a vast, exhaustive, extraordinary facility detailing the history and engineering of rail travel in Britain. The enormous museum contains more than 50 locomotives dating back to the early 1800s, all still in working order, along with gorgeously restored railcars that date back to the 1700s – some splendid and rich, others definitely second class. There's memorabilia galore, with posters, charts, adverts and bits and pieces of rail history sure to have trainspotters refusing ever to leave.

Around York

Within an hour's drive of York the countryside changes, as the flat farmland gives way to the rolling hills of the moors. Between the city and the hills are a series of charming villages, reminders of wealth past and ancient edifices. **Castle Howard** ⓘ *T01653-648444, www.castlehoward.co.uk. Feb-Nov, house 1100-1600, grounds 1000-1630, house and grounds £9, concessions £8, children £6, gardens and grounds only, £6, children £4,* is a fantastic building among the farmland about 15 miles north of York (off the A64, 11 miles northeast of York, well-signposted). It has an irresistible lure to anybody who followed breathlessly the trials and tribulations of the upper classes in the series *Brideshead Revisited*. The extraordinary manor house that served as a backdrop to that 1970s programme was Castle Howard. With its domed roof and Grecian-style statues, this vast building stands as proof that some people have more money than sense. Not a castle at all, but a mansion with ambition, the Baroque building was designed in 1699 by Sir John Vanbrugh and Nicholas Hawksmoor for Charles Howard, the third Earl of Carlisle. The inside of the building is, if anything, even more over the top than the exterior, filled as it is with paintings by Rubens and Van Dyck, along with so many Chippendale chairs sitting below friezes and plasterwork frills that the mind boggles. Not all of the building is open to visitors, as members of the Howard family still live here, but there's enough to be seen to satisfy. The thousand acres of grounds are better, really, than the house. Even before you reach the building you drive through one unnecessary- but-beautiful archway after another. In the front of the house, a huge fountain gushes amidst statuary and perfectly manicured hedges.

Sleeping

York *p402, map p405*

York is a tourist town, so hotels abound, and B&Bs even more so. While accommodation is scattered about, Bootham and Clifton streets have the highest concentration, and is a good place to look for a room if you've arrived without reservations. The tourist office in the train station will also book a room for you.

A **The Grange Hotel**, 1 Clifton, T01904-644744, www.grangehotel.co.uk. This grand building has large, gorgeous rooms with all the modern amenities along with a friendly staff and some of the best restaurants in York. It's located in easy walking distance of the centre.

B **Judges Lodging Hotel**, 9 Lendal, T01904-638733, www.judges-lodging.co.uk A short stroll from the Minster in a listed Georgian townhouse on the tourist track. Many of its rooms have 4-poster beds.

B **Royal York Hotel**, Station Rd, T01904-653681, www.principalhotels.co.uk. Has three acres of landscaped gardens. It is designed to pamper in historic elegance.

C **Alhambra Court Hotel**, 31 St Mary's, Bootham, T01904-628474, www.alhambra courthotel.co.uk Well-appointed rooms with period furnishings within walking distance of the centre.

C **Wheatlands Lodge Hotel**, 75-85 Scarcroft Rd, T01904-654318, wheatlodge@aol.com. A large, friendly facility near the train station with all the modern conveniences, along with a pleasant bar and handy restaurant.

D **23 St Mary's**, 23 St Mary's, T01904-622738. A sweet, centrally located hotel near St Mary's Abbey – family owned.

D **The Golden Fleece**, 16 Pavement, T01904-627151, goldenfleece@fibbers.co.uk. A few rooms in a historic pub, it's also well located with views of the Minster and the Shambles. The place is said to be haunted.

D **Bootham Guesthouse**, 56 Bootham Cres, T01904-672123, F672123. A friendly, quiet place tucked inside a period building, walking distance from the centre, with cheery owners and massive breakfasts.

D **Bronte Guesthouse**, 22 Grosvenor Terr, T01904-621066, F653434. In a period building with charming rooms with en suite bathroom, walking distance from the centre.

D **Carlton House Hotel**, 134 The Mount, T01904-622265, www.carltonhouse.co.uk An elegant Georgian house with modern accoutrements 5 mins from the centre.

D **Friar's Rest Guesthouse**, 81 Fulford Rd, T01904-629823, www.friarsrest.co.uk Has 7 rooms (bathroom en suite) in an historic monastery 10 mins' walk from the centre.

D **Crook Lodge**, 26 St Mary's, T01904-655614, www.crooklodge.co.uk Historic building with 7 rooms (bathroom en suite) 500 yds from the centre.

Eating

York *p402, map p405*
It seems like the only thing there's more of than churches in York is restaurants. Choose carefully from the ranks, and you can have a very good meal here.

$$$ **Blue Bicycle**, 34 Fossgate, T01904-673990, serves fabulous gourmet dishes with a seafood emphasis in a gorgeous building that once served as a brothel. Don't even think about going if you haven't booked, though.

$$$ **The Grange Hotel** 1 Clifton, T01904-644744. Modern European dishes in an unashamedly posh atmosphere. Prices are unsurprisingly steep at both restaurants.

$$ **Melton's Too**, 25 Walmgate, T01904-634 341. A good option for an excellent dinner or just an afternoon nibble, offers modern dishes in a 1690s building.

$$ **Rubicon**, 5 Little Stonegate, T01904-676076. This isn't your parents' vegetarian restaurant. Rubicon is modern, elegant and cool, and you'll only notice the lack of meat if you, erm, well, look at the menu. The bustling atmosphere here is all business, the food is creative and international in scope.

$$ **Russells Restaurant** 34 Stonegate, 01904 641432. Dinner for two around £30. There's almost always a crowd gathered round the big plate-glass windows out front of this place on touristy Stonegate, watching the carvers in big chefs' hats cutting enormous legs of beef and lamb on to large plates. This place packs 'em in, night after night, for meaty meals from carving stations.

$$ **St Williams Restaurant**, College St, T01904- 634830. Offers modern British cuisine in the grand setting of one of York's most historic buildings right next to the Minster.

$ **Caesars Pizzeria & Ristorante** 27-9 Goodramgate, T01904-670914. Inauspiciously located at the foot of the Minster, this casual Italian may be filled with tourists, but the food is good traditional fare and the atmosphere is laid back.

$ **Café Concerto**, 27 High Petergate, T01904-610 478. Creative fusion cuisine at a reasonable price in this sunny café, although it's even better for a piece of cake and a cup of coffee in the afternoon.

$ **The Patio**, 13 Swinegate Court East, T01904-627879. This breezy, cheery restaurant has as many tables outdoors as in, and its menu is basic reliable food, with an emphasis on English dishes and a wide array of salads and sandwiches for lunch.

$ **Plunkets**, 9 High Petergate, T01904-637722. Offers American dishes with a southwestern flavour at moderate prices, although booking is essential at weekends.

Pubs, bars and clubs

York *p402, map p405*
Some of York's pubs are almost too historic and quaint. You feel like it's a put on.

The Black Swan, Peasholme Green, T01904-686911, is one of these. In a distinguished medieval timber-frame house, the pub dates back to 1417. Understandably, it is believed to be haunted, so look out for a filmy but beautiful girl staring anxiously into the fireplace.

The Blue Bell, Fossgate. Two dinky rooms surround the little bar. The amiable staff will look out for you, and there are occasional (and challenging) pub quizzes on Sun nights.

The Olde Starre Inne, 40 Stonegate, T01904-623063. The sign is one of the easiest to spot in town, as it stretches clear across Stonegate. The sign itself dates from 1733, while the tavern preceded it by a couple of hundred years. Despite its spot on the tourist path, this is a lovely boozer with lots of wood panelling, open fireplaces and etched glass.

Old White Swan, Goodramgate, T01904-540911. This is one of the largest pubs in town and it spreads over a warren of nine medieval, timber-framed buildings. The lunches here are particularly good.

Snickleway Inn, Goodramgate, T01904-656138. When you enter its historically perfect rooms, with open fireplaces and a real sense of history, it won't seem surprising that this is believed to be one of the most haunted pubs in York. Scared yet?

Entertainment

York *p402, map p405*

Cinema

City Screen, 13-17 Coney St, T01904-541155, has transformed York's cinema life to include art-house films in a riverside setting with a posh café and bar packing them in every night.

Odeon, Blossom St, T01425-954742. For mainstream films.

Theatre

Grand Opera House, Cumberland St, T01904-671818, offers a variety of productions including ballet, theatre, musicals and opera.

The Theatre Royal, St Leonard's Pl, T01904-623568, is where the locals go for musicals, pantos and mainstream theatre.

Festivals

York *p402, map p405*

Jul York's Early Music Festival, is justifiably famous, and historically based musical groups travel here from all over the world to perform. The fabled York Mystery Plays are held every 4 years in the Museum Gardens, T01904-551800, with the next one set for summer 2004.

Transport

York *p402, map p405*

Bus

National Express, T08705-808080, run directly from **London Victoria** (5 hrs), **Birmingham** 1 daily (3 hrs), **Manchester** 2 daily (3 hrs), **Leeds** (1 hr), **Sheffield** 1 daily (2 hrs 30 mins).

Car

Europcar, York Station, T01904-656161; Practical Car and Van Rental, 5 mins' walk from the station on Rougier St, T01904-624277.

Taxi

Castle Cars, 22 Fetter Lane, T01904-611511; Station Taxis, Station Rd, T01904-623332.

Rail

Virgin Trains run services to York from **London King's Cross** (2 hrs) and **Birmingham New Street** (2 hrs 30 mins). Arriva run direct services from **Manchester Piccadilly** (1 hr 30 mins), **Leeds** (30 mins), **Sheffield** (1 hr 15 mins).

Directory

York *p402, map p405*

Hospital York District Hospital, Wigginton Rd, T01904-631313. **Internet** Internet Exchange, 13 Stonegate, T01904-638808.

North York Moors →*Colour map 4*

The stark beauty of the moors never fails to impress. Were there no signs at all telling you that you had reached them, you would still know that you were there. The view changes from emerald green farmland to the dark – almost black-green – hue of the heather. In summer, when it is in flower, the vista is tinted dark pink as far as the eye can see. At the farthest points of the North York Moors, you can drive for miles without seeing anything but roaming sheep, which, occasionally, you must shoo from the road in order to continue on your way. The villages here tend to be small and quaint, and in the middle of nowhere. The names of villages – Goathland and Hutton-le-Dale – reflect the languages of centuries of invaders and there is a comfortable sense here that little has changed, or will change, as the decades go by. ⏩ *For Sleeping, Eating and other listings, see page 414.*

Ins and outs

Getting around The **Moorsbus**, T01439-770657, www.moorsbus.net, connects many of the towns, in its brief operating season, otherwise a car is absolutely necessary to get to the smaller villages. Run by the National Park Authority, and intended to make the very limited transport through the region more convenient, the Moorsbus runs throughout the North York Moors in the high season. The service is limited, operating only Sun and bank holidays from Apr-Oct, and daily from late Jul-1 Sep. You can pick up timetables in all area tourist offices. The routes are from Helmsley to Sutton Bank, Osmotherley, Rieveaulx, Coxwold and Kilburn; Pickering to Hutton le Hole and Castleton; Danby to Rosedale Abbey and Dalby Forest; and Helmsley to Pickering. There's also long-distance service to Beverley, Darlington, Hartlepool, Hull, Middlesbrough, Northallerton, Redcar, Saltburn, Scarborough, Stockton, Thirsk and York. ▸▸ *For further details, see Transport, page 414.*

Information Helmsley TIC ⓘ *T01439-770173, Easter-Oct 0930-1700 daily, Nov-Easter 1000-1600 Sat, Sun*, in the town hall is helpful for all your questions about how to get around, things to see in the area and where to stay. It sells information, maps and guides for walks in the moors and the Cleveland Way.

North York Moors National Park (West)

Osmotherley

The little stone village of Osmotherley sits with medieval charm about 10 miles north of Thirsk. Once an agrarian centre, it is now best known to ramblers who wander by it while hiking the ambitious Cleveland Way. Well-marked walks from here include one to the priory (about 2 miles), or you can have a go at the stretch of the **Cleveland Way** walk to the 982-ft summit of **Scarth Wood Moor** and on to **Cod Beck Reservoir** about 3 miles away.

Most people choose the short route to **Mount Grace Priory** ⓘ *Apr-Sep 1000-1800 daily, Oct 100-1700 daily, Nov-Mar 1000-1300, 1400-1600 Wed-Sun, £3, can be reached either by foot or car, just off the A19,* and for good reason. Its simple structure and lovely setting make it a uniquely beautiful place. Historians consider it to be the most important and best-preserved Carthusian ruin in Britain, and its modest structure stands in stark contrast to the more spectacular Cistercian ruins, such as Rievaulx. Built in 1398, its simple design is explained by the equally simple life led by Carthusian monks, who lived lives of solitude. Rather than living in grand shared houses, each Carthusian monk was given his own stone hut and a garden to tend, with a church (the tower of which still remains) in the middle of the large grounds. Despite their proximity to one another, they lived in isolation – even their homes were hidden from one another by stone walls. While most of the huts lie in ruins, one has been reconstructed to give an idea of their appearance. There's also a herb garden, landscaped to fit the monks' descriptions of their own gardens. There's an on-site information centre and shop.

Coxwold

The sweet little village of Coxwold, with its quaint stone buildings and flowering window boxes, has been attracting tourists for as long as the writer Laurence Sterne has been dead. Sterne, author of *The Life and Opinions of Tristam Shandy*, served as vicar at the church of St Michael's from 1760 until he died in 1768, and is buried in the churchyard. While the tombstone standing above his grave is damaged, there's another stone on the porch from his first grave in London.

Along with the curiosity of Sterne's grave, Coxwold also offers the charms of **St Michael's Church**, with its unusual octagonal tower and medieval stained-glass windows. Up the road is Sterne's home, **Shandy Hall** ⓘ *T01347-868465, house May-Sep Wed 1400-1630, Sun 1430-1630, gardens May-Sep, daily except Sat 1100-1630, house and garden £4.50, children £1.75, garden only £2.50, children £1.25,* which has been converted into a museum to his life, filled with books and memorabilia. The aptly named home was where Sterne lived when he wrote the controversial *Tristam Shandy*, and his travel tales *A Sentimental Journey through France and Italy*.

Helmsley

Teetering at the edge of the North York Moors, Helmsley is a picture-perfect village, complete with flowering window boxes, stone cottages, arched bridges across streams, picturesque churchyards and the ruins of a Norman castle. There's a handy public car park in the central **town square**, which is an excellent starting base for an exploratory wander. The square is surrounded by shops (there's a useful tourist office in the town hall) and is the scene of the weekly market each Friday. The cross at the centre of the square marks the start of the **Cleveland Way** ⓘ *For information on the Cleveland Way, ask at the Helmsley tourist office (see below) or contact The Cleveland Way Project, T01439-770657*, the famed walking path that starts at Helmsley and crosses the North York Moors, the Cleveland Hills and the coastal cliffs before ending in Scarborough.

Beyond the square the town's medieval lanes are lined with twee shops likely to warm the heart of any grandmother. If you're looking for pink hand-knitted jumpers or garden gnomes, you'll be in heaven. Just past the shops, the stark ruins of **Helmsley Castle** ⓘ *Apr-Sep 1000-1800 daily, Nov-Mar 1000-1300, 1400-1600 Wed-Sun, £2.40*, overlook the town from a well-tended green field. While not a great deal is left of this Norman castle, what remains is quite evocative. You enter via a wooden bridge over the moat, past remnants of the walls. The one standing tower makes for a dramatic photo, while more recent 15th-century structures are also intact, and you can wander through them at will.

Rievaulx Abbey

ⓘ *T01439-798228. Apr-Sep 1000-1800 daily; Jul-Aug 0930-1800 daily; Oct, Feb 1000-1700 daily; Nov-Mar 1000-1600 daily. £3.60 (Terrace £3.40). Getting there: there is a well-signposted walking path from Helmsley to Rievaulx (about 3 miles), otherwise you can take the Moorsbus, T01439-770657 in season, or drive the brief distance following the clear signs that lead you there.*

Several miles from Helmsley – just inside the North York Moors – are the remains of one of the most spectacular abbeys in all of England. Once the most important Cistercian abbey in the country, Rievaulx was founded in 1132 by French Cisctercians seeking to expand their sect into Britain. At its peak, Rievaulx was home to 140 choir monks and 500 lay brothers and lay servants. From the 13th century on, however, the population in the abbey declined, as political changes made it difficult for the abbey to prosper. By the time Rievaulx was suppressed in 1538, only 22 monks still lived on the grounds.

The ruins of Rievaulx are impressively complete, and the look of the place – with the jagged arched walls juxtaposed against green wooded hills – is breathtaking. Enough is left of the buildings to give an awe-inspiring indication of how magnificent it all must have been when it was complete.

North York Moors National Park (East)

Hutton-le-Hole

Hutton-le-Hole is undeniably precious, with perfect stone cottages and colourful gardens framing a quiet stream with grassy banks upon which lovers woo and children gambol. Everybody knows about this place, so it's packed to the gills with tourists and in such a little village, the crowds can be downright oppressive. The locals who run the *Barn Hotel and Tearoom* and the *Crown* pub try to keep up, but are quickly overwhelmed and then submerged in the waves of hungry and thirsty travellers. As these are the only options for food and drink, it would not be a bad decision to see Hutton-le-Hole and then go eat somewhere else. Still, it's charming, and worth a quick wander. Its proximity to Helmsley, just 8 miles away, is probably as responsible for its popularity as are its pretty gardens. Along with the sheer charm of the place, the

 Ryedale Folk Museum ⓘ *T01751-417367, daily 1000-1630, £3.50, children £2, family £9*, is the biggest draw in town. This 2-acre museum is respected for its efforts to recreate and preserve historic rural life. Inside you can watch metal being hammered in a 16th-century blacksmith's shop, and glass being blown in a glass furnace. There's a traditional herb farm, a Tudor cottage, craft workshops, and that's just the start. The museum's gift shop has information on the area and on local walks for amblers.

Rosedale

It's best to approach Rosedale from the north, as from that direction you top a high hill with an extraordinary view of rolling moors that extends for miles. From a distance the old mining village is obscured by trees, and thus it appears suddenly in front of you as you drive up. It's a less charming and more gangly town than Lastingham or Hutton-le-Hole, where nature seems to be taking over; no sheep wander its streets keeping the grass tidy, houses are hidden away behind thick foliage. Built as it is on the side of a steep hill, in places its streets are precipitously vertical, and the signs telling you where to find **Rosedale Abbey** are hard to see, and difficult to understand. If you do successfully find your way to the town – which took its deceptive name from a long-gone Cistercian monastery – you'll find there's not much there except for the beautiful countryside. The remains of the abbey were largely scavenged to build **St Lawrence's** parish church. Still, the crowds pour in to Rosedale village on summertime weekends, mostly just to sit around the *Milburn Arms*, a busy pub (and rather overpriced inn) with a good view.

Pickering

One of the biggest market towns in the moors, Pickering, like Helmsley, is a hub of sorts. Although it's a rather charmless town, it offers lots of places to stay, impressive castle ruins, and, of course, the fabulous **North Yorkshire Moors Railway**. Once a splendid royal home used primarily as a hunting lodge, **Pickering Castle** ⓘ *Apr-Sep 1000-1800 daily, Oct 1000-1300, 1400-1700 daily, Nov-Mar 1000-1300, 1400-1600 Wed-Sun, £2.50*, dates back to William the Conquerer, although most of what remains was built in the 12th century. The motte (a man-made hill on which the keep was built) was ordered built by William himself, in order that he could defend the castle from attacks coming from the surrounding territory. His 11th-century defences make for excellent 21st-century views – from the top you can see for miles. Aside from the walls and the motte, there's not much left of the castle, but what remains is impressive.

You can see the steam from the undeniably pretty **North Yorkshire Moors Railway's** ⓘ *T01751-472508, www.northyorkshiremoorsrailway.com, £10 for an all-day adult pass, concessions £8.50, children £5, family £25*, engines from the top of the castle's motte. A short walk downhill takes you to the quaint station, which – right down to the advertisement posters on the walls – has been restored to look as it did in 1937. This is what most people are in Pickering to see, and if you come across no tourists elsewhere in town, you will surely find plenty on the colourful train platform, where the crowd surges forward to see the old engines pull in, puffing mightily, in an utterly authentic swirling cloud of steam and cinders. The train takes an 18-mile journey from Pickering to Grosmont, stopping along the way at Levisham Station in the scenic Newton Dale Valley, then at Newton Dale Halt and Goathland Station. The train is particularly popular with walkers, as a variety of paths pass near those stations, so you can easily leave the train at one stop and walk to the next.The train follows one of the oldest lines in England; trains travelled this route from 1835 to 1965. After being closed down, the line was reopened as a private operation in 1973. Days and times of operation vary from month to month, although service is hourly during the summer. Timetables can be picked up at the station or at any TIC in the area.

Dalby Forest

A favourite with hikers, the thick expanse of wilderness includes a number of paths. The most popular walks pass near the car park at **Low Stain Dale**; the best known of these is the **Bridestones Trail** which features many of the mysterious sandstone boulders that appear throughout the moors, and whose origin is not really known. There are a number of well-marked paths to choose, but if you'd rather drive, there's a 9-mile toll road through the forest (£4, road open 0700-2100 daily) that ends near the town of Hackness. Whichever way you travel, it's a good idea to visit the visitors' centre, at **Low Dalby** ⓘ *T01751-460295, www.forestry.gov.uk, May-Sep 1000-1700 daily, Oct and Apr 1000-1600 daily, closed winter*, where you can get information on trails, wildlife and the history of the forest.

Hole of Horcum

This extraordinary gorge just off the A169 north of Levisham is so breathtaking that local officials had a car park built opposite it to stop motorists running one another off the road as they gazed at it. A deep, heather-covered indentation in the hills, much lore surrounds the Hole, which is also called the Devil's Punchbowl. Legend holds, for instance, that a giant named Wade scooped the Hole when he grabbed a handful of dirt to throw at his wife during one of their rows. The clod missed her, and fell a mile away, forming the hill known as **Blakey Topping**. The view from the edge is stunning, also a number of paths lead down into the depths of the valley, and across to the nearby hills.

Goathland

If you feel like you've seen this place before – with its plain stone houses, bright red roofs and close-cropped village green – you probably have. The town of Goathland stands in for the imaginary 'Aidensfield' in the popular television series *Heartbeat*.

The town's name sounds like 'Goatland' but it's actually a corruption of the word *gaut*, which meant 'gorge'. Carved by the movement of water, Goathland is surrounded by natural water features, including several waterfalls. The best of the bunch is the impressive 70-ft **Mallyan Spout**, which can be reached by a footpath that starts next to the *Mallyan Spout Hotel*, T01947-896486, not a bad place to stay the night, or just to have a lazy drink. You can also pick up the **North Yorkshire Moors Railway** here, and take a ride courtesy of steam power. From Goathland you can also hike up to the tiny village of **Beck Hole**, accessible only by foot. The mini-village features an equally small pub, the **Birch Hall Inn**, which is highly rated by pub experts. It also serves as a store and sandwich shop, and its home-baked pies are legendary.

Lealholm

Despite other claims to the contrary, it is entirely possible that this is the prettiest village in Yorkshire. On a narrow country lane, the town appears as the road dips down into a small valley. Thick green trees surround the cottages gathered at the edge of the shallow River Esk. There really is nothing here at all, except for the rare simple beauty of the place. The river is crossed downstream by a bridge of peach-tinged stone, while a short stroll away a stepping stone bridge in the same subtle pastel hue offers a more amusing way to cross from one bank to the other. Three or four buildings make up the centre of town; there's a little antiques shop and the *Shepherd's Inn*, which has a few rooms, acres of chintz and a good restaurant. Across the bridge, *Cameron's Inn* has a charming restaurant and tearoom with views over the river.

Most houses in this farming village have the same enigmatic symbol above their doors, and some bear the inscription, "Ancient Society of Shepherds".

Sleeping

Helmsley

Many B&Bs line Ashdale Rd (just up Bondgate from the square). If you prefer a hotel, there are fewer options, though one of the best is the slightly expensive

C **Feversham Arms**, just behind the old church, 1 High St, T01439- 770766. Another is the more pricey

B **Black Swan** on Market Pl, T01439-770466, which has lovely gardens, pub and restaurant. The Feversham Arms has an excellent bar and restaurant as well, and serves modern European cuisine.

North York Moors Park (East)

The TIC near the Eastgate car park has helpful lists of B&B availability, T01751-473791. Apr-Oct 0930-1800 Mon-Sat, 0930-1700 Sun; Nov-Mar 1000-1630 Mon-Sat.

C **Forest and Vale Hotel**, Malton Rd, T01751-472722, www.forestandvale hotel.co.uk. An 18th-century manor house a little way out of town.

D **The Black Swan**, 18 Birdgate, T01751-472286, F472928, An 18th-century coaching inn with 4-poster beds and a good restaurant downstairs.

D **Crossways Hotel**, 134 Eastgate, T01741-472804, F472804. Has a good location and is a lovely Victorian building.

D **Barn Hotel**, Hutton-le-Hole, T01751-417311, is usually booked months in advance in the summertime. As is the lovely B&B

D **Hammer and Hand**, Hutton-le-Hole, T01751-417300. Alternatively ask at the folk museum for more advice on B&Bs in the area.

D **The White Swan** T01751-472288, www.white-swan.co.uk Among the better hotels in town, this is a charming, old inn located right on the marketplace.

Transport

Helmsley

Bus

Local There is a service between Helmsley and other nearby towns including York and Scarborough, T0870-6082608, as well as the Moorsbus T01439-770657, which runs regular service from late Jul to early Sep.

Coxwold

Bus

Local You can get to Coxwold by (relatively infrequent) bus from York – Mon, Fri and Sat only). There is also a seasonal Moorsbus, T01439-770657, www.moors bus.net, that runs a regular service daily to towns and significant sites in the area between Jul and 1 Sep, and on Sun and bank holidays from Mar-Oct.

Car

Coxwold is off the A170 five miles east of Thirsk, or off the A19 down a series of winding country roads.

Yorkshire Coast

→Colour map 4

From the edge of the moors you can look into the distance and see the deep blue – almost midnight blue – of the North Sea. The black-purple hills roll right to the edge of land, and the sudden appearance of the flat expanse of sea is almost startling. Mysterious moors stones give way to mischievous whalebone sculptures. The shrieking of gulls replaces the vibrato of sheep. Gentle hills are truncated by threatening cliffs. Similarly, the stolid stone villages of the moors disappear, and colourful towns like Scarborough, with its creams and yellows, Whitby, with its blue and russet hues, and Robin Hood's Bay, with its vivid red rooftops, gleam. This is a different Yorkshire in many ways, but the seaside promenades, rock candy and silly hats are also accompanied by ancient ruins of castles and abbeys that tell the tale of the history of this land. » For Sleeping, Eating and other listings, see pages 422-423.

Ins and outs

Getting around It's relatively difficult to travel around here by train, as only Scarborough and Whitby have stations. **Trains** to Scarborough run from Hull every 2 hrs, and from York every 45 mins. There are 4 trains daily to Whitby from Danby, Grosmont and Middlesbrough. A series of coastal **roads** skirt the ocean and connect to one another – the A174 in the north, the A171 in the centre and the A165 in the south. Keep an eye out for signs, as many towns along the coast have only one entrance road and if you miss it, you've missed it. There are regular **buses** between Scarborough and Helmsley, Hull, Leeds, Milton, Middlesbrough, Pickering, Robin Hood's Bay and Whitby. **Traveline,** T0870-6082608. For information on the periodic Moorsbus service. ▸▸ *For further details, see Transport, page 423.*

Staithes

The northernmost village on the Yorkshire coast, little Staithes clings tenaciously to the edge of the land. It's easy to miss the turnoff from the A174, so keep an eye out for the signs, and don't be put off by the first somewhat grim view of the town. After you park in the public car park and walk down the cliff to the town, you'll understand why you came this far. (Don't make the mistake of driving into the town; the signs are true – you really can't park down there, and you don't even want to think about trying to turn a car around on its claustrophobically narrow streets.) It's a wonder this weatherbeaten town still exists, considering the strength of the storms that regularly slam against it. But it's a good thing that it hangs on, as Staithes is probably the most historically authentic fishing village in the region. In fact, it has changed little since Captain James Cook came here as a boy to bide his time before he could take to the sea. While some coastal towns are fairy tale pretty, Staithes is rugged, yet not without charm.

To learn more about Captain Cook, head to the High Street for the **Captain Cook and Staithes Heritage Centre** ⓘ *daily 1000-1730, £1.75,* which not only tells the story of his life, but includes a recreation of an 18th-century Staithes street, complete with shops. Otherwise, there's not much to do here except to wander around and take in the sights and sounds. Just north of town you can hike up the **Boulby Cliffs,** which tower at 650 ft, making them the highest on the coast. Or you can follow the cars with surfboards sticking out the windows to the nearby beaches said to offer some of the best waves in England.

Whitby and around

Erstwhile home to both Bram Stoker and Captain Cook, Whitby is a town with two distinct personalities. The waterfront promenade with novelty shops, candy floss and fish and chip shops is one Whitby, while the other is manifested in the grim clifftop church and the skeletal abbey which loom above the town like an admonishment. This is one of the most interesting towns in all of Britain – a beautiful and paradoxical place. For centuries, Whitby was cut off from the rest of the country by its isolated location at the foot of cliffs. By the 18th century, however, it had become a prosperous major port and a northern leader in shipbuilding, fishing and whaling. Its wealth lasted through the 19th century and is demonstrated in the row of fine Georgian houses on the top of the west cliff, built by and for successful shipbuilders. Most of the town, though, is more modest, with whitewashed cottages and humble shops built for fishermen.

Ins and outs

Getting there Whitby is on the Esk Valley line and **trains** run once daily to Middlesbrough (1 hr 30 mins) from the station on the harbour near the town centre. Getting there from London King's Cross involves 2 changes at Darlington and Middlesbrough (4 hrs 45 mins). Whitby is on the A174, and is well signposted. There

Dracula's town

The Irish author Bram Stoker was searching for a hit when he visited Whitby on holiday in 1893. He was working with Sir Henry Irving at the time, running the London Lyceum Theatre, and he longed to write a play that would bring attention to the theatre and to himself. Instead, of course, he ended up writing a novel that has continued to attract readers – and filmmakers – for more than a century. Staying at No 6 Royal Crescent, Stoker was taken by the dark beauty of the town and its ruins. Searching for a villain, he discovered the name 'Dracula' while reading in the old Subscription Library near where Pier Road meets Khyber Pass. He based the Count's shipwreck arrival in Whitby – wherein his vessel crashes into the rocks near the pier – on an actual shipwreck that occurred here in 1885. He would later have one of the characters in the novel describe the abbey he could see from his own window as "a most noble ruin, of immense size, and full of beautiful and romantic bits". He placed the novel's heroines Mina and Lucy, as well as Count Dracula's attorney, in houses on East Crescent. And describes the town in detail, as Mina races down the western cliff, across the bridge, up Church Street, then climbs the stairs to the churchyard in her bid to save her friend. While there is certainly a kind of cult of Dracula in Whitby, and visitors could be forgiven for thinking the town cultivates this, in fact, the reverse is true. The town is not gloomy because Stoker based Dracula here. The feel of the place hasn't changed in centuries and it seems entirely probable that if he had not based a horror novel here, somebody else would have.

are large **car** parks next to the train station. You can catch most buses at the bus station, next to the train station, others, including the **Yorkshire Coastliner,** T01653-692556, services which connect Leeds and York with the coast and **National Express,** T08705-808080, buses from London (7 hrs 45 mins) and York (2 hrs) arrive on Langborne Rd, around the corner from the train station.

Getting around The River Esk divides the town as it flows out to sea. This provides a handy geographical division of the town's two personalities: Whitby Abbey stands on the east cliff above the oldest section of Whitby, while a statue of Cook and a massive arch of whalebones dominate the more modern west side. The town is quite small, and best handled on foot. There are a very few local buses, with a stop near the train station, but these are only useful if you're going out of town, as walking is simply the best way to get around.

Information Whitby TIC ⓘ *corner of Langborne Rd and New Quay, near the bus station. T01947-602674. May-Sep 0930-1800 daily; Oct-Apr 1000-1230, 1300-1630 daily.* It offers maps, information on tours and an accommodation booking service.

Sights

As you cross the swing bridge toward eastern Whitby, looking out to sea the two piers on either side of the river reach out into the water like pincers, with a small lighthouse in the centre of each. Cobblestone streets that twist and turn up the eastern cliffside are flanked on either side by tourist-orientated shops, restaurants and pubs. Because there was limited space at the base of the cliffs, buildings were constructed very close together and they crowd up the steep sides of the hills, connected by medieval pedestrian alleyways (called ginnels) and stone staircases. **Church St** is the main route on this side, and it is filled with jewellery shops peddling Whitby jet – the famed glossy black stone (actually fossilized wood) that was so fashionable among the funereal set in Victorian times – antique stores and clothing shops. Tiny **Grape Lane**, which branches off to the right, has buildings dating back to the 17th and 18th centuries. Nearby is the former home of Captain John Walker, a ship owner under whom Captain Cook served his apprenticeship from 1746-49. The house has been converted into the **Captain Cook Memorial Museum** ⓘ *T01947-601900, www.cookmuseum whitby.co.uk, Apr- Oct 0945-1700 daily, Mar 1100-1500 Sat, Sun, £2.80, concessions £1.80*, and contains a number of pieces of memorabilia, although some of it is only distantly related to Cook's life.

The cobbled area at the intersection of Church and Grape streets was once the Tollgate where, until 1540, the abbot of Whitby gathered his dues. The **Salt Pan Well Steps** leading off of Church St climb up to the old ropery which once made rigging for shipbuilders. Following the path to the **Boulby Bank** (once used by monks from the abbey to move goods down to the seafront) and past the old **Seamen's Hospital** leads to a gallery with wide views across the town and harbour. Nearby is **Elbow Terrace**, which once held a busy smuggler's tunnel, long ago filled in and replaced with houses. Back at the top of Church Street is the curved base of the famous **199 steps** up to the Gothic **St Mary's Church**. Bram Stoker memorialized the steps in his novel *Dracula*, in which Mina, in a frantic effort to save Lucy, rushes up the steps to the churchyard above. Climbing to the top is the equivalent of climbing an 11-storey building, so most people don't rush up; they creep, pausing to take in the view and grab a breath along the way. It's easy to see why the steps struck Stoker – they were originally built for pallbearers carrying coffins up to the churchyard at the top. It must have been a spectacularly dark sight, the black-clad people silently carrying a body up the long stairway as the church bell tolled. The windswept churchyard reaches to the very edge of the high seafront cliff and is almost too gloomy to be real, with long grass bending in the constant wind past the blackened tombstones.

Through the churchyard to the back is a lane leading to the abbey, which is directly behind St Mary's. Over the years, **Whitby Abbey** ⓘ *T01947-603568, Apr-Sep 1000-1800, Oct 1000-1700, Nov-Mar 1000-1600, £3.80, children £1.90, family £9.50, note, if the stairs are a problem, there is a car park at the top of the cliff behind the abbey; follow the brown signs off the A171*, has been one of the most photographed ruins in the country, and it is an astonishingly bleak combination of terrain and architecture that can be seen from miles away. An abbey has stood here since the seventh century, when the Northumbrian king, Osway, first founded a monastery – unusually, one that was for both men and women – on this site. The most impressive part of the structure that still remains is the 13th-century choir, with its soaring east wall and banks of arched windows. In the grass inside the choir are deep markings showing where the original church ended in a rounded apse. The 13th-century north transept stands at the site of the church's crossing, and still has a medieval inscription carved into its northern arcade column crediting a monk with carving a long lost altar.

> *The first known poem in English, The Song of Creation', was written here by Caedmon, a monk.*

The western side of the town is mostly a 19th-century development, created when Whitby became a popular seaside resort, and the mood of holiday frivolity couldn't be more different from the town's east side. Along the waterfront all the usual noisy arcades, chip shops and 'kiss me quick' hats are present and accounted for. Further down Pier Rd is the more serious attraction of the **Whitby Lifeboat** Museum ⓘ *T01947-602001/606094, Easter-Oct daily 1000-1600 (subject to weather), donations requested*, which has an interesting exhibition on the death-defying work of lifeboat crews. Up above on West Cliff are elegant houses and Georgian crescents as well as the much-photographed whalebone arch and statue of Captain Cook. At Pannett Park is the unique **Whitby Museum** ⓘ *May-Sep 0930-1730 Mon-Sat,*

 1400-1700 Sun, Oct-Apr 1030-1300 Mon, Tue, 1030-1600 Wed-Sat, 1400-1600 Sun, £2, a wonderful, old-fashioned place in which some objects are still explained in script on yellowing notecards. Much of the museum is devoted to the city's heritage among seafarers and whalers. There's still more Cook memorabilia here, including objects his crew brought back from their trips, alongside some unusual fossils – including some from the Jurassic period – that had been discovered in the area.

Robin Hood's Bay

One of those rare towns that lives up to its fairy tale name, Robin Hood's Bay huddles on the side of sheer cliffs as if it's trying to hide from view. There's not much in the way of traditional sights here – no museums or castles – its just a peaceful and pretty place in which to wander and get lost on its tangled staircases emerging, suddenly, on the windswept headland. Its trademark bright red rooftops seem to stack one on top of each other as the whitewashed stone cottages are built on nearly perpendicular rocks that reach inexorably for the sea. For sun worshippers, there's a sandy **beach** to one side of the town, and a rocky strip of coast on the other. When the tide is out, this is said to be a good place to find fossils.

Ravenscar

A few miles south of Robin Hood's Bay, some of the best views on the coastline can be had at the ill-fated 'town' of Ravenscar. On red-stone cliffs that soar hundreds of feet above the dark blue sea, the gorgeous view stretches for miles. The area looks like a flat, grassy park, until you study it further and notice that it is arranged like a cul-de-sac. In fact, a developer named John Septimus Bland planned to turn the area into a resort town, and laid out the roads, put in a drainage system and built a couple of shops and houses before realising it was a terrible idea. The perch is too high, the route down to the sea too precarious, and the competition from Whitby and Scarborough too intense for it ever to have worked. He dropped the idea, and the abandoned development now provides handy parking spaces from which to stroll to the isolated *Raven Hall Hotel*, T01723-870353, which once acted as George III's hideaway when the mental demons were acting up. The views from the hotel, where the cliffs reach 800 ft high, are extraordinary.

Scarborough and around

Scarborough is one of those towns that looks best from afar: from a distance it glows like a cream-coloured mirage against the backdrop of dark blue sea and green hills. Up close, it's more tacky, particularly along the waterfront, where casinos, arcades and souvenir shops fight for space with hamburger stands and candy shops. Above it all, the ancient fortifications of Scarborough Castle bristle anachronistically. The castle might be the only attraction here, were it not for a woman named Elizabeth Farrow, who, upon drinking a glass of local spring water in 1620, and noting its mineral taste, pronounced it medicinal. Over the subsequent years, thousands poured into the town to take 'the cure', and the town was built up to cater to them. By the time Queen Victoria took the throne, Scarborough was one of the country's most popular resort towns among the moneyed classes.

Ins and outs

Getting there The **rail** station is conveniently located in the centre of town at the top of the hill on Westborough. Trains leave daily for Hull (1 hr 20 mins), Leeds (1 hr 30 mins) and York (1 hr). You can get to Scarborough from London King's Cross by way of York (3 hrs). If you're going by **car** down the coast, Scarborough is on the A165. If you're driving in from Central Yorkshire it's on the A170. **Coaches** and buses arrive at the train station including the **Yorkshire Coastliner**, T01653-692556, services which connect Leeds and York with the coast, and **National Express**, T08705-808080, buses from London and York.

Getting around Scarborough is sprawling, but walkable, if you've got the time. If you prefer to ride, there is a handy park-and-ride bus system that will shuttle you to major sights in town – look for the signs near any of the 12 car parks in the town centre. This is a better option than attempting to drive from one sight to another, as traffic is congested, parking is competitive (lots often fill up early) and the general frustration of trying to find a streetside parking place can take the fun out of the day. Trains run from Filey Station to Bridlington, Hull and Scarborough. There's also an hourly bus service connecting Filey with Bridlington and Scarborough.

Information TIC ⓘ *Pavilion House on Valley Bridge Rd, T01723-373333. May-Sep 0930-1800 daily; Oct-Apr 1000-1630 daily* is just across the road from the train station. There's another office on the waterfront at Sandside. Easter-Oct only (no phone enquiries).

Sights

Along the waterfront the amusements are quite obvious. The **North Bay** offers the most places to spend your money with its water slides, games and miniature North Bay Railway. At the far north end, the **Sea Life Centre** ⓘ *T01723-376125, daily 1000-1600, £6.95, concessions £5.95, children £4.75*, has hands-on aquatic exhibits with aquariums filled with sealife and rockpools. All along the waterfront are carnival rides and games rooms, as well as myriad opportunities for ocean cruises and speedboat rides. On the curve of the headland, there's nothing but sea views – an acknowledgement of the power of the sea that prevents any development here. On the other side, the beaches on the **South Bay** are wider and more popular than are those on the north. Here, too, are more silly seaside amusements, but there are also grown-up options in the form of the lush **South Cliff Gardens** to which a hydraulic lift ascends (Jul and Aug only), offering great views of the town and sea. From the gardens you can branch out across the clifftop neighbourhoods to explore the city's lovely Victorian architecture. For fans of Victoriana, the house known as **Wood End** ⓘ *The Crescent, Jun-Sep 1000-1700 Tue-Sun, Oct-May 1100-1600 Wed, Sat, Sun*, is now a museum dedicated to that time. It was once the holiday home of the Sitwell family, famed as writers and philosophers.

Virtually all of the city's museums are at this end of town. The unique round Georgian building on Vernon Road that holds the **Rotunda Museum** ⓘ *Jun-Sep 1000-1700 Tue-Sun, Oct-Apr 1100-1600 Tue, Sat, Sun, a £2 ticket known as a Museum S Pass, can be purchased at any of Scarborough's museums, and provides entrance to all of them*, is hard to miss. The best museum in town, the Rotunda holds interesting archaeological remains that have been discovered in the area, including the 3500-year-old body that has come to be known as Gristhorpe Man. On Albion Road, the church of **St Martin on the Hill** is home to a collection of pre-Raphaelite art. The pulpit features panels by Rossetti, while other pieces are by Burne-Jones and William Morris.

According to local lore, King Richard III so loved the views from **Scarborough Castle**, ⓘ *T01723-372451, Apr- Sep 1000- 1800 daily, Oct 1000- 1700 daily, Nov-Mar 1000-1600 daily, £2.80, concessions £2.10, children £1.40, family £7.00*, that his ghost still returns here today. For nearly 900 years, the castle's rambling ruins have dominated the northern headland, but use of the site as a fortress has been traced back much further than a millennium. Archaeological digs have uncovered items from the Bronze and Iron ages. The Romans used it as a signalling station in the fourth century. The structure that remains dates from 1136, when it was built by William de Gros to replace a wooden fort. Today the barbican, walls and three-storey keep gives an idea of the vastness of the structure that once stood here.

Filey

About 8 miles south of Scarborough, Filey is one of the most underrated towns on the coast. This is somewhat understandable, considering that it lacks Scarborough's glitz and Whitby's fame, but with its long expanse of dark sand beach, Edwardian architecture and a general sense of decorum that eludes other seaside towns, Filey has much to offer. Its natural setting – surrounded by dark stone cliffs and green hills – is its primary charm and its **beach** is undeniably the best on the coast, stretching for miles down as far as Flamborough Head to the south. Just north is **Filey Brigg**, with its pleasant nature trails that wander through the hills and down to the shore. For information on **walks** in the area stop in at the **Visitors' Centre** ⓘ *John St, T01723-518000, May-Sep 1000-1700 daily, Oct-Apr 1000-1500 Sat, Sun.*

Bempton Cliffs and Flamborough Head

The sheer white cliffs at Bempton, on the B1229 off the A165, plunge hundreds of feet straight down into the chill waters of the North Sea and seem the most inhospitable of places in which to live, but in the summer, thousands of seabirds call them home. The **Bempton Cliffs RSPB nature reserve** was set up to protect the cliffs and to allow safe vantage points for watching the birds in action. From a series of viewing stations along the clifftops you can watch big white gannets wheeling through the skies in search of supper. Between May and early July this is one of the best places in the country to see impossibly adorable puffins, with their colourful beaks and penguin-like bodies. They nest here in the spring and early summer, but by August their young have grown large enough to head out to their winter grounds. Other birds to be seen include kittiwakes, guillemots and razorbills. Helpful displays help amateurs separate one from another, but binoculars are necessary for a good view. Just south of the Bempton Cliffs, the cliffs at **Flamborough Head** offer equally spectacular views of chalky white rock and deep blue sea. The lighthouse at Flamborough village dates back to the 1700s. You're not allowed to go inside, but it still makes for a lovely photograph.

Hornsea to Spurn Head

From Flamborough the coastline becomes more empty and forbidding. Hornsea is the last village of any size, and it is known primarily for the eponymous **pottery** that is made here. If you're a fan, there's a factory on the main road, the B1242, which is open for tours and has a shop. ⓘ *0930-1800 daily.* Near the village is the vast, freshwater **Hornsea Mere**, the largest lake in Yorkshire. It is another RSPB bird sanctuary, and is home to flocks of herons. South of Hornsea is mile after mile of empty beach. About 7 miles down the road near Aldbrough, is **Burton Constable** Hall ⓘ *T01964-562400, Mar-Oct 1300-1700 Mon-Thu, Sat, Sun, £6*, a manor house that dates back to Elizabethan times. The lovely building – which was altered in the 18th century – has been fitted with period furnishings and is open to the public most afternoons. Among its 'decorations' are paintings by Renoir, Pissarro and Gainsborough. Its vast grounds were landscaped by Capability Brown.

The end of the Yorkshire coast comes at **Spurn Head**, a thin spit of beach that reaches out into the sea, then curves back as if it has changed its mind. It is now a Yorkshire Wildlife Trust nature reserve, and is reached down a toll road from the village of Easington on the B1445. Except for a few animal lovers, you'll often have the whole thing to yourself; well, that is, you and the seals, floating butterflies and seabirds that live protected lives there.

Hull and around

Hull – which is much better suited to its truncated nickname than by its rarely used full name of Kingston- upon-Hull – is certainly not a tourism hub. It sits at the mouth of the River Humber, an old port city with a disreputable edge, and only recently was voted Britain's 'crappest town'. Hull was England's biggest port for centuries, and is still a busy seaport, although these days some of its major docks have been renovated into expensive flats and shining modern shopping malls.

Ins and outs

Getting there The **train** station is on busy Ferensway St on the west side of town. There are regular trains to Leeds (1 hr 30 mins), London King's Cross (3 hrs, with trains every 30 mins), Scarborough (1 hr 20 mins) and York (1 hr 15 mins). By **car**, rom the north, the A1079 and the A165 both go to Hull. It is about 10 miles south of Beverley and 45 miles southeast of York. There is a convenient central car park at the Princes Quay shopping centre – it's well signposted. The **bus** station is just to the north of the train station, and served by **National Express**, T08705-808080, coaches. If you're driving from the west, Hull is on the A63. From the east it's on the A1033. **P&O North Sea Ferries**, King George Dock, Hedon Rd, T08705-202020, from Rotterdam and Zeebrugge arrive at the **ferry** port on the eastern side of town, and there are shuttlebuses from the dock to the town centre. ⏩ *For further details, see Transport, page 423.*

Getting around Hull is a busy city with a useful bus system. There is a park and ride scheme from Walton St and Anlaby Rd (signposted on main routes into the city) with shuttles every 3 mins from Mon-Sat. Fare £1. Otherwise you can catch buses near the train station and the bus station, or from main streets in the city centre. Once you're in the city centre, you can walk to the main sights in the old city and along the waterfront. But a good map is necessary, and the tourist office can offer guidance to get you started.

Information Hull TIC ⓘ *Queen Victoria Sq, T01482-223559, www.hullcc.gov.uk, 0900-1800 Mon-Sat, 1100-1500 Sun*. You can pick up information and maps available and the office also offers very good guided tours for £2.50. **Beverley** TIC ⓘ *34 Butcher Row, T01482-391672. 0930-1730 Mon-Fri, 1000-1700 Sat, 1000-1400 Sun (closed Sun from Sep-May).*

Sights

Princes Quay in particular is now the town's shopping pride and joy – a sparkling modern shopping mall, it has all the high street shops on several levels. Nearby on the waterfront is **The Deep** ⓘ *Tower St, T01482-381000, www.thedeep.co.uk, 1000-1700 daily, £6, children £4, families £18*, the city's gleaming new aquarium. It's a massive and absorbing place with every imaginable form of sealife. The town's maritime history dates back to the 13th century, and you can learn absolutely everything there is to know about that at the **Town Docks Museum** ⓘ *T01482- 613902, 1000-1700 Mon-Sat, 1330-430 Sun, free*, on Queen Victoria Square near the Princes Quay. Appropriately located in the old town Docks Office, the well-designed museum traces the seafaring side of Hull back to the days of Edward I. It also goes into some detail on Hull's whaling history, including hundreds of pieces of (now politically incorrect) whaling technology and memorabilia. There are elaborate whalebone carvings made by sailors, and massive equipment used to handle the giant mammals. It's all quite fascinating if you're not squeamish. Along with the sea you often get those whose artistic soul is struck by the ocean, and Hull was once home to Philip Larkin, who didn't like it much, and before then the 17th-century poet Andrew Marvell who did. **Wilberforce House** ⓘ *25 High St, T01482-613902, 1000-1700 Mon-Sat, 1330-1630 Sun, free*, was the former home of William Wilberforce, who was the leading campaigner for abolition of slavery in the British Empire. The Jacobean house is now a monument to the anti-slavery movement and includes a small but interesting collection of memorabilia and information on Wilberforce's work. Behind the house on the waterfront you can climb onto a restored fishing boat, the **Arctic** Corsair ⓘ *T01482-613902 for a free tour that gives you an idea of what it was like for those who lived and worked on the sea.*

Beverley

It's easy to see that this bustling, mid-sized town 10 miles north of Hull was once a market centre for the region, and though the streets have been widened, and the old shopfronts replaced with modern high street façades, you can still see how the streets once curved around to a broad open-air market. That fact, and its beautiful church, are the main reasons for a visit.

Today, aside from the interesting layout of the town, and the lovely minster, Beverley manages not to *feel* historic – quite a feat for a town in which 350 buildings are listed. This town – the childhood home of Mary Wollstonecraft (1759-97) – still feels like a modern town, and so things like the old **North Bar** – the only of the city's medieval gates still standing – come as something of a surprise. While not as elaborate as York's gates, the gate at the busy corner of Hengate and North Bar, is quite pretty, and gives you some idea of how very much the town has changed since its 14th-century construction.

Most people who come to Beverley are drawn by its **Minster** ⓘ *Mar-Apr, Sep and Oct 0900-1700 Mon-Sat, 1400-1600 Sun, May-Aug 0900-1800 Mon-Sat, 1400-1600 Sun, Nov-Feb 0900-1600 Mon-Sat, £2 donation requested*, which is on the other side of the town centre from **St Mary's**. You can't really miss it, as its twin towers are the tallest structures in the city. Once a humble chapel, it became a monastery in the eighth century, under the leadership of a monk called John of Beverley. His body lies still under the nave, and after he was canonized, pilgrims made regular journeys to the church to worship and to donate money. Kings from Athelstan to Henry V credited their pilgrimages here with victories in battle, and so they showered the church with gifts. All of this funded constant expansions until the church grew to its current jaw-dropping size. The west front, which dates from the early 15th century, is considered by many to be the most beautiful part of the building. Inside, the Saxon sanctuary chair was built in the 10th century. The 16th-century oak choir is one of the most perfectly preserved in the country. The Percy Tomb on the north side of the altar – believed to be the tomb of Lady Idoine Percy (who died in 1365) – is a masterpiece of medieval art. Behind the minster, on Friars Lane, are a few buildings that were once part of the Dominican friary founded in 1240. The Beverley friary is namedropped by Chaucer in his *Canterbury Tales.* Some of the buildings are now used as a youth hostel, that allows curious members of the public to have a wander.

Sleeping

Whitby and around *p415*

D **Bagdale Hall Hotel,** 1 Bagdale St, T01947-602958. A beautiful Tudor mansion, Bagdale has 6 bedrooms with en suite bathrooms, some with 4-poster beds, and one of the best restaurants in town.

D **Stakesby Manor Hotel**, High Stakesby, T01947-602773. With 13 comfortable rooms in a converted Georgian manor house with extensive grounds, Stakesby overlooks both Whitby and the moors.

E **Cliffemount Hotel,** Runswick Bay, T01947-840103. This 1920s hotel perches on the cliff above town and offers panoramic views of the countryside. Most of its rooms have en suite bathrooms, many have sea views.

E The Grove, 36 Bagdale, T01947-603551. This family-run guesthouse offers 7 rooms in a lovely building near the town centre.

E **The Old Ford**, 1 Briggsworth, T01947-810704. Three rooms in a charming cottage in a bucolic setting at the edge of the River Esk.

F Whitby YHA, East Cliff, T01947-602878. This excellent hostel has a spectacular location beside the abbey at the top of the east cliff overlooking Whitby, the sea and the moors. Most beds in dorms.

Robin Hood's Bay *p418*

There are many B&Bs here, but the most desirable accommodation is the self-catering cottages. There is a list from the tourist office in Whitby or at www.robin-hoods-bay.co.uk.

C **Victoria Hotel**, at the top of the hill, T01947-880205. A grand Victorian structure with views of the sea, and a popular bar.

E **Bay Hotel**, sits right at the water's edge, and offers lovely views, T01947-880278.

E **Boathouse Bistro**, at the foot of the cliff, T01947-880099. Has one of the best restaurants in town, and rents out a few comfortable rooms, as well as the pretty Little House, a tiny self-catering cottage.

F **YHA hostel**, in an old corn mill on the path from Robin Hood's Bay to Boggle Hole, a mile down the coast, T08707-705704.

Scarborough *p418*

There are quite a few B&Bs clustered in the area around the train station.

B **The Crown**, The Esplanade, T01723-357424, www.scarboroughhotel.com The most elegant hotel in Scarborough, this is a lovely 19th-century building with excellent views, outstanding facilities and fabulous indoor swimming pool surrounded by statues.

B **The Royal Hotel**, St Nicholas St, T01723-364333, F500618. A beautiful Regency building overlooking the South Bay and with a gorgeous central lobby.

C **Wrea Head Country House Hotel**, Barmoor Lane, Scalby, just outside Scarborough, T01723-3788311, F355936. A stunning place offering peace and beauty on 11 acres of secluded woodlands.

D **Bradley Court Hotel**, 7-9 Filey Rd, T01723-360476, F376661. A frilly, white period building, but excellent value for money, and has a quality restaurant.

E **The Old Mill Hotel**, Mill St, off Victoria Rd, T01723-372735, www.windmill-hotel.co.uk. Surely the most unique hotel in Scarborough offering, as the name implies, 11 rooms inside an 18th-century windmill near the centre of Scarborough.

F **Scarborough YHA**, Burniston Rd, Scalby Mills, T01723-361176. Located in a picturesque old watermill outside the town centre on the A165 and conveniently perched at the edge of the popular Cleveland Way walking path.

Eating

Whitby *p415*

££ **Bagdale Hall**, 1 Bagdale St, T01947-602958. Offers excellent traditional European cuisine in a gorgeous historic setting at surprisingly reasonable prices.

££ **Green's**, 13 Bridge St, T01947-600284. The kitchen offers creative modern cuisine using local fish and game. Booking is essential at weekends.

££ **Huntsman Inn** in the tiny village of Aislaby (about 15 mins' drive away) is highly rated for its excellent affordable cuisine.

£ **Magpie Café**, 14 Pier Rd, T01947-602058. This has to be one of the world's largest fish and chips shops. Unfortunately, the queues are enormous in the high season.

£ **White Horse & Griffin** Church St, T01947 604 857. Probably the best bet in town for good pub grub, and the atmosphere is top.

Pubs, bars and clubs

Whitby *p415*

The Duke of York, Church St, near the 199 steps, offers excellent views and good food.

Middle Earth Tavern, 26 Church St has regular music nights and seats outside in the summer.

Entertainment

Hull *p421*

The Hull Truck Theatre Company, Spring St, T01482-323638, has made quite a name for itself, and its performances are often ground-breaking.

Transport

Hull *p421*

Car

Budget, 70 Manchester St, T01482-323862; **Thrifty**, 2-4 Cleveland St, T01482-219561.

Directory

Hull *p421*

Hospitals Hull and East Yorkshire Hospital, Hedon Rd, T01482- 376215.

Internet The Cyber Café, St Margaret's Church, Shannon Rd Long hill Estate, T01482-795040; **MIJ Internet Express**, 327a Beverley Rd, T01482-474422.

Sheffield

→ Colour map 4

The unofficial capital of South Yorkshire, Sheffield has gone from feast to famine over the course of the last century. Once the affluent industrial centre of the country, its modern, and largely unattractive appearance is a result of the fact that it was nearly obliterated by German bombs during the Second World War. Reconstruction after the war was hurried and paid little attention to aesthetics, and the city developed a sterile and ugly appearance, so much so that it acquired the local motto of 'the city that Hitler built on his

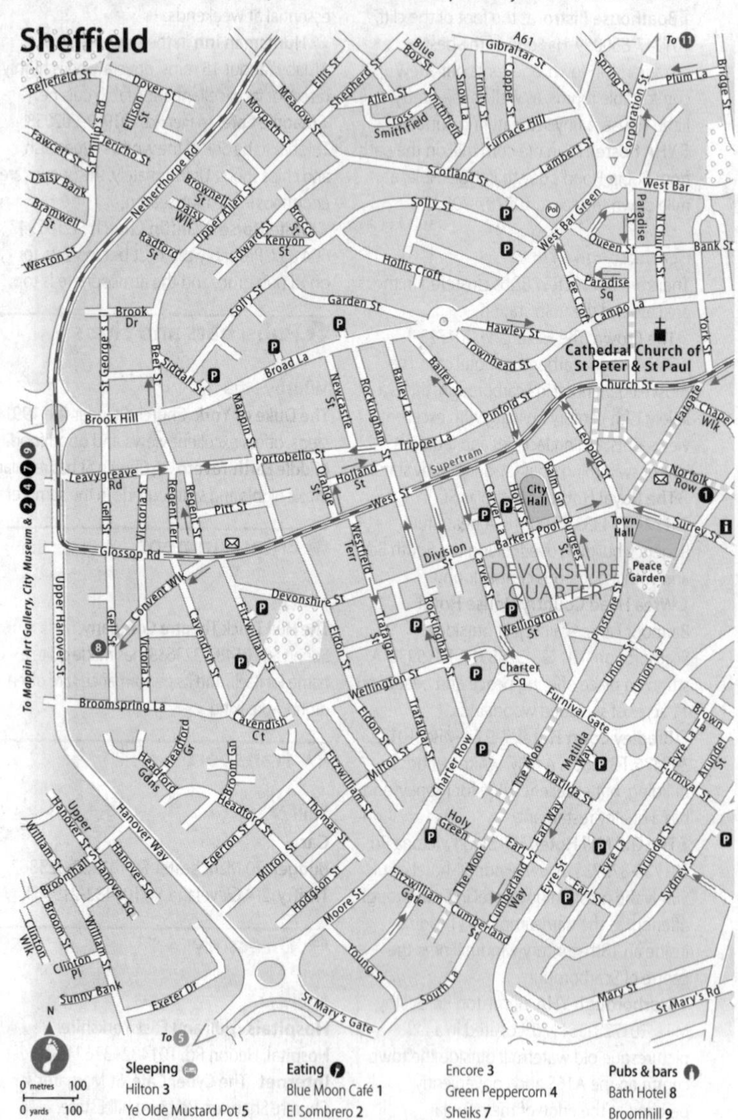

way home'. Still, it has some remnants of its old beauty, in dark, red-brick Victorian buildings, that dot its hilly streets, and spawned one of the great British cinematic hits of recent years, 'The Full Monty'. » *For Sleeping, Eating and other listings, see pages 426-427.*

Ins and outs

Getting there Sheffield's **train** station is about 15 mins' walk east of the centre of town near Sheaf Square. There is a regular service to Leeds (1 hr), London (King's Cross 2 hrs 30 min) and York (1 hr). By **car**, Sheffield is on the A57 from the east or west and on the A629 from the north, and the A61 from the south. The Sheffield Interchange bus station is on Pond St, and here you can catch **National Express**, T08705-808080, services to London (4 hrs 30 mins) Leeds, (1 hr), York (2 hrs 30 mins), Manchester (3 hrs), Liverpool (3 hrs) and many other cities. » *For further details, see Transport, page 427.*

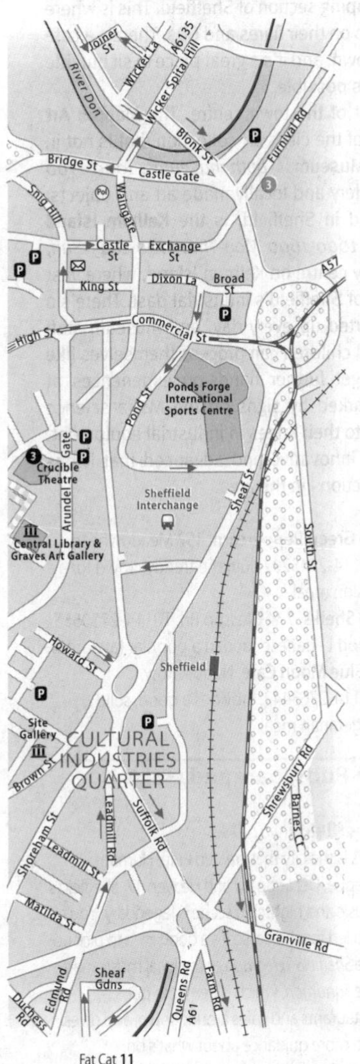

Getting around Sheffield is a big, bustling city, and walking is generally not an option, particularly because many of its museums are on the outskirts of the city. You can walk the city centre, however, and a good place to start is at the tourist office on Tudor Square (see below), which is just a few minutes' walk from both the train and bus stations. Local public transport includes numerous buses and the handy **Supertram**, T0114-2728282. Most buses depart from the High St. Fare and timetable information are available at the Travel Information Centre in the Interchange. 0800-1730 Mon-Fri, 0830-1700 Sat, 0900-1700 Sun. A one-day pass is £4.95 and allows unlimited travel throughout the area, while a day pass for the Supertram is £1.90.

Information Sheffield TIC ⓘ *Tudor Sq, T0114-2211900, www.sheffieldcity.co.uk, 0930-1715 Mon-Fri, 0930-1615 Sat.* It will, bury you in maps, brochures and guides.

Sights

Winning the gold star for 'most improved part of Sheffield' – and the obvious place to start any tour – is the **Cultural Industries Quarter**. This is the newly renovated section of town near the train station filled with trendy nightclubs and art galleries, as well as the offices of IT companies that have opened here over the last few years. One of the best of the galleries in this area is the **Site Gallery** ⓘ *Brown Street, 1100-1800 Tue-Fri 1100-1730 Sat, free*, with its acclaimed collection of photography. More art collections worth your attention can be found in the centre of town. The **Graves Art Gallery** ⓘ *T0114-2782600, 1000-1700 Mon-Sat, free*, is on the top floor of the City Library on a rather grim section of Surrey Street. It has a surprisingly solid collection of works by European artists including pieces by Matisse, Turner and Nash in a modern setting. The library is located near the Gothic-Victorian **Town Hall** on Pinstone Street, which gets its distinctive dark look from the Derbyshire stone from which it is made. The green space in front of the town hall is the **Peace Garden**, with its fountains and summertime flowers.

If you head south down Division Street from the town centre you enter the **Devonshire Quarter,** which is the hippest shopping section of Sheffield. This is where the students from Sheffield University stock up on their flares and CDs. There's a café culture here that you won't find elsewhere in town, and it's a great place to sit outside and sip a cappuccino, while looking as cool as possible.

There are yet more art museums to the west of the town centre. The **Mappin Art Gallery** is in Weston Park, and houses much of the city's art collection that is not in the Graves Gallery. While, next door, the **City Museum** ⓘ *both museums, 1000-1700 Tue-Sat, 1100-1700 Sun, free*, holds more cutlery and locally made art and objects. Better than these, for those really interested in Sheffield, is the **Kelham Island Museum** ⓘ *T0114-2722106, www.simt.co.uk, 1000-1600 Mon-Thu, 1100-1645 Sun, £3, child £2, family £8*, a mile north of the city centre on Kelham Island, where vast exhibitions display objects that tell the story of Sheffield's industrial past. There's a 12,000 horsepower steam engine that is started up every day, and museum staff show how steel was pounded into shape, and children can process themselves like steel in the interactive exhibits. Kids can get further hands-on experiences at **Magma** ⓘ 1000-1700 daily, £6, it is well marked by signs off the M1, a science adventure centre where little ones can get up to their knees in industrial equipment, musical devices and more. This place is so innovative and advanced that it has quickly become one of the most popular attractions in the area.

Sleeping

Sheffield *map p424*

B **Sheffield Marriott**, Kenwood Rd, T0114-2583811. Located in a handsome old buildings on landscaped grounds, and has all the luxuries and essentials.

C **Hilton**, Victoria Quays, T0114-2525500. With a location on the canals and great views, and with all of its usual luxuries – not a bad choice.

D **Ye Olde Mustard Pot**, Mortimer Rd, T01226-761155. A 17th-century inn offering good inexpensive accommodation just at the edge of town.

Eating

Sheffield *map p424*

$$ **El Sombrero**, 27 Regent Terr, T0114-272 9587. Casual Mexican fare, popular.

$$ **Encore**, in the Crucible Theatre on Tudor Sq, T0114-275 0724. Modern British food with a pre-theatre bent, a reasonable choice.

$$ **Green Peppercorn**, 352 Meadowhead, T0114-2745202. Join the trendy crowd for a fusion meal.

$$ **Sheiks**, 274 Glossop Rd, T0114-2750555. Good Lebanese food in a popular favourite.

$ **Blue Moon Café**, Norfolk Row, T0114-2763443. Provides a good, solid vegetarian meal.

Pubs, bars and clubs

Sheffield *map p424*

This is the city that created Pulp, Human League, Def Leppard and Heaven 17. Sheffield's music and nightclub scene is legendary. You're spoiled for choice, so it's a good idea to pick up the *Sheffield Telegraph* or the local music mag, *The Sandman*, which is free from pubs, restaurants and cafés around town, and gives you more guidance about what's on.

Area 51, 14 Matilda St, is a warehouse converted into an unbeatable nightclub, **Bath Hotel**, 66 Victoria St, off Glossop Rd, is where you can get a good pint of real ale.

Broomhill, 484 Glossop Rd, the student hub which has great music playing virtually whenever its doors are open.
The Fat Cat, 23 Alma St, is a great but tiny pub, a very local joint quite a way out from the centre on Kelham Island.
Leadmill, 6-7 Leadmill Rd, T0114-2754500. A little underground venue with Playstations in a nook at the back. Also has live music.
Republic 112 Arundel St, T0114- 2766777, a great place to dance in this old factory.

Transport

Sheffield *map p424*
Car
Europcar, NCP Car Park, Matilda Way, T0114-2768802; Sixt Kenning, 198a Gibraltar St, T0114-2766050. Thrifty, Parkway Av, T0114-2443366.

Taxi
Abbey Taxis Ltd, 20 Bedford St, T0114-2751111. Central Cab Company, 240 Woodbourn Rd, T0114-2769869. Sheffield Taxi Services Ltd, 20 Bedford St, T0114-2558888.

Directory

Sheffield *map p424*
Hospitals The Royal Hallamshire Hospital, Glossop Rd, T0114-2711900. **Internet** Bar Matrix, 4 Charter Sq, T0114-2754100; Havana Internet Cafe, 32-34 Division St, T0114-2495452; Refresh Cafe, 198 Whitham Rd, T0114-2667979.

Leeds

→ *Colour map 4*

The cultural centre of Yorkshire, Leeds is still living down a reputation as a northern industrial town. For years that reputation was deserved, but recently much has changed. Over the last decade, central Leeds has been refurbished, and its grand Victorian buildings restored. Industrial sections have been converted into posh modern shopping and residential arcades. Everywhere there are cafés with outdoor tables (in defiance of the weather), cool, modern bars and upscale department stores. The presence of thousands of university students adds a constant infusion of youth – along with crowded nightclubs, excellent music shops and cheap used clothing stores – while the many museums, the West Yorkshire Playhouse and Opera North provide an acclaimed art sector. ▸▸ *For Sleeping, Eating and other listings, see pages 430-432.*

Ins and outs

Getting there **Leeds/Bradford International Airport**, T0113-2509696, www.lbia.co.uk/contact/index.shtml, is approximately 10 miles northwest of Leeds City centre and has a variety of rail, bus and road links. It has regular flights throughout Britain and to western Europe. The impressively big and busy Leeds City **Rail** Station is in the town centre in front of City Square. There are regular services from several major UK cities. The **bus** and coach station is nearby on St Peter's St behind Kirkgate Market. You can catch **National Express,** T08705-808080, coaches as well as regional services to York and the North Yorkshire Moors from here. Local buses also set out from here, as well as from stops throughout Leeds. The **Metro Travel Centre** at the bus station can get you going in the right direction (Mon-Fri 0830-1730, Sat 0900-1630) and advise you which travel card will work for you. **Metroline,** T0113-2457676, 0800-2000 daily, has free bus travel advice for the confused and lost.

Getting around Leeds has an extensive bus system, but most of the sights are in the compact city centre, and few tourists ever need the buses, unless they're going to the few far-flung sights. The train station makes an easy starting point for a walking tour, but buses can be caught on St Peter St, a short walk from the train station. The tourist office has helpful maps and information about transport. Taxis are plentiful and affordable, and there's a rank adjacent to the train station. » *For further details, see Transport, page 432.*

Information Leeds TIC ⓘ *inside the train station, T0113-2425242. 0930-1800 Mon-Sat, 1000-1600 Sun.* A large and helpful tourist office which can weigh you down with free maps, brochures, guides and advice.

Sights

Central Leeds

The area around the train station provides the best examples of Leeds' massive Victorian architecture. From the second you step out of the station you are surrounded by the statues and overly elaborate bronze gas lamps that the Victorians so loved. The area directly in front of the station is the recently renovated **City Square**, at an intersection of several busy streets. Recent renovations have pedestrianized the square and added new cafés with views of 19th-century statues, which include the Black Prince on horseback and Joseph Priestley, James Watt, John Harrison and Dean Hook. The Gothic church on the east side of the square is the **Mill Hill Chapel** where

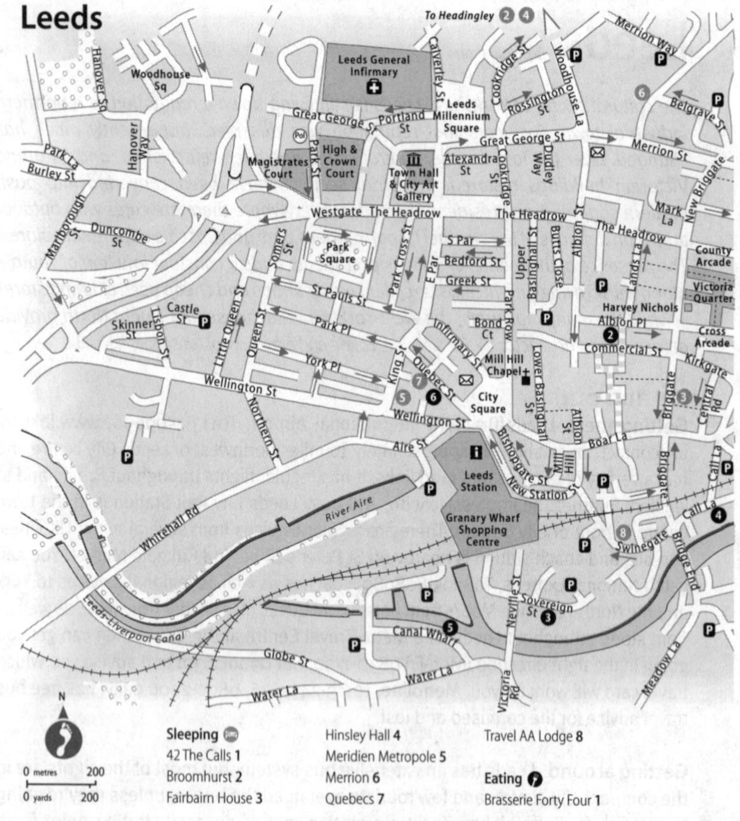

Priestley was minister in the mid-1700s. The obvious next stop on any wander around central Leeds is down Park Row, past a row of well-restored 19th-century office buildings then continuing up The Headrow to the domineering **Leeds Town Hall,** just a few blocks away. The enormous 19th-century building has every imaginable decoration – stone lions, a clocktower, sculptures and columns. Architect Cuthbert Brodrick used everything in his bag of architectural tricks on this one. Next door to the Town Hall, the **City Art Gallery** ⓘ *Mon-Sat 1000-1700, Wed 1000-2000, Sun 1300-1700, free*, is the biggest and best art collection in the north of England. It has a clear British emphasis with a constantly changing display of selections from its vast permanent collection of mostly 19th- and 20th-century art including works by Courbet, Sisley, Constable and Crome. Particularly notable is its collection of works by Henry Moore (who studied at the Leeds School of Art). The adjacent **Henry Moore Institute** ⓘ *Mon-Sat 1000-1700, Wed 1000-2000, Sun 1300-1700, free*, features more works and information on the sculptor and changing exhibitions of sculptures by other artists. The institute also features a study of the art of sculpture and a library.

East of here, **Briggate** is a pedestrianized lane of shops and businesses in 19th-century buildings with all the filigree, stained glass and marble you could dream of. This section of town has been elegantly restored, and best of all is the frilly arcade of the **Victoria Quarter** where *Harvey Nichols* has planted its northern flag – along with other expensive shops – to the eternal joy of local ladies who lunch. While its clothes are a draw, as in London, its posh café – with its odd mixture of low-cal dishes and high-cal desserts – is the biggest attraction for many visitors. Beyond Vicar Lane, Eastgate continues to Quarry Hill Mount to the acclaimed **West Yorkshire Playhouse**. Known for its quality productions, if there's a show on here while you're in town, it is worthwhile to try to catch it. Follow Vicar Lane down to Duncan Street to reach the vast **Corn Exchange** (open daily). Yet another market, this one has an emphasis on the needs of the university crowd, with its hand-made jewellery, art, antique clothes and CDs. Just behind the exchange is one of Leeds' trendiest neighbourhoods. The **Exchange Quarter** is filled with cool cafés, upscale restaurants, arty stores and hip bars.

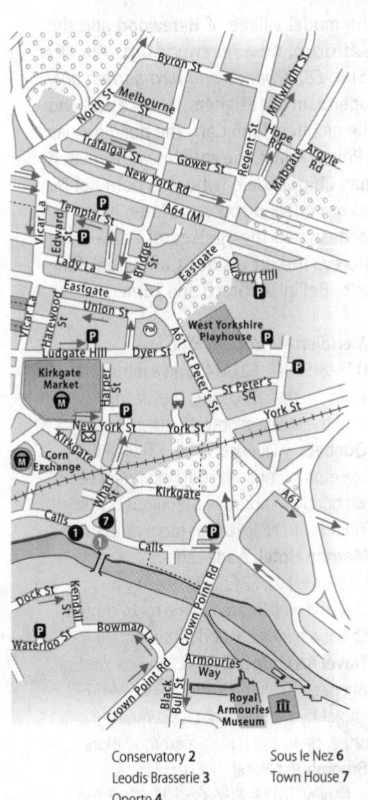

Conservatory **2**
Leodis Brasserie **3**
Oporto **4**
Rascasse **5**
Sous le Nez **6**
Town House **7**

On the water

The once grim industrial section of Leeds along the Leeds-Liverpool Canal was a symbol for urban blight. Today, however, it stands as a shining tribute to renewal and renovation, as the formerly empty and decrepit old warehouses and brownfield sites have been converted into expensive loft flats, and along with those have come the Siamese triplets of such developments – expensive restaurants, open-air cafés and trendy bars. A waterside footpath connects pricey apartment complexes with dozens of entertainment options, all close to the town centre. Much further along the canals at Armouries Way and Crown Point Road stands one of Leeds' best museums – the **Royal Armouries** ⓘ *T0113-2201940, www.armouries.org.uk, 1000-1700 daily, £4.90*. Designed to hold the armour and weaponry from the Tower of London, it has been cleverly expanded into an interactive museum with a educational collection that spans 3,000 years. There are excellent displays, costumed demonstrations, dramatic interpretations and live action events daily, along with well-made films and hands-on technology. It is almost impossible not to learn something here.

Around the city

Just a couple of miles outside the city centre off the A65, the walls of **Kirkstall Abbey** stand gloomily in a large green park on the River Aire. Considered the best preserved of all the Cistercian houses in the north of England, Kirkstall was founded in 1152 by monks from Fountains Abbey looking for a place of their own. It has stood empty for nearly 500 years since Henry VIII shut it down, and so it is astonishing how intact it remains. Its **church** is particularly interesting, even with its collapsed tower. The Norman **chapter house** is nearly perfect, in defiance of time, while the 13th-century **abbot's lodging** is simply beautiful. The 12th-century **gatehouse** has been restored and turned into the **Abbey House Museum** ⓘ *Dawn to dusk daily, free, from central Leeds take bus 732, 733, 734, 735 or 736*, and is mostly devoted to Victoriana, with toys and games and reconstructed Victorian streets with an eye for detail in its shops, cottages and homes.

About 7 miles north of central Leeds is the model village of **Harewood** and the mansion known as **Harewood House** ⓘ *T0113-2181010, www.harewood.org, Apr-Oct 1100-1630 daily, Nov-Mar 1100-1630 Sat and Sun, £8, grounds and bird garden only £6.25*. The house was built from 1759-72 by a superteam of designers, landscapers and architects assembled by the respected Yorkshire architect John Carr. The building was designed by Carr and modified and finished by Robert Adam, the gardens were created by Capability Brown and the furniture by Thomas Chippendale (who was born not far from here in Otley). Even when the building was remodelled 100 years later, it was by the best of the best – Sir Charles Barry (who designed the Houses of Parliament) remodelled the façade and added the third storey. The art inside is an astonishing collection that includes works by Titian, Tintoretto, Bellini, El Greco and Turner.

Sleeping

Leeds *map p428*

With its universities and busy business centre, Leeds has plenty of places to stay – from lush expensive modern properties, to low-cost B&Bs. Most expensive places are in the town centre, while most B&Bs are in the Headingley neighbourhood, which is easily accessible by bus.

A **42 The Calls**, 42 The Calls, T0113-2440099, www.42thecalls.co.uk. If the name is the same as the address, you can almost guarantee it's going to be trendy and expensive. Fits the bill on both counts. A modern boutique hotel in a historic townhouse overlooking the waterfront, this is the hottest hotel in town. Weekend packages can make this place slightly more affordable.

A **Meridien Metropole**, King St, T0113-2450841, F2341430. In a terracotta building in the city centre, the *Meridien* is one of the loveliest hotels in town.

A **Quebecs**, 9 Quebec St, T0113-2448989, www.etontownhouse.com Another of Leeds' posh boutique hotels in a fabulous Gothic building with 45 luxurious rooms and suites.

B **Merrion Hotel**, Wade Lane, T0113-2439191, F2423527. Slightly less pricey and well located in the town centre. Also has a handy bar and restaurant.

C **Travel AA Lodge**, Blayds Ct, Blayds Yard, off Swinegate, T08700-850950, F0113-2445793. It's hotel-by-numbers, but it's centrally located, clean and basic accommodation.

D **Broomhurst Hotel**, 12 Chapel Lane, Headingley, T0113-2786836, F2307099. Just over a mile from the city centre in the pleasant Headingley neighbourhood.

D **Fairbairn House**, 2 Lower Briggate, T0113-2436454, F2434241. This grand Victorian edifice is owned by the University of Leeds. It's well located, pleasant, quiet and good value for money.

D **Hinsley Hall**, 62 Headingley Lane, T0113-2618000, F2242406. This extraordinary 19th-century manor house is worth a visit in its own right. Owned by the Diocese of Leeds, it sits on tranquil grounds 2 miles from the city centre.

Eating

Leeds *map p428*

Here you get London food at Leeds prices – even many of the top restaurants here price most main courses below £15.

£££ **Brasserie Forty Four**, in the posh 44 The Calls Hotel, T0113-2343232, was recently listed as the best brasserie in Leeds by the *Good Food Guide*, its trendy atmosphere and French-style food are unbeaten here. Prices are correspondingly high.

£££ **Leodis Brasserie**, Victoria Mill, Sovereign St, T0113-2421010. Another highly rated place. Located in an old mill it offers beautiful views along with English and French food.

££ **Fourth Floor Café** at *Harvey Nichols*, Briggate, T0113 -2048000. One of the hottest places in town, it packs in shoppers and non-shoppers for light lunches and traditional British dinners.

££ **Oporto**, 31-33 Call Lane, T0113-2454444. Less trendy, but just as good, *Oporto* offers casual fusion meals combining European and Asian cooking techniques in the Exchange Quarter, or come later in the evening and drink yourself silly until 0200.

££ **Rascasse**, Canal Wharf, Water Lane, T0113-2446611. A stylish, modern waterfront restaurant with Anglo-French cooking.

££ **Sous le Nez**, The Basement, Quebec House, Quebec St, T0113-2440108. Another highly rated restaurant that serves expertly crafted seafood to a trendy crowd.

£ **Harry Ramsden's**, White Cross, Guiseley, T01943-879531, has been selling fish and chips many consider to be the best in town, for decades. It's in the 'burbs though, but you can find your way there on buses 732, 733, 734 or 736. Expect to queue.

Cafés

£ **The Conservatory**, Albion Pl, T0113-2051911. It's a cellar bar where you can have an excellent breakfast or lunch, or just sip a coffee in its refined atmosphere.

£ **Harvey Nichols Espresso Bar**, Victoria Quarter, T0113-2048000, which serves impressively expensive morning coffee, lunches, snacks and afternoon tea.

£ **Town House**, Assembly St, T0113-2194000, has good coffee and equally good beer along with light meals during the day, and turns itself into a remarkably hip bar at night.

Pubs, bars and clubs

Leeds *map p428*

Creation, 55 Cockridge St, T0113-2800100. Here there's a mix of touring international and local bands.

The Elbow Room, 64 Call Lane, T0113-2457011. For quality jazz acts.

Milo, 10-12 Call Lane, ranks as one of the most unpretentious bars in town. Depending on the night, you can catch a quality local band, dance to DJ-spun tunes or sit gabbing lazily with your friends.

Norman, 36 Call Lane, is all glitz and some glamour and claims to have been voted one of the 100 best bars in the world.

The Observatory, a unique Victorian building with a domed ceiling and two levels of bars and dancing. Its interior balcony allows you to be above it all. It's quite popular with the student population.

The Ship on Ship Inn Yard off Briggate, where you can get a very nice pint or a bit of pub grub.

Velvet, 11 Hirst's Yard, which brags about its 'rigorous door policy'. If you've got the look, go on to dance the night away.

Victoria on Great George St. For a taste of frilly Victorian pub life.

The Vine, 11 The Headrow, T0113-2031820, is a traditional Bass pub that acts as sort of a pub/club combination. Its regular disco nights put paid to the idea of it being a normal pub, however.

Whitelocks on Turk's Head Yard, which is known for its traditional pub décor and enormous crowds. Fot the slightly older or more famous...

Entertainment

Leeds *map p428*

Theatre

West Yorkshire Playhouse, Quarry Hill Mount, T0113-2137700, which puts on a range of highly rated performances in its two theatres.

Grand Theatre and Opera House 46 New Briggate, T0113-2226222, with regular season of professional performances put on by *Opera North* and the *Northern Ballet Theatre*.

Leeds Town Hall, The Headrow, T0113-2476962. . More classical music is produced frequently at this glorious venue.

Transport

Leeds *map p428*

Bus

National Express, 08705-808080, serve Leeds from **London Victoria** (4 hrs 30 mins) almost hourly throughout the day, also services from **Manchester** (1 hr 30 mins), **York** (1 hr), **Birmingham** (3 hrs 30 mins), **Sheffield** (1 hr) as well as many other destinations.

Car

Avis, Roseville Rd, T0113-2439771 and at the airport, T0113-2503880; **Europcar**, Aspley House, 78 Wellington St, T0113-2376855.

Taxi

A Metro Cars Private Hire, 66a New Briggate, T0113-2444031; New Headingley Cars, 1 Royal Park Rd, T0800-0155454.

Train

Leeds is served by regular GNER trains from **London King's Cross** (2 hrs 20 mins) as well as from **Birmingham** (2 hrs), **Liverpool** (2 hrs), **Manchester** (1 hr), **Sheffield** (1 hr) and **York** (25 mins).

Directory

Leeds *map p428*

Hospitals Leeds General Infirmary, Great George St, T0113-2432799.

Bradford, Haworth and around

→Colour map 4

Another northern industrial town, Bradford is not known for its beauty, but it has some attractive sections that are often overlooked by those outside of Yorkshire, most of whom would never think of coming here as a tourist. It's a very modern town. Including its suburbs, it's the fourth largest metropolitan area in England, and remains a very lived-in city. Just beyond its western fringes are the Pennine Hills and the little village of Haworth, famous the world over as the centre of Brontë country. ▸▸ *For Sleeping, Eating and other listings, see page 434.*

Ins and outs

Information **Bradford TIC** ⓘ *City Hall, Centenary Square, T01274-753678, Mon-Fri 0900-1730, Sat 0900-1700*, offers helpful advice, more maps than you need, and more brochures than you might think possible.

Bradford

The City Hall precinct on the inner ring road is a good place to start, with the Gothic **City Hall** built in the late 19th century, and the neoclassical **St George's Hall**, dating from 1853 and dominating the corner of Bridge Street. Both buildings were designed by the same architecture firm, and yet each is very different from the other. Nearby the creamy columns of the **Alhambra Theatre** lures with its pure linear structure, showing the transition of architectural mores from Victorian style to new modern lines at the time of its construction in 1914. Now beautifully restored, its interior is as gorgeous as its exterior.

From the front of the theatre you can see the excellent **National Museum of Photography, Film and Television** ⓘ *T01274-202030, www.nmpft. org.uk, Tue-Sun and public holidays 1000-1800, free*, which represents the main reason many tourists make their way to Bradford. Opened in 1983, it holds the largest cinema in Britain, where there are daily IMAX screenings. The ground floor holds the Kodak Gallery, which traces the history of photography, using the film company's private collection as illustrations. The rambling museum holds room after room of exhibitions on cameras and equipment, the art of film photography and the history of television. You can spend hours here, so it's lucky there's a café for sustenance, and a shop filled with prints, movie posters and clever souvenirs.

Heading back to the city centre, the Gothic **Wool Exchange** on Market Street – once again by Lockwood and Mawson, who designed the City Hall – is one of few indications you'll find around town that Bradford was once the world's largest producer of worsted cloth and wool production. The old exchange has been renovated and converted into a shopping and dining mall. Above the exchange, the tower of the beautiful **Bradford Cathedral** stands on nearby Stott Hill. The 14th-century building was much altered during the 20th century, but still contains a 15th-century font cover and 19th-century stained glass in the Lady Chapel. Opposite the Wool Exchange stands the **Peace Museum** ⓘ *10 Piece Hall Yard, T01274-7754009, www.peacemuseum.org.uk, Wed-Fri 1100-1500, free*, a one-of-a-kind facility with informative displays devoted to world leaders who espouse non-violence, tactics by which violence can be avoided, and conflict resolution. This worthy facility has an outreach element that offers tutorials on peace.

Haworth

The little village at the edge of the Pennines has long ago had its way of life subsumed by the world's seemingly limitless curiosity about the reclusive, Brontë sisters who wrote tales of repressed passions on heather-strewn moors. It seems that every street they once walked on, and every building they ever entered, has been turned into some sort of Brontë memorial, but the biggest is the **Brontë Parsonage Museum** at the top of the main street. Located in the simple house in which they grew up, the displays inside tell the family's sad tale. The house is filled with pictures of the children and the furniture remains the same as it did when they lived here. There are extensive original documents written by the girls, starting when they were children and working up to their successful novels. This is a good museum, but crowded in the high season. ⓘ *T01253-642323, www.bronte.org.uk Daily Apr-Sep 1000-1730; Oct- Mar 1100-1700. Adult £4.80, concessions £3.50, child £1.50* Also popular is the **parish church** adjacent, in which all of the family, except Anne, are entombed in the family vault. Nearby is the **Sunday school** where the sisters taught when they weren't writing, down the road is the pharmacist where their brother Branwell bought the opium to which he was addicted. This has been converted into a souvenir shop, and the *Black Bull Inn*, where he often drank himself into a stupor, is still open for business.

The countryside around Haworth is beautiful, and there are numerous **walks** along the paths that so inspired the Brontës. The tourist office (2 West Lane, at the top of Main Street, T01535-642329, 0930-1730 daily) will give you maps and directions. The most interesting of the walks is the one to **Top Withens**, a ruined, gloomy building out in the hills that many determinedly believe was the model for *Wuthering Heights*. Further along is **Ponden Hall**, which could well have been the building she called Thrushcross Grange in her novel.

Hebden Bridge and Heptonstall

A few miles south of Haworth, the A646 dips into the valley of the River Calder, and the Pennine Way walking path crosses the road by the stark **Stoodley Pike obelisk**. Nearby sit the twin tiny mill towns of **Hebden Bridge** and **Heptonstall**. In the 19th century, when these were bustling towns producing enormous amounts of textiles, the mills in

Hebden Bridge ran constantly, while the workers lived up the hill in Heptonstall. The mills were long ago silenced, and these are now quiet villages, but the two towns are still connected by a path that once was used by packhorses moving fabric and wool. Hebden Bridge still has a rare working clog mill that is open to visitors. The sight of it groaning into life offers an interesting perspective on how life must have once been in this section of Yorkshire when hundreds of such mills ran non-stop. Heptonstall is a handsome village, much less crowded with tourists than Haworth (as the Brontë's never came here). At its centre is an old ruined church, as well as a slightly newer (18th-century) Wesleyan chapel. But its main draw is the grave in the newer of its two churchyards in which the American poet Sylvia Plath lies buried. Her husband, Ted Hughes, was born in nearby Mytholmroyd, and grew up in and around Heptonstall. He frequently wrote about the towns, not the least in the poem *Heptonstall Churchyard*.

Sleeping

Bradford *p432*

B **Midland Hotel**, Forster Sq, T01274-735735. The height of Victorian luxury and conveniently located near the train station.

B **Quality Victoria Hotel**, Bridge St, T01274-728706. Equally lush and designed by the same slick team that did the trendy *42 The Calls* in Leeds.

C **Jarvis Bankfield Hotel**, Bradford Rd, Bingley, just outside of town, T01274-567123. Less central but equally deluxe it's located in a gorgeous manor house with 103 elegant rooms where you can rest in style.

D **Ivy Guest House**, 3 Melbourne Pl, T01274-727060. Provides affordable, nice enough accommodation in the city centre.

D **New Beehive Inn**, 169 Westgate, T01274-721784. A charming, gaslit inn with Edwardian character and cheap rooms.

Haworth *p433*

There are plenty of B&Bs in town, but they book up quickly, even in the low season, so plan well in advance. You can get a full list from the tourist office.

C **Weavers**, 15 West Lane, T01535-643822. The most upscale guesthouse in town, it's a lane of old weavers' cottages that have been converted into guestrooms with antiques.

D **The Apothecary**, 86 Main St, T01535-643642. There are excellent views from the windows of this charming guesthouse in the centre of the village.

E **Heather Cottage**, 25 Main St, T01535-644511. A small guesthouse with tearooms.

E **Old White Lion Hotel**, Main St, T01535-642313. A picturesque, rambling old inn right next to the parsonage. It has 2 charming old bars and a handy restaurant.

Eating

Bradford *p432*

Bradford's curry restaurants are legion and renowned. If you don't fancy curry, however, you might be in a bit of trouble, as there's not much to choose from.

££ **Bombay Brasserie**, Simes St, T01274-737564, which offers elegant versions of gourmet curry-based dishes in a lovely setting.

££ **Kashmir**, 27 Morley St, T01274-726513. Established and renowned for its good food at reasonable prices.

Haworth *p433*

££ **Black Bull** on Main St is a popular option for lunch or a pint. It was a favourite of Branwell Brontë's as well.

££ **The Old White Lion** has two pubs inside as well as a restaurant that can get quite crowded at lunchtime.

Transport

Haworth *p433*

Bus

Local Haworth is located off the A6063, and it is well signposted. From **Bradford** there are regular buses throughout the day, including buses 663, 664, 665 and 699.

Train

Best of all, though, is the **Keighley and Worth Valley Railway**, T01535-647777, which runs a steam-engine train from **Keighley** to **Oxenhope**, stopping at Haworth. You can catch trains to Keighley from **Leeds** and **Bradford** and then switch to the steam train. Services run daily in the summer, and Sat and Sun Sep-Jun. £5-£8.

The Yorkshire Dales

→Colour map 3-4

The western equivalent of the North York Moors, the Yorkshire Dales are just as beautiful and, if anything, even more dramatic. Seeing one without taking in the other is like hearing half the story. The word 'dale' comes from the Viking word for valley – and while the moors are marked by gently rolling hills layered one upon another, the dales are more rugged, the hills steeper and more frequent, culminating in the three peaks of Pen-y-ghent, Ingleborough and Whernside. The old spa town of Harrogate, meanwhile, has hardly changed at all in the last century, except to change the signs from welcoming the upper class to welcoming the business class. » *For Sleeping, Eating and other listings, see pages 442-444.*

Ins and outs

Getting there The best **rail** access into the Dales is via the **Settle to Carlisle Railway,** which offers glorious views into the bargain. There are connections to the line from Skipton and Leeds. By **car**, from Leeds, the A65 provides easy entrée to the Dales, heading through Ilkley and on to Skipton. From York, the A59 heads through Harrogate and on to Skipton. Once in the Dales, however, the most scenic route is on the small country roads that wind and sprawl across the empty miles. The dales are well covered by **bus** service, especially in the summer, although service is patchy on Sun and some holidays. If you're travelling by bus, the **Dales Explorer** bus timetable is absolutely essential. You can pick one up at any tourist information office in the region.

South Dales

Ins and outs

Getting there Ilkley is connected to Leeds and Bradford by **train** and **bus**, both of which arrive at the central station. Skipton is a transport hub in the South Dales, so there is train service to Skipton Station from Leeds, Bradford, Keighley, Carlisle, Lancaster and Morecambe. The station in Skipton is near the centre on Broughton Rd. You can also connect to the Settle-Carlisle Railway, www.settle-carlisle.co.uk, directly from here. The bus station is on Keighley Rd, where many B&Bs are also clustered, at the bottom of the High St. There is regular **National Express coach** service from London, as well as regional buses from Bradford and Keighley, Leeds, Ilkley, Harrogate and York.

Information Ilkley TIC ⓘ *opposite the train station on Station Rd, T01943-602319. 0930-1730 Mon-Sat, 1300-1700 Sun.* Has walking maps. **Skipton TIC** ⓘ *Coach St, T01756- 793809, www.skiptononline.co.uk Mon- Sat 1000-1700; Sun 1130-1400 1530- 1700.* Has information on local B&Bs, good local walks, history and more.

Ilkley

Heading into the dales from Leeds on the A65, the charming town of Ilkley is the first of any size that you come to. One of several spa towns, the town's grand buildings owe their existence to Ilkley's 19th-century popularity among the upper classes (not much has changed) as a place to retreat for rest and 'healing' waters. Its best-known building is the dark grey **Manor House** ⓘ *T01943-700066, 1100-1700 Wed-Sat, 1300-1600 Sun.* Built between the 15th and 17th centuries, it is reached through a stone archway from Church Street. It's been converted into a museum that traces the history of the village back to prehistoric times.

Skipton

Just a few miles from Ilkley, the bigger town of Skipton is a bustling place whose name – which means 'Sheeptown' – rather gives away what the main business here once was. Today it could be called Castletown as the well-preserved **Skipton** Castle ⓘ *Mar-Sep Mon-Sat 1000-1800, Sun 1200-1800, Oct-Feb Mon-Sat 1000-1600, Sun 1200-1600, £4.40, children £2.20, family £11.90*, is one of the town's biggest tourist draws. A castle has stood on this site since 1090, although most of the current structure was built in medieval times. The thick 14th-century walls have endured more than time. They have survived a three-year siege by Parliamentarians during the Civil War. So sturdy was the squat little fortification with its rounded battlements (in places, its walls are 12 ft thick), that Cromwell ordered the roof to be removed, as it had survived one bombardment after another. When the castle's owner, Lady Anne Clifford, later asked to replace the roof, he allowed her to do so, as long as it was not strong enough to withstand cannon fire. Today the buildings are so complete that you cannot help but get the feel for what life was like for the villagers who worked and lived in its shadow, and under its protection.

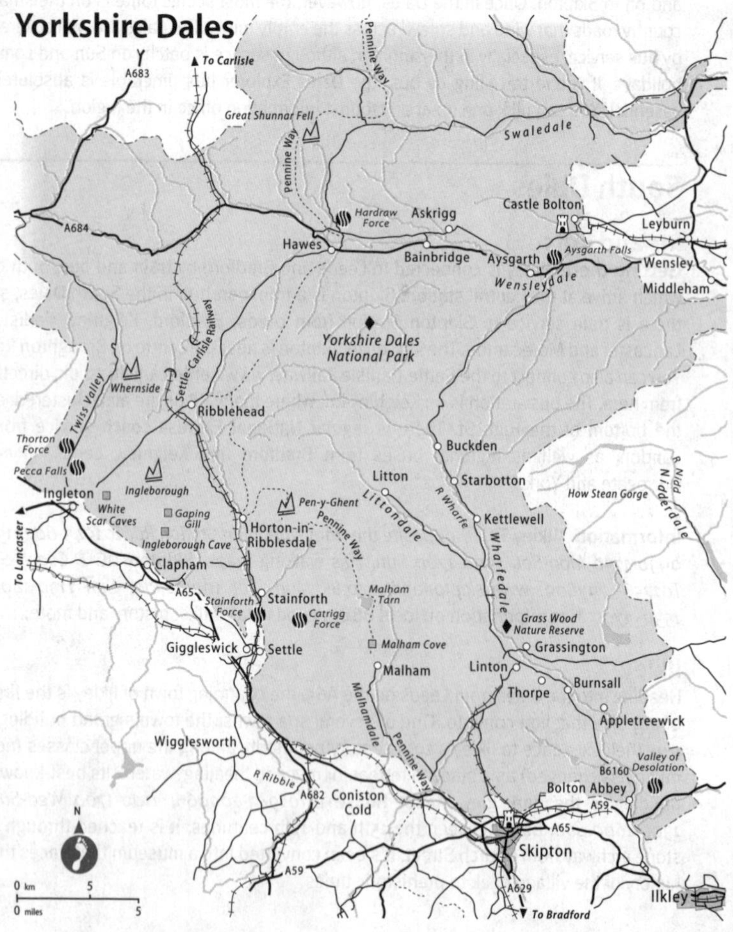

Bolton Abbey

This is another one of those towns that has taken its name from an old monastery. In this case, unlike in some towns, at least the abbey ruins still exist. In fact, the scant remains of the **Bolton Priory** are the primary attraction here. The priory once formed part of a wide-ranging Augustinian network of churches and monasteries throughout the region. The building was started in 1150, and stood complete until the Dissolution when it was abandoned. The ruins were once much bigger – it was painted by Turner – but now all that remains is the nave, which has survived in good nick because it was used as the parish church for years.

Grassington and around

Heading north from Bolton Abbey on the B6160 into an old lead-mining region, there's one tiny charming dales village after another. Built on the edge of a picturesque river, Grassington is too big to be really pretty, but it has a mixture of handsome touches sometimes overshadowed by a rather high twee factor. Perhaps the best part of the town is the setting, with the **Grass Wood nature reserve** providing a backdrop to the Georgian houses at the centre, the cobbled streets and olde inns.

Grassington also has the main **National Park Information Centre,** Hebden Road, T01746-752774, where you can get help booking a room, find maps for walks in the area and explore the history of Wharfedale. Even without a park service map you can drive the few miles from Grassington to the scenic village of **Linton**, with its lovely parks. This is a fantastic place for a picnic on a summer's day. Its small stream is crossed by both an ancient packhorse bridge and an old clapper bridge, and with its perfect 12th-century church, it is the picture of bucolic peace.

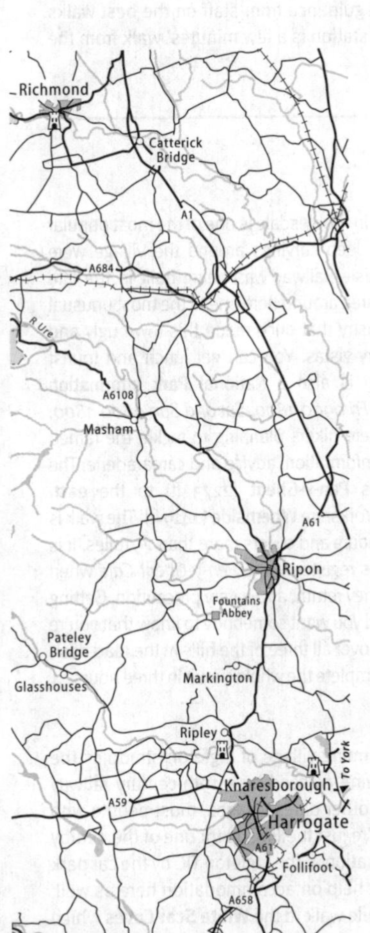

Around Malham Village

Due west of Linton you cross from Wharfedale into **Malhamdale** and enter one of the prettiest regions of the dales. The heather is permeated more frequently by limestone here, as this is a rocky region of striking high stone cliffs. It's a favourite with walkers, and the **Pennine Way** wanders through here, bringing a steady stream of ramblers. The biggest and busiest hub for these backpack toters is Malham Village. In the summertime, you simply cannot move for the walkers in this tiny village with its quaint stone cottages. In fact, by some estimates, half a million people a year make their way here. That means that, unless you are using this town as a setting off point yourself, there's too much of a crush here for it to actually be pleasant. If you're walking, there's a handy car park where you can leave your car and set off, and there's a **National Park Information Centre** ⓘ *T01729-830363, Easter-Oct daily 1000-1700, Nov-Easter Sat, Sun 1000-1600*, stocked with maps and advice on where to stop off on a multiple-day hike. The main attraction here, aside from the pub meals and comfy B&B rooms is the proximity to nearby walking trails. Walking north on a well-marked path you can travel about a mile to the stunning **Malham Cove**, the misnamed geological formation along the Mid-Craven Faultline created by movement of the earth's plates, it is a massive limestone amphitheatre that towers hundreds of feet above the surrounding countryside.

Settle

Heading just a few miles west from Malhamdale to Settle, you cross over into the dark, dramatic moors of **Ribblesdale**. Settle is the biggest village in this area, and the terminus of the gorgeous Settle-Carlisle rail line, which passes through some of the most consistently beautiful countryside in Britain. As Malham does in Malhamdale, Settle makes a popular base for walkers in Ribblesdale. With the added attraction of the railroad, this small town can get quite crowded as well in the summer. And, similarly, there's not much here save for B&Bs and pubs. Walkers usually head directly to the TIC in the town hall on Cheapside off the market, T01729-825192, 1000-1700 daily, to pick up maps and to get guidance from staff on the best walks around the village. The well-signposted train station is a few minutes' walk from the tourist office and the town centre.

Around the Three Peaks

Horton-in-Ribblesdale

Along with Settle, the old quarry town of Horton-in-Ribblesdale is one of the most popular stops for walkers in the Dales. Many of the deep carvings around the village were scratched into the stone when the Settle-Carlisle Railway was being built in the late 1800s. The deep cuts and rocky hills make the area around here one of the most unusual you're likely to see in the North. The very industry that once made this town ugly and utilitarian has, over time, created extraordinary vistas. You can get lunch and tourist information at the *Peny-y-Ghent Café*, which is also a **National Park Information** Centre ⓘ *T01729-860333, May-Sep Mon, Wed-Fri 0900-1800, Sat and Sun 0800-1800, Oct-Apr Mon and Wed 0900-1800*. This is where hikers planning to tackle the famed **Three Peaks Walk** often gather beforehand for information, advice and camaraderie. The three peaks in question are the mountains **Pen-y-Ghent** (2273 ft) to the east, **Ingleborough** (2373 ft) and the highest point in Yorkshire **Whernside** (2419 ft). The walk is a gruelling path around all three that takes 12 hours and covers more than 25 miles. It is only for fit and experienced hikers. Most hikers register at the *Pen-y-Ghent Café* when they head out for the path, and check in when they return, as a safety precaution. Getting lost or getting hurt are possibilities up there, and you want somebody to know that you're missing. Each April dozens of true fanatics race over all three of the hills in the mad dash known as the **Three Peaks Race**. Fast runners complete the whole circuit in three hours.

Ingleton

The furthest west point in the dales, the charming village of Ingleton straddles the junction of two picturesque streams in a ravine crossed by a 19th-century railway viaduct. Although the town is lovely, as with other dales villages, most people who come here aren't here to see the village. They're just fuelling up for one of the nearby hikes. Before setting out, get maps and information at the Ingleton TIC by the car park on Main St, T01524-241049. You can also get help on accommodation here as well. The most popular hike is the one and a half mile walk to the **White Scar Caves** which are, if anything, more spectacular than the Ingleborough Cave. An internal waterfall provides a constant rumble that grows to a roar as you get closer to it. A series of walkways have been erected to make the tour through the depths safer, but it's still a cave, so there's a section where the walls are only about a foot apart, and another where they're less than 5 ft high. A tour here is not for the unfit. At the centre of the cave is the massive **Battlefield Cavern** ⓘ *T01524-241244, 1000-1700 daily, £6.25,* 300 ft long and 100 ft high. All tours into the cave are guided, and it's not cheap, but it's well worth it.

East Dales

Litton to Kettlewell

Heading east from the Three Peaks, you enter **Littondale,** where more small villages and good walks can be found. In the little stone village of Litton there's a very small but useful **National Park Information Point** inside the post office where you can get maps and guidance. Litton makes a good base for climbing Pen-y-Ghent, but be aware that the villages here are so tiny that it gets harder to find accommodation or restaurants, so either bring your own tent and provisions, or drive back to one of the larger villages at the end of the day. Just beyond Litton the countryside is particularly beautiful, with rolling hills and deep valleys.

Pateley Bridge

Heading into the eastern Dales, the focus remains on rural walks, gorgeous countryside and charming villages like little Pateley Bridge. Small this village may be, but it's extremely important for walkers interested in taking in the scenery. You don't have to go far, a short stroll takes you up to the ruins of the church of **St Cuthbert** perched overlooking it all from a nearby hilltop. The ruins are striking and the view of the surrounding moors is simply spectacular. But that's not enough for most visitors, so it's handy that the TIC, 18 High St, T01423-711147, Easter-Oct only, has maps, information, advice and guidance for those interested in striking out. Before you head off, staff in hand, stop in at the **Nidderdale Museum** ⓘ *Apr-Oct 1400-1700 daily, Nov-Mar 1400-1700 Sat, Sun, £1.50,* which can help you brush up on local history, complete with a recreated 18th-century village street.

Harrogate and around

The best known town in the Dales, everything Harrogate has it owes to water. A specific kind of water that rises from Tewit Well, to be precise. The sulphur springs were discovered in 1571 and the rest is history. In the spa boom of the 18th and 19th centuries, Harrogate soon rose to the top, and the town boomed around the springs in an explosion of austere and grand architecture, befitting the class of those who flocked to the town to drink the water, soak in the water, be electrified in the water, and all the other strange things they did back then in the name of 'health'.

Ins and outs

Getting there The **train** station is on Station Parade near the town centre. There are regular trains from Leeds and York. Harrogate is on the A59 from Skipton and the A61 from Leeds. It's well located for access to the Dales. The bus station is just down the street from the train station, with local and regional services. **National Express buses** drop off and pick up on Victoria Av, near the library.

Information Harrogate TIC ⓘ *inside the Royal Baths on Crescent Rd, T01423-537300, May-Sep Mon-Sat 0900-1800, Sun 1200-1500, Oct-Apr Mon-Fri 0900-1715, Sat 0900-1230*. They can help you book guided tours of the town, and offer guidance on accommodation and good restaurants in town.

Sights

So well-preserved is the town that you can walk in the footsteps of 19th-century society starting at the **Royal Baths Assembly Rooms** ⓘ *Crescent Road, T01423-556746*. Plunge right in by taking a bath yourself. Just around the corner from the baths is the **Royal Pump Room**, ⓘ *Crown Place, Apr-Oct Mon-Sat 1000-1700; Sun 1400-1700, Nov-Mar Mon-Sat 1000-1600, Sun 1400-1600, £2*. It stands over the well that provides sulphurous water for the baths, and has been converted to include an interesting museum. The big building that stands across from the baths is the 19th-century **Royal Hall**, where those in town for the waters would catch ballets and symphonies in the evening. Down the road from the Pump Room, the **Mercer Art Gallery,** just a short distance away on Swan Road, is in the oldest pump building in town.

Around Harrogate

A worthwhile daytrip from Harrogate, **Knaresborough** – just four miles away – may well be one of the most underrated cities in England. Sitting as it does in the shadow of its famous neighbour, it's not well known despite its dramatic location above the River Nidd, its well-preserved townhouses, traditional pubs and colourful gardens. Even the railroad viaduct that crosses the ravine makes for an extraordinary view. Along with the lovely setting, Knaresborough has a modest **castle** ruin in a most picturesque location, towering above it all on a desolate hilltop. The remains of the Norman castle are mostly limited to its keep, but it's worth a visit if only because of its historic importance, which is well documented in the **Old Court House Museum** ⓘ *Castle Yard, Easter-Sep 1030-1700 daily, £2*. Best of all, you're given freedom to wander the dark old tunnels that run under the castle. On the river bank is the strange **Chapel of Our Lady of the Crag**, a mysterious shrine carved into the rocks – apparently around 1400 – that contains the figure of a knight. Across the river from the castle in the **Dropping Well Estate** is a mysterious cave that was once home to the famed 15th-century prophet known as Mother Shipton. She is said to have predicted many of the events of the subsequent 500 years, from the Great Fire of London to the phenomenon of world wars. **Mother Shipton's Cave** ⓘ *Easter-Oct 0930-1745 daily, Nov-Easter 1000-1645 daily, £3.95*, is filled with strange memorabilia and spooks the punters. It's located very near the other punter puller, the quite cool **Petrifying Well**, where the natural lime-rich waters turn everything they touch to stone. People have been putting objects here for years – from clothing to toys – and they are petrified in weeks.

Fountains Abbeyⓘ *Fountains Abbey and gardens Apr-Sep 1000-1900 daily; Oct, Feb, Mar 1000-1700 daily; Nov-Jan 1000-1700 Sun-Thu. £4.50*. It's difficult to decide what's more beautiful – the remains of the Cistercian abbey or the wooded setting in the valley of the River Skell. Surrounded by the water gardens known as **Studley Royal**, which were designed in the 19th century to compliment the rambling, jagged ruins of the abbey, the whole scene is simply extraordinary – equalled only by the hillside ruins at Rievaulx (see page 411). Fountains Abbey was founded by a rebellious group of Benedictines from York in 1132, but was taken over by the Cistercians within three years. Over the next century it grew into the most successful of the Cistercian monasteries in England, and that is reflected in the size of the ruins that remain today, growing out of the hillside in castle-like proportions of stone turrets and archways. Unlike many other Yorkshire abbeys, the ruins here are very substantial, including much of the **nave**, and the pointed **arcade** towering above Norman piers. The filigree remains of the **Chapel of the Nine Altars** gives some idea of how extraordinary this building must have been when complete. The **dormitory** where the lay workers slept is still largely intact, and it's clear that it was once massive, as it would have needed to be in order to house the hundreds of workers who lived and worked here, alongside the monks. John Aislabie stopped the destruction of the abbey, and designed the stunning gardens that now surround it, with a mixture of flowers, woods, deer parks and lakes. The most unusual of the features designed by Aislabie is the water gardens that include ponds, cascades and lakes, all integrated perfectly into the wild, wooded landscape. Despite the occasional wrong note hit by enthusiastic owners over the years, the combined effect of ruins and gardens is breathtaking.

The pretty town of **Ripon** sit a few miles from Fountains Abbey and about 11 miles north of Harrogate. For more than 1,300 years, its main draw has been its small but exquisite **cathedral** ⓘ *Daily 0800-1830, £2 donation requested*. From the outside, it looks much like any other parish church, but inside the architecture dates back to its foundation by St Wilfrid in 672. Even a decade before then, though, there was a monastery on this site, mentioned by the ancient historian Bede in his writings of that time. The labyrinthine crypt, with its arched passageways and mysterious shadows has been dated to that period, and is, without question, the most extraordinary part of the building. A number of relics – including the Ripon jewel (discovered in 1976 and dated back to the building's earliest years) – are on display down here. The Danes destroyed the rest of that first building in the ninth century. The chapel was built in the 11th century, and much of the rest of the building dates from the 12th century, although the twin towers at either side are 13th-century structures. There are regular chamber concerts here, usually on Monday evenings, and the Ripon Cathedral Choir is justifiably famous, and any chance to catch one of their performances should be grabbed. There's also an annual celebration in honour of St Wilfrid, as a procession moves regally down the streets in his name on St Wilfred's Feast the Sunday before the first Monday in August.

Northeast Dales

Ins and outs

Information Richmond TIC ⓘ *Friary Gardens, Victoria Rd T01748-850252 Apr-Sep 0930-1730 daily, Oct-Mar 0930-1630 Mon-Sat*. In addition to providing maps and advice for walks in the area, it will also help you find B&B accommodation in the rural area around Richmond.

Aysgarth and Askrigg

The hilltop village of **Aysgarth** is blessed with a gorgeous setting at the edge of the River Ure, which streams by on its limestone bed and then tumbles over impossibly picturesque **waterfalls**. In the summer, the little village fills with walkers, parking their cars, picking up maps at the **National Park information centre** T01969-663424 and striking up the surrounding hills. The paths are well marked, both the **Upper Falls** and the **Lower Falls** are a short walk from the town centre through thick woods. And the views are extraordinary. A few miles west is the village of Askrigg, which may look familiar if you watched the TV series of the James Herriott book *All Creatures Great and Small*, which was filmed here and around. Aside from looking for buildings you recognize, there are walks from here to the ruggedly beautiful **Whitfield Force** and **Mill Gill Force**, each well marked and fairly short – neither is more than a mile from the town centre. The jewel-like town of **Bainbridge** is just a couple of miles southwest of Askrigg, and has a historic nightly ceremony in which a horn is sounded on the village green at 2100, to call travellers in from the surrounding moors. The haunting horn sound is extremely evocative, and if you hear it without getting goosepimples, you're harder than most. The best place to be when the horn sounds is the 15th-century coaching inn, the *Rose & Crown Hotel*, T01969-650 225, which has a magnificent pub, and a few pleasant rooms.

Hawes

The little mountain town of Hawes is an unlikely tourist hub. It is home to just 1,300 souls, isn't particularly pretty and is primarily a centre of business and shopping for nearby farmers. But it is also surrounded by hills and waterfalls that act like flame to a moth for hikers. At 800 ft, Hawes claims to be the highest market town in Yorkshire, and its weekly market on Tuesday is crammed with cheeses and locally made jams and fresh butter. The **Wensleydale Creamery** on Gayle Lane is a regular stop for visitors stocking up before heading home. Cheese has been made in Hawes since the Cistercians started making it here in the 12th century, and it is sold everywhere in town. Before you head out on a walk, stop by the **National Park information centre** for maps and advice. It is located inside the surprisingly good **Hawes Ropemakers Museum** ⓘ *T01969-667450, Jul-Oct 0900-1730 Mon-Fri, 1000-1730 Sat, Nov-Jun 0900-1730 Mon-Fri, free*, which offers free demonstrations on the local skill of ropemaking.

Richmond

Just at the edge of the furthest eastern border of the dales, and about eight miles from Castle Bolton, the splendid castle town of Richmond provides a fitting ending to the dales, with its market square, Georgian architecture and bright gardens. At the centre of it all is the 11th-century **castle** ⓘ *Apr-Oct 1000-1800 daily, Nov-Mar 1000-1300, 1400-1600 daily, £2.70*, which stands guard from a steep precipice above the river. Lore connects this castle to England's most famous mythical king, as King Arthur is said to lie in a nearby cave, waiting for the time when England needs him again. Unlike many Yorkshire castles, the gloomy walls of Richmond Castle still hold many of its original Norman buildings including its gatehouse, keep (one of very few surviving Norman keeps in the country, and perhaps the eldest) and curtain wall. Along with all of this you get dramatic views from the sheer cliffs atop which it stands.

At the edge of Richmond stand the ruins of **Easby Abbey** ⓘ *dawn to dusk daily, free*, which was founded in 1152, and once was home to hundreds of Premonstratensian canons. Access to the site is free, and there is an easy, well-marked path here from the town centre. And there are few sights more beautiful than the jagged ruins of this abbey at sunset.

Sleeping

Skipton *p436*

C **Hanover International Hotel**, Keighley Rd, T01756-700100, www.hanover-international.co.uk. The biggest hotel in town, it has all the necessary luxuries along the Leeds-Liverpool Canal.

D **Coniston Hall Hotel**, Coniston Cold, T01756-748080, www.conistonhall.co.uk. Set on acres of private parkland is a beautiful hotel with its own lake and promises of "shooting, fishing, archery, corporate activities".

D **Highfield Hotel**, 58 Keighley Rd, T01756-793182. This small and centrally located hotel is very handy and affordable.

D **Maypole Cottage**, Blackburn House Farm, Thorpe, T01756-720 609. A detached old stable converted to form private self-catering accommodation which can be rented by the week.

E **Craven Heifer Inn**, Grassington Rd, just outside Skipton, T01756-792521, www.cravenheifer.co.uk. A grand old barn that has been converted into a rural guesthouse with a good bar and restaurant.

E **Skipton Park Guest 'Otel**, 2 Salisbury St, T01756-700640. Friendly and cheap best describes this place.

Bolton Abbey *p437*

L-A **Devonshire Arms**, T02756-710441. If you want to spend some serious money while you're in the area, spend the night here, at the ancestral home of the Duke and Duchess of Devonshire, it's a gorgeous manor house just south of Bolton Abbey, filled with antiques.

Around Malham Village *p437*

In general, especially if you arrive without booking in advance, you're better off trying any of the nearby villages, which are less crowded, book up less quickly and are slightly less expensive.

C **Riverhouse Hotel**, on the main road, T01729-830315. A Victorian country house that's been converted into a decent hotel with a good restaurant.

D **Miresfield Farm**, by the National Park office, T01729-830414. Lovely and friendly, this is one of the best places to stay.

E **The Buck Inn**, a traditional country inn with basic rooms and a good pub downstairs.

Settle *p438*

D **Yorkshire Rose**, Duke St, T01729-822032. A small and friendly place, out of the town centre.

D **Husbands Barn**, in Stainsforth, T01728-822240. A stone farmhouse and B&B.

D **Plough Inn**, in nearby Wigglesworth, T01729-840243, F840243. Offers lovely views and a fine restaurant.

E **Penmar Court Guest House**, T01729-823258. Again outside the town yet affordable and handy.

F **Stainforth Youth Hostel**, T01729-823577.

Horton-in-Ribblesdale *p438*

D **Crown Hotel**, T017239-860238, offer decent rooms, as well as good food and a convivial evening atmosphere as everyone relaxes over a few drinks after an exhausting day. There's also the somewhat more upscale

Camping

E **Holme Farm**, a tents-only campsite, T01729-860281.Just outside of town.

Ingleton *p438*

There's quite a bit of accommodation to choose from, although booking ahead in the summer is essential.

D **Bridge End Guest House**, Mill Lane, T01424-241413. Handy and attractive.

D **Moorgarth Hall**, New Rd, T01524-241946. Handsome building outside of town which has good views of the surrounding countryside.

Camping

Moorgaarth Farm, T01524-241428.

Stacksteads Farm, T01524-241386, both about a mile outside of town. *Stacksteads* also has a bunkhouse barn.

Harrogate and around *p439*

Harrogate is filled with hotels and B&Bs for every budget. The best areas to troll for a room are on King's Rd and Franklin Rd, where they stand shoulder to shoulder.

A **Rudding Park Hotel**, Rudding Park, Follifoot, T01423-871350, www.ruddingpark.com. A converted manor house just outside of town on the A661, one of the most elegant hotels in the area. It also has an excellent restaurant and gorgeous bar.

B **The Imperial**, Prospect Pl, T01423-565071. One of the town's grande dames, perfectly located and absolutely gorgeous. Worth the money if you can swing it.

D **Ascot House Hotel**, 53 King's Rd, T01423-531005, www.ascothouse.com For much of the glamour at less of the price, try this rambling, turreted house on lovely grounds and has a fabulous bar.

D **Fountains Hotel**, 27 King's Rd, T01423-430483. Friendly and family-run and offering basic comfort at a reasonable price.

D **Hob Green Hotel**, Markington, T01423-770031, F771589. About 5 miles north of Harrogate on vast, beautiful grounds with wonderful views and period furnishings, as well as an excellent restaurant.

Richmond *p442*

C **King's Head Hotel** Market Pl, T01748-850220, www.kingsheadrichmond.co.uk. Georgian building stocked with antiques. Its pub and restaurant are among the best in town.

D **Bridge House Hotel**, Catterick Bridge, T01748-818331, sits at the edge of the water, and offers gorgeous views. It also has a good bar and two restaurants.

D **Old Brewery Guesthouse**, 29 The Green, T01748-833460, is, as the name implies, a converted old brewery just below the castle.

D **Willance House**, 24 Bridge St, T01748-824467. Lovely 17th-century building, but only has a couple of rooms.

Eating

Skipton *p436*
££ **Le Caveau**, 86 High St, has modern European cooking in an elegant atmosphere.
£ **Wooly Sheep Inn**, has a good selection of beer and a not-bad selection of pub food.

Settle *p438*
£ **Ye Olde Naked Man Café**, has good food and a wonderful sign to take somebody's picture in front of.

Harrogate and around *p439*
££ **Clock Tower**, Rudding Park, T01423-871350, has good modern British cuisine, or you can just sip a drink in its very nice bar.
££ **Court's**, 1 Crown Pl, T01423-536336, ideal for sip a glass of wine in its posh environs.
££ **Courtyard**, 1 Montpellier Mews, T01423-530708. For an upscale modern European meal.
£ **Betty's**, 1 Parliament St, T01423-502746, which has stood on this spot for 80 years. Tea and scones for two about £10. You will never have a better chance to stuff yourself with scones. The best tea place in town, by popular acclaim.
£ **Drum and Monkey**, 5 Montpellier Gardens, T01423-502650, provides outstanding fish and chips, with a similar historic pedigree.
£ **Garden Room Restaurant** in the Botanical gardens, T01423-505604. For smaller crowds and a good view, you can get an excellent cream tea or lunch.

Richmond *p442*
££ **Restaurant on the Green** on Bridge St, which offers good food in a pleasant atmosphere.
££ *Unicorn*, on Newbiggin. A little ways out from the castle, and therefore not as crowded as some of the closer places. Here you can get a pint of real ale and a good meal.

North of England

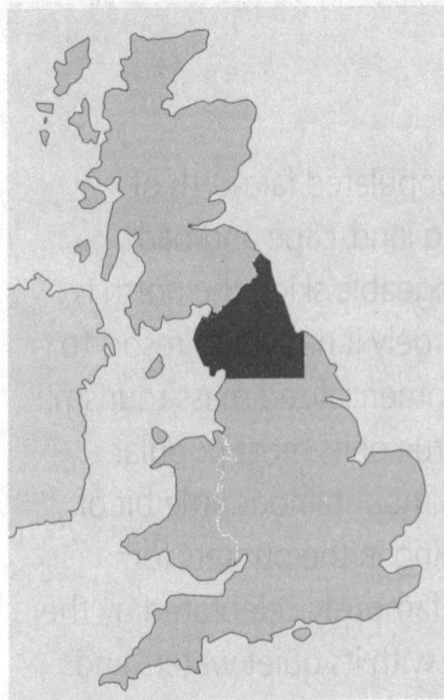

Introduction

First impressions of the sparsely populated far north of England are likely to involve its big landscape and bad weather. Spread wide under changeable skies, the north is hard-bitten but open-hearted. Largely it has yet to resort to the more cynical trappings of commercialized mass tourism, though that's no longer entirely true of its most popular destination, the Lake District. This mountainous little bit of Cumbria off the M6 has been pulling in the punters for centuries. Here, the landscape so famously celebrated by the Romantic poets, still stirs the soul with its quiet waters and wild scenery but the roads winding through it are often terribly overcrowded. The rest of Cumbria offers more peaceful touring, hiking and strolling, especially through the valleys of the rivers Eden and Lune. To the north, Carlisle, close to the Scottish border, makes a good base for exploration of the country's longest and most lasting Roman landmark, Hadrian's Wall. At the other end of the wall, the city of Newcastle upon Tyne is the largest in the north and is reinventing itself as a happening European cultural centre with a spirit of architectural revival on the banks of the Tyne. To its south, Durham rests on its laurels boasting one of the most spectacular pieces of old architecture in the UK in the shape of its hilltop Norman cathedral. Further north than all these, one of the least spoiled or hyped counties in England, Northumberland seems determined to keep it that way. Sometimes chilly and bleak perhaps, it also rains less often here than almost anywhere else. Mile upon mile of deserted beaches make for holiday heaven around Alnwick, while the crowds still flock to the Holy Island of Lindisfarne.

★ Don't miss...

1. Visit **Blackwell**, a renovated Arts and Crafts villa overlooking peaceful Lake Windermere, page 452 .
2. Explore the history of the Border Reivers before checking out the remains of the Roman answer to the problem in the shape of **Hadrian's Wall**, page 466.
3. Blink in astonishment at the transformation of **Newcastle Gateshead's** Quayside district, complete with its 'blinking bridge' across the Tyne, page 471.
4. Amble around **Alnwick** and see what the Duchess of Northumberland has been up to in her castle garden, page 481.
5. Take a train trip on the spectacular **Leeds-Settle-Carlisle railway**, stopping at Kirkby Stephen to find the oldest known representation of the devil in human form, page 461.

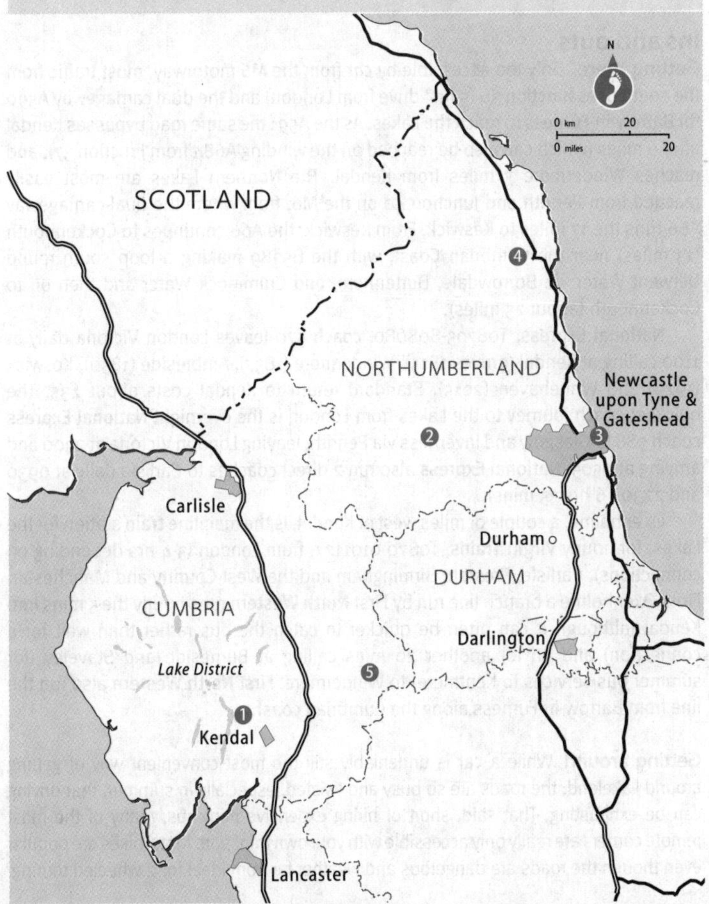

Cumbria and the Lake District

→Colour map 5

The north by northwestern corner of England comes as quite a surprise. Cumbria embraces the wildest and most spectacular scenery in England. The M6 motorway slices through on its way to Glasgow and even traffic hurtling along this high road gets a taste of the region's bleak beauty. Rising suddenly from sea level to about 3000 ft, the Lake District National Park is no more than 100 miles in circumference but contains 64 lakes, at least 15 of them impressive in their scale, brooded over by about 200 mountains over 2000 ft. To the east of the M6, lonelier fells roll off towards County Durham, studded by sturdy pockets of civilization, small market towns like Sedbergh, Kirkby Stephen and Appleby-in-Westmorland. Westmorland was the old county that bordered Lancashire to the north until the 1970s but its name lives on throughout the southern part of the new region, wonderful walking country usually soft underfoot. Cumberland, its grim northern neighbour, also included the mining communities on the coast and the border country up to Hadrian's Wall and Carlisle, now the county town of Cumbria. ▸▸ *For Sleeping, Eating and other listings, see pages 456-460.*

Ins and outs

Getting there Only too accessible by *car* from the M6 motorway, most traffic from the south uses Junction 36 (5 hrs' drive from London) and the dual carriageway A590 for Barrow-in-Furness to reach the Lakes. As the A591 the same road bypasses Kendal after 6 miles (which can also be reached on the winding A684 from Junction 37), and reaches Windermere 7 miles from Kendal. The Northern Lakes are most easily reached from Penrith and Junction 40 on the M6, from where the dual-carriageway A66 runs the 17 miles to Keswick. From Keswick, the A66 continues to Cockermouth (13 miles) near the Cumbrian Coast, with the B5289 making a loop south round Derwent Water via Borrowdale, Buttermere, and Crummock Water and then on to Cockermouth (about 25 miles).

National Express, T08705-808080, **coach** 570 leaves London Victoria daily at 1100 calling at Kendal (arrives 1815), Windermere (1837), Ambleside (1850), Keswick (1920) and Whitehaven (2015). Standard return to Kendal costs about £35. The quickest coach journey to the Lakes from London is the overnight **National Express** coach 588 to Glasgow and Inverness via Penrith, leaving London Victoria at 2300 and arriving at 0505. **National Express** also run 2 direct coaches to Carlisle daily at 0930 and 2230 (6 hrs 35 mins).

Oxenholme, a couple of miles west of Kendal, is the mainline **train** station for the Lakes, for hourly **Virgin Trains**, T0870-0101127, from London (3-4 hrs depending on connections), Carlisle, Preston, Birmingham and the West Country and Manchester. From Oxenholme a branch line run by **First North Western** runs hourly the 5 mins into Kendal (although it can often be quicker to catch the bus rather than wait for a connection) and on for another 20 mins calling at Burneside and Staveley (for summer bus services to Kentmere) to Windermere. **First North Western** also run the line from Barrow-in-Furness along the Cumbrian coast.

Getting around While a **car** is undeniably still the most convenient way of getting around Lakeland, the roads are so busy and twisted, especially in summer, that driving can be exhausting. That said, short of hiring expensive minicabs, many of the most remote corners are really only accessible with your own transport. Motorbikes are popular even though the roads are dangerous and weather far from ideal for 2-wheeled touring.

The same applies to cycling, although mountain-biking is still increasing in popularity. With enough time, easily the best way to explore is on foot, and luckily the local bus network is just about comprehensive enough to make this a practical alternative, especially if you want to avoid circular walks. All the main towns are connected by regular bus services, except on Sun. Kendal, Windermere, Ambleside, Keswick, Hawkshead and Coniston are all connected by at least 1 bus in any 2 hrs Mon-Sat throughout the year. A variety of special tickets are available, for example **Explorer Tickets** giving unlimited travel on *Stagecoach* in Cumbria buses for 1 day £7, 4 days £16, 7 days £23. For anyone using public transport, Cumbria County Council publish a booklet on getting around Cumbria and the Lake District, available from most information centres, complete with timetables, maps, and ticket prices.

Information **Lake District National Park** ⓘ *Murley Moss, Oxenholme Rd, Kendal, T01539-724555*. The main National Park Visitor Centre is at the **Brockhole Visitor Centre** ⓘ *on the eastern shore of Lake Windermere, T01539-446601, www.lake-district.gov.uk, daily Apr-Oct 1000-1700*. **Lake District Weatherline** ⓘ *T01768-775757 (local or national call rate, sponsored by Hawkshead clothing)*. **Kendal TIC** ⓘ *Kendal Town Hall, Highgate, T01539-725758, www.southlakeland.gov.uk* **Windermere** TIC ⓘ *Victoria St, T01539-446499, www.lakelandgateway.info, daily 0900-1700 (-1830 Jul and Aug)*. **Bowness Bay National Park Information Centre** ⓘ *Glebe Rd, T01539- 442895, Apr-Oct daily 0930-1730*. **Ambleside TIC** ⓘ *Central Buildings, Market Cross, T01539-432582 www.lakelandgateway.info, daily 0900-1700*. **Waterhead National Park Information Centre** ⓘ *Nr Ambleside, T01539-432729, daily Apr-Oct 1000-1700*. **Grasmere National Park Information Centre** ⓘ *Red Bank Rd, T01539-435245, Apr-Oct daily 0930-1700*. **Glenridding National Park Information Centre** ⓘ *Ullswater, T01768-482414*. **Pooley Bridge National Park Information Centre** ⓘ *The Square, T01768-486530*. **Hawkshead National Park Information Centre** ⓘ *Main Car Park, T01539-436525*. **Coniston National Park Information** Centre ⓘ *Main Car Park T01539-441533*. **Keswick TIC** ⓘ *Moot Hall, T01768-772645, www.keswick.org, daily Apr-Oct 0930-1700; Nov-Mar 0930-1630*. **Seatoller Barn National Park Information Centre** ⓘ *Borrowdale T01768-777294*.

Sights

Kendal and around

Just outside the boundary of the National Park, Kendal is called the 'Gateway to the Lakes' thanks to its proximity to the M6 and the main west coast railway line at Oxenholme.This doughty old market town was built largely out of local limestone and became known as the 'auld grey town'. It's the capital of southeastern Cumbria, most famous for Kendal Mint Cake – a hard-bitten sugar and peppermint sweet favoured by mountaineers – but also closely associated with the 18th-century portrait painter George Romney. (One best-selling brand of Kendal Mint Cake is called Romney's.) Kendal makes a pleasant and relatively inexpensive base from which to explore the Lakes and remains a proper working town, some 7 miles east of all the tourist activity at Windermere and Bowness.

Kendal's main street is Highgate, where the impressive **Town Hall** is home to some Victorian debating chambers, seriously antique public lavatories and the small TIC. But Kendal's main attraction is the **Abbot Hall Art Gallery**, by the river near the bottom of Highgate where it becomes Kirkland. One of the country's cutest public art galleries, in an elegant Georgian villa by the river, as well as two almost life-size late-17th-century portraits of the indomitable Lady Anne Clifford, it holds works by local man George Romney, as well as Lakeland scenes by Turner, Ruskin and contemporary art by Lucien Freud and Bridget Riley. ⓘ *T01539-722464, www.abbothall.org.uk Daily 1030-1600, £3.75, children £1.75*.

The Lake District

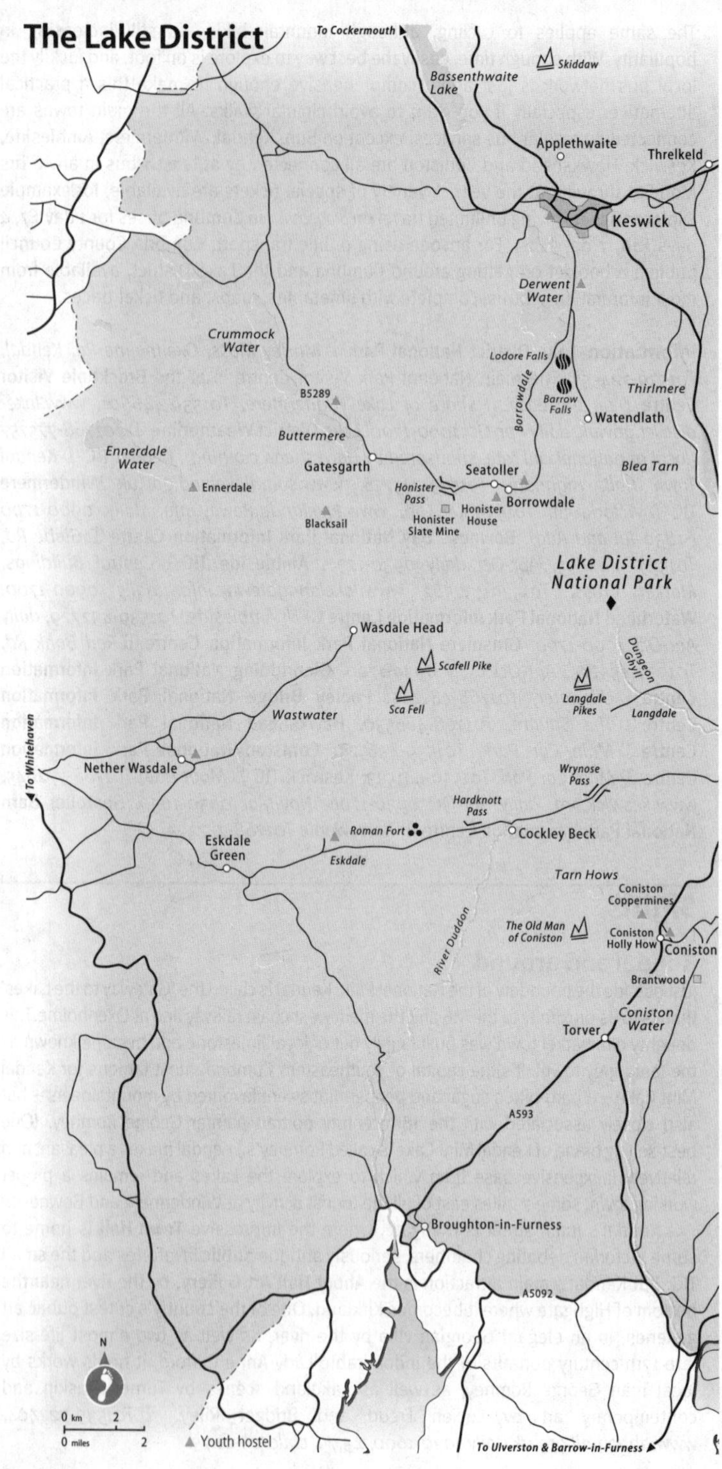

To Cockermouth
Skiddaw
Bassenthwaite Lake
Applethwaite
Threlkeld
Keswick
Derwent Water
Crummock Water
Lodore Falls
Borrowdale
Barrow Falls
Thirlmere
B5289
Watendlath
Buttermere
Ennerdale Water
Gatesgarth
Seatoller
Blea Tarn
Ennerdale
Honister Pass
Borrowdale
Honister House
Honister Slate Mine
Blacksail
Lake District National Park
Wasdale Head
Dungeon Ghyll
Scafell Pike
Langdale Pikes
Sca Fell
Langdale
Wastwater
To Whitehaven
Nether Wasdale
Wrynose Pass
Hardknott Pass
Roman Fort
Cockley Beck
Eskdale Green
Eskdale
Tarn Hows
Coniston Coppermines
River Duddon
The Old Man of Coniston
Coniston Holly How
Coniston
Brantwood
Coniston Water
Torver
A593
Broughton-in-Furness
A5092
N
0 km 2
0 miles 2
Youth hostel
To Ulverston & Barrow-in-Furness

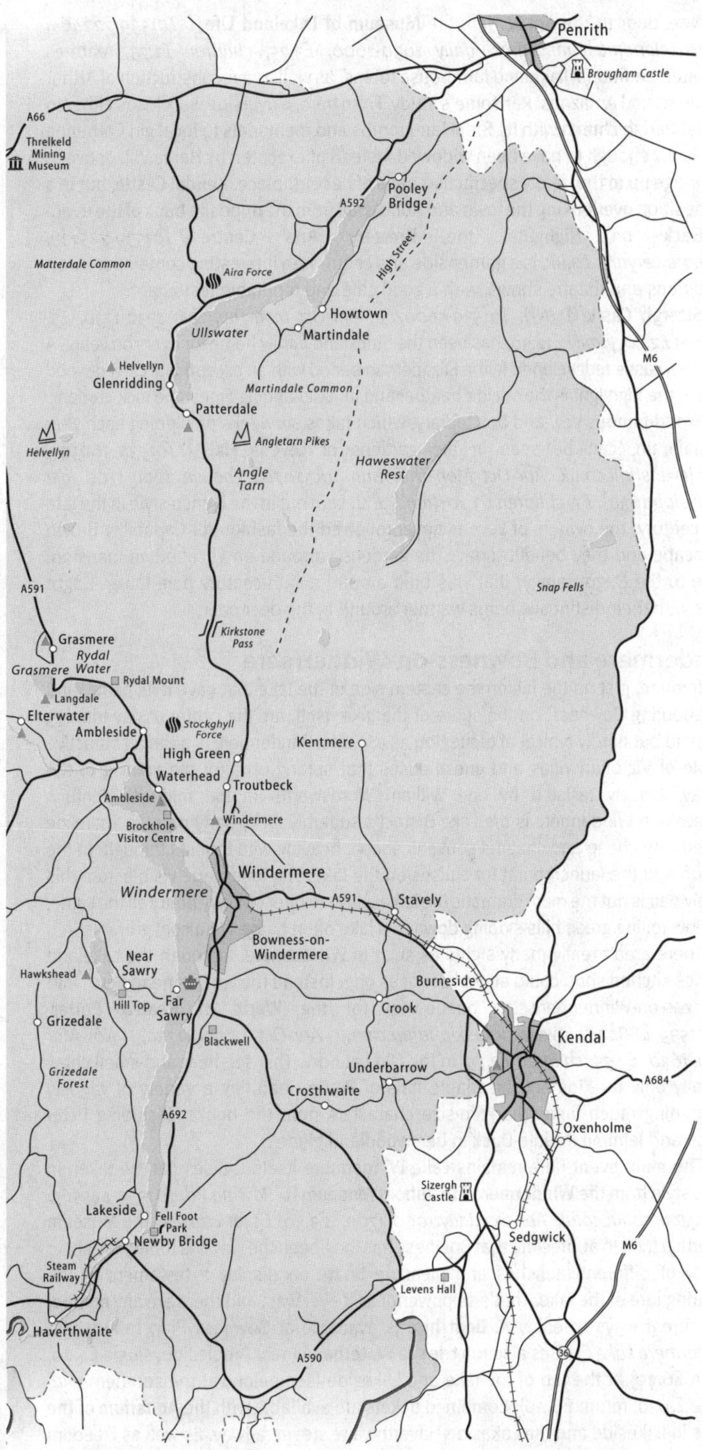
Penrith
Brougham Castle
A66
Threlkeld Mining Museum
Pooley Bridge
A592
High Street
Matterdale Common
Aira Force
Howtown
Ullswater
Martindale
M6
Helvellyn
Glenridding
Martindale Common
Patterdale
Helvellyn
Angletarn Pikes
Haweswater Rest
Angle Tarn
Snap Fells
A591
Kirkstone Pass
Grasmere
Rydal Water
Grasmere
Rydal Mount
Langdale
Elterwater
Ambleside
Stockghyll Force
Kentmere
High Green
Waterhead
Troutbeck
Ambleside
Brockhole Visitor Centre
Windermere
Windermere
Windermere
A591
Stavely
Bowness-on-Windermere
Near Sawry
Hawkshead
Hill Top
Far Sawry
Burneside
Crook
Grizedale
Blackwell
Kendal
Grizedale Forest
Underbarrow
A684
Crosthwaite
A692
Oxenholme
Sizergh Castle
Lakeside
Fell Foot Park
Sedgwick
Newby Bridge
M6
Steam Railway
Levens Hall
Haverthwaite
36
A590

Next door to the Abbot Hall, the **Museum of Lakeland Life** ⓘ *T01539-722464, www.lakelandmuseum.org.uk, daily 1030-1600, £3.75, children £1.75*, features recreated traditional Lakeland farmhouse rooms, as well as a reconstruction of Arthur 'Swallows and Amazons' Ransome's study. From here, a riverside walk leads either to **Kendal Parish church** with its Strickland tombs and memorials to local girl Catherine Parr, lucky enough to have been widowed instead of executed by Henry VIII, or over a footbridge up to the hardly spectacular ruins of her birthplace, **Kendal Castle**, but in a fine position overlooking the town and Abbot Hall from the opposite bank of the river.

Back on Highgate, the **Brewery Arts Centre** ⓘ *T01539-725133, www.breweryarts.co.uk*, is a gardenside arts centre with interesting contemporary art exhibitions and theatre shows, with a good café and reputable restaurant.

Sizergh Castle ⓘ *(NT), T01539-5600700, Apr-Oct Mon-Thu, Sun 1330-1730, £5, children £2.50, family £12.50*, has been the Strickland family home for over 700 years. A medieval castle redeveloped in the Elizabethan period with an exceptional carved-wood interior, the highlight is the Inlaid Chamber and an outstanding limestone rock garden.

World-famous yew and box topiary, which takes six weeks of clipping each year to maintain, can be seen in the gardens of **Levens Hall** ⓘ *T01539-560321, www.levenshall.co.uk, Apr-Oct Mon-Thu, Sun 1000-1700 (house 1200-1700 last admission 1630), £7, children £3.70, family £21*. Laid out in the French style in the late 17th century, the owners of Levens never followed the fashion for Capability Brown landscape and they benefit today. The gardens surround an Elizabethan mansion, home to the Bagot family, that was built around a 13th-century pele tower. Bagot goats with their distinctive horns wander around in the deer park.

Windermere and Bowness-on-Windermere

Windermere, just up the hill on the eastern side of the lake that gave it its name, and neighbouring Bowness, on the shore of the lake itself, are the centre of day tripping Lakeland but hardly typical of the region as a whole. Windermere is quite an attractive jumble of Victorian villas and guesthouses that sprang up after the coming of the railway (fiercely resisted by one William Wordsworth) in the mid-19th century. Bowness-on-Windermere is the Lake District's superbly tacky party prom, a shoreline riddled with cheap and cheerful souvenir shops, heaving with tourists throughout the season and the launch point for cruises on the lake. The landscape visible from this unholy pair is not the most dramatic the Lakes have to offer but very pretty all the same, with low rolling green hills sloping down to a lake often bathed in a cool grey mist.

There aren't really many sights as such in Windermere, although the Lakeland Plastics kitchen shop could almost count as one. Instead the crowds head down into Bowness-on-Windermere to queue up for the **World of Beatrix Potter** ⓘ *T01539-488444, www.hop-skip-jump.com, Apr-Oct 1000-1730, Nov-Mar 1000-1630, £3.75, children £2.75*, in the Old Laundry. This see-hear-and-smell show is really only for kids and insatiable fans of Potter, featuring a variety of vaguely threatening much larger-than-life-size characters from the books, including Peter Rabbit and Jemima Puddle-Duck in her 'woodland glade'.

The main event here remains Lake Windermere itself. Cruises can be taken in some style from the **Windermere Steamboat Museum** ⓘ *Rayrigg Rd, T01539-445565, www.steamboat.co.uk, Apr-Oct daily 1000-1700, £3.50, £5 for cruises*. The Museum is worth a look to appreciate that Bowness has long been the way it is today, the sheer variety of different launches and pleasure boats on display a testament to the enduring lure of the lake. That's as powerful as it ever was, and there are any number of different ways to enjoy it. **Boat hire** is available at Bowness Pier, from where *Windermere Lake Cruises* also run **trips to Waterhead** (near Ambleside, single £4.20, return £6.20) at the top of the lake and Lakeside (see below, at the southern end, single £4.30, return £6.40). Combined tickets are available with the **Aquarium of the Lakes** in Lakeside and the Lakeside-Haverthwaite steam railway, as well as Freedom of the Lake tickets (round the lake from any pier) costing £11, valid for 24 hours. A ferry runs across to **Ferry House**, from where it's a long steep climb up to Beatrix Potter's study house at Hill Top in Near Sawrey (see page 454).

Just over a mile south of Bowness, just off the A5074 on the B5360, **Blackwell** ⓘ *T01539-446139, www.blackwell.org.uk, daily 1000-1700 (-1600 in Feb, Mar, Nov, Dec, closed Jan-mid-Feb). £4.50, under-16s and concessions £2.50, family £12*, is an immaculate Arts and Crafts house built for the Manchester brewer Sir Edward Holt in a beautiful position looking towards Coniston Old Man in the last two years of the 19th century. Restored and reopened by the Lakeland Arts Trust in 2001, it now represents one of the finest examples extant of the design movement founded by William Morris in pursuit of locally sourced materials, skills and inspiration.

Seven miles south of Bowness, **Fell Foot Park** is a Victorian lakeside pleasure garden restored by the National Trust at the southern end of Lake Windermere. The gardens are at their best in spring or autumn, and there's a tearoom with rowing boat hire in season (Apr-Oct). Round the corner on the opposite side of the lake, beyond Newby Bridge in Lakeside, the **Aquarium of the Lakes** ⓘ *T01539-530153, www.aquariumofthelakes.co.uk, daily 0900- 1800 (-1700 Nov-Mar, last admission 1 hr before closing)*, is a good wet-weather attraction, a very comprehensive freshwater aquarium tracing a local river from its source to the sea. Here's the chance to see what ducks get up to while they're underwater, meet an otter or come face to face with a fearsome pike.

The **Lakeside and Haverthwaite Steam Railway** ⓘ *T01539-531594, May-Oct, £4.10 return*, runs 20-minute trips up the Leven Valley from Lakeside, with combined steam and boat trips on the Victorian gondola *MV Tern*.

Ambleside

Five miles north of Windermere, beyond the Lake District's main visitor centre at Brockhole and the small village of Troutbeck, Ambleside is the other half of Lakeland's pulsating heart and not very aptly named: this is where the tough get going. None of the ambling lazy pleasures of Bowness and Windermere here. This is a serious hiker town with a fairly forbidding grey- stone look to go with. That said, Ambleside does have a polite and rather sedate side, best appreciated down by the lake where it becomes Waterhead, and has a vaguely Bohemian atmosphere in its pubs and cafés. Part of the reason for the town's cachet with hikers is that it's within (serious) walking distance of Windermere station and several strenuous, rewarding climbs can be made right out of the town centre itself.

Back on the main A591, half way between Windermere and Ambleside, the **National Park's main visitor centre** ⓘ *T01539-446601, www.lake-district.gov.uk, daily Apr-Oct 1000-1700*, at Brockhole is surrounded by lakeside gardens and contains the latest interactive wizardry to elucidate and entertain visitors about the National Park, including a three-dimensional model of the central massif and a gift shop.

Ambleside itself is introduced by **Waterhead**, at the head of the lake, with a Youth Hostel and landing stages for the steamer services and boat hire, about a mile from the centre of the town. The A561 becomes Lake Road as it heads into town, round the one-way system and up to the Market Cross, passing **Zeffirelli's Cinema**, an unusual combination of pizzeria and two-screen cinema. Nearby, and equally unconvential, is the **Homes of Football** ⓘ *100 Lake Rd, T01539-434440, www.homesoffootball.co.uk, daily 1000-1700 (-1900 Jun, Jul, Aug), free*, a free exhibition of offbeat photographs of football grounds great and small around the country, focusing on the people that inhabit them, both fans and players.

Since the renovation of the old bus station, the centre of town has moved away from the gloomy Market Place into the open area called **Market Cross**, surrounded by shops and cafés that almost manage an Alpine buzz. The rivulet of Stock Ghyll flows into town from the east here, crossed by the Bridge House, apparently built to evade land tax. Further up Rydal Road, the **Armitt Museum** ⓘ *T01539-431212, www.*

 armitt.com, daily 1000-1700 (last admission 1630), £2.50, concessions £1.80, families £5.60, is the town's interesting local history museum, with finds from Galava Roman Fort and displays on the 19th-century writers and artists that once made Ambleside such a vibrant place: Charlotte Mason, Beatrix Potter, and the Collingwoods. Founded in 1912, the museum is named after Mary Louisa Armitt who gave her library to the town.

Beyond the Langdale Valley, the tortuous **Wrynose Pass** climbs up to Cockley Beck at the head of the Duddon Valley before the even steeper **Hardknott Pass** beneath Sca Fell. The road runs by **Hardknott Roman Fort**, an awe-inspiring spot for a legionary outpost overlooking beautiful Eskdale, on the Cumbrian Coast. From Eskdale Green a tiny road runs round to **Nether Wasdale** at the foot of **Wast Water**, the deepest, most remote and mysterious of the Lakes, with precipitous scree slopes on its southern side. A difficult road runs along its northern shore all the way to **Wasdale Head**, the most isolated settlement in the entire region. The pub here is suitably serious (many of its customers have walked miles to reach it) and the little church is a moving place too.

Grasmere

Four miles up the road from Ambleside, Grasmere is an undeniably pretty stone-built village five minutes' walk from its own little lake. And it's also the most popular in the Lakes thanks to one William Wordsworth and his younger sister Dorothy, whose homes at Dove Cottage, in the village itself, and at Rydal Mount, on the road up from Ambleside, have been preserved as shrines to the spirit of Lakeland. Although it always becomes very busy with day-trippers in summer, and occasionally dismissive in its attitude to tourists, Grasmere still makes a good base for serious walkers, with wonderful trails west leading up Sour Milk Gill to Easdale Tarn, the Langdale Pikes and over to Borrowdale; or east on to the flanks of Helvellyn, the Lake District's most famous mountain.

First stop from Ambleside on the Wordsworth trail is **Rydal Mount** ⓘ *T01539-433002, Mar-Oct daily 0930- 1700, Nov-Feb Mon, Wed-Sun 1000-1600, £4, concessions £3, children £1.50*. The Wordsworths moved into this comfortable whitewashed stone house in 1813 and lived here until 1850. Still owned by their descendants, highlights include the attic room where Wordsworth worked once he was Poet Laureate (although not where he did his best work), the cosy dining room and airy library adding up to an evocative insight into the early Victorian literary life and one of Lakeland's better wet-weather options. The sloping garden was designed and much loved by the great man himself, and his original plantings have been respected. The main road skirts the shoreline of **Rydal Water** on its way into Grasmere. The best views of the small lake are not from this road though but from the fells above, reached on the Grasmere-Eltwater road.

Fans thirsting for more information on the poet, his sister and famous friends will want to press on to **Dove Cottage** ⓘ *T01539-435544, www.wordsworth.org.uk, daily 0930-1650 (museum -1730), £5.80, children £2.60, concessions £4.50*. They lived here from 1799-1808 and the enormously enthusiastic 20-minute guided tours every half hour fill in much of the information missing at Rydal Mount. Coleridge stayed with them here and the eight-room cottage has been restored to look pretty much as it might have done at the turn of the 19th century. Ticket price includes a modern art gallery and the Wordsworth Museum, packed with memorabilia and trivia related to the influential Lakeland literary circle. Weather-permitting, the garden is included on the tour too.

Hawkshead and Coniston

West of Ambleside, or reached by ferry across Lake Windermere, Hawkshead and Coniston are relatively quieter and less frequented villages. Hawkshead is an attractive place, sitting at the top of tiny Esthwaite Water, below the heights of Near Sawrey (where Beatrix Potter's Hill Top House is the main attraction) and Far Sawrey (for the ferry to Bowness). Coniston is set some way back from Coniston Water itself, a more sedate version of Ambleside, but equally popular with hikers wanting to tackle the Coniston Old Man looming above the village.

As Grasmere is to William Wordsworth, so Coniston is to John Ruskin (1819-1900), and it's not too fanciful to think that the differences in the two villages says something about the difference between the two men. Ruskin was inspired by the works of Turner and Wordsworth to find a place of his own in the Lake District. Instead of Rydal Mount, with its cosy situation, he settled at **Brantwood** ⓘ *T01539-441396, www.brantwood.org.uk, mid-Mar to early Nov daily 1100-1730, mid-Nov to early Mar Wed-Sun 1100-1730, £4.75, concessions £3.50, children £1, family £10*. He famously described it as "little more than a hut" when he arrived, but the breathtaking beauty of its position ensured that he perservered until he was inhabiting the fairly grand house it is today. Some way along the eastern shore of the lake, best reached on the splendid steam yacht *Gondola* from Coniston itself, Brantwood is one of the most remarkable houses in the Lake District. Quite apart from the wealth of information on Ruskin's life and work, the place was lived in recently enough for it to remain powerfully redolent of his character. The gardens also command magnificent views over the lake.

In Coniston itself, the **Ruskin Museum** ⓘ *T01539-441164, www.ruskinmuseum.com, Easter to mid-Nov daily 1000-1730, mid-Nov to Easter Wed-Sun 1030-1530, £2.50, concessions £2*, gives an insight into the man and his works, including his attempts to improve the local economy and ideas on art and life. Ruskin is buried in the churchyard.

Hawkshead is often trumpeted as the 'prettiest village in the Lake District', a claim that could well be justified thanks to the measures that have been taken to keep it that way. Consequently the whole place has an unreal atmosphere: traffic-free, overpriced and often overcrowded. Hawkshead also boasts the **Beatrix Potter Gallery** ⓘ *(NT), T01539-436355, Apr-Oct Mon-Wed, Sat, Sun 1030-1630, £3, children £1.50, entry by timed ticket*, in the tiny house that was once her husband's law office, little altered since his day, putting on changing displays of her original artwork for her stories.

In Near Sawrey, **Hill Top** ⓘ *(NT), T01539-436269, Apr-Oct Mon- Wed, Sat, Sun 1100-1630 (1030-1730 Jun-Aug), £4.50, children £1, family £10, advance booking advisable*, was the house where Beatrix Potter wrote many of her best-loved stories, and has been kept exactly as she left it, complete with her furniture and china. Mrs Tiggywinkle would feel quite at home here, but she'd have to join the queue like everyone else, unless she'd been a sensible little hedgehog and booked ahead.

South of Hawkshead stretch the 9000 green acres of **Grizedale Forest**, home to the Grizedale sculpture trail, where over 60 contemporary artists have transformed bits of the wood with startling responses to the natural environment since the 1970s.

Keswick and around

Keswick is the capital of the Northern Lakes, a lively market town with few pretensions and very popular with fell walkers. The business end of the Lake District, at the head of lovely Derwent Water on the River Greta, Keswick retains the atmosphere of a hard-working Cumbrian town and makes a good base for exploring Borrowdale, Watendlath and Buttermere. It also has a variety of fairly half-baked attractions to kill time if the weather's bad. Scafell Pike, the highest mountain in England, is usually tackled from here or from Langdale. To the north, Skiddaw presents a worthwhile challenge, overlooking peaceful Bassenthwaite Lake.

The centre of Keswick is the **Moot Hall**, home to the National Park Information Centre, where the most comprehensive array of leaflets on the Northern Lakes is available. Top of the range of Keswick's attractions is the **Cumberland Pencil Museum** ⓘ *T01768-773626, www.pencils.co.uk, daily 0930-1630*, an unusual and intriguing insight into the history of the humble pencil. The industry in the town as a whole was killed off by technological advances, but one factory remains, manufacturing high-quality graphite Derwent pencils. Somehow inevitably, the museum boasts the world's largest pencil. Kids though would probably be happier looking into the **Cars of the Stars Motor** Museum ⓘ *Standish St, T01768-773757, www.carsofthestars.com, daily 1000-1700*, featuring original and replicas of various celebrity motor vehicles, from Chitty Chitty Bang Bang, via Herbie, to Knightrider's Kitt.

Three miles east of Keswick off the A66 the **Threlkeld Mining Museum** ⓘ *Threlkeld Quarry and Mining Museum, 3 miles west of Keswick, T01768-779747, Mar-Oct daily 1000-1700, museum £3, under-14s £1.50, mine tour £4, children £2*, is one of the best places to get to grips with the Lake District's industrial heritage. As well as a huge variety of different mining implements, large and small, tours of the workings are given by experienced guides and there's even a chance to pan for gold.

Another more spectacular mine tour is at the **Honister Slate** Mine ⓘ *T01768-777230, www.honister-slate-mine.co.uk, mine tours daily 1030, 1230, 1530 (and 1400, 1700 in summer), £7, children £4, family £20*, on Honister Pass above Borrowdale, 9 miles from Keswick, where the Westmorland Green Slate has been mined for centuries.

South of Keswick, the B5289 skirts Derwent Water and heads up into **Borrowdale**, many people's favourite Lakeland valley. Sights on the way include the famous **Falls of Lodore**, a waterfall praised to the skies by Robert Southey; the **Barrow Falls**, on the road up to Watendlath, another popular beauty spot, with trails up on to the hills overlooking the mystical little Blea Tarn; and the **Bowdler Stone**, an enormous erratic boulder on top of which people climb around. The village of Borrowdale itself is often mobbed with tourists pausing before making the steep ascent up **Honister Pass** beyond Seatoller. After 3 miles the road descends to **Buttermere** and **Crummock Water**, a pair of the most windswept lakes in the district.

Ullswater

The second largest and most northeasterly of the lakes, Ullswater has a special kind of menacing charm that was much appreciated by Wordsworth. Even though roads run down either shore, it often seems unnaturally quiet here. Relatively one of the least congested of the lakes, the road from Pooley Bridge to Glenridding is the most impressive approach by road to Helvellyn (3116 ft), the mountain climbers' favourite challenge.

From Pooley Bridge a tiny road runs along the southern shore of the lake to Howtown and then to **Martindale** with its lonely chapel and then on to Dale Head Farm. From Howtown a lovely walk leads up on to **Martindale Common. Angle Tarn,** beneath the twin Angletarn Pikes, is one of the most picturesque mountain pools or tarns in the Lake District, with its oddly irregular shape, small islands and popularity with the local herds of red deer.

Three miles before Glenridding, **Aira Force** is an impressive 70 ft waterfall that tumbles down the south face of **Matterdale Common** (where Wordsworth is supposed to have seen his host of nodding daffodils) to the north of the lake. It's a short walk up from the car park on the A5091.

Sleeping

Youth hostels and camping barns

The Lake District is packed with self-catering options, from mansions to bothies. Endless different campsites are on offer, details from the local tourist office. Freerange camping is not exactly encouraged, but if done carefully on National Trust land (most of the central range) without disturbing the environment in any way at all, no one's likely to mind. The other option is one of the 25 Youth Hostels. They usually need to be booked well in advance and many are not open in winter, so it's best to ring first. Facilities also vary quite widely. More basic still, but in the most glorious positions, are the range of **YHA Camping Barns**. There are at least 10 dotted around the Lake District, many within walking distance of each other, but they too need to booked ahead some time in advance especially in high season. Not all are open all year. Contact Lakeland Barns Booking Office, Moot Hall, Market Sq, Keswick, CA12 4JR, T01768-772645.

Kendal and around *p449*

C **Burrow Hall Country Guest House**, Plantation Bridge, Staveley, T01539-821711, www.burrowhall.co.uk Two miles outside Kendal, an old Lakeland house, tastefully furnished in peaceful countryside, £50.
C **Heaves Hotel**, Nr Levens Hall, Sedgwick, T01539-560269, www.heaveshotel.co.uk. Has 13 very good value rooms in a superb country house hotel in the old manor house of Heaves. Recommended.
C **Lakeland Natural**, Queen's Rd, Kendal, T01539-733011. Provides non-smoking, vegetarian accommodation in an elegant Victorian home within beautiful gardens.
D **Garnett House Farm**, ¼ mile from Burneside station, 2 miles out of Kendal towards Windermere, T01539-724542, www.garnetthousefarm.co.uk. A 15th-century farmhouse on a working farm with some rooms en suite.
D **The Glen**, Oxenholme, Kendal, T01539-726386, www.glen-kendal.co.uk, a small friendly guesthouse on outskirts of town. Above Oxenholme station, close to the pub.
D **Hill Crest Bed & Breakfast**, 98 Windermere Rd, Kendal T01539-727851, family-run with good views from the front room to Shap and en suite bathrooms.
F **Kendal YHA**, 118 Highgate, Kendal, T01539-724066. With 54 beds in the middle of town close the Brewery Arts Centre.

Windermere and Bowness-on-Windermere *p452*

L **Gilpin Lodge**, Crook Rd, Windermere, T01539-488818, www.gilpin-lodge.co.uk. With very friendly service, not overly formal, there's a small country house atmosphere at this hotel with top-notch food at around £45 a head.
L **Miller Howe**, Rayrigg Rd, Windermere, T01539-442536, www.millerhowe.com. The smart option in Windermere, a 'luxury hotel' with a reputation for its excellent food. Great views over fells and lake.
A **Holbeck Ghyll**, Holbeck Lane, between Windermere and Ambleside, T01539-432375, www.holbeckghyll.com. A romantic country house hotel with superb views and thoroughly competent kitchen.
C **The Coppice Guest House**, Brook Rd, Windermere, T01539-488501, www.thecoppice.co.uk. Guesthouse with quality food, all home prepared and leisure club membership included in the price. Well-behaved pets welcome. Non smoking.
C **The Cottage Guest House**, Elleray Rd, Windermere, T01539-444796, www.thecottageguesthouse.com. A family-run guesthouse, most rooms have en suite bathrooms. Close to station.
F **Windermere YHA**, Bridge Lane, Troutbeck, T01539- 443543. With 69 beds in a panoramic position above the town, good for gentle walks through the woods.

Ambleside *p453*

A **Rothay Manor Hotel**, Ambleside, T01539-433605. Traditional Ambleside hotel with good restaurant and comfortable rooms.
B **Wasdale Head Inn** Wasdale Head, T01946-726229. Venerable walkers and climbers pub with a serious atmosphere and comfortable rooms.
C **Claremont House**, Compston Rd, Ambleside, T01539-433448, www.claremontambleside.co.uk. Family-run, friendly atmosphere, 8 rooms most with en suite bathrooms.
C **Lingmell House**, Wasdale Head, T01946-726261. Booking well ahead advised for this charming B&B in remote Wasdale.
F **Ambleside YHA**, Waterhead, Ambleside, T01539-432304. With 245 beds in 43 2-5-bedded rooms and 16 6-8 bedded rooms, near the landing stages for the lakes.
F **Elterwater YHA**, Elterwater, nea Ambleside, T01539-437245. With 45 beds in the last village in Langdale, very popular with climbers.
F **Langdale YHA**, High Close, Loughrigg, near Ambleside, T01539-432304. With 96 beds in a Victorian mansion owned by the National Trust, lower than the other Langdale hostel.
F **Wastwater YHA**, Wasdale Hall, Wasdale, T01946-726222. 50 beds in an imposing National Trust property on the edge of Wastwater. One of the most dramatically situated in the Lakes.

Grasmere p454

A **The Grasmere Hotel**, Broadgate, Grasmere, T01539-435277, www.grasmerehotel.co.uk. Quiet location with 13 rooms, Victorian house renowned for quality of its food.

A **Lancrigg Country House Hotel**, Easedale Rd, T01539-435317, www.lancrigg.co.uk. Snuggled into the Easedale valley, with a particularly good vegetarian restaurant.

A **Michael's Nook**, Grasmere, T01539-435496. Michelin-starred cuisine at this Victorian country house hotel. Dress smart.

B **Bridge House Hotel**, Church Bridge, Grasmere, T01539-435425, www.bridgehousegrasmere.co.uk. Family-owned hotel beside the River Rothay with peaceful woodland gardens.

B **Old Dungeon Ghyll Hotel**, Great Langdale, T01534-937272, www.odg.co.uk. Basic but practical enough, with 14 bedrooms and the hiker's bar in a magnificent position beneath the Langdale Pikes.

B **Traveller's Rest Inn**, Grasmere on the outskirts on the A591, T0800-0199740. 16th-century inn at foot of Helvellyn, real fires, home-cooked food.

C **The Harwood**, Red Lion Sq, Grasmere, T01539-435248, www.harwoodhotel.co.uk. Small, family-run quiet guesthouse in the centre of the village with 7 rooms.

F **Grasmere Butterlip How YHA**, Easedale Rd, Grasmere, T01539-435316. With 82 beds close to the heart of the village and very popular with walkers.

F **Grasmere Thorney How YHA**, Easdale Rd, Grasmere T01539-435316. With 53 beds, smaller and more secluded than the other Grasmere hostel, also a favourite with ramblers.

Hawkshead and Coniston p454

B **Coniston Lodge Hotel**, Station Rd, Coniston, T01539-441201, www.coniston- lodge.com. Award-winning 6-room hotel with superb cooking, set back from the village.

B **Waterhead Hotel**, Coniston, T01539-441244 www.pofr.com. A 21-room hotel lying in its own grounds with private jetty and rowing boats. Owned by the Post Office Fellowship of Remembrance.

C **Arrowfield Country Guest House**, 1½ miles towards Torver, T01539-441741. A 5-bedroomed house in a quiet location, lovely views, log fires and delicious breakfast.

F **Coniston Coppermines YHA**, Coniston, T01539-441261. With 28 beds in a beautiful mountain setting above Coniston village, ideal for the taking on the Coniston Old Man.

F **Coniston Holly How YHA**, Far End, Coniston T01539-441323. With 60 beds and within walking distance of the village.

F **Hawkshead YHA**, Hawkshead, T01539-436293. With 109 beds in a Regency mansion overlooking Esthwaite Water, popular with families.

Keswick and around p455

L **Underscar Manor**, Applethwaite, T01768-775000. Reputable, expensive restaurant and stunning lake views from this Italianate Victorian mansion.

A **Lyzzick Hall**, Under Skiddaw, T01768-772277. More superb views and a beautiful garden at this old manor house hotel with a swimming pool.

C **Greystones Hotel**, Ambleside Rd, Keswick, T01768-773108. Small, well-appointed guesthouse within walking distance of both town centre and lake.

C **Hazeldene Hotel**, The Heads, Keswick, T01768-772106. Views over the fells on the outskirts of town, family-run, and good food.

F **Borrowdale YHA**, Longthwaite, Borrowdale, T01768-777257. With 88 beds in 2,4,6 and 8-bedded rooms, a cedarwood cabin beside the river.

F **Buttermere YHA**, Buttermere, T01768-770245. With 70 beds in an old farmhouse at the foot of Honister Pass.

F **Derwentwater YHA**, Barrow House, Borrowdale, Nr Keswick, T01768-777246. With 88 beds, in an 18th-century mansion overlooking the lake.

F **Ennerdale YHA**, Cat Crag, Ennerdale, T01946-861237. With 24 beds, basic facilities at the head of the lake.

F **Honister Hause YHA**, Seatoller, Nr Keswick, T01768-777267. With 26 beds, high up on Honister Pass, within strenuous walking distance of the highest summits in the Lakes.

F **Keswick YHA**, Station Rd, Keswick, T01768-772484. With 91 beds close to the river and the centre of town.

F **Thirlmere YHA**, Old School, Stanah Cross, near Keswick, T01768-773224. With 28 beds in an old schoolhouse.

Ullswater *p456*

L **Sharrow Bay Country House Hotel**, T01768-486301. A 4-star hotel on the lake shore with a solid and traditional Michelin-starred restaurant. 26 bedrooms in 4 different locations near the lake.

A **Glenridding Hotel**, T01768-482228, www.glenriddinghotel.co.uk. Surrounded by mountains and the lake, warm friendly atmosphere, with a swimming pool.

A **Howtown Hotel**, Howtown, on Ullswater, T01768-486514, www.howtownhotel.co.uk. Traditional and friendly hotel in a fabulous position on the southern shore of the Lake. £58 per person for dinner, B&B. Recommended.

C **Netherdene Guest House**, Troutbeck, T01768- 483475, www.netherdene.co.uk. Traditional Lakeland country house, great views, rooms with en suite facilities.

C **White Lion**, Patterdale, T01768-482214. About a mile from the end of Ullswater, a very popular pub with walkers.

F **Helvellyn YHA**, Greenside, Glenridding, T01768-482269. With 64 beds at 900 ft, base camp for the mountain above Ullswater.

F **Patterdale YHA**, Patterdale, T01768-482394. With 82 beds in a Scandinavian-looking building.

F **Skiddaw House YHA**, Bassenthwaite, near Keswick T01697-478325. With 20 beds beneath the summit of Skiddaw.

Camping Barn, Swirral, on the Helvyllyn Range, near the routes to Striding Edge and Ullswater. Sleeps 8.

Eating

Kendal and around *p449*

£££ **Moon**, 129 Highgate, T01539-729254. A long-standing local favourite doing modern European cooking in a civilized environment (about £30 a head).

££ **Déjà Vu**, 124 Stricklandgate, T01539-724843. A small French restaurant doing vegetarian and Spanish evenings as well, with starters at about £5, mains around £11. Booking essential at the weekends.

££ **Paulo Gianni's**, 21a Stramongate, T01539-725858. Popular local Italian with good pizzas and pasta as well as daily specials of Mediterranean food.

££ **Shang Thai**, 54 Stramongate, T01539-720387. The only Thai restaurant in Kendal, very laid-back and reasonably priced.

Windermere and Bowness-on-Windermere *p452*

££ **Jambo**, Victoria St, is close to the station, Windermere, T01539-443429. Freshly prepared British food with fine wines.

££ **Jericho's**, Birch St, T01539-4442522. Well-prepared modern British food in the middle of town (about £12 main courses).

££ **Oregano**, 4 High St, T01539-444954. Don't only do Italian food but what they do they do well (mains about £12).

Ambleside *p453*

££ **Glass House**, Rydal Rd, T01539-432137. Modern imaginative menu and décor in a lovely setting, unfussy and reasonably priced.

££ **Lucy's on a Plate**, Church St, Ambleside, T01539-431191. Café by day (bacon and goat's cheese rösti £6), and other eclectic fare, 'tickled trout' £13.

££ **The Queen's Head**, Townhead, Troutbeck, T01539-432174. A 17th-century inn with excellent food.

££ **Zeffirelli's**, Compston Rd, Ambleside, T01539-433845. Wholesome wholefood pizzeria unusually enough with a 2-screen cinema attached, right in the village centre.

£ **Apple Pie**, Rydal Rd, Ambleside, T01539-433679. Excellent home-made cakes, breads and sandwiches in this popular little café.

£ **Mr Dodds Restaurant**, Rydal Rd, Ambleside, T01539-432134. Morning coffee, lunch or evening menu, vegetarian dishes, pizza to eat in or take-away.

Grasmere *p454*

£££ **Michael's Nook Hotel**, see above, T01539-435496. Gourmet option, about £50 a head, dress smart and booking essential.

££ **Cumbria Carvery**, Stock Lane, Grasmere, T01539-435005. Daytime canteen and nightime table service for some decent English food, about £15 a head.

££ **Rowan Tree**, Church Bridge, Stock Lane, Grasmere, T01539-435528. About £20 for a 3-course vegetarian meal just off the main road. Booking weekends advisable.

Keswick and around *p455*

££ **Luca's** Greta Bridge, High Hill, T01768 774621. Popular local Italian restaurant, family- owned and run, with home-made pizzas & pastas, as well as steaks, fish and vegetarian menu (about £20 a head).

££ **Morrel's**, 34 Lake Rd, T01768-772666. Well-respected traditional British restaurant on the road down to the theatre, (starters £5), braised oxtail (£12.50) and plenty of vegetarians. Weekend booking essential.

Entertainment

Keswick and around *p455*

Alhambra Cinema, St John's St, with interesting screenings of mainstream and arthouse films by the Keswick Film Club, T01768-772398 www.keswickfilmclub.org.

Theatre by the Lake, Lakeside, Keswick T01768-774411, www.theatrebythelake.com Middle scale touring productions at one of the most prettily situated theatres in the UK.

Festivals and events

Windermere and Bowness-on-Windermere *p452*

Mid-Sep-Oct Bowness Theatre Festival, www.oldlaundrytheatre.com or find details from the The World of Beatrix Potter. Usually features some top names in performance, with poetry readings, films and interesting talks.

Activities and tours

Hawkshead and Coniston *p454*

Coniston Boating Centre, T01539-441366. Day boats for hire.

Coniston Launch, T01539-436216, www.conistonlaunch.co.uk also operate trips right round the lake.

National Trust Steam Yacht Gondola, Coniston to Brantwood T01539-463850. Round-trip £5. Apr-Oct 5 sailings daily 1100, 1200, 1400, 1500, 1600 from Coniston. The National Trust also operates a free bus service on Sun Apr-Oct between Hawkshead, Tarn Hows and Coniston.

Directory

Bike hire Biketreks Cycle Centre, Compston Rd, Ambleside, T01539-431245. **Country Lanes Cycle Centre**, Windermere Railway Station, Windermere, T01539-444544. **Easy Riders**, Waterhead, Ambleside, T01539-432902. **Grizedale Mountainbikes**, Holehird Farm, Patterdale Rd, Windermere, T01539-447302..

The Lune and Eden Valleys

→*Colour map 3 & 5*

Much less visited than the more dramatic Lake District on the other side of the M6, the valleys of the Lune and the Eden are a lovely pair, embracing one of the most charming forgotten corners of the country. The Lune rises on the Shap Fells in the western Lake District, flowing south through beautiful Borrowdale and down the western flank of the rolling Howgill Fells. It passes below the mountain town of Sedbergh, through doughty little Kirkby Lonsdale and on to the sea at Lancaster. The Eden rises in Mallerstang and flows north past Kirkby Stephen, round the northern edge of the Howgills, through Appleby-in-Westmorland, around Penrith and on to meet the sea beyond Carlisle in the Solway Firth. As well as the wonderful walking country on the fells above, it's the small towns like Sedbergh, Kirkby Stephen, and Appleby-in-Westmorland that make a holiday here so rewarding. Among the most unspoiled in the country, almost untouched by 19th-century heavy industry or 20th-century development, they have so far also managed to resist the worst excesses of 21st-century commercialization. Penrith sits on the northeastern edge of the Lake District on the M6, a convenient and businesslike market town but not much else. To its northwest, reached along a spectacular road, Alston is a high, riverside old town near the meeting of three counties ▸▸ *For Sleeping, Eating and other listings, see pages 462-463.*

Ins and outs

Getting there By **road**, both valleys are surprisingly easily reached off the M6 motorway from the south. From the east the A66 dual carriageway follows an old packhorse route, roaring across the North Pennines from Scotch Corner, near Richmond in North Yorkshire, to Penrith via Appleby. The A685 and then A683 are scenic roads south of the A66 at Brough passing through Kirkby Stephen, Sedbergh and Kirkby Lonsdale. **Stagecoach Darlington** run the 564 3 times a day Mon-Sat from Kendal and Oxenholme mainline station to Sedbergh, Kirkby Stephen, Brough and Darlington. More frequent **buses** link Brough with Appleby and Penrith (also on the West Coast Main Line). The Leeds-Settle-Carlisle **railway**, one of the most scenic in England, is run by **Arriva Train Northern**, T01729-822007. Useful stations are Appleby, Kirkby Stephen, and Garsdale (near Sedbergh). Kirkby Stephen station is a mile and a half south of the town itself, on the A685. Garsdale is the closest station to Sedbergh, but the town is most easily reached by bus from Kirkby Stephen, the next stop up the line towards Carlisle, or from Oxenholme mainline station near Kendal. Penrith (about 4 hrs from London Euston via Preston) is the on the same line as Oxenholme, a useful stop for Ullswater and the northeastern Lake District.

Getting around The local **bus** network is reliable but not frequent. Unfortunately a car is really the only convenient way to explore the area. Cycling is a workable option in the summer, but the big roads can be intimidating. Cycle hire from **Stephen McWirter**, Station Yard, Kirkby Stephen, T01768-372442.

Information Appleby TIC ⓘ *Moot Hall, Boroughgate, T01768-351117, www.applebytown.org.uk, Apr-Oct daily 1000-1700, Nov-Mar Fri, Sat 1000-1500.* **Kirkby Stephen** TIC ⓘ *Market Square, T01768-371199, www.visiteden.co.uk, Easter-Oct daily 1000-1700, Nov-Mar Mon-Sat 1000-1300.* **Yorkshire Dales National Park and TIC** ⓘ *72 Main St, Sedbergh, T01539-620125.* **Penrith TIC** ⓘ *Penrith Museum, T01768-867466. Easter-Oct daily 0930-1700, Nov-Easter Mon-Sat 0930-1600.* **Alston TIC** ⓘ *Town Hall, T01434-3882244. Easter-Oct daily 0930-1700, Nov-Easter Mon, Wed-Sat 0930-1200.*

Sedbergh to Kirkby Stephen

Sedbergh is a very attractive place, a mountain market town at the meeting point of four valleys and four rivers and very popular with hikers. Hidden away up Garsdale in the valley of the River Dee, 5 miles southeast of Sedbergh, is the small village of **Dent**. Once a centre of the local knitting industry – wonderful Herdwick wool sweaters – it's still a popular corner with woolly ramblers, in the far northwest of the Yorkshire Dales National Park, and accessible on the Leeds-Settle-Carlisle railway. The station is a 4-mile walk from the village, in the lea of **Widdale Fell**.

The lovely A683 continues for another 14 miles up to Kirkby Stephen, a solid-looking town which is still very much the working centre of its region, yet to have its character completely altered by the demands of tourism. On the main Market Square a Georgian loggia stands in front of the impressive church, which contains a mysterious eighth-century Anglo-Danish relic called the **Loki Stone**. The only one of its type in England, it's a remarkable survival, apparently the earliest known depiction of the devil in human form – the troublemaking Norse god Loki in horns and chains.

The source of the river Eden lies some 10 miles south up the Mallerstang valley via Outhgill on the B6259. The river is already a significant obstacle as it flows past the east side of the town. Three miles down this mysterious and lonely valley road are the ruins of little **Pendragon Castle**. On a small mound beside the river, this was supposedly where King's Arthur's father Uther was poisoned. Like the castles at Brough, Appleby and Brougham, it was restored in the 17th century by the indefatigable wandering medievalist Lady Anne Clifford. Since then it has become a very quiet and picturesque ruin.

Appleby-in-Westmorland

Tucked into a loop in the river 12 miles northwest of Kirkby, Appleby-in- Westmorland is a delightful old red stone riverside town, solid and castellated. Once the county town of Westmorland, it's a sort of mini-Edinburgh with its castle (closed for redevelopment at time of writing) at the top of its cobbled main street, Boroughgate, columns at either end marking the extent of the market and battered old church behind a colonnade at the bottom. The church, like the castle, was restored by Lady Anne Clifford, and contains one of the oldest organ cases in the country, as well as the memorial chapel to the great woman herself. The draped effigy of her mother was apparently carved by the same hand as that of Elizabeth I in Westminster Abbey.

Penrith and around

Sitting next to junction 40 on the M6, Penrith is a fairly unprepossessing market town on the main west coast railway line that makes a useful launch pad for Ullswater and the northeastern Lakes. There's not a huge amount to see in the town, apart from the small Penrith Museum, T01768-867466, and the ruined castle, but its specialist shops make for some rewarding browsing. Southeast of town, however, **Brougham Castle** ⓘ *(EH), T01768-862488, Apr-Sep daily 1000-1800, Oct daily 1000-1700, £2.20, concessions £1.70, children £1.10*, is beautifully situated on the banks of the River Eamont. The castle was involved in border disputes throughout its early history, and the ruin was taken in hand by Lady Anne Clifford in the late 17th century. Today it remains one of the most impressive examples of her restorations.

Northwest of Penrith, the A686 heads up on to the North Pennines via the village of Melmerby (famous for its organic bakery) affording spectacular views over the Lakeland hills and Eden Valley before it reaches Alston, the highest market town in England. It's a serious stone-built old-fashioned place in the middle of nowhere on the South Tyne River and the Pennine Way, close to the meeting of Cumbria, Northumberland and County Durham.

Sleeping

Sedbergh to Kirkby Stephen *p461*

B **Augill Castle**, South Stainmore, near Kirkby Stephen, T01768-341937, www.stayinacastle.com. Wonderfully converted old castle with friendly hosts, fluffy towels in the bathrooms and happy breakfast atmosphere in the old dining room. Recommended.

B **The Black Swan Hotel**, Ravenstonedale, near Kirkby Stephen, T01539-623204, www.blackswanhotel.com. Privately owned, comfortable hotel in a Victorian building in the middle of a quiet village. Recommended.

D **Croglin Castle Hotel**, South Rd, Kirkby Stephen, T01768-371389. Decent pub hotel with good food, convenient for the station.

F **Bents Camping Barn** T01768-371760. £4 per person per night, £48 for sole use, with 12 beds. A 17th-century barn on the edge of the Howgill Fells, 5 miles from Kirkby Stephen railway station, on the Coast to Coast walk.

F **Dentdale YHA**, Cowgill, Dent, Nr Sedbergh, T01539-625251. An old shooting lodge a couple of miles from Dent station, with 38 beds in 2 8-bedded, one 10-bedded and one 12-bedded room.

F **F Kirkby Stephen YHA**, Market St, Kirkby Stephen, T01768-371793. Right in the middle of town, a mile and a half from the station, in a converted chapel with 44 beds in 2, 4, 6, and 8 bedded rooms.

Appleby-in-Westmorland *p462*

B **Royal Oak**, Bongate, Appleby, T01768-351463. The best bet for staying above a pub, does good and imaginative pub food freshly prepared daily. Recommended.

B **Tufton Arms Hotel**, Market Sq, Appleby, T01768-351593. Rambling old hotel right in the middle of town, with good value lunchtime snacks, comfortable rooms and conservatory restaurant.

C **Old Hall Farmhouse**, Bongate, Appleby, T01768-351773. A smaller B&B operation on the outskirts of town.

D **Bongate House**, Bongate, Appleby, T01768-351245. A large family-run guesthouse in a fine Georgian building on the northern edge of town.

Eating

Sedbergh to Kirkby Stephen *p461*

££**Croglin Castle Hotel**, Kirkby Stephen, T01768-371389. Does a very good modern British menu in the evenings, and for lunch on Fri, Sat and Sun.

£**Sun Inn**, Dent, T01539-625208. A cosy, beamed pub with reliable food and its own-brew ales.

Appleby-in-Westmorland *p462*

££**Hoagy's Bistro**, High Wiend, Appleby, T01768- 352368. Quiet and friendly with a varied menu served evenings only.

£**Royal Oak**, Bongate, Appleby, T01768-351463. Does good and imaginative pub food freshly prepared daily.

Festivals

Appleby-in-Westmorland *p462*

Jun Appleby Horse Fair. A traditional Gypsy horse fair that usually takes place at the end of the first week of the month, contact TIC for details. See the ponies being washed in the Eden ready for sale.

The Cumbrian Coast

→ *Colour map 3 & 5*

Between the Lakeland mountains and the Irish Sea, the Cumbrian Coast is a strange, embattled, but in places very beautiful region, largely overlooked by many Lakeland tourists. Most immediately attractive and accessible are its southern fringes, known as the Furness Peninsulas. This broken, heavily indented coastline spreads out into the sandflats of Morecambe Bay around the shipbuilding and gas-terminal port of Barrow-in-Furness, defined by the silted estuaries of the rivers Kent, Leven and Duddon. The village of Cartmel is still the main attraction, along with the famous gardens at Holker Hall. The larger promontory to the west boasts the lively market town of Ulverston before petering out at with industrial sprawl of Barrow at its tip. The port does draw in a few visitors with its interesting dockside museum, some superb nature reserves and small boat trips out to Piel Island and its ruined castle. Broughton-in-Furness is a dignified little town that sits at the root of the peninsula near the mouth of the Duddon. The coast road and railway then sneak round the bulk of Black Combe, with its panoramic views, and head north, past Ravenglass, where Eskdale meets the sea, to St Bees Head, the starting point for Wainwright's Coast-to-Coast walk. ▸▸ *For Sleeping, Eating and other listings, see pages 465-466.*

Ins and outs

Getting there From Junction 36 on the M6 the A590 leads to Ulverston and Barrow-in-Furness. Off this big **road**, the A595 is reached via the A5092 and runs all the way round the coast back to Carlisle at the top of the M6. **National Express**, T08705-808080, run **coaches** to Kendal from where the X35 runs to Ulverston and Barrow-in-Furness. Cartmel can be reached by bus from Grange-over-Sands. The Furness Line from Lancaster to Carlisle also runs right round the coast, calling at Grange-over-Sands, Ulverston, Barrow-in-Furness, Ravenglass, Seascale, St Bees, Whitehaven, and Maryport, among other places.

Getting around Once again, a **car** is the most convenient way of exploring the coast, although the rail and bus service is more reliable than elsewhere in Cumbria.

Information Grange-over-Sands TIC ⓘ *Victoria Hall, Main St, T01539-534026.* **Barrow-in-Furness TIC** ⓘ *Town Square, T01229-894784, www.barrowtourism.co.uk* **Ulverston TIC** ⓘ *Coronation Hall, T01229-587120. Mon-Sat 0900-1700, www.lakelandgateway.info* **Cockermouth TIC** ⓘ *01900-822634.*

Cartmel and around

Cartmel is the most popular and also one of the most attractive little villages in these parts, clustered around the remains of its 12th-century **priory** ⓘ *(NT) Cartmel Priory Gatehouse, Cavendish St, T01539-536874, Easter-Oct Wed-Sun 1000-1600, Nov-Mar Sat, Sun 1000-1600*. The church survived the Dissolution, thanks to also being the place of worship for the parish, and is still a very fine building indeed. Restored by the Preston family of Holker Hall in the 17th century, its bell tower sits at an angle to the main church. Inside, highlights include the stained glass, medieval chancel, Jacobean screen and carved choir stalls. The gatehouse of the priory is also still standing, thanks to being a grammar school in the 17th and 18th centuries, and is now in the care of the National Trust, containing displays on the history of the village, priory and the peninsula.

Five miles west of Grange on the B5277, the main part of **Holker Hall** ⓘ *T01539-558328, www.holker-hall.co.uk, Apr-Oct Mon-Fri, Sun 1000-1800, £7.25, children £4.50*, was built in the 1870s for William Cavendish, the Seventh Duke of Devonshire, and represents Victorian country house style at its best. Still the home of Lord and Lady Cavendish, the interior of the house is warm and welcoming, decorated with antiques and Old Masters, but it's the gardens that have made the house famous. They feature a limestone cascade, sunken garden and a fountain, as well as the **Lakeland Motor Museum** ⓘ *T01539-558509, www.lakelandmotormuseum.co.uk, open same hours as hall, inclusive tickets available*, where a variety of veteran vehicles share space with an exhibition devoted to Donald Campbell, the waterspeed recordbreaker. The **garden festival** held in the first week of June is one of the most prestigious in the country.

Ulverston

From Holker Hall, the shifting sands of the Leven estuary can be crossed on foot with the guidance of Mr Raymond Porter, T01229-580935. It's a wonderful and bracing way to reach Ulverston or Conishead Priory on the opposite bank. Ulverston is a delightful old market town, complete with cobbled streets, ancient alleys and a vigorous local life. The town is overlooked from the north by the monument to the founder of the Royal Geographical Society, Sir John Barrow, on Hoad Hill, which commands fine views. The other great man associated with Ulverston is George Fox, who founded Quakerism at Swarthmoor Hall to the south of the town. The **Cumbria Way** is a long-distance footpath that runs from here to Carlisle for 70 miles.

Barrow-in- Furness

At the end of the peninsula Barrow-in-Furness was developed in the mid-19th century by William Cavendish of Holker Hall as a port for iron ore and then steel. It became one of the main shipbuilding yards in the country and now relies on the handling of nuclear fuel and gas for most of its income. The town's main attraction is the **Dock Museum** ⓘ *T01229-894444, Apr-Oct Tue-Fri 1000-1700, Sat, Sun 1100-1700, Nov-Mar Wed-Fri 1030-1600, Sat, Sun 1100-1630, free*, with models of the ships that have been constructed here, and interesting displays on the development of the town.

The other main draw from Barrow is the 14th-century **Piel Castle**, T01229-835809, now in ruins, built to defend Furness Abbey from the Scots. It sits lonely and remote on Piel Island, reachable by an erratic small-boat ferry from Roa Island. On the island, which was given to the people of Barrow by the Duke of Buccleuch in memory of their dead in the First World War, the *Ship Inn* provides hearty refreshments.

Around Black Combe

Just within the National Park, at the top of the peninsula, **Broughton-in- Furness** is an old stone-built town with an attractive market square where the fish slabs, stocks and obelisk celebrating the coronation of George III still survive. From here the A593 runs up into the Lake District and Coniston Water, a small road branching off left up the relatively unexplored valley of the river Lickie with walks above Broughton Mills.

Just before Duddon Bridge, on the main A595 coast road, another small road leads north up the Duddon Valley to **Ulpha**. A favourite of Wordsworth's, the rolling fells embracing the Duddon Valley remain surprisingly undiscovered compared to much of the Lake District. The coast road continues through Whicham, from where an easy path leads up to the **Black Combe**, rising to 1970 ft and providing one of the most spectacular views in the country from its heathery summit. On a clear day the panorama includes the Isle of Man and Ireland beyond to the west, as well as the main peaks of the Lake District to the east.

Eskdale

Ten miles further up the coast, **Ravenglass** ⓘ *T01229- 717171, www.ravenglass-railway.co.uk, Apr-Oct daily, Nov-Dec and Mar Sat, Sun, phone for running times, £7.80, concessions £6.90, children £3.90*, is a little village sitting at the bottom of Eskdale. From here the road climbs up the valley of the Esk and into the Lakes via Hardknott and Wrynose passes, the only road eastwards and hence often jammed. (The only other way back into the Lakes is all the way round to the north via Cockermouth and Keswick). The valley of the Mite, next door to the Esk, carries a miniature railway 7 miles from Ravenglass to Boot, originally built to carry iron ore, and known as **La'al Ratty**. It's a big hit with kids.

More family fun is on offer at **Muncaster Castle** ⓘ *Muncaster Castle, T01229-717614, www.muncaster.co.uk, Mar-Oct Gardens and Owl Centre daily 1030-1800 (or dusk if earlier), Castle Mon-Fri, Sun 1030-1800 (or dusk if earlier) Castle and Gardens,£7.80, children £5, family £21*, home of the World Owl Centre, the largest collection of the wise birds in the world, and there's also the opportunity of taking an interactive wand tour of the castle's interior, still home to the Pennington family after 800 years.

St Bees Head

Somehow there's a bleak and sadly unprepossessing tone to the rest of the Cumbrian Coast to the north. The relatively dramatic cliffs of St Bees Head are a glorious exception, popular with puffins and seals, and there's an excellent little overhanging cave system at **Fleswick Beach**. This is close to the start of Wainwright's Coast-to-Coast walk to Robin Hood's Bay on the North Yorkshire coast.

Cockermouth

Thirteen miles northeast of Whitehaven and 7 miles inland, Cockermouth is a hard-bitten but good-looking farming town. Its main visitor attraction is the National Trust's **Wordsworth House** ⓘ *Main St, T01900-824805*, where Dorothy and William were born. Their large house has been filled with a few momentoes, but it's not the most engaging of stops on the Wordsworth trail. Monthly changing exhibitions by accomplished local artists can be seen at the impressive Georgian home of the **Castlegate House Gallery** ⓘ *T01900- 822149, www.castlegatehouse.co.uk*.

Sleeping

Cartmel and around *p464*

B **Aynsome Manor Hotel**, Cartmel, T01539-536653, F536016. A small family-run country house hotel, cosy and wood-panelled with glorious views from the garden and good food in the quiet restaurant.

C **Cavendish Arms**, Cartmel, T01539-536240. An old locals' pub with character in the middle of the village, fine real ales (including their own brew) and a back garden.

C **Masons Arms**, Strawberry Bank, Cartmel Fell, T01539-568486, www.masonarms.co.uk. A very popular own-brew pub with comfortable good value rooms, reliable food and views all around.

Ulverston *p464*

A **Bay Horse Hotel**, Canal Foot, Ulverston, T01229-583972, www.thebayhorsehotel.co.uk. Overlooks the estuary and has a confidently ambitious but quite expensive restaurant (about £40 a head).

Eskdale *p465*

C **Brookhouse Inn**, T01946-723288, www.brookhouseinn.co.uk, on the Eskdale Green to Hard Knott Road is a popular choice with walkers.

D **Ross Garth Guest House**, Main St, Ravenglass, T01229-717275. Has comfortable rooms, also in the middle of the village.

F **Eskdale YHA**, T01946-723219. The local youth hostel.

Camping

Hollins Farm Campsite, at the other end of the Esk valley, in Boot, T01946-723253. Idyllic pitches for about £5 a night.

Hadrian's Wall

→*Colour map 5*

Built by the Romans and their slaves, Hadrian's Wall marked the northern boundary of their empire in the second and third centuries AD and was their most impressive engineering achievement in Northern Europe. Strategic considerations at the time of its construction mean that its route still commands some of the best views between Carlisle and Newcastle. Carlisle advertises itself as a 'great border city' with some justification. This strategic town near the mouth of the River Eden was continually at the centre of border disputes right up to the rebellion of Bonnie Prince Charlie in 1745. Today it's the county town of Cumbria and still a fairly forbidding place despite a clutch of attractions worth an afternoon of anyone's time: the cathedral, castle and local museum and art gallery called Tullies House. Stretching away to the east of Carlisle and really the best reason for a visit to the city, the World Heritage Site of Hadrian's Wall is a crumbling relic, 73 miles long, still standing up to 6 of its original 10 ft in some places, hugging the high ground all the way to Newcastle. The most complete remains of forts are at Birdoswald, Housesteads and Chesters, with a superb stretch of the wall itself near Walltown Crags. Hexham is a good-looking Abbey town close to the wall above the river Tyne. Further east, Newcastle upon Tyne is the most vigorous city in the North, with a wealth of new developments and an optimistic, forward-looking spirit born out of the ashes of industrial decline. ▸▸ *For Sleeping, Eating and other listings, see pages 468-469.*

Ins and outs

Getting there By **road** Carlisle is at the top of the M6 motorway, a little over 300 miles from London, about 5 hrs' drive. Hadrian's Wall is easily reached along the impressive A69 to Newcastle upon Tyne (46 miles to the east). Most of the major Roman sites are reached along the B6318, a minor road following the course of the one built by General Wade to suppress the Scots under Oliver Cromwell. **National Express** run 2 coaches to Carlisle from London Victoria at 0930 and 1030 arriving at 1610 and 1745 respectively, as well as a nightcoach leaving at 2230 arriving at 0505. **Coaches** also run from Carlisle to Leeds, Manchester and Birmingham, T08705-143219. Carlisle is on the main eastcoast line to Glasgow from London Euston. A branch line runs to Brampton, Haltwhistle, Reburn, Haydon Bridge, Hexham and Newcastle. The Leeds-Settle-Carlisle **railway** is easily the most scenic route to the city, www.settle-carslisle.co.uk. **Virgin Trains** serve Carlisle direct from London Euston (3 hrs 40 mins) or more frequently with a change at Preston (4 hrs 30 mins).

Getting around The centre of Carlisle is easily small enough to be explored on foot. Buses to Hadrian's Wall leave from Warwick Rd and the bus station on Lonsdale St. Hadrian's Wall **Bus** run by **Stagecoach** in Cumbria, T01434-322002, www.hadrians-wall.org. May-Sep links Carlisle with Hexham, Haltwhistle, Brampton and most of the main Roman sites. By *train*, the Tyne Valley Line to Newcastle from Carlisle calls at Brampton, Haltwhistle, Bardon Mill and Haydon Bridge.

Information Carlisle Visitor Centre ⓘ *Old Town Hall, T01228-625600, www.historic-carlisle.org.uk, Apr, Sep, Oct Mon-Sat 0930-1700, (May also open Sun 1030-1600); Jun, Jul, Aug Mon-Sat 0930-1730, Sun 1030-1600.* For cycle routes, bike hire and accommodation. **Haltwhistle TIC** ⓘ *Railway Station, Sation Rd, T01434-322002, open all year.* **Hexham TIC** ⓘ *Wentworth Car Park, T01434-652220, open all year.*

Carlisle

From Court Square in front of the train station, the round towers of the 19th-century **Citadel**, modelled on a gate erected by Henry VIII, make an imposing entrance to the town centre down English Street. A further 100 yds down, this pedestrianized area opens out into the market square. The cross from which Bonnie Prince Charlie proclaimed his father king still stands, as does the Elizabethan town hall, now home to the helpful Carlisle Visitor Centre. Next door is the **Guildhall**, T01228 534781, which has a small museum on the history of the building, dating from 1405.

Carlisle **cathedral** ⓘ *Carlisle Cathedral, T01228-48151, Mon-Sat 0730-1815, Sun 0730-1700, Prior's Kitchen, T01228-543251, open until 1630 Mon-Sat in summer, in the medieval undercroft of the Fratry*, is largely a 19th-century concoction although a fair amount of the medieval building survives. Built out of distinctive red sandstone, highlights of the interior include the East Window with its 14th-century stained glass images of the Last Judgement in the tracery lights, and the Brougham Triptych: a carved Flemish altarpiece depicting the Passion in St Wilfrid's Chapel.

Just down the road from the cathedral, the **Tullie House Museum** ⓘ *Castle St, T01228-534781, www.tulliehouse.co.uk, Apr-Oct Mon-Sat 1000-1700 (-1800 Jul and Aug), Sun 1200-1700 (1100-1800 Jul and Aug), Nov-Mar Mon-Sat 1000-1600, Sun 1200-1600, £5.20, concessions £3.60, children £2.60, family £14.50*, is an award-winning local history museum and art gallery. Vivid and imaginative interactive displays trace the history of the city from the Romans to the present day. As well as a reconstruction of part of Hadrian's Wall, there's a particularly strong section on the Border Reivers, the lawless families that terrorized this part of Britain for centuries.

Hadrian's Wall

Hadrian's Wall was built by order of the Emperor Hadrian following his visit to Britain in AD122. It was planned as a continuous wall with a mile castle every Roman mile, with two turrets between each castle, running some 80 miles from Maia (Bowness-on-Solway) past Luguvalium (Carlisle) to Segedunum (Newcastle upon Tyne). A new 81-mile National Trail now follows its entire length, through some of the bleakest landscape in Britain. The wall itself survives most visibly east of Birdoswald and west of Chesters along the military road built by General Wade, now the B6318.

At **Birdoswald** ⓘ *Birdoswald Roman Fort T01697-747602, Mar-Oct daily 1000-1730 (last admission 1700), Nov-Feb exterior only, £3, concessions £2.50, children £1.75, family £7.75*, the remains include a unique drill hall or basilica as well as the outline of granary buildings, at what was once a large fort designed for 1000 legionaries. The masonry of the fort's west gate is particularly impressive. There's also an interactive visitor centre.

At **Greenhead**, 'Gateway to Hadrian's Wall', the A69 becomes a spectacular road as it enters Northumberland, with distant views north and south over apparently endless wastes. The 400-m-long section of the wall at **Walltown Crags** is one of the most impressive: here it's still at least 7 ft wide and 5 ft high in places as it clings to the precipitous edge of the crags, including the remains of a turret.

Close to the Walltown Crags is the entertaining **Roman Army Museum** ⓘ *T01697-747485, www.vindolanda.com, daily mid-Feb to mid-Nov 1000-1700 (-1600 Feb, Nov, -1730 Apr, Sep, -1800 May, Jun, -1830 Jul, Aug), £3.30,* *concessions £2.90, children £2.20 (£6 with Vindolanda),* ideal for a rainy day. Exhibits include a Roman Army recruitment video, an Eagle's Eye View from a chopper along the wall, as well as some real Roman pottery amid the replicas of legionaries' uniforms and weaponry.

Two and a half miles northeast of Bardon Mill on the B6318, **Housesteads Roman Fort** ⓘ *Housesteads Roman Fort (EH and NT), T01434-344363, Apr-Sep daily 0930-1800, Oct daily 1000-1700, Nov-Mar daily 1000-1600, £3.10, concessions £2.30, children £1.60,* is the most complete of its type to survive in the UK. Four gates, the commandant's house, barracks, granaries, hospital and latrines can all be clearly discerned. Superb views from the site too.

Half a mile west of Chollerford on the B6318, is one of the best-preserved examples of a **cavalry fort** ⓘ *Chesters Roman Fort (EH), T01434-681379, Apr-Sep daily 0930-1800, Oct daily 1000-1700, Nov-Mar daily 1000-1600, £3.10, concessions £2.30, children £1.60,* featuring the remains of the baracks, bath-house and HQ. In a beautiful riverside setting, it overlooks the remains of the bridge that carried the wall over the Tyne. The **Clayton Collection** of the altars and sculptures found along the wall is also here.

Twenty miles west of Newcastle, **Hexham** is a dignified old town on the River Tyne blessed with a remarkable Abbey Church. The best approach by car is from the north and the A69, over an impressive bridge across the Tyne. The train station is on this side of town too, along with the Tynedale Retail Park, T01434-607788, full of discount high street stores. It's a short walk uphill beyond this eyesore into the town, up cobbled Hallgate (past the TIC) from the Safeway's car park. The first sight as such is the **Old Gaol**, the oldest recorded one of its type in England, purpose-built in 1332. It now contains the interesting **Border History Museum** ⓘ *T01434-652349, Apr-Oct daily 0930-1600, Nov, Feb, Mar Mon, Tue, Sat 0930-1600, £2, children £1, family £5,* where you can listen to the medieval punishment commentary, hear about cross border marriages in 1587 and find out what a Pele tower is'. Next up is the **Moot Hall** (which sometimes holds craft fairs, contact TIC for details) with a gateway into the main Market Place, with the **Abbey Church** ⓘ *Hexham Abbey, T01434- 602031, Oct-Apr daily 0930-1700, May-Sep 0930-1900,* on its far side, and an attractive public park behind. Founded in 674, the ruddy stoned old building dominates the town and contains rare Roman and Saxon carvings. One of the more remarkable commemorates a Roman standard bearer called Flavinus of the Cavalry Regiment of Petriana stationed on the wall, who died aged 25 during the first century AD. The Saxon Crypt of St Wilfrid also survives, open at 1100 and 1530 daily.

Sleeping

Carlisle *p467*

B **Number Thirty One**, 31 Howard Pl, Carlisle, T01228-597080, www. number31. freeservers.com. Three rooms in an elegant and tastefully decorated Victorian townhouse in the middle of the town. Book well ahead.

D **Langleigh House**, 6 Howard Pl, Carlisle, T01228-530440, www.langleighhouse .co.uk. Comfortable and roomy B&B in a pleasant part of town.

F **Carlisle YHA**, Old Brewery Residences, Bridge Lane, Caldewgate, Carlisle, T01228-597352. With 56 beds in single bedrooms, a university hall of residence.

Hadrian's Wall *p467*

L **Farlam Hall**, near Brampton, T01697-746234, www.farlamhall.co.uk. A Victorian country house hotel with amazing terraced gardens and very good walks round about.

B **Beaumont Hotel** Beaumont St, Hexham T01434-602331. Right in the middle of town, close by the abbey, with comfortable rooms.

C **Angus Hotel**, 14 Scotland Rd, Stanwix, T01228- 523546. 11 comfortable rooms with en suite bathrooms on the edge of the town.

C **Broomshaw Hill Farm**, a mile outside Haltwhistle, T01434-320866, www.broom shaw.co.uk. Farmhouse B&B near the wall.

D **West Close House**, Hextol Terrace, Hexham, T01434-603307. A non-smoking fairly central 1920s guesthouse off Allendale Rd, a 10-min walk east of the Abbey.

F **Greenhead YHA**, Greenhead, near Brampton, T01697-747401. With 40 beds in a converted Methodist chapel close to Hadrian's Wall.

F **Once Brewed YHA**, Military Rd, Bardon Mill, T01434- 344360. With 90 beds mainly in 4-bedded rooms, close to Vindolanda.

Eating

Carlisle *p467*

££ **Almond's Bistro**, 16 Scotland Rd, Stanwix, Carlisle, T01228-523546. Open until 2100 Mon-Sat. English and continental food served in the evenings with internet access thrown in.

££ **The Lemon Lounge**, 18 Fisher St, Carlisle, T01228-546363. Mediterranean food in a cheerful atmosphere with a bar area attached.

Hadrian's Wall *p467*

£ **Milecastle**, Military Rd, near Haltwhistle, T01434- 320682. An isolated and welcoming real ale pub with very decent pub grub, both at the bar, and in more sophisticated style in the restaurant.

£ **Wallace Arms**, Rowfoot, south of Haltwhistle off the A69 towards Alston, T01434-321872. A lovely old pub with excellent food and fine real ales.

Newcastle and Gateshead

➔*Colour map 5*

As Nottingham is to the East Midlands, so Newcastle upon Tyne is to the Northeast: on the up and up. In quite a spectacular position above the Tyne River, the once coal-blackened and grimey hub has become an upbeat weekending destination with twenty-somethings thanks to injections of European and lottery cash, a vigorous nightlife and the energy of its citizens, known as Geordies. First impressions are still unlikely to be very favourable: apart from its dramatic multilevel river crossings, including the famous mini prototype of Sydney Harbour bridge, the city is a mess of roundabouts, big roads and building sites. That said, it doesn't take long to discover what all the excitement is about: the opening of the Gateshead Millennium Bridge and Baltic Centre for Contemporary Art has confirmed the boom along the riverside in Newcastle and its fiercely competitive neighbour on the south bank, Gateshead, that's been underway for the last few years. It may be the latest addition to Newcastle's attractions, but even the older parts of the city centre have been caught up in the wave of optimism sweeping the region. Some say it all started with the Angel of the North, a giant gliderman sculpture perched above the A1. The rusty red steel thing sings in the wind, a potent symbol of this once heavily industrialized corner of the UK's vibrant hope for a less gritty future. ➧ *For Sleeping, Eating and other listings, see pages 473-475.*

Ins and outs

Getting there **Newcastle airport**, T0191-2144444, www.newcastleairport.com, is 6 miles northwest of the city centre at Woolsington, with a 25-min metro link into the city centre. Direct **flights** to destinations all over Europe. **Ferries** dock and depart from the International Ferry Terminal, Royal Quays, North Shields (7 miles east of Newcastle upon Tyne). **Fjord Line,** T0191-2961313, www.fjordline.com, operates car ferries to Bergen, Stavanger, and Haugesund in Norway. **DFDS Seaways,** T08705-333000, www.dfdsseaways.co.uk, sail to Kristiansand in Norway, Gothenberg in Sweden and Amsterdam in Holland. Bus 327 runs out to the terminal from Central Station, Gallowgate and the Youth Hostel prior to ferries' departure. The Percy Main Metro station is a 20-min walk from the terminal. Newcastle upon Tyne is a main stop on the London-York-Edinburgh **train** line. London King's Cross (3 hr 30 mins to 4 hrs), Edinburgh (1 hr 40 mins). Newcastle is on the A1, about 275 miles north of London, usually reached in 6 hrs on that **road**, sometimes less on the M1 via Leeds. **National Express,** T08705-808080, run coaches to most major towns and cities in the UK from Newcastle. Service 425 runs 5 times a day and once a night to London, taking about 7 hrs. » *For further details, see Transport, page 474.*

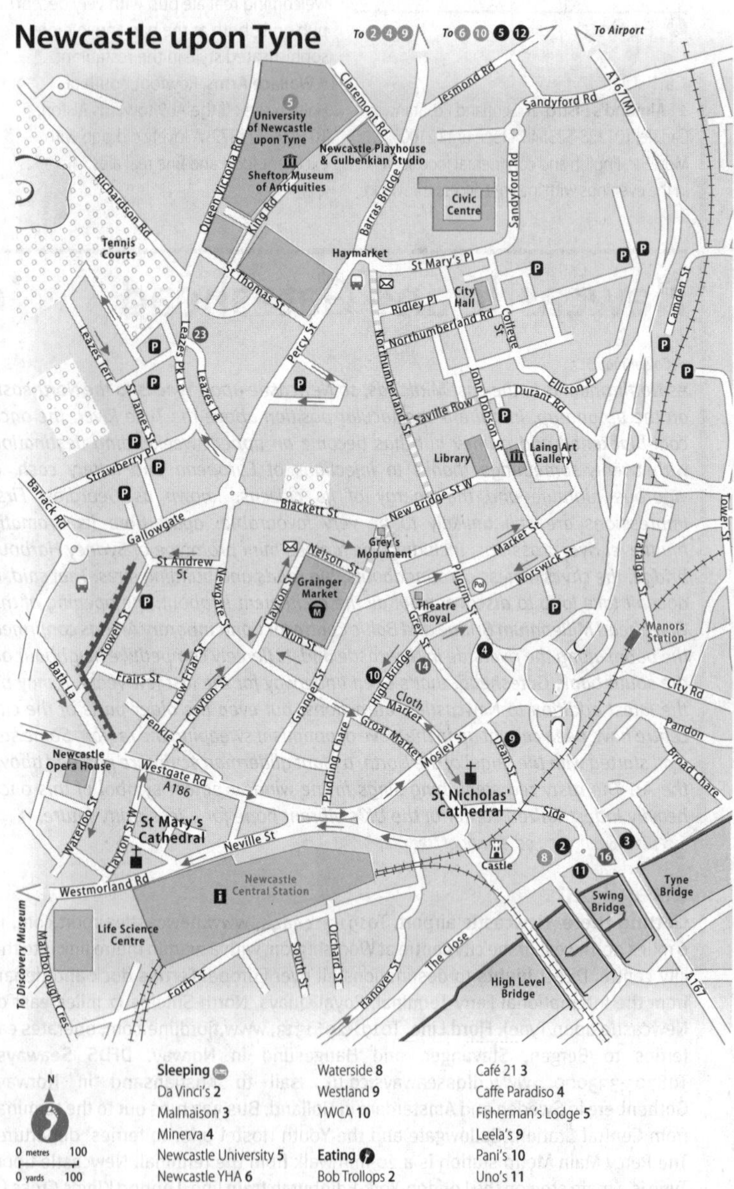

Getting around Although the areas of most interest to visitors are within walking distance of each other, the Newcastle **Metro** can be very useful for reaching Jesmond, the student district to the north of the universities. Regular buses operated by **Arriva Northumbria**, run to Hexham and Carlisle from the Haymarket bus station. The scenic route 888 run by **Wright Bros**, T0191-2778000, connects Newcastle with Keswick in the Lake District via Alston. The Kielder Bus Service 714 run by *Arriva* is a summer service on Sun to Keilder Water.

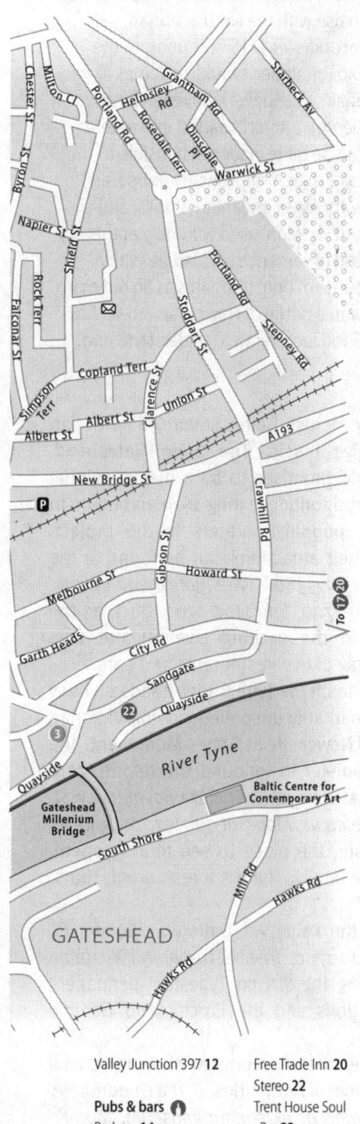

Valley Junction 397 **12**

Pubs & bars

Barluga **14**

Chase **16**

Cluny **17**

Free Trade Inn **20**

Stereo **22**

Trent House Soul Bar **23**

Information Newcastle TIC ⓘ *Central Station Concourse, Neville St, T0191-2778000. Mon-Sat 0930-1700. Also at 132 Grainger St. Mon-Sat 0930-1730 (Thu – 1930, Easter-Sep also Sun 1000-1600). www.newcastle.gov.uk*

Sights

Newcastle **Central Station** is quite a sight in itself: a grand survival of the city's industrial heyday, with lavish Victorian waiting rooms that have been converted into salubrious bars. Its main entrance is on Neville Street, which is a 10-minute walk away from most of the city's main sights.

From the Swing Bridge downstream to the new **Gateshead Millennium Bridge**, both banks of the Tyne have become the epicentre of 'Newcastle Gateshead', their wealth of new developments really 'buzzin'. The **Tyne Bridge**, symbol of the city, was completed in 1928 and looks beautiful at night. It's taken 70 years for it to be upstaged by the Gateshead Millennium Bridge half a mile upstream. The world's only tilting bridge, designed to look like a blinking eye, it too is impressively lit at night throwing patterns across the river. The footbridge leads over the river to the massive contemporary visual art space in the converted Baltic Flour Mill. The **Baltic Centre for Contemporary** Art ⓘ *South Shore Rd, Gateshead, T0191-4781810, www.balticmill.com, Mon-Sat 1000-1900, Thu 1000-2200*, houses temporary exhibtions and provides studio space for artists. Definitely worth a look with its restaurants, cafés, bar, bookshop, and library, it's the north's answer to Tate Modern in London, although without the permanent collection of modern art.

Northern accents

Although parodied by southerners as a succession of 'by gums, by 'eck and such like, the way people speak 'up North' is very finely differentiated. Within the space of any 20 square miles there are likely to be several different words for even the most common features of the local landscape. In Lancashire for example they call the hills 'fells', unlike the 'moors' of Yorkshire. Generally agreed upon across the region though are a 'beck' or stream, 'force' or waterfall, 'gill' or ravine, and 'tarn' or pond among many others mainly of Scandinavian origin. A law unto themselves are the Geordies. Regularly voted the most trustworthy telephone accent in the British Isles, Geordie is the native tongue of the citizens of Newcastle upon Tyne. Apparently the name, diminutive for George, dates back to the city's refusal to rise with the Northumbrian Jacobites in 1715 in support of the Old Pretender, would-be James III, against the new Hanoverian King George I. At its broadest, the accent can be quite incomprehensible to the English or Americans. Its peppered with 'Alreet' meaning Alright, and 'But' or 'Mon' used willy nilly at the end of sentences. A 'gadgie with a bottle of dog' translates as an old man with a bottle of Newcastle Brown Ale. Good luck trying to understand him.

Also on the Gateshead side of the river, across Baltic Square, Sir Norman Foster's glassy facility for all kinds of live music, **The Sage Gateshead**, T0191-4434555, is due to open in 2004/5 and promises to be a major regional centre for music-making of all kinds, with an auditorium seating 1670 and home to the Northern Sinfonia and Folkworks, the founding partners in the project. Information on the new developments and their attractions can be found at the **Gateshead Quays Visitor Centre** ⓘ *T0191-4775380, www.gateshead.gov.uk, Mon-Thu 0830-1700, Fri 0830-1630, Sat 1000-1700, Sun 1100-1700.* Back on the Newcastle bank, the **Quayside** is home to the exciting Live Theatre (see entertainment, below) as well as a glinting array of new restaurants and bars.

A walk up into town from the Quayside beneath the Tyne Bridge heads up busy Side and Dean Streets into Grey Street, a remarkably unspoiled curving Victorian greystone street that leads up to the centre of Newcastle at **Grey's Monument**. The statue was put up when Earl Grey was Prime Minister, in honour of the Reform Act of 1832. From around the same time is the **Theatre Royal** ⓘ *Theatre Royal, Grey St, T0870-9055060, www.theatre-royal-newcastle.co.uk, Mon-Sat 0900-2000*, with its lovely Victorian auditorium by Frank Matcham, the place to see touring opera, ballet, theatre and various spectacles for the family. There's a restaurant, tours, poetry and discussions and tearoom.

A short walk down New Bridge Street, the **Laing Art Gallery** ⓘ *Higham Pl, T0191-2327734, Mon-Sat 1000-1700, Sun 1400-1700, free*, is the grand Victorian repository of the city's art collection, including the 'Art on Tyneside' permanent collection, silver, glass and costume collections and the Proctor and Gamble Children's Gallery.

A good 15-minute walk further north, some other museums worth a look are all part of Newcastle University. The **Shefton Museum of Antiquities** ⓘ *The Quadrangle, University of Newcastle, T0191-2228996, www.ncl.ac.uk/shefton-museum, Mon-Fri 1000-1600, free*, is the major archaeological museum of the region, including artefacts found at Hadrian's Wall and a model of the thing itself.

Two other attractions close to the train station are the new **Life Science Centre** ⓘ *Times Sq, Scotswood Rd, T0191-2438223, www.centre-for-life.co.uk,*

Mon-Sat 1000-1800, Sun 1100-1800, £6.95, children £4.50, concessions £5.50, family £19.95, which promises 3-4 hours of entertainment, with motion rides, interactive touch-tellies and games broadly based on the subject that was once called biology. Great for kids, and adults who wouldn't recognize a double helix if it bit them, it's based around a cutting-edge life science research institute. The place becomes an open-air ice rink in winter.

A hundred yards west, the **Discovery Museum** ⓘ *Blandford Sq, T0191-2326789, Mon-Sat 1000-1700, Sun 1400-1700, free*, is a recently refurbished interactive museum telling the story of Newcastle from the Romans to the present day. Filled with reconstructions, it offers the chance to re-enact the tales of its characters and includes the Turbina Display – built on the Tyne, she was the first ship to be powered by steam turbines and was the fastest of her time. In the Science Maze, there are hands-on demonstrations of scientific and engineering principles, including the waterpower inventions of celebrated Geordie William Armstrong.

Sleeping

A **Malmaison**, 104 Quayside, T0191-2455000, www.malmaison.com. Some weekend special offers. Creamy natural walls, crisp white sheets, rich royal spreads and throws, this place is only 6 years old. Chicly developed from old co-op warehouse with modern rooms. French restaurant with view onto river. Eggs benedict, wild mushrooms polenta, roasted sea bass are on offer in the restaurant.

B **The Waterside**, 48-52 Sandhill, T0191-2300111, www.watersidehotel.com. An acceptable 3-star hotel, the rooms are not exactly modern and not exactly antique. Breakfast not included in the price: £10.50 English breakfast, £6.50 continental breakfast.

C **Da Vinci's Hotel**, 73 Osbourne Rd, Jesmond, T0191-2815284, www.davincis.co.uk. A clean and comfortable place in the Jesmond district with a decent Italian restaurant attached.

C **Westland Hotel**, 27 Osbourne Av, T0191-2810412, www.westland- hotel.co.uk. Cheaper rooms without bathroom available. A 14-bedroom hotel in a large double-fronted Victorian house, 20 mins' walk into town. It's family run, provides TV, and hairdryers and refurbishment is underway. Good value, comfortable and clean.

D **Minerva Hotel**, 105 Osborne Rd, Jesmond, T0191-2810190, F2870119. Breakfast included. A fairly ordinary B&B on 3 floors with rooms facing the road or a back yard. Comfortable but nothing special.

E **YWCA**, Jesmond House, Clayton Rd, T0191-2811233, F2120070. Hostel built in 1985. No rooms with bathrooms. Weekend deal £106.68 incl breakast and dinner.

E **Newcastle University Student Halls of Residence**, T0191-2226296. Offers student rooms in the summer vacation, as does the **University of Northumbria**, T0191-2274204.

F **Newcastle YHA**, 107 Jesmond Rd, T0191-2812570, F2818779. Has 60 beds in a large townhouse, divided into 2-bedded rooms and dormitories. It also offers single rooms in University of Newcastle halls of residence for £15 a night in Jul, Aug.

Eating

££ **Bob Trollops**, 32 Sandhill, T0191-2611037. An incongruous 17th-century timber-framed building surviving amid Quayside's redevelopment, home to a characterful vegan/vegetarian restaurant and bar.

££ **Caffe Paradiso**, 1 Market Lane, T0191-2211240. Live piano music to enhance the atmosphere of this cerebral and reflective restaurant and bar.

££ **Café 21**, 19-21 Queen St, Princes Wharf, Quayside, T0191-2220755. Generally regarded as one of the best restaurants in the city with its bistro-style fusion menu. A meal here could cost anything from £10-£30 or more.

££ **Fisherman's Lodge**, Jesmond Dene, T0191-2813281. In Heaton Park, a lakeside setting and wooded seclusion as well as serious cuisine make this one of the city's grandest dining experiences.

££ **Leela's**, 20 Dean St, T0191-2301261. A recommended South Indian restaurant with top-rate vegetarian options and affable staff. More expensive than the average curry house though.

£ **Pani's**, 61-65 High Bridge, T0191-2324366. A much-loved and authentic Italian café-restaurant, near Grey St.

£ **Uno's**, 18 Sandhill, Quayside, T0191-2615264. Another popular choice for Italian food and surprisingly affordable given the celebrity cult that's grown up around it. Booking advisable.

£ **Valley Junction 397**, The Old Station, Archbold Terr, T0191-2816397. An unusual and exceptional curry house in a converted junction box and railway carriage.

Pubs, bars and clubs

Barluga, 35 Grey St, T0191-2302306. Mood lighting, soul music and soft, soft furnishings.

Chase, 13 Sandhill, Quayside, T0191-2450055. This 70s-themed designer bar is still one of the city's most striking pre-club warm-up destinations. Has a beer garden beneath the Tyne Bridge. Spot the footballer but do not disturb.

The Cluny, 36 Lime St, T0191-2304474. A 15-min walk from the centre, a huge converted warehouse that's become a live-music venue and riverside art gallery of some note.

Free Trade Inn, St Lawrence Rd, T0191-2655764, has large beer gardens with fabulous views over the city from a bog-standard boozer doing great sandwiches.

Nice at the Playrooms, Low Friar St, T0191-2302186. Saturday here is one of the most popular and happening garage and house nights in the city.

Revolution, Collingwood St, T0191-2616998. Close to the Bigg Market and a massive hit with locals at weekends.

Stereo, Sandgate, Quayside, T0191-2300303, currently one of the hippest bars in the city, with its furnishings and fishfinger sandwiches.

Stone Love at Foundation, 57-59 Melbourne St, T0191-2618985. Favoured by Indie rockers and glamourpusses. Thursday night's the night.

Trent House Soul Bar, 1-2 Leazes Lane, T0191-2612154. A little underground style bar with a tangible air of multicultural cool.

Entertainment

Cinema

Side Cinema, Courtesy of Side Gallery, 5/9 Side, T0191-2610066. Small cinema showing art and good independent films.

Tyneside Cinema, 10 Pilgrim St, T0191-2321507, www.tynecine.org For the film buff, showcase for London Film Festival tours.

Live music

Newcastle Opera House, Westgate Rd, T0191-2320899, www. newcastleopera house.org Capacity of 1100. Live mainstream rock, folk, pop and jazz venue.

Telewest Arena, Arena Way, T0191-2605000, www.telewestarena.co.uk Booking on T0870-7078000, www.telewest arena.co.uk, for any big gigs.

Trillions, Princess Sq, T0191-2321619. Has quality local rock/metal/ska/whatever bands on most nights.

The Cluny Warehouse, Lime St, Nr Byker Bridge, T0191-2304474. Good beer, staff and great for alternative music. Monthly jazz from big jazz stars and plenty of gigs from up and coming local bands.

Theatre

Live Theatre, 27 Broad Chare, Quayside, T0191-2321232, www.live.org.uk. Café live run by *Café 21*. Small city centre venue for new plays, music, dance and new writing, often with touring productions by national companies.

Newcastle Playhouse and Gulbenkian Studio, Barras Bridge, T0191-2305151, www.northernstage.com Middle-scale innovative classic and contemporary drama by the resident Northern Stage Company as well as touring productions. With non-smoking bar.

Theatre Royal, Grey St, T0870-9055060. Plays host to major touring companies like the RSC and National Theatre as well as ballet, opera and dance.

Transport

Bus

Long distance National Express, T08705-808080, serve Newcastle from most major UK cities, including: **Manchester** (5 hrs), **York** (2 hrs 30 mins), **London** (6 hrs 40 mins), **Durham** (30 mins), **Leeds** (2 hrs 30 mins) and **Edinburgh** (3 hrs).

Car

Argyle Garage Ltd, Coquet St, T0191-2322905; **MD Jowetts Ltd**, 8a Marlborough Cres, T0191-2325735; **Hutton Hire Service**, 133 Sandyford Rd, T0191-2811920.

Taxi

ABC Taxis, 1-3 Cross St, T0191-2323636; Central Taxis, Prudhoe St, Haymarket, T0191-2716363; Noda Taxis, Central Station, Neville St, T0191-2221888.

Train

GNER serve Newcastle from **London King's Cross** frequently (3 hrs 30 mins). Also direct services from **Birmingham** (3 hrs 45 mins), **Leeds** (1 hr 20 mins), **York** (1 hr), **Edinburgh** (1 hr 40 mins) and **Durham** (10 mins). From **Liverpool** and **Manchester**, change at Leeds.

Directory

Hospitals The Royal Victoria Infirmary, Queen Victoria Rd, T0191-2325131. **Internet** Internet Exchange, 26-30 Market St, T0191-2301280. **Police** Newcastle City Centre Police Station, Market St, T0191-2146555. **Post office** St Marys Pl, T0845-7223344. C.L.E.O., 23 Newbiggin Hall Centre, T0191-2862694.

Durham and around

→ *Colour map 5*

Durham presents passing train travellers with a wonderful spectacle: stacked up half a mile away on a ridge in a tight loop of the River Wear, its massive cathedral towers up behind the castle, a grey-brown stone fantasy of a place. Visually it's unlikely to disappoint day-trippers either, although there's not a huge amount more to do than wander over the river on to the 'peninsula' and up to the cathedral, enjoying the compact and cobbled centre of this university town. The recent opening of the Gala centre in Millennium Place beside Millburngate Bridge is supposed to address that problem with a state-of-the-art visitor centre, theatre, cinema, library and café complex. Chances are that it will provide an entertaining night out following the mandatory appreciation of what is arguably the most impressive Romanesque cathedral in Europe. After soaking up the atmosphere of this mighty achievement of the Norman church, the tour of the castle might come as a bit of a disappointment. Otherwise Durham makes a reasonable base from which to explore the hillwalking delights of Weardale and Teesdale in the Pennine hills to the west. ▸▸ *For Sleeping, Eating and other listings, see pages 478-479.*

Ins and outs

Getting there By **road**, Durham is just off the A1 (M) linking it to north and south, about 260 miles from London, a journey that usually takes about 5 hrs. From the west, the A68 'holiday route' crosses Northumberland and Border Country. **National Express** service 425 runs 5 times a day to Durham from London Victoria, including a nightbus, leaving at 0830, 1230, 1500, 1730 and 2330. The journey takes just over 6 hrs. Durham is also connected by **coach** to Newcastle and York. **GNER** run about 17 express west coast trains to Durham from London King's Cross daily, taking about 2½-3 hrs.

Getting around The medieval centre of Durham can easily be negotiated on foot. All the main sights are located within half a square mile on the peninsula of the river Wear. In fact, Durham pioneered congestion charging in Britain with its £2 charge for cars using the town centre from Mon-Sat 1000-1600. The paypoint is next to St Nicholas' church at the entrance to the market place. Durham Cathedral Bus no 40 runs from the Coach Park and train station to the cathedral via the Market Place, every 20 mins Mon-Fri 0805-1725, Sat 0905-1725, Sun 0945-1645. Local buses run out to the university campus and Durham Art Gallery. ▸▸ *For further details, see Transport, page 479.*

Information Durham TIC ⓘ *Millennium Pl, T0191-3843720, www.durham tourism.co.uk. Mon-Sat 0930-1730, Sun 1100-1600.* All the usual tourist information services, and during the season the visitor centre shows a short film about St Cuthbert called the 'Sacred Journey', on a giant screen.

Sights

From the station, on high ground in the west of the city, after taking a moment to enjoy the view it's a 15-minute walk downhill over the river to the cathedral. The most direct route is also the best, heading down North Road past the bus station to pedestrianized Framwelgate Bridge. From here there are more fine views of the castle walls up above, before the steep climb up to the Market Place via Silver Street. As well as the grand Town Hall and Victorian covered market, the Market Place boasts a fine statue of Neptune, God of the Sea. The spire of **St Nicholas Church** at the entrance to Market Place is a useful landmark.

Cathedral

ⓘ *T0191-3864266, www.durham cathedral.co.uk. Mon-Sat 0930-dusk (varies, phone for details), Sun 1230-dusk (varies, phone for details). The Cathedral's Treasures of St Cuthbert: Mon-Sat 1000-1630, Sun 1400-1630. £2.50, concessions £20, children £0.70, family £6. Tower: Apr-Sep Mon-Sat 1000-1600 (last entry 1540); Oct-Mar Mon-Sat 1000-1500 (last entry 1440). £2.50, children £1.50, family £7. Monk's Dormitory: Apr-Sep Mon-Sat 1000-1530, Sun 1230-1515. £1, concessions £0.30. Guided tours: mid-Apr-Sep Sat 1100, 1430 (also 1815 and Sun 1700 mid-Jul, Aug); late Jul-Sep Mon-Fri 1100, 1430. £3.50, concessions £2.50, children free.*

A right turn from here leads up Saddler Street towards the heart of the peninsula. Down to the left, Elvet Bridge slopes off across the river again to the Elvet district, the city's administrative centre with its classiest hotels, *The Royal* and the *Three Tuns*. Cobbled Owengate on the right again climbs the short distance up to Palace Green, the wide open lawn dividing cathedral and castle at the top of the hill. Durham Cathedral is the most superb Norman survival in England, a fact recognized by its designation as a World Heritage Site, but its striking position, remarkable state of preservation and sheer size are what make first impressions so immediately rewarding. A powerful statement of the authority of the Norman Conquest, this is still a place with presence. On the north door, the main entrance, hangs a replica (the original is in the Treasures of St Cuthbert Museum in the cloisters) of the Sanctuary Knocker, used by criminals and exiles seeking safe haven and passage to the coast. Once inside, the eye is drawn down the long nave toward the round east window by the huge columns supporting the vault of the nave: this was the first church in Europe to be rib-vaulted throughout, its piers alternately rounded or clustered, the round ones decorated with geometric patterns. Approaching the high altar they spiral up towards heaven. Highlights of the interior, apart from the overall impression, include the **Galilee Chapel** at the west end, which contains the tomb of the Venerable Bede, (his *Ecclesiastical History of the English People*, written in the eighth century, long set the benchmark for early histories of the country); the tombs of the powerful **Neville family**; **Prior Castell's Clock**, an early-16th-century clock restored in 1938; the **Bishops Throne** in the choir, that of Prince Bishop Hatfield (1345-1381); the **Miners Memorial** in the nave; and beyond the Frosterley Marble Bar, marking the limit of women's permitted access to the monastic church, the **shrine of St Cuthbert** himself in the Chapel of Nine Altars. The shrine was demolished during the Reformation, and the saint now lies buried beneath a marble slab. South of the main body of the cathedral, the original monastic buildings clustered around the cloisters, built in the early 15th century. The monk's dormitory with its fine timber roof can be seen, although more interesting perhaps are the **Treasures of St Cuthbert**, a revamped exhibition of the cathedral's valuables, including a piece of the saint's coffin and some of the relics found inside. Look out too for the original **Sanctuary Knocker** and some extraordinary illuminated manuscripts. Finally, the views from the top of the **tower** on a fine day are well worth the modest charge.

Castle

Opposite the north side of the cathedral, a couple of hundred yards away across Palace Green, the castle was started in the early 1070s, a key element in William the Conqueror's subjugation of the north. Although the arch of the gateway is original, additions and renovations to the whole castle were undertaken in the 19th century when it became the first college of the university. Like Oxford and Cambridge, **Durham University** ⓘ *Durham Castle, T0191-334 2000, www.durhamcastle.com, Jul-Sep daily 1000-1230, 1400-1630, Oct-Jun Mon, Wed, Sat, Sun 1400-1600, guided tours for about 40 mins, £3.50, concessions £3, children £2.50*, operates a collegiate system. Guided tours of the place include the Great Hall, with its 14th-century roof, the late 17th-century Black Staircase and the Norman chapel.

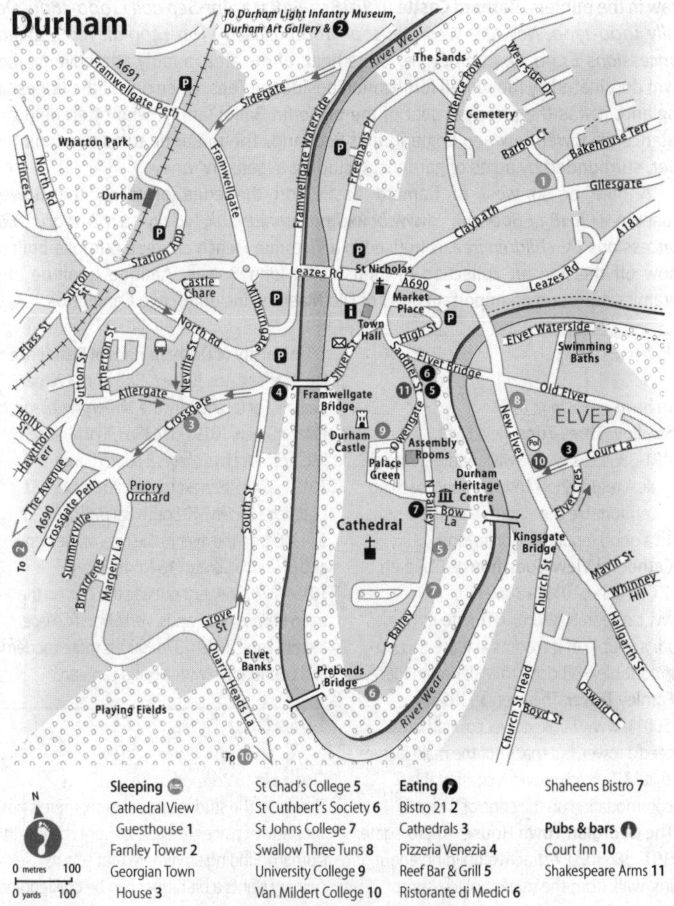

Other sights in the city

On the east side of the peninsular, in the old church of St Mary-le-Bow overlooking little Kingsgate bridge, the **Durham Heritage Centre** ⓘ *St Mary-Le-Bow, North Bailey, T0191-3845589, Apr, May, Oct Sat, Sun, bank holidays 1400-1630, Jun daily 1400-1630, Jul, Aug, Sep daily 1100-1630*, is a local history museum with displays on the mining industry, crime and punishment and medieval Durham.

With more time you could also visit the **Durham Light Infantry Military Museum** ⓘ *Aykley Heads, T0191-3842214, daily Apr-Oct 1000-1700, Nov-Mar 1000-1600, £2.50, concessions £1.25, family £6.25*, which traces the heroic history of the regiment from 1758-1968, and is combined with interesting temporary exhibitions in the art gallery.

Around Durham

West of the city, the A690/A689 runs through the Pennine valley of the Wear, Weardale, to the Cumbrian market town of Alston. There aren't many sights as such en route, but the road passes through some impressively wild and remote scenery, popular with hillwalkers. Almost parallel with the valley of the Wear to the south, Teesdale is similar but more touristy. Visitors come here to walk, but there are also waterfalls like **High Force**, certainly true to its name when the river's in spate, which draw in the punters. **Barnard Castle** ⓘ *T01833-638212, Apr-Sep daily 1000-1800, Oct daily 1000-1700, Nov-Mar Wed-Sun 1000-1600 (closed 1300-1400 all year), £2.50, concessions £1.90, children £1.30*, is the heart of the area, a fairly attractive market town dominated by the ruined fortification beside the Tees. Once one of the largest in England, it was the principal seat of the powerful Baliol family, who often held the balance of power between England and Scotland. The romantic ruins overlook the river, surrounded by acres of gardens, including a 'sensory' one.

A mile or so west of Barnard Castle, on the edge of town, the **Bowes** Museum ⓘ *T01833-690606, www.bowesmuseum.org.uk, daily 1100-1700, £6, concessions £5, children free*, is housed in a Victorian French chateau purpose-built to show off the fine art collection of industrialist John Bowes. Antique furniture and ceramics surround an important array of Old Masters, including two Canalettos.

Sleeping

Durham *p476, map p477*

B **Swallow Three Tuns**, New Elvet, T0191-3864326, www.swallowthreetuns.ntb.org.uk. A refurbished 16th-century coaching inn, comfortable but slightly characterless, with a good reputation for its food.

C **Cathedral View Guesthouse**, Claypath, 212 Gilesgate, T0191- 3869566, www.cathedralview.com. True to its name from a couple of its rooms at least, this is a comfortable B&B close to Millennium Place.

C **Farnley Tower**, The Avenue, T0191-3750011, www.farnleytower.co.uk. There is indeed a tower, but that's not the main feature of this B&B, which provides comfortable accommodation on the edge of the city.

C **The Georgian Town House**, 10 Crossgate, T0191- 3868070. Attractive building about 5 mins' walk from the market place, some rooms with views of the cathedral.

D **University of Durham Halls of Residence** late Mar-late Apr, Jul-Sep. B&B from £20 per person. For location try the *University College*, Palace Green, T0191-3743863, in the castle itself, or *St Johns College*, 3 South Bailey, T0191-3743598, next to the cathedral, or *St Cuthbert's Society*, 12 South Bailey, T0191-3743464, on the river in the crux of the bend, and *St Chad's College*, 18 North Bailey, T0191-3743364. Just outside the city, on the main university campus, *Van Mildert College*, Mill Hill Lane, T0191-3743900, is more modern and comfortable with a good canteen.

Eating

Durham *p476, map p477*

Thanks to the student population, there's no shortage of places to eat a lot very cheaply in Durham. Finding anywhere that sets its culinary sights a bit higher can be challenging.

£ **Bistro 21**, Aykley Heads House, Aykely Heads, T0191-3844354. Probably the best mid-range option. It does good value English food in a cosy place, but it's some way from the centre, near the Durham Art Gallery and Light Infantry Museum.

£ **Cathedrals**, Court Lane, T0191-3709632. The former Durham city police station converted into a large airy restaurant with a bar on the ground floor and a bistro and restaurant above.

£ **Ristorante di Medici**, 21 Elvet Bridge, T0191-3861310. Italian joint doing pizza or pasta deals for £3, popular with students.

£ **Pizzeria Venezia**, 4 Framwellgate Bridge, T0191-384 6777. Even more mobbed, an authentic family-run Italian.

£ **The Reef Bar and Grill**, Saddler St. A dive bar popular with law students but does very good Belgian beers and chips.

£ **Shaheens Bistro**, The Old Post Office, 48 North Bailey, T01913-860960 is an accomplished and friendly Indian restaurant.

Pubs, bars and clubs

Durham *p476, map p477*

The Court Inn, Elvet, has a cult following with sporty students because of its filling grub.

Shakespeare Arms, Saddler St, T0191-3869709. An unbeatably authentic traditional locals' pub with very good beer.

Transport

Durham *p476, map p477*

Car

Enterprise Rent-a-Car Ltd, Enterprise Premises, Darlington Rd, Nevilles Cross, T0191-3868666; **S Jennings**, High St, Carrville, T0191-3846655.

Taxi

Direct Taxis, The Warehouse, Rennys Lane, T0191-3862002; **Pratts Taxis**, Maven House, Frankland Lane, T0191-3860700.

Directory

Durham *p476, map p477*

Bike hire Specialist Cycles, within Meadowfield and District Soc, Frederick St South, Meadowfield, T0191-3783753. **Hospitals** University Hospital, Lancaster Rd, T0191-3332300. **Internet** Saints Bar, Chop House and Internet Café, Back Silver St, T0191-3867700. **Police** Durham Police HQ, Aykley Heads, T0191-3864929. **Post office** 33 Silver St, T0845-7223344.

Northumberland

→Colour map 5

North of Newcastle and also embracing the best bits of Hadrian's Wall, the wilds of Northumberland are a remote haven for naturalists, historians and hikers. Still the least densely populated of English counties, from Alnwick to Berwick, the coast plunges in and out of the North Sea around rocky headlands, ruined castles and windswept fishing villages. Offshore, the Farne Islands support an extraordinary variety of seabirds, while Holy Island provided sanctuary for the early Celtic Christian church in the seventh century. Alnwick itself was voted by Country Life readers the most desirable town in the UK in which to live, going some way towards explaining the popularity of green wellies, working dogs and conservative attitudes throughout the county. Its castle is still the ancestral home of the Duke of Northumberland, and the gardens recently given a multimillion pound Millennium makeover by the Duchess. On the border with Scotland, Berwick-upon-Tweed has an embattled charm born of its deeply disputed history. Inland, much of the rest of the county is taken up with the Northumberland National Park, an ancient granite plug surrounded by mile upon mile of the kind of carboniferous limestone that forms the bedrock of Ireland. Recent campaigns by conservationists have encouraged the return of indigenous wild flowers and grasses across many parts of this beautiful moorland. ▸▸ *For Sleeping, Eating and other listings, see pages 485-486.*

Alnwick and the coast

Walking or driving along anywhere between Alnwick and Berwick is a rare pleasure: few cars, fewer walkers and miles of superb empty beaches, though swimming and sunbathing are perhaps only for the hardiest. The coast unfolds a landscape of spectacular beauty, dotted with the country's finest selection of castles and home to a wide variety of birds and wild flowers. The long swathes of sand are punctuated by rocky promontories and quiet fishing villages that are gradually turning into quiet resorts and retirement homes as the fish disappear and, though not picturesque, they get on with the job as unobtrusively as possible. Out to sea, the Farne Islands promise prolific birdlife while across the causeway on Holy Island lies the bleak outpost that produced the vigorous flower of early English Christianity.

Ins and outs

Getting there The A1 **road** runs between Newcastle and Berwick while the scenic route hugs the coast more closely. Newcastle to Alnwick takes 45 mins and Alnwick to Berwick the same again. To the southwest, the B3642 runs down to Rothbury, Hexham and The Wall and the B6346. **National Express coach** from London (10 hrs) calls at Newcastle (2 hrs) and Alnwick, before heading north to Edinburgh (1 hr 30 mins). **National Express** service X18 runs between Newcastle and Berwick, making a stop at Alnwick, also calling at Warkworth and Alnmouth for connections to the **train**. Intercity and local services run along the mainline Edinburgh to London route, fast trains calling 4 times a day at Alnmouth, about 5 miles from Alnwick itself. Berwick (30 mins), Newcastle (40 mins) and Edinburgh (40 mins). Newcastle has frequent trains from London (4 hrs).

Getting around **Arriva**, T0191-2123000, run a good if infrequent network of local buses along the coast. Cycling is very popular locally, and there are cycle routes in abundance along the flattish coast.

Information **Alnwick TIC** ⓘ *The Shambles opposite the market place, T01665-510665. 0900-1700 Mon-Sat, 1000-1600 Sun.* **Northumbria Tourist Board** ⓘ *www.ntb.org.uk*, has a wealth of tourist and orientation information. **Berwick TIC** ⓘ *106 Marygate, T01289-330733. 0900-1700 Mon-Fri, 1000-1700 Sat. Try www.berwickonline.org.uk* For comprehensive local information, www.northumberland.gov.uk for the bigger picture.

Alnwick

This charming town quite simply has it all: a magnificent castle, cobbled streets, a breezy local welcome, spectacular views over the Cheviot Hills and bright, clean air. Though small enough to easily find your way around, Alnwick (pronounced Annick) wears its rich historical grandeur with grace yet is far enough away to avoid overcrowding even in high season. Elizabeth I felt sufficiently uncomfortable about the wealth of the Dukes of Northumberland and their distant estates centred round Alnwick that for many years the earl was forbidden to visit his lands on pain of death. Stroll round the market place and take in the characteristically ambitious new gardens laid out for the millenium when the sun shines, or lose yourself in the castle's palatial interior and enjoy the fast, good natured banter in one of the town's many pubs when the sharp northeasterlies blow through and you cannot help but notice the strong, almost feudal sense of pride and independence.

The **Castle** ⓘ *T01665-510777, daily end Mar-end Oct, 1100- 1700 (last admission 1615), £7.50, £6.50 concessions, children free*, like its town, comes complete in medieval splendour with all the trimmings: imposing gatehouse, majestic lions and cobbled courtyards. It has been in the Percy family since 1309 and in active military use for the following 250 years, playing an important part in the incessant border wars. In the 18th century, the first duke – they had been humble earls until then – undertook the first of several rounds of restoration thereby making it into one of the grandest statelys on the circuit. After Windsor it is the largest inhabited castle in the country and there is certainly a luxurious if not royal feeling of grandeur about the place. Lofty state rooms with Adam interiors are hung with paintings by Canaletto, Van Dyck and Titian, high windows overlook a Capability Brown landscape, elegant cabinets overflow with Meissen in the dining room while the library boasts one of the finest collections of books in the country. Watch out for Harry Potter fans on pilgrimage to locations used in the film.

The **Alnwick Gardens** ⓘ *£4, concessions £3.50, children free but must be accompanied by an adult*, reopened in 2002 after a £7 million redig, were masterminded by the current Duchess. A monumental cascade takes centre stage, its fountains periodically erupting in great bursts while paths meander along the planted beds in the walled garden above. The huge scale might initially seem stark but given time, the garden should grow into its own, delighting rather than overpowering the senses.

Book lovers and train enthusiasts will find rich pickings at **Barter Books** ⓘ *T01665-604888, www.barterbooks.co.uk, 0900-1900 daily*, housed in the former Alnwick Station. Starting off in what was the ticket and parcel office, the bookshop has expanded down the platforms and through the waiting rooms, until it now covers over one-quarter of the whole station site. Over 8000 sq ft, 350,000 books, three miles of shelving and a model train that runs round the lot. Cakes, tea and coffee for the sore of foot or eye.

Around Anwick

The town's port at **Alnmouth** has a picturesque harbour which had a bustling trade with Norway, Holland and London during its heyday in the 18th century. Now it sits happily at the mouth of the River Aln welcoming holiday makers, walkers, hardy swimmers and cream tea enthusiasts with colourful warmth. A must for the die-hard bucket and spade brigade.

A 5-mile walk south along a beautiful stretch of sand will bring you to the small town of **Warkworth**, dominated by a particularly impressive **castle** ⓘ *T01665-711423, Apr-Sep daily 1000-1800, Oct 1000-1700, Nov-Mar 1000-1600 (closed 1300-1400), £3.20, concessions £2.50, children £1.70, family £7.70*, dating from the 14th century, proud on a hill above a bend in the River Coquet. Also owned by the Percy family, it's understandable that even they were unable to keep up two such establishments so close to each other. The unrestored ruins here, however, give a good idea of how a purely military castle gradually changed into a fortified house: note particularly the enormous fireplaces and spartan bed chambers. Its dramatic setting is put to good use in Shakespeare's *Henry IV*.

The ruins of the 14th-century **Dunstanburgh Castle** ⓘ *(EH), T01665-576231, Apr-Oct 1000-1800 daily, Nov-Mar 1000-1600 Wed-Sun. £2.20, children £1.10*, sitting high above the waves on a rocky outcrop are among the most evocative and romantically positioned of any in the country. Built by John of Gaunt, it was fortified during The Wars of the Roses only to fall into disuse thereafter. Although only the gatehouse and some of the walls remain, the 30-minute walk up to the castle from Craster and the longer stretches beyond along the Bays of Embleton and Beadnell are richly rewarding whatever the weather. In fact, dark clouds and rain suit Dunstanburgh as diamonds would the Ritz.

Bamburgh

Bamburgh's village green complete with pub, hotel, butcher, church, baker et al is quintessentially English and its pedigree is impeccable. In Anglo-Saxon times, it was the royal capital of the Kingdom of Northumbria and looking up at the castle, its Norman keep still standing proud and its high walls crowning a magnificent natural fortress, you'll see why. The panoramic view from the top is knockout, sweeping in most of the coastline and a good deal of the beautiful country inland, though the chilly interior has little of interest except the comprehensive collection of **Victorian kitchenware** ⓘ *T01668-214515, Apr-Oct 1100-1700 daily, £5, children £2,* in its bare scullery. The village also comes with a towering Victorian heroine in the shape of **Grace Darling**, the brave daughter of a lighthouse keeper who rowed across stormy seas to save nine people from a sinking steamboat in 1838. The house of her birth has a small **museum** ⓘ *T01573-223333, free.*

Farne Islands

ⓘ *(NT), trips to the islands can be made throughout the year from nearby Seahouses, though the best 'birding' is to be had during the breeding season from May-Jul. T01665-720308, www.farne-islands.com or the TIC near the pier for other operators. £8, children £6 for 1 hr 30 min tour. Landings all year round on Inner Farne and Staple Island (at captain's discretion in bad weather) an additional £4 for adults and £2 for children. Deep sea fishing and diving also available.*

These bare islands beloved of birds and hermits are one of the few places in the world where visitors can get so close to such a variety of breeding seabirds. As many as 28 species crowd on to the inhospitable rocks some 4 miles off the mainland, their numbers including an estimated 70,000 puffins, half a million fulmar as well as 3000-odd grey seals. Guillemots, razorbills, cormorants and shags jostle for space with oyster catchers and eider duck, known locally as Cuddy duck, after St Cuthbert who spent his dying days here in 687. A chapel commemorates the community of monks who lived here until Henry VIII's Dissolution when the tower on the island was briefly used as a government fort.

Lindisfarne

Low-lying Holy Island is a strange mixture: the beautiful isolated setting, the picturesque ruins of the priory and the island's legacy of inspired artistry sit at odds with the concerned, almost apologetic air and limp handshake characteristic of contemporary Christianity and the inevitable tourist trappings. Linger a while, however, and wander round when the crowds return to the mainland with the high tide and the island's graceful inspiration may return.

St Aidan established the first community here in the seventh century hoping that the isolated position would provide protection and inspiration for his monks. Invited by King Oswald of Northumbria, he arrived from Iona in 635 making the island a base for active conversion of first the northeast and then farther afield. It became a place of considerable scholarship, encouraging literacy and a flourishing of the arts. The Benedictine monks of Lindisfarne produced wonderful illuminated texts of which the Lindisfarne Gospels, with their interlaced patterns of intricate birds and animals are the most outstandingly beautiful. Dedicated to St. Cuthbert, the island's most famous hermit and reluctant abbot, they left with the monks who feared renewed attack in 875 and are now in the British Museum.

The Priory ⓘ *T01289-389200, www.lindisfarne.org.uk, daily, all year, 1000-1600 (1800 from Apr-Sep and 1700 in Oct; 1600 Nov-Mar), £3, children £1.50,* whose splendid Romanesque ruins stand today, was built in the late 11th century and run by a handful of monks from Durham as a branch house until 1537. The nave of the church is particularly impressive with the stark outline of its one remaining arch, monumental columns and towering west window. The **Visitor** Centre ⓘ *T01289-389244, Apr-Oct 1200-2000 daily, longer when tide suits, £4,* has a strong display and good introduction to the island's history while the 12th-century Parish Church of St Mary is also well worth a visit. Lindisfarne Castle, largely built with stone from the abandoned Priory in 1550, followed the local pattern of brief active service and lengthy decline until it was restored by Lutyens in 1903. It has a small walled garden by Gertrude Jekyll.

Berwick-upon-Tweed

Berwick's graceful bridges and elegant high street belie its tempestuous border past, at the height of which the town changed hands between Scots and English no less than 13 times, making it apparently second only to Jerusalem as the most fought over city worldwide. Its famous walls have stood the test of time, however, and the oldest of the three bridges, finished in 1624, was certainly built with law and order in mind. A traveller in 1799 remarked, "The sixth pillar separates Berwick from the county of Durham. The battlements at this pillar, higher than the others, are always covered with sods as a guide to constables and others in the execution of warrants for the apprehension of delinquents." Walking across today you may be hissed at by a swan dallying on The Tweed but otherwise passage should be uneventful, leaving you to enjoy the fine views and the prospect of a warm welcome on the other side.

Though nothing remains of the medieval walls begun by Edward II, the town's fine **Elizabethan walls** ⓘ *Guided tours 1115 Mon-Sat, 1430 Sun*, were the most sophisticated that the 16th century could muster, built to an Italian design with protection from light artillery and gunfire in mind. However, as the Border Wars gradually became less ferocious, little dent was made in the 12 ft thick walls and you can still walk almost all the way round (1hr 30 mins). The medieval castle faired less well, though more from builders than soldiers, for the Border Bridge, the Parish Church and the Barracks are all built with its stone and it was finally demolished to make way for the 19th-century railway station.

The **Barracks** ⓘ *T01289-304493, daily 1000-1600 (1700, Oct, 1800 Apr – Sep), closed Mon-Tue Nov-Mar, £2.80*, designed by Vanbrugh, were the first purpose-built in England in answer to the people's protests at having soliders billeted on them. They now house a number of exhibitions including the Berwick Borough Art Gallery which includes paintings by Degas and Japanese 'Arita' pottery on loan from the Burrell collection in Glasgow.

Northumberland National Park

Some of the most dramatic and beautiful moorland in the country stretches unspoilt from Hadrian's Wall in the south to the wide expanse of Kielder Water and the prominent peak of The Cheviot in the north. The walking is exhilarating and inspiring whether you tackle the challenges of the famed Pennine Way or opt for something more gentle around Wooler or Rothbury. The paths are well-kept and clearly signed but a large scale Landranger Map or one of the more detailed walking guides is indispensable for a longer tramp. For the indoor bound, Chillingham and Cragside are well worth a visit, their wonderful gardens offering nature close at hand rather than the wilder scenery elsewhere.

Ins and outs

Getting there The A69 **road** runs east-west along the south side of the park while the A697 borders the east going up to Wooler from Morpeth and the A68 comes from Jedburgh and the north. Minor B roads criss-cross the park but look out for the signs indicating military or MOD activity. **Bus** services are limited although the **National Express** coach from Newcastle to Edinburgh runs twice a day with stops at Otterburn, Byrness, Jedburgh and Melrose.

Getting around Walking is highly recommended for those without transport as the scenery is unparalleled and long waits likely at the infrequent bus stops. However, local service includes postbus from Hexham to Bellingham and **Arriva**, T0191-2123000, service 880. Also Newcastle to Rothbury via Morpeth once a day.

Information National Park TIC ⓘ *T01665-578248.* **Rothbury TIC** ⓘ *T01669-620887.* **Otterburn TIC** ⓘ *T01830-520093.* **Wooler TIC** ⓘ *T01668-282123.* Go online at www.nnpa.org.uk, for more details on guided walks and other events throughout the year, and www.kielder.org

Around the park

Nearly 400 square miles of empty moorland, bog and rushing water make up the park, lying in isolated splendour on both sides of the border. Contested and viciously fought over in the Middle Ages, few villages prospered and those inhabitants who did not leave tended towards the more hospitable and easily defendable lowland areas. Aspiring romantics and the outward bound will find inspiration and challenges a plenty. The **Pennine Way** ⓘ *www.thepennineway.co.uk, includes details of accommodation and luggage taxi*, follows the border south from Kirk Yetholm, skirting the summit of The Cheviot, turning south at Byrness and proceeding down through Bellingham to Hadrian's Wall. **St Cuthbert's Way** ⓘ *www.stcuthberts way.fsnet.co.uk*, follows the monk's 65-mile journey from Melrose Abbey in Scotland to Holy Island. For the less steely limbed, the 2-hour walk from **Bellingham up to Hareshaw Linn** has wonderful views as does the walk up to **Yavering Bell from Wooler** while getting to the top of **The Cheviot** and back will take about 4 hours all in, but do check with the Wooler TIC, T01668-282123, for weather conditions as low cloud and mist swoop down with unexpected speed.

The beautiful country around the wide open expanse of **Kielder** Water ⓘ *T01434-250312, www.kielder.org*, can seem bleak and austere in poor weather and is prone to intense midge activity from May to September making walks tough going unless there is a stiff wind or copious repellent to hand. The **Border Forest Park**, however, breaks up the moorland and offers riding as well as pleasing variety to the eye and as the most capacious man-made lake in Europe, the Water itself has the full range of fishing, boating, and other watersports available at **Leaplish Waterside Park**.

Bellingham is a pretty town standing on the North Tyne river and makes a good base for touring the surrounding country. You'll find thorough descriptions of good walks, and cheap guides for sale, at www. shepherdswalks.co.uk, T01670-774675; while www.birdwatchnorthumbria.co.uk arranges birding for the novice watcher. The post-walk bath will undoubtedly benefit from the plant oils and organic herbs that go into the handmade goodies from **The Natural Soap Shop**, T01434-220548. The 12th-century **church** here is particularly fine with its stone roof consisting of hexagonal ribs overlaid with stone slabs. Medievalists may want to visit the **Percy Cross Memorial** commemorating the Battle of Otterburn (1338) where Harry Hotspur fought a moonlit battle against a Scots raiding party led by Earl Douglas.

To the east, **Rothbury** ⓘ *(NT), T01669-620333, Apr-Oct 1030-1900, house only in the afternoon, closed Sun*, is unremarkable except for the Victorian mansion of Cragside, built by the pioneering engineer Lord Armstrong who used it as a place to test his engineering theories, giving the house a worldwide first in the hydro-electric light stakes. The Terraced Garden contains an Orchard House and restored 19th-century clock tower.

Wooler is a good base for walking but otherwise unrewarding although **Chillingham Castle** ⓘ *T01668-215359, www.chillinghamcastle.com, daily 1200-1700 Jul and Aug, Wed-Mon May, Jun and Sep, £4.50, child free*, to the southeast is delightful. Dating from the 12th century, it has been in the hands of the Grey family since 1245 and been lovingly and imaginatively restored by its current owners. An impressive, eclectic collection complements garden, state rooms, dungeons and torture chamber. The handsome **Chillingham Wild Cattle** ⓘ *T01668-215250, Apr-Oct 1000-1200, 1400-1700 Wed-Sun (afternoons only)*, roam in the park where they have done so for the past 700 years, isolated from other herds and rarely touched by human hand. Their remarkable endurance and nobility may be due to the fact that the fittest and strongest bull becomes 'King' and the leader of the herd. He remains so for just as long as no other bull can successfully challenge him in combat, and has the pleasure of siring all the calves that are born, thus ensuring only the best available blood is carried forward. Winner, as they say, takes all.

Sleeping

Alnwick *p480*

C **The White Swan**, Bondgate Within, T01665-602109. The dining room here has been kitted out with the ceiling, stained glass and panelling from the *Titanic's* sister ship, the *Olympic* though the rooms upstairs are very much au style touristique.

D-E **The Georgian Guest House**, Hotspur St, T01665-602398, GeorgianGuestHouse@eggconnect.net Very good value accommodation close to the castle.

Self-caterering

Holiday cottages available for week bookings in summer, weekends Nov to mid-Mar from The Duke Of Northumberland's Estate Office, T01665-510777.

Berwick-upon-Tweed *p483*

C **The Cobbledyard Hotel**, 40 Walkergate, T01289-308407. More modest though friendly.

C **The King's Arms Hotel** in Hide Hill, Berwick, T01289-307454. Twenty individually furnished rooms in an old coaching inn which has a warm welcome.

Northumberland National Park *p483*

B **Otterburn Tower Hotel**, T01830-520620, www.otterburntower.co.uk Pull the stops out at an old country house with three stars, known for its food, with 17 bedrooms.

B **Riverdale Hall Country House Hotel**, Bellingham, near Hexham, T01434-220254. Decent rooms with a good fish and game restaurant. Self-catering also a possibility.

C **The Percy Arms Hotel**, Otterburn, T01830-520261. As it sounds, an old-fashioned charmer on the edge of the National Park .

C **The Tankerville Arms Hotel**, Cottage Rd, Wooler, T01668-281581, www.tankervillehotel.co.uk. A similar style and offers fishin', shootin' and even huntin' though covers its back with a good vegetarian menu.

D **Bridgeford Farm**, Bellingham, T01434-220940. Does good rural B&B.

D **Mrs J A Scott** up at Kelder, is a contender for national best, wowing visitors year in year out with her hospitality and breakfasts, T01434-250254.

Self-catering

C **Ridd Cottage**, sleeps 6 from £500 a week and has been well-kitted out, T0191-2533714, www.northumberlandcottageholidays.co.uk

D **Dunns Houses**, Bellingham, T01830-520677, www.northumberlandfarmholidays.co.uk. Pets welcome, stable facilities for horses and has fishing.

D **Chillingham Castle**, T01668-215359. If you want to indulge in a bit of medieval fancy then book a suite here and don't hold back.

D **Conheath Farm Cottages** sleep 5 from £230 per week upwards, T01434-220250, www.conheath.co.uk.

Eating

Berwick-upon-Tweed *p483*

££ **Foxton's Restaurant and Bar**, Hide Hill, T01289-303939. With an acceptable Mediterranean menu.

£ **Barrels Ale House**, Bridge St, T01289-308013. A no-frills menu at this lively pub.

£ **Cannons**, 11 Castlegate. For fish and chips.

£ **The Market Shop**, High St is a good bet if the sun is shining and you fancy a picnic.

For an explanation of the sleeping and eating price codes used in this guide, see the inside front cover. Other relevant information is provided in the Essentials chapter, page 36.

Northumberland National Park *p483*

££ The Cheviot Hotel, Bellingham, T01434-220696. For a hearty steak or lasagne.

££ The Coquet Vale Hotel, Rothbury, T01669-620305, for good filling fare.

££ The Ryecroft Hotel, 28 Ryecroft Way, T01668-281459, gives a warm welcome.

£ The Blackcock Inn, Falstone, T01434-240200, will stoke you up for walking or wind you down in the evening.

Northwest England

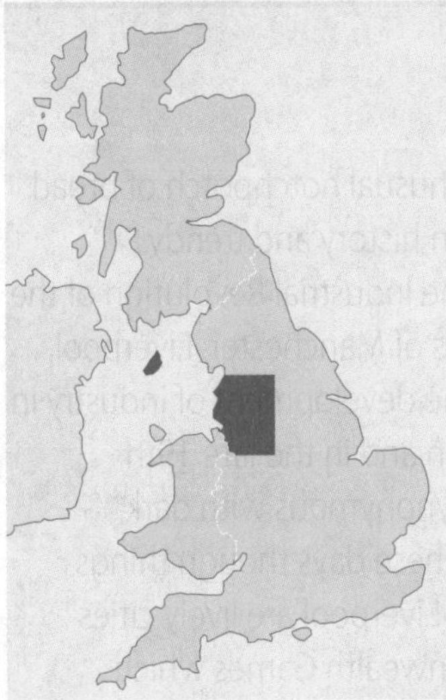

Introduction

The northwest of England is an unusual hotchpotch of broad plains, industrial cities, Pre-Roman history and trendy post-industrial chic. Shaped by the Industrial Revolution of the 18th and 19th centuries, the areas of Manchester, Liverpool and Lancashire were central to the development of industry in England. The bubble burst though and in the late 19th century the Northwest became synonymous with dark, desolate mills and urban decay. These days though things have moved on. Manchester and Liverpool are lively cities much aided by the 2002 Commonwealth Games which allowed the almost total redevelopment of Manchester city centre and the creation of new museums like the Imperial War Museum of the North. They are two of the country's hot spots for nightlife, but that's not to say that there's nothing to do round here during the day. The Peak District National Park is the jewel of the region, curving around the spine of the Pennines with scenic views and wonderful walking country within an hour's journey of the city. The Cheshire Plain to the southwest is lush pasture, countryside with a depth of history like the Roman town of Chester, an ideal stop-over on the way to the Lake District.

★ Don't miss...

1. Escape the rain of **Manchester** in one of the city's inspiring museums. When the sun clears up the rain, marvel at their architectural genius too, page 491.
2. Dream of Arthurian legends, wizards and underground tunnels in the ancient woodland of **Alderley Edge**, Cheshire, page 511.
3. Nurture your crush on Mr Darcy. Visit that lake at **Lyme Park**, Cheshire, where a soaking Colin Firth caused a thousand hearts to skip a beat, page 511.
4. Take a magical mystery tour around **Liverpool** and visit the Cavern, Penny Lane and the Albert Dock to worship at the altar of the Fab Four, page 515.
5. Rev up for the races on the **Isle of Man**. Alongside the world-famous TT motorcycle event held every May, you can also see – or participate in – the World Tin Bath championships and Viking Longboat races in August, page 528.

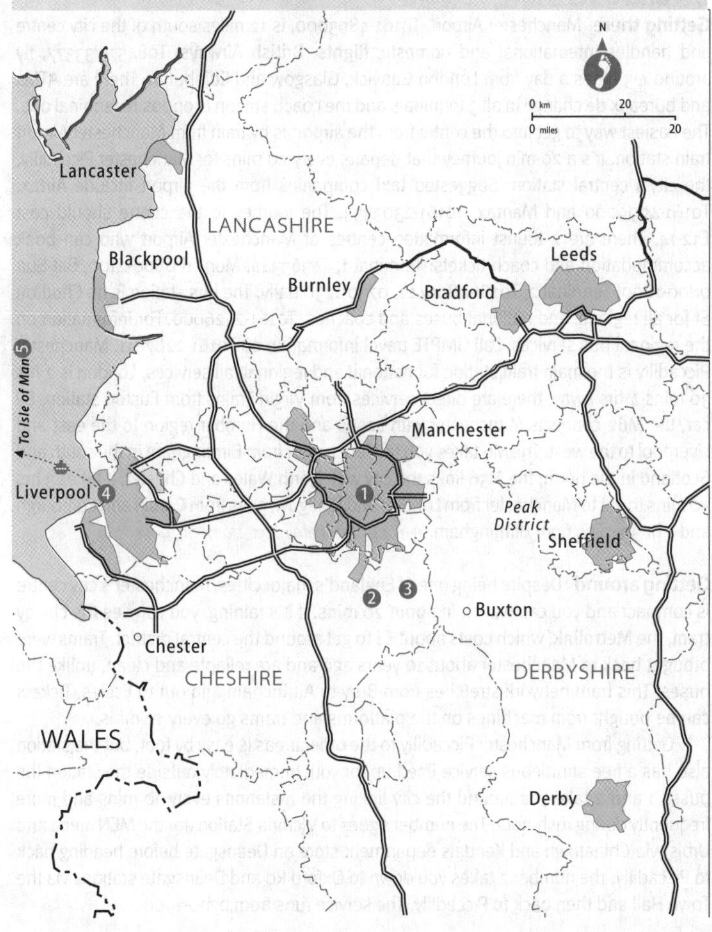

Manchester

→Colour map 3

Manchester, so said French footballer Eric Cantona, is a city in love with "le football, la fete et la musique". Many things have changed since the mid-90s when he played for Manchester United, but the city still prays to that holy trinity of sport, music and partying. Manchester was at the forefront of the industrial revolution of the 18th and 19th centuries but that image is receding fast. The Commonwealth Games of 2002 brought a huge influx of money and allowed Manchester to transform itself into the city it is today; the Victorian workhouses are now being celebrated for their architecture and have been redeveloped into luxury flats, offices and nightclubs.

Urbis, the world's first museum about city life, and the Imperial War Museum North are two exceptionally confrontational glass and steel structures that shape the city like the Guggenheim has Bilbao. There's stiff competition from Leeds and Liverpool for the title of best clubbing town in England, but it's just got the edge over its rivals with three universities and a thriving gay scene. Manchester's a warm-hearted, fast-moving city full of history, humour and high-spirits. ▸▸ *For Sleeping, Eating and other listings, see pages 495-499.*

Ins and outs

Getting there Manchester Airport, T0161-4893000, is 12 miles south of the city centre and handles international and domestic **flights**. **British Airways**, T08457-733377, fly around 4-5 times a day from London Gatwick, Glasgow and Edinburgh, There are ATMs and bureaux de change in all 3 terminals and the coach station is opposite terminal one. The easiest way to get into the centre from the airport is by train from Manchester Airport train station. It's a 20-min journey that departs every 20 mins for Manchester Piccadilly, the city's central station. Suggested **taxi** companies from the airport include **Airtax**, T0161-4999000 and **Mantax**, T0161-2303333. The journey to the centre should cost £12-14. There are 2 tourist information centres at Manchester Airport who can book accommodation and coach tickets: Terminal 1, T4363344, Mon-Fri 0800-2100, Sat-Sun 0800-1800; Terminal 2, T0161-4896412, 0730-1230 daily. The **bus** station is on Chorlton St for all regional and national buses and coaches, T0161-2426000. For information on the regional bus services, call **GMPTE** travel information on T0161-2287811. Manchester Piccadilly is the main **train** station for national and regional rail services, London is 2 hrs 30 mins-4 hrs away, there are direct services from Virgin Trains from Euston station. By **car**, the M62 connects Manchester with Leeds and the Humber region to the east and Liverpool to the west. The M6 takes you to Manchester from Birmingham in the south and Scotland in the north; the M56 links the city with North Wales and Chester. It takes 3 hrs 30 mins to get to Manchester from London and Glasgow, 3 hrs from Cardiff and Edinburgh and 1 hr 30 mins from Birmingham. ▸▸ *For further details, see Transport, page 499.*

Getting around Despite being one of England's major cities, Manchester's city centre is compact and you can walk it in about 20 mins. If it's raining, you can see the city by **tram**, the **Metrolink**, which costs about £1 to get around the central district. Trams were brought back to Manchester about 10 years ago and are reliable and clean, unlike the buses. This tram network stretches from Bury to Altrincham and out to Eccles. Tickets can be bought from machines on the platforms and trams go every 12 mins.

Getting from Manchester Piccadilly to the other areas is easy by foot, but the station also has a free shuttlebus service lined up for you. Immediately outside the station the buses 1 and 2 take you around the city linking the 4 stations every 10 mins and more frequently during rush-hour. The number 1 goes to Victoria Station (for the MEN arena and Urbis) via Chinatown and Kendals department store on Deansgate before heading back to Piccadilly; the number 2 takes you down to Oxford Rd and Deansgate stations via the Town Hall and then back to Piccadilly. The service runs from 0700-1900.

Information The main **tourist office** ⓘ *town hall extension, Lloyds St, St Peter's Sq, daily Mon-Sat 1000-1730, Sun 1100-1600 except 25 and 26 Dec and 1 Jan, T0161-2343157, www.manchester.gov.uk/visitorcentre*, can arrange accommodation, city walking tours, theatre and coach tickets and car hire. **Salford Quays TIC** ⓘ *1 the Quays, T0161-8488601, Mon-Sat 0830-1630, Sun 1000-1600*, provides information about Old Trafford, The Lowry and the Imperial War Museum of the North.

The websites www.destinationmanchester.com and www.manchester.com provide useful, up-to-date listings about the area. Your best bet if you've come to Manchester for a short break is to pick up a copy of *Citylife*, the city's glossy listings magazine which is in the mould of London's *Time Out*. It's published fortnightly on a Tue and is good for all things young, fun and Mancunian, www.citylife.co.uk. *The Manchester Evening News* is the regional daily newspaper with listings, and *The Metro* is a free daily commuter paper with digested national news and local listings.

Sights

Salford Quays

Not so long ago, the Quays area was shabby and run-down, a relic of the industrial period that was still in use. Now though, it's the place to be seen at, with an art gallery and museum that have been instrumental in Manchester's reinvention as a city of dynamism and culture. It's also spitting distance from Manchester's main claim to fame, the home turf of Manchester United at Old Trafford. Salford Quays is about a mile and a half to the southwest of the city centre and easily reached by Metrolink from Harbour City and Old Trafford tram stops.

Tickets to see Man United play are like gold dust even if you are a member, but you can console yourself with a look round the changing rooms and down on to the pitch at the **Manchester United Museum and Tour** ⓘ *North Stand, Old Trafford, Sir Matt Busby Way, T0870-4421994 www.manutd.com, Mon-Sun 0930-1700, closed on match days and the day before champions' league games, museum, £5.50, concessions £3.75 and the combined museum and tour price is £8.50, £5.75 concessions*. There's a lot to see here, from Busby's babes to glittering trophies, Best, Beckham and boots and plenty of stats and history for the die-hard fan.

Just one stop away on the Metrolink will take you to Harbour City and the Quays itself. It's a tough call, but of the two museums here, **The Lowry** ⓘ *Pier 8, T0161-8762000, www.thelowry.com, Mon-Wed 1100-1700, Thu-Fri 1100-1930, Sat 1000-1930, Sun 1100-1700, free, except for special exhibitions*, is probably the best, although you can easily visit this and the Imperial War Museum of the North (see below) in an afternoon. Salford's most illustrious son painted scenes of Manchester and the surrounding area in the first half of the 20th century and his depiction of the workers with eyes red-rimmed from the dust and malnourished children speak more about the city than any of the museums. The Lowry exhibition is permanent and there are also rotating exhibitions by local and national artists, two theatres, a café, a restaurant and beautiful views across the quays.

Across the bridge from The Lowry you can see the stunning **Imperial War Museum of the North** ⓘ *Trafford Wharf, T0161-8364000, www.iwm.org.uk, daily 1000-1800 all year round, free*, arcing across the sky. The building itself, designed by the architect Daniel Libeskind and opened in 2002, is as much a draw as what's inside. He decided to represent conflict on the three planes of air, water and land with the three shards of glass and steel which divide your view here, modelled on a broken teacup, and it certainly works as a confrontational structure. The focus of the museum is on the way that war shapes people's lives over a variety of different conflict situations and it contains thought-provoking and state-of-the-art exhibits.

Manchester

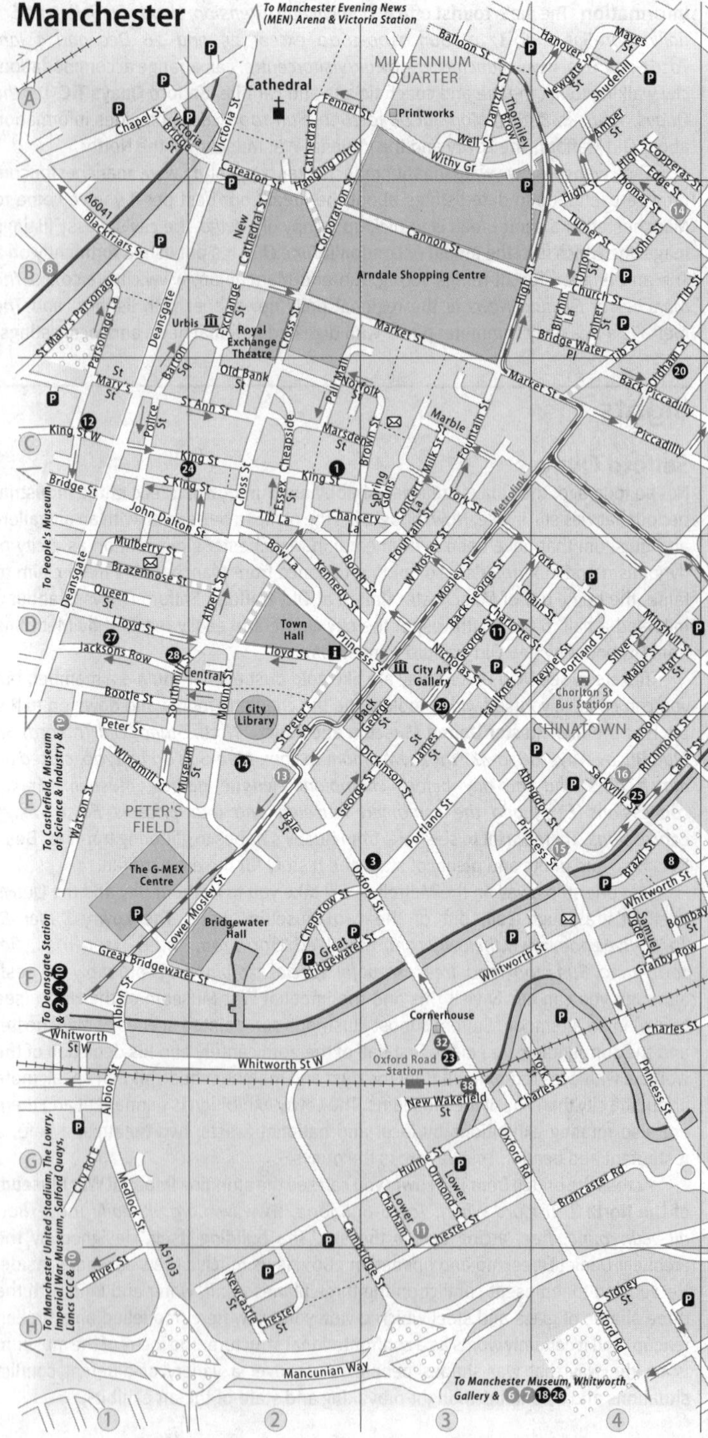

Northwest England Manchester

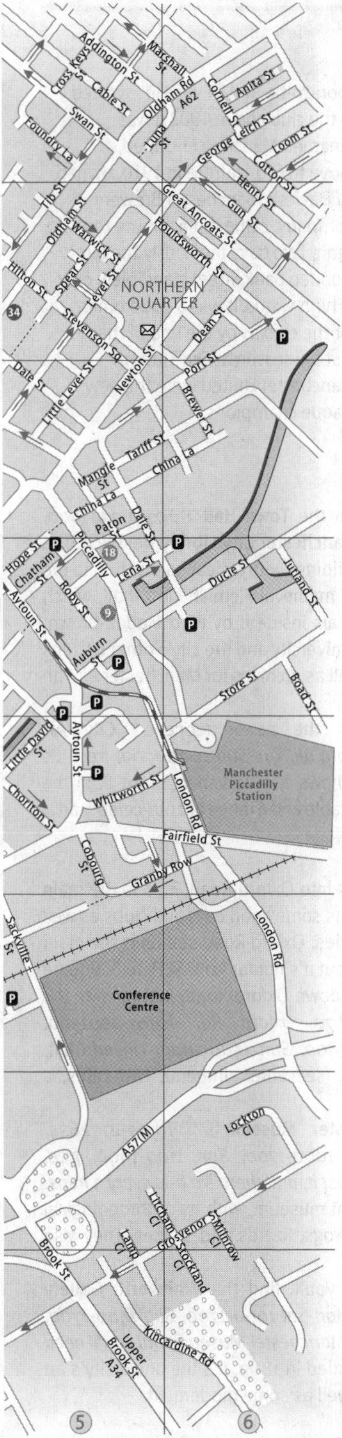

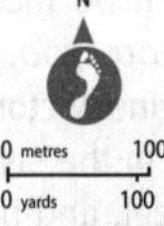

Sleeping

Grafton **6** *H4*
Imperial **7** *H4*
The Lowry **8** *B1*
Malmaison Manchester **9** *D5*
Manchester Backpackers **10** *H1*
Manchester Student Village **11** *G3*
Midland **13** *E2*
Millstone **14** *B4*
New Union **15** *E4*
Rembrandt **16** *E4*
Rossetti **18** *D5*
Walkabout Inn **19** *E1*

Eating

39 Steps **1** *C2*
Atlas **2** *F1*
Beaujolais **3** *E3*
Dimitri's **4** *F1*
Gaia **8** *E4*
Jowata **10** *F1*
Kailash **11** *D3*
Koreana **12** *C1*
Livebait **14** *E2*
Monsoon Nights **18** *H4*
Pure Space **23** *F3*
Reform **24** *C1*
Sarasota **25** *E4*
Shere Khan **26** *H4*
Simply Heathcote's **27** *D1*
Tampopo **28** *D1*
Yang Sing **29** *D3*

Pubs & bars

Cornerhouse **32** *F3*
Dry **34** *B5*
Revolution **38** *G3*

Humble beginnings

Manchester United is perhaps the most famous football club in the world, with a huge following across the globe. Its beginnings, however, were rather less auspicious, starting out in 1878 as a local works football team, Newton Heath Lancashire and Yorkshire Railway. It joined the fledgling football league in 1892 and soon ran into financial difficulty. But a chance encounter by the captain's dog and local brewery owner John Henry Davies found a saviour for the soon-to-be Red Devils. He invested in the club and in 1902 it was renamed Manchester United. A move to Old Trafford in 1910, owned by Davies's Manchester Brewery Company, came not a minute too soon. Two days previously the old wooden Bank Street stand blew over in high winds. It was a good omen for the club as by the end of their first full season at Old Trafford, Manchester United were the new league champions.

St Peter's Square and around

Step outside the TIC and you'll be faced with the **Town Hall** ① *T0161-2341900, Mon-Thu 1000-2000, Fri-Sat 1000-1700*, and **Manchester City Library** beside it. The town hall is one of the city's original Victorian buildings with a clear connection to the Cottonopolis days. It was built in the style of a medieval Flemish cloth hall, which gives the square a European feel, and has murals inside it by Ford Madox Brown. Manchester Library is the central library for the university and the city's other citizens and has a beautiful frescoed ceiling inside as well as archives for Manchester and an extensive music library.

Across the road on Mosley Street is the newly reopened **City Art** Gallery ① *T0161-2358888, www.cityartgalleries.org.uk, Tue-Sun 1000-1700, free*. It's recently undergone a £35 million facelift and shows a wide variety of art from the Pre-Raphaelites to the Renaissance, Turner, Constable and a range of 20th-century art.

Oxford Road and around

Peter Street running alongside the Library turns into Oxford Road. This is the main student area in Manchester and consequently has some good bars and clubs as well as a number of art galleries and university facilities. Oxford Road station is the main way to reach this area if you don't fancy a walk, but it's not far from St Peter's Square at all. All buses except the no. 47 will take you down Oxford Road. Just outside the station is the avant-garde **Cornerhouse** ① *70 Oxford Rd, T0161-2001500, www.cornerhouse.org, galleries Tue-Sat 1100-1800, Sun 1400-1800, closed Mon, free*, containing three galleries, three cinemas (see Entertainment), two cafés, a bookshop and a bar.

Further down Oxford Road is **Manchester Museum** ① ① *T0161-2752634, F2752676, www.museum.man.ac.uk, Mon-Sat 1000-1700, Sun 1100-1600, free, virtually every bus going in this direction goes past it, and there's a bus every 3 mins*, at the University of Manchester. It's a traditional museum, with its anthropological and natural history exhibits and gallery of live frogs, lizards and snakes. They also have a range of well-preserved mummies.

Opposite the Manchester Royal Infirmary you'll find the **Whitworth Gallery** ① *T0161-2757450, www.whitworth.man.ac.uk, Mon-Sat 1000-1700, Sun 1400-1700, free, about 10 mins further down Oxford Rd from Manchester Museum, but you'll need to drive or take the bus, it's too far to walk*. Founded in 1889, it's the university's art gallery and has a large collection of Turners as well as some modern art.

Castlefield

Castlefield, the oldest part of Manchester, has a couple of exceptional older museums that are particularly family-friendly, but after dark it's one of the main party areas with classy bars overlooking the canals. The Roman fort of Mamucium was situated here 2000 years ago and in later years the canals and railways helped to drive the industrial revolution. It became Britain's first urban heritage park in the 1980s and retains many original Victorian buildings like an 1830s warehouse down towards the river. Take the train to Deansgate station and then take a left to find Castlefield; otherwise try the GMEX Metrolink stop.

It's no surprise given this area's industrial heritage that the **Museum of Science and Industry** ⓘ *Liverpool Rd, T0161-8322244, 8321830, www.msim.org.uk, daily 1000-1700, free, turn left out of Deansgate Station*, is here. It tells of Manchester's industrial history and even offers you the chance to smell the Victorian sewers, reconstructed of course. Housed partly in old Victorian buildings, look out for the excellent air and space gallery with a host of aviational and astronomical models and interactive features.

The **People's Museum** ⓘ *T0161-8396061, Tue-Sun 1100-1630, free on Fri, all other days £1*, around the corner at The Pumphouse on Bridge Street, tells the story of the ordinary people involved in industry in the city through to the present day. There are a lot of trade union banners and it's an interesting look at how England's social fabric has developed over the years.

The Millennium Quarter

Up in the north of the city is the newly named Millennium Quarter, a substantially redeveloped area around Victoria station, reachable by train and Metrolink. The first thing you'll see as you pitch up at the station is the massive **Manchester Evening News** (MEN) **Arena**, a huge stadium which hosts all manner of things from Manchester Storm ice hockey team on a Sunday to touring rock and pop acts. Directly across from this is **Chetham's**, Manchester's top classical music academy, and **Urbis** ⓘ *Urbis, Cathedral Gardens, T0161-9079099, www.urbis.org.uk, daily 1000-1800, £5, £3.50 concessions*, an immense £30 million 'glass-skinned' building which has, inevitably caused controversy amongst that tawdry band of media luddites who raise their ugly heads every time an architect tries to be bold and innovative in this country. The self-conscious modernity of the building is its real draw, with a great glass elevator and exhibits that don't just involve you but use your participation to continually develop the way that it portrays city life.

Sleeping

Accommodation in the centre of Manchester is expensive and generally business-orientated. There are a few nice retreats though, and down Canal St there are a couple of characterful gay hotels. The best bet for B&Bs is to look a little further out of town on Oxford Rd. For a charge of £2.50 the TIC can secure 10% discounted rates on featured places.

A **The Lowry Hotel**, 50 Dearman's Pl, Chapel Wharf, T0161-8274000, enquiries@thelowryhotel.com. Manchester's first 5-star hotel and one of only two in the Northwest area is the most exclusive and expensive place to stay. It's a Rocco Forte hotel with all that you'd expect of a top new modern hotel, including a Marco Pierre White restaurant (which doesn't quite live up to the hype) and a great location. They even organize shopping and spa breaks for you here, and you'll be seriously pampered.

A **Malmaison Manchester**, T0161-2781000, manchester@malmaison.com. Right in the middle of the not-so-exclusive Piccadilly area, opposite the station, this is a seriously chic, light and airy place to stay. Minimalist without being distant or pretentious. A gym, spa and brasserie and the additional attraction of a CD library for guests, all of which makes up for the fact that it's in a bit of a dodgy area.

A **The Midland Hotel**, Peter St, T0161-2363333, F9324100. This Edwardian hotel, run by Crowne Plaza, is one of the most imposing buildings in the city. Decorative marbled halls, huge 4-poster beds, a gym and an excellent French restaurant are some of the attractions.

A **The Rossetti Hotel**, 107 Piccadilly, T0161-2477744. Newly opened boutique hotel across the road from *Malmaison* with a young and hip vibe, ideal for weekenders. There's a warm and welcoming glow about the place, funky cushions, an Italian café/restaurant and a jazz lounge downstairs.

D **Walkabout Inn Hotel**, 13 Quay St, T0161-8174800, F8174804. A small hotel attached to a bar and restaurant and a cheaper option without moving from this prime location. Good if you're after a lively night.

D-E **Manchester Student Village**, Lower Chatham St, T0161-2361776, info@thesv.com Double rooms and cheaper and plainer singles around the corner from Oxford Rd station and the bars and clubs around it. Room quality ranges from passable to bog-standard. There are a number of cheaper and smaller hotels and B&Bs to the south of the city.

E **The Grafton Hotel**, 56 Grafton St, beside the University off Oxford Rd, T0161-2733092, F2743653. A medium-sized friendly family-run B&B within walking distance of the city and its restaurants.

E **The Imperial**, 157 Hathersage Rd, Rusholme, 10 mins by bus from the city centre, T0161-2256500, F2256500. It sounds like a restaurant but isn't. The small hotel offers B&B and an evening meal if you want it and is fairly hectic.

E **Manchester Backpackers Hotel**, 64 Cromwell St, Stretford, T0161-8659296, www.manchesterback packershostel .co.uk This small hostel is in a characterful terraced Victorian house with dorm and private rooms, a kitchen and TV lounge. A train ride from the centre but close to Stretford station.

E **The Millstone Hotel**, 67 Thomas St, T0161-8390213, F8390213. A coaching inn dating back to 1700. It's recently been refurbished and is a bargain price for its location in the heart of the shabby-retro-chic of the Northern Quarter. Expect standard pub/B&B treatment and a number of locals sitting in the corner of the bar.

E **The New Union Hotel**, at the junction of Princess St and Canal St, T0161-2281492, F2280341. Not posh or classy, but a gay-friendly hotel with plenty of atmosphere and loud blaring music. A good value option and they serve breakfast on your return from your all-night partying.

E **Rembrandt Hotel**, 33 Sackville St, T0161-2361311, rembrandthotel@aol.com. Right in the thick of the action and very popular. If you head down to the bar you might catch the resident drag queen on the karaoke machine – this is not a place where you'll get much sleep either, but is maximum camp fun.

Eating

Manchester has all the culinary variety you'd expect of a multicultural modern city. Chinatown and Rusholme have excellent Chinese and Indian restaurants respectively and on the curry mile many are open till 0100. Deansgate has a real mixture of restaurants from chain Italian café-restaurants to exclusive plush dining rooms, while studenty Oxford Rd is where to head for cheap and cheerful grub.

£££ **39 Steps**, 39 South King St, T0161-8332432. Serving gourmet fish Mon-Sat in Manchester's finest and most recommended seafood restaurant is a classy, upmarket place to eat. Booking essential.

£££ **French Restaurant** in the *Midland Hotel* on Peter St (see sleeping above), T0161-2363333. The most exclusive French restaurant in Manchester, it's booked up weeks in advance and serves the best of Gallic cuisine in a dimly lit, classy environment.

£££ **Koreana Restaurant**, 40A King St West, T0161-8324330. One of the leading Asian restaurants outside Chinatown. The Korean barbecue is a particular speciality.

£££ **Livebait**, 22 Lloyd St, T0161-8174110. Another of the city's snazzy fish restaurants, serving shellfish, including whelks, as well as tuna and swordfish.

£££ **The Reform**, King St, T0161-8399966. A relatively new restaurant serving contemporary English food. An intimate, plush, red velvety dining room attracts local celebrities, including Coronation St stars and footballers.

£££ **Simply Heathcote's** Jackson's Row, Deansgate, T0161-8353536. 'Celebrity chef' Paul Heathcote is famous for his northwest English cuisine, so expect black pudding, pies and hotpots, all in a modern, classy restaurant.

£££ **Yang Sing**, 34 Princess St, Chinatown, T0161-2362200. Looks distinctly ordinary from the outside, but this has been rated by food critic Jonathan Meades as "not only the finest Chinese restaurant in Britain, but one of the finest restaurants in Britain, full stop".

£££ **Beaujolais Restaurant**, 70 Portland St, T0161-2369626. A small French restaurant with impeccable service.

££ **Dimitri's** in Campfield Arcade by Deansgate station, T0161-8393319. Greek taverna with a small Mediterranean-based menu and has long been a favourite with locals, especially on a Fri and Sat evening when it serves up jazz along with the *dolmades*. Book in advance for weekends.

££ **Gaia**, 46 Sackville St, T0161-2281002. A fashionable mixed restaurant-bar venue with dim lights, comfortable sofas and European food. It's another place to spot Manchester's actors and musicians and has a young, funky vibe. Downstairs there are DJs on a Fri night. Open daily till 2300 for food.

££ **Jowata**, Sackville St, an intimate restaurant serving traditional pan-African cuisine and wine and a variety of vegetarian dishes. It's a friendly and fairly casual dining experience with superb food. Open Tue-Sat, 1800-2430, credit cards not accepted.

££ **Kailash**, 34 Charlotte St, T0161-2361085. Nepalese restaurant serving gently spiced curries and other ghee-free delicacies.

££ **Pure Space**, 11-13 New Wakefield St by Oxford Rd station, T0161- 2364899. An arty, minimalist place to eat with stripped wooden floorboards and wholesome bar food. It turns into a trendy club later in the evening and has a fresh feel to it. They've even got a roof-garden and modern art on the walls.

££ **Sarasota**, 46 Canal St, T0161-2363766, With a rooftop bar serving British fusion cuisine, this place is also very fashionable and friendly. This being Manchester, the roof can come back on if the weather's not behaving, and you get a great view of the canals.

££ **Tampopo**, 16 Albert Sq, T0161-8191966. Well-priced, minimalist pan-Asian restaurant with specials from Thailand, Singapore, Japan and Malaysia.

£ **Atlas**, 376 Deansgate, T0161-8342124, by Deansgate station, overlooking the canal. One of the city's best bar-cafés, where delicious wholesome home-made food is served until 1430 daily. Then it turns into a clubby bar later, open till 0200.

£ **Monsoon Nights**, 108 Wilmslow Rd, T0161-2246669. New and sophisticated.

£ **Shere Khan** across the road has impeccable service, the milky drink *lassi* and balti specials.

Pubs, bars and clubs

Manchester comes alive after dark with clubs and bars of every description. The city's huge student population makes it a lively place to be, coupled with the distinct musical heritage of the place that brought you the likes of New Order, the Happy Mondays and Oasis. The train service between Piccadilly and Oxford Rd and Deansgate means that it's hop around between bars and clubs. Generally, bars in Manchester open until around 0200 at the weekends and 1100-1200 during the week, longer if they are hosting events. Many of the bars have music and dancing. Oldham St is a good place to sip a foreign beer in a trendy bar. Keep an eye on *Citylife* or the *Manchester Evening News* to find out what's on.

The Brickhouse, arch 66 off Deansgate, T0161-2364418, has been running for a lot longer than most, with Motown and soul anthems.

The Contact Theatre, Oxford Rd, T0161-2740600, For something more avant-garde and a bit of R'n'B or hip-hop, hosts club nights on Fri and Sat and a few gay nights which are similarly cool.

Cornerhouse Bar, Oxford St, opposite the station. Chrome surfaces and continental beers, attracting an older, more cultured group of people than some of the other bars round here.

Dry Bar, Oldham St, T0161-2369840. Where the designer bar revolution all started off in the early Nineties, when it was owned by Factory Records and New Order.

Night and Day Café, Oldham St, T0161-2364597, a daytime café serving Mexican dishes and a night-time bar. A laid-back vibe – more designer jeans and trainers than high heels and fake tan.

North, T0161-8391989, on the corner of Tib St and Church St plays funky house and garage in a more chilled-out atmosphere. Open till 0400 on Sat night/Sun morning.

The Paradise Factory, also on Princess St, T0161-2735422, is the city's most well-known gay club on a Sat with 3 floors of dance and all sorts. During the week it's open for student nights. People come from all over the north for the weekends here.

Revolution, further along Oxford Rd, is a successful vodka bar, with others now in Liverpool, London and Deansgate Locks. The music is loud and clubby, attracting professionals and students.

Soundtrack to the City

In the late 1980s, Factory Records and New Order decided that there were no clubs in Manchester that catered for their tastes. So they came up with one of their own. The Hacienda was a popular haunt with the musical sense to book Madonna for her first UK appearance. An explosion of local talent followed and with the crossover of the dance music and indie music scenes, 'Madchester' took off. People all over the country started laying claim to Mancunian blood and the university was massively oversubscribed with students wanting to spend their three years partying. You could spot Mancunian music a mile off with the swirling Hammond organ of the Inspiral Carpets right through to the swagger of the Stone Roses and the Happy Mondays who dominated the charts. The scene, like The Hacienda, boomed and then bust, but not without laying the foundations of the new local and national independent music scene.

Recommended listening:
Love Will Tear Us Apart – Joy Division
This Is How It Feels – The Inspiral Carpets
Regret – New Order
How Soon Is Now – The Smiths
Kinky Afro – Happy Mondays
Come Home – James
The Only One I Know – The Charlatans
Getting Away With It – Electronic
Waterfall – Stone Roses
Supersonic – Oasis

Sankey's Soap, T0161-6619668. In an old mill, Beehive Mill, on Jersey St, it's head and shoulders above the rest for house and dance music. It's a place for high heels and short skirts rather than the scruffy student look, so make an effort and don't wear sportswear or you won't be allowed in. They have various touring top named DJs on a regular basis.
Sofa Central, again on Princess St, T0161-2737336, is another venue for R'n'B and soul, fairly trendy with leather sofas and a bar feel.

Entertainment

Cinema and theatre

The Cornerhouse cinema, 70 Oxford Rd, T0161-2001500, has 3 screens that show the best of foreign and independent films.
Filmworks at the The Printworks, Exchange Sq in the Millennium Quarter is expensive but has more screens than you can count, showing mainstream cinema, T08700-102030.
Royal Exchange, T0161-8339833, www.royalexchange.co.uk. Described by Tom Courtenay as "a smaller world inside a greater one", the intimate theatre puts on superb productions from Oscar Wilde to Shakespeare and is highly recommended. They also have a bookshop, craft shops and a café and restaurant inside the complex. Beg, borrow or steal a ticket for a show here – they're worth it.

Live music

The Bridgewater Hall, an impressive glass building on Lower Mosely St near the GMEX tram stop, T0161-9079000, www.bridgewater-hall.co.uk, is the home of Manchester Camerata and the Halle Orchestra. Expect nothing but the best in this venue with superb acoustics and a serene environment. There are also guided tours taking you backstage and around the building, £5.
Manchester Academy, just down from the university at 296 Oxford Rd, T2752930.
Manchester Apollo, Stockport Rd, T0161-2422560, are both venues holding around 200-300 sweaty bodies for the latest rock and pop acts.
MEN Arena, T0870-1535353, www.men-arena.com. Up by Victoria Station, is the 1000-seater place for screaming teens coming to see their pop idols, and screaming mums coming to see the likes of Tom Jones.

Transport

Bus

National Express run 11 services a day from Chorlton St bus station to and from **London Victoria** (5 hrs). They go 12 times a day to **Birmingham** (3 hrs), 6 times to **Edinburgh** (7 hrs), 6 times to **Gatwick airport** (7 hrs 10 mins via **Birmingham** and **Heathrow**) and 12 times to **Heathrow** (5 hrs 30 mins). Services to **Liverpool** are hourly (1 hr) and there are 7 daily services to **Stansted airport** (6 hrs 30 mins).

Car

Easycar, NCP car park, Chatham St, www.easycar.com, T09063-333333. **Hertz**, Auburn St across from Piccadilly Station, T08708-484848 (closed Sun), www.hertz.com. **Sixt Kenning**, Manchester Airport Terminals 1, 2 and 3, T4892666, www.e-sixt.co.uk.

Train

Virgin Trains are the main service to and from Manchester, T0870-0101127, www.virgintrains.co.uk. They go hourly to **London Euston** from Manchester Piccadilly, Mon-Sat until 2000, taking 3 hrs. Trains to **Birmingham** go regularly, take 1 hr and to **Liverpool** it takes 1 hr. From Manchester Piccadilly you can also get to **Glasgow** in 4 hrs.

Directory

Chemists Boots, Market St, **Moss Chemists** at the top of Oxford St opposite Thomas Cook. **Hospitals** Manchester Royal Infirmary, Oxford Rd, T0161-2361234. **Internet** Debenhams, Market St, T0161-8328666, £1 for 30 mins, **Easy Everything**, 8 Exchange Sq, T0161-8329200, £1 for 45 mins. **Manchester YHA**, Potato Wharf, T0161-8399960. **Police station** Bootle St behind the library, T0161-8725050. **Post office** Spring Gardens off Market St, Piccadilly.

The Peak District

→*Colour map 3*

At the southern end of the Pennine Hills between Manchester and Sheffield sits the Peak District National Park, an oasis in the heart of the Northwest's built-up areas. In 1932 the ninth Duke of Devonshire, the biggest private landowner in the Peak District, set his gamekeepers on trespassers venturing here on his grouse moors on Kinder Scout and sparked off a furore. Five of them were subsequently jailed for up to six months, but it was this trespass and the resulting outrage which brought about the existence of this and Britain's 10 other national parks. Nowadays of course, you're free to roam over the 555 square miles of moorland, dales, rocky cliffs and skyline-shattering tors which sit between six counties. ▸▸ *For Sleeping, Eating and other listings, see pages 505-508.*

Ins and outs

Getting there **Manchester airport**, T0161-4893000, is the closest international and domestic airport, about 25 miles away by road. You can get to the Peak District from here on the train service changing at Manchester Piccadilly for Buxton. Situated between Manchester, Sheffield and Derby, the **road** access here is good. The Peak District is linked to Manchester and Derby by the A6, Chesterfield by the A619 and Sheffield by the A625. Buxton is an hour's drive from Manchester, Nottingham, Sheffield and Derby. **National Express**, T08705-808080, have a coach service to Buxton from London via Derby, Leicester and Loughborough. The **local bus network** runs through the Peak District via Buxton between Manchester, Derby and Nottingham and from Sheffield, Stoke-on-Trent, Ashbourne and Macclesfield. Macclesfield is on the London Euston-Manchester intercity route, from where you can reach Buxton. **Trains** go several times a day. The Peak District, served by the **Hope Valley** train line (see Getting around, below) is also accessible from Chesterfield, Derby and Sheffield. ▸▸ *For further details, see Transport, page 508.*

The Peak District

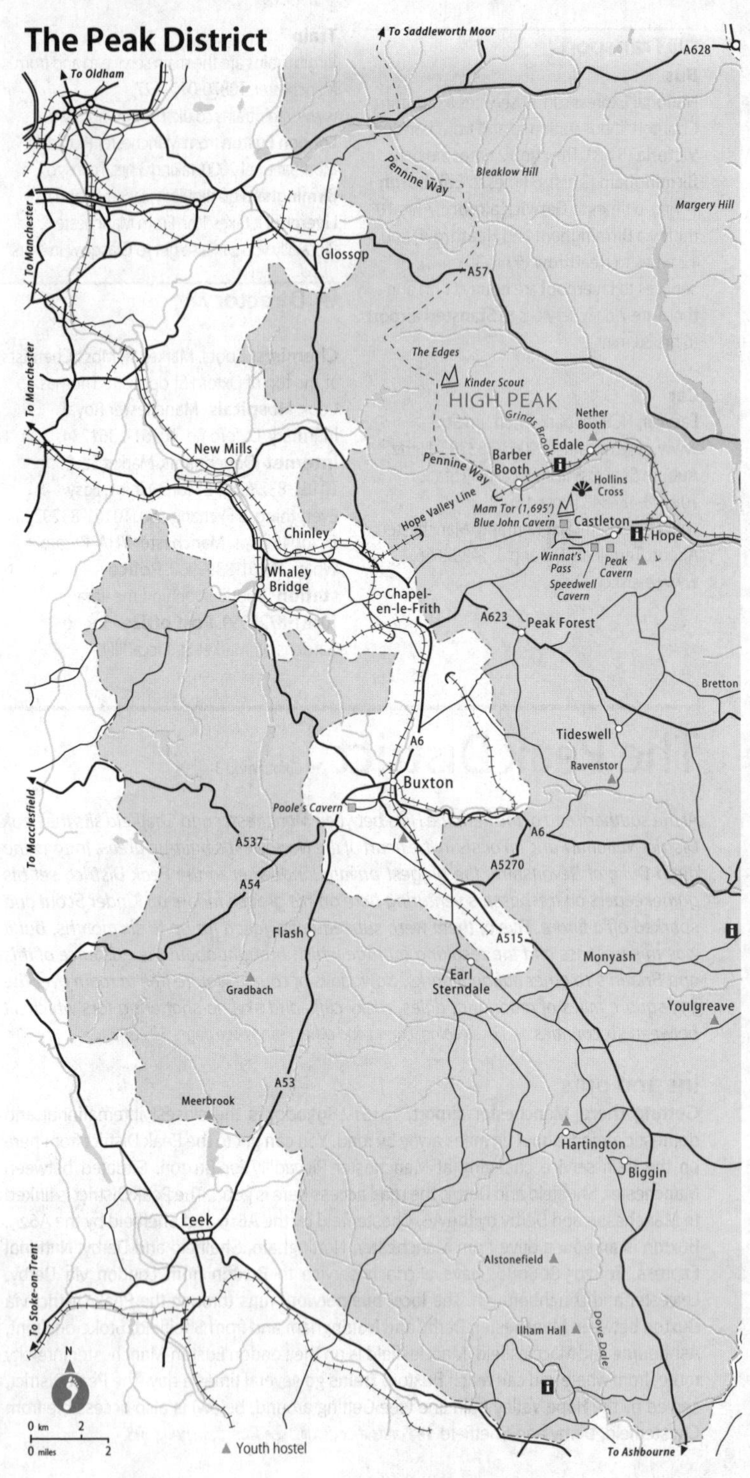
To Saddleworth Moor
A628
To Oldham
To Manchester
To Manchester
Pennine Way
Bleaklow Hill
Margery Hill
Glossop
A57
The Edges
Kinder Scout
HIGH PEAK
Grinds Brook
Nether Booth
Edale
Barber Booth
Pennine Way
New Mills
Hollins Cross
Hope Valley Line
Mam Tor (1,695')
Blue John Cavern
Castleton
Hope
Chinley
Winnat's Pass
Peak Cavern
Speedwell Cavern
Whaley Bridge
Chapel-en-le-Frith
A623
Peak Forest
Bretton
Tideswell
A6
Ravenstor
Buxton
To Macclesfield
Poole's Cavern
A537
A6
A5270
A54
Flash
A515
Monyash
Earl Sterndale
Gradbach
Youlgreave
A53
Meerbrook
Hartington
Biggin
Leek
Alstonefield
To Stoke-on-Trent
Ilham Hall
Dove Dale
N
0 km 2
0 miles 2
Youth hostel
To Ashbourne

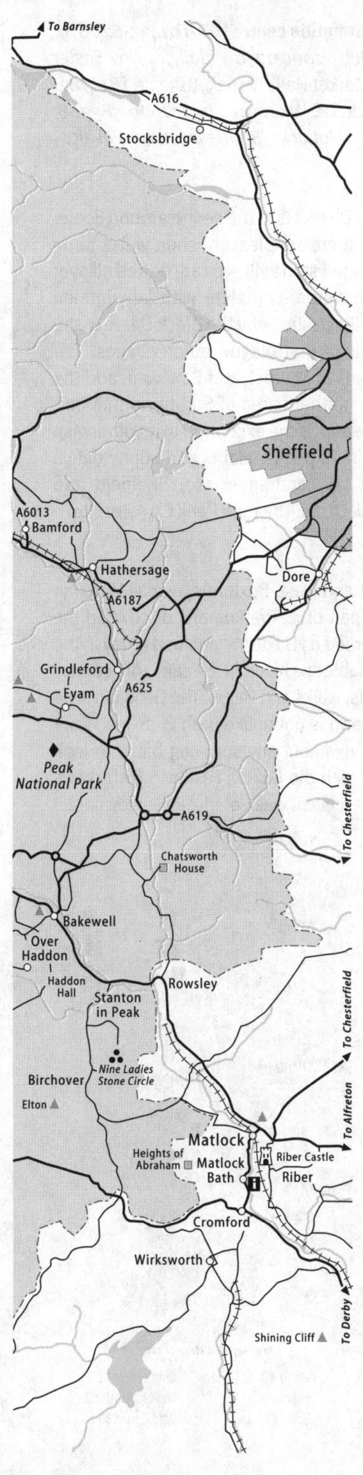

Getting around The public transport network in the Peak District is not too bad at all, especially considering that all the locals have cars to get around in. The bus and train services are especially useful if you're doing a non-circular walk. If you're driving, be aware that the 500,000 drivers a year that this area attracts have an enormous environmental impact on the scenery, so toll roads (costing £3) are to be introduced in certain areas including the Upper Derwent Rd in the north. The Derbyshire Wayfarer Ticket gives you a day's unlimited travel on buses and trains in Derbyshire, which you can buy at most TICs and **bus** travel offices for £7.50 adult and £3.75 concessions and dogs. It's a good idea if you want to cover a lot of ground quickly, and you can get from Buxton to Sheffield on this service easily, taking in all the little villages in between. The **Transpeak** bus service runs every 2 hrs between Nottingham and Manchester, calling at Derby, Belper, Matlock, Bakewell, Buxton and Manchester. **National Express** also run a daily coach service to Matlock from London Victoria. By car, Matlock is 25 miles north of Derby on the A6, 10 miles southwest of Chesterfield on the A632 and 8 miles west of Alfreton on the A632. By **train** there's the **Hope Valley line** which runs from Manchester to Sheffield calling at New Mills, Chinley, Edale, Hope, Bamford, Hathersage, Grindleford and Dore. Trains run a couple of times an hour in both directions with the last train at around 2200. From Manchester Piccadilly it takes just over an hour to get to Sheffield, and it takes 45 mins to New Mills Central. From Buxton, you need to take a train to New Mills to join the Hope Valley Line, a service that runs at least 3 times an hr and takes 30 mins. The Manchester-Sheffield train stops at Hope and Edale where linking buses take you into Castleton.

Information Buxton TIC ⓘ *0930-1700 daily. T01298-25106, www. highpeak. gov.uk, www.peakdistrict-tourism.gov.uk*, is in the old hall just beside The Crescent and contains informative displays and exhibitions by local artists and craftsmen. They can book accommodation and are the main TIC for the Peak District. **Castleton information centre** ⓘ *T/F01433-620679, castleton@peakdistrict-npa.gov.uk, Easter-Oct 1000-1730 daily, Nov-Easter 1000-1700 Sat-Sun only.* **Bakewell TIC** ⓘ Old Market Hall, T01629-813227, F814782, www.peakdistrict.org 0930-1730 daily. **Matlock TIC** ⓘ *Crown Sq, T01629-583388, www.derbyshiredales.gov.uk, and also at Matlock Bath in the Pavilion, T01629-55082, 0930-1730 daily.*

Orientation The major **walking** area in the Peak District is in the centre around Edale. Dovedale in the south is also very popular and there are pleasant short walks to be had all over the national park as you'd expect. Small stone villages are dotted all over the place, with the most interesting being Castleton, complete with labyrinthine caves through the limestone hills and Eyam, a village struck by the Black Death in the 17th century which has avoided tourist trappings that plague other villages. The southeast of the park has the small market towns of Matlock and Bakewell, and the only place not really worth checking out is the northern area of Saddleworth Moor, unless you're a big fan of bleak, misty barren areas. It's the exception in an otherwise geologically interesting area with wide variety in its peaks, plains and sunny dales.
Maps Ordnance Survey Buxton and Matlock OS Landranger 119; Sheffield and Huddersfield OS Landranger 110; The White Peak OL 24; The Dark Peak Explorer OL1.

Buxton

Enclosed by the national park to the south, east and west, Buxton is a small Victorian town central to the district although not strictly part of it. The Romans discovered the mineral springs here in AD 78 which are still regarded as Buxton's lifeblood today in the form of Buxton Mineral Water. It became a fashionable spa resort in the early 19th century when the Duke of Devonshire improved the hotels, walks and baths. The Georgian style Crescent was built in imitation of Bath and the town is not unlike Bath in its feel – but without the hordes of tourists, and unfortunately without any surviving baths to look round. Buxton really comes alive in the summer with the Buxton Festival which draws artists and enthusiasts from miles around for an excellent week of musical enjoyment.

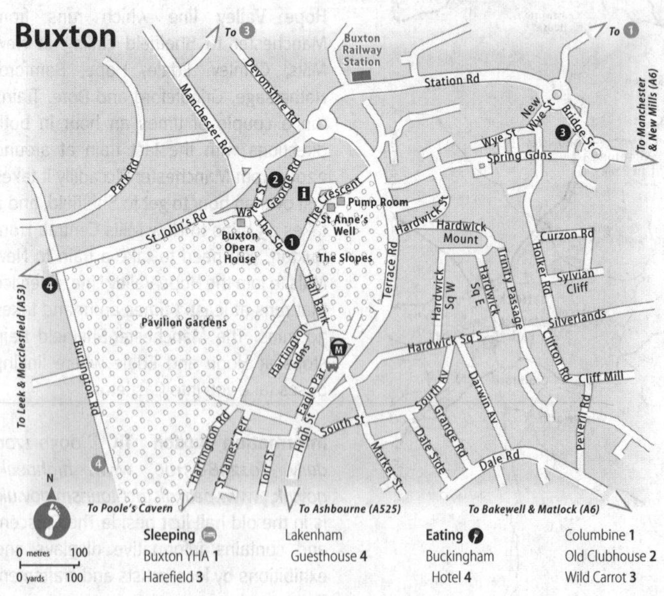

The Crescent, undeniably Buxton's most dominant architectural presence and built in 1780-84, intended to rival the famous Royal Crescent in Bath. It's now a listed building undergoing massive refurbishment by English Heritage. Directly opposite is a small fountain, **St Anne's Well**, a public pump built by the eighth Duke of Devonshire to let the people of Buxton have a free supply of their famous water. It comes out of the pump at 28 degrees centigrade and usually has a stream of locals standing beside it filling containers. Next to that is the **Pump Room** where once visitors took the thermal waters; it is now used to display the work of local artists. Behind that you've got **The Slopes**, public gardens on a bit of a hill with a view of the cobblestone town from one side and the shadow of the Peaks on the other.

Next door to the TIC is the **Old Hall**, Buxton's oldest building dating from 1573 and now a hotel. Mary Queen of Scots stayed here when she visited the town to take the waters in a bid to alleviate her rheumatism. Walking past this, you come to **Buxton Opera House**, the town's main attraction, designed by Frank Matcham in 1903. It's popular in the summer as it holds the **Buxton Opera Festival** and also the **International Gilbert and Sullivan Festival**, www.buxtonfestival.co.uk. **The Pavilion Gardens** beside it are classic Victorian landscaping.

Castleton

This beautiful, if touristy, village in the heart of the Peak District has underground caves, a Norman castle and the dramatic entrance through Winnat's Pass, a steep descent of 1300 ft. The pass is rocky, treacherous and with a heart-stopping view. To put it in context, if you were to drive down it on a bike, you'd be in Sheffield before you had to start pedalling. The area was heavily mined for lead and the mineral **Blue John**, found nowhere else in the world, and the resulting caves and caverns are now top tourist attractions, taking you deep into the middle of the earth, while the stone now twinkles in the window of every single tourist shop in the village. The area is a great base for walking and outdoor activities too and the caverns are worth visiting if you need to shelter from the rain.

Put the brakes on as you come to the bottom of Winnat's Pass and you'll find the best of the four underground caves in Castleton. The **Speedwell** Cavern ⓘ *T01433-620512, www.speedwellcavern.co.uk, daily except Christmas Day, 0930-1700 high season, 1000-1530 low season, £6, concessions £5, children £4, take a jumper, it's cold and damp down there*, takes you down through an airlock and on to a boat to explore the underground world. The guides are fun and informative and you can see where the miners carved out claustrophobic tunnels as well as the natural caves and stalactites and stalagmites.

Further into the village you'll find the **Peak Cavern**, trumpeting about its alternative name, *The Devil's Arse* ⓘ *T01433-620285, www.devils arse.com, Apr-Oct daily 1000-1700, Nov-Mar weekends only, 1000-1700, £5.50, concessions £4.50, children £3.50*, where you walk into the limestone gorge below Peveril Castle on an hour-long tour.

Overlooking Castleton is all 1695 ft of **Mam Tor**. Meaning "mother mountain", it's known locally as the 'shivering mountain', because it is composed of crumbling layers of gritstone and shale which produce frequent, small landslips. It's an easy walk up because it has a stepped footpath, ideal if you're not a true walker.

Edale and The Pennine Way

A pleasant walk from the centre of Castleton to Hollin's Cross will take you to Edale. It's also reachable by train on the Hope Valley line from Hope station and, as the beginning of the Pennine Way, is undoubtedly the most popular place to walk in the Peaks. The Way stretches from here through the High Peak, into the Yorkshire Dales beyond, into the Cheviot Hills and ends right up in the Scottish Borders. Opened in 1965 as the UK's first long distance path, it's a walk of 289 miles (463 km) up the backbone of England from Edale to Kirk Yetholm in the Scottish borders. It takes at least two weeks of solid walking across moorland and is a truly rewarding hike, but you need to be prepared for it. The high rainfall in the upland area and possibility of heatwaves make it unpredictable as far as the weather is concerned and you need to know how to use a map and compass. The best time of year to go is in the summer between late May and September. A number of walkers' books are available about the route, including Wainwright's *Pennine Way Companion*.

Eyam

Pronounced *eem*, don't be surprised if you can't find anywhere to park in this small village or if you're assailed by hordes of schoolchildren waving clipboards at you on a weekday. Eyam is famous for being the plague village where from 1665-6 the villagers underwent a voluntary quarantine to protect others from catching the Black Death, see box, and primary schoolchildren know the story better than anyone. It's a pretty place to explore and there are lovely walks to be had in this area.

The best place to begin your exploration of Eyam is the **Eyam** museum ⓘ *T01433-631371, Easter-Oct Tue-Sun 1000-1630, closed Mon, £1.75, concessions/children £1.25*, at the top of the village. It explores the early history of plague in the village in detail with a strong anecdotal focus on how it affected individuals. Downstairs is a smaller display about the silk and cotton industries alongside mining and quarrying which make up the more recent history.

From the museum you can walk into town where you'll find the **Plague cottages**, pretty, residential stone cottages with plaques on the outside walls with gruesome death tallies. The medieval **Eyam Parish Church** is also just off the main road and has a small exhibition inside about the plague. It has a far older history than this though, with a Saxon font and a Saxon cross in the graveyard outside. Don't be shy about looking round, it's all trampled by schoolchildren on a daily basis as they hurdle gravestones in search of plague victims. From the church there's a pleasant walk (1 km) across the fields to **Mompesson's well** on the outskirts of the village.

Bakewell

The best thing about Bakewell, roughly 5 miles from Eyam, is its major claim to fame – the delicious almond pastry cakes, Bakewell tarts, which came about when someone trying to bake a Christmas cake got it wrong. Originally an old Saxon market town, it's now a large village or small town, easily reached from Buxton or Chesterfield, with a small shopping centre, public gardens and a river running through it under a stone bridge. But the major sights in the area, Haddon Hall and Chatsworth House, just outside the town, are what often bring people here.

Two miles south of Bakewell on the A6, **Haddon Hall** ⓘ *T01629-812855, www.haddonhall.co.uk, Mar-Sep daily 1030-1700, Oct Thu-Sun 1030-1630, £7.25, concessions £6.25, children £3.75*, is a real delight in an idyllic setting. It's a beautiful medieval hall with Tudor additions set high on the hill with views of the surrounding area and a babbling offshoot of the River Wye passing under a stone bridge. Owned by the Manners family for 800 years, the walled gardens are very romantic and inside the hall you can walk round the Tudor bedrooms and the medieval chapel with its original heraldic wall paintings pretending to be a lord or lady taking some exercise in the long gallery. It's a quintessentially English scene and totally unmissable on a lovely day and compared with its neighbour, Chatsworth House, Haddon Hall is much more intimate and manageable in size.

Chatsworth House and Gardens ⓘ *T01246-582204, www.chatsworth.org, house and garden, Mar-Dec daily 1100-1730, £8.50, concessions £6.50, children £3, garden only, £5, concessions £3.50, children £2, farmyard and adventure playground, Mar-Dec daily, 1100-1730, £3.90, park open year round, free, leave plenty of time to explore this palatial residence, which could easily take all day and wear some comfortable shoes*, 8 miles north of Bakewell, is a huge 16th-century country estate known as the Palace of the Peak. The 105-acre garden is 450 years old and contains a maze, cottage gardens, 5 miles of wooded walks with rare trees and shrubs and a 200 m cascading waterfall. There's also a brilliant adventure playground up amid the trees and a working farmyard for children. The Duke and Duchess of Devonshire still live here and are actively involved in its upkeep. There are hundreds of richly decorated rooms, historic paintings and sculptures including works by Holbein, Rembrandt and Gainsborough. The Orangery in the gardens has some lovely craft shops and a café.

Matlock and Matlock Bath

Matlock is one of the larger towns in the Peak District. Surrounded by hills, and overlooked by a folly, Riber Castle, it's reasonably picturesque with a few good places to stay and eat but little in the way of tourist attractions – the real treasures lie outside the town. Matlock Bath, on the other hand, a couple of miles down the road, has plenty of child-friendly attractions – a cable car to a cave-riddled tourist centre, a Gulliver's Kingdom and an aquarium. Although its setting is undoubtedly striking, in a gorge with the River Derwent running through, these days it is awash with chip shops, amusement arcades and tacky trinket shops. In summer it becomes a haven for motorbikers attracted by the challenging, sweeping Derbyshire roads.

The Edwardian spa town became less popular towards the end of the 19th century and there's not much left to see of the actual spa today. On a rainy day, you could visit the **Aquarium** ⓘ *T01629-583624, F760793, 110 North Pde, Easter-Oct 1000-1730, Nov-Apr weekends 1000-1700, closed during the week, £1.80*, found in the old Matlock Bath Hydro, complete with a marble staircase and thermal pool which now comforts the aches and pains of the koi carp rather than the ladies and gents of the town.

Also in Matlock Bath is the **Peak Mining Museum and Temple Mine** ⓘ *The Pavilion, T01629-583834, www.peakmines.co.uk, museum, Easter-Oct daily 1000-1700, Nov-Apr daily 1100-1500, temple mine, daily Easter-Oct 1200-1600, Nov-Apr only weekends, 1200-1600, museum or mine £2.50, concessions £1.50, joint museum and mine ticket £4, concessions £2.50*, with hands-on exhibits and a maze of twisting tunnels. It's a real insight into the industry which has shaped so much of the area.

Riber Castle, at the top of the hill, is a ruined 19th-century castle built and designed by local textile designer John Smedley who founded Matlock's hydros. It has been unoccupied for many years, hence its romantic and ruined appearance. Take a walk up the hill to see it for yourself. A couple of miles to the south of Matlock Bath is **The Heights of Abraham** ⓘ *T01629-582365, www.heights-of-abraham.co.uk, Feb daily 1000-1630, Mar Sat-Sun only, 1000-1630, Apr-Nov daily1000-1700, £7.50, concessions £6.20, children £5.20*, where cable cars take you up above the Derwent River Valley to a limestone cliff. At the top you can go underground into the show caves and find out more about the mining history of the area. There's also an adventure playground for children and the view is breathtaking. Really it's a fully organized and commercial take on the countryside which you can see just as well by going for a walk independently, although the cable cars are fun.

Sleeping

Buxton *p502, map p502*

C **Biggin Hall**, Biggin-by-Hartington, 11 miles from Buxton, T01298-84451, www. bigginhall.co.uk. A fabulously romantic 17th-century pile which boasts air so pure that it supposedly soothes asthmatics and insomniacs. The bedrooms are stunning, huge low-beamed affairs with 4-poster beds and antiques, as well as log fires in the sitting rooms and a library. There's also traditional farmhouse cooking.

D **Lakenham Guesthouse**, 11 Burlington Rd, T01298-79209. One of many places overlooking Pavilion Gardens, it's a small place with period furniture and antiques.

E **Barms Farm**, a mile north of Buxton at Fairfield, T01298-77723, F78692. The pick of the bed and breakfasts round here. The good value but luxury rooms are light and airy in this non-smoking country farmhouse.

E **Fernydale Farm**, just 5 miles from Buxton at Earl Sterndale, T01298-83236, F83605. Bed and hearty breakfasts are on offer at this pretty white stone cottage on a small working farm. From Buxton, take the A515 to Ashbourne for about 3 miles and it is signposted from there.

E **Harefield**, 15 Marlborough Rd, T01298-24029, www.harefield1.freeserve.co.uk. A quiet and spacious Victorian home with a croquet lawn, run by fun-loving hosts. It's only a little walk from the town centre with gardens that meet the moors and a real log fire.

F **Buxton YHA**, Sherbrook Lodge, T/F01298-22287, buxton@yha.org.uk It's in wooded grounds 1½ miles from the station. Open from 1700.

Castleton *p503*

C **The Castle Hotel**, Castle St, T01433-620578. Really an old pub in the centre of the village, this is the only luxury accommodation here, 6 of its rooms containing jacuzzis, and 4-poster beds. It is 350 years old, has wholesome pub food and welcomes walkers.

E **Cryer House B&B**, is a charming homely small stone house with a cottage garden right next door to the Castle Hotel, T01433-620244.

F **Castleton YHA**, Castle St, T01433-620235, castleton @yha.org.uk. Hostel contained in a large stone farmhouse with a drying room, internet access, games rooms and information about local walks. They can also provide information about activities in the area like hang-gliding and pot-holing.

Camping

F **Losehill Caravan Club Site**, T01433-620636.

Edale *p503*

F **Edale YHA**, Rowland Cote, Nether Booth on the wooded hillside of the Kinder plateau, T01433-670302, edale @yha.org.uk, is particularly good for activities and activity groups. In the middle of a network of footpaths. There are also numerous farms who will let you pitch your tent in a field for a small price. No mod cons here, but at least it's cheap.

Eyam *p504*

E **The Old Rose and Crown**, on the main road, T01433-630858. The only place to stay in Eyam village. A charming white stone cottage, formerly the old village inn, now a B&B with lovely views of the area and 4 rooms.

F **Bretton YHA**, 2 miles from Eyam, T01433-631856, bookings T01629-592707, a small remote stone farmhouse with 18 beds.

F **Eyam YHA**, Hawkhill Rd, just out of town, T01433-630335, eyam@yha.org.uk. An eccentric turreted Victorian building just up the road from the village with 60 beds, open from 1700. They also have crazy golf.

Bakewell *p504*

D-C **Rutland Arms Hotel**, T01629-812812, F812309. A grand old establishment in the centre of Bakewell, which has played host to Wordsworth, Coleridge and Turner in the past, this is the home of the original Bakewell Pudding. It's the only hotel in the centre of Bakewell and has a welcoming restaurant serving traditional English food.

D **Haddon House Farm**, Haddon Rd just out of Bakewell, T01629-814024, www.haddon-house.co.uk. Quiet, spacious and a touch of romance with 2 luxurious double rooms.

E **Croft Cottage**, Coombs Rd, T01629-814101. A gorgeous 17th-century stone cottage with a luxury private suite in the converted barn. Comfortable and welcoming.

E **Melbourne House**, Buxton Rd, T01629-815357. A private Georgian house offering a variety of home-cooked breakfasts and a warm welcome.

Camping

F **Chatsworth Park Caravan Club Site**, T01246-582226 (Mar-Dec). In an old walled garden. You can also camp at

F **Haddon Grove Farm**, near Over Haddon on Monyash Rd, 4 miles west of town, T01629-812343.

Matlock and Matlock Bath *p505*

A **Riber Hall**, Riber, Matlock, T01629-582795, www.riber-hall.co.uk. An exceptional historic country house in a tranquil upmarket setting, with period furniture and exquisite detail, where you'll receive first class treatment.

C-D **The New Bath Hotel**, New Bath Rd, Matlock Bath, T0870-4008119, www.heritage-hotels.com. The Victorian hotel is the only place where you can still take to the healing water, it has indoor and outdoor pools and 5 acres of grounds, and is run by the Forte Hotel Group.

D **Hogkinson's Hotel**, 150 South Pde, Matlock Bath, T01629-582170, enquiries@hodgkinsons-hotel.co.uk. A place with a dash of Victorian elegance, terraced gardens and a restaurant.
D **The Temple Hotel**, Temple Walk, Matlock Bath, T01629-583911, www.templehotel.co.uk Another historic stone building with comfortable accommodation and a bar with real ale on tap. Lord Byron wooed one of his mistresses here and the restaurant is named after him. It's comfortable and friendly, but if Byron were around today, he'd probably stay at the more exclusive *New Bath Hotel* instead.
E **Middlehills Farm**, by Grange Hill in Matlock, T01629-650368. Cheap and quirky stone farmhouse with home-baked bread and genial hosts. You can also make friends with a potbellied pig.
E **The Old Sunday School**, New St, Matlock, T/F01629-583347. If you want something a little different from your usual B&B try this converted ex-chapel with, despite its history, a friendly home-from-home atmosphere.
F **Matlock YHA**, 40 Bank Rd, T01629-582983, T0870-7705690, matlock@yha.org.uk With charming laid-back staff, this medium-sized hostel used to be the Hydropathic Hospital. Has loads of information on the area as well as a bar. They also have information on inter-hostel walking trails which are a really good way to see around the Peak District as they're only between 9 and 17 miles apart.

Camping

F **Middle Hills Farm**, Grange Hill, Matlock, T01629-650368, l.lomas@btinternet.com. Camping and caravan site with toilets and showers and half a mile from the nearest pub.
F **Wayside Farm** on Matlock Moor, T01629-582967, there is also camping here although it's wilder and with few mod cons.

Eating

Buxton *p502, map p502*

££ **The Buckingham Hotel** 1 Burlington Rd, T01298-70481. Traditional English carvery menu most nights of the week, smoked salmon starters and a range of fish and vegetarian dishes too. Grilled chicken with goats' cheese and avocado, fillet steak and roast lamb are typical.
££ **Columbine Restaurant**, 7 Hall Bank, T01298-78752, is the town's best restaurant. Very reasonably priced for fresh local produce, there's a range of meat and fish dishes including venison in Guinness, and friendly service in a classy restaurant. Closed Sun and Tue Nov-Apr.
££ **Old Hall Hotel** on the Square just across from the Opera House, T01298-22841, serving English Sunday lunch style roasts within its historic wood-panelled walls. They have a pre- and post-theatre menu and accommodation.
£ **The Old Clubhouse**, Water St, T01298-70117, is a traditional warm pub with an open fire serving pub grub. It also has a garden for the summer months.
£ **The Wild Carrot**, 5 Bridge St, T01298-22843, a small licensed vegetarian cafe with home-cooked food. Open Wed-Sun. There's also a wholefood shop downstairs, open Mon-Sat.

Entertainment

Buxton *p502, map p502*

Buxton Opera House, T01298-72190, www.buxton-opera.co.uk. There are regular shows here throughout the year of various genres from book adaptations and poetry readings to opera, ballet and newly commissioned plays including *The Full Monty*. The **Old Hall Hotel** contains **The Pauper's Pit Theatre**, with more fringe productions. **The Buxton Buzz Comedy Club** on the first Fri in the month upstairs at the **Old Clubhouse** from 2030. On the last Thu in each month **Club Acoustic Concerts** are also held upstairs in the *Old Clubhouse*, T01298-25954.

Activities and tours

Outdoor pursuits

Derwent Pursuits, Cromford Mill, Mill Lane, Cromford just outside Matlock, T01629-824179, info@derwent-pursuits.com. Offer a range of courses from a full day to weeks where you can make the most of the outdoors with orienteering, caving, climbing and abseiling. It's one of the few places where you can have a go without committing yourself to a full all-action week. Otherwise you could try the *YHA*, who provide information on outdoor pursuits in the area.

Riding

Ladybooth Trekking Centre, T01433-670205. Full and half-day treks through the Peak District, and lessons for beginners. A 2½-hr ride over the moors costs £18 Apr-Sept only.

Northfield Farm Riding and Trekking Centre in Flash, just outside Buxton, have rides by the hr or the day for all abilities. T01298-22543, F27849. A 2-hr trek costs £20 and it's £37 for a full day.

Walking

Peakland Walking Trails, based in Tideswell, Derbyshire. For the more experienced walker, can organize self-guided tours and also offer year-round weekend walking tours with an experienced guide from about £170 including accommodation in Tideswell, T01298-872801, www.walkingholidays.org.uk

Transport

Bus

Buses go from Castleton to **Bakewell** 5 times a day and 6 times a day to **Buxton**. The village is 3 miles from the nearest station in Hope, see Hope Valley Railway page 501. The no. 200 bus runs from Castleton bus station to **Edale** station hourly from 0853 and takes 20 mins. There's also a service from **Castleton** to **Bakewell** via **Buxton**, the 173 bus which takes 50 mins and runs every 2 hrs.

Directory

Buxton *p502, map p502*

Bicycle Peak Cycle Hire in Hayfield, just outside Buxton on the A624, hire out bikes and have information on cycle trails throughout the Peak District, T01663-746222, F741581.

Cheshire

→Colour map 3

Contained within Cheshire's boundaries, which stretch from North Wales to Manchester and Derbyshire, are an inordinate number of country houses, medieval hunting estates and the small town of Prestbury, housing more millionaires per head than any other town in England. Small wonder that a lot of Cheshire's residents have delusions of grandeur – this is an upmarket area with a very desirable postcode. Chester, the much-visited Roman city with fantastic shopping and museums, is worth a visit, as is the lush countryside that the wealthy landowners liked so much. Cheshire is a serious bit of posh amid the metropolitan areas of the Northwest and its residents wouldn't want you to forget it. » *For Sleeping, Eating and other listings, see pages 511-513.*

Chester

Chester is a walled Roman city on the Welsh borders and the Romans still rule the roost here today. Don't be surprised if you see the odd centurion or two sitting around having a coffee in one of the many cafés in the centre of town – as you'll realize within five minutes of being here, tourism is the main industry. Despite the Roman theme, your first impressions are likely to be of the beautiful black and white Tudor-style architecture, particularly the Rows, the half-timbered shopping precincts unique to Chester. While browsing the many shops, your ears will be assailed by any number of regional accents, buskers and odd gabble of Welsh – the language still thrives a couple of miles away across the border. Walking around the walls, taking a boat trip on the Dee and enjoying the historic pubs after a shopping spree around the Rows are some of the best ways to spend your day here.

Ins and outs

Getting there Manchester Airport is 40 mins away on the M56 and M53 from Chester for international and domestic flights, T0161-4898000. Liverpool John Lennon Airport in Liverpool is also 40 mins away by road T0151-2884000. Chester is well-linked with the M53 and M56 for getting to and from Liverpool and Manchester. The bus station is on Delamere St for all regional and national buses. Be warned that the local buses in this area aren't particularly direct or reliable. You can get to North Wales from here by bus and around Cheshire, but you'll need to check the timetables closely. **National Express** run coach services around England, Wales and Scotland and **Cheshire Traveline** has further information on local buses, T01244-602666. There are high speed rail services run from London Euston and Paddington to Crewe and Chester, also from Glasgow on the West Coast Main Line. It's also easy to get here from Manchester's Piccadilly and Oxford Rd stations and Birmingham New St. The station is a 15-min walk from the centre. ▸▸ *For further details, see Transport, page 512.*

Getting around It only takes 20 mins to walk from one side of Chester to the other and going by foot is your only option as the centre of town is pedestrianized. Naturally, there are plenty of well-signposted car parks, mainly to the north of the town and a number of park and ride options at the far edges of the city.

Information Just outside the city walls to the southeast of the city is the excellent **Chester Visitor Centre** ⓘ *Vicar's Lane overlooking the amphitheatre, T01244-402111, www.chestertourism.com, Apr-Sep Mon-Sat 0900-1730, Sun 1000-1600, Oct-Mar Mon-Sat 1000-1700, Sun 1000-1600*, there you can book accommodation for a £3 charge, which will give you a 10% discount. Upstairs is an excellent historical exhibition and the chance to do some brass rubbing and candlemaking. **Chester** TIC ⓘ *Town hall on Northgate St, T402111, Apr-Sep Mon-Sat 0900-1730, Sun 1000-1600, Oct-Mar 1000-1700.*

Sights

Starting at the TIC at the town hall, walk under the 14th-century archway to the left of the cathedral into Abbey Square and through the northwest corner to find the **city wall**. Walking along the wall away from town will take you to the **Northgate** with its canals and locks behind it.

This is the beginning of a 40-minute walk into town which takes in most of the sights of Chester. To your left here the **cathedral** ⓘ *Daily 0730-1830, £2 donation*, stands where there has always been a church since AD 907. The cloisters are very atmospheric and it has a very good information trail including a manuscript of Handel's *Messiah* which he practised here en route to Ireland.

Next, the **Eastgate**, once the main entrance to the city is now a bridge over the main shopping street, Eastgate Street, with the second most photographed clock in England after Big Ben, commemorating 60 years of Queen Victoria's reign. Walking on, you reach **Newgate** from which there is a view over the **Roman amphitheatre** to the left, and the Chester visitor centre beyond it. It's not that impressive and has only been half excavated, but held between six and seven thousand spectators in its day. Beyond it is **Grosvenor Park**, a local beauty spot and ideal for a picnic.

Just beyond Newgate is the river, reached easily if you go down **the wishing steps**. Folklore has it that if you run up and down and then up again without drawing breath, your wish will come true. There aren't all that many of them, but they're uneven in depth which makes it a tricky one and may have you looking for a casualty ward if you're not careful.

Walking from here into town along the walls will take you to the Southgate, known locally as **Bridgegate** as it's opposite the 14th-century bridge out of town.

Around Chester

The borough of **Macclesfield** in north Cheshire is the largest district in the county, comprising Alderley Edge, Knutsford, Poynton and Wilmslow, and is easily the most affluent. Accessible on the London-Manchester intercity rail link or from the M6, 'Macc' is known for its 18th and 19th century silk industry. At that time it was the greatest silk weaving town in England. The **Silk Museum** ⓘ *T01625-613210, Mon-Sat 1100-1700, Sun 1300-1700, £3, £2 children*, at the heritage centre on Roe St tells the story of the town, whose football team are still known as the Silkmen.

Prestbury

The B5087 from Macclesfield to Alderley Edge turns north to the picturesque village of Prestbury. The river Bollin runs through this historic town complete with half-timbered Tudor buildings, and it's no wonder that so many affluent people have chosen to live around here. It's known in the area for being the village with the most millionaires per mile in the county, if not the country.

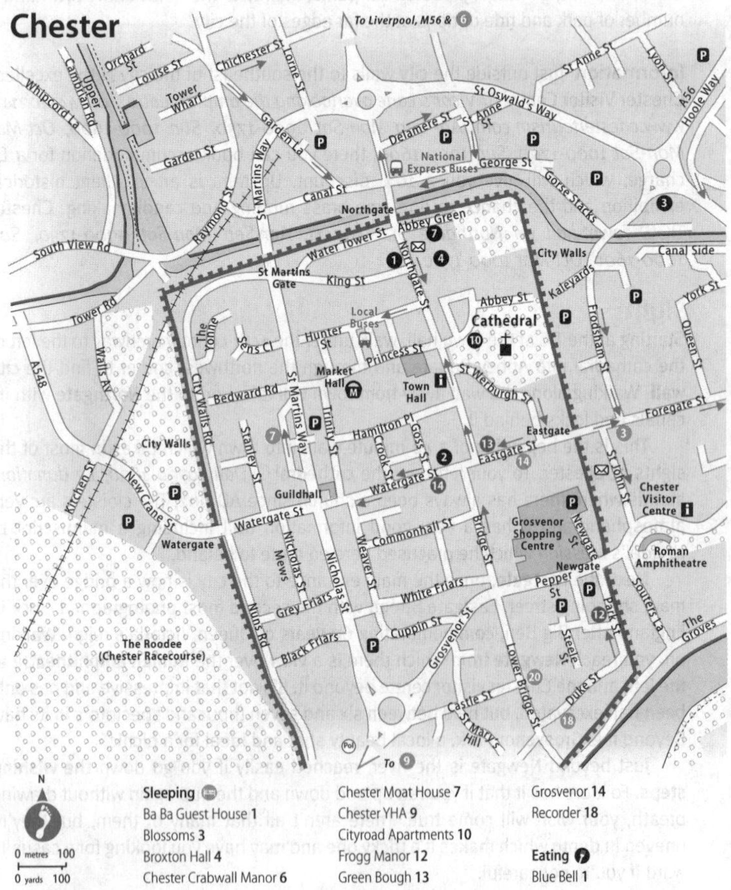

Alderley Edge

From Prestbury you can wind round the village roads past Mottram St Andrews to Alderley Edge, home of David Beckham. The town is nothing special, but just before is an area of outstanding natural beauty. Try to stop for a walk to the **Edge**, 250 acres of sandstone ridge with views out over the Cheshire Plain as far as the Peak District. It's a place which inspired Alan Garner's children's book, *The Weirdstone of Brisingamen*.

Lyme Park

Take the A523 from Macclesfield to Hazel Grove and then the A6 to High Lane and you'll find Lyme Park. In the borough of Stockport, it's the largest country house in Cheshire. With Ionic pillars, Greek marbles and an Elizabethan drawing room, the 16th-century house itself is very grand and not surprisingly frequently used as a backdrop for period dramas. Walks around the grounds along a number of well-marked trails are free and worth the effort. From the car park you can easily walk to **The Cage** ⓘ *T01663-762023, hall and gardens, Apr-Oct Fri-Tue 1300-1700, £5.50, park Apr-Oct daily 0800-2030, Nov-Mar 0800-1800, free for walkers, £3.50 per car, you can also reach the park by train and a short walk from Disley station*, the folly at the top of the nearest hill from where the ladies of the house used to watch the hunt. You can see the Peak District from the top of the hill and the many red and fallow deer across the estate. More gruesomely, the lower part of the cage was used to jail poachers.

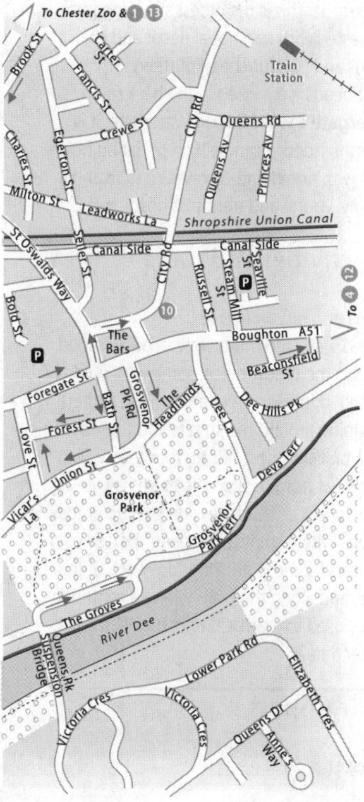

Brasserie **3**
Elliot's **4**
La Boheme **2**
Mediterranean **7**
Refectory **10**

Pubs & bars
Albion Inn **12**
Boot Inn **13**
Watergate's **14**

Sleeping

Chester *p508, map p510*

A **Chester Moat House**, Trinity St, T01244-899988, F316118. A little less individual with a country hotel feel, but younger and with a great spa complex.

A **The Grosvenor Hotel** on Eastgate, T01244-324024. Bang in the centre of town and very plush, this place is owned by the Duke of Westminster and one of the two 5-star hotels in the Northwest. It is traditional with leather armchairs and 4-poster beds.

B **Chester Crabwall Manor**, Parkgate Rd, Mollington, T01244-851666, www.marstonhotels.com. A country manor retreat set in private grounds with a swimming pool and elegant individually designed rooms.

C **The Green Bough Hotel**, 60 Hoole Rd, T01244-326241, greenboughhotel@cwcom.net. A boutique-style hotel with 4-poster beds and luxurious fabrics in elegant, rooms. There's also a restaurant here, *The Olive Tree*, and antique furniture.

C **Frogg Manor**, Nantwich Rd in Broxton, a short drive from Chester, T01829-782629, F782459. Flounces and frills and an overdose of romance in this eccentric place with mad 1930s and 40s-style bedrooms.

D **Blossoms Hotel**, St Johns St just off Eastgate, T01244-323186, F346433. Traditional and reasonably priced hotel but not particularly exciting. Has a restaurant and decent-sized rooms.
D **The Broxton Hall Hotel**, Whitchurch Rd, Broxton, T01829-782321, reservations @broxtonhall.co.uk. A stunning black and white 17th-century hall with landscaped gardens, fishing, riding and log fires.
E **Ba Ba Guest House**, 65 Hoole Rd, T01244-315047, www.babaguesthouse.co.uk. An elegant Victorian townhouse, it's one of the most friendly and welcoming B&Bs in town.
E **Recorder Hotel** right in the centre of Chester at 19 City Walls, overlooking the river Dee, T01244-326580, www.recorderhotel.co.uk. A stately guesthouse with individually designed bedrooms (12 guest rooms named after the signs of the zodiac), it also has 4-poster and Victorian beds and the location is perfect.
F **Chester YHA**, Hough Green House, 40 Hough Green, T01244-680056, chester @yha.org.uk A Victorian house with a laundry, internet and kitchen facilities. It's bigger than it looks with around 100 beds and offers evening meals.
F **Cityroad Apartments**, 18 City Rd, T01244-313651 daytime, www.chesterooms.com. Very basic student room-style accommodation plus an optional breakfast. Even cheaper than the YHA.

Eating

Chester *p508, map p510*
£££ **Blue Bell restaurant**, 65 Northgate St, T01244-317758. Highly recommended and serves local produce in a medieval inn with a great wine list. It's very relaxed and friendly.
££ **The Brasserie**, Brookdale Pl just off Frodsham St across the canal, T01244-322288, looks like an identikit pub from the outside but serves fantastic British and Mediterranean cooking in a trendy minimalist environment, blowing the cobwebs from most of Chester's older establishments.
££ **Elliot's**, T01244-329932, at 2 Abbey Green just off Northgate St beyond the town hall serves delicious organic and vegetarian food.
££ **La Boheme**, 58 Watergate St, T01244-313721, is an unusual fusion of Swedish and French cuisine, very good value and served in an elegant minimalist restaurant.
££ **The Mediterranean Restaurant** in Rufus Court just around the corner, T01244-320004, is particularly good for fish and has the atmosphere of a Greek taverna.
£ **The Refectory** in Chester Cathedral is a cheap and wholesome affair, seated on school canteen type benches but with much nicer home-made snacks, T01244-313156.

Pubs, bars and clubs

Chester *p508, map p510*
The Albion Inn is a great stopping point along the walls just after Newgate but only if you're also 'hostile to kids' as it proclaims itself to be. It serves outstanding pub grub and has a warming log fire in winter.
The Boot Inn, on the right-hand side of Eastgate St. This is the oldest surviving pub in Chester, with traditional décor and oak beams and pub lunches. Fourteen roundheads were killed in the back room.
Watergate's Wine Bar on Watergate St is recommended, a candlelit crypt dating from 1120 with nooks and crannies to sit in and a friendly, young and trendy atmosphere.

Activities and tours

Chester *p508, map p510*
Guided walks around town can be arranged through the tourist office, some with guides dressed in full Roman gear leading children whooping around the streets and there's also a brilliant ghost hunter tour (every Thu, Fri and Sat from outside the town hall at 1930, Jun-Oct). This takes you past a number of pubs where spirits have been spotted over the years by those drinking too much of the same, and along the walls where a centurion is supposed to roam. Contact the TIC for further details.

Transport

Chester *p508, map p510*
Bus
There are 10 **National Express** coach services daily to **London** (6 hrs), 8 to **Birmingham** (2 hrs), 6 to **Cardiff** (5 hrs), 8 to **Gatwick** (8 hrs), 8 to **Liverpool** (1 hr), 6 to **Manchester** and **Manchester** airport (1 hr). For **Edinburgh** there are 4 services a day (11 hrs) and buses run to **Glasgow** twice daily (7 hrs).

Car
Avis 128 Brook St, T311463, **Budget**, The Bridgegate, Lower Bridge St, T313431, **Hertz**, Trafford St, T374705, **Europcar**, 143 Brook St, T312893, **Eurodollar**, Sealand Industrial Estate, T390008.

Train
Central Trains, www.centraltrains.co.uk, run from Chester to **Birmingham** (2 hrs) and **London Euston** (4 hrs). First Northwestern run the stopping service from Chester to **Manchester** via **Knutsford** (1 hr 15 mins) and services into Wales including to **Holyhead** for the boat to **Dublin** (1 hr 30 mins).

Liverpool

→Colour map 3

Liverpool's trying hard to shrug off its image as a city full of scallies, shell suits and curly perms, not least by becoming the European Capital of Culture for 2008. Built around the docks and the River Mersey, it's a small city with the vibrant blend of cultures that its history as a major port has produced. There's an exceptional modern art scene nestled in a town with its fair share of rough areas, as well as museums, the Albert Dock and, of course, the Beatles. You could be forgiven for thinking that Liverpool has stood still after the demise of the four cheeky scousers: through the Cavern Quarter to the Albert Dock you'll find tours and trips to satisfy the worst of Beatlemaniacs. The overdose of Beatles culture can be righted with a trip to Cream, the UK's most popular nightclub and the Ropewalks area, throbbing with clubs and bars and not a shell suit in sight. Perfect for a hard day's night. ▸▸ *For Sleeping, Eating and other listings, see pages 518-521.*

Ins and outs

Getting there The newly renamed **Liverpool John Lennon Airport**, T0151-2884000, is 7 miles southeast of the city centre in Speke. There are now budget easyJet flights to destinations including Paris and Barcelona from here as well as services to Ireland. The **airport** has currency exchange facilities and ATMs in the main terminal. The express bus 500 is the only way to reach the centre of Liverpool by public transport as there's no train station. **National Express coach** services run from Norton St to all major UK cities and towns from the station north of Liverpool Lime St station. By **car**, Liverpool is 35 miles from Manchester on the M62 and M60, 215 miles from London and 102 miles from Birmingham on the M6. From the M6 follow the M56 or M62. The main *ferry* terminal, for ferries to the Isle of Man and Ireland, is at Pier Head to the west, within walking distance of the centre. The **Seacat** service, T0870-5523523, connects Liverpool with Dublin in 4 hrs and the **Isle of Man Steam Packet** service, T08705-523523 (UK), T1800-551743 (Ireland), connects with Douglas, and **Norse Merchant Ferries** links with Dublin and Belfast, T0870-6004321. **Train** connections to London, Manchester and other major cities is at Liverpool Lime St station, well-signposted just north of the centre of town. ▸▸ *For further details, see Transport, page 521.*

Getting around Finding your way around Liverpool isn't too difficult. It's a manageable size and you can orientate yourself easily by looking up to the Radio City tower, St John's Beacon, which has the TIC in Queen Sq below it, or looking out towards the Royal Liver building and the docks. The Pier Head and the Albert Dock are a 15 min walk from the TIC, or 2 mins in a taxi or a bus, running also from Queen Sq bus station. The **smart bus** network extends all over the city, taking you down to the Albert Dock on the no.1 from the Queen Sq bus station.

 Information TIC ⓘ *Queen Sq, T0906-6806886 (calls cost 25p per minute), askme@visitliverpool.com, can book transport and accommodation for you. Book free on T0845 6011125, www.visitliverpool.com.* Blue badge walking tours also leave from outside at various pre-arranged times. Mon, Wed-Sat 0900-1730, Tue 1000-1730, Sun 1030-1630. There is a smaller **TIC** ⓘ *T0906-6806886, www.albertdock.com 1000-1730 daily*, inside the Albert Dock, again with an accommodation booking service,

Sights

Albert Dock

The Albert Dock, once the main quayside for the influential port in the 19th century, is now the city's main tourist attraction. You'll no longer see sacks of spices and exotic produce in the complex but some impressive museums telling the story of the city, from the slave trade through to the Beatles, amid cafés and a few touristy shops.

Just before you enter the Albert Dock along the Wapping Road that runs parallel to the dock, you'll see two modern sculptures, both bright yellow. One is the **Yellow Submarine**, cheery and recognizable from the cartoon, welcoming you to the city's biggest and best Beatles museum, The Beatles Story, inside the dock. The other is **SuperLambBanana**. It's basically a giant 18 ft yellow lamb morphing into a banana, the work of Japanese artist Taro Chiezo. It's a weird sight, set against the background of disused 19th-century warehouses, and it's one of many modern street sculptures you'll see in the city.

The entry point to the Albert Dock at Britannia Pavilion blasts a selection of Beatles' hits at you – it's the unmissable **Beatles Story** ⓘ *T0151-7091963, www.beatlesstory.com, daily 1000-1800, £7.95, £5.45 concessions*. Walk through mocked up streets of Liverpool and Hamburg, including a fake Cavern, and check out Lennon's white 'Imagine' piano. This is the city's finest tribute to the Fab Four from beginning to end. Set in the basement vaults it's a must if you're a fan. You'll be singing harmonies all day long and you can visit the gift shop stuffed full of memorabilia if you don't fancy paying the entry fee.

Walking through the docks around the square to the right, you'll find the small TIC in the Atlantic Pavilion. On Hartley Quay the **Merseyside Maritime Museum** ⓘ *all museums, T0151-4784499, daily 1000-1700, free*, incorporates the **HM Customs and Excise Museum** and the **Museum of Liverpool Life**. The customs museum on the ground floor has plenty of interactive features allowing you to experience a-day-in-the-life-of a customs officer while the Museum of Liverpool Life is housed on the other side of the Canning Dock with displays about the personality of Merseyside as well as a history of the city and its workers. The real gem here is in the basement of the Merseyside Maritime Museum itself. If you don't have time to visit any other attraction in Liverpool, make sure you don't miss the deeply moving **Transatlantic Slavery Gallery**. The exhibition, opened by Maya Angelou in 1992, explores this area of history in a personal and affecting way.

Tate Liverpool ⓘ *T0151-7027400, www.tate.org.uk /liverpool, Tue-Sun 1000-1800, closed Mon except bank holidays, free with a charge for special exhibitions*, is the original Tate Modern, with four floors of modern art and regular exhibitions by major international artists including exhibitions touring from the London Tate Modern. There's something about it that doesn't work quite so well – the building has nothing of Bankside Power Station's buzz, and the low ceilings make it feel a little flat – they do host some interesting artist talks though.

Magical Mystery Tour

In 1960 four local Scouse lads changed the face of music forever. Hailing from Liverpool, John, Paul, George and Pete Best, soon to be replaced by Ringo Starr, spent the 60s singing about the places they'd remember all their lives, from Strawberry Fields to Penny Lane. Some places have changed and some remain the same, but here's a few of the places you can visit:

The Beatles Story, Albert Dock, T7091963. They've got the white *Imagine* piano on loan from George Michael in this museum, as well as a complete history of the band from Hamburg to the present day.

20 Forthlin Road, Speke, T427 7231. Paul McCartney's childhood home and the kitchen where he and Lennon wrote *Love Me Do*. Now owned by the National Trust.

Mendips, 251 Menlove Avenue, where Lennon lived with his aunt until he was 23, has recently been bought by Yoko Ono and donated to the National Trust. Tours leave from the Albert Dock and Speke Hall.

The Cavern, Cavern Quarter, T0871-2221957. The Cavern witnessed 300 performances from the Beatles here in the 1960s as well as a final gig of the century from Paul McCartney in December 1999.

Mathew Street Gallery, above The Beatles shop, Cavern Quarter, T2360009. See the Astrid Kirchherr and Klaus Voorman black and white portraits here alongside displays and exhibitions about the life and times of the Beatles.

Pier Head

From the Albert Dock you can take a walk along the Mersey on the **Riverside Walk** to Pier Head. It only takes a few minutes and you'll walk past one of Liverpool's most famous buildings, the **Liver Insurance Building** (pronounced like 'driver' rather than 'river'). It was built in 1910 as one of the world's first multi-storey reinforced concrete buildings and its clock, 'The Great George', has the largest face of any of Britain's clocks. At the top of the building are the Liver Birds, one of the city's symbols. The mythical species of bird owe their creation to an ancient corporation seal of the town which originally featured an eagle. Local legend says that if they fly away, the city will cease to exist. Pier Head is along the dock past the Liver Building, the home of **Mersey Ferries** ① *Heritage cruises Mon-Fri 1000-1500, Sat-Sun 1000-1800, T0151-3301444, www.merseyferries.co.uk, £4.50, concessions £3.30*. A 50-minute tour of the river is the best way to see the city from the murky Mersey and takes you through 850 years of the city's history.

Cavern Quarter

More like a tiny fraction than a quarter with its three small streets, this area has had a disproportionately huge impact on the city as a whole. It's the home of the Cavern Club where the Beatles first found fame, providing more photo opportunities than anywhere else in the city. You can slink your arm around a young bronze John Lennon on Mathew Street as he lounges against a wall covered in the names of bands who have rocked the Cavern since 1957. **The Cavern Club** opposite is a dingy little bar and club that's still going strong, see Live music.

Nothing to do with the moptops is the intimate **View Two Gallery** ① *Thu-Sat 1200-1600, free*, three floors of modern art in a townhouse on Mathew Street. It's got wooden floorboards, white space and a particularly good gallery on the third floor. A calm environment away from the blatant tourism of the street below.

Liverpool

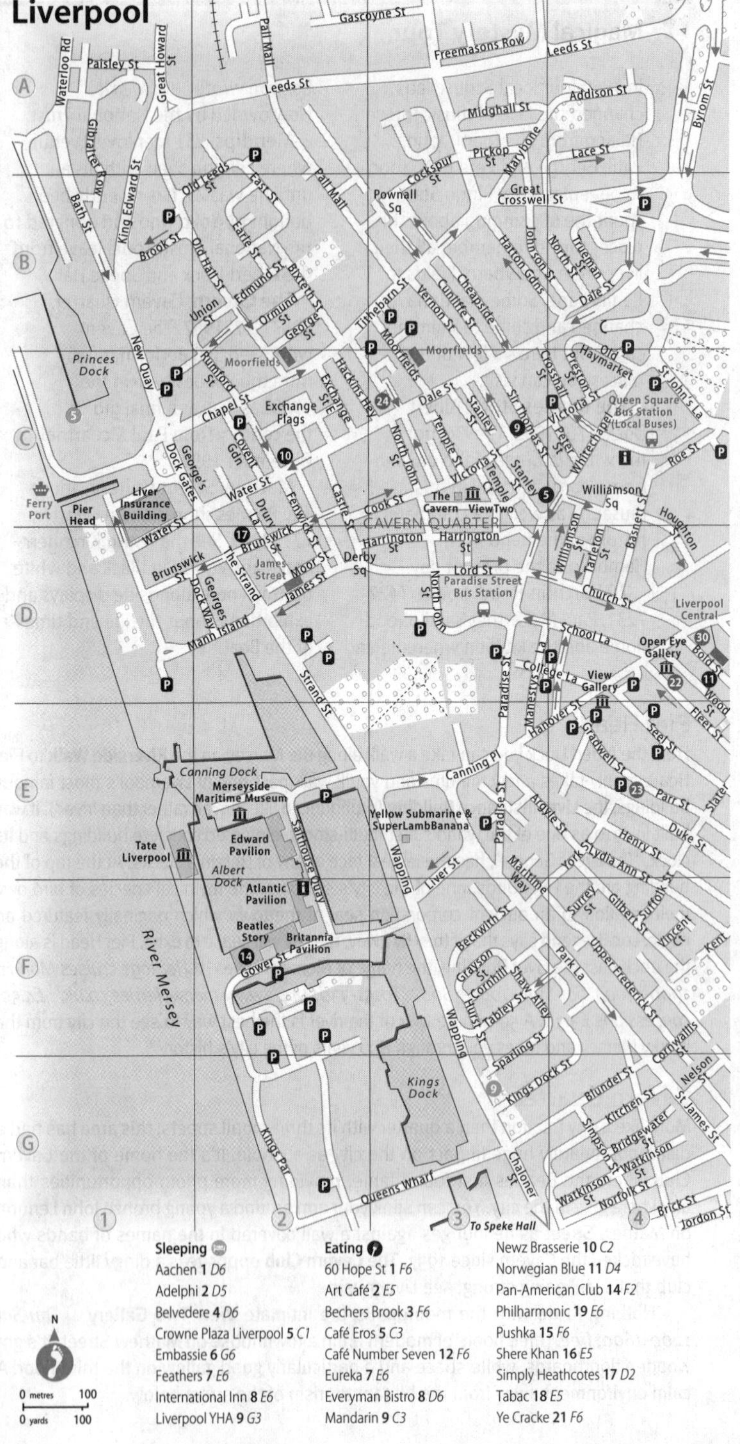

Gascoyne St
Freemasons Row
Leeds St
Pall Mall
Paisley St
Great Howard St
Waterloo Rd
Addison St
Midghall St
Byrom St
Lace St
Pickop St
Marybone
Cockspur St
Gibraltar Row
King Edward St
Old Leeds St
East St
Great Crosswell St
Pownall Sq
Bath St
Brook St
Old Hall St
Earle St
Hatton Gdns
Johnson St
North St
Trueman St
Bixteth St
Edmund St
Union St
Ormund St
George St
Tithebarn St
Vernon St
Cunliffe St
Cheapside
Dale St
New Quay
Princes Dock
Rumford St
Moorfields
Old Haymarket
Preston St
St John's La
Hackins Hey
Exchange St E
Exchange Flags
Chapel St
Covent Gdn
Tempest Hey
Stanley St
Crosshall St
Queen Square Bus Station (Local Buses)
Temple St
Victoria St
St Thomas St
Peter St
Whitechapel
Roe St
George's Dock Gates
North John St
Water St
Fenwick St
Castle St
Cook St
The Cavern
View Two
Temple Ct
Williamson Sq
Houghton St
Ferry Port
Pier Head
Liver Insurance Building
CAVERN QUARTER
Drury La
Brunswick St
Harrington St
Williamson St
Tarleton St
Basnett St
The Strand
James Street
Moor St
Derby Sq
Lord St
Paradise Street Bus Station
Church St
Liverpool Central
Georges Dock Way
James St
Mann Island
School La
Open Eye Gallery
Bold St
College La
View Gallery
Wood St
Manestys La
Paradise St
Strand St
Hanover St
Fleet St
Seel St
Gradwell St
Canning Dock
Canning Pl
Merseyside Maritime Museum
Parr St
Slater St
Yellow Submarine & SuperLambBanana
Argyle St
Duke St
Henry St
Tate Liverpool
Edward Pavilion
Albert Dock
Salthouse Quay
Wapping
Liver St
Maritime Way
York St
Lydia Ann St
Atlantic Pavilion
Beatles Story
Britannia Pavilion
River Mersey
Gower St
Surrey St
Gilbert St
Suffolk St
Vincent Ct
Beckwith St
Kent St
Grayson St
Cornhill
Shaw St
Alley
Park La
Upper Frederick St
Hurst St
Tabley St
Sparling St
Cornwallis St
Kings Dock
Kings Dock St
Nelson St
Blundel St
Kitchen St
St James St
Simpson St
Bridgewater St
Kings Par
Queens Wharf
Chaloner St
Watkinson St
Norfolk St
Brick St
Jordon St
To Speke Hall
Sleeping
Aachen 1 D6
Adelphi 2 D5
Belvedere 4 D6
Crowne Plaza Liverpool 5 C1
Embassie 6 G6
Feathers 7 E6
International Inn 8 E6
Liverpool YHA 9 G3
Eating
60 Hope St 1 F6
Art Café 2 E5
Bechers Brook 3 F6
Café Eros 5 C3
Café Number Seven 12 F6
Eureka 7 E6
Everyman Bistro 8 D6
Mandarin 9 C3
Newz Brasserie 10 C2
Norwegian Blue 11 D4
Pan-American Club 14 F2
Philharmonic 19 E6
Pushka 15 F6
Shere Khan 16 E5
Simply Heathcotes 17 D2
Tabac 18 E5
Ye Cracke 21 F6
N
0 metres 100
0 yards 100

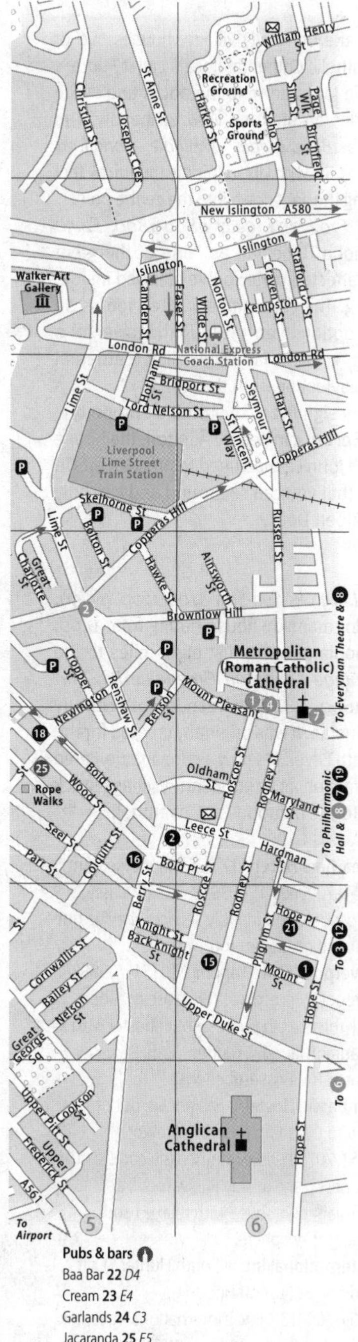

Pubs & bars
Baa Bar **22** *D4*
Cream **23** *E4*
Garlands **24** *C3*
Jacaranda **25** *E5*
Late Room **30** *D4*

Walker Art Gallery

Adjacent to Liverpool Lime Street station on William Brown Street stands the grand **Walker Art Gallery** ⓘ *T0151-4784199, www.walkerartgallery.org.uk, Mon-Sat 1000-1700, Sun 1200-1700, free*. Unlike most of Liverpool's art galleries, the Walker has a varied collection of paintings and sculptures dating from before 1950, including masterpieces by Rembrandt and a selection of impressionist paintings. There's only a small collection of modern art here, but that's pretty special too, with David Hockney hanging beside Gilbert and George. It's the city's biggest and most varied collection and one of the institutions that's driving Liverpool's bid to be the European Capital of Culture in 2008.

Around Hanover Street

From the outside, the Gostins Building on Hanover Street looks like so many of those around it – a little dishevelled and ramshackle office block – but inside it's a treasure trove. The ground floor houses **The View Gallery** ⓘ *T0151-7097273, Mon-Fri 1000-1700, Sat 1200-1600, Sun closed, free*, View Two's big brother and a former furniture showroom. It's a private art gallery with quirky pieces of furniture and contemporary paintings going back far into the building. The modern paintings, predominantly by professional artists from the Northwest, are very interesting, particularly the owner's own politically slanted photo-collages. It's got all the atmosphere that the Tate Liverpool is crying out for – and you're likely to get a personal tour and a glass of wine too.

Just off Concert Square on Wood Street in the very centre of Liverpool is the **Open Eye Gallery** ⓘ *T0151-7099460, www.openeye.org.uk, Tue-Fri 1030-1730, Sat 1030-1700, closed Sun and Mon, free*. It was developed to exhibit photography, film and video and has survived being flooded, burnt out and prosecuted for obscenity to become one of the best photo and new media galleries in England.

Other sights in the city

Finally, the Hope Street area which leads up to the university village, houses two of Liverpool's landmarks. At one end, the Roman Catholic Cathedral (locals call it *Paddy's wigwam*) with its spiky crown and concrete façade looks down to the docks and at the other the tower of the Anglican cathedral provides an amazing view of the city. The **Metropolitan Cathedral** ⓘ *T0151-7099222, 0800-1800, guides available, donations encouraged*, is a distinctive building built 1962-1967 with an inspiring theatrical feel inside with Mondrian-inspired stained glass filtering the light down into the centre point.

The Anglican Cathedral ⓘ *T0151-7096271, F7027292, daily 0800-1800, £2.50 donations encouraged*, was described by Sir John Betjeman as "one of the great buildings of the world" and it's hard not to feel affected once you've stepped inside. The sheer volume of space inside is astounding. The cathedral's vaulted roof is so high that you feel swallowed up and there's an option to go 331 ft up the tower for a view of the city (*costing £2 adults, £1 concessions*). It's the largest Anglican cathedral in Europe and the bells have the highest and heaviest peals in the world.

The National Trust recently purchased a very significant Liverpudlian property – **20 Forthlin Road** ⓘ *Mar-Oct Wed-Sat, Nov-Dec Sat only*, in nearby Allerton, the house where Paul McCartney grew up and where he and John Lennon used to practise riffs in the kitchen. It's the only original Beatles house that you can see round and can only be reached by minibus from Speke Hall or the Albert Dock.

Around Liverpool

Speke Hall ⓘ *T0151-427 7231, www.spekehall.org.uk, Tue-Sun 1100-1700. £5.50, children £3.50*, is a beautiful half-timbered Tudor mansion house dating from 1490, surrounded by a maze and some gorgeous woodland walks just eight miles to the south of the city centre. **Port Sunlight** ⓘ *Heritage Centre on Greendale Rd, Port Sunlight Wirral, T0151-6446466, daily 1000-1600*, is a picturesque 19th-century village just outside Bebington on the Wirral Peninsula. It was originally created for the workers of Lever's soap factory by William Hesketh Lever. It's now a conservation area with landscaped gardens, primarily a tourist attraction as a 19th-century village stuck in time, all the more strange for being so close to the metropolis of Liverpool.

Sleeping

A **Crowne Plaza Liverpool**, Princess Dock, Pier Head, T0151-2438000, F2438111. The only hotel in this price bracket, the Crowne Plaza is down on the waterfront with all that you'd expect from the chain of stylish modern hotels.
B-C **The Adelphi Hotel**, Ranelagh Pl, T0151-7097200, F7080743. It's a Liverpool landmark which featured in a documentary series *Hotel*. A massive Victorian hotel based on an oceanliner layout. It used to be the poshest hotel in the city, but the fame that the series brought has made it feel a little ridiculous.
D **Aachen Hotel**, 89-91 Mount Pleasant, T0151-7093633, F7091126. Recently voted the best small hotel in Liverpool. It's a small, central, friendly place with a huge all-you-can-eat breakfast.
D **Belvedere Hotel** at 83 Mount Pleasant, small family-run hotel close to the city's attractions, T0151-7095239, F7097169.
D **Feathers Hotel**, 117-125 Mount Pleasant, T0151-7099655, F7093838. A fairly classy atmosphere and friendly service. They've got a bar and restaurant too.
E **Liverpool YHA**, Wapping, T0151-7098888, liverpool@yha.org.uk Very close to Albert Dock this is a big purpose-built hostel with a restaurant, laundry, games room. Perfectly situated for most attractions.
F **Embassie Hostel**, 1 Falkner Sq, out of town to the south past Chinatown, T0151-7071089, www.embassie.com. It's the cheapest place to stay in Liverpool, a Georgian townhouse with relaxed and friendly atmosphere.
F **International Inn**, 4 South Hunter St off Hardman St (just off Hope St), T0151-7098135, info@internationalinn.co.uk. Set in a Victorian warehouse this place is friendly, more centrally located and very modern in design.

Eating

Chinatown's Nelson St is lined with Chinese restaurants and the Albert Dock caters for tourists during the day with cheap cafés and the more selective crowd in its underground vaults in the evening. The most fashionable and new restaurants are clustered around Victoria St, and Hope St, just off the Ropewalks, also has some exclusive places to eat.

£££ **60 Hope Street**, T0151-7076060. Down the road towards the Anglican cathedral is a modern restaurant in a Georgian townhouse. It serves pancetta-wrapped kidneys and grilled sea bass upstairs and has a cheaper bistro in the same style with steak and chips and good chocolate brownies downstairs. It's fairly exclusive but not snooty. Closed on Sun.

£££ **Bechers Brook** Hope St, T0151-7070005. A classy modern restaurant, serving award-winning British cuisine like venison cutlet, beef and lobster. There's a cheaper lunch and pre-theatre menu. You'll need to make a reservation as the locals love it too.

£££ **Newz Brasserie**, down towards Pier Head and the Albert Dock at 18 Water St, T0151-2362025. A mixture of a coffee lounge, bar and deli during the day and a delicious eaterie in the evening. The tablecloths are starched, the food is French and it's altogether a pretty glamorous affair.

£££ **Simply Heathcotes**, 25 The Strand, Beetham Plaza (across from the Albert Dock), T0151-2363536. Serves up celebrity chef Paul Heathcote's trademark no-nonsense northwest cuisine in a select and stylish environment.

££ **Cafe Number Seven**, 7 Falkner St, T0151-7099633. Just off Hope St, this is the city's best arty veggie option. It's minimalist, casual and art-studenty, serving things like home-made spicy parsnip soup and marmalade crumble cake. 0800-1900 Mon-Fri.

££ **Eureka**, 7 Myrtle Pde, T0151-7097225, is a really popular place with the locals, it's a Greek restaurant that's cheap, cheerful and complete with chirpy Greek pop soundtrack.

££ **Everyman Bistro** under the Everyman Theatre on Hope St, T0151- 7089545, is an arty option, serving French food in a contemporary restaurant.

££ **Mandarin Restaurant**, 73-79 and 40 Victoria St, T0151-2279011. Delicious Cantonese and Peking food – the best in Liverpool – in the centre of town.

££ **Norwegian Blue** is more central in Concert Sq, a funky modernist bar-café with interesting global cuisine to share like Tempura Shrimp and Mini Lobster Tails as well as burgers and sandwiches. The dance anthems get turned up really loud later on and then from 0230-0600 it's open as a chillout haven.

££ **The Shere Khan**, 17-19 Berry St, T0151-7096099, is one of the 5 Shere Khans in the Northwest and this one has a difference: the interior. The restaurant has the feel of a brasserie with a modern and contemporary design but thankfully still serves the highly-rated Indian food. Open to 0100 Fri and Sat.

££ **Tabac**, 126 Bold St, T0151-7099502, is one of the city's award-winning trendy options with home-made soup and reasonably priced Sunday roasts with a twist just at the bottom of this price category.

£ **Art Cafe**, 9-13 Berry St, just off Bold St. It exhibits local and recent Liverpool graduates contemporary artwork and does a good line in herbal teas and cheap muffins. Down-to-earth prices and a happy vibe.

£ **Cafe Eros**, the Conservation Centre, Whitechapel, uses the feel and white space of an art gallery well, T4784994. It's good for Sunday brunch 1000-1600, and is open every day for expensive sandwiches and more reasonable tea and scones.

£ **The Pan-American Club** in Britannia Pavilion, at the Albert Dock, T0151-7091156. Has a real New York atmosphere, fashionable with stone floor, burgers and steak-style food and dimly lit booths.

£ **The Philharmonic** 36 Hope St. For something slightly different, try this imposing Victorian pub, built in imitation of the gentlemen's club. There are a lot of pubs in Liverpool, but nowhere else will you find William Morris wallpaper, Art Nouveau tiling and marble urinals.

£ **Pushka**, 16 Rodney St, T0151-7088698, is a funky little European café serving Euro food with vegetarian options in a friendly, young atmosphere. It's just down the hill from Hope St towards the Ropeworks.

£ **Ye Cracke** on Rice St near Hardman St. In his art school days, John Lennon used to hang-out here. It's a very cheap pub with cozy snugs and value greasy-spoon meals.

Pubs, bars and clubs

Liverpudlians are proud of their nightlife and concentrated in a small area you can find everything you could want from cozy pubs to sophisticated bars and the trend-setting club, *Cream*. Don't forget *Garlands* either, the hugely popular mixed and gay venue.

Baa Bar, 43-45 Fleet St, T0151-7070610, Liverpool's original trendy bar with some bargain drink offers and 2 floors of music. One of many trendy bar-clubs on this street.

The Camel Club, a Moroccan themed bar-club on Wood St above *Revolution*. It's got the whole souk thing going on – draped fabric, candlelit alcoves to smooch in and dancefloors to flail about on to the funk and breakbeat, T0151-7071933. The bar below, *Revolution*, serves vodka in a million different flavours.

Cream in Wolstenholme Sq, off Slater St in the centre of the Ropeworks. Open every Sat 2200-0400. Britain's most popular superclub is a massive dance music venue with many spin-offs including a record label. The resident DJs are the best in the UK and it's always packed on a Sat. T0151-7091693, www.cream.co.uk, entrance fee £10-15, NUS discount.

Garlands at 8-10 Eberle St, T0151-7078385. It's a riot of colour and attitude, a mixed gay and straight crowd dressed flamboyantly and out for a good time. It's an antidote to big warehouse clubs, broken down into smaller rooms, and the sort of place you expect to see a drag queen or two. Sat night's the night to go. £10 entry.

G-bar,1-7 Eberle St, T0151-2581230, has a kitschy crowd: gay, straight and everything in between, all dressed up to the nines.

Jacaranda, on Slater St, T0151-7078281, is a relaxed low-key cellar bar with murals painted by Lennon and Sutcliffe. It's popular with the students and not as pretentious as most of the clubbier bars.

The Late Room, T0151-7072333. Underneath the *Life Cafe* on Bold St is this late night lounge bar in the basement. It's got a relaxed atmosphere and has a comedy club too.

Velvet Lounge on Bold St, is another ultra-fashionable cherry and chocolate leather sofa kind of place. The wooden floors, intimate booths and soft lighting make it a luxurious place to shake your booty.

Entertainment

Cinema and theatre

The Everyman Theatre, 5-9 Hope St, T0151-7094776. A top venue for anything from small touring productions, classic theatre and Shakespeare to new plays, poetry and comedy.

The FACT Centre, Wood St, T0151-7092663, www.fact.co.uk A new addition to Liverpool's arts scene. Catering for Film and Creative Technology, the centre is a leading agency for the support and development of film, video and new media projects and is painfully cutting edge.

The Picturehouse, galleries, internet access and a bar. An independent cinema situated inside the complex.

The Liverpool Playhouse, Williamson Sq, T0151-7094776, www.everymanplayhouse.com. This is a more grown-up theatre, at the Shakespeare end and not so experimental but attracting big name actors and touring productions.

Odeon Cinema on London Rd up by Lime St Station, T08705-50007, is your best bet for new releases and mainstream films, .

The Philharmonic Hall, Hope St, T0151-7093789, info@liverpoolphil.com. An unusual Art-Deco hall showing classic films, music and comedy. There's also a regular programme of classical music here with the Royal Philharmonic, see live music listings.

The Unity Theatre, 1 Hope Pl, T0151-7094988. An intimate space with a varied programme of dance, music and film.

Live music

Blundell Street, 57 Blundell St, the Albert Dock, T0151-7095779, www.blundellstreet.co.uk A kind of lounge bar/easy listening music venue with an authentic 50s vibe, skilfully circumventing the kitsch image of the genre with small candlelit booths and a classy atmosphere. There are live acts here most nights for you to listen to while sipping cocktails, and they serve food too. Tue-Sat.

The Cavern, Mathew St, T0151-2221957. Has live music most days of varying quality with a stone floor and a slightly grotty feel. There's a lot of wannabees here and it doesn't really live up to its image as the first step on the ladder to fame.

The Picket, 24 Hardman St, T0151-7085318. Liverpool's favourite live music venue where you're most likely to catch the next big thing. They have a wide range of performers from the latest chart sensations to young breakthrough indie bands and Peruvian banjo players.
The Royal Liverpool Philharmonic, Hope St, T0151-7093789, info@ liverpoolphil.com Home to the city's orchestra, the Phil, have a regular programme of classical music and a Schumann festival in Jan and Feb each year. If you want to hear classical music, this is the best place, and it's a quirky hall with its Art Deco design.

Festivals

Aug International Beatle Week, T0871-2221963, runs from 22-27 Aug and is the biggest celebration of Beatles music in the world, with numerous sound- and look-alike bands. It incorporates the **Mathew St Festival**, a free music festival with over 200 bands playing from 24-26 Aug.
Aug The dance music festival **Creamfields** is hosted by Cream every year on the Aug Bank Holiday weekend and is regularly voted the best dance event in the UK. The dance version of Glastonbury. T0151-7091693, tickets sell out fast.

Activities and tours

Magical Mystery Tours run 2-hr trips in vintage buses showing where the Fab Four grew up with landmarks including John Lennon's childhood home on Penny Lane and Strawberry Fields before finishing at the Cavern. Daily tours from the Albert Dock at 1400 and 1500 and Queen Sq outside the TIC at 1340 and 1440, T0151-2369091, F2368081, £10.95.
Liverpool Ducks, odd yellow vehicles taking you from Atlantic Pavilion in the Albert Dock around the city's waterfront, city and dock areas. T0151-7087799, enquiries@liverpoolducks.co.uk. £9.95 for adults, £7.95 concessions, for which you get an hr long land and sea tour. Tours run mid Feb-Christmas daily 1030-1800, approximately every hr.

Transport

Bus

National Express have regular services to major towns and cities in Britain from the Norton St Coach Station. **London Victoria** 12 times daily (5 hrs), **Birmingham** 12 times daily (3 hrs), **Manchester** 19 times daily (1 hrs 30 mins), **Blackpool** 8 times daily (1 hr 45 mins), **Edinburgh** 7 times daily (8 hrs).

Car

Skydrive UK, South Terminal Lennon Airport, T0151-4480000, F4481044; **Avis**, 113 Mulberry St, T0151-7094737; **Easycar**, NCP car park Paradise St, www.easycar.com.

Train

From Liverpool Lime St you can reach most major UK destinations, including **Manchester**, (1 hr), **Birmingham** (1 hr 30 mins) and **London Euston**, (3-4 hrs), on Virgin trains, www.virgintrains.com.

Taxis

Mersey Cabs, T0151-2982222, T2072222 or the ranks up by Lime St station, on Whitechapel or Clayton Sq.

Directory

Chemists Moss Chemists, 68-70 London Rd. **Hospitals** Royal Liverpool University Hospital, Prescot St, T0151-7062000. **Internet** Planet Electra Internet Cafe, London Rd, T0151-7080303; STA Travel, Bold St, 0930-1730 Mon-Fri, 1000-1730 Thu, 1100-1700 Sat shut Sun. **Police** just off Clayton Sq on Church St, T0151-7096010. **Post office** The Lyceum, Bold St and 23-33 Whitechapel.

For an explanation of the sleeping and eating price codes used in this guide, see the inside front cover. Other relevant information is provided in the Essentials chapter, page 36.

Lancashire

→ Colour map 3

Lancashire is a diverse mix of the constituent parts of the North of England. To the north, the county borders Cumbria with stunning views, lakes, mountains and moors; in the south, Manchester spreads into the dark mill towns of Preston, Blackburn and Burnley. The county town of Lancaster in the northwest is historic and beautiful with wide cobbled streets and country pubs. The working castle in the town is the final destination of the Pendle Witch Tour, tracing the steps of 10 witches from the eastern part of the county who were condemned to hang during the 17th century. This eastern part of the country borders Yorkshire where the Lancashire forests meet the dales. There is, however, one spot in the county that gets more than its fair share of attention: the Las Vegas of the North, Blackpool. It's a traditional seaside resort that has got out of hand with its largest rollercoaster in Europe and its Golden Mile of arcades and flashing lights. ▸▸ *For Sleeping, Eating and other listings, see pages 526-527.*

Ins and outs

Getting around The best and easiest way of exploring the region, particularly the charming country villages, is by car. Local buses run in Lancashire but are not always as frequent or regular as necessary. Train services between major towns in Lancashire, however, are very regular every day except Sun and coach connections from Liverpool and Manchester to Blackpool are reliable, going every hour or more frequently. Manchester and Liverpool are the main coach, bus and air transport hubs in the Northwest, including Lancashire. ▸▸ *For further details, see Transport, page 527.*

Blackpool

Blackpool is synonymous with all things tacky. This unashamedly bold, brash and bawdy seaside resort has devoted itself to the pursuit of pleasure – preferably with 16 pints of lager, a dodgy kebab and perhaps a street brawl thrown in for good measure. Now almost exclusively the preserve of the stag and hen brigade, its long promenade is littered in the summer with drunken bodies and often awash with gallons of vomit. It's not all alcohol and infamy, though. Blackpool has the biggest glitterball in the world and a host of other claims to fame including the Pleasure Beach, a huge park with amusement arcades and rollercoasters. Blackpool has also repackaged itself as the 'Las Vegas of Britain' and the sounds of young revellers retching in the streets is almost drowned by the constant ching of slot machines paying out.

Ins and outs

Getting there Blackpool is easily reached by car from Manchester on the M61, M6 and M55, Leeds on the M62, M6 and M55 and the rest of Lancashire on the M6 and M55. **National Express** run regular coach services from Manchester and Liverpool. The coach stop is on Lonsdale Rd in summer and Talbot Rd during the winter season.

Information Blackpool TIC, 1 Clifton St near the North Pier, T01253-478222, tic@blackpool.gov.uk, www.blackpool.gov.uk, www.blackpooltourism.co.uk Mon-Fri 0900-1700. They can book accommodation and tickets into the main tourist attractions are discounted here. There is also a smaller TIC on the promenade between the North and Central Piers. Mon-Fri 0915-1700, Sun 1015-1530. They can also book accommodation and offer discounted entry to the attractions.

Sights

The 518 ft of **Blackpool Tower** ⓘ *Blackpool Tower, Bank Hey St, T01253-292029, www.theblack pooltower .co.uk, daily until Nov 3, 1000-2300, £11.50, children £7.50, £8.50 adults and children after 1900*, contains a family-orientated circus, souvenir stalls and the Tower Ballroom. It might well be one of Blackpool's most famous features but it's a very pricey trip up to the top to look over the sand and grey sea.

The **Pleasure Beach** ⓘ *Blackpool Pleasure Beach, Ocean Boulevard, T0870 4445566, www. blackpool pleasurebeach.co.uk, weekends only Jan-Mar 2, daily from 23 Mar-Nov 3, times subject to change, a 1-day wristband costs £26, individual rides £1-5*, is the real attraction in Blackpool with huge rollercoasters overlooking the sea and the southernmost end of the town. Admission into the park is free and you can either pay per ride or per day. The **Big One** is Europe's tallest and fastest rollercoaster at 235 ft high and 87 mph, a massive structure that is closed on windy days. There are lots of other white-knuckle rides as well as arcades, candy floss stalls, cafés and tacky musical shows.

You cannot consider yourself a true English seaside town unless you've got at least one pier. Blackpool, true to form, has gone over the top and has three. There isn't much to pick between them, except that you have to pay £0.25 to visit the North Pier, which has a short tram ride on it to take you to the end. All three piers are garish and have more arcades and stalls than is strictly necessary; the Central Pier also has a big wheel and other rides amid the Blackpool rock stalls. Alongside the promenade it is possible to take pony and trap rides along the Golden Mile. Unlike other tourist resorts that view the end of August as the end of the season, Blackpool takes it as a cue to begin enticing visitors back to the town. The Illuminations, famed in 1879 for being like "artificial sunshine" and now for being an immense gaudy display of neon and plastic, are switched on at the end of August and carry on until the beginning of November. Just outside Blackpool, the **Zoo** ⓘ *Blackpool Zoo, East Park Drive, T01253-830830, www.blackpoolzoo.org.uk, daily 1000-1630, £7.95, children £5.75, free bus 21 from outside the Tower goes to the zoo and it can easily be reached by car just 2 miles from the seafront*, was recently voted one of the UK's top five zoos and has a particular speciality in the Gorilla Mountain as well as over 400 animals in captivity here including dolphins, orang-utans and elephants. It's fairly spacious as British zoos go.

Lancaster

Lancaster is the historic county town of Lancashire and was recently granted city status. The main feature of the town is its Norman castle, used today as a court and prison. It has held some notorious inmates in its time including the Pendle witches and the Birmingham Six. The town centre is compact and charming with wide cobbled streets and cosy traditional pubs. All in all the city is a pleasant place to stop on the way to or from the Lakes, just south of the Cumbrian border.

Ins and outs

Information Guided walks around Lancaster telling of ghosts and murderers, pubs, the Pendle witch trail and the town's history leave from the castle gates at 1930 on Thu evenings in Aug and Sep, T01524-792089, www.catwalks-lancaster.co.uk. £3, children £0.50. **Lancaster TIC** *29 Castle Hill, T01524-32878, www.lancaster.gov.uk, 1000-1700 daily*. The TIC has more information on other walks throughout the year including Halloween walks and torchlit Old Calendar walks and can book accommodation.

Sights

Lancaster Castle ⓘ *Lancaster Castle, Castle Hill, T01524-64998, F847914, daily mid Mar-Dec 1000-1700, guided tours leave half hourly from 1030-1600, £4, concessions £2.50, entrance through the back of the castle, not through the imposing John of Gaunt*

The Pendle Witches

In 1612 under the reign of Protestant King James I, the greatest number of witches ever caught were found in the Pendle area and hung at Lancaster Castle. James was obsessed with witchcraft and the Catholic area of Lancashire was seen as a hotbed for this kind of heresy. The Pendle witchcraft trials centred on two peasant families headed by two old crones, Demdike and Chattox. They were believed to have magic powers, and their daughters and sons likewise, using them to do harm and to consort with the devil. Many locals testified to their evil-doings and, most remarkably of all, the witches confessed to their crimes unlike in other trials of the time. One of the witches, the wonderfully named Alice Nutter, was convicted on the evidence of a nine-year-old child. Her grave is in nearby Newchurch where the graveyard has an eye of God in it to prevent her evil harming others.

Witchcraft was also practised in this time in a healing capacity and local people were paranoid about the existence of witches. Growing bluebells in your garden was said to be a sign of witchcraft, as witches used the flowers to lure fairies to their houses so that they could pick their brains.

Today, the only remaining evidence about the Pendle witches is the transcript of the court proceedings and many a story has been created in the region to fill in the missing background.

gate, the main entrance for the prison, is the dominant building in Lancaster and has been since it was built in 1093. The hill on which it stands was used as a fort by the Romans around AD 79 and in 1093 a Norman baron, Roger of Poitou, built a motte and bailey castle here. Fifty years later that was replaced by a stone keep, some of which survives today. The castle is currently a fully working castle that you cannot walk round independently. There are around 250 inmates detained in the prison and the courthouse is still in use. Tours of the castle, an hour-long trail around the courts, the oldest parts of the castle, the old cells, hanging corner, are well worth taking.

Lancaster Priory ⓘ *Castle Hill, T01524-65338, www.priory.lancaster.ac.uk, daily 1000-1630*, is adjacent to the castle and was originally a Benedictine priory in 1094. It is now a parish church and contains carved stones and crosses from the 9th-11th centuries. There is a refectory inside the church serving teas and coffees. To the rear of the church on the hill are the remains of the old Roman baths.

In the centre of town and originally home to one of the witch hunters, Thomas Covell, the **Judges' Lodgings** ⓘ *Judges' Lodgings, Church St, T01524-32808, www.bringinghistoryalive.co.uk, free*, is a beautiful Grade I listed Georgian building. It has also been home to the chief jailor and afterwards became the residence of judges visiting the Assize courts. Inside the house is a Museum of Childhood with dolls, toys and games from the 18th century, a mcollection of Lancaster's delicate Gillow furniture and a portrait collection depicting the town's connections with the slave trade.

In the former customs house of Lancaster, the **Lancaster Maritime** Museum ⓘ *Lancaster Maritime Museum, Custom House, St George's Quay, T01524-64637, F841692, daily Easter-Oct 1100-1700, Nov-Easter 1230-1600*, explores the history of Lancaster as a port, the Lancaster canal, fishing and the nearby Morecambe Bay. The exhibitions are brought alive with audio-visual stimuli, smells, sounds and reconstructions and provide an interesting history of the city's development.

The Ribble Valley

The east of Lancashire is an undiscovered gem with wonderful walking trails around the Forest of Bowland, charming stone cottages and country pubs. With more of the feel of rural Yorkshire, it all seems a lot further away from the old industrial towns of south Lancashire than it really is. Pendle Hill dominates the area with the town of Clitheroe and its 12th-century castle. The area is well known in the county as the home of the Pendle Witches, hung in 1612 at Lancaster Castle. From Clitheroe you can follow their path around the district. Alongside the River Ribble around Clitheroe you can also follow geology and sculpture trails in the open countryside.

Ins and outs

Getting there The town of Clitheroe is 7 miles north of Blackburn on the A666/A59. Local **buses** run to the town from Preston, Bury, Skipton in Yorkshire and Manchester. There is a train station in Clitheroe with a regular **rail** service to Blackburn and Manchester every day but Sun.

Getting around By far the most convenient way to explore this area of Lancashire is by car, which allows you to reach the more out-of-the-way spots.

Information TIC ⓘ *14 Market Pl, Clitheroe, T01200-425566. Mon-Sat 0900-1700.*

Clitheroe and the Forest of Bowland

Clitheroe is a small country town presided over by a 12th-century **Norman castle** with an unusual hole in the wall of its keep. The town has a nice array of pubs and a few places to stay as well as a charming arts and crafts gallery in a refurbished railway building.

Climb up the steep and winding path around the formal garden and you will reach the castle keep of **Clitheroe Castle** ⓘ *Daily until 2200, free.* It was built in 1186 by Robert De Lacy to protect his estate and is made of limestone and sandstone. There's a great view of Pendle Hill from 35 m above the limestone bed as well as the surrounding rural area.

Housed in one of the Georgian stone buildings in the courtyard behind the castle, the castle **museum** ⓘ *T0120-0424635, www.ribblevalley.co.uk, Easter-Oct daily 1100-1630, Nov- mid Dec Sat-Sun 1100-1630, closed Jan, weekends only Feb, Mar-Easter Sat-Wed 1100-1630*, has displays on local history, including the Pendle witches, geology and a sound system to provide an authentic experience of life in an Edwardian kitchen. Upstairs is a reconstructed 18th-century lead mine with whistling and coughing miners to keep you company.

The TIC in Clitheroe sells guides to the **Pendle Witches Trail** around the area. It is a 45-mile route that traces the path taken by the 10 convicted witches from the Pendle area to their final destination at Lancaster Castle. Begin at **Pendle Heritage Centre**, Park Hill, Barrowford, Nelson, T01282-661701. It's a 17th-century hall with a video about the witches which will start you off. The trail continues via a number of small country towns and Clitheroe to Lancaster Castle, contact TIC for further details. The **Ribble Way** is a 70-mile long path along the River Ribble from its source to the estuary. You can pick up the trail at various locations and it takes you through limestone gorges, marshland and moorland. The best map to take for the area is the OS Explorer OSL41 Forest of Bowland and Ribblesdale and further information about the path can be found at the Clitheroe TIC.

 Sleeping

Blackpool *p522*

C **Carlton Hotel**, 107 Hornby Rd, T01253-621347. Small well-kept 3 star hotel in central Blackpool, with en suite bathrooms and a seaside atmosphere. Pets welcome.

D **The Derwent Private Hotel**, 42 Palatine Rd, T01253-620004. Eleven-bedroomed small family hotel with en suite bathrooms and welcoming friendly hosts. Dinner is available for £7 as well as B&B.

D **The Granville Hotel**, 12 Station Rd, T01253-343012. Pleasant small hotel catering particularly for families and groups with en suite bathrooms, a licensed bar and home-cooked meals.

D **The Kimberley**, 25 Gynn St, T01253-352264. Comfortable frilly B&B with en suite bathrooms and no stag or hen parties in a slightly quieter part of town.

D-E **Baricia Hotel**, 40-2 Egerton Rd, T01253-623130. Family-run small B&B hotel close to the station. Cosy rooms, en suite bathrooms also available.

D-E **Beachcomber Hotel**, 78 Reads Av, T01253-621622, beachcomber@euphony.net. Comfortable family guesthouse with small rooms, a restaurant and car park.

D-E **Manor Grove Hotel**, 24 Leopold Grove, T01253-625577. Friendly hotel/guesthouse with cosy rooms, standard B&B and an evening meal if required.

E **Raffles Hotel**, 73-5 Hornby Rd, T01253-294713, raffleshotelblackpool.co.uk. Smart with full English breakfast, top service and as much elegance as you can find in Blackpool. Friendly and pleasant.

F **Arncliffe Hotel**, 24 Osborne Rd, South Shore, T01253-345209, arncliffe.hotel@virgin.net. Small, licensed family-run hotel catering for families and couples and no, repeat no, stag or hen parties.

Lancaster *p523*

B **Royal Kings Arms**, Market St, T01524-32451, F841698, www.menzies-hotels.co.uk. A 3-star period hotel on one of Lancaster's wide cobbled streets, the King's Arms is modern, relaxed and welcoming. Charles Dickens stayed here in 1854 and 1862 and although much of the interior has been modernized, the stained-glass windows and features like the Minstrel's Gallery remain.

D **The Farmer's Arms Hotel**, Penny St, T01524-36368, farmersarmslancaster@btinternet.com. Small hotel priding itself on creating a comfortable, relaxed atmosphere.

D **Greenbank Farmhouse**, Abbeystead, T/F01524-792063, www.greenbankfarmhouse.co.uk. Just outside Lancaster in the rolling countryside, 15 mins from the city centre at junction 3 of the M6. Well-kept grounds, good location for walking and fishing.

D **Railton Hotel**, 2 Station Rd, T01524-388364, F388364. Reasonably priced B&B close to the station with basic facilities and en suite rooms.

D **Shakespeare Hotel**, 96 St Leonardgate, T01524-841041. Popular and award-winning bed and breakfast on the outskirts of town with top-class service.

E **Castle Hill House**, 27 St Mary's Pde, Castle Hill, T01524-849137, gsutclif@aol.com.uk. B&B in the centre of Lancaster beside the castle with quiet and comfortable rooms.

Ribble Valley *p525*

A-C **Mitton Hall Country House Hotel**, Mitton Rd, Whalley, Nr Clitheroe, T01254-826544, www.mittonhall.com. Grand and beautiful old country house with historic interior, large fireplace, lovingly decorated with antlers, and antique furniture. There are 4-poster beds for the ultimate in romance and luxury; golfing, fishing and executive breaks also catered for.

C **Hotel Don Dino**, 78-82 Whalley Rd, Clitheroe, T01200-424450. Not the mafia hang-out its name would suggest, a hotel attached to the local Italian restaurant with clean, modern rooms, full English breakfast, all en suite.

C **Old Post House Hotel**, 44-8 King St, Clitheroe, T01200-422025, www. posthousehotel.co.uk. Townhouse in the centre of Clitheroe town with cosy and charming décor and friendly service. Recommended.

D **Brooklands**, 9 Pendle Rd, Clitheroe, T/F01200-422797, kenandjean @tesco.net. Homely 3-bedroomed Victorian B&B on the outskirts of Clitheroe near to the train station. Rooms are large, comfortable and en suite.

D **Petre Lodge**, Northcote Rd, Langho near Clitheroe, T01254-245506, www.petrelodge.co.uk. Large stone cottage-style hotel on the edge of the Ribble Valley a short drive from Clitheroe. B&B with the option of evening meals, quality service and upmarket décor.

Eating

Lancaster p523

£££ **The Castle Restaurant**, *Royal Kings Arms Hotel*, Market St. Large wine list, good service and traditional English food served in this historic hotel overlooked by a minstrel's gallery. The best place to eat out in Lancaster.
££ **The Old John O'Gaunt** 53 Market St. Quaint and charming pub with stained-glass windows and snugs. They serve traditional pub food and real ale and boast of having *strange staff*.
££ **Pizza Margherita**, 2 Moor Lane, T01524-36333, is a large, airy and bright Italian restaurant operating as a café, bar and restaurant. It's the classiest of the Italian restaurants in the town.
£ **The Sun**, Church St, is another traditional pub serving home-cooked food in a warm and cosy atmosphere.

Ribble Valley p525

££ **Browns Bistro**, 10 York St, Clitheroe, T01200-426928. Intimate French restaurant with an intimate atmosphere on the edge of Clitheroe. Open for evening meals through the week and lunch on Fri, closed on Sun.
££ **Hotel Don Dino**, 78-82 Whalley Rd, Clitheroe, T01200-424450. High class Italian food served in a warm and friendly environment showing fans of identikit chains what they're missing out on.
££ **Penny Black Restaurant**, 44-48 King St, Clitheroe, T01200-422025. Traditional English restaurant and coffee house serving lunches 1200-1400 and evening meals 1900-2100. Ideal for a roast on a Sun in a relaxed, upmarket atmosphere or pan-fried lamb, grilled gammon and other meat dishes during the week.
£ **The Apricot Meringue**, 15 King St, Clitheroe, T01200-426933. Elegant teashop just off the high street serving high tea, home-made cakes and vegetarian dishes.
£ **Bashall Barn**, Bashall Town, Clitheroe, T01200-428964. On the road out of Clitheroe towards Bashall, this dairy barn has been converted into a café, craft workshop and walking centre serving home-cooked snacks.
£ **Halfpenny's of Clitheroe**, Old Toll House, 1-5 Parson Lane, Clitheroe, T01200-424478. Listed building housing a traditional English teashop serving sandwiches, roasts, cream teas and pastries. Welcoming and homely.

Transport

Lancaster p523

Bus

By bus there are twice-hourly services to **Preston** (1 hr 10 mins), **Blackpool** (1 hr 15 mins) and **Kendal** (1 hr 20 mins), **Windermere** (1 hr 30 mins) and **Keswick** (2 hrs 30 mins) in the Lake District.

Train

From Lancaster there are regular train services to **Preston** (25 mins) where you can change to get to **Liverpool** (1 hr), **Manchester** (45 mins) and **London** (2 hrs 40 mins). You can also reach **Carnforth** (10 mins) by rail.

Ribble Valley p525

From Clitheroe it is easy to reach the Yorkshire Dales by road and towns to the south of Lancashire.

Bus

Local buses run to **Accrington** (35 mins), **Manchester** (1 hr 25 mins), **Blackburn** (35 mins), **Bolton** (1 hr 15 mins) and **Preston** (35 mins). For further information about rail and bus services in the region, T01200-429832.

Train

There are regular trains to **Blackburn** (20 mins), **Blackpool** (1 hr 15 mins) and **Manchester** (1 hr 15 mins).

Directory

Blackpool p522

Banks Birley St, Corporation St and Victoria St have branches of all the high street banks. **Chemists** Lloyds Pharmacy, Talbot Rd, open until 2100, T01253-627932. **Hospitals** Victoria Hospital, Whinney Heys Rd, T01253-300000. **Police station** Bonny St, turn left opposite the central pier, T01253-293933.

Ribble Valley p525

Cycle hire Pedal Power, Waddington Rd, Clitheroe, T01200-422066. Mon-Fri 0900-1730, Sat 0900-1630, closed Sun. They can advise on nearby cycle routes through the Forest of Bowland and the Ribble Valley.

The Isle of Man

→Colour map 3

The Isle of Man is a place of its own in many different ways. It's a self-governing kingdom, an island a mere 33 miles long and 13 miles wide, 60 miles off the Lancashire coast in the Irish Sea. It's classified as a 'crown dependency', neither belonging to the UK nor the EU, with its own parliament, laws, traditions, stamps, currency and language. Everyone in the country speaks English, however, and English money is accepted.

The island is often unfairly stereotyped and ridiculed when it should be celebrated for retaining its eccentricity. Perhaps the island is stuck behind in the fifties, a haven for tax dogers, while the rest of the UK is hip, modern and trail-blazing. There are grouse moors and mountains, wide romantic beaches and leafy woodland dells, ruined castles and an ancient stone circle. ▸▸ *For Sleeping, Eating and other listings, see pages 530-532.*

Ins and outs

Getting there Flights to Ronaldsway Airport, T01624-821600, in the southeast of the island are available on **British Airways**, T0870 8509850. **Flybe** also fly to the Isle of Man, T08705- 676676, (return flights from London City, Bristol and Belfast cost from £100 return) www.flybe.com. The small airport is well served by buses into Douglas and there are a number of car hire operatives. The Isle of Man Steam Packet Company run **ferry** crossings across the rough stretch of the Irish Sea from Heysham and Liverpool into Douglas taking around 2 hrs 30 mins, T08705-523523 (UK), T1800-551743 (Republic of Ireland) www.steampacket.com (return from £21 for a foot passenger day trip and from £118-185 for a car plus one passenger). Booking in advance for cheaper deals is recommended. ▸▸ *For further details, see Transport, page 532.*

Getting around The Isle of Man is blessed with some unconventional and quaint forms of transport, many with a Victorian heritage, T01624-662525 for timetable enquiries for all. The ferry company also offers island explorer deals including free unlimited travel on all the island's public transport from £28 per adult for a day, £14 children.

It is easy to get around the island on the reasonably priced bus service which serves all towns. However, hiring a car is one of the best ways of exploring the island, especially if you want to discover the glens. The centre of the Isle of Man is only barely reachable by road and is mainly uninhabited. Beware of motorcyclists – even outside the TT season there are more around than you would expect. Bike hire is available in Douglas and Ramsey for exploring the island in a more leisurely fashion. Surprisingly, you cannot hire a motorbike on the Isle of Man due to license restrictions.

In the south from Douglas to Castletown, Port St Mary and Port Erin there is a rail link with steam trains that inspired the *Thomas the Tank Engine* stories. From Douglas to Laxey and Ramsey in the north there is an electric railway link and it is possible to reach the top of the island's highest mountain Snaefell by the Snaefell Mountain Railway.

The island has some idyllic scenery to walk through on a number of marked long distance footpaths (see TIC pamphlet). The undulating countryside has sand dunes, marshland, mountains and meadows of wild flowers to delight all comers.

Information Douglas TIC ⓘ *Sea Terminal Building, Douglas, T01624-686766, www.visitisleofman.com, summer 1000-1900 daily, Oct-May Mon-Thu 0900-1730, Fri 0900-1700*, is the central information point for the island. The *Story of Mann Heritage Pass* is available from the TIC and each individual attraction included on it. For £10 adults get admission to four of the following sites: The Old House of Keys, Castle Rushen, The Nautical Museum, Rushen Abbey, Cregneash Folk Museum, Peel Castle, The House of Manannan, The Great Laxey Wheel, The Grove Rural Life Museum. Children and family tickets also available and the adult saving is £5.25 overall.

Sights

Douglas

The Victorian seaside resort of Douglas is the administrative and banking capital of the island as well as being its main hub for hotels and shops. A yellow sand beach lies at the foot of a sweeping promenade still busy with 19th-century horse-drawn trams. It isn't as pretty as any of the island's other towns but it's the most developed and has many restaurants and hotels.

The **Manx Museum** ⓘ *The Manx Museum, Douglas, T01624-648000, Mon-Sat year round, free*, contains the National Art Gallery, Geology, Archaeology, Social History and TT race displays. It also has some beautiful glass beads believed to belong to a Viking noblewoman found at Peel Castle. Allow a couple of hours to explore the museum thoroughly. The best place in Douglas to escape the rain and entertain children with fairy folklore and multimedia displays.

Just two miles out of the town past the suburb of Onchan is the **Groudle Glen Railway** ⓘ *T01624-670453, the glen is two miles along the coast road from Douglas to Laxey, trains run at half hourly intervals on Sun 5 May-29 Sep 1100-1630, and on Wed evenings 3 Jul-14 Aug 1900-2100, £2.50, children £1.50*, a late Victorian narrow gauge railway service that takes you down through beautiful woodland and beach scenery to Sea Lion Rocks.

Castletown

An hour by bus from Douglas, Castletown, a large village with a beach and pretty harbour in the south of the island, is dominated by the large **Castle Rushen** ⓘ *The Quay, 29 Mar-Oct 1000-1700 daily, £4.25, children £2.25*, which dates back to the 12th century. The limestone fortress was the home of the former Kings and Lords of Mann, including the last Norse monarch, King Magnus in 1265. Having been an administrative centre, prison and law court amongst other things in the past, it is now a fabulous museum. Walking around the walls and down to the dungeons is also well worth it.

The long and turbulent history of the Isle of Man's political independence is explored in the **Old House of Keys** ⓘ *Old House of Keys, Parliament Sq, T01624-648000, 29 Mar-Oct daily 1000-1700, guided presentations run on the hour, £3, children £1.50*. It has been restored to its 1866 glory as the parliament house and debating chamber.

Port St Mary and Port Erin

Port St Mary and Port Erin, charming neighbouring coastal towns at the south of the island, are often called the sisters of the south. Port St Mary is a quaint and pretty place with a small harbour and beach that's perfect for rockpooling. A walk along the coast beside the palm trees for about five minutes takes you to **Chapel Beach**, a sandy stretch just a little out of the way. Along the coast in the other direction will take you to the cliffs and the **Chasms**, dramatic vertical rifts in the rocks. Not far from the town is the **Cregneash Folk Museum** ⓘ *Cregneash Village Folk Museum, Cregneash, Port St Mary, T01624-648000, 29 Mar-Oct, 1000-1700 daily, £3, children £1.50*, which represents the way that crofters lived and worked in the 19th century.

Daily boat trips from Port Erin take you to the bird sanctuary of **Calf Island** ⓘ *Calf Island Cruises, Raglan Pier, T01624-832339, Apr-Oct weather permitting, 1015, 1130 and 1300*, a 616-acre islet off the southern tip of the Isle of Man.

Peel

Nowadays Peel is the main fishing town of the island and has a **Kipper Museum** ⓘ *Mill Rd, T01624-843622, Apr-Oct Mon-Fri 1000-1700*, to prove it. But Peel is also one of the oldest cathedral cities in the British Isles, dating back to the sixth century. Its narrow winding streets are historic and pretty if you overlook the ugly power station and chimney to the top of the town. The unmissable **House of Manannan** ⓘ *Mill Rd, T01624-648000, open all year 1000-1700, £5, children £2.50*, is a multimedia feast of Viking, Celtic and Manx history with sights, sounds, talking waterfalls and excellent short films bringing each period alive.

Peel Castle stands on the St Patrick's Isle, used as a fortress since the Celtic Iron Age and a former Viking stronghold. The crumbling sandstone walls enclose an 11th-century church and round tower, **St Germain's Cathedral** ⓘ *St Patrick's Isle, T01624-648000, 29 Mar-Oct 1000-1700 daily, free*, and ruins of the later apartments of the Lords of Mann. The island used to be completely cut off from the mainland at high tide but when the causeway was built to link the island a small sandy beach, Fenella's Beach, was created naturally on one side. On the road from Peel to Douglas, the **Tynwald Hill** is the site of the oldest continuous parliament in the world. The name derives from the Norse word *Thing-voeller* meaning Parliament Fields, and the site is a small circular area of stepped grass crowned with a flag.

Snaefell

The mountain of Snaefell is one of the highlights of the Isle of Man. At 2036 ft Snaefell means "Snow Mountain" and it is said that from the top of the mountain you can see the six kingdoms: England, Ireland, Scotland, Wales, Mann and the Kingdom of Heaven. You can reach the top by walking all the way, taking the tram halfway and walking the rest or by taking the 100-year-old **Snaefell Mountain Railway** ⓘ *Laxey Station, T01624-663366, 20 Apr-29 Sep, fares from Laxey to the summit return £6, one child free per fee-paying adult, all others £3*, all the way to the top. There's a small café at the top to rest yourself or commiserate when all you can see is a large blanket of mist.

Sleeping

Douglas *p529*

A-D **Admiral House Hotel**, 12 Loch Promenade, T01624-629551, www.admiralhouse .com Luxury seafront hotel with excellent service and a choice of modern rooms or 4-poster-bed suites. Also a bar serving food and a Mediterranean restaurant in the basement. Recommended.

C **The Empress Hotel**, Central Promenade, T01624-661155, www.theempresshotel.net. Grand Victorian seafront hotel with a health club, marble bathrooms, a high standard of service and a fine sea view.

C-D **Mount Murray Hotel and Country Club**, Santon, T01624-661111, www.mountmurray.com. Just out of Douglas, the island's most luxurious timbered hotel with a full health complex, golf course and acres of beautiful scenery.

D **Claremont Hotel**, 18-19 Loch Promenade, T01624-698800, www.sleepwellhotels.com. Young, modern seafront hotel with 28 luxury rooms, pine-floored designer bar and restaurant serving Mediterranean and French food.

E **Allerton Guest House**, 29 Hutchinson Sq, T01624-675587, www.allerton.ttfans.com. Small family B&B in the centre of town overlooking sunny garden square. Very good value.

Castletown *p529*

D **The George Hotel**, The Parade, T01624-822533. Central large traditional Georgian hotel with a classy ambience.

E **Ballaquinney Farm**, Ronague nr Castletown, T01624-824125. Manx farmhouse B&B with evening meals in the countryside near to Castletown.

For an explanation of the sleeping and eating price codes used in this guide, see the inside front cover. Other relevant information is provided in the Essentials chapter, page 36.

Port St Mary and Port Erin *p529*

D **Falcon's Nest Hotel**, The Promenade, Port Erin, T01624-834077, www.falconsnest.co.uk. Pleasant family-run hotel just off the promenade with cosy rooms and mod cons. It's above a traditional Manx pub serving local ale in the glow of an open fire. Very friendly.

D **Ocean Castle Hotel**, The Promenade, Port Erin, T01624-836399, hotel@oceancastle.co.uk. Excellent sea view from this traditional Victorian seaside hotel. They also have self-catering apartments. 1950s bistro-style restaurant serves Manx food. Eat-as-much-as-you-like Sunday lunch is served in the carvery from 1200-1430.

D-E **Rowany Cottier**, Spaldrick near Port Erin, T01624-832287, F835685. Spacious, elegant house with a large garden and extensive Manx breakfast menu. Family-run with high quality service.

E **Beachcroft Guest House**, Beach Rd, Port St Mary, T01624-834521, crompton @beachcroft1.fsnet.co.uk. Secluded family-run guesthouse with lovely views of the surrounding countryside.

Peel *p529*

D **Ballacallin House**, Dalby, T01624-841100. A little out of town, Ballacallin House is a large old whitewashed Manx farmhouse with wonderful views, 4-poster beds and a lounge bar and restaurant.

E **The Fernleigh**, Marine Parade, T01624-842435. Comfortable small hotel with a family feel offering B&B.

E **The Merchant's House**, 18 Castle St, T01624-842541. Georgian merchant's house with a walled garden with B&B accommodation.

E **The Waldick Hotel**, Promenade, Peel, T/F01624-842410. Friendly family-run hotel on the promenade in Peel overlooking the beach.

Isle of Man

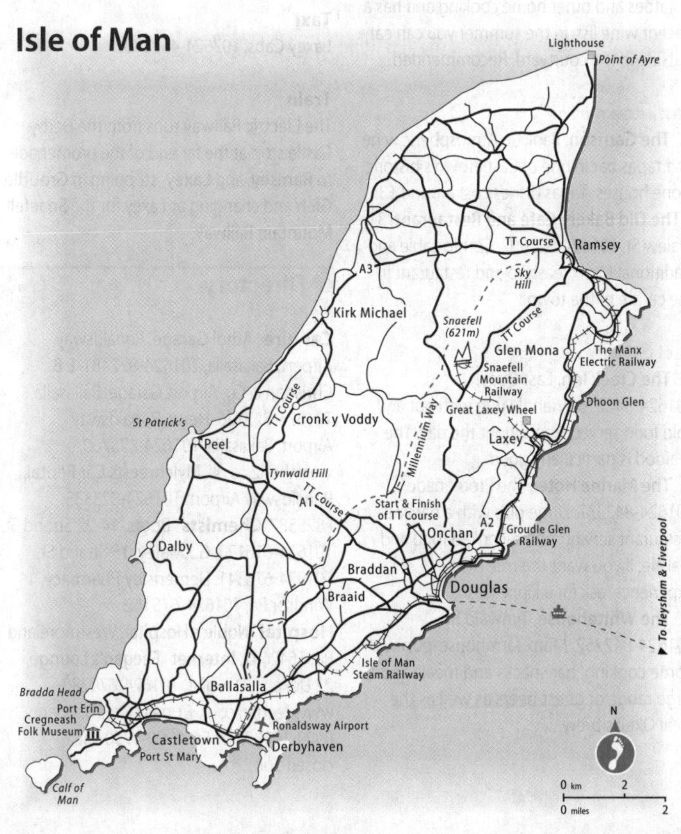

Eating

Douglas *p529*

£££ **Waterfront Restaurant**, North Quay, T01624-673222. At the lower end of this price bracket and very good value for money. It's run by television chef Kevin Woodford and is warm and friendly. With a menu of traditional Manx-English food like sausage and mash with red onion gravy, Dover sole and Manx rarebit and a classy atmosphere, it's the best restaurant in Douglas by some way.

££ **La Brasserie**, Empress Hotel, Central Promenade, T01624-661155. French restaurant inside the *Empress Hotel* which is a copy of an authentic French Brasserie near the Gare du Nord in Paris. Various menus available including a Sunday roast in a stylish and traditional restaurant.

££ **Scotts Bistro**, 7 John St, T01624-623764. Smart warm bistro inside the oldest house in Douglas. The bistro specializes in jacket potatoes and other home cooking and has a decent wine list. In the summer you can eat outside in the courtyard. Recommended.

Castletown *p529*

££ **The Garrison**, Bank St. Atmospheric wine and tapas bar in one of Castletown's historic stone houses. Tapas dishes cost around £3.

£ **The Old Bakery Café and Restaurant**, 31 Malew St, T01624-823092. Comfortable and traditional Manx teashop and restaurant in the centre of the town.

Peel *p529*

££ **The Creek Inn**, East Quay, T01624-842216. Friendly pub with hot and cold food served throughout the day. The seafood is particularly good.

££ **The Marine Hotel**, The Promenade, T01624-842337. Large pub with a bar and restaurant serving home-cooked food and real ale. If you want the true Manx experience, ask for a kipper dish.

££ **The Whitehouse**, Tynwald Rd, T01624-842252. Manx farmhouse-pub with home cooking, bar snacks and meals and a large range of guest beers as well as the local Okell's brew.

Festival and events

The International Tourist Trophy (TT) motorcycle race has been held on the Isle of Man since 1904 and is one of the world's most famous motorsport events. Every year on the last week in May and first week in Jun the island comes alive with passionate fans watching the contenders fly by. The circuit is 37.73 miles long and leading riders can make speeds of 120 mph/200 kmph. If you're planning to watch, accommodation is hard to come by and you are advised to book in advance. ,www.iomtt.com

Transport

Douglas *p529*

Bus

Bus numbers 4,5,6,8 and 10 run to **Peel** from the bus station on North Quay; buses 1 and 2 run to **Port St Mary**, **Port Erin** and **Castletown**.

Taxi

Laxey Cabs, T07624-432343.

Train

The **Electric Railway** runs from the Derby Castle stop at the far end of the promenade to **Ramsey**, and **Laxey**, stopping in **Groudle Glen** and changing at Laxey for the Snaefell Mountain Railway.

Directory

Car hire Athol Garage, Ronaldsway Airport, Ballasalla, T01624-822481. E B **Christian & Co**, Airport Garage, Ballasalla, T01624-822126. **Hertz**, Ronaldsway Airport, Ballasalla, T01624-823760, www.hertz.co.uk. **Mylchreests Car Rental**, Ronaldsway Airport, T01624-823533, F825587. **Chemists** Boots, 14-22 Strand St, T01624-616120. **G.J.Maley**, 15 Strand St, T01624-676341. **Hemensley Pharmacy**, 1 Windsor Rd, T01624-675162.

Hospital Noble's Hospital, Westmoreland Rd, T642642. **Internet** Feegan's Lounge, 22 Duke St, Douglas, T01624-679280, www.feegan.com. £1 per 15 mins, open 0900-1900 Mon-Fri, 0900-1700 Sat, closed Sun.

South Wales

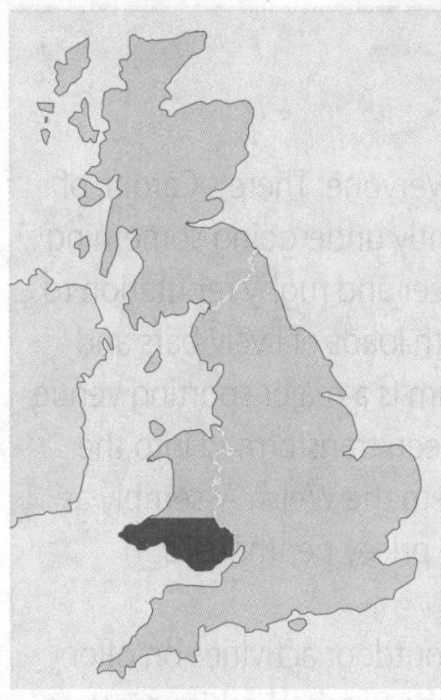

Introduction

South Wales has something for everyone. There's Cardiff, of course, the capital which is currently undergoing something of a renaissance, shaking off its beer and rugby reputation to become a great shopping city with loads of lively bars and restaurants. Its Millennium Stadium is a major sporting venue and the former docklands have been transformed into the shiny new Cardiff Bay area, home to the Welsh Assembly as well as a five-star hotel and some pricey penthouses.

Then there is the huge variety of outdoor activities on offer: from surfing and coasteering on the Pembrokeshire coast, to hill-walking and mountain biking in the rugged Brecon Beacons National Park. Those who prefer something a bit less active can visit some of the south's great historic sites like Tintern Abbey, which inspired romantic painters and poets, or the impressive Roman remains at Caerleon. Alternatively they can browse in the second-hand bookshops that dominate the border town of Hay-on-Wye – home to the famous Hay Festival which attracts the literati from all over the world.

West of Cardiff is the Gower Peninsula, Britain's first designated Area of Outstanding Natural Beauty, and Laugharne, the small village that became home to the hard drinking poet Dylan Thomas. Furthest west is Pembrokeshire, a county ringed by superb sandy beaches. This is where you'll find one of Britain's most spiritual spots, the tiny city of St David's, as well as one of its most picturesque and enjoyable seaside resorts, the Victorian town of Tenby.

★ **Don't miss...**

1. Watch the sun set off **Rhossilli**, on the Gower Peninsula, page 568.
2. Try to spot the 'green men' in the ceiling of **St David's Cathedral**, page 575.
3. Walk a section of the Pembrokeshire Coastal Path, page 572.
4. Visit **Dylan Thomas' Boatshouse** in Laugharne, page 580.
5. Go shopping in **Cardiff**, page 536.

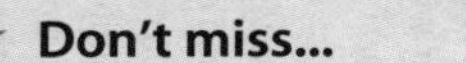

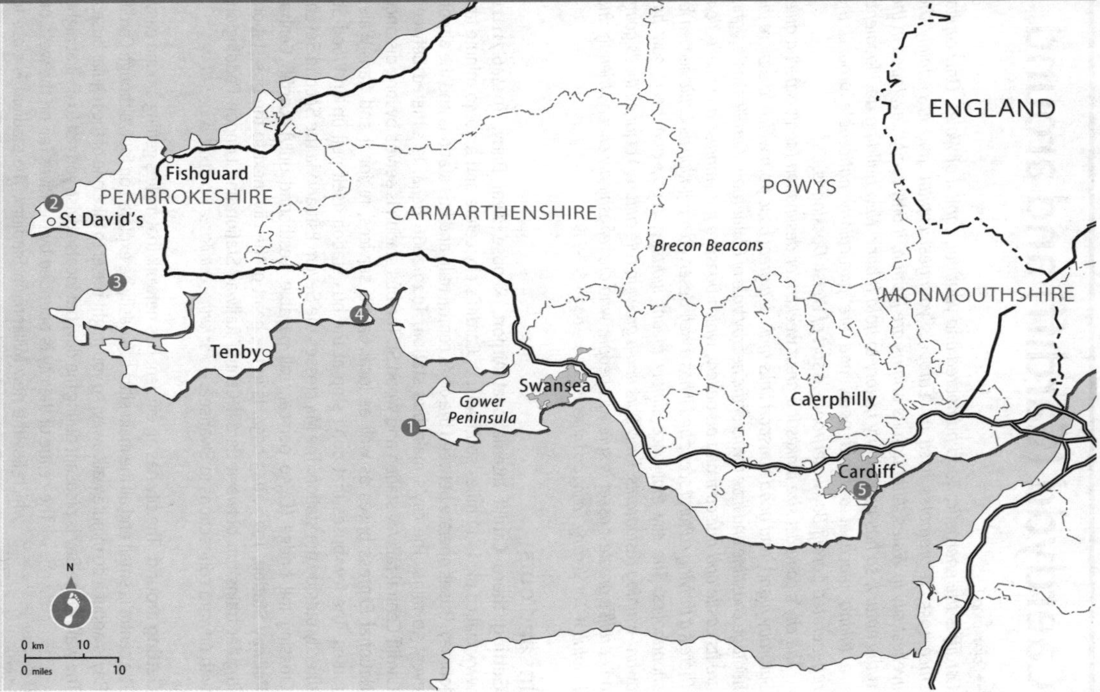

Caerdydd (Cardiff) and around

→Colour map 1

Cardiff is the energetic, good humoured and youthful, capital of Wales. Only capital since 1955, it promotes itself as 'Europe's youngest capital' and is certainly the liveliest city in Wales. Although its origins are Roman, it only really developed in the 19th-century, so has no weighty history to hold it back. New building developments are taking place at a rapid pace, and are particularly noticeable around the regenerated Cardiff Bay waterfront – a sort of Welsh Docklands.

The city's compact size makes it a great weekender destination (don't expect a quiet Saturday night), and good transport links make it a great base from which to explore the heritage coastline and little towns of the nearby Vale of Glamorgan . Cardiff's main sights are its castle and museum and art gallery, which boasts a fine Impressionist collection. There's a thriving cultural scene and it has a well-deserved reputation as Celtic heaven for shopaholics. The city that once simply meant industry, rugby and beer, now has award-winning restaurants, lively bars and a growing café culture. Yet for all that's going on Cardiff's greatest asset is surely its people, who are refreshingly cheery, friendly and helpful. ▸▸ *For Sleeping, Eating and other listings, see pages 542-549.*

Ins and outs

Getting there Cardiff International Airport, Rhoose, near Barry, T01446-711111, www.cial.co.uk, is 12 miles southwest of Cardiff's city centre and a 30-40 minute taxi journey. Buses operate between the city's central train and bus stations and the airport every 30 mins. The city's main **bus station**, T029-2066 6444, is situated between Cardiff Central railway station and Wood St. The bus station is served by long distance **National Express** buses as well as local Cardiff services, regional and trans-Wales routes. The few buses that don't stop at the bus station itself pull up on Wood St, directly outside the station. The M4 crosses the Severn Estuary via the Second Severn Crossing toll bridge (£4.50 per car, toll payable westbound only). **Cardiff Central Railway Station,** T029-2043 0554, is in the heart of the city, next to the bus station. Regular trains run between Cardiff Central Railway Station and London Paddington, with onward connections to Swansea. ▸▸ *For further details, see Transport, page 548.*

Getting around The city has an efficient bus network that makes getting around easy. The centre is small and all the main sites can easily be explored on foot, although Cardiff Bay is about a 20 minute walk away, so you might prefer to take one of the regular buses. The walk to the Bay is pleasant during the day, but locals advise you not to do it at night. The centre of the city is bounded by the River Taff on the west, on which lies the new Millennium Stadium. The stadium is close to Cardiff Castle, which is separated from the Taff by the green parklands of Bute Park. East of the park, north of the centre, is the university and the studenty/arty Cathays and Roath districts. West of the Taff, close to the city centre, is increasingly exclusive Pontcanna, popular with Welsh media mafia. South of centre is the revitalised docklands area of Cardiff Bay.

There is a strong possibility the Visitor Centre will move to the Old Library, The Hayes in Spring 2004.

Information Cardiff Visitor Centre ⓘ *16 Wood St, T02920-227281, www.visitcardiff.info, Mon – Sat 1000 -1800 and Sun 1000-1600 Sun all year.* Has information on both Cardiff and the rest of Wales, with plenty of leaflets/book on activities. Here you can buy the great value Cardiff Card (www.cardiff-card.co.uk), £11, giving a day's unlimited travel with Cardiff Bus and Valley Line trains, as well as discounts to selected restaurants and free admission to a wide range of attractions including Cardiff Castle, the National Museum and Gallery and the Big Pit Museum.

24 hours in Cardiff

Start the day like the sportier locals, with a gentle jog or stroll through Bute Park on the River Taff. Head back to your hotel for a leisurely breakfast, then put on a pair of comfy shoes and head off to the National Museum and Art Gallery to admire the collection of Impressionist paintings. Now it's just a short walk back to the heart of the city for some lunch – try the contemporary Welsh food at Blas. Then head to the cashpoint or flex your credit card and treat yourself to an afternoon of retail therapy in the arcades. If you start to flag there are plenty of cafes to revive you. There'll be time for an early evening drink at the trendy Ha Ha Bar, before you head off to a restaurant in Cardiff Bay for something to eat overlooking the water. If you've got the energy after that, go clubbing – Club Ifor Bach's a good choice.

Sights

City centre

Cardiff Castle ⓘ*Castle St, T02920-878100, www.cardiffcastle.com, daily Mar-Oct 0930-1800, Nov-Feb 0930-1700, last entry and tour 1 hr before closing, grounds only £3, children £1.90, family £8.80, grounds and tour £6, children £3.70, family £17.60,* is situated in the heart of the city, and is the historic heart of Cardiff, though it seems slightly incongruous so close to the busy shops and bars. Once inside the high stone walls you can see the motte, or artificial hill, on which is perched the ancient Norman keep, the oldest part of the castle buildings dating back to the 11th-century (though the site was in used even earlier). In the Middle Ages, successive owners reinforced and added to this ancient fortification but many of their additions were demolished in the late 18th-century by Capability Brown, leaving the keep looking, in the words of one contemporary visitor, like 'a deserted pigeon house on the top of a truncated sugar loaf '. Climb the well-worn steps for a great panoramic view of the city and surrounding countryside.

In the 1420s separate lodgings were built, which became the main living quarters. As the need for defences decreased the house was extended and gradually became more luxurious and comfortable – although it fell into disrepair after the Civil War. Eventually the castle came into the possession of the Bute family, the wealthy Scots who owned vast areas of land in south Wales. By the time the elaborately monikered John Patrick Crichton-Stuart, 3rd Marquess of Bute (1847-1900), inherited the family had more money than they knew what to do with – so the Marquess was able to indulge his architectural whims by upgrading the house. He commissioned architect William Burges, who shared his passion for the gothic, and the two worked together to create a medieval fantasy. To see the lavish interior you have to take one of the guided tours, but it's worth it. Among the riotously colourful rooms are: the Winter Smoking Room in the Clock Tower, with stained glass windows and a carved chimney piece; the Bachelor Bedroom with a marble bath; the Eastern influenced Arab Room, Lord Bute's gilded bedroom with a mirrored ceiling, and the Banqueting Hall where Royals, from Edward V11 to Charles and Diana, were entertained. Quiet good taste it isn't but it's certainly worth seeing.

National Museum and Gallery ⓘ *Cathays Park, T02920-397951, www.nmgw.ac.uk, Tue-Sun 1000-1700, free.* This excellent museum and art gallery could hold its head up anywhere in the world. It covers everything from a hi-tech, interactive look at the Evolution of Wales – a good spot for children on a rainy day – to conventional displays of art. The story of Wales is told through its archaeology and natural history. There are galleries on animals and the environment, Roman relics found in Wales, Celtic jewellery, displays on the early church and around 3000 pieces of Welsh pottery and porcelain.

The art collection is excellent. It is intended to illustrate the art history of Wales and put it in context – and as you would expect contains many works by Welsh artists from Thomas Jones and Richard Wilson to Augustus John and Ceri Richards. Wales also features as the subject of many works, including **LS Lowry**'s view of the Six Bells Colliery, Abertillery. But this is not a parochial collection, there are also works by **Poussin, Cuyp, Claude** and **Gainsborough**. Pre Raphaelites such as **Dante Gabriel Rossetti, Ford Madox Brown** and **Burne- Jones** are well represented. The jewel in the gallery is the Davies collection of 19th and early 20th French art. Room 12 contains several sculptures by **Rodin**, including a large copy of *The Kiss*; a **Degas** bronze of a dancer, and paintings by **Renoir, Boudin, Manet, Monet, Pisarro**. Room 13 has **Van Gogh**'s *Rain-Auvers* 1890, as well as paintings by **Cezanne**. Gallery 14 and 15 focus on 20th-century art, with **Magritte, Lucien Freud, Stanley Spencer**, and others all being represented. There's also a gallery that has a changing collection of contemporary art, which features Welsh artists as well as the likes of sculptor Rachel Whiteread.

Tours of the Millennium Stadium are available, see page 548.

Cardiff Bay

About a mile from the city centre, is Cardiff's former docklands area, built in the 19th-century by the Bute family and the key to city's growth and wealth (see history). It's separated from the city by parallel streets: Bute Street – to the west of which are the poor, multi-racial areas of Butetown and Grangetown; and Lloyd George Avenue, a characterless stretch lined with bland – and pricey -new housing. Once better known as Tiger Bay, (birthplace of Shirley Bassey) this was a cosmopolitan, working class area, home to everyone from Somalis and Scandinavians to Russians and Ukranians. After the decline of the docklands the area became increasingly run down, but has now been given a serious – and expensive – facelift. Like similar developments in Britain (London's Docklands, Edinburgh's Leith) the shiny new buildings, retail outlets and rash of bars and restaurants have certainly helped regenerate the area, but with a consequent loss of its working class character and sense of community. Property here is expensive – Charlotte Church bought one of the showpiece flats here, only to discover that she was right on the tourist bus route. There's enough to see and do to occupy you for the best part of a day and it's an area that is changing all the time.

It's worth starting with a visit to **Butetown History and Arts Centre** ⓘ *4/5 Dock Chambers, Bute St, T02920-256757, www.bhac.org, Tue-Fri 1000-1700, Sat, Sun 1100-1630*, a small gallery which focuses on the multi-racial history of the Bay. There are changing exhibitions of photographs and documents, with a lot of emphasis on local memories and stories.

Close by there's a huge steel fountain, on the other side of which is the new face of Cardiff Bay – the **Wales Millennium Centre**, due to open Nov 2004. This will be an international arts centre, home to Welsh National Opera and a venue for everything from ballet to musicals. Next to this, on the waterfront, is the lovely redbrick Victorian Pierhead Building, topped with a distinctive clock tower and containing fine stonework and tiling. Built in 1897 as home for the Bute Dock Company, this is currently home to the **National Assembly Exhibition** ⓘ *T02920-898200, www.wales.gov.uk, Mon-Thur 0930-1630, Fri 1000-1630, Sat, Sun 1000-1700, free.* This is an informative exhibition on the background to the setting up of the Assembly, an explanation of devolution and how the Assembly operates. There's also a scale model of the new Assembly building, which is currently being erected on adjacent land: work, some say, will finish late in 2005. For now the Assembly functions from a nearby building and tours to see it in action can be arranged (T02920-898477).

Further east round the waterfront is the **Goleulong Lightship** ⓘ *T02920-487609*, an old lightship that also contains a Chapel and Christian café, and a tinny looking tube housing the **Cardiff Bay Visitor Centre** ⓘ *T02920-463833, Mon-Fri 0930-1700, Sat and Sun 1030-1700*, which has a scale model of the Bay, plenty of information and also sells parking vouchers. The most striking building is the **Norwegian Church** (T02920-454899) a Norwegian Seamen's Mission which was rebuilt here from a former site in the Bay. It's now an arts centre and café (see Entertainment).

The centre of the waterfront is taken up with the shops, bars and restaurants of the new Mermaid Quay development. From here you can get boat trips into the Bay and out to the Barrage (see Activities and sport). East of this is **Techniquest** ⓘ *Stuart St, T02920-475475, www.techniquest.org, Mon-Fri 0930-1630, Sat, Sun 1030-1700, £6.50, children £4.50, family £18*, a family friendly, interactive science centre with a whole load of 'hands-on' exhibits covering everything from firing a rocket to forecasting the weather. There's also a planetarium, and a discovery room aimed at younger children. Further east round the waterfront is the glistening 5 star St David's Hotel and Spa (where non residents can book spa treatments). Further developments are taking place on the Ferry Road site, where a £700 million International Sports Village is planned. The first phase of this will involve construction of an Olympic standard swimming pool, with plans for a snowdome and an ice arena.

On the other side of the Bay is the controversial **Cardiff Bay Barrage** ⓘ *T02920-877900, Apr-Sept daily 1000-2000, reduced hours in winter*, built across the Taff and Ely estuaries to keep the tide out and create the enormous lake which forms the heart of the development. The barrage, an advanced piece of engineering with locks, sluice gates and a fish pass, meant that a huge expanse of mudflats – a precious habitat for thousands of wading birds, disappeared. You can take tours to see the Barrage (see Activities and sport).

Outside the city

Llandaff Cathedral ⓘ *T02920-564554, www.llandaffcathedral.org.uk, buses from city centre*, is Cardiff's most important religious site, situated in the pretty village of Llandaff, a couple of miles north west of the centre along Cathedral Road. It stands on the site of a 6th-century church, founded by St Teilo, although the present building dates from the 12th-century when the Norman stone church was built by Bishop Urban. The cathedral suffered following the Reformation and by the 18th-century was almost a ruin. However it was saved by restoration work, particularly in the mid 19th-century, when Pre-Raphaelite artists made a great contribution to its renewal. There's a triptych, *The Seed of David* by **Dante Gabriel Rossetti** and stained glass by William Morris and Burne-Jones. The cathedral was badly bombed in 1941 and further restoration and rebuilding was undertaken. A **Jacob Epstein** statue, *Christ in Majesty*, was added during this period. The former Bishop of Llandaff, Rowan Williams, is now the Archbishop of Canterbury.

Museum of Welsh Life ⓘ *St Fagans, T02920-573500, daily 1000-1700, free, buses to the site are infrequent, especially on Sun, taxi costs around £10.* This excellent open air museum is 4 miles west of the city centre, in the grounds of St Fagans Castle, and could easily take up a full day – especially if you've got kids. The museum brings to life 500 years of Welsh social history. The indoor galleries (handy if it's raining) include a wide collection of agricultural implements; a costume gallery with traditional Welsh clothing; a fascinating section on folklore – including elder tree crosses, believed to give protection against witches, and displays of gruesome looking old surgical instruments. Outdoors, around 44 acres (18 ha) of grounds have been given over to a collection of 40 period Welsh buildings, moved from their original locations and carefully rebuilt here. They come together to give an evocative glimpse of old Wales. The buildings range from tiny Nant Wallter Cottage, a 2-room, 18th-century thatched cottage with walls made of clay mixed with straw and stone dust, to Kennixton Farmhouse, a comfortable 17th-century farmhouse with red painted walls – for protection against evil spirits. There's also a chapel, a cockpit, a mill, a Victorian school and a recreated Celtic village. Perhaps most fascinating are the Rhyd-Y-Car iron worker's houses, a 19th-century terrace from Merthyr Tydfil

Cardiff

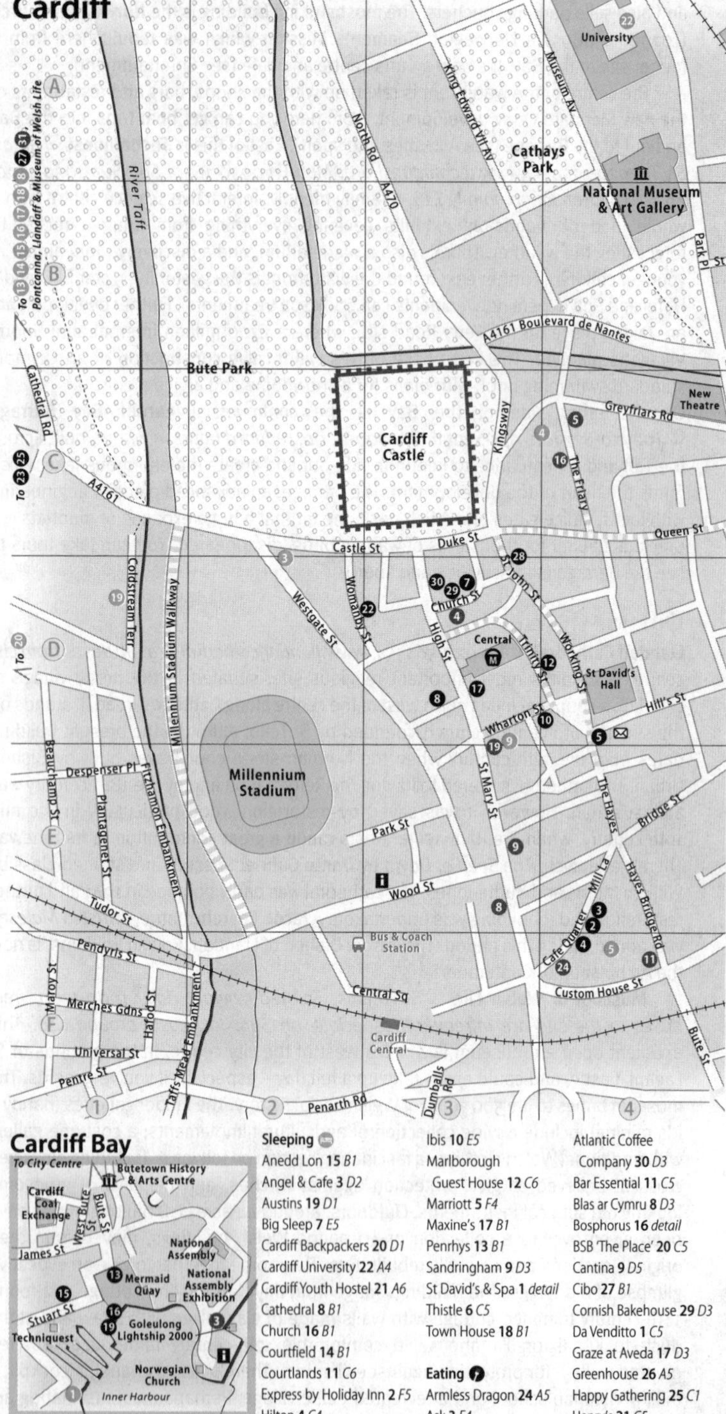

Sleeping

Anedd Lon **15** *B1*
Angel & Cafe **3** *D2*
Austins **19** *D1*
Big Sleep **7** *E5*
Cardiff Backpackers **20** *D1*
Cardiff University **22** *A4*
Cardiff Youth Hostel **21** *A6*
Cathedral **8** *B1*
Church **16** *B1*
Courtfield **14** *B1*
Courtlands **11** *C6*
Express by Holiday Inn **2** *F5*
Hilton **4** *C4*
Ibis **10** *E5*
Marlborough Guest House **12** *C6*
Marriott **5** *F4*
Maxine's **17** *B1*
Penrhys **13** *B1*
Sandringham **9** *D3*
St David's & Spa **1** *detail*
Thistle **6** *C5*
Town House **18** *B1*

Eating

Armless Dragon **24** *A5*
Ask **3** *E4*
Atlantic Coffee Company **30** *D3*
Bar Essential **11** *C5*
Blas ar Cymru **8** *D3*
Bosphorus **16** *detail*
BSB 'The Place' **20** *C5*
Cantina **9** *D5*
Cibo **27** *B1*
Cornish Bakehouse **29** *D3*
Da Venditto **1** *C5*
Graze at Aveda **17** *D3*
Greenhouse **26** *A5*
Happy Gathering **25** *C1*
Henry's **21** *C5*

South Wales Cardiff & around

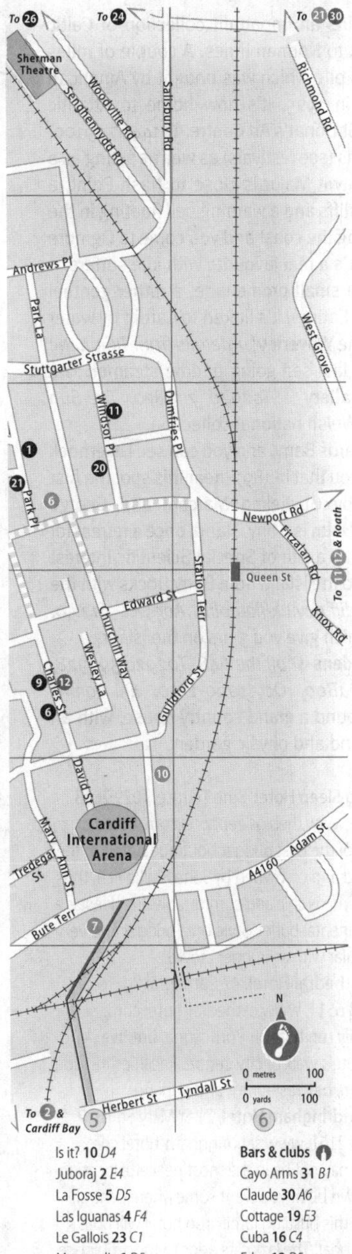

Is it? **10** *D4*
Juboraj **2** *E4*
La Fosse **5** *D5*
Las Iguanas **4** *F4*
Le Gallois **23** *C1*
Metropolis **6** *D5*
Salt **13** *detail*
St John the Baptist Church **28** *C3*
Terra Nova **19** *detail*
Toad at the Exhibition **12** *D4*
Topo Gigio **7** *D3*
Union Undeb **22** *D2*
Woods Brasserie **15** *detail*

Bars & clubs
Cayo Arms **31** *B1*
Claude **30** *A6*
Cottage **19** *E3*
Cuba **16** *C4*
Edge **12** *D5*
Golden Cross **11** *F4*
Ha!Ha! **5** *C4*
Life **8** *E3*
Moloka **24** *F4*
Old Arcade **4** *D3*
Sodabar **9** *E3*
Waterguard **3** *detail*

complete with gardens and sheds. Each of the houses is furnished in a different period, from 1805 to 1985. Nearby there's a postwar pre-fab bungalow, an example of the kit homes made to replace houses bombed in the war.

An extremely popular area of the museum are the Victorian Gwalia Stores from Bridgend, with shelves filled with things like bile beans, Sloan's liniment, loose biscuits and tins saying things like: Ringer's Shag – The Old Favourite. Next door is a shop selling traditional items like laverbread, Welsh cheeses and Welsh cakes, while upstairs is a tea room. When you've exhausted all the buildings you can also explore the lovely Castle Gardens, with terraces, 18th century fishponds and a recently restored Italian Garden.

Around Cardiff

The gentle, pastoral scenery of the **Vale of Glamorgan** is easily accessible from Cardiff, with trains to Bridgend, buses to towns like Cowbridge and a water bus to Penarth. The heritage coastline is varied, with the fish, chips and fairground rides resort of Barry mingling with the pleasant but snoozy Victorian town of Penarth. There are craggy cliffs, some award winning beaches and good walks – notably the coastal walk around Dunraven Bay. Inland is **Cowbridge**, a pretty and very prosperous town filled with independent shops, including lots of antique shops, and some good places to eat. A great place to stroll around and window shop. Near Porthcawl is the **Kenfig Nature Reserve** ⓘ *information at 79 Eastgate, Cowbridge, T01446 772901, Mon, Thu, Fri 0845-1300, 1400-1630, closes at 1600 Fri*, where a lake and dunes provide a habitat for migratory birds.

If you're interested in church history head out to the little town of **Llantwit Major**, where you'll find St Illtud's Church, off Burial Lane. St Illtud founded a church and religious school on this site around 500 AD. It was the first Christian college in Britain – and alumni are said to include St David and St Patrick. Local kings were buried here and the church contains an important collection of Celtic stones. The building you see today dates back to Norman times. A couple of miles from the town is St Donat's Castle, a medieval pile which was bought by American newspaper tycoon William Randolph Hearst in 1925. It's now home to Atlantic College, the international school, and also the St Donat's Art Centre, T01446 799100, www.stdonats.com, which hosts various festivals (see festivals) as well as acting as a venue for theatre, film and dance events. Llantwit Major is close to Nash Point, a lovely lonely spot with two lighthouses, craggy cliffs and a warning bell floating in the bay, clanging eerily in the wind. Travel west along the coast and you come to Ogmore by Sea, where there's a lovely sandy beach that's a real favourite with kite surfers.

Penarth is a Victorian seaside town with a small promenade, a rather genteel little pier and a good vegetarian restaurant (see Eating). It's linked to Cardiff by water bus and in summer you can also take trips on the **Waverley** ⓘ *details from TIC on the pier, T02920 708849, Easter-Sep*, the world's last sea going paddle steamer. The town also contains the **Turner House Art Gallery** ⓘ *T02920 708870, Tue-Sun 1000-1700*, which displays paintings from the Welsh national collection.

Travel a couple of miles along the coast, towards Barry, and you can see **Lavernock Point**. A plaque by the little church here informs you that in 1897 'near this spot the first radio waves were exchanged across water by Guglielmo Marconi and George Kemp/Between Lavernock and Flat Holm...'. **Flat Holm** is a tiny island, once a retreat for monks, as well as a refuge for smugglers. Now it's a site of Special Scientific Interest (SSSI) and is rich in wildlife. There are boat trips to the island from Barry Docks with the **Flat Holm Project** ⓘ *T01446 747661, www.cardiff.gov.uk/flatholm, Apr-Oct, £12.50, children £6.25, family £35, booking essential*, which give you 3 hrs on the island.

Garden lovers should make for **Dyffryn Gardens** ⓘ *off the A48, T02920 593328, www.dyffryngardens.org.uk, Easter-Sep 1000-1800, Oct 1000-1700, £3, family £6.50, free in winter*, Grade 1 listed gardens around a grand country house, with an herbaceous border, Italian garden, arboretum and and physic garden.

Sleeping

City Centre *p537, map 540*

L **Angel Hotel**, Castle St, T029 2064 9200, www.paramount-hotels.co.uk. Victorian hotel sandwiched between Cardiff Castle and Cardiff Arms Park. A mere Gareth Edwards sidestep from the shops , it is a perennial favourite with locals and regular visitors.

A **Hilton Hotel**, Kingsway, T029 2064 6300, www.hilton.com. Elegant and tasteful, this hotel attracts the great and the good (and its fair share of star guests). Has a Health Club with 20 metre pool as well as a gym and spa.

A **Marriott Hotel**, Mill Lane, T029 2039 9944, www.marriott.com. Standing cheek by jowl with Cardiff's Cafe Quarter, this four star hotel claims to be Cardiff's premier hotel and offers the standard facilities you'd expect of a major chain. Not funky but reliable.

B **Thistle Hotel**, Park Place, T029 2038 3471, 0870 333 9257, www.thistlehotels.com/cardiff. Restored to its Victorian splendour, with comfy furnishings, the location in the pedestrianised zone makes it handy for shopping.

C **Big Sleep Hotel**, Bute Terrace, T029 2063 6363,www.thebigsleephotel.com. Listed as one of the best budget boutique hotels in the world and co-owned by John Malkovich, this high rise is chic and comfortable. Breakfast is a continental buffet. Style on a budget and very popular with a younger crowd.

C **Cathedral Hotel**, 47 Cathedral Rd, T029 2023 6511, www.cathedral-hotel.com. Family run hotel in Pontcanna, but five minute's walk of city centre. Facilities include a gym, bar, restaurant and parking.

C **Sandringham Hotel**, 21 St Mary St, T029 2023 2161, www.sandringham-hotel.com. This may not be in the most peaceful location in town but if you want somewhere central, then this bustling family run hotel will float your boat. The jazz cafe adds to the ambience.

C **Marlborough Guest House**, 98 Newport Rd, Roath, T029 2049 2385. A well tended front garden welcomes you to accommodation in a roomy Victorian end of terrace.

C **Penrhys Hotel**, 127, Cathedral Road, Pontcanna, T029 2023 0548. Family run hotel offering ensuite rooms with TV and even a four poster. The Victorian building boasts a splendid tower and dining room complete with stained glass and dark wood.

C-D **Courtfield Hotel**, 101 Cathedral Rd, Pontcanna, T/F 029 2022 7701. Well-run B&B set up in 1950 and still going strong. Some ensuite rooms, off street parking and a licenced bar – handy before a day's rugby watching or after a hard day's shopping.

D **Anedd Lon**, 157 Cathedral Rd, T029 2022 3349, F 029 20644 0885. Pretty hanging baskets welcome you to this comfortable B&B offering no smoking ensuite accomodation in sedate Pontcanna.

D-F **Cardiff Backpackers**, 98 Neville St, Riverside, T029 2034 5577, www.cardiffbackpackers.com. Funky and friendly hostel accommodation about half a mile from Cardiff Central station. Cheerful single, double, triple and bunk bedroom options are available. The bright and welcoming communal areas include cafe -style chairs and tables, a fully licensed bar and squashy sofas.

D **Church Hotel**, 126 Cathedral Rd, Pontcanna, T029 2034 0881. Vegetarian friendly accommodation recently taken over by Charlotte Church's parents. All rooms ensuite with colour TV, but no off road parking. Vegetarian breakfasts by advance request.

D **Maxine's**, 150, Cathedral Rd, T029 2022 0288, F 029 2034 4884. Straightforward B&B in light, bright surroundings offering value for money in the leafy Pontcanna district. Handy for the smart parade of local stores further up Cathedral Rd.

D **Town House**, 70 Cathedral Rd, Pontcanna,T029 2023 9399, F 029 2022 3214. Pleasant rooms in an imposing and recently restored three storey Victorian mock gothic townhouse. All rooms ensuite, off road parking – vegetarian breakfasts available.

E **Austins**, 11, Coldstream Terrace, T029 2037 7148, F 029 2037 7158 Clean and simple accommodation in a great central location across the River Taff just opposite the mighty Millennium Stadium but tucked away on a relatively quiet road.

E **Cardiff Youth Hostel**, 2 Wedal Rd, Roath Park, T029 2046 2303, www.yha.org.uk. Handily placed near an Indian and Italian restaurants, the student district of Cathays, several bus stops and 2 miles north of the city centre. Popular hostel, continental breakfasts available.

E **Cardiff University**, Cathays, T029 2087 5508, www.cardiff.ac.uk, Thousands of rooms, 50% ensuite, available during vacation season (Jun-Sep) – room only, B&B, self-catering all options.

Cardiff Bay *p538, map p540*

L **St.David's Hotel and Spa**, Havannah Street, Cardiff Bay, T029 2045 4045, F 029 2031 3075, www.rfhotels.com. Local wags would have you believe that the rf stands for 'really fancy' but it is Rocco Forte's luxurious waterfront hotel which dominates the Bay's skyline. Spa, fitness centre and Marco Pierre White inspired restaurant.

C **Express by Holiday Inn Hotel**, Longueil Close, Schooner Way, Cardiff Bay, T029 2044 9000, www.exhicardiff.co.uk. Less pricey (and less luxurious) than St David's, the modern rooms are ideal if you are looking for easy access to the Bay.

Around Cardiff *p541*

A **The Great House**, Laleston, Bridgend, T01656 657644, www.great-house-laleston.co.uk. Reminders of old Wales in this restored 16th-century building, complete with oak beams and mullioned windows.

B **Egerton Grey Country House**, Porthkerry, Barry, T01446 711666, www.egertongrey.co.uk. Plush 7th-century country house, filled with antiques, oak panelling and period detail. Secluded gardens, yet convenient for the nearby airport.

C **Court Colman Manor**, Pe-y-Fai, Bridgend, T01656 720212, www.court-colman-manor.com. Grand old manor house set in its own grounds, with a pleasantly eccentric mixture of styles: open fires and comfy sofas in the wood paneled public rooms and themed bedrooms decorated in anything from traditional Indian to Moroccan styles.

Eating

City Centre *p537, map 540*

£££ **The Armless Dragon**, 97-99 Wyeverne Rd, Cathays, T02920 382357, Tue-Fri noon-1400, Mon-Wed 1900-2100, Fri, Sat 1900-2130, booking advised. Dull exterior hides an award winning restaurant offering a new twist on traditional Welsh dishes. Lots of fresh lamb and fish – as well as choices for veggies like – er – laverballs.

£££ Union Undeb, 23 Womanby St, T02920 343433. The hot place to be seen, this private members' club in a lofty Victorian building, is Cardiff's answer to London's Soho House. The restaurant serves contemporary Welsh food and is open to non-members in the evenings on pre booking.

£££-££ Da Venditto, 7-8 Park Place, T02920 230781, Award winning Italian restaurant close to the theatre. Mains might include Gressingham duck with pea and broad bean risotto, or ravioli with spinach, baby courgettes and parmesan. Special lunch set menus- 2 courses £14.50, 3 courses for £18.

££ Juboraj, 10 Mill Lane, T02920 377668, Mon-Sat 1200-1400 (not Fri) and 1800-midnight, closed all day Sun. Highly rated South East Asian restaurant in the Café quarter.

££ La Fosse, 9-11 The Hayes, T02920 237755, Mon-Sat 1200-1430, 1800-0030, closed Sun. This contemporary seafood restaurant/oyster bar, all blue glass and chrome, is housed downstairs in the former fish market.

££ Metropolis, 60 Charles St, T02920 344300, bar/restaurant 1200-1500, 1800-2300 daily, Sleek wooden floors, beige seats and cool customers, and a surprisingly reasonably priced menu. Mains might include pork and leek sausages with colcannon, or stuffed aubergine and feta. Good puds too.

££ Topo Gigio, Church St T02920 344794, Mon-Fri 1200-1500, 1730-2300, Sat 1200-2330, Sun 1200-2300. Enduringly popular Italian offering a wide range of tasty pastas and pizzas-some with a Welsh twist.

££-£ The Greenhouse, 38 Woodville Rd, Cathays, T02920 235731, Tues-Sat 1830-2200, Fri 1200-1500, Sun 1100-1600. A good vegetarian restaurant offering imaginative dishes.

£ Blas ar Cymru, Old Library, The Hayes, Tues-Sat 1000-1600. Lovely contemporary café, all blonde wood and chrome, showcasing the best Welsh produce. A huge screen shows you everything that's going on in the open kitchen. Recommended. At the time of writing this was only their temporary home.

£ Cantina, 48 Charles St, T02920 382882, Tues-Fri 1100-1530, plus Thu, Fri evenings 1830-2230, Sats 1100-2230. Lovely Mediterranean style café/bistro, with trendy yellow and lilac seats and a little garden for warm days. Good value pastas, pizzas and lunchtime ciabatte.

£ Cibo, 83 Pontcanna St, T02920 232226, Mon 1200-2100, Tues-Sun 1000-2200, booking advisable. Great Italian place, good for daytime or evenings. Good value ciabatta, pizzas and pastas in friendly atmosphere.

Cardiff Bay *p538, map p540*

£££ Tides, St David's Hotel and Spa, Havana St, T02920-313018, Mon-Thu 1200-1430, 1800-2200, Fri, Sat 1230-1430, 1800-2230, Sun 1230-1500, 1800-2200. Marco Pierre White oversees this sophisticated restaurant in the 5 star hotel overlooking Cardiff Bay. The place to bring folk you want to impress.

£££ Woods Brasserie, Pilotage Building, Stuart St, T02920-492400, booking required. Upmarket brasserie with excellent food. Plenty of seafood on the menu.

££ Bosphorus, Mermaid Quay, T02920-487477, Mon-Fri 1200-1500, 1800-2400, Sat, Sun 1400-1700, 1800-2400. Perched on a jetty this glass sided Turkish restaurant has great views around the Bay. The food's a reminder that Turkish cuisine isn't limited to a doner kebab after the pub.

££-£ Salt, Mermaid Quay, Stuart Street, T02920-494375 (see bars) This slick bar/restaurant offers a range of pasta dishes and sharing plates in the heart of the revitalised Bay.

Around Cardiff *p541*

££ Tomlins, 46 Plassey St, Penarth, T029 2070 6644, Tues-Sat from 1900 plus Fri, Sat 1200-1430, open alternate Suns 1200-1430. High quality veggie restaurant serving imaginative food such as pea cannelloni with blue cheese sauce.

££ Valentino's, 44 High St, Cowbridge, T01446 771155, Thurs-Sat 1215-1445, 1730-2200. Italian restaurant serving the usual pizzas, pastas and meaty mains. Lunch and early bird menus for £4.95.

££-£ Bar 44, 44c High St, T01446 776630, Mon 1200-2100, Tues-Sat 1200-2300, Sun 1200-2230. Lively tapas bar on the main street.

££-£ Bokhara Brasserie, Court Colman Manor, Pen-y-Fai, Bridgend T01656 721122, Tues-Fri 1230-1430, 1900-2300, Sat 1900-2300, Sun 1200-1430. Great Indian cuisine in the unlikely setting of a rambling former manor house that's now an hotel. Very good value.

Pubs, bars and clubs

Most of the constantly changing bars, pubs and clubs are in the city centre and Cardiff Bay. Mill Lane, otherwise known as the 'Café Quarter', offers a fair choice of eating options and bars. Gay venues focus on Charles St and elsewhere on the city's southern fringe. Wednesday night sees the university crowds descend on the town for student nights at various venues.

City Centre *p537, map 540*

Bar Essential, Windsor Place, T02920 383762, food from 1200. One of Cardiff's many busy café/bars. This one serves sandwiches, pasta dishes and things like steak and chips. At night it's the choice of the city's young professionals and visiting businesspeople.

Is it?, 12 Wharton St, T02920 413600, food daily 1000-2100, open until 0030 Sun-Wed, 0100 Thu, Fri, 0200 Sat. Large, self consciously, trendy café/bar with an enormous mirror behind the bar and a seating area upstairs as well as down. Sandwiches, including BLTs from £2.95, salads, pasta dishes and mains like burgers or mussels.

Cayo Arms, 36 Cathedral Road, Pontcanna, T029 20391910. Named after a commander of the Free Wales Army, this pub is popular with those who, in ale terms, like to keep it real. Several Camra awards, excellent beer and food.

Cuba, Unit 9, The Friary, T02920 397967, closed Sun. Small bar gets cramped towards the weekend with drinkers, gawpers and people shaking their thing to salsa and merengue.

The Edge, 35, Charles St, T029 2040 0876 Usually packed, friendly and full of clubbers getting ready for a big night at Club X close by.

Golden Cross, 238 Hayes Bridge Rd, T029 2039 4556 This is a popular drinking and watering hole and pre-club venue on the southern edge of the city centre, set in the best preserved Victorian pub in Cardiff.

Ha!Ha! Bar and Canteen, The Friary, Cardiff, T029 2039 7997. This bar is perfect for chilling out after a hard day's shopping or for posing after dark – aims to be all things to all (thirtysomething) people. A wide selection of snacks, main meals and desserts is also on offer – one of Cardiff's best new bars.

Henry's, Park Chambers, T02920 224672. Food Mon-Thu 0900-2100, Fri, Sat 0900-1930, Sun 1200-1800. Busy 80s style chain café/bar popular with shoppers and the post work crowd – who come for the cocktails.

Moloka, 7 Mill Lane, T02920 225592, daily. Lively vodka bar doing a popular line in cocktails too. Regular DJ nights.

The Old Arcade, 14 Church Street, T029 2023 1740 is an old-fashioned pub serving Brains beer as well as bar food. Packed on rugby international days.

The Glassworks, 4 Wharton St, T02920 222114 Large pub in former glass factory offering 4 guest real ales, in addition to Greene King brews. Real ale 'happy hour' weekdays 1700-1900. Also serves bar food and all day breakfasts.

Life, St Mary St, T029 2066 7800 is popular with young professional types who are thirsty but wouldn't be seen dead in one of Life's pub chain neighbours. This still does not explain the long queues on Fri and Sat.

The Sodabar, 41 St Mary Street, Cardiff, T029 2023 8181, www.thesodabar.com. Pitching for the more discerning end of the clubbing market, its chic interior is packed to the gunnels with Italian furniture on flagstone floors. Great DJ's and an excellent sound system add to the buzzy atmosphere.

Union-Undeb, 23 Womanby Street, T029 2034 3433 (see eating). Private members club in converted warehouse with several bars and a restaurant. Residents of the St Davids Hotel and Spa can use the facilities during their stay. Honorary members include Cerys Matthews and Ioan Gruffudd.

Cardiff Bay *p538, map p540*

Salt, Mermaid Quay, Stuart Street, Cardiff Bay, T029 2049 4375. New England style bar, complete with arty driftwood over two floors, complete with stylish comfortable sofas.

Terra Nova, Mermaid Quay, Stuart Street, Cardiff, T029 2045 0947. Set on 4 levels, the building is shaped like a ship's bow. A seating area on the top floor resembles a crows nest.

The Waterguard, Harbour Drive, Cardiff Bay, T029 2049 9034. The main bar area is modern and open with comfy sofas in light and airy surroundings. As an independent pub, its cellar represents a welcome change from the norm. Bar meals and snacks.

Around Cardiff *p541*

The Bush Inn, St Hilary, T01446 772745 This ancient inn is popular with locals as it serves good bar meals and real ales. There's a real fire in winter.

Plough and Harrow, Monkash off B4265 near Nash Point, T01656 890209, Pub that's full of character (it's an old Welsh longhouse with an inglenook fireplace) with a good range of real ales. Serves good food too.
The Vale of Glamorgan, High St, Cowbridge T01446 772252. Good traditional pub with real fires, real ales and a good atmosphere.
The Victoria Inn, Sigingstone, on B4270 near Cowbridge, T01446 773943. Popular pub serving good bar and restaurant meals. Noted for its Sunday lunches.

Clubs

Club X, 35-39 Charles Street, T02920 2040 0876, www.clubx-cardiff.com. The biggest gay club in Wales has had yet another new facelift with a newly extended beer garden, games room, pool room and balcony area.
Clwb Ifor Bach, 11 Womanby Street, T029 2023 2199, www.clwb.net is situated over three floors and is open every night. It is regarded as one of the 'coolest' clubs in Cardiff thanks to a popular mix of regular live music and DJs. Saturday is for members only (be they Welsh speaking or Welsh learners).
The Emporium, 8-10 High Street ,T029 2066 4577, dance club that hosts a variety of club nights with visiting big-name DJs, spread over two floors. Something for everyone, especially the diehard clubmonster.
Evolution, UCI building, Atlantic Wharf, Cardiff Bay, T029 2046 4444 is the biggest club in Cardiff and offers cheap booze and party anthems and mainstream house and dance. There is a free bus service to collect would-be groovers from outside the New Theatre in the city, every 15 minutes from 2115. You may well wonder why.
Liquid, Imperial Gate, St Mary Street, T029 2064 5464 is bright, breezy and invariably busy. If strobing, a mixed bag of sounds and playing sardines on the dancefloor is your thing, you'll love it here.
Toucan Club, 95-97 St Mary's St, Cardiff, 029 2037 2212, www.toucanclub.co.uk. A unique and independent venue in Cardiff, this chilled yet friendly club hosts live music with an eclectic global flavour upstairs and it often features salsa and Latin American music. It also serves original Mediterranean food in the Cafe Bar downstairs Tue- Sun from 1700-0200.

Entertainment

The local press have details of what's happening in the city. Also look out for Buzz, a free, informative, monthly guide to listings on gigs, galleries, film etc. Information on the arts in Cardiff is available from 0800 389 9496, www.arts4cardiff.co.uk

Cinema

Chapter Arts Centre, Market Road, Canton, T029 2031 1050 – art house as well as mainstream cinema, 2 screens, showing many foreign films
UGC, Mary Ann Street, T0870 9070 739- mainstream city centre multiplex
UCI, Atlantic Wharf, Cardiff Bay, T0870 010 2030, www.atlanticwharf-cardiff.com – 12 screen multiplex showing almost exclusively mainstream movies.

Comedy

The Glee Club, Mermaid Quay, Cardiff Bay T0870 241 5093, www.glee.co.uk. Cardiff's main comedy club, regularly stages live acts from comedy circuit regulars. Once the acts are over, the laughs continue as the club morphs into a boozy dance venue.

Live music

Live music is easy to find. Classical music is generally staged at St David's Hall. Cardiff Male Voice Choir rehearses at Cowbridge Rd Methodist Church, Canton, Wed and Fri 1930-2130, T02920 594497 –check beforehand.
St David's Hall, The Hayes, T02920 878444, www.stdavidshallcardiff.co.uk. This concert hall dominates much of the city centre. It's the prime venue for classical concerts as well as the Welsh Proms and other large scale events.
Café Jazz, Sandringham Hotel, St Mary Street, T029 2038 7026, www.cafejazzcardiff.com is home to the Welsh Jazz Society and hosts top local performers as well as international acts. Costs depend on acts – call ahead to check.
Cardiff International Arena, Mary Ann Street T029 2022 4488, www.uk.cc.com/cia and occasionally the Millennium Stadium, Westgate Street T029 2082 2228 are the prime venues for big name rock and pop acts: past performers have included Atomic Kitten, Tom Jones, Blue, Iron Maiden, Holiday on Ice, The Strokes – so pretty varied. Prices upwards of £20, depending on the act.

Wales Millennium Centre, Cardiff Bay – at the time of writing they're still building this arts venue, part of the new face Cardiff is presenting to the world. Due to open 2004 for everything from opera and ballet to musicals.
Barfly Club, Kingsway, T02920 667658/ 0870 9070999, www.barflyclub.com This bar hosts a range of live bands, both local and visiting. Check gig guides in local press or chance it.
University Student's Union, Park Place, Cathays Park T029 2078 1458, www.cardiff.ac.uk. Many events are restricted to NUS card-holders but others are open. Attracts a wide range of big name bands and dance acts.
Cardiff Coal Exchange, Mount Stuart Square, Cardiff Bay, T029 2049 4917, www.coalexchange.co.uk. The former commercial centre is now a hub for live performances.

Theatre

New Theatre, Park Place, T029 2087 8889, www.newtheatrecardiff.com Traditional Edwardian theatre offers everything from opera, ballet, musicals, drama – and the odd pantomime at Christmas. It's currently home to the Welsh National Opera (www.wno.org.uk) when in town.
Sherman Theatre, Senghennydd Rd, T029 2064 6900, www.shermantheatre.co.uk, concentrates on more serious drama, programmes for children and avant garde productions. Welsh and English language productions here.
Chapter Arts Centre, Market Rd, Canton T02920 311050, box office 02920 304400, www.chapter.org (see Cinema). Home to several experimental theatre companies and offers actors' workshops as well as a range of full performance pieces. Very lively programme.
Norwegian Church Arts Centre, Harbour Drive, Cardiff Bay, daily 0900-1700, plus evenings for performances, T02920 454899, norwegian.church@talk21.com. This attractive little church, where author Roald Dahl was christened, is a venue for all sorts of exhibitions, workshops and concerts. Also has a good café.
Ffotogallery, T02920 708870, www.ffotogallery.org. Arts organisation dedicated to promoting photography in Wales. As well as running courses they stage exhibitions – at the time of writing these are in the temporary venue of Turner House Gallery, Plymouth Rd, Penarth, Wed-Sat, 1100-1700, free.

Festivals and events

Feb Celtic Festival of Wales, Vale of Glamorgan – Celtic music and dance festival, T01656 782103.
Jun Cardiff Singer of the World, BBC Wales bi-ennial singing competition.
International Festival of Musical Theatre, biennial event alternating with the Singer of the World comp.
Jul International Storytelling Festival, St Donat's Castle, T01446 799100.
Late Jul, early Aug Cardiff Festival, T02920 872087, www.cardiff-festival.com. Annual free arts festival aiming to be the new Edinburgh Fest, with theatre, music, street entertainment and fairground. Culminates in the Big Weekend.
End Nov-early Jan Winter Wonderland, Cardiff celebrates Christmas and the New Year with an open air ice rink, music and fireworks, www.cardiff.gov.uk/winterwonderland.

Shopping

Cardiff is an excellent city for shopping. The centre is compact, so you can get around easily on foot, and while there are all the usual high street chains (a huge Next, Waterstones, HMV, Gap- you name them) you'll also find a great choice of smaller, specialist outlets selling everything from cigars to guitars. As well as modern, characterless malls there are also some splendid Edwardian and Victorian arcades. Pedestrianised Queen St is the main drag, followed by St Mary St. Late opening night is Thursday when most large outlets are open until 2000.

Activities and tours

Boat trips

Bay Island Voyages, from Mermaid Quay, Cardiff Bay, T02920 484110, www.bayisland.co.uk, offer high speed boat trips out to the barrage and the bay, as well as longer, more leisurely trips to Flatholm and Steepholm Islands £18.50 for 2 hrs).
Cardiff Bay Cruises, from Mermaid Quay, T02920 472004, www.cardiffbaycruises.com. Operate half hour cruises of the Bay on an 'African Queen' lookalike (£3), and 1hr trips in the Bay, the rivers Taff and Ely and the barrage, on the Canberra Queen former lifeboat £6.

Water Bus, Cardiff Cats, T02920 488842, www.cardiffcats.com, run trips between Cardiff Bay and Penarth and to the barrage.

Bus tours

Guide Friday tour buses Apr-Nov, www.city-sightseeing.com/cardiff, £7, £2.50 concessions or free with a Cardiff Card open top bus tours do a fifty minute loop from the Castle, taking in 9 stops. You may hop off at any point before joining a later tour within a 24 hour period.

Cycling

Taff Trail Cycle Hire centre T029 2039 8362 is off Cathedral Rd, near the Cardiff Caravan Park and by Pontcanna Fields. Bikes are available for day rental from £9, £6.50 children and £28 for a family ticket (2 adults and 2 children). The Taff Trail extends from Cardiff Bay to Brecon, 87km (54 miles) to the north.

Rugby

The Millennium Stadium, Westgate St, T02920 822228, www.millennium stadium.co.uk is the sporting venue in Wales, with seating for 72,500 spectators and a retractable roof. The home of Welsh rugby (www.wru.co.uk). Hosts matches in the annual Six Nations Championships rugby, as well as international football matches. In the embarrassing absence (for the English) of a stadium at Wembley it is also the location for major English footballing events including the FA Cup Final. Tours of the stadium are available daily, entrance gate 3, booking advised. £5, £2.50 children, £15 family. Cardiff Rugby Club T0870 013 5213 play at the Arms Park, Westgate St, by the Millennium Stadium.

Train trips

Cardiff Barrage Crossing, from Mermaid Quay, Cardiff Bay T02920 512729, keeftrain@ntlworld.com, 1100-1700, £4 return, £2 return child, £10 return family. Family friendly trip, with commentary, on a little train taking you from the Quay to the Port of Cardiff and on to the Barrage. Single or return journeys.

Walking Tours

Creepy Cardiff, Ghost Tours, T07980 975135, www.creepycardiff.com, £5, 1hr ghost tours of the city, starting from steps of the National Museum

Guided tours of Cardiff, by local historian John May, T02920 811603, £5, 1½ hr walking tour taking in all the city's main sights

Transport

Air

In addition to the many charter flights, there are now direct scheduled flights to a number of UK and European destinations, through Air Wales (T0870-7773131, www.airwales.co.uk.) and budget airline bmibaby (T0870-264 2229, www.bmibaby.com) and many worldwide connections are available via the following gateway airports: **London City**, **Amsterdam**, **Paris**, **Brussels** and **Dublin**. The taxi office is in the arrivals hall and taxis are prebookable on 01446 710693, approx. £20-25 per journey. Buses operate between the city's central train and bus stations and the airport every 30 minutes, approx.£2.90 per 30-40 minute journey (Mon-Sat, 06.53-18.58), then every 60 minutes 1936-2236. An hourly service operates on Sundays, 08.15-21.35.

Bus

Cardiff Bus (TTraveline Cymru 0870 608 2 608, www.cardiffbus.com) runs services all over the city from its base in Wood St and its green, white and orange buses generally operate between 05.30 and 23.20 with a reduced service at the weekend and on public holidays. Prices vary according to the system of colour coded fare zones, Zone A (red) being the city centre, where tickets cost from 60p. Exact change is usually needed and tickets may be bought on the buses. The main routes between the city centre and the Bay area include 6 Bay Xpress www.cardiff.gov.uk/bayxpress (from **Central Station**), 35 (**Wyndham Arcade** on St Mary St to **Mermaid Quay**) and 8 (**Wood St** to **Atlantic Wharf**) and these services run every 15 minutes 0730-2300. A 24- hour CityRider pass, costing £3.20, gives unlimited travel on all Cardiff Buses within Cardiff and its near neighbour **Penarth**. Can be purchased on the buses or from the bus sales office in Wood St.

Taxi

Taxis can be found in the ranks at Central Station, Queen St station and on Duke St by the castle. A taxi from Central Station / Wood St Bus Station to Cardiff Bay costs around £4 one way. Taxis may be hailed on the street or, alternatively, can be ordered by telephone from dozens of firms, including **Dragon Taxis** (T029 2033 3333), **Capitol Cars** (T029 2077 7777), **Black Cab** (T02920 222999), Castle (T02920 344344) and Premiere (T02920 555555/565565).

Train

First Great Western T08457 484950 runs hourly services from **London Paddington** to **Cardiff**: journey time approx. two hours. Regional railways provide a direct link to **Cardiff** from **Manchester** and the **North West**, from **Birmingham** and the **Midlands** and from the West Country and England's South Coast. Suburban and Valley Lines trains also use the station, linking this station with Cardiff Queen St. **Valley Lines** run most local train services (T029 2023 1978, www.valleylines.co.uk) which run between 0500 and 2430 on weekdays, with a reduced service on weekends /public holidays. A shuttle train service takes three minutes to run from Queen Street station in the city centre to Bute Street station, from where Cardiff Bay is a five minute walk. There are four services per hour on weekdays, two per hour on Saturdays but no service on Sundays(from £1.30 off-peak). Travelling to Bute St from Central Station costs the same but takes around 15 minutes, including a change at Queen St. Valley Lines also offer a Day Explorer pass for £6, allowing for one day of unlimited travel on their train services, **Stagecoach** buses and discounts to tourist attractions around the Valleys to the north of Cardiff.

Parking City centre parking is heavily restricted and the presence of eagle eyed traffic wardens encourages the use of the pay and display NCP car parks spread around the city centre as well as the use of the voucher parking system. Vouchers can be bought in advance from local shops (80p-£1 for one hour).

Directory

Hospitals University of Wales Hospital, Heath Park T02920 747747.
Internet Internet Exchange, 8 Church St, T02920 236047, Mon-Thurs 0900-2100, Fri, Sat 0900-2000, Sun 1100-1900. Non members £1 per 15 mins, day pass for £7 if bought before midday. **Urban Retreat**, 104 Crwys Rd, Cathays, T02920 302803, daily. Internet access and café in the studenty zone. Free access at **Central Library** (best to reserve), Frederick St (see directory).
Laundry Launderama, 60 Lower Cathedral Rd. **Library** Cardiff Central Library, Frederick St Mon-Sat 0900-1730 T02920 382116. **Post Office** Main Post Office, The Hayes, Mon-Fri 090—1730, Sat 0900-1230.
Police Cardiff Police Station, King Edward V111 Avenue, Cathays Park T02920 222111.
Travel Agencies STA Travel, 11 Duke St and Cardiff University Students Union, Park Place, T02920 382350, www.statravel.co.uk.

Caerphilly and The Valleys

➔ *Colour map 1*

Most tourists by- pass the Valleys for the more conventional attractions of the beaches of the Pembrokeshire coast or the mountains of Snowdonia. Yet these distinctive communities, with their rows of terraced houses squeezed into the valleys of the mountains that lie between Cardiff and the Brecon Beacons, are full of history. These were the coal and iron producing heartlands of the Industrial Revolution; where close working class communities lived harsh lives under the gloomy shadow of hills scarred and blackened with slag heaps.

When the coal mining industry died, so to a large extent did the Valleys, with unemployment devastating the population. But the slag heaps have now gone or been greened over, some coal mines are now museums and Blaenavon, a world heritage site, is re-inventing itself as a booktown. The towns are still poor, but the people very friendly; the surrounding hills are stunning and the glimpse of the industrial past is fascinating. ▸▸ *For Sleeping, Eating and other listings, see pages 552-554.*

Ins and outs

Getting there Eight miles north of Cardiff, Caerphilly is easily reached by **road** from J32 of the M4, by taking the A470 and then following signs for Caerphilly. There are good **train** and **bus** links from Cardiff to Caerphilly and the main towns in the valleys like Merthyr Tydfil. The half hourly Cardiff to Bargoed or Rhymney service from Valley Lines serves Caerphilly railway station about a quarter of a mile from the visitor centre opposite the castle. The trip takes about 20 minutes. **Trains** run right along the Rhonda and also go to Merthyr Tydfil. Valley Line Traina www.valleylines.co.uk. Cardiff Bus service No 26 runs hourly from Cardiff Bus station in Wood St, takes about 45 minutes and will stop at Caerphilly Railway Station and on Castle St near Caerphilly Visitor Centre.

Getting around Towns like Merthyr Tydfil and Caerphilly are small enough to explore on foot. If you want to travel from valley to valley without returning to Cardiff it is easier to go by car.

Information Caerphilly Visitor Centre ⓘ *Lower Twyn Square, Caerphilly, T029 2088 0011, tic@caerphilly.gov.uk, Apr-Sep 1000-1800,Oct-Mar 1000-1700,* **Blaenavon TIC** ⓘ *North St, The Ironworks, T01495 792615, blaenavon.ironworks@btopenworld.com, Apr-Oct Mon-Fri 0930-1630, Sat 1000-1700, Sun 1000-1630*, as well as tourist information they can also help people to trace their local family history. **Merthyr Tydfil TIC** ⓘ *14a Glebeland St T01685 379884, merthyrtic@hotmail.com , Apr-Sep 0930-1730 Mon-Sat, Oct-Mar 0900-1700 Mon-Sat* **Pontypridd TIC** ⓘ *Bridge ST, T01443 490748, bdavies@pontypriddmuseum.org.uk, Mon-Sat 1000-1700.*

Caeffili (Caerphilly)

Caerphilly Castle ⓘ *Caerphilly, T029 2088 3143, www.cadw.wales.gov.uk, 09.30-1800, Jun-Sep, 0930-1700, Apr, May, Oct, 0930- 1600, Nov-Mar, 1100-1600, Sun, £2.50, £2 children, £7 family CADW.* This vast medieval fortress is the second largest castle in Europe and stands comparison with even the mightiest of the castles built by Edward I. It was built from 1268 by Red (as he was known after the fiery colour of his hair) Gilbert de Clare, Earl of Gloucester, one of Henry III's most powerful and ambitious barons, to prevent the area falling into the hands of the Welsh leader Llywelyn the Last. The castle is vast, spread over some 30 acres of land, moving the poet Tennyson to write: 'It isn't a castle – it's a town in ruins'.

Llancaiach Fawr Manor ⓘ *T01443 412248, on B4254 near Nelson, north of Caerphilly, Mar-end Oct Mon-Fri 1000-1700, Sat, Sun 1000-1800, closed Mon Nov-Feb, £4.50, £3 children, £12 family.* This lovely old manor house was built in 1530 and is now a living history museum. It focuses on the year 1645 – the Civil War – when then owner Col Edward Prichard changed his allegiance from the Royalist to the Parliamentarian cause. The informative guides are dressed in period costume and speak and act as they would have in the 17th-century (works well – honest). The rooms have been restored and furnished to the period and there are also 17th-century style gardens.

Castell Coch ⓘ *west of Caerphilly, T02920 810101, £3, £2.50 children, £8.50 family, Jun-end Sep daily 0930-1800, Apr-Jun, Oct 0930-1700, Nov-Mar 0930-1600 Mon-Sat, 1100-1600 Sun, CADW.* Like Cardiff Castle, the lavishly eccentric interiors of this castle are a result of the partnership of the Marquis of Bute and architect William Burges. Their joint love of gothic fantasy and Bute's vast fortune allowed them to create extravagant rooms, with gilded ceilings, walls painted with golden apples, monkeys and peacocks and elaborate furniture and fittings.

The Valleys

Blaenavon

In 2000 the industrial town of Blaenavon was designated a UNESCO World Heritage Site – a recognition of the important role it played in the Industrial Revolution. **Blaenavon Ironworks**ⓘ *T01495 792615 (hrs as Blaenavon TIC), £2, £1.50 concessions, £5.50 family pre book for guided tours min £20*, are one of the best preserved 18th-century ironworks in Europe. Established in 1788 – the site being chosen for its abundance of coal, iron-ore, limestone and water – they were at the cutting edge of technology, using steam rather than water to power the furnaces. By 1796 Blaenavon was the 2nd largest producer of iron in Wales. In later years the metallurgist Sidney Gilchrist Thomas worked from here, spawning the mighty steel industry. As well as the remains of the works, there's a little terrace of iron workers cottages – inhabited until 1973.

Blaenavon is now in the process of re-inventing itself as a book town (www.booktownblaenafon.com), on the same lines as Hay-on-Wye. The force behind it is the energetic James Hanna, who is full of plans. To date 11 book shops have opened selling everything from cookery books to travel titles – and cafes, bars and places to stay are all in the pipeline. The town also plans to have its first book festival in 2004.

Blaenavon wasn't just an iron working centre, it was also a coal mining town as you can see at **Big Pit National Mining Museum**ⓘ *approx 1 miles west of Blaenavon, T01495 790311, www.nmgw.ac.uk mid Feb – end Nov daily 0930-1700, 1st tour 1000, last 1530, free*. This historic mine, high on the moors, gives an excellent insight into the life of the Valleys' coal miners. This mine opened in the mid 19th-century and was one of the few in the Valleys that did not experience a major disaster. Coal was mined from 1880 until 1980 – the site opening as a museum in 1983. In its heyday it employed 1300 men and produced more than 250,000 tons of coal a year. The highlight of a visit is the tour, which takes you 3000 ft (90m) underground. You don a helmet, cap-lamp and battery pack and, guided by ex-miners, go down to the coal face where you see the miserable conditions under which people worked. Not just people either – the underground stables still bear the names of the pit ponies who spent their lives in darkness. The last ponies around here were only brought to the surface in 1972.

The Big Pit is undergoing a £7million redevelopment and more surface attractions are being added. You will be able to see the listed 1930s Pithead Baths, learn about the social history of the area and see a gallery focusing on modern mining. There's a café too.

Merthyr Tydfil (Merthyr Tudful)

The name of Merthyr Tydfil is synonymous with the industrial past, although the town has roots dating back to Roman times if not before. The town's name refers to Tydfil, a Welsh princess who was martyred for her Christian beliefs in the 5th-century. In the 18th-century the town was transformed when its rich supplies of iron ore and limestone were discovered and exploited. It became the most important iron producing town in the world. The population swelled rapidly as workers swarmed in – being housed as cheaply as possible by their wealthy masters. The appalling working conditions and poor cramped housing led to a wave of radicalism: in 1831 there was a violent workers uprising (when the Red Flag was raised for the first time) and in 1900 it became the first town in Britain to elect a Socialist MP- Keir Hardie. When the industry declined in the 20th-century Merthyr suffered terribly from the consequent depression.

Today the history of the town, and the gulf that existed between the iron masters and their workers, can best be understood by visiting two contrasting sites. Joseph Parry's Cottage, T01685 721858, Apr-Sept Thur-Sun 1400-1700, free at 4 Chapel Row is a preserved ironworkers cottage, part of a terrace built in 1825 for skilled workers employed in the Cyfartha Ironworks. The ground floor rooms are furnished simply, as they would have been in the 1840s. Upstairs there's an exhibition about composer Joseph Parry who was born here and wrote a well known Welsh tune -Myfanwy.

Not far away, on the high ground, is the lavish **Cyfartha Castle** ⓘ *Brecon Rd T01685 723112, daily Apr-Sep 1000-1730, Oct-Mar 1000-1600 Tue-Fri, 1200-1600 Sat, Sun, free*, built at a cost of £30,000 in 1825 by the Crawshay family, who owned the Cyfartha Ironworks. It stands in 160 acres of parkland. Part of this opulent pile is now a school, the rest an excellent museum and art gallery. There are displays on singer Paul Robeson, who had strong links with the miners – he helped raise money for them in 1929. There's a good collection of pottery and ceramics, including local Nantgarw ware; Egyptain and Roman artefacts collected by a local man; displays on Male Voice Choirs, the Iron Industry, Welsh Nationalism and the miners strike of 1984-85. You can also see paintings by artists such as Jack Butler Yeats (brother of the poet), Kyffin Williams, Cedric Morris – and George Frederick Harris, Rolf Harris' grandfather who was born in Merthyr. There's a nice café too.

Rhonda Heritage Park ⓘ *Coed Cae Rd, Trehafod T01443 682036, www.netwales.co.uk/rhondda-heritage, daily 1000-1800, last tour 1630, closed Mon Oct-Easter, £5.60, £4.30 children, £16.50 family*. Based at the former Lewis Merthyr Colliery there's an interesting exhibition looking at life in the valleys, with recreated shops and house interiors. Panels tell the story of the colliery and the appalling Tynewydd Colliery disaster in 1877 when the pit was flooded and many men trapped underground. Tours of the site are available and there's also a good selection of books on life in the Valleys, and a café and gallery upstairs.

Margam Stones Museum ⓘ *near Port Talbot, T02920 500200, Wed-Sun 1000-1600, £2, £1.50 children, £5.50 family Abbey, T01639 871184*, is small but fascinating, situated next to Margam abbey church, it contains a fine collection of early Christian sculptured stones. There's the Bodvoc Stone, which once sat on Margam mountain set into a line of prehistoric barrows; 10th and 11th century crosses found at a nearby farm, and a 6th century memorial stone to Pumpeius Carantorius, with Ogham inscriptions which look rather like Morse code. The church itself is well worth a visit and contains 16th and 17th century tombs. **Margam Park** ⓘ *reached by junction 38, M4, T01639 881635, www.neath-porttalbot.gov.uk/margampark, daily Easter-end Sep 1000-1730, winter 1000-1630, free, £2 car park* is delightful parkland surrounding an elaborate 19th-century house and the romantic ruins of Margam Abbey. In the gardens is an elegant 18th-century Orangery, designed by Antony Keck to house a citrus collection of around 100 orange and lemon trees. There's a walled garden, fuchsia collections, play area for children – and contemporary artworks by artists such as Paul Williams and Elizabeth Frink are dotted around the grounds.

Sleeping

The Valleys *p551*

B Heritage Park Hotel, Coed Cae Rd, Trehafod, near Pontypridd, T01443 687057, www.heritageparkhotel.co.uk. Comfortable business geared hotel that makes a good base for exploring the valleys. Friendly staff and good facilities including a swimming pool.

C Mill Farm, Cwmafon, Pontypool T01495 774588. Farmhouse B&B with en-suite rooms, log fires and a small indoor heated swimming pool.

D Tyn-y-Wern Country House, Ynysybwl, Rhonnda Cynon Taff, near Pontypridd, T01443 790551 Victorian mine manager's house with 3 rooms, 1 en-suite. Dinner available by arrangement.

Caerphilly *p550*

C Cottage Guest House, Pwll-y-pant, Caerphilly, T029 2086 9160, www.s-h-systems.co.uk/hotels/cottagegh This 300 year old cottage is only a mile from Caerphilly Castle. Friendly welcome and hearty breakfasts.

D Dugann B&B, Springfield Bungalow, Rudry, Caerphilly, T029 2086 6607, 2 ensuite rooms welcoming non smokers only. Family friendly 2 star guesthouse about 1.5m from town centre.

Eating

Caerphilly *p550*
£ Glanmor's, Unit 30, Castle Court, Brynau Rd, T029 2088 8355. A great sandwich shop, close to the castle, serving homemade pastries.
£ Traveller's Rest, Thornhill Rd, Thornhill, T029 2085 9021, sits astride the hill summit between Caerphilly and Cardiff. Essentially a chain pub, it does so-so food in pretty and quaint surroundings – still better than much of what Caerphilly itself can offer.

The Valleys *p551*
££ Heritage Park Hotel, Coed Cae Rd, Trehafod, near Pontypridd, T01443 687057, 1200-1400, 1900-2200 daily. This hotel restaurant is worth checking out if you want a change from pub grub. Lots of steaks and roast meats, as well as some good veggie choices.
£ Cyfartha Castle Tearoom, Cyfartha Castle, Merthyr Tydfil, T01685 723112, Apr-end Sep, daily 1000-around 1700; Oct-end Mar, Tues-Fri 1000-around 1530, Sat, Sun 1200-1530. As it's free entry to the castle it's worth going just for this little tearoom.
£ Cook in the Books, 86 Broad St, Blaenavon daily 1000-1700, Sun 1100-1600 Due to open at the time of writing this café plans to offer coffees, cakes and light meals in the centre of Blaenavon.

Pubs
Aberaman Hotel, Brynheulog Terrace, Aberaman T01685 874695 Typical valleys pub serving real ales and bar meals.
Capel, Park Place, Gilfach Fargoed, T01443 830272 Traditional pub serving several real ales.
Falcon Inn, 1 Incline Row, Cwmaman T01685 873758 Popular pub on the riverside. Serves real ales and bar meals.
Glan Taff, Cardiff Rd, Quakers Yard, T01443 410822 Popular inn on the River Taff, serving real ales and good bar meals.

Festivals and events

The Big Cheese – two day event late **July**/ early **August** to celebrate Caerphilly, the pale, salty and mild cheese, once so popular with miners who needed to top up their salt levels. Cheese races, a medieval themed fair, live music, crafts and costumed events.

Activities and tours

Train trips
Pontypool and Blaenavon Railway, T01495 792263, www.pontypool-and-blaenavon.co.uk. Steam engines trips, Easter-end Sep weekends

Climbing
Welsh International Climbing Centre, Taff Bargoed Centre, Trelewis, Treharris, sth of Merthyr Tydfil, T01443 710749, www.mountaineers.net/BaseCamp/Everest/WelshClimbing Centre, / www.indoorclimbingwalls.co.uk, offers indoor climbing (largest indoor climbing wall in Europe), caving, abseiling, high ropes courses and mountain bike hire – 2hr and ½ day introductory tasters, adult lessons and longer breaks. Also have bunkhouse accommodation.

Cycling/mountain biking
National Cycle Route runs from Blaenavon through Pontypool and into Cwmbran, using old railway lines and canal towpaths. Further Details from Countryside Section, Development Department, Floor 4, County Hall, Cwmbran, NP44 2WN, T01633 648034.
The Taff Trail (55 miles/93 km route from Brecon to Cardiff) passes through Merthyr Tydfil and Pontypridd, information hotline 0800 243731, celtic-trail@tsww.com.
Cwmcarn Forest Drive, Visitor Centre and Campsite, Cwmcarn, Crosskeys, T01495 272001, cwmcarn-vc@caerphilly-gov.uk, www.caerphilly.gov.uk/visiting Mountain biking track the Twrch Trail in former coal mining area. There is also a visitor centre, forest drive (£3 charge per car), guided and self guided walks, and a campsite.

Horse riding
Groeswen Riding stables, Ty Canol Farm, Caerphilly, T02920 880500, www.groeswenstables.com – escorted trekking from 1 hr to full day.

Walking
Walking leaflets describing walks around Pontypool available from Torfaen County Borough Council, County Hall, Cwmbran, Torfaen, NP44 2WN.

Directory

Caerphilly *p550*
Internet Caerphilly TIC but expensive at £1 for 10 minutes. A better bet might be free access in Caerphilly library, Morgan Jones Park, CF83 1AP,T029 2085 2543, near the town centre 09.30-1800 Mon,Wed, Thu, 09.30-13.30 Tue, 09.30-1900 Fri, 09.30-1700 Sat.

The Valleys *p551*
Library Blaenavon Library, Lion St, T01495 790367, free access Mon, Thu, 0930-1300, 1400-1730, Tues, 1400-1900, Sat 0900-1300.

Monmouthshire

→*Colour map 1*

When George Borrow wrote his famous travelogue 'Wild Wales', Monmouthshire was considered to be English rather than Welsh. Although now officially part of Wales, the county still feels less immediately Welsh than do the borderlands further north. Once it was the scene of fierce fighting, as locals resisted first Roman and then Norman incursions on their land. There are vivid reminders of those times in the extensive Roman remains at Caerleon and the 'don't mess with me' Norman castle at Chepstow. The west of the county, particularly around the city of Newport, is industrialised, but as you move east it becomes increasingly green. There are good golf courses here- in 2010 the Ryder Cup is coming to Newport. The most beautiful area is the lush, green Wye Valley: an area of Outstanding Natural Beauty formed as the River Wye ripples along the border from Monmouth to Chepstow. The valley, an excellent area for walking and canoeing, is home to one of the most celebrated sites in Wales – Tintern Abbey, a picturesque ruin, right on the border with England. »» *For Sleeping, Eating and other listings, see pages 556-557.*

Ins and outs

Getting there By **road**, Monmouth is easily reached from Cardiff and the South West by exiting at J24 of the M4 and taking the A449 and A40. From the Midlands and the North, leave M5 at J8 and follow the M50 and A40. Chepstow is just off the M48 and Newport off the M4. Newport is linked to Cardiff and Chepstow by **train**, as well as the Midlands. **Stagecoach** service No 65 or 69 runs hourly between Monmouth and Chepstow and the journey takes about 50 minutes. **National Express** also operates coaches to and from Chepstow and Monmouth – 08705 808080, www.gobycoach.com A useful booklet, Discover the Wye Valley on foot and by bus is available for 30p from TICs.

Information Chepstow TIC ⓘ *Castle Car Park, Bridge St, T01291 623772, chepstow.tic@monmouthshire.gov.uk, daily 1000-1730, closed 1hr at lunch.* **Monmouth Visitor Centre** ⓘ *Shire Hall, Agincourt Sq, NP5 3DY, T01600 713899, F 01600 772794 www.monmouth.gov.uk (Easter-Oct 1000-1730, Oct- Easter 1000-1300, 1400-1700).* **Newport TIC** ⓘ *Museum and Art Gallery, John Frost Square, T01633 842962, newport.tic@newport.gov.uk, Mon-Sat 0930-1700.* **Wye Valley Tourism** ⓘ *T01600 715781, www.wyevalleytourism.co.uk.* **Wye Valley AONB** ⓘ *www.wyevalleyaonb.co.uk.* **Monmouthshire** ⓘ *www.visitwyevalley.com; www.monmouthshire.gov.uk.*

Cas-Gwent (Chepstow)

Chepstow deserves the title 'gateway to Wales': it's the first town you come to if driving to Wales from the south and is strategically situated on the Wye, which here marks the border with England. The main reason for stopping here is to visit the magnificent **Castle** ⓘ *T01291 624065, Apr, May, end Sep-late Oct , 0930-1700 daily, Jun-end Sep 0930-1800 daily; late Oct-end Mar 0930-1600 Mon-Sat, 1100-1600 Sun, last entry 30* *mins prior to closing, £3, £2.50 children, £8.50 family, CADW,* the first stone castle built in Britain. It occupies a superb position on a bend of the Wye, and you get views along the river as you wander round. During the Civil War it was held by the Royalists and came under siege, surrendering in 1645 – events recalled in an exhibition inside. The castle grew over the years as its fortifications were strengthened but you can still see the oldest part – the Great Tower, dating back to 1067.

Chepstow Museum ⓘ *Bridge St, near the castle T01291 625981, summer Mon-Sat 1030-1730, Sun 1400-1730, winter Mon-Sat 1100-1700, 1400-1700 Sun, free,* has displays on the town and local history, including the story of local man Able Seaman Williams who won the VC at Gallipoli. Upstairs is a room containing a variety of old machines, including a 'permanent waving machine' c1940 that bears a strong resemblance to an instrument of torture.

The most spectacular site is **Tintern Abbey** ⓘ *T01291 689251, 1 Apr-1 Jun, 29 Sep-26 Oct 0930-1700 daily; 2 Jun-28 Sep 0930-1800 daily, 27 Oct–31 Mar 0930-1600 Mon-Sat, 1100-1600 Sun, £2.50, £2 concessions, £7 family, CADW, bus 69 from Chepstow,* founded in 1131 for Cistercian monks. The abbey became increasingly wealthy and its power was reflected in a grand rebuilding programme in the late 13th-century. It flourished until dissolution in 1536 – then gained a new lease of life as a romantic ruin in the 18th-century, its picturesque beauty and glorious setting inspiring both Wordsworth and JMW Turner. The abbey, a beautiful shell, with soaring archways, and delicate stonework, still attracts bus loads of tourists today, so try to visit early in the morning or late in the day. To really see the ruins at their best you should cross the Wye at a nearby bridge and follow the path to view the abbey from the opposite bank. A mile from the abbey is Tintern Old Station, T01291 689566, Apr-Oct daily 1030-1730, a Victorian station now converted into a visitor and information centre, with a camping area nearby.

Trefynwy (Monmouth) and around

North of Tintern, where the Wye joins the Monnow, is the handsome town of Monmouth. The heart of the town is Agincourt Square, a reminder that Henry V was born here and won the Battle of Agincourt (1415) with the help of Welsh archers. There's a statue here of Charles Rolls of Rolls Royce fame – holding a model of an aircraft. He was also a pioneer aviator and in 1910 became the first person to make a double crossing of the Channel. A month later he was killed when his plane crashed at an airshow. His mother, Lady Llangattock, was a distant relative of Lord Nelson and her collection of Nelson memorabilia can be seen at the **Nelson Museum and Local History Centre** ⓘ *Priory St, T01600 71351,9 Mon-Sat 1000- 1300, 1400-1700, Sun 1400-1700, £1, 50p concessions.* Among the exhibits are various fake personal effects, manufactured to profit from the cult of Nelson that flourished after his death. Nelson made not infrequent visits to Monmouth. The official reason was to break his journey to the Pembrokeshire forests supplying wood for his ships, although the presence of a certain local heiress – Lady Emma Hamilton – was no doubt an added attraction.

Monnow Bridge was built in the thirteenth century to replace an earlier wooden crossing. The fortified medieval bridge spans the River at the west end of Monnow Street and the stone gatehouse is the only complete example of its kind in Britain.

Raglan Castle ⓘ *T01291 690228, Apr-late Oct 0930-1700 daily, late Oct-end Mar 0930-1700, Mon-Sat, £2.50, £2 concessios, £7 family,* is an attractive mixture of castle and palace. Work began in 1435 and the owner, Sir William ap Thomas took the opportunity to show off his wealth and status.

The little town of Usk has several good places to eat and drink, and pretty buildings. The **Usk Rural Life Museum** ⓘ *New Market St, T01291 673777, Easter-end Oct, Mon-Fri 1000-1700, w/es 1400-1700, £2, £1 children,* is a fascinating museum housed in three converted barns. It focuses on rural life from 1850 to the end of WW11 and has a vast collection of old farming implements, with ploughs, tractors, scythes and grim items like castrating irons. There are also recreated domestic interiors like a farmhouse kitchen.

Newport and around

On the outskirts of Newport, Caerleon was a Roman town – Isca – and was founded in 75AD. It became a major base for the Roman legions – one of only three in Britain. Around 6,000 troops of the 2nd Augustan Legion were housed here, in a sophisticated garrison complete with amphitheatre, baths and shops. The **amphitheatre** ⓘ *open, free*, which seated 6,000 and had boxes for VIPS, is impressive and it is not too difficult to imagine bloodthirsty contests between gladiators and wild animals. It was only excavated in the 1920s – before this it was concealed by a grassy mound – once thought to be King Arthur's Round Table.

By the Bull Hotel car park are the **Fortress Baths** ⓘ *T01633 422518, daily 0930-1700 Apr-late Oct, late Oct-end Mar 0930-1700 Mon-Sat, 1300-1700 Sun, £2.50 , £2 child, £7 family, CADW*, once a 'leisure centre' for the soldiers with a swimming pool, heated changing rooms, hot and cold baths and a gymnasium. Finds from local excavations are displayed in the **Roman Legionary Museum** ⓘ *T01633 423134, daily, free*. The new agey Ffwrrwm Centre, approx 0930-1730 focuses on Caerleon's Arthurian links and has a courtyard filled with wooden sculptures, as well as little shops and a bistro.

Sleeping

Chepstow *p554*

D Castle View Hotel, 16 Bridge Street, T01291 620349, www.hotelschepstow.co.uk. Hotel dating back 300 years, in the centre of town. Comfortable and very convenient for the castle – as the name suggests.

Monmouth and around *p555*

B-A Glen-Yr-Afon-House, Pontypool Rd, Usk, T01291 672302, www.glen-yr-afon.co.uk. Secluded country house in its own grounds, just a few minutes walk from the centre of Usk. Home cooked food and bar.

B The Bell at Skenfrith, Skenfrith, Monmouthshire, T01600 750235, www.thebellatskenfrith.co.uk. On the banks of the River Monnow, this romantic former coaching inn has been restored to its 17th century glory. 8 smart bedrooms complete with widescreen TVs and DVDs.

B Cwrt Bleddyn Hotel and Country Club, Llangybi, near Usk T01633 450521, www.cwrt-bleddyn-hotel.co.uk, This is a private member's club but residents of the hotel can use all the spa and leisure facilities.

C Riverside Hotel, Cinderhill St, T01600 715577, riverside@compass-rose.org.uk. Originally a 19th century coaching inn, this hotel is set in a quiet corner of Monmouth. Two bedrooms are on the ground floor, ideal for guests who are less mobile.

D Burton House, St James Sq, T01600 714958, www.burtonhousemonmouth.co.uk. Child friendly, family run and cosy B&B.

Newport and around *p556*

D Pendragon, 18 Cross Street, T01633 430871 Friendly and accommodating B&B. Rooms are clean and comfy, and you eat breakfast at a large wooden table – homemade bread, lots of fresh fruit if you want and veggies catered for. Packed lunches if you ask.

C-B The Inn at the Elm Tree, St Brides, Wentlooge, near Newport, T01633 680225, www.the-elm-tree.co.uk. Tucked away among flatlands and reed beds, in an area that looks more like Holland than Wales is this refreshingly comfortable 5 star inn. The rooms are individually designed, and there are books, pot plants and magazines dotted around.

Eating

Chepstow *p554*

££ The Boat Inn, The Back, T628192, Mon-Sat 1200-1500, 1830-2130, Sun 1200-1500. With a lovely waterside setting, outdoor seats and an old beams this inn is the best place in town for a drink, a snack or a good bar meal. From Sun-Thurs early bird rates apply with £10.95 for 2 courses and £12.95 for 3.

££ Castle View Hotel, 16 Bridge Street, T01291 620349, daily 1200-1430, 1830-2100. Relaxed, hotel serving tasty light meals during the day, such as ploughman's lunches and jacket potatoes, and more substantial evening meals that range from pork steaks to roast duck.

££ The Grape, 24 St Mary's Street, T620959, food 1200-2130. This wine bar/bistro serves baguettes, sandwiches and snacks during the day – as well as wine of course. There's a restaurant upstairs.

££ **Wye Knot**, The Back T622929, Tues-Fri 1230-1430, 1900-2200, Sat 1900-2200, Sun 1230-1430. Winner of 2 AA rosettes, this restaurant down by the river is the best place to eat in Chepstow. Sunday lunch here is a local favourite, with choices such as leg of lamb or sirloin of beef.

Monmouth and around *p555*
£££ The Bell at Skenfrith, Skenfrith, Monmouthshire, T01600 750235. The 2 AA Rosette dining room at this popular inn offers a range of modern dishes using largely seasonal and locally sourced ingredients and a fab award-winning wine list.
££ The Bush House Bistro, 15 Bridge Street, Usk T01291 672929, evenings only. Brightly coloured tablecloths and terracotta walls make this good quality restaurant a cheery choice on a damp evening. Dishes range from Mediterranean to Welsh and might include sea bass roasted in rock salt or Cornish cod stuffed with smoked cheese. Mains vary from £9.95-15.50. Vegetarian options available.
££ French Horn Brasserie, 24 Church St, T01600 772733, Tue-Sat. This small restaurant offers equally small prices at lunch: soup, such as Mediterranean tomato, and crusty bread costs around £3, and the fish dish of the day around £7. At dinner, mains move into the £10-15 bracket.
££ **Three Salmons Hotel**, Bridge St, Usk, T01291 672133, daily lunchtimes and 1800-2130 (1830-2200 Sat). Lunchtimes snacks like BLTs and ploughmans with a varied menu in the evening ranging from veggie dishes like cannelloni with wild mushrooms and goats cheese or meaty choices such as breast of goose.

Newport and around *p556*
£££-££ The Inn at the Elm Tree, St Brides, Wentlooge, near Newport, T01633 680225, Mon-Sat 1200-1430, 1730-2100, Sun 1200-1500. High quality food at this 21st century inn. You can have a light lunch like wild boar and apple sausages, or broadbean and tomato risotto for £7.50, or splash out and eat on crisp white linen in the restaurant in the evening. Mains are strong on fish and local produce. Good vegetarian dishes too.

Entertainment

Chepstow Male Voice Choir rehearse at Dell School, Welsh St, Chepstow, on Mon and Thu 1930-2115.

Activities and tours

Canoeing
Monmouth Canoe and Activity Centre, Castle Yard, Monmouth, T01600 713461, www.monmouthcanoehire.20m.com. Offer canoe hire and kayaking on the Wye.
Wye Valley Canoes, Glasbury-on-Wye, Herefordshire, T01497 847213, www.wyevalleycanoes.co.uk – over the border in England, offer canoeing and kayaking on the Wye

Cycling/Mountain biking
Pedalabikeaway Cycle Centre, Cannop Valley, near Coleford (just over the border), T01594 860065, www.pedalabikeaway.com. Bike hire, maps and information, as well as mountain bike trails
Pedalaway, Trereece Barn, Llangarron, Ross-on-Wye, T01989 770357, www.pedalaway.co.uk, mountain bike trails and routes for casual cyclists, range of bikes to hire

Directory

Chepstow *p554*
Internet Chepstow Library, Manor Way, T01291 635730. Free access.

Monmouth and around *p555*
Internet Bookable internet access is available at **Monmouth library** (T01600 775215) On Whitecross St (£1.25/ 30 mins, £2/60 mins).

For an explanation of the sleeping and eating price codes used in this guide, see the inside front cover. Other relevant information is provided in the Essentials chapter, page 36.

Brecon Beacons National Park

→ Colour map 1

Covering 520 square miles of wild countryside in south east Wales, the Brecon Beacons National Park is a magnet for lovers of the outdoors. While none of the mountains is over that magical 3000ft, this still isn't 'walking for softies' country and the terrain can be rugged and windswept: it's not for nothing that the SAS train here, sending hopefuls up and down the highest peak Pen-y-fan (2907ft, 886m) in order to wear them down both physically and mentally. The wildest part of the National Park is in the west where Fforest Fawr, a former hunting forest, now an area of lonely uplands and waterfalls, leads to the bleak and barren expanse of Black Mountain – the least visited area with the most challenging walks. The central area is occupied by the eponymous Brecon Beacons range, to the north of which is the busy town of Brecon, a popular base for a wide range of outdoor activities. The Monmouthshire and Brecon Canal offers some undemanding walks, before the National Park stretches out to Abergavenny, and the famous book town of Hay-on-Wye, both of which are great bases for exploring the brooding Black Mountains in the east. ▸▸ *For Sleeping, Eating and other listings, see pages 561-565.*

Ins and outs

Getting there and getting around The only town with a train station is **Abergavenny,** with trains running from Newport: the only other station is in **Merthyr Tydfil,** south of the National Park, which is linked to Cardiff. Bus services are better, most run by **Stagecoach,** but they only link major towns like Abergavenny, Brecon and Hay-on-Wye. Sunday services and those between villages are poor or non existent, especially if you are travelling out of season. The nearest station to Hay-on-Wye is Hereford, from where bus 39 runs to Hay and on to Brecon. Just on the edge of the wilder western reaches of the National Park are stations at Llandeilo and Llandovery. In summer, Beacons Bus, an all encompassing term for local services, runs from mid May to mid Aug, with some services on Sun, and links Carmarthen, Swansea, Bridgend, Cardiff, Newport and Hereford to Brecon. Cardiff and Swansea services have cycle trailers. The bus will drop you off at various points en route. T01873 853254, www.visitbreconbeacons.com.

Information National Park Information Centre and Brecon TIC ⓘ *Cattle Market Car Park, Brecon, T01874-623156, brecon.ic@breconbeacons.org, www.brecon beacons.org.* **Abergavenny TIC** ⓘ *Swan Meadow, Cross St, Abergavenny, T01873- 857588, www.abergavenny.co.uk. Daily Apr-Oct 1000-1730, Nov-Mar 1000-1600, closed for 1 hr at lunch.* **Crickhowell TIC** ⓘ *Beaufort Chambers, Beaufort St, T01873 812105, cticktic@powys.gov.uk, www.crickhowell.org.uk, Apr-end Sep Mon-Sat 0930-1700, Sun 1000-1600 (this may be moving to a different location in town in 2004)*. **Hay on Wye** TIC ⓘ *Craft Centre, Oxford Rd, Hay-on-Wye, T01497 820144, post@hay-on-wye.info, www.hay-on-wye.co.uk, daily Easter-Nov 1000-1300, 1400-1700, rest of year 1100-1300, 1400-1600.www.tourism.powys.gov.uk, www.silurian-retreats.com.*

Western Brecon Beacons

The Black Mountain and Fforest Fawr are noted for their wild, unspoilt landscapes. The main visitor attraction – and a good place to take kids on a rainy day – is the **Dan-yr-Ogof Showcaves** ⓘ *off the A4067, T01639 730801, www.showcaves.co.uk, daily Apr-Oct 1000 around 1600 (varies with season), £8.* Discovered in 1912 by two local farmers the 3 caves contain stalactites, underground waterfalls and exhibits on Bronze Age and Age life aimed at children. There's also a dinosaur park and dry ski slope.

Aberhonddu (Brecon)

The undoubted hub of the National Park, the solid market town of Brecon can trace its roots back to pre-Roman times, but development only really began when the Normans arrived and built the castle and a Benedictine Priory – which later became the cathedral. The town continued to grow in importance, becoming the capital of the old county of Brecknockshire, and a centre of the cloth trade. Plenty of Georgian buildings still stand in the centre, which tends to be peopled by a mix of local farmers and visiting walkers. The highest peak in the National Park, Pen-y-Fan, can be reached easily from here, as can the Brecon Beacons Mountain Centre and the indoor climbing centre at Llangorse (see activities). The town is the northern end of the Monmouthshire and Brecon canal, which runs 33 miles from Brecon to Pontypool and you can take trips along the calm waters (see activities).

Brecon Cathedral ⓘ *Priory Hill, T01874 625222, 0830-1800, free*, stands on a site that is reckoned to have been used for Christian worship for around 1000 years. In 1093 a Benedictine Priory was established here and you can still see the Norman font in the cathedral today. In the 15th century it became a focus of pilgrimage, as the central crucifix in the rood screen (destroyed during the reformation) was believed to have healing properties. After the dissolution of the monasteries the building became a Parish church, and was made the cathedral in 1923. After you've wandered round the cathedral you can visit the small **Heritage Centre** ⓘ *Mar-Dec, Mon-Sat 1030-1630, Sun 1200-1500, free*, which has exhibits on the cathedral.

Brecknock Museum and Art Gallery ⓘ *Captain's Walk, T01874 624121, Mon-Fri 1000-1700, Sat 1000-1300, 1400-1700, also Sun 1200-1700 from Apr-Sept, £1*. Exhibits include a dugout canoe discovered in Llangorse lake, a carved four poster bed in which Charles 1 is said to have slept when he came through Brecon in 1645, and various recreated aspects of old Wales such as a smithy, village schoolroom and courtroom.

Other attractions in Brecon: **Oriel Jazz Gallery** ⓘ *The Watton T01874 625557, Mon-Sat 1100-1700, and Suns in summer with audio visual material and photographs looking at the development of jazz- and the town's thriving annual Jazz Festival*; and the **South Wales Borderers Museum** ⓘ *The Watton, T01874 623111, Apr-Sept 0900-1700 daily, Oct-end Mar 0900-1700 Mon-Fri, £3, under 16 free* – one for anyone who's a fan of the film Zulu (1964), as this is the regiment that fought the famous battle at Rorkes' Drift in 1879.

About 4 miles out of town the **Water Folk Canal Centre and Museum** ⓘ *Llanfrynach, T01874 665382, daily except Fri 1000-1700, £1.50*, has exhibits and memorabilia on the history of the canal and also offers horse drawn boat trips on a narrow boat ⓘ *Wed and weekends Easter-Oct, plus daily in Aug, 1200 and 1500, £4*).

Crug Hywel (Crickhowell)

With plenty of places to eat, drink and sleep, the pretty little town of Crickhowell is an excellent base for exploring the eastern Beacons. Its most prominent feature is the 16th-century Usk Bridge, which distinctively has 12 arches on one side and 13 on the other. Once an important stop for stagecoaches, the town is squeezed between the Usk and Table Mountain – on the summit of which is the 'crug' or hillfort, of Hywel – hence the town's name. It's a great place for walkers, with a choice of routes going up Table Mountain, along the river, or into the Black Mountains to the east. It's also easy to arrange activities such as para-gliding, canoeing and caving.

Tretower ⓘ *(Tre-twr), 3 miles north of town, T01874 730279, Mar-Oct daily 1000-1700, £2.50 , £2 concessions, £7 family*. The first settlement here was a Norman earthwork castle, built around 1100 to guard an important route through the Black Mountains. In the 13th-century a stone structure replaced it – and although this was eventually abandoned in favour of the house, the round keep is still standing today. The house itself is a fine late medieval home with a galleried courtyard and well preserved Great Hall, with a huge hearth and high ceiling. The old kitchen contains displays various herbs commonly used in medieval times – including dandelion, nettle, sage and sorrel. The main bedchamber is thought to have had a secret opening in the wood panelling so that the occupant could keep an eye on events in the Great Hall below. There's a re-created medieval garden too.

Y Fenni (Abergavenny)

Just on the edge of the National Park, Abergavenny is surrounded by delightful countryside and makes an excellent base for exploring and walking. There has been a settlement here since Neolithic times and the Romans later established a fort known as Gobannium. Development really took off when the Normans built the inevitable castle here around 1090 and in later years the town became an industrial centre, with flourishing tanning and weaving industries, as well as a busy market.

Perhaps its most famous resident was Hitler's deputy, Rudolf Hess, who was imprisoned at Maindiss Court near the town after the plane in which he was flying crashed in Scotland in 1941. He was allowed out once a week for walks in the hills – and became a regular at a local pub.

The castle is now ruined but was the scene of an infamous massacre at Christmas in 1175 when the Norman lord, William de Braose, invited local Welsh chieftains to a banquet – and then murdered them. A hunting lodge, built in the 19th-century from the castle's keep is now a small **museum** ① *T01873 854282, Mon-Sat 1100-1300, 1400-1700, Sun 1400-1700, closes at 1600 and on Suns Nov-Feb, £1*, with exhibits on the town's history including a recreated Victorian farmhouse kitchen and grocer's shop.

St Mary's church, Monk Street, was founded around 1090 as a Benedictine priory. It contains an important selection of medieval monuments and a 15th-century carving of Jesse, the father of King David, which was once part of an altarpiece showing Christ's family tree.

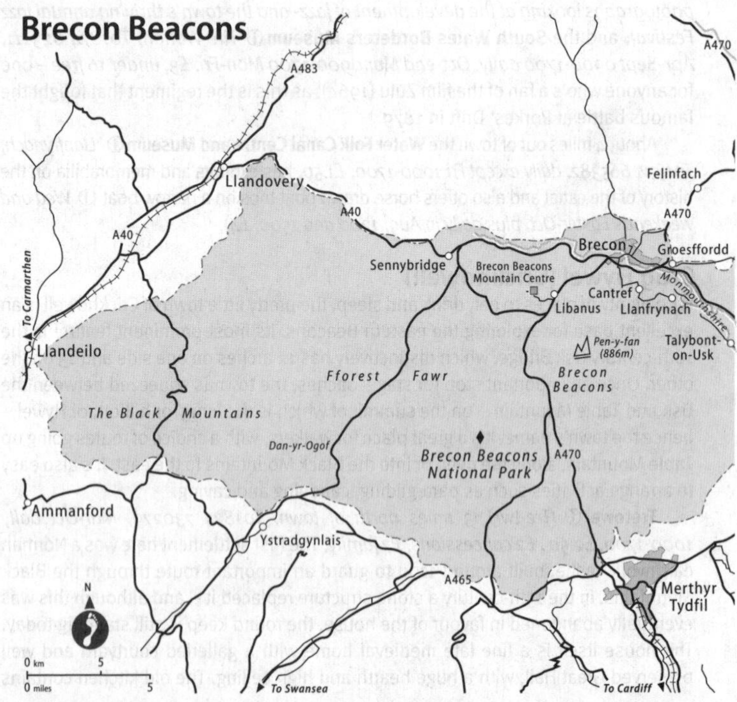

Around Abergavenny are the hills of Blorenge (1834ft) to the south west– a favourite with paragliders and hang gliders; Skirrid-Fawr (1596ft/486m) in the north east and Sugar Loaf (1955ft, 596m north west.

From Abergavenny there is a wonderful scenic drive to the famous Welsh booktown of Hay-on-Wye – an effortless way of enjoying the striking beauty of the Black Mountains. You can pick up the road at Llanfihangel Crucorney, north of the town and then follow the unclassified road as it leads you to Llanthony Priory, then on to the hamlet of Capel-y-Ffin, past the viewpoint at Hay Bluff and down into Hay-on-Wye. It's single track much of the way.

Llanthony Priory (CADW, free), now a picturesque and sleepy ruin, was founded in 1108, probably on the site of a 6th-century hermitage. The medieval traveller Giraldus Cambrensis described it as 'truly calculated for religion' and the description still holds true today and there is a sense of peace and spirituality here that is missing from better known and more commercialised sites, such as Tintern Abbey. There's a hotel/inn built into the ruins but it doesn't seem to spoil the beauty of the site. Capel-y-Ffin was once the home of sculptor and type-face designer Eric Gill who lived here with various family members and artistic friends, from 1924-1928.

Y Gelli (Hay-on-Wye)

From a lone second hand bookshop in 1961, Hay-on-Wye now has over 30, specialising in everything from apiculture to erotica – the town is bliss for bibliophiles. The former cinema alone has a stock of around 200,000 books and every other building in town, including the old castle, seems to be filled with wonderful piles of dusty tomes, old school annuals and rare first editions. The widest selection of all is at Richard Booth's Bookshop, Lion St, with over 400,000 titles for sale. Booth was the force behind Hay's rejuvenation as a booktown, opening the first secondhand bookshop here and promoting Hay to the extent that it is now known throughout the world as a centre for secondhand books. In 1977, on April 1st, Booth declared Hay, right on the border of England and Wales, an independent state – proclaiming himself king in the process. The town is busiest during the annual Hay Festival, an excellent literary festival that attracts the biggest names in literature.

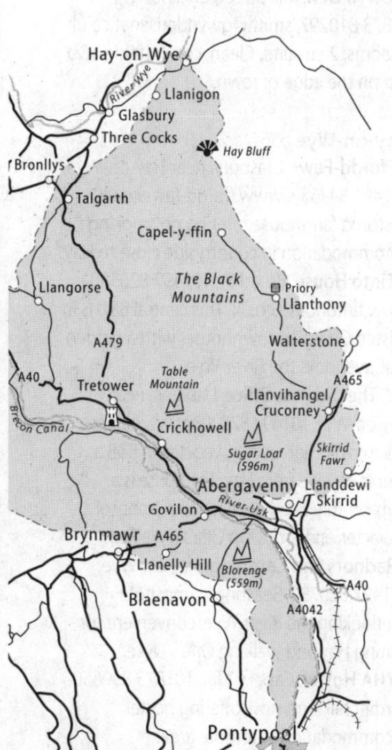

Sleeping

Brecon *p559*

B Felin Fach Griffin, near Brecon, T01874 620111, www.eatdrinksleep.ltd.uk. This lovely refurbished pub 3 miles north of Brecon on the A470 has 7 individually designed, simple bedrooms. Contemporary, unfussy style.

C Beacons Guest House, 16 Bridge Street, T/F 01874 623339, www.beacons.brecon.co.uk. Non smoking, situated just over the Usk bridge, a few minutes from the centre of town.

C Blaencar Farm, Sennybridge, near Brecon, T01874 636610, www.blaencar.co.uk. This is a working farm offering good quality B&B in a refurbished farmhouse.

C Castle of Brecon Hotel, Castle Square, Brecon, T01874 624611, F 623737, www.breconcastle.co.uk, Rather old fashioned hotel that grew out of the remains of Brecon castle in the 17th century. Has its own gardens and is a few minutes walk from the centre of town.

C **George Hotel**, George Street, Brecon, T01874 623421, F 611579, www.george-hotel.com, 17th century building which retains some original features such as the 300 year old staircase. Some suites available which have Jacuzzi baths.

C **Pickwick House**, St Johns Road, Brecon, T01874 624322, www.pickwick-house.brecon.co.uk, 3 en suite rooms. Non smoking B&B in estate just minutes from the centre of town. Has small conservatory residents can use and drying facilities for walkers and cyclists.

F **Bikes and Hikes Bunkhouse**, The Elms, 10 The Struet, Brecon, T01874 610071, www.bikesandhikes.co.uk. Central bunkhouse that has cycle lock up and also does bike rental.

F **Canal Barn Bunkhouse**, Ty Camlas, Canal Bank, Brecon, T01874 625361, www.canal-barn.co.uk. 24 beds at this at this bunkhouse not far from the town centre. Must book in advance.

F **Cantref Bunkhouse**, Upper Cantref Farm, Cantref, near Brecon, T01874 665223, www.cantref.com. This farm bunkhouse about 3 miles from Brecon has dormitory accommodation and also grounds where you can pitch a tent.

Abergavenny *p560*

A **Allt-yr-Ynys Country House Hotel**, Walterstone, near Abergavenny, T01873 890307, www.allthotel.co.uk. Technically this comfortable and reliable hotel is in England – by about a foot. It's a secluded location, with many rooms in converted outbuildings dotted around the grounds, giving you extra privacy.

B **The Angel Hotel**, 15 Cross St, Abergavenny, T01873 857121, F 858059, www.angelhotelabergavenny.co.uk, Famous old coaching inn in the centre of Abergavenny offering plush rooms, one with a four poster bed.

D **Pentre House**, Brecon Rd, T01873 853435, treardonsm@aol.com. This attractive B&B is out of town at the turning for Sugar Loaf mountain. There are 3 rooms, one en suite and very attractive gardens.

F **Black Sheep Backpackers**, Station Rd, T01873 859125, www.blacksheepbackpackers.com. This bunkhouse by the station offers dormitory accommodation. Price includes a light breakfast.

Crickhowell *p559*

B-A **The Bear Hotel**, Crickhowell, T01873 810408, www.bearhotel.co.uk. Lovely old coaching inn dating back to 1432, the Bear has individually decorated rooms – some with Jacuzzi baths or four poster beds. The bar has lots of character with oak beams and a flag stone floor. Recommended.

C **The Manor Hotel**, Brecon Road, Crickhowell, T01873 810212, www.manorhotel.co.uk. Swish hotel perched on a hill outside Crickhowell, which also has leisure facilities. Dark wooden floors and heraldry shields on the walls downstairs, while bedrooms are lighter and brighter.

C **Ty Croeso Hotel**, Dardy, near Crickhowell, T01873 810573, www.wiz.to/tycroeso. This small hotel overlooks the Usk Valley and close to the Brecon and Monmouthshire Canal. There's a good quality restaurant and a welcoming atmosphere.

D **Gwyn Deri**, Mill Street, Crickhowell, T/F 01873 810297, smith@gwynderi.fsnet.co.uk, 3 rooms, 2 en suite. Clean, comfortable b&b just on the edge of town.

Hay-on-Wye *p561*

C **Ffordd-Fawr**, Glasbury, near Hay-on-Wye, T01497 847332, www.ffordd-fawr.co.uk. Restored farmhouse offering no smoking accommodation in countryside close to Hay.

C **Tinto House**, Broad St, T01497 820590, www.tintohouse.co.uk. This central B&B is in a listed Georgian townhouse, with a garden that overlooks the River Wye.

D-C **The Old Post Office**, Llanigon, near Hay-on-Wye, T01497 820008, www.oldpost-office.co.uk. High quality, vegetarian B&B a couple of miles from Hay. The house is a 17th-century listed building with plenty of character, and is close to Offa's Dyke Path.

F **Radnors End Camping**, Hay-on-Wye, T01497 820780. Seasonal campsite overlooking the River Wye, convenient for visiting Hay and walking Offa's Dyke.

F **YHA Hostel**, Capel y Ffin, T01873 890650. Former hill farm now offering hostel accommodation in remote area.

Eating

Brecon *p559*

£££-££ Felin Fach Griffin, near Brecon,3 miles out of town on A470 T01874 620111 One of a new wave of highly rated 'gastropubs' in Wales. The interior is an eclectic mix of oak beams, stone floors and laid- back leather sofas, and the food is based on fresh local produce such as saltmarsh lamb, cheeses and locally grown salad leaves. Even A A Gill liked it.

£££-££ The White Swan, Llanfrynach, a few miles south of Brecon, T01874 665276, www.the-white-swan.com. Another revitalised pub, serving high quality food, tucked away in the countryside outside Brecon. Features fresh produce and has a daily 'specials' menu that features many fish dishes, also has several veggie choices.

££ Beacons Guest House, 16 Bridge Street, T01874 623339, Tues-Sat 1830-2100. Guest house restaurants serving non residents. Mains might include halloumi cheese with tomato and black olive sauce, or pork hock in fruit compote for around £9.95.

££ Castle of Brecon Hotel, Castle Square, T01874 624611, food Thurs-Sat 1200-2130, Mon-Wed 1200-2100, Sun 1800-2100. Sandwiches and salad available during the day, and heartier dishes such as beef and stilton pie (£8.25), good old cod, chips and peas (£8.95). Some veggie choices available.

££-£ The Puzzle Tree, opposite museum, T01874 610005, Mon-Wed 1100-1100, Thu 1100-midnight, Fri, Sat 1100-0100, Sun 1200-2230. Large modern looking place attracting a younger crowd. Does a bit of everything, serving breakfasts from 0900-1200, cream teas in the afternoon, and meals such as curries, steaks and veggie choices from around £6.95-13.95.

£ Bull's Head, 86 The Struet, Brecon, T01874 622044 food 1200-1430, 1830-2130. Good traditional pub serving bar meals, with some veggie and vegan choices – all around £5.95. Real ales also on offer.

£ The Café, 39 High Street, Brecon Mon-Sat 1000-1700. Busy, popular licensed café with nice bright décor of white painted floors and shocking pink chairs. Serves fair trade coffees, soups, cakes and baguettes stuffed with filling like brie and grape, beef and horseradish or goats cheese, rocket and pine nuts.

Crickhowell *p559*

££ The Bear Hotel, Crickhowell, T01873 810408, daily 1200-1400, evenings Mon-Sat 1900-2130. Wide choice of very good food, with several vegetarian choices. Mains in the bar cost around £7-9 and might include homemade faggots in onion gravy; restaurant mains such as fillet of salmon with asparagus around £14.50.

££ Nantyffin Cider Mill Inn, Brecon Road, Crickhowell, T01873 810212, food 1200-1400 and 1830-2100 (1900-2100 in winter) – sometimes shuts on Mon or Tues. Lovely old, pink painted inn on the A40 out of Crickhowell, serving excellent food and real ales. Mains might include baked vegetable tart (£10.50) or roast duck (£14.95), and scrummy puds such as lemon tart. Very popular so worth booking.

£ Dragon Hotel, High Street, Crickhowell T01873 810362, Mon-Sat 1000-1400, 1800-2100. Coffees and light lunches, with more substantial traditional food in the evening like steak and kidney pie or West Indian lamb.

Abergavenny *p560*

£££ The Walnut Tree Inn, Llandewi Skirrid, Abergavenny, T01873 852797, www.thewalnutreeinn.com, closed Sun, Mon. Well established and highly rated restaurant that has been attracting food pilgrims (with healthy credit cards) for years.

££-£ The Angel Hotel, 15 Cross St, Abergavenny, T01873 857121, bar meals 1200-1430 and 1830-2200, restaurant 1900-2200. You can choose formal meals in the restaurant of this revamped hotel, which offers mains like duck breast with red cabbage £13.90 or lighter bar meals. 2 course lunches for £7.80.

Hay-on-Wye *p561*

£££-££ Kilverts, The Bullring, Hay-on-Wye, T01497 821042, food 1200-1400, 1900-2130. Very popular pub that serves great bar food. Seats outside on fine days.

£££-££ Old Black Lion, Lion St, Hay-on-Wye, T01497 820841, food 1200-1430, 1830-2130. Highly rated food (awarded a Michelin star) in this atmospheric old inn. You can splash out in the restaurant or eat more cheaply in the bar.

££-£ Blue Boar, Castle Street, T01497 820884. Coffees from 0930, light meals 1200-1800, more expensive choices in the evening. Friendly café/bar where you can get things like hummous with pitta bread, sandwiches, cakes or mains like Tuscan bean casserole with cous cous (£7.95).

£ The Granary, Broad St, Hay-on-Wye, T01497 820884, food daily 1000-2100 Another very popular, relaxed self service café, with green plastic cloths on the tables, wooden floors and good food. Great spot for soup, salads, sandwiches or just a coffee, cake and a read of the newspaper. Plenty of veggie and vegan main meal choices.

£ Oscars, High Town, Hay-on-Wye, T01497 821193, daily 1030-1630. Very busy, good value self service café, with scrubbed pine tables and wooden floors – hard to get a seat at peak times. Great place for bowls of soup, delicious cakes, or substantial main meals. Always plenty for veggies.

Pubs, bars and clubs

Abergavenny *p560*

Hen and Chickens, 7 Flannel Street, T01873 853613, food daily 1100-1500, 1900 on. Nice traditional pub with lots of old pictures and fittings. During the day you can get 'doorstep sandwiches' such as beef or beef with dripping for £2.70, or larger meals for around £5.25. Sunday lunches and live jazz every Sunday night, folk music every other Tuesday.

The Lounge, 21a High Street, T01874 611189, Mon-Wed 1100-2300, Sun 1200-2230. Newly opened café/ bar serving cocktails and coffees – popular new spot with locals.

King's Head, Cross St, T01873 853575. Popular bar serving real ales and offering bar lunches during the week. Live music on Friday evening.

Entertainment

Brecon *p559*

Male voice choirs

Male voice choirs rehearse on the following nights and visitors are welcome (not Aug) – Brecon, Fri 1930-2100, Llanfaes Primary School – T01874 624776; Talgarth Male Voice Choir, Mon 2000-2200 – not late July or Aug), Gwemyfed Rugby Club, Talgarth, T01874 625865; Ystradgynlais Male Voice Choir, Wed and Fri, 1900-2100, Coronation club, Glanrhyd, Ystradgynlais, T01639 843845

Theatr Brycheiniog, Canal Wharf, Brecon, T01874 611622, www.theatrebrycheiniog.co.uk, stages a wide range of concerts, dance, opera and plays.

Festivals and events

Mar Three Peaks Challenge, annual sporting challenge over 3 main peaks around Abergavenny, T029 2023 8576.

May Hay festival, Hay-on-Wye, internationally known literary festival – past speakers have included Bill Bryson – and Bill Clinton, T01497 821217, www.hayfestival.co.uk.

Aug Brecon Jazz Festival, Brecon, international jazz festival attracting all the great names in jazz over the years, T01874 625557, www.breconjazz.co.uk.

Sep Abergavenny Food Festival, a celebration of the area's local produce, with demonstrations and entertainment T01873 851643, www.abergavennyfoodfestival.co.uk.

Activities and tours

Boating/sailing/canoeing

Monmouthshire and Brecon Canal, near Rich Way, Brecon, T07831 685222, www.dragonfly-cruises.co.uk, 2 ½ hr cruise on the Dragonfly canal boat , £5, Mar-end Oct, twice daily.

Brecon Boats, Travellers Rest Inn, Talybont on Usk, near Brecon, T01874 676401. Self drive boat hire on Monmouthshire to Brecon Canal. Llangorse Lake, near Brecon,. The lake is a general outdoor activity area, good for sailing, rowing, canoeing or fishing. Camping available at Lakeside, T01874 658226, www.lakeside-holidays.net.

PGL Llangorse Sailing School, T01874 658657, Llangorse Sailing Club T01874 658596. Paddles and Pedals, 15 Castle St, Hay-on-Wye, T01497 820604, www.canoehire.co.uk.

Canoe and kayak hire

Celtic Canoes, Newport St, Hay-on-Wye T01497 847422, www.canoehireuk.com. Canadian canoe hire, instruction and tours.

Wye Valley Canoes, The Boat House, Glasbury-on-Wye, Hereford, T01497 847213, www.wyevalleycanoes.co.uk. Canoeing on the Wye, suitable for families.

Caving

Good caves for beginners are Porth yr Ogof, near Ystradfellte and Chartist Cave on the Llangyndir Moors. Permission is needed and you should go as part of a group/course. More on caving from www.caving.uk.com.

Robert Jeffery Centre, Abergavenny, T01873 831185. Caving operator.

Crickhowell Adventure Sports T01873 810020 is a specialist shop.

Climbing

Llangorse Rope Centre, Gilfach Farm, llangorse, T01874 658272, www.activityuk.com. Indoor climbing centre with natural rock faces, climbing walls and facilities for kids. Also do range of other activities including horse riding. Open Mon-Sat 0930-2200, Sun 0930-1800, 2hr climbing/acitivity session £13, 1 hr climbing taster £11; trekking from £11 1 hr to £32 full day for beginners. Also has bunkhouse accommodation.

Cycling/mountain biking

Pedalaway, Hopyard Farm, Govilon, near Abergavenny, T01873 830219, www.pedalaway.co.uk.

Brecon Cycle Centre, 10 Ship St, Brecon, T01874 622651, www.breconcycles.com – bicycle hire.

Horse riding

Cantref Riding Centre, Upper Cantref Farm, Cantref T01874 665223, www.cantref.com. Offer everything from 1 hr to full day rides on the Brecon Beacons.

Grange Trekking Centre, Capel-y-Ffin, near Abergavenny, T01873 890215. Trekking holidays in the Black Mountains. Apr-Oct.

Llanthony Riding and Trekking, Court Farm, Llanthony, T01873 890359, www.llanthony.co.uk. Trekking for beginners and hacks for more experienced riders. Apr-Oct.

Mills Bros, Newcourt Farm, Felindre, Three Cocks, T01497 847285, half and full day treks in the Black Mountains.

Tregoyd Mountain Rides, Three Cocks, near Hay-on-Wye, T01497 847351, www.tregoydriding.co.uk. Hourly or full day rides and treks. Accommodation available.

Wern Riding Centre, Llangattock Hillside, Crickhowell, T01873 810899, www.wiz.to/wern, Apr-Oct. Trekking, hacking and trail riding.

Mountain activities

Black Mountain Activities, Three Cocks, near Hay-on-Wye, T01497 847897, www.blackmountain.co.uk. 1-5 day multi activity breaks, with white water rafting, mountain biking, caving etc. Mountain bike and canoe hire.

Kevin Walker Mountain Activities, 74 Beacons Park, Brecon, T01874 625111 – runs mountain craft, climbing and caving courses in the Brecon Beacons

Mountain and Water, 2 Uppe Cwm, Nant Gam, Llanelli Hill, T01873 831825, www.mountainandwater.co.uk. All sorts of activities including abseiling, coasteering and caving. Days, holidays and courses.

Paragliding

Welsh Hang Gliding and Paragliding Centre, T01873 850910, www.hg-pg.com, for information about paragliding at Blorenge mountain near Abergavenny.

Walking

Brecon Beacons Mountain Centre, Libanus, (6 miles from Brecon off A470), T01874 623366, www.breconbeacons.org, daily March-June, Sep, Oct 0930-1700, July, Aug 0930-1800, Nov-Feb 0930-1630, free. This centre has plenty of maps, guides and information on outdoor activities in the area and is a good starting point for walks, whether gentle or challenging. There's a good café and an exhibition on the National Park.

Taff Trail, 0800 243731, the Taff Trail is a 55 miles (93km) cycling/walking route that starts in Brecon and runs through the Valleys to Cardiff. Free leaflets are available from TICs

Directory

Internet Free internet access from **Crickhowell Library**, T01873 810856, Tues 1000-1300, 1530-1900, Thu 1000-1230, 1330-1730, Fri 1000-1230, 1330-1630, Sat 0930-1300; **Brecon library**, T01874 623346, Mon, Wed, Thu, Fri 0930-1700, Tues 0930-1900, Sat 0930-1300; **Hay-on-Wye library**, Chancery Lane, T01497 820847. **Crickhowell Resource and Information Centre**, currently in Market Hall (location may change 2004), has internet access all day for £10, and shorter chargeable slots, Mon-Fri 1000-1600, T01873 811970

Swansea, the Gower and the Carmarthenshire coast

→Colour map 1

This is, above all, Dylan Thomas territory. The poet was born in the industrial city of Swansea and spent his final years further west in the evocative village of Laugharne, where his last home, the simple Boathouse, is set on a glorious silvery spot on the Taf Estuary. Most of his greatest works, including his 'play for voices' Under Milk Wood, were written and inspired by this little chunk of Wales and if you're a fan of his work – or want to learn more about it – then this is the place to come.

Swansea itself has some worthwhile museums and the nearby resort of Mumbles, now famous as the birthplace of Catherine Zeta Jones, offers a great choice of places to eat and drink. Best of all, for anyone looking for accessible yet unspoiled countryside, is the Gower peninsula, a tourist hotspot that famed for its award winning beaches – great for surfing – in the south, and its quieter marshlands in the north. This is a place best explored leisurely on foot or by bike. » *For Sleeping, Eating and other listings, see pages 569-572.*

Ins and outs

Getting there Swansea Airport (www.swanseaairport.com) lies just west of Swansea. **Air Wales** (T0870 777 3131, www.airwales.co.uk) now operates 3 flights daily to **London City Airport** and the journey takes about 80 minutes, stopping in arch rival **Cardiff** en route. It is also possible to fly to **Cork, Dublin** and **Plymouth**. Visitors from overseas can fly to **Cardiff Airport** and then travel by train direct to Swansea station from Cardiff Central. The train journey will take approximately 40 minutes. **National Express** run coaches to Swansea from most major towns and cities. **First Cymru** (T0870 6082608) operate the Swansea area routes, as well as a **shuttle bus** between Swansea and Cardiff. Swansea is served by **First Great Western** trains from **London** (Paddington) via **Reading, Bristol** and **Cardiff**, the journey from London taking approximately 3 hours. From the **Midlands** and **North**, Intercity services, with **Virgin Cross Country & Wales Trains** and **West Passenger Train**'s regional networks also provide services to the city. Daily **sailings** during peak seasons to and from **Cork** in the Republic of Ireland are provided by **Swansea Cork Ferries** (T01792 456116, www.swansea-cork.ie) from the ferry terminal by the mouth of the Tawe river about 1 m east of town.

Getting around Swansea can easily be explored on **foot** – the **train station**'s at the top of the High St, around 10-15 mins walks from the main attractions. The Gower is well served with **buses**.

Information Mumbles TIC ⓘ *2 Dunns Lane, Mumbles, T01792 361302, www.mumbles.info, open Mar-Oct, Mon-Sat 1000-1600 and longer hours in school holidays and Jul and Aug.* Very helpful office with books on walking in the Gower. **Swansea Tourist Information Centre** ⓘ *off West Way by bus station, T01792 468321, tourism@swansea.gov.uk, www.swansea.gov.uk, Mon-Sat 0930-1730, July/Aug Sun 1000-1600. www.visitswanseabay.com, www.dylanthomas.org, www.neath-port talbot.gov.uk/attractions/index.html, www.gogwa.com – Gower Watersports*

Abertawe (Swansea) and around

Swansea, the second city of Wales, is a far more Welsh place than its great rival, the capital Cardiff, and Welsh is spoken by far more people. It origins go back to Norman times at least, when a castle was built here as part of William the Conqueror's strategy to suppress the troublesome Welsh. Its maritime location and proximity to Wales' rich coalfields led to its inevitable development as an industrial town. By the 18th-century it was a thriving coal port, as well as a copper smelting centre. The city was very badly damaged by bombing in the Second World War and most of its historic heart was flattened. It was described by Dylan Thomas as an 'ugly, lovely town, crawling, sprawling by the side of a long and splendid curving shore'. Ugly is a moot point but it's a relaxed city with a welcoming atmosphere. Thomas himself later described it as 'marble town, city of laughter, little Dublin'.

If you've only a day to spend here try not to make it Monday – nearly all the sights close.

Today Swansea is trying to re-invent itself as a tourist spot, making use of natural features like its seemingly endless arc of sand, which stretches from Swansea Pier in the east to Mumbles Pier in the west. The city centre and Maritime Quarter (the former docks) have some fine collections in the art galleries and museums. You can see everything from contemporary installations to traditional crafts and Egyptian relics.

Dylan Thomas Centre ⓘ *Somerset Place, Swansea, T01792 463980, www.swansea.gov.uk/dylanthomas, www.dylanthomas.org, 1030-1630 Tue-Sun,* This beautiful colonnaded Victorian listed building celebrates Thomas through memorabilia like original manuscripts and letters and also hosts literature festivals, author readings, lectures and discussions. Dylan Thomas pilgrims should walk up to his birthplace at 5 Cwmdonkin Drive, Uplands where a blue plaque is affixed to the wall. He was born here in the upstairs front bedroom on 26 October 1914. The house can be visited by special arrangement with the Dylan Thomas Centre.

Plantasia ⓘ *Parc Tawe shopping/cinema complex T01792 474555, 1000-1700 Tue-Sun £2.30 £1.60 child,* Swansea's hot house is home to 850 species of tropical and sub-tropical plants as well as Tamarind monkeys, rainforest birds and butterflies and other exotic animals. There are 3 different climate zones where you can find bananas, coconuts, giant bamboo, a wonderful lush collection of ferns and plenty of prickly cacti.

Attic Gallery ⓘ *14 Cambrian Place, Swansea, T01792 653387,www.atticgallery.co.uk,* Wales' longest established private gallery is located in the historic Old Maritime Quarter where it highlights the work of some of the principality's most important artists and promotes new artists. **Glynn Vivian Art Gallery** ⓘ *Alexandra Rd, T01792 655006, Tue-Sun 1030-1730, free,* has a good collection of work by 20th-century Welsh artists. There's also an international collection of porcelain and china.

Maritime and Industrial Museum ⓘ *Swansea Marina, T01792 650351, Tue-Sun 1030-1730, free,* collection focusing on Swansea's maritime and industrial history. You can see the world's first passenger train, which ran between Swansea and Oystermouth, an old tram and a steam tug. In 2005 the National Waterfront Museum is due to open here. Check!!

Swansea Museum ⓘ *Victoria Rd, T01792 653763, Tue-Sun 1030-1730, free,* The oldest museum in Wales (Dylan Thomas called it 'a museum that should be in a museum'), it's best known for its ancient mummy of a priest of Isis, but also has a good collection of Nantgarw pottery and porcelain. More Egyptian antiquities at the Egypt Centre, Taliesin Arts Centre, Swansea University, T01792 295960, www.swansea.ac.uk/egypt Tues-Sat 1000-1600, free. There are over 1000 artefacts dating as far back as 3500BC, with statues of gods and goddesses, jewellery and painted coffins.

Outside the town, **Singleton Botanical Gardens** ⓘ *T01792 298637, daily until 1630 later in summer,* have glass houses for Temperate and Tropical regions, as well as a herb garden and ornamental gardens. **Clyne Gardens** ⓘ *T01792 401737, daily, www.swansea.gov.uk/leisure/allparks.html,* cover 50 acres of landsurrounding Clyne Castle, purchased in 1860 by millionaire William Graham Vivian. As well as a great collection of rhododendrons and azaleas there's a bog garden, wildflower meadow and bluebell wood.

Mwmbwls (Mumbles)

West of Swansea Bay and the gateway to the Gower, is the cheery stretch of seafront known, unenticingly, as Mumbles (Dylan Thomas called it 'a rather nice village, despite its name'). This name originally referred to a couple of little offshore islands and is a corruption of the name mamelles (breasts) that French sailors gave them. Today it's a general term for the village of **Oystermouth** (Ystumllwynarth), an historic oyster fishing port, and the long stretch of seafront to Mumbles Lighthouse and the blue flag beach **Bracelet Bay**. It's noted for its generous number of pubs (some patronized by the ever thirsty Mr Thomas) and has some great places to eat (see Eating, page 570). Nearby Caswell Bay offers some great urban surfing. The winding streets behind the promenade contain the ruins of **Ostermouth Castle** ⓘ *Apr-end Sep, £1, con 80p*, a former Norman stronghold. Mumbles most famous daughter is Catherine Zeta Jones, who still returns occasionally to see her family.

Gower

West of Mumbles is the 19 mile long Gower (Gwyr), a small and scenic peninsular, which resembles a toe dipping tentatively into the Bristol Channel. The Gower was Britain's first designated Area of Outstanding Natural Beauty and much of the coastline is owned by the National Trust. Its lovely beaches have become a favourite with surfers and windsurfers (for surfing try Llangennith, especially if you're a beginner; for windsurfing try Oxwich Bay – again good for learners, Horton and Llangennith). And its cliff tops and narrow lanes offer some good walking – there's a Gower Coastal Path and cycling. The peninsula is sprinkled with ancient churches, small villages and lovely heathlands. If you want to escape the crowds make for the north coast, where there are lonely stretches of grazed saltmarshes, rich in rare plants.

Three Cliffs Bay is the closest of the Gower beaches to Swansea. At nearby Parkmill, on the main A4118 is the **Gower Heritage Centre** ⓘ *T01792 371206, www.gowerheritagecentre.co.uk, daily Apr-Oct 1000-1730, 1000-1600 Nov-Mar, £3.60, £2.50 children, £11 family*, a child orientated attraction based around an old water powered corn mill, with craft workshops and displays and a tea shop. They also offer guided walks for groups and have plenty of leaflets on the area.

Oxwich Bay is a National Nature Reserve encompassing dunes, marshes and woodlands, as well as a popular sandy beach. Here you'll find **St Illtyd's** Church ⓘ *generally open 1100-1500*, which stands on the site of a sixth-century Celtic monastic cell. From popular Port Eynon, a Blue Flag beach, you can walk a lovely stretch of coastline round to **Rhossili**. Rhossili is a stunning area – the Land's End of the Gower (but without the ghastly commercialism that has ruined the one in Cornwall). Much of it is owned by the National Trust and there's a NT information centre. You can walk from here to **Worms Head** rocks, home to seals and seabirds – tide allowing, or along the glorious beach where you can sometimes see the wreck of the **Helvetia**, which went down in 1887. On fine days the sunsets here can be superb – well worth the trip to the Gower alone.

Inland you can visit the church at **Llangennith**, dedicated to St Cenydd who founded a priory here in the sixth-century. Even older is the massive dolmen near Reynoldston known as **King Arthur's stone**, which sits alone on a windy ridge. A giant capstone, weighing around 25 tons, balanced on smaller rocks, it marks a Neolithic burial chamber. The views from this isolated spot are superb.

Carmarthenshire Coast (East)

Carmarthenshire is far more typically Welsh than the south east of Wales, with the language being spoken far more frequently. The coastline has a different character to the interior. As you travel west from the Gower along the A484 over the Loughor estuary, you come to the excellent **National Wetland Centre** ⓘ *Penclacwydd, Llwynhendy, near Llanelli T01554 741087, www.wwt.org.uk, daily 0930-1700 summer, 0930-1630 winter, £5.50, £3.50 child, £14.50 family*. This covers 500 acres around the Burry Inlet, with salt marshes, mudflats – and a landscaped area that's home to flamingos, geese and ducks. Hides give you the opportunity to see a wide range of wildfowl and wading birds – in winter around 50,000 birds come here. Species you might spot include herons, Ringed Plovers and Little Egrets. There's also a good interactive Discovery Centre and a café.

Further west, just off the A484, is one of Wales' lesser known castles, well preserved **Kidwelly** ⓘ *T01554 890104, daily 0930-1700 Apr, May end Sept-end Oct, 0930-1800 Jun-end Sep, Mon-Sat 0930-1600, Sun 1100-1600 end Oct-end Mar, £2.50, £2 concessions, £7 family, CADW*. Founded by the Normans – who else, the castle was a link in a chain of coastal strongholds. Its most prominent feature is the great gatehouse, completed in 1422 – you can see the arches through which rocks were chucked onto assailants.

Sleeping

Swansea and around *p479*

L Morgan's Hotel, Somerset Place, T01792 484848, www.morganshotel.co.uk. Catherine and Michael's hotel of choice. Individually designed bedrooms furnished in silk and satin with plasma TVs set into the walls.

B-C Beaumont Hotel, 72-73 Walter St, T01792 643956, www.beaumonthotel.co.uk. Family-run hotel with well furnished and comfortable bedrooms. The executive rooms are larger and have sunken bath tubs; some have four-poster beds.

C Windsor Lodge Hotel, Mount Pleasant, T01792 642158, www.windsor-lodge.co.uk Small and friendly hotel in a welcoming grade II listed building has the air of a country hotel yet in the city. Elegant ensuite rooms, smart restaurant, convenient parking.

C White House Hotel, 4 Nyanza Terrace, www.thewhitehousehotel.co.uk. Beautifully refurbished and maintained Victorian hotel located one mile from the city centre. Comfortable and warm ensuite rooms.

D Bayswater Hotel, 322 Oystermouth Rd, T01792 655301, F 01792 643463. Value accommodation for non smokers in amongst the many sea front guest houses. Some ensuite, some rooms with sea view.

D Cefn Bryn Guest House, 6 Uplands Crescent, Uplands, Swansea, T01792 466687, www.cefnbryn.co.uk Conveniently located in sedate suburban Uplands, yet just 1 mile from the station and close to the city centre, a genuinely warm welcome awaits in this smart late Victorian setting. Non smokers only.

Mumbles *p568*

B Hillcrest House Hotel, 1 Higher Lane, Langland, Mumbles, T01792 363700, www.hillcresthousehotel.com. Small, comfortable hotel with individually themed rooms (lots of daffodils for the Welsh room for instance), all en suite.

C Glenview Guest House, 140 Langland Rd, Mumbles, T01792 367933, www.mumblesglenview.co.uk. B&B in Victorian house, with en suite rooms, gardens and real fires in the lounge in winter.

C Tides Reach, 388 Mumbles Rd, Mumbles, T01792 404877, www.tidesreachguesthouse.co.uk. High quality B&B on the seafront. All rooms en suite. Furnished with antiques and very clean and comfortable.

Gower *p568*

A-L Fairyhill, Reynoldstone, Gower, T01792 390139, www.fairyhill.net This is the Gower's only 5 star hotel. Tucked away in the quiet of the countryside it's a great place to luxuriate and treat yourself – if you can afford it.

C King Arthur Hotel, Higher Green, Reynoldston, Gower, T01792 390775, www.kingarthurhotel.co.uk. Lovely newly refurbished rooms at this warm and popular inn, situated on the village green. Ask for a room in the lovely new annexe and you don't have to worry about noise from the bar.

B-C Oxwich Bay Hotel, Oxwich Bay, Gower, T01792 390329, www.oxwichbayhotel.co.uk. Large, traditional hotel with great situation overlooking by Oxwich Bay. Try and get a room with a sea view.

C **Woodside Guest House**, Oxwich, Gower T01792 390791, www.oxwich.fsnet.co.uk. 4 star guest house, situated near Oxwich beach.

C **Surf Sound Guest House**, Long Acre, Oxwich, Gower, T01792 390822, www.surfsound.co.uk. Good value B&B convenient for Oxwich beach.

C-D **Parc-le-Breos**, Parkmill, Gower, T01792 371636, www.par-le-breos.co.uk. 19th century hunting lodge set in its own grounds. The rooms are clean, with en suite facilities and many have pleasant views of the gardens. Popular with those on riding, surfing or walking holidays. Evening meals available.

D **Headlands**, 28a East Cliff, Southgate, Gower T01792 234912, headlandsgower@talk21.com. Good value B&B on the clifftop.

D **Highfield**, Highfield, Port Eynon, Gower, T01792 390357. Old house in its own grounds, with rooms overlooking Port Eynon Bay.

D **Tallizmand**, Llandmadoc, Gower, T01792 386373. Small, comfortable B&B, with 2 en suite rooms and 1 with shared bathroom. In the quiet village of Llandmadoc and convenient for nearby beaches and walks. Evening meals and packed lunches available.

F **Port Eynon Youth Hostel**, Old Lifeboat House, Port Eynon T01792 390706, porteynon@yha.org.uk, 28 bed seasonal hostel close to the beach.

Carmarthenshire Coast (East) *p568*

D **GlanGwendraeth Farm**, Priory St, Kidwelly, T01554 890309, www.glangwendraeth.co.uk. Clean and comfortable farmhouse B&B, all rooms en suite, some with views of Kidwelly's stunning castle. Good value.

Eating

Swansea and around *p566*

Swansea's salty maritime heritage means you can try local grub such as fresh cockles with loads of vinegar and pepper from the bustling market by the Quadrant Shopping Centre - also renowned for its laverbread and bacon (Swansea's breakfast dish) and freshly baked welshcakes. Joe's Ice Cream, also available in nearby Mumbles, where they even queue in the winter, is proclaimed by locals (and many visitors) to be the best ice cream in the whole world. £Govindas, 8 Cradock St, T01792 468469, 1000-1800. Established veggie diner offering good value grub.

Mumbles *p568*

£££-££ **Knights Restaurant**, 614-616 Mumbles Rd, T01792 363184, Mon 1830-2130, Tues-Sat 1200-1400, 1830-2130, Sun 1200-1400. Lively, contemporary restaurant with extensive fish menu, as well as lots of unusual meat choices like wild boar, ostrich or guinea fowl. Separate veggie menu.

££ **Patrick's with Rooms**, 638 Mumbles Rd, T01792 360199, Mon-Sun 1200-1400, Mon-Sat 1830-2150. Imaginative British cuisine in very popular restaurant.

£ **Café Valance**, 50 Newton Rd, Mumbles, T01792 367711, Mon-Sat 0800-1800. Great café with lots of comfy sofas and a good choice of filled baguettes, panini, cakes and coffees.

£ **Claudes**, 93 Newton Rd, T01792 366006, www.claudes.org.uk, Mon-Fri 1200-1430,1800-2200, Sat 1200-1430, 1800-2145, Sun 1200-1500. Inventive Welsh cuisine with dishes such as home made meatballs, roast cod with red pepper sauce, or saffron risotto. 2 course set lunch for £7.50, 2 course set dinner £12.50, 3 courses £15.

£ **G&Ts Bistro**, 602 Mumbles Rd, T01792 367309, Mon 1830-2130, Tues – Sat 1200-1400, 1830-2130, Sun 1200-1500, 1900-2130. Warm red interior and flickering candles at this bistro which serves mains like Welsh beef and lamb, as well as tapas.

£ **Verdi's Knab Rock**, Mumbles Rd, T01792 369135, www.verdis-café.co.uk, Daily 1000-2100 (2200 July and Aug), earlier closing Mon-Thurs in winter. Relaxed Italian ice cream parlour and restaurant, with great views across Swansea Bay. Great for relaxing outside with an ice cream sundae, pizzas, foccacia or just coffee.

Gower *p568*

£££ **Fairyhill Reynoldstone**, Gower, T01792 390139. If you can't afford to spend the night at this luxurious country hotel you can still enjoy some of its comforts in the restaurant, which uses local produce and serves classical food with a contemporary twist. Good choice of wines too.

££ **Welcome to Town Inn**, Llanrhidian, Gower, T01792 390015, www.thewelcometotown.co.uk. Tues-Sun 1200-1400, Tues-Sat 1900-2130. Highly acclaimed food at this award winning bistro. Lots of Welsh produce on the menu. Good value set lunches with 2 courses for £11.75 and 3 for £14.95.

££-£ King Arthur Hotel, Higher Green, Reynoldston, Gower, T01792 390775, 1200-1430, 1800-2100 (2130 at weekends). Lively inn on the village green, with a nautical theme in the cosy bar. Wide choice of bar meals with several veggie options.
££-£ Oxwich Bay Hotel, Oxwich Bay, Gower, T01792 390329, food available all day. Plenty of choice here with dishes like baked potatoes, sausages or burgers as well as pricier food like steaks and seabass. The terrace offers a great outlook over the beach.
£ King's Head, Llangennith, T01792 386212, food 1100-2130 Mon-Sat, Sun 1200-2130. Popular pub serving bar meals like lamb balti, goulash or sweet and sour chicken. Good selection of real ales.
£ Three Cliffs Coffee Shop, 68 Southgate Rd, Penard, T01792 233885, daily 1030-1800. Outside seating and good homebaking at this lovely little café tucked away on the south Gower coast. Serves a good selection of filled baguettes, snacks and coffees.

Pubs, bars and clubs

Swansea *p566*

Cafe Mambo, 46 The Kingsway, T01792 456620. Primarily a restaurant, the bar section is very small yet the atmosphere is very good in this Latino themed bar offering cocktails by the glass or pitcher.
Escape, Northampton Lane, T01792 652854, www.escapegroup.com. Balearics come to Swansea Bay in this venue hosting varied club nights. 2200-0400 weekends.
Monkey Cafe Bar, 13 Castle St, T01792 480822, www.monkeycafe.co.uk. Cool bar offering DJ nights and live music as well as good pub grub in relaxed surroundings.
No Sign Wine Bar, 56 Wind St, T01792 465300. One of the oldest bars on Wind Street and yet another of Dylan Thomas' old haunts. The warm atmosphere of this cafe bar tends to attract an eclectic mix of local drinkers, D.T.fans and clubbers.
Palace, 156 High St, T01792 457977, www.thepalaceswansea.co.uk. Loud house in club handily close to railway station.

Mumbles *p568*

Antelope, Mumbles Rd One of those 'Dylan Thomas drank here' pubs along the popular Mumbles Mile. Has a beer garden.

Gower *p568*

King's Head, Llangennith, T01792 386212. Good selection of real ales as well as bar meals.
Greyhound Inn, Oldwalls, T01792 391027. Traditional pub said to serve the best beers on the Gower. Selection of real ales, and pub grub.

Entertainment

Swansea and around *p479*

Theatre

Swansea Grand Theatre, Singleton Street, Swansea, T01792 475715. Drama, pantomime, opera, ballet, concerts.
Taliesin Arts Centre, University of Wales, Mumbles Rd, Swansea, T01792 236883, www.taliesinartscentre.co.uk. The centre is home to a wide variety of performances, exhibitions, activities and events, with a cinema, gallery and conference facilities.

Festivals and events

Swansea and around *p479*

27 Oct-9 Nov Dylan Thomas Festival, events to celebrate the poet and his work, T01792 463980, www.dylanthomasfestival.org
May-Sep Swansea Bay Summer Festival, events run through the summer months, www.swanseabayfestival.net
Oct Swansea Festival of Music and the Arts, everything from opera to jazz, www.swanseafestival.co.uk.

Activities and tours

Boat trips

Gower Coast Adventures, T07866 250440, www.gowercoastadventures.co.uk. Jet boat trips from Port Eynon Bay to Worms Head (2hrs, £20) and Knab Rock, Mumbles to Three Cliffs Bay (1 ½ hrs, £14).

Cycling

The Millennium Coastal Park has a 20km cycle trail along the Loughor Estuary and runs from Bynea in the east to Pembury in the west.
Swansea Cycles, 10 Wyndham St, Swansea, T01792 410710. Hire, half day £8, full day £14.
Schmoos Cycles, Lower Oxford St, Swansea T01792 410710. Cycle hire.
Pedalabikeaway, North Dock, Llanelli, T01554 780123, www.pedalabikeaway.com, mountain bikes to tandems for hire.

General activities

Clyne Farm, Westport Ave, Mayals, Swansea, T01792 403333, www.clynefarm.com run weekend and school holiday activity days for all ages from 8 upwards. Can include archery, riding, indoor climbing – booking necessary. Also offer hacks and beach rides.

Horse riding

Pitton Moor Trekking, Pilton Cross, Rhosilli, Gower T01792 390554, WTRA approved trekking on the Gower. Parc le Breos, Parkmill, Gower, T01792 371636, www.parc-le-breos.co.uk Daily rides and pony trekking holidays.

Walking

Gower Guided Walks, T01792 652040, www.gowerguidedwalks.co.uk, variety of guided walks on the Gower.

Watersports

Bay Watersports, Oystermouth Rd, T01792 534858, www.baywatersports.co.uk. Offer windsurfing lessons and kit hire. 1 lesson £20, 2 day course (4 lessons) £65.
Euphoria Sailing, T0870 7702890 or 07812 774701, www.watersports4all.com offer a variety of watersports in Oxwich Bay from sailing and windsurfing to wakeboarding.
Hot Dog Surf Shop, Kittle, Gower T01792 234073, www.higdogsurf.com. For surfing gear.
PJs Surf Shop, Llangennith, Gower T01792 386669 good range of wetsuits and surfboards for hire, (from £9) also have a surf hotline 0901 603 1603 (60p per minute).
Welsh Surf School, Llangennith, Gower, T01792 386426, www.wsfsurfschool.co.uk Run surfing lessons from Apr-Oct in Rhossili Bay (Llangennith).

Directory

Swansea

Internet Swansea library, Alexandra Rd, T01792 516757 for £1.50 per half hour, Mon-Sat 09.30-1700.

Pembrokeshire and Carmarthenshire

→ *Colour map 1*

Pembrokeshire, the most westerly county in Wales, is also one of the most beautiful. Its coastline of dramatic sea cliffs, glorious beaches and secluded coves has been attracting tourists for years – and its importance was recognised in 1952 when it was designated a National Park. Punctuating this rugged coastline are pretty villages and seaside towns: on the south coast is the traditional – but far from tacky – bucket and spade resort of Tenby; on the north coast is the quietly comfortable little town of Newport. Far to the west is delightful St David's – Britain's smallest city and a spiritual centre since the sixthcentury. Today the best way to appreciate this unspoilt landscape is on foot: the Pembrokeshire Coast Path clings to the coastline as much as possible and provides some of the best walking in Britain. East of Pembrokeshire lie the green hills, farms and ancient castles of Carmarthenshire, extending out to the edge of the brooding Black Mountains. It's a quiet county full of history and mystery – the Romans mined gold here and legend has it that it's the birthplace of Merlin the magician. ▸▸ *For Sleeping, Eating and other listings, see pages 580-586.*

Ins and outs

Getting there Haverfordwest serves as a hub for public transport- both **bus** and **trains**, and the main towns of Tenby, Pembroke and Fishguard are all on railway lines. St David's can only be reached by bus. Carmarthen has good public transport links with Swansea, Haverfordwest and Cardiff. ▸▸ *For further details, see Transport, page 586.*

Getting around During the summer public transport along the coastal path is pretty good with bus services linking the main areas. As you go inland it's generally easier to get around if you've got your own transport.

Information Tenby TIC ⓘ *The Croft, Tenby, T01834 842404, tenby.tic@pembrokeshire.gov.uk, daily Apr-May 1000-1700, Jun-Sep 1000-1730, Jul, Aug 1000-2100, Oct 1000-1700, Nov-Apr 1000-1600.* **Pembroke Visitor Centre** ⓘ *The Commons Rd, Pembroke, T01646 622388, pembroke.tic@pembrokeshire.gov.uk, daily Jun-end Sep 1000-1730, otherwise 1000-1700.* **Newport TIC** ⓘ *Long St, T01239 820912, Apr-Sept Mon-Sat 1000-1730, shuts for lunch.* **St Davids TIC/National Park Visitor Centre** ⓘ *The Grove, St David's, T01437 720392, dianea@stdavids.pembrokeshirecoast.org.uk, www.stdavids.co.uk, daily Apr-Oct 0930-1730, Mon-Sat Nov-Mar 1000-1600.* **Fishguard TIC** ⓘ *The Square, SA65 9HA, T01348 873484, F 01348 875246, www.fishguard.tic@pembrokeshire.gov.uk, Summer: open 7 days Easter-May 1000-1700, Jun-Sep 1000-1730. Winter: open Mon-Sat Oct 1000-1700, Nov-Easter 1000-1600.* **Fishguard Harbour TI C** ⓘ *Ocean Lab, T01348 872 037, F 01348 872528, www.fishguardharbourtic@pembrokeshire.gov.uk, daily1000-1800 Easter-Oct, 1000-1600 Nov-Easter.* **Haverfordwest Visitor Centre** ⓘ *Old Bridge St, T01437 763110, F 01437 767738. Mon-Sat 1000-1700,Easter-Oct and Sun 1000-1600 mid Jul-Aug, open 1000-1600 Mon-Sat at all other times.* **Carmarthen TIC** ⓘ *113 Lammas Street, T01267 231557, www.carmarthenshire.gov.uk. Near the Crimea Monument, daily: Easter-Oct 0930-1300, 1400-1730 Mon-Sat, Jun-Aug 0930-1730 daily, Nov-Easter 1000-1630.* **Carmarthen TIC** ⓘ *at Middleton Gardens T01558 669084 Jun-Sep 1000-1730 daily, Nov-Easter Mon-Sat 1000-1640. Websites: www.pembrokeshirecoast.org, www.visitpembroke shire.com, www.activitypembrokeshire.com, www.stdavids.pembrokeshirecoast.org.uk.*

Trefdaeth (Newport) and around

Lovely little Newport makes a great base for exploring the northern part of Pembrokeshire. The town's small streets, which stretch either side of the A487, give easy pedestrian access to the Pembrokeshire Coast Path to the north. Head south and you can walk up the distinctive, brooding hill known as Carn Ingli – or 'Hill of Angels' – which was once topped with an Iron Age hillfort. There are more reminders of Newport's pre-historic past at Carreg Coeltan, a Neolithic burial chamber reached via Feidr Pen-y-Bont. Inevitably it was once claimed to be the burial spot of King Arthur. The TIC has plenty of information on walks and cycle routes in the area.

Around two miles east of Newport is the little village of Nevern, site of the fascinating church of St Brynach, which as founded in the 6th-century. Dark yew trees line the path, one of which (the 2nd on the right) is known as the 'bleeding yew' on account of the reddish sap that oozes from it. Legend has it that a man was hanged from the tree for stealing church plate. The churchyard is older than the church and beside the porch is an ancient stone known as the Vitalianus Stone, a bilingual 5th century stone inscribed both in Latin and in Ogham (an Irish branch of Celtic then used in parts of Wales) and commemorating a British chieftain, or a Briton who served in the Roman army. The churchyard also contains the Great Cross, a Celtic Cross 13ft high, probably carved in the 10th-century. Inside the church is another bilingual stone, the Maglocunus Stone and a Celtic carved Cross Stone. From the church you can bear right and uphill to visit Pentre Ifan, a vast Neolithic burial chamber that is probably one of the finest in Wales.

Unclassified roads that stretch between Nevern and Cardigan bring you to hidden sections of stunning coastline. Head for Moylegrove and you can get to Ceibwr Bay, where you can walk a section of the Coastal Path or simply gaze at the dramatic cliffs and swooping sea birds. Further north, a little road leads from St Dogmaels to the beach at Poppit Sands, then to a tranquil estuary and Cemaes Head.

Four miles east of Newport, just off the A487, is **Castell Henllys** ⓘ *T01239 891319, www.castellhenllys.com, daily Easter- early Nov, 1000-1700, guided tours at 1130 and 1430, £2.80, £1.90 concession, £7.50 family*, a fascinating reconstructed Iron Age village, built on the site of an original hillfort. A footpath through the woods takes you to the circle of thatched roundhouses, where smoking fires burn and informed staff give demonstrations of weaving and other crafts. This is a working archeological site and more is being discovered all the time – it's a great place for both children and adults.

Cwm Gwaun (Gwaun Valley)

This must be one of the least explored areas of Pembrokeshire, easily reached if you take the A487 from Newport towards Cardigan, and turn first right after the Golden Lion pub. A couple of miles further on there's a t-junction, where you turn right again and into the heart of this deep, wooded valley. Part way along you can turn off to visit lovely **Penlan-Uchaf gardens** ⓘ *T01348 881388, Mar-Nov 0900-dusk, £2.50*, where there are 3 acres of landscaped grounds with views to die for – it's a great spot for tea and homemade cake too. Further along is exquisite Pontfaen church – a real ecclesiastical jewel. The church was founded in 540AD but after the dissolution was neglected and was almost ruined by the 19th-century. However it was later lovingly restored. In the churchyard are two pre-Conquest Latin crosses, while inside is a glistening icon – a copy of 'The Tabernacle of the Madonna of the Stars' by Fra Angelico. On the road near the church is the blue painted, and wonderfully time-warped, Dyffryn Arms (see pubs).

Shortly after this you can take the B4313 left, to reach the eccentric village of Rosebush, intended to be a Victorian spa – but never successful. The Tafarn Sinc, is a corrugated iron pub, erected as temporary hotel (see pubs) and trading ever since.

Abergwaun (Fishguard)

Fishguard is rarely regarded as anything more than a stop-off to and from the nearby ferry port serving Ireland. Its Lower Town was used extensively as a film location when Richard Burton made *Under Milk Wood* in the early seventies and it attracts its fair share of Dylan Thomas fans.

The town was the location of one of Wales's most remarkable and historic battle victories when in 1797, an army of local women forced the surrender of French troops, the last invading army to land on the British mainland. Having arrived at nearby Carreg Wastad, legend has it that the invading troops mistook the traditional Welsh dress (black stovepipe hats and red flannel dresses) of local women marching towards them for the outfit of British soldiers and instantly capitulated. One woman, pitchfork wielding Jemima Nicholas, a 47-year-old cobbler, is known to have single-handedly captured fourteen of the French soldiers. She is buried in the local church. At the time of writing, the Fishguard Tapestry depicting this episode, is out of public view, but will probably be displayed during the school summer holidays at the junior school on West St (check TIC for details).

OceanLab ⓘ *Goodwick, SA64 0DE, T01348 874737*, www.ocean-lab.co.uk, daily 1000-1800 Easter – Oct, 1000-1600 Nov – Easter, features an exhibition gallery about sea and shore life and displays of fossils. Other facilities include a cyber café, soft play area for under 5's, and coffee shop.

Tyddewi (St David's) and around

No visit to Pembrokeshire is complete without a trip to St David's, Britain's smallest city famed for its magnificent cathedral, founded in AD550 by St David, who was born and baptised near here. The city is the most important religious site in Wales and has been a place of pilgrimage since the sixth-century attracting saints, sinners and sightseers – yet although it gets extremely busy, it somehow never loses its air of tranquillity. It's a lovely place to stay, with plenty of decent accommodation, and some good pubs and restaurants.

St David's Cathedral ⓘ *T01437 720199, www.stdavidscathedral.org.uk, 0800-1900 daily, donations welcome, for guided tours T01437 720691*, is one of the oldest in Britain. It is built on the spot St David selected for his monastery, an area known as Glyn Rhosyn in Welsh, meaning 'valley of the little marsh'; it would have been a wild, deserted spot but well hidden from raiders. Early pilgrims included William the Conqueror, who came here in 1081, and Henry 11 who visited twice in 1171 and 1172. You can still see St David's shrine, although it was damaged during the Reformation. Set in its own grassy hollow on the edge of the city, the cathedral is a delightful place to explore, with lots of tombs, statues and ornate carvings to examine.

The building you see today dates back to the late 12th century, although there were many later additions and alterations – an earthquake damaged the building around 1247/48 and the floor of the nave has a discernible slope. As you enter you are struck by the fine carved ceiling, made of Irish oak it was built in the late 15th-century to conceal restoration work – when the building again looked in danger of collapse. If you look carefully you can see several Green Men carved here – the attendants can help you spot them. The carved misericords in the choir are also worth a look, and include a particularly vivid depiction of a man being sick over the side of a boat. The choir contains a stall reserved for the monarch, unique in Britain – the Queen being an automatic Canon of the cathedral. Behind the choir the presbytery has a brilliantly coloured 15th-century ceiling, which was restored and repainted in the 19th-century by Sir George Gilbert Scott.

Close to the cathedral is the **Bishop's Palace** ⓘ *T01437 720517, Apr-1 June, 29 Sept-26 Oct daily 0930-1700, 2 June-28 Sep 0930-1800 daily, 27 Oct–31 Mar 0930-1600 Mon-Sat, 1100-1600 Sun, £2.50, £2 concessions, £7 family, CADW*. This is a magnificent ruin, built between 1328-47 by Bishop Henry de Gower, who pulled out all the architectural stops to create a building that reflected the power and wealth of the church – and the bishop. You can see the remains of many of the fine carvings, ornate windows and grand state rooms, and there is also an exhibition on the life of the palace.

From the city you can walk to St Non's Bay, the spot at which St Non was said to have given birth to David – a spring suddenly appearing in the ground when he was born. There's a shrine here that still attracts pilgrims and the ruins of a 13th-century chapel, as well as a 20th century chapel. The finest beach here is **Whitesands Bay** ⓘ *£2 car parking, no dogs May-Sep*, a clean, sandy stretch popular with surfers and windsurfers. The coast north of St Davids is less visited and dotted with interesting little villages and beaches. Loveliest is Porthgain, a former village port surrounded by the ivy covered, remains of its former brickworks. By the little harbour is a great pub The Sloop Inn as well as a restaurant (see Eating, page 583) and you can also take boat trips (see Tours and activities, page 585).

St Bride's Bay

To the south, the Coast Path takes you round the curve of St Bride's Bay, past some stunning scenery. There are endless sands at Newgale beach, an excellent spot for all sorts of watersports, and several good places to eat in the picturesque little village of Solva. There are plenty of camping and caravanning spots, with rather lively holiday villages such as Broad Haven, and a glorious cliff top walk, accessible from the NT car park (£2) at Marloes, from where you can reach the quieter sandy beach of Marloes Sands. The village of Dale is a popular watersports centre while Martins Haven, near Marloes, is the usual starting point for trips to the islands of Skomer, Skokholm and Grassholm: nature reserves populated by huge numbers of seabirds in the spring and summer months. The boats usually run from April to October, weather permitting. Contact the **Wildlife Trust West Wales (WTWW)** ⓘ *T01437 765462* or **Dale Sailing Company** ⓘ *T01646 601636, www.dale-sailing.co.uk*, for details.

Skomer, Skokholm and Grassholm islands

St David's is a good spot from which to take boat trips (see Activities, page 585) out to nearby **Ramsey Island**, noted for its rich bird life, while the waters are great for spotting seals, whales and dolphins. **Skomer** is home to one of the most the most easily accessible of all seabird colonies in northwest Europe, and has been a National Nature Reserve (NNR) since 1959. Puffins and Manx shearwaters are the island's most famous residents, to be seen throughout the summer until August. There is a huge range of other wildlife including grey seals, which pup in September, the common porpoise and dolphins. To the south is **Skokholm**. Walkers may enjoy guided trips in the summer around this WTWW reserve to view the puffins, Manx shearwaters and storm petrels up close.Lying 11 miles off the coast is **Grassholm**, an RSPB reserve housing 35,000 breeding pairs of gannets. These give rise to the island's nickname the 'Wedding Cake' as, from a distance, it appears to be covered in a white icing. Landing is not allowed.

Hwlffordd (Haverfordwest) and Arberth (Narberth)

The main transport hub and shopping centre of Pembrokeshire, Haverfordwest offers little in the way of tourist attractions, though there's a ruined castle and small museum and art gallery. The 12th-century castle was the focus around which the town developed, later becoming a prosperous port in the 17th and 18th centuries. If you head three miles east of town, off the A40, you'll find **Picton Castle and Woodland Gardens** ⓘ *The Rhos, T/F 01437 751326, www.pictoncastle.co.uk, Tue-Sun 1030-1700, £3.95*, a 13th- century castle set in 40 acres of beautiful grounds, including woodlands and a walled garden. The Walled Garden contains a large collection of culinary and medicinal herbs labelled with their herbal remedies.

Scolton Manor Museum and Country Park ⓘ *Spittal, SA62 5QL, T01437 731328 (Museum), T01437 731457 (park), Visitor centre 10.30-1730 Apr-Oct. Park 0900-1730 Apr-Oct, 0900-1630 Nov-Mar, £2.* Only 4 miles northeast of Haverfordwest, there's a museum and visitor centre housed within this early Victorian manor house. It's set in 60 acres of grounds, with gardens and a nature reserve. The museum concentrates on the history and natural history of Pembrokeshire. There are country trails, picnic sites and play areas.

The town of **Narberth** lies at the hub of the Landsker Borderlands. It was one of the homes of the Princes of Dyfed and is even mentioned in the Mabinogion, an early collection of Welsh folk-tales. Among the art studios in town is the **Creative Cafe** ⓘ *Spring Gardens, Narberth, SA67 6BT, T01834 861651, www.thecreativecafe.co.uk*, a studio/café with a difference. Kids can enjoy painting designs on ready-made pottery – leave it with the experts to glaze and fire, and collect one to three days later (postal service available). Also tea, coffee, baguettes and cakes.

Out of town is **Oakwood Park** ⓘ *Canaston Bridge, Narberth, T01834 891660, www.oakwood-leisure.com, 1000-1700 Apr-Sep, until 2200 end Jul-Aug, £12.95*, family concessions, is Wales' answer to Alton Towers. Oakwood claims to have Europe's longest watercoaster, largest skycoaster and largest wooden rollercoaster. CC2000 is a new all-weather family complex including a Crystal Maze and a ten-pin bowling alley.

Penfro (Pembroke) and around

On Pembrokeshire's south coast is the pleasant, but rather uninspiring, market town of Pembroke, which developed after the building of a castle here in 1093 – the mightiest of the Norman castles in the south west of Wales. The heart of the town is the Main Street, an attractive jumble of Georgian and Victorian buildings that runs downs from the fine castle – undoubtedly the main reason for visiting.

Pembroke Castle ⓘ *T01646 681510, www.pembrokecastle.co.uk, daily Apr-end Sep, 0930-1800, Mar, Oct 0930-1700, Nov-Feb 1000-1600, £3, £2 children, £8 family,* was first built in 1093 by Roger de Montgomery, cousin of William the Conqueror. This first building was timber, but was strong enough to withstand a long siege from the Welsh. In 1204 work began to reconstruct the castle in stone, a task finished around 1247. In 1452 Jasper Tudor was granted the castle, and in 1457 his nephew, the future Henry V11 and first Tudor king, was born here. During the Civil War the castle withstood another long siege, until the garrison surrendered – after which much of the building was destroyed on Cromwell's orders. Today the ruins you see have been restored. There's a Keep or Great Tower, a Norman Hall, dating from c 1150-1170, and a spiral staircase leading to Wogan's Cavern, an unexpectedly large, dank cave that was used as a shelter as far back as the Palaeolithic Period, and continued intermittently into the Mesolithic age.

Opposite the castle is the quirky little **Museum of the Home** ⓘ *7 Westgate Hill, T01646 681200, May-Sept, Mon-Thurs 1100-1700, £1.20, 90p concessions*, a house containing a fascinating private collection of all sorts of household oddities from the 'unstately' home. Cases are filled with toys and games (including Roman dice), kitchen utensils, washboards, oddments such as a 'moustache soup spoon' (to protect whiskers from hot liquids) and even a pocket sputum bottle. Closes for good in September 2004.

South of Pembroke is a gloriously unspoiled coastline. The Stackpole Estate is owned by the National Trust and encompasses sheer cliffs and quiet beaches. Stackpole Quay, a tiny natural harbour, has a good tearoom (see eating) and is a good starting point for walks on the cliffs. From here you can follow an easy path for ½ miles over the clifftops to Barafundle Bay, a lovely stretch of sand and dunes. Footpaths continue to Stackpole Head, Broad Haven and Bosherston – where the rugged offshore rock formation known as Stack Rocks teems with birdlife, including a large colony of guillemots. Just inland, near Bosherston, are Bosherston Lakes, a series of man made lakes created in the late 18th and early 19th-centuries. They now support a range of wildlife, including otters, toads and kingfishers. Further west the land is owned by the MOD. A Coastal Cruiser bus service runs between Pembroke and Broadhaven, Stackpole and Lamphey, £3 return.

The A4139 south east of Pembroke takes you first to the ruined **Bishops Palace** ⓘ *Lamphey, T01646 672224, daily 1000-1700, £3, £2.50 concessions, £8.50 family, CADW*. This was the country retreat of the bishops of St Davids, which came with everything from fishponds to orchards. Further along the road you come to a turn off for Manorbier (bus 349), where there's a lovely ruined castle overlooking a sandy beach. **Manorbier Castle** ⓘ *Easter-end Sep daily 1030-1730, £3, £1.50 children*, was the birthplace in 1146 of Giraldus Cambrensis, or Gerald of Wales, the medieval churchman who travelled widely through Wales and chronicled the country and its people.
East of Pembroke is **Carew Castle and Tidal Mill** ⓘ *T01646 651782, www.carewcastle.com, daily Easter-end Oct 1000-1700, £2 castle, £2.95 both*. The castle was built by the Normans but altered and extended over the years, eventually becoming an Elizabethan country mansion. It's now ruined but is often used as the setting for events in summer. The Tidal Mill was built in Elizabethan times and was powered by the force of the tides. It is one of only 3 in Britain, and retains the original machinery.

Dinbych y Pysgod (Tenby)

Tenby must qualify as one of the most delightful seaside towns in Britain. Perched on a rocky promontory above endless sandy beaches, with a fringe of pastel coloured buildings round a cosy harbour it has a genteel, but lively, charm. The town's mix of award winning beaches, winding medieval streets, and busy bars and restaurants allow it to appeal to a wide range of people, whether young surfers, weekending city slickers or holidaying families. It's also an important stop on the Pembrokeshire Coast Path, and there's plenty of accommodation and entertainment for weary walkers.

The town's Welsh name means 'Little Fort of Fishes'. It grew up around the Norman castle, first mentioned in 1153, the remains of which are perched on the headland. In the 13th –century the town was partly enclosed by protective walls, which were later extended and strengthened. Tenby gradually developed into a thriving port and although trade declined during the Civil Wars, enjoyed a new incarnation in the 18th century as a salt water spa. The arrival of the railway in the 19th-century brought large numbers of visitors keen to enjoy the health giving benefits of the seaside. It became a fashionable Victorian resort and attracted a wide range of people, from the naturalist P H Gosse to artists and authors like Lewis Carroll, George Elliot and JMW Turner.

In the heart of the town, is St Mary's Church, with its 152 ft spire. Among those commemorated is Robert Recorde c.1510, a mathematician, born in Tenby who was said to have invented the 'equals' sign. On Quay Hill is the **Tudor Merchant's House** ⓘ *T01834 842279 NT*, one of the oldest buildings in town dating back to the 15th-century. A former wealthy merchant's house it is on three floors. You can see the remains of Tudor frescoes on the walls and get an idea of how the family would have lived.

In the remains of the castle is the **Museum and Art Gallery** ⓘ *T01834 842809, www.tenbymuseum.free-online.co.uk, Easter-early Dec daily 1000-1700, early Dec-Easter Mon-Fri 1000-1700, last admission 1630, £2*. This includes exhibits on the towns geology, maritime and social history, and has a permanent art collection which includes works by locally bred artists Augustus and Gwen John and Nina Hamnett.

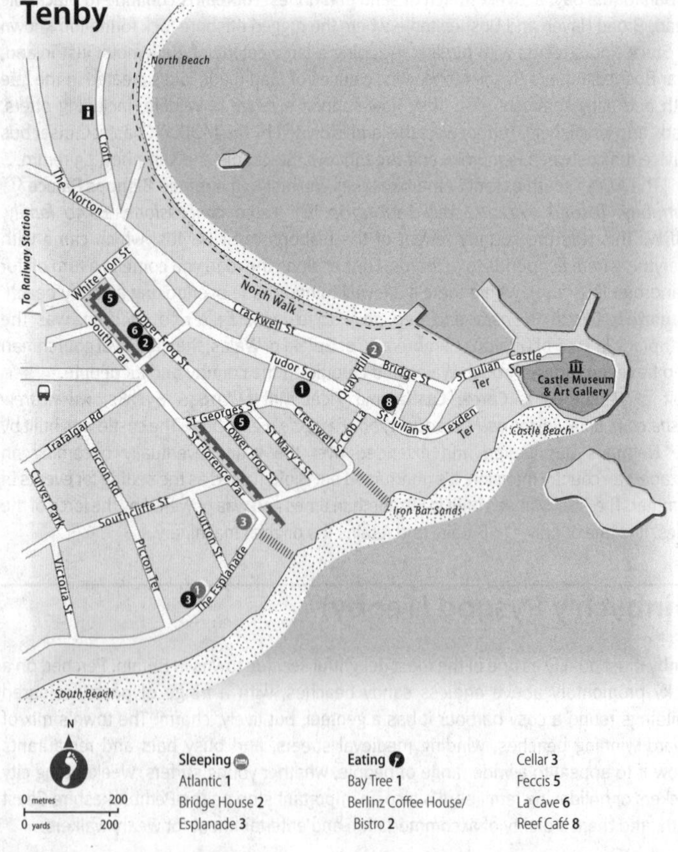

Caldey Island, just a few miles offshore, has been a monastic settlement since around the 6th-century and is now a popular destination for **boat trips** ⓘ *T01834 844453, www.caldey-island.co.uk, Easter-Oct, Mon-Sat, £7.50*, from Tenby, . In the early Middle Ages a Benedictine order founded a priory here, but it was deserted after the Dissolution. The island is now home to a small community of monks of the Reformed Cistercian Order, who manufacture a range of products including perfumes and toiletries made from the islands wild flowers, gorse and herbs.

Caerfyrddin (Carmarthen) and around

Often regarded as the gateway to West Wales, the town on the River Tywi (also known by its anglicised name, Towy) is the ancient capital of the region. Although it was founded as a Roman fort, legend claims that it is the birthplace of Merlin (Myrddin). Once a busy trading port and wool town, Carmarthen's a flourishing market town and stronghold of the Welsh language.

Heritage Centre ⓘ *Quay Side, T01267 223788, Wed-Sat 1100-1600, free*. Tucked away down by the river, this is a good little place to catch up on the history of the town. **Oriel Myrddin** ⓘ *Mon-Sat 10.30-1700 free*, a craft centre and imaginative gallery showcasing local artists. **Carmarthenshire County Museum** ⓘ *Bishop's Palace, Abergwilli, T01267 231691 Mon-Sat 1000-1630, free*. Two miles east of Carmarthen, the former seat of the Bishop of St David's between 1542 and 1974 now houses the regional history museum. This interesting and eclectic exhibition covers well-presented displays of local castles, pottery and archaeological finds, wooden dresser, and he origins of one of Wales's first eisteddfodau (Welsh cultural festivals), held nearby in 1450.

Middleton Garden (National Botanic Garden of Wales) ⓘ *T01558 668768, www.middletongardens.com/ www.gardenofwales.org.uk, Llanarthne, summer daily 1000-1800, winter 1000-1630, £6.95, £3.50 children, £17.50 family*. Opened in May 2000, this is one of Wales' most important millennium projects – its own botanic garden. It's a bit like a mix of Kew and the Eden Project – though on a smaller scale. The Middleton estate on which it's built dates from the 1600s and the old double walled garden (cleverly designed so as to produce more heat) has been restored and has beds containing all sorts of vegetables and flowers, with interesting old varieties like yellow raspberries and funny shaped tomatoes. There's an excellent exhibition on the Physicians of Myddfai – the name referring to a line of Welsh physicians who used natural remedies to cure people. It has displays on herbal remedies/treatments from all over the world: opium, you learn, was first recorded on Sumerian tablets from the 4th millennium BC. There's also a 19th-century apothecaries hall from Anglesey – complete with bottles with labels like 'Dr Rooke's Solar Elixir and Reanimating Balm of Life'. Heart of the garden is the newly built Great Glasshouse designed by Norman Foster. This is divided into different climate zones, with plants from Australia, South Africa, the Medierranean, Canary Islands, Chile and California. Gardens obviously take a long time to get established and Middleton still feels very new – the plan is to gradually extend it –although at the time of writing its very future is under threat – which would be a great pity.

Aberglasney Gardens ⓘ *Llangathen, T01558 668998, www.aberglasney.org.uk, daily summer 1000-1800, winter 1030-1600, (last entry 1hr before closing) £5.50, £2.50 child, £14 family*. East of Middleton, off A40 near Llandeilo, is Wales' answer to Heligan – a lost garden surrounding a fine manor house, both of which had suffered badly from neglect and looked doomed to disappear. Both the house- a listed building– and the weed choked grounds, were saved in the mid 1990s and a unique garden was discovered – now carefully restored. The formal Cloister Gardens are a rare and authentic Jacobean survival – almost all such gardens were swept away in the 18th-century. You can also see Victorian aviaries, a Pool Garden, Kitchen Garden and an atmospheric Yew Tunnel. There's a good café where you can sit outside on fine days.

Dinefwr Castle and Park and Newton House, *T01558 823902, near Llandeilo, house and park Apr-Oct Thu-Mon 1100-1700, £3.50, £1.70 child, £8.30 family, park only £2.30, £1.20 child, £5.80 family, unrestricted access to castle.* Legend has it that the first castle at Dinefwr was built in 877AD by Rhodri Mawr, King of Wales. It became the principal court of Hywel Dda (the 'Good') who in 920AD ruled much of South West Wales, known as Deheubarth. He was responsible for creating the first uniform legal system in Wales. The ruined stone castle you can see today was built on the same site and was the 12th-century stronghold of Lord Rhys, who united Welsh rulers against the English.

In the 17th-century the more comfortable Newton House was built (about a 25 minute walk across parkland from the castle), and the park was landscaped in the 1770s by Capability Brown. The house is gradually being restored by the National Trust and you can see the period rooms, hung with paintings. The park is notable for its indigenous rare White Park cattle, which are white with long horns and black noses. They have a lineage stretching back to the time of Hywel Dda – in the event of any injury to the King of Deheubarth tribute had to be paid in the form of these cattle.

South east of Llandeilo, near Trapp is **Carreg Cennen Castle** ⓘ *T01558 822291, Apr-Oct 0930-1730 daily, Nov-end Mar 0930-dusk daily, £3, £2.50 child, £8.50 family, CADW* probably the most dramatically situated castle in Wales, high on a precipitous crag above the River Cennen. The views down the valley are stunning. Legend has it that a castle was built here by King Arthur's knights – and one of them is still said to sleep under the existing structure, a seemingly impenetrable stone stronghold which dates from around 1300. It was dismantled by the Yorkists in the Wars of the Roses and is now a romantic ruin. A visit here includes taking a torch and walking along the dark passageway that leads to a cave beneath the fort.

Talacharn (Laugharne)

The undoubted high point of the Carmarthenshire coast is Laugharne, described by Dylan Thomas as 'a legendary lazy little black magical bedlam by the sea' – and the most likely inspiration for fictional Llareggub of Under Milk Wood which he wrote here. It is here, on the Taf Estuary, that you can most easily feel the spirit of the poet. He came here several times, once to chase after Caitlin – whom he later married, and lived in several houses around the town until in 1949 his benefactor Margaret Taylor, bought him and his family the famous Boathouse where he lived until his death in 1953. **The Dylan Thomas Boathouse** ⓘ *T01994 427420, www.dylanthomasboathouse.com, daily May-Oct 1000-1730, Nov-Apr 1030-1530, £2.95, £1.25 children, £7 family*, is a simple building with an idyllic location, perched on the clifftop with glorious views over the estuary and its 'heron-priested shores'. It's reached by a narrow track from the town and his little writing shed, originally a garage, is laid out much as it was when Thomas worked here. Downstairs in the house itself is the simply furnished living room, with some copies of his manuscripts and other memorabilia, and upstairs there's a video presentation. Nearby, in the village is St Martins Churchyard, where Thomas and his wife are buried.

Close to the Boathouse, on the shore, is **Laugharne Castle** ⓘ *T01994 427906, Apr-Sept daily 1000-17000, £2.50, £2 concessions, £7 family*, an atmospheric ruin built in the mid to late 13th-century. In Elizabethan times it was turned into a mansion but after the Civil War fell into decline. JMW Turner painted it and Dylan Thomas sometimes worked in its summerhouse. A short drive inland from Laugharne is the village of St Clears, where there's a good craft centre and excellent contemporary café (see eating).

Sleeping

Newport and around *p556*

B **Tregynon Farmhouse and Country Cottages**, Gwaun Valley, T01239 820531, www.online-holidays.net/tregynon. Award winning serviced B&Bs and self catering cottages, with great views of the Gwaun Valley. Wonderful base for walking.

C **Cnapan Hotel**, East St, Newport, T01239 820575. Well established and very popular four star hotel, noted for its good food.

C Llysmeddyg, East St, Newport, T01239 820008, louise@llysmeddyg.freeserve.co.uk. Lovely large, airy rooms in this clean, friendly guesthouse. Breakfast from local and organic foods, with imaginative veggie options. Restaurant due to open 2004.

Fishguard *p574*

B-A Fishguard Bay Hotel, Quay Rd, Goodwick, T01348 873571, www.smoothound.co.uk/hotels/fighguar.htm Originally a mansion converted to accomodate passengers on the mail steamers to Ireland, this renovated grande dame of a hotel is comfortable and rather old-fashioned in its faded elegance and the views of Fishguard Bay are stunning.

B Three Main Street, 3 Main Street, Fishguard, T01348 874275. This excellent restaurant just off Market Square has three stylish rooms and the breakfasts are great. (For sale at time of writing so future uncertain.)

C Glanmoy Lodge Guesthouse, Tref-Wrgi Road, Goodwick, T01348 874333, www.glanmoylodge.co.uk. Ten minutes' walk from the port, comfortable and clean ensuite rooms in a secluded location. Chance to watch badgers at night.

E Hamilton Backpackers Lodge, 21-23 Hamilton St, T01348 874797. Just a minute's walk from the tourist office. Some ensuite rooms, doubles as well as dorm accommodation available.

Camping

Fishguard Bay Caravan and Camping Park, Garn Gelli, Fishguard, T01348 811415, www.fishguardbay.com, Mar-Dec

St David's and around *p574*

B Warpool Court Hotel, St David's, T01437 720300, warpool@enterprise.net. Pay the extra for a sea view if you can, at this comfortable, friendly hotel on the edge of town. Relaxing gardens and 3000 exquisite hand-painted tiles dotted all over the hotel.

C Old Cross Hotel, Cross Square, T01437 720387, www.oldcrosshotel.co.uk. Rather old fashioned but comfortable hotel in the centre of St Davids. Closed Christmas to beginning of Feb. Good food and pleasant garden.

C The Square, Cross Square, T01437 720333, closed Jan and Feb. Small but cool B&B with stripped wooden floors, sleek chrome fittings and lush pot plants. Egyptian cotton sheets on the beds and imaginative breakfasts.

C Y-Gorlan, 77 Nun St, T01437 720837, www.stdavids.co.uk/gorlan, Clean and comfortable B&B. 2 rooms have a view over Whitesands Bay, as does the large residents lounge. Serves healthy options for breakfast.

B Crug-Glas Country House, Abereiddy, T01348 831302, www.crug-glas.co.uk. On large working farm, with carefully designed, comfortable rooms and en suite bathrooms. Luxurious base for exploring the coast.

Camping

There are plenty of camping sites available – among them are:

F Newgale Camp Site, Wood Farm, Newgale, T01437 710253, www.newgalecampingsite.co.uk. Mar-Oct. Camp in the field just across the road from gorgeous Newgale beach.

F Caerfai Farm Camp Site, St Davids, T01437 720548, www.caerfai.co.uk, close to Caerfai Bay, toilets and showers, end May-end Sep.

Pembroke and around *p576*

C Poyerston Farm, Cosheston, near Pembroke T01646 651347, www.poyerston-farm.co.uk. Lovely clean and comfortable rooms on this friendly working farm. Flowery fabrics and traditional touches throughout. Breakfast is taken in the conservatory.

D Beech House, 76-78 Main St, T01646 683740. Very pretty little B&B with lots of flowers outside in summer.

Tenby *p577, map p578*

B-A Atlantic Hotel, The Esplanade, T01834 842881, www.atlantic-hotel.uk.com. Traditional flowers and flounces at the swishest hotel along the sea front. Worth paying a bit extra to get a sea view. Two restaurants, spa, sauna and pool.

B The Esplanade Hotel, The Esplanade, T01834 842760, www.esplanadetenby.co.uk. Traditional seafront hotel, cheaper but less luxurious than the Atlantic.

C Bridge House, Bridge St, T01834 843893, Easter-Oct. Only one rooms en suite, but the others are large and airy with stunning sea views. Very clean and comfortable.

Haverfordwest *p576*

C The County Hotel, Salutation Square, T01437 762144, F 01437 762504. Reasonably cosy ensuite rooms in family run establishment.

D College Guesthouse, 93 Hill St, St Thomas Green, T01437 763710. Decent B&B in former Baptist college about 1 mile from town centre.

Carmarthen and around *p579*

C **Boar's Head**, Lammas St, T01267 222789, F 01267 222289. Reasonably priced clean ensuite rooms in a quaint old coaching inn in central location.

C **Allt y Golau Uchaf**, Felingwm Uchaf, T01267 290455, www.visit-carmarthenshire.co.uk/alltygolau. Comfortable and clean accommodation in restored farmhouse in peaceful location. No TV in rooms, but immaculate residents lounge.

D **Drovers Arms**, Lammas St, T01267 237646, F 01267 237097. A family run hotel proud of its long history with the early cattle drovers who travelled long distances from rural Wales to the important cattle markets. Comfortable en-suites, cosy bar and open fire in pub serving real ale.

Eating

Newport and around *p556*

£££-££ **Cnapan Hotel**, East St, T01239 820575, coffee 1000-1200, lunch 1200-1400, dinner 1845-2045, closed Tues. Highly rated restaurant using fresh local produce. Expect to pay around £13.50-15.50 for a main course.

£-££ **Beehive Café**, Bridge St, T01239 820372, daily 0930-1400, and 1900-2030 (not Thu or Sun). Friendly little café/restaurant serving good fresh food. Daytime for breakfasts, light meals and cakes, while evening choices might be beef in red wine, or crab salad.

£-££ **Café Fleur**, Market St, T01239 820131, Wed-Sat 1030-1700, Sun 1100-1500 and Fri, Sat from 1930. Good café/restaurant which serves a wide range of sweet and savoury pancakes, paninis and more substantial meals in the evening. Plenty of veggie dishes.

££-£ **Fronlas Café**, Market St, T01239 820351, Tues-Sat 1030-1600, Fri, Sat from 1930. During the day it's a café, at night it's a seafood restaurant. You could find anything from sole to sea bass on the menu, with mains ranging from £14.95-17.50. Veggie choice available. Unlicensed.

£ **Penlan-Uchaf Gardens**, Gwaun Valley, 5 miles from Newport, T01348 881388, Mar-Nov daily until dusk. Outstanding views across the valley from the tea rooms of this garden. Homemade cakes and hot drinks, and ploughman's lunches in winter.

£ **Old Post Office Tea Rooms**, Rosebush, T01437 532205, Tues-Sun lunchtime and Tues-Sat 1830-2300. Pretty little tea rooms tucked away behind the distinctive corrugated iron buildings of Rosebush.

£ **Tafarn Sinc**, Rosebush, T01437 532214. Tues-Sat 1200-1430, 1800-2100 and Sun lunch. Atmospheric pub serving traditional dishes like faggots in gravy or Glamorgan sausages.

St David's and around *p574*

£££ **The Old Pharmacy**, Main St, Solva, T01437 720005, daily from 1800, booking recommended. Best place to eat round here, with lots of local dishes. Several veggie choices and selection of desserts. You don't have to have a main meal – dessert and coffee in the garden is fine.

£££ **Warpool Court Hotel**, St Davids, T01437 720300. For formal dining in St Davids come to the restaurant of this comfortable hotel. Mains like guinea fowl casserole, or roast teal and several veggie options.

£££-££ **Morgan's Brasserie**, 20 Nun St, St Davids, T01437 720508, Tues-Thurs 1900-2100, Fri, Sat 1830-2100. Booking essential at this popular brasserie. There's a blackboard menu for fresh fish dishes, while other mains might include salt marsh lamb and puy lentils or aubergine, spinach and cashew millefeuille.

£££-££ **The Shed**, Porthgain, T01348 831518, daily 0900-1800 Apr-Oct, Wed-Sat. This tea room/bistro serves snacks, light meals and cream teas, as well as set meals. Lots of fish, booking recommended.

££ **The Nest Bistro**, Grove Pl, Little Haven, T01437 781728, daily from 1900. Lots of fish on the menu here. Mains cost around £13-15, with veggie choices slightly cheaper.

££ **Williams Restaurant and Deli**, courtyard off Main St, Solva T01437 720802, Thur-Sun 1230-1530, 1830-2030. You're advised to book if you want dinner at this cosy restaurant with serves dishes like mussels in white wine, or salmon and sea bass fishcakes. Veggie options available. Rooms also available (www.williamsofsolva.co.uk). Recommended.

££-£ The Sloop Inn, Porthgain, T01348 831449, food Mon-Sat breakfasts 0930-1130, bar meals 1200-1430, 1800-2130, Sun food until 1430. Dating back to 1743, this great inn serves a good range of bar meals, and pricier specials such as monkfish and tomato fondue (£13.95). Maritime theme inside with old ropes, floats etc. Serves real ales.

£ Cantref, 22/23 Cross Square, St Davids, T01437 720422, 1100-1430, 1830-2100, closed Fri and in winter. Good choice for old favourites like jacket potatoes and burgers, as well as filled yorkshire puds and veggie dishes.

£ The Square, Cross Square, St Davids Tues-Sun 1030-1700, closed Jan, Feb. Lovely little café, hung with the owner's artworks and serving cakes, light lunches and all sorts of sandwiches (even peanut butter and tomato).

Fishguard *p574*

£££ Three Main Street, 3 Main Street, T01348 874275 An excellent restaurant with rooms overlooking the Bay serving modern European cuisine with its focus on top class seafood, set in a Georgian townhouse. Beautiful interiors, fresh flowers and comfortable chairs.

£ Royal Oak, Market Square,T01348 872514. Near the town hall, this old inn has a brass memorial plaque outside which gives information about the invasion and has memorabilia dating back to the actual event – including musket balls and muskets. Great pub food and folk music nights on Tuesdays.

Pembroke and around *p576*

££-£ Renaissance Bar One, Main St, T01646 687895, Mon-Thurs 1000-1700, Fri 1000-2300, Sat 1000-late. Lively bar/bistro serving drinks, and Mediterranean style light meals and salads during the day, as well as more substantial dishes in the evening.

£ Boathouse Tearoom, Stackpole Quay, T01646 672058, daily 1030-1730, 1200-1530, closes Nov-Easter but sometimes open from Boxing Day for 2 weeks. Lovely licensed tea room close to beautiful Barafundle Bay. Homemade cakes, filled baguettes and jacket potatoes and imaginative dishes like tomato and chive tart with feta.

£ Henry's Coffee Shop, Main St, T01646 622293, Mon-Sat 0900-1700, Fri, Sat 1900-2130. Hidden away at the back of a gift shop this tea shop caters for those just wanting slices of cake, or light meals during the day. At night it offers dishes such as brie, basil and sundried tomato cheesecake or Peculiar Pie – beef casserole with Old Peculiar since you're asking.

£ Rowlies, 2 Main St, T01646 686172, Mon-Wed 0900-2000, Thurs-Sat 0900-2100. Award winning fish and chips that you can take away or sit in and eat.

Tenby *p577, map p578*

££ La Cave, Upper Frog St, T01834 843038, daily from 1830. Good wine bar/bistro offering a good range of veggie dishes as well as meaty mains that range in price from £7.95 to £15.95 (for tournados).

££ The Cellar, The Esplanade, T01834 845566, daily 1200-1430, 1800-2200. Bistro of the swish Atlantic hotel offering modern Welsh dishes. For more formal dining try The Carrington, also in The Atlantic, which has 4 course table d'hote meals for £18.

££ The Reef Café, St Julian St, T01834 845258, daily 1100-1600, and from 1800. Lively Mediterranean style café with wooden tables and lots of seasidey blue paint. Dishes like squid in chilli sauce or risotto.

££-£ The Bay Tree, Tudor Square, T01834 843516. From 1800. One of the most popular of the mid range places to eat, with plenty of veggie choices and meat dishes.

££-£ Berlinz Coffee House/Bistro, Upper Frog St, T01834 842143, daily 1000-1700 and 1800-2230. Lots of pasta dishes, stakes and chicken at this café/ bistro.

£ Feccis, Upper Frog St, St Georges St, Tenby Well established Italian ice cream parlours where you can settle down to a huge knickerbocker glory at a table, or buy a cone to slurp on the beach. Also have a fish and chip shop on Lower Frog St.

Carmarthen and around *p579*

£££ The Four Seasons Restaurant, Nantgaredig, T01267 290238, booking essential, closed Sun. This restaurant with rooms offers a 4 courses set menu for £25. Mains like rabbit with Dijon mustard, or spinach and Caerphilly pancakes.

£££-££ Y Polyn, Nantgaredig, T01276 290000, lunches 1200-1500, evenings from 1800. Lots of Welsh produce on the menu in this pub which has both a restaurant and bar. Serves real ales too.

££ Glasfryn, Brechfa, T01267 202306, evening meals by arrangement. This B&B happily cooks for non residents if you book. You eat in the conservatory, the food is freshly cooked– mains cost around £8.50 and might be lamb in redcurrant sauce, or cheese and parsnip roulade with apricot stuffing.

££ Halfway Inn, Nantgaredig, T01558 668337, Tue-Sat 1130-1430, 1800-2130, Sun 1200-1345. Pub offering standard bar lunches, as well as more filling meals like roast duck or steak and mushroom pie. Some veggie choices.

££ Quayside Brasserie, Coracle Way, Carmarthen T01267 223000 closed Sun. Well prepared and presented fresh food on the Tywi quay.

££-£ Y Capel Bach Bistro at The Angel, Rhosmaen St, Llandeilo T01558 822765, lunch and dinner, not Sun. Popular pub with a restaurant at the back that serves good food at modest prices. Tapas and sangria on Fridays, and all you can eat pasta for £4.95 on Thu.

£ Barita, 139 Rhosmaen St, Llandeilo, T01558 823444, Mon-Sat from 0930-approx 1700. Excellent deli/café serving great coffee, cakes and imaginative tarts, filled rolls and baguettes. Try your chosen cheese from the counter with sticky onion marmalade. Recommended.

£ The Plough, Felingwm-uchaf, T01267 290019, food Mon-Fri 1800-2100, Sat 1200-1500, 1800-2100. Great traditional pub with oak beams and a real fire in winter. Serves 'farmers' portions' of food, some veggie choices and a good selection of real ales.

£ The Railway Inn, Nantgaredig, from 1800. Unpretentious, but great value food at this family run pub. Good curries and steak and chips.

Laugharne *p580*

££-£ Portreeve Restaurant and Tavern, Market Square, Laugharne, T01994 427476, daily 1215-1430, and Tues-Sat 1830-2130, and Sun 1215-1430. Booking advised. Good bar meals, with lots of Welsh produce as well as pizzas and other dishes. Real ales.

£ Talents Coffee House, Pentre Rd, St Clears, T01994 231826, Mon-Sat 1030-1630 and Bank Hols. Great contemporary café serving fresh local produce like Salt Marsh lamb hot pot, or Welsh black beef casserole, as well as veggie dishes, filled baguettes, juices, local ice cream and homemade cakes. Recommended.

Pubs, bars and clubs

Newport and around *p556*

Dyffryn Arms, Ponfaen, open daily 1100-2300, winter 1200-2300. Fantastic old pub untouched by the 20th, let alone 21st century. Bessie, the landlady, whose family has owned it since 1845, serves beer poured into jugs from behind a serving hatch. Simple living room lined with seats and a real fire in winter.

Tafarn Sinc, Rosebush, T01437 532214. Red corrugated iron exterior hides a great little pub inside, with sawdust on the floor, old settles and lots of old photos. Serves real ales.

Fishguard *p574*

Ship Inn, Newport Rd, Lower Town, Cluttered yet cosy, this rather eccentric little inn is a great place to while away a couple of hours.

St David's and around *p574*

Farmers Arms, Goat St, T01437 720328. The liveliest and most popular pub in St Davids. Serves real ales and has a garden. Bar meals available lunchtimes and evenings.

Druidston Hotel, Druidston T01437 781221. Bohemian hotel and bar high up on the cliffs with great views.

Pembroke and around *p576*

The Watermans Arms, 2 The Green, Pembroke, T01646 682718, food 1200-1400, 1800-2100 daily. Situated just over the bridge, this pub has a verandah where you can sit and look over the water nursing a pint or eating one of their bar meals.

Haverfordwest *p576*

The Fishguard Arms, Old Bridge Close, T01437 768123. Excellent food at reasonable prices and real ales in a friendly atmosphere with live music (jazz, folk, soul) nearly every night.

Carmarthen and around *p579*

The Plough, Felingwm-uchaf, T01267 290019. Real fires and real ales.

The Salutation, Llandeilo, T01558 823325, Traditional pub serving real ales with live music. Jazz on Tues, folk on Wed, bluegrass on Thu and tunes on the piano on Sat.

New Three Mariners, Market St, Laugharne, T1994 427426. Established pub now refurbished and part owned by actor Neil Morrissey. Serves bar food too.

Festivals and events

May or early Jun St Davids Cathedral **Festival**, annual classical music festival, T01437 720271, www.stdavidscathedral.org.uk.

July Fishguard International Music Festival, T01348 873612 – week long classical and popular music festival.

Mid Aug Pembrokeshire County Show, County showground, Haverfordwest, T01437 764331, 3 day agricultural show.

Sep Tenby Arts Festival, annual week long music and arts festival, T01834 84229, www.tenbyartsfest.com.

Activities and tours

Boat trips

Porthgain Boat Trips, Quayside, Porthgain, T01348 831518, www.porthgainboats.ndo.co.uk. Coastal cruises and fishing trips on small, traditional boat. 1 hr dolphin search trip. Times vary so check when booking.

Thousand Islands Expeditions, Cross Square, St Davids, T01437 721721, www.thousandislands.co.uk RSPB cruises to Ramsey Island wildlife reserve, opportunity to land on the islands and chance to see various sea birds as well as basking sharks, pilot whales and dolphins.

Voyages of Discovery, 1 High St, St Davids, T0800 854367, www.ramseyisland.co.uk, whale and dolphin watching and tours of the coast.

Cycling

The western section of the long distance Celtic Trail (220 miles from Chepstow to Fishguard) runs through Pembrokeshire. Information from T0800 243 731, celtic-trail@tsww.com. General information on cycling in Pembrokeshire is contained in a 'Freewheeling Pembrokeshire' pack available from TICs.

Mead Bike Hire, The Mead, Manorbier Newton, Tenby, T01834 871267.

Mikes Bikes, 17 Prendergast, Haverfordwest, T01437 760076, Cycle hire for whole family, open Mon-Sat 0900-1730.

Newport Cycle Centre, Llysmeddyg, East St, Newport, T01239 820008, repairs and hire.

Diving

There are several diving centres/ schools in Pembroke:

Celtic Diving, Main St, Goodwick T01348 874752, www.celticdiving.co.uk. Courses for all in snorkelling, scuba and specialist courses.

Dive Pembrokeshire, The Old School House, Walton West, Little Haven, T01437 781117, www.divepembrokeshire.com, SSI training centre, dive charters and specialist courses.

Pembrokeshire Dive Charters, Neyland Marina, T01646 602941, www.gopdc.co.uk – dive charters and courses.

St Davids Scuba Diving Centre, Caerfai Bay Rd, St davids, T01437 721788, www.dive wales.com –boat charters, dive school, scuba courses and holiday packages.

West Wales Divers, Hasguard Cross, near Little Haven, T01437 781457, www.westwales divers.co.uk. Diving gear for sale and hire.

Horse riding

East Nolton Riding Stables, Nolton, Haverfordwest, T01437 710360, www.eastnolton.com. Riding for all abilities, also have accommodation.

Sycamore Ranch Western Riding Centre, Llawhaden, Narberth, T01437 541298, www. americanhorseriding.com. Western style treks and trails, from 2 hours to all day. Pre book..

Outdoor activities

Sealyham Activity Centre, Wolfcastle, Haverfordwest, T01348 840763, www.sealy ham.com. Run courses from 1- 5 days in kayaking, surfing, rock climbing, coasteering or dinghy sailing. Pre booking needed.

Tyf Adventure, 1 High St, St Davids, and 16 Julian St, Tenby, T0800 132588, 01437 721611, www.tyf.com. Offer coasteering, surfing, kayaking and climbing – taster sessions, half day, full day and longer programmes available.

Sailing

Solva Sailboats, 1 Maes-y-Forwen, Solva, T01437 720972, www.solva.net/solvasailboats. Two hour taster sailing sessions, accompanied sails and longer courses in dinghy and keelboat sailing. Powerboat courses also available.

Surfing

Newsurf, Newgale, T01437 721398, www.newsurf.co.uk, daily surf reports T01437 720698, hire out and sell surf skis, surfboards, body boards and wet suits, and also offer instruction.

Ma Simes Surf Hut, 28 High St, St Davids, T01437 720433, www.masimessurfhut.co.uk andwww.whitesandssurfschool.co.uk. Do surf hire and surfing lessons, on Whitesands beach, also sell surfing kit. From £20 for 2 ½ hrs.
West Wales Wind, Surf and Sailing, Dale, T01646 636642, www.surfdale.co.uk – variety of watersports for all levels – from half day windsurfing and catamaran sailing, to full week courses. Also offer powerboat courses and have a surf school. Equipment for hire.

Walking

The Pembrokeshire Coast Path is a waymarked National Trail that runs 186 miles (300km) around the coast. An annual coast park walk is held – usually each May: a two week guided walk along the route, details as before. There are plenty of opportunities to walk short sections of the route, using buses (summer) to get back to your starting point – details of the Poppit Rocket, Strumble Shuttle and Celtic Coaster service available from TICs or www.pembrokeshiregreenways.co.uk.
Pembrokeshire Discovery, T01437 710720, www.pembrokeshirediscovery.co.uk. For guided walking tours.
Pembrokeshire Walking Holidays T01437 760075, www.pembrokeshire-walking-holidays.co.uk. Self guided walking, includes transfers to the footpath and luggage transfer.
Pembrokeshire Greenways Holidays, T01834 860965, www.pembrokeshire-greenways holidays.co.uk, offer walking packages with luggage transfer, as well as self guided walks using public transport – a special Walk and Ride leaflet is available T01437 776313

Transport

Car

Good road links via the A40 from Haverfordwest to Fishguard, and the M4 beyond to the south. The A487 leads north east up the coast towards Cardigan Bay and Aberystwyth.

Bus

Local bus services run by Richards Brothers (T01239 613756) link **Haverfordwest** with **Fishguard** every 2 hours, **St David's** every hour and **Cardigan** every hour. National Express coaches run from **London** and **Birmingham** to **Pembrokeshire** T08705 808080. Coastal buses operate May-Sep, Puffin Shuttle between **Milford Haven** and **St Davids**, details from www.pembrokeshire.gov.uk/puffin-shuttle; and Celtic Coaster, www.pembrokeshire.gov.uk/celtic-coaster. Pembrokeshire Greenways promotes the use of public transport locally, T01437 7766313. Carmarthen bus station is on Blue Street, just on the north side of the bridge. Services run to **Swansea**, **Cardigan** and **Haverfordwest**.

Train

Fishguard station is next to the ferry terminal on Quay Road. Currently, there is a twice daily service to and from **London Paddington**. **Haverfordwest** train station (01437 746361) is a ten minute walk east of the town centre. Up to 7 daily services link the town with **Swansea**, **Cardiff** and **London Paddington**. Carmarthen train station lies over Carmarthen Bridge, on the south side of the river and about 500m from the bus station. Six daily services link the town to Swansea and Cardiff, two hours away. The Heart of Wales line runs through Carmarthenshire linking the area with **Shrewsbury** and **Swansea**. www.heart-of-wales.co.uk,

Ferry

Fishguard's ferry terminal is in **Goodwick** (Wdig) about a mile from the town centre and is served by rail and bus connections. Stena Line ferries (T0870 570 7070, www.stenaline.com), operates two types of vessel between **Rosslare** in Ireland and **Fishguard**: a high speed catamaran which completes the crossing in just under 2 hours and a conventional superferry which completes the journey in about 3h30. Buses usually meet ferries. A taxi (T01348 874491) into town costs around £3-5

Directory

Internet Public internet access is available at Fishguard TIC in the CyberCafe, £2 per 30 mins. Tenby library, Greenhill Rd, Mon-Fri 0930-1300, 1400-1700, Sat 0930-1230 has free access as does Newport Library, Bridge St, Mon 1400-1700, Wed 1000-1300, Fri 1000-1200, 1400-1700.

Mid Wales

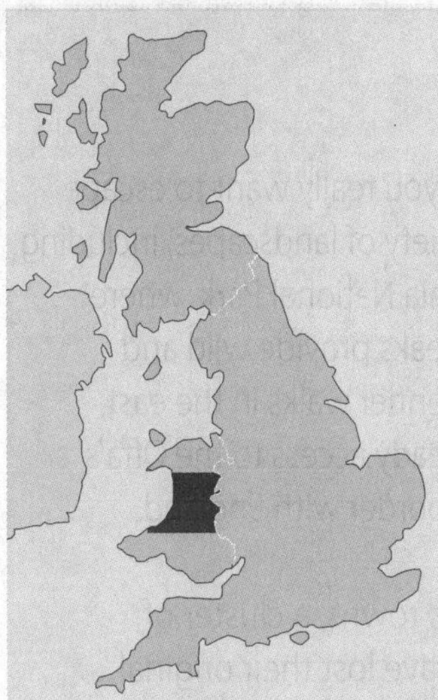

Introduction

Mid Wales is the place to come if you really want to escape the crowds. It encompasses a variety of landscapes, including the southern part of the Snowdonia National Park, where Cadair Idris and its surrounding peaks provide wild and challenging walking. There are gentler walks in the east, where towns like Knighton give ready access to the Offa's Dyke Path, which runs along the border with England.

It is here that you'll find the Wells towns, a cluster of Victorian spa towns that might have lost their original lustre but still retain an air of faded grandeur. And then there's Rhyader, gateway to the Elan Valley – the lakeland of Wales, with enormous reservoirs that can easily be explored on foot or by bike.

Rhyader is also a great place for wildlife watching, its surrounding hills now home to a thriving population of red kites – distinctive birds of prey that have all but disappeared from the rest of Britain. Remote farms operate as feeding stations and you can watch from hides as hundreds of kites swoop down to feed.

There are more wildlife watching opportunities along the coast, where plenty of operators run boat trips that give you the chance to see dolphins, porpoises and seabirds. It's along this stretch of coastline that you'll find places like Harlech, famed for its well preserved castle; Aberystwth, famed for its university; and fishing villages like Aberaron and New Quay which aren't famed for anything but are charming all the same.

★ Don't miss...

1. Visit the **Centre for Alternative Technology**, page 592.
2. Have a meal at the Harbourmaster Hotel, **Aberaeron**, page 599.
3. Go for a drive along the **Abergwesyn Pass**, page 605.
4. Explore the **Elan Valley**, page 604.
5. Picnic on **Harlech** beach, page 591.

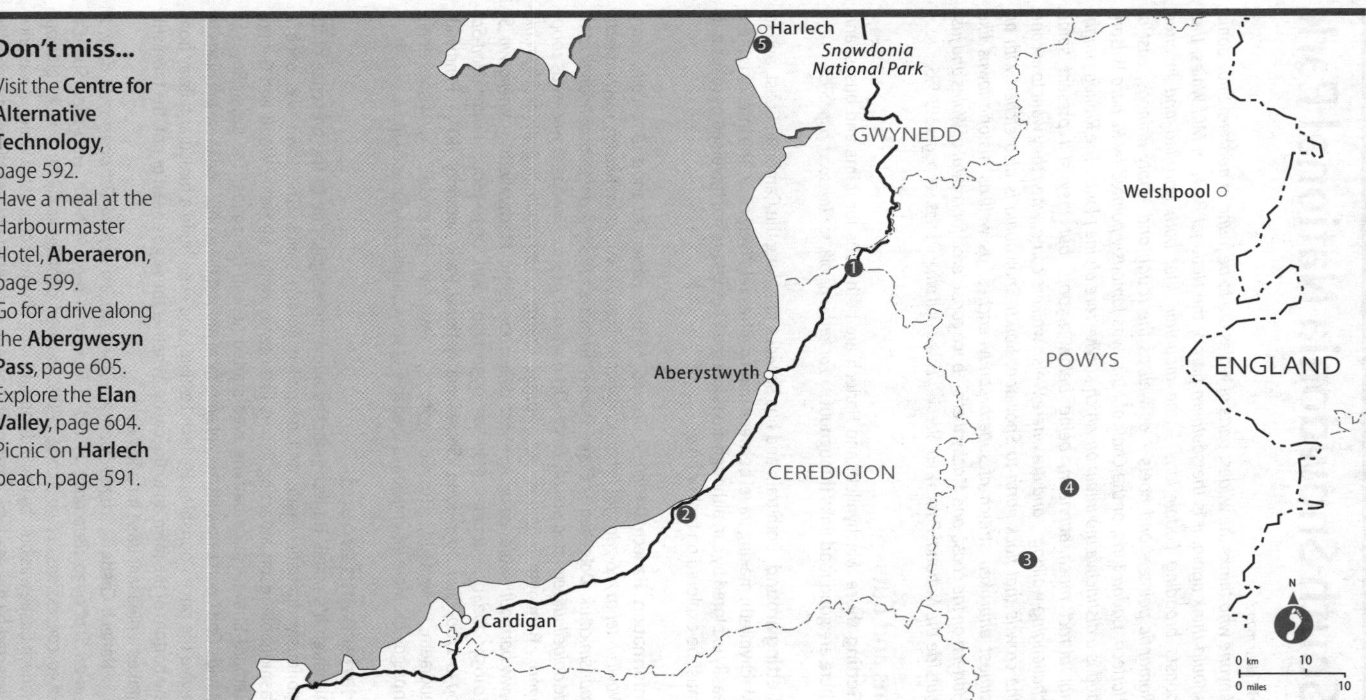

South Snowdonia National Park

➔ *Colour map 3*

Anyone who thinks the wildest parts of Wales are to be found in northern Snowdonia should think again. It is the southern part of the National Park, in Mid Wales, that boasts brooding Cadair Idris – the mountain that both horrified and inspired Romantic painters and poets – as well as the rough and empty Rhinogs, east of Harlech. Cadair Idris, or the Chair of Idris, was famously painted by Richard Wilson, and is a distinctive mountain on which survive rare alpine plants. The Rhinogs might not attract much attention, being below 2,500ft, but they still present some challenging walking – and are where Welsh walkers come, when they want to escape the crowds that flock north to Snowdon. South Snowdonia is also etched with an almost unbroken stretch of superb sandybeaches, as well as historic towns like Harlech on the coast, and Machynlleth – once considered for capital of Wales and just outside the National Park. ➤➤ *For Sleeping, Eating and other listings, see pages 593-595.*

Ins and outs

Getting there Machynlleth and Harlech are both hubs for trains and buses, and there are good road links throughout. ➤➤ *For further details, see Transport, page 595.*

Getting around Both train and bus services run along the Cambrian Coast, and to Machynlleth, making travel between main centres relatively easy. The interior is most easily explored by car, although areas like the Rhinogs are not traversed by roads and must be explored on foot or bike.

Information **Harlech** ⓘ *High St, T01766 780658, Easter-Oct 1000-1800 daily, (from Nov-Feb tel 01766 780356) ticharlech@hotmail.com, www.harlech-i.com, www.harlech-tourism.co.uk.* **Dolgellau** ⓘ *Eldon Square, T01341 422888, ticdolgellau@hotmail.com, tic.dolgellau@eyri-npa.gov.uk, Easter-Oct daily 1000-1800, Nov-Easter weekends 1000-1700.* **Barmouth** ⓘ *Station Rd, T01341 280787, barmouth.tic@gwynedd.gov.uk, www.barmouth-wales.co.uk Apr-Sept daily 1000-1800.* **Machynlleth** ⓘ *Maengwyn St T01654 702401, summer Mon-Sat 0930-1730, Sun 0930-1600; winter Mon-Sat 0930-1700, Sun 0930-1600.* **Snowdonia National Park Authority HQ** ⓘ Penrhyndeudraeth, Gwynedd, T01766 770274, www.eryri-npa.gov.uk; www.snowdonia-npa.gov.uk. More information is available at www.secretsnowdonia.co.uk.

Harlech and around

Although it's small, Harlech punches above its weight, due to the presence of its gloriously dramatic castle and unspoiled golden sands. The town was once a fashionable resort attracting figures like Gustav Holst, Sir Henry Wood and George Bernard Shaw – nude bathing even started here in the 1930s. The swish Royal St Davids Golf Course now attracts players from around the world, and there are plans to revive the once flourishing Harlech Festival, and even build a funicular railway from the bottom of the town up to the castle. Whether these go ahead or not, the town still makes a pleasant base for a few days.

Harlech Castle ⓘ *T01766 780552, 1 Apr-1 Jun, 29 Sep-26 Oct 0930-1700 daily, 2 Jun-28 Sept 0930-1800 daily, 27 Oct-31 Mar 0930-1600 Mon-Sat, 1100-1600 Sun, £3, £2.50 concessions, £8.50 family, CADW.* Perched photogenically on a rocky outcrop, Harlech Castle was built by Edward 1 around 1283 after his conquest of Wales. It was once protected by the sea (which has now receded), but despite its seemingly impregnable position was captured more than once and had to withstand several long sieges. Owain Glyndwr took it in 1404, it was recaptured, then was held by the Lancastrians for 7 years during the Wars of the Roses – a feat that inspired the famous song 'Men of Harlech'. The castle's battlements are extremely well preserved, and the short climb (on a clear day) is well worth it for the views across the sea and over to Snowdon.

Harlech's beach is excellent, with soft, clean golden sand – the sort of place where kids still make sand castles and paddle without missing their computer games. The Morfa Harlech National Nature Reserve of sand dunes and estuary protects land where you can see wildlife such as redshank, shelduck and ringed plover.

A couple of miles away, set into the sand dunes at Llandanwg, is the fascinating little church of St Tanwg. The church is Early Middle Ages, but gravestones have been found here dating back to the 5th-century. The church was used until 1845 but then fell into disrepair. However it was later restored and candelit services are sometimes held here. Further south is **Llanbedr** ⓘ *www.llanbedr.com*, where there's a good pub and where a narrow road leads down to **Shell Island** ⓘ *T01341 241453, www.shellisland.co.uk, daily 1 Mar-30 Nov, £5 per car high season, £4 low season*, a peninsula cut off at high tide where you can go boating, birdwatching or fishing. There's also a restaurant and camp site.

There are a number of impressive prehistoric sites in this part of Wales, some of which can be seen south of Llandanwg at Dyffryn Ardudwy on the A496. A little path leads behind a school to the Dyffryn Burial Chamber, two Neolithic communal burial chambers sited close together.

Barmouth

Barmouth was once a busy port and there are reminders of its maritime heritage in the Ty Gwyn Museum (summer, daily, free) with finds from local shipwrecks. It was here that Henry Tudor's Uncle plotted his campaign against Richard III – resulting in Henry becoming Henry VII after the Battle of Bosworth. When the railway came to Barmouth in 1860, maritime trade declined and the town became a fashionable resort for genteel Victorians, attracted by the town's picturesque setting, squeezed beneath the cliffs at the mouth of the Mawddach Estuary. Today the town is more populist than picturesque, a bustling resort with a mish mash of amusements, busy bars and gift shops – in addition to the excellent Blue Flag beach and unspoiled surrounding countryside. It's popular with sailors, particularly each June when the **Three Peaks Yacht Race** ⓘ *T01341 280298*, starts here.

Dolgellau

At the head of the Mawddach Estuary, Dolgellau was accurately described in 1932 by HV Morton as 'a hard little mountain town. Its houses are made of the mountains. They look ...as though they were made to endure forever.' With its stone buildings and narrow streets, this pleasant market town seems to have changed little. It's full of history: Owain Glyndwr assembled a parliament here in 1404, and in the 19th-century it became a Welsh Klondike when the discovery of gold in the local rocks sparked a mini gold rush. Today it attracts walkers and outdoor enthusiasts seeking a good base from which to explore nearby Cadair Idris, go cycling along the Mawddach Trail, fish in the rivers, or go birdwatching in the **Mawddach Valley** ⓘ *RSPB, Dolgellau, T01341 422071*. There are plenty of walks to choose from including the Torrent Walk, along the banks of the Clywedog river, or the Precipice Walk round Llyn Cynwch.

Make time to seek out **Our Lady of Sorrows** church, Meyrick St, built due to a determined Maltese priest, Fr Francis Scalpell. He came to the town in 1939 when it was mainly Welsh speaking and began celebrating mass in an old stable. He eventually built a makeshift church with the help of Italian POWs but, determined to build something better, wrote 25,000 letters all over the world asking for funding. The money was eventually supplied by an anonymous stranger and the church opened in 1966.

A couple of miles north of town are the ruins of **Cymer Abbey** ⓘ *Daily 1000-1600, CADW free*, a once isolated abbey (now sadly next to a caravan site). It was founded in 1198 by the Cistercians, an order that sought remote locations.

South of Barmouth

You'll find the resort towns of Aberdovey (Aberdyfi) and Tywyn, close to the green and scenic Dyfi Valley. Aberdyfi is the prettier of the two, while Tywyn is home to the **Talyllyn Railway** ⓘ *T01654 710472, www.talyllyn.co.uk, daily end Mar-early Nov, some days in Feb, Mar and Dec, £9.50 day rover, 5-15 yrs £2 if accompanied, 8 day runabout fare £28, £14 child*, a narrow gauge railway that steams 7 miles through the countryside to the mountain halt of Nant Gwernol, Abergynolwyn. You can use the train to get to the starting point of a number of walks in the area, such as the Pendre station walk (4 miles), and the Dolgoch Falls.

Machynlleth

Pronounced Mah-hun-kthleth and just outside the Snowdonia National Park, this busy market town is a good base for exploring southern Snowdonia. With a reputation for being 'a bit hippy', 'Mac' as it's known to locals is a mix of galleries, pubs, wholefood shops and historic buildings. **Parliament House** ⓘ *Maengwyn St, T01654 702827, Easter-Oct, Mon-Sat 1000-1700, other times by arrangement, free*, is a 15th century building where Owain Glyndwr assembled a Welsh parliament in 1404. Displays cover Glyndwr's life and explain his importance in Welsh history.

Plas Machynlleth, is a 17th-century mansion that now houses **Celtica** ⓘ *T01654 702702, www.celticawales.com, daily 1000-1800, last admission 1640, £4.95, £3.95 children, £15 family*, which aims to bring to life the history and culture of the Celts. It focuses mainly on the Celts in Wales, but also includes the Cornish, Manx, Bretons, Scots and Irish. Downstairs is a 'trip through time' tour, where you don a headset and walk past figures and scenes from Britain's Celtic past – so you can hear, see and smell life as it was. Upstairs are interesting and educational displays, with exhibits on everything from language (you can hear recordings of six Celtic languages), art and the Celts place in history. The section on Celtic beliefs explains the importance of water. Offerings were frequently made to it, which explains the importance of the Lady of the Lake in Arthurian legend, and human sacrifice was common: unfortunate victims were often left in bogs, their remains being preserved for centuries by the acidic, oxygen free environment.

> *Dyfi Valley Days tickets are joint tickets for Celtica, the Centre for Alternative Technology and King Arthur's Labyrinth. It can save up to £5, and also gives 20% discount on the Talylln Railway. Tickets available at any of the 3 sites, www.DyfiValleyDays.com*

The Museum of Modern Art (MOMA), ⓘ *Penralt St, T01654 703355, www.tabernac. dircon.co.uk, Mon-Sat 1000-1600, free*, is a cultural and performing arts centre which has permanent displays of modern Welsh art and regular temporary exhibitions.

Three miles north of Machynlleth on the A487 (and the Sustrans 8 cycle route) is the **Centre for Alternative** Technology ⓘ *T01654 705950, www.cat.org.uk, daily 1000-1700 or dusk, Jan-Easter £5, £3 child, £15 family; Easter-end Oct £7, £4 child, £20 family*, which deserves its reputation as one of the premiere attractions in Wales – and despite its worthy sounding name, is certainly not just aimed at people who spin their own wool and know 101 ways with tofu. The Centre was established in 1974 on an abandoned slate quarry, the idea being to build a self sufficient community, both embracing and promoting 'green' technologies. You reach the centre via an extraordinary water balanced cliff railway, similar to a cable car, and then watch an introductory video on the centre's establishment and ethos. The rest of the site is taken up with demonstrations of 'alternative' technologies and how they can be applied to modern urban living. There's a prototype low energy house, with displays asking you to think about everything from the distance your food has travelled, to using plants to improve air quality. Working organic plots demonstrate the principles of productive organic gardening, there are working solar panels and wind energy pumps, even a selection of eco toilets. There's also a good value vegetarian café doing hearty soups, cakes and salads – allow a good half day for your visit.

Sleeping

Harlech p590

B **Castle Cottage**, High Street, opp TIC, Harlech, T780479, F 781251, www.castlecottageharlech.co.uk. Family run restaurant with rooms in the centre of Harlech. The modern Welsh cuisine of the restaurant is a feature.

B **Cemlyn**, High Street T780425, www.cemlynrestaurant.co.uk, 2 en suite rooms, Very comfortable and attractively furnished rooms above excellent restaurant. Try and get the room with the wonderful views of the castle.

C **Hafod Wen**, 1 mile south of Harlech on A496, T780356, www.harlechguesthouse.co.uk, Delightful Edwardian house set in 8 acres of grounds, with private steps leading down to the beach. Some rooms have balconies and glorious views of the bay. Rooms are individually furnished and the atmosphere is comfortable and welcoming. Meals available.

D **Gwrach Ynys**, Talsarnau, on A496, 2 miles north of Harlech, T01766 780742, F 01766 781199, www.gwrachynys.co.uk, Lovely Edwardian house with great views over the mountains, and spacious and tasteful rooms. It's very welcoming and makes a relaxing base for walking and exploring nearby Portmerion and the beaches of Harlech.

D **Pensarn Hall**, on A496, near Llanbedr, T01341 241236, www.pensar-hall.co.uk. Spacious and cosy Victorian house set in lovely gardens, with good views over the Artro Estuary. A good base for walkers as the owners are happy to dry your gear and do you a packed lunch. There's also a self catering cottage.

F **YHA hostel**, Plas Newydd, Llanbedr, T01341 241287, open Apr-Oct. Dormitory accommodation in the centre of the village.

Barmouth p591

C **Ty'r Graig Castle**, Llanaber Road, Barmouth, T01341 280470, F 281260, www.tyrgraig.castle.btinternet.co.uk, Striking Victorian house built as a summer retreat on a rock overlooking the town. Lovely stained glass windows and wood panelling, and comfortable rooms. 2 have balconies where you can sit and watch the sun go down over the bay. Recommended.

Machynlleth p592

L **Ynyshir Hall**, Eglwysfach, near Machynlleth, T01654 781209, F 781366, www.ynyshir.hall.co.uk, 7 suites. For real indulgence you can splash out at this luxurious hotel set in its own tranquil grounds, close to the Ynys-hir RSPB reserve. Only suites are available, all individually decorated with thick carpets, swagged curtains and plump cushions. Special breaks that include dinner are better value than one night's stay and worth investigating.

D **Penrhos Arms Hotel**, Cenmaes, near Machynlleth T/F 01650 511243. Lovely elegant rooms in this popular pub a few miles from the centre of town. Décor is light and bright, with antiques dotted around: one room has a 4 poster.

Eating

Harlech p590

£££ **Castle Cottage**, High Street, opp TIC, Harlech, T01766 780479, restaurant with rooms serving evening meals, specialising in Welsh produce. Dishes might include local lamb or steak. 3 course meal for £24.50.

£££ **Cemlyn**, High Street, Harlech T01766 780425, teas Tues-Sun from 1100, dinners from 1900. Light lunches like Welsh rarebit available during the day, while evening meals might include red sea bream, liver and bacon casserole, or lentil pie. 2 courses £21, 3 courses £23.

£££ **Hafod Wen**, 1 mile south of Harlech on A496, T01766 780356, dinner at 1900. Dine by candlelight in this romantic guesthouse which holds 'dinner party' meals where residents all dine together – along with locals 'in the know'. It's a set 3 course meal (£21), and includes home grown vegetables and freshly made bread. Vegetarians happily catered for – reservations essential.

££ **Yr Ogog Bistro**, High Street, Harlech T01766 780888, daily from 1900. Bistro serving range of steaks, chicken dishes and some veggie options.

££-£ **Yr Hen Feudy**, Llanbedr, T01341 241555, just off the main road, Mon-Sat 1000-1600. Outdoor seats for summertime tea and cakes, and filling main meals like curries, steaks and steak and kidney pie.

Cafés

£££ **Cemlyn**, High Street T780425, teas Tues-Sun from 1100, dinners from 1900. Voted top tea place in Wales for 2003, this tasteful teashop/restaurant serves a wide variety of teas including Rose Congou, Russian Caravan and Formosa Oolong – team a pot with a rich brownie or freshly baked tiffin and relax on the little terrace. Recommended.

£ **Weary Walkers Café**, High street, Harlech Mon 1000-1700, Wed closed, rest 0900-1700. Range of snacks and light meals in busy café.

Barmouth *p591*

££ **Greeners at Ty'r Graig Castle**, Llanaber Road, Barmouth, T01341 280470, Mon-Sat 1900-2030 (2100 on Sat), plus Sunday lunch. Good selection of modern Welsh dishes, as well as veggie choices, in this quality restaurant. 3 course Sunday lunch available for £12.50. Traditional Welsh dishes on Monday nights.

££ **The Bistro**, Church Street, Barmouth T01341 281009 1900-2100, closed Wed. Rustic bistro décor and good range of dishes, including some veggie options.

££ **The Indian Clipper**, Church Street, Barmouth T01341 280252. Summer daily 1800-2200, Nov-Apr, Thurs-Sat only 1800-2200. If nothing but curry will do, this highly rated balti house is worth seeking out.

Cafés

£ **Wannabe's Coffee Bar**, High Street, Barmouth T01341 280820. Have coffee and cakes then browse in the adjoining outdoor gear shop.

Dolgellau *p591*

£ **Lemon Grass**, Finsbury Square, T01341 421300, Sun-Thurs 1200-1400, 1700-2330; Fri, Sat 1200-1400, 1700-2345. Indian restaurant, offers 'eat as much as you like' buffet on Sundays for £9.95.

££ **Y Sospan**, Queen's Square, T01341 423174. The tea room serves cream teas for around £3, while the restaurant upstairs serves main courses like lamb from 1830.

Cafés

£ Yr Hen Efail, by car park , Dollgellau T01341 422977. Tea rooms with outside seating area serving light meals such as toasties, jacket potatoes and egg and chips.

Machynlleth and around *p592*

£££ **Ynyshir Hall**, Eglwysfach, near Machynlleth, T01654 781209, daily 1200-3130, 1900-2030, booking essential. If you can't afford to stay at this swish hotel you can maybe stretch to one of their highly rated meals. Set menus only, lunch 3 courses for £28.50, dinner £42. Tell them in advance if you're veggie.

££ **Penrhos Arms Hotel**, Cenmaes, near Machynlleth T01650 511243, food Mon-Fri 1830-2100, Sat 1200-1400, 1830-2100, Sun 1200-1400. The interior of this great pub is modern and simple, with plain wooden tables, stone walls and a fire in winter. Bar meals such as Welsh black beef and mushroom pie £5.95, while mains in the restaurant might include Eastern spiced lamb £8.50 or grilled trout £9.50. Veggie choices available. There's a lovely garden for summer nights.

£ **Wholefood Café**, Maengwyn St Mon-Sat 0900-1700, Sun 1000-1600 (shorter hours in winter). If you're after some dandelion coffee, a baked potato or a veggie meal, then you can try this wholefood café in this centre of Machynthlleth.

£ **Taj Mahal**, T01654 703088. The pink swathes on the ceiling, chandeliers and plump pink chairs seem slightly out of place among the grey stone that dominates the town, but is a cheery sight.

£ **Y Bwtri**, Maengwyn St Eat in or takeway at this veggie café. As well as beans on toast, sandwiches, and salads there are veggie pancakes for £4.95.

££-£ **Victoria Inn**, Llanbedr, T01341 241213. Likeable, busy inn offering a good range of meals. Beer garden is popular in summer.

£ **Wynnstay Arms**, Maengwyn St, Machynlleth T01654 702941. Busy pub which also serves decent food.

For an explanation of the sleeping and eating price codes used in this guide, see the inside front cover. Other relevant information is provided in the Essentials chapter, page 36.

Entertainment

Harlech *p590*

Harlech Dispersed Gallery, artworks change every 2 months and are displayed throughout Harlech, in galleries, shops and gardens, T01341 241348.

Theatr Ardudwy, films, plays and musicals, T01766 780667, theatr.ardudwy@virgin.net.

Festivals and events

Jul Barmouth Music Festival. Live music with everything from folk to jazz, T01341 281112.

Mid-Jul Sesiwn Fawr, Dolgellau, the 'big session' is a music festival with live bands performing in venues all over town, www.sesiwnfawr.demon.co.uk.

Early Sep Barmouth Arts Festival, established festival that includes music and cabaret, T01341 280392.

Late Sep Barmouth Festival of Walking, week of guided walks in Barmouth area, details from Barmouth TIC.

Activities and tours

General outdoor activities

CMC Pensarn Harbour, Llanbedr, T01341 241646, www.cmcpensarn.org.uk Outdoor pursuits centre that doing residential activities.

Golf

Aberdovey Golf Club, seaside links, T0800 0962057, **www.aberdovey.co.uk.**

Royal St Davids Golf Club, Harlech, T01766 780361, www.royalstdavids.co.uk, championship links, said to be the most difficult par 69 in the world.

Mountain biking

Greenstiles, 4 Maengwyn St, Machynlleth, T01654 703543 mountain bike hire, as well as selling gear and accessories. Information on mountain biking around Machynlleth from www.mach-off-road.org.uk.

Rhiw Goch Ski and Mountain Bike Centre, Bronaber, Trawsfynydd, T01766 540578, www.skiinguk.com, daily, mountain bike hire.

Pony trekking

Abergwynant Farm and Pony Trekking Centre, Penmaenpool, Dolgellau T01341 422377 2 hr and 1 hr treks.

Quad biking

Madian Quads, Ty Mawr, Penegoes, Machynlleth, T01654 702746, www.madianquads.co.uk offer 1 and 2 hr treks at £25 and £45, also 1 hr trek for children £20.

Skiing

Rhiw Goch Ski and Mountain Bike Centre, Bronaber, Trawsfynydd, T01766 540578, www.skiinguk.com, dry ski slope open daily, snowboard lessons for beginners.

Walking

The area offers everything from challenging walks on Cader Idris and the Rhinogs, to gentle strolls through Bron Y Graig park, near Harlech.

Transport

Bus

Buses run between the major towns, and Crosville Wales coaches run from South Wales to **Dolgellau**. T0870 608 2608.

Car

The M4 from the south links to the A470 to **Dolgellau** and close to Machynlleth, while the northern stretch of the A470, linked to both the A55 and A5, joins the A496 which runs along the coast.

Train

Services from the Midlands run to **Machynlleth** and link up with the **Cambrian Coaster** which stops at **Harlech** and **Barmouth**. Trains also run to **Twyn**.

Directory

Internet Free access at Barmouth library, Talbot Square. Free access at Twyn library, Neptune Rd, T01654 710104, closed Wed, Sat afternoon and Sun. Free access at **Machynlleth library**, Maengwyn St Tues, Wed 1000-1300, 1400-1700, Fri 1100-1300, 1400-1900, Sat 0930-1300. Free access at **Harlech library**, off Fford Isaf beaches, as well as historic towns like Harlech on the coast, and Machynlleth – once considered for capital of Wales and just outside the National Park.

Ceredigion Coast

→ Colour map 3

The area know today as Ceredigion stretches south of the Dyfi Estuary to Cardigan, a ribbon of coastal communities stretched out along Cardigan (Ceredigion) Bay. This western coast is the haunt of seals, sailors and students, dotted with hidden bays and pretty fishing villages. It's a great place to come for marine wildlife watching and there are some lovely beaches too. The main settlement is the Victorian resort of Aberystwyth, now a lively student town. But if you take your time you'll also discover pretty seaside villages which feel almost Cornish in character, such as Georgian Aberaeron and bustling New Quay – a favourite haunt of the poet Dylan Thomas. ▸▸ *For Sleeping, Eating and other listings, see pages 599-602.*

Ins and outs

Getting there Trains from the Midlands run to Machynlleth, where you can then travel on to Aberystwth. Express buses run from Bristol and Cardiff to Aberystwyth. ▸▸ *For further details, see Transport, page 602.*

Getting around The narrow gauge steam Vale of Rheidol railway can take you inland from Aberystwyth to Devils Bridge, otherwise it is difficult to explore the more remote areas without your own transport. Trains don't run between Aberystwyth and Cardigan and you'll have to rely on buses, which link towns along the coast such as Cardigan, New Quay, Aberaeron and Aberystwyth.

Information Aberystwyth TIC ⓘ *Terrace Rd, T01970 612125, aberystwythtic @ceredigion.gov.uk, Jun-Aug daily 1000-1800, rest of year Mon-Sat 1000-1700.* **New Quay TIC** ⓘ *Church St, T01545 560865, newquaytic@ ceredigion.gov.uk, Jul-early Sep daily 1000-1800, Apr-Jun, Oct Mon-Sat 1000-1700, closes for lunch.* **Aberaeron** TIC ⓘ *The Quay, T01545 570602, aberaerontic@ ceredigion.gov.uk, Mon-Sat 1000-1800, Apr-Oct, 1000-1700 Nov-Mar, opens Sun at peak times, closes for lunch.* **Cardigan TIC** ⓘ *Theatr Mwldan, Bath House Rd T01239 613230, cardigantic@ceredigion.gov.uk, www.visitcardigan.com, www.ceredigion. gov.uk, Jul-Aug 0900-1800 daily, closes for lunch, Sep- Jun Mon-Sat 0900-1300, 1400-1700.* More information on Ceredigion can be found at www.ceredigion.gov.uk and www.pumlumon. org.uk and www.caridganshirecoastandcountry.com. Cardigan Bay also has a conservation website www.cardiganbaysac.org.uk.

Aberystwyth

Aberystwyth is both a student town and a resort. The university, founded in the 19th-century, is now centred on a modern campus above the town, close to the National Library of Wales. The town grew from what is now the suburb of Llanbadarn Fawr, a settlement dating back to the 6th-century when St Padarn established a monastic settlement here. It became a popular seaside resort from the early 19th-century onwards, the numbers of visitors being swelled still more after the coming of the railway in 1864: its promenade, seafront Regency terraces and dowager hotels are constant reminders that this was once the 'Brighton of Wales'. Today it's a resort with a radical edge: a Nationalist town, home of the Welsh Language Society and a place with a thriving art and music scene.

The former Coliseum theatre is now the opulent home of Aberystwyth's TIC, and **Ceredigion Museum** ⓘ *Terrace Rd, T01970 633088, Mon-Sat 1000-1700, free*, which provides an unusual setting for a permanent collection on life in Victorian Wales, and changing exhibitions of art and crafts.

From here you can walk along Marine Terrace to Constitution Hill, which rises 450ft and is topped with a Camera Obscura: a cross between a telescope and a CCTV system, this has a 14in lens and allows you to look over the mountains and sea, and watch what's happening in town. It can be reached on foot or by the **Cliff Railway** ⓘ *T01970 617642, mid Mar-early Nov, daily 1000-1700 (1800 July and Aug) £2.25 return,* which opened in 1896 and is the longest in Britain. Now powered by electricity it was originally water balanced when it opened for Victorian pleasure trippers.

At the other end of town are the remains of Aberystwyth Castle (CADW, free), built by Edward I in the late 13th-century. It saw plenty of action, withstanding several sieges including holding out for the king during the Civil War, until 1646 when its forces surrendered to Parliament.

Out of town at the university campus is the **National Library of Wales** ⓘ *Penglais Hill, T01970 632834, www.llgc.org.uk, Mon-Sat 1000-1700, closed first full week Oct, free*, where extensive collections give a good insight into aspects of Welsh culture. Exhibits include the oldest surviving manuscripts in the Welsh language. Further up the hill is the **Arts Centre** ⓘ *T01970 622882, Mon-Sat 1000-2000 (galleries shut at 1700), summer Suns 1400-1700*, which houses the university's ceramic collection.

Penglais Road leads to the **Penglais Nature Reserve** set in a former quarry. It has a variety of tree and plant life, with a fine display of bluebells in the spring. Not far from the railway station in a fine Edwardian building, is the university's **School of Art,** ⓘ *Buarth, Mon-Fri 1000-1300, 1400-1700, www.aber.ac.uk, free,* where you can see some fine examples of Welsh art from the university's permanent collection.

Vale of Rheidol

East of Aberystwyth is the Vale of Rheidol, a lush wooded valley most famous as the location of the Devil's Bridge and waterfalls – described by George Borrow in Wild Wales as 'one of the most remarkable locations in the world' and a long standing tourist trap. You can easily reach Devil's Bridge from Aberystwyth on the **Vale of Rheidol Railway** ⓘ *Park Avenue, T01970 625819, www.rheidolrailway.co.uk, Apr-Oct, £11, £2 child*, a narrow gauge steam railway built in 1902 to serve the lead mines and passengers of the valley. The journey through the gorgeous valley takes about an hour.

Devil's Bridge consists of 3 bridges stacked on top of one another, above the Mynach river. There's the 20th-century road bridge, below which is the Middle Bridge, erected in 1753, and the original Pont-y-gwr-Drwg (Bridge of the evil man) which was built in the 11th-century by monks from a nearby Cistercian Abbey. Access to the bridges and the Devil's Punchbowl is by a turnstile (£1 coin). On the opposite side of the road is the entrance to a nature trail and path which lets you see the bridges and the stunning **Mynach Falls** ⓘ *Easter-end Oct 0945-1700, £2.50, £1.25 child paid to attendant, otherwise £2 in coin operated turnstile.*

Bwlch Nant Yr Arian visitor centre ⓘ *Ponterwyd, T01970 890694, daily 1000-1700 summer, 1000-dusk winter* gives access to waymarked walks and mountain bike trails, as well as a café. From the visitor centre you can see red kites swooping in to be fed (ⓘ *daily 1500, 1400 in winter*) – in fact if you're on the A44 around that time you'll see the birds flying low over the roadway. You can do more bird watching further north off the A487 at the RSPB's Ynys-hir Reserve (see activities).

Llywernog Silver-lead Mines ⓘ *Ponterwyd, T01970 890620, mid Mar-end Oct 1000-1800 Tue-Sun and Mons in Jul, Aug, last admission 1600, £5.50, £3.50 children, £16 family*. Speculators came to this area in the 1860 and you can join a 45 min underground tour and try your hand at panning for minerals.

Aberaeron

Aberaeron comes as something of a surprise in this most Welsh of areas, as it looks distinctly English. It's a neat, orderly Georgian planned town, built almost from scratch in the 19th-century, with wide streets and houses painted in cheery colours, round a pretty harbour. It was built by the Rev Alban Gwynne, who spent his wife's considerable inheritance creating the village – designed by John Nash. His intention was to create a new port for mid Wales.

About 2 miles away on the A482 is **Llanerchaeron** ⓘ *T01558 825147, mid Mar-early Nov, Wed-Sun, house 1130-1630, farm and garden 1100-1700, £4, £2 child, £10 family, NT*, a Welsh 18th-century gentry estate, once common in the area. The house, designed by John Nash, has been restored and is furnished in Edwardian style, with fascinating servants' quarters and a service courtyard with a dairy, laundry and brewery. The estate operates as a working organic farm.

New Quay

There's a salty tang to New Quay, a little village squeezed in picturesque Cornish fashion around a harbour. Dylan Thomas often visited – and drank in the pubs, even living here for a time in 1944-45. It was here that he started work on Under Milk Wood, so the town has a good claim to be the fictional Llareggub in the play. One of the pubs, The Black Lion, witnessed a fight between Thomas and William Killick, a friend who had returned from war service to discover that his wife, Vera, had been using his army pay to support Thomas and Caitlin. Killick suspected some sexual shenanigans, and they argued. Killick then got a machine gun and hand grenade, went to Majoda, the house the Thomas' were renting and fired. He was arrested and tried for attempted murder. He got off and Thomas sensibly left New Quay soon after. You can pick up a good, free Dylan Thomas walking trail of the village in the TIC. The village is very lively in summer, you can go on dolphin watching boat trips (see activities) and there are plenty of pubs and places to eat.

A couple of miles away is **New Quay Honey Farm** ⓘ *T01545 560822 May-Oct daily 1000-1730, £2.75, £1.60 children, £7.20 family*, with a small but informative exhibition on the life of the honey bee. Glass cases allow you to see bees coming and going to a huge honeycomb, and there are panels explaining the different ways they communicate. There's also a great café open all year (see cafes).

South of New Quay

The coastline here takes on an even more Cornish character, with stunning beaches and hidden coves linked by a maze of narrow, high banked lanes teeming with wild flowers. **Llangrannog** (parking £2 in peak season) is a charming little village with a tiny beach, bustling old pub, cafe and a little shop selling surfing gear and buckets and spades.

Then there's **Penbryn beach**, owned by the National Trust, where trails lead to the Corbalani stone, burial site of a 5th-century chief; Tresaith (parking £1 in field above), another unspoiled cove where a waterfall cascades down from the cliffs, and the busier, more popular beach at Aberporth. The most beautiful and unspoiled spot along here is **Mwnt** (parking £1.50), a remote headland owned by the National Trust, with a secluded, sandy beach below, reached by steep steps. Mwnt was a stopping place for the bodies of saints being taken to Bardsey Island, their traditional burial ground and was also on a pilgrims route to St Davids. There's a lonely little church Holy Cross Y Mwnt, the oldest in Ceredigion. It's a 13th-century building, but built on much older foundations. If you go in you can see that a small window on the north side has been walled up. It's thought that this let lepers, and others not allowed into the building, observe the service from outside.

Cardigan

With such a gorgeous coastline to explore you are unlikely to want to linger long in Cardigan, though it's pleasant enough. Of most interest is the **Cardigan Heritage Centre** ⓘ *T01239 614404, Apr-Oct daily 1000-1700, 1100-1600 Nov- mid Mar, £2, £1 child, £5 family*, on the ground floor of an 18th-century warehouse. It tells the story of the town, once one of the principal ports on Wales' west coast, right back to its pre-Norman days.

Outside the town, a short drive on the B4548 to Gwbert, is the **Cardigan Island Coastal Farm Park** ⓘ *T01239 612196, www.cardiganisland.com, mid Mar-early Nov £3*, where you can walk (or take a tractor ride) to a viewing point to spot seals that breed in the caves below. There are also various farmed animals such as wallabies, a llama, emus, ponies etc some of which children can feed if they wish (special feed is for sale). There's also a café with seats looking out to sea (no seat indoors so not one for a rainy day).

Cenarth

The A484 from Cardigan leads to pretty, but supremely touristy, Cenarth. This little village is famed for its tumbling rapids and salmon leap (car park £1.50), easily accessed from the road, and first mentioned by a 12th-century traveller Gerald Cambrensis, who passed through the village recruiting for the crusades and wrote of salmon 'leaping as high as the tallest spear'. It was high on the Victorian's 'must see' list. You can also visit the **National Coracle Centre** ⓘ *T01239 710980, www.coraclecentre.co.uk, Easter-end Oct Sun-Fri 1030-1730, £3, children £1.50*, which contains coracles (small round boats dating back to the ice age) from around the world. Cenarth was once a centre for coracle fishing. The centre is housed in a 17th-century flour mill, and you can still see the water wheel. The village has a craftshop, several pubs and a tea shop.

One of the best places for wildlife watching is at the Welsh Wildlife Centre, tucked away off the A478 at **Teifi Marshes Nature Reserve** ⓘ *Cilgerran, T01239 621600, reserve open all year, visitor centre Apr-Oct 1030-1700, free, £3 parking*. The reserve encompasses river, marshland and woods and has walking trails which give you the opportunity to spot (if you're lucky) their resident otters, the rare Cetti's warbler, 18 species of dragonfly and visitors such as sedge warblers and wildfowl. The visitor centre has a very good café (1030-1700) and you can also join guided walks (1415 Wed and Sun), or canoe or kayaking trips (see activities).

Sleeping

Aberystwyth *p596*

A **Conrah Country House Hotel**, Chancery, Rhydgaled, Aberystwyth, T01970 617941, 624546, www.conrah.co.uk, Aberystwyth's most luxurious hotel, set in its own grounds about 3 miles from town. Fresh flowers from the garden, antiques dotted around and all the comforts you'd expect.

D **Bodalwyn Guest House**, Queen's Avenue, T01970 612578, , hilary.d@lineone.net, Comfortable rooms in this large, Welsh speaking guest house just off the promenade.

D **Harry's**, 40-46 North Parade, Aberystwyth, T01970 612647, , www.harrysaberystwyth.com, Look for the bright orange awnings outside and that's Harry's, a town centre restaurant with rooms that is gradually being refurbished.

D **Llethr Melyn Country Farmhouse**, Trawsgoed, near Aberystwyth, T/F 01974 261400, www.welsh-breaks.co.uk. 17th century farmhouse in the country close to Aberystwyth, set in 20 acres with horses, and other farm animals. Evening meals available.

E-D **Yr Hafod**, 1 South Marine Terrace, T01970 617579, F 636835, johnyrhafod@aol.com, Reliable guest house on the seafront, offering good value accommodation.

F **University of Wales**, Penglais, T01970 621960, www.aber.ac.uk/visitors. Single rooms in university flats (self catering) from mid June-mid Sept.

Aberaeron *p597*

B **The Harbourmaster**, Pen Cei, T01545 570755, F 570762, www.harbour-master.com, Brilliant cool and contemporary rooms with great views of the harbour. There's a fresh seaside feel throughout, with white and aquamarine décor, fine white sheets and CD players. Recommended.

D **Arosfa**, Cadwgan Place, T01545 570120, www.arosfaguesthouse.co.uk. Three star guest house by the quay, serving award winning breakfasts.

New Quay *p598*

C-D **Ty Cerrig**, 3 Hengell Uchaf, T01545 560850. All rooms are en suite at this clean, comfortable modern house on the outskirts of New Quay. Will take dogs.

D **Summat Else**, New Road, T01545 561418. Next door to Ty Cerrig, this modern four star guest house also has en suite rooms.

Cardigan *p598*

D **Black Lion Hotel**, High St, T01239 612532. Right in the centre of town, clean and comfortable ensuite rooms. Restaurant and pub attached.

Eating

Aberystwyth *p596*

£££ **Conrah Country House Hotel**, Chancery, Rhydgaled, Aberystwyth, T01970 617941. This is the place to come for a formal meal in lovely surroundings. Food is modern British and local produce, including vegetables from the hotel garden, are used as much as possible. 2 AA rosettes.

££ **Agra Indian Restaurant**, 36 North Parade, T636999, Mon-Thurs 1200-1345, Fri 1730-2230, Sat, Sun 1730-2230. Indian food with veggie options – bring your own wine.

££ **Harry's**, 40-46 North Parade, Aberystwyth, T01970 612647, daily 1200-1400, Mon-Fri 1830-2115, Sun 1830-2030. Harry's bills itself as a restaurant with rooms and main courses are a mixture of traditional British dishes like fish and chips, or ham hock with mash, as well as some pasta and veggie dishes.

££-£ **Le Figaro**, Alexandra Road, T01970 624242, Mon-Sat 1000-1400, 1800-2200. Mediterranean style dishes at this restaurant near the station. Coffees and light meals served during the day.

££-£ **La Taberna**, 1 New Street, T01970 627677, daily 1800-2230. Tapas bar offering tapas or more substantial main courses.

££-£ **Rendez Vous**, 31 Pier Street, T626444, Mon-Wed 1100-1900, Thurs-Sat 1900-2300, Sun 1200-1700. Vegetarian and vegan cuisine, with choices like herb nut roast, vegetable and hazelnut en croute, or lighter filled rolls and wraps during the day.

Cafés

£ **Blue Creek Café**, Princess Street, T615084, Tues-Sat 1000-1730. Cosy but uncluttered café. Lots of good choices for veggies, with choices like bean burgers at £4.50. Other dishes include 'posh beans on toast' served with bacon, rocket and parmesan £3.50, as well as cakes and hot drinks.

£ **Clock Tower**, 2 Pier Street, T626269, daily 1000-2200. Café with restaurant upstairs, serving dishes from around £5-6.

£ **Home Café**, 13-15 Pier Street, T01970 617417, Mon-Fri 0730-2030, Sat, Sun 0800-2100 in summer; shuts as about 1800 in winter. Cheap, cheerful and good value café popular with locals. Serves cakes, toasted sandwiches, BLTs and hot meals.

£ **Raw Bar**, 18 Pier Street, T01970 627268, Mon-Sat 0930-1830. Freshly squeezed juice, or soup and sandwiches.

£ **Upper Limit Café**, 27 North Parade, T07814 786863, Mon-Fri 0730-1700, Sat 0800-1600. Good café fare with cooked breakfasts, jacket potatoes and various veggie options.

Aberaeron *p597*

££ **The Harbourmaster**, Pen Cei, T01545 570755, food Tues-Sun 1200-1500, Mon-Sat 1800-2300. Great contemporary bar and restaurant offering modern Welsh cuisine. Mains like tuna and plaice with sundried tomato mash or Welsh lamb in smoked bacon. Veggie options available.

££-£ **The Hive on the Quay**, Cadwgan Place, T01545 570445, 1030-1700 (Aug 1000-2100). Famed for its delicious honey ice cream, this restaurant overlooking the water also serves fish dishes such as haddock chowder.

Cafés

££-£ **Isfryn Foods**, Regent St, T01545 571588, Mon-Fri 1100-1600, Sat 1000-1700, Tues-Sat from 1900. Home made cakes, light lunches and imaginative dishes like mackerel with gooseberry sauce (£4.95), and veggie dishes.

New Quay *p598*

££ **The Hungry Trout**, 2 South John Street, New Quay, T01545 560680, Wed-Sat coffee1000-1400, lunch 1200-1400, tea 1400-1600, a la carte 1800-2130, also Mon evening, Sun 1030-1400. Good restaurant by the harbour with lots of fish dishes and good veggie choices like black eye bean and squash stew (£10.75).

££-£ **The Black Lion**, Glanmor Terrace, T01545 560209, food 1200-2130. One of Dylan Thomas' many haunts, with a collection of photos and posters inside. Traditional bar meals, as well as pricier restaurant food. Choices for veggies and vegans.

Cafés

£ **Café Connect**, the harbourside, www.cafeconnect.biz, daily from 1000. Internet café also serving hot drinks and food.

£ **New Quay Honey Farm Tea Room**, Cross Inn, outside New Quay, daily 1000-1730, winter shorter hours. Lovely smell of honey and freshly made cakes, soups and sandwiches.

Cenarth *p599*

££ **Three Horse Shoes**, Cenarth, T01239 710119, food daily 1200-1400, 1800-2100. This pub is the best place to eat in Cenarth. It specialises in fish but also does old favourites like chicken curry as well as veggie options like roast veg and squash filo tart for £6.35.

Cardigan *p598*

£ **Red Lion Hotel**, Pwllhai, T01239 612482 serves a decent pint and pub grub in lively surroundings, often backed by live rock.

Around Cardigan *p598*

£ **The Royal Oak**, 30 North Rd, T01545 570233, food 1200-2100. Pleasant pub serving pub grub with several seafood options.

£ **Welsh Wildlife Centre**, near Cilgerran, food 1030-1700. Good views over the reserve in this café above the visitor centre. Serves, cakes and hot drinks, as well as hot meals between 1200-1430.

Entertainment

Aberystwyth Arts Centre, Penglais, Aberystwyth, T01970 622882, www.aber.ac.uk/ houses a theatre, concert hall and wide range of exhibitions.

The Black Lion, Glanmor Terrace, New Quay has live jazz on Sunday nights in winter, and 60/70s music on Fridays/Saturdays in winter.

Male Voice Choir, rehearse Thurs, Tabernacle Chapel, Mill St, Aberystwyth, 1930 not Aug.

Theatr Mwldan, Cardigan, T01239 621200, www.mwldan.co.uk, venue for theatre, music and cinema.

Festivals and events

Oct Cardigan Walking Festival, T01239 621200, popular festival of guided walks

Activities and tours

Bird watching

Bwlch Nant Yr Arian, Ponterwyd, T01970 890694, www.forestry.gov.uk, red kite feeding.

Hafod Lodge, Cwmstwyth, Aberystwyth, T01974 282247, www.midwalesbird watching.co.uk. 2-7 day birdwatching trips.

Ynys-hir RSPB reserve on Dyfi Estuary, 1.5km off A487 Machynlleth-Aberystwyth rd, T01654 781265, daily 0900-dusk, £3.50, large nature reserve. Chance to see pied flycatchers, redstarts, wood warblers, White fronted geese, as well as otters, dragonflies and other species.

Boat trips

Cardigan Boat Charters, trips along the Teifi Estuary and into Cardigan Bay, as well as self hire boats, T01239 614050.

New Quay boat trips, along the coast, 1 hr on ERMOL 6 or 2 hrs on ERMOL 5, T01545 560800, Apr-Oct, £5 1hr £10 2 hr.

Canoeing

Heritage Canoes, Teifi Marshes Nature Reserve, Cilgerran, T01239 613961, open canoe trips on River Teifi and kayaking adventure trips – £15.

Cycling/mountain biking

New Image Bikes, Pwllhai, Cardigan T01239 621275, tom@newimagebicycles.fsnet.co.uk cycle hire, half day £11.75, full day £17.63.

Teifi Trails, at Mapstone Newsagents, Pendre, Cardigan, T01239 614729, mountain bike hire by day, week or hour as well as route planning and advice.

Dolphin watching

Aberaeron Sea Aquarium, 2 Quay Parade, Aberaeron, T01545 570142, www.coastalvoyages.co.uk, offer trips in Cardigan Bay viewing dolphins, seals and birds.

Dolphin Survey Boat Trips, New Quay, T01545 560032, offers 4 and 8 hr boat trips from New Quay on scientific survey boats equipped with hydropohones.

Horse riding

4 Trek, Bontgoch, Aberystwyth, T01970 832291, centre offering hourly and day accompanied rides: also do quad biking and mountain biking.

Castellan Riding School, Blaenffos, Boncath, Cardigan, T01239 841644 Mar-Nov, hourly rides, hacks or pony trekking.
Cwmtydu Riding and Trekking Centre, Pantrhyn, New Quay, T01545 560494, pony trekking for all the family, with 1, 2 or 3 hr treks.

Skiing

Llangrannog Ski Centre, 1 mile out of village on B4321, T01239 654656, www.llangrannog.org, Mon-Thur 1700-2000, Sun 1400-1500, dry ski slope.

Walking

Ceredigion Council have a series of guided walks during the season taking in everything from challenging coastal walks to evening pub strolls. Information leaflet in TICS or T01545 572142, www.ceredigion.gov.uk.

Watersports

New Quay Watersports Centre, The Sandy Slip, The Harbour, New Quay, T01545 561460, www.newquaywatersports.org.uk, taster sessions and courses in sailing, windsurfing and kayaking, as well as power boat courses.

Shopping

Crafts

Curlew Weavers Woollen Mill, Rhydlewis, near Newcastle Emlyn, T01239 851357, family mill producing items like throws, shawls and bedspreads.
Custom House Shop and Gallery, 44-45 St Mary St, Cardigan, T01239 615541, www.customhousecardigan.com, has artworks, gifts, furniture and accessories.
The Forge Blacksmiths, Gwenlli, near Synod Inn, hand crafted iron work, T01559 363430, www.fored4u.co.uk.
Rhiannon Celtic Design Centre, Main Sq, Tregarron, T01974 298415, www.rhiannon.co.uk, Celtic design jewellery

Transport

The A487 trunk road runs between the main towns on this stretch of coastline linking Cardigan to **Aberystwyth** to the north and to Fishguard and Haverfordwest. Local bus company Richards (T01239 613756) and Arriva Cymru (T01970 617951) use the bus stand on Finch Square.

Directory

Health centre Cardigan health centre, 01239 612021, Police station 01239 612209. **Internet** Aberystwyth Library, Constitution St, and Cardigan Library, off Pendre, also Aberaeron Library, County Hall, both with free access. Café Connect, Harbourside, New Quay internet café and gallery.

Central Wales

→ *Colour map 3*

Squeezed between the bulk of the Cambrian mountains to the west and the rolling English border to the east, Central Wales consists of the old counties of Radnorshire and Monmouthshire, now lumped together with the Brecon Beacons under the rather unwieldly umbrella of Powys. It is probably easier to escape the crowds here than anywhere else in Wales. Much of the area is sparsely populated and it receives far fewer visitors than honeypots like Snowdonia. In the past it was the setting for much of the most ferocious fighting between the English and Welsh, notably the battle fought at Pilleth in 1402 when over 1000 English troops were killed by Owain Glyndwr's men. The landscape is wonderfully varied with mountains, reservoirs, rolling pastures and narrow winding lanes. There are plenty of remote hamlets and little villages to explore, and the towns all have their own distinctive characters, ranging from genteel Victorian spas to bustling market towns. Red kites, rare in other parts of Britain, can be readily spotted and the possibilities for walking, biking and other outdoor activities are endless. ▸▸ *For Sleeping, Eating and other listings, see pages 605-608.*

Ins and outs

Getting there **Trains** run to the main towns like Welshpool and Llandrindod Wells, but links between them aren't good and you'll need to rely on **buses.** ▸▸ *For further details, see Transport, page 608.*

Getting around To reach many places, such as the Elan Valley, you must rely on rural buses or occasional postbuses (www.postbus.royalmail.com). There is no doubt it is best to have your own transport to reach the most remote area – roads in Wales are well maintained.

Information **Welshpool TIC** ⓘ *Vicarage Gardens Car Park, Church St, T01938 552043, www.welshpool.org, daily Apr-Oct 0930-1730, Nov-Mar 0930-1700.* **Llandrindod Wells** ⓘ *Old Town Hall, Memorial Gardens, Temple St, T01597 822600, llandtic@powys.gov.uk, Easter-Oct Mon-Fri 0930-1700, Sat, Sun 0930-1600; Nov-Easter Mon-Sat 0930-1700.* **Rhayader TIC** ⓘ *Leisure Centre, North St, T01597 810591, www.rhayader.co.uk. Daily Apr-Oct 1000-1730, Nov-Mar Mon-Wed and Fri, Sat 1000-1700.* **Elan Valley Visitor Centre** ⓘ *off B4518 from Rhayader T01597 810898 mid Mar-Nov, daily 1000-1730, www.elanvalley.org.uk.* **Lake Vyrnwy TIC** ⓘ Vyrnwy Craft Workshops, Lake Vyrnwy, T01691 870346, laktic@powys.gov.uk Apr-Oct 1000-1700, Nov-Mar 1000-1600.

Welshpool and around

Welshpool has been a market town since the 13th-century and with a strategic position on the River Severn, has been one of the main entry points to Wales for centuries. It's only three miles over the border and the architectural influences are more English than Welsh, with half timbered Tudor buildings rubbing shoulders with Georgian and Victorian styles.

The town's main attraction is magnificent **Powis Castle** ⓘ *T01938 551944, Castle, garden and museum, early Apr-end June, Sep-early Nov, Wed-Sun 1300-1700; July, Aug Tues-Sun, castle and museum 1300-1700, garden 1100-1800, last admission 30 mins before closing, £8, £4 child, £20 family, NT, 1 mile south of town, accessible by pedestrian path from town centre.* This imposing red stoned pile was originally a medieval fortress for Welsh princes, but in 1587 it was bought by an English nobleman Sir Edward Herbert, who started turning it into an extravagant mansion. In 1784, Edward Clive, son of Clive of India, married into the family and today the Clive Museum contains a stunning collection of treasures from India, including Mughal armour, ivory playing cards and the tent of the Sultan of Mysore. The state rooms contain carved oak panelling, lavish painted ceilings and fine furniture. Among the many paintings are portraits by Reynolds and Gainsborough, and a landscape of Verona by Bernardo Bellotto, a relative of Canaletto. Allow time to explore the Italianate terraced gardens, virtually unchanged since they were first created in the 17th century and early 18th century, and now Britain's finest example of a baroque garden. There is topiary so smooth it looks like velvet, lush herbaceous borders, a small fountain garden and wooded walks. The views from the terraces are superb. There's a good tea room and restaurant by the castle.

From the town centre you can take a trip on the Montgomery Canal (see activities) next to which is the little **Powysland Museum** ⓘ *T01938 554656, May-Sept Mon, Tues, Thurs, Fri 1100-1300, 1400-1700, Sat 1000-1300, Sun 1400-1700, Oct-Apr weekday as before, Sat 1400-1700, closed Sun,* housed in a former warehouse. It focuses on local history from prehistoric times to the 20th-century. About ½ a mile's walk from town is the narrow gauge **Welshpool and Llanfair Railway** ⓘ *Raven Square station, T01938 810441, www.wllr.org.uk, Easter, late May-Aug daily, Apr-late May, Sept, Oct weekends,* which runs steam trains to the little village of Llanfair Caereinion.

North of Welshpool is a series of Little villages, largely unexplored by visitors. These include tongue twisting Llanfihangel yng Ngwynfa, birthplace of Welsh hymn writer Ann Griffiths who died age 29, Meifod, an important centre of learning in the Dark Ages, and Llanerfyl, where the churchyard has an ancient yew tree and the font in the church still bears the marks where Oliver Cromwell's soldiers sharpened their swords against the stone. They are good starting points for walks. **Lake** Vyrnwy ⓘ *T01691 870278, www.stwater.co.uk, 17 miles from Welshpool*, is a reservoir created in 1877 to provide water for Liverpool – flooding the original village of Llanwddyn in the process. Today it's a good spot for birdwatching, walking and cycling and there's also a sculpture trail to follow.

South of Welshpool

Newtown, the largest town in the area, and an important centre of the textile industry during the 19th-century. The **Textile Museum** ⓘ *Commercial St, T01686 622024, free,* covers the history of industry and its importance to the town. The town's most famous son was the industrialist and social reformer Robert Owen, who was born here in 1771 and later founded the model industrial village of New Lanark in Scotland. His birthplace is now a **museum** ⓘ *Broad St, T01686 626345, free*. It has a good street market, held here since 1279.

Prettier, and a more attractive base than Newtown is **Llandiloes**, a small market town once an active centre for Chartism, a movement that campaigned for the rights of the weavers. There's a local museum (its most famous exhibit being a two headed lamb) and several pubs and places to eat. From Llandiloes there's a superb scenic drive: follow the B4518 just past Staylittle then bear left along the unclassified road to Dylife and on to Machynlleth. There's a lovely, eye-stretching viewpoint near Dylife that also serves as memorial to the writer and broadcaster Wynford Vaughan-Thomas (1908-87).

Rhyader is a bustling crossroads in the heart of the countryside and makes a good base for enjoying outdoor activities and visiting two of Central Wales' main attractions: the Elan Valley and the red kite feeding station. During the 19th-century the town was the centre of the famous Rebecca Riots when local men, dressed up as women, went on the rampage smashing the tollgates that encircled the town. Half a mile south of town off the A470, is the **Gigrin Farm Red Kite Feeding Station** ⓘ *T01597 810243, www.gigrin.co.uk, daily feeding 1500 summertime, 1400 winter (GMT) £2.50, children £1*. Feeding started here in winter 1994 and now there are several hides where you get close up views of red kites, once almost extinct from Wales, swooping down to eat – on some days as many as 150 birds can be seen. Try and arrive about 30 mins before feeding, that way you get a chance to enjoy the views, watch the films of both kites and badgers feeding, and look at the small exhibition.

The enthusiasm with which the English flooded large areas of Wales is in evidence at the Elan Valley (B4518 south west of Rhayader) where a series of four enormous reservoirs were built between 1893 and 1904, to supply the rapidly growing city of Birmingham. A fifth reservoir was added at Claerwen in 1952. Beneath one of the reservoirs, Caban Coch, is the house in which the poet Shelley stayed when he visited the area with his wife. The Victorian dams now make a striking addition to the landscape, and the estate contains nature trails, and paths suitable for walkers and cyclists – including the Elan Valley Trail, an 8 mile (13km) path from Rhayader to Craig Goch Dam. Call in to the Elan Valley Visitor Centre first to pick up maps, details of routes and guided walks, and look at the exhibition on the area. There's also a café and toilets.

Knighton is as old as Offa's Dyke, and a good starting point for walks along this 8th-century earthwork, which served as both customs point and a dividing line between Wales and King Offa of Mercia's lands. It is home to the **Offa's Dyke** Centre ⓘ *West St, T01547 528753, www.offasdyke.demon.co.uk, Easter-Oct daily*

0900-1730, Nov-Easter Mon-Fri 0900-1700. Nearby Presteigne, a former county town, has a good **museum** ⓘ *Broad St, T01544 260650*, in the former Judge's Lodging, the courtroom and residence of visiting judges.

The Wells Towns

This is the collective name given to four Victorian spa towns in the south of the area. The best preserved is **Llandrindod Wells**, where a profusion of confident Victorian buildings, wrought iron work and green parkland leaves you in doubt of the town's heritage. You can still taste the waters (not delicious) at the renovated pump room in the town's **Rock Park** ⓘ *T01597 822997*, and there's also a small **museum** ⓘ *Temple St, T01597 824513, Apr-Sept Tue-Thur 1000-1300, 1400-1700, Fri 1000-1300, 1400-1630, Sat 1000-1700, Sun 1300-1700; rest of year closes at 1300 Sat and shut Sun*, which has an eclectic mix of exhibits from hospital surgical instruments to a 12th-century log boat.

Builth Wells is now most famous as the home of the agricultural extravaganza that is the Royal Welsh Show, while sleepy little **Llangammarch Wells** reached its zenith in the 19th century when the great and the good came to taste its barium rich waters. Best base for activities is **Llanwrtyd Wells** (**TIC** ⓘ *T01591 610666, www.llanwrtyd-wells.powys.org.uk*) set in stunning countryside and a good base for walking and mountain biking. It stages a number of off-the-wall events each year including a man versus horse race in May and the World Bog Snorkelling Championships (see Festivals and events, page 607). From here there's another wonderfully scenic drive, along an old drovers' road the Abergwesyn Pass. This cover 14 miles of wild countryside from nearby Abergwesyn over the mountains to Tregaron.

Sleeping

Welshpool and around *p603*

L-A **Lake Vyrnwy Hotel**, Llanwddyn, T01691 870692, www.lakevyrwy.com. Grand hotel where you can spoil yourself with a touch of luxury. Rooms are individually decorated, there are antiques, log fires and a wide range of outdoor activities on off.

B **Buttington Country House**, Buttington, near Welshpool, T01938 553351. Georgian rectory set in large garden, offering evening meals by arrangement.

C **Lower Trelydan**, Guilsfield, near Welshpool T01938 553105, www.lowertrelydan.com. High quality B&B on working farm a couple of miles from Welshpool. Riding holidays available.

D **Cwm Llwynog**, Llanfair Caereinion, T01938 810791. Working dairy farm set out in the country west of Welshpool. Lots of low beams, an inglenook fireplace and home cooking.

D **Trefnant Hall**, Berriew, near Welshpool, T01686 640262, jane.trefnant@virgin.net. A couple of miles from Powis Castle this listed farmhouse, on a working farm offers B&B and also has a self catering unit. Mar-Nov

South of Welshpool *p604*

B **Milebrook House Hotel**, Milebrook, near Knighton, T01547 528632, www.milebrookehouse.co.uk. Family run hotel in own grounds beside the River Teme. Grow their own vegetables which are served in the restaurant. Good for walking, birdwatching and fishing.

B **The Talkhouse**, Pontdolgoch, near Caersws, T01686 688919, www.talkhouse.co.uk. Old coaching inn now noted for its modern Welsh cuisine. Make you sure like Laura Ashley fabrics – the rooms are full of them as the original factory is nearby.

C **Elan Valley Hotel**, Elan Valley, near Rhyader, T01597 810448, www.elanvalleyhotel.co.uk. Family run hotel offering good food and 2 star accommodation. Special break rates available.

D **Brynafon Country House**, South St, T01597 810735, F 810111, www.brynafon.co.uk, Just on the edge of Rhyader this former Victorian workhouse is now a 3 star hotel. It has comfortable accommodation and is willing to take dogs.

D **Lower Ffrydd**, Caersws, T01686 688269, www.lowerffrydd.co.uk. Just 3 rooms at this 4 star 16th-century farmhouse.

E **Gigrin Farm**, Rhyader T01597 810243, F 810357, www.gigrin.co.uk, 2 rooms, none en suite. If you're keen to watch the red kites you won't get a better chance than here, at Gigrin Farm, where the kites are fed twice daily. It's a working farm with great views over the surrounding countryside.

Self catering

Glyngynwydd Farm Cottages, Cwm Belan, Llanidloes, T01686 413854, www.glyngynwydd.co.uk, 5 star cottages converted from traditional stone barn. 5 cottages, sleep 2 – 18, £130-£342 per week
Nannerth Fach, Rhyader, T01597 811121, www.nannerth.co.uk. 5 star self catering that sleeps 4. Price from £185-383 per week.
Elan Valley Trust has 2 self catering properties: **Penglaneinon Farmhouse** that sleeps 6 and **Llannerch y Cawr**, a 15th century longhouse that is divided in two with accommodation for 6 above and 4 below. Both are in the heart of the Elan Valley. Contact Elan Valley Estate Office, Elan Village, Rhyader, T01597 810449, F 811276, www.elanvalley.org.uk

The Wells Towns *p605*

L **Llangoed Hall**, Llyswen, T01874 754525, www.llangoedhall.com. Created by Sir Bernard Ashley, husband of the late Laura Ashley, this mansion gives you a taste of life in a grand country house. Come for a treat.
B **The Metropole**, Temple Street, Llandrindod Wells, T01597 823700, F 824828, www.metropole.co.uk, 122 en suite rooms. Grand Victorian building in the heart of town, with comfortable rooms, very much geared to the conference market. There are leisure facilities and friendly and helpful staff. Best town centre hotel.
C **Acorn Court**, Chapel Rd, Howey, near Llandrindod Wells, T01597 823543, www.acorncourt.co.uk Country B&B convenient for wildlife watching and golfing on the outskirts of the town.
C **Brynhir Farm**, Chapel Rd, Howey, near Llandrindod Wells, T01597 822425, www.brynhir.farm.btinternet.co.uk. Friendly working farm just a mile from the town.
C **Guidfa House**, Crossgates, near Llandrindod Wells, T01597 851241, www.guidfa-house.co.uk. Lovely Georgian guesthouse set in its own grounds a few miles from Llandrindod Wells and serving high quality food.
C **Holly Farm**, Howey, near Llandrindod Wells, T01597 822402, www.ukworld.net/hollyfarm. Restored Tudor farmhouse on working farm, offering 5 star accommodation.
D **Dolberthog Farm**, off Howey Rd, near Llandrindod Wells, T01597 822255, www.ukworld.net/dolberthogfarm. Working farm with en suite rooms catering for walkers and cyclists.
E **Brynllys Guest House**, High Street, Llandrindod Wells, T01597 823190, 3 rooms all en suite. Cosy and clean B&B just a couple of minutes walk from the station. Will do evening meals on request.

Eating

Welshpool and around *p603*

£££ **Lake Vyrnwy Hotel**, Llanwddyn, T01691 870692 High class hotel restaurant overlooking Lake Vyrnwy. Menu uses local produce including game. Come for afternoon tea if you can't run to dinner.
££ **The Corn Store**, 4 Church Street, T01938 554614. Downstairs is tearoom serving everything from breakfast to quiches, while the wine bar/restaurant upstairs opens in the evening and serves things like crab salad and local beef in whisky and cream.
££ **The Royal Oak**, Severn Street, T01938 552217. Good value in traditional coaching inn. Other pubs worth trying are Mermaid and the Talbot, both on the High Street.
£ **Fortune Court**, 42 High Street, T01938 558899, Tues-Thurs 1200-1400, 1700-midnight, Fri, Sat 1200-1400, 1700-0030, Sun 1700-midnight. Take away Cantonese with a restaurant upstairs.

South of Welshpool *p604*

£££-££ **Lloyds Hotel and Restaurant**, Cambrian Place, Llandiloes, T01686 412284. Established restaurant offering a fixed price menu.
£££-££ **Yesterdays Restaurant with Rooms**, Severn Square, Newtown, T01686 622644. Acclaimed restaurant serving Welsh dishes made with fresh local produce, as well as vegetarian dishes. Accommodation also available.
££ **Elan Valley Hotel**, Elan Valley, near Rhayader, T01597 810448. Family run hotel and restaurant which serves bar meals, as well as imaginative restaurant food. Veggies catered for. Real ales.
££-£ **The Radnorshire Arms**, High St, Presteigne, T01544 267406. Attractive pub with black beamed bar serving meals in both the bar and the restaurant.

The Wells Towns *p605*

££ **The Metropole**, Temple Street, Llandrindod Wells, T01597 823700, light bar snacks or main meals in the restaurant of this slightly faded, grand old hotel. Veggie choices available.

£ **The Llanerch**, off Waterloo Rd, Llandrindod Wells, T01597 822086. Food 1200-1415, 1800-2115 daily. Good choice of bar meals in this popular 16th-century inn. Light bites such as omelettes with chips served at lunchtime only, while more substantial dishes are always available.

£ **The Rock Park restaurant**, Rock Park, T01597 829267, Tues-Sun 1000-1700, Thurs-Sat 1830-2130. Like everywhere else in Llandrindod Wells, this restaurant/café is slightly faded but has a very pleasant setting in the middle of the former spa gardens. Coffees, cakes, light meals – as well as Sunday lunches at £5.95.

£ **Upstairs Downstairs**, Spa Road, Llandrindod Wells, T01597 824737, daily 1000-1630. There's a relaxing atmosphere at this pleasant café, which has wooden floors and old settles inside, as well as some seats outside. As well as cakes and coffee you can get Welsh rarebit (£3.25), salads or veggie burgers (£4.75).

Pubs, bars and clubs

The Wells Towns *p605*

Hundred House Inn, Hundred House, near Builth Wells, T01982 570231. A former drovers inn, with real fires. Serves good bar food.

Laughing Dog, Howey, near Llandrindod Wells T01597 822406. This pub has a games room and offers several real ales.

Llanerch Inn, Llanerch Lane, near Llandrindod Wells, T01597 822086. Former coaching inn, with an inglenook fireplace. Serves food.

Red Lion, Llanafan Fawr, near Llandrindod Wells, T01597 860204. This 12th-century pub is possibly the oldest in Wales. It serves real ales and food.

Entertainment

Theatr Hafren, Newtown, T01686 625007, www.theatrhafren.co.uk, stages drama and a wide range of musical events.

Oriel 31, Newtown, T01686 625041, gallery with temporary exhibitions and workshops

Festivals and events

Jun **Mid Wales Music Festival**, Gregynog Hall, near Newtown, T01686 623538.

Jul **Royal Welsh Show**, Builth Wells, T01982 553683, www.rwas.co.uk, agricultural show.

Jul **World Bog Snorkelling Championships**, Llanwrtyd Wells, T01591 610666, snorkelling – as the title suggests – in a bog.

Aug **Llandrindod Wells Victorian Festival**, T01597 823441, www.victorianfestival.co.uk. Biggest event in the town with street theatre, drama and music all with a Victorian theme.

Aug **Presteigne Festival of Music and the Arts**, T01544 267800, www.presteignefestival.com.

Nov **Mid Wales Beer Festival**, Llanwrtyd Wells, T01591 610666. Over 60 real ales, as well as guided walks and evening entertainment.

Activities and tours

Canal cruises

Montgomery Canal Cruises, Canal Yard, Welshpool, T01938 553271, www.montycanal.co.uk, offer full day boat hire or 1 ½ hr cruises along the Montgomery Canal.

Fishing

Rhayader and Elan Valley Angling Associates, T01597 810383, fly fishing and coarse fishing, permits required, from Daisy Powell Newsagents, Rhayader T01597 810451.

General outdoor activities

Elan Valley Lodge, Elan Village, Rhayader, T01597 811143, www.elanvalleylodge.co.uk, adult outdoor centre offering everything from climbing and canoeing to mountain biking.

Horse riding

The Lion Royal Trekking Centre, Lion Royal Hotel, Rhayader, T01591 810202, pony trekking May-Sept, booking essential.

Lletty Mawr Trekking Centre, Lletty Mawr, Llangadfan, Welshpool, T01938 820646 pony trekking from £10 per hour.

The Mill Trekking Centre, Aberhafep, Newtown, T01686 688440, offer pony trekking and off road karting aimed at children, booking essential.

Cycling/Mountain biking

Artisans Mountain Bikes, Old Sawmill, Lake Vyrnwy, Llanwddyn, T01691 870317.
Brooks Cycles, 9 Severn St, Welshpool, T01938 553582, cycle shop which also hires out bikes.
Builth Wells Cycles, Smithfield Rd, Builth Wells, T01982 552923, mountain bike hire and guided rides, from £8 half day, £12 full day.
Cycles Irfon, Maesydre, Beulah Rd, Llanwrtyd Wells, T01591 610710, www.cycleirfon.co.uk, mountain bike hire from £10 half day, £15 full day, also do guided tours.
Elan Cyclery, Cwmdauddwr Arms, West St, Rhayader, T01597 811343, www.clivepowell-mtb.co.uk, bike hire from £3 per hr and £12 per day, also do guided weekends breaks.
Freewheeling Wales, circular day routes in Mid Wales, details from T01874 612275.
Red Kite Mountain Centre, Neuadd Arms Hotel, Llanwrtyd Wells, T01591 610236, mountain bike hire along waymarked routes.

Quad biking

Border Quad Trekking, Bulthy Hill Farm, Middletown, near Welshpool, T01743 884694, www.borderquadtrekking.com, offer quad biking and grass karting, booking required.

Wildlife watching

Gilfach Nature Discovery Centre, Gilfach Nature Reserve, St Harman, Rhayader, T01597 870301, hill farm nature reserve with walks, picnic area and disabled access, on the Wye Valley Walk.

Transport

The **Cambrian** railway line (www.walesandborderstrains.co.uk) serves the northern part of this area, with trains running from Shrewsbury to **Welshpool** and **Newtown**. The rural **Heart of Wales** line (T01597 822053, www.heart-of-wales.co.uk) also runs between Shrewsbury and Swansea, running through towns like **Knighton**, **Llandrindod Wells** and **Llanwrtyd Wells.**

Directory

Internet Free access is available from **Knighton library**, West St, T01547 528778, **Rhayader library**, West St, T01597 810548, **Presteigne library**, The Old Market Hall, Broad St, T01544 260552, **Newtown library**, Park Lane, T01686 626934 and **Welshpool library**, Brook St, T01938 553001.

North Wales

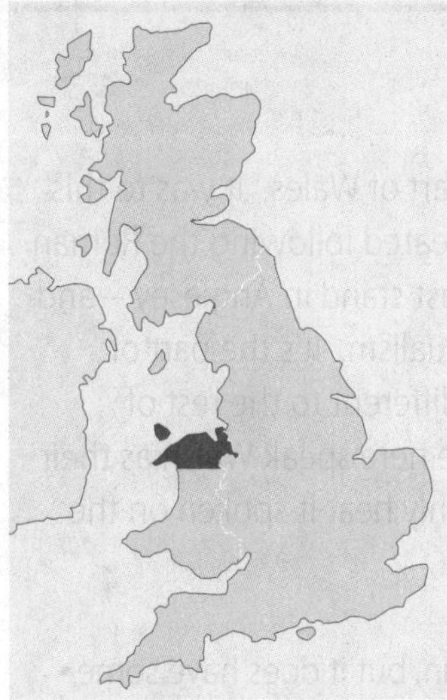

Introduction

North Wales is the most Welsh part of Wales. It was to this area that the ancient Britons retreated following the Roman invasion – the Druids had their last stand in Anglesey – and it still retains a distinctive individualism. It's the part of Wales that feels most culturally different to the rest of Britain. Large numbers of people here speak Welsh as their first language and you will certainly hear it spoken on the streets and in the shops.

North Wales is not noted for its sun, but it does have some striking scenery. Its greatest attraction are the hills and mountains of the Snowdonia National Park, which draw thousands of walkers, climbers and mountain bikers each year. Snowdon, the heart of the area, is the highest peak in Britain outside Scotland. Dotted through the National Park are towns and villages such as busy Betws-y-Coed, which teems with visitors in walking boots and waterproofs, and delightful Beddgelert, one of the most picturesque towns in Wales.

If you're not an outdoor type you can still find things to do here. The north coast is notorious for its raucous 'kiss me quick' strip of caravans and amusement arcades, but it does contain one jewel in Llandudno, a Victorian resort that still has plenty of traditional charm. The eastern corner, closest to the border, is dotted with attractive towns, like historic Ruthin and St Asaph, home to the smallest cathedral in Britain. Go west and you can explore great castles like Carnarvon; neolithic stones on the pastoral isle of Anglesey, and the fantasy village of Portmerion.

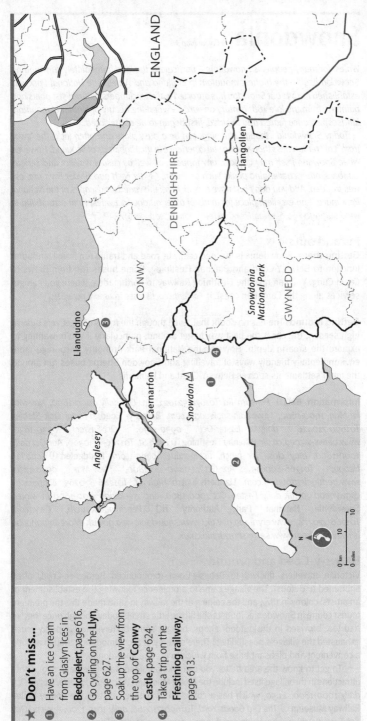

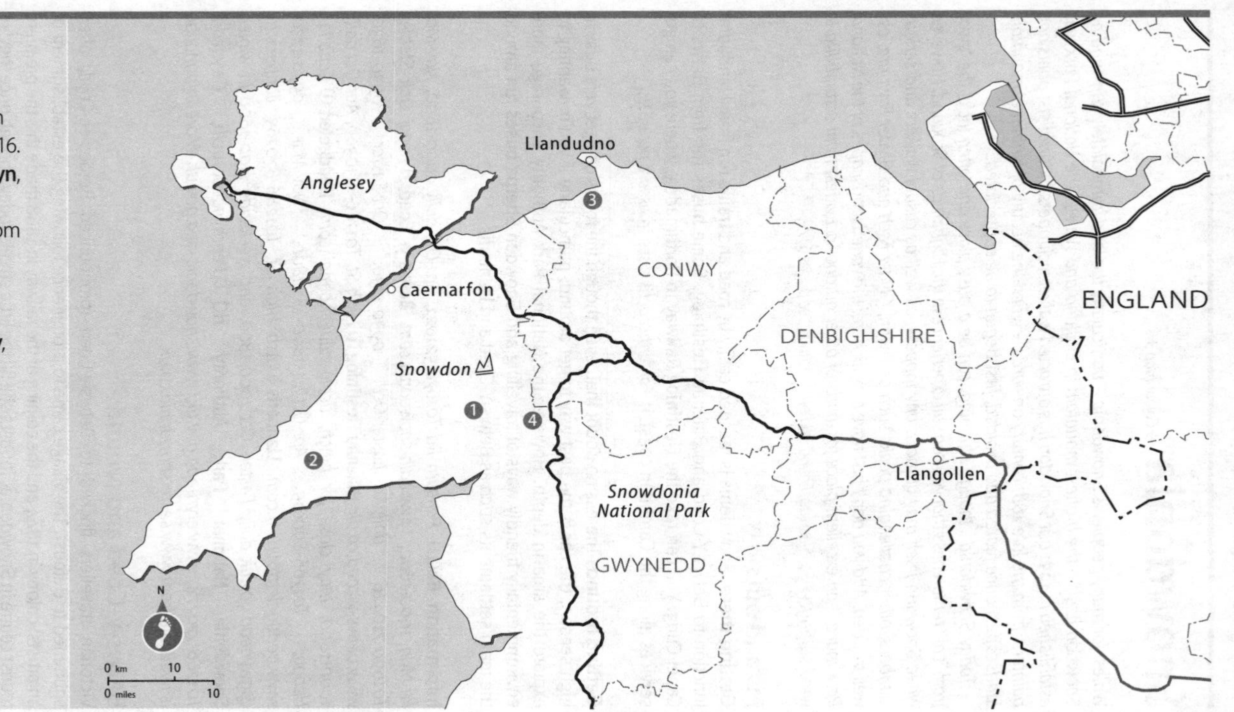
★ Don't miss...
1 Have an ice cream from Glaslyn Ices in **Beddgelert**, page 616.
2 Go cycling on the **Llyn**, page 627.
3 Soak up the view from the top of **Conwy Castle**, page 624.
4 Take a trip on the **Ffestiniog railway**, page 613.
Anglesey
Llandudno
Caernarfon
Snowdon
CONWY
DENBIGHSHIRE
ENGLAND
Llangollen
Snowdonia National Park
GWYNEDD
N
0 km 10
0 miles 10

Snowdonia

→Colour map 3

Wales, for many people, is Snowdonia – particularly the land immediately surrounding Snowdon itself – the highest mountain in England and Wales. The National Park was established in 1951 but Snowdon has attracted walkers, climbers, naturalists, poets and painters, from the late 18th century onwards – when the beauty of 'sublime' mountain landscapes, once feared and avoided, first began to be appreciated.

Today Snowdonia , though stunning, can be a busy place and often lacks the 'away from it all' remoteness that you can still experience in the Highlands of Scotland. However, while Snowdon itself may attract many trippers, as well as casual walkers and serious climbers, other challenging peaks such as Tryfan, Glyder Fach and Glyder Fawr are less well trodden. And you don't just have to walk here: the varied landscapes of the National Park make it an excellent place for loads of other outdoor activities, from scrambling to wind surfing. ►► *For Sleeping, Eating and other listings, see pages 617-619.*

Ins and outs

Getting there Snowdonia is reached easily by **road** and **trains** run from Llandudno Junction to Betws-Y-Coed and Blaenau Ffestiniog. Some **buses** run from Betws to Capel Curig. You can take the **Ffestiniog Railway** to Porthmadog, where you can get services along the Cambrian coast. ►► *For further details, see Transport, page 619.*

Getting around There is no doubt that, even though the roads can get very busy in high season, the **car** is the best way to get around, particularly if you're wanting to explore the area in depth. However the National Park Authority encourage more environmentally friendly ways of travelling and **Snowdon Sherpa buses** run around the main settlements such as Betws-Y-Coed and Llanberis.

Information Bala ⓘ *Pensarn Rd T01678-521021, Apr-Oct daily 1000-1800, Nov-Mar Fri-Mon 1000-1600, www.bala-snowdonia.com.* **Betws-y- Coed** ⓘ *Royal Oak Stables T01690-710426 daily Easter-Oct 0930-1730, Oct-Easter 0930-1630, www.betws-y-coed.co.uk.* **Blaenau Ffestiniog** ⓘ *High St, T01766- 830360, Apr-Oct daily 1000-1800, may close for lunch, ticblaenau@hotmail.com.* **Beddgelert** ⓘ *Canolfan Hebog, T01766-890615 Apr-Oct 1000- 1800, Nov-Mar 0930-1730, www.beddgelerttourism.com.* **Llanberis** ⓘ *41b High St, T01286-870765, llanberis.tic @gwynedd.gov.uk daily Easter- Oct 1000-1800, and weekends 1100-1600 in winter.* **Snowdonia National Park Authority HQ** ⓘ *Penrhyndeudraeth, Gwynedd, T01766-770274, www.eryri-npa.gov.uk; www.snowdonia-npa.gov.uk. More information is available from www.secretsnowdonia.co.uk.*

Betws-y-Coed and around

Victorian travellers flocked to Betws-y-Coed (pronounced Betoos-ee-Coyd, often shortened to Betoos). The village came to prominence following the establishment of an artists' colony in 1844 and the coming of the railway in 1868 made this the premiere tourist centre in Snowdonia. Tourists still fill the little streets today, though once they've had tea, browsed in the outdoor shops, bought some pottery, they've pretty much exhausted the village's possibilities. There's plenty of accommodation though and it's a convenient and pleasant base from which to explore Snowdonia.

To get to know the area better you can take a guided walk (see page 619). Other attractions in the village itself include the **Motor Museum** ⓘ *T01690-710760, Easter-Oct, daily 1000-1800, £1.50*, which has a collection of vintage cars and the **Conwy Valley Railway Museum** ⓘ *The Old Goods Yard, T01690-710568, daily 1015-1700, Apr-end Oct, Sat-Tues in winter*, where kids can ride on a miniature steam railway.

The rail thing

There are six major paths to the summit of Snowdon, the routes varying in difficulty. Before you tackle any of them, or do any serious walking in Wales, make sure you properly prepared with boots, warm and waterproof clothing (even in summer), maps (the best for walkers are OS Explorer 1:25,000), compass, food and water. Check weather conditions before setting off (T 09068-500449, www.metoffice.com). To give you an idea of how severe conditions can get think about this: Snowdon get 200 inches (508cm) of rain each year, the temperature can reach –20C in winter, and the wind speed can reach 150mph. A leaflet, Stay Safe in Snowdonia, is available from TICs.

The most popular, and easiest, ascent is the Llanberis Path, which follows the Snowdon Mountain Railway and takes about 3 hrs (descent about 1-2 hrs). The other paths are the Miners' Track, the Pyg Track, the Rhyd Ddu Path, the Snowdon Ranger Path and the Watkin Path. There is also a serious ridgewalk, the Snowdon Horseshoe.

Of course you don't have to walk to reach the top of Snowdon (to the disgust of legions of outdoorsy types). Llanberis, starting point for many of the classic ascents of Snowdon, is also the starting point for the Snowdon Mountain Railway ⓘ *T0870-458 0033, www.snowdonrailway.co.uk, daily mid Mar-Oct, weather permitting, £18,* the narrow gauge railway (Britain's only rack and pinion railway) that runs nearly 5 miles up the mountain and has been operating since 1896. Once on the summit you can have a hot drink at the café (yes, a café, designed by Clough William-Ellis of Portmeirion fame) and in half an hour make the return journey. Do try and book in advance in summer.

The village is really a base for walking and mountain biking. The best biking trails are in the Gwydir Forest Park (see sports/activities), while all types of walks are readily accessible, from tough climbs in the surrounding mountains to gentle woodland strolls.

A couple of miles west of the village, along the A5, is one of the area's most visited attractions Swallow Falls. A draw since Victorian times, this pretty waterfall can only be reached through a turnstile (ⓘ *£1 coin, correct money only*). Further along the road is **The Ugly House** or **Ty Hyll** ⓘ *T01690-720287, www.snowdonia-society.org.uk, Apr-Oct daily 0930-1730, £1*, a cottage made from a haphazard arrangement of stones – it's said to date from 1475, when a house would be yours if you built it overnight and had smoke coming from the chimney by morning. It's now the headquarters of the Snowdonia Society and has a little garden, woodland walk and nature trail.

From here the road leads to **Capel Curig**, the little village known to all walkers and climbers in Snowdonia. Standing at the gateway to the Llanberis and Nant Francon passes, it is a good base for exploring the surrounding mountains and there are several places to eat and stay, all heavily geared to hearty rucksack wearers. The village is the location of the National Mountain Centre, Plas Y Brenin.

After Capel Curig the A4086 branches off to **Llanberis** (www.llanberis.org), the busy lakeside village, once a centre of slate production, that is the starting point for the Snowdon Mountain Railway (see Snowdon, page 590) as well as the most popular walking route up the peak. Attractions include **Electric Mountain** ⓘ *T01286-870636, www.electricmountain.co.uk, Apr, May, Sep, Oct daily 1030-1630, Jun-Aug daily 0930-1730, Feb, Mar, Nov, Dec Wed-Sun 1030-1630, last underground tour 1 hr before closing, £6 tour high season, £5 low season*, the lakeside visitor centre for the Dinorwig Power Station, a hydro-electric station housed in enormous caverns underground. An

Snowdonia

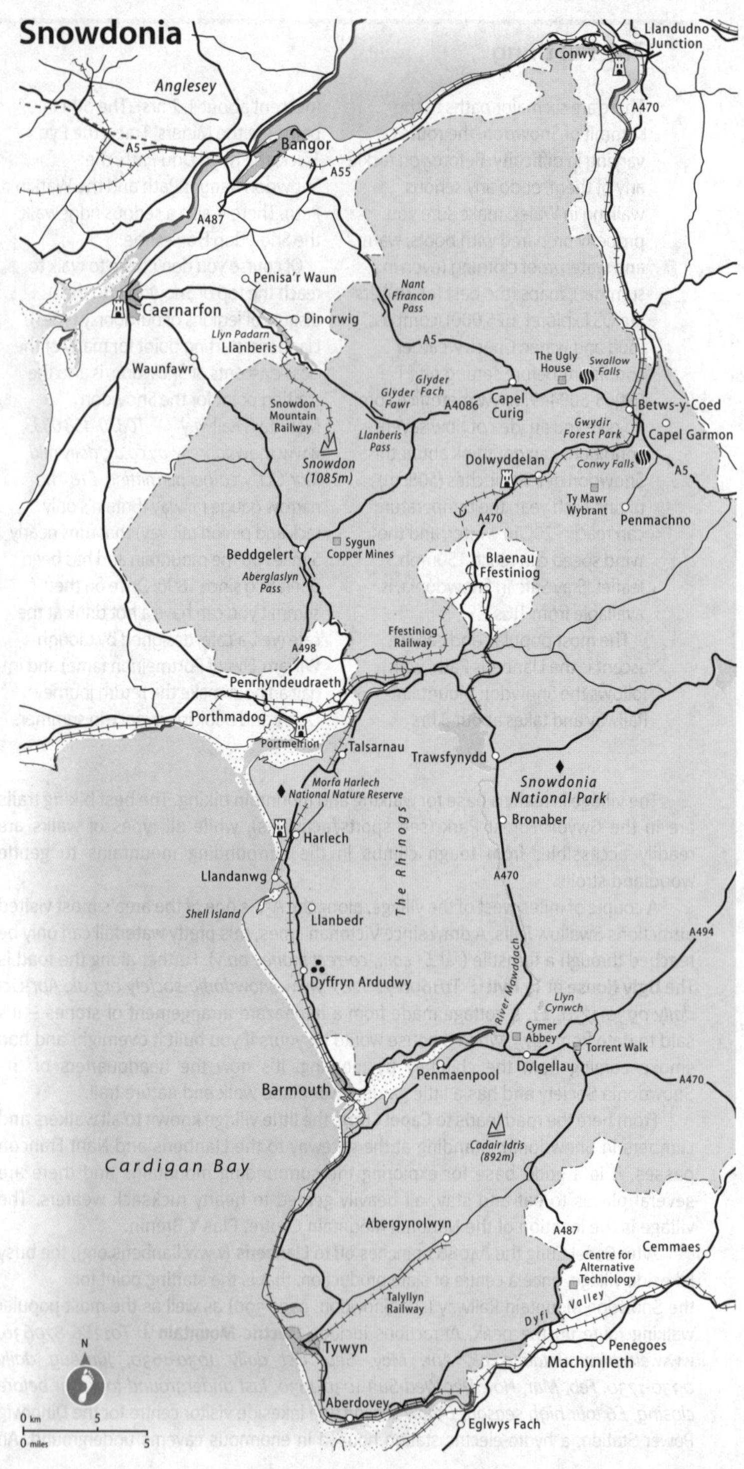
Anglesey
Bangor
A5
A55
A487
Conwy
Llandudno Junction
A470
Penisa'r Waun
Nant Ffrancon Pass
Caernarfon
Dinorwig
Llyn Padarn
Llanberis
Waunfawr
A5
The Ugly House
Swallow Falls
Glyder Fach
Glyder Fawr
A4086
Capel Curig
Betws-y-Coed
Snowdon Mountain Railway
Llanberis Pass
Gwydir Forest Park
Capel Garmon
Snowdon (1085m)
Dolwyddelan
Conwy Falls
A5
Ty Mawr Wybrant
A470
Penmachno
Beddgelert
Sygun Copper Mines
Blaenau Ffestiniog
Aberglaslyn Pass
Ffestiniog Railway
A498
Penrhyndeudraeth
Porthmadog
Portmeirion
Talsarnau
Trawsfynydd
Morfa Harlech National Nature Reserve
Snowdonia National Park
Harlech
Bronaber
Llandanwg
The Rhinogs
A470
Shell Island
Llanbedr
A494
Dyffryn Ardudwy
River Mawddach
Llyn Cynwch
Cymer Abbey
Torrent Walk
Dolgellau
Penmaenpool
A470
Barmouth
Cadair Idris (892m)
Cardigan Bay
Abergynolwyn
A487
Cemmaes
Centre for Alternative Technology
Talyllyn Railway
Dyfi
Valley
Penegoes
Tywyn
Machynlleth
N
Aberdovey
Eglwys Fach
0 km
5
0 miles
5

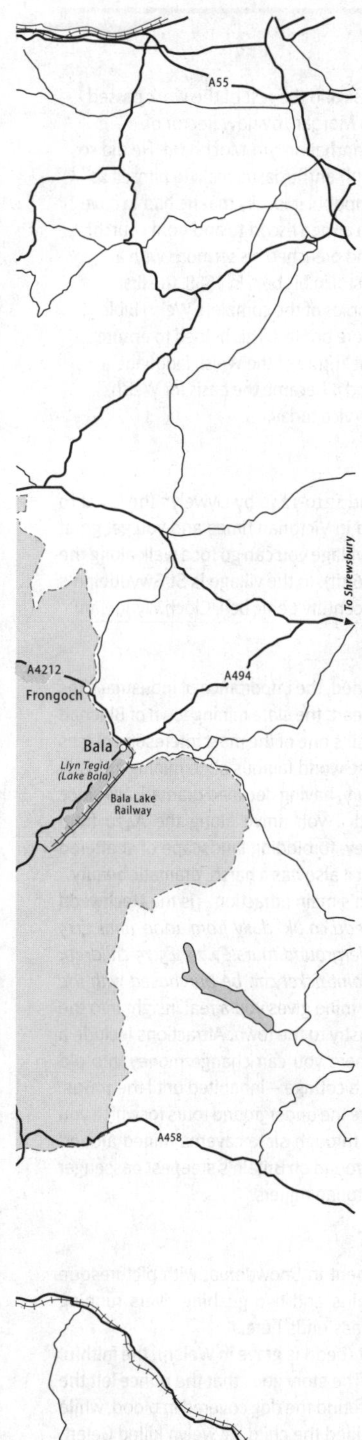

exhibition displays the 16th-century Peris Boat, and a 12th century dugout canoe, unearthed during the building of the power station. Free entry to the displays and cafes; the underground tour takes an hour – book in advance.

Padarn Country Park ⓘ *T01286-870892*, is an 800 acre park around the shores of Lake Padarn, on land once part of the Dinorwig Slate Quarry, which employed over 3000 local men until its closure in 1969. The workshops are preserved in the **Welsh Slate** Museum ⓘ *T01286-870630, www.nmgw.ac.uk,daily Easter-Oct 1000-1700, Nov-Easter, Sun-Fri 1000-1600, free*, as well as a reconstructed terrace of quarrymen's houses and a huge waterwheel. Also in the park is the **Llanberis Lake** Railway ⓘ *T01286- 870549, www.lake-railway.co.uk, daily Easter-Oct, £4.50*, a steam railway originally built to transport slate from the quarry. You can take a trip on the lake in a **pleasure steamer** ⓘ *T07974-716418, £4*, in summer. Trips start from a jetty near the Slate Museum.

South of Betws-y-Coed

To visit **Conwy Falls** ⓘ *T01690-710696, www.conwy-falls.co.uk, £1 coin admission*, you enter through a turnstile by a pink painted café, designed by Sir Clough William-Ellis and can then walk down to see the stunning waterfalls and the remains of a Victorian fish ladder.

Northwest of Penmachno village, is **Ty Mawr Wybrant** ⓘ *A5 S of Betws, then B4406 to Penmachno, 2½ miles from Penmachno, T01690-760213, Apr-Sep, Thu-Sun 1200-1700, Oct 1200-1600, £2.20, £1.10 child, family £5.50, NT*. This cottage is reached via a single track road that seems to last forever. It is an isolated spot, worth visiting for the delicious sense of remoteness alone. The cottage itself was the home of Bishop William Morgan (1545-1604), the man who first translated the whole of the bible into Welsh (see box, page 616). The house has been restored to its 16th century appearance and has a display of Welsh Bibles inside.

Dolwyddelan Castle ⓘ *1 Apr-29 Sept 0930-1830 daily, 29 Sep-31 Mar 0930-1600 Mon-Sat, 1100-1600 Sun,*

A labour of love

Born in Ty Mawr, Penmachno in 1541, Morgan studied at Cambridge, just a few years after an Act of Parliament was passed in 1563 by Elizabeth I to allow the translation of the Bible into Welsh 'because the English tongue is not understood [by]… her majesty's...obedient subjects inhabiting Wales.' The first Welsh New Testament was produced by Bishop William Salesbury, Richard Davies and Thomas Huet, in 1567. However they did not continue their task and the rest of the work passed to Morgan, by now Rector of Llanrhaedr- ym-Mochnant. He did so with enthusiasm, making himself so unpopular locally that he had to have an armed escort to and from church, and preached his sermons with a pistol in his belt. In 1588, the first copies of the complete Welsh Bible were printed. This helped to ensure the future of the Welsh language and it became the basis for Welsh service today.

£2, *concessions £1.50, family £5.50,* built around 1210-1240 by Llywelyn the Great to guard a mountain pass. The castle was restored in Victorian times and you get great views from the battlements. From Dolwyddelan village you can go for a walk along the river, or hike to the summit of Moel Siabod (2,862ft). In the village is St Gwyddelan's church, built early in the 16th-century with a 7th-century Celtic bell, Cloch Wyddelan.

Blaenau Ffestiniog

When the Snowdonia National Park was established, the importance of industrial sites was not recognised. So although it's right at its heart, the slate mining town of Blaenau Ffestiniog isn't part of the National Park itself. Yet it's one of the most interesting places to visit. It's essentially a living museum today, the world famous slate mining industry that brought the town prosperity in the 19th-century, having declined dramatically since the 1960s. Slate still dominates the area, and if you arrive along the A470 from Betws-y-Coed the sudden appearance of this grey, forbidding landscape of shattered slate heaps can be depressing in the extreme. But it also has a harsh, dramatic beauty.

Other than the **Ffestiniog Railway** – the town's main attraction – is the **Llechwedd Slate Caverns** ⓘ *T01766-830306, http://llechwedd.co.uk, daily from 1000 until 1715 Mar-Sept, 1615 Oct-Feb, free above ground, underground tours £7.75, £5.75 children: buses run from the town to the caverns and a joint ticket can be purchased with the railway,* which sounds dull – but isn't. This slate mine gives you a real insight into the life of the miners and the importance of the industry to the town. Attractions include a Victorian mining village, with a sweet shop, where you can change money into old currency and purchase sweets like gobstoppers, a cottage – inhabited until the 1960s, and the working Miners' Arms pub. The big pull are the underground tours for which you don hard hats: the Miners' Tramway takes you through slate caverns mined around 1846, while the Deep Mine tour takes you underground on Britain's steepest passenger railway, where you learn about the life of the Victorian miners.

Beddgelert

Beddgelert is easily the most attractive settlement in Snowdonia, with picturesque stone houses surrounded by majestic mountains and two gushing rivers running through the village. The beautiful Aberglaslyn Pass ends here.

The most famous sight is the grave of Gelert (bedd is grave in Welsh), the faithful dog who was said to belong to Prince Llywelyn. The story goes that the prince left the dog to guard his child, but when he returned he found the dog covered in blood, while the child was missing. Assuming the dog had killed the child, Llywelyn killed Gelert, then found the child lying safe with a dead wolf (that Gelert had bravely killed) nearby. You can see Gelert's grave under a lone tree, but it's believed the tale was made up in the 18th-century by a local publican trying to attract tourists to the area – the place name instead referring to the grave of Celert, an early saint.

A short distance out of the village is the **Sygun Copper Mine** ⓘ *01978-01766-510101, www.syguncoppermine.co.uk, usually daily, Oct, Mar 1030 (Sun 1100)-1600; Nov-Feb 1100-1530, Easter-Sep Mon-Sat 1000-1700, Sun 1100-1600, £4.95,* where you can do an underground tour through tunnels veined with coloured ores, and chambers of stalactites and stalagmites.

Bala

East of Blaenau Ffestiniog, reached via the A4212 is Bala, on the edge of the National Park. It sits by the largest freshwater lake in Wales Llyn Tegid (Lake Bala), a noted spot for all sorts of watersports (see sports/activites). Just out of town is the **Bala Lake Railway** ⓘ *T01678-540666, www.bala-lake-railway.co.uk, £7.50 return,* a narrow gauge, steam railway.

Sleeping

Betws-y-Coed and around *p612*

C **Pengwern**, Allt Dinas, Betws-y-Coed T01690-710480, www.snowdonia accommodation.com. Lovely house about a mile south of Betws-y-Coed, once used by visiting artists. Rooms individually furnished and very comforable. The Richard Gay Somerset room must boast the best loo-with-a-view in Britain. A former artist's studio has also been turned into a self catering cottage. Recommended.

C **Henllys** (The Courthouse), Old Church Road, Betws-y-Coed, T01690-710534, www.guesthouse-snowdonia.co.uk. Former courthouse, now B&B, that retains some of its old features – including an old holding sell that is now a single room.

C **Penmachno Hall**, near Penmachno, T01690-760410, www.penmachnohall.co.uk. 4 star country house in lovely rural setting.

C-D **Plas Coch Guest House**, High St, Llanberis, T01286-872122, www.plas-coch.co.uk. Comfortable accommodation and good breakfasts.

D **Afon View**, Holyhead Road, Betws-y-Coed, T01690-710726, www.afon-view.co.uk. Friendly, clean and comfortable B&B close to the river in Betws-y-Coed. Non smoking.

D **Bryn Tyrch Hotel**, Capel Curig, on A5, T01690-720223, www.bryntyrch-hotel.co.uk. 17 rooms, 10 en suite. Recently refurbished hotel, ideally situated for walkers and cyclists, and with a pleasant, relaxed atmosphere. Evening meals and lunches available too.

D **Glyntwrog House**, just south of Waterloo Bridge,15 mins walk from the village, T01690-710930, www.glyntwrogsnowdonia.co.uk. Award winning, with clean and comfortable rooms. Walkers and cyclists welcome.

D **Marteg B&B**, High St, T01286-870207, Llanberis, http://mysite.freeserve.com/ martegllanberis. Spacious rooms in 4 star B&B happy to cater for walkers and cyclists.

E **Swn-y-Dwr**, Pentrefelin, T01690-710648. Pleasant guesthouse, with lovely garden.

F **Jesse James' Bunkhouse**, Buarth y Clytiau, Penisarwaun, T01286-870521. Established bunkhouse a few miles outside Llanberis.

F **YHA Hostel**, Capel Curig, T0870-770-5746, www.yha.org.uk. Hostel with family bunkrooms

Beddgelert *p616*

C **Tanronnen Inn**, Beddgelert, T01766-890347. Comfortable and cosy inn, with some rooms that overlook the river, others the mountains. Meals available and packed lunches can be made up on request.

D **Sygun Fawr**, off A498, near Beddgelert, T/F 01766-890258, www.sygunfawr.co.uk. 9 rooms, all en suite. Lovely old manor house in pretty gardens, close to Beddgelert village. Rooms cleans and comfortable, some with views over the mountains. Well worth seeking out. 4 course dinner available for £16.95.

E **Plas Colwyn**, Beddgelert, on A4085, T01766-890458. 6 rooms, 3 en suite. Clean and friendly guest house set in lovely gardens, with log fires in winter. Possible to walk to Snowdon from the garden.

Eating

Betws-y-Coed and around *p612*

££ **Bryn Tyrch Hotel**, Capel Curig, on A5, T01690-720223. Food 1200-1700 and 1800-2100 daily. Bustling bar serving wide range of meals, including an excellent choice of veggie/vegan dishes. An aduki beanburger and chips will set you back around £6.75, a vegetable lasagne £8.75.

££ **Stable Bar**, Royal Oak, T01690-710219. The hub of the village. You can sit outside in summer and there's a wide range of food available. Live jazz on Thursday nights in summer, and venue for local male voice choir on Fridays.

££ **Talking Point**, Holyhead Road, T01690-710957. Tue-Sun 1830-2100, reservation recommended. Popular local bistro serving dishes like pan fried red mullet with turmeric tagliatelle £11.50.

££ **Ty Gwyn**, on A5, T01690-710383 Attractive inn serving good bar meals and very popular with locals as well as visitors. Best to reserve.

££ **White Horse Inn**, Capel Garmon, T01690-710271. About 1 ½ miles from Betws-y-Coed, this pub serves highly rated, homemade food and good beer.

Beddgelert *p616*

££ **Sygun Fawr**, off A498, near Beddgelert, T/F 01766-890258. You'll need to book if you want to eat at this house set in its own grounds. Non residents can join guests (see sleeping) for a 4 course, home cooked meal for £16.

£ **Tanronnen Inn**, Beddgelert, T01766-890347. Food 1230-1430, 1900-2100 daily. Good choice of bar meals with mains costing around £7.50. Popular with locals and visitors.

£ **Beddgelert Bistro**, Beddgelert, T01766-890543. Serves traditional tea and cakes as well as more substantial meals.

Glaslyn Ices, Beddgelert. Award winning ice cream shop. Home made sorbets and every flavour of ice cream from good old vanilla to chocolate and ginger or coffee and rum.

Pubs, bars and clubs

Stable Bar, Royal Oak, Betw-y-Coed T710219 Bustling pub in the heart of the village. The local male voice choir sings here every Friday.

Shopping

Betws-y-Coed *p612*

Betws-y-Coed is the main shopping centre for outdoor gear. Outlets include a **Cotswold**, Holyhead Rd, T01690-710710 and **Stewart R Cunningham**, T01690-710454 and **Snowdon Ranger**, in a converted church.

Activities and tours

Canoeing

Boulder Adventures, T01248-870556, www.boulderadventures.co.uk, hire out canoes on Llyn Padarn, Llanberis in summer

Climbing

Beacon Climbing Centre, Waunfawr, west of Llanberis, T01286-650045, www.beaconclimbing.com, has an indoor climbing wall and offers short, taster sessions.

General outdoor activities

Plas Y Brenin, Capel Curig, T01690-720214, www.pyb.co.uk, runs residential courses in everything from rock climbing and mountaineering to kayaking, canoeing and skiing. Also 2 hr sessions of climbing, canoeing or skiing – geared to kids but adults welcome. Indoor climbing wall and ski slope.

Surf Lines Adventure Shop, 57 High St, Llanberis, T01286-879080, www.surf-lines.co.uk. Offer activities from coasteering to climbing, also guided trips to Snowdon. Canoe hire.

Horse riding

Ty Coch Farm, Penmachno, half to full day rides, T01690-760248

Dolbadarn Pony Trekking Centre, by Dolabadarn Hotel, High St, Llanberis, T01286-870277

Mountain biking

Beics Beddgelert, T0800-2985835, www.beics.com. Beics Betws, mountain bike hire, full day from £16, T01690-710829, beicsbetwshire@btconnect.com.

Gwydir Forest, near Betws-y-Coed, offers biking including the 25 km Marin Trail. Further information from *Forest Enterprise*, T01341-422289, www.mbwales.com.

Paragliding

Snowdon Gliders, Mynydd Llandygai, T01248-600330. Paragliding for all levels.

Rowing

Padarn Boats, on Llyn Padarn, Llanberis hire out rowing boats in summer, go to the green hut by the playground

Walking

Guided walks round Betws-y-Coed and the surrounding area, start from TIC at 1000, Thu-Sun, and Bank Hol Mon, Apr-Sep, around 6-8 miles, £3.50. Snowdon guided walks can also be arranged using Sherpa Bus, £5, book in advance, T0151-4880052

Watersports

Bala Adventure and Watersports, by TIC at Bala lake, T01678-521059, www.balaadventureandwatersportscentre.co.uk, do windsurfing, kayaking, canoeing and landyachting.

Whitewater rafting

National Whitewater Centre, Frongoch, Bala, 2hr to full day experiences, T01678-521083, www.ukrafting.co.uk, white water rafting and kayaking.

Transport

Bus

Snowdon Sherpa buses run at busy times – and it's worth contacting Bus Gwynedd, T01286-679535, www.gwynedd.gov.uk/bwsgwynedd. Freedom of Wales Flexi Passes allow unlimited travel on all mainline rail services and buses including the Snowdon Sherpa. Buses to **Beddgelert** run from Caernarfon and Porthmadog T08705-808080

Car

Snowdonia is reached easily by road, with links from the M6 to the M56 and A55 from the north, while the A487 and A470 get you there if coming from the south. The A5 runs through the heart of the area, from Shrewsbury across the border in England, direct to the bustling centre of **Betws-y-Coed**.

Llangollen and around

→Colour map 3

Llangollen is best known as the venue for the International Musical Eisteddfod. Close to Wrexham and the border with England, the area is often bypassed by people in a hurry to reach Snowdonia. But it's a likeable place, surrounded by mountains and forests, with the lively River Dee running through its heart and is a good base for outdoor activities like canoeing and walking – it's within easy reach of the Offa's Dyke Path for instance. The surrounding countryside is delightful, particularly the Ceiriog Valley which seems like a secret world, dotted with small communities and laced with varied walks. ▸▸ *For Sleeping, Eating and other listings, see pages 622-623.*

Ins and outs

Getting there **Road** links to Llangollen are good but there's no station here. Nearest transport hub is Wrexham. ▸▸ *For further details, see Transport, page 623.*

Getting around Llangollen is easily explored on **foot**, but if you want to get out into the lovely Edeyrnion and Ceiriog valleys you will certainly need your own transport.

Information **Llangollen TIC** ⓘ *Castle St, Llangollen, T01978-860828, Easter-Oct daily 1000-1800, Nov-Easter, closed Wed, 0930-1630. www.borderlands.co.uk.*

Llangollen

Llangollen's a lively place, with a good range of pubs, restaurants and cafes. The river and the canal run through the town and seem to give it extra life: the canal towpath being a particularly good place for families with young children to stroll.

Llangollen International Musical Eisteddfod

For the last 56 years the pretty little Denbighshire town of Llangollen has hosted the International Musical Eisteddfod. For six days each July the normally sedate streets throng with as many as 50,000 visitors, who come to see 5,000 competitors from all corners of the globe partake in a broad spectrum of performing arts. Amateur musicians, singers and dancers from places as diverse as Mongolia and the USA compete in 20 very different events. Many are decked out in their national costumes, so the eisteddfod takes on a carnival air. Although the event has grown in prestige, its essence has remained the same since its inauguration in 1947. The eisteddfod's purpose is as much about creating a glorious visual spectacle and promoting international friendship as it is about competing. For some of today's mega stars, the eisteddfod was the place they cut their performing teeth. Luciano Pavarotti and Placido Domingo among them. Amateur events are interspersed with professional concerts given by such luminaries as the above mentioned tenors, Kiri Te Kanawa, Lesley Garrett, Bryn Terfel and Monserrat Caballe. Diversity is the name of the game, and it's not surprising to find Shirley Bassey, jazz heroes Cleo Laine and John Dankworth, and the Harlem Gospel Choir on the same bill. And for the who fancy something slightly different, there's even a fringe festival. For further information, have a look at www.international-eisteddfod.co.uk.

Plas Newydd Hill St ⓘ *T01978-861314, www.denbighshire.gov.uk, daily 1000-1700 (last admission 1615) Easter-Oct, £3, £2 children, £8 family*, is a mock Tudor building famed as the home of the Ladies of Llangollen, a lesbian couple who came here in 1780 and lived together contentedly for 50 years. Sarah Ponsonby and Lady Eleanor Charlotte Butler were a well bred couple who met at boarding school in Ireland and later eloped, dressed in men's clothing, with Sarah carrying a pistol. They were intercepted and returned to their families but ran away again, and were allowed to set up home together. Although they shared a bed they never admitted to having anything other than a loving friendship. Whatever its precise nature, their relationship fascinated fashionable society and they received a remarkable number of well-connected visitors. The Duke of Wellington was a particular favourite and came to the house several times – the ladies describing him as 'a charming young man, handsome, fashioned tall and elegant'. Other visitors included Josiah Wedgwood, Sir Humphrey Davy, Sir Walter Scott and William Wordsworth. The house itself was originally a cottage but the ladies transformed it into an elaborate 'gothic' creation with an overwhelming abundance of ornate dark oak carvings, many of which were presents from visitors. The house is left largely empty today, although the ladies' bedchamber has been refurbished as it was in 1832, a year after Sarah, the last surviving 'lady', died.

The town is the starting point for the **Llangollen Railway** ⓘ *T01978-860979, www.llangollen-railway.co.uk, core service Apr-Oct, also some services out of season, £8.50 return*. This steam railway runs from quaint Llangollen Station, where Queen Victoria arrived when she visited in 1889, for 8 miles, stopping at carefully restored stations like Berwyn (from where you can walk to the Horseshoe Falls), Glyndyfrdwy and Carrog.

f you've got young kids in tow it's worth checking out the **Llangollen Exhibition Centre** ⓘ *Mill St, T01978-860584, www.dapol.co.uk, daily 1000-1700, combined £9.75*, which houses several attractions. For the dedicated Dalek lover there's the Dr Who Experience which has original costumes and other memorabilia from the long running TV series – children used to today's sophisticated special effects will no doubt find much of it amusing. Train spotters and model builders can make for Model Railway World, which has over 20 working model railways. There's also a Model Factory where you can watch models and toys being made.

On the outskirts of the town is the **Motor Museum** ⓘ *T01978-860324, www.llangollenmotormuseum.co.uk, Apr-Sept Tues-Sun 1000-1700, Oct-Mar Wed-Sun 1100-1600, £2.50*, which houses a collection of 20th-century cars and motor cycles, as well as an exhibition on the canal. From here you continue along the A542 to the romantic ruins of **Valle Crucis Abbey** ⓘ *Apr-Sept 1000-1700 daily £2, £1.50 concessions, £5.50 family (free in winter 1000-1600)*. Although the approach to this once isolated Cistercian Abbey is sadly ruined by a tacky camping and caravaning site it still has plenty of picturesque charm, with a fine rose window, carved doorway and the monk's original fishpond. Founded in the 13th-century, the abbey was deserted after the Dissolution, its crumbling charms later captured on canvas by Turner. The abbey ('the abbey of the cross') was named after a nearby stone cross Eliseg's Pillar, erected in the 9th century in memory of a Welsh prince. Some researchers claim that Valle Crucis lies on a site associated with King Arthur, excavations in the 19th-century having revealed late Roman and Saxon finds. Other Arthurian links eagerly pointed out by local historians are the remains of a stone cross near the Llangollen Canal, known as Gueineveres' Cross, and a nearby spring called Arthur's Well.

Corwen

Little town west of Llangollen, from where Owain Glyndwr set out in his bid to wrest Wales from English rule. There's a statue of him in the town centre, while a few miles east the hump known as Owain Glyndwr's Mount is thought to be the site of his fortified manor. Just west of Corwen are two interesting churches, both in the care of CADW. **Rug Chapel** ⓘ *off the A494, T01490-412025, Apr-Sept daily 1000-1700, £2.50, concessions £2, family £7*, is a private 17th-century chapel, founded by Col William Salusbury, royalist governor of Denbigh Castle in the Civil War. In the 19th-century a carved rood screen was added, separating the clergy from the congregation. The architect Sir Edwin Lutyens visited the chapel and claimed that he was much influenced by what he saw. **Llangar Chapel**, off the B4401 (contact Rug Chapel for entry) is a medieval building, built on the remains of an earlier structure. It includes some 15th-century wall paintings, box pews and a painting of a large skeleton, representing death. Excavations in the early 1970s were said to have revealed the mysterious remains of 170 bodies beneath the church floor.

A pretty drive is the B4401 from Corwen to Bala, through the gentle Vale of Edeyrnion. About half way along is the little hamlet of Llandrillo, a good starting point for walks in the Berwyn Hills to the south.

Chirk

South of Llangollen, Chirk is notable for its famous **Castle** ⓘ *(NT) T01691-777701, castle Apr-early Nov, Wed-Sun, 1200-1700 (till 1600 Oct-Nov), garden 1100-1800 (till 1700 Oct-Nov) £5.80, £2.90 children, £14.50 family)*. Built around 1295 on behalf of Edward 1, it was the last in the great chain of castles built to subdue Wales. It was never quite completed and in 1595 was bought for £5000 by Sir Thomas Myddelton, a wealthy merchant whose family still live here. Today it feels more like a stately home than a castle with swish rooms filled with fine furniture, portraits and tapestries. There are also large gardens to explore and some elaborate gates, made by the Davies brothers in the early 18th-century. Chirk guards the head of the beautiful **Ceiriog Valley**, a wonderfully pastoral, unspoiled place with great walks and pubs.

North of Llangollen

Erddig ⓘ *2 miles south of Wrexham, T01978-315151 (NT), Sat-Wed, house end Mar-end Sept 1200-1700, Oct-early Nov 1200-1600; garden end Mar-end Jun 1100-1800, Jul, Aug 1000-1800, Sept 1100-1800, Oct-early Nov 1100-1700, £6.60, children £3.30, family £16.50.* This stately home was owned by the Yorke family from 1733 until the 1970s and remained almost unchanged during their years of occupancy. The 'upstairs' rooms contain some fine 18th -century furniture, as well as paintings and more commonplace items, while the 'below stairs' quarters are particularly well preserved with kitchens, servants' hall and, most unusually, portraits of the staff. The walled garden is one of the most important 18th-century gardens in Britain, and contains lots of rare fruit trees as well as around 150 different types of ivy.

Sleeping

Llangollen *p619*

D **Cornerstones**, 19 Bridge Street, T01978-861569, www.cornerstones-guesthouse.co.uk. 2 en suite rooms. 3 star B&B, good base for walkers and cyclists.

D **Gales of Llangollen**, Bridge Street, T01978-860089, F861313, www.galesofllangollen.co.uk. 15 rooms all ensuite. Situated above Gales wine bar, comfortable rooms handy for the town centre.

D **Oakmere**, Regent St, T01978-861126, www.oakmere.llangollen.co.uk. This large house is set in its own grounds a short distance from the town centre. Four of the six rooms are en suite.

D **The Grange**, Grange Rd, T01978-860366, www.thegrangellangollen.co.uk. Spacious house set in large, peaceful garden. No single supplement.

D **Tyn Celyn Farmhouse**, Tyndwr, near Llangollen, T01978-861117, www.borderlands.co.uk/tyn-celyn. This B&B is surrounded by lovely countryside on the outskirts of the town. Three rooms, all en suite.

F **YHA Youth Hostel**, Tyndwr Rd, T0870-7705932, llangollen@yha.org.uk. Good standard of hostel in large house about a mile out of town.

Chirk *p621*

A **The West Arms Hotel**, Llarmarnon Dyffryn Ceiriog, T01691-600665, F600622, www.thewestarms.co.uk. You won't find much more character than at this ancient inn, situated in a tranquil valley. The bedrooms are comfortable and there are all sorts of nooks and crannies in the public rooms downstairs, with settles, huge fireplaces and low beams. Pricey, but a great setting.

B **The Hand Hotel**, Llanarmon Dyffryn Ceiriog, T01691-600666, www.handhotelanarmondc.co.uk. Cheaper but less characterful than the West Arms Hotel, this inn is deep in the Ceiriog Valley. Log fires in winter.

Corwen *p621*

C **Tyddyn Llan**, on B4401 Llandrillo, near Corwen T01490-440264, www.tyddynllan.co.uk. There's a lovely, relaxed atmosphere at this Georgian house, set in a secluded valley. You can have afternoon tea on the lawn, or curl up on a sofa in the lounge with a book.

D **Powys Country House**, Holyhead Rd, Bonwym, near Corwen, T01490-412367, www.powyscountryhouse.co.uk. Large country house in 3 acres of gardens. Also has 2 self catering cottages.

Self catering

The Olde Granary, Maerdy Mawr, Gwyddelwern, near Corwen, T0771-4186943, www.maerdymawr-cottages.co.uk. Converted granary, with 4 self catering cottages on sheep farm. Open Apr-Oct.

Eating

Llangollen *p619*

££ **The Corn Mill**, Dee Lane, T01978-869555, 1200-2130. Lovely riverside setting and outdoor decking area make this converted mill the liveliest place to eat in town. Style is café/bistro so sandwiches and salads are available, as well as more filling mains like pork and apple sausage with mash, or fried halloumi with roasted vegetable cous cous.

££ **Gales Wine Bar**, Bridge Street T01978-860089, Mon-Sat 1200-1400, 1800-2200. Great choice of wines at this cosy wine bar that also offers a range of good value meals, such as fillet of sea bream.

£ **The Bull Inn**, Castle St. Popular, youthful pub with a beer garden serving bar meals.

£ **River View Bistro**, Bridge St. Tea room and bistro beside the river, offering tea, cakes and light meals such as crab and spinach flan

£ **Sun Inn**, Rhewl, about 3.5 miles from Llangollen on B103, T01978-861043. 14th-century drovers' inn, with low beams and period features. Serves real ale and good bar meals.

Chirk *p621*

£££-££ **The West Arms Hotel**, Llarmarnon Dyffryn Ceiriog, T01691-600665. Award winning fresh food at this lovely old inn. Cosy atmosphere in the bar where you can have delicious bar meals such as local pork sausages in Yorkshire pudding (£8.95), or good veggie options. There's also an acclaimed restaurant.

Corwen *p621*

£££ **Tyddyn Llan**, on B4401 Llandrillo, near Corwen T01490-440264. Dinner only, must book. Crisp white tablecloths, fresh flowers and an air of relaxed elegance. Choose from a full menu (£35) with imaginative canapes, homemade breads, 4 courses, cheese and coffee, or go for 2 courses (£27) or 3 (£32). Mains might include Welsh black beef or turbot with leek risotto, and delicious desserts vary from blackberry and almond tart to homemade ice cream. Vegetarians are well catered for. Recommended.

Entertainment

Welsh male voice choirs can be heard at: **Neuadd Edeyrnion**, Corwen every Wed at 2000 (not Aug), T01490-412604; **Neuadd Goffa**, Stryd Uchaf, Glyn Ceiriog, Wed 2000, T01691-600242, and at the **Hand Hotel**, Llangollen on Fri (not Aug) at 1930, T01978-860303.

Festivals and events

Early Jul International Musical Eisteddfod, Llangollen. World famous festival of music, song and dance, T01978-862001, www.international-eisteddfod.co.uk.

Late Aug Balloon Festival, Llangollen, hot air balloon fest, T08700-115007

Activities and tours

Boating

Llangollen Wharf, Llangollen Wharf, Wharf Hill, T01978-860702, www.horsedrawnboats.co.uk. Horse drawn narrowboat trips on the canal (£4) and 2 hr cruises across the Pontcysyllte aqueduct (£7.50)

Canoeing

JJ Canoeing and Rafting, near Llangollen, T01978-860763, www.jjraftcanoe.com.

General adventure

Adventure activity Solutions, Castle St, Llangollen, T01978-860634, www.Adventure-Solutions.co.uk. Range of activities from kiting to climbing. Half day taster sessions available.

Mountain biking

Llangollen Bike Hire, Castle St, Llangollen, T01978-860605, www.northwalesbikehire.co.uk. Mountain bike hire for everything from 1 hr to 1 week.

Transport

Car

From the north the M56, then M53 takes you to Chester, from where you take the A55, then A483 to Wrexham, then the A539. From the south, the A5 from Shrewsbury runs straight to Llangollen. The scenic route is the A525, then A542 from Ruthin,

Train, bus and boat

There is no station at Llangollen, the nearest is **Ruabon**, south of Wrexham, where you can pick up bus 94 or 95 to **Llangollen**. www.chester2shrewsburyrail.net. Buses from **London** (National Express) run to **Wrexham**. The canal system links **Llangollen** to **Shropshire**, so it's also possible to arrive by **narrowboat**.

Directory

Internet Free access is available at **Llangollen Library**, and at **Corwen Library** and **One Stop Shop**, Tue 1430-1900, Wed 1000-1200, Thur 1000-1400, Fri 1430-1900.

Conwy and the Northwest Corner

→Colour map 3

The Northwest corner feels a world away from the chips and caravans of the north coast resorts. This is the most Welsh part of Wales, where the language is spoken widely and where the Celtic past never seems far away. You sense a difference as soon as you see the brooding beauty of Conwy Castle and stroll the streets of this neat little walled town – the best base for exploring the area. Further along the coast you come to the busy university town of Bangor and then to the heartland of Welsh nationalism, Caernarfon, famous for its castle. This corner of Wales also includes the two most characterful and isolated parts of the country; the beautiful Llyn peninsula and the pastoral isle of Anglesey, last refuge of the Celts and rich in prehistoric sites. ▸▸ *For Sleeping, Eating and other listings, see pages 629-632.*

Ins and outs

Getting there Conwy is reasonably well served with **buses** and **trains.** Trains and buses also run to Bangor and the **North Wales Coast Line** runs to Holyhead on Anglesey. There is a station at Pwhelli on the Llyn. ▸▸ *For further details, see Transport, page 632.*

Getting around The main towns of Conwy, Bangor and Caernarfon are small enough to be explored on foot. Buses run to the main places in Anglesey and the main towns in the Conwy Valley by train. However it is much easier with your own transport.

Information Conwy Castle Visitor Centre ⓘ T01492-592248, conwy.tic@virgin.net, Apr-Sep daily 0930-1700, Oct-Mar, Mon-Sat 0930-1600, Sun 1100-1600. **Porthmadog Tourist information Centre** ⓘ *High St T01766-512981, Apr-Oct daily 1000-1800, Nov-Mar 1000-1700.* **Holyhead TIC** (Anglesey) ⓘ Stena Line Terminal, T01407-762622 holyhead.tic@virgin.net, daily 0830-1800, www.anglesey.gov.uk. **Caernarfon** TIC ⓘ *Oriel Pendeitsh, Castle St T01286-672232, daily Apr-end Oct 1000-1800, Nov-Mar daily except Wed 1000-1630, caernarfon.tic@gwynedd.gov.uk, www.caernarfon.com.*

Conwy

Conwy's a gem: a pretty little walled town dominated by a stunningly photogenic castle. With its well preserved medieval charms, and picturesque setting on the Conwy estuary, it's easy to see why its a World Heritage Site. The town's history stretches back to Roman times at least, with settlers being attracted to the mussels that are still harvested there today. The castle is certainly the biggest draw but there are enough other attractions, shops and places to eat to occupy you for a day or two.

Constructed between 1283 and 1287, **Conwy Castle** ⓘ *T01492-592358, www.cadw.wales.gov.uk, Apr-1 Jun 0930-1700 daily, 2 Jun-28 Sept 0930-1800 daily, 29 Sept-26 Oct 0930-1700 daily; 27 Oct-31 Mar 0930-1600 Mon-Sat, 1100-1600 Sun, £3.50, concessions £3, family £10,* was one of the key fortresses in the 'iron ring' of castles built by Edward 1 to contain the Welsh. It took just four years to build at a cost of around £15,000 – about £9 million today, and its exterior, with eight huge round towers, is still largely intact. It's easy to see why it has long been a favourite subject for artists, including JMW Turner who painted it many times. Once inside, make sure you go up to the battlements, from which you'll get striking views of the surrounding mountains and of Conwy's well preserved town walls, which stretch for around three quarters of a mile (1 ¼ km) and are studded with 22 towers.

You can also see Conwy's old **Suspension Bridge** ⓘ *T01492-573282, 27 Mar-31 Oct 1000-1700 daily, £1.20, children £0.60*,b uilt by Thomas Telford and opened in 1826. The bridge today is only used by pedestrians. Your fee gets you into the old Toll House, furnished as it would have been when inhabited around 1891.

From the bridge you can walk along **Conwy Quay**, where **boat trips** ⓘ *T01492-592830, £3.50*, on the Queen Victoria leave along for Llandudno or up river for views of the Conwy Valley, or visit the **Smallest House in Great** Britain ⓘ *Apr-end Oct 1000-1700, later in summer, £0.50, children £0.30*. This tiny dwelling has just two rooms yet was inhabited until 1900, the last resident being a 6ft 3in fisherman. You can squeeze inside and see the conditions for yourself.

A short walk away is the quirky **Teapot World** ⓘ *Castle St, T01492-593429, www.teapotworld.co.uk, Easter-Oct, Mon-Sat 1000-1730, Sun 1100-1730; £1.50, concessions £1, family £3.50*. This private collection of teapots fills just one room but contains many rare pieces ranging from Wedgwood, Clarice Cliff and Susie Cooper pots, to a 'War against Hitlerism' pot given from 1939-45 to people who donated their aluminium pans for the war effort.

The oldest house in Conwy is **Aberconwy House** ⓘ *Castle St, T01492-592246, Mar-Oct, daily except Tue, 1100-1700, £2.40, child £1.20*. Built as a merchants' house it dates back to the 14th century and has rooms furnished in various periods of its long history. However, the most interesting property is fabulous **Plas Mawr** ⓘ *High St, T01492-580167, daily 1 Apr- 1 June, 1-28 Sept, 0930-1700; 2 June-31 Aug 0930-1800, 29 Sep-26 Oct 0930-1600, £4.50, concessions £3.50, family £12.50, joint tickets with Conwy Castle £6.50, concessions £5.50, family £18.50*, a superbly preserved Elizabethan house, built 1576-85 for Robert Wynn, a prosperous Welsh merchant. Many of the rooms are decorated with elaborate plasterwork, designed to impress visitors in a 'come up and see my ceiling' sort of way. You can get an audio tour of the house, and there's also an exhibition containing horribly fascinating details of the contemporary diet – kids love it.

Art lovers should go to the **Royal Cambrian Academy** ⓘ *off High St, Tue-Sat 1100-1700, Sun 1300-1630, free*, nearby. It has changing exhibitions and displays contemporary paintings by artists such as Kyffin Williams, Maurice Cockrill, and Ishbel McWhirter. As you go upstairs you're rewarded with a striking view of the castle.

Conwy

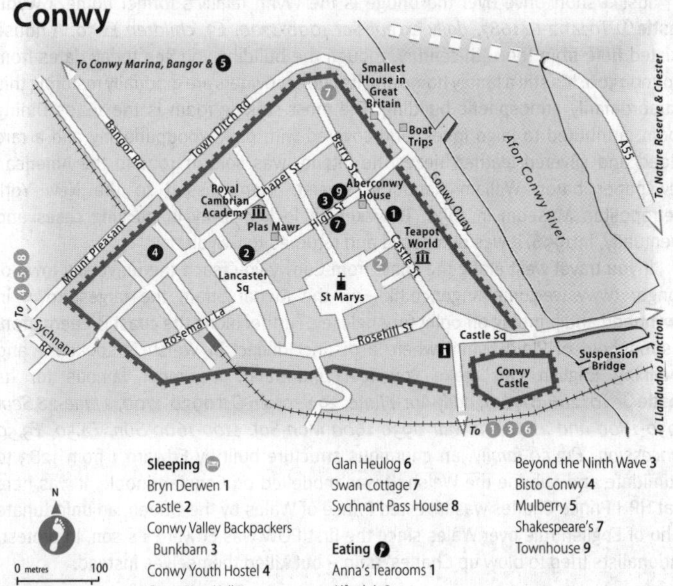

Just outside town is an **RSPB Nature Reserve** ⓘ *Llandduno Junction, T01492-584091, www.rspb.org.uk, daily 1000-1700, £2.50, children £1, concessions £1.50, family £5*, where there are extensive reedbeds, with hides and walks allowing you to spot reed buntings, reed warblers and sedge warblers, as well as many waders.

Vale of Conwy

The lovely Vale of Conwy stretches from Conwy into the Snowdonia National Park to Betws-Y-Coed. It's dotted with interesting villages and hamlets and has several good places to eat. Sites to visit are: **Bodnant Garden** ⓘ *near Tal-y-Cafn, T01492-650460, Mar-early Nov daily 1000-1700, £5.20) which covers 80 acres of ground*, and **Trefiw Wells** ⓘ *T01492-640057, Mon-Sat Oct-Easter, 1000-dusk, Sun 1200-dusk; Easter-Sep daily 1000-1730, £3 for self guided tour*, an ancient spa, with iron rich waters, believed to have been discovered by the Romans and later used by Victorian visitors.

Llanrwst

A pleasant market town with several good places to eat and drink. The Pont Fawr, is an arched bridge attributed to Inigo Jones. It's often called the Buttermilk Bridge as the central arch, incorrectly fitted by drunken builders, collapsed soon after opening in 1636. The men were restricted to drinking buttermilk until it was safely rebuilt. The lovely ivy clad building by the bridge is Tu Hwnt I'r Bont, which dates back to the 17th-century and was once the courthouse. Now it's a busy tea room. Do take time to pop into **Gwydir Chapel**, beside St Grwst church. Ascribed to Inigo Jones, it's the memorial chapel of the local Wynn family and contains a fascinating jumble of tombs, brasses and marble tablets. Look out for the stone effigy of a knight, and the underpart of the stone coffin of Llewelyn ap Iowerth (the Great), the son in law of King John whose coffin was brought here after the dissolution of Conwy Abbey. No one knows what happened to his body.

Just a short drive over the bridge is the Wynn family's former home, **Gwydir Castle** ⓘ *T01492-641687, daily except Sat 1000-1700, £3, children £1.50*. A house existed here from the 14th-century, though the building you see today dates from around 1500. It's still a family home and its current owners are gradually restoring this extraordinarily atmospheric building. The most striking room is the 1640s Dining Room, attributed to Inigo Jones, and covered with dark woodpanelling and a rare gilded and silvered leather frieze. The interior was sold in 1921 to the American newspaper baron William Randolph Hearst, then passed to the New York Metropolitan Museum in 1956. They kept it locked away in packing cases and eventually, in 1996, it was purchased and returned to Gwydir.

If you travel west along the coast from Conwy you reach the university town of Bangor (www.welcomebangor.co.uk), on the Menai Strait, the largest town in Gwynnedd and jumping off point for Anglesey. Further along the coast is Caernarfon, a stronghold of Plaid Cymru where a distinct dialect of Welsh is spoken – and speaking English can make you feel unpopular. It's most famous for its **Castle** ⓘ *T01286-677617, daily Apr-1 June, 29 Sept-26 Oct 0930-1700, 2 June-28 Sept 0930-1800 and 27 Oct-31 Mar 0930-1600 Mon-Sat, 1100-1600 Sun, £4.50, £3.50 concession, £12.50 family*, an enormous structure built by Edward 1 from 1283 to intimidate and subdue the Welsh. It was modelled on Constantinople. It was here that HRH Prince Charles was invested Prince of Wales by the Queen, an unfortunate echo of English rule over Wales since the first POW was Edward 1's son. In protest, nationalists tried to blow up Charles' train – but killed themselves instead.

Ynys Mon (Anglesey)

Across the Menai Strait is the Isle of Anglesey, linked to the mainland by the Menai Suspension Bridge, built by Thomas Telford in 1826, and the Britannia Tubular Bridge the brainchild of Robert Stevenson, built in 1850. The landscape is pastoral and so fertile that it was known as the breadbasket of Wales. It's a great place to come if you're into prehistoric sites – the island is covered with them. Just a few of the island's sites are:

Biwmares (Beaumaris)

Once the capital of Anglesey, the name is thought to mean 'beautiful marsh' in old French. **Moated Beaumaris Castle** ⓘ *T01248-810361, www.cadw.wales.gov.uk, daily 0930-1800, £3, children £2.50, family £8.50*, was never completed – the money ran out – but is a technical triumph. It defences include fourteen deadly obstacles, including cunning arrow-slits and 'murder holes' to defend entrances. Also here is the **Beaumaris Victorian Gaol & Courthouse** ⓘ *T01248-810921, 1030-1700, Easter to end of Sep, £2.75, children £1.75, family £7*, comprising Victorian punishment cells, dark secrets and dimly lit corridors.

Llanddwyn Island (Ynys Llanddwyn) a peninsular in the southern corner, derives its name from Saint Dwynwen, the Welsh equivalent of St Valentine. The ruins of Dwynwen's Chapel can still be seen. The island lies within the Newborough Nature Reserve. Canada geese, shelduck and red-breasted merganser are frequent visitors and over 550 different plant species including Sea Spurge Euphorbia paralias, and Dune Pansy Viola curtisii have been recorded.

Llanfairpwll

The most exciting thing about Llanfairpwllgwyngyllgogerychwyrndrobwllllantysilio-gogogoch, Llanfair PG or simply Llanfair (as it's known to locals) is its name – the longest in Europe. In English it's 'The Church of St Mary in the hollow of the white hazel near the rapid whirlpool and the church of St Tysilio near a red cave'. It was contrived as a marketing ploy by a 19th-century tradesman.

Plas Newydd ⓘ *(NT) 1 ½ miles from Llanfair PG, A4080, T01248-715272, Mar-Oct (closed Thu and Fri), house 1200-1700, gardens 1100-1730, £5, children £2.40, family £12, gardens: £2.80, children £1.40*. Built by James Wyatt. This magnificent 18th-century building was the home of the Marquis of Anglesey. It's surrounded by extravagant gardens and houses a military museum and tea room.

Holyhead

Holyhead, with its busy port, mainly serving Ireland, and bustling market day (Mondays 0800-1600) is the largest town on the island. There's not a huge amount to detail the tourist, save the **Holyhead Maritime Museum** ⓘ *T01407-769745, Tue -Sun 1300-1700, £2.50, children £0.50, concessions £1.50, family £5*.

The Llyn

The Llyn Peninsula has a wonderful untamed appeal, particularly along the northern coast and remote tip, yet many visitors never get further than Porthmadog, nearest town to the famous and gloriously eccentric village of Portmeirion. The area's main beauties are its unspoilt beaches, high banked lanes and sleepy churches – it's the sort of place to explore on foot or by bike.

Porthmadog and around

Porthmadog takes its name from its founder, the MP William Madocks, who created a port linked by rail to the slate quarries at Ffestiniog, allowing vast quantities of slate to be shipped overseas. Rather unprepossessing, it's most notable as the southerly terminus of the delightful Ffestiniog Railway (see Snowdonia page 616). It's also a convenient base from which to explore the unique holiday village of **Portmeirion** ⓘ *T01766-770000, www.portmeirion-village.com, daily 0930-1730, £5.50, children £2.70, family £13*. This was the creation of the architect Clough Williams-Ellis, and a fulfilled a boyhood ambition to build an idealised village in a coastal setting. Work began in 1926, centring the village round an Italian style piazza and sprinkling it with a Liquorice Allsorts mix of buildings, with Gothic, Classical and Italianate styles mixed with arches, fountains and statues. The brightly coloured buildings make an arresting sight – but try and get here early in summer to avoid the coach parties. Many visitors are Prisoner groupies, fans of the 60's cult TV series, The Prisoner, starring Patrick McGoohan, which was set here. As well as the village, there are 70 acres of woodland to explore.

Criccieth

This is a pretty Victorian holiday resort which snuggles beneath its ruined **Castle** ⓘ *T01766-522227, daily 2 Jun- 28 Sep 1000-1800, 1 Apr-1 Jun and 29 Sep-26 Oct 1000-1700, £2.50, £2 concessions, £7 family; rest of year free access CADW*. Originally built by Llywelyn the Great around 1230-1240, the castle was later taken over by Edward 1, who extended and refortified it. It was eventually captured and burned by Owain Glyndwr in 1404. There are panoramic views from the top and on a hot day it's worth bring a book and settling down for a lazy hour or two.

You can also visit the **Chapel of Art** ⓘ *T01766-523570, www.the-coa.org.uk, Tue-Sat 1300-1700*, which is a restored chapel that shows contemporary Welsh art.

Llanystumdwy

A mile west of Criccieth is the boyhood home of David Lloyd George, the charismatic Welsh social reformer who became British Prime Minister during WW1. His home is now part of the **Lloyd George Museum** ⓘ *T01766-522071, www.gwynedd.gov.uk/museums, Easter, 1030-1700, May Mon-Fri 1030-1700, Jun Mon-Sat 1030-1700, Jul-Sep daily 1030-1700, Oct Mon-Fri 1100-1600, £3, £2 concessions, £7 family*. There's a film on his life, as well as memorabilia ranging from Lloyd George teapots, to political cartoons – even the thick yellow pencil with which he wrote his war memoirs. In the garden is the little cottage in which he was brought up, furnished much as it would have been during his lifetime.

Llanbedrog, is a small but pleasant village with a lovely beach. It's notable for **Plas Glyn-Y-Weddw** ⓘ *T01758-740763, www.oriel.org.uk, daily 1100-1700 Jul, Aug, closed Tue rest of year, £2.50, £1 concessions, £5 family*, a Victorian Gothic mansion that is now an art gallery. With eye stretching views out to sea, the house provides a grand setting for its changing exhibition of contemporary Welsh and Polish paintings (many Poles settled here after the Second World War and there are strong connections with Poland) and sculpture. In the Andrews Room is the permanent collection of porcelain, with Swansea and Nantgarw pieces.

The A499 road ends at Abersoch, a yachties haven, leaving the tip of the Llyn to be explored by a lovely maze of B and unclassified roads. Worth looking out for on the south coast is Plas-yn-Rhiw, Rhiw, once home to acclaimed Welsh poet R S Thomas and the little village of Aberdaron, where Thomas was minister. Off the tip of the Llyn is Bardsey Island, an important place of pilgrimage since the 6th-century and now a nature reserve, noted for its birdlife.

The north coast is less populated than the south, and dotted with quiet beaches and sleepy churches. One of the loveliest is the **church of St Beuno** (May-Oct 1000-2000) at Clynnog Fawr, situated on an old Pilgrims' Route. Surprisingly large (Dr Johnson praised it as 'very spacious and magnificent for this country' 1774) given its remote setting, it's a Tudor building but Christians have worshipped here since the 7th-century. Inside are informative panels on the church and its history, as well as a parish chest of 1600, and some dog tongs, used to control badly behaved dogs in church. Nearby, at the crossroads at Aberdesach, a little road runs right down to a delightful hidden beach, a mix of golden sand, stones and seaweed. There's nothing but a few beach huts – it's a perfect place to paddle, stroll or just gaze out to sea.

Sleeping

Conwy *p624*

B **Castle Hotel**, High St, Conwy T01492-582800, www.castlewales.co.uk. This former coaching inn is conveniently situated right in the centre of Conwy and claims to have hosted illustrious guests such as Wordsworth and Thomas Telford.

B **Sychnant Pass House**, Sychnant Pass Road, near Conwy T01492-596868, www.sychnant-pass-house.co.uk. Wonderful and welcoming, award winning country house – dogs, cats, books, squashy sofas and individually decorated rooms, all very high standard. Meals on request.

D **Crows Nest Hall**, Sychnant Pass, near Conwy T572956, www.crowsnesthall.co.uk. Lovely old house in isolated country pass, great location for walking.

E **Bryn Derwen**, Llanwrst Rd, Conwy T01492-596134, www.conwy-wales.com/ brynderwen. Reliable B&B, dotted with Grecian style pots and knick-knacks.

E **Glan Heulog**, Llanrwst Rd, Conwy T01492-593845, www.walesbandb.com. Good, clean and friendly B&B just outside the town walls.

E **Swan Cottage**, 18 Berry Street, Conwy T01492-596840, www.swancottage.btinternet.co.uk. 3 rooms in basic B&B in town centre. Two of the rooms have lovely views over the estuary.

F **Conwy Valley Backpackers Bunkbarn**, Pyllau Gloewen Farm, T01492-660504, www.pyllaufarm.co.uk. About 6 miles out of Conwy this farm offers basic bunk facilities and camp/caravan site.

F **Conwy Youth Hostel**, Larkhll, Sychnant Pass Road, near Conwy T01492-593571. 24 rooms – sleeps 80-100. 4 star youth hostel a short walk from the town centre.

Vale of Conwy *p626*

B **The Groes Inn**, 2 miles from Conwy on B5106, T01492-650545, www.groesinn.com. This old coaching inn claims to be the first licensed house in Wales, dating back to 1573. All rooms are individually furnished and the inn retains its character with log fires and wooden beams.

D **Gwydir Castle**, on B5106 just outside Llanrwst, T01492-641687, www.gwydircastle.co.uk. 2 rooms Extremely atmospheric, haunted medieval manor house with oak panelling, antique furniture and baths so deep you could practically swim in them.

The Llyn *p627*

L-A **Portmeirion Hotel**, Portmeirion, Gwynedd, T01766-770000, www.portmeirion-village.com. Plush rooms, suites and serviced cottages in the main hotel and dotted around the village of Portmeirion. Special breaks available.

L-A **Castell Deudraeth**, Portmeirion, Gwynedd T01766-772400, www.portmeirion-village.com. Castle on the edge of Portmeirion: cool, sleekly styled rooms and suites, less fussy and flowery than the main hotel and very comfortable.

D **Yr Hen Fecws**, 16 Lombard Street, Porthmadog T514625, F 514865, www.henfecws.com. Once a bakehouse, this central restaurant with rooms has a comfortable, contemporary style.

D **Wern Fawr Manor Farm**, Llanbedrog, T/F 01758-740156, www.wernfawr.co.uk. High quality B&B in this Grade 11 listed , 16th century manor house set in over 6 acres of grounds. Freshly laid free range eggs and home made bread and jams for breakfast, and evening meals available in winter. There are also self catering cottages from £230 (sleeps 2) to £690 (sleeps 8)- lower rates apply out of high season.

For an explanation of the sleeping and eating price codes used in this guide, see the inside front cover. Other relevant information is provided in the Essentials chapter, page 36.

Eating

Conwy *p624*

££ **Alfredos**, Lancaster Sq, T592381. Mon-Sat 1800-2200, Sun 1800-2130, lunch Fri-Sun 1200-1400. Popular local Italian joint serving usual range of pizzas for £5-6, and pasta dishes for around £7.

££ **Bistro Conwy**, Chapel St, T596326. 1130-1400 Tue-Sat, 1900-2100 Tue-Thu and 1900-2130 Fri, Sat, closed Sun. New bistro tucked away under the old town walls. Serves tasty lunches like baked herb rolls with filling, and contemporary British main meals in the evenings like liver with red onion and orange sauce.

££ **The Mulberry**, Conwy Marina, T583350. Mon-Thu 1200-1500, 1800-2130, Fri-Sun 1200-2130. Pub serving pricey meals, but with good views over the new marina.

££ **Shakespeare's**, High St, T582800. Award winning restaurant in the Castle Hotel, serving fresh Welsh produce in a formal setting.

£ **Anna's Tearooms**, 9 Castle Street, Conwy T01492-580908, open 1000-1700 daily. Stock up on walking gear in the outdoor shop below, then pop upstairs to this good quality tea room for some soup or filling cheese and potato pie.

£ **Beyond the Ninth Wave**, 4 High Street, Conwy T01492-582212. Wed-Sat 1030-1630. Light modern café, on the ground floor of a pottery shop. As well as coffees and cakes it serves dishes like feta and olive salad.

£ **Townhouse Restaurant**, 2 High St, T596436. Tue-Sun 1100-1500, Wed-Sat from 1830. Light lunches such as jacket potatoes or lamb burgers, evening meals are British with a Welsh flavour, such as lamb with garlic and rosemary.

Vale of Conwy *p626*

££ **The Austrian Restaurant**, Capuelo, 2 miles out of Conwy, T01492-622170. Wed-Sat from 1800, Sun lunch from 1200. Authentic Austrian restaurant, slightly incongruous in rural Wales, but serving sustaining dishes like wiener schnitzel and apfel strudel.

££ **Eagles Hotel**, Llanrwst. Daily 1200-1400 and 1800-2030 Sun,Thu, 1800-2100 Fri, Sat, This hotel is popular with locals and serves bar meals, Sun lunches and good thick chips.

££ **Groes Inn**, Tyn-y-Groes, on B5106 about 2 miles from Conwy, T01492-650545. Daily 1200-1415, Sun-Fri 1830-2100, Sat 1800-2100. Lovely 16th-century inn serving everything from sandwiches to steak and mushroom pie. Desserts include rose petal ice cream.

££ **Pen-y-Bont**, Rowen, 4 miles out of Conwy off B5106. T01492-650022. 1200-1700 daily and evenings at weekends. Secluded tea room and restaurant in the pretty village of Rowen.

££ **The Tannery**, Llanrwst T01492-640172. Mon-Sat 100-1700, 1900-2100, Sun 1100-1600. Lovely contemporary café/bistro with a wooden deck overlooking the river. Good coffee and cakes, and imaginative dishes such as grilled goats cheese with a strawberry dressing, or broccoli and stilton tart. Mains £6.95-£13.95.

£ **Tu Hwnt I'r Bont**, by Pont Fawr in Llanwryst. Tue-Sun 1030-1700, Literally 'the house beyond the bridge' this riverside, ivy-covered tearoom has friendly staff, lovely location and great value cream teas.

£ **La Barrica**, Ancaster Sq, Llanrwst. Apr-Oct 0930-1600, closed Tue, good Italian style coffee stop also serving Mediterranean snacks, patisserie and hot filled baguettes for around £2.75.

Anglesey *p627*

££ **Tafarn Y Bont**, Menai Bridge, T01248-716888. 1100-2100. Within a stone's throw of Menai Suspension Bridge – wide range of fish specialities.

££ **The Waterfront Restaurant**, Treaddur Bay; T01407-860006. Chef Wayne Roberts transforms local produce into culinary delights.

£ **Liverpool Arms Hotel**, Menai Bridge T01248-810362. Summer 0700-1000 and 1200-2100, winter 0700-1000, 1200-1400 and 1800-2100. A busy but friendly pub that provides good wholesome food and has a range of fish specialities.

£ **Tafarn Y Rhos**, Rhostrehwfa, near Llangefni; at the centre of Anglesey, T01248-724404,1200-1430 and 1645-2130. A popular meeting place, with delicious bar meals, games room, lounge bar and a friendly smile.

The Llyn *p627*

£££ **Castell Deudraeth**, Portmerion T01766-772400. 1200-1400, 1800-2130. Brasserie style food in lovely setting. Welsh twist on meals with mains such as Llyn crab and Anglesey turbot.

££££ **Portmerion Hotel**, Portmerion T01766-770228. 1200-1400, 1830-2100. Upmarket, formal restaurant in the Portmerion hotel. Modern Welsh cuisine using local, fresh produce. No jeans, best to reserve. Around £35 for dinner.

££ **Yr Hen Fecws**, 16 Lombard Street, Porthmadog T514625. Mon-Sat 1800-2200. Excellent, lively bistro, with wooden beams and slate tablemats. Starters such as Thai fish cakes £4.53, and mains of fish, meat and imaginative vegetarian choices like herb pancakes with roquefort and sundried tomatoes £9.35

££ **Ponds Bistro**, High Street, Porthmadog T512333. Tue-Fri 1800-2100, Sat 1800-2130. Popular meals, booking advised in season.

££ **The Galley**, by the beach at Llanbedrog, off A499 T01758-740730. Daily from 1100, Mar-Oct. Busy bistro with seats overlooking the beach. Serves soups, filled ciabatta, and mains like curries, pizzas and roast beef.

£ **Café Lawrence**, Snowdon Lodge, Church St, Tremadog, T01766-515354. Lawrence of Arabia's birthplace, now a café where you can fill up with sandwiches, baguettes and cakes.

£ **The Ship Inn**, Bryn-y-Gro, just outside Llanbedrog T01758-740270. Daily 1200-1430, 1700-2100. Pleasant pub with beer garden, offering meals like steaks, pasta and pizza at around £6.80

Criccieth *p628*

£££-££ **Tir a Mor**, Mona Terrace, Criccieth T01766-523084. Best place for a special meal, but you'll have to book. Mains might include roast local lamb £13.95, or ravioli with wild mushrooms £12.95.

££ **Granvilles**, High Street, Criccieth T01766-522506. Coffee shop/ bistro, evening meals from 1800-2100. Tiled floor, terracotta walls and large mirrors make it relaxed and bright. Daytime – cakes, snacks and light meals. Evenings come for fish dishes like monkfish with tagliatelle, sea bass with herb risotto, or veggie risotto of leeks, broccoli and herbs.

££-£ **Poachers Restaurant**, 66 High Street, Criccieth T01766-52251. Mon-Sat from 1800. French style bistro/restaurant offering set meals and some vegetarian choices.

£ **Caffi Cwrt**, Y Maes, Criccieth. Best choice for traditional teas, scones and cakes in atmospheric old building with wooden beams and a little tea garden.

Pubs, bars and clubs

Vale of Conwy *p626*

The Fairy Glen, Capuelo, 2 miles out of Conwy, food served Mon-Fri 1200-1345, 1800-2045, Sat, Sun 1200-2045. Pub serving good food.

Ty Gwyn, Rowen, 4 miles out of Conwy off B5106. Village pub that serves good bar meals.

The Old Ship, Trefiw, T01492-640013. Traditional pub offering bar meals.

The Llyn *p627*

££ **Brondanw Arms**, Garreg, Llanfrothen T01766-770555, food 1200-1400, 1800-2100 Mon-Fri, Sat, Sun 1200-2100. Family friendly pub serving bar meals.

££ **Coach Inn**, on A499, Clynnog Fawr, T01286-660212, pleasant inn offering bar meals, across from St Bueno's church.

££ **The Griffin**, Penrhyndeudraeth, at crossroads in village T01766-771706, food 1200-1430, 1800-2100 daily. Friendly local serving good pub grub.

Festivals and events

Jun Criccieth Festival, with jazz, chamber music and art.

Jul Conwy Bluegrass Festival, T01492-580454.

Aug Bryn Terfel's Faenol Festival, Faenol Estate, Bangor, www.brynfest.com. Music Festival.

Activities and tours

Climbing

Ropeworks, Greenacres, Black Rock Sands, Morfa Bychan, Porthmadog, T01766-515316, www.ropeworks.co.uk.

Cycling/Mountain biking

Conwy Valley Cycle Route: Llanrwst to Conwy loop 25 miles, Llanrwst to Penmachno loop 21 miles, www.conwy. gov.uk/countryside.

Gwydyr Forest has lots of new Single-track links and challenging climbs, www.forestry.gov.uk

Fishing

Sea angling trips can be booked from the Harbour Office in Conwy, T01492-596253. Game fishing is possible at Llyn Crafnant, T01492-640818.

General outdoor activities

Artro Adventure, T01341-241275, www.prthmadog.co.uk/artroadventure – canoeing, scrambling, walking.

Horse riding

Pinewood Stables, Conwy, T01492-592256.

Sailing

Conwy School of Yachting does RYA practical and shore based courses, T01492-572999, www.conwy-yachting.com. **Conwy Yacht club**, Deganwy, T01492-583690, www.conwyyachtclub.com. **North Wales Cruising Club**, Conwy, T01492-593481, www.nwcc.info.

Walking

Conwy Valley Ramblers has information on T01978-855148, and there is a pack on Walks in the Conwy Valley from T01492-575361.

Transport

Road

Conwy on the main A55 road. To the Conwy Valley, take the A470 or B5106. **Buses** that run along the north Wales coast stop at Conwy. National Express coaches run to **Bangor**, **Caernarfon** and **Holyhead** as well as **Pwllheli**.

Train

Regular trains run from London, Birmingham and Manchester to **Llandudno Junction**, where you change for **Conwy** station; some trains stop at Conwy itself. Conwy Valley railway, runs between **Llandudno** on the coast and **Blaenau Ffestiniog** in Snowdonia, stopping at places like **Llanrwst** and **Betws-y-Coed** en route, www.conwyvalleyrailway.co.uk. The **North Wales Coast** line runs from Chester to **Bangor** and **Holyhead**. Cambrian Coaster trains run to **Porthmadog** and **Pwhelli**.

Directory

Internet Free at Conwy library, Castle Street open Mon, Thur, Fri 1000-1730, Tues 1000-1900, Wed, Sat 1000-1300. Free at **Porthmadog library**, Chapel St. Free at **Caernarfon library**, Bangor St. **Criccieth** – Roots, High Street, Criccieth daily in season 1000-1700, access (5p per minute) and small coffee bar, also has some tourist leaflets. **Post office** Porthmadog Post Office, corner of High St and Bank Place. North Wales Police T01286-673347

Northeast Wales

→*Colour map 3*

The Northeast corner of Wales covers all shades of the tourist spectrum. It's best known for its sandy coastline which includes the genteel Victorian town of Llandudno, as well as lively, and frankly tacky, resorts like Colwyn Bay and Rhyl: full of caravans, bingo halls and the smell of chips. But venture inland and you'll find little gems that many visitors fail to explore: Britain's smallest cathedral at St Asaph; the pretty market town of Ruthin; the excellent art collection at Bodelwyddan Castle, and gentle walks in the Vale of Clywd. And on the Dee Estuary, the ancient pilgrimage site of Holywell. ➤ *For Sleeping, Eating and other listings, see pages 637-640.*

Ins and outs

Getting there There are good **road** links (A55) to the Northeast Corner, which is also well served with **buses** and **trains** along the coast. Travelling inland is not as easy by public transport. ➤ *For further details, see Transport, page 640.*

Getting around The railway line that runs along the coastal stretch makes it relatively easy to explore the coast by train, and also to reach Wrexham. To reach towns like Ruthin and smaller villages you will have to take buses, which link the largest settlements like Ruthin and Denbigh. Timetables are available at TICs and bus stations.

Information Ruthin TIC ⓘ *just on the edge of the town centre on Park Road, T01824-703992, ruthin@nwtic.com, daily 1000-1730 summer, 1000-1700 Oct-Easter.* **Mold TIC** ⓘ *Earl Rd by Daniel Owen statue, T01352-759331, mold@nwtic.com or mold.tic@virgin.net, Mon-Sat 0930-1300, 1330-1700 (might be shorter in summer).* **Holywell Town information** ⓘ *T01352-711757, www.holywell-town.gov.uk.* **Denbigh library/TIC** ⓘ *Hall Square, T01745-816313, www.denbighshire.gov.uk/libraries, Mon, Wed 0930-1900, Tue, Thu, Fri 0930-1700, Sat 0900-1200. Free Internet access in library.* **St Asaph** ⓘ *www.stasaph.co.uk.* **Prestatyn TIC and Offa's Dyke Centre** ⓘ *Central Beach, daily 1000-1600, Easter-Sep, T01745-889092, www.prestatyn.org.uk,* are housed in the same building and there are plenty of walking leaflets, books and maps available. **Llandudno TIC** ⓘ *1-2 Chapel St, T01492-876413, www.llandudno-tourism.co.uk, Easter-end Sep Mon-Sat 0900-1730, 0930-1600 Sun, closed Sun out of season.* Ask for a copy of the Town Trail. **Flintshire** ⓘ *www.visit.flintshire.com.*

Rhuthun (Ruthin) and the Vale of Clwyd

The lush Vale of Clwyd lies beneath the Clwydian hills, tucked between the industrial areas of the Dee Estuary and the coastal resorts of Prestatyn and Rhyl. It's not spectacular scenery but is pretty and pastoral, dotted with interesting little churches: good for gentle walks and lazy drives. Ruthin, the main town, was besieged by Owain Glyndwr in 1400 and has some interesting historic sites and several good places to eat and drink. It's the best base for exploring the area.

Ruthin Gaol ⓘ *Clwyd St, T01824-708250, www.ruthingaol.co.uk, May-Oct 1000-1700 daily except Thu when open till 1900, Nov-Mar as before but closed Mon, last admission 1hr before closing. £3, children £2, family £8* was used from 1654 to 1916, but focuses on conditions for prisoners in Victorian times – when a wing was built modelled on Pentonville in London. You can explore the cells, find out how prisoners lived and how they were punished. You also learn about former inmates such as the Welsh 'Houdini', John Jones who escaped from Ruthin by making a rope from his bedclothes but died of shock after being shot while on the run.

Siop Nain, on Wells St, was where the first copies of the Welsh National Anthem were printed.

Ruthin Castle is now a hotel and the grounds private. However you can pop in for tea or coffee to get a peek at this former medieval fortress. Among the animals heads and ornate carved fireplaces, are photographs of Edward V11 at Ruthin, when still Prince of Wales. Castle Street contains one of the oldest houses in North Wales, dating back to the 16th century, and the house with railings around it was once home to Cynthia Lennon, who was living here when news of John's murder came out.

Yr Wyddrug (Mold) and the Dee Estuary

Mold, though having origins dating back to Norman times, has many unsympathetic 20th-century developments. It is largely notable as the boyhood home of the artist Richard Wilson, who is buried in the churchyard. Less well known is the writer Daniel Owen 1836-1895, remembered in a statue opposite the Post Office. Owen wrote in Welsh, his subject matter being the lives of ordinary people.

Near Mold is **St Deiniol's Library** ⓘ *T01244-532350, Church Lane, Hawarden, www.btinternet.com/-st.deiniols/homepage.htm, Mon-Sat free,* a residential library and the National Memorial to former Prime Minister, William Ewart Gladstone. Gladstone married into the family who owned nearby Hawarden Castle The church has a memorial window by Burne-Jones.

North of Mold, on the Dee Estuary, is the former port of Flint (Y Fflint), of which Henry Wyndham, travelling in 1781 said disparagingly: "It is scarcely worth the traveller's while to visit the poor town of Flint". Only come to see Flint Castle (CADW, free) built by Edward I and now a pleasant ruin down by the shore. Built on 'Y Flynt', an early English term for any hard rock, the castle was largely destroyed in 1647, when taken by Parliamentarians in the Civil War. It is most famous as the place where Richard I was taken after being ambushed and captured by Henry Bolingbroke.

The hills around the town of Flint were once known as the 'Peru of Wales', as they were sources of lead and silver, and were once the richest lead mines in Wales. *Loggerheads Country Park ⓘ T01352-810614, www.loggerheads-wales.com, bus B5 and X10*, is a good spot for kids to let off steam, with walks, nature trails, picnic seats and facilities for abseiling. Opposite is the We Three Loggerheads pub, whose original sign was said to have been painted by celebrated landscape artist Richard Wilson in the 1770s. The picture recalls a local boundary dispute.

Treffynnon (Holywell)

This is an ancient place of pilgrimage: 'The Lourdes of Wales'. **St Winefride's Well** ⓘ *T01352-713054, daily Apr-Sep 0900-1730, Oct-Mar 1000-1600, £0.60, £1.50 family, bathing times Mon-Sat 0900-1000 Apr-Sep*, is down a steep hill about half a mile out of town. Legend has it that Winefride, the only child of a nobleman, was killed by a chieftain who was trying to rape her. He cut off her head when she resisted, and a spring appeared where it fell. St Bueno put her head back on, restoring her to life and she became a nun. Mmm. A chapel was later built around the well, which was said to have curative properties. Hundreds of pilgrims still come each year, particularly around 22 June , which is St Winefride's Day. Pilgrims who wish to bathe wade through the waters of the well three times, a tradition that probably derives from the Celtic rite of baptism by triple immersion. Dr Johnson came in 1774 and was put out to find that: 'the bath is completely and indecently open: a woman bathed while we all looked on'.

From St Winefride's Well you can follow a walkway along an old railway line, which runs through the **Greenfield Valley Heritage Park** ⓘ *Visitor Centre, Farm and Museum, T01352-714172, www.greenfieldvalley.com/, mid Mar-end Oct, daily 1000-1630, £2.50, children £1.50, family £6*. This area was the heart of local industry in the 18th century, producing copper for the colonies and spinning cotton. These old works are largely ruined but at the bottom of the valley is an interesting farm and museum, with reconstructed farm buildings from all over North Wales, which have been saved from demolition. Nearby is **Basingwerk Abbey** (CADW, free), a picturesque ruin which was founded around 1131 and moved to this location in 1157. It belonged to the Cistercian Order, and around the middle ages the area became home to several Welsh poets.

Just a short drive from Basingwerk Abbey, standing in a field between Whitford and Trelogan, is Maen Achwyfan (CADW, free, 1.6 miles north of A151). This 12ft high Celtic cross is said to be the tallest wheel cross in Britain and has been described as 'the most remarkable stone monument in North Wales'. The cross was probably erected around 1000AD, to commemorate a person or event, or to mark a site of particular importance. The decorations on it include patterns copied from Viking art.

The Vale of Clwyd

The fertile Vale of Clwyd stretches from Ruthin down to Rhyl and is dotted with some attractive little towns and ancient churches. Llanrhaedr is a tiny hamlet in the Vale, site of St Dyfnog's Church which is notable for its fine stained glass Jesse Window. The name is a reference to the subject matter, the family tree of Christ showing his ancestors right back to Jesse, the father of King David. Jesse is shown reclining at the bottom and the window is regarded as the finest in Wales. As you enter the church, on the right hand side, is a huge organ, built in 1899 and famed among those in the know as the only surviving example of a 'Hope-Jones' organ – Robert Hope-Jones being the father of the cinema organ.

Known since Roman times and now one of the 'Seven Wonders of Wales', Holywell spring has been a place of pilgrimage since the 7th century...

If you walk to the far corner of the churchyard, go through a gap in the wall, over a small bridge and turn right to follow the path through the woods, you'll soon come to St Dyfnog's Well, a holy well once noted for its healing properties. You can still see the bath, in among the trees. Opposite the church, in the old smithy, is the **Anvil** Pottery ⓘ *T01745-890532, Mon-Sat 0900-1700*, where you can watch pots being made and buy goods to take home.

Dinbych (Denbigh)

'Dinbych', means 'little fortress' in Welsh, and is a pleasant market town that dates back to the 11th century and retains many of its medieval buildings. It was the birthplace of Henry Morton Stanley (1841-1904), the Victorian explorer of 'Dr Livinstone I presume' fame. The garden of nearby **Gwaenynog Hall** ⓘ *T01745-812066, Jun-end Aug, by appointment, £2*, was the inspiration for Beatrix Potter's 'The Tale of the Flopsy Bunnies'.

Denbigh Castle ⓘ *T01745-813385, Apr-Sep, Mon-Fri 1000-1730, Sat, Sun 0930-1730, £2.50, children £2, family £7*, is one of the largest in Wales. Denbigh grew up as a centre of Welsh power and was a residence of Welsh princes. Dafydd ap Gruffudd (brother of Llywelyn 'the Last') sparked a revolt against the English Crown, which led to Edward 1's final assault on the north. His stronghold here withstood a month's siege before falling to the English in 1282. Dafydd was captured and put to death in the Tower of London in 1283, and the castle erected as part of Edward's anti-Welsh campaign. The medieval town, enclosed by its walls, grew up at the same time. Walking up to the castle you first see a rather lonely tower, all that remains of St Hilary's Chapel, built around 1300 but demolished in 1923. Then you enter the castle through the enormous triple towered gatehouse, built by Edward's architect Master James of St George, who built all Edward's main castles in the north. The views from here are great.

Llanelwy (St Asaph)

St Asaph seems like a large village yet it is a city, due to the presence of its lovely **cathedral** ⓘ *High St, daily 0800-1830*, the smallest in Britain. The site has been a place of worship since 560AD, when the church was founded by St Kentigern, later succeeded by his pupil Asaph. It survived the Civil War, when Cromwell's soldiers took it over and used the font as a watering trough, and was restored by Gilbert Scott in 1870. The church is notable for the Welsh Bibles on display, to the left of the altar. One is by William Morgan 1588, who made the first complete translation of the Bible into Welsh. Only 800 of these were produced, and the revised edition by Richard Parry, from 1620, is also on display. They are commemorated outside the cathedral in the 'Translators' Memorial' monument. To the right of the altar, set into the wall in the Lady Chapel, is a tiny Madonna, said to have come from the Spanish Armada. Morgan is buried in an unknown spot in the churchyard, as is the composer William Mathias (1934-1992) who composed an anthem for the wedding of Charles and Diana.

East of St Asaph is Tremerchion, close to which is **St Beuno's College** where Jesuit priests were trained, and now a centre for retreats. Poet Gerard Manley Hopkins (1844-1889) trained here and several of his sonnets where written here. He was much inspired by the local landscape.

One of the area's greatest attractions is **Bodelwyddan Castle** ⓘ *T01745-585060, www.bodelwyddan-castle.co.uk, mid Apr-end Sep daily 1030-1700, rest of year 1030-1600 closed Mon and Fri, 4.50, children £2, family £12*. A castle has stood on this site since 1640, but the grand structure you see today was mainly built in the 19th-century. Once a family home it now functions as an outpost of the National Portrait Gallery, with over 100 pictures from the collection hung throughout the house, in rooms that are decorated in Victorian style and feature furniture from the Victoria and Albert museum. For kids suffering from computer withdrawal symptoms, there's a room upstairs that has on-line links to the whole of the National Portrait Gallery's collection. The grounds have a play area , woodlands walks and plenty of space for ball games and picnics.

Opposite the castle is the stunning Marble Church, which contains Florentine marble. In the graveyard are the graves of Canadian soldiers who were billetted here after the Second World War. Some died of illness, but many others were shot during the Kinmel Riot. This took place in 1919 when many soldiers mutinied, angry that they had still not been sent home. Many were wounded and some shot dead, but for years events were hushed up to avoid scandal

Llandudno and the North Coast

If you're looking for seaside sophistication you're best to steer well clear of the coastal area that stretches from Prestatyn and on through the cheap and cheerful resorts of **Rhyl** and **Colwyn Bay**. Some people have suggested that the reason the A55 was made into a dual carriageway was to allow you to whizz past as fast as possible and unless you've got kids in tow who are desperate to play on the sand, or spend your money in the garish amusement arcades, that's probably the best thing to do. Llandudno however, is a lively but still rather decorous seaside town, with a lingering air of Victorian grandeur.

Prestatyn is the best of the bunch, with some decent places to eat, as well as being the starting point for the 182 mile Offa's Dyke Path, the waymarked walk which goes from Prestatyn to Chepstow.

Llandudno, further along the coast, is classier, retaining much of its Victorian character, when its dramatic setting, beaches, grand hotels and shops attracted the great and the good. It's lively, but not tacky. The seafront sweeps in a lovely arc around Llandudno Bay and its sandy and pebbly beaches are overlooked by the mighty summit of the Great Orme. **Oriel Mostyn** ⓘ *12 Vaughn St, T01492-879201, www.mostyn.org, Mon-Sat 1030-1730, free*, is a contemporary art gallery, which has changing exhibitions of contemporary artworks, which could include film, installations and photographs.

Alice in Wonderland Centre ⓘ *3-4 Trinity Square, T01492-860082, www.wonderland.co.uk, Easter-end Oct Mon-Sat 1000-1700, Sun 1000-1600; Nov-Easter closed Sun £2.95*, is a low key attraction which relives the Lewis Carroll story – the connection being that Alice Liddell, who inspired the books, used to holiday here with her family.

The **Llandudno Museum** ⓘ *17-19 Gloddaeth St, T01492-876517, Easter-Oct, Tues-Sat and Bank Hols, 1030-1300, 1400-1700, Sun 1415-1700, Nov-Easter, Tue-Sat 1330-1630, £1.50*, has various exhibits associated with the town, from a footprint on a Roman tile to paintings and sculpture donated to the town. There's more on the past at the **World War II Home Front Experience** ⓘ *New St, T01492-871032,www.homefront-enterprises.co.uk, Mar-Nov Mon-Sat 1000-1630, Sun 1200-1600, £3, £2 children, £7.50 family*, which focuses on civilian life in Britain during the Second World War. There's an old Anderson bomb shelter, a recreated wartime street, and plenty to learn about the work of the Home Guard, as well as rationing and the blackout.

The **Great Orme** itself, a huge limestone outcrop, can be reached on foot, by **tramway** ⓘ *T01492-575275, www.greatormetramway.com, daily late Mar-late Oct*, or by cable car (T01492-877205). From here you get stunning views along the coast. It was settled as far back as Neolithic times and its rich mineral stores were mined as far back as the Bronze Age. **The Great Orme Bronze Age Copper Mines** (the clue's in the name) ⓘ *T01492-870447, www.greatorme.freeserve.co.uk, Feb-end Oct daily 1000-1700, £4.50*, tram from Victoria tram station or short walk from cable car gives you the chance to don hard hats and go underground to explore these mines that were worked over 4,000 years ago. There's a Visitor Centre depicting life in the Bronze Age.

The **Great Orme Country Park Visitor Centre** ⓘ *T01492-874151, www.conwy.gov.uk/countryside, Easter-end Oct, daily 0930-1730*, has displays and video on the area's history, geology and rich wildlife – over 400 types of plants grow here, some extremely rare. There's a live camera link up with a nearby seabird colony and information on the walks and nature trails on the Great Orme. At the Summit Complex (T01492-860963) there are places to eat and drink. There's also a Ski and Snowboard Centre (see Activities and tours, page 640).

Sleeping

Ruthin *p633*

B-A Ruthin Castle, Corwen Road, T01824-702664,, www.ruthincastle.co.uk. 58 en suite rooms in a former castle, now a large hotel. Set in its own grounds a few minutes from the centre.

C Castle Hotel, St Peters Sq, T01824-702479, enquiries@castlehotel.co.uk. Comfortable, family run hotel on the main square in Ruthin.

C Firgrove Country House, Llanfwrog, Ruthin, T/F01824-702677, www.firgrovecountryhouse.co.uk. 2 en suite rooms and self catering cottage. Charming Georgian house and lush gardens, just a mile out of Ruthin. Owners are friendly and welcoming and offer excellent home cooked meals, with wine, by arrangement for £15-25. Recommended.

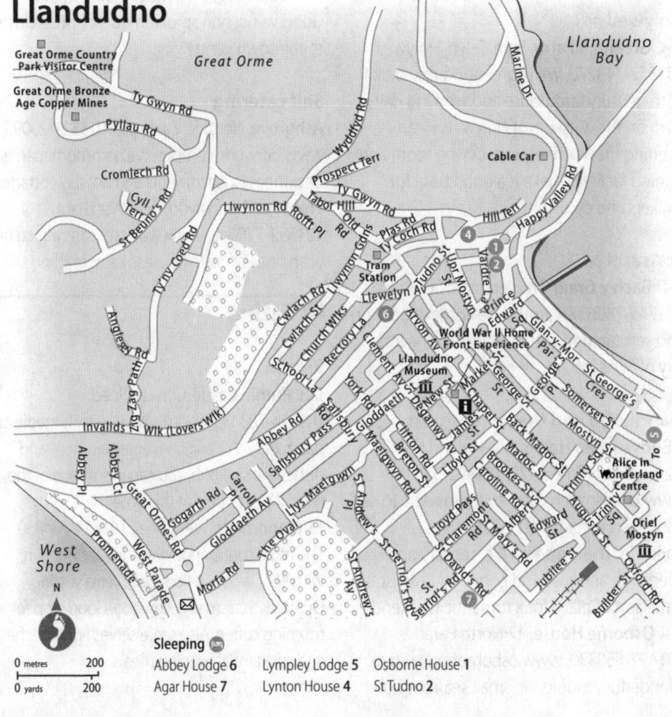

C **Manorhaus**, Well St, T01824-704830, www.manorhaus.com. A Georgian townhouse that is gradually being revamped to offer comfortable, contemporary style rooms, all with DVD/CD players. A good town centre option.
D **Gorphwysfa**, Castle Street, T01824-707529. 3 rooms, 2 en suite. Town centre B&B with original features like wood panelling and huge fireplaces.

Denbigh *p635*

C **Hafod Elwy Hall**, Bylchau, near Denbigh on A543, T01690-770345, www.hafodelwyhall.co.uk. Right out on the Denbigh Moors is this former shooting lodge, now a home on a smallholding. Good 'get away from it all' spot.
D **Cayo Guest House**, 74 Vale Street, Denbigh, T01745-812686., 6 rooms, 4 en suite. Clean and pleasant guest house in central Denbigh. Dogs are welcome.

Mold *p633*

F **Maeshafn Youth Hostel**, Maeshafn, T01352-810320 has 31 beds and no en suite facilities. Easter, July and Aug only. Close to Loggerheads Country Park

Holywell *p634*

D-C **Greenhill Farm**, Bryn Celyn, Holywell, T01352-713270, www.greenhillfarm.co.uk. 16th-century farmhouse and working dairy farm on the outskirts of Holywell. Hearty evening meals on request. Drying room and ironing facilities make it a good base for walkers and cyclists.

St Asaph *p635*

C-D **Bach y Graig**, Tremerchion, St Asaph, T01745-730627. Farmhouse accommodation and self catering cottage, close to the little city of St Asaph.

Llandudno and the North Coast *p636*

L **Bodysgallen Hall**, 3 miles inland from Llandudno off the A470, T01492-584466, www.bodysgallen.com. 19 rooms and 16 self contained cottages set in 200 acres of parkland. The house is 17th-century and filled with antiques and comfy squashy sofas – the sort of place for a romantic weekend.
L-A **Osborne House**, 17 North Parade, T01492-860330, www.osbornehouse.co.uk. Wonderfully indulgent, small seafront hotel that has suites with cast iron beds, Egyptian cotton sheets, Victorian fireplaces, luxurious bathrooms and widescreen TV with DVD.
A **St Tudno Hotel**, North Parade, Promenade, T01492-874411, www.st-tudno.co.uk. Small, swish, luxurious hotel with great location on the seafront. You can ask to stay in the suite used by Alice Lidell (Alice in Wonderland) and her family when they stayed here. Some rooms have sea views.
C **Abbey Lodge**, 14 Abbey Road, T01492-878042, www.abbeylodgeuk.com. Comfortable non smoking B&B with garden.
C **Barratt's at Ty'n Rhyl**, 167 Vale Rd, Rhyl T01745-344138, E.Barratt@aol.com. Lovely old house in its own grounds, with comfortable bedrooms and food from an award winning chef. All rooms are en suite.
C **Lynton House Hotel**, 80 Church Walks, TT01492-875009. Centrally located, comfortable B&B, among several others on Church Walks.
D **Lympley Lodge**, Colwyn Road, Craigside, T01492-549304, www.lympleylodge.co.uk. This 5 star B&B is set in its own grounds and has great views over the sea.
E **Agar House**, 17 St David's Road, T01492-875572, www.agarhouse.co.uk. Good value, non smoking guest house close to the town centre.

Self catering

Ashgrove, North St, Caerwys, T01352-720095, www.ourworld.compuserve.com/homepages/dewithomas. Apartments and holiday cottages.
Treetops, Llanfynydd, near Wrexham, T01352-770648, www.walesselfcatering.co.uk. Scandinavian style houses, 4 star grading.

Eating

Ruthin *p633*

£££ **Ruthin Castle**, Corwen Road, T01824-703435. If you're keen to try a medieval banquet with traditional entertainment and dishes like syllabub, you can join in one of the special nights held at this hotel.
££ **Manorhaus**, Well Street, T01824-704830. The most contemporary restaurant in town, with light wooden floors and retro seating. Operates as a small gallery too. Good stop for a morning coffee. Also serve serves light lunches and substantial evening meals.

££ **Cross Keys**, nearly 1 mile out of Ruthin on B5105, T01824-705281. Good family pub serving a range of food. Popular with the locals.

Mold *p633*
££ **We Three Loggerheads**, on A494 west of Mold, opposite Loggerheads Country Park, T01352-830337. Food daily 1200-2100 (2200 in summer). Good choice of bar meals like fish and chips and curries in this old inn.

St Asaph *p635*
££ **Barrow Alms**, High Street, St Asaph T01745-582260. Serves food from 1800 in the restaurant. 3 courses for £19.95 or 2 courses in the bistro for £9.95.
££ **New Inn**, Dyserth T01745-570482. Food served all day. Friendly pub serving wide range of baguettes and sandwiches at lunchtime, in addition to soups and meaty main courses.

Llandudno and the North Coast *p636*
£££ **Red Lion Inn and Restaurant**, Llanasa, near Whitford. Bar meals 1200-2200 (2100 Sun), resaurant 1200-1430, 1830-2200 (2100 Sun). In the pretty, prosperous looking village of Llanasa this pub serves basics like filled jacket potatoes, as well as steaks and veggie options like leek and mushroom crumble.
£££ **Bodysgallen Hall**, off A470 near Llandudno, T584466. High quality British food in posh country house hotel. Dishes might include braised guinea fowl with polenta, or loin of venison with red cabbage and celeriac fondant. 3 courses for £36.
£££ **St Tudno**, North Pde, Llandudno T874411 This hotel's restaurant is highly rated and offers expensive, sophisticated, French style food. Desserts might include rhubarb cheesecake with ginger ice cream. Main courses cost around £18. Also noted for its afternoon teas.
£££ **Osborne's Café and Grill**, 17 North Pde, T860330. Tue-Sat. Situated in Osborne's hotel, good food and full A La Carte menu. Lots of fish and imaginative pasta.
££ **Archies Wine Bar and Bistro**, 145 High St, Prestatyn, T01745-855106. Best to book if you want an evening meal at this bistro, away from the hubbub at the seafront.
££ **Nant Hall**, Nant Hall Road, Prestatyn T01745-856339. Food 1200-2130. Large family friendly restaurant on Prestatyn outskirts, with garden and play area. Serve sandwiches and salads at lunchtime, as well as chargrilled steaks, fish and stir fries – as well as chicken nuggets and chips for kids.
££ **Nikky Ip's**, 57 Station Road, Deganwy, T01492-596611, Popular Chinese restaurant, with contemporary interior and large pink sofa in the window. Dishes such as pan fried pork with ginger for around £6.80. Service can be rather snooty.
££ **Paysanne**, Station Road, Deganwy, T01492-582079, open Tues-Sat. A little bit of France in North Wales in this country style French restaurant. Vegetarian food requires advance notice (very French).
££ **Sands**, 59-63 Station Road, Deganwy, T01492-592659, open Tues-Sun 1200-1430, pm from 1800. Attractive bistro with tiled floors and relaxed atmosphere. Dishes might include pasta with butternut squash and borlotti beans, or blackened tuna with saffron pilaff.

Entertainment

Male voice choirs
Regular choir concerts at St John's Methodist Church, Mostyn St, and at the English Presbyterian Church, Chapel – both Llandudno

Theatre
North Wales Theatre, Promenade, Llandudno, T01492-872000, www.nwtheatre.co.uk. Theatre staging everything from musicals and opera to ballet and comedy.
Theatr Colwyn, Colwyn Bay, T01492-872000 or 532668. Small theatre and cinema.

Festivals and events

Jun Llandudno Festival, www.llandudnofestival.org.uk.
Sep North Wales International Music Festival, St Asaph Cathedral, T01745-584508, www.northwalesmusicfestival.co.uk. Usually held in the last wek of September.

Shopping

Crafts
The Craft Centre and Gallery, at the TIC Park Road, Ruthin, Jun-Sep daily 1000-1700, Oct-May Mon-Sat 1000-1700, Sun 1200-1700, T01824-703992 is a great place for gifts or for

treating yourself. Contemporary work from all over the UK is for sale, with glassware, jewellery and silverware. In the courtyard are independent craft studios, with units for everything from upholstery and furniture making to jewellery and ceramics.

Activities and tours

Cycling

Snowdonia Cycle Hire, Llandudno, T01492-878771, www.snowdoniacyclehire.co.uk, cycle hire and guided weekend cycling breaks.
West End Cycles, Conway Rd, Colwyn Bay, T01492-530269, bike hire

Horse riding

Linden Farm, Rhes-Y-Cae, Holywell T01352-780539. Hourly, half or full day rides.

Sailing

Llandudno Sailing Club, T01492-876083 or call the Harbour Master's Office T01492-596253

Skiing

Llandudno Ski and Snowboard Centre, Wyddfyd Rd, Great Orme, Llandudno, T01492-874707, www.jnll.co.uk, daily 1000-2200. Dry slope skiing, snowboarding, snowblading and snowbobbing. 750m toboggan run

Walking

Offa's Dyke Path Association T0547-528753, has information on the long distance Offa's Dyke Path. Useful walking leaflets worth picking up include 5 inspired by Welsh naturalist Thomas Pennant. The Pennant Group Walks range from 3 to 6 miles and can be obtained from the Greenfield Valley Heritage Park Visitor Centre, Greenfield, Holywell T01352-714172. A useful range of leaflets detailing walks around the Clwydian hills, called Beyond the Offa's Dyke Path, call Denbighshire Countryside Service T01352-810614 or try TICs. There are several walks around Tremerchion. For a small charge you can walk the nature trail through the forest around Bach-y-graig, T01745-730627. There are also trails through Y Graid Nature Reserve.

Transport

Bus

There is a rail link bus route between Chester, Buckley and **Mold** (3/4/X44/X55). **National Express** services link Chester to **Rhyl** and **Wrexham**. **Coast Rider** buses also serve the coastline, and other buses link **Ruthin**, **Denbigh** and **Mold**. Buses run between the main towns and in summer link **Ruthin** to the **Loggerheads Country Park**. Get hold of the **Clwydian Ranger Leisure Bus** timetable for summer travel details. Bus information from **Traveline** 0870-6082 608, **Denbighshire** T01824-706968, **Flintshire** T01352-704035, **Wrexham** 01978-266166. The main towns in the Vale of Clwyd can be explored by **Vale Rider** buses (T01824-706968), or if you have your own transport, the A525 and B5429 roads.

Car

The A55 road is the main driving route from England to the northeast coast of Wales, and then on to **Angelsey**. To reach towns like **Wrexham** turn off on the A541, and **Ruthin** take the A494

Train

North Wales Coast line runs from Chester to **Rhyl** and on to **Llandudno** Junction, where there are onward connections to **Snowdonia**. Trains run hourly. There are also services from Chester to **Wrexham** every 2 hrs Mon-Sat.

Directory

Dentist Emergency dentist 01745-887098. **Hospital** Glan Clwyd, Bodelwyddan, near St Asaph T01745-583910. **Internet** Free at **Ruthin library**, Record Street. **Library** Holywell library, North Rd, Mon 0930-1700, Tues 0930-1900, Wed 0930-1300, Thu, Fri 0930-1900, Sat 0930-1230. Internet available. **Police** 01745-343898.

Edinburgh

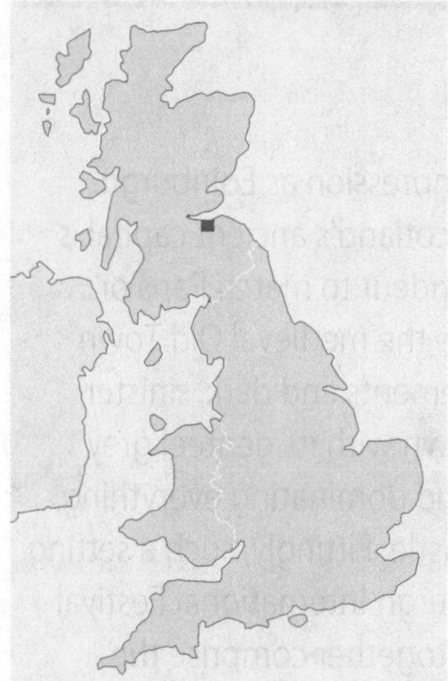

Introduction

Few cities make such a strong impression as Edinburgh. Dubbed the 'Athens of North', Scotland's ancient capital is undeniably beautiful, with a grandeur to match Paris or Prague, Vienna or Rome. There is the medieval Old Town with its labyrinth of soaring tenements and dark, sinister alleyways; the Georgian New Town with its genteel grey façades and wide, airy streets; and dominating everything, the brooding presence of the Castle. Fittingly, such a setting provides the stage for the Edinburgh International Festival and its various offshoots, which together comprise the biggest arts event on the planet. But Edinburgh is more than just the sum of its arts. Its Hogmanay party is the biggest celebration in the northern hemisphere, and the arrival of the new Scottish Parliament has brought confidence and vitality to a city that was always thought of as being rather straight-laced. Edinburgh, once the most puritanical of places, has learned how to have fun, how to be stylish, and, heaven forbid, even how to be just a wee bit ostentatious.

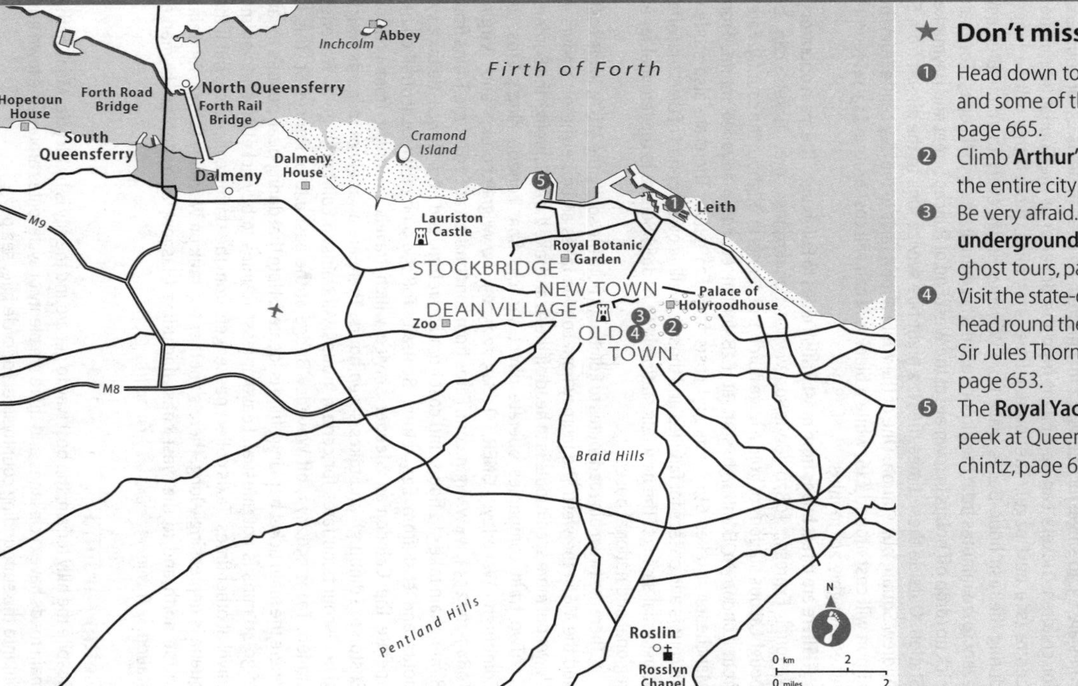

★ Don't miss...

1. Head down to **Leith** for an al fresco summer drink and some of the finest seafood in the country, page 665.
2. Climb **Arthur's Seat** for the wonderful views over the entire city and beyond, page 652.
3. Be very afraid... when you visit the **haunted underground city vaults** on one of the city's many ghost tours, page 672.
4. Visit the state-of-the-art **Museum of Scotland**, then head round the corner to the ghoulishly entertaining Sir Jules Thorn Exhibition of the History of Surgery, page 653.
5. The **Royal Yacht Britannia** where you can take a peek at Queenie's bedroom and admire all that chintz, page 659.

Ins and outs

Getting there

Edinburgh international airport, T0131-333 1000 (general enquiries), T0131 344 3136 (airport information), is eight miles west of the city centre. Terminal facilities include a tourist information desk, Bureau de Change, ATMs, restaurants and bars (first floor) and shops (ground floor and first floor). The tourist information desk is located in the international arrivals area, and will book accommodation and car hire. The main international car hire companies are located in the terminal in the main UK arrivals area. The airport is easily reached by car, just off the A8. Car parking costs £1.70 per hour short term, or £4.70 per day long term. There is an Airlink bus to the airport from Waverley Bridge, T0131-555 6363, www.flybybus.com Fares are £3.30 single for adults, £2 for children. An open return is £5 for adults, £3 for children. Tickets can be bought from the driver or at the Tourist Information Centre (see next page). The journey time is 25 mins, though this will be longer during the rush hour. Buses leave from Waverley Bridge every 10-20 minutes and every 10-20 minutes from the airport to the city centre from 0450 till 0025. The main pick up/drop off points in town are at the West End of Princes Street and Haymarket Station. Outside these times the N22 night bus service runs to the airport from St Andrew Square bus station. One of the white airport taxis to the city centre from the airport will cost around £16, while a black taxi cab will cost around £13-14. Journey time is roughly 20-30 mins.

There are direct **buses** from most British cities to Edinburgh. The main operator is National Express, T0870-5808080, www.nationalexpress.com. Tickets can be bought at bus stations or from a huge number of agents throughout the country. Fares from London to Edinburgh start at £28 for an economy advance return. From Manchester it takes 6½ hours and costs from £21 return. There are also student discounts and passes for families and those travelling over a period of days that offer substantial savings. The new bus station in St Andrew Square is the terminal for all regional and national buses.

There are two main **road** routes to Edinburgh from the south: the M1/A1 in the east; and the M6 in the west. The journey from London takes around eight to 10 hours. A slower but more scenic route is to head off the A1 and take the A68 through the Borders.

Two **train** companies operate direct services from London King's Cross to Edinburgh Waverley: **GNER**, T0845-7225225, www.gner.co.uk; and **Virgin**, T0845-7222333, www.virgin.com. Fares from London start at £29 return. Trains from Birmingham take 5½ hours and cost from £29 return, and from Newcastle take 1½ hours and cost from £23 return. **Scotrail**, T0845-7550033, www.scotrail.co.uk, operate the **Caledonian Sleeper** service which travels overnight from London Euston to Edinburgh and takes seven hours. There are a variety of railcards which give discounts on fares for certain groups. All trains to Edinburgh go to Waverley station, T0131-5562477, off Waverley Bridge at the east end of Princes St. This is where the main ticket booking office is located. Note that during peak periods a wait of 30-40 mins is not unusual. Leave at least 10 mins to buy tickets for immediate travel at other times. Taxis collect passengers from the station concourse, but if the queue is depressingly long, there's another taxi rank on Waverley Bridge. All trains to the north and to the west coast, including Glasgow, also stop at Haymarket station. » *For further details, see Transport, page 672.*

Getting around

Despite the hilly terrain, the best way to get around the city is by **bicycle**. Many of the main roads have cycle lanes and there are plenty of cycle routes around the town and out into the surrounding countryside. For cycle hire, see p673.

Public transport is generally good and efficient. The frequency of **bus** service depends on the route, but generally speaking buses run every 10-15 mins on most main routes Mon-Fri 0700-1900. Outside these peak times, services vary so it's best to check timetables. Princes Street is Edinburgh's main transport hub and you can get a bus to any part of the city from here. Fares range from £0.60-£1 and there's a raft of saver tickets which can be bought can be bought from the driver. Night buses run every hour from 0015 till 0315, leaving from Waverley Bridge. A flat fare of £2 (£1 with Ridacard) applies on all night bus routes and allows one transfer to another Night Bus at Waverley Bridge free of charge. An excellent way to see the sights is to take one of the city bus tours, see page 671.

Edinburgh is one of the least **car**-friendly cities in Britain. The main routes into town have been turned into 'greenways', which give buses priority, and on-street parking is limited to 10 mins. The centre of town is a complicated system of one-way streets designed to ease congestion. The privatized traffic wardens are ruthless in their dedication to duty. Parking in or near the city centre is expensive and restrictive. It can cost £2 per hour to park in George St. There are large NCP car parks behind Waverley train station (entered via East Market Street), beside the St James Centre (entered from Elder Street), on King Stables Road and on Morrison Street, near the junction with Lothian Road.

Although Greater Edinburgh occupies a large area relative to its population of less than half a million, most of what you'll want to see lies within the compact city centre which is easily explored on **foot**. Though most of the main sights are within walking distance of each other, Edinburgh is a hilly city and a full day's sightseeing can leave you exhausted.

The council-imposed city **taxi** fares are not cheap, costing from around £3 for the shortest of trips up to around £6 from the centre to the outskirts. There are far more people wanting to get home late on Fri or Sat night than there are cabs on the streets, so be prepared to wait, walk or book ahead.

Information

Edinburgh's main **tourist office** ⓘ *3 Princes Street on top of Waverley Market T0131-473 3800, F0131-473 3881, www.edinburgh.org (Apr and Oct Mon-Sat 0900-1800, Sun 1100-1800; May and Sep Mon-Sat 0900-1900, Sun 1100-1900; Jun Mon-Sat 0900-1900, Sun 1000-1900; Jul and Aug Mon-Sat 0900-2000, Sun 1000-2000; Nov-Mar Mon-Sat 0900-1800, Sun 1000-1800.* It gets very busy during the peak season and at Festival time, but has the full range of services, including currency exchange, and will book accommodation, provide travel information and book tickets for various events and excursions. There's also a tourist information desk at the **airport** ⓘ T0131-333 2167. (Apr-Oct Mon-Sat 0830-2130, Sun 0930-2130; Nov-Mar Mon-Fri 0900-1800, Sat 0900-1700, Sun 0930-1700, in the international arrivals area. Another useful tourist information resource is the **Backpackers Centre** ⓘ *6 Blackfriars Street, T0131-557 9393*, which will provide information about hostels and tours and will book coach tickets. The City Council has produced a free map of the different bus routes around Edinburgh. This is available from the TIC or from the **LRT ticket centres** ⓘ *31 Waverley Bridge, T0131-2258616, Easter-Oct Mon-Sat 0800-1800, Sun 0900-1630; Nov-Easter Tue-Sat 0900-1630; or 27 Hanover St, T0131-5556363, Mon-Sat 0830-1800*. Both offices sell travel cards. Traveline runs a public-transport information service for Edinburgh, East Lothian and Midlothian: T0800-232323 (local calls) or T0131-2253858 (national calls), Mon-Fri 0830-2000. Their office is at 2 Cockburn St, near Waverley Station.

Sights

→ Colour map 5

The city centre is divided in two. North of Princes Street is the neoclassical New Town, built in the late 18th and early 19th centuries to improve conditions in the city. South of Princes Street, across the Princes Street Gardens, is the Old Town, a warren of narrow alleys inhabited by the ghosts of Edinburgh's past, and the inspiration for Stevenson's Dr Jekyll and Mr Hyde. The best place to start a tour of Edinburgh is in the medieval Old Town, where you'll find most of the famous sights, from the **castle,** down through the **Royal Mile,** to the **Palace of Holyroodhouse.** South of the Royal Mile is the **Grassmarket,** the **Cowgate** and **Chambers Street,** site of the **University of Edinburgh** and two of the city's best museums, the **Royal Museum of Scotland** and the **Museum of Scotland.** The **New Town** also deserves some exploration, in particular the **National Gallery, Royal Scottish Academy** and **National Portrait Gallery.** A bit further out from the centre are the **Royal Botanic Garden** and the **Gallery of Modern Art.** Though in theory you could 'do' the Old Town in a day, you really need several days to do it justice, and to leave yourself enough energy to explore the rest of the city. You should also leave enough time to enjoy the wild, open countryside of **Holyrood Park** and take a stroll up **Arthur's Seat,** from where you get stupendous views of the city and beyond.

Every day (except Sundays, Christmas Day and Good Friday) since 1851, the 'One o'clock gun' has been fired from the Mill's Mount Battery as a time-check for the city's office workers.

The Old Town

Edinburgh Castle

ⓘ *T0131-225 9846 (HS), Apr-Sep daily 0930-1800, Oct-Mar 0930-1700. Last admission 45 mins before closing. £8.50, concessions £6.25, children £2.*

The city skyline is dominated by the Castle, sitting atop an extinct volcano, protected on three sides by steep cliffs. Until the 11th century the Castle *was* Edinburgh, but with the founding of Holyrood Abbey in 1128 and development of the royal palacefrom the early 16th century, the Castle slipped into relative obscurity. Though largely of symbolic importance, it is worth a visit, if only for the great views over the city from the battlements.

The castle is entered from the top of the Royal Mile, via the Esplanade. Dotted around the Esplanade are memorial plaques to members of the Scottish regiments who fell in overseas wars, and several military monuments. A drawbridge leads to the 19th-century **Gatehouse,** which is flanked by modern statues of Sir William Wallace and Robert the Bruce. The main path then leads steeply up, to the **Argyll Battery** then the **Mill's Mount Battery.** The steep road continues up to the summit of Castle Rock and **St Margaret's Chapel,** the oldest surviving building in the castle. The chapel is said to have been built by Margaret herself, but the Norman style suggests it was constructed later. In front of the chapel is the **Half Moon Battery,** which offers the best views of the city.

South of the chapel is **Crown Square,** its eastern side taken up by the **Palace,** begun in the 15th century and remodelled in the 16th century for Mary, Queen of Scots. Later, in 1617, the Palace buildings were extended with the addition of the Crown Room, where the **Honours of Scotland** are now displayed – the royal crown, the sceptre and the sword of state. There is no more potent a symbol of Scottish nationhood than these magnificent crown jewels, which were last used for the coronation of Charles II in 1651. The jewel-encrusted crown contains the circlet of gold with which Robert the Bruce was crowned at Scone in 1306, and was remade for James V in 1540.

On the south side of the square is James IV's **Great Hall,** once the seat of the Scottish Parliament and later used for state banquets. It now houses a display of arms and armour. On the west side of the square is the 18th-century **Queen Anne Barracks**, which now contains the Scottish United Services Museum. On the north side stands the neo-Gothic Scottish National Monument, a testament to the many tens of thousands of Scottish soldiers killed in the First World War. From the western end of Crown Square you can descend into the **Vaults**, a series of dark and dank chambers, once used as a prison for French captives during the Napoleonic Wars. One of the rooms contains Mons Meg, the massive iron cannon forged here in the reign of James IV (1488-1513). It was said to have had a range of nearly a mile and a half and was used for salutes on royal occasions.

Royal Mile

The narrow uppermost part of the Royal Mile nearest the castle is known as Castlehill. At 354 Castlehill is the **Scotch Whisky Heritage Centre**, ⓘ *T0131-2200441, www.whisky-heritage.co.uk, daily Jun-Sep 0930-1800, Oct-May 1000-1730, £7.50, children £3.95, concessions £5.50*, where you can find out everything you ever wanted to know about Scotland's national drink. The best part is the bond bar, where you can sample some of the vast range of malt whiskies on offer before buying a bottle in the gift shop. Across the street is the **Edinburgh Old Town Weaving Company** ⓘ *T0131-2261555, daily 0900-1730, free entry to mill and a small charge for the exhibition*, which has a real working mill where you can see tartan being woven and a small exhibition.

A few doors further down, on the corner of Ramsay Lane, is the **Outlook Tower** ⓘ *T0131-2263709, daily Apr-Oct 0930-1800 (later in Jul/Aug), Nov-Mar 1000-1700, £5.75, children £3.70, concessions £4.60*, which has been one of the capital's top tourist attractions since a **camera obscura** was set up in the hexagonal tower by optician, Maria Theresa Short, in 1854. The device consists of a camera which sweeps around the city and beams the live images onto a screen, accompanied by a running commentary of the city's past. There's also an exhibition of photographs taken with a variety of home-made pinhole cameras and the rooftop viewing terrace offers fantastic views of the city.

A little further down, on the opposite side of the street is the **Tolbooth Kirk**, whose distinctive spire is the highest in the city and a distinctive feature of the Edinburgh skyline. Originally intended to house the General Assembly of the Church of Scotland, it was converted into **The Hub**, which houses the ticket centre for Edinburgh International Festival (see Festivals and events). The Hub also stages various events and is home to the excellent *Café Hub* (see Eating). Opposite is the neo-Gothic **New College and Assembly Hall**. Built in 1859, it is the meeting place of the annual General Assembly of the Church of Scotland and is also used during the Festival to stage major drama productions. It is now the temporary home for the Scottish Parliament. You can arrange tickets to visit the Debating Chamber when Parliament is sitting (Wednesday afternoons and Thursdays) at the Visitor Centre, on the corner of the Royal Mile and George IV Bridge.

The Tolbooth Kirk and Assembly Hall mark the top of the Lawnmarket, a much broader street named after the old linen market which used to be held here. At number 477b, is **Gladstone's Land** ⓘ *T0131-2265856 (NTS), 1 Apr-end-Oct Mon-Sat 1000-1700, Sun 1400-1700, £3.50, concessions £2.60, children fee if accompanied by an adult*, the most important surviving example of 17th-century tenement housing in the Old Town, where the cramped conditions meant that extension was only possible in depth or upwards. The magnificent six-storey building, completed in 1620, contains remarkable painted ceilings and was the home of an Edinburgh burgess, Thomas Gledstanes. The reconstructed shop booth on the ground floor has replicas of 17th-century goods and the first floor of the house has been refurbished as a typical Edinburgh home of the period.

Further down Lawnmarket, steps lead down to Lady Stair's Close, where you'll find **Lady Stair's House**, another fine 17th-century house, though restored in pseudo-medieval style. It is now the home of the **Writer's Museum** ⓘ *T0131-5294901, Mon-Sat 1000-1700 and Sun 1400-1700 during the Festival only, free* dedicated to the three giants of Scottish literature, Burns, Scott and Stevenson.

Further down the street on the opposite side is **Brodie's Close,** named after the father of one of Edinburgh's most nefarious characters, Deacon Brodie. He was an apparent pillar of the community by day and a burglar by night, until his eventual capture and hanging in 1788. Robert Louis Stevenson co-wrote a play about his life, which was to provide the inspiration for *Dr Jekyll and Mr Hyde*.

Across George IV Bridge, at the top of the High Street, stands the **High Kirk of St Giles,** ⓘ *T0131-2259442, Easter-Sep Mon-Fri 0900-1900, Sat 0900-1700, Sun*

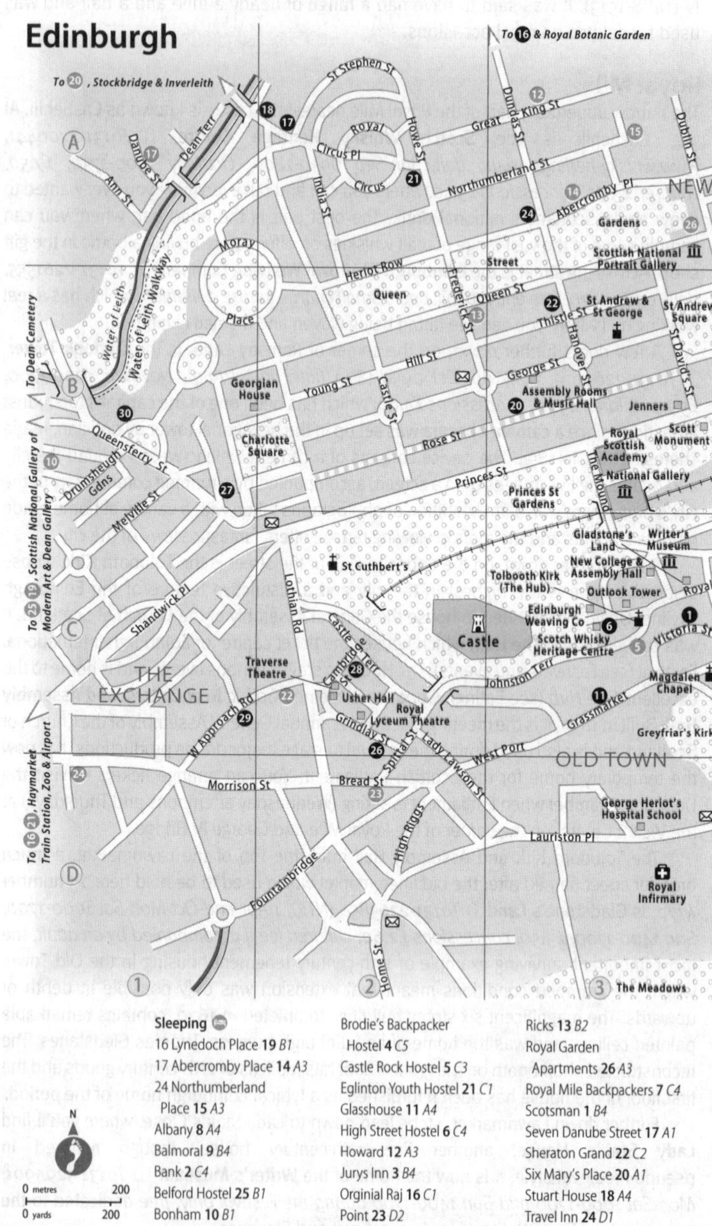

1300-1700, Oct-Easter Mon-Sat 0900-1700, Sun 1300-1700, free (donations welcome), the only parish church of medieval Edinburgh and the home of Presbyterianism, where the firebrand preacher John Knox launched the Scottish Reformation. The Kirk is mistakenly called St Giles Cathedral. This is because Charles I called it so when he introduced bishops into the Church of Scotland and the name stuck, even after Presbyterianism was re-established. The church was given a major face-lift in the 19th century, covering most of its Gothic exterior, but parts of the original medieval

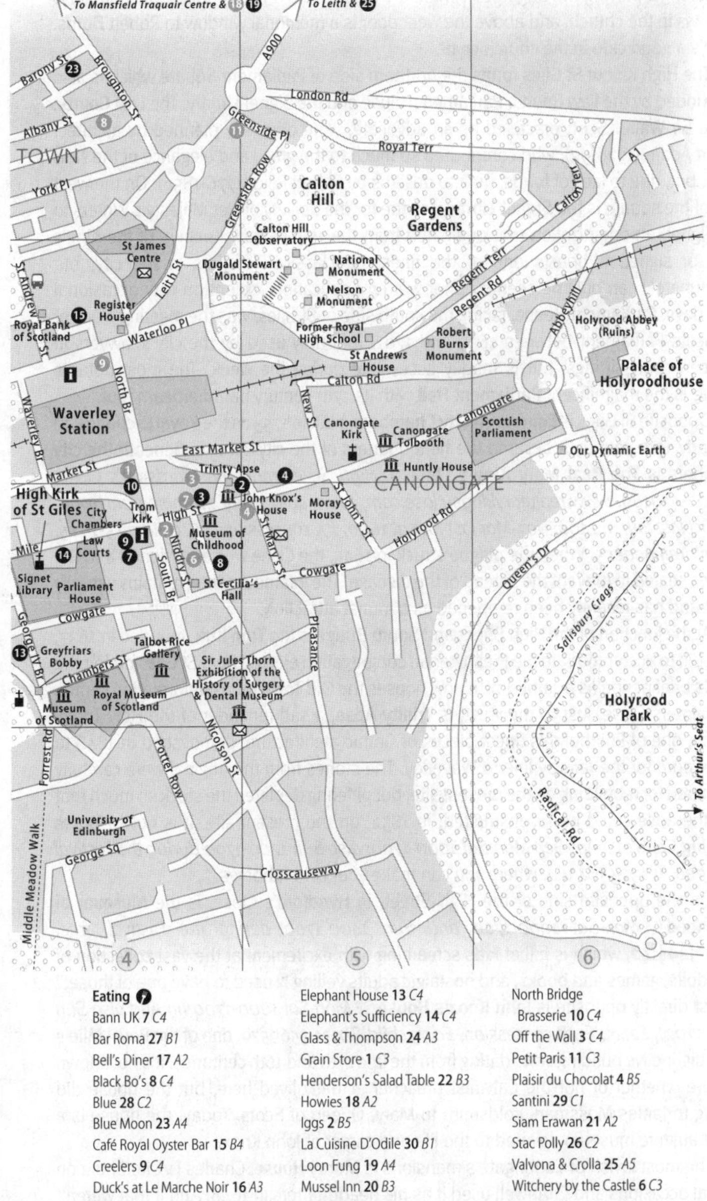

 building still survive, most notably the late-15th-century crowned tower. The four huge octagonal pillars which support the central tower are thought to date back to the previous Norman church, built in 1120 and razed to the ground by English invaders in the late 14th century.

There have been many additions to the High Kirk since its restoration. One of these is the very beautiful **Thistle Chapel**, the Chapel of the Most Ancient and Most Noble Order of the Thistle (Scotland's foremost order of chivalry). It was designed by Sir Robert Lorimer and built in 1911. The elaborate ornamentation and fine carvings are exquisite (look out for the angel playing the bagpipes). There are also several Pre-Raphaelite stained-glass windows in the church, and above the west door is a memorial window to Robert Burns. There's a good café in the church crypt.

The High Kirk of St Giles forms the northern side of Parliament Square which is also surrounded by the Law Courts, Parliament House and the Signet Library. The **Law Courts**, where Sir Walter Scott practised as an advocate, were originally planned by architect Robert Adam (1728-92), who contributed so much to the grace and elegance of the New Town, but, due to lack of funds, built to designs by Robert Reid (1776-1856). On the west side of the square is the **Signet Library**, centre for the Society of Her Majesty's Writers to the Signet, an organization that originated from the 15th-century Keepers of the King's Seal, or signet. It boasts one of the finest neoclassical interiors in the city, but unfortunately can only be seen by prior written application, except on very occasional open days. **Parliament House**, facing the south side of St Giles, was the meeting place of the Scots Parliament between 1639 and 1707. It is now used by the city's lawyers in between court sittings, but is readily accessible during the week. The most notable feature is the magnificent **Parliament Hall** with its 17th-century hammerbeam roof.

Opposite St Giles is **Edinburgh City Chambers**, built in 1753 as the Royal Exchange. In the early 19th century it became the headquarters of the city council. Beneath the city chambers is **The Real Mary King's Close** ⓘ *High St, entrance on Warriston's Close, T08702-430160, www.realmarykings close.com, tours daily every 20 mins from 1000, Apr-Oct last tour at 2100; Nov-Mar last tour at 1600, £7, concessions £6, children 5-15 £5, no children under 5*. When the plague struck in 1645, the Close was abandoned and the houses sealed to prevent the spread of the disease. The infamous street remains virtually intact and has recently been re-opened as a tourist attraction.

At the junction of the High Street and South Bridge is the **Tron Kirk**, founded in 1637, and built to accommodate the Presbyterian congregation ejected from St Giles during the latter's brief period as a cathedral. It now houses the Old Town tourist information centre. In Chalmers Close, just to the west, is **Trinity Apse**, a sad reminder of the Holy Trinity Church, one of Edinburgh's finest pieces of Gothic architecture, demolished in 1848 to make room for the railway line to Waverley. The stones from the original were carefully numbered for rebuilding on the present site, but pilfering depleted the stock so much that only the apse could be reconstructed, in 1852, on the present site. It is now a **Brass Rubbing Centre** ⓘ *Apr-Sep Mon-Sat 1000-1700; also Sun 1200-1700 during the Festival only, free, T0131-5564364*, where you can make your own rubbings.

On the opposite side of the High Street, in Hyndford's Close, is the **Museum of Childhood** ⓘ *Mon-Sat 1000-1700 and Sun 1400-1700 during the Festival, free, T0131-5294142*, which is full of kids screaming with excitement at the vast collection of toys, dolls, games and books, and nostalgic adults yelling "I used to have one of those!" Almost directly opposite is **John Knox's House** ⓘ *Mon-Sat 1000-1700 (in Aug also Sun 1200-1700), £2.25, £1.75 concession, £0.75 child, T0131-5569579*, one of the Royal Mile's most distinctive buildings and dating from the late 15th and 16th centuries. It's not known for sure whether or not the Calvinist preacher actually lived here, but the house did belong to James Mossman, goldsmith to Mary, Queen of Scots. Today, the house is a rather austere museum devoted to the life and career of John Knox.

The most lavish of Canongate's mansions is **Moray House**. Charles I visited here on several occasions and Cromwell used it as his headquarters in 1648. And if that weren't enough historical significance, in 1707 the Treaty of Union was signed in a summerhouse in the garden. A little further east is the 16th century **Huntly** House ⓘ *T0131-5294143, Mon-Sat 1000-1700 and Sun 1400-1700 during the Festival, free*, the city's main local history museum, but disappointing nevertheless. Among the highlights is the original copy of the National Covenant of 1638.

Opposite Huntly House is the late-16th-century **Canongate Tolbooth**, the original headquarters of the burgh administration, as well as the courthouse and burgh prison. It now houses **The People's Story** ⓘ T0131-5294057, Mon-Sat 1000-1700 and Sun 1400-1700 during the Festival, free, a genuinely interesting museum which describes the life and work of the ordinary people of Edinburgh from the late 18th century to the present day. The museum is filled with the sights, sounds and smells of the past and includes, among others, reconstructions of a prison cell, a workshop and a pub.

The Palace of Holyroodhouse

ⓘ *1 Apr-31 Oct daily 0930-1800; 1 Nov-31 Mar 0930-1630 (guided tour). Closed to public during state functions and during the annual royal visit in Jun and Jul. £6.50, £3.30 child, £5 concession, £16.50 family. T0131-5561096, www.royal.gov.uk.*

At the foot of the Royal Mile lies Holyrood, Edinburgh's royal quarter. The palace began life as the abbey guest house, until James IV transformed it into a royal palace at the beginning of the 16th century. The present palace largely dates from the late 17th century when the original was replaced by a larger building for the Restoration of Charles II, although the newly crowned monarch never actually set foot in the place. It was built in the style of a French chateau, around a large arcaded quadrangle and is an elegant, finely proportioned creation. Designed by William Bruce, it incorporates a castellated southwest tower that balances perfectly the northwest original.

Inside, the oldest part of Holyroodhouse is open to the public and is entered through the **Great Gallery**, which takes up the entire first floor of the north wing. Here, during the '45 rebellion, Bonnie Prince Charlie held court, and it is still used for big ceremonial occasions. The walls are adorned with over one hundred portraits of Scottish Kings, most of them mythical, beginning with 'Fergus I, BC 330' and ending with James VI.

The **Royal Apartments**, in the northwest tower, are mainly of note for their association with Mary, Queen of Scots and in particular for the most infamous incident in the palace's long history. It was here that the queen witnessed the brutal murder, organized by her husband, Lord Darnley, of her much-favoured Italian private secretary, David Rizzio. He was stabbed 56 times, on a spot marked by a brass plaque.

The later parts of the palace, known as the **State Apartments**, are less interesting, though decorated in Adam Style, with magnificent white stucco ceilings. These are associated with later monarchs, such as George IV, who paid a visit in 1822, dressed in flesh-coloured tights and the briefest of kilts, rather appropriately perhaps, given the length of time he actually spent here. But it was Queen Victoria and Prince Albert who returned the palace to royal favour, as a stopover on their way to and from Balmoral. This custom has been maintained by her successors and the present queen still spends a short while here every year at the end of June and beginning of July.

In the grounds of the palace are the ruins of **Holyrood Abbey**. At its height the abbey was a building of great importance and splendour, and this is hinted at in the surviving parts of the west front. Much of it was destroyed, as were many of the county's finest ecclesiastical buildings, during the Reformation. During the reign of Charles I it was converted to the Chapel Royal and later to the Chapel of the Order of the Thistle, but it suffered severe damage once more, this time during the 1688 revolution. Some restoration work was attempted in the 18th century, but this only caused the roof to collapse in 1768, and since then the building has been left as a ruin. In the Royal Vault beneath the abbey are buried several Scottish Kings, including David II (son of Robert the Bruce), James II, James V and Lord Darnley, 'King Consort' to Mary, Queen of Scots.

Scottish Parliament

Opposite the Palace of Holyroodhouse is the new Scottish Parliament building, still under construction at the time of going to press but scheduled for completion by May 2004. The controversial building was designed by visionary Barcelona architect, Enric Miralles, who died in 2000, the same year that Donald Dewar, architect of the Scottish Parliament and the first First Minister of Scotland, also died. It incorporates symbols of Scottish economic and artistic heritage: the roof is a series of up-turned fishing boats, while the windows are based on an abstract shape of Sir Henry Raeburn's *Skater on Duddingston Loch*, and the crow-stepped gables are a paradigm of Scots vernacular architecture married to modernist principles. The parliament building has not been without its critics, however, in particular over the spiraling costs, which now stand at nearly £400 mn. The adjoining **visitor centre** ⓘ *Daily 1000-1600, free*, includes the original architectural designs and models and a 15-minute film of its development from the conceptual stage. Until the building is complete, the Scottish Parliament sits in the Church of Scotland headquarters in Milne's Court. A visitor centre on George IV Bridge provides information about the workings of the parliament (T0131-348 5411, www.scottish.parliament.uk).

Holyrood Park and Arthur's Seat

Edinburgh is blessed with many magnificent green, open spaces, and none better than Holyrood Park (Queen's Park) – a 650-acre rugged wilderness of mountains, crags, lochs, moorland, marshes, fields and glens – all within walking distance of the city centre. This is one of the city's greatest assets, and it's easy to wander around till you're lost from the eyes and ears of civilization.

The park's main feature, and the city's main landmark, is **Arthur's Seat**, the igneous core of another extinct volcano, and the highest of Edinburgh's hills (822ft). Another dominating feature of the Edinburgh skyline is the precipitous **Salisbury Crags**, lying directly opposite the south gates of the palace. The best walk in the city is to the summit of **Arthur's Seat**, from where you get the very best view of the city, as well as the Pentland Hills to the south, the Firth of Forth and of Fife to the north, and, on a clear day, to the Highland peaks, 70 or 80 miles away. The walk to the top is a popular one, and easier than it looks. There are several different routes, all of which take less than an hour. One starts opposite the palace car park and winds up by the foot of Salisbury Crags. This is the **Radical Road**, built in 1820 and so called because Sir Walter Scott suggested it be constructed by a group of unemployed weavers from the west, who were believed to hold radical political views. This is where James Hutton is said to have dreamt up the idea of geology by looking at the rock formations. The road traverses the ridge below the crags and continues on grass through "Hunter's Bog" and up to the summit.

Our Dynamic Earth

ⓘ *T0131-5507800, www.dynamicearth.co.uk. Apr-Oct daily 1000-1800; Nov-Mar Wed-Sun 1000-1700. £8.45, children and concessions £4.95, family £22.50*

Edinburgh's very own mini-dome is multi-million pound, multi-media exhibition which takes you on a journey through space and time. Using the state-of-the-art technology and special effects, you'll experience every environment on Earth and encounter many weird and wonderful creatures. An absolute must if you've kids in tow and you're guaranteed to find out things about our planet that you never knew.

Cowgate and Grassmarket, Victoria Street and Greyfriars

The Cowgate is one of Edinburgh's oldest streets and one of its least salubrious. It runs almost parallel to the High Street, but on a much lower level. In recent years the Cowgate has become one of the city's major nightlife streets, lined with bars and clubs. At the corner of Niddry Street is the exquisite **St Cecilia's Hall**, built in 1763 for the Edinburgh

Musical Society. The interior is beautiful, with a music hall and concave elliptical ceiling. Further west along the Cowgate is **Magdalen Chapel** ⓘ *Mon-Fri 0930-1630; other times by arrangement, T0131-2201450, free*, founded in 1541. The unremarkable façade is Victorian but the interior is Jacobean and worth a look, to see the pre-Reformation Scottish stained glass still in its original position.

The Cowgate passes beneath George IV bridge to become the Grassmarket, a wide cobbled street closed in by tall tenements and dominated by the castle looming overhead. The Grassmarket, formerly the city's cattle market, has been the scene of some of the more notorious incidents in the city's often dark and grisly past. At the west end, in a now vanished close, is where **Burke and Hare** lured their hapless murder victims, whose bodies they then sold to the city's medical schools. The gruesome business finally came to an end when Burke betrayed his partner in crime, who was duly executed in 1829. Today, the Grassmarket is one of the main nightlife centres, with lots of busy restaurants and bars lining its north side. At the northeastern corner of Grassmarket is **Victoria Street**, an attractive two-tiered street with arcaded shops below and a pedestrian terrace above. This curves up from the Grassmarket to **George IV Bridge**.

Greyfriars and around

At the southwestern end of George IV Bridge, at the top of Candlemaker Row, is the statue of **Greyfriars Bobby**, the faithful little Skye terrier who watched over the grave of his master John Gray, a shepherd from the Pentland Hills, for 14 years until his own death in 1872. The little statue, modelled from life and erected soon after his death, is one of the most popular, and sentimental, of Edinburgh's attractions. The grave that Bobby watched over is the nearby **Greyfriars Kirkyard**, one of Edinburgh's most prestigious burial grounds. Greyfriars also has its its sinister tales. Most notorious of all is the tale of George 'Bloody' Mackenzie, former Lord Advocate, who is interred here. Greyfriars is particularly associated with the long struggle to establish the Presbyterian church in Scotland. The kirkyard was the first place where the National Covenant was signed, on 28 February 1638. Later, in 1679, over 1,200 Covenanters were imprisoned by Mackenzie in a corner of the kirkyard for three months, and many died of exposure and starvation. The prison, known as the 'Black Mausoleum', behind the church on the left, is said to be haunted by Mackenzie's evil presence and is visited as part of one of the city's ghost tours (see Activities and tours). **Greyfriars Kirk,** somewhat overshadowed by the graveyard, dates from 1620 and was the first church to be built in Edinburgh after the Reformation.

The Museums and the University

Across the road from Greyfriars Bobby, running between George IV Bridge and South Bridge, is Chambers Street, home of two of the best museums in Scotland, the **Museum of Scotland** and the **Royal Museum of Scotland** ⓘ *T0131-2474422, www.nms.ac.uk, Mon-Sat 1000-1700 (Tue till 2000), Sun 1200-1700, free, full disabled access to all floors, free guided tours at 1415 (and 1800 on Tue)*. The former is a striking contemporary building housing a huge number of impressive Scottish collections which were transferred from the National Museum of Antiquities. The museum is a veritable treasure trove of intriguing and important artefacts, including Roman gold and silver, Pictish and Gaelic carved stones and medieval armour. One of the most popular exhibits is 'The Maiden', Edinburgh's once-busy guillotine. The Museum also contains an excellent rooftop restaurant, *The Tower* (see page 662).

Further east along Chambers Street, on the same side, is the **Royal Museum of Scotland**. The extensive and eclectic range of collections on display include everything from Classical Greek sculptures to stuffed elephants, from whale skeletons to Native North American totem poles. It's all here, beautifully-presented in a wonderful Victorian building, designed by Captain Francis Fowkes of the Royal

 Engineers (architect of the Royal Albert Hall in London) and built in 1888 in the style of an Italianate palace. The magnificent atrium soars high above and makes a very impressive entrance to what is probably the most complete museum in the country.

Hemmed in by Chambers Street, South Bridge, West College Street and South College Street is Edinburgh University Old College, whose main courtyard is reached through the massive arch on South Bridge. Built between 1789 and 1834, the Old College, was originally designed by Robert Adam, but on his death in 1792 very little had been completed and his grandiose plans had to be abandoned due to lack of funds. Nevertheless, it is magnificent architectural achievement and one of the finest neoclassical interiors in Scotland. It is now mainly used for ceremonial occasions but can be viewed by guided tour in the summer. The Upper Museum, which housed the Royal Museum before it moved to its present site, is now the home of the **Talbot Rice Gallery** ⓘ *T0131-650 2210, Tue-Sat 1000-1700 (daily during the Fesitval), free*, which features the University's collection of Renaissance European painting as well as several temporary exhibitions every year. There are also free lunchtime guided tours of the Old College (from 19 July-28 August, Monday-Saturday, starting at 1300 at the reception). For more details of University tours, contact the **University of Edinburgh Centre** ⓘ *7-11 Nicolson St, T0131-650 2252, Mon-Fri 0915-1700.*

Almost opposite the Festival Theatre and hidden behind the Royal College of Surgeons, at 19 Hill Square, is the **Sir Jules Thorn Exhibition of the History of Surgery and Dental Museum** ⓘ *Mon-Fri 1400-1600, free, T0131-5271600*, a bit of a mouthful but a hidden gem which outlines the history of surgery in the city since the early 16th century. It's all a bit ghoulish but great for kids.

The New Town

The neoclassical New Town was built in a burst of creativity between 1767 and 1840. The New Town was conceived by Edinburgh's Lord Provost (Lord Mayor), **George Drummond,** who wanted his city to be a tribute to the Hanoverian-ruled United Kingdom, which he had helped create. In 1760 a competition was announced for the plans and the winner was an unknown 22-year-old architect, **James Craig.** His design symbolized the union of Scotland and England. The grand central thoroughfare of the First New Town, as the area came to be known, is **George Street**, named in honour of the king. It links two great civic squares, **St Andrew** in the east and St George's in the west. On either side of George Street, and running parallel to it, are two long lanes, **Thistle Street** and **Rose Street,** symbolizing the national emblems of the two countries. Traversing George Street are **Hanover Street** and **Frederick Street.**

Princes Street to Queen Street

The southernmost terrace of the New Town is Princes Street, one of the most visually spectacular streets in the world, with uninterrupted views of the Castle Rock, across the valley now occupied by Princes Street Gardens. The north side of the street has lost any semblance of style and is now an undistinguished jumble of modern architecture. Princes Street may be Edinburgh's equivalent of Oxford Street in London, but at least the magnificent view makes walking its length a more pleasant experience.

Everything worthwhile in Princes Street is on the south side, with a few notable exceptions. At the far northeast end of the street is **Register House** (1774-1834), one of Adam's most glorious buildings and now the headquarters of the Scottish Record Office, which stores historical and legal documents – including birth, marriage and death certificates, wills and census records – dating as far back as the 13th century.

Running along most of the south side of Princes Street are the sunken **Princes Street Gardens,** which were formed by the draining of Nor' Loch in the 1760s and are now a very pleasant place to sit and relax during the summer. Standing in East Princes

Street Gardens, is the towering **Scott Monument**, ⓘ *Mar-May and Oct Mon-Sat 0900-1800, Sun 1000-1800; Jun-Sep Mon-Sat 0900-2000, Sun 1000-1800; Nov-Feb 0900-1600, £2.50*, over 200ft high and resembling a huge Gothic spaceship, and built in 1844 as a fitting tribute to one of Scotland's greatest literary figures. Beneath the archway is a statue of Sir Walter Scott, and there are also 64 statuettes of characters from his novels. The monument is open to the public, and a 287-step staircase climbs to a platform near the top of the spire, from where you get wonderful views.Opposite the Scott Monument is the other notable building on the north side of Princes Street, the elegant 19th-century department store, **Jenners**, Edinburgh's answer to Harrods.

A little further west, Princes Street gardens are divided in two by **The Mound**. At the junction of The Mound and Princes Street are two of Edinburgh's most impressive neoclassical public buildings, the **Royal Scottish Academy** and the **National Gallery of Scotland** ⓘ *T0131-624 6200, www.nationalgalleries.org, daily 1000-1700, Thu till 1900, free (charge made for special loan exhibitions), wheelchair access, lifts*. The latter houses the most important collection of Old Masters in the UK outside London. Begun originally by the old Royal Institution in the 1830s, the collection was given international credibility in 1946 by the loan of the Duke of Sutherland's collection, one of the finest in the UK, including major works by Titian, Raphael and Rembrandt and renowned Scottish painters such as Ramsay, Raeburn and Wilkie. If you visit the gallery in January you have the rare opportunity to see its excellent collection of Turner watercolours. The National Gallery's neighbour, the Royal Academy, was built to house the Society of Antiquaries and the Royal Society. In 1911 it was converted into the headquarters of the Royal Scottish Academy and is now used as a temporary exhibition space. It also acts as an overspill during the Festival when the National Gallery stages much larger exhibitions. At the time of going to press, the RSA is closed for refurbishment as part of the £26 million Playfair Project. It is due to reopen in August 2003 when it will stage a major Monet exhibition. Work is also well underway on the other part of the Playfair Project, an undergound link between the two galleries which will include a lecture theatre, shop and restaurant. This is due for completion in 2005.

On the other side of The Mound is **West Princes Street Gardens**, beautifully located right under the steep sides of Castle Rock. At the far western corner, below the junction of Princes Street and Lothian Road, is **St Cuthbert's Church and Churchyard**. This is the oldest church site in the city, dating back to the reign of Malcolm III, though the present church was mostly built in the 1890s. The churchyard is worth visiting and a peaceful refuge from the Princes Street traffic. Here lies Thomas de Quincey (1785-1859), author of *Confessions of an English Opium Eater*, a classic account of drug addiction in the early 19th century. De Quincey spent the last years of his life in Edinburgh.

Running to the north and parallel to Princes Street is once venerable **George Street**, which has made the move from finance to fashion and is now lined with upmarket shops, bars and restaurants. At the eastern end is **St Andrew Square**, surrounded by insurance companies and financial institutions. The most impressive building, on the eastern side of the square, is the headquarters of **The Royal Bank of Scotland**. This handsome 18th-century town house was originally the home of Sir Laurence Dundas, but was remodelled in the 1850s when the wonderful domed ceiling was added. In the centre of the square is the massive 100 ft pillar, carrying the statue of the lawyer and statesman Henry Dundas, first Viscount Melville (1742-1811).

A few hundred yards along George Street the **Assembly Rooms and Music Hall** (1787) once the social hub of the New Town and now a major Fringe venue. Opposite is the oval-shaped St Andrew's Church, now known as the **Church of St Andrew and St George**. The church is famous as the scene of the 'Great Disruption' of 1843, when the Church of Scotland was split in two. At the western end of the street is **Charlotte Square**, designed by Robert Adam in 1791 and considered by most to be his masterpiece. It is now the heart of the city's financial community, home to bankers, investment-fund managers, stockbrokers, corporate lawyers, accountants and insurance executives. At Number seven is the **Georgian House** ⓘ *T0131-2263318 (NT),1 Mar-31 Oct Mon-Sat 1000-1700, Sun 1400-1700; Nov-Dec Mon-Sat 1100-1600, Sun 1400-1600, £5, £3.75 concession*which gives a fascinating insight into how Edinburgh's gentry lived in the late 18th century. The house has been lovingly restored by the NTS and is crammed with period furniture and hung with fine paintings, including portraits by Ramsay and Raeburn. The National Trust for Scotland has its head offices on the south side at number 27.

Parallel to George Street, and slightly downhill from it, is **Queen Street**, the most northerly terrace of James Craig's New Town plan, bordered by Queen Street Gardens to the north. The only public building of interest here is the **Scottish National Portrait Gallery**, ⓘ *T0131-6246200, Mon-Sat 1000-1700, Sun 1400-1700 (till 1800 and from 1100 on Sun during the festival, free*, at the far eastern end of the street, a huge late-19th-century red sandstone building, modelled on the Doge's Palace in Venice. The gallery contains a huge range of pictures of notable Scots from the 16th century to the present day. It also has a good café.

Calton Hill and around

Another of the absolute musts for visitors to Edinburgh is to climb to the top of **Calton Hill**, via the stairs at the east end of Waterloo Place. The views from the top are simply stunning, especially up the length of Princes Street and the sweep of the Forth Estaury.The slopes of Calton Hill are covered with many fine buildings, which probably earned Edinburgh the epithet 'Athens of the North'. You could take a circular route, clockwise right round the hill, starting from Leith Walk and heading along **Royal Terrace**, **Calton Terrace, Regent Terrace, Regent Road** and **Waterloo Place**, which leads into the east end of Princes Street. The best of the buildings are to be found in the magnificent sweep of Regent Terrace, hailed as the most beautiful of all Regency terraces in Britain, with fantastic views across to Arthur's Seat and Salisbury Crags.

On Regent Road, 200 yards east of the junction with Regent Terrace, is the former **Royal High School**, perhaps the finest of all Edinburgh's Greek temples. It was built in 1825-29 by Thomas Hamilton, a former pupil of the school and architect of the **Robert Burns Monument**, which stands on the opposite side of the road. The Royal High is the oldest school in Scotland, dating back to the 12th century, and its long list of famous former pupils includes Robert Adam, Sir Walter Scott and Alexander Graham Bell. Further west on Regent Road, on the south side, is **St Andrews House**, a massive Art Deco structure housing government offices, built on the site of **Calton Jail**.

The monuments at the top of Calton Hill are also worth the climb. They form the four corners of a precinct and make for a strange collection. Most famous is the **National Monument**, built to commemorate the Scots who died in the Napoleonic Wars. The project was carried out on a massive scale and, not surprisingly, in 1822, three years after it had begun, funds ran out with only 12 columns built. However, this was in keeping with the original contract drawing, so what we see today was the architect's intention – a deliberate folly. Though it caused much controversy and was labelled 'Scotland's disgrace', it did serve to inspire all subsequent building in the 'Athens of the North'. On the west side of the hill, overlooking the St James Centre, is the old **Calton Hill Observatory**, also built by Playfair in 1818. It was abandoned in 1894 when light pollution became too great, and relocated to Blackford Hill. Since 1953 it has been home to the Astronomical Society of Edinburgh. It is open most Friday nights, if the skies are clear enough, and visitors with an interest in astronomy are welcome (www.astronomyedinburgh.org). Southwest of the observatory is the **Monument to Dugald Stewart** (1753-1828), a Playfair construction commemorating an obscure

Arthur Conan Doyle, who created world's most famous fictional detective, Sherlock Holmes, was born at 11 Picardy Place in 1859.

University professor. Completing the quartet of monuments is **Nelson's Monument** ⓘ *Apr-Sep Mon 1300-1800, Tue-Sat 1000-1800, Oct-Mar Mon-Sat 1000-1500, £2.50*, a 108-ft tower in the shape of an upturned telescope, built in 1816 to celebrate Nelson's victory at the Battle of Trafalgar. In the mid-19th century the Astronomer Royal for Scotland introduced a time signal for sailors at Leith.

Broughton Street and the streets around it form Edinburgh's so-called 'pink triangle', heart of the city's thriving gay scene. With an atmosphere redolent of New York's East Village, Broughton Street is home to many of the city's hippest bars, clubs, cafés and restaurants. On the corner of Broughton Street and East London Street is the **Mansfield Traquair Centre** (ww.mansfieldtraquairturst.org.uk), a late 19th-century neo Norman edifice which is home to a stunning series of Pre-Raphaelite murals by Phoebe Traquair, a leading light in the Scottish Arts and Crafts Movement. She created them over an eight-year period (1893-1901), and though they suffered badly due to years of neglect, they have been restored to their original glory thanks to the dedication of the Mansfield Traquair Trust. Contact them for details of public viewing days and guided tours. Her work can also be seen on the walls of the Song School at St Mary's Cathedral.

Stockbridge and Inverleith

Over the years, Edinburgh's New Town spread out beyond its original plan to swallow up a series of quaint little villages. One of these, the once bohemian Stockbridge, is the perfect antidote to all that perfect symmetry and neoclassical grandeur. Stockbridge has been home to many artists and writers over the years, among them the painter Sir Henry Raeburn (1756-1823) and 19th-century junkie Thomas de Quincey (1785-1859), author of Confessions of an English Opium Eater (see also p). Though Stockbridge has all but lost its rakish charm, it remains one of Edinburgh's most beguiling corners and is an interesting place to explore with its jumble of antique shops and second-hand bookstores. Further north, beyond the northern boundary of the New Town and the Water of Leith, is the district of Inverleith, where you'll find Edinburgh's gorgeous **Royal Botanic Garden** on Inverleith Row ⓘ *T0131-5527171, Nov-Feb daily 1000-1600, till 1800 Mar-Apr and Sep-Oct, till 2000 May-Aug, free, but voluntary donations welcome, take buses 8, 17, 23 and 27 from city centre*. Contained within its 72 acres is a mind-boggling variety of plants and trees, as well as walkways, ornamental gardens, various hothouses and huge open spaces, with not a dog poo in sight. There's an awful lot to enjoy, but particularly notable are the outdoor rock garden, the huge Victorian Palm House, the amazing Glasshouse Experience and the new Chinese Garden, featuring the largest collection of Chinese wild plants outside China. The Terrace Café is a good place for lunch, with stupendous views across the New Town to the castle.

West Edinburgh

Stretching from Princes Street and Lothian Road out towards the city bypass and the airport is West Edinburgh, an indefinable sprawl of mostly residential streets, which on the surface appears to offer little to visitors. This part of the city was once its main engine room, with dozens of breweries and the water-borne trade from the Union Canal. The old industries have mostly disappeared and the area around Lothian Road and the West Approach Road, called The Exchange, has reinvented itself as Edinburgh's new financial district. At the west end of Princes Street is the start of Lothian Road, one of Edinburgh's busiest thoroughfares, which runs south to Tollcross. At weekends Lothian Road becomes a seething mass of drunken bodies pouring out from the many bars that line its route. Ironically, however, it is also very close to three of the city's main cultural venues: the Usher Hall, the Royal Lyceum Theatre and the Traverse Theatre (see page 669).

Queensferry Street follows the old coaching route to South Queensferry (see page 675) and soon reaches the wooded valley of the **Water of Leith**, the little river which flows from the Pentland Hills to the port of Leith where it enters the Firth of Forth. One of the best ways to escape the traffic fumes is to take a stroll along the Water of Leith, which can be walked beside for most of its length. The walkway runs from Roseburn, past the Gallery of Modern Art, through Dean Village, past the Royal Botanic Garden, then a short walk along the road at Canonmills before passing Warriston cemetery and on down to Leith docks. Particularly charming is the walk upstream from Stockbridge, into the verdant gorge under the Dean Bridge, where the running water blocks out any traffic noise. At Dean Village you can either continue up the riverside towards the Gallery of Modern Art, or turn right, up the steep slope of Dean Path to **Dean Cemetery**, one of Edinburgh's finest places of final rest. The cemetery houses the graves of the likes of architect William Playfair, pioneering photographer Octavius Hill, and Dr Joseph Bell, who is said to have been the flesh-and-blood inspiration for Arthur Conan Doyle's character Sherlock Holmes.

A free shuttle bus runs between the National Gallery and RSA, the Portrait Gallery, the Gallery of Modern Art and the Dean Gallery, leaving from the National Gallery every hour on the hour from 1100 till 1600 (from 1200 on Sun).

About 10 minutes' walk from Dean Village, is the **Scottish National Gallery of Modern Art** ⓘ *Mon-Sat 1000-1700, Sun 1400-1700, free,*which is definitely worth visiting, even if you know *nada* about Dada. The hugely-impressive permanent collection features everything from the Impressionists to Hockney and is now second in Britain only to the Tate Museums in London. It is particularly strong on Expressionism, with works by Picasso, Cezanne, Matisse, Magritte, Mondrain, Henry Moore, Kandinsky, Klee, Giacometti and Sickert all displayed, among many other important names, including many contemporary Scottish artists. Don't miss the excellent café, especially if the sun is shining. Across the street is the new **Dean Gallery** (same times as above), featuring the work of Edinburgh-born artist Sir Eduardo Paolozzi. It also houses a major Dada and Surrealist collection and exhibitions of contemporary art.

Three miles west of the city centre, is **Edinburgh Zoo** ⓘ *T0131-3349171, www.edinburghzoo.org.uk, Apr-Sep daily 0900-1800; Oct and Mar 0900-1700, Nov-Feb 0900-1630, £8, concessions £6, children £5, numerous buses from Haymarket and Princes St*, by far the largest in Scotland, set in 80 acres on the side of Corstorphine Hill. Whatever you think of zoos, this one is highly respected for its serious work as well as being an enormous amount of fun. There are over 1,000 animals from all over the world, but the zoo is best known for its penguins – the largest breeding colony of Antarctic penguins anywhere outside Antarctica itself. You can watch the famous penguin parade at 1400 daily (March-October weather permitting) and see them swimming underwater in the world's largest penguin pool.

Leith

Leith Walk leads from Princes Street down to the port of **Leith**, which has a distinct flavour all of its own. Leith became a burgh in its own right in 1833 and only became integrated into the city of Edinburgh in 1920. In its heyday, Leith was Scotland's major port but in the 1960s, when fishing and shipping trade decanted south, the heart was ripped out of Leith. Much of its old centre was replaced with grim housing schemes and the port area fell into decay. However, the old port's fortunes have changed in recent years and Leith has been turned around. Millions have been spent on restoring many of its fine historic buildings, and it is now one of the best parts of the city for eating and drinking, with scores of fashionable restaurants, bistros and bars (see Eating and Bars, pubs and clubs). At the same time private developers have been converting old warehouses and office buildings into expensive dockside flats. The old port still has its rough edges, and you'll need to be careful after dark, but it's worth a visit, especially **The Shore**, the road which follows the last stretch of the Water of Leith before it reaches the Firth of Forth.

Leith's main attractions is the **Royal Yacht Britannia** ⓘ *T0131-5555566, www.royalyachtbritannia.co.uk, Oct-Mar daily 1000-1530; Apr-Sep daily 0930-1630, closes 1½ hrs after last admission, £8, concessions £6, children £4, family £20, Brittania Tour bus from Waverley Bridge or buses 11, 22, 34, 35 and 36 from Princes St,* which is now moored at its own purpose-built Ocean Terminal, complete with swanky restaurants, bars and shops. The old ship is well worth visiting, despite the rather steep entrance charge, and a genuine insight into the lives of the royals. It's like stepping into a 1950s time warp and you'll be amazed (or appalled) at the sheer ordinariness of it all.

Sleeping

As you'd expect in Scotland's major tourist city, Edinburgh has a huge selection of places to stay. Many of the **hotels** are concentrated in the New Town and the West End, particularly around Princes St, Calton Hill and the streets north of Haymarket station. There are also hundreds of **guest houses** and **B&Bs** dotted all over the city. There are several areas which have a particularly high concentration, all within about 2 miles of the centre and all on main bus routes, such as Bruntsfield and Mayfield, both south of the centre, Pilrig, east of the city centre heading towards Leith, and west from Haymarket along the Corstorphine Rd.

There are also 4 official **SYHA hostels** and several **independent hostels**, most of which are convenient, and a couple of **campsites** which are not too far from the centre. Most of the universities and colleges offer **campus accommodation**, but this is neither cheap nor centrally located. Another option, if you're staying a week or more, is **self-catering**, which is cost-effective, or you can **rent** a room or flat.

If you arrive in Edinburgh without a reservation, particularly during the festival, or at Hogmanay, the chances are you won't find a room anywhere near the centre. It pays to book well in advance. The Tourist Information Centre sends out its accommodation brochure for free so that you can book a place yourself, or their Central Reservations Service, T0131-4733855, centres@eltb.org, will make a reservation for you, for a non-refundable fee of £5.

The Old Town *p646*

L **Scotsman Hotel**, North Bridge, T0131-5565565, www.scotsmanhotel.co.uk. 68 rooms and suites. Each room has been furnished with attention to detail, with original art, DVD and internet. Services and facilities include valet parking, screening room, bar, brasserie and restaurant, breakfast room, private dining rooms and a Health Club and Spa with a stainless steel pool.

L **The Witchery by the Castle**, Castlehill, Royal Mile, T0131-225 0973, F0131-220 4392, www.thewitchery.com. Upstairs from the acclaimed restaurant are six suites of Gothic theatrical excess, with velvet drapes, four-poster beds, 18th-century oak paneling, marble bathrooms, antiques and historic portraits. Additional touches include a complimentary bottle of champers, home-made cookies, DVD and CD library. Four new suites have recently been opened across the road in 17th-century Sempill's Court.

A **Bank Hotel**, 1 South Bridge, T0131-556 9043, F558 1362, www.festival-inns.co.uk. Nine individually themed rooms, each based on a famous Scot, from the poetry of Robert Burns to the designs of Charles Rennie Mackintosh, and all tastefully done. Hotel reception is in Logie Baird's bar at street level and this is also where breakfast is served. A good deal for this part of town.

A **Jurys Inn** , 43 Jeffrey St, T0131-200 3300, F0131-200 0400, bookings@jurysdoyle.com. 186 en suite rooms. Huge converted office block. Functional but comfortable and an unbeatable location close to the Royal Mile, Princes Street and Waverley Station. Some rooms have been adapted for disabled visitors. On-street parking. Cheaper during the week (Sun-Thu) when the stags and hens have departed.

E **Brodie's Backpacker Hostel**, 12 High St, T/F0131-556 6770, W.brodieshostels.co.uk. Smaller and cosier than the other city centre hostels, with only four dorms. Friendly and good range of facilities.

E **Castle Rock Hostel**, 15 Johnston Terr, T0131-225 9666, F0131-226 5078, castle-rock@ scotlands-top-hostels.com. Prime location below the Castle. Vast building with 250 beds in 20 dorms. No singles or doubles.

E **High Street Hostel**, 8 Blackfriars St, T0131-557 3984, high-street@scotlands-top-hostels.com. Long-established backpacker hang-out. 16 dorms. Cheap, lively and right in the thick of the action, between the sights of the Royal Mile and nightlife of the Cowgate. They also run their own (free) Old Town tour.

E **Royal Mile Backpackers**, 105 High St, T0131-557 6120, royalmile@scotlands-top-hostels.com. Small, cosy hostel with 38 beds in five dorms. Same group as the Castle Rock and High Street hostels (see above). Open 24 hours and offer an optional breakfast for under £2.

The New Town *p654*

L **Albany Hotel**, 39-43 Albany St, T0131-5560397, F0131-5576633, 1237@compuserve.com. 21 rooms. New Town Georgian elegance and bourgeois charm only a few minutes from Princes Street. High degree of intimacy created by the rich furnishings and discreet attention. Excellent basement restaurant, *Haldane's*.

L **Balmoral Hotel**, 1 Princes St, T0131-5562414, F0131-5573747, W.roccofortehotels.com/balmoral. 188 en suite rooms. Century-old Edinburgh landmark above Waverley station. From the modern and luxurious entrance hall to the magnificent city views in the upper rooms, the Balmoral oozes class. Its main restaurant, **Number One**, is excellent and the brasserie, Hadrian's, less grand but good value.

L **The Bonham**, 35 Drumsheugh Gdns, T0131-226 6050, F0131-226 6080, www.thebonham.com. 48 rooms. This trio of Victorian townhouses was turned into a hotel in 1998. Rooms are all decorated individually in cool, yet elegant contemporary styles. The suites have lofty ceilings and the baths and four-poster beds are so big you could get lost in them. The superb restaurant serves Scottish cuisine with an international twist.

L **The Glasshouse**, 2 Greenside Pl, T0777-6003890, www.theetongroup.com. 65 rooms. This new luxury boutique hotel, which opened in May 2003, is on the top floor of the Omni leisure complex and is entered via the original façade of a Victorian church. Most rooms have their own balconies and great views. Features a two-acre roof garden with superb views and a rooftop bar. The rooms are stylish and contemporary, complementing the sleek glass exterior.

L **The Howard**, 34 Great King St, T0131-5573500, F0131-5576515, www.thehoward.com. 18 en suite rooms. Beautiful Georgian townhouse, the epitome of quiet, understated New Town elegance and famous for its chintzy luxury. Such privilege doesn't come cheap, however, and The Howard is more expensive than most. Its basement restaurant, **36**, serves the very best of modern Scottish cuisine in contemporary, minimalist surroundings.

A **Ricks**, 55a Frederick St, T0131-622 7800, F0131-622 7801, www.ricksedinburgh.co.uk. Not so much a hotel as a restaurant with rooms. The 10 very sleek and stylish rooms are accessed via a staircase at the rear of the bar-restaurant, but sound-proofing means that late-night revellers don't keep you awake. Decor is subtle, furnishings unfussy and in-room entertainment includes CD and DVD players and minibar. Book well ahead during the Festival and Hogmanay.

A **17 Abercromby Place** 17 Abercromby Pl, T0131-5578036, F0131-5583453. 9 rooms. Classic townhouse hotel and former home of renowned New Town architect, William Playfair. Sumptuous style and superb views.

A **24 Northumberland Place**, 24 Northumberland Pl, T0131-556 8140, F0131-556 4423 www.ingrams.co.uk, run by David and Theresa Ingram, very friendly, welcoming and engaging hosts who offer a quality of service lacking in most B&Bs. Three en suite rooms, all very comfortable and tastefully decorated, as you'd expect from a former antique dealer. Crucially, there's parking at the rear, a rarity in the New Town. No sign outside so very discreet. Booking ahead essential.

A **The Original Raj**, 6 West Coates, T0131-346 1333, F0131-337 6688, originalrajhotel@aol.com. 17 rooms. A mile from Princes Street on the airport road. Indian theme hotel, which is immediately apparent from the large white elephants guarding the entrance. Indian furniture and soft furnishings grace the airy, spacious rooms. The suites are a bit more expensive but very large and good value. Staff are friendly and accommodating. No car park, but being this far out of town street parking is not a great problem.

A **Seven Danube Street**, 7 Danube St, T0131-332 2755, F0131-343 3648, seven.danubestreet@virgin.net. Three en suite rooms. Exceptional, award-winning B&B in a salubrious part of town. Big and airy rooms, despite being in the basement; double and twin have four-poster beds. Unusually, the single is the same price per head. They have a self-contained basement flat round the corner which sleeps up to six. As with everywhere else in the New Town, parking is an issue. Booking essential.

A **Stuart House**, 12 East Claremont St, T0131-5579030, www.stuartguesthouse.co.uk. Five en suite rooms. Comfortable and well-furnished rooms in Georgian-style townhouse. A short walk from Broughton Street and New Town.

A **16 Lynedoch Place** , 16 Lynedoch Pl, T0131-225 5507, F0131-226 4185, www.16lynedochplace.co.uk. Three rooms. Great location between the West End and New Town, though parking might be an issue. Lovely Georgian townhouse with a double, twin and single room, plus small sitting room for guests. Excellent breakfast and hospitality sets it apart from the competition.

B **Six Mary's Place**, 6 Mary's Pl, Raeburn Pl, T0131-3328965, info@sixmarysplace.co.uk. 8 rooms. Eight rooms. Non-smoking guesthouse on busy Stockbridge street. Handy for neighbourhood shops and restaurants. Friendly, informal atmosphere. Offers good vegetarian cooking. Internet access in rooms.

E **Eglinton Youth Hostel**, 18 Eglinton Cres, West End, T0131-3371120. SYHA hostel in a quiet street about 1 mile west of the centre, near Haymarket train station. 160 beds, most in dorms but also 12 rooms for 4. Includes continental breakfast. Doors closed at 0200 and hostel closed in Dec.

West Edinburgh *p657*

L **Sheraton Grand Hotel**, 1 Festival Sq, T0131-229 9131, F0131-228 4510, www.sheraton.com/grandedinburgh. 261 rooms. Enormous business hotel with few aesthetic qualities, but since the creation of The Exchange it has become less incongruous. Very central and with excellent facilities and service. Some rooms have great views of the Castle. Their Grill Room restaurant is highly acclaimed and the equally acclaimed Santini (see p) is on its doorstep. The new One Spa is the best in the city and the ultimate in pampering (see p).

A **Point Hotel**, 34 Bread St, T0131-2215555, F0131-2219929, www.point-hotel.co.uk. 140 en suite rooms. This former Co-op department store has been stylishly refurbished and is now the height of contemporary chic and minimalist elegance. The suites are huge and some have jacuzzis. Handily placed for the castle and Royal Mile. Its bar and grill, **Mondobbo**, is equally stylish.

D **Travel Inn** , 1 Morrison Link, T0131-228 9819, F0131-228 9836, www.travelinn.co.uk. 128 en suite rooms. Huge, converted office block offering the kind of facilities you get at motorway service stations. Not pretty, but to secure a bed at this price in the city centre requires sacrificing a few frills. Some rooms adapted for wheelchair users. Parking.

D-E **Belford Hostel**, 6-8 Douglas Gdns, T0131-225 6209, F0131477 4636, info@hoppo.com. 98 beds in small dorms (F), also double rooms (E). Huge red sandstone ecclesiastical edifice about a mile from the West End near Dean Village and the Gallery of Modern Art. Plenty of entertainment and facilities and no curfew. It may be a converted church, but don't expect any quiet reflection.

Leith *p658*

L-A **Malmaison Hotel**, 1 Tower Place, Leith, T0131-4685000, F0131-4685002, www.malmaison .com. 101 rooms. Parking. Award-winning and designer hotel in Leith's waterfront quarter, still providing the benchmark for urban style. Rooms are the epitome of sleek sophistication and cool, contemporary chic with CD in every room (good selection at reception). Suites at front are the most expensive but have the best views. Stylish brasserie and café-bar on ground floor.

Camping

E Edinburgh Caravan Club Site, Marine Dr, T0131-3126874. Open all year. Run by the Caravan Club of Great Britain, with good facilities. 5 miles northwest of the centre in Silverknowes. Take a 28 bus from town.

D-E Mortonhall Caravan Park, 38 Mortonhall Gate, Frogston Rd East, T0131-6641533, enquiries@mortonhallcp.demon.co.uk. Open Mar-Oct. Well-equipped site about 6 miles southwest of town. From the city bypass take the Lothianburn or Straiton junction, or take a 7 or 11 bus from Princes Street.

Serviced apartments

L-A Royal Garden Apartments, York Buildings, Queen St, T0131-625 1234, www.royalgarden.co.uk. Opposite the Scottish National Portrait Gallery and handy for Broughton village and George Street. Sumptuously furnished self-catering apartments with bags of space, satellite TV, a CD player, designer fitted kitchen and views across the Firth of Forth, and access to Queen Street Gardens. Limited parking. Café serving breakfast and snacks. Great for families.

Eating

Edinburgh has a wide range of culinary options, everything from Creole to Cantonese. Scottish cuisine is also well represented, from traditional fare to more contemporary eclectic cuisine. Most of the upmarket restaurants are in the New Town, though there are also some excellent places to be found around the Royal Mile and in Leith, with its many fish restaurants and bistros located around the refurbished dockside. The area around the University campus, in Southside, is where you'll find the best-value eating in town, especially for vegetarians. BYOB is a commonly used abbreviation meaning bring your own bottle.

The Old Town *p646*

£££ The Grain Store, 30 Victoria St, T0131-2257635. Mon-Thu 1200-1400, 1800-2200; Fri and Sat 1200-1500, 1800-2300; Sun 1200-1500, 1800-2200. High quality Scottish ingredients in the exuberant menu featuring fish, game and meat. Wide selection of less orthodox starters which can be eaten combined with each other, tapas-style. A real find, and popular with those in the know.

£££ Iggs , 15 Jeffrey St, T0131-5578184. Mon-Sat 1200-1430, 1800-2230. Closed Sun. Superb Spanish restaurant with a formidable reputation. Combines the flavour of the Mediterranean with contemporary Scottish cuisine. Excellent tapas at lunch, though you may be better off trying the cheaper tapas bar, Barioja, next door (Mon-Sat 1100-2400).

£££ Off the Wall, 105 High St, T0131-558 1497. Mon-Sat 1200-1400, 1730-2200. Closed Sun. Combines the finest Scottish produce with flair and imagination, so the fillet of beef with soft braised fennel and crisp Parma ham is tender and pink (as all good Scottish beef must be). Vegetarians are also well-catered for and the puddings are luscious in the extreme. The wine list is upmarket but with low mark-up.

£££ Plaisir du Chocolat, 251-253 Canongate, T0131-556 9524. Tue, Wed and Sun 1000-1800, Thu-Sat 1000-2230. No smoking. Not content to be one of the city's best French restaurants, it is also its finest tearoom, offering some 180 varieties of tea, hot chocolate, cakes and biscuits, sandwiches, brioche and petit fours. Now open in the evenings at weekends when the menu includes such classics as tarte tatin, fondue and superb foie gras. Their bread, is for sale in the *épicerie* across the road, along with the many other temptations.

£££ The Tower , Museum of Scotland, Chambers St, T0131-225 3003. Daily 1200-2300. No smoking. Still the place to be seen among the corporate set, the superb Scottish menu and magnificent views across the city skyline from the rooftop terrace are hard to beat. This is modern dining at its sophisticated best.

£££ The Witchery by the Castle, 352 Castlehill, T0131-225 5613. Daily 1200-1600, 1730-2330. The reputation here has spread far and wide and is frequented by the likes of Jack Nicholson and Michael Douglas. But though eating here is more of a life experience than simply a meal, style does not take precedence over content. The wine list is phenomenal, with over 900 available. Downstairs, in a converted schoolyard, is the impossibly romantic Secret Garden, which shares the same glorious Scottish menu.

££££ **Bann UK**, 5 Hunter Sq, T 0131-226 1112. Daily 1100-2300. Bann's is still one the city's leading vegetarian eateries with an effortlessly cool, minimalist look and a lifestyle menu to match. They offer an imaginative and adventurous range of dishes, taking veggie food far away from the tedious, sandal-wearing days of old. This is a popular street performing venue during the Festival, so great for an al fresco lunch, if that's your cup of herbal tea. Busy but laid-back and generally good value.

££ **Black Bo's**, 57-61 Blackfriars St, T0131-5576136. Mon-Sat 1200-1400, 1800-2230, Sun 1800-2230. Vegetarian restaurant that is one of the city's truly great culinary experiences. So good even the most fanatical carnivore might even give up meat. Supremely imaginative use of various fruits gives the delicious dishes a real splash of colour. Their lunch is superb value at under £10. The bar next door serves the same food.

££ **Creelers**, 3 Hunter Sq, T0131-220 4447. Sun, Mon and Thu 1200-1400, 1700-2230; Tue-Wed 1200-1400 (May-Oct only), 1700-2230; Fri-Sat 1200-1400, 1700-2300. No smoking. From the owners of the famous Arran restaurant and smokehouse, the capital version serves the same wonderfully fresh seafood, with outdoor seating in the summer. Highlights include the sensational smoked or cured salmon and lip-smacking langoustines grilled in garlic butter.

££ **North Bridge Brasserie** , 20 North Bridge, T0131-662 2900. Daily 1215-1430, 1815-2230. Bar open Sun-Thu 1000-2300, Fri-Sat till 0100. No smoking. Located in the swanky Scotsman Hotel, erstwhile home of **The Scotsman** newspaper. Excellent brasserie menu features grilled meats and seafood, plus sushi and vegetarian choices, though a definite minus are the highly priced starters.

££ **Petit Paris**, 38-40 Grassmarket, T0131-226 2442. Daily 1200-1500, 1730 till late. Francophiles will fall in love with this place. Everything about it is French to the core, from the chequered tablecloths to the coquettish waitresses. The food is delectable and includes classic dishes such as Toulouse sausages and coq au vin. All in all, a wonderful experience, despite the squeeze.

Great lunchtime bargains with a selection of mains for only £5 and pre-theatre deals. BYOB Sunday-Thursday, £2 corkage.

Cafés

Café Hub, Castlehill, T0131-473 2015. Sun-Mon 0930-1800; Tue-Sat 0930-2200. No smoking. The relaxing blues and yellows of this stylish, chilled-out café provide a soothing backdrop to the tasty and inventive food. Seating outside on the terrace in summer.

Elephant House, 21 George IV Bridge, T0131-220 5355. Daily 0800-2300. Very studenty – a great place to linger over coffee and bagels or one of many cheap snacks and main courses. Café-bar by evening with live music. Mellow vibe and lots of pachyderms but not a mahout in sight.

Elephant's Sufficiency, 170 High St, T0131-220 0666. Mon-Fri 0800- 2200; Sat and Sun 0900-2200; till 1700 in winter months. Perennial favourite with locals and tourists. Great value, with a huge selection of breakfasts and lunches. It gets totally crazy at lunchtimes, so prepare to wait or try somewhere a less popular.

The New Town *p654*

£££ **Café Royal Oyster Bar**, 17a West Register St, T0131-5564124. Daily 1200-1400, 1900-2200. An Edinburgh institution and much-loved by numerous celebrities. The ornate tiles and stained-glass windows create an atmosphere of Victorian elegance and opulence. There are better (and cheaper) seafood restaurants in town but none are as classy. The adjoining Bistro Bar is just as impressive and less damaging on the bank balance.

£££ **Duck's at Le Marche Noir**, 2-4 Eyre Pl, T0131-558 1608. Mon-Fri 1200-1430, 1800-2230, Sat 1800-2230, Sun 1800-2130. Classic French provincial cooking married to the best of Ecossais served with precision in sumptuous surroundings. Perhaps Edinburgh's finest French? Complemented by an extensive wine list.

££ **Bell's Diner**, 7 St Stephen St, Stockbridge, T0131-225 8116. Open Mon-Fri 1800-2300, Sat/Sun 1200-2300. The best burgers and steaks in town. This diner is popular with the locals, students and tourists alike who come for its honest, filling and great value food in an informal atmosphere.

££ Howies, 4-6 Glanville Pl, T0131-225 5553. Daily 1200-1430, 1800-2230. Something of an Edinburgh institution, this chain of bistros hits the spot every time with imaginative Scottish food that is always tasty and great value (BYOB policy), in an informal atmosphere. The others are at 29 Waterloo Place, 208 Bruntsfield Pl, and 10-14 Victoria St.
££ Loon Fung, 2 Warriston Pl, T0131-5561781. Mon-Thu 1200-2330, Fri 1200-0030, Sat 1400-0030, Sun 1400-2330. Still one of the great Oriental eating experiences in town, this Cantonese restaurant is an old favourite, with a wide selection of dim sum and seafood dishes.
££The Mussel Inn, 61-65 Rose St, T0131-225 5979. Mon-Thu 1200-1500, 1800-2200, Fri and Sat 1100-2200. What could be better than a huge pot of steaming fresh mussels and a bowl of fantastic chips? Not much, judging by the popularity of this place, in the heart of pub-land. A must for seafood-lovers.
££ Siam Erawan, 48 Howe St, T0131-226 3675. Daily 1200-1430, 1800-2245. Edinburgh's original Thai restaurant and still the best, according to many. The cosy basement ambience encourages you to take your time. The same people have two other branches: Erawan Express, 176 Rose St, T0131-220 0059; and Erawan Oriental, 14 South St Andrew St, T0131-556 4242.
£ Henderson's Salad Table, 94 Hanover St, T0131-225 2131. Mon-Sat 0800-2230. This basement vegetarian self-service restaurant is the oldest in the city and still one of the best. It can get very busy but manages to combine efficiency with comfort. Excellent-value two-course set lunch. Upstairs is their deli and takeaway and round the corner is **Henderson's Bistro**, which provides the same excellent food but in more intimate surroundings, with table service and at only slightly higher prices.

Cafés

Blue Moon, 1 Barony St, T0131-5562788. Mon-Fri 1100-0030, Sat and Sun 0900-0030. Gay café in the city's 'pink triangle'. Good selection of cakes, also snacks and meals. Gets busy later in the evening with pre-clubbers.
Glass & Thompson, 2 Dundas St, T0131-5570909. Mon-Fri 0830-1830, Sat 0830-1730, Sun 1100-1630. Coffee shop and deli with the emphasis on quality food. Popular with local residents who know a good thing when they see (and taste) it.
The Queen Street Café, The Scottish National Portrait Gallery, 1 Queen St, T0131-5572844. Mon-Sat 1000-1630, Sun 1400-1630. The best scones and caramel shortcake in town, not to mention excellent value snacks and light meals, served in grand surroundings. No smoking.
Valvona & Crolla, 19 Elm Row, T0131-556 6066. Mon-Sat 0800-1700. More authentically Italian than almost anything you'd find in New York. Great home cooking and the best cappuccino in town. Needless to say, somewhere this good is very, very popular. No smoking.

West Edinburgh *p657*

£££The Atrium, 10 Cambridge St (same building as the Traverse Theatre), T0131-228 8882. Mon-Fri 1200-1400, 1800-2200, Sat 1800-2200. Award-winning Scottish cooking in elegant modern surroundings. This outstanding restaurant is one of the best in town, but by no means the most expensive.
£££ Stac Polly, 8-10 Grindlay St, T0131-229 5405. Mon-Fri 1200-1430, 1800-2200, Sat/Sun 1800-2200. Elegant Scottish restaurant famous for its now legendary haggis in filo pastry, as well as numerous other mouth-watering native dishes with a gallic touch. Also has a subterranean sister at 29-33 Dublin St.
££ Bar Roma, 39a Queensferry St, T0131-2262977. Mon-Thu and Sun 1200-2400, Fri and Sat till 0100. Traditional Italian serving a huge variety of pasta and pizza to huge numbers of late-night revellers in a fun atmosphere.
££ blue, 10 Cambridge St, T0131-2211222. Tue-Sat 1200-0100, Sun and Mon till 1200. The stylish and minimalist interior of this leading city bistro attracts the arty and media types as well as the more sober suits. Sister to the outstanding **Atrium** (downstairs) so not surprisingly the food on offer is a substantial cut above the rest. Also a great place for a drink, its well-stocked bar boasts a satisfying selection of malts and excellent service.
££ Santini, 8 Conference Sq, T0131-221 7788. Mon-Fri 1200-1430, 1830-2230, Sat 1830-2230. Bar Mon-Fri 1200-1500, 1700-2400, Sat 1700-2400. With such a sleek, chic interior, this is the smartest Italian restaurant in town. With two branches in London and one in Milan, Mr

Santini knows how to wow the punters. Everything is cooked to perfection. The bistro, Santini Bis, is more informal with its own menu.

£ **La Cuisine D'Odile**, 13 Randolph Cres, T0131-225 5685. Tue-Sat 1200-1400 only. Hidden away in the French Institute, this is a real find. Genuine quality French cuisine at amaz-ingly low prices. Great views from the terrace in the summer.

Cafés

Terrace Café, Royal Botanic Garden, Inverleith Row, T0131-5520616. Daily 0930-1800. Set in the grounds next to Inverleith House, this is little more than a school canteen, but the views of the castle, Old Town and Arthur's Seat take some beating. No smoking.

Leith *p658*

£££ **(fitz)Henry**, 19 Shore Pl, T0131-555 6625. Mon-Fri 1200-1430, 1830-2230, Sat 1830-2230.This stylish warehouse brasserie is incongruously located close to some seedy looking tenements but don't be put off. It has received awards for its genuinely original and excellent Scottish cooking and is up there with the city's finest.

£££ **Restaurant Martin Wishart**, 54 The Shore, T0131-553 3557. Tue-Fri 1200-1400, 1900-2200; Sat 1900-2200. Multi award-winning restaurant serving French-influenced cuisine at its very finest. A meal here is a truly memorable experience, as you'd expect from such a renowned chef as Martin Wishart, the only one in the city to receive a coveted Michelin star.

£££ **Skippers**, 1a Dock Pl, T0131-554 1018. Mon-Sat 1230-1400, 1900-2200. This nautical bistro is small and intimate, and very popular, so you'll need to book. Many in the know would say this is the best place to eat seafood in town.

£££ **The Vintners Rooms**, 87 Giles St, T0131-554 6767. Mon-Sat 1200-1400, 1900-2230. These former wine vaults dating from the 17th century now house a restaurant and bar, both lit by candlelight and oozing historic charm and romance. The food is French provincial and excellent, as is the service. Meals in the bar at lunchtime are cheaper.

££ **Fishers**, 1 The Shore, T0131-5545666. Daily 1215-2230. This is one of Edinburgh's finest fish restaurants, in an area packed full of them. It's housed in the tower at the end of The Shore.

££ **Malmaison Brasserie**, 1 Tower Pl, T0131-468-5000. Mon-Fri 0700-1000, 1200-1400, 1800-2230 (Sat from 0800, Sun till 2200). Attached to the acclaimed Malmaison Hotel (see 'Sleeping'). Excellent French brasserie food in stylish surroundings.

££ **The Shore**, 3-4 The Shore, T0131-5535080. Mon-Sat 1100-2400, Sun 1230-2300. One of the city's best fish restaurants with a real fire and huge windows overlooking the Water of Leith. No smoking. You can eat from the restaurant menu in the adjoining bar.

Pubs, bars and clubs

Edinburgh boasts an inordinate amount of watering holes, from centuries-old pubs brimming with history, to the latest in contemporary chic. There's a bar for everyone in this town. And if that weren't enough, the city is blessed with liberal licensing laws, which are relaxed even further during the Festival in Aug and over Christmas and New Year. It is not a problem finding bars open till past midnight any night of the week and some are open till 0300 at weekends.

A good area for bars is around the **Grassmarket**, in the Old Town, which gets very lively at weekends and is particularly popular with students. Those looking for more hip and happening places should head for George St, or the area between George IV Bridge and the High Street in the old town, or the cluster of cool bars around **Broughton Street**, at the east end of the New Town. This is in the 'pink triangle', the centre of the city's gay scene, though many of the bars are not exclusively gay. Most bars are open from 1100-0100 Mon-Fri and 1230-0100 Sun. During the Festival and the Xmas/ New Year period all premises get the opportunity to open an extra 2 hours, so many stay open till 0300.

The Old Town *p646*

Beluga Bar, 30a Chambers St, T0131-624 4545. Vast basement drinking den, regularly rammed with the city's toothsome twenty-somethings. Stylish decor and furnishings but the clientele are more interested in getting trousered than admiring each others' gear. Food in the ground floor bistro is fairly predictable and a tad pricey. DJs at weekends and live jazz on Sun.

The Beehive Inn, 18-20 Grassmarket, T0131-225 7171. Typically rowdy Grassmarket pub downstairs, but the restaurant upstairs is surprisingly intimate and serves good Scottish fare. Starting point for Literary Edinburgh tours (see page 672).

City Café , 19 Blair St, T0131-220 0125. The daddy of Edinburgh's style bars and still the busiest and most vibrant pre-club venue in town. Done out like an American diner with chrome-topped bar and booth seating. Humungous platefuls of food served all day (chilli, burgers, etc) and a couple of pool tables. Set on two floors with a large bar area with pool tables to the rear on the top (ground) floor and smaller bar downstairs where funky House/Garage DJs play at weekends.

EH1, 197 High St, T0131-2205277. Attracts workers from the High Street area during week and popular with tourists sitting in the sun. In the vicinity of the main clubs which are situated around the Cowgate/Royal Mile area and is a modern furbished bar with a small area at the back where DJ's play on Fri-Sat nights.

Iguana, 41 Lothian St, T0131-2204288. Refurbished from old student haunt the Bristo Bar. Smart deco and DJ's Fri/Sat night. Large video screens. Can be too noisy to maintain any form of conversation. Popular with clubbers going to Potterrow which is a Student Venue. The food is excellent and the menu imaginative, but it gets busy at night, so book if you want to be sure of a table.

Negociants, 45-47 Lothian St, T0131-2256313. Is it a bar, is it a bistro? Both, actually. Great for a relaxing lunch-time beer or coffee and popular with students and professionals alike. At night it's a fave late-night watering hole with DJs and dancing downstairs. The menu is international in flavour, excellent value and available till 0230. Good place for a relaxing Sun brunch.

Clubs

The Bongo Club, 14 New St, T0131-556 5204. Cabaret-style venue for a wide variety of performing artists, aimed very much at the arty, bohemian crowd. Innovative, eccentric and pretentious in equal measure. Music nights include funky breakbeat, trip hop and Latin. Operates a full and varied list of live acts every evening Monday-Thursday.

Cabaret Voltaire , 36 Blair St. Formerly home of The Honeycomb and Peppermint Lounge. Now refurbished and aiming to host a variety of performance art and avant garde acts during the week with club nights at weekends. The funky house Ultragroove has relocated from the burnt-out La Belle Angèle and runs fortnightly Saturdays.

Massa , 36-39 Market St. There are two sides to this venue, on a Friday from 1700 onwards its TFI Friday night is the most popular post-work venue for the city's office workers, and half price drinks are served till 2000 to a backdrop of Wham, Abba, young secretaries and leering bosses – not for the faint hearted. It also hosts the gay nights, Eye Candy and Tackno.

The Honeycomb , 15 Niddry St. Formerly The Vaults, some £100 million has been spent on its refurbishment. It was set to be sold early this year until most of its surrounding opposition was destroyed in the great fire of December. Hosts on alternative Saturdays Audio Deluxe and Do This Do That (the latter night which often sees big name DJs visiting Edinburgh once again). The long-running Friday drum'n' bass night, Manga, has relocated from the fire-ravaged La Belle Angèle.

The Liquid Room , 9c Victoria St (top end), T0131-225 2564. Now a very popular venue. Attracting many acts for gigs Monday-Thursday (particularly old punk acts) and hosting some of the city's biggest club nights at the weekends. Saturdays rotate between the long-running gay-friendly night Luvely, 70's cheese Rewind, live acts and Colours (which attracts many big name DJs). Sundays host the popular gay-friendly night Taste.

The New Town *p654*

The Abbotsford, 3 Rose St, T0131-2255276. Big, old reliable pub in a street that's largely lost its drinking appeal. Good, solid pub lunches and a restaurant upstairs that's open in the evenings.

Barony Bar, 81-85 Broughton St, T0131-5570546. Stylish and lively place where you won't feel like you've gatecrashed your young nephew's party. Very busy at weekends. Good bar food.

Baroque, 39-41 Broughton St, T0131-5570627. Brightly coloured decor that's not quite as loud as the young party lovers who frequent this popular bar. Usual range of trendy grub and a great selection of juices.

The Basement, 10-12a Broughton St, T0131-5570097. This Broughton Street original feels like it's been around for ever and is just as hip and happening as ever. Good bistro food with a mainly Mexican flavour.

Café Royal Circle Bar, 19 West Register St, T0131-5564124. You can't help feeling spoiled in these elegant and civilized surroundings. Adjacent to the **Café Royal Oyster Bar** (see Eating). Treat yourself to the seafood menu.

Café Royal Bistro Bar, next door upstairs is thea big favourite with the rugger fraternity.

Candy Bar , 113-115 George St, T0131-225 9179. Cosy and classy subterranean bar with a warm, unpretentious feel and good cocktail list. Simple, clean lines and an attractive design make it easy on the eye.

CC Blooms, 23-24 Greenside Pl, T0131-556 9331. Ever-popular gay bar and club next to the Playhouse Theatre. Upstairs is the bar – lots of mirrors and neon; downstairs is the sweaty dance floor. Packed to the gunnels late at night and weekends.

The Cumberland Bar, 1 Cumberland Street, T0131-5583134. Classic New Town bar that oozes refinement and respectability. Fine selection of real ales, a beer garden and some decent nosh. A good place to kick back and while away an hour or several.

Opal Lounge, 51a George St, T0131-226 2275. Cavernous subterranean bar and bistro with three other bar areas, sunken lounges for dining and dancing. Comfortable and relaxed vibe despite the high pose quotient, created by the sultry lighting, dark wood decor and chocolate furnishings. The menu is Oriental in flavour and decent value.

The Outhouse, 12a Broughton St La, T0131-557 6668. Under the same management as Ego night club, this small dark bar is not very plush but does fill up quickly and has a good atmosphere. A firm fave with pre-clubbers. Good beer garden in the summer months.

Pivo Caffé, 2-6 Calton Rd, T0131-5572925. At the top of Leith Walk opposite the St James Centre. Czech-themed bar offering a thick slice of Prague. Very good czech beer and huge portions of grub. Lively buzz in evenings when it's full of students on their way to **The Venue**.

Planet Out , Greenside Pl, T0131-524 0061. Friendly, happy, award-winning gay bar which attracts a loyal following for its various weekly activities including DJs and a quiz. Voted 'Best Pub in Scotland' by NOW UK magazine.

Clubs

Ego, 14 Picardy Pl. Refurbished casino hosting various well-established club nights such as Velvet, a monthly lesbian night, Vibe (every Tue), the monthly Wiggle and long-running gay night Joy. Fridays tend to host new clubs in the smaller Cocteau Lounge. Club nights in the summer months sometimes utilize the Outhouse's beer garden.

The Venue , 17-23 Calton Rd (behind Waverley Station), T0131-557 3073. Recently refurbished and under new management, Venue now hosts a variety of new up and coming soul, hip hop and house nights with a variety of live acts on week nights.

West Edinburgh *p657*

Bennet's Bar, 8 Leven St, T0131-2295143. Not strictly West, more South and next to the King's Theatre. Marvel at the carved wooden gantry, the stained-glass windows, the huge mirrors, and the glass-topped tables with inlaid city maps while you enjoy a great pint of beer and perhaps some good old-fashioned (and cheap) food (served in the back room at lunch-times only). One of the city's finest traditional pubs.

Bert's Bar, 29-31 William St, T0131-2255748. A better class of rugby bar which attracts the more refined aficionado as well as the occasional Charlotte Street mafioso. A pie and a pint doesn't get much better than this.

Indigo Yard , 7 Charlotte La, T0131-220 5603. This converted and covered courtyard has been transformed into an immensely popular bar and restaurant. The menu is cosmopolitan (Thai, Mexican, French, Italian etc) and the food excellent. It has a good cocktail list and popular with weekend pre-clubbers. One of the places to be seen drinking in.

Mondobbo, 34 Bread St, T0131-2215555. Part of the supremely stylish **Point Hotel**, and don't it show. Popular with local office workers for a sophisticated light lunch or after work for happy-hour cocktails.
Traverse Bar Café, Traverse Theatre, 10 Cambridge St, T0131-2285383. Very stylish bar that's popular with luvvies, suits and students. Excellent and affordable food served at all times and regular special drinks offers.

Leith *p658*

Bar Java , 48-50 Constitution St, T0131-467 7527. Groovy little bar that opens early for breakfast, has a beer garden for those rare warm summer evenings, good food, live music and even rooms for B&B upstairs.
The Pond, 2 Bath Rd, T0131-467 3825. Make no mistake, this place looks weird, but makes for an interesting drinking experience, and also effortlessly laid-back.

Entertainment

As host of the World's premiere arts festival, Edinburgh is well endowed with various cultural venues. But don't be mistaken in thinking that when the Festival packs its bags and leaves in early Sep the city hibernates till Aug comes round again. The city's cultural scene is thriving throughout the year, catering equally well for the avid culture vulture or hedonistic night owl. The many fine **theatres** and **concert halls** have full and varied programmes. Club culture in the capital has improved greatly in the last few years and Edinburgh now boasts some of the UK's best club nights, many of which go on until 0400 or 0500. These change frequently but tend to use the same venues, which are listed below. Those who prefer their music live, can take advantage of the liberal licensing laws and check out **jazz**, **folk** and **rock** bands any night of the week in many of city's 700-plus bars. The main live music venues are listed below, but also see under 'Bars'. The city's vibrant **gay scene** has been centred around the Playhouse Theatre at the top of Leith Walk, the 'pink triangle', for many years. It has continued to develop around Broughton St, with new places constantly opening up, be they exclusively gay or gay-friendly. A large percentage of the city's trendiest bars, cafés and clubs can now be found on or around Broughton St, making Edinburgh an easy city for the gay tourist to visit.

To find out **what's on** in the city, pick up a copy of *The List*, the fortnightly listings magazine that tells you what's happening and where in both Edinburgh and Glasgow. Alternatively, the local evening paper, the *Edinburgh Evening News*, appears daily except Sun and gives details of what's going on the city on that day. Tickets and information on all events are available at the **Tourist Information Centre**. You can also find flyers (promotional leaflets) for various events at the main concert halls and theatres and in many of the bars and cafés in the centre of town. For a full list of what's on, visit www.edinburghevents.com

Cinemas

The Cameo, 38 Home St, T0131-2284141. In the Tollcross. 3 screens showing new arthouse releases and cult classics. Late showings at weekends and a good bar with video screen showing short films, comfy seating and snacks. Great place for movie buffs to hang out. Bar open Sun-Wed 1230-2300, Thu-Sat till 0100.
Filmhouse, 88 Lothian Rd, T0131-2282688. Three screens showing a wide range of movies, including new arthouse releases, obscure foreign films and old classics. Good café-bar. Hosts the annual Film Festival, so you never know who you might bump into.
UGC Cinemas, Fountainpark, Dundee St, T0870-9020417. Vast 13-screen complex which also includes bars, restaurants, gym and nightclub.

Comedy

During the 80s, alternative comedy was king and any aspiring comedian had to play the Edinburgh Festival if they wanted to make an impact. This is now less so, as more and more comedians preview their Edinburgh shows in London, but playing The Fringe is still de rigueur for any self-respecting funny person and the Perrier Award, given to the brightest new comedy talent, remains the ultimate goal for all budding comedians. The legendary Gilded Balloon Theatre was tragically burned down in the terrible fire of December 2002, but it lives on in spirit at a series of alternative venues (listed on the next page).

Jongleurs Comedy Club, Unit 6/7, Omni Leisure Developent, Greenhouse Pl, T0870-7870707, www.jongleurs.com*Comedy Thu-Sun till 2300* Opened in 2003.

The Stand Comedy Club, 5 York Pl, T0131-558 7272, www.thestand.co.uk. *Mon-Thu 1200-2400, Fri 1200-1900, 1930-0100, Sat 1930-0100, Sun 1230-2400.* This is the showcase for emerging comedy talent seven nights a week. By day it's a popular café-bar serving budget lunches, and on Sunday there's free comedy with your lunch.

Dance

Dance Base, T0131-225 5525, www.dancebase.co.uk The facilities include four studios and the largest dance space available for public use in the UK.

Concert halls

For details of current performances, see *The List* or Sat's *Scotsman* newspaper. Classical music played by one of the national orchestras can be heard at the main civic concert hall, the **Usher Hall**, Lothian Rd and Grindlay St, T0131-2281155. Smaller classical ensembles, as well as jazz, blues, folk, rock and pop groups, play at **Queen's Hall**, 89 Clerk St, T0131-6682019. Less frequent performances are held at **Reid Concert Hall**, Bristo Sq, T0131-6504367, **St Cecilia's Hall**, Cowgate and Niddry St, T0131-6502805.

Live music venues

Good places to catch up-and-coming young **indie bands** are The Liquid Room and The Venue, which are listed above under 'Clubs'. The Liquid Room has established itself as good place to see touring acts such as Moby and Mogwai. They also host the T on The Fringe music festival. The **Playhouse Theatre** (see below) is a favourite with old codgers like Lou Reed and Van Morrison.

Live **jazz** can be heard in Henry's Cellar Bar, Morrison St, T0131-2211228. Also know as the **Jazz Joint**, this tiny cellar bar shows a vast range of acts. Occasional jazz concerts, as well as a growing number of top rock and pop gigs, also take place at the *Queen's Hall* (see above). One of the best places to hear authentic grassroots **folk music** is The Royal Oak, 1 Infirmary St. Another good bet is the **Tron Ceilidh House**, 9 Hunter Square, behind the Tron Kirk, T0131-2201550. Below the ground floor bar are two basement levels, with regular folk sessions and a comedy club. Open Sun-Thu till 2400, Fri/Sat till 0100. Nighthawks should head down to **Whistlebinkies**, Niddry St, T0131-5575114, where you can listen to raucous folk till 0300.

Theatre

Festival Theatre, Nicolson St, T0131-5296000. The city's showcase theatre with a varied programme including the world's leading companies.

King's Theatre, 2 Leven St, T0131-2291201. Refurbished Edwardian theatre showing everything from Shakespeare to panto.

Netherbow Arts Centre, 43 High St, T0131-5569579. Home to the Scottish Storytelling Centre, with children's shows in the day and drama for adults in the evenings.

Playhouse Theatre, 18-22 Greenside Pl, T0131-5572950. Vast 3,000-seater theatre for all the West End productions as well as the occasional rock star. Used during the official Festival for dance and opera.

Pleasance Theatre, 60 The Pleasance, T0131-5566550. One of the top Fringe venues staging comedy and drama. The outdoor cobbled courtyard is a great place to hang out during the Festival for a bit star-spotting.

Royal Lyceum, 30 Grindlay St, T0131-2299697. Lovely old Victorian theatre staging mainstream drama all year round. **Theatre Workshop**, 34 Hamilton place, T0131-2265425. Small, accessible and amenable theatre down in bohemian Stockbridge with a reputation for innovative and daring productions.

Traverse Theatre, 10 Cambridge St, T0131-2281404. Internationally renowned theatre dedicated to new writing talent. Consistently good entertainment. Also blessed with the excellent restaurant, *The Atrium*, in the foyer and *blue* bistro upstairs (see 'Eating'), as well as a good bar (see 'Bars').

Festivals

For full information about the International Festival events, and for access to the websites of all the Edinburgh Festivals visit the official festival site: www.go-edinburgh.co.uk.
The free daily listings magazine, *The Guide*, is a good way to find out what's on and where. *The List* and *The Scotsman* also give comprehensive coverage.

Edinburgh not only hosts the world's greatest arts festival in Aug, but also stages several other notable events throughout the rest of the year. The most renowned of these is **Edinburgh's Hogmanay**, which has grown to become one of the world's major winter events and which was the largest Millenium celebration in the northern hemisphere. It starts on the 29 Dec with a torchlit procession through the city centre followed by four days of various events, including pop and rock concerts. The highlight is the giant street party on the 31st (which is for ticket holders only). Accommodation is always fully booked at this time. For information contact **The Hub**, or www. edinburghshogmanay.org.

Edinburgh International Festival Box office: The Hub, Castlehill, T0131-4732000, www.eif.co.uk.

Edinburgh Festival Fringe Box office: 180 High Street, T0131-2265257, www.edfringe.com.

Edinburgh International Film Festival Box office: Filmhouse, 88 Lothian Road, T0131-2292550, www.edfilmfest.org.uk.

Edinburgh International Jazz & Blues Festival Box office: 29 St Stephen St, T0131-2252202, www.jazzmusic.co.uk.

International Book Festival Box office: 137 Dundee St, T0131-2285444, www.edbookfest.co.uk.

Edinburgh Military Tattoo Box office: 32 Market St, T0131-2251188, www.edintattoo.co.uk.

International Science Festival Box office: Roxburgh's Court, off 323 High St, T0131-2605860, www.sciencefestival.co.uk.

The **Folk Festival**, at the beginning of **Apr**, is a massive event and draws performers from near and far, T0131-5543092.

The **Scottish International Children's Festival** is the UK's largest performing arts festival for children and is held at the end of **May** (Box office: 45a George St, T0131-2258050, www.imaginate.org.uk).

At the end of **Jun** is the **Royal Highland Show**, at the Royal Highland Centre, Ingliston, T0131-3356200. It's a sort of display of the best of rural Scotland, with pedigree livestock competitions, flower shows, craft fairs and showjumping, amongst other things.

Also in **Jun**, usually in the 1st week, is the **Caledonian Beer Festival**, held at Edinburgh's own Caledonian Brewery on Slateford Road (see Bars, pubs and clubs). The event features dozens of real ales, food and live music (mostly jazz) in the brewery's Festival Hall. See local press for details, or T0131-3371286.

The **Filmhouse** (see 'Cinemas') also hosts a number of foreign film seasons, most notably French (in **Nov** and Italian, in **Apr**. There's also a gay film season, in **Jun**. For details, T0131-2282688.

Shopping

Edinburgh's shops are best known for traditional Scottish souvenirs and upmarket goods, food products in particular. The main shopping street is Princes Street, where you'll find all the main department stores such as **Debenhams, Frasers, BHS, Marks & Spencers**. Two independent department stores are **Jenners**, also on Princes Street, and **Aitken & Niven**, at 77-79 George St. George Street is the place to come for fashionistas as it's lined with chic clothes shops, with that temple to conspicuous consumption, Harvey Nicks, now open in St Andrews Sq, darling. Good places to look for second-hand and antique art, jewellery and books are around the **New Town** (St Stephen St, Northwest Circus Pl, Thistle St), **Broughton St, Victoria St** and the **Grassmarket**. Shopping hours are now more relaxed and many of the main city centre outlets are open till 1930-2000 on Thu and on Sun.

Edinburgh's festivals

Every year Edinburgh plays host to the world's biggest arts festival when the capital bursts into life in a riot of entertainment. Edinburgh during its Festival has been variously described as "simply the best place on Earth" and "the cultural hub of the world".

The Edinburgh Festival is actually a collection of different festivals running alongside each other, from the end of July through to the beginning of September. The **International Festival** tends to be a fairly highbrow affair and features large-scale productions of opera, ballet, classical music, dance and theatre performed in the larger venues. It ends with an open air concert and spectacular fireworks display in Princes Street Gardens. The **Festival Fringe** began life in 1947 as an adjunct to the International, or "official" Festival, but has since grown so large it now overshadows its big brother and threatens to outgrow the city. Last year over 500 companies performed in nearly 200 venues; everything from the country's leading comedians at the Assembly Rooms to a group of existentialist students staging "Waiting for Godot" in Mandarin in a draughty church hall. Over the years the Fringe has been a major showcase for fresh talent and the likes of Billy Connolly, Maggie Smith, Emma Thompson, Rowan Atkinson and Harry Enfield all started out here. The Fringe continues to be the launching pad for many of our greatest actors, comedians, writers and directors as well as pushing back the boundaries of art and entertainment. A good opportunity to preview many of the Fringe performers for free is Fringe Sunday, which takes place in Holyrood Park, at the foot of the Royal Mile.

The **International Jazz and Blues Festival** kicks the whole thing off in July and features some of the world's leading performers, as well as many lesser known ones, playing in just about every pub in the city centre. The **International Film Festival** is the UK's most important film festival and screens many brilliant new movies long before they reach London and the rest of the country. It is also the longest continually running event of its kind in the world. The **International Book Festival**, meanwhile, may look like a just a bunch of tents in Charlotte Square, but the marquees are full of some of the biggest names in literature holding readings, discussions, interviews and a whole range of workshops for adults and children. Although it's a separate event, the **Military Tattoo**, set against the magnificent backdrop of Edinburgh Castle, is very much part of the Festival. It's an unashamedly kilt-and-bagpipes event, featuring Massed Pipes and Drums, display teams, dancers and bands from all over the world.

Activities and tours

Bus tours

One of the best ways to see the city sights is to take a guided bus tour on board an open-top double decker bus. These depart from Waverley Bridge every 15 minutes, the first one leaving around 0900 and the last one between 1730 and 2000, depending on the time of year. The complete tour lasts an hour, stopping at the main tourist sights, but tickets are valid for the full day and you can hop on and off any of the company's buses at any of the stops. **Guide Friday** tours are recommended and cost £8.50 per person (students £7/children £2.50); Guide Friday Tourism Centre, 133-135 Canongate, Royal Mile, T5562244, www.guidefriday.com. **Lothian Regional Transport** (LRT) run similar guided bus tours; £7.50 (students £6/children £2.50). Tickets and further information from their city centre offices.

Climbing

Adventure Centre, Ratho village, off A8, 10 mins west of airport, T0131-229 3919, www.adventurescotland.com. Massive rock climbing and sports training venue based in a converted quarry. This is the largest climbing arena in the world, with outdoor rock cliffs and wall. Home to the National Rock Climbing Centre. Includes Air Park, a suspended aerial adventure ropes ride, and an adventure sports gym. Bars, restaurant and accommodation.

Football

Edinburgh has 2 Scottish Premier League teams, who play at home on alternate Saturdays during the league season. **Heart of Midlothian**, or Hearts, play at Tyncastle, on the Gorgie Road about a mile west of Haymarket, and **Hibernian** (Hibs) play at Easter Road, east of the centre near Leith. Rivalry between the two is fierce, but thankfully free from the religious bigotry of their Glasgow counterparts.

Health and fitness

Escape, at the Scotsman Hotel (see Sleeping), T622 3800, www.escapehealthclubs.com. State-of-the-art gym and fitness centre, beauty spa, sauna and 16-m stainless steel pool.
One Spa, 8 Conference Sq, T0131-221 7777, www.one-spa.com. The ultimate in pampering, from a simple back massage (£38) to the full Ayurverdic Holistic Body Treatment (£110).

Horse riding

Edinburgh & Lasswade Riding Centre, Kevock Rd, Lasswade, T0131-6637676.
Pentland Hills Icelandics, Rodgersrigg Farm, Carlops (south of Hillend Ski Centre), Midlothian, T01968-661095.
Tower Farm Riding Stables, 85 Liberton Drive, T0131-6643375.

Rugby

Scotland's national side play at Murrayfield Stadium, a few miles west of the city centre and reached from Corstorphine Rd or Roseburn St. For tickets T0131-3645000, though these are scarce for major internationals.

Skiing

Midlothian Ski Centre, at Hillend, take the A702 off the City Bypass at the Lothianburn exit, T0131-4454433 (open Mon-Sat 0930-2100, Sun 0930-1900). Artificial ski slope for ski and snowboarding practice and instruction. Also downhill mountain bike trail and chairlift.

Walking tours

There are various guided walking tours of Edinburgh, which fall into roughly two categories: historical tours of the medieval closes and wynds of the Royal Mile during the day, and spooky, nocturnal tours of the city's dark and grisly past. Some of the latter tours include a visit to the 200 year-old haunted vaults hidden deep beneath the city streets. There are several versions of these tours, but the main operator is
Mercat Tours, T/F2256591, who leave from the Mercat Cross by St Giles Cathedral.
City of the Dead Haunted Graveyard Tour, T0771-5422750, leaves from the Mercat Cross nightly at 2030 and involves being locked in a haunted graveyard with the notorious Mackenzie poltergeist. Most of these guided walking tours last around two hours and cost £6-7 per person.
Edinburgh Literary Pub Tour, a witty exploration of the city's distinguished literary past, which starts at the Beehive Inn in the Grassmarket. The two-hour tour costs £7 per person (students £5). Tickets can be booked at the tourist office or direct from The Scottish Literary Tour Company, T0131-2266665, www.scot-lit-tour.co.uk

Transport

Air

There are flights to Edinburgh from Europe, Ireland and the UK. Flights from North America arrive via Glasgow. (For flight details, see page 644). There is one daily flight from Edinburgh to **Inverness**, which takes 45 mins.

Bus

There are numerous bus services from London and prices are very competitive. There are also links with other English cities, such as **Newcastle**, **Manchester**, **Birmingham** and **York**. (For details of these services, see p644).

Buses leave from St Andrew Square bus station to most of the major towns in Scotland. Most west coast towns are reached via Glasgow. There are buses to and from **Glasgow**. There are also regular daily buses to: **Aberdeen** (4 hrs); **Dundee** (2 hrs 10 mins, or 1 hr 25 mins direct); **Perth** (1½ hrs, or 1 hr direct); **Inverness** (4½ hrs, or 3 hrs 40 mins direct), via Pitlochry and Aviemore. One of the main operators is **Scottish Citylink**, T08705-505050, with buses to virtually every major town in Scotland. For bus services to and from English towns and cities, contact **National Express**.

Car hire

The main national car-hire companies can all be found at the airport. The following are local companies which may offer better deals: **Arnold Clark**, Lochrin Pl, T0131-2284747. **Melville's**, 9 Clifton Terr, Haymarket, www.melvilles.co.uk. **Condor Self Drive**, 45 Lochrin Pl, Tollcross, T0131-229 6333, sales@condorselfdrive.com **Enterprise** Rent-a-Car, Block B, Unit 15, Sighthill shopping Centre, T0131-442 4440.

Cycle hire

Central Cycle Hire, 13 Lochrin Pl, T0131-2286333, F0131-2283686. £15/day. Open Mon-Fri 0930-1800, Sat 0930-1730, Sun 1200-1700. **Edinburgh Cycle Hire**, 29 Blackfriars St, T0131-5565560. £10-12/day. Open daily 0900-2100.

Train

There are regular daily services to and from London King's Cross. (For details of frequency and fares, see pXXX.) **ScotRail** runs regular daily train services to **Inverness** (3¾ hrs), via **Stirling** (45 mins), **Perth** (1¼ hrs), **Pitlochry** and **Aviemore** (3 hrs). Also to **Aberdeen** (2¾ hrs), via **Kirkcaldy** and **Dundee** (1¾ hrs). There are trains every 30 mins to and from **Glasgow** (50 mins; £8-10 day return). There is also a regular service to **North Berwick** (35 mins).

Directory

Banks

Bank opening hours are Mon-Fri from 0930 to between 1600 and 1700. Some larger branches may also be open later on Thu and on Sat mornings. You can withdraw cash from selected banks and ATMs (or cashpoints as they are called in Britain) with your credit/debit card. Visa card holders can use the **Bank of Scotland, Clydesdale Bank, Royal Bank of Scotland** and **TSB** ATMs; Access/MasterCard holders can use the Royal Bank and Clydesdale; Amex card holders can use the Bank of Scotland.

Gay and Lesbian

Lothian Gay and Lesbian Switchboard, T556 4049. Daily 1930-2200. Helpline for lesbians and gay men.

Hospitals

Edinburgh's 24-hr walk-in accident and emergency department is at **The Royal Infirmary of Edinburgh**, 1 Lauriston Place, T0131-5361000. If it's not an emergency but you still need to see a doctor look in the *Yellow Pages*, or call the Primary Care department, T0131-5369000.

Internet

There are cybercafés throughout the city, but two of the best are **Cyberia**, 88 Hanover St, T0131-2204403, open Mon-Sat 1000-2200, Sun 1100-2000, prices from £2.50 per ½hr (£2 concession) and **Web 13**, 13 Bread St, T0131-2298883, open Mon-Fri 0900-2200, Sat 0900-2000, Sun 1100-2000, prices from £2.50 per ½hr at peak times (1200-1700 Mon-Sat) and £3.50 all other times. **Easy Everything**, Hanover Buildings, 58 Rose St, T0131-2203580. Open 24 hrs and cheap at £1 per hr.

Libraries

Central Library, George IV Bridge, T0131-2255884. Open Mon-Fri 0900-2100, Sat 0900-1300. Excellent Scottish and local reference sections. **National Library of Scotland**, George IV Bridge, T0131-2264531. Open Mon-Fri 0930-2030, Sat 0930-1300. Superb copyright library, for research purposes only. Reference facilities at the **Map Room**, 33 Salisbury Pl; open Mon-Fri 0930-1700, Sat 0930-1300.

Pharmacies
Boots the Chemist, 48 Shandwick Place, T0131-2256757. Open Mon-Sat 0800-2100, Sun 1000-1700. In an emergency outside these times, go to The Royal Infirmary.

Police
If you are robbed or assaulted and need to report the crime, call 999. The police information centre is at 188 High St, T0131-2266966, open daily 1000-2200.

Post office
The central post office, at 8-10 St James Centre, is open Mon 0900-1730, Tue-Fri 0830-1730, Sat 0830-1800. There's also a main office at 7 Hope St. Other post offices are open Mon-Fri 0900 to 1730 and Sat 0900 to 1230 or 1300. Smaller sub-post offices are closed for an hour at lunch (1300-1400) and keep the same half-day closing times as local shops. There is a late collection from the post box at the Royal Mail head office, 10 Brunswick Rd (one third of the way down Leith Walk).

Around Edinburgh

→ *Colour map 5*

The Pentland Hills
South of the Braid Hills, beyond the City Bypass, are Edinburgh's Pentland Hills, a serious range of hills, remote in parts, rising to almost 2,000 ft and which stretch around 16 miles from the outskirts of Edinburgh to Lanarkshire. The hills offer relatively painless *climbs* and you'll be rewarded with magnificent views once you reach the top.

There are many paths up to the various Pentland summits and round the lochs and reservoirs. One of the many walks is described above, but if you want to explore more fully there are many books about the Pentlands, including *25 Walks in Edinburgh and Lothian* (HMSO, 1995). Ordnance Survey Landranger Map no 66 covers the area.

The main access is by the A702, which passes the *Midlothian Ski Centre* at **Hillend**. There's a marked walking trail up to the ski slope, or you can take the chair lift. At the top of the slope it's a short walk to **Caerketton Hill** for fantastic panoramic views of Edinburgh, the Firth of Forth and the hills of Fife and Stirlingshire.

Lauriston Castle, Cramond and Dalmeny
About five miles northwest of town is **Lauriston Castle,** ⓘ *Apr-Oct Sat-Thu 1100-1300 and 1400-1700; Nov-Mar Sat/Sun 1400-1600. £7.50, concession £5. T0131-3362060*, a fine Edwardian country mansion set in lovely grounds overlooking the Firth of Forth. The original tower house is late 16th century, with many neo-Jacobean additions by William Burn in the 19th century. It was once the home of John Law, who founded the first bank in France and obtained sole trading rights in the Lower Mississippi, which he christened Louisiana in honour of the French King. The interior contains fine collections of period furniture and antiques.

One mile further west is the lovely little coastal village of **Cramond**, situated where the River Almond flows into the Forth. The 18th-century village of whitewashed houses is the site of an ancient Roman fort, a large part of which has been excavated. The most recent discovery was a magnificent sandstone sculpture of a lioness dating from the second century BC. In addition to being steeped in ancient history, Cramond boasts a pleasant promenade, a golf course and a lovely, wooded walk along the banks of the Almond river towards the 16th century **Old Cramond Brig**. And if that weren't enough to tempt you, there's also **Cramond Island**, which can be reached via a raised walkway when the tide is out. Just make sure you keep an eye on the time or you may find yourself stuck there for longer than you anticipated. Tide times are posted on the shore, and are also available from the Tourist Information Centre.

A local passenger **ferry service** ⓘ *0900-1300 and 1400-1700 in summer, till 1600 in winter, closed Fri*, still crosses the River Almond at Cramond From the other side of the river it's a two-mile walk to **Dalmeny House** ⓘ *Jul and Aug Sun 1300-1730, Mon and Tue 1200-1730 (last admission 1645), £4, £2 children, T0131-3311888*, the Earl of Rosebery's home for over 300 years. The present house, built in 1815 in Tudor Gothic, contains a superb collection of 18th-century French furniture, porcelain and tapestries and paintings, including portraits by Gainsborough, Raeburn, Reynolds and Lawrence. There is also a fascinating collection of Napoleon Bonaparte memorabilia, assembled by the fifth Earl of Rosebery, a former Prime Minister.he house can also be reached via the village of Dalmeny, eight miles west of Edinburgh, on the A90 then B924. There's a bus service from St Andrew Square to Chapel Gate, one mile from the house, or you can take a train which stops at the village station. The main point of interest in the village is the wonderful 12th-century church.

Roslin

Seven miles south of Edinburgh, in the county of **Midlothian**, just off the A701 to Penicuik, lies the little village of Roslin, home of the mysterious 15th-century **Rosslyn Chapel** ⓘ *Mon-Sat 1000-1700, Sun 1200-1645. £4, £3.50 concession. T0131-4402159, www.rosslynchapelt.org.uk. Take one of the regular buses for Penicuik from St Andrews Sq.* Perched above the North Esk, the magnificent and unique chapel has a richly carved interior full of Biblical representations and pagan and masonic symbols and has been described as "a fevered hallucination in stone". Foundations were laid in 1446 for a much larger church which was never built. What exists is the Lady Chapel, inspiration of Sir William Sinclair, who himself supervized masons brought from abroad who took 40 years to complete it to his design. According to legend, his grandfather, the adventurer Prince Henry of Orkney, set foot in the New World a century before Columbus. This is backed up by the carvings of various New World plants. One of the most fascinating sights in the church, and the most elaborate carving, is the **Prentice Pillar**. Legend has it that while the master mason was away in Rome making additional drawings to complete the pillar, an apprentice finished it for him. On the mason's return he murdered the apprentice in a fury.

Speculation as to the purpose of the chapel dwells on esoteric secrets and a plethora of recent books claims that the Holy Grail, supposedly brought from the East by the Knights Templar, is buried here. Whether or not you believe this, you'll still find its architecture and atmosphere fascinating. Once you've seen the chapel, there are some pleasant walks in nearby Roslin Glen, for great views of Roslin Castle.

South Queensferry

Less than a mile from Dalmeny is the ancient town of South Queensferry, which gets its name from the 11th-century St Margaret, who used the town as the crossing point during her trips between her palaces in Edinburgh and Dunfermline, which was Scotland's capital at that time. The town's narrow main street is lined with picturesque old buildings, most striking of which is the row of two-tiered shops. If you fancy a drink, or a meal, or perhaps a bed for the night, try the historic *Hawes Inn*, which was featured in Stevenson's *Kidnapped*. The town is dominated by the two great bridges that tower overhead on either side, spanning the Firth of Forth at its narrowest point. The massive steel cantilevered **Forth Rail Bridge**, over a mile and a half long and 360 ft high and is a staggering monument to Victorian engineering. It was built in 1883-90 and 60,000 tons of steel were used in its construction. Beside it, is the **Forth Road Bridge**, a suspension bridge built between 1958 and 1964, which ended the 900-year-old ferry crossing between South and North Queensferry. The Road Bridge is open to pedestrians and it's worth walking across for the views of the Rail Bridge.

To get to South Queensferry from Edinburgh, take buses 43, X43, 47 or 47a from St Andrew Sq

From Hawes Pier, right underneath the Rail Bridge, you can take a variety of **pleasure boat cruises** on the Forth. **Jet Boat Tours** ⓘ, *T0131-3314777, prices are around £5-10 per person, cruises run Apr/May/Sep/Oct weekends and public holidays 1000-1800; Jun-Aug daily 0930-2000,* have cruises up the River Almond at Cramond, looking out for dolphins, seals and porpoises en route, as well as 'Bridge Tours' and 'Jet-Boat fun rides'.

Inchcolm Abbey

There are also Sealife Cruises on board the *Maid of the Forth* ⓘ *Sailings from Easter to Oct, evening jazz and ceilidh cruises throughout the summer on Fri, Sat and Sun evenings, £11, £9 concession, £4.50 child, T0131-3314857,* as well as Evening Cruises beneath the bridges with jazz and folk accompaniment. The most interesting cruise of all, and the most popular, is the cruise to the island of Inchcolm, whose beautiful ruined **abbey**, founded in 1123 by King Alexander I, is the best-preserved group of monastic buildings in Scotland. The oldest surviving building is the 13th-century octagonal chapter house. You can also climb the tower for great views of the island, which is populated by nesting seabirds and a colony of seals.

Hopetoun House

ⓘ *Daily Apr-end of Sep, and every weekend in Oct, 1000-1730. £6, concessions £5, children £3, T0131-3312451, www.hopetounhouse.com.*

Two miles west of South Queensferry is Hopetoun House, which thoroughly deserves its reputation as 'Scotland's finest stately home'. Set in 100 acres of magnificent parkland, including the Red Deer park, the house is the epitome of aristocratic grandeur and recently celebrated its 300th birthday. Hopetoun House is perhaps the finest example of the work of William Burn and William Adam. It is, in fact, two houses in one. The oldest part was designed by William Bruce and built between 1699 and 1707. In 1721 William Adam began enlarging the house by adding the facade, colonnades and grand State Apartments. It was built for the Earls of Hopetoun, later created Marquesses of Linlithgow and part of the house is still lived in by the Marquess of Linlithgow and his family. The house contains a large collection of art treasures and the grounds are also open to the public. You could come here and pretend you're a member of the aristocracy for the day, then go back to your tiny B&B and weep.

Southern Scotland

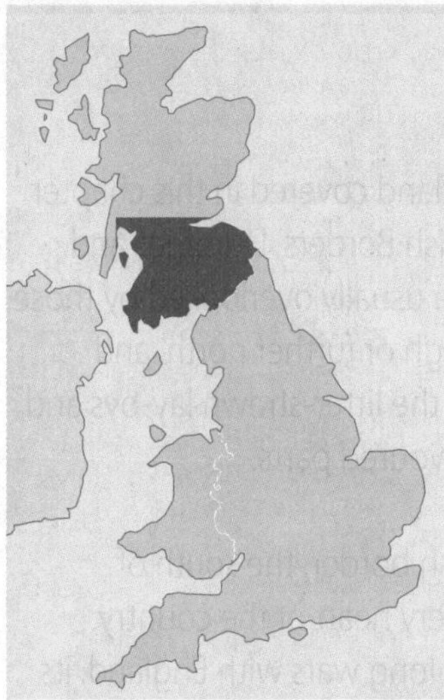

Introduction

The vast swathe of Southern Scotland covered in this chapter comprises East Lothian, the Scottish Borders, Dumfries and Galloway and Ayrshire. It's an area usually overlooked by those on their way to Glasgow, Edinburgh or further north, and consequently relatively free from the litter-strewn lay-bys and crowded beauty spots of more favoured parts.

Despite its proximity to the English border, the south of Scotland is in many ways at the very heart of the country. Under constant threat during the long wars with England, its people were at the front line in the defence of Scottish nationhood. It is therefore no coincidence that Scotland's two greatest literary figures, Robert Burns and Sir Walter Scott, were born and lived here.

Southern Scotland is divided neatly by the A74(M), the main route from England to Scotland. To the east of this line the main tourist focus is the Borders region, with its peaceful little mill towns, in particular lovely little Melrose. To the north are the narrow ranges of the Lammermuir, Moorfoot and Pentland Hills. North of the Lammermuirs is East Lothian, with its sandy bays and rugged coastline.

The landscape becomes ever more wild and mountainous as you head west from the Tweed Valley across the Southern Uplands. The most spectacular scenery is west of Dumfries, in the Galloway Forest Park. The Solway coast, from Dumfries to the Mull of Galloway, is equally appealing. North of Galloway is the Ayrshire coast, lined with seaside resorts and some great golf courses, and best known for its associations with Robert Burns, especially Alloway, where he was born.

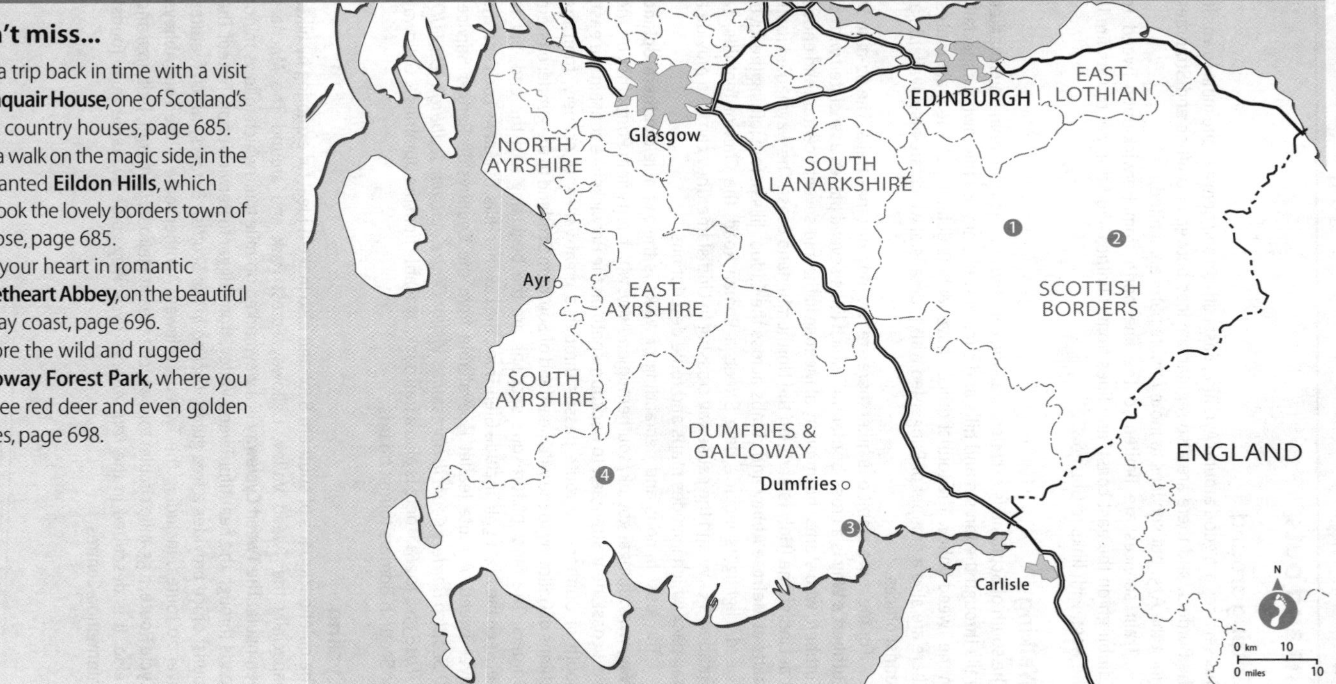

★ Don't miss...

1. Take a trip back in time with a visit to **Traquair House**, one of Scotland's great country houses, page 685.
2. Take a walk on the magic side, in the enchanted **Eildon Hills**, which overlook the lovely borders town of Melrose, page 685.
3. Lose your heart in romantic **Sweetheart Abbey**, on the beautiful Solway coast, page 696.
4. Explore the wild and rugged **Galloway Forest Park**, where you can see red deer and even golden eagles, page 698.

Ins and outs

Getting around

Bus services are good around Ayrshire, East Lothian and between the main towns in the Borders, and there are also regular services between Dumfries and Stranraer, along the A75, but services to more remote parts are limited.

Train services are limited to the line north from Berwick-upon-Tweed to Edinburgh on the east coast, and lines from Dumfries and Stranraer to Ayrshire in the west, with links to Glasgow.

Walking

The south of Scotland is excellent walking country, and there are numerous marked trails through the forests and hills and circular walks around the towns, especially in the Tweed Valley. The tourist offices have leaflets detailing all the main routes. There are also a number of Ranger-led walks, details of which are also available at tourist offices.

For the more ambitious hiker there are two long-distance trails. The 62-mile **St Cuthbert's Way** is a cross-border trail which links several places associated with St Cuthbert, who started his ministry at Melrose in the mid-seventh century and ended it at Lindisfarne (Holy Island), on the Northumberland coast. The waymarked route starts at **Melrose Abbey** and climbs across the Eildon Hills before joining the River Tweed. Highlights include Dere Street, a Roman Road, the Cheviot foothills, St Cuthbert's Cave and the causeway crossing to Lindisfarne. They can also provide a trail pack which includes maps and route descriptions.

The most famous and demanding of walks is the 212-mile **Southern Upland Way**, www.dumgal.gov.uk/southernuplandway, which runs from Portpatrick on the west coast, near Stranraer, to Cockburnspath on the Berwickshire coast in the east, south of Dunbar. The route passes through a great variety of scenery, from the Rhinns of Galloway to the wild heartland of Southern Scotland to the gentler eastern Borders. The most picturesque sections are the beginning and the end, but in between the highlights include Glen Trool, the Lowther Hills, St Mary's Loch and the River Tweed. A route leaflet is available from the Countryside Ranger Service, ⓘ *Scottish Borders Council, Harestanes Visitor Centre, Ancrum, Jedburgh TD8 6UQ, T/F01835-830281*. There is also a trail pack, available from the Dumfries & Galloway or Scottish Borders tourist boards.

Cycling

The quiet backroads of southern Scotland also make it ideal for exploring by bike, especially the Tweed Valley, Galloway Forest Park and around The Machars peninsula. The **Tweed Cycleway** is a waymarked 90-mile route which follows minor roads through the beautiful Tweed Valley, from Biggar to Berwick-upon-Tweed. The tourist office provides a free guide, *Cycling in the Scottish Borders*, which features over 20 routes, including the Tweed Cycleway. Another route is the **Four Abbeys Cycle Route**, a 55-mile circular tour which takes in Melrose, Dryburgh, Jedburgh and Kelso. It is described in the *Four Abbeys Cycle Way* guide available from Tourist Information Centres.

East Lothian

→Colour map 5

East Lothian stretches east from Musselburgh, to the east of Edinburgh, along the coast to North Berwick and Dunbar. This is real golfing country, with a string of excellent courses running the length of the coast, and there are miles of sandy beaches. The East Lothian coast is also home to huge colonies of seabirds, especially on the Bass Rock, a dramatic volcanic islet off North Berwick. Inland is the attractive historic market town of Haddington, and further south the village of Gifford is the gateway to the Lammermuir Hills, which form the boundary with the Borders region and offer good walking opportunities. ▸▸ *For Sleeping, Eating and other listings, see pages 682-683.*

Ins and outs

There are good transport links with Edinburgh and most of the main sights can be visited in a few day trips from the capital. **Trains** from Edinburgh stop in Musselburgh, Prestonpans, North Berwick and Dunbar. There are also regular **buses** to all the main towns. For more information on East Lothian and for a free accommodation, contact **Edinburgh and Lothians Tourist Board** ⓘ *T0131-4733800, www.eltb.org*, or East Lothian TICs in Musselburgh, North Berwick and Dunbar. ▸▸ *For further details, see Transport, page 683.*

Musselburgh to North Berwick

Six miles east of Edinburgh, across the River Esk, is the town of **Musselburgh**. It's a fairly humdrum place, but may be of interest to golfing enthusiasts as the original home of golf; Royal Musselbugh is one of the oldest clubs in the country. About 10 miles further east is **Gullane**, a resort town with an exclusive air which is hopelessly devoted to **golf**. There are no fewer than four golf courses surrounding Gullane; Nos 1, 2 and 3 and the world-famous **Muirfield**, where you need an introduction to play. Between Gullane and North Berwick is the attractive little village of **Dirleton**, dominated by the ruins of **Dirleton Castle** ⓘ *Apr-Sep daily 0930-1830; Oct-Mar Mon-Sat 0930-1630, Sun 1400-1630, £3, £2.30 concession*. The original castle dates from the 12th century and was added to over the following three centuries, until it was destroyed by Cromwell's army. The very lovely **gardens**, which date from the 16th century, are well worth a visit. At the eastern end of the village a road runs north for a mile or so to **Yellowcraigs**, one of the very best beaches in the country, with great views across to **Fidra island**. Access is from the car park (£1.50), an easy five-minue walk along the woodland and dune path.

North Berwick

The dignified and slightly faded Victorian seaside resort of North Berwick is 23 miles east of Edinburgh and easily visited as a day trip from the capital. The biggest attraction is the **Scottish Seabird Centre** ⓘ *T01620-890202, www.seabird.org, summer daily 1000-1800; winter Mon-Fri 1000-1600, Sat, Sun 1000-1730, £4.50*, on the harbour. It's a bit like a hi-tech hide, with remote control cameras on the Bass Rock transmitting live pictures to screens placed in the visitor centre. You can control the cameras yourself, rotating, panning and zooming so that you can get the best view possible. Cameras are also trained on Fidra, so that you can watch the puffins too. If you come during the winter, when the gannets and puffins have left, you can watch the grey seals that pup on the nearby Isle of May in December. There's also a very popular café here, with great views across the water.

Three miles east of town, off the A198, are the mid-14th-century ruins of **Tantallon Castle** ⓘ *Apr-Sep daily 0930-1830, Oct-Mar Mon-Wed and Sat 0930-1630, Thu 0930-1200, Fri and Sun 1400-1630, £3, £2.30 concession, take the Dunbar bus from North Berwick*, perched dramatically on the edge of the cliffs, looking out to the Bass

 Rock. This formidable fortress was the stronghold of the 'Red Douglases', Earls of Angus, until Cromwell's attack in 1651, which left only the massive 50-ft high curtain wall intact. There's a great beach a few miles south of Tantallon which is well worth the slight detour. Turn left off the A198 at Auldhame farm, follow the road for about a mile to the gate (£1 toll charge) and beyond to the car park, then walk.

Three miles offshore is the 350-ft high **Bass Rock**, a massive, guano-covered lump of basalt, used as a prison in the 17th century but now home to millions of nesting gannets and other seabirds including guillemots, razorbills and fulmars. There are also puffins nesting on the nearby island of **Fidra**.

Twelve miles southeast of North Berwick, just off the main A1 from Edinburgh to the south, is the little fishing port of Dunbar. A few miles south of Dunbar on the A1, past Torness Nuclear Power Station, is the turn-off for the beautiful long strand of **Thorntonloch Beach**, almost hidden behind the rocky outcrop of Torness Point and backed by shallow dunes. Here, you can windsurf, swim or just admire the views south to the Berwickshire cliffs. A geology trail starts from the car park at Whitesands Bay and there's lots to interest the keen twitcher.

Haddington and around

Handsome Haddington, the archetypal prosperous country town, is very attractive and makes for a pleasant stroll. No fewer than 129 buildings have been listed as historically interesting, including the graceful **Town House**, in tree-lined Court Street, which was built in 1748 by William Adam, father of Robert. At the east end of the High Street, Church Street leads to **St Mary's Collegiate Church**, ⓘ *01620-T823109, Apr-Sep Mon-Sat 1100-1600, Sun 1400-1630, free (donations welcome)*, the largest parish church in Scotland, dating from the 14th century and restored in the 1970s. It's a particularly beautiful ecclesiastical building, with lots of interesting nooks and crannies, and enjoys a lovely setting on the river. Buried in the churchyard is Jane Welsh (1801-66), wife of essayist and historian Thomas Carlyle. The **Jane Welsh Carlyle House**, ⓘ *2 Lodge St, T01620-823738, Apr-Sep Wed-Sat 1400-1700, £1.50, £1 concession*, was her home until her marriage, and part of it is open to the public.
A mile south of Haddington is **Lennoxlove House**, ⓘ *T01630-823720, Easter-Oct Wed, Thu and some Sats and Sun 1400-1630, £4, £2 concession*, seat of the Duke of Hamilton. The sprawling confection of styles consists of a medieval tower house with additions over the centuries. Inside the house are paintings and furniture, but the *pièce de résistance* is the death mask of Mary, Queen of Scots, and a casket in which she kept her letters, given to her by her first husband, Francis II of France.

Sleeping

Musselburgh to North Berwick *p681*

L **Greywalls Hotel**, Gullane, T01620-842144, open Apr-Oct, a charming and elegant country house designed by Sir Edwin Lutyens. It overlooks Muirfied golf course and has an enviable reputation for superb cuisine. If you can't afford a meal, call in for tea and shortbread. It's not cheap (£7.50), but it does give you a chance to enjoy the house – and the lovely gardens designed by Gertrude Jekyll.

A **Open Arms Hotel**, Direlton, T01620-850241. A traditional country house hotel opposite the castle, it's a friendly and comfortable place with a highly rated, and expensive, restaurant.

North Berwick *p681*

A **Craigview**, 5 Beach Rd, T01620-892257, 3 rooms, overlooking West Beach, friendly, healthy breakfasts with vegetarian options.

A **The Marine Hotel**, Cromwell Rd, T01620-892406, F01620-894480. 83 rooms. North Berwick's premier hotel, overlooking

For an explanation of the sleeping and eating price codes used in this guide, see the inside front cover. Other relevant information is provided in the Essentials chapter, page 36.

the seafront and with an open-air pool.

B **The Glebe House**, on Law Rd, T/F01620-892608, excellent guesthouse.

There's a **campsite** at **Tantallan Caravan Park**, T01620-893348, open Mar-Oct, on Dunbar Rd, near to Glen golf course.

Eating

Musselburgh to North Berwick *p681*

£££ **La Pontinière**, Gullane, T01620-843214. This cosy French bistro was the best place to eat in Gullane but has changed hands.

Haddington and around *p682*

££ **Drover's Inn**, East Linton, T01620-860298. A great place for a pub lunch where you can sit outside on a sunny day, or stay inside in the cosy bistro. Either way, the food is excellent and worth the trip alone.

££ **The Waterside**, T01620-825674, by the river near Nungate Bridge, where you can enjoy excellent French bistro-style food. Open 1200-1400, 1730-2200 (1200-2200 at weekends).

Activities and tours

North Berwick *p681*

There are **boat trips** from North Berwick, weather permitting, to the Bass Rock and Fidra, daily between May and Sep with **Fred Marr**, T01620-892838. Trips cost £5.00 per person and last about 1¼ hrs. You can also arrange in advance to be dropped off on Bass Rock and picked up 3 hrs later for £10 per person, but you'll need to be a dedicated bird-watcher to put up with the stench of guano.

Transport

North Berwick *p681*

The train station is a 10-min walk east of the town centre. There's a frequent rail service to and from **Edinburgh** (30 mins). There are also regular buses (X5, 124) from **Edinburgh**, via **Aberlady** and **Gullane**. These stop on the High St. There are also regular buses from **Edinburgh** to **Dunbar** via **Haddington** (X6/106). First Edinburgh buses, T0131-6639233.

Haddington *p682*

First Edinburgh run regular buses to and from **Edinburgh**, T0131-6639233. There are also hourly buses to **North Berwick** (Mon-Sat, less frequently on Sun; 45 mins) and hourly buses to **Gifford** (20 mins).

The Borders

→ *Colour map 5*

The Scottish Borders covers a huge swathe of southern Scotland to the east of the M74. It's an unspoiled wilderness of green hills, rushing rivers and bleak, barren moors, and it has an austere beauty which would surprise those who think that real Scotland starts somewhere north of Perth. The Borders' proximity to England also gives it a romantic edge and makes it even more essentially Scottish. This is a region which is drenched in the blood of countless battles with the English, and its many ruined castles and abbeys bear witness to Scotland's long, turbulent relationship with its belligerent southern neighbour. It should come as no surprise, then, that this southern corner of Scotland has so inspired the country's greatest poets and writers. Robert Burns and John Buchan often spoke of its rare charms, but it is Sir Walter Scott, inspired not only by the stark beauty of the countryside but also by its lore and legends, who is most closely associated with the region.

The wildest and most spectacular scenery is to be found in the southern part of the region, along the Yarrow Water, between Selkirk and Moffat, the upper reaches of the Tweed valley, south of Peebles, and in Liddesdale, southwest of Jedburgh. But it is along the central valley of the River Tweed, between Peebles in the west and Kelso in the east, where you'll find most of the historic attractions, including the fascinating Traquair House, Sir Walter Scott's mansion at Abbotsford. Together with Selkirk, and the textile-producing towns of Galashiels and Hawick, these towns form the heart of the Borders. ▸▸ *For Sleeping, Eating and other listings, see pages 690-692.*

Ins and outs

Getting around There's a good network of **buses** serving the region's main towns. Bus timetables are available from local tourist offices. For all bus information, call the **Borders Council Transport Division,** T01835-825200. The main operator is **First Edinburgh,** T0131-6639233. There are numerous buses running between the main towns of **Galashiels, Melrose, Peebles, Hawick, Selkirk, Jedburgh** and **Kelso.** There are also buses connecting the Border towns with **Edinburgh** and **Berwick-upon-Tweed.** There are regular buses from **Berwick-upon-Tweed** (**Traveline** T0870-6082608). **National Express,** T08705 808080, runs services from **Newcastle** to **Edinburgh** via **Jedburgh, Galashiels** and **Melrose.**

The regular bus service is supplemented during the summer months (Jul-Sep) by the **Harrier Scenic Bus Services.** Buses make round-trip tours once a week on the following routes: **Melrose-Moffat,** via **Galashiels, Selkirk, Bowhill House, Yarrow, St Mary's Loch** (on Thu); **Selkirk-Eyemouth** via **Galashiels, Melrose, Kelso, Coldstream, Berwick-upon-Tweed; Hawick-Eyemouth** via **Jedburgh, Town Yetholm, Berwick-upon-Tweed.** Current timetables are available at local tourist offices.

The best way to see the Borders, though, is on **foot** or by **bike**. The 90-mile *Tweed Cycleway* runs past the most important sights, while the *Southern Uplands Way* takes you through the region's most beautiful and spectacular scenery.

The main **London-Edinburgh railway** line follows the east coast from **Berwick-upon-Tweed** north to **Dunbar** in East Lothian. There is no rail link with the Border towns, so you'll have to get off at Berwick and take a bus from there.

There are plenty of opportunities for **walking** in the Borders, whether it's a gentle stroll or a serious hike across open country. There's a comprehensive network of paths and forest trails plus a programme of Ranger-led walks. For more details see *Walking in the Scottish Borders* and *Ranger-led Walks*, both available free at tourist offices.

Information There are nine tourist information centres throughout the region. The ones in **Jedburgh** and **Peebles** are open all year, and the others (in **Coldstream, Eyemouth, Galashiels, Hawick, Kelso, Melrose** and **Selkirk**) are open from Apr to Oct. Details are given under each town. For any of their free publications call T0870-6070250, and for information on Borders festivals, such as the Melrose Rugby Sevens or the Ridings, call the Events Line, T01750-20054. Alternatively, visit www.scot-borders.co.uk, or call the information line, T01835-863435

Sights

Peebles and the Tweed Valley

Due south of Edinburgh is the neat and tidy town of Peebles, on the banks of the river Tweed, surrounded by wooded hills. The **Tweeddale Museum** ① *Apr-Oct Mon-Fri 1000-1200 and 1400-1700, Sat 1000-1200, 1400-1600, winter hours vary, free,* on the High Street is housed in the Chambers Institute, which was a gift to the town from William Chambers, a native of Peebles and founding publisher of the Chambers Encyclopaedia. Just to the west of town, on the A72, is **Neidpath Castle,** ① *T01721-720333, May-early Sep, Mon-Sat 1030-1630, Sun 1230-1630. £3, £2.50 concession, £1 children*, perched high on a rocky bluff overlooking the Tweed. The medieval Tower House enjoys an impressive setting, but there's little to see inside which would justify the entrance fee. The castle can be reached by following the trail along the River Tweed from Hay Lodge Park in town. The walk passes a beautiful picnic spot beneath the castle and you can swim in the river (but take care). The trail continues through lovely wooded countryside and you can cross the river and return at Manor Bror (a three-mile round trip) or further on at Lyne footbridge (an eight-mile round trip). Seven miles east of Peebles is the village of

Innerleithen, home of **Robert Smail's Printing Works** ⓘ *T01721-830206 (NTS). Mar-Jun and Sep-Oct Thu-Mon 1200-1700, Sun 1300-1700, Jun-Aug Thu-Mon 1000-1800, Sun 1300-1700. £3.50, £2.60 child/concession*, on the main street, where you can see how printing was done at the beginning of the 20th century. You can watch the printer at work on the original machinery and even try your hand at typesetting.

Traquair House

ⓘ *T01721-830323, www.traquair.co.uk, Apr, May and Sep daily 1200-1730; Jun-Aug 1030-1730; Oct 1100-1600. £5.60, £5.30 concession, £3.10 child. Bus No C1 runs once a day to Traquair from Peebles.*

The big attraction in these parts is the amazing Traquair House, one of Scotland's great country houses. It lies about a mile south of Innerleithen, on the south side of the Tweed. Traquair is the oldest continually inhabited house in the country and is still owned by the Maxwell Stuarts, who have been living here since 1491. Its history goes much further back, however, and parts of the house are believed to date from the 12th century. The original Tower House was added to over the next five centuries, and most of what you see today dates from the mid-17th century. It has been visited by no fewer than 27 monarchs, including Mary, Queen of Scots, who stayed here with her husband, Darnley, in 1566. The place is steeped in Jacobite history, but the family paid for its Catholic principles. The fourth earl was imprisoned in the Tower of London, and sentenced to death, for his part in the Jacobite rising of 1715, but managed to escape with the help of his wife who smuggled him out disguised as a maid. The fifth earl served two years in the Tower of London for his support of Bonnie Prince Charlie in 1745 and the famous Bear Gates, which have remained closed ever since the Pretender passed through them on his way south, bear testament to his undying support. By the turn of the 18th century the family had lost most of its estates and had neither the money nor the motivation to undertake any major rebuilding.

Also worth seeing are the **gardens**, where you'll find a maze, craft shops, a cottage tearoom and an 18th-century working **brewery** producing several ales including *Bear Ale* and *Jacobite Ale*, which can be purchased in the tearoom and gift shop. There's also B&B accommodation available (see below for contact details). A **craft and music fair** is held in the grounds of the house every August.

Melrose and around

Nestled at the foot of the mystical Eildon Hills, by the banks of the Tweed, is little Melrose, the loveliest of all the Border towns. It's an engaging mix of cute little shops and cottages and dignified Georgian and Victorian houses, and boasts one of the most famous ruins in Scotland (see below). Melrose makes a great base for exploring the beautiful landscapes of the middle stretch of the Tweed which so inspired Sir Walter Scott, the famous son of the Borders.

The bitter wars that ravaged the Scottish borders for centuries did irrevocable damage to **Melrose Abbey**, ⓘ (*HS*) *Apr-Sep Mon-Sat 1000-1730, Sun 1330-1730, Oct-Dec Mon-Sat 1000-1600, Sun 1330-1600, £3, £2.50 concessions, £1.20 children*, but even in ruins it remains toweringly beautiful and impressive. It was founded in 1136 by the prolific David I (who helped to found all four of the great Border Abbeys) and was the first Cistercian monastery in Scotland. It was attacked in 1322 by Edward II, but soon restored thanks to the financial assistance of Robert the Bruce. In 1385 it was largely destroyed by Richard II of England, then completely rebuilt, only to be ravaged again, this time by Henry VIII, in the mid-16th century. The abbey's real claim to fame is that the **heart of Robert the Bruce** was buried here, at his request, after it had been taken to the Holy Land to help in the Crusades. The lead casket believed to contain the heart was finally excavated in 1996 and now takes pride of place in the abbey museum, in the **Commendator's House**, next to the church.

One of the Borders' top tourist attractions is **Abbotsford House,** ⓘ *T01896-750043, mid-Mar to May and Oct Mon-Sat 0930-1700, Sun 1400-1700, Jun-Sep daily 0930-1700, £4, £2 children, take the Melrose-Galashiels bus and get off at the Tweedbank traffic island. From there it's a 15-min walk,* home of Sir Walter Scott from 1812 to 1832 and a must for the novelist's many admirers. Scott spent a small fortune transforming the original farmhouse into a huge country mansion befitting a man of his status and, though Abbotsford may not be to everyone's taste, the house is an intriguing mix of styles and enjoys a beautiful setting. The house is still lived in by Scott's descendants, and the library and study have been preserved much as they were when he lived here, including the collection of over 9,000 antiquarian books. There's also an amazing assortment of Scottish memorabilia, including Rob Roy's purse, Bonnie Prince Charlie's drinking cup and Flora MacDonald's pocketbook. The house is well worth visiting and sits in pleasant grounds, about three miles west of Melrose between the Tweed and the B6360.

Five miles southeast of Melrose on the B6404, near the village of St Boswells, is **Dryburgh Abbey,** ⓘ *T01835-822381, Apr-Sep 0930-1830, Oct-Mar Mon-Sat 0930-1630, Sun 1400-1630, £3, £2.30 concession,* the most beautifully idyllic, romantic and evocative of the Border abbeys. It dates from around 1150, when it was founded by Hugh de Morville for Premonstratensian monks from Alnwick in Northumberland. The 12th- and 13th-century ruin is remarkably well-preserved and complete, and was chosen as the burial place for Sir Walter Scott. His final resting place is in the north transept of the church. Close by lies Field Marshal Earl Haig, the disastrous First World War commander.

North of Melrose on the main A68 is **Thirlestane Castle** ⓘ *T01578-722430, end Mar-end Oct daily (except Sat) 1030-1700 – last admission 1615, £5.30, £3 child,* one of Scotland's oldest and finest castles, which stands on the eastern edge of town. The castellated baronial house is the seat of the Earls of Lauderdale and has been owned by the Maitland family since the 16th century.

Selkirk and around

About six miles southwest of Melrose, on the A7 to Hawick, is the little town of Selkirk, standing on the edge of the Ettrick Forest which rises steeply from the Ettrick Water. Selkirk has been a textile centre since the early 19th century when the growing demand for tweed could no longer be met by the mills of Galashiels.

Three miles west of Selkirk, where the B7009 turns south off the A708, is the entrance to **Bowhill House and Country Park,** ⓘ *House open Jul daily, 1300-1630. £4.50, £2 children, wheelchair users free, country Park Apr-Jun and Aug daily except Fri 1200-1700, Jul daily 1200-1700, £2,* home of the Scotts of Buccleuch and Queensberry since 1812. They were once the largest landowners in the Borders and fabulously wealthy, a fact made evident by the fantastic collection of French antiques and European paintings on display. There are works by Canaletto, Guardi, Reynolds and Gainsborough. The wooded hills of the Country Park can be explored via a network of footpaths and cycle trails. There's no public transport to Bowhill, but the weekly *Harrier Scenic Bus Service* runs near Bowhill from Selkirk and Melrose in the morning, returning in the afternoon. It runs from July to September (see page 684).

The A707 heads southwest from Selkirk to Moffat, following the beautiful **Yarrow Water** to **St Mary's Loch**, where the road is crossed by the **Southern Upland Way**. A few miles west of Selkirk is the turning south on to the B7009 which follows the course of the Ettrick Water to meet the B709, which continues south, past the village of **Ettrick**, to **Eskdalemuir** and on to **Langholm** (see page 693). This is one of the most remote and beautiful parts of Scotland, and an area inextricably linked with **James Hogg** (1770-1835), 'The Ettrick Shepherd', who was a great friend of Sir Walter Scott. Hogg was a notable writer himself and his most famous work, *The Confessions of a Justified Sinner*, is important in Scottish literature. Hogg was born in Ettrick and spent his entire life in the Ettrick and Yarrow valleys. He and Scott would often meet in *Tibbie Shiels Inn* (see Eating page 690).

Jedburgh

Ten miles from the English border is the attractive little town of Jedburgh, straddling the Jed Water at the edge of the northern slopes of the wild, barren Cheviot Hills. Jedburgh was strategically the most important of the Border towns, due to its proximity to England, and as a result received the full brunt of invading English armies. These days the only invaders are tourists. Jedburgh is the most visited of the Border towns and there are a number of interesting sights. The town is dominated by **Jedburgh Abbey**, ⓘ *T01835-863925, May-end Sep daily 0930-1830; Oct-Mar Mon-Sat 0930-1630, Sun 1400-1630, £3.50, £2.50 concession, £1.20 child,* founded in 1138 by David I for Augustinian canons from northern France. The site had much older religious significance, however, and stonework in the abbey's museum dates from the first millennium AD. Malcolm IV was crowned here and Alexander III married his second wife in the abbey in 1285. Their wedding feast was held at nearby Jedburgh Castle (see below) and, like the castle, the abbey came under attack during the many English invasions, most devastatingly in 1523 when it was bombarded and burned. Despite this, the abbey church is remarkably complete, particularly the tower. Excavations have recently uncovered the remains of the cloister buildings, and among the finds is the priceless 12th-century 'Jedburgh comb', which is on display in the excellent **visitor centre** which brilliantly tells the abbey's long and fascinating history.

Nearby, at the top of the Castlegate, is **Jedburgh Castle Jail and Museum**, ⓘ *T01835-864750, Easter-end Oct Mon-Sat 1000-1630, Sun 1300-1600, £1.50, £1 concession,* which was formerly the county jail. It was built in 1823 on the site of the 12th-century castle, which changed hands many times until it was destroyed by the Scots because of its value to the English. The displays in the cell blocks depict prison life in the 19th century, and there's an exhibition on the town's history.

At the other end of the town centre is **Mary, Queen of Scots House** ⓘ *T01835-863331, Mar-Nov Mon-Sat 1000-1630, Sun 1200-1630, £2.60, £1.50 concession,* a beautiful 16th-century building of rough-hewn stone which contains a small bedroom occupied by Mary during her stay at Jedburgh in 1566. She spent several weeks here recovering from illness after her famous 30-mile ride to Hermitage Castle (see below) to visit her injured lover, the Earl of Bothwell. The ensuing scandal was only exacerbated by the murder of her husband Darnley the following year at Holyrood Palace in Edinburgh. Many years later, during her long incarceration, Mary regretted the fact that she hadn't died while staying in Jedburgh. This episode in Scottish history is told through a series of displays, and there are various artefacts associated with Mary.

Hawick and around

Fourteen miles southwest of Jedburgh and 12 miles south of Selkirk is Hawick (pronounced 'Hoyk'), the largest town in the Borders and centre of the region's knitwear and hosiery industry for over 200 years. Hawick is not a place noted for its great beauty, but it does attract lots of visitors who come to shop at its many factory outlets where you can buy all the classic brand names in knitwear.

A few miles north of **Newcastleton**, the B6357 meets the B6399 which runs north back to Hawick. Four miles north of the junction is the turning to **Hermitage Castle** ⓘ *T01387-376222 (HS), Apr-Sep daily 0930-1830, £2.20, £1.60 concession,* one of the great Border strongholds. The oldest part of the castle dates from the 13th century and it was in the hands of the Earls of Douglas until 1492, when it passed to the Earls of Bothwell. The fourth Earl of Bothwell, James Hepburn, was the third husband of Mary, Queen of Scots, following the murder of her second husband, Darnley, and is thought to have been behind the plot to murder him. It was to Hermitage that Mary made her famous ride to visit her future husband who had been injured in a border raid. Mary's marriage to Bothwell in 1566 was ill-advised and only succeeded in uniting their enemies; and led ultimately to her imprisonment in Lochleven Castle. Bothwell meanwhile fled to Norway, where he was captured and later died a prisoner himself, in 1578. Hermitage became largely irrelevant following the Union of Crowns in 1603 and fell into disrepair. Much of what you see today dates from the 19th century when the Duke of Buccluech ordered its repair. The vast and eerie ruin is said to be haunted, which is not surprising given its grisly past. One owner, William Douglas, starved his prisoners to death in the ghoulish dungeons, which can still be seen.

Kelso and around

The little market town of Kelso, at the confluence of the Tweed and Teviot rivers, is one of the most picturesque of the Border towns, with its cobbled streets leading into a wide market square bounded by elegant, three-storey 18th- and 19th-century town houses. The countryside around Kelso is worth exploring, for here you'll find some of Scotland's finest stately homes.

Kelso Abbey ⓘ *Apr-end Dec daily (Sun afternoon only), free,* was once the largest and richest of the Border abbeys, but suffered the same fate as its counterparts, Jedburgh, Dryburgh and Melrose. Kelso was a strategic point in the Border wars between the Scots and the English and the abbey, founded in 1138 by King David, was laid to waste by successive English invasions, most devastatingly in 1545 by the Earl of Hertford. This latter attack was part of Henry VIII's so-called 'Rough Wooing', when the king took exception to the Scots' refusal to ratify a marriage treaty between his son and the infant Mary Stuart. Today, little remains of the abbey, and it is the least complete of those in the Borders.

Floors Castle ⓘ *T01573-223333, mid Apr to end Oct daily 1000-1630 (last admission 1600), £5.50, £4.75 concession,* the vast ancestral home of the Duke of Roxburghe, stands imperiously overlooking the Tweed, about a mile northwest of the town centre. The original Georgian mansion was designed by Robert Adam and built in 1721-26, though it was later remodelled by William Playfair in the 1840s, with the addition of many flamboyant features. Only 10 rooms are open to the public but they are undeniably elegant and palatial, and amongst the many family items on display are outstanding collections of European furniture, porcelain and paintings by Picasso, Matisse and Augustus John, and a 15th-century Brussels tapestry. Floors is the largest inhabited castle in Scotland and the current occupier, the 10th Duke of Roxburghe, is a close personal friend of the royal family. The house also has a restaurant and a coffee shop.

Six miles northwest of Kelso on the B6397 is the village of Smailholm, where a turning leads to **Smailholm Tower** ⓘ *T01573-460365, Apr-Sep daily 0930-1830, Oct-Mar Sat 0930-1630, Sun 1400-1630, £2, £1.50 concession,* a classic Scottish tower house and an evocative place full of history and romance. The 15th-century fortified farmhouse, built by the Pringles, squires to the Earls of Douglas, stands on a rocky pinnacle above a small lake. Sir Walter Scott's grandfather owned the nearby farm and the young Scott came here as a sickly child in the 1770s to improve his health. So began the writer's long love affair with the lore and landscapes of the Scottish Borders which inspired so much of his poetry and prose. Scott would write a ballad about this gaunt tower house – *The Eve of St John* – as part of a deal with the owner to save it. Today Smailholm houses a small, unremarkable museum relating to some of Scott's works, but the views from the top of the tower are rewarding.

Northwest of Kelso, on the A6089 to Gordon, is the signpost for **Mellerstain House** ⓘ *T01573-410225, Easter weekend and May-Sep Sun-Mon 1230-1700, £5, £4.50 concession,* home of the Earl of Haddington and one of Scotland's great Georgian houses. This 18th-century architectural masterpiece was designed by William Adam and his son Robert and perfectly characterizes the elegant symmetry of the period. The superb exterior is more than matched by the exquisitely ornate interiors. There is also furniture by Chippendale and Hepplewhite, as well as paintings by Constable, Gainsborough, Veronese and Van Dyck. The formal Italian gardens, laid out in the early 20th century, are equally impressive.

Duns and around

The quiet market town of Duns lies in the middle of Berwickshire, surrounded by the fertile farmland of the Merse. Duns is best known as the birthplace of Jim Clark (1936-68), a former farmer who went on to become world motor racing champion twice in the 1960s and who remains one of Britain's greatest ever racing drivers. His successful career was tragically cut short when he was killed in a crash while practising at Hockenheim in Germany. The **Jim Clark Room**, ⓘ *44 Newton St, T01361-883960, Apr-Sep Mon-Sat 1000-1300 and 1400-1630, Sun 1400-1600, Oct Mon-Sat 1300-1600, £1.30, children free,* is a museum dedicated to his life.

Two miles east of Duns, on the A6015, is **Manderston House,** ⓘ *T01361-883450, www.manderston.co.uk mid-May to Sep Thu and Sun 1400-1700, £6.50 (£3 concession) house and gardens, £3.30 (£1.50 concession) gardens only,* described as the finest Edwardian country house in Scotland. No expense has been spared in the design and decoration and the whole effect, from the silver staircase to the inlaid marble floor in the hall, is one of quite staggering opulence. Take a good look at the staircase – it had tarnished badly over the years (one panel is left to show how black it was) and was voluntarily and lovingly cleaned up by a retired couple. The 56 acres of beautiful gardens should not be missed. There are wonderful displays of rhododendrons late in May.

Twelve miles east of Duns, and five miles west of Berwick-upon-Tweed off the B6461 to Swinton, is **Paxton House,** ⓘ *House open Easter-Oct daily 1115-1700 (1615 last tour), £5, £4.75 concession, grounds open Apr-Oct 1000 till sunset,* a grand neoclassical mansion designed by John and James Adam, the less-famous brothers of Robert, for Patrick Home,who had fallen in love with a Prussian aristocrat at the court of Frederick the Great. She was a great favourite of Frederick's and he strongly opposed the marriage, which never went ahead. She and Patrick corresponded for years and vowed never to marry anyone else while the other was alive. Both kept their promise. Inside there's an impressive display of Chippendale and Regency furniture, and the Picture Gallery is an outstation of the National Gallery of Scotland. In the 80 acres of grounds beside the River Tweed is a Victorian boathouse and a salmon-fishing museum.

Berwickshire coast

The Berwickshire coast is not exactly a name on the tip of every Scottish tourist's tongue. Tucked out of the way, these wild and woolly cliffs are often deserted and home to a number of excellent coastal **walks**, particularly the seven-mile **Burnmouth to St Abbs walk** described below. The waters around Eyemouth are excellent for scuba diving. They form part of the **St Abbs and Eyemouth Voluntary Marine Reserve,** one of the best dive sites in Scotland, with a wide variety of marine life and the spectacular **Cathedral Rock.**

Five miles north of the border on the Berwickshire coast is the busy fishing port of Eyemouth. Fishing has been the life and soul of Eyemouth since the 13th century and the **Eyemouth Museum** ⓘ *£1.75, £1.25 concession,* in the Auld Kirk on Market Place, has displays on the town's fishing heritage. The centrepiece is the Eyemouth Tapestry, made by local people in 1981 to mark the centenary of the Great Disaster of 1881, when 189 local fishermen were drowned during a violent storm.

Three miles north of Eyemouth on the A1107 is the village of **Coldingham,** notable only for its medieval **priory,** founded by King Edgar in 1098, then rebuilt in the 13th century before suffering further attacks in 1545 and 1648. The remaining sections have been incorporated into the present parish church. Here the B6438 turns north and winds its way down to the picturesque little fishing village of **St Abbs,** nestled beneath steep cliffs. There's a little museum and a Visitor Centre for the Marine Reserve in the Old School House – open summer, hours vary with volunteer staff. St Abbs is also a good base for divers wishing to explore the **St Abbs and Eyemouth Voluntary Marine Reserve** (see above).

Just north of the village is the **St Abb's Head National Nature Reserve** (NTS), which comprises almost 200 acres of wild coastline with sheer cliffs inhabited by large colonies of guillemots, kittiwakes, fulmars and razorbills. To get to the reserve, follow the trail from the car park at Northfield Farm on the road into St Abbs. The path ends at the lighthouse, about a mile from the car park. An excellent coastal walk, from Burnmouth, south of Eyemouth, to St Abbs is described below. A side road turns off the B6438 at Coldingham and leads a mile down to the coast at **Coldingham Sands**, a tiny resort with a fine sandy beach. It's a popular spot for **surfing** and **diving**.

Sleeping

Peebles and the Tweed Valley *p684*

A **Castle Venlaw Hotel**, Edinburgh Rd, Peebles, T01721-720384, www.venlaw.co.uk, an old baronial castle with good views over the town.

A **Cringletie House Hotel**, 2 miles north of Peebles just off the A703 to Edinburgh. T01721-730233, www.cringletie.com, Lovely 19th-century baronial house set in 28 acres of grounds, with an excellent restaurant (see below) and friendly service.

A **Peebles Hotel Hydro**, Innerleithen Rd, Peebles, T01721-720602, www.peebleshotelhydro.co.uk. One of Scotland's oldest and grandest hotels, the Hydro has made a concerted effort to meet modern demands with an excellent pool and a health and beauty suite offering a huge range of therapies. Also provides a whole host of activities for kids and baby-sitting service. Prices include dinner in the grand, but rather formal dining room. Their bistro, *Lazels*, is more realxed. Various deals on offer so best to call and ask for the best prices.

C **Grey Gables**, on Springwood Rd, T01721-721252, uses organic produce and can provide vegetarian breakfasts.

There's a **campsite** at **Tweedside Caravan Park** on Montgomery St, T01721-831271, open Apr-Oct. Note that accommodation is usually fully booked during the Traquair Fair in Aug (see below).

Melrose and around *p685*

A **Burts Hotel**, on Market Sq, T801896-22285, www.burtshotel .co.uk. This refurbished traditional 18th-century inn is the best option, very comfortable and renowned locally for its excellent modern Scottish cuisine (see Eating below).

C **Kilkerran House**, High St, T01896-822122, www.kilkerran.net. One of the best guesthouses. Nicely furnished and in the centre of town. There's a very good and very popular E **Youth Hostel**, in a mansion on the edge of town, overlooking the abbey from beside the A6091 bypass, T01896-822521, open all year.

There's also a **campsite** at **Gibson Park**, T01896-822969, at the end of the High St opposite the Greenyards rugby ground.

Selkirk and around *p686*

A **Philipburn Country House Hotel**, Linglie Rd, T01750-720747, www.philipburnhousehotel.co.uk. Upmarket accommodation and good food.

B **Glen Hotel**, Yarrow Terr, T/F01750-20259, www.glenhotel.co.uk, refurbished Victorian house with good views of the hills and river.

B-C **Tibbie Shiels Inn**, T01750-42231, on the narrow strip of land separating St Mary's Loch from the ethereal Loch of the Lowes. It's still a famous watering hole and popular stop along the Southern Upland Way. It also serves bar meals (Easter-Nov daily; Nov-Easter closed Mon, Tue, Wed).

C **Hillholm**, 36 Hillside Terr, T01750-21293. Good value. 5 mins walk from town.

D **SYHA Broadmeadows Youth Hostel** at Yarrowford, T01750-76262; open end-Mar to end Sep, 5 miles west of Selkirk on the A708, beyond Bowhill (see below).

Jedburgh *p687*

A **Jedforest Hotel**, in the village of Camptown, 6 miles south of Jedburgh, on the A68, T01835-840222, www.jedforesthotel.freeserve.co.uk. The self-proclaimed 'First Hotel in Scotland' is very comfortable, with a fine restaurant. Dinner, B&B also available (A).

B **Glenfriars House**, The Friars, T01835-862000, www.edenroad.demon.co.uk. A lovely house near the north end of the High St.

C **Hunalee House**, T/F01835-863011, sheila.whittaker@btinternet.com. Open Mar-Oct. This early 17th-century house is a mile south of town on the A68, set in 15 acres of gardens and woodlands. Unmatched for style and value-for-money.

B-C **Ancrum Craig**, T/F01835-830280, ancrumcraig@clara.net. Open Jan-Dec. A quiet 19-century country house 2 miles from the A68 near the village of Ancrum. Great value.

Hawick and around *p687*

A **Glenteviot Park** , Hassendeanburn, T01450-870660. 5 rooms. New hotel overlooking the Teviot river, faultless design and exceptional service, strictly for grown-ups in search of some indulgence and pampering.

Kelso and around *p688*

L **The Roxburghe Hotel & Golf Course**, at the village of Heiton, a few miles from town on the A698 to Hawick, T01573-450331,www. roxburghe.net. This country mansion, owned by the Duke of Roxburgh, is the most luxurious place to stay hereabouts. It stands in hundreds of acres of park and woodlands on the banks of the Teviot, and offers grand style, superb cuisine and a championship golf course.

A **Ednam House Hotel**, on Bridge St, T01573-224168, F226319. Less salubrious but nevertheless highly recommended and slightly more affordable. A family-run Georgian mansion overlooking the Tweed and close to the town centre. Excellent food served all day (lunch cheap; dinner mid-range) in a restaurant with great views over the river.

B **Bellevue House**, Bowmont St, T/F01573-224588, bellevue.kelso@virgin.net. Fine non-smoking guesthouse.

B **Border Hotel**, Kirk Yetholm, T01573-420237, overlooking the village green, which marks the end of the Pennine Way. Kirk Yetholm was once the home of the king of the gypsies (you can still see his pretty little cottage by the green) and the bar is full of pictures of the former gypsy inhabitants. It serves a welcome pint of ale and good food, too.

E **Youth Hostel** in Kirk Yetholm, T01573-420631, open mid-Mar to end Oct.

There's a caravan park (no tents) at **Kirkfield Caravan Park**, on Grafton Road in Town Yetholm, T01573-420346, Apr-Oct.

Duns and around *p689*

B **Wellfield House**, Preston Rd, Duns, T01361-883189, www.wellfieldhouse.com, a traditional Georgian house offering great value (no smoking).

Berwickshire coast *p689*

L **Churches**, Albert Rd, T018907-750401, www.churcheshotel.co.uk. 6 rooms. Such a serious wow factor is suprising here. Stylish without a hint of pretension. The restaurant (see Eating) is the best for miles.

C **Castle Rock Guest House**, Murrayfield, St Abbs Head, on the cliffs above the harbour, T01890-771715, is excellent.

D **The Rock House Dive Centre**, T01890-71288, bunkhouse accommodation right on the harbour.

D **Dunlaverock Country House Hotel**, at Coldingham Sands, T01890-771450, a small, comfortable hotel offering excellent food.

There are a few **campsites**, including **Scoutscroft Holiday Centre**, T01890-771338, open Mar-Nov, which also rents diving equipment and offers courses.

Eating

Peebles and the Tweed Valley *p684*

£££ **Cringlethie House Hotel**, is the best place to eat. Serves delicious Scottish cuisine. Open 1230-1400, 1900-2100.

Melrose and around *p685*

£££ **Burt's Hotel** (see above), Best of all. Dine in style in the dining room or opt for their excellent pub grub.

££ **Marmions Brasserie**, T01896-822245, on Buccleuch St near the abbey A good French-style bistro, daily 0900-1800, 1830-2200.

Duns and around *p689*

£££ **Wheatsheaf at Swinton** in the village of Swinton, about 5 miles south of Duns on the A6112, T01361-860257, www.wheatsheaf-swinton.co.uk. The best place to eat in the area. The food is 1st-class. Open Tue-Sun 1200-1400, Tue-Sat 1800-2100.

Berwickshire coast *p689*

£££ **Churches**, Albert Rd, Eyemouth, T018907-750401. Run by Rosalind and Marcus, who also have the eponymous hotel (see Sleeping). Superior cooking served with aplomb in chic surroundings.

Festivals and events

Feb Jedburgh Hand Ba' game, a bruising and exhausting contest between the 'uppies' (those born above the Market Place) and the 'downies' (those born below), who endeavour to get a leather ball from one end of the town to the other.

Apr The week-long **Melrose Sevens** sees the town taken over by rugby fans from all over the world for the acclaimed seven-a-side rugby tournament which has been going since 1883.

Jun The week-long **Beltane Fair**, the great Celtic festival of the sun which marks the beginning of summer, is held in Peebles. **Selkirk Gathering** is the largest of the Border Ridings, an ancient ritual which dates back to the Middle Ages when young men, or 'Callants', would ride out to check the boundaries of common lands owned by the town. Jedburgh's Common Riding, the **Callant's Festival**, takes place in **late Jun/early Jul**.

Jul The week-long **Herring Queen Festival** takes place in Eyemouth. The **Border Union Agricultural Show** and the **Riding of the Marches** both take place in Kelso.

Activities and tours

Diving

There are a number of boats at St Abbs Head offering dive charters as well as birdwatching boat trips. Try **Peter Gibson**, T018907-71681, **Alistair Crowe**, T018907-71412, **Billy Atkinson**, T018907-71288, or ask at the harbour. The dive shop at *Scoutscroft Holiday Centre*, T01890-71669 (see Sleeping), rents out equipment and runs diving courses.

Horse riding

Horse riding is available for experienced riders at **Ferniehurst Mill Lodge**, T01835-863279, 2 miles south of Jedburgh on the A68. They offer accommodation and tailor-made riding holidays.

Mountain biking

Two miles east of town on the A72 is **Glentress Forest**, which is fast becoming a top mountain biking destination with some of the best singletrack anywhere in the UK. There are dozens of tracks through the forest, graded according to level of difficulty.

The Hub in the Forest, T01721-721736, www.thehubintheforest.co.uk, open Mon-Fri 1000-1800, Wed till 2200, Sat and Sun *0900-1900*, is an official partner of Forest Enterprise and hires out ountain bikes for £12 per half day and £16 per day, as well as providing route maps and spares. There's also a good café where your bike can have a post-ride hosedown while you tuck into coffee and cake.

Dumfries and Galloway

→ Colour map 5

Dumfries and Galloway is one of Scotland's forgotten corners, forsaken by most visitors for the cities of Edinburgh and Glasgow or the grandeur of the Highlands. But the southwest has much to offer those prepared to leave the more-beaten track. Away from the main routes west from Dumfries to Stranraer and north to Glasgow, traffic and people are notable by their absence, leaving most of the region free from the tourist crush of more popular parts.

Some of the most beautiful scenery is to be found along the Solway coast, west from Dumfries to the Mull of Galloway. Here you'll find the romantic ruins of Caerlaverock Castle, Threave Castle and Sweetheart Abbey, along with Whithorn Priory, known as the 'Cradle of Christianity' in Scotland. Also on this lovely coast is the beguiling town of Kirkcudbright, inspiration for some of Scotland's most famous artists and still a thriving artistic colony. Rising behind the coastline are the Galloway Hills which form part of the 150,000-acre Galloway Forest Park, a vast area of mountains, moors, lochs and rivers, criss-crossed by numerous trails and footpaths suitable for all levels of fitness. Running right through the heart of the Galloway Hills is the 212-mile Southern Upland Way, one of the country's great long-distance walks. The southwest also has strong literary associations. The great poet, Robert Burns, lived and died here, in Dumfries, and the town boasts several important Burns sights. ▸▸ *For Sleeping, Eating and other listings, see pages 701-705.*

Ins and outs

Getting around The region has a good network of **buses**. The main operators are **Stagecoach Western**, T01387-253496, and **McEwan's**, T01387-256533. **National Express**, T08705-808080, has long-distance coaches from **London**, **Birmingham**, **Glasgow** and **Edinburgh** to **Stranraer**, for the ferry crossing to **Belfast** and **Larne** in Northern Ireland. P&O ferries to Larne (T08705-980666, www.poirishsea.com) leave from **Cairnryan**, 5 miles north of Stranraer on the A77. Bus No 358 and X58 runs to Cairnryan from Stranraer. There are two train routes from **Carlisle** to **Glasgow**, via **Dumfries** and **Moffat**. There's also a line from **Stranraer** to **Glasgow**. For rail information, T08457-484950. Dumfries & Galloway council has a travel information line, T08457-090510, for all public transport services. Open Mon-Fri 0900-1700. ▸▸ *For further details, see Transport, page 705.*

Information The **Dumfries and Galloway Tourist Board** ⓘ *64 Whitesands, Dumfries, T01387-245550, www.visit-dumfries-and-galloway.co.uk*, have a range of free brochures and guide books for the region, including *Accommodation*, *Birdwatching*, *Cycling*, *Fishing*, *Walking and Golfing*. There are also tourist offices in **Stranraer**, **Castle Douglas**, **Gatehouse of Fleet**, **Gretna Green**, **Kirkcudbright**, **Moffat** and **Newton Stewart**.

Sights

Annandale and Eskdale

The first place you encounter across the border is the nondescript little village of **Gretna Green**. It's not a particularly interesting place to visit, but Gretna Green has been synonymous with marriage ceremonies for many years and thousands of couples still come here to tie the knot. The **World Famous Old Blacksmith's Shop** ⓘ *T01461-338224, www.gretnagreen.com, Jan-Mar and Nov-Dec daily 0900-1700; Apr-May and Oct daily 0900-1800; Jun and Sep daily 0900-1900; Jul and Aug daily till 2000, £2, £1.50 concession,* houses a visitor centre with a small exhibition on Gretna Green's history as well as gift shops. There's also a rival blacksmith's shop, the **Gretna Hall Blacksmith's Shop**, ⓘ *T01461-337635, Apr-Oct daily 0900-2000, Nov-Mar daily 0900-1700. £0.80, children free,*at the *Gretna Hall Hotel*. This was where better-off runaway couples would come to maintain a class distinction.

Nine miles northwest of Gretna Green on the A74(M) is the neat little village of Ecclefechan, birthplace of the great writer and historian **Thomas Carlyle** (1795-1881), one of the most powerful and influential thinkers in 19th-century Britain. His old home, The Arched House, is now a tiny museum known as **Carlyle's Birthplace** ⓘ *T01461-300666, Apr-30 Sep Fri-Mon 1330-1700, £2.50/£1.70,* and features a collection of personal memorabilia.

Langholm and around

Langholm sits at the confluence of three rivers – the Esk, Lewes and Wauchope – on the A7, one of the main routes north to Edinburgh, and a less stressful alternative to the A74(M). During the 18th century Langholm became a thriving textile town and is still a major centre of the Scottish tweed industry. This is clan Armstrong country and the **Clan Armstrong Trust Museum** ⓘ *T01387-380610, Easter-Oct Tue-Sun 1400-1700, £1.50,*is a must for anyone with that particular surname.

Langholm was also the birthplace of the great **Hugh McDiarmid** (1892-1978), poet and co-founder of the Scottish National Party. He is also buried here, against the wishes of the local nobs, who took great exception to his radical views. On the hill above the town is the **McDiarmid Memorial**, a stunning modern sculpture which looks like a giant metallic open book.

A scenic route from Langholm to the Borders region is the B709. It runs northwest to the tiny village of **Eskdalemuir**, 14 miles from Langholm, then north through the Eskdalemuir and Craik forests to **Ettrick**, where it follows the valley of the Ettrick Water to Selkirk (see page 686). About 1½ miles north of Eskdalemuir is the **Kagyu Samye Ling Tibetan Monastery** ⓘ *T01387-373232, www.samyeling.org, daily 0900-1800 (tearoom and shops daily 1000-1700 and 1900-2200 at weekends), all inclusive 8-day retreats £300, weekend courses £45, bus No 112 from Lockerbie stops at the centre.* This Tibetan Buddhist centre was founded in 1967 for study, retreat and meditation, and incorporates the Samye Temple, the first Tibetan Buddhist monastery in the west. There are guided tours for visitors, regardless of faith (prices vary from £2-5), and a programme of retreats and weekend courses. There's also a café for vegetarian meals (pre-booking advised) and shops on site and pleasant walks through the gardens.

Moffat and around

Just to the east of the A74(M), at the northern end of Annandale, is the neat and tidy market town of Moffat. Once a fashionable spa town, Moffat is now a centre for the local woollen industry, as clearly evidenced by the statue of a ram on its wide High Street. The **TIC** is on Ladyknowes, off the A701 heading into town from the A74 ⓘ *T220620, open daily Apr-Oct.* Near the TIC is the **Moffat Woollen Mill**, ⓘ *T01683-220134, Mar-Oct daily 0900-1730, Nov-Feb daily till 1700, free,* where you can see a demonstration of traditional weaving and trace your Scottish ancestry.

Moffat makes a convenient base from which to explore the Lowther Hills to the west and the wild and barren southwest Borders to the east, either by car or on foot. The A708 to Selkirk is a very beautiful route which passes through the most stunning parts of the Southern Uplands. Ten miles northeast of Moffat on this road is the spectacular **Grey Mare's Tail** waterfall, which plunges 200 ft from a glacial hanging valley. It's only a five-minute walk from the car park up a series of steps to the base of the falls. More serious walkers can take the path which crosses the stream and climbs steeply up to **Loch Skeen**, the source of the falls. It's about an hour to the loch. From Loch Skeen experienced walkers can climb to the summit of **White Coomb** (2,696 ft).

Dumfries

Dumfries is the largest town in southwest Scotland, straddling the River Nith, a few miles from the Solway Firth. Known as the 'Queen of the South', Dumfries has long been a thriving market town and seaport for a large agricultural hinterland, and its strategic position made it a prime target for English armies. Its long history of successive invasions began in 1306, when Robert the Bruce committed the first act of rebellion against Edward I by capturing Dumfries Castle, which led to the Wars of Independence. But it was town planners in the 1960s who did more to destroy the town centre than invading armies. Nevertheless, Dumfries is a pleasant and convenient base from which to explore the beautiful Solway coast, and its associations with Robert Burns, who spent the last years of his life here, also make it worth a visit in its own right. There are many interesting sights lying within easy distance of Dumfries, including **Caerlaverock Castle** to the southeast, **Drumlanrig Castle** to the north in Nithsdale as well as some of the best mountain biking trails in Scotland, particularly in Mabie Forest, south of town on the road to New Abbey.

Most of the town's attractions and facilities are on the east side of the river. A tour of the main sights should begin on the pedestrianized High Street, at the **Burns Statue**, at its northern end. It shows the great bard sitting on a tree stump with his faithful dog at his feet. A few minutes' walk along the High Street is the **Midsteeple**, built in 1707 to serve as a courthouse and prison. Nearby, at 56 High Street, is the **Globe Inn**, T252335, one of Burns' regular drinking haunts, where you can sit in the poet's favourite chair and enjoy a drink (see 'Eating' below). Continue down the High Street and follow the signs for **Burns' House**, in Burns Street, where the poet spent the last few years of his life, and died in 1796. It contains some interesting memorabilia, including original letters and manuscripts. ⓘ *Apr-Sep Mon-Sat 1000-1700, Sun 1400-1700; Oct-Mar Tue-Sat 1000-1300, 1400-1700, free, T01387-255297.* Just to the south is the red sandstone **St Michael's Church**. In the churchyard is the **mausoleum** where Burns lies buried.Pick up a copy of the free Burns Trail leaflet from the TIC.

On the other side of the river, on Mill Road, is the award-winning **Robert Burns Centre** ⓘ *T01387-264808, Apr-Sep Mon-Sat 1000-2000, Sun 1400-1700; Oct-Mar Tue-Sat 1000-1300 and 1400-1700, free, audio-visual £1.50, concession £0.75,* housed in an old water mill. It tells the story of Burns' last years in the town. On the hill above, centred around an 18th-century windmill tower, is **Dumfries Museum** ⓘ *Apr-Sep Mon-Sat 1000-1700, Sun 1400-1700; Oct-Mar Tue-Sat 1000-1300 and 1400-1700, free, T01387-253374,* which has good local history, natural history and anthropology displays. On the top floor of the windmill tower is a **Camera Obscura**. ⓘ *Apr-Sep (also open Mar weather permitting), Mon-Sat 1000-1700, Sun 1400-1700, £1.50, £0.75 concession.* Also on the west bank of the river, at the west end of the 15th-century Devorgilla Bridge, is the dinky **Old Bridge House** ⓘ *T01387-256904, Apr-Sep Mon-Sat 1000-1700, Sun 1400-1700, free.* Built in 1660 and the town's oldest house, it is now a rather disjointed museum.

Around Dumfries

Eight miles from Dumfries, on the east bank of the Nith estuary where it enters the Solway Firth, is the magnificent ruin of **Caerlaverock Castle,** ⓘ *(HS), T01387-770244. Apr-Sep 0930-1830; Oct-Mar Mon-Sat 0930-1630, Sun 1400-1630. £3, concession £2.30, child £0.80 To get there, take Stagecoach Western bus No 371 from Dumfries,* the ultimate defensive fortress and one of the best-preserved medieval castles in Scotland. The unusual triangular-shaped castle, which dates from around 1277, was the stronghold of the Maxwells, the Wardens of the Western Marches. But though surrounded by a moat and impregnable-looking, it has fallen several times over the course of its long history. It was first besieged and captured in 1300 by Edward I of England during the Wars of Independence, then destroyed by Robert the Bruce. It was repaired in the 1330s, then 300 years later refurbished in the trendy Renaissance style by Robert Maxwell, first Earl of Nithsdale. But several years later it was attacked again, this time by the Covenanters, who captured it after a 13-week siege and proceeded to trash the place. Caerlaverock was never occupied again. A nature trail runs behind the castle and through the woods to the site of the original castle, built in the 1220's and abandoned within 50 years as it was too close to the salt marshes of the Solway Firth. There's also a siege exhibition, a gigantic model Trebuchet (a medieval siege engine) and café.

A few miles further on is the **Caerlaverock Wetlands Centre** ⓘ *T01387-770200, www.wwt.org.uk, daily 1000-1700. £4, children £2.50, WWT members free,* the largest wetland reserve in Britain and an absolute must-see for birdwatchers. The 8,000 ha of mudflats and merse attract many thousands of birds, most notably barnacle geese, migrating here in the winter. A series of hides and observation towers allow you to get very close to the birds, and during the summer months there are nature trails through wildflower meadows, where you may see the rare natterjack toad. There's also a Visitor Centre and a Fair-Trade coffee shop.

West of Dumfries, off the A75 to Castle Douglas, is **Glenkiln Reservoir**, where you'll find an extraordinary collection of **sculptures** scattered amongst the hills, woods and meadows of Glenkiln Estate. There are six works in all, the easiest ones to find being *John the Baptist* by Rodin, which stands at the head of the reservoir, and *Standing Figure* by Henry Moore. There are other works by Moore as well as one by Epstein, which is hidden in a copse of Scots Pine. Heading west on the A75, take the turning right for Shawhead, about 9 miles west of Dumfries. From Shawhead, follow signs for the reservoir.

Six miles northwest of Dumfries, on the A76 at Hollywood, is **Ellisland Farm,** ⓘ *T01387-740426, www.ellislandfarm.co.uk, Apr-Sep Mon-Sat 1000-1300 and*

 1400-1700, Sun 1400-1700; Oct-Mar Tue-Sat 1000-1700. £2.50, £1 concession, child free. This was the home of Robert Burns from 1788 to 1791, during which time he built the farmhouse and tried to introduce new farming methods. Ultimately, this venture collapsed and he moved to Dumfries, but not before writing his famous ghost story, *Tam o' Shanter*, and Hogmanay favourite, *Auld Lang Syne*. The farmhouse is now a museum displaying various personal items.

About 14 miles north of Dumfries is **Thornhill**, where the A702 heads eight miles west to the peaceful little conservation village of **Moniaive**. Bus No 202 runs to Moniaive from Dumfries. Four miles north of Thornhill is the turning for **Drumlanrig Castle** ⓘ *T01848-330248, www.drumlanrigcastle.org.uk, castle Easter and May to early Sep MonSat 1100-1600, Sun 12001600, gardens Easter- end Sep daily 1100-1700, £6, concessions £4, child £2. Drumlanrig is 1½ miles from the A76*, more French château than Scottish castle. This sumptuous stately home of the Duke of Buccleuch and Queensberry is renowned for its superb art collection, which reflects the mind-boggling wealth of its owners. Included are works by such luminaries as Rembrandt, Leonardo Da Vinci, Holbein, Breughel and Van Dyck, as well as numerous family portraits by Allan Ramsay and Godfrey Kneller. After all that you may need to clear your head with a stroll round the extensive **country park**. You can also hire mountain bikes and explore a network of trails. There's also a **bicycle museum**, commemorating the fact that the bicycle was invented nearby, at Keir Mill. Drumlanrig became front page news on August 27 2003 when thieves walked off with Leonardo Da Vinci's *Madonna with Yarnwinder*, worth a cool £40 million.

New Abbey and around

Seven miles south of Dumfries, in the endearing little village of New Abbey, are the graceful red sandstone ruins of **Sweetheart Abbey** ⓘ *T01387-850397 (HS) Apr-Sep daily 0930-1830; Oct-Mar Mon-Wed and Sat 0930-1630, Thu 0930-1200, Fri and Sun 1400-1630, £1.80, concession £1.30, child £0.75*, founded by Cistercian monks in 1273. The abbey gets its name from the extreme marital devotion of its patron, Lady Devorgilla de Balliol, wife of John, who founded Balliol College, Oxford. On his death she had his heart embalmed and carried it around with her, until her own death in 1290. Now both she and the heart are buried in the presbytery. The ruins can be appreciated just as easily from outside the perimeter fence, or even better, from the patio of the Abbey Cottage tearoom. On the northern edge of the village is **Shambellie House Museum of Costume** ⓘ *Apr-Oct daily 1100-1700. £2.50, concession £1.50, T01387-850375*, a Victorian country house set in beautiful gardens, which houses a collection of period costumes from the late 18th to the early 20th centuries. A few miles south of New Abbey, at **Kirkbean**, is the turning for the **John Paul Jones Cottage** ⓘ *Apr-Jun Tue-Sun 1000-1700; Jul and Aug daily 1000-1700. £2 (£1), T01387-880613*, birthplace of the US naval hero. It's now a small museum and includes an exhibition and audio visual of his amazing life. While you're here don't miss a visit to the **Steamboat Inn** (see page 704) in the tiny hamlet of Carsethorn, at the end of the single-track road.

The A710 turns west south of Kirkbean and parallels the Solway Coast, past the wide expanse of the perfectly-named **Sandyhills Bay**, to **Colvend**. About a mile beyond, a side road turns off to the impossibly cute little village of **Rockcliffe**, its row of whitewashed cottages facing a rocky cove and beach at the mouth of the Urr estuary. On a sunny day it's almost too perfect. From Rockcliffe you can walk about 1½ miles to neighbouring Kippford, a popular sailing centre, along the **Jubilee Path** (NTS). The path passes the **Mote of Mark**, an ancient Celtic hillfort. Another path runs south from Rockcliffe along the cliff tops, to **Castlehill Point**. From Kippford, at low tide, you can walk across the causeway to **Rough Island**, a 20-acre offshore bird sanctuary owned by the NTS. During May and June, when the terns and oystercatchers are nesting, it's out of bounds.

Kirkcudbright

Kirkcudbright (pronounced 'kir-koo-bree') sits at the mouth of the river Dee and is, without doubt, the most attractive town in the southwest. Kirkcudbright has an airy and spacious feel to it, its wide streets lined with elegant Georgian villas and Victorian town houses. The Glasgow Boys (see below) started to come here in the late 19th century and established an artists' colony, and ever since then Kirkcudbright has been a favourite haunt of artists – the Scottish equivalent of St Ives in Cornwall. The town's name comes from the now-vanished Kirk of Cuthbert, which relates to St Cuthbert, who converted much of southern Scotland to Christianity.

Near the harbour is **MacLellan's Castle**, ⓘ *T01557-331856 (HS), Apr-Sep daily 0930-1830, £2, concession £1.50, child £0.75,* which is a castellated town house rather than a defensive fortress. It was built in the 1570s by the then-provost, Thomas MacLellan of Bombie, using stone from the adjoining ruined monastery. Nearby, at 12 High Street, is the wonderful **Broughton House** ⓘ *T01557-330437 (NTS), house closed for restoration, may open in 2004, check details at TIC, garden open Apr-Oct daily 1300-1700, opens at 1100 in Jul (hrs may vary), £2, concession £1 (honesty box)*, the Georgian town house which was bought in 1901 by E A Hornel, the renowned artist and member of the 'Glasgow Boys', an influential late 19th-century group of painters who established an artists' colony in Kirkcudbright. Many of Hornel's works are on display here, in the Hornel Gallery. Het also designed the **Japanese Garden**, which leads from the house to the river.

Only a few minutes' walk along the High Street is the early 17th-century **tolbooth**, which now houses the **Tolbooth Art Centre** ⓘ *T01557-331556, all year Mon-Sat 1100-1600 and Sun 1400-1700, free.* As well as featuring a display of works by Hornel and his fellow 'colonists', including local artist Jessie King, the centre also tells the story of the town's artists colony from the late 19th century to the present day, and there are temporary exhibitions of local arts and crafts and photography. Another of the town's art galleries is the **Harbour Cottage Gallery**, which hosts a variety of shows throughout the year. ⓘ *Mar-Nov Mon-Sat 1030-1230, 1400-1700, Sun 1400-1700, £0.80, concession £0.50, child free.* From art to artefact, one of the town's more eclectic attractions is the **Stewartry Museum** ⓘ *St Mary Street, T01557-331643, all year Mon-Sat 1100-1600 and Sun 1400-1700, free*, a diverse collection of exhibits reflecting the social and natural history of this part of the Solway coast, once known as the Kirkcudbright Stewartry because it was administered by the kings' stewards during the 14th and 15th centuries.

About seven miles southeast of Kirkcudbright are the ruins of **Dundrennan Abbey** ⓘ *T01557-500262 (HS), Apr-Sep daily 0930-1830, Oct-Mar Sat 0930-1630 and Sun 1400-1630, £1.80, concession £1.30, child £0.75. Bus No 505 between Kirkcudbright and Dumfries passes through Dundrennan, or if you're feeling energetic it's a lovely five-mile walk along quiet country roads*, a 12th-century Cistercian establishment standing in a beautifully bucolic setting in a secluded valley. You may not be too surprised to learn that the abbey has associations with Mary, Queen of Scots. She spent her last night on Scottish soil here. A mile further east is the lovely wee village of Auchencairn and, between here and **Palnackie** (see Festivals and events, page 704), is the turn-off for the 15th-century **Orchardton Tower** ⓘ *(HS) Apr-Sep daily 0930-1830, Oct-Mar Mon-Sat 0930-1630, free, key available locally*, the only circular tower house in Scotland.

Castle Douglas

The neat little town of Castle Douglas, standing on the edge of lovely little **Carlingwark Loch**. There's nothing of note in the town itself, but it makes a good alternative base for exploring Galloway Forest Park (see page 698) and the surrounding sights. The A713 runs north from Castle Douglas along the shores of long and skinny **Loch Ken**, a popular watersports centre, with sailing, windsurfing, water-skiing, canoeing, rowing and fishing (see Activities and tours on page 705). There's also an RSPB nature reserve on the west bank, and walking trails.

A mile southwest of town, off the A75 or reached by the lochside road, is **Threave Garden and Estate** ⓘ *T01557-502575 (NTS), gardens daily all year from 0930 till sunset, visitor centre Apr-Oct daily 0930-1730, Feb-Mar and Nov-Dec daily 1000-1600, house Mar-Oct Wed-Fri and Sun 1100-1600, guided tours only, house and garden £9, concession £6.50, family £23, garden only £5, concession £3.75, family £13.50,* the NTS horticultural school's magnificent floral extravaganza. The best time to visit is early spring when over 200 types of daffodils burst into bloom, but it's a very colourful experience at any time of the year. Threave House is also now open to the public. There's a very good self-service restaurant in the Visitor Centre.

Two miles further west at Bridge of Dee, a country lane branches north (right) and leads for about a mile to the start of a footpath which takes you to the gaunt tower of **Threave Castle,** ⓘ *T0131-6688800 (HS), 1 Apr-30 Sep daily 0930-1830, last boat back at 1800, £2.20, concession £1.60, child £0.75,* standing alone on an island in the middle of the River Dee. Threave was built in the 14th century by Archibald 'the grim', third Earl of Douglas, and head of the 'Black' Douglas line. The Douglases were one of Scotland's most powerful baronial families and the main line, the 'Black' Douglases, were descended from 'the Good' Sir James, trusted friend of Robert the Bruce. The outer wall of the castle was added in 1450 in an unsuccessful attempt to defend it against King James II, who was determined to break the power of the maverick Border family. The Covenanters reduced Threave to its present ruinous state in 1640, and little remains of the interior. It's a romantic ruin nevertheless, especially as you have to be ferried across to the island. It's a 1 km walk from the car park, then ring the bell for the custodian to take you across in a small rowing boat. There's a tearoom at the car park.

Gatehouse of Fleet

The quiet little town of Gatehouse of Fleet lies 10 miles west of Kirkcudbright, a mile or so north of the A75. It's an attractive place on the banks of the Water of Fleet, surrounded by forested hills. On the main street, opposite the TIC, is the **Mill on the Fleet Museum** ⓘ *T01557-814099, Easter-Oct daily 1030-1700, £1.50, concession £1, child £0.50,* housed in a restored 18th-century cotton mill complete with working water wheel. The museum traces the history of the town's cotton industry which lasted from the mid-18th century until the early 19th century. There are walks in the surrounding countryside, including to **Cardoness Castle**, ⓘ *T01557-814427 (HS), Apr-Sep daily 0930-1830, Oct-Mar Sat 0930-1630 and Sun 1400-1630, £2.20, concession £1.60, child £0.75, about 1½ miles to the south*, standing on a hill overlooking the B796 which connects Gatehouse with the main A75. The ruin was the home of the MacCullochs and is a classic example of a 15th-century tower house.

Galloway Forest Park and New Galloway

Between the Solway Firth and the Ayrshire coast lies Galloway Forest Park, the largest forest park in Britain, covering 300 square miles of forested hills, wild and rugged moorland and numerous lochs. It's a vast and beautiful area criss-crossed by waymarked Forestry Commission trails and longer routes, such as the **Southern Upland Way**. It's also home to a rich variety of fauna, such as feral goats, red deer, falcons and even golden eagles. The best way to see the park is on foot or by bike. Those wishing to hike in the park should be properly equipped and buy the relevant Ordnance Survey maps. The OS Outdoor Leisure Map No 32 covers Galloway Forest Park. **National Cycle Route 7** incorporates 30 miles of off-road trails through the park, as well as the **Raider's Road** (see below). Newton Stewart TIC (Dashwood Sq, just off the main street and opposite the bus station) can provide lots of information on walking and cycling in Galloway Forest Park. See also their free guide to Ranger led walks and activities. There are Visitor Centres at Glentrool, Kirroughtree and Clatteringshaws (see below). The Forestry Commission regional office is at Creebridge ⓘ *east of Newton Stewart, T01671-402420, www.forestry.gov.uk/gallowayforestpark.*

The A712 runs northwest from Newton Stewart, cutting through the southern section of the Galloway Forest Park, to New Galloway. This 19-mile stretch of scenic road is known as **The Queen's Way**. Seven miles southwest of New Galloway the road skirts **Clatteringshaws Loch.** On the shores of the loch is the **Clatteringshaws Forest Wildlife Centre**, which gives an introduction to the park's flora and fauna. ⓘ *T01557-420285, Apr-Oct daily 1030-1700, free.* About a mile southwest of the Forest Wildlife Centre, opposite the massive Clatteringshaws dam, is the turning for the **Raiders' Road**, a 10-mile timber road and erstwhile cattle rustlers' route which runs from the A712 and follows the Water of Dee southeast to Stroan Loch and then turns north to meet the A762 just north of Mossdale. The Raider's Road is only open between April and October, and there's a toll charge. It can be driven but is best enjoyed on two wheels. The A762 heads north along the western shore of Loch Ken back to New Galloway, making a circuit of about 20 miles, starting and ending in New Galloway. About three miles southwest of Clatteringshaws Loch along The Queen's Way is the **Galloway Red Deer Range**, where you can get close up to the deer, stroke them and take photos. ⓘ *T07771 748401, end Jun to mid-Sep Tue and Thu 1100 and 1400, Sun 1430, £2.50, £1 child.*

About three miles east of Newton Stewart, near Palnure, is the **Kirroughtree Visitor Centre** ⓘ *T01671-402165, Apr-Sep daily 1030-1700, Oct closes at 1630*, the southern gateway to Galloway Forest Park. A series of waymarked trails and cycle routes lead from here into the forest. There's also a tea room serving light mealsOne of the most accessible and loveliest parts of Galloway Forest Park is **Glen Trool**. Ten miles north of Newton Stewart at **Bargrennan**, on the A714, a narrow road winds its way for five miles past Glen Trool village to **Loch Trool**, hemmed in by the wooded slopes of the glen. Halfway up the loch is **Bruce's Stone**, which marks the spot where Robert the Bruce's guerrilla band ambushed the pursuing English force in 1307, after they had routed the main army at Solway Moss.

There are a number of excellent **hiking trails** which start out from here, including the one to the summit of **Merrick** (2,766 ft), the highest peak in southern Scotland. It's a tough climb of about four hours, but fairly straightforward and well worth the effort. There are also numerous Forestry Commission trails for the less fit/ experienced/adventurous. On the road to Loch Trool, about a mile from the village, is the **Glen Trool Visitor Centre.** ⓘ *T01671-402420, Apr-Oct daily 1030-1730.*

One of the most convenient entry points for Galloway Forest Park is New Galloway, a pleasant little village of whitewashed houses nestled in the valley of **The Glenkens**, which runs north from Loch Ken.

Newton Stewart

The amiable little town of Newton Stewart is a popular base for **hiking** in the hills of Galloway Forest Park, especially around **Glen Trool**. Set on the west bank of the River Cree at the junction of the main A75 and the A714, amidst beautiful wooded countryside, Newton Stewart is also a major centre for **salmon and trout fishing**. The season runs from March till mid-October. Permits, guides and the hire of fishing gear can all be arranged at the fishing tackle shops in town. Four miles north of town, reached via the A714, is the **Wood of Cree Nature Reserve** ⓘ *T01671-402861*, the largest ancient woodland in southern Scotland. This RSPB reserve is home to a huge variety of birdlife, including pied flycatchers, redstarts and wood warblers. There are nature trails running for two miles through the forest in the Cree Valley. Southeast of town, just beyond Palnure, on the A75, is **Creetown**, standing on the east shore of Wigtown Bay, overlooked by the distinctive bulk of Cairnsmore of Fleet hill (2,330 ft). Creetown is most notable for its **Gem Rock Museum,** ⓘ *T01671-820357, www.gemrock.net, Easter-Sep daily 0930-1800, Oct and Nov daily 1000-1600, Dec-Feb Sat and Sun 1000-1600. £3.25, concession £2.75, child £1.75, family £8.25,* which has a wide range of precious stones on display.

The Machars

South of the A75 is the peninsula of fertile rolling farmland known as the Machars. It's a somewhat neglected corner of the southwest but has strong early-Christian associations, and there are many important sites. The disconsolate little town of **Wigtown** sits on the northwesterly shore of Wigtown Bay and is notable for its large number of bookshops (18 at the last count). It is now gaining a reputation as Scotland's National Book Town with festivals held throughout the year, www.wigtown-booktown.co.uk. If you need to buy a book in the southwest, then this is the place to do it.

Eleven miles south from Wigtown is the village of **Whithorn**, which occupies a crucially place in Scotland's history. It was here in the fifth century, that **St Ninian** established a mission and built the first Christian church north of Hadrian's Wall. The church, which he called **Candida Casa** ('bright shining place'), has not survived but after Ninian's death a priory was built to house his tomb. This became a famous seat of learning and an important place of pilgrimage for penitents from England and Ireland, as well as from Scotland.

The **Whithorn Story** ⓘ *T01988-500508, Apr-Oct daily 1030-1700, £2.70, concessions £1.50,* features artefacts uncovered by the archaeological dig in the ruins of the 12th-century priory and an audio-visual display telling the story of the area's development. The adjacent **Priory Museum** contains some important interesting archaeological finds and early-Christian sculpture, including the Latinus Stone which dates from 450 AD and is the earliest Christian memorial in Scotland.

Four miles away is the misnamed **Isle of Whithorn**, which isn't an island at all but an atmospheric old fishing village built around a natural harbour. The village is the site of the ruined 13th-century **St Ninian's Chapel**, built for pilgrims who landed here from England and Ireland. Along the coast to the west of the village is **St Ninian's Cave**, said to have been used by the saint as a private place of prayer. It is reached via a footpath off the A747 before entering the Isle of Whithorn.

From Whithorn the A747 heads west to meet the coast and then runs northwest along the east shore of **Luce Bay** for 15 miles till it meets the A75 at the pretty little village of Glenluce. Two miles north of the village, signposted off the A75, is **Glenluce Abbey** ⓘ *Apr-Oct 0930-1830; Oct-Mar Sat 0930-1630, Sun 1400-1630, £1.80, £1.30 concession, buses 430 and 500 between Newton Stewart and Stranraer stop in Glenluce village and you can walk from there,* founded in 1192 by Roland, Earl of Galloway for the Cistercian order. The remains, set in a beautiful and peaceful valley, include a handsome early 16th-century Chapter House with a vaulted ceiling noted for its excellent acoustics. The abbey was visited by Robert the Bruce, James IV and, you guessed it, Mary, Queen of Scots.

Stranraer

Stranraer wins no prizes for beauty or tourist appeal, but as Scotland's main ferry port for Northern Ireland it's an important town which sees a lot of through traffic. It sits on the shores of sheltered Loch Ryan on the **Rhinns of Galloway**, a windswept peninsula shaped like the head of a pick-axe at the end of the Solway coast.

The main attraction is the medieval tower which is all that remains of the 16th-century **Castle of St John** ⓘ *T01776-705544, Apr-mid Sep Mon-Sat 1000-1300 and 1400-1700, £1.20, concession £0.60,* one of the main headquarters of Graham of Claverhouse, the fanatical persecutor of the Protestant Covenanters in the late 17th century. Many of them died in the castle dungeons. It was later used as a prison in the 19th century. Inside, an exhibition traces the castle's history. Also worth a peek is the **Stranraer Museum** ⓘ *T01776-705088, Mon-Fri 1000-1700, Sat 1000-1300, 1400-1700, free,* which features displays on local history and has a section devoted to the life of Arctic explorer Sir John Ross (1777-1856), whose expeditions to find the Northwest Passage to the Pacific led to the discovery, in 1831, of the North Magnetic Pole. His house, called North West Castle, is now a hotel (see below). Three miles east of Stranraer are **Castle Kennedy Gardens** ⓘ *T01776-702024, Apr-Sep daily 1000-1700, £3, £2 concession,* famous for their riotous rhododendrons and magnificent monkey puzzle trees. The 75 acres of landscaped gardens are set on a peninsula between two lochs and two castles (Castle Kennedy and Lochinch Castle).

Portpatrick to the Mull of Galloway

Nine miles southwest of Stranraer on the windswept and rugged west coast of the Rhinns is the extremely photogenic old port of Portpatrick. Until the mid-19th century it was the main departure point for Northern Ireland but is now a peaceful little holiday resort and a good base from which to explore the southern part of the peninsula. You can arrange **sea fishing trips** from Portpatrick ⓘ £8 for half a day, T01776-810468. Portpatrick is also the starting point for the **Southern Upland Way,** the 212-mile coast-to-coast route which ends at Cockburnspath on the Berwickshire coast. From Portpatrick the road runs south to the Mull of Galloway through lush, green farmland which receives high average rainfall. The Rhinns are also warmed by the Gulf Stream which gives the peninsula the mildest climate in Scotland and means it's almost frost-free. This is beautifully demonstrated at **Logan Botanic Garden,** ⓘ *T01776-860231. Apr-Sep daily 1000-1800, Mar/Oct 1000-1700. £3, concession £2.50 , children £1, bus No 407 from Stranraer passes through Port Logan on its way to Drummore,* an outpost of Edinburgh's Royal Botanic Garden, about a mile north of the tiny village of **Port Logan.** The garden boasts a vast array of exotic, subtropical flora from the southern hemisphere, including tree ferns and cabbage palms. Five miles further south is the **Mull of Galloway,** a dramatic, storm-lashed headland and Scotland's most southerly point, only 25 miles from Ireland and the Isle of Man. The narrow isthmus is an **RSPB nature reserve** and the home of thousands of seabirds such as guillemots, razorbills and puffins. There's a small information centre. ⓘ *Late May-Aug, T01671-402861.*

Sleeping

Langholm and around *p693*

A **Riverside Inn**, Canonbie, T01387-371512, www.langholm .com/riverside, serves superb pub food and is also a good place to stay.

Moffat and around *p694*

B **Well View Private Hotel**, Ballplay Rd, T01683-220184, www.wellview.co.uk. Overlooking the town is this lovely Victorian house with an excellent restaurant (see Eating).

B-C **Hartfell House**, Hartfell Cres, T01683-220153, robert.white@virgin.net. Elegant and supremely comfortable guesthouse, a 10-minute walk from the High St.

C **Kirkland House**, Well Rd, T01683-221133, www.kirkland-moffat.co.uk. 4 spacious rooms, 2 en suite. Former manse, only a few minutes from the High St. Parking. Friendly and comfortable. Caters for vegetarians.

Dumfries *p694*

A **Station Hotel**, 49 Lovers Walk, T01387-254316, www.stationhotel.co.uk. 32 rooms. Refurbished classic Victorian hotel, very handy for the train station and has a good restaurant.

B **Edenbank Hotel**, 17 Laurieknowe, T01387-252759, www.edenbankhotel.co.uk. 10 en suite rooms. A short walk west of the town centre, where you'll find several places to stay.

B **Redbank House**, New Abbey Rd, T01387-247034, www.redbankhouse.co.uk. 5 en suite rooms. Lovely country house set in 3 acres of gardens. Non-smoking.

Around Dumfries *p695*

A **Comlongon Castle**, T01387-870283, www.comlongon.com. For a bit of luxury, try this 14th-century, family-owned castle and adjacent mansion house hotel. To get there, head north from Ruthwell for about a mile to Clarencefield, where a signposted road turns left (west) for another mile to the castle.

A-B **Speddoch**, large country house, a short drive from the sculptures at Glenkiln Reservoir, T01387-820342, www.wolsey-lodges.co.uk. Has been owned by the same family for 300 years. The family is very hospitable, there are cosy log fires and good home cooking – if you choose to eat there you'll dine with the family at night. It's a Wolsey Lodge – private homes offering accommodation where you're treated like a family guest.

B **Buccleuch and Queensberry Hotel**, 112 Drumlanrig St, Thornhill, T/F01848-330215, www.buccleuchhotel.co.uk. 19th century coaching inn in the centre of the village.

B **Trigony House Hotel**, Closeburn, Thornhill, 01843-331211, www.trigonyhotel.co.uk. Former shooting lodge for Closeburn Castle, Trigony combines the traditional estate living with the cosy hospitality of a family home. Ideal base for fishing and walking holiday but it is the food that really sets it apart. Everything is home-made, using organic produce from their own garden and the best in local game and fish. Highly recommended.

New Abbey and around *p696*

A **Cavens**, Kirkbean, T01387-880234. Country house hotel, once owned by tobacco baron, Robert Oswald. The perfect place to get away from whatever it is you want to get away from, and superb food (see Eating).

B **Craigbittern House,** at Sandyhills, about a mile east of Colvend, T01387-780247. Baronial splendour at affordable prices. Also has self-contained cottage for rent.

Camping and self-catering There are some good campsites in the area, including **Kippford Holiday Park**, T/F01387-620636, www .kippfordholidaypark.co.uk, and **Castle Point Caravan Site**, T01387-630248, open Mar-Oct, near Rockcliffe. Pick of the bunch is the wonderfully-sited **Sandyhills Bay Leisure Park**, T01387-780257, open Apr-Oct. There's a lot of self-catering accommodation in Rockliffe. Contact the tourist board for further details. The **National Trust for Scotland** have a lovely cottage right on the beach, sleeps 5, £250-550 per week, see page 32 for details.

Kirkcudbright *p697*

A **Selkirk Arms Hotel**, High St, T01557-330402, www.selkirkarmshotel.co.uk. 17 rooms. The top hotel in town. Beautifully refurbished Georgian building with attractive rooms and also has the town's finest restaurant (see Eating).

A **Balcary House Hotel**, Auchencairn, T01556-640217, www.balcary-bay-hotel.co.uk. 20 rooms. Open Mar-Oct. Luxurious, family-run country house hotel set in 3 acres of garden, overlooking lovely Auchencairn Bay. Excellent restaurant (see Eating below).

B **Baytree House**, 110 High St, T01557-330824, www.baytreehouse.net. 3 en suite rooms, 1 on ground floor. Unmissable peach-coloured Georgian house with nice touches throughout. Good food available. No smoking. Great value.

B **Fresh Fields**, Arden Rd, Twynholm, a few miles north of Kirkcudbright, T01557-860221, open Jan-Oct. 5 en suite rooms. Friendly, attractive rooms, guest lounge, good breakfasts.

B **Gladstone House**, 48 High St, T01557-331734, hilarygladstone@aol.com. 3 en suite rooms. This wonderful, superior guesthouse has a secluded garden and also offers afternoon tea. No smoking. A cracking place to stay, fantastic value.

B **Mrs McLaughlin**, 14 High St, T01557-330766. 2 en suite rooms, open Apr-Sep. Very comfortable rooms and good views of the river.

C **The Rossan**, Auchencairn,T01556-640269, www.the-rossan.co.uk. 3 rooms. Vegetarian-friendly B&B offering dinner at a modest extra charge. Easy-going and informal atmosphere, ludicrously cheap considering the levels of cuisine and comfort. Carnivores and special diets also catered for. No smoking. Recommended.

Camping

Silvercraigs Caravan & Camping Site, T01557-503806, open Easter to late-Oct, is on an elevated site overlooking the town, about a 10-min walk from the centre; and **Seaward Caravan Park**, T01557-870267, open Mar-Oct, is part of a new leisure complex at Brighouse Bay, with a wide range of facilities including heated pool, 9-hole golf course and pony trekking.

Castle Douglas and around *p697*

A **Craigadam**, 11 miles out of town, on the A712 near Crockettford, T/F01557-650233, www.craigadam.com. 6 en suite rooms. Elegant country house and working farm where you can enjoy good home cooking (**A** with evening meal).

A **Longacre Manor**, Ernespie Rd, T01557-503576, www.longacremanor.co.uk. 4 rooms. Very comfortable country house set in gardens overlooking the town. Fine reputation for their home cooking.

Camping

Lochside Caravan & Camping Site, beside the loch, T01557-503806, open Easter-late Oct.

Loch Ken Holiday Park, by the village of Parton, T01644-470282, www.lochkenholiday park.freeserve.co.uk, open late Mar-early Nov (see also Activities and tours below).

Gatehouse of Fleet *p698*

A **Cally Palace Hotel**, T01557-814341, www.callypalace.co.uk. Set in 500 acres grounds, this very exclusive Georgian mansion and former home of local laird James Murray, offers luxury and top-class facilities, including private 18-hole golf course and indoor pool.

A **Murray Arms Hotel**, Ann St, T01557-814207, www.murrayarms.com. A bit more down-to-earth but lots of character and good bar meals (see Eating).

New Galloway *p698*

D **Leamington Hotel**, High St, T01644-420327, www. leamington-hotel.com. Small and comfortable, does evening meals.

E **Youth Hostel** at Kendoon, T01644-460680, 5 miles north of Dalry on the B7000, close to the Southern Upland Way and the A713. It's open mid-Mar to early Oct. Take the Castle Douglas-Ayr bus and ask to get off near the hostel.

Newton Stewart *p699*

L **Kirroughtree House**, T01671-402141, www.kirroughtreehouse.co.uk. 17 rooms. This grand 18th-century country mansion is set in its own grounds and offers impeccable standards of comfort and service. It's superb restaurant (see Eating page 703) has a well-deserved reputation for its gourmet Scottish cuisine.

A **Creebridge House Hotel**, across the river in the village of Minnigaff, T01671-402121, www.creebridge.co.uk. 19 rooms. Nice location, good food in restaurant or bistro.

D **Oakbank**, Corsbie Rd, T01671-402822, open Feb-Nov. 3 rooms. Very comfortable Victorian house, good breakfasts. Evening meals by arrangement. No smoking.

D **Stables Guest House**, Corsbie Rd, T01671-402157, www.stablesguesthouse.com. 6 rooms. Comfortable no smoking guesthouse.

D-E **Kilwarlin**, 4 Corvisel Rd, T01671-403047, open Apr-Oct. Friendly and welcoming, caters for cyclists.

E **SYHA Youth Hostel**, T01671-402211, open mid-Mar to end-Oct, in the village of **Minnigaff**, which is on the other side of the river, across the bridge.

The Machars *p700*

A **Corsemalzie House Hotel**, about 11 miles west of Whithorn, near the village of Port William, T860254, www.corsemalzie-house. ltd.uk Sumptuous and highly rated hotel and restaurant. Open Mar-Jan.

B-C **Steam Packet Inn**, Isle of Whithorn, T01988-500354, a popular fishermen's pub with rooms on the quayside, which serves good, cheap bar meals.

Stranraer *p700*

L **Corsewall Lighthouse Hotel**, 11 miles northwest of town at Corsewall Point, T01776-853220, corsewall-lighthouse@ msn.com. 6 rooms. This hotel is housed in a working lighthouse, set in 20 acres of grounds on the wild and windy clifftops. The owners can arrange transport from Stranraer.

A **North West Castle Hotel**, T01776-704413, www.northwestcastle.co.uk. 73 rooms. The former home of Sir John Ross (see page 700) also offers leisure facilities and excellent cuisine.

F **Sally's Hoose**, Balyet Farm, Cairnryan Rd, T01776-703395. It only has 6 beds but is open all year.

Portpatrick to the Mull of Galloway *p701*

L **Knockinaam Lodge Hotel**, T01776-810471. By far the best place to stay in this area, a wonderful place which offers great sea views, exquisite and unmatched cuisine (see below) and impeccable service. It is rated as one of the best hotels in the south of Scotland.

A **Fernhill Hotel**, T01776-810220, www.fernhillhotel.co.uk. Those without the means to enjoy the splendours of Knockinaam Lodge can try the Fernhill which overlooks the village. Its restaurant has a fine reputation (see below).

Eating

Moffat *p694*

£££ **Well View Hotel,** see Sleeping page 701. Locally-renowned for its excellent use of the best of local produce. 6-course dinner is lavish and expensive, lunch is mid-range and served Sun-Thu.

££ **The Lime Tree**, High St, T01683-221654, www.limetree-restaurant.co.uk. Open for dinner Tue-Sat. Very popular restaurant with a varied menu that always hits the mark. Best to book in advance.

Dumfries *p694*

££ **Benvenuto**, 42 Eastfield Rd, T01387-259890. Very popular Italian-style restaurant some way from the centre of town. Tue-Sun 1700-late. Pizza and pasta under £5 1700-1830.

££ **Bruno's**, 3 Balmoral Rd, T01387-255757. Good, honest Italian food. Pizza/pasta supper special at £9 for 2 courses. Open 1700 till late.

££ **Hector's Kitchen**, 20a Academy St, T01387-256263. International menu featuring such diverse temptations as Tempura vegeable salad and pan-crusted sea bass, also tex-mex and pasta. Cheap lunches. Shiny, happy decor matched by the friendliness of the owners. Mon-Sat 0900-1500 and 1730-2130. No smoking.

££**Hullabaloo**, on Mill Rd, T01387-259679, above the Burns Centre in a converted old water mill. Chilled atmos by day with good selection of wraps, baguetted and bagels, by night menu features pastas, steaks and salads plus daily specials and decent wine list. Beer garden for those rare summer rays. Mon 1100-1600, Tue-Sat 1100-1600 and 1800-2200, Sun 1100-1500.

New Abbey and around *p696*

££ **Anchor Hotel**, Kippford, T01387-620205. Serves superb pub food and is the perfect spot for a great pint of real ale after the walk from Rockcliffe.

££ **Criffel Inn**, New Abbey, T01387-850244. Great village pub serving good bar meals. Beer garden and good selection of ales. Food daily 1200-1400 and 1700-2000.

££ **Steamboat Inn**, Carsethorn, T01387-880631, www.steamboatinn carsethorn.co.uk. Food daily 1200-1430, 1830-2300. Location alone would be enough for the Steamboat to be included, sitting at the end of a dead-end road looking across the Solway Firth, but blow me if they don't go and serve some of the best pub grub this side of Hadrian's Wall. On top of all that, they have a good selection of beers and malts. And that beer garden out front. People drive hundreds of miles for this sort of thing.

Kirkcudbright *p697*

£££ **Balcary House Hotel**, see Sleeping page 702. Enjoy the modern Scottish dinner menu or Sunday lunch in the conservatory. Either way, this is a rare treat. Mon-Sat dinner by arrangement, Sun 1200-1400.

£££ **Selkirk Arms Hotel**, see Sleeping, p 702. The best place to eat in town, the highly skilled chef is something of local celebrity. Restaurant specialises in local fish and seafood while the bistro offers a more affordable alternative. Food served daily 1200-1400 and 1800-2130.

££ **Auld Alliance Restaurant**, 5 Castle St, T01557-330569. As the name suggests, it's a mixture of Scottish and French culinary styles, and features delights such as local queen scallops in garlic butter with smoked Ayrshire bacon and Galloway cream, also whisky, honey and oatmeal ice cream.

New Galloway *p698*

£ **Kitty's Tearoom** , on the main street. Tue-Sun 1100-1700. A local insitution and the best place around for lunch or a coffee break. Great cakes.

Newton Stewart *p699*

£££ **Kirroughtree House**, see Sleeping page 703. Worth the expense to eat here.

Portpatrick to the Mull of Galloway *p701*

£££ **Knockinaam Lodge** see Sleeping page 703. The best place to eat here and one of the very best in the south of Scotland.

£££ **Waterfront Hotel and Bistro**, on the seafront, T01776-810800. Good value lunch and dinner featuring local seafood.

Entertainment

Dumfries *p694*

RBC Film theatre, in Burns Centre, T01387-264808. Good programme of arthouse and mainstream cinema. £4, concession £3.

Festivals and events

May The Scottish and British **Gold Panning Championships** are held in Wanlockhead during the second last weekend in May. **Dumfries Book Fair** at the beginning of May.

Jun/Jul Kirkcudbright Jazz Festival, held in

mid Jun. Check out www.summerfestivities.com **Langholm's Common Riding** takes place on the last weekend in Jul.

Aug First Saturday in **Aug** Palnackie hosts the **World Flounder Tramping Championships**, an unusual event which involves trying to catch the biggest flounder – with your feet! The **Langholm & Eskdale Festival of Music and Arts** is held in the last week in **Aug**. **Kirkcudbright Arts Festival**, takes place over two weeks in late **Aug** and early **Sep** in venues throughout the town.

Castle Douglas hosts the **Scottish Alternative Games** on the first Sun in **Aug**. The various traditional Scottish games include the world finals of the Gird'n'Cleek competition, whatever that may be.

Activities and tours

Boat trips

GM Marine Services, T331557. Run wildlife cruises up and down the River Dee on the *Lovely Nellie*. Leave from the marina (behind Broughton House). Contact TIC for times. £5, concession/child £2.50.

Mountain biking

Four miles south of Dumfries is the turn-off to **Mabie Forest**, a large area criss-crossed by forest paths and mountain bike trails of varying degrees of difficulty. The 9-mile *Rik's Red Route* offers some of the best single track in the country. You can hire bikes at **Riks Bike Shed**, T01387-270275, rik@riksbikes.co.uk, open Mon-Sat 1000-1800, Sun 1000-1600. Bikes cost from £10 per person per half day. They have a bike shop and the staff will advise you well. They also have a hire-only site at Drumlanrig. Mabie Forest is part of the 7 Stanes project. Just south of Dalbeattie, off the A710 to Kippford, is the start of the **Hardrock Trail**, a must for all mountain bike enthusiasts.

Watersports

Loch Ken Marina, hires boats (£15 per day), canoes (£5 per day), bikes (£12 per day) and issues fishing permits (£5 per day). Easter-31 Oct daily 0900-1700.

Galloway Sailing Centre, also at Parton, T01644-420626, www.lochken. co.uk, offers tuition and hire for windsurfers, canoes and dinghies, as well as other activities such as quad biking and gorge scrambling. Also hot showers, snacks and basic dormitory accommodation (**F**). Apr-Oct daily 0900-1900, Nov-Mar daily till 1700.

Transport

Dumfries *p694*

There are regular **buses** to **Kirkcudbright** (Nos 76, 501, X74). No 500 and X75 go twice daily to **Newton Stewart** (1 hr 20 mins) and **Stranraer** (2 hrs), for the ferry to **Belfast**. National Express, T08705-808080, runs a daily service between **London** and **Belfast**, via Dumfries and **Stranraer** and towns in between. Stagecoach Western, T01292-613500, has 2 buses daily to and from **Edinburgh** (No 100; 2 hrs 20 mins). There are buses to **Carlisle** (No 79; 50 mins) and to **Moffat** (No 114 or X74; 1 hr). Bus No 500 runs to **Castle Douglas** (45 mins) and No 246 to **Cumnock**, via **Sanquhar** (50 mins). There are also buses to **Thornhill, Dalbeattie** via **Rockcliffe, Moniaive, Glencaple/Caerlaverock Castle** and **Annan** via **Ruthwell**. Bus No 372 runs from Dumfries to **Dalbeattie**, stopping in **New Abbey, Kirkbean, Rockcliffe** and **Kippford**, T710357. Frequent **trains** Mon-Sat to and from **Carlisle**(35 mins) and several daily (Mon-Sat) to and from **Glasgow** (1 ½ hrs), via **Kilmarnock**, where you change for trains to **Stranraer**. Reduced service on Sun.

Directory

Dumfries *p694*

Car hire Arnold Clark, New Abbey Rd, T01387-247151. Open Mon-Fri 0800-1800, Sat 0830-1700, Sun 1100-1700. **Cycle hire** Nithsdale Cycle Centre, 46 Brooms Rd, T01387-254870. Daily 1000-1700. **Kirkpatrick** Cycles, 13-15 Queen St, T01387-254011. Bike repairs and parts. Riks Bike Shed in Mabie Forest (see page 705). **Internet** Ewart Library, Catherine St, T01387-253820. Mon- Wed and Fri 0915-1930, Thu and Sat 0915 -1700.

Kirkcudbright *p697*

Cycle hire W Law, 19 St Cuthbert St, T01557-330579.

Castle Douglas *p697*

Cycle hire Castle Douglas Cycle Centre, 11 Church Street, T01557-504542. £10 per day for mountain bikes and hybrids. Mon-Wed, Fri, Sat 0900-1230, 1330-1700.

Ayrshire
→ Colour map 5

The region of Ayrshire is best known as the birthplace of Robert Burns, Scotland's great poet, loved and revered the world over. The vast majority of visitors come here to visit the many sights associated with the great bard, but the Ayrshire coast is also famed for its excellent golf courses, such as Turnberry, Troon and Prestwick. There are a few other reasons for visiting Ayrshire, most notably Culzean Castle to the south of Ayr, one of Scotland's top tourist attractions. ▸▸ *For Sleeping, Eating and other listings, see pages 708-708.*

Ins and outs

Getting around There are frequent buses and trains to Ayr from Glasgow, Dumfries and Stranraer. There are **trains** every 30 mins to and from Glasgow Central (50 mins), and several daily to **Stranraer** (1¼ hrs). ▸▸ *For further details, see Transport, page 708.*

Information The **Tourist Information Centre** ⓘ *22 Sandgate near, Town Hall, Ayr, T01292-678100, also offices in Irvine, Largs, Girvan and Millport (open Easter-Oct).*

Ayr

The largest town in southwest Scotland, looking west out on to the Firth of Clyde and Arran, Ayr has been a popular seaside resort since Victorian times. The town's 2½ miles of sandy beach, together with Scotland's most important racecourse, continue to attract hordes of visitors from nearby Glasgow. Ayr is best known for its many connections with Scotland's national poet, **Robert Burns**, who was born in the neighbouring village of **Alloway** and who famously praised the town for its 'honest men and bonnie lasses'.

Most of Ayr's important sights are contained within the **Burns National Heritage Park** in Alloway a few miles south of the town centre, ⓘ *www.burnsheritagepark.com, Apr-Sep daily 0930-1730, Oct-Mar daily 1000-1700. Combined ticket for all sites (valid for 3 days) £5, concessions £2.50, family £12.50, audio guide £0.50. Buses run from Alloway to Ayr (No 361) regularly.* The best place to start is the **Burns Cottage and Museum**, the low, thatched, whitewashed 'auld clay biggin' where the poet was born on 25 January 1759 and spent the first seven years of his life. The museum contains original manuscripts, books, paintings and other memorabilia, plus a brief history of his life. Nearby is the **Tam o' Shanter Experience**, a building housing an audio-visual theatre telling the story of *Tam o' Shanter*, a funny and frightening poem and a cautionary tale of the consequences of alcoholic over-indulgence. There's also a well-stocked gift shop and a restaurant.

Across the road are the ruins of **Alloway Kirk**, where Robert Burns' father, William, is buried. This was the setting for the famous scene in *Tam o' Shanter* when Tam stumbles across a wild orgy of witches, warlocks and demons. When he gets carried away watching one particularly winsome witch, Nannie, and screams out his encouragement, the ghouls give chase and Tam and his mare, Meg, narrowly escape, minus Meg's tail, across the **Brig o' Doon**, the 13th-century humpbacked bridge which still stands nearby, spanning the River Doon. Overlooking the bridge is the **Burns Monument**, a Neoclassical temple which houses a display.

Culzean Castle and Country Park

ⓘ *Castle Easter-Oct daily 1100-1700 (last admission 1630); Visitor centre open Easter-Oct daily 1030-1730. Country Park open all year daily 0900-sunset. Castle and park £9, concession £6.50; park only £5, concession £3.75. Guided tours of castle daily at 1530, also at 1100 in Jul and Aug; tours of grounds Apr-Jun daily at 1430, Jul-Aug daily at 1100 and 1430, Sep 1430. T01655-884455. Accommodation is available (L) in six double bedrooms on the top floor. There's also a top-class, and very expensive, restaurant for residents only.*

Twelve miles south of Ayr is Culzean (pronounced 'cullane'), one of Scotland's great castles and the National Trust for Scotland's most visited property. It is one of Ayrshire's few non-Burnsian attractions and well worth a detour if you're in the vicinity. Culzean enjoys a magnificent setting, perched high on a clifftop above a rocky shore and surrounded by 563 acres of country park. The scale of the house and the country park is overwhelming and you should allow more than a few hours to do it justice.

Culzean was designed by Robert Adam and built in 1772-90 for David Kennedy, 10th Earl of Cassilis, as a replacement for the original 15th-century castle. The grand exterior gives no hint of the almost overweening opulence inside. Adam's customary meticulous attention to detail and love of classical embellishment reaches its zenith here. The magnificent oval staircase is regarded as one of his greatest achievements, and the perfect symmetry of the circular saloon is a deliberate counter-balance to the seascapes on view from the windows. The castle contains a collection of paintings and 18th-century furniture and an armoury, and there's an Eisenhower Room, which celebrates the former US President's military career and his association with Culzean. He stayed several times as a guest of the Kennedys, and the top floor was given to him by the erstwhile owners.

The vast **country park** is also well worth exploring and was Scotland's first, created in 1969. It features a network of woodland paths, clifftop trails and the shoreline below, formal gardens, the ice house, pagoda and the beautiful Swan Pond. There's also a walled garden with a Victorian vinery. The best place to start is the **visitor centre** housed in the Home Farm buildings, with a café, shop and exhibits. Here you can pick up free leaflets and maps to help you find your way around, or you can take a guided tour.

Kirkoswald and Crossraguel Abbey

A few miles inland from Culzean, on the A77, in the tiny village of Kirkoswald, is the refurbished **Souter Johnnie's Cottage** ⓘ *Apr-Sep daily 1130-1700; also weekends in Oct 1130-1700, £2.50, concessions £1.70, T01655-760603. There's an hourly bus service between Ayr and Girvan which stops in Kirkoswald,* which was the home of John Davidson, village souter (shoemaker), who was the original Souter Johnnie of Robert Burns' *Tam o' Shanter*. Life-sized stone figures of the souter, Tam himself, the innkeeper and his wife are in the restored ale-house in the garden, and there are Burns' relics in the cottage. Two miles south of **Maybole** on the A77 are the ruins of **Crossraguel Abbey** ⓘ *T01655-883113, Apr-Sep daily 0930-1830. £2.20, concession £1.60,* a Clunaic establishment founded in the 13th century by the Earl of Carrick, and much rebuilt during the next three centuries. The remarkably complete remains include the church, cloister, chapter house and much of the domestic premises. About five miles northwest of Maybole on the A719 coastal road to Ayr, you'll pass a curious local phenomenon known as the **Electric Brae**. Because of an optical illusion, it appears that you're travelling uphill rather than down.

Largs and Great Cumbrae

The most attractive town on the North Ayrshire coast is the resort of Largs, backed by high wooded hills and facing the island of **Great Cumbrae**, a few miles offshore and reached by ferry from Largs. The town is not only a traditional family holiday centre, but its extensive **marina** is popular with yachties, and the **Sportscotland National Centre** at Inverclyde, T01475-674666, hosts numerous national indoor competitions.

The award-winning **Vikingar!** ⓘ *T01475-689777, www.vikingar.co.uk, Apr-Sep Mon-Fri and Sun 1030-1730, Sat 1230-1530; Oct and Mar Mon-Fri and Sun 1030-1530, Sat 1230-1530; Nov and Feb Sat 1230-1530, Sun 1030-1530. £3.80, children £2.90,* at the north end of the promenade is a multi-media exhibition which fully describes the Viking influence in Scotland, which ended with the Battle of Largs in 1263 (see below). Hidden away in Largs' Old Kirk on Bellman's Close, just off the High Street, is **Skelmorlie Aisle**, ⓘ *Jun-Aug Mon-Fri 1400-1700; keys from museum next door, free,* an absolute gem of Renaissance architecture unique in Scotland.

Only a few minutes from Largs by ferry is the hilly island of **Great Cumbrae**. At only four miles long and a couple of miles wide, it's ideally suited for a day or half-day trip from Largs and is best explored on foot or by bike. Great Cumbrae is a major water sports centre and Millport beach is a popular place for **windsurfing**. The only settlement of any size is **Millport**, which is home to Europe's smallest cathedral, the beautiful **Cathedral of the Isles** ⓘ *daily 1100-1600 except during services*. built in the mid-19th century. About a mile east of town is the **Marine Life Museum** ⓘ *T01475-530581, Mon-Fri 0930-1215 and 1400-1645; Jul-Sep also Sat. £1.50, £0.75 children*, part of Glasgow University Marine Biology department, which contains an excellent aquarium. The nicest parts of the island are away from Millport and are best explored by bike. The 14-mile main road runs right round the edge of the island, or there's a narrow Inner Circle Road which passes **The Glaidstone** (417 ft), the highest point on the island. More information on these cycle routes is available from the TIC.

Sleeping

Ayr *p706*

There are numerous comfortable guesthouses and B&Bs in the Victorian new town, in the streets and squares between Alloway Pl and the Esplanade, especially along Queens Terr.

L **Fairfield House Hotel**, 12 Fairfield Rd, T01292-267461, www.fairfieldhotel.co.uk. 45 rooms. Near the seafront, luxury facilities and excellent restaurant and conservatory brasserie.

L **Turnberry Hotel**, 5 miles north of Girvan, T01655-331000, www.turnberry.co.uk, one of the most luxurious and prestigious hotel in the country, overlooking the world-famous gold course.

A **Ivy House**, Alloway, T01292-442336, www.theivyhouse.uk.com. 5 rooms. This comfortable country house is convenient for the Burns Trail and has a good restaurant. Another high-class hotel is the

Largs and Great Cumbrae *p707*

A **Brisbane House Hotel**, on the seafront promenade, T01475-687200, www.maksu-group.co.uk. Comfortable and offers very fine Scottish cuisine at mid-range prices.

Eating

Ayr *p706*

£££ **Fouters**, 2a Academy St, T01292-261391. This bistro/restaurant in a converted bank basement opposite the town hall offers superb French-influenced cuisine using the very best of local fish, seafood, game and beef.

££ **Tudor Restaurant**, 8 Beresford Terr, T01292-261404. More of a café really and serves great home-cooked meals and high teas. Mon-Sat 0900-2000, Sun 1200-2000.

Largs and Great Cumbrae *p707*

£££ **Brisbane House Hotel** (see Sleeping) is the best place in town for a full-blown meal.

££ **Nardini's**, on the promenade, T01475-674555. This Italian café is reckoned to be the best in Scotland. The ice cream is a magical experience. Also good Italian food and coffee.

£ **Ritz Café** has been serving great ice cream, chips and cappuccino for almost a century.

Activities and tours

Horse racing

Ayr Racecourse is at 2 Whitletts Rd, T01292-264179, www.ayr-racecourse.co.uk. The premier racecourse in Scotland, holding the Scottish Grand National in mid-Apr.

Transport

There are several daily **trains** to and from **Ayr** and **Stranraer**. There's a **bus** service (No 923) between **Glasgow** and **Stranraer** which passes through Ayr. **Ferries** leave **Largs** every 15 mins during the summer and every 30 mins in winter for the 10-min sailing to the slip on the northeast shore. **Buses** meet the ferry for the 4-mile trip to **Millport**. The return fare is £3.15 per person and £13.35 per car, or £3.60 and £15.70 respectively at peak times. Bikes cost £2 return. For more information, contact CalMac, T08705-650000, or at Largs pier, T674134.

Directory

Bike hire In Millport at Mapes & Son, 3-5 Guildford St, T530444, for £4 per day.

Internet Carnegie Library, 12 Main St, Ayr, T01292-286385, jcastle@lib.south.ayrshire.gov.uk

Glasgow

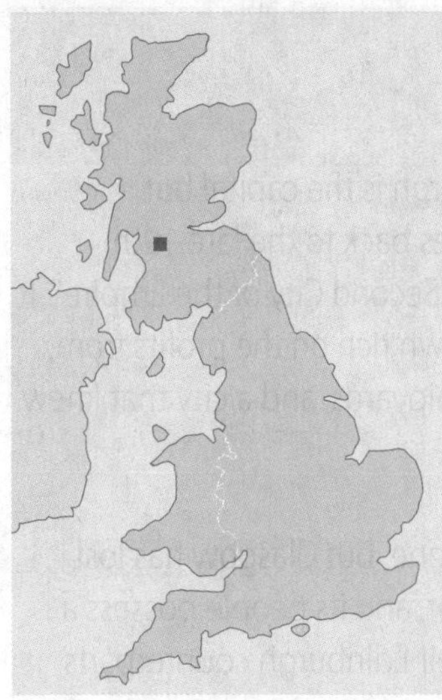

Introduction

There's an old saying that Edinburgh is the capital but Glasgow has the capital. This dates back to the late 19th century, when Glasgow was the "Second City of the Empire". It was a thriving, cultivated city grown rich on the profits from its cotton mills, coal mines and shipyards, and a city that knew how to flaunt its wealth.

The heavy industries have long gone, but Glasgow has lost none of its energy and excitement, and its people possess a style and swagger that makes their Edinburgh counterparts look staid and stuffy by comparison. Just take a stroll round the revived Merchant City or along Byres Road in the West End, and sit in one the countless stylish bars and restaurants, and you'll witness a degree of posing that is Continental in its fervency. The licensing laws may not be Continental but they're more liberal than they are in London and the atmosphere is infused with those vital Glasgow ingredients missing from so many large British cities – warmth and humour. Glasgow is without doubt the friendliest of Britain's large cities. Perhaps that's because it doesn't feel British. Glasgow is often described as European in character; for the remarkable diversity of its architecture, for the accessibility of its art, and for the optimism and openness of its people. It is also compared with North America; for its gridiron street system and for the wisecracking of its streetwise citizens.

★ Don't miss...

1. See an amazing show at the world-renowned **Citizens' Theatre**, page 734.
2. Find out all about the city's fascinating history through the eyes of its people at the **People's Palace**, page 717.
3. Take a tour round the **School of Art**, Charles Rennie Mackintosh's Art Nouveau masterpiece, page 719.
4. Wander round the **Barras** market listening to the famous Glasgow East End patter and maybe you'll unearth a hidden treasure, page 717.
5. Experience the unique atmosphere of an **'Old Firm'** game, the world's most competitive football match, page 735.
6. Get your freak on at the **Arches**, home to some of Glasgow's best club nights, page 731.

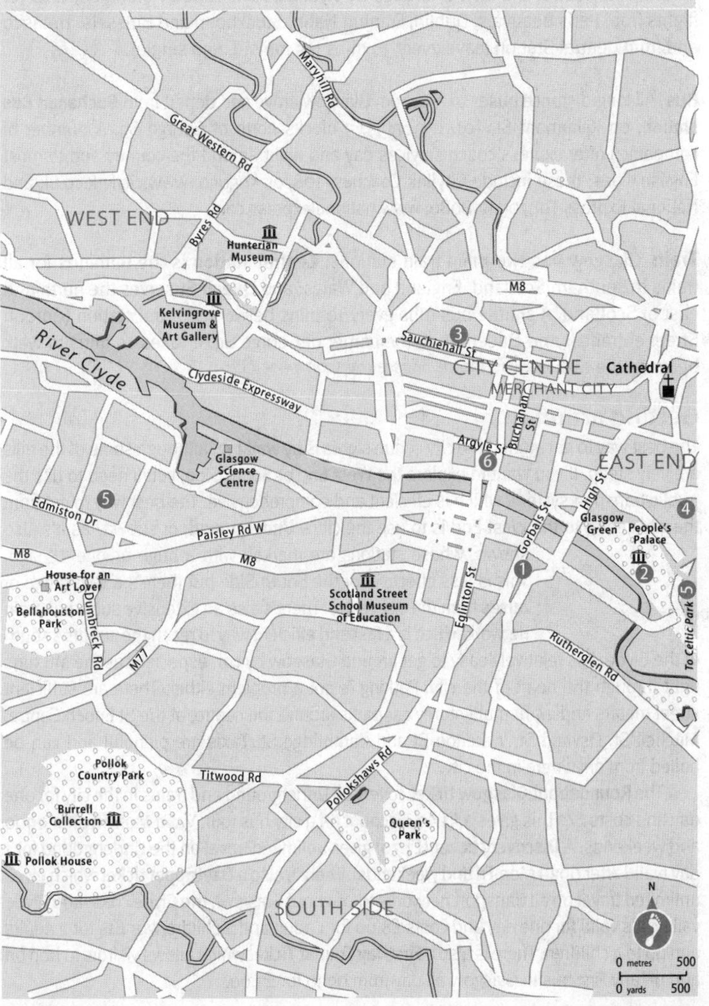

Ins and outs

Getting there

Air Glasgow International airport, T0141-8871111, www.baa.co.uk/glasgow is 8 miles west of the city, at junction 28 on the M8. It handles domestic and international flights. Terminal facilities include car hire, bank ATMs, currency exchange, left luggage, tourist information (T0141-8484440) and shops, restaurants and bars. There's also a **Travel Centre** in the UK Arrivals concourse, T0141-8484330 (open daily 0800-2200 in summer and till 1800 in winter) and a Thomas Cook Hotel and Travel Reservations desk in the International Arrivals concourse, T0141-8877220. To get into town take a Glasgow Airport Link bus from outside Arrivals. They leave every 10-15 mins to Buchanan bus station, with drop-off points at Central and Queen St train stations; 25-30 mins, £3.30 single, £5 return. Tickets can be bought from the driver. Buses to the airport leave from Buchanan St bus station and stop outside the main TIC (see below). A taxi from the airport to the city centre costs around £16.50. **Glasgow Prestwick**, T01292-511000, www.gpia.co.uk, is 30 miles southwest of the city. It is used by **Ryanair** from London Stansted, also for flights from Paris Beauvais, Dublin, Franfurt Hahn, Stockholm and Brussels. Trains to and from Central Station leave every 30 mins (45 mins; £2.50 single).

Bus All long-distance buses to and from Glasgow arrive and depart from **Buchanan Bus station**, on Killermont St, T0141-3327133, 3 blocks north of George Sq. A number of companies offer express coach services day and night around the country and to most English cities; these include **Citylink Coaches**, T08705-505050, www.citylink.co.uk and **National Express** T08705-808080, www.nationalexpress.com.

Train Glasgow has two main train stations: **Central station** is the terminus for all trains to southern Scotland, England and Wales; and **Queen St** serves the north and east of Scotland. A shuttle bus runs every 10 mins between Central station (Gordon Street entrance) and Queen St, at the corner of George Sq. It takes 10 mins to walk between the two. *For further details, see Transport, page 735.*

Getting around

The best way to get around the city centre sights is by **walking**, although some of the hills are very steep. If you want to explore the West End or South Side, you'll need to use the public transport system, which is efficient and comprehensive. The best way to get from the city centre to the West End is to use the city's **Underground**, or subway as it's also known, whose stations are marked with a huge orange 'U' sign. This is less effective for the South Side but there's a vast range of **buses** from the city centre. There's also an extensive suburban train network which is a fast and efficient way to reach the suburbs south of the Clyde. It is relatively easy to get around Glasgow by **car**, especially as the M8 runs right through the heart of the city. Parking is not a problem either. There are sufficient street meters and 24-hr multi-storey car parks around the centre, at the St Enoch Centre, Mitchell St, Oswald St, Waterloo St and Cambridge St. **Taxis** are plentiful and can be hailed from anywhere in the city.

Further details available from the Strath clyde Travel Centres (see below)

The **Roundabout Glasgow ticket** covers all Underground and trains in the city for one day and costs £4. This gives a £1.50 discount on a city bus tour. Valid Mon-Fri after 0900 and weekends. A **Discovery ticket** (£1.70) gives unlimited travel on the Underground for 1 day (valid after 0930 Mon-Fri and weekends). There's also a **Daytripper ticket** which gives unlimited travel on all transport networks throughout Glasgow, the Clyde coast and Clyde valley. It's valid for one day and costs £8.00 for 1 adult and 2 children, or £14 for 2 adults and up to 4 children. There is also a **FirstDay Tourist Ticket** which allows visitors to hop on and off any First bus in Glasgow all day from 0930 for £3.00.

Information

Tourist Information Centre ⓘ *11 George Sq, T0141-2044400, www.seeglasgow.com, May daily 0900-1800, Jun and Sep daily 0900-1900, Jul and Aug daily 0900-2000, Oct-Apr Mon-Sat 0900-1800.* They provide a wide selection of maps and leaflets and a free accommodation booking service. You can also buy travel passes, theatre tickets, arrange car rental and exchange currency at their bureau de change.

South of George Sq, in front of the giant St Enoch Centre, is the **Strathclyde Travel Centre** ⓘ *T0141-2264826, open Mon-Sat 0830-1730.* They can provide maps, leaflets and timetables. Their free Visitor's Transport Guide includes a particularly useful map of the city. There are other travel information centres at **Buchanan Bus station** ⓘ T0141-3327133, open Mon-Sat 0630-2230, Sun 0700-2230, **Hillhead Underground Station** ⓘ *Byres Rd, T0141-3333673, open Mon 0800-1730, Tue-Sat 0830-1730*, and at **Glasgow airport** (see page 712).

Sights →Colour map 5

To the east of George Square is the **Merchant City**, where the Palladian mansions of the Tobacco Lords have been cleaned up and reclaimed by the professional classes as a fashionable place to eat, drink and play. Further east, in almost surreal contrast, is the **East End**, a traditional working-class stronghold, and to the north is the oldest part of Glasgow, around the medieval **cathedral**.

West of George Square is **Buchanan Street**, one of the city's principal shopping thoroughfares, along with **Sauchiehall Street**, at its northern end, and the more downmarket **Argyle Street**, at the southern end. From here the streets rise towards **Blythswood Square**, a much quieter area of elegant late Georgian buildings filled with office workers. Beyond **Charing Cross**, across the ugly scar of the M8, is the city's **West End**, an area of grand Victorian townhouses and sweeping terraces and home of some of the city's best **museums**.

On the city's **South Side**, across the River Clyde, is **Pollok Country Park**, home of two of Glasgow's finest museums, the **Burrell Collection** and **Pollok House**. The **River Clyde** itself has been added to the list of visitor attractions. The **Clydeside Walkway**, running from Victoria Bridge in the east to the River Kelvin in the west, is an attempt to direct Glasgow's great river towards a post-industrial future of leisure and tourism.

Perhaps not surprisingly, given the origins of its name, Glasgow boasts quite a few green spaces – more per head of population than any other city in Europe. There are more than 70 parks in all, from **Glasgow Green** in the East End to **Kelvingrove Park** in the West End, and **Queen's Park** and **Pollok Country Park**, both in the South Side.

City centre

George Square and around

The heart of modern Glasgow is George Square, which makes the obvious starting point for a tour of the city centre, as the **Tourist Information Centre** is located here, on the south side. Amongst the many statues which adorn the square are those of Queen Victoria, Prince Albert, Sir Walter Scott, Robert Burns, Sir Robert Peel and James Watt. The square was named after George 111 and laid out in 1781. The square is surrounded by fine Victorian buildings, most notable of which is the grandiose **City Chambers** ⓘ *T0141-2872000, free guided tours of the City Chambers, Mon-Fri at 1030 and 1430*, which fills the east side, a wonderful testament to the optimism and aspiration of Victorian Glasgow. It was designed in Italian Renaissance style by William Young and the interior is even more impressive than its façade. The imposing arcaded marble entrance hall is decorated with elaborate mosaics and a marble staircase leads up to a great banqueting hall with a wonderful arched ceiling, leaded glass windows and paintings depicting scenes from the city's history. One wall is covered by a series of murals by the Glasgow Boys.

Just to the south of George Square, facing the west end of Ingram Street, is **Royal Exchange Square**, which is almost completely filled by the **Gallery of Modern Art (GOMA)** ⓘ *T0141-2291996, www.glasgow.gov.uk, Mon-Thu and Sat 1000-1700, Fri and Sun 1100-1700, free*, one of the city's newest, and its most controversial, art venues, drawing

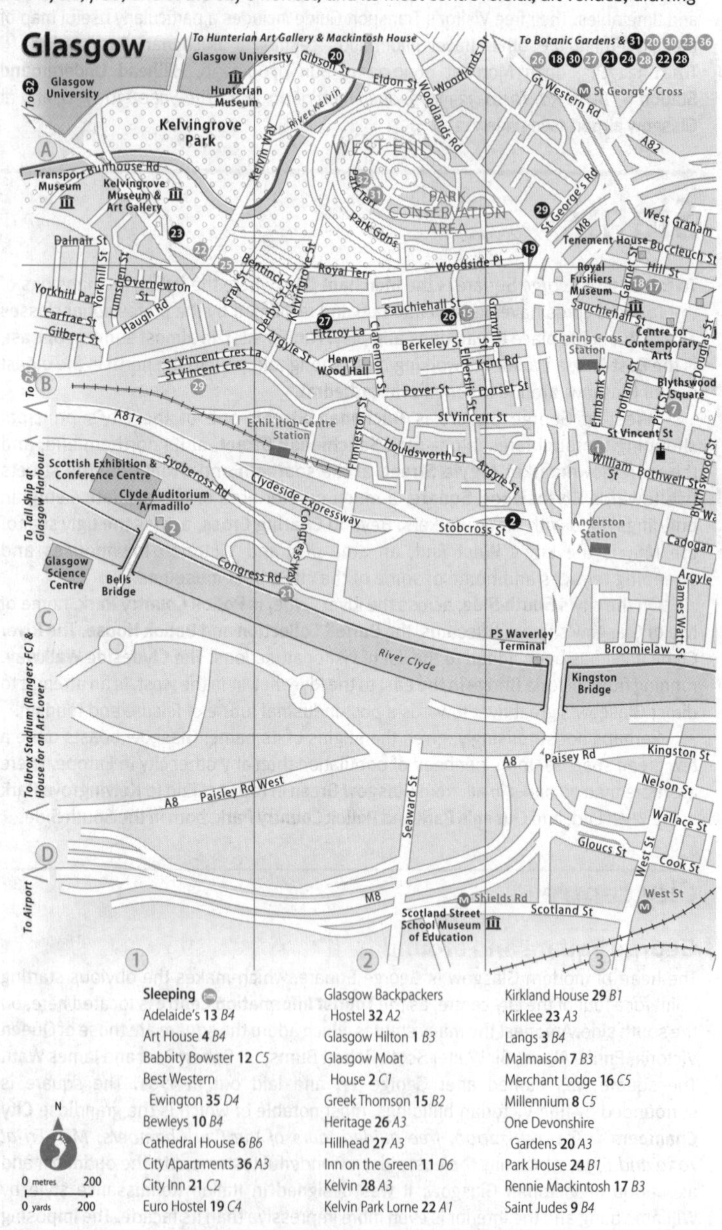

the ire of many a critic for its unashamed eclecticism and populism. The gallery features contemporary works from artists worldwide over three themed levels: the **Earth Gallery** on the ground floor; the **Water Gallery**; and the **Air Gallery**. It's an innovative art space, making excellent use of the original interior. The works you can see are varied and include powerful paintings by Peter Howson, the Imperial War Museum's war artist in Bosnia; photographs by Henri Cartier-Bresson, and Beryl Cook's jolly work 'By the Clyde'.

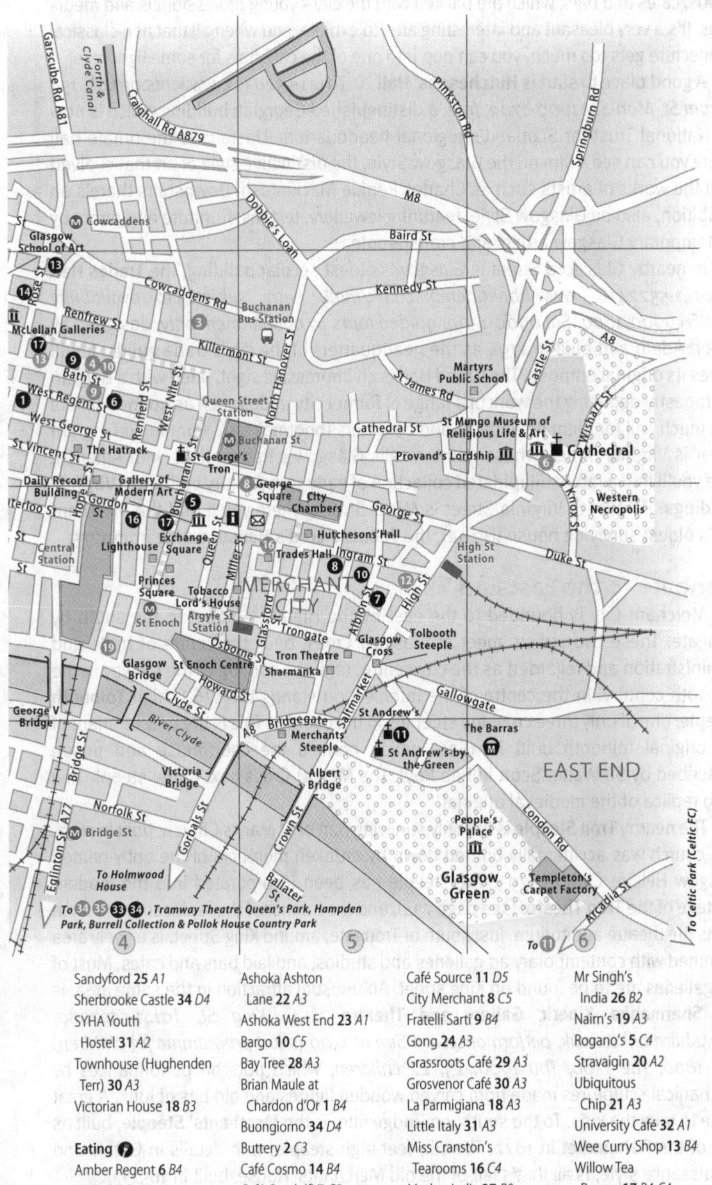

Sandyford **25** *A1*
Sherbrooke Castle **34** *D4*
SYHA Youth Hostel **31** *A2*
Townhouse (Hughenden Terr) **30** *A3*
Victorian House **18** *B3*

Eating
Amber Regent **6** *B4*
Arigo **33** *D4*
Ashoka Ashton Lane **22** *A3*
Ashoka West End **23** *A1*
Bargo **10** *C5*
Bay Tree **28** *A3*
Brian Maule at Chardon d'Or **1** *B4*
Buongiorno **34** *D4*
Buttery **2** *C3*
Café Cosmo **14** *B4*
Café Gandolfi **7** *C5*
Café Source **11** *D5*
City Merchant **8** *C5*
Fratelli Sarti **9** *B4*
Gong **24** *A3*
Grassroots Café **29** *A3*
Grosvenor Café **30** *A3*
La Parmigiana **18** *A3*
Little Italy **31** *A3*
Miss Cranston's Tearooms **16** *C4*
Mother India **27** *B2*
Mr Singh's India **26** *B2*
Nairn's **19** *A3*
Rogano's **5** *C4*
Stravaigin **20** *A2*
Ubiquitous Chip **21** *A3*
University Café **32** *A1*
Wee Curry Shop **13** *B4*
Willow Tea Rooms **17** *B4, C4*

The Merchant City

The grid-plan of streets to the east of George Square as far as the High Street form the Merchant City, where the Tobacco Lords built their magnificent Palladian mansions and made Glasgow the most important tobacco trading city in Europe. This part of the city was once a bustling trade centre and money has been poured into the restoration of its 18th century warehouses and homes in an attempt to revitalise and regenerate the city's old historic core. Though many of the buildings are little more than façades, the investment has succeeded in attracting expensive designer clothes shops and a plethora of stylish bistros, cafés and bars, which are packed with the city's young professionals and media types. It's a very pleasant and interesting area to explore, and when all that neo-classical architecture gets too much, you can pop into one of the café-bars for some light relief.

A good place to start is **Hutchesons' Hall** ⓘ *T0141-5528391, www.nts.org.uk, 158 Ingram St, Mon-Sat 1000-1700, free*, a distinguished Georgian building which is now the National Trust for Scotland's regional headquarters. Upstairs is the ornate hall where you can see a film on the Glasgow Style, the distinctive style of art that evolved from the works of artists such as Charles Rennie Mackintosh. Downstairs there's an exhibition, also on Glasgow Style, featuring jewellery, textiles, furniture and prints by contemporary Glasgow artists and craftspeople.

In nearby Glassford Street is Glasgow's oldest secular building, the **Trades Hall** ⓘ *T0141-5522418, www.bbnet.demon.co.uk/thall, entry subject to availability Mon-Fri 0900-1800, Sat 0900-1300, guided tours by appointment only*, designed by Robert Adam and built in 1794 as the headquarters of the city's trade guilds. It still serves its original purpose. The Grand Hall is an impressive sight, lined with a Belgian silk tapestry depicting the work of a range of former city trades such as bonnetmakers (not much call for them nowadays) and cordiners (bootmakers). Running off Ingram Street is Virginia Street, whose name recalls Glasgow's trading links with America. Here you'll find a rather dilapidated collection of early 19th century buildings, **Virginia Buildings**. Parallel to Virginia Street is Miller Street, where you'll find the Merchant City's oldest surviving house (No 42), the **Tobacco Lord's House**, dating from 1775.

Trongate to the East End

The Merchant City is bounded to the east by the High Street and to the south by Trongate. These two streets meet at Glasgow Cross, once the centre of trade and administration and regarded as the city centre, until the coming of the railway in the mid-19th century. In the centre of the intersection stands the 126 ft-high **Tolbooth Steeple**, one of only three crowned steeples in the country. This is the only remnant of the original tolbooth built in 1626, which housed the courthouse and prison (described by Sir Walter Scott in Rob Roy). The **Mercat Cross** next to the steeple is a 1929 replica of the medieval original.

The nearby **Tron Steeple** is the only surviving part of St Mary's Church, built in 1637. This church was accidentally burned down by drunken members of the aptly-named Glasgow Hellfire Club in 1793. The steeple has been incorporated into the modern frontage of the **Tron Theatre** (see page 734), and the interior of the replacement church forms the theatre auditorium. Just south of Trongate, around King Street, is a lively area crammed with contemporary art galleries and studios, and laid bars and cafes. Most of the galleries are to be found on King street. An unusual attraction in the same area, is the **Sharmanka Kinetic Gallery and Theatre** ⓘ *14 King St, T0141-5527080, www.sharmanka.co.uk, performances on Sun at 1500 (short programme for children) and 1800, Tue 1300, Thu 1900, £3, £2 children*, which puts on performances by mechanical sculptures made from carved wooden figures and old bits of junk. A great place to take the kids. To the south, on Bridgegate, is the **Merchants' Steeple**, built as part of the **Fishmarket** in 1872. The 164 feet-high steeple, with details in Gothic and Renaissance style, is all that's left of the old Merchants' House, built in 1651-59.

East of Glasgow Cross, Gallowgate and London Road lead into the city's **East End**, only a stone's throw from the Merchant City. It may look shabby and rundown by comparison but this is where you can sample a slice of pure Glasgow, especially in **The Barras** (The Barrows), ⓘ *every weekend, 1000-1700*, and the entrance is marked by the huge red gates on Gallowgate, a huge market spread out around the streets and alleys south of Gallowgate. A lot of it's junk (dodgy computer games, pirate videos etc) but there are plenty of bargains to be found and there's every chance of unearthing some valuable antique. The real attraction, though, is the unique atmosphere of the place and wit and repartee of the market traders.

Glasgow Green and People's Palace

South of The Barras is the wide expanse of Glasgow Green, said to be the oldest public park in Britain. It has been common land since at least medieval times and Glaswegians still have the right to dry their washing here. The Green has always been dear to the people of Glasgow and some of the city's major political demonstrators have held meetings here, including the Chartists in the 1830s and Scottish republican campaigners in the 1920s. There are various **monuments** dotted around the park, including a 144 feet-high monument to Lord Nelson, erected in 1806, and one to James Watt. Just to the north of the Green are two of the city's oldest churches, dating from the mid-18th century. In St Andrew's Square is **St Andrew's Church**, one of the finest classical churches in Britain. Sadly neglected for many years, it has now been restored to its Georgian splendour. It no longer functions as a church but has been cleverly converted to house a sleek café (Café Source) downstairs and a Scottish music venue upstairs. You can go upstairs and see the stunning original stained glass windows and intricate plaster work. Concerts and ceilidhs are staged throughout the year – tickets available from *Café Source*, T0141-5486020.

On the edge of the green, to the east of the People's Palace (see below), is **Templeton's Carpet Factory**, a bizarre but beautiful structure designed in 1889 by William Leiper in imitation of the Doges' Palace in Venice. Once described as the 'world's finest examples of decorative brickwork, it's Britain's best example of polychromatic decoration (in other words, very colourful). The building is now used as a business centre.

On the northern end of the green, approached from London Road, is the **People's Palace** ⓘ *T0141-5540223, Mon-Thu and Sat 1000-1700, Fri and Sun 1100-1700, free*, which gives a real insight into the social and industrial life of this great city from the mid-18th century to the present day. Its galleries display a wealth of artefacts, photographs, cartoons and drawings, and a series of films, music and people's anecdotes. A visit to the People's Palace should be on everyone's itinerary, particularly if you're interested in scratching beneath the city's surface and getting to know it better. Equally recommended is the **Winter Gardens**, a huge conservatory at the rear of the museum, where you can enjoy a cup of tea or coffee and a snack in tropical surroundings.

The Cathedral area

At the top of the High Street stand the two oldest buildings in the city, **Glasgow Cathedral** and **Provand's Lordship** ⓘ *T0141-5526891, www.historic-scotland.gov.uk. Apr-Sep Mon-Sat 0930-1800, Sun 1400-1700, Oct-Mar Mon-Sat 0930-1600, Sun 1400-1600, free*. The rather severe-looking early Gothic structure is the only complete medieval cathedral on the Scottish mainland. It was built on the site of St Mungo's original church, established in AD 543, though this has been a place of Christian worship since it was blessed for burial in AD 397 by St Ninian, the earliest missionary recorded in Scottish history. Most of the building was completed in the 13th century though parts were built a century earlier by Bishop Jocelyn. The choir and crypt were

Glasgow city centre's trademark grid-layout inspired town planners in the USA.

added a century later and the building was completed at the end of the 15th century by Robert Blacader, the first Bishop of Glasgow.

Behind the cathedral looms the **Western Necropolis**, a vast burial ground overlooking the city from the top of a high ridge. It's the ideal vantage point from which to appreciate the cathedral in all its Gothic splendour and many of the tombs are wonderfully-ornate. Interred here are the great and the good (and not so good) of Victorian Glasgow, – there was no discrimination; anyone could be buried here – as long as they could afford it.

In front of the cathedral is the weetabix-coloured **St Mungo Museum of Religious Life and Art**, ⓘ *T0141-5532557, Mon-Thu and Sat 1000-1700, Fri and Sun 1100-1700, free*, which features a series of displays of arts and artefacts representing the six major world religions, as well as a Japanese Zen garden in the courtyard outside – great for a few moments of quiet contemplation. Highlights include Salvador Dalí's astounding painting Christ of St John of the Cross, purchased by the city from the artist in 1951. There's also a bookshop and café serving hot meals, snacks and drinks. Across the street the **Provand's Lorship** ⓘ *same phone number and opening hours as above*, the oldest remaining house in Glasgow, built in 1471 as part of a refuge for the city's poor and extended in 1670. Now it's a museum devoted mainly to medieval furniture and various domestic items. In the grounds is a specially created medieval garden.

Buchanan Street to Charing Cross

Glasgow's commercial heart is the area between Buchanan Square and the M8 to the west. It is home to the city's main shopping streets and arcades, as well as its businesses and financial institutions and also where you'll find many of its architectural treasures. A short walk north on Buchanan Street is **Princes Square**, one of the most stylish and imaginative shopping malls in Britain. Even if you're not buying or looking, it's worth going in to admire this beautifully-ornate Art Nouveau creation. A little further north, on the opposite side of the street, is a branch of the famous **Willow Tea Rooms** (see below) with replicas of Mackintosh designs.

Lovers of architecture should head west into Gordon Street and then south (left) into Mitchell Street, where you'll find **The Lighthouse** ⓘ *T0141-2216362. Mon, Wed, Fri and Sat 1030-1730, Tues 1100-1700, Thurs 1030-1700, Sun 1200-1700, £2.50, £2 concessions*. It was designed by the ubiquitous Charles Rennie Mackintosh in 1893 to house the offices of the Glasgow Herald. The Herald vacated the premises in 1980 and it lay empty, until its recent transformation into **Scotland's Centre for Architecture, Design and the City**, a permanent legacy of the Glasgow's role as UK City of Architecture and Design in 1999. This stunning 21st century building contains the **Mackintosh Interpretation and Review Gallery**, on the third floor, which features original designs and information on the life and work of the great architect. From this gallery you can reach the Mackintosh Viewing Tower. Reached by a 135 step spiral staircase, it was part of the original building and offers unbeatable, panoramic views of the city. There's also a shop and café on the fifth floor and another café on the ground floor.

Further north on Buchanan Street, close to Buchanan Street Underground, are two more interesting buildings: **St George's Tron Church**, designed in 1808 by William Stark and the oldest church in the city centre, and the **Athenaeum**, designed in 1886 by JJ Burnet and showing early signs of his later modernism. Running west from George Square, between Argyle Street and Sauchiehall Street, is St Vincent Street, where you'll find two of the city's extraordinary buildings. **The Hatrack**, at No 142, was designed in 1902 by James Salmon Jnr. It's a very tall, narrow building, like many in the city centre, with a fantastically-detailed roof which looks like an old hat stand.

Further along St Vincent Street, near the intersection with Pitt Street, is one of the jewels in Glasgow's architectural crown, the **St Vincent Street Church**, designed in 1859 by Alexander 'Greek' Thomson, the city's "unknown genius" of architecture. Much of his work was destroyed in the 1960s and this is his only intact Romantic Classical church, now on the World Monument Fund's list of the 100 most endangered sites. The Presbyterian church is fronted by Ionic columns like those of a Greek temple and the church also shows Egyptian and Assyrian decoration. The main tower is Grecian in style while the dome could have come straight out of India during the Raj.

On Sauchiehall Street is Charles Rennie Mackintosh's wonderful **Willow Tea Rooms**, ⓘ *The tea rooms are open from 0930 to 1630* (see also Cafés), at No 217, above Henderson's the Jewellers. This is a faithful reconstruction on the site of the original 1903 tea room, designed by CRM for his patron Miss Kate Cranston, who already ran three of the city's most fashionable tea rooms, in Argyle Street, Buchanan Street and Ingram Street. Mackintosh had already worked with Miss Cranston on her other tea rooms, but Sauchiehall Street was their tour de force. Sauchiehall means "alley of the willows" and this theme was reflected not only in the name, but throughout the interior. Mackintosh was allowed free rein to design the fixtures and fittings; everything, in fact, right down to the teaspoons. Visitors today can relive the splendour of the original tea rooms as they relax in the distinctive high-backed chairs with a cup of tea, brought to them by the specially selected high-backed waitresses.

A few yards west, on the opposite side of the street, are the **McLellan Galleries** ⓘ *T0141-5654137, www.glasgowmuseums.com, open Mon-Thur & Sat 1000-17000; Fri and Sun 1100-1700, free,* another fine example of classical architecture. While Kelvingrove Art Gallery and Museum is closed for refurbishment (until late 2005) these galleries are hosting a display of the most important artworks from the collection. Further down the street, on the same side, is the **Centre for Contemporary Arts (CCA)** ⓘ *T0141-3327521. www.cca-glasgow.com, centre Mon-Sat 0900-2400; Sun 1200-1900, galleries Mon-Sat 1100-1800, Sun 1200-1700, free,* housed in the Grecian Buildings, a former commercial warehouse designed by Alexander 'Greek' Thomson in 1867-68. The centre presents a changing programme of contemporary theatre, dance and other cultural events. It also has two excellent café-bars.

Glasgow School of Art

ⓘ *T0141-3534526, www.gsa.ac.uk. Tour times Oct-Jun Mon-Fri at 1100 and 1400, Sat 1030 and 1130; Jul-Sep Mon-Fri 1100 and 1400, Sat/Sun 1030, 1130 and 1300. Closed late Jun for graduation and from Christmas through to New Year. £5, £3 students. Booking is advised.*

A very steep walk up from Sauchiehall Street, at 167 Renfrew Street, is the Glasgow School of Art, one of the city's most important buildings, and one of the most prestigious Art Schools in the country. The building was designed by Charles Rennie Mackintosh, after his proposal won a competition set to find a design for the school, in 1896.

The school is regarded as Mackintosh's architectural masterpiece and gives full expression to his architectural ideals. It is rooted in tradition, with a thoroughly modern-looking exterior of extreme austerity, and there are medieval, castle-like features such as turrets and curving stair wells. The interior is both spacious and utilitarian and shows perfectly his desire to create a unified and harmonious working environment for both students and teachers. The studio walls and high ceilings are painted white, with huge windows allowing light to pour into the spaces. The corridors and staircases are decorated with glazed coloured tiles to help guide students and staff around the massive building. In the spectacular two-storey library Mackintosh also designed the light fittings, bookcases and the oak furniture. There are symbols of nature everywhere throughout the building, used to inspire the students to produce their own works of art. And who could fail to be inspired in such a stunning environment. Entry to the school is by guided tour only which visits the main rooms containing many of the well-known pieces of furniture and includes the famous library. It is still a working art school, so take note of the annual closing.

Other Mackintosh buildings

Aside from the Mackintosh buildings listed separately, there are a number of his lesser known works scattered around the city centre. These include the **Martyrs' Public School** (1895), at Parson Street, just off the High Street and M8 (open Mon-Sat 1000-1600, Sun 1100-1600, free), the former **Daily Record Building** (1901), at 20-26 Renfield Lane (external viewing only), the **Royal Fusiliers Museum** (c1903), at 518 Sauchiehall Street (ring for opening times, T0141-3320961), **Ruchill Church Hall**, Shakespeare Street (Monday-Friday 1030-1430, closed July/August, free) and the former **Glasgow Society of Lady Artists' Club** (1908), at 5 Blythswood Square (external viewing only). At 870 Garscube Road is **Queen's Cross Church**, ⓘ *T0141-9466600, Mon-Fri 1000-1700, Sun Mar- Oct 1400-1700, £2, £1 concession, buses 21, 61 and 91 from Hope St (west side of Central station), or Underground to St George's Cross and walk 10 mins on Maryhill Rd*, CRM's only church and a fascinating piece of architecture. Beautifully simple, with echoes of the symbolism of his other buildings, it now functions as the headquarters of the Charles Rennie Mackintosh Society (T0141-9466600, www.crmsociety.com).

The Tenement House

ⓘ *T0141-3330183, www.nts.org.uk, Mar-Oct, daily 1300-1700, £3.50, £2.60 concession.*

A few hundred yards northwest of the School of Art, down the other side of the hill, at 145 Buccleuch Street, is the Tenement House, a typical late Victorian tenement flat. This was the home of Miss Agnes Toward, a shorthand typist, for 50 years until she moved out in 1965. It's a fascinating time-capsule of life in the first half of the 20th century and retains most of the original features such as the bed recesses, kitchen range and coal bunker. The whole experience is a little voyeuristic, as the flat includes many of Agnes' personal possessions, and in the parlour the table is set for afternoon tea, lending a spooky atmosphere redolent of the Marie Celeste. On the ground floor is an exhibition on tenement life. The property is owned by the NTS.

The West End

On the other side of the M8 is the West End, an area which contains many of the city's major museums, as well some of its finest examples of Victorian architecture. During the course of the 19th century the West End grew in importance as wealthy merchants moved here, away from the dirt and grime of the industrial city. By the middle of the 19th century the **Park Conservation Area** had been established and was described as one of the finest pieces of architectural planning of the century. Perhaps the most impressive of all the terraces in the conservation area are **Park Quadrant** and **Park Terrace**, with glorious views across **Kelvingrove Park**. Soon after, in 1870, the **university** also moved west, to its present site overlooking Kelvingrove Park, and in 1896 the Glasgow District Subway was extended west. In 1888 the park was used to stage an international exhibition and the profits were used to build the **Kelvingrove Museum and Art Gallery**, which housed the second international exhibition, in 1901. The museum is closed for refurbishment until late 2005. Artworks from the collection are temporarily on display at the McLellan Galleries, Sauchiehall Street (see page 719).

Transport Museum

ⓘ *Mon-Thu and Sat 1000-1700, Fri and Sun 1100-1700, free, T0141-2872720.*

Opposite the Kelvingrove Museum and Art Gallery and behind the **Kelvin Hall**, just off Argyle Street, is the Transport Museum, whose name may lack appeal but which is one of the country's most fascinating museums. There are collections of trams, trains, motor cars, horsedrawn vehicles, bicycles, motorbikes, as well as a whole room dedicated to models of Clyde-built ships. There's also a reconstruction of a 1938 cobbled street, an old Underground station and a cinema showing old films of Glaswegians heading "doon the watter". Something for everyone, as they say in the tourist brochures. A new, larger museum is planned for the future – to be located on the Clyde.

Glasgow University and the Hunterian Museum

ⓘ *T0141-3304221, www.hunterian.gla.ac.uk, Mon-Sat 0930-1700, free.*

The university's roots go back to 1451 when Pope Nicholas V authorised William Turnbull, Bishop of Glasgow to found a seat of learning in the city. At first there was just an Arts faculty and lectures were held in the cathedral crypt and neighbouring monastery. In the 17th century the university moved to new premises in the High Street, but these became too small and, in 1870, it moved to its present site, on Gilmorehill, overlooking Kelvingrove Park. The Gothic buildings were designed by Sir George Gilbert Scott, though the Lion and Unicorn balustrade on the stone staircase opposite the Principal's Lodging is a relic of the old High Street colleges, as is the stonework of the lodge gateway. Bute Hall, which is now used for graduation and other ceremonies, was added in 1882. The **university chapel** is also worth seeing.

Contained within the university buildings is the **Hunterian Museum**, named after William Hunter (1718-83), a student at the university in the 1730s. His bequest to the university of his collections led to the establishment of the Hunterian Museum in 1807, Scotland's oldest public museum. It has displays of history, archaeology and geology and includes Roman relics from the Antonine Wall and one of the largest coin collections in Britain. Beneath the museum is the **University Visitor Centre**, which features interactive displays on the university and a coffee bar. There's also a **Zoology Museum**, housed in the Graham Kerr Building, a few minutes' walk from the main museum.

Hunterian Art Gallery and Mackintosh House

ⓘ *T0141-3304221, www.hunterian.gla.co.uk, Mon-Sat 0930-1700, Mackintosh House closed daily 1230-1330, free, take buses 44 and 59 from the city centre (Hope St), or the Underground to Hillhead and walk.*

Across the road, at 82 Hillhead Street, is the Hunterian Art Gallery, a modern building containing the more interesting part of Hunter's bequest, the fabulous art collection. The gallery holds an important collection of European paintings including works by Rembrandt, Koninck, Rubens, Pissaro and Rodin, as well as 18th century British portraits by Ramsay and Reynolds. There is also a fine collection of Scottish 19th and 20th century paintings including works by McTaggart, Guthrie and Fergusson. The piece de resistance is the huge collection of works by the American painter, James McNeill Whistler. There are some 70 paintings and a selection of his personal possessions (including his specially made long-handled paintbrushes) on show, making it the largest display of his work outside the USA. Among the works are many of his distinctive full-length portraits and some moody depictions of the Thames.

Attached to the gallery is the **Mackintosh House**, a stunning reconstruction of the main interiors from 78 Southpark Avenue, the Glasgow home of Charles Rennie Mackintosh and his wife, Margaret MacDonald, from 1906 to 1914. A stairway leads to an introductory display containing numerous drawings and designs, including those for his major buildings, furniture and interiors. From there you are led into the cool, soothing rooms, lovingly reconstructed and exquisitely furnished with some 80 original pieces of his furniture. These give the perfect example of just why this innovative designer and architect is so revered. Among the highlights are the Studio Drawing Room, decorated in white and flooded with natural light, and the guest bedroom from Northampton, a later commission, with its bold and dazzling geometric designs.

Botanic Gardens

ⓘ *Gardens open daily 0700 till dusk, free, Kibble Palace and all glasshouses open daily 1000-1645 in summer, 1000-1615 in winter.*

At the top of Byres Road, where it meets the Great Western Road, is the entrance to the Botanic Gardens, a smallish but perfectly formed park where you can lose yourself along the remote paths that follow the wooded banks of the River Kelvin. They were created to provide medical and botanical students at the university with fresh plant material, but soon became a fashionable place to promenade. There are two large hothouses in the park, one of which is the **Kibble Palace**, built as a conservatory for the Clyde Coast home of Glasgow businessman, John Kibble, and then shipped to its present site in 1873. It was once used for public meetings and British Prime Ministers William Gladstone and Benjamin Disraeli both gave their rectorial addresses here when they became Rectors of the University. The domed glasshouse, contains the national collection of tree ferns and temperate plants from around the world.The **main glasshouse** is more attractive, and has 11 sections featuring plants such as cacti, palms, insectivorous plants and palms. Its collections of orchids and begonias are outstanding. The central bed has plants that have been used in the past in Scotland. Look out for Meadowsweet, used for headaches; Coltsfoot used for coughs and chest complaints, and Yellow Flag iris – the leaves of which give a bright green dye and the rhizomes a black dye which were traditionally used in the Harris tweed industry. In the Outer Hebrides the black dye was used for the cloth for the suits worn on Sundays.

South of the Clyde

South of the River Clyde is a part of Glasgow largely unknown to most visiting tourists, except for three of the city's most notable attractions, the **Burrell Collection** and **Pollok House**, both set in the sylvan surrounds of **Pollok Country Park – as well as the sleek new Science Centre on the Clyde.** There are other reasons to venture south of the river, however, not least of these being to see Charles Rennie Mackintosh's **House for an Art Lover** in nearby Bellahouston Park. Further east is another stop on the Mackintosh trail, the **Scotland Street School Museum of Education**. To the south, in Cathcart, is **Holmwood House**, Alexander 'Greek' Thomson's great architectural masterpiece.

After all the years of neglect, it is good to see that Glasgow's newest, most dazzling development is to be found on the Clyde. The £75 million **Glasgow Science Centre** ⓘ *50 Pacific Quay, T0141-4205000, www.gsc.org.uk, Science Mall daily 1000-1800, IMAX Theatre Sun-Wed 1100-1700, Thu-Sat 1000-2030 (hours subject to change), Science Mall £6.95, £4.95 concessions, IMAX or Glasgow Tower £5.95, £4.45 concessions, Arriva buses 23 and 24 go to the Science Centre from Jamaica St.* This enormous complex aims to demystify science, bringing it life with imaginative displays and interactive exhibits covering everything from the human body to the internet. The kids love it – as do their fathers. The heart of the Centre is the Science Mall, with 3 floors of themed exhibits. The 1st floor looks at how we experience the world, the 2nd floor looks at science in action and the 3rd floor looks at how science affects your daily life. You can find anything here from laboratories where you can study your own skin or hair through a microscope, to an infra-red harp which you play with a beam of light. The Glasgow Tower, the tallest free standing building in Scotland at 300ft, has experienced some engineering problems and at the time of writing it's shut. But when it reopens it's worth a look as each of its floors has a theme and takes a serious look at aspects of science, from the basic rules of nature to cloning and genetic modification. At the top there's a viewing cabin and great views over Glasgow and the Clyde. The Centre also contains an IMAX theatre.

Opposite the Science Centre is the **Scottish Exhibition and Conference Centre (SECC)**, built in 1987 on the site of the former Queen's Dock and now the country's premier rock and pop venue. Next door is the controversial **Clyde Auditorium**, known locally as the "Armadillo", which was designed by Sir Norman Foster and built in 1997.

Further west, also on the north bank of the Clyde, is a romantic looking sailing ship, the SS Glenlee – otherwise known as the **Tall Ship at Glasgow Harbour** ⓘ *100 Stobcross Rd, T0800-3281373, www.thetallship.com, Mar-Oct daily 1000-1700, Nov-Feb daily 1100-1600 £4.50, £3.95 concessions.* Launched in 1896, this three masted ship was built on the Clyde and is one of only 5 Clydebuilt sailing ships that remain afloat in the world. She circumnavigated the globe 4 times and carried cargo as varied as coal, grain – and even guano, which was transported from Chile to the European ports of Antwerp and Rotterdam to be used as fertiliser. The ammonia fumes from the guano were so pungent they corroded the lining of sailor's noses and even killed the occasional ship's cat. The Glenlee was saved from the scrapyard in 1992 and has now been restored. Exhibitions on board provide a vivid insight into the daily lives of the sailors and the conditions on board ship in 1896. Further west still, at Braehead, is **Clydebuilt,** at junction 25a (westbound) off the M8 or can be reached on the **Clyde waterbus** ⓘ *T0141-8861013, Mon-Thu, Sat 1000-1800, Sun 1100-1700, £3.50, £1.75 concessions, see page 735,* a museum charting the close relationship between Glasgow and the Clyde. There's an audio-visual presentation on the history of shipbuilding and displays on a whole range of themes related to the river, from the cotton and tobacco trades, to emigration and immigration.

Scotland Street School Museum of Education

ⓘ *T0141-2870500. Mon-Thu and Sat 1000-1700, Fri and Sun 1100-1700. Free. Underground to Shields Rd, or buses 89, 90, 96 and 97 from the city centre.*

Directly opposite Shields Road Underground is another of Charles Rennie Mackintosh's great works, the Scotland Street School, which opened in 1906 and closed in 1979. The entire school has been preserved as a museum of education and is a wonderfully evocative experience. The school has been refurbished and now includes an audio-visual theatre and has computer activities for children. There's a fascinating collection of school memorabilia and reconstructed classrooms from Victorian times up to the 1960s, as well as changing rooms, science room and headmaster's office (straighten your tie and comb your hair before entering). This was the most modern of Mackintosh's buildings and is notable for its semi-cylindrical glass stair towers, the magnificent tiled entrance hall and his customary mastery of the interplay of light and space.

The Burrell Collection

ⓘ *T0141-6497151, www.glasgow.gov.uk, Mon-Thu and Sat 1000-1700, Sun 1100-1700, free. Buses 45, 47 and 57 from the city centre (Union St) pass the park gates on Pollokshaws Rd. From the gates it's a 10-min walk to the gallery, or there's a twice hourly bus service. There are also regular trains from Central station to Pollockshaws West station. A taxi from the city centre costs £6-7.*

Three miles southwest of the city centre is Glasgow's top attraction and a must on any visit, the Burrell Collection, standing in the extensive wooded parklands of Pollok Country Park. The magnificent collection contains some 8,500 art treasures, donated to the city in 1944 by the shipping magnate, William Burrell (1861-1958) who sold his shipping interests in order to devote the remainder of his life to collecting art. He began collecting in the 1880s, and in 1917 bought Hutton Castle near Berwick-on-Tweed to house his collection. There it stayed, even after his bequest to the city, as he stipulated that all the works in his collection be housed in one building in a rural setting – since he was concerned about the possible damage caused by the pollution that then blackened Glasgow. It wasn't until the Clean Air Act of the 1960s and the council's acquisition of

Pollok Park that a suitable site was found and the award-winning gallery could be built – with the £450,000 donated by Burrell. The building opened to the public in 1983.

The collection includes ancient Greek, Roman and Egyptian artefacts, a huge number of dazzling oriental art pieces, and numerous works of medieval and post-medieval European art, including tapestries, silverware, textiles, sculpture and exquisitely-lit stained glass. The tapestries are particularly fine and date from the late 15th and 16th centuries. There's also an impressive array of paintings by Rembrandt, Degas, Pissaro, Bellini and Manet amongst many others. Look out too for Rodin's famous sculpture Thinker which – like many film stars and TV personalities you've only seen in pictures, is smaller than you expect.

The gallery is a stunning work of simplicity and thoughtful design, which allows the visitor to enjoy the vast collection to the full. The large, floor-to-ceiling windows afford sweeping views over the surrounding woodland and allow a flood of natural light to enhance the treasures on view. Some sections of the gallery are reconstructions of rooms from Hutton Castle and incorporated into the structure are carved stone Romanesque doors. There's also a café and restaurant on the lower ground floor.

Pollok House and Country Park

ⓘ *T0141-6166410, www.nts.org.uk. Daily 1000-1700. £5, £3.75 child/concession, Nov-Mar free. Entry to the park is from Pollokshaws Road, or Haggs Road if you're on foot. Car parking is at the Burrell Collection and costs £1.50.*

Also in Pollok Country Park, a 10-minute walk from the Burrell, is **Pollok House**, designed by William Adam and finished in 1752. This was once the home of the Maxwell family, who owned most of southern Glasgow until well into the last century. It contains one of the best collections of Spanish paintings in Britain, including works by Goya, El Greco and Murillo. There are also paintings by William Blake, as well as glass, silverware, porcelain and furniture. The most interesting part of the house are the servants' quarters downstairs, which give you a real insight into life 'below stairs' – with rows of bells waiting to summon servants to any part of the house. There's a good tearoom in the old kitchens. If the weather's fine, the park is worth exploring. There are numerous trails through the woods and meadows and guided walks with the countryside rangers. There are two golf courses within the park grounds, as well as a herd of highland cattle.

House for an Art Lover

ⓘ *T0141-3534770, www.houseforanartlover.co.uk. Apr-Sep Mon-Wed 1000-1600, Thur-Sun 1000-1300; Oct-Mar Sat-Sun 1000-1300; call for weekday access times. £3.50, £2.50 concession. To get there take the Underground to Ibrox station and walk (15 min), or bus 91 from Hope St.*

A short distance north of Pollok Park is Bellahouston Park, site of the most recent addition to the Charles Rennie Mackintosh trail, the House for an Art Lover. Although the building was designed in 1901 as an entry to a competition run by a German design magazine, the brief being to create a lavish country house for an art lover. The interior and exterior had to be a coherent work of art. Building never went ahead during Mackintosh's lifetime and it was not until 1989 that construction began following his original drawings. It was not completed until 1996, when it became a centre for Glasgow School of Art postgraduate students, though rooms are open to the public. Mackintosh worked with his wife on the design of the house and there is distinctive evidence of her influence, especially in the exquisite **Music Room** with its elaborate symbolism, particularly the rose motif, which is used throughout. But though the detail is, as ever, intense, the overall effect is one of space and light. The exterior of the house is equally impressive and totally original.

East of Pollok Park

To the east of Pollok Country Park, by Pollokshaws Road, is **Queen's Park**. It's a pleasant place for a stroll and the views north across the city make it even more enjoyable. Close by, in Mount Florida, is **Hampden Park**, home of Scottish football and now also the home of the new **Scottish National Football Museum** ⓘ *T0141-6166139, www.scottishfootballmuseum.com, Mon-Sat 1000-1700, Sun 1100-1700, £5, £2.50 concession, Tour of the stadium £2.50 (£5 if not visiting museum), regular trains to Mount Florida station from Central station (turn left out of station and head straight downhill till you see the stadium, or buses 5, 12, 31, 37 or 44A*, which describes the history of the game in Scotland. This may strike some as a rather masochistic idea given some of the more infamous and embarrassing episodes, but there have been highs (Wembley '67 and Lisbon '69) as well as lows (Wembley '66 and Argentina '78). The museum is large and includes a huge range of football memorabilia. You can also get a guided tour of Hampden Park.

Holmwood House

ⓘ *T0141-6372129, Apr-31 Oct, daily 1200-1700, but access may be restricted at certain times; phone in advance. £3.50, £2.60 child/concession. Trains every ½ hr to Cathcart from Central station, or take buses 44 and 46 from the city centre to Cathcart bridge, turn left onto Rannon Rd and walk 10 mins to gates.*

South of Queens Park and Hampden, at 61-63 Netherlee Road in Cathcart, is Holmwood House, designed by Alexander "Greek" Thomson, Glasgow's greatest Victorian architect. Holmwood was built for James Couper, a paper manufacturer, between 1857 and 1858 and is the most elaborate and sumptuously decorated of all the villas Thomson designed for well-to-do industrialists on the outskirts of Glasgow. It was rescued from decline by the National Trust for Scotland in 1994 and is well worth a visit.

The building is a work of genuine originality and has become a monument of international importance, as Thomson was the first modern architect to apply a Greek style to a free, asymmetrical composition. The house also includes features reminiscent of Frank Lloyd Wright, which pre-date the great American architect by some forty years. Thomson designed everything in the house and conservation work is revealing very beautiful and elaborate stencilled decoration and friezes with Greek motifs. The best description of Holmwood comes from Thomas Gildard who wrote in 1888: "If architecture be poetry in stone-and-lime – a great temple an epic – this exquisite little gem, at once classic and picturesque, is as complete, self-contained and polished as a sonnet".

Sleeping

Glasgow has a good range of accommodation. Most of the hotels, guest houses, B&Bs and hostels are in the city centre and the West End or south of the river, around Queen's Park. The best area to find good value mid-range accommodation is the West End, around Kelvingrove Park and the university. A large number of big chains have opened up in the city, offering everything from deluxe accommodation to simple low cost lodging – meaning that there are often good deals available to travellers prepared to shop around. The city also has several boutique hotels, offering stylish accommodation with more character than the international chains. Finding accommodation can be difficult during the major festivals (see page 734) and in Jul and Aug and it's best to book ahead at these times. The Tourist Information Centre can help find somewhere to stay and does a free accommodation guide

City centre *p713*

L-A **Glasgow Hilton**, 1 William St, T0141-2045555, www.hilton.co.uk 319 rooms. Gigantic, futuristic-looking luxury hotel regarded as one of the city's best. Full facilities include leisure centre and shopping mall. Their restaurant, Cameron's, is also widely held to be one of the finest around (see Eating).

L-A **Glasgow Moat House**, Congress Rd, T0141-3069988, www.moathousehotels.com. 283 rooms. Next to the SECC and 'Armadillo' on the banks of the Clyde. 2 excellent restaurants, Mariner's and Dockside No 1.
L-A **Langs Hotel**, 2 Port Dundas Pl, T0141-3331500, www.langshotel.co.uk Has 110 contemporary bedrooms, a trendy bar and Californian inspired restaurant.
A **The Art House**, 129 Bath St, T0141-2216789, www.arthousehotel.com. Stylish refurbishment of former education authority building. Well located and good value. Features Scotlands's first Japanese Teppan-yaki grill.
A **The Brunswick Merchant City Hotel**, 106-108 Brunswick St, T0141-5520001, www.scotland2000.com/brunswick 21 rooms. Chic minimalism in the heart of the Merchant City. Ideal for cool dudes wishing to sample the delights of Glasgow nightlife. Their excellent bar-restaurant boasts style and quality.
A **Cathedral House**, 28/32 Cathedral Sq, T0141-5523519, www.cathedralhouse.com. 8 rooms. Overlooking the cathedral. Wonderfully atmospheric old building with comfortable rooms and very good moderately priced restaurant.
A **Malmaison**, 278 West George St, T0141-5721000, www.malmaison.com. 72 rooms. Sister hotel of the one in Edinburgh and equally chic and stylish. Superior in every way. Their brasserie is also highly recommended.
A **Millennium Hotel**, George Sq, T0141-3326711, www.millennium-hotels.com. 117 rooms. Huge 18th century hotel in the heart of the city, next to Queen St station. Conservatory bar on the ground floor is good for people-watching.
A **Saint Judes**, 190 Bath St T0141-3528800, www.saintjudes.com. An intimate boutique hotel with only 6 bedrooms and a fine dining restaurant.
B **Bewleys Hotel**, 110 Bath St, T0141-3530800, www.bewleyshotel.com One of the well-known Irish chain hotels which opened in Jul 2000. 103 rooms all priced at £59 year-round.
B **The Inn on the Green**, 25 Greenhead St, T0141-5540165, www.theinnonthegreen.co.uk Well-established small, hotel featuring hand-crafted furniture quirky rooms.
B-C **Babbity Bowster**, 16-18 Blackfriars St, T0141-5525055, F5527774. 6 rooms. A local institution and one of the first of the Merchant City townhouses to be renovated. Typical Glaswegian hospitality, a near-legendary pub (see page 728) and an excellent restaurant. Babbity Bowster, in case you were wondering, is an old Scottish country dance.
B-C **Adelaide's**, 209 Bath St, T0141-2484970, www.adelaides.co.uk 8 rooms. Beautiful 'Greek' Thomson restoration, with 8 rooms in the heart of the city centre.
B-C **The Townhouse Hotel**, 21 Royal Cres, T0141-3329009, www.hotels.glasgow.com. 19 rooms. Elegantly-restored Victorian townhouse, set back off Sauchiehall St. Good value.
C **Greek Thomson** , 140 Elderslie St, T0141-3326556, www.renniemackintosh hotels.com, 17 rooms. Named after Glasgow's less-famous architectural son. Good value, city-centre guest house.
C **The Merchant Lodge**, 52 Virginia St, T0141-5522424, www.themerchantlodge. sagenet.co.uk, 40 rooms. Renovated old building in quiet side-street close to the Merchant City's stylish bars and restaurants.
C **Rennie Mackintosh Hotel**, 218-220 Renfrew St, T0141-3339992, www.renniemackintoshhotels.com, 24 rooms. A small hotel offering friendly service and superb value for money.
C **The Victorian House**, 212 Renfrew St, T0141-3320129, www.thevictorian.co.uk 50 rooms. Large, friendly lodge very close to the art college. Superb location and just about the best value in the city centre.
D-E **Euro Hostel**, 318 Clyde St, T0141-2222828, F2222829, www.euro-hostels.com 364 beds, all rooms with en suite facilities, includes continental breakfast. A huge multi-storey building overlooking the Clyde.

West End *p720*

L **One Devonshire Gardens**, 1 Devonshire Gdns, T0141-3392001, www. onedevonshire gardens.co.uk. 36 rooms. Highly-acclaimed hotel with last word in style and comfort. There is no classier places to stay in the country.
A **City Inn**, Finnieston Quay, T0141-2401002, www.cityinn.com Situated on the Clyde and convenient for the SECC. 164 rooms all with a contemporary feel. Emphasis is on providing business facilities, with ISDN and modem points in every room.

A **Kelvin Park Lorne Hotel**, 923 Sauchiehall St, T0870 609 6138, www.corushotels.com. 100 rooms. Dependable old stalwart and well located for galleries, museums etc.
B **Kirklee Hotel**, 11 Kensington Gate, T0141-3345555, www.kirkleehotel.co.uk. 9 rooms. Lovely Edwardian townhouse with beautiful garden. Close to bars and restaurants on Byres Road and the Botanic Gardens.
B **Park House**, 13 Victoria Park Gardens South, T0141-3391559, www.parkhouse glasgow.co.uk. 3 rooms offering 4 star B&B.
B **The Sandyford Hotel**, 904 Sauchiehall St, T0141-3340000, www.sandyfordhotelglasgow.co.uk. 55 rooms. Comfortable and good value lodge convenient for the SECC and art galleries.
B-C **Heritage Hotel**, 1 Alfred Terr, by 625 Great Western Rd, T0141-3396955, www.goglas gow.co.uk. 26 rooms. Good value Victorian townhouse close to the West End action.
B-C **Hillhead Hotel**, 32 Cecil St, T0141-3397733, www.hillheadhotel.co.uk 11 rooms. Small hotel ideally placed for the Byres Rd nightlife and close to Hillhead Underground.
B-C **Kelvin Hotel**, 15 Buckingham Terr, Great Western Rd, T0141-3397143, www.kelvinhotel.com. 21 rooms. Comfortable guest house in lovely Victorian terrace near Byres Rd and Botanic Gardens.
B-C **Kirkland House**, 42 St Vincent Cres, T0141-2483458, www.kirkland.net43.co.uk. 5 rooms. Small, family-run guest house with that little bit extra. Close to Kelvingrove Park.
B-C **The Townhouse**, 4 Hughenden Terr, T0141-3570862, F3399605, www. thetown houseglasgow.com. 10 rooms. Just off the Great Western Rd. Lovely Victorian townhouse offering comfort, hospitality and great value.
E **SYHA Youth Hostel**, 7/8 Park Terr, T0870 0041119, www.syha.org.uk. 135 beds. This former hotel has been converted into a great 4 star hostel, all rooms with en suite facilities (being refurbished, opens June 2004). Price includes continental breakfast. It gets very busy in Jul/Aug so you'll need to book ahead. Open 24 hrs. It's a 10-min walk from Kelvinbridge Underground station, or take bus 44 or 59 from Central station and get off at the first stop on Woodlands Rd, then head up the first turning left (Lynedoch St).
E **Glasgow Backpackers Hostel**, 17 Park Terr, T0141-3329099, www.scotlands-top-hostels 90 beds. Open Jul- Sep. Independent hostel housed in university halls of residence.
E **Glasgow Backpackers**, until early 2005 there is a temporary hostel sleeping 26 at 163 North St, Charing Cross while other hostels are being renovated. After that two large hostels on Berkeley St, Charing Cross, will open up, together with a proposed new hostel near Central Station. T0141-2217880/2045470, www.glasgowhostels.com. 120 beds. Take a 57 bus from the city centre and get off near the Mitchell Library.

South of the Clyde *p722*

A **Sherbrooke Castle Hotel**, 11 Sherbrooke Av T0141-4274227, ww.sherbrooke.co.uk, is a small hotel (25 rooms) with a bit more character than the chains. It's a good base for exploring the attractions of the south side as it's only about a mile from the Burrell collection.
A **Best Western Ewington**, Balmoral Terr, 132 Queen's Dr, T0141-4231152, www.countryhotels.net. 43 rooms. Friendly and comfortable hotel in a secluded terrace facing Queen's Park. Their restaurant, Minstrels, is superb value and worth a visit in its own right.

Campus accommodation

Glasgow's universities open their halls of residence to visitors during the summer vacation (late June to September), and some also during the Easter and Christmas breaks. Many rooms are basic and small, with shared bathrooms, but there are also more comfortable rooms with private bathrooms, twin and family units and self-contained apartments and shared houses. Full-board, half-board, B&B and self-catering options are all available. Prices for bed and breakfast tend to be roughly the same as for most B&Bs, but self-catering can cost as little as £50 per person per week. For the University of Glasgow, contact the Conference and Visitor Services, 3 The Sq, T0800-027 2030, www.cvso.co.uk. Local tourist offices have information, or contact the British Universities Accommodation Consortium, T0115-9504571 for a brochure,

Self-catering and serviced accommodation

There is plenty of Scottish Tourist Board (STB) approved self-catering accommodation available. The minimum stay is usually one week in the summer peak season, or three days or less at other times of the year. Expect to pay from around £300 to over £1000 per week in the city. Much of this self catering and serviced accommodation in the city is quite upmarket.

City Apartments, 401 North Woodside Rd, T0141-3424060, www.glasgowhotelsand apartments.co.uk Close to Kelvinbridge Underground. Have 4 apartments to let from £330 per week, £48 per night.

The Serviced Apartment Company, SACO House, 53 Cochrane St, T0845 1220405, F0117 9237571, www.saco apartments.co.uk.12 apartments in the Merchant City. Weekly rates from £525-630.

Eating

The greatest concentration of eating places is around **Byres Road** in the West End, which is heavily populated by students and therefore the best area for cheap, stylish places to eat. The **Merchant City** contains most of the designer brasseries, which are more expensive, but many of the bars serve good food at reasonable prices. Some of the places listed below also appear in the **Bars** section. **Cafés** are often good value places to eat, and these are also listed separately below.

City centre *p713*

£££**Brian Maule at Chardon d'Or**, 176 West Regent St, T0141-2483801. Opulent venue catering very much to well lunched businessmen. Head chef was formerly at Le Gavroche in London.

£££**The Buttery**, 652 Argyle St, T0141-2218188. Victoriana abounds in this old favourite with its clubby atmosphere. Consistently rated as one of the best in the city, with an emphasis on the finest Scottish fish, seafood and game. Good high-quality wine list. Open Tue-Fri 1200-1400, 1900-2200; Sat 1800-2200.

£££**Cameron's**, 1 William St, T0141-2045511. In Glasgow's Hilton Hotel. Sublime Scottish/French cuisine. Pricey but well worth it. No smoking area. Open Mon-Fri 1200-1400, 1900-2200; Sat 1900-2200.

£££**St Judes**, 190 Bath St, T0141-3528800. Part of the chic small hotel but open to non residents. Very much the in-place for Glasgow's movers and shakers. Modern Scottish food with lots of char-grilled fish and meat and very good puddings. Open Mon-Fri 1200-1500; Mon-Sun 1800-2230.

£££ **Rogano's**, 11 Exchange Pl, T0141-2484055. A Glasgow culinary institution. Designed in the style of the Cunard liner, Queen Mary, and built by the same workers. Looks like the set of a Hollywood blockbuster and you'll need a similar budget to pay the bill, but the seafood is truly sensational. Open daily 1200-1430, 1830-2230. Downstairs is **Café Rogano**, which offers a less stylish alternative, but it's a lot easier on the pocket. Open Sun-Thu 1200-1430, 1830-2230.

££**Amber Regent**, 50 West Regent St, T0141-3311655. Plush and very upmarket restaurant serving classic Chinese cuisine. Those on a tight budget can also indulge themselves, with half price main courses before 1900 Wed-Fri and all night Mon/Tue. BYOB. Open Mon-Thu 1200-1415, 1730-2300; Fri 1200-1415, 1730-2330; Sat 1200-2330.

££ **Café Gandolfi**, 64 Albion St, T0141-5526813. The first of Glasgow's style bistro/brasseries back in 1979, which almost makes it antique by today's contemporary design standards. Still comfortably continental, relaxed and soothing. Good place for a snack or a leisurely late breakfast. Open Mon-Sat 0900-2330, Sun 1200-2330.

££ **City Merchant**, 97-99 Candleriggs, T0141-5531577. The best of Scottish meat and game but it's the fish and seafood which shine. Absolutely superb. It's at the top end of this price range but their two- and three-course set menus are more affordable and excellent value (available 1200-1830). Very popular and a good atmosphere. No smoking area. Open Mon-Sat 1200-2230.

££ **Fratelli Sarti**, 121 Bath St, T0141-2040440. Everything you'd expect from a great Italian restaurant, and a lot more besides. Good value food in authentic Italian surroundings.. No wonder it's always busy – service is often slow then. No smoking area. Open Mon-Sat 0800-2230; Sun 1200-2230.

£ **Babbity Bowster**, 16-18 Blackfriars St, T0141-5525055. You can't get away from this place, and why would you want to? Buzzing café-bar housed in a magnificent 18th century building in the heart of the Merchant City. Traditional Scottish and French dishes served with flair. Outrageously good value. The bar is one of the city's perennial favourites (see Pubs, bars and clubs). Open Mon-Sat noon-2300; Sun 1000-2300.

£ **Bargo**, 80 Albion St, T0141-5534771. Impressively stylish designer bar serving excellent value bar snacks and meals of superior quality. Definitely a place to be seen in (see 'Bars'). Open Mon-Sat 1200-1900; Sun 1230-1900 (bar open until midnight).

£ **Café Source**, 1 St Andrews Sq (in the church) T0141-5486020, Mon-Thur 1100-2300, Fri, Sat 1100-midnight, Sun noon-2300. (no food 1500-1700 Mon-Fri). Great contemporary café offering everything from fishcakes to savoury vegetarian tart. Or just chill out with a latte and read the papers. Live music every Wed from 2100.

£ **Tempus at the CCA**, 350 Sauchiehall St, T0141-3327959. Set in the recently refurbished Centre for Contemporary Arts this café/restaurant serves contemporary Scottish dishes. The menu is flexible and you can just drop in for a coffee and a snack if you don't want lunch. Upstairs (also reached via Scott St) is the **CCA Bar** which serves sandwiches and coffees. It is notable for its decor, designed by artist Jorge Pardo, which is a psychedelic creation with lots of bright colours and carved wood. Daily 1100-midnight (last order for food 2130).

£ **Wee Curry Shop**, 7 Buccleuch St, T0141-3530777. Son of Mother India (see below). Small in every sense except flavour and value. Quite simply the best cheap curry this side of Bombay, in a cosy, relaxed atmosphere. Good vegetarian options and incredible value 3-course buffet lunch. BYOB. Open Mon-Sat 1200-1400, 1730-2230.

Cafés

Café Cosmo, 12 Rose St. T0141-3326535. Part of the Glasgow Film Theatre (see 'Entertainment') and definitely worth knowing about, even if you're not a movie buff. It's a great cheap lunch venue, especially for vegetarians. Open daily 1200-1700, bar open till 2100.

The Doocot Café and Bar, The Lighthouse, 11 Mitchell Lane, T0141-2211821. There's a 1950s retro look at this café on the top of the Lighthouse (see sights). Stop for soups, sandwiches and light meals before immersing yourself in the world of architecture.

Miss Cranston's Tearooms, 33 Gordon St T0141-2041122. You could miss this traditionally run tea-shop as it's hidden above a baker's shop. This is the place to come for a full blown afternoon tea with sandwiches, scones, cakes and gallons of tea.

Willow Tea Rooms, 217 Sauchiehall St, T0141-3320521. A recreation of the original Miss Cranston's Tearooms, designed by Charles Rennie Mackintosh and filled with many of his original features. Most visitors come here for the interior design, but they also offer a good selection of reasonably-priced teas, sandwiches, cakes and scones, as well as hot meals. Open Mon-Sat 0900-1630, Sun noon-1530. There's also a sister branch at 97 Buchanan St (T2045242), which is licensed. No smoking area. Open Mon-Sat 0930-1700; Sun 1200-1700.

West End *p720*

£££ **La Parmigiana**, 443 Great Western Rd, T0141-3340686. This sophisticated Italian restaurant is one of Glasgow's finest eating establishments. Good for special occasions. Open Mon-Sat 1200-1430, 1800-2300.

£££ **Nairn's**, 13 Woodside Crescent, T0141-3530707. Much-hyped restaurant run by TV chef Nick Nairn, but deserving of all the praise. Exceptional cuisine and superb value. Open Tue-Sat 1200-1345, 1800-2145.

£££**Stravaigin**, 28-30 Gibson St, T0141-3342665. Hard to define but difficult to resist. An eclectic mix of flavours and prime Scottish ingredients to produce the most sublime results. Expensive but you won't get better value for money in this category and totally justifies its many awards. Upstairs is a café-bar where you can sample some of that fabulous food at more affordable prices. Open Tue-Thu , 1700-2230; Fri-Sun 1200-1430, 1700-2300.

£££**The Ubiquitous Chip**, 12 Ashton La, T0141-3345007. A ground-breaking, multi award-winning restaurant and still the city's favourite place for Mctastic Scottish food, especially venison and seafood. All served in a plant-filled, covered courtyard patio. Open Mon-Sat 1200-1430, 1730-2300; Sun 1230-1500, 1830-2300. Upstairs is their bistro, **Upstairs at the Chip**, which doesn't make you feel quite as special but is much easier on the wallet. Open daily 1200-2300.

££**Ashoka Ashton Lane**, 19 Ashton La, T0141-3371115. First-class Indian restaurant, part of the famous west coast chain. Very popular with students and Byres Road trendies. Open Mon-Thu 1200-2400; Fri/Sat

1200-0030; Sun 1700-2400. Also run **Ashoka West End**, 1284 Argyle St, T0141-3393371.

££ **Gong** , 17 Vinicombe St, T0141-5761700. Sleek new venture housed in an old cinema that is already proving popular with the locals. Lots of sharing platters and Italian and Mexican influences. Brunch served at weekends. Mon-Thur 1700-2230, Fri, Sat, noon-1500, 1700-0200, Sun 1200-1500, 1700-2230, bar open longer.

££ **Gingerhill**, 1 Hillhead St, T0141-9566515. Well off the beaten track in posh Milngavie, but well worth the trip. Has a reputation as one of Glasgow's best seafood restaurants. It's an awfy wee place so you'll have to book well in advance. Open Wed-Sun 1930-2130. No smoking. BYOB (no licence).

££ **Mr Singh's India**, 149 Elderslie St, T0141-2040186. Imagine good Punjabi cooking brought to you by kilted waiters with a background wallpaper of disco music. If that sounds like your cup of char then get on down here and join in the fun. Many celebs have, so you never know who might pop in for a popadum. Open Mon-Sat noon-midnight Sun 1430-midnight. Very child friendly.

££ **Mother India**, 28 Westminster Terr, Sauchiehall St, T0141-2211663. Exquisite Indian cooking at affordable prices. Friendly and informal atmosphere. Strong vegetarian selection. Cheap set lunch and good banquet menus. BYOB . Open Mon, Tue 1730-2230; Wed,Thu 1200-1400, 1730-2230; Fri 1200-1400, 1700-2300; Sat 1300-2300; Sun 1630-2200.

£ **The Bay Tree**, 403 Great Western Rd, T0141-3345898. Rather basic self-service café serving food with a Middle Eastern emphasis. Open Mon-Sat 0930-2100; Sun 1000-2000.

£ **Grassroots Café**, 97 St Georges Rd, T0141-3330534. Vegetarian and vegan food at this intimate café near St Georges Cross. Lots of soups and salads and filling main courses. Mon-Sun 1000-2200.

Cafés

Grosvenor Café, 31 Ashton La, T0141-3391848. Behind Hillhead Underground. A perennial favourite with local students who come for the wide selection of cheap food (filled rolls, soup, burgers, pizzas, etc). Cosy and friendly atmosphere. Open Mon , Tue 0900-1600; Wed-Sat 0900-2200; Sun 1000-1800.

Little Italy, 205 Byres Rd, T0141-3396287 is a convenient and buzzy refuelling stop that never seems to close. Great pizza and strong espresso. Mon-Thur 0800-2200, Fri, Sat 0800-1145, Sun 1000-2200.

University Café, 87 Byres Rd, T0141-3395217. A gloriously authentic Italian Art Deco café, where grannies and students sit shoulder-to-shoulder enjoying real cappuccino, great ice cream and good, honest and cheap mince and tatties, pie and chips, sausage rolls, gammon steak and all the other golden oldies. Open Mon-Thur 0900-2200; Fri, Sat 0900-2230; Sun 1000-2200.

South of the Clyde *p722*

££ **Arigo**, 67 Kilmarnock Rd, T0141-6366616. Good Italian restaurant offering high quality fresh food. The sort of place that doesn't need to advertise. Mon-Fri noon-1430, 1700-2230, Sat, Sun noon-2230.

£ **Buongiorno**, 1021 Pollokshaws Rd, T0141-6491029. The best pizza in Glasgow – at these prices? Impossible, surely. Well, check it for yourself. Impeccable Italian family cooking, with cosy ambience to match. They even have a pre-theatre two-for-one deal! Are they crazy? Simply unbeatable, so book ahead. Open Mon-Sat 0900-2300; Sun 1000-2200.

Cafés

Art Lovers' Café, Bellahouston Park, Drumbreck Rd, T0141-3534779. Housed in CRM's exquisite House for an Art Lover. A nice place to chill and a good selection of light snacks and hot and cold meals. Also live jazz on Sat nights in the bar. No smoking. Open Sun-Fri 1000-1700; Sat also 1830-2400.

Pubs, bars and clubs

Glasgow is bursting at the seams with bars and pubs to suit all tastes, from ornate Victorian watering holes to the coolest of designer bars, where you can listen to thumping dance beats before heading off to a club. DJs normally start at 2100 till 2400 and entry is usually free, with some places charging after 2300 when they transform into clubs. One of the best areas for the sheer number and variety of pubs and bars is the **West End**, with its large student population. A number of style bars have also opened up along Bath St. Glagow's **club** scene is amongst the most vibrant in the UK. Opening times are pretty much the same all over with doors opening from 2300-0300.

City centre and Merchant City *p713*

The Arches Café Bar, 253 Argyle St. Part of the legendary club, this stylish basement bar is the perfect place to linger over a Belgian beer or enjoy their food.

Babbity Bowster, 16-18 Blackfriars St. Prime Merchant City pub that has everything; lively atmosphere, wide selection of real ales and good food (see also 'Eating').

Bar 10, 10 Mitchell St. This converted warehouse is Glasgow's original style bar and still as cool as ever. Good food on offer and a popular pre-club meeting place at weekends with regular Djs.

Blackfriars, 36 Bell St. Merchant city favourite which pulls in the punters with its vast range of international beers and lagers. Also a wide range of excellent grub, live music and comedy at weekends and that inimitable Glasgow atmosphere (see also 'Comedy' and 'Live music venues' below).

Candy Bar, 185 Hope St. Billed as one of the city's coolest bars, this is the place to flaunt those new clothes you splashed out on in Princes Square.

The Horse Shoe Bar, 17 Drury La, between Mitchell St and Renfield St, near the station. Classic Victorian Gin Palace that is still one of the city's favourites. Its much-copied island bar is the longest continuous bar in the UK, so it shouldn't take long to get served, which is fortunate as it gets very busy. Incredibly good-value food served Mon-Sat 1200-1930, Sun 1230-1700 and perhaps the cheapest pint in town. If you only visit one pub during your stay, then make sure it's this one.

Kelly Cooper Bar, 158-166 Bath St, T3314060. Style conscious newcomer on the Glasgow scene – dress to impress. Downstairs is Lowdown, which is another cool hangout that majors on cocktails.

Rab Ha's, 83 Hutcheson St. This old Merchant City stalwart still packs 'em in. It has an enviable reputation for its food and is above the restaurant of the same name.

Spy Bar, 153 Bath St, T0141-221 7711. Another sleek style bar on Bath St and popular with a pre club crowd. Food ranges from sandwiches and soups to more substantial fare. Food until 2000.

The Victoria Bar, 159 Bridgegate. Real traditional howff in one of Glasgow's oldest streets. Seemingly unchanged since the late 19th century and long may it stay that way. One of the city's great pubs, where entertainment is provided free, courtesy of the local wags.

West End *p720*

Firebird, 1321 Argyle St. Yet another of the city's style bars, but this one has the distinct advantage of providing excellent food, especially their pizzas. DJs most nights.

The Halt Bar, 160 Woodlands Rd. T5641527. This erstwhile tram stop (hence the name) is one of Glasgow's great unspoiled pubs with many of the original Edwardian fixtures intact. Also a good place to see live music two or three times a week (see 'Live music venues' below).

Lock 27, 1100 Crow Rd. If the weather's fine – and it sometimes is – there are few nicer places to enjoy a spot of al fresco eating and drinking than this place by the Forth and Clyde Canal in Anniesland. Good food served until 2100 and kids are made welcome. You could take a stroll along the towpath afterwards.

Tennent's, 191 Byres Rd. Big, no-nonsense, old West End favourite, serving a range of fine ales to a genuinely mixed crowd. It's also a great place for a chat (no loud music) and some very cheap food.

Uisge Beatha, 232 Woodlands Rd. The "water of life" is one of those pubs you go into for a wee drink and you're still there many hours later, the day's plans in ruins around your feet. Looks and feels like a real Highland hostelry. Cosy and welcoming and serving ridiculously cheap food. Scottish in every sense, and 135 whiskies to choose from too.

Clubs

Alaska, 142 Bath La, T0141-2481777. Everything from funk and soul to house music.

Archaos, 25 Queen St, T0141-2043189. A younger more dressy crowd come here for house, techno and club classics in this massive venue.

The Arches, 253 Argyle St, T0901-0220300, www.thearches.co.uk. Cavernous space under Central station. Glasgow's finest and always at the cutting edge of the UK dance scene.

Babaza, 24 Royal Exchange Sq, T0141-2040101. Unusual interior, up-for-it crowd who love their R&B and hip hop.

Cathouse, 15 Union St, T0141-2486606. Big rock n roll and grunge venue.

Cube, 34 Queen St, T0141-2268990. Increasingly popular plays host to a musical mix of club nights 5 nights a week.

Fury Murry's, 96 Maxwell St, T0141-2216511. Behind the St Enoch Centre. An eclectic crowd get down to a mix of dance and student faves.

The Garage, 490 Sauchiehall St, T0141-3321120. Downbeat, sticky student haunt featuring the usual cheesy retro stuff that they seem to love, and cheap drinks, which always go down well. Occasional live bands. More of an old-fashioned getting bevvied up and copping off kind of place.

Havana, 50 Hope St, T0141-2484466 (see also 'Bars'). More of a bar with dancing, and only open till 0100 at weekends, but they play the hottest Latin grooves you can find.

MAS, 29 Royal Exchange Sq, T0141-2216381. Fool's Gold on Wed is indie and rock n' roll night, techno and house mix on Thurs, Mon is Burn, free to staff of pubs n clubs.

The Sub Club, 22 Jamaica St, T0141-2484600. One of the city's favourite clubs. House, techno, dance and anything else that's going.

The Tunnel, 84 Mitchell St, T0141-2041000. A new Millennium and still going strong as one of the city's prime club venues.

Entertainment

It's been a few years now since Glasgow was chosen as 'City of Culture' but the legacy lives on and the city continues to enjoy a wide span of art, theatre, film and music. The majority of the larger **theatres, concert halls** and **cinemas** are concentrated in the city centre, though its two most renowned theatres, the Citizens' and the Tramway, are to be found south of the Clyde.

Details of all the city's events are listed in the two local newspapers, *The Herald* and the *Evening Times*. Another excellent source of information is the fortnightly listings magazine *The List*, www.list.co.uk, which also covers Edinburgh and which is on sale in most newsagents. To book **tickets** for concerts or theatre productions, call at the Ticket Centre, City Hall, Candleriggs (open Mon-Sat 0900-1800; Sun 1200-1700). Phone bookings T0141-2874000 (Mon-Sat 0900-2100; Sun 0900-1800). Note that some of the **live music venues** don't have their own box office. For tickets and information go to Tower Records, on Argyle St, T0141-2045788.

Art galleries

Apart from the large, main galleries listed under 'Sights', there are many small, independent galleries showcasing contemporary local, Scottish and international artists. The Glasgow Galleries Guide, www.glasgowgalleries.co.uk, free from any of the galleries, lists all current exhibitions. The following galleries are amongst the most interesting.

Art Exposure Gallery, 19 Parnie St (behind the Tron Theatre), T0141-5527779. Open Mon-Sat 1200-1700.

Collins Gallery, 22 Richmond St, T0141-5482558. Part of Strathclyde University campus. Open Mon-Fri 1000-1700; Sat 1200-1600.

Compass Gallery, 178 West Regent St, T0141-2216370. Open Mon-Sat 1000-1730.

Cyril Gerber Fine Art, 148 West Regent St, T0141-2213095. Open Mon-Sat 0930-1730.

Intermedia, T0141-5522540, 18 King St, Mon-Sat noon-1800, an exhibition space which frequently has works on show by local artists.

Glasgow Print Studio Galleries, on the 1st floor of 25 King St, T0141-5520704, www.gpsart.co.uk, Tue-Sat 1000-1730, are one of the largest publishers of original prints in the UK. They display and sell etchings, lithographs and screenprints by over 300 artists including names like Elizabeth Blackadder, Ken Currie, Peter Howson and Adrian Wiszniewski.

Streetlevel, T0141-552 2151, 26 King St, Tue-Sat 1000-1700 which specialises in photographic works.

Café Cossachok, T0141-553 0733, Tue-Sat 1130-late, 10 King St. It's a Russian café with a gallery exhibiting the work of Soviet artists. Many of the works in these galleries are for sale.

Cinemas

Glasgow Film Theatre (**GFT**), at 12 Rose St, T0141-3328128, with an excellent programme of art-house movies and a good bar for discussion later.

Grosvenor, in Ashton La, off Byres Rd, T0141-3398444. An old 2-screen cinema recently refurbished, showing art-house and mainstream films.

Comedy venues

The Stand Comedy Club, 333 Woodlands Rd, T0870-6006055, www.thestand.co.uk. Top notch comedy Thu-Sun.
Blackfriars, 36 Bell St, T0141-5525924. Regular slots on Sun nights. Also live jazz (see below).
The State Bar, 148 Holland St, T0141-3322159. Good comedy club on Sat nights. Also live blues on Tue and a good selection of real ales. Not a bad pub, actually.

Concert halls

City Halls, Candleriggs, T0141-3538000. Smaller-scale classical music events. Home of the Scottish Chamber Orchestra.
Henry Wood Hall, 73 Claremont St, T0141-2253555, www.rsno.org.uk. HQ of the Royal Scottish National Orchestra.
Royal Concert Hall, 2 Sauchiehall St, T0141-3538080, www.grch.com. Prestigious venue for orchestras and big rock, pop and soul acts.
The Royal Scottish Academy of Music and Drama, 100 Renfrew St, T0141-3324101, www.rsamd.ac.uk. Varied programme of international performances.
Theatre Royal, Hope St, T0141-3323321, www.theatreroyalglasgow.com. The home of the generally excellent Scottish Opera and Scottish Ballet, also regularly hosts large-scale touring theatre and dance companies and orchestras.

Gay clubs and bars

Bennet's, 90 Glassford St, T0141-5525761. Glasgow's main gay club. Wed-Sun 2300-0330.
Delmonica's, 68 Virginia St, T0141-5524803. Daily 1200-2400. Free. A fun place and crowd. DJs at weekends, karaoke Sun nights.
Revolver, 6a John St, T0141-5532456. Mon-Sun 1200-2400. Free jukebox. Sexy new bar with interesting theme nights.
Polo Lounge, 84 Wilson St, T0141-5531221. Mon-Thu 1700-0100, Fri-Sun 1700-0300. Happy Hour . Very classy bar popular with young professionals. Very busy at weekends.
Sadie Frost's, 8-10 West George St, T0141-3328005. Mon-Sat 1200-2400, Sun 1300-2400. Free. Underneath Queen St station. Very busy and noisy. Sappho's is a women only bar.
Merchant Pride, 20 Candleriggs, T0141-5641285, Mon-Sun 1200-2400. Sociable bar with karaoke nights and jazz sessions on Sat.

Live music venues

Barrowlands, Gallowgate, T0141-5524601. Famous old East End ballroom and now Glasgow's liveliest and best-loved gig venue. Popular with acts just breaking through and big names trying to rediscover what it's all about.
Cathouse, 15 Union St, T0141-2486606. Glasgow's only rock club. Ideal for seeing bands before they make it big.
Clutha Vaults, 167 Stockwell St, T0141-5527520. Well-known pub which has live music nights from a wide range of local talent.
Cottier's, 93-95 Hyndland St, T0141-3575825. Good venue for more esoteric music acts, also jazz and blues (see also 'Eating').
The Garage, 490 Sauchiehall St, T0141-3321120. Medium-sized venue for bands on the verge of a breakthrough.
King Tut's Wah Wah Hut, 272a St Vincent St, T0141-2215279. Glasgow's hallowed live music venue. Many a famous band has made the break in this cramped, sweaty club. Good bar downstairs for a pre-gig drink.
Nice 'n' Sleazy, 421 Sauchiehall St, T0141-3330900. Great bar and music venue. Everything from indie to rock downstairs while musos hang out in upstairs bar.
The Scotia Bar, 112 Stockwell St, T0141-5528681. A Glasgow institution and home of Glasgow's folk scene.
Scottish Exhibition and Conference Centre (SECC), Finnieston Quay, T0141-2483000. Gigantic multi-purpose venue with all the atmosphere of a disused aircraft hangar. Plays host to the likes of Robbie Williams and Pavarotti.
13th Note Café , 50-60 King St, T0141-5531638. Another major player on the alternative live music scene. Popular and lively venue for up-and-coming indie/rock bands. Also good veggie food in the bar upstairs (see 'Eating').

Theatre

The Arches, 30 Midland St, T0141-5651023. In the railway arches under Central station. Presents more radical and experimental theatre. Also home to one of the city's major clubs (see Clubs above).
Centre for Contemporary Arts (CCA), 350 Sauchiehall St, T0141-3524900. Hosts contemporary dance and theatre, as well as staging various art exhibitions.

Citizens' Theatre, 119 Gorbals St, T0141-4290022, www.citz.co.uk. Just across the river. Home to some of the UK's most exciting and innovative drama. Main auditorium and two smaller studios. Big discounts for students and the unemployed.
King's Theatre, 294 Bath St, T0141-2401300, www.kings-glasgow.co.uk. The city's main traditional theatre presenting musicals, panto and that kind of thing.
Mitchell Theatre, 6 Granville St, T0845 3303501. At Charing Cross. Stages various drama productions as well as occasional jazz concerts.
Theatre Royal (see 'Concert Halls' above). Primarily a concert hall but also stages high-brow theatre, darling.
Tramway Theatre, 25 Albert Drive, T0845 3303501/4222023. Just off Pollokshaws Rd. Internationally-renowned venue with varied programme of innovative and influential theatre, dance, music and art exhibitions.
Tron Theatre, 63 Trongate, T0141-5524267. Major contemporary theatre productions. Also musical performances and big-name comedy acts. Home to a very fine bar and restaurant.

Festivals and events

Glasgow doesn't like to be overshadowed by Edinburgh, and has a few notable festivals of its own. Things kick off in the last 2 weeks of **Jan** with the **Celtic Connections** music festival, featuring artists form around the world. It is held in the various venues (T0141 -3538000, www.celticconnections.co.uk). The city's biggest festival is the **West End Festival**, 2 weeks of music, theatre and various free events held over 2 weeks in **Jun** (T0141-3410844, www.westendfestival .co.uk). Other festivals include the **RSNO Proms**, at the Royal Concert Hall in **Jun**, the **Glasgow International Jazz Festival** (T0141-5523552, www.jazzfest.co.uk) in **Jul**, and the **World Pipe Band Championships** (T0845 241 4400) which are held in **mid-Aug**. **Glasgay** is Britain's largest lesbian and gay arts festival held in various venues from **late Oct** to **early Nov**, T0141-3347126, www.glasgay.co.uk. For further information, check the website at www.seeglasgow.com

Shopping

Glasgow is a shopaholic's paradise. The best city in the UK after London provides endless opportunities for retail therapy. **Merchant City** is the home of the **Italian Centre**, Glasgow's most upmarket shopping area. This is the home of Armani and Versace, as well as some other upmarket shops, cafés and restaurants. There's also a branch of **Cruise** on Ingram St. Not far away is **Innhouse** on Wilson St, which has lots of contemporary designer homeware by names like Alessi.

On **Buchanan St** the possibilities are endless. You can not only find all the usual high street stores, but designer names and some specialist stores. At the top of Buchanan St, just minutes from Queen St station, is the city's newest shopping centre **Buchanan Galleries**. Off Buchanan St is the **Argyll Arcade** a specialist shopping centre with over 30 jewellery shops. For more standard high street chains there is the **St Enoch** shopping centre at the very bottom of Buchanan St, and there's also Argyle St which again has high street stores.

Antique hunters should make for **West Regent St** and **Victorian Village** where a selection of traders sell lovely costume jewellery, antiques and retro clothing. For the widest range of retro clothing go to **Saratoga Trunk**, 4th floor, 62 Hydepark St (Mon-Fri only, do call first T0141-2214433). (Also has a small outlet in Victorian Village). It's an enormous Aladdin's cave of a warehouse stuffed with the most extraordinary range of clothes, from beautiful beaded dresses to swirly 60s gear. The staff are very friendly and they also have brilliant jewellery and accessories. They supply gear for film and tv crews, which is why you need to check they can see you beforehand. Well worth the journey if you like great vintage clothes.

The West End is a great place for browsing as it's full of quirky, off beat shops. There are several good jewellery shops. **Bethsy Gray** is a jewellery designer with a shop/workshop in Starry Starry Night on Dowanside Rd. She specializes is working with silver. **Orro** on Bank St is a sleek contemporary jewellers'. You can also find jewellery, as well as antiques, pottery,

'Glasgow Style' artefacts etc in **De Courcey's Arcade** in Cresswell La, which has a brilliant selection of goods from different traders.

If you're a booklover there are plenty of good second hand bookshops to explore. **Bookpoint**, on Hyndland Rd has lots of books on Scotland and Glasgow, while **Voltaire and Rousseau** on Otago St is an old established antiquarian bookstore. For academic books there's a branch of **John Smith and Son** on University Av. The **Oxfam Bookshop** on Byres Rd is also worth trying.

Activities and tours

Boat trips

At Anderston Quay, east of the Science Centre, is **The Waverley**, T0141-2218152, www.waverleyexcusions.co.uk, the world's last ocean going paddle steamer and one of a former fleet of pleasure boats that used to take Glaswegians on trips 'doon the watter' to Clyde coast resorts. She has now completed a £7 million refit and has been restored to her original glory. You can take still take day trips on the Waverley along the Clyde to destinations like Dunnoon, Largs, the Kyles of Bute and Arran. Sailings take place from Easter-mid May and from Jun to late Aug, Fri-Mon. Office open summer Mon-Fri 0900-1700, Sat 0900-1300, winter Mon-Fri 0900-1700. Trips range from £10-30.

Next to the Tall Ship is **Seaforce**, T0141-2211070, www.seaforce.co.uk, a company offering high speed powerboat trips along the Clyde. Trips range from a 15 min 'taster' (£3) to a 4 hr trip to the village of Kilcreggan (includes a chance to visit the village) £35, £15 concession. There's also a mystery tour which goes to, well, it's a surprise. £50, lunch included, £25 concession, open all year, trips must be booked. Office hours 0800-2200.

Clyde Waterbus, T07711 250 969 , www.clydewaterbusservices.co.uk, Pride of the Clyde, is a riverbus that runs along the Clyde between Broomielaw and Braehead (where there is the large Braehead shopping centre and Clydebuilt maritime museum). Trips go about every 1½ hrs and include a commentary on the history of the river. Services run Mon-Fri from 1045-1815, Sat from 1115, Sun from 1145. £3, £5 return, concession £2, £3.50 return.

Football

Celtic Football Club are based at Celtic Park, 95 Kerrydale St, T0141-5562611, off the London Rd in the East End.

Their bitter opponents, **Rangers**, play at Ibrox Stadium, 150 Edmiston Dr, T0141-4278500, in the South Side. Tickets for league matches start at around £15-20.

Walking

Several companies offer guided walking tours of Glasgow.

Alexander Thomson Society offers guided tours that take in all the main sites associated with Glasgow's 'other' architect Alexander 'Greek' Thomson. T0141-6372129, www.greekthomson.com.

Mercat Glasgow offer themed on walks on various aspects of Glasgow's history. T0141-5865378, www.mercat-glasgow.co.uk.

Or try a self guided tour with **Walkabout Tours**. You pick up one of their audio machines from the Tourist Office in George Square, then use it to guide you around.

Transport

Long distance

Air Glasgow International airport is the main departure point in Scotland for flights to North America. There are also flights to European destinations and many domestic flights. Also flights to **Glasgow Prestwick**.

Bus Scottish **Citylink** has buses to most major towns in Scotland. There are buses to **Edinburgh** every 15 mins (1¼ hrs); hourly buses to **Stirling** (45 mins) and **Inverness** (4 hrs); 15 buses daily to **Aberdeen** (4 hrs); 4 daily to **Oban** (3 hrs); 4-5 daily to **Fort William** (3 hrs); 3 daily to **Portree** (7 hrs); and hourly to **Perth** (1½ hrs) and **Dundee** (2¼ hrs). **Midland** Bluebird (T01324-613777) runs buses to **Milngavie**, at the start of the West Highland Way (30 mins).

Train Scotrail operates the West Highland line from Queen Street north to **Oban** (3 daily, 3 hrs), **Fort William** (3 daily, 3¾ hrs) and **Mallaig** (3 daily, 5¼ hrs). **ScotRail** also runs services to **Edinburgh** (every 30 mins, 50 minutes, £7.50 cheap day return), **Perth** (hourly, 1 hr), **Dundee** (hourly, 1 hr 20 mins), **Aberdeen** (hourly, 2½ hrs), **Stirling** (hourly, 30 mins) and **Inverness** (3 daily, 3½ hrs).

Local

Bus Routes are shown on the Visitor's Transport Guide. For short trips in the city fares are £0.80. On most buses you'll need to have exact change. After midnight, till 0400, there's a limited night bus service (more frequent at weekends). Full details from Travel Centres. A good way to get around town is to buy a ticket for one of the guided bus tours.

Taxi There are taxi ranks at Central and Queen Street train stations and Buchanan bus station. To call a cab, try **Glasgow Taxis** (T0141-4292900), who also run city tours. Minimum fare around the city centre is £1.50-2. To the Burrell collection from the city centre (about three miles) should cost around £6-7.

Train Trains leave from **Glasgow Central** mainline station to all destinations south of the Clyde, including to **Greenock** (for ferries to **Dunoon**), **Wemyss Bay** (for ferries to **Rothesay**), **Ardrossan** (for ferries to **Arran**) and to **Prestwick airport**. There's a low-level station below Central station which connects the southeast of the city with the northwest. This cross-city line serves the SECC and a branch runs north to **Milngavie**, at the start of the West Highland Way. There's also a line from **Queen Street** which runs west all the way to **Helensburgh**, via **Partick** and **Dumbarton**. Branches of this line run to **Balloch**, at the south end of Loch Lomond, and **Milngavie**.

Underground Locals affectionately call it the "Clockwork Orange", as there's only one circular route serving 15 stops and the trains are bright orange. It's easy to use and there's a flat fare of £0.90, or you can buy a day ticket for £2.50. Trains run roughly every 5-8 mins from approximately 0630 till 2235 Mon-Sat and from 1100 till 1750 on Sun.

Directory

Car hire Arnold Clark, 188 Castlebank St, T0141-339 98861 (also at the airport, T0141-8480202), www.arnoldclark.com. **Avis**, 70 Lancefield St, T0141-2212877 (also at the airport, T0141-8872261), www.avis.co.uk. **Hertz**, 138 Hydepark St, T0141-2487736 (also at the airport, T0141-8877845), www.hertz.co.uk. **Enterprise**, 45 Finnieston St, Unit 4, T0141-2212124, www.enterprise.com **Cycle hire** Dales, 150 Dobbies Loan, T0141-3322705. Close to Buchanan bus station. **West End Cycles**, 16 Chancellor St, T0141-3571344, at the south end of Byres Rd. £12 per day for mountain bikes, £50 per week. ID and £50 deposit required. **Dental** For emergencies go to the **Glasgow Dental Hospital**, 378 Sauchiehall St, T0141-2119600. **Gay and lesbian contacts** Lesbian and Gay Switchboard, T0141-3328372, open daily 0700-2200. **Stonewall Scotland**, LGBT Centre, 11 Dixon St, T0141-2040022. **Hospitals** Glasgow **Royal Infirmary** is at 84 Castle St, T0141-2114000, near the cathedral. The **Southern General Hospital** on Govan Rd, T0141-2011100, is the main South Side hospital. **Internet** EasyEverything, 57 St Vincent St, huge facility and the cheapest service in town. **The Internet Café** is at 569 Sauchiehall St, T0141-5641052. It charges £2-2.50 per ½ hr on line. **Internet Exchange**, 136 Sauchiehall St, T0141-3530535. **Café Internet**, 153-157 Sauchiehall St, T0141-3532484. **Post office** is at 47 St Vincent St, T0345-222344. Services include poste restante, currency exchange and cash withdrawal at the **German Savings Bank**. Open Mon-Fri 0830-1745, Sat 0900-1900. Also branches at 85-89 Bothwell St, 216 Hope St and 533 Sauchiehall St. Post offices in some supermarkets are open on Sun. **Police** 945 Argyle St, T0141-5323200. Free emergency numbers are T999 or T112.

Argyll and the Inner Hebrides

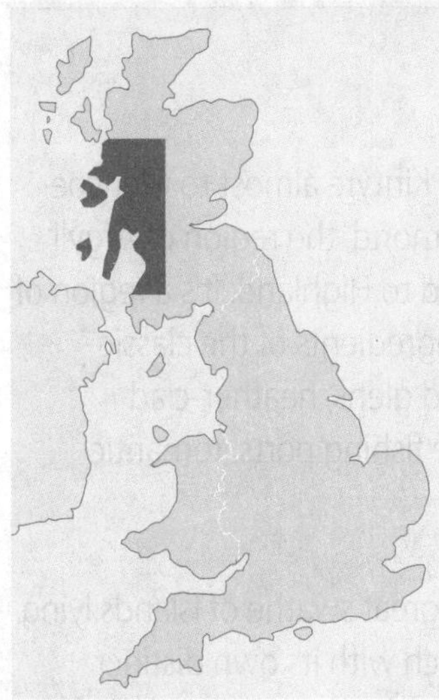

Introduction

Stretching north from the Mull of Kintyre almost to Glencoe and east to the shores of Loch Lomond, the region of Argyll marks the transition from Lowland to Highland. It's a region of great variety, containing all the ingredients of the classic Scottish holiday: peaceful wooded glens, heather-clad mountains full of deer, lovely wee fishing ports, romantic castles and beautiful lochs.

The Inner Hebrides comprise the great swathe of islands lying off the western coast of Argyll, each with its own distinct appeal. The most accessible of the islands is Mull, a short ferry ride from Oban. The variety of scenery on offer is astounding and its capital, Tobermory, is the most attractive port in western Scotland. A stone's throw from Mull is tiny Iona, one of the most important religious sites in Europe, with some divine beaches. Boat trips can be made to the dramatic island of Staffa, looming out of the sea like a great cathedral and the inspiration for Mendelssohn's 'Hebrides Overture'. Further west, windswept Coll and Tiree offer miles of unspoilt beaches and some great windsurfing and, to the south, Colonsay is a stress-free zone that makes Mull seem hectic.

Those who enjoy a good malt whisky should head for Islay, famed for its distilleries, while neighbouring Jura is a wild and beautiful place, perfect for some off-the-beaten-track hiking. If you're after some peace and quiet on Jura then you're in good company, for this is where George Orwell came to write '1984'. Furthest north are the "small islands" of Eigg, Muck, Rùm and Canna, reached from Mallaig, but ignored by most tourists. People come here for the fine bird watching and superb walking.

★ Don't miss...

1. Take a cruise on **Loch Etive**, inaccessible except by boat, and one of Scotland's great hidden treasures, page 750.
2. Explore the archaeological treasures of **Kilmartin Glen**, page 748.
3. Drive down to **Tighnabruaich** in Southwest Cowal and enjoy the wonderful views across the Kyles of Bute, page 746.
4. Take a look round the magnificent Gothic fantasy of **Mount Stuart**, page 747.
5. Take a boat trip to the spectacular island of **Staffa** and the cathedral-like Fingal's Cave, which inspired Mendelssohn, page 755.
6. Brave the treacherous waters of the **Corryvreckan**, one of the world's largest whirlpools, page 745.

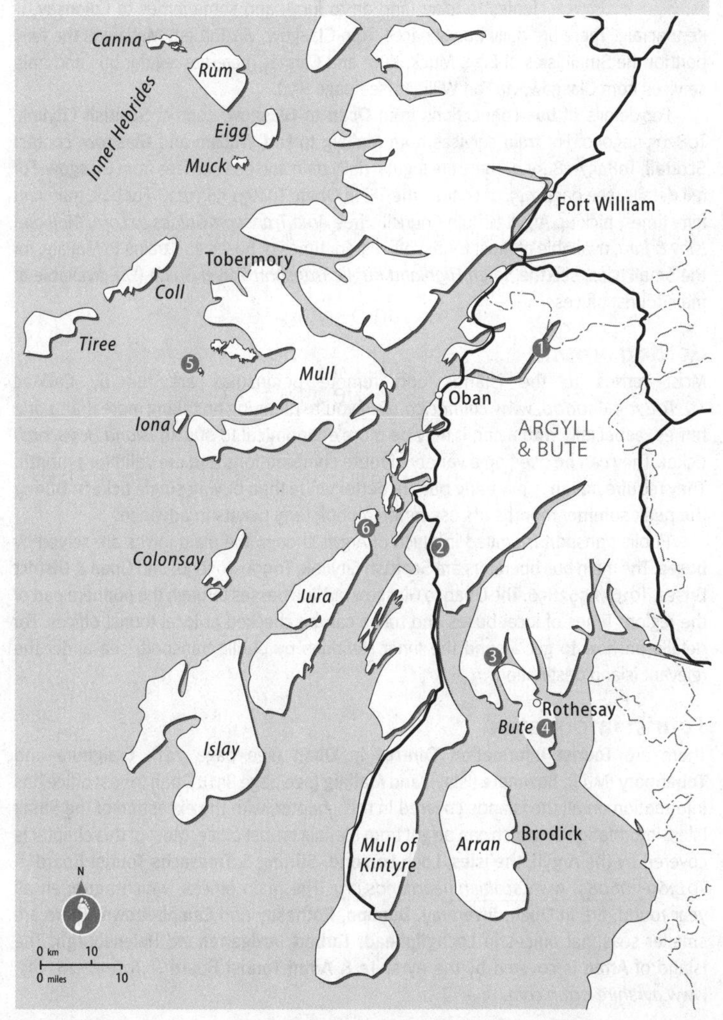

Ins and outs

Getting there

There are **flights** from Glasgow to Port Ellen (**Islay**): 2 daily Mon-Fri and 1 on Sat (40 mins), all year round. From Glasgow to **Tiree**: 1 flight daily Mon-Sat (45 mins), all year round. For flight times, call **British Airways Express**, T08457-733377, the local **Tourist Information Centres**, or **Port Ellen airport**, T01496-302022, and **Tiree airport**, T01879-220309.

CalMac car and passenger **ferries** sail to and from Mull, Islay, Coll, Tiree, Colonsay and Gigha, and passenger-only ferries sail to Iona and the Small Isles (Eigg, Muck, Rùm and Canna). The departure point for ferries to Mull, Coll, Tiree and Colonsay is **Oban**. Ferry times change according to the day of the week and time of the year. Services listed below under each separate island are for the summer period (2 Apr-16 Oct). For full details see the *CalMac Ferry Guide* or call **CalMac** ⓘ T08705-650000, reservations@calmac.co.uk; T01475-650100, www.calmac.co.uk (general enquiries). The departure point for ferries to **Islay** (and on to **Jura**), and some ferries to **Colonsay**, is Kennacraig. There are daily bus services from Glasgow, via Tarbert. **Mallaig** is the ferry port for the Small Isles of Eigg, Muck, Rùm and Canna. There are regular bus and train services from Glasgow, via Fort William (see page 851).

Car space on ferries is limited during the summer months, so it's advisable to book ahead.

For details of **bus** connections from **Oban** to **Glasgow**, contact **Scottish Citylink**, T08705-505050. For **train** services from **Mallaig** to **Fort William** and **Glasgow**, contact **Scotrail**, T08457-484950. There are regular daily train and bus services from **Glasgow**. For full details, see page 745, or contact the TIC in **Oban**, T01631-563122. For bus, train and ferry times, pick up Argyll & Bute Council's free *Area Transport Guides to Lorn, Mull and Islay & Jura*, available at most tourist offices. For times of buses and trains to Mallaig, for the Small Isles, see the *South Highland Public Transport Travel Guide* (£1), available at main tourist offices.

Getting around

Most **ferries** to the islands and remote peninsulas are run by **CalMac** ⓘ *T08705-650000, www.calmac.co.uk*. If you're planning on taking more than 1 or 2 ferries, especially with a car, it may be more economical to buy an *Island Hopscotch* ticket. They can be used on a variety of route combinations and are valid for 1 month. They require advance planning but are better value than buying single tickets. During the peak summer months it's essential to book ferry tickets in advance.

Public transport is limited in much of Argyll, though the main towns are served by **buses**. The main bus operators are **Scottish Citylink**, T0990-505050, and **Oban & District Buses**, T01631-562856. The Oban to Glasgow rail line passes through the northern part of the region. Times of local buses and trains can be checked at local tourist offices. For details on how to get around the Inner Hebrides by public transport, see under the relevant island destination.

Tourist information

There are **Tourist Information Centres** in **Oban** (see page 741), **Craignure** and **Tobermory** (Mull), **Bowmore** (Islay), and **Mallaig** (see page 851). Oban tourist office has information on all the islands covered in this chapter, with the exception of the Small Isles, information on which can be got from Mallaig tourist office. Most of this chapter is covered by the **Argyll, the Isles, Loch Lomond, Stirling & Trossachs Tourist Board** ⓘ *T01369-706085, www.scottish.heartlands.org*. The main offices, which are open all year round, are in **Oban**, **Inveraray**, **Dunoon**, **Rothesay** and **Campbeltown**. There are smaller seasonal offices in **Lochgilphead**, **Tarbert**, **Ardgarten**and **Helensburgh**. The island of **Arran** is covered by the **Ayrshire & Arran Tourist Board** ⓘ *T01292-262555, www.ayrshire-arran.com*.

Oban and around

→Colour map 5

Oban lies at the centre of the northerly part of Argyll, known as Lorn, which stretches north as far as Appin, south to Ardfern and east to the shores of Loch Awe. It also comprises several relatively peaceful islands, including Lismore, Kerrera, Seil and Luing. It's a busy little place: not only is it the largest port in northwest Scotland and the main departure point for ferries to the Hebrides, it is also the main tourist centre in Argyll. Not surprisingly, it gets very crowded in summer, with passing traffic and people using it as a base for exploring the region. It has a wide range of hotels, guest houses, B&Bs, restaurants and shops, and a number of tourist attractions, which is useful to know if you're stuck here in bad weather. The town lies in the beautiful setting of a wide, crescent-shaped bay, backed by steep hills, with the island of Kerrera, just offshore, providing a natural shelter. ▸▸ *For Sleeping, Eating and other listings, see pages 744-745.*

Ins and outs

Getting there Oban is reasonably well served by **buses** and **trains** from Glasgow, Fort William and Inverness, and there are a number of west coast local bus services to and from Lochgilphead, Dalmally and Kilmartin. ▸▸ *For further details, see Transport, page 745.*

Getting around There are regular local **buses** around town and around Lorn, including to Clachan Seil, North Cuan, Isle of Luing, North Connel, Dalavich, Bonawe, and Ganavan Sands. These are mostly operated by **Oban & District Buses** or **Royal Mail Postbuses**, T01463 -256200.

Information **Oban Tourist Information Centre** ⓘ *Argyll Sq, T01631-563122, and has internet access. Open 1-29 Apr Mon-Fri 0900-1700, Sat-Sun 1000-1700; 30 Apr-17 Jun Mon-Sat 0900-1730, Sun 1000-1700; 18 Jun-1 Jul Mon-Sat 0900-1830, Sun 1000-1700; 2 Jul-2 Sep Mon-Sat 0900-2000, Sun 0900-1900; 3-23 Sep Mon-Sat 0900-1830, Sun 1000-1700; 24 Sep-28 Oct Mon-Sat 0900-1730, Sun 1000-1600; 29 Oct-31 Mar Mon-Fri 0930-1700, Sat/Sun 1200-1600.*

Sights

The town's great landmark is **McCaig's Folly**, an incongruous structure that resembles Rome's Coliseum and which dominates the skyline. The tower was built by local banker John Stuart McCaig in the late 19th century, as a means of providing work for unemployed stonemasons. Unfortunately, McCaig died before the project was complete, and to this day no one is quite sure of his intentions. There's not much to see, apart from the exterior walls, but the views of the town and bay are quite magnificent and well worth the climb up.

Dunstaffnage Castle ⓘ *Apr-Sep daily 0930-1830; Oct-Mar daily Sat-Wed 0930-1630. Castle grounds open all year round. Adult £2, concession £1.30, children £0.75, T01631-562465*, three miles north of Oban, off the A85, is a 13th-century fort built on an impressive site, and much of the curtain wall remains intact. The ruins of the little chapel nearby are worth a look. The castle served as a temporary prison for Flora MacDonald.

Two miles east of Oban along the Glencruitten Road is the **Rare Breeds Farm Park.** ⓘ *Late Mar to late Oct daily 1000-1730 (mid-Jun to end of Aug till 1930). Adult £5, concession/children £3.50. There are 3 buses daily Mon-Fri to and from Oban train station, T01631-770608.* It's a fun place, especially for kids, with lots of strange-looking, yet familiar animals native to these shores. The animals are in pens, or roam free, and are very friendly and approachable.

If the weather's bad you can take a tour round the **Oban Distillery** ⓘ *at the end of Stafford Street, which is opposite the North Pier, Easter to Oct Mon-Fri 0930-1700, and Sat 0930-1700; Jul-Sep Mon-Fri 0930-2030, £4, T01631-572004.*

Around Oban

A good place to get away from the crowds and enjoy some peace and quiet and some fine walking is the island of Kerrera, which protects Oban Bay. It's only five miles by two, so can be explored easily on foot or by bike. The highest point on the island is 600 ft, from where there are great views across to Mull, the Slate Islands, Lismore and Jura. Otherwise, there's a good trail down to the ruins of **Gylen Castle**, built by the MacDougall's in 1582, which is perched on a cliff-top on the south coast. A mile northwest of the ferry jetty is **Slatrach Bay**, a nice sandy beach and a great place for a picnic.

Five miles north of Oban an impressive steel cantilever bridge carries the A828 across the mouth of Loch Etive at **Connel**. It's worth stopping here to see the **Falls of Lora**,

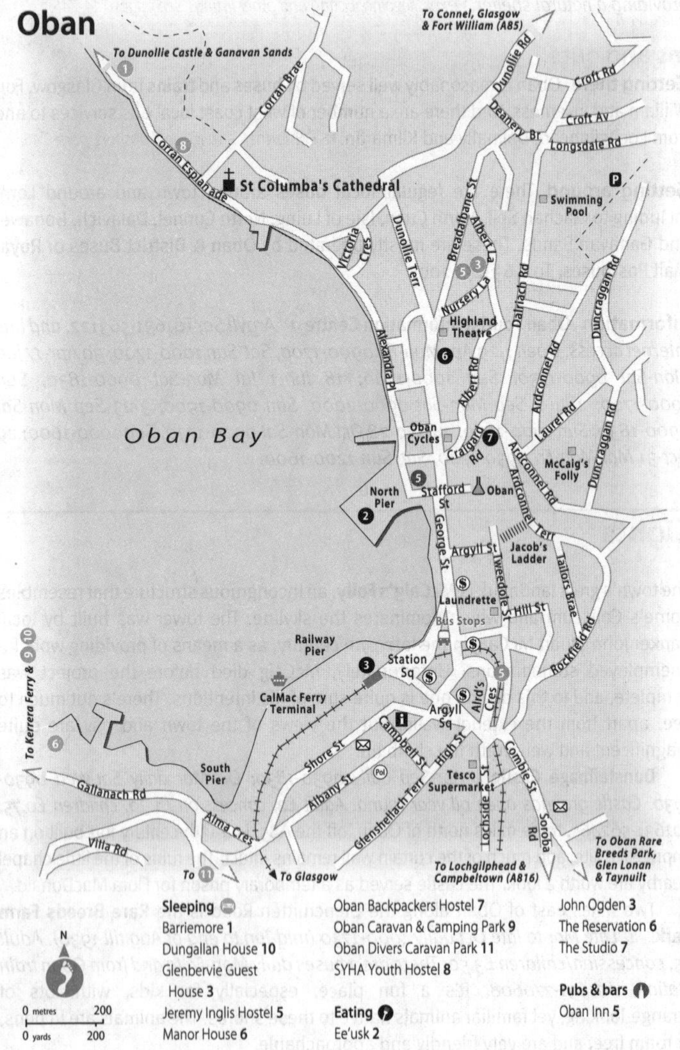

a wild tide-race created by the narrow mouth of the sea loch and the reef that spans most of it, thus restricting the flow of water. The result is the impressive rapids, which are best seen from the shore in the village or from halfway across the bridge. Continue on this road to reach **Barcaldine Castle** ⓘ *Jul-Aug Tue-Sun 1200-1700. £3.25, T01631-720598*, built by the Campbells in the late 16th century. The tower house is still occupied by Campbells, having been sold in the mid-19th century and then bought back as a ruin 50 years later. It's now open to the public and, though there are no real treasures, there are interesting stories to be told, a dungeon (with obligatory ghost) and a tearoom where you can try Mrs Campbell's home baking.

Near Barcaldine Castle, on the main A828, is the **Oban Sealife Centre** ⓘ *Daily 0900-1800 (1000-1700 in the winter months), £6.50, concession £5.50, children £4.50. Various discount vouchers are in operation. Ask at the TIC or phone directly; T01631-720386. Buses to from Oban to Fort William pass by the Sealife Centre (see page 745)*, on the shore of Loch Creran. It's enormous fun and also environmentally friendly as they rescue seals and other aquatic life and then release them back into the wild at the end of the season. You can see lots of strange underwater creatures at close quarters and even touch some of them.

The road runs around Loch Creran and enters the district of Appin, made famous in Robert Louis Stevenson's *Kidnapped*, which was based on the 'Appin Murder' of 1752. A road turns southwest off the main Fort William road to Port Appin, on the western tip of the peninsula, the departure point for the passenger ferry to **Lismore**. To the north of Port Appin is the irresistibly photogenic Castle Stalker. Standing on its own tiny island with a background of islands and hills, it's probably second only to the famous Eilean Donan in its portrayal of Scotland's romantic image. It was built in the 16th century by the Stewarts of Appin before falling into Campbell hands after the ill-fated 1745 rebellion. The current owners open it to the public for a limited period in July and August. Check opening times at the tourist office in Oban.

The island of **Lismore** lies only a few miles off the mainland, in Loch Linnhe, yet feels a world away. It makes an ideal day trip and offers great opportunities for walking and cycling, as well as wonderful views across to the mountains of Morvern and Mull, the Paps of Jura to the south and Ben Nevis to the north. It's a fertile little island (the name *leis mór* is Gaelic for "the big garden") and once supported a population of 1,400, though the present population is about a tenth of that. Lismore has a long and interesting history. It was the ecclesiastical capital of Argyll for several centuries and the **Cathedral of St Moluag** was founded here in the 12th century, just north of Clachan. All that remains is the choir, which is now used as the parish church. Not far from the church, is the 2,000-year-old **Broch of Tirefour**, one of the best-preserved prehistoric monuments in Argyll, with surviving circular walls up to 16-ft high.

Eight miles south of Oban the B884 turns west off the A816 to the tiny Slate Islands, so called because in the mid-19th century, the island's slate quarries exported millions of roofing slates every year. The quarrying industry has long since gone, leaving behind dilapidated old buildings as well as pretty little villages of whitewashed cottages built for the slate workers.

The most northerly of the Slate Islands is Seil, which is reached from the mainland across the impressive Clachan Bridge, better known as the 'Bridge over the Atlantic', built in 1792, with its elegant, high arch to allow ships to pass beneath. Two miles south, at **Balvicar**, the road turns right and climbs up and over to the main village of **Ellanbeich**, an attractive wee place with rows of white cottages around the harbour. This was once a tiny island itself until the intensive slate quarrying succeeded in silting up the narrow sea channel. The village is also, rather confusingly, known by the same name as the nearby island of **Easdale**, so renowned was the latter for its slate deposits. Another road runs south from Balvicar to **North Cuan**, from where the car ferry sails across the treacherous Cuan Sound to **Luing** (see below).

Easdale is separated from Seil by a 500-yd-wide channel which has to be dredged to keep it open. The island, only 800 yds by 700 yds, was the centre of the slate industry and the old dilapidated workers' cottages can still be seen. There was once a population of over 450 here, but the quarries were flooded during a great storm in 1881 and the industry collapsed. The present population numbers around 50. The old quarries can still be seen, filled with water, with the derelict work buildings standing forlorn as the surrounding vegetation takes over. The fascinating history of the island is explained at the **folk museum** ⓘ *Apr-Oct daily 1030-1730, £2, T01852-300370.*near the main square in the village.

The long, thin island of Luing (pronounced 'Ling') once had a population of around 600 which was drastically reduced during the Clearances to make way for cattle. The island is small, six miles by two, and mostly flat, making it ideal for exploring by bike. Bikes can be hired in the pretty little village of **Cullipool**, a mile or so southwest of the ferry (contact *Isle of Luing Bike Hire*, T01852-314256).

South of the turn-off to the Slate Islands is **Arduaine Gardens** ⓘ *Daily all year 0930 till sunset, adult £3, concession £2, children £1, T01852-200366*, a beautiful place and an absolute must for all gardening enthusiasts. The 20-acre garden, now owned by the National Trust for Scotland, is best visited in May and June when you can enjoy the spectacular rhododendrons, but there are also beautiful herbaceous borders, ponds filled with water lilies, woodland and sweeping lawns to admire, as well as great views across to Jura and the Slate Islands.

Sleeping

Oban *p741, map p742*

Oban is the main ferry port for the islands and gets busy in the summer with traffic. It's often an idea to get the tourist office to find a place, which costs more, but saves time and effort.

A **Dungallan House Hotel**, Gallanach Rd, T01631-563799, dungallanhotel- oban.co.uk 13 rooms, open Jan, Mar-Oct and Dec. A Victorian house set in 5 acres of woodland, offering great views, hospitality and fine food.

A **Manor House Hotel**, Gallanach Rd, T01631-562087, F563053. 11 rooms, open Feb-Dec. Overlooking the bay on the road south out of town towards the Kerrera ferry. Offers comfort, style and superb cuisine.

B **Barriemore Hotel**, Corran Esplanade, T/F01631-566356. 13 rooms, open Mar-Nov. More of a guesthouse, and a superior one at that. Great views and a friendly atmosphere.

C **Glenbervie Guest House**, Dalriach Rd, T01631-564770, F566723. 8 rooms. Lovely house high above the town on a street full of good accommodation, good value.

D **SYHA Youth Hostel**, T01631-562025, open all year from Mar, is on Corran Esplanade, just beyond St Columba's Cathedral.

D **Oban Backpackers**, T01631-562107, on Breadalbane St. Mar-Oct and Dec 21-Jan 14.

D **Jeremy Inglis Hostel**, T01631-565065, at 21 Airds Cres, opposite the TIC. Cheaper and with breakfast included, smaller and quirkier.

There are 2 **campsites** nearby:

Oban Divers Caravan Park, T/F01631-562755, open Mar-Nov, on the Glenshellach Rd, about 1½ miles south of the ferry terminal; and **Oban Caravan & Camping Park**, T01631-562425, F566624, open Apr to mid-Oct, on Gallanach Rd, 2 miles south of town near the Kerrera ferry.

Around Oban *p742*

L **Airds Hotel**, Port Appin, T01631-730236, F730535. 12 rooms. This classy little roadside hotel boasts one of the very best restaurants in the whole country.

A **Pierhouse Hotel**, Port Appin, T01631-730302, F730400. Sitting right by the tiny pier, this cosy little hotel has a deserved reputation for excellent, moderately priced local seafood.

Eating

Oban *p741, map p742*

£££ **Ee'usk**, North Pier, T01631-565666. Glass-fronted fish restaurant which has the edge over its competitors. Superb. Open daily 1100-1600 and 1800-2130.

££ **The Reservation**, 108 George St, T01631-563542. Very popular with an emphasis on meat and fish. Open summer daily 1130-2200.

££ **The Studio**, Craigard Rd, T01631-562030. Good-value 3-course set dinner and good à la carte menu, popular with locals, so you'll need to book, open daily 1700-2200 (cheap 'early bird special' served 1700-1830). For a cheap snack look no further than John Ogden's world famous green shed by the ferry terminal. His prawn sandwiches are widely held to be the best on the planet (£2.50). Open 0930-1800.

Pubs, bars and clubs

The town is not exactly the party capital of Scotland, so don't expect much in the way of late-night diversion. Your best bet is the **Oban Inn**, by the north pier, which is the nicest pub in town and serves bar food.

Festivals

Apr The Highlands & Islands Music & Dance Festival is held at the end of Apr/beginning of May.
Aug Argyllshire Gathering (Oban Games) is held at the end of Aug in Mossfield Park.

Activities and tours

Boat trips
Boat trips can be made from Oban, to **Mull, Iona**, **Staffa** and **The Treshnish Islands** with Gordon Grant Tours, on Railway Pier, T01631-562842. There are other operators around the harbour, on the North, South and Railway Piers. You can rent from Borro Boats, Dungallan Parks, Gallanach Road, T01631-563292. For some excitement, check out Seafari Adventures, T01852-300003, www.seafari.co.uk, who use 300hp RIBS (rigid inflatable boats) to take you on a thrilling ride across the Corryvreckan (see page 764). Trips leave from Easdale Island on Seil (see below) but can be booked in advance at Oban TIC.

Diving
Puffin Dive Centre, Gallanach Port, Gallanach Rd, T01631-566088. Diver training centre and facilities (open 0800-2000).

Watersports
At **Lettershuna**, just beyond Port Appin, is the Linnhe Marine Watersports Centre, where you can hire motor boats, sailing dinghies or windsurfing boards, take sailing or windsurfing lessons, or try water-skiing, pony trekking or even clay pigeon shooting. May-Sep 0900-1800. T01631-730227, 0421-503981.

Transport

Ferry
Oban is the main ferry port for many of the Hebridean islands. The **CalMac** ferry terminal, T01631-566688, is on Railway Pier, to the south of the town centre. Only 100 yds away is the train station which is next to the bus terminal. The departure point for ferries to **Kerrera** is 1½ miles along the Gallanach Rd. They leave several times daily between 0845 and 1800 (between 1030 and 1700 on Sun). The **CalMac** car ferry from Oban lands at **Achnacroish** on Lismore (2-4 daily Mon-Sat; 50 mins. A passenger ferry leaves from **Port Appin** pier to the island's north point (daily every 1-2 hrs; 10 mins). A tiny passenger ferry sails from Ellanbeich on Seil to **Easdale**, making the 5-min trip at regular intervals between 0745 and 1900 Mon-Sat (between 0930 and 1500 on Sun), partly to schedule, partly on request. A car ferry to **Luing** (South Cuan) sails from South Cuan on Seil (5 mins), Mon-Sat every 15-30 mins from 0745 to 1815 (later in summer) and on Sun every 30 mins from 1100 to 1800. Check times at Oban tourist office.

Train
There are 3 trains daily to **Glasgow**, via Crianlarich, where the Oban train connects with the Mallaig/Fort William-Glasgow train.

Directory

Banks All the major banks have branches with ATMs in the centre and you can change foreign currency at the TIC. **Car hire** Flit Van & Car Hire, Glencruitten Rd, T/F01631-566553. From £33.50 per day. **Practical Car & Van Rental**, Robertson's Motor Repairs, Lochavullin Industrial Estate, T01631-570900. From £36 per day. **Hazelbank Motors**, Lynn Rd, T01631-566476, F566783. From £35 per day. **Cycling** You can rent bikes from **Oban** Cycles, 9 Craigard Rd, T01631-566966. For details of cycle routes through the forests of Argyll, see the Forest Enterprise leaflet, *Cycling in the Forest*, available at the tourist office. **Internet** Oban Backpackers charge £1.50 for 15 mins.

Mid and South Argyll

→Colour map 5

Southern Argyll has its own particular attractions in the shape of its numerous prehistoric sites. Much of the region was once part of the ancient Kingdom of Dalriada, established by the Irish Celts (known as the Scotti, hence Scotland) who setteld here in the fifth century. ▸▸ For Sleeping, Eating and other listings, see pages 749-750.

Ins and outs

Information **Helensburgh TIC** ⓘ *in the clock tower on the waterfront, T01436-672642. Apr-Oct.* **Bute TIC** ⓘ *Promenade, Rothesay, T01700-502151, open year round.***Iveraray Tourist Information Centre** ⓘ *Front St, T01499-302063. Open year round.***Lochgilphea Tourist Information Centre** ⓘ *Lochnell St, T01546-602344, Apr-Oct.* **Tarbert Tourist Information Centre** ⓘ *Harbour St, T01880-820429.* **Campbeltown Tourist Information Centre** ⓘ *Old Quay, T01586-552056.*

Helensburgh

Overlooking the Clyde is the town of Helensburgh, its wide, grid-plan streets lined with elegant Georgian houses. The town is most famously known for its connection with the great Glasgow architect, **Charles Rennie Mackintosh**. In the upper part of the town, on Upper Colquhoun Street, is **Hill House** ⓘ *T01436-673900, Apr-Oct daily 1330-1730, adult £6, concession/children £4.50. To get there from the Central Train Station, walk about a mile and a half up Sinclair St, then turn left at Kennedy St and follow the signs. From Helensburgh Upper Station (see below) it's a 5-min walk*, one of the best examples of Mackintosh's work. The house was designed for Glasgow publisher Walter Blackie in 1902-04, and is now owned by the National Trust for Scotland. The house is a masterpiece of balanced perfection and artistry and there's much to admire. The attention to detail, the use of natural light, the symbolism of the floral patterns and use of light and dark – hallmarks of his personal Art Nouveau style – are all very much in evidence. After exploring the house, you can visit the kitchen, which has been tastefully converted into a tearoom (open 1330-1630).

Cowal Peninsula

The northern part of the peninsula is largely covered by the sprawling **Argyll Forest Park** which extends from Loch Lomond south to Holy Loch. This area contains the most stunning scenery in Cowal, and includes the **Arrochar Alps**, a range of rugged peaks north of Glen Croe which offer some of the best climbing in Argyll. The most famous of these is Ben Arthur (2,891 ft), better known as **"The Cobbler.**

The A83 runs down through **Glen Kinglas** to reach the village of **Cairndow**, at the head of Loch Fyne. A mile or so further on towards Inveraray, at **Clachan**, at the head of Loch Fyne, is the highly acclaimed Loch Fyne Oyster Bar. At the southern end of Loch Eck, at **Benmore**, is the **Younger Botanic Garden** ⓘ *1 Mar-31 Oct daily 0930-1800, £3, concession £2.50, children £1, T01369-706261,* a lovely woodland garden and offshoot of the Royal Botanic Garden in Edinburgh. Its 140 acres are laid out with over 250 species of rhododendrons and feature an avenue of Giant Redwoods.

One of the most beautiful parts of Argyll is the southwest of Cowal, particularly the route down to the little village of **Tighnabruaich**. The A8003 runs down the west side of Loch Riddon and there are few lovelier sights than the view from this road across the **Kyles of Bute**, the narrow straits that separate Cowal from the island of Bute. Tighnabruaich gets busy in the summer with visitors who come here to enjoy the best sailing on the west coast. A few miles southwest of Kames, is **Portavadie**, on the west coast of Cowal. A *CalMac* car and passenger **ferry** sails from here to **Tarbert**, on the Kintyre Peninsula, saving a lot of time if you're heading for the islands of **Islay, Jura** or **Colonsay.**

Isle of Bute

Barely a stone's throw off the south coast of Cowal is the island of Bute, another favourite holiday destination for people from Glasgow and Ayrshire, who come here in droves during the busy summer months. But though the island is small (15 miles long by five miles wide), it's deceptively easy to escape the hordes, who tend to congregate around the east coast resort of Rothesay, leaving the delights of the sparsely populated west coast free for those who enjoy a bit of peace and quiet.

The sole town on Bute is **Rothesay**, with its handsome period mansions lining the broad sweep of bay, its elegant promenade lined with palm trees and the distinctive 1920s **Winter Gardens**, now refurbished and housing a cinema and restaurant, as well as the TIC. **Rothesay Castle** ⓘ *Apr-Sep Mon-Sat 0930-1830, Sun 1400-1830, Oct-Mar Mon-Sat 0930-1630, Sun 1400-1630 closed Oct-Dec Thu and Fri, Jan-Mar Thu afternoons, Fri and Sun morning , £2.50, concession £1.90, children £0.75.*

One of Bute's main attractions is **Mount Stuart** ⓘ *T01700-503877, www.mountstuart.com, Easter weekend and May-Sep/Oct daily except Tue and Thu, gardens 1000-1800, house 1100-1700, hours vary every year so check in advance, house/gardens £7, children £3*, a unique Victorian Gothic house set in 300 acres of lush woodland gardens, three miles south of Rothesay. This magnificent architectural fantasy reflects the Third Marquess of Bute's passion for astrology, astronomy, mysticism and religion, and the sheer scale and grandeur of the place almost beggars belief. This is truly one of the great country houses of Scotland and displays breathtaking craftsmanship in marble and stained glass, as well as a fine collection of family portraits and Italian antiques. Much of the existing house dates from 1877, and was built following a terrible fire which destroyed the original, built in 1719 by the Second Earl of Bute. Equally impressive are the **landscaped gardens** and woodlands, established by the Third Earl of Bute (1713-92), who advised on the foundation of Kew Gardens in London, and the stunning new Visitor Centre. It's worth spending a whole day here in order to take in the amazing splendour of the house and to explore the beautiful gardens. And if the weather's fine, why not bring a picnic and enjoy the wonderful sea views.

Inveraray and around

One of Argyll's most famous castles, **Inveraray Castle** ⓘ *Apr-Jun, Sep-Oct Mon-Thu and Sat 1000-1300 and 1400-1745, Sun 1300-1745; Jul-Aug Mon-Sat 1000-1745, Sun 1300-1745, £5.50, concession £4.50, children £3.50, T01499-302203*, has been the clan seat of the Campbells for centuries and is still the family home of the Duke of Argyll. The present neo-Gothic structure dates from 1745, and its main feature is the magnificent armoury hall, whose displays of weaponry were supplied to the Campbells by the British government to quell the Jacobite rebellion. **Inveraray Jail** ⓘ *T01499-302381, Apr-Oct daily, 0930-1800, Nov-Mar daily 1000-1700, £5.75, concession £3.75, children £2.80*, the Georgian prison and courthouse in the centre of the village has been brilliantly restored as a fascinating museum that gives a vivid insight into life behind bars from medieval times up till the 19th century.

Another worthwhile diversion, especially if you've got kids in tow, the **Inveraray Maritime Museum** ⓘ *Apr-Sep daily 1000-1800, Oct-Mar daily 1000-1700, £3.60, concession £2.60, children £2, T01499-302213*, housed in the *Arctic Penguin*, one of the world's last iron sailing ships, which is moored at the loch-side pier. Below decks are lots of interesting displays on Clyde shipbuilding and the Highland Clearances, as well as various 'hands-on' activities. South of Inveraray is **Crarae Gardens,** ⓘ *T01546-886614, Mar-Oct 0900-1800, from dawn till dusk in winter, £3.50, children £2.60*, one of Scotland's best public gardens, set in a deep wooded glen on the shores of Loch Fyne.

Loch Awe and Loch Etive

The A819 north from Inveraray joins the A85 at the northeastern tip of Loch Awe, between the villages of of **Dalmally** and **Lochawe**. A few miles west of Lochawe, and almost a mile inside Ben Cruachan (3,695 ft) is the underground **Cruachan Power Station** ⓘ *Apr-Nov 0930-1700; Jul-Aug 0930-1800, £3.50, children £1.50,* or "Hollow Mountain". From the visitor centre on the shores of Loch Awe, a bus trip takes you into the heart of the mountain through tunnels until you reach the generating room.

Further west, and 12 miles east of Oban, is the tiny village of Taynuilt, near the shore of Loch Etive. North of the village on the shores of Loch Etive is **Bonawe Iron Furnace** ⓘ *T01866-822432, Apr-Sep, daily 0930-1830, £3, concession £2.30, children £1,* Founded in 1753 by a group of Cumbrian ironmasters, Bonawe used the woodlands of Argyll to make charcoal to fire its furnace. At its height, it produced 600-700 tonnes of pig-iron a year. This was then shipped to the forges of England and Wales.

Kilmartin Glen and Crinan Canal

North of Lochgilphead, on the A816 to Oban, is Kilmartin Glen, one of the most interesting and least-known prehistoric sites in Europe. The entire area is littered with Neolithic and Bronze-Age chambered and round cairns, stone circles, rock carvings, Iron-Age forts and duns, Early-christian sculptured stones and medieval castles. Most notable of all is the **linear cemetery**, a line of burial cairns that stretch southward from Kilmartin village for over two miles.

Before exploring this fascinating area, it's a good idea to stop off at **Kilmartin House** ⓘ *Daily all year 1000-1730, adult £3.90, concession £3.10, children £1.20, T01546-510278.* the multi award-winning interpretive centre, housed in the old manse next to the parish church in the tiny village of Kilmartin. The imaginative and interesting museum helps to explain the bewildering array of prehistoric sites lying all around, and includes artefacts from the various sites and prehistoric music. The café/restaurant does not disappoint either, and serves cheap snacks and meals, using local produce, and excellent coffee from 1230 till 1700. Next door in the church graveyard are the **Kilmartin crosses**, dating from as far back as the ninth and 10th centuries. Also within the graveyard is one of the largest collections of medieval grave slabs in the West Highlands. A few miles south of Kilmartin village is the Iron-Age hill fort of Dunadd, which stands atop a rocky outcrop and dominates the surrounding flat expanse of Moine Mhór (Great Moss), one of the few remaining peat bogs in the country and now a Nature Reserve. Dunadd Fort became the capital of the ancient kingdom of Dalriada around 500 AD and is one of the most important Celtic sites in Scotland.

Kilmartin Glen is bordered to the south by the **Crinan Canal**, a nine-mile stretch of waterway linking Loch Fyne at Ardrishaig with the Sound of Jura. You don't need to come in a boat to appreciate the canal. You can walk or cycle along the towpath that runs the entire length of the canal, from Ardrishaig to Crinan, and watch boats of all shapes and sizes negotiating a total of 15 locks. The best place to view the canal traffic is at **Crinan**, a pretty little fishing port on Loch Crinan at the western end of the canal (see Acitivities and tours).

Kintyre

The long peninsula of Kintyre is probably best known as the inspiration for Paul McCartney's phenomenally successful 1970s dirge, 'Mull of Kintyre', but don't let that put you off. Kintyre has all the usual Highland ingredients, such as great scenery, wildlife, bags of history, golf and whisky, but also has the added attraction of being one of Scotland's least explored spots.

The fishing village of **Tarbert** sits at the head of East Loch Tarbert, in a sheltered bay backed by forested hills, and is one the most attractive ports on the west coast. Tarbert attracts its share of yachties, particularly in May when the village hosts the second largest racing series in the UK after Cowes attracting hundreds of boats.

The small island of **Gigha** (pronounced "Gee-a" with a hard "g") translates from Norse as "God's Island". A grand claim, perhaps, but there's no question that this most accessible of islands is also one of the loveliest. It's only a 20-minute ferry ride away, and only six miles by one mile, so it can be visited easily in a day, which is just about enough time to appreciate why the Vikings loved it so much. The island's single greatest attraction is the wonderful **Achamore Gardens** ⓘ *T01583-505254, daily all year 0900 till dusk, £2,* one mile south of the ferry terminal. Thanks to Gigha's mild climate, the 50-acre woodland garden has an amazing variety of tropical plants, including rhododendrons, azaleas, camellias as well as other, more exotic, species.

At the southern end of the Kintyre Peninsula is **Campbeltown**. This may be the largest town by far in this part of Argyll, but it has a real end-of-the-line feel, due in part to its geographical isolation, but also because the town has long since lost its raison d'être – whisky. Six miles from Campbeltown, on the west coast of Kintyre, is Machrihanish, site of Campbeltown's airport and a magnificent beach – five miles of glorious unspoiled sand backed by dunes and washed by gigantic Atlantic breakers. Not surprisingly, this is a cracking place for windsurfing and surfing; one of the very best in the country, in fact. It also boasts a dramatic 18-hole championship golf course. The beach can be approached either by walking north from the village, or south from the car park on the main A83 to Tayinloan and Tarbert, where it leaves the coast.

Sleeping

Cowal Peninsula *p746*

A **Kames Hotel**, Kames, T01700-811489, F811283, tcandrew@aol.com, with great views, and live music in the bar.

A **The Royal Hotel**, Tighnabruaich, T01700-811239, F811300, royalhotel@btinternet.com, on the waterfront, with a multi-gym and sauna, and restaurant.

D **SYHA youth hostel**, T01700-811622, open Apr-Sep, sits high above the village with great views across the Kyles and is often full.

Isle of Bute *p747*

A **Cannon House Hotel**, Battery Pl, Rothesay, T01700-502819, F505725. A comfortable Georgian townhouse. Convenient for the ferry.

C-D **Ascog Farm**, 3 miles south of town, at Ascog, T01700-503372. Feng shui farmhouse offering excellent-value. Very friendly.

Inveraray and around *p747*

A **Fernpoint Hotel**, T01499-302170, fernpoint.hotel@virgin.net, a lovely Georgian house overlooking the loch.

B **George Hotel**, Main St, T01499-302111. Cosy hotel offering good value. Also does good bar meals.

Loch Awe and Loch Etive *p747*

L **Ardanaiseig Hotel**, T01499-833333, www.ardanaiseig-hotel.com. 3 miles east of Kilchrenan village on an unclassified road. Open Feb-Dec. The most luxurious place to stay, and the best place to eat.

A **Taychreggan Hotel**, T01499-833211. Not as grand as the **Ardanaiseig Hotel**, but with equally wonderful views and superb cuisine.

Kilmartin Glen and Crinan Canal *p748*

L **Crinan Hotel**, T01546-830261, www.crinanhotel.com. One of the most beautifully located hotels in the country, and its restaurants are amongst the best.

A **Cairnbaan Hotel**, T01546-603668, F606045, a lovely 18th-century coaching inn overlooking the Crinan Canal in the village of Cairnbaan, just north of Lochgilphead.

C **Kilmartin Hotel**, opposite the church in Kilmartin village, T01546-510250, F606370. Comfortable and serves meals all day.

Kintyre *p748*

L-A **Stonefield Castle Hotel**, 3 miles north on the A82 to Lochgilphead, T01880-820836, F820929. Price includes dinner. A Baronial Victorian mansion set in acres of woodland garden, with great views across the loch.

A **Columba Hotel**, on East Pier Rd, T/F01880-820808, www.columbahotel.com. 10 rooms. On the waterfront with restaurant and bar.

A **Gigha Hotel**, at Ardminish, T01583-505254, F505244, open Mar-Oct, offers comfort, great views and good bar food.

A **Kilberry Inn**, west of Tarbert on the B8024, T01880-770223, www.kilberryinn.com. 3 rooms, open Easter-Oct. Offers superb food.

A **Tayinloan Inn**, at the ferry port of Tayinloan, 01583-T441233, a small and cosy 18th-century coaching inn.

C **Post Office House**, T01583-505251, a short walk from the ferry. The McSporrans also run the post office and general store, provide good home cooking and even rent out bikes.

Eating

Isle of Bute *p747*

£ **West End Café**, 1-3 Gallowgate, T01700-503596. It is a must while you are on Bute to sample the fish and chips at this award-winning chippie. It's open for takeaways all year round, and for sit-down meals Easter-Sep 1200-1400 and 1600-2400 (closed Mon).

Inveraray *p747*

££ **Loch Fyne Oyster Bar**, T01499-600264, about 9 miles east of town on the A83 near Clachan. This restaurant, shop and smokehouse is the best for miles. Open Nov-Mar daily 0900-1800, from mid-Mar onwards 0900-2100 (booking essential at weekends).

Festivals and events

May The Isle of Bute Jazz Festival is held during the May Bank Holiday weekend.
Jul There's also the **Isle of Bute International Folk Festival and World Ceilidh Band Championships,** a massive festival of music and dance held over the third weekend in Jul.
Aug If you're around Campbeltown at the end of Aug, don't miss the **Mull of Kintyre Music Festival,** 3 days of the best in traditional Celtic music, held throughout the town.
Sep Tarbert hosts an excellent **folk music festival,** over a weekend at the end of September (for details, T01880-820343).

Activities and tours

Boat trips

Beyond the Bonawe Heritage Site is the departure point for **Loch Etive Cruises**, T01866-822430, cruises depart at 1000, 1200 and 1400 (except Easter-30 Apr, Sat-Sun, 1-14 Oct, at 1400 only), £9, children £5, no booking necessary but arrive in plenty of time. The loch is inaccessible except by boat, and the 3-hr cruise is worth it.
You can take a boat trip with **Gemini Cruises**, based at Crinan harbour, T/F830238, who offer 2-hr wildlife spotting cruises round Loch Craignish (£9 per person), or longer trips out to the Gulf of Corrievreckan.

Transport

Air

There are 2 flights daily (35 mins), all year round from Glasgow to **Machrihanish** airport. For times and reservations, contact British Airways Express, T08457-733377.

Bus

There are buses from Lochgilphead to **Cairnbaan**, **Crinan**, **Achnamara** and **Tayvallich** several times daily Mon-Sat. There are buses and taxis to **Oban** via **Kilmartin** (Mon-Sat) and a postbus to **Inveraray** (Mon-Sat). There's a service to and from **Ardrishaig**. For taxi details, contact Mid Argyll Taxis, 4 Slockavullin, Kilmartin, T01546-510318. There are several daily buses from Glasgow to **Campbeltown** (4½ hrs), via Inveraray, Lochgilphead, Kennacraig and Tarbert. There are buses from Campbeltown to **Machrihanish** (hourly Mon-Sat, 3 on Sun; 15 mins), to **Carradale** (45 mins) and **Saddell** (4 daily Mon-Sat, 2 on Sun; 25 mins), to **Southend** (several daily; 25 mins).

Ferry

To Bute Daily every 45 mins from 0715 till 1945 (later on Fri, Sat and Sun). For times, T01700-502707. There's also a ferry to **Rothesay** from Brodick on **Arran** (2 hrs), once a day on Mon, Wed and Fri in the summer. **Bute** can also be reached from the **Cowal Peninsula**. A car/passenger ferry makes the crossing from **Colintraive** to **Rhubodach**, at the northern end of Bute, daily every half hour or hour; from 0530-1955 Mon-Sat and 0900-1955 Sun in the summer (21 Apr-27 Aug).
To and from Kintyre There is a car and passenger ferry from Portavadie on the Cowal peninsula to **Tarbert** (25 mins), which leaves daily every hour in summer, less frequently in winter. There are ferries from Tarbert to **Lochranza** on Arran and a summer ferry (Apr to mid-Oct) goes to Lochranza from **Claonaig** on the west coast of Kintyre, south of Kennacraig (see page 751). Ferries leave from **Kennacraig**, 5 miles south of Tarbert, to **Islay** (see page 762) and to **Colonsay** (see page 760). The small **CalMac** car and passenger ferry leaves from Tayinloan to the ferry pier at Ardminish, daily all year round (hourly 0800-1800 Mon-Sat, 1100-1700 Sun).

Isle of Arran

→ Colour map 5

In the wedge of sea between Ayrshire and Kintyre lies the oval-shaped and very beautiful island of Arran. It manages to combine the classic features of the Northwest Highlands with the more sedate pleasures of the Southern Lowlands, thus earning the sobriquet, "Scotland in Miniature". This obvious appeal, coupled with its easy accessibility, makes Arran a very popular destination, but it remains unspoiled, and at 25 miles long is big enough never to feel crowded. ▸▸ For Sleeping, Eating and other listings, see pages 752-753.

Ins and outs

Getting there The main **ferry** route to Arran is from the distinctly unappealing Ayrshire town of Ardrossan to the island's main town, **Brodick**. The **CalMac** car/passenger ferry makes the 55 min journey 6 times daily Mon-Sat, 4 times on Sun. There's a regular train connection between Ardrossan and Glasgow Central. There's also a bus connection to/from Edinburgh. By **car**, from the south the main route to Arran is from the M74 motorway, on to the A71 via Kilmarnock, to Irvine and Ardrossan. For more ferry information, contact Ardrossan ferry office, T01294-463470, or Brodick, T01770-302166.

The other **ferry** routes to Arran are from Claonaig, near Skipness, to **Lochranza** in the north of the island. The non-bookable car/passenger ferry makes the 30-min trip 8-11 times daily during the summer (Apr-Oct), less frequently in winter. There is also a service from Tarbert to Lochranza (1 hr 35 mins). For ferry times, T08705-650000, www.calmac.co.uk; for reservations on sailings to Lochranza, T01880-730253.

Getting around It's possible to explore the island using public transport, as there are regular **bus** and postbus services. There are regular daily buses from Brodick to **Blackwaterfoot** (30 mins) via "The String"; to **Lamlash** (10 mins) and **Whiting Bay** (25 mins) and on to **Blackwaterfoot** (1 hr 10 mins); to **Corrie** (20 mins), **Sannox** (25 mins), **Lochranza** (45 mins), **Catacol** (50 mins), **Pirnmill** (1 hr), **Machrie** (1 hr 10 mins) and **Blackwaterfoot** (1 hr 20 mins). There's also a **postbus** service from Brodick to Corrie, Sannox, Lochranza, Catacol, Pirnmill, Machrie, Blackwaterfoot and back to Brodick; and from Brodick to Lamlash, "The Ross", Kildonan, Whiting Bay and back to Brodick. Arran is best appreciated on a **bike**, however, and for details of bike hire, see below under Brodick. For details of bus services to **Claonaig**, T01546-604695.

Information Brodick Tourist Information Centre ⓘ *beside the ferry pier and bus terminal, T01770-302140, F302395, www.ayrshire-arran.com Mar-Sep Mon-Sat 0900-1930, Sun 0900-1700, also open daily in winter, all hours vary so check beforehand.*

Brodick

The largest and busiest settlement on Arran, and main ferry port, is Brodick, lying in a wide bay (hence its Norse name breidr vik, meaning "broad bay") backed by a range of steep crags. It's not the most attractive village on the island, and consists of little more than one long street that sweeps round the bay, but you'll find a wide range of tourist facilities and services here. A few miles north of town is the impressive **Brodick Castle** ⓘ *T01770-302202, castle and restaurant open 1 Apr-30 Jun and 1 Sep-31 Oct, daily 1100-1630; 1 Jul-31 Aug, daily 1100-1700. Garden and country park open all year, daily 0930-1700 (country park – sunset). £7, £5.25 concession); garden and country park only £3.50, £2.60,* one of the island's top sights and a flagship NTS property. Until recently this was the family seat of the Dukes of Hamilton, erstwhile owners of the island. The oldest part of the castle dates from the 13th century, with extensions added in the 16th, 17th and 19th centuries. The hour-long tour of the sumptuously furnished rooms and kitchens is interesting and can be rounded off with a visit to the castle restaurant, where you can enjoy home-cooked meals or light snacks. On a good day you can sit outside on the castle terrace and have lunch whilst admiring the views. The walled garden is worth a look, and the surrounding country park includes 11 miles of way-marked trails.

South Arran

The south of Arran is a fertile landscape of rolling hills and pretty little seaside villages, where you'll find the bulk of the island's population and tourists. A few miles south of Brodick is Lamlash, a quiet and attractive place set in a wide, sheltered bay but with an unappealing mud beach. Lying just offshore is the humpbacked **Holy Island**, which is owned by a group of Scottish Buddhists who have retired here for peace and meditation. A ferry runs to and from the island several times daily from 1 May to 4 September (limited service 5 September to 30 October). The first ferry departs Lamlash at 1000 and the last one returns at 1715, leaving you just enough time to climb up to the highest point, **Mullach Mór** (1,030 ft).

The little fishing village of Blackwaterfoot is set round a bay with a tiny harbour. Two miles north along the coast are the **King's Caves**, where, according to legend, Robert the Bruce watched a spider try, try and try again and was thus inspired to secure his own and Scotland's destiny. It's a 45-minute walk from where you leave the car to the cathedral-like main cave, which has an iron gate to keep out wandering sheep. Four miles north of Blackwaterfoot, off the main coast road, is **Machrie Moor**, site of the most impressive of Arran's Bronze-Age **stone circles**. Park by the *Historic Scotland* sign and then walk for one and a half miles along the farm track to reach an area boasting no fewer than six stone circles. Many of them are barely visible above the ground, but the tallest is over 18 ft high. A few miles further on, just south of the turn-off to Machrie village, is another Historic Scotland sign, this time for **Moss Farm Road Stone Circle**, which lies about a half mile walk along the farm track.

North Arran

The north half of Arran contrasts sharply with the southern part. It looks and feels more like the Scottish Highlands – desolate, unspoiled and much of it accessible only to the serious hill-walker. But though the north is scenically more spectacular, it attracts few visitors. Six miles north of Brodick is Arran's loveliest village, Corrie. Corrie has a couple of hotels and B&Bs, a good pub, and makes an attractive alternative to Brodick as a starting point for the ascent of Goatfell. The main coastal road continues north from Corrie to **Sannox,** with its sandy beach, then it cuts inland and climbs northwest towards Lochranza. It's worth taking your time to admire the view and on the other side of the pass, in **Glen Chalmadale,** you can see red deer heading down to the shore at dusk.

The most spectacular introduction to Arran is to arrive at Lochranza, the most northerly village and second ferry port. This charming village is guarded by its ruined 13th-century castle and backed by looming mountains. **Lochranza Castle** can be visited free of charge (the key is available from the *Lochranza Stores*). Lochranza is also the site of Scotland's newest distillery, **Isle of Arran Distillers** ⓘ *T01770-830264, www.arranwhisky.com Mar-Oct daily 1000-1800, guided tours held throughout the day. £3.50, £2.50 child,* which opened in 1995 and is the first legal whisky distillery on the island for over 150 years. There are guided tours of the distillery, followed by the obligatory dram, and also an excellent restaurant (see below).

Sleeping

Brodick *p751*

A **Kilmichael Country House Hotel,** Brodick, T01770-302219, www.kilmichael.com. 7 rooms. Take the road north towards the castle, turn left at the golf course and follow the signs for about a mile. Refined elegance in the island's oldest house. Their award-winning restaurant is the best on the island. Booking is essential for non-residents. No children under 12.

A **Auchrannie Country House Hotel,** just beyond the turning to Kilmichael, T01770-302234, www.auchrannie.co.uk. 28 rooms (also self-catering and time-share lodges). May lack the charm of Kilmichael but makes up for it with superb facilities and leisure complex. It also has a 36-bedroom spa resort. Their *Garden Restaurant* is also highly rated and the Brambles Bistro offers less expensive bar meals. There is also **B&B** accommodation, including:

C **Glen Cloy Farmhouse**, Glen Cloy Rd, T01770-302351, which is a cut above the rest. The nearest **campsite** is **Glen Rosa**, T01770-302380, open Apr-Oct, two miles from town on the road to Blackwaterfoot.

South Arran *p752*

A **Argentine House Hotel**, Whiting Bay, T01770-700662, www. argentinearran.co.uk. 5 rooms, on the seafront and recognisable by the flags flying outside. Excellent cooking.

A-B **Burlington Hotel**, T01770-700255, www.milford.co.uk/go/ burlingtonarran.html. 9 rooms, open Easter-Oct. Comfortable rooms and a reputation for superb seafood; moderately priced set 3-course dinner in dining room or à la carte in bistro.

North Arran *p752*

B **Corrie Hotel**, Corrie, T01770-810273. Friendly and good value with a lively bar.

B **Apple Lodge**, Lochranza, T/F01770-830229. A lovely country house with four double rooms, offering home cooking for residents.

C **Castlekirk**, Lochranza, T01770-830202, a converted church opposite the castle.

There's a **campsite** next to the golf course in Lochranza, with facilities, T01770- 820273, office@lochgolf. demon.co.uk, Apr-Oct.

Eating

Brodick *p751*

£££-££ **Creelers Seafood Restaurant**, at the Home Farm, a mile or so north of town on the road to the castle, T01770-302810. Some of the best seafood in the whole country.

££-£ **Brodick Bar**, behind *Wooley's bakery* and opposite the post office. Superior pub grub served in the bar or restaurant next door.

North Arran *p752*

££ **Harold's Restaurant**, T01770-830264, arranvc@aol.com, in the distillery visitor centre. Here you can enjoy innovative Scottish/Caribbean cuisine. Open till 2100.

Directory

Brodick *p751*

Banks Brodick has banks with ATMs but these are the only ones on the island. **Car and cycle hire** Whiting Bay Garage, T/F01770-700345, for car hire, taxis, or island tours. Whiting Bay Hires, on the jetty, T01770-700382, for cycle hire. **Post office** Just off the seafront, opposite the petrol station and pharmacy.

Mull and Iona

→Colour map 7

The island of Mull is the third largest of the Hebridean islands and, after Skye, the most popular. Everyone has their own favourite island, but Mull has enough going for it to appeal to most tastes: spectacular mountain scenery; 300 miles of wild coastline; castles; wildlife; a narrow-gauge railway; some of the best fishing in Scotland; and some of the prettiest little villages; all in an area roughly 24 miles from north to south and 26 miles from east to west. It's worth spending time on Mull to fully appreciate its pleasures and take the time to make a pilgrimage to tiny Iona, the most spiritual of places and one of the loveliest. ▸▸ *For Sleeping, Eating and other listings, see pages 757-759.*

Ins and outs

Getting there Mull is served by **ferry** services. From Oban to **Craignure** (40 mins) 6-8 times daily Mon-Sat and 5 times daily on Sun. CalMac offices: Oban, T01631-566688, and Craignure, T01680-812343. Kilchoan to **Tobermory** 7 times daily Mon-Sat and 5 times daily on Sun (Jun-Aug). Lochaline to **Fishnish** (15 mins) hourly 0700-1910 Mon-Sat and 0900-1800 Sun. Some ferries from Oban to Coll and Tiree call in at Tobermory.

Getting around You can get to most parts of the island by **bus**. Services given below are for Apr-Oct. Winter services are less frequent. There's a bus from Tobermory post office to **Dervaig** and **Calgary**, 5 times a day Mon-Fri and twice on Sat (operated by RN Carmichael, T01688-302220). The Craignure to **Tobermory** via Salen service runs 5 times a day Mon-Fri, 8 times on Sat and 3 times on Sun (operated by **Bowman's Coaches,** T01680-812313, and **Highlands & Islands Coaches,** T01680-812510). There's a bus from Craignure to **Fionnphort** (for Iona) 6 times a day Mon-Fri, 4 times on Sat and 1 on Sun (**Bowman's** and **Highlands & Islands**). There's also a **postbus** service from Salen to **Burg** (Kilninian) via the **Ulva Ferry** twice a day Mon-Sat (Royal Mail, T01463-256200). For bus times, contact the operators or pick up the *Mull Area Transport Guide* at the tourist office in Oban, Tobermory or Craignure. This also includes ferry times. Tobermory is a 30-40 min drive north from the ferry pier at Craignure. There are daily buses from Craignure which coincide with ferry arrivals. **To Iona,** a passenger-only **ferry** leaves from Fionnphort, Mull (5 mins) frequently 0845-1815 Monday-Saturday and hourly 0900-1800 Sun.

Information Craignure TIC, opposite the pier in the same building as the **CalMac** office ⓘ *T01680-812377. Easter-end Oct.* **Tobermory** TIC is in the same building as the **Calmac** office ⓘ *at the far end of Main St, T01688-302182. Apr-Sep.*

Craignure to Tobermory

The arrival point for visitors is the village of Craignure. One and a half miles south of Craignure is **Torosay Castle** ⓘ *T01680-812421, Easter-mid Oct daily 1030-1730. Gardens open all year daily 0900-1900, house and gardens £4.50, children £1.50; gardens only £3.50, child £1,* more of a baronial family home than a full-blown castle. The best way to arrive at the castle is by the **Mull and West Highland Railway** ⓘ *open Easter-mid Oct (T01680-812494 for times), £2.50 single, £3.50 return.*

A couple of miles east of Torosay is **Duart Castle** ⓘ *T01680-812309, May-mid Oct daily 1030-1800, £3.80, concession £3, children £1.90,* the 13th-century ancestral seat of the Clan Maclean stands imperiously at the end of a promontory, commanding impressive views over Loch Linnhe and the Sound of Mull. The castle's main feature is the tower house, built in the late 14th century when it became the main residence of the Macleans of Duart. Today it's a fascinating place to visit, with many relics and artifacts on display. There's also an excellent tearoom serving delicious home-baked scones.

Tobermory

There is no prettier port in the west of Scotland than Tobermory, Mull's main village. The brightly painted houses that line the harbour front date from the late 18th century when the British Fisheries Society built Tobermory as a planned herring port. It never really took off as a fishing port, however, and nowadays you're more likely to see pleasure yachts anchored in the protected waters of the natural harbour. Lying at the bottom of the harbour is a galleon of the Spanish Armada, which sank in mysterious circumstances, along with its treasure of gold doubloons which has eluded salvage crews ever since.

At the foot of the main road down to the harbour is the tiny **Tobermory Distillery** ⓘ *T01688-302645, Easter to end-Oct Mon-Fri 1000-1700, £2.50, concession £1, children 18 free,* which offers a guided tour rounded off with a sampling of the island's single malt.

The west coast

Mull's west coast is where you'll find some of the island's most stunning scenery. The B8073 winds its way anti-clockwise from Tobermory in a series of twists and turns as it follows the contours of the coastline. The road climbs west from Tobermory then makes a dramatic descent, with hairpin bends, to Dervaig. Dervaig is a lovely village of whitewashed cottages, beautifully situated at the head of Loch Cuin.

It has two very notable features. One is **Kilmore Church,** which has an unusual pencil-shaped spire. Dervaig's claim to fame, though, is the **Mull Little**

Theatre ⓘ *T01688-400245, May-September,* the smallest professional theatre in Britain, with only 43 seats. It puts on an impressive programme of plays in the summer. One mile beyond Dervaig take the turn-off to Torloisk to reach the **Old Byre Heritage Centre** ⓘ *T01688-400229, Easter to end-Oct daily 1030-1830, £3, concession £2, children £1.50*, which stands out as one of the few genuinely interesting examples of these places. It also features a video of Mull's history and a tearoom (see below).

Five miles west of Dervaig is **Calgary Bay,** Mull's most beautiful beach ringed by steep wooded slopes with views across to Coll and Tiree. Calgary in Alberta, Canada was named after the former township. Many emigrants were forcibly shipped to Canada from here during the Clearances. There are some wonderful paths through Calgary Wood, just past Calgary Farmhouse Hotel, including a half hour circular walk.

Isle of Ulva

ⓘ *A small bicycle/passenger-only ferry makes the 2-min crossing on demand from Ulva Ferry, Apr-Oct Mon-Fri 0900-1700, and on Sun Jun-Aug. This includes entry to the Boathouse Heritage Centre, Sheila's Cottage (a musuem of island life) and access to all walks. At other times call to make arrangements, T01688-500226.*

If you have the time and need to escape the hectic bustle of Mull, then take a day out on idyllic Ulva (meaning 'wolf island' in Norse), just off the west coast. You won't see any wolves around, but you're almost guaranteed to spot deer, golden eagles, buzzards and seals offshore. There are several woodland and coastal trails across the island, including one to the southwest where there are basalt columns similar to those on Staffa, or you can follow the trail to the top of the hill for views across to the Cuillins on Skye (on a clear day), or cross to Ulva's even smaller neighbour **Gometra** by a causeway. For more information on the island walks and on its history, visit the **Boathouse Heritage Centre** ⓘ *T01688-500241, ulva@mull.com, Easter-Oct Mon-Fri 0900-1700 and Sun Jun-Aug only. The entry price is included in the ferry fare (see below)* close to the ferry slip on Ulva. There's also a tearoom where you can try the local oysters with Guinness.

Staffa and the Treshnish Isles

The tiny uninhabited island of Staffa, five miles off the west coast of Mull, is one of the most spectacular sights not just in Scotland but anywhere in the world. It consists of immense, hexagonal, basalt pillars which loom up out of the sea, like a giant pipe organ. Staffa was formed 60 million years ago by the slow cooling of Tertiary basalt lavas. These have been carved by the pounding sea into huge cathedral-like caverns such as the mightily impressive **Fingal's Cave**. The sound of the sea crashing against the black crystalline columns made such an impression on Felix Mendelssohnn in 1829 that he immortalized the island in his *Hebrides Overture*. The composer was obviously aware of its original name in Gaelic, which means 'The Melodious Cave'. You can land on the island – if the weather is good enough – and walk into the cave via the causeway; an experience not be missed. But even if the seas are too rough, it's worth making the 90-minute boat trip just to witness the columns and cave.

South Mull

From Ulva Ferry the B8073 heads east along the north shore of **Loch na Keal** then enters a wide flat valley, where the road forks east to Salen and west along the south shore of Loch na Keal. This part of Mull is dominated by **Ben More** (3,170 ft), the island's highest mountain. All around is a spectacular region of high jutting mountains and deep glens, extending west to the **Ardmeanach Peninsula**. The peninsula may look impenetrable, but with the proper walking gear can be explored on foot. On the north coast, about a mile from the road, is the massive entrance to **MacKinnon's Cave,** which runs for about 100 yards back under the cliffs. Make sure to visit only at low tide. The area around the headland, now owned by the National Trust for Scotland, is known as **'The Wilderness'**.

 Near the headland is **MacCulloch's Tree**, a remarkable fossilized tree 40 ft high and thought to be 50 million years old, which was discovered in 1819. The tree is only accessible by a seven-mile footpath which begins at Burg Farm. You should call in at the farm to let them know of your intentions and also to get directions. You should have a map of the area and also time your arrival with low tide.

Mull's southernmost peninsula stretches west for 20 miles from the head of Loch Scridain as far as Iona. Most visitors use it merely as a route to Iona but there are a couple of interesting little detours along the way. A twisting side road leads south from Pennyghael over the hills and down to **Carsaig Bay**, from where you can head east or west along the shore for some dramatic coastal scenery. Two roads lead south from Bunessan. One leads to **Scoor**, near where is a great beach at Kilveockan. The other road splits near the coast: the left branch leads to **Uisken Bay**, where there's a nice beach; the righthand branch leads to **Ardlanish Bay**, which also has a good beach.

The road ends at **Fionnphort**, the departure point for the small passenger-only ferry to Iona, just a mile across the Sound of Iona. The village is little more than a car park, a row of houses, a pub and a shop, but there are several inexpensive B&Bs for those arriving too late to make the crossing. Even if you're not staying, it's worth stopping off in the village to visit the **Columba Centre** ⓘ *Mid-May to end-Sep Mon-Sat 1000-1800, Sun 1100-1800, £2, children £1,* a museum which relates the saint's life story.

A road runs south from Fionnphort to **Knockvologan**, opposite **Erraid island**, which is accessible at low tide. The island has literary connections, for it was here that Robert Louis Stevenson is believed to have written *Kidnapped*. **Balfour Bay** on the south of the island is named after the novel's hero who was shipwrecked here.

Iona

Iona is a small island – barely three miles long and a little over a mile wide – but its importance to Christianity is out of all proportion to its size. Iona's place in religious history was guaranteed when St Columba arrived with his 12 disciples and founded a monastery there in 563 AD. The Irish monk then set about converting practically all of pagan Scotland and much of northern England. Iona went on to become the most sacred religious site in Europe and has been a place of pilgrimage for several centuries. Today that pilgrimage has turned into more of an invasion, with daytrippers making the five-minute ferry trip from Mull to visit the abbey. Few, however, venture beyond the main village, **Baile Mór**, and it's easy to find a quiet spot, particularly on the west coast with its sparkling silver beaches washed by turquoise sea. It's worth spending a day or two here to soak up the island's unique spiritual peace.

The **abbey** ⓘ *Open all year and at all times, free but give a donation at the entrance, where you can pick up a plan of the abbey*, dates from around 1200, though it has been rebuilt over the centuries and completely restored in the 20th century. The oldest part is the restored **St Oran's Chapel**, to the south of the abbey on the right, which is plain and unadorned save for its splendid 11th-century Norman doorway. Surrounding the chapel is the **Reilig Odhrain**, the sacred burial ground, which is said to contain the graves of 48 Scottish kings, including Macbeth's victim, Duncan, as well as four Irish and eight Norwegian kings. The stones you see today are not the graves of kings but of various important people from around the West Highlands and Islands.

Beside the **Road of the Dead**, which leads from the abbey church to St Oran's Chapel, stands the eighth-century St Martin's Cross. This is the finest of Iona's Celtic high crosses and is remarkably complete, with the Pictish serpent-and-boss decoration on one side and holy figures on the other. In front of the abbey entrance is a replica of St John's Cross, the other great eighth-century monument. The original is in the Infirmary Museum, at the rear of the abbey, along with a collection of medieval gravestones.

No part of St Columba's original buildings survives, but to the left of the main entrance is **St Columba's Shrine**, the small, steep-roofed chamber which almost certainly marks the site of the saint's tomb. You get a good view of the whole complex from the top of the small grassy knoll opposite the abbey entrance. This is **Torr an Aba**, where Columba's cell is said to have been. The **Abbey** itself has been carefully restored to its original beautiful simplicity and inside, in a side chapel, are marble effigies of the eighth Duke of Argyll and his third wife, Duchess Ina.

The passenger ferry from Fionnphort on Mull lands at **Baile Mór**, Iona's main village, which is little more than a row of cottages facing the sea. There are over a dozen places to stay but, as demand far exceeds supply during the busy summer season, it's best to book in advance at one of the tourist offices on Mull, or in Oban. There's also a post office, a very good craft shop and general store in the village. Just outside the village, on the way to the abbey, are the ruins of the **Augustinian nunnery**. Just to the north, housed in the parish church manse, built by Thomas Telford, is the **Iona Heritage Centre** ⓘ *Apr-Oct Mon-Sat 1030-1630, £1.50,* which features displays on the island's social history. Nearby stands the intricately carved 15th-century **Maclean's Cross.**

On the west coast are some lovely beaches of white sand and colourful pebbles. The best of the lot is the **Bay at the Back of the Ocean**, beside the golf course, and only a mile and a half walk from the ferry. This was one of John Smith's favourite places and it's easy to see why. At the southern tip of the island is another sandy beach at **St Columba's Bay**, believed to be the spot where the saint first landed. Another good walk is to the top of **Dun I**, the only real hill, which rises to a height of 300 ft.To get there, continue on the road north from the abbey, past MacDougal's Cross, then go through a gate to the right of Bishop's Walk Farm and follow the fence up to where you join a footpath up to the top. It's only about half an hour up and down and there are great views from the top of the entire island and the coastline of Mull.

Sleeping

Craignure to Tobermory *p754*

B **Craignure Inn**, T01680-812305, www.craignure-inn.co.uk 3 rooms, open all year. Its cosy bar serves decent cheap-moderately priced food and is a good place to seek refuge on a wet day.

B **Old Mill Guest House & Restaurant**, 3 miles south of Craignure, at Lochdon, T/F01680-812442. 3 rooms. Their cosy little restaurant has a deserved reputation for fine cuisine, so you'll need to book in advance.

Tobermory *p754*

L **Western Isles Hotel**, T01688-302012, F302297. 23 rooms. Open all year, the biggest and grandest hotel on the island, set high above the harbour with great views from the comfortable rooms, has 3 excellent restaurants, including the lovely conservatory bar.

C **Mishnish Hotel**, Main St, T01688-302009, www.mishnish.co.uk Open all year, 10 rooms. Its bar is the live music focus of the town and social hub (see below).

C **Baliscate Guest House**, a short walk from town, T01688-302048, F302666. 4 en suite rooms. They also organize fishing and wildlife trips (see below).

D **Failte Guest House**, Main St, T/F01688-302495. Open Mar-Oct, 7 rooms. Best of the guesthouses, excellent.

The west coast *p754*

A **Druimard Country House Hotel**, T01688-400291, www.druimard.co.uk 6 rooms, open end Mar-Oct. This Victorian country house is right beside the Mull Little Theatre; the room rate includes dinner.

B **Calgary Farmhouse Hotel**, T01688- 400256. 9 rooms, open Apr-Oct. This farmhouse is one of Mull's gems, and the adjoining *Dovecote Restaurant* serves excellent food (££). There's also a tea-room, *The Carthouse*, which offers light lunches and home baking.

South Mull *p755*

B **Pennyghael Hotel,** Pennyghael, overlooking the loch, T01681-704288, F704205, which is open from Easter to October and has an excellent restaurant.

C **Achaban House**, just before Fionnphort, T01681-700205, www.achabanhouse.co.uk. 7 rooms. This former manse is comfortable and well-furnished, and also offers dinner.

C **Uisken Croft**, Uisken Bay, T01681-700307, open Apr-Oct. Idyllic.

Iona *p756*

A **Argyll Hotel**, T01681-700334, www.argyllhoteliona.co.uk. 17 rooms, open Apr-Oct. This is the better of the island's 2 upmarket hotels, and its good restaurant serves lunches 4-course dinners.

D **Iona Hostel**, T01681-700642, an exceptional hostel with views to the Treshnish Islands about a mile from the ferry along the path past the abbey. It's best to book ahead in summer.

Eating

Tobermory *p754*

The best eating in town is to be had in the **Western Isles Hotel** (see above), where you can choose between 3 restaurants. A 3-course à la carte in the dining room or the oriental **Spices Bistro** is expensive to mid-range, while cheap bar meals are served in the **Conservatory Bar**. The harbour front is filled with places to eat, including the bar of the **Mishnish Hotel**. A worthwhile detour is to walk to the edge of town to the **Green Barn** which is run by **Isle of Mull Cheese**.

Festivals and events

Apr A great time to be on Mull is during the annual **Mull Music Festival**, known as the *Whisky Olympics*, is held on the last weekend of Apr, when you can enjoy a feast of Gaelic folk music and, of course, whisky. The focus of the festival is the bar of the *Mishnish Hotel* in Tobermory (for details T01688-302383).

Jul Another great musical event is the **Mendelssohn on Mull Festival**, held over 10 days in early Jul to commemorate the famous composer's visit here in 1829. The **Tobermory Highland Games** take place annually on the 3rd Thu in Jul.

Sep **The Sound of Mull**, a day long celebration of local rock and pop acts, takes place at the end of Sep.

Oct Rally enthusiasts should not miss the **Tour of Mull Rally** held in early Oct.

Activities and tours

Boat trips

Trips to **Staffa** and the **Treshnish Isles** leave from Oban, Dervaig, Ulva Ferry, Iona or Fionnphort, weather permitting. A full-day cruise including Staffa and the Treshnish Isles costs £33 per person (£17 for children); a cruise to Staffa only costs around £15.

Turus Mara, T08000-858786 (freephone), www.turusmara.com, leave from Ulva Ferry, daily May-Sep and Sep-Oct subject to weather and demand. They also run this trip from Oban; £35 including ferry and courtesy bus form Craignure to Ulva Ferry.

Inter-island Cruises leave from Croig near Dervaig, T/F01688-400264. They're a little bit more expensive than the others, but also have trips to Coll and Muck.

Alternative Boat Hire, T01681-700537, offer trips around the coastline and handline fishing on a traditional wooden boat. You can hire by the hour or for an afternoon, May-Oct, from Fionnphort and Iona.

Cycling

There are many places to rent bikes. In **Tobermory** there's **Tom-a' Mhuillin** on the Salen Rd, T01688-302164, **Brown's Hardware** shop on Main St, T01688-302020, or try the **youth hostel** in Tobermory. In **Salen** there's **On Yer Bike**, T01680-300501, which also has a shop by the ferry terminal in **Craignure**, T01680-812487.

Diving

Diving trips and courses are available with **Seamore Diving**. Book through Seafare Chandlery & Diving Service, Main St, Tobermory, T/F01688-302277.

Fishing

Fishing trips can be made with **Amidas Sea Fishing & Wildlife Trips**, based at Baliscate House (see 'Sleeping' above), or book at **Tackle & Books**, T01688-302336. Trips cost around £15 for 3 hrs, or £30 for a full day. Permits for trout fishing are available from **A Brown & Son**, 21 Main St, Tobermory, T01688-302020, F302454. For more details pick up the *Tobermory Angling Association* leaflet from the tourist office.

Wildlife tours

These can be made from Aros, just to the north of Salen, with Richard Atkinson at **Island Encounter Wildlife Safaris**, Arla-Beag, Aros, T01680-300441. Full-day wildlife safaris with a local guide cost £25 including lunch. You'll see golden eagles, white-tailed sea eagles, hen harriers, divers, merlins, peregrine falcons, seals and porpoises, to name but a few. Whale and dolphin watching trips can be made from Tobermory with **Sea Life Surveys**, T01688-302787. A full-day tour costs £45 (£48 in Jul/Aug), and there's a maximum of 12 people per trip. You can find out more at the **Hebridean Whale and Dolphin Trust**, a charity which aims to protect the marine environment through education, at 28 Main St, Tobermory, T01688-302620, www.gn.apc.org/whales open daily 1000-1700 all year round. **Isle of Mull Landrover Wildlife Expeditions**, at Ulva House Hotel, T01688-302044 (David Woodhouse).

Directory

Banks Mull's only permanent bank is the **Clydesdale Bank** on Main St. There's also a mobile bank which tours the island; for details T08457-826818.

Coll, Tiree and Colonsay

→ Colour map 7

The low-lying, treeless and windswept island of Coll offers the simple pleasures in life. There's little to do here other than stroll along the magnificent, deserted beaches. Tourism, though, remains low on the list of priorities, and those who do come prefer it that way. Even by Hebridean standards there are few facilities, and accommodation is scarce. Tiree, meanwhile, claims to be the sunniest place in Scotland, but it's also one of the windiest places in the country. So windy, in fact, that Tiree has become the windsurfing capital of Scotland and is known as the 'Hawaii of the North'. Colonsay is the epitome of the island haven: remote, tranquil and undemanding. It has abundant wildlife, beautiful plants and flowers and glorious beaches. All this has become accessible to daytrippers, with a ferry round trip (see below), leaving you six hours ashore. This does scant justice to the island's peculiar charms, however, and judging by the ever-growing number of holiday homes and self-catering accommodation on Colonsay, it's a view shared by many. ▸▸ *For Sleeping and other listings, see page 761.*

Ins and outs

Getting there **To Coll**: there's a **ferry** from Oban to Coll (2 hrs 40 mins) and Tiree (55 mins) once daily on Mon, Tue, Wed, Fri and Sat. **To Tiree**: Tiree has an **airport** and there are regular daily flights (except Sun) all year round from Glasgow. The airport is at The Reef, Crossapol (T01879-220309). There are **CalMac** car and passenger **ferries** to the island from Oban, via Coll and, occasionally, Tobermory. The ferry port is at Scarinish (T01879-220337). From Oban to Tiree (55 mins) once daily on Mon, Tue, Wed, Fri and Sat. **To Colonsay**: There are **ferry** sailings from Oban (2 hrs) once daily Wed, Fri and Sun, arriving at Scalasaig on the east coast. From Kennacraig there is 1 sailing (3 hrs 35 mins) on Wed. From Port Askaig there is 1 sailing (1 hr 10 mins) also on Wed. Ferries need to be booked well in advance during the summer months.

Getting around **Tiree**: there's a **shared taxi** service which operates on request Mon-Fri 0930-1500 (limited service on Sat), also Mon-Wed and Fri 1600-1730. There's also a Tue evening service for arriving ferries, but only in the summer. For private taxi hire call **Island Cabs**, T01879-220344 (evenings and weekends only). There's a **postbus** service around the island, including to and from the airport. The timetable is available at Scarinish Post Office. **Bicycle hire** is available at the **Tiree Lodge Hotel** (see below), or contact Mr N Maclean, T01879-220428. Colonsay: there's a limited bus and postbus service around the island Mon-Sat, for those without their own transport. On Wed in the summer, a tour bus meets the ferry and takes visitors round the island. As the island is only 8 miles long by 3 miles wide, you might want to consider hiring a bicycle. Bike hire from A McConnel, T01951-200355.

Coll

The best of Coll's beaches are on the west coast, at **Killunaig**, **Hogh Bay** and **Feall Bay**. The latter is separated from the nearby **Crossapool Bay** by giant sand dunes up to 100 ft high. These are now owned by the RSPB to protect the resident corncrake population. The CalMac ferry from Oban calls in at Coll's only village, **Arinagour**, where half of the island's population live and where you'll find the post office and a few shops. There's no petrol station, but you should leave the car behind anyway. The island is only 13 miles long by 4 miles wide and the best way to get around is on foot or by bike.

It's worth taking a walk up **Ben Hogh** (341 ft), the island's highest point, overlooking Hogh Bay on the west coast, to get a good overview. The east coast, north from Arinagour to **Sorisdale**, is an uninhabited wilderness which is ideal for some gentle hillwalking.

Tiree

Tiree is a low, flat island, only about 11 miles long and six miles across at its widest, and is also known by the nickname *Tir fo Thuinn*, or "Land below the waves". When seen from a distance most of it disappears below the horizon, save its two highest hills, **Ben Hynish** (462 ft) and **Beinn Hough** (390 ft), on the west coast. Being flat and small, it obviously makes good sense to explore it by bicycle, but remember that the constant wind varies from strong to gale force. The ferry port is at **Gott Bay**, half a mile from **Scarinish**, the island's main village and home to a *Co-op* supermarket, post office and bank (there's a garage at the pier head). About four miles from Scarinish, is Vaul Bay, where the well-preserved remains of **Dun Mor**, a Pictish Broch built around the first century AD, stand on a rocky outcrop to the west of the bay.

The island's main road runs northwest from Scarinish, past the beautiful beach at **Balephetrish Bay** to **Balevullin**, where you can see some good examples of restored traditional thatched houses. Just to the south, at **Sandaig**, is the **Thatched House Museum** ⓘ *Jun-Sep Mon-Fri 1400-1600*, which tells of the island's social history.

In the southwestern corner of the island is the most spectacular scenery of all, at the headland of **Ceann a'Mara**, or Kenavara. The massive sea cliffs are the home of thousands of sea birds and you can see seals on the rocky shore. East from here, across the golden sands of Balephuil Bay, is the island's highest hill, **Ben Hynish**, topped by a radar-tracking station resembling a giant golf ball. Despite this, it's worth the climb to the top for the magnificent views over the island and, on clear days, across to the Outer Hebrides. Below Ben Hynish, to the east, is the village of **Hynish**, where you'll find the **Signal Tower Museum**, which tells the fascinating story of the building of the **Skerryvore Lighthouse** (1840-44) by Alan Stevenson, an uncle of Robert Louis Stevenson. This incredible feat of engineering was carried out from Hynish, where a dry dock/reservoir was built for shipping materials by boat to the Skerryvore reef, 10 miles to the southwest.

Colonsay

Colonsay's population lives in the three small villages, the largest of which is **Scalasaig**, the ferry port. A few miles north of the ferry, in the middle of the island, is **Colonsay House**, dating from 1772. The house was sold, along with the rest of the island, in 1904 to Lord Strathcona, who had made his fortune in Canada with the Hudson Bay Company and went on to found the Canadian Pacific Railway. The house is not open to the public but the lovely gardens and woods, full of rhododendrons, giant palms and exotic shrubs, are worth a stroll. The estate cottages are now self-catering holiday homes.

There are several standing stones, the best of which are **Fingal's Limpet Hammers**, at Kilchattan, southwest of Colonsay House. There are also Iron Age forts, such as **Dun Eibhinn**, next to the hotel in Scalasaig (see below). Colonsay is also home to a wide variety of **wildlife**. You can see choughs, one of Britain's rarest birds, as well as corncrakes, buzzards, falcons, merlins and perhaps even the odd golden eagle or sea eagle. There are also otters, seals and wild goats (said to be descended from the survivors of the Spanish Armada ships wrecked in 1588). The jewel in the island's crown, though, lies six miles north of Scalasaig, past Colonsay House, at **Kiloran Bay**. The beach here is described as the finest in the Hebrides, and who could argue. The magnificent half mile of golden sands, backed by tiers of grassy dunes, with massive breakers rolling in off the Atlantic, is worth the two-hour ferry crossing alone.

Just off the southern tip of Colonsay is the island of Oronsay, two miles square with a population of six and one of the highlights of a visit to Colonsay. The name derives from the Norse for 'ebb-tide island', which is a fitting description as Oronsay can be reached on foot at low tide, across the mud flats known as 'The Strand'. It takes about an hour to walk from the south end of Colonsay to the ruins of a 14th-century **Augustinian Priory**. This was the home of some of the most highly skilled medieval craftsmen in the Western Highlands. A surviving example of their work is the impressive Oronsay Cross and the beautifully carved tombstones, on display in the **Prior's House**. Make sure you take wellies for the walk across The Strand and check on the **tides**. Tide tables are available at the hotel or shop. Spring tides (new and full moon) allow about three to four hours to walk across and back, which is just enough time to see the priory but little else.

Sleeping

Coll *p760*

A **Coll Hotel**, Arinagour, T01879-230334, F230317. A family hotel with a good restaurant.

C **Achamore**, T01879-230430. A lovely old farmhouse a few miles west of the village.

Tiree *p760*

A **Kirkapol House**, in a converted church overlooking Gott Bay, T/F01879-220729.

B **The Glassary Guest House & Restaurant**, at Sandaig, T/F01879-220684. 4 en suite rooms, open all year, very good food (mid-range).

Colonsay *p760*

Accommodation on Colonsay is limited and must be booked up well in advance.

A **Isle of Colonsay Hotel**, T01951-200316, www.colonsay.org.uk A few hundreds yards from the ferry, 11 rooms, a cosy inn with a friendly bar and excellent food; they also arrange various trips around the island.

C **Seaview**, T01951-200315, at Kilchattan, near the standing stones. Open Apr-Oct.

D **Colonsay Backpacker's Lodge**, T01951-200312, www.colonsay.org.uk. An old keeper's cottage 2km from the ferry, sleeps 16 and open all year, phone for lift from ferry.

Activities and tours

Windsurfing tuition is available at Loch Bhasapol, Tiree, T01879-220559 (summer only). The major windsurfing event is the **Wave Classic**, held annually in Oct.

Islay and Jura

→Colour map 5

Islay (pronounced eye-la), the most southerly of the Hebridean islands and one of the most populous, with around 4,000 inhabitants, has one very important claim to fame – single malt whisky. Islay produces a very distinctive, peaty malt and connoisseurs are in for a treat, as the island has no fewer than seven working distilleries. Aside from whisky, people also come here to watch birds. The island is something of an ornithologists' wonderland, and from October to April plays host to migrating barnacle and white-fronted geese flying down from Greenland in their thousands for the winter. The short ferry crossing from Islay takes you to Jura; another world, pervaded by an almost haunting silence. The words 'wild' and 'remote' tend to get overused in describing the many Hebridean islands, but in the case of Jura they are, if anything, an understatement. Jura has one road, one hotel, six sporting estates and 5,000 red deer, which outnumber the 200 people by 25:1, the human population having been cleared to turn the island into a huge deer forest. Rather appropriately, the name Jura derives from the Norse 'dyr-ey', meaning deer island. ▸▸ For Sleeping and eating, see page 765.

Ins and outs

Getting there Islay can be reached by **air** from Glasgow (for details, see page 740). The airport is at **Glenegedale**, a few miles north of Port Ellen on the road to Bowmore. The **ferry** to Islay (and Jura) from Kennacraig to **Port Ellen** (2 hrs 10 mins) sails 1 daily on Mon and Sun and 2 daily on Tue, Thu, Fri and Sat; and to **Port Askaig** (2 hrs) 1 daily on Tue, Wed, Thu, Fri and Sat and 2 daily Mon. The ferry from Oban to **Port Askaig** sails on Wed (4 hrs 15 mins). From Colonsay to **Port Askaig** (1 hr 10 mins) there is a sailing on Wed. **CalMac** offices ⓘ *Kennacraig, T01880-730253; Port Ellen, T01496-302209.* A small car and passenger **ferry** makes the regular 5-min crossing daily to **Jura**, from Port Askaig on Islay to Feolin Ferry. For times, contact Cerco Denholm, T01496-840681.

Getting around For those without their own transport, there's a regular bus service around the island, with **Islay Coaches**, T01496-840273, and **Royal Mail Postbuses**, T01246-546329. There are buses from Portnahaven to **Port Ellen**, via **Port Charlotte**, **Bridgend**, **Bowmore** and the airport; from Port Askaig to **Port Ellen** via **Ballygrant**, **Bridgend**, **Bowmore** and the **airport**; from Port Ellen to **Ardbeg**, **Bowmore**, **Port Askaig** and **Portnahaven**, and also a **postbus** to **Bunnababhain**. Buses run regularly at least from Mon-Sat, but only once on Sun. There is a **bus** service on Jura, which runs from Feolin Ferry to **Craighouse** several times a day, Mon-Sat. A few buses continue to **Lagg** and **Inverlussa** and return to Craighouse. Note that some journeys are by request only and must be booked the day before, T01496-820314.

Information Islay's only official **Tourist Information Centre** is in **Bowmore** ⓘ *T01496-810254. Apr-Jun Mon-Sat 0930-1700 (and Sun 1400-1700); Jul-Sep Mon-Sat 0930-1730, Sun 1400-1700; Sep and Oct Mon-Sat 1000-1700, Oct-Mar Mon-Fri 1200-1600.* They'll find accommodation for you.

Port Ellen and around

Port Ellen is the largest place on Islay and the main ferry port, yet it still has the feel of a sleepy village. There are many day trips from Port Ellen. A road runs east out to **Ardtalla**, where it ends. Along the way, it passes three distilleries, first **Laphroaig**, then **Lagavulin** and lastly, **Ardbeg**, all of which offer guided tours (see page 764). Between the Lagavulin and Ardbeg distilleries is the dramatically sited 16th-century ruin of **Dunyvaig Castle**, once the main naval base and fortress of the Lords of the Isles. A mile further on is the impressive **Kildalton Cross**, standing in the graveyard of the ruined 13th-century chapel. The eighth-century cross is well preserved and one of Scotland's most important Early Christian monuments, and the carvings depict biblical scenes.

Southwest of Port Ellen a road runs out to a little, rounded peninsula known as **The Oa**, an area of varied beauty, both wild and pastoral, and with a wonderful coastline. The road runs as far as **Upper Killeyan**, from where it's about a mile uphill to the spectacular headland at the **Mull of Oa**. Here you'll see the strange-looking **American monument**. The obelisk commemorates the shipwrecks offshore of two US ships, the *Tuscania* and the *Ontranto*, both of which sank in 1918 at the end of the war. There's a great walk north from the Mull of Oa up to Kintra, but it's best to start out from Kintra (see below).

A turn-off from the road to The Oa leads north to **Kintra**, at the south end of **The Big Strand** at Laggan Bay, with five miles of sands and dunes. There's a restaurant and accommodation here, and it's a great place for camping (see below). The restaurant is at the end of the road, with the beach on one side and on the other a wild and spectacular coastal walk to the **Mull of Oa**. There's a detailed map of the route in the restaurant. Just to the north of Kintra is the **Machrie golf course**, a memorable golfing experience.

Bowmore and the Rinns of Islay

The A846 runs north from Port Ellen, straight as a pool cue, to Bowmore, the island's administrative capital and second largest village. Founded in 1768 by the Campbells, it's an appealing place, laid out in a grid plan with the main street running straight up the hill from the pier to the unusual **round church**, designed to ward off evil spirits, who can hide only in corners. Thankfully, the nice spirit stayed behind and can be found at the **Bowmore Distillery**, just to the west of Main Street. This is the oldest of the island's distilleries, founded in 1779, and the most tourist-friendly.

North of Bowmore, at **Bridgend**, the A846 joins the A847 which runs west to the hammerhead peninsula known as the Rinns of Islay ("rinns" is derived from the Gaelic for promontory). A few miles west of Bridgend the B8017 turns north to the **RSPB Reserve** at **Loch Gruinart**. The mudflats and fields at the head of the loch provide winter grazing for huge flocks of barnacle and white-fronted geese from Greenland, arriving in late October. There's an RSPB visitor centre at **Aoradh** (pronounced "oorig") which houses an observation point with telescopes and CCTV, and there's a hide across the road. There are about 110 species of bird breeding on Islay, including the rare chough and corncrake.

The coastal scenery around the Rinns is very impressive, particularly at **Killinallan Point**, a beautiful and lonely headland at the far northeast of Loch Gruinart. Also impressive is **Ardnave Point**, west of Loch Gruinart, and further west along the north coast, **Sanaigmore.** The best beaches are at **Saligo** and **Machir Bay** on the west coast, past Loch Gorm. Both are lovely, wide, golden beaches backed by high dunes, but swimming is forbidden due to dangerous undercurrents.

Port Charlotte is without doubt the most charming of Islay's villages, with rows of well-kept, whitewashed cottages stretched along the wide bay. Here, the **Islay Wildlife Information and Field Centre** ⓘ *T01496-850288, Easter-Oct Mon, Tue, Thu, Fri and Sun 1000-1500, £2,* is a must for anyone interested in flora and fauna. It's very hands-on, with good displays on geology and natural history, a video room and reference library. It's also a great place for kids, and has activity days when staff take tours of the surrounding area. Also worth visiting is the compact **Museum of Islay Life** ⓘ *Easter-Oct Mon-Sat 1000-1700, Sun 1400-1700, £2,* to the east of the village, where you can find out all about illegal whisky distilling on the island. It also has interesting archival material. At the southern end of the Rinns is the picturesque little fishing and crofting village of Portnahaven, its Hebridean cottages rising steeply above the deeply indented harbour.

Around Port Askaig

Port Askaig is Islay's other ferry port, with connections to the mainland and to the islands of Jura and Colonsay. It's little more than a dock, a car park and a few buildings huddled at the foot of a steep, wooded hillside. A short walk north along the coast is the **Caol Ila distillery**, and a couple of miles further north, at the end of the road which branches left before you enter Port Askaig, is the beautifully situated **Bunnahabhain Distillery.**

The A846 runs east from Bridgend out to Port Askaig passing through **Ballygrant**, just to the south of **Loch Finlaggan.** Here, on two crannogs (artificial islands), were the headquarters of the Lords of the Isles, the ancestors of Clan Donald. The MacDonalds ruled from Islay for nearly 350 years, over a vast area covering all of the island off the west coast and almost the whole of the western seaboard from Cape Wrath to the Mull of Kintyre. There's a new **visitor centre** ⓘ *Easter-Oct Tue, Thu and Sun 1400-1630, £1.50,* to the northeast of the loch, where you can see some of the archaeological remains. You can walk across the fen to **Eilean Mor,** where there's a collection of carved gravestones near the ruins of a medieval chapel. A smaller island, **Eilean na Comhairle** ('The Council of the Isle'), is where the Lords of the Isles met to decide policy.

Jura

Jura is one of the last, great wildernesses in the British Isles and perfect for some real off-the-beaten-track walking. Its main attractions are the beautiful **Paps of Jura,** three breast-shaped peaks that dominate not only the island itself but also the view for miles around. From Kintyre, Mull, Coll and Tiree, and from the mountains of mainland Scotland from Skye to Arran, they can be seen on the horizon.

The Whisky Trail

Though the whisky distilling process is basically the same everywhere, some distilleries have more beautiful locations and more interesting tours. Islay's seven distilleries enjoy the most scenically stunning settings and are full of character and history. Islay also offers the unique opportunity to visit several of Scotland's most impressive distilleries in one day, and their distinctive peaty malts are considered to be among the finest.

Laphroaig (pronounced 'la-froyg') is the closest to Port Ellen, and its wonderful setting is summed up by its name, meaning "The beautiful hollow by the broad bay" in Gaelic. According to many this is the ultimate in malt whisky and is at its best after dinner. The free distillery tours are by appointment only, T302418.

Lagavulin (pronounced 'laga-voolin') is a mile along the shore by the romantic ruin of Dunyveg Castle. Their 16-year-old single malt is one of the classics and also makes the ideal after-dinner tipple. They also offer a very interesting tour (£3), Monday-Friday by appointment only, T302400.

Ardbeg distillery is a mile further east and produces a robust and powerful single malt. Established in 1815, it was closed for a while, but was recently acquired by Glenmorangie and runs tours (£2) Monday-Friday from 1030 till 1530, and also on Saturday and Sunday June-August, T302244.

Bowmore is the oldest distillery on Islay and still uses all the old traditional methods to produce its fine single malt, also at its best after dinner. Their hour-long tours are the most professionally done and even include a video. Tours (£2) all year round from Monday-Friday at 1030 and 1400, in the summer months at 1030, 1130, 1400 and 1500, T810441.

Caol Ila (pronounced 'coal-eela') was founded in 1846 and lies close to Port Askaig, with great views across the Sound of Islay to Jura. Unlike most of its island peers, this single malt is best before dinner. Tours of the distillery (£3) all year round by appointment only, T840207.

Bunnahabhain (pronounced 'bun a havan') is the most northerly of the distilleries, set in a secluded bay with great views across to Jura. Free tours are also by appointment only, T840646.

Bruichladdich (pronounced 'brook-laddie') is in the village of the same name on the road south to Port Charlotte. Recently voted distillery of the year by the readers of America's Malt Advocate. They offer tours (£3) all year round Mon-Sat at 1030, 1130 and 1430, www.bruichladdich.com.

One of the island's main draws is the Corryvreckan whirlpool at the very northern tip, between Jura and the uninhabited island of **Scarba**. The notorious whirlpool, the most dangerous tide race in Scotland, is best appreciated one hour after low tide, and its awesome roar can be heard long before you reach it. To get there, follow the rough track from **Ardlussa** to **Kinuachdrach**, or get someone to drive you, then it's a two-mile walk. Before setting out, ask at the hotel for information and directions.

Also in the north of the island is **Barnhill**, the completely isolated and forlorn-looking cottage where **George Orwell** wrote *1984* between 1946 and 1948 (hence the book's title). Though the house attracts literary pilgrims, it remains closed, although it can be rented from £400 per week from April to December; T01786-850274. The only village on Jura is Craighouse, eight miles from Feolin Ferry on the southeast coast. Here you'll find the **Jura distillery**, which welcomes visitors. Tours are by appointment, T820240.

Sleeping and eating

Islay *p762*

A **Glenmachrie**, by Machrie golf course, T/F01496-302560. 5 rooms. A genuine farmhouse offering genuine hospitality and superb food. The price includes dinner, and you'd be crazy to book B&B only and deny yourself the pleasure.

A **Port Charlotte Hotel**, Port Charlotte, T01496-850361, F850361. 10 rooms. Restored Victorian inn with gardens and conservatory on seafront; their restaurant features local seafood and is the best around.

B **Harbour Inn**, Main St, Bowmore, T01496-810330, F810990. 4 rooms. Completely refurbished to a high standard, great views across the bay and superb food in their acclaimed restaurant (**£££**)

B **Kilmeny Farmhouse**, near Port Askaig, T/F01496-840668. Comfort, style, excellent food and a warm, friendly atmosphere. The only drawback is that there are only 3 rooms, so book well in advance.

B **Lochside Hotel**, Shore St, Bowmore, T01496-810244, F810390. 8 rooms. Friendly and good-value hotel with a mind-boggling selection of single malts.

C **The Bothy**, 91 Lennox St, Port Ellen, T01496-302391, mickstuart@thebothyislay.freeserve.co.uk. Run by Mick Stuart who hires out bikes and acts as a wildlife guide.

Jura *p763*

A **Jura Hotel**, T01496-820243, F820249, the one and only hotel, overlooking the small isles bay. They'll provide information on island walks, and the pub is the social hub.

The Small Isles

→*Colour map 7*

The Small Isles is the collective name given to the four islands of Eigg, Muck, Rùm and Canna, lying south of Skye. Seen from the mainland, they look a very tempting prospect, especially the jagged outline of Rùm and the curiously shaped Eigg. But visiting the islands is not easy, as ferry transport is designed for the inhabitants and not geared towards the convenience of island-hopping tourists. Furthermore, the island populations are small, and accommodation and facilities are limited. But anyone with time on their hands will be well rewarded, particularly on mountainous Rùm, with its superb walking and abundant wildlife. ▸▸ *For Sleeping, see page 766.*

Ins and outs

Getting there A **CalMac** passenger-only **ferry** sails from Mallaig to all four islands. From Mallaig to **Eigg** (1½ hrs) on Mon, Tue, Thu and Sat; Mallaig to **Muck** (2 ½ hrs) on Tue, Thu and Sat; Mallaig to **Rùm** (1¾ -3½ hrs) on Mon, Wed and Sat; Mallaig to **Canna** (3 hrs) on Mon, Wed, Fri and Sat. From May-Sep the **CalMac** ferries from Mallaig are supplemented by cruises from Arisaig with **Arisaig Marine**, T01687-450224. For details, see page 853.

Getting around There are ferries between Eigg, Muck, Rùm and Canna; for details contact **CalMac** office in Mallaig, T01687-462403. On Sat in the summer a ferry leaves at 0500 and sails **Mallaig-Canna-Rùm-Muck-Eigg**, allowing those with little time to at least see the islands from close up. A second ferry leaves on summer Sat, making it possible to spend either 9½ hrs on Canna, or 7½ hrs on Rùm, or 5 hrs on Muck, or 3½ hrs on Eigg.

Eigg

Having endured a succession of absentee landlords, the 65 remaining islanders on Eigg (pronounced 'egg'), seized the moment and bought the island themselves, in conjunction with the Scottish Wildlife Trust. Now everyone can enjoy the island's wildlife, which includes otters, seals, eagles and many other birds, such as the Manx shearwater, guillemots and black-throated divers.

The island is dominated by **An Sgurr**, a 1,289 ft flat-topped basalt peak with three vertical sides. It can be climbed by its western ridge. Sitting in the shadow of the Sgurr, at the southeastern corner, is the main settlement, Galmisdale. This is where the ferries drop anchor (passengers are transferred to a smaller boat), and there's a post office, shop and tearoom, all by the pier. At the northern end is the township of Cleadale, on the Bay of Laig. Just to the north are the "Singing Sands", a beach that makes a strange sound as you walk across it.

Muck

Tiny Muck is the smallest of the four islands and is flat and fertile, with a beautiful shell beach. It has been owned by the MacEwan family since 1879. The island gets its unfortunate name (*muc* is Gaelic for pig) from the porpoises, or "sea pigs", that swim round its shores. The ferry drops anchor near **Port Mór**,

Rùm

Rùm, or Rhum, is the largest of the Small Islands and the most wild, beautiful and mountainous. The island is owned and run by Scottish Natural Heritage as an enormous outdoor laboratory and research station, and most of the 30 or so inhabitants are employed by them. Studies of the red deer population are among the most important areas of their work, and access to parts of the island is restricted. This is not prohibitive, though, and there are many marked nature trails, walks and bird-watching spots. The island is a haven for wildlife, and perhaps its most notable resident is the magnificent white-tailed sea eagle, successfully re-introduced on to Rùm in the 1980s and now spreading beyond the island. Rùm is also home to golden eagles and Manx shearwaters.

Though it looks like a wilderness, Rùm once supported a population of 300. Most of them were shipped off to Canada in the mid-19th century, leaving behind an uninhabited deer forest for sporting millionaires. One of these, John Bullough, bought it in 1888 and passed it on to his son, Sir George Bullough, who built the extravagant and extraordinary **Kinloch Castle**. No expense was spared on this massive late-Victorian mansion, constructed of red sandstone from Arran in a bizarre combination of styles; to describe it as over-the-top would be a gross understatement. It is currently undergoing a £14 mn refurbishment.

Canna

Canna is the most westerly of the Small Isles and is owned by the National Trust for Scotland. It's a small island, five miles long by one mile wide, bounded by cliffs and with a rugged interior, fringed by fertile patches. The main attraction for visitors is the fine walking. It's about a mile from the ferry jetty up to the top of **Compass Hill** (458 ft), so called because its high metallic content distorts compasses. The highest point on the island is **Carn a' Ghaill** (690 ft). In summer, a day trip from Mallaig allows you over nine hours in which to explore Canna and enjoy the fantastic views across to Rùm and Skye.

Sleeping

Accommodation on the islands is limited: most people visit on a day trip. If you plan to stay longer than a day, book well in advance. There are a couple of cheap and basic bothies (D) on **Rùm** and you can stay at B **Port Mór House**, T01687-462365. The price includes dinner which is also available to non-residents. Alternatively, you can ask permission to camp at the tearoom, which does snacks and sells fresh bread.

Those wishing to stay on **Canna** can camp rough, with permission from the National Trust for Scotland, or rent out their self-catering cottage, T0131-226 5922.

On **Eigg**, 2 croft houses at Cleadale offer B&B: B **Lageorna**, T01687-482405, www.isleofeigg.org, also offers full board with packed lunch, and caters for vegetarians; and B **Laig Farm**, T01687-482437. There's also an independent hostel with 24 beds, D **The Glebe Barn**, T01687-482417, open Apr-Oct.

Central Scotland

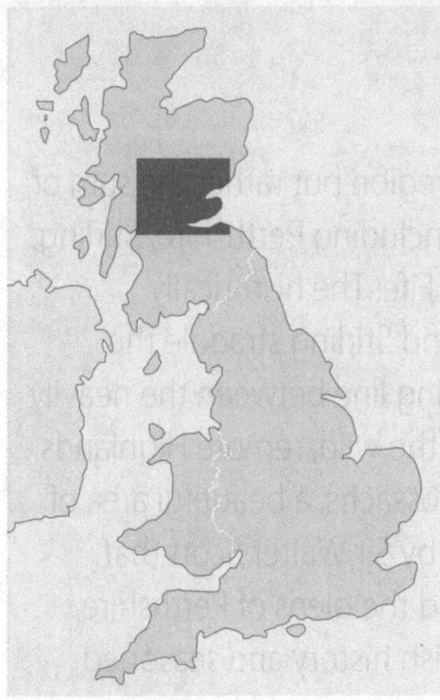

Introduction

Central Scotland is not a distinct region but rather the sum of disparate parts of other regions, including Perthshire, Stirling, the Trossachs, Loch Lomond and Fife. The historically important regions of Perthshire and Stirling straddle the Highland Boundary Fault, the diving line between the heavily populated Central Lowlands and the wild, remote Highlands. Just across this 'border' are the Trossachs, a beautiful area of mountains and forests eulogized by Sir Walter Scott that stretches west from Callander, and the glens of Perthshire, steeped in the rich broth of Scottish history and seasoned with lochs and mountains.

To the east, bounded by the Firth of Tay to the north and the Firth of Forth to the south, is the Kingdom of Fife, once isolated from the rest of the country. Even since the building of the Forth and Tay bridges, the region has managed to retain its own peculiar flavour. The small peninsula juts out into the North Sea like the head of a little terrier dog. Rather apt, given the proud Fifers' fight to preserve the identity of their own 'Kingdom' when it was threatened by local government reorganization in 1975 and 1995.

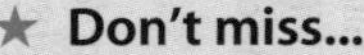

Don't miss...

1. Find the Roman in the gloamin' at the lovely Perthshire village of **Fortingall**, said to be the birthplace of Pontius Pilate, page 775.
2. Travel the road from Aberfoyle to Callander, through the spectacular **Duke's Pass**, one of the most beautiful routes in the country, page 787.
3. Play hunt the royal in **St Andrews**, medieval university town and ancient home of golf, page 792.
4. Explore historic **Stirling**, home of Braveheart and scene of Scotland's greatest military triumph, page 779.
5. Meander through the string of pretty fishing villages in the **East Neuk of Fife**, page 794.

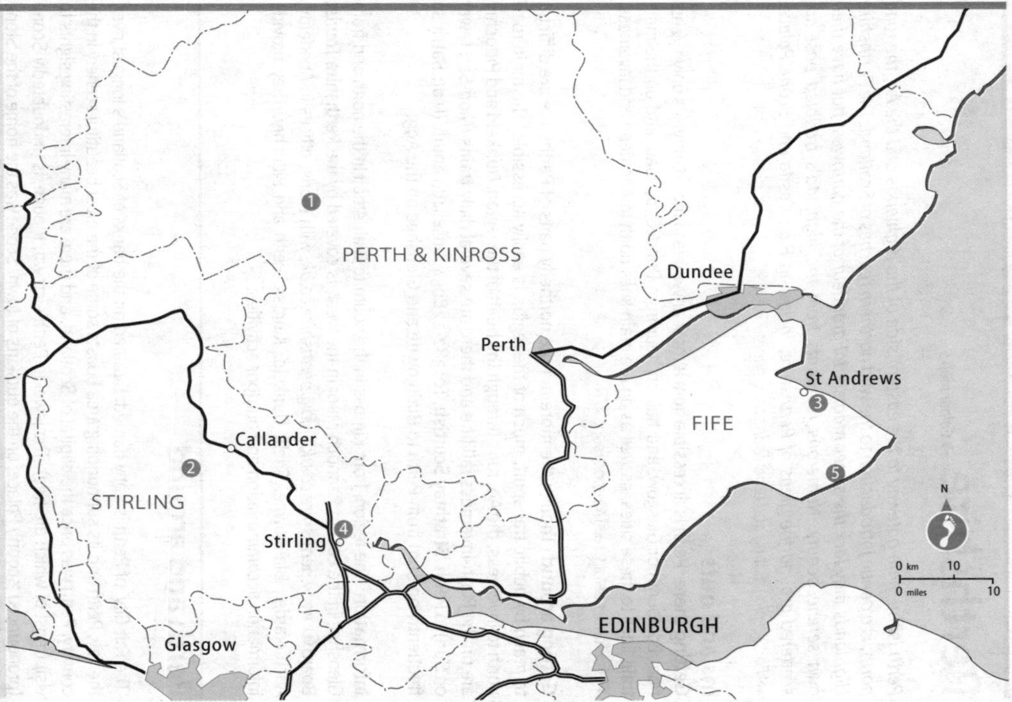

Perthshire → *Colour map 5*

Perth is the main gateway to the eastern side of the Highlands and the A9, the road north, is a gentle introduction to the wild northern reaches of Scotland. The Perthshire Highlands may lack the sheer magisterial grandeur of the northwest but have their own serene beauty. Numerous remnants from the highland's troubled past are scattered around the glens of Perthshire, including Blair Castle and Scone Palace.
▸▸ *For Sleeping, Eating and other listings, see pages 776-779.*

Ins and outs

Getting there Perth is accessible from almost anywhere in the country. It's only 1½ hrs from Edinburgh or Glasgow, and half an hour from Dundee, by **road**, and on the main **train** lines to these cities, as well as on the main lines north to Aberdeen and Inverness.
▸▸ *For further details, see Transport, page 778.*

Getting around Though the more remote northerly parts of Perthshire are difficult to reach by public transport, much of the region is easily accessible. The main road north to Inverness, the A9, runs through the heart of the region. Dunkeld and Pitlochry are on the Perth-Inverness rail line and there are several daily **trains** (Mon-Sat; fewer on Sun) to Perth. **Strathtay Scottish**, T01382-228054, buses run hourly (Mon-Sat, less frequently on Sun) from Perth to Blairgowrie and Glenshee on the A93.

Information The region, from Kinross in the south to Blair Atholl in the north and from Glenshee in the east to Rannoch Moor in the west, is covered by the **Perthshire Tourist Board** ⓘ *www.perthshire.co.uk, info@perthshire.co.uk*, with tourist offices in Aberfeldy, Auchterarder, Blairgowrie, Crieff, Dunkeld, Kinross, Perth and Pitlochry. They provide information accommodation and outdoor activities.

Perth and around

'The Fair City' of Perth is aptly named. Situated on the banks of Scotland's longest river, the Tay, Perth and its surrounding area boasts some of the most beautiful scenery in the country. Perth was once the capital of Scotland, and there are many interesting sights to visit (most of which are free). The jewel in Perth's crown, though, is undoubtedly Scone (pronounced 'scoon') Palace, on the outskirts of town. Scone was the home of the Stone of Destiny for nearly 500 years, and the site where every Scottish king was crowned. Perth is also well-placed for other outdoor activities such as walking, cycling and skiing.

Ins and outs

Getting around The train and bus stations are almost opposite each other at the west end of town, where Leonard St meets Kings Pl. The town centre is very compact and it's easy to get around on foot, but Scone Palace and many of the B&Bs are on the eastern bank of the river, so you may wish to take a bus. Local buses are run by **Stagecoach**, T01738-629339. An enjoyable way to see the sights is to use the **Guide Friday** bus tour of Perth. Tour tickets are valid all day, so you can get on and off as often as you please and you can join the tour at various locations throughout the city. T0131-5562244 for more details, or contact the tourist office.

Information **Perth TIC** ⓘ *Lower City Mills, West Mill St, T01738-450600. Apr-Jun, Sep and Oct Mon-Sat 0900-1730, Sun 1100-1600; Jul and Aug Mon-Sat 0900-1830, Sun 1100-1700; Nov-Mar Mon-Sat 0900-1600.*

Sights

A few minutes' walk north of the High Street, on North Port, is the **Fair Maid's House**, the fictional home of Sir Walter Scott's virginal heroine in his novel, *The Fair Maid of Perth*. Close by, at the corner of Charlotte Street and George Street, is the **Museum and Art Gallery** ⓘ *T01738-632488, Mon-Sat 1000-1700, free,* with displays on local history, art, archaeology, natural history and whisky.

In the 18th century the world-famous Black Watch regiment was raised in Perth, and the **Black Watch Museum** ⓘ *T0131-310 8530, May-Sep Mon-Sat 1000-1630, closed last Sat in Jun, Oct-Apr Mon-Fri 1000-1530, free,* housed in the 15th-century Balhousie Castle, is well worth a visit even to the most un-military minded. The museum is on Hay Street, on the edge of the North Inch, to the north of the town centre. Back in the town centre, in West Mill Street is Lower City Mills (also home to the tourist office), a restored and working 19th-century oatmeal mill powered by a

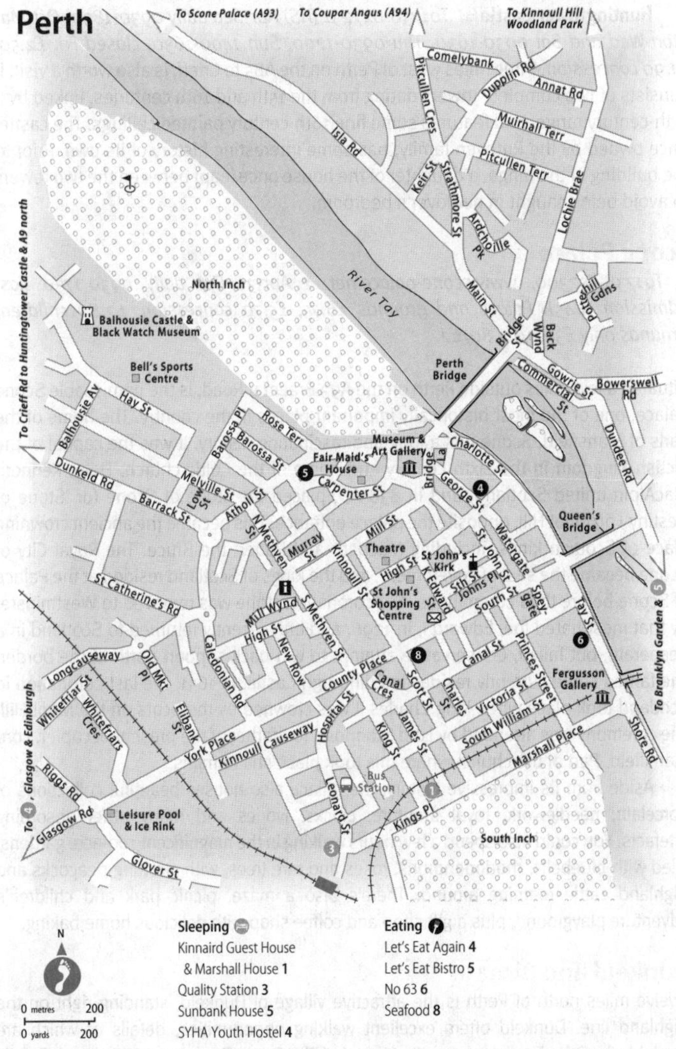

huge water wheel (closed to visitors at the time of writing). Perth's other museum contains the excellent **Fergusson Gallery** ⓘ *T01738-441944, Mon-Sat 1000-1700, free*, a display of works by the renowned Scottish colourist, John Duncan Fergusson. The gallery is found at the south end of Tay Street, near South Inch, in a splendid neo-classical building which was once Perth's waterworks.

For those with more horticultural leanings, **Branklyn Garden** ⓘ *116 Dundee Rd, T01738-625535 (NTS), Mar-Oct daily 0930-sunset, £5, £3.75 concession*, has been described as 'the finest two acres of private garden in the country'. With an impressive collection of rare and unusual plants, it includes superb examples of Himalayan poppies. Well worth a visit at any time of year, many of the plants grown there are on sale in the shop. **Kinnoull Hill Woodland Park** is a beautiful wooded area on the outskirts of the city. The trip to the top of Kinnoull Hill (783 ft) itself affords an astounding view across Perth, down to the Tay estuary and through Fife to the Lomond hills. To the north, the views stretch from Ben More in the west to Lochnagar in the northeast.

Huntingtower Castle ⓘ *T01738-627231 (HS) Apr-Sep daily 0930-1830; Oct-Mar Mon-Wed and Sat 0930-1630, Thu 0930-1200, Sun 1400-1630, closed Fri. £2.50, £1.90 concession*, three miles west of Perth on the A85 to Crieff, is also worth a visit. It consists of two complete towers dating from the 15th and 16th centuries, linked by a 17th-century range, and features some fine 16th-century painted ceilings. The castle, once owned by the Ruthven family, has some interesting history of its own. Prior to the building of the range, a daughter of the house once leapt between the two towers to avoid being caught in her lover's bedroom.

Scone Palace

ⓘ *T01738-552300, www.scone-palace.net, 1 Apr-31 Oct daily 0930-1730 (last admission 1645). Palace and grounds £6.75, £5.70 concession, £3.80 children; grounds only £3.40/£2.80/£2.*

Situated a few miles outside Perth on the A93 Braemar Road, is the unmissable Scone Palace, one of the most historically important places in the country. The home of the Earls of Mansfield, Scone has a long and fascinating history. It was the capital of the Pictish Kingdom in the sixth century and home of the Celtic church. Here, Kenneth MacAlpin united Scotland, and in 838 AD, placed the stone of Scone (or 'Stone of Destiny') on Moot Hill, opposite the palace entrance. This became the ancient crowning place of Scottish kings, including Macbeth and Robert the Bruce. The Royal City of Scone became the seat of government, and the kings of Scotland resided at the Palace of Scone before their coronations. The coronation stone was removed to Westminster by that most hated foe, Edward I, in 1296, and only recently returned to Scotland in a desperate, but failed, Conservative attempt to win back support north of the border. The famed stone currently resides in Edinburgh Castle. In 1651, the last coronation in Scotland took place when King Charles II was crowned by the Scots on the Moot Hill. The ceremony was attended by Lord Stormont, forefather of the present occupier, Lord Mansfield. Part of the church where this took place still remains.

Aside from its impressive history, the palace also houses beautiful collections of porcelain, needlework, royal furniture, clocks, ivories and many other absorbing artefacts. You could also spend a few hours walking in the magnificent 100-acre gardens, filled with bluebells, rhododendrons, roses and rare trees, with strutting peacocks and Highland cattle roaming around. There's also a maze, picnic park and children's adventure playground, plus a gift shop and coffee shop with delicious home baking.

Dunkeld and Birnam

Twelve miles north of Perth is the attractive village of Dunkeld, standing right on the Highland line. Dunkeld offers excellent walking opportunities, details of which are available from the Tourist Information Centre at The Cross (T01350-727688). It's definitely worth making a stop here, if only to admire the **cathedral,** ⓘ *Apr-Sep 0930-1830, free,* in the most idyllic situation on the banks of the fast-flowing, silvery Tay. Half of it is still in use as a church and the other half is in ruins. The oldest part of the cathedral is the 14th-century choir, which now forms the parish church, while the 15th-century nave and tower are also still standing. Much of the original was damaged during the orgy of ecclesiastical destruction that accompanied the Reformation. It was damaged again in the Battle of Dunkeld in 1689, fought between supporters of the protestant William of Orange and the Stuart monarch James VII.

Across the bridge from Dunkeld is **Birnam,** made famous in Shakespeare's *Macbeth*. Birnam was the inspiration for another famous literary figure, **Beatrix Potter,** who spent her childhood summers here. Visitors can explore the origins of the *Peter Rabbit* stories at the **Beatrix Potter Exhibition** ⓘ *Daily 1000-1700, free.* A short distance north of Dunkeld on the A9 is the turning to **The Hermitage**. A marked woodland walk starts from the car park and follows the river Braan to the Black Linn Falls, overlooked by Ossian's Hall, an 18th-century folly built by the Duke of Atholl. It's a lovely spot, which has inspired the likes of Wordsworth and Mendelssohn. Further on is Ossian's Cave. Buses to Pitlochry (see below) stop at the turning for The Hermitage.

Pitlochry and around

Despite being one of the busiest Highland tourist towns in the summer, Pitlochry's setting on the shores of the River Tummel, overlooked by Ben y Vrackie, makes it a pleasant enough base for exploring the area, especially out of season. The town also has a few notable attractions of its own.

Pitlochry's main attraction is the **fish ladder**, part of the **power station and dam** which formed man-made **Loch Faskally** when it was constructed on the River Tummel. The ladder allows salmon to swim up to their spawning grounds and you can watch them leaping spectacularly in the spring and summer. The best months are May and June. The fish ladder is across the river, a short distance from the *Pitlochry Festival Theatre* (see below). **In summer 2002 the Scottish Plant Collectors Garden will open in the grounds of the theatre. Contact the theatre for further information.**

There are two excellent whisky distilleries to visit. The larger of the two is Bell's **Blair Atholl Distillery,** ⓘ *T01796-482003, www.malts.com, Easter-Sep Mon-Sat 0930-1700, Sun 1200-1700; Oct Mon-Fri 1000-1600, Nov-Easter Mon-Fri 1300-1600, tours every 20 mins, £4, redeemable in shop*, at the southern end of town, heading towards the A9 to Perth. A couple of miles east of town, on the A924, is the **Edradour Distillery** ⓘ *T01796-T472095, www.edradour.com, Jan and Feb Mon-Sat 1000-1600, Sun 1200-1600, Mar-Oct Mon-Sat 0930-1800, Sun 1130-1700, Nov and Dec Mon-Sat 0930-1700, Sun 1200-1700, free,* the smallest in Scotland, which can be a blessing or a curse, depending on how busy it is.

Around Pitlochry

Four miles north of Pitlochry the A9 cuts through the **Pass of Killiecrankie,** a spectacular wooded gorge which was the dramatic setting for the Battle of Killiecrankie in 1689, when a Jacobite army led by Graham of Claverhouse, Viscount 'Bonnie Dundee', defeated the government forces under General Hugh Mackay. One government soldier allegedly evaded capture by making a jump of Olympic gold medal-winning proportions across the River Garry at **Soldier's Leap**. An NTS **visitor centre** ⓘ *T01796-473233, Apr-Oct daily 1000-1730, free (honesty box; £1 donation advised)* has displays on the battle and the local natural history.

Seven miles from Pitlochry, and a mile from the village of Blair Atholl, is **Blair Castle** ⓘ *T01796-481207, Apr-Oct 1000-1800 (0930 in Jul and Aug), house and grounds £6.25, grounds only £2,* traditional seat of the Earls and Dukes of Atholl. This whitewashed, turreted castle dates from 1269 and presents an impressive picture on first sight. This is the headquarters of Britain's only private army, the Atholl Highlanders, and one of them usually pipes in new arrivals. Thirty-two rooms in the castle are open for public viewing and are packed full of paintings, furniture, armour, porcelain and much else besides, presenting a startling picture of aristocratic Highland life in previous centuries. The surrounding landscaped grounds are home to peacocks and Highland cattle, and there are woodland walks and a walled Japanese water garden to enjoy.

Eight miles from Blair Atholl, just off the A9, are the **Falls of Bruar**. There's a short walk from the car park to the lower falls, but it's worth continuing to the more dramatic upper falls, which are less visited (see above). By the car park is the excellent **House of Bruar**, a huge shopping emporium designed like a Victorian hunting lodge where you can buy just about any kind of souvenir and enjoy some very fine Scottish cooking.

The B8019 turns off the B8079 road from Pitlochry to Blair Atholl and runs west along the shores of beautiful lochs Tummel and Rannoch, best seen in the autumn when the trees change their colours. At the eastern end of Loch Tummel is **Queen's View**, a spectacular viewpoint which looks down the loch and across to Schiehallion. There's a **visitor centre** ⓘ *T01796-473123, Apr-Oct daily 1000-1730, free, £1 parking charge*, here, with displays and audio-visual programmes about the area. **Schiehallion** (3,552 ft) is one of Scotland's best-loved mountains, whose distinctive conical peak made it ideal for use in early experiments in 1774 to judge the weight of the earth. These were not an unqualified success, but led to the invention of contour lines as an aid to surveying the mountain. The walk to the summit is fairly straightforward, except for the very rocky final stretch. You'll need to be properly clothed and equipped and take a map and compass. The route to the summit starts at the car park on the B846 Kinloch Rannoch to Aberfeldy road, near Braes of Foss. OS sheet No 51 covers the route. Beyond Loch Tummel is the little village of **Kinloch Rannoch**, where backpackers can stock up on supplies before heading into the hills. Sixteen miles west of the village the road ends at Rannoch station, where you can catch trains north to Fort William or south to Glasgow.

Aberfeldy and Loch Tay

The little town of Aberfeldy stands on the banks of the River Tay, on the A827 which runs between the A9 and Loch Tay. It's well placed geographically for exploring the northern part of Perthshire, though Pitlochry has better tourist facilities. The 14-mile-long Loch Tay is surrounded by some of the loveliest scenery in Perthshire and is well worth exploring.

Aberfeldy

Just outside Aberfeldy is **Dewar's World of Whisky** n *T01887-822010, www.dewars.com/worldofwhisky, Apr-end Oct Mon-Sat 1000-1800, Sun 1200-1600, Nov-Mar Mon-Fri 1000-1600, £5, concession £3, children £2.50*, one of a new breed of distillery visitor centres. The tour is always interesting, though the hard sell may not be to everyone's taste. A mile west of Aberfeldy, across the Tay at Weem, is **Castle Menzies** ⓘ *T01887-820982, Apr-mid Oct Mon-Sat 1030-1700, Sun 1400-1700, £3.50, £3 concession*, an impressive, restored 16th-century 'Z-plan' fortified tower-house, the former seat of the chief of Clan Menzies. A popular local walk is to the **Falls of Moness**, through the famous **Birks of Aberfeldy**, forever associated with the poet Robert Burns who was inspired by the birks (birch trees) to write his eponymous song. It's a fairly easy walk along a marked trail up to the impressive falls, and the views of Strathtay and the surrounding hills on the descent also make it worthwhile. It's about four miles there and back.

Around Loch Tay

At the northeast end of Loch Tay is **Kenmore**, a neat little village of whitewashed cottages dominated by a huge archway which stands at the gateway to Taymouth Castle, built by the Campbells of Glenorchy in the early 19th century and now a very fine **golf course**, T01887-830228. Near the village, on the southern bank of the loch, is **The Scottish Crannog Centre** ⓘ *T01887-830583, Mar and Nov daily 1000-1600; Apr to mid-Oct 1000-1730, £4.25, concession £3.85,*an authentic reconstruction of a *crannog*, an artificial Bronze-Age island-house built for the purpose of defence. Loch Tay is a major **watersports** centre, see Activities and tours page 778.

For those with their own transport, two of the least-known and loveliest routes in the country are at hand. The first is the spectacular road which winds its way south from Kenmore high up into the mountains, across a bleak and barren plateau and down the other side to the tiny hamlet of **Amulree**. This road is often closed in the winter and there are gates at either end. From Amulree you can continue south to Crieff (see below), through the gentler, but equally stunning scenery of the **Sma' Glen**. Alternatively, you could head north to Aberfeldy and then complete the circuit back to Kenmore.

A few miles west of Kenmore a minor road turns off the A827, which runs along the north bank of the loch, and heads to **Fortingall**, a tiny village of classic beauty which features on many a calendar. It's little more than a row of thatched cottages which wouldn't even get a mention were it not for two amazing claims. The 3,000-year-old yew tree in the churchyard is claimed to be the oldest living thing in Europe. More astonishing is the claim that this is the birthplace of **Pontius Pilate**, said to be the son of a Roman officer who was stationed here. Furthermore, it is believed that Pilate returned here to be buried, and a gravestone in the churchyard bears the initials 'PP'. If you have your own transport, make a detour up **Glen Lyon**, one of the most beautiful of all Scottish glens. On a summer's day there can be few lovelier places on earth, as the River Lyon tumbles through corries and gorges and through flowering meadows, with high mountain peaks on either side and eagles soaring overhead. It's no surprise that Wordsworth and Tennyson waxed lyrical over its qualities. The road from Fortingall runs all the way to the head of the glen, at Loch Lyon. This is walking and fishing paradise. There are several Munros to 'bag' and fishing permits are available at the **Fortingall Hotel** (see page 777).

Crieff and around

The well-groomed town of Crieff sits on the slopes of the Grampian foothills overlooking the wide Strathearn valley. It's a popular tourist centre and a good base for exploring the western part of Perthshire and the Trossachs. A mile from town, just off the A85 to Comrie, is the superb **Glenturret Distillery** ⓘ *T01764-656565, www.glenturret.com, Jan-Dec daily 0900-1800 (last tour 1630), Jul and Aug daily 0900-1830 (last tour 1730), £6, concessions £5, under 12s free.*, Scotland's oldest distillery, established in 1775. Glenturret is the most visited whisky distillery in Scotland and its easy to see why, combining as it does the best of tradition and modernity. It has a good restaurant which serves food all day.

Two miles south of Crieff, on the A822 to Muthill, is the turning to the very wonderful **Drummond Castle Gardens** ⓘ *T01764-681257, Easter weekend and May-Oct daily 1400-1800 (last entry 1700), £3.50, £2.50 concession, take bus No 47 towards Muthill and get off at the gates, then walk 1 mile up the castle drive*, one of the finest formal gardens in Europe. Even the most horticulturally ignorant of people could not fail to be amazed by the graceful harmony and symmetry, in particular the magnificently laid-out flower beds celebrating family and Scottish heraldry. If you have the feeling you've seen them before, that's because they were featured in the film Rob Roy.

Sleeping

Perth and around *p770, map p771*

A **Ballathie House Hotel**, at Kinclaven, near Stanley, 2 miles north of Perth, just off the A9, T01250-883268, www.ballathiehouse hotel.com. 43 rooms. Pick of the bunch. This elegant, award-winning 19th-century former hunting lodge has a reputation for superb Scottish cuisine (£££).

A **Huntingtower Hotel**, T01738-583771, F583777, www.huntingtowerhotel.co.uk, 1 mile west of Perth off the A85 to Crieff, 34 rooms. Another excellent option. Elegant country house hotel in its own landscaped gardens, good food in the dining room (££) and bar meals in the conservatory (£).

A-B **Quality Station Hotel**, next to the train station, on Leonard St, T01738-624141, admin@gb628-u-net.com. 70 rooms. A grand old Victorian edifice close to the town centre.

B-C **Sunbank House Hotel**, 50 Dundee Rd, T01738-624882, F442515. 9 rooms. A lovely little hotel overlooking the Tay and close to Branklyn Garden and Kinnoull Hill, great value.

D **Kinnaird Guest House**, 5 Marshall Pl, which overlooks the South Inch, T01738-6280121, www.Kinnaird-guesthouse.co.uk.

E **Achnacarry Guest House**, 3 Pitcullen Cres, on the A94 Coupar Angus road, T01738-621421. Good choice on a road full of B&Bs.

F **SYHA Youth hostel** is at 107 Glasgow Rd, T01738-623658, open Mar-Oct, about half a mile west of the town centre (take bus No 7). There's a campsite at **Cleeve Caravan Park**, on Glasgow Rd, near the ring road, about 2 miles from town, T01738-639521, open Apr-Oct. There's also the **Scone Palace Camping & Caravan Club Site**, T01738-552308, open Apr-Oct.

Dunkeld and Birnam *p772*

L **Hilton Dunkeld**, Dunkeld, T01796-727771, www.dunkeld.hilton.com. Luxurious former home of the Duke of Atholl, now with full leisure and outdoor activity facilities.

L **Kinnaird House**, at Dalguise, about 8 miles north via the A9 and the B898, T01796-482440. The top hotel in the area. The setting, the style, the service and the restaurant are all excellent.

There are also lots of cheaper options, including: C **The Bridge B&B**, 10 Bridge Street, T727068, www.visitscotland.com/thebridge. C-D **The Pend**, 5 Brae St, T727586, www.thepend.com; andD **Birnam Guest House**, 4 Murthly Terr, Birnam, T727201.

E **Western Caputh Independent Hostel**, at Caputh, 5 miles east of Dunkeld, on the A984 to Coupar Angus, T01738-710617. It has 18 beds and is open all year.

Pitlochry *p773*

A **Pine Trees Hotel**, Strathview Terr, T01796-472121, www pinetreeshotel.co.uk. The best hotel in town is this superb Victorian country house set in 10 acres of gardens away from the tourist bustle. Its *Garden Restaurant* has a fine reputation.

A-B **Killiecrankie Hotel**, a few miles north of Pitlochry, in the village of Killiecrankie, T01796-473220, www.killiecrankiehotel.co.uk. Open Mar-Dec. 10 rooms. It's a quiet, cosy country house hotel which offers quite possibly the very finest food in the area.

B-C **Dunfallandy Country House Hotel & Restaurant**, T01796-472648, dunfalhse@aol.com. A mile out of town on the road to Logierait. 8 rooms. Top-class hotel. Georgian mansion offering great views, peace and quiet and superb cuisine, no smoking, excellent value.

There are numerous guesthouses and B&Bs, far too many to list here. The tourist office will provide a full list. Among the most recommended are: C-D **Craigroyston House**, 2 Lower Oakfield, T472053; D **Arrandale House**, Knockfarrie Rd, T472987; and D **Craigatin House & Courtyard**, 165 Atholl Rd, T472478.

E **SYHA Youth Hostel**, T472308, on Knockard Rd overlooking the town centre is open all year.

Around Pitlochry *p773*

B-C **Atholl Arms Hotel**, near the train station in Blair Atholl village, T481205, does B&B and serves bar meals.

D **Bunrannoch House**, T01882-632407, www.bunrannoch.co.uk, a former Victorian shooting lodge which offers good cooking.

Aberfeldy *p774*

L-A **Farleyer House Hotel** in Weem, T01887-820332, 100127.222@compuserve.com. Best of the hotels around town. Magnificent 15th-century building.

A **Guinach House**, T01887-820251. Family run country house hotel in a lovely setting by the Birks and with a superb restaurant (expensive).
B **Weem Hotel** T01887-820381, in Weem, about a mile west of Aberfeldy on the B846 to Strathtummel. Very friendly welcome.
B **Ailean Chraggan**, Weem, T01887-820346. Serves very good food in the bar (££).
D **Tigh'N'Eilean Guest House**, on Taybridge Dr, T01887-820109. Recommended and offers good value.

Around Loch Tay *p775*

B **Kenmore Hotel**, Kenmore, T01887-830205. Claims to be Scotland's oldest coaching inn, dating from 1572. Whether or not this is true, there's no denying that it's full of character and very comfortable. Excellent food is to be had in the lovely bar (££).
C **Fortingall Hotel**, next to the churchyard in Fortingall, T01887-830367, hotel@fortingall.com. Wonderful and very popular.

Crieff and around *p775*

L **Crieff Hydro**, turn off the High Street at the Drummond Arms Hotel then continue uphill and follow the signs, T01764-655555, www.crieffhydro.com. First opened in 1868 as the *Strathearn Hydropathic*. The best place to stay in Crieff. It offers a huge range of leisure activities and a fine restaurant.
L **Gleneagles Hotel**, T01764-662231, www.gleneagles.com. A luxury 5-star hotel and leisure resort with 3 top-class golf courses. If you can afford it, there is no better way to pamper yourself. The restaurant, **Andrew Fairlie at Gleneagles** (T694267), is equally impressive and expensive.
A **Royal Hotel**, Melville Sq, Comrie, T01764-679200, www.royalhotel.co.uk. Very comfortable, has a good restaurant and great pub round the back serving real ales.
D **Merlindale**, Perth Rd, Crieff, T01764-655205. Best of the cheaper accommodation.
F **Braincroft Bunkhouse**, T01764-670140, an independent hostel 2 miles east of Comrie on the road to Crieff.

Eating

Perth and around *p770, map p771*

££ **Let's Eat Bistro**, Kinnoull St, T01738-643377. Tue-Sat 1200-1400, 1830-2130. Very classy establishment which provides a modern Scottish menu with Mediterranean influences, all meals cooked fresh to order. Its sister restaurant, **Let's Eat Again** is at 33 George St and open till 2145.
££ **No. 63**, 63 Tay St, T01738-441451. Tue-Sat 1200-1400, 1830-2100. Swish restaurant down by the river at which serves contemporary Scottish food.
££ **The Seafood Restaurant**, 168 South St, T01738-449777. Specializes in fish and game.

Pitlochry *p773*

£££ **East Haugh Country House Hotel & Restaurant**, a couple of miles south of Pitlochry on the old A9 road, T01796-473121, www.easthaugh.com, a 17th-century country house with excellent and elegant dining and great bar lunches.
£££ **Killiecrankie Hotel** (see above) is expensive but the best place to eat.The bar is less formal and cheaper than the restaurant.
££ **Port-na-Craig Inn & Restaurant**, T01796-472777, which is just below the Festival Theatre on the banks of the River Tummel. It offers great Scottish cooking in a bistro ambience.
£ **Moulin Inn**, a few miles north of Pitlochry, at Moulin on the A924, T01796-472196, www.moulin.u-net.com. Food daily till 2130. Serves good, cheap pub food and fine real ales (try their 'Braveheart') in a great atmosphere.

Around Pitlochry *p773*

£££ **Loft**, Golf Course Rd, Blair Atholl, T01796-481377, www.theloftrestaurant.co.uk. The best food hereabouts. Superior Modern Scottish/Mediterranean food.

Crieff and around *p775*

££ **The Bank**, 32 High St, T01764-656575. Other than the hotels in town and the Glenturret Distillery (see above), there isn't a huge choice of good places to eat. This is the pick of the lot and offers modern food.

Entertainment

Perth and around *p770, map p771*

Perth Theatre, 185 High St, T01738-621031, is a beautiful Victorian-era theatre with an excellent reputation for high-class productions.

Playhouse cinema at 6 Murray St, T623126, offers a dose of escapism on the big screen.

Pitlochry *p773*

Pitlochry Festival Theatre, T01796- 484626, is across the river from the town centre. It stages a different play every night for 6 nights a week from May to Oct.

Festivals and events

The **Perth Highland Games** are held on the second Sun in **Aug**, on the same weekend as the **Perth Show**, which takes place on South Inch. There are also regular jump racing events during the summer at **Perth Racecourse**, near Scone Palace, T01738-551597. The **Crieff Highland Gathering** takes place on the penultimate Sun in **Aug**.

Activities and tours

Cycling

Crieff Ski Shop, 66 Commissioner St, Crieff, T01764-654667. Escape Route, 8 West Moulin Rd, Pitlochry, T/F01796-473859. Touring and off-road bikes for £14 per day. **Atholl Mountain Bikes**, Blair Atholl, 01796-T473553, have a leaflet listing various cycle routes, including the Glen Tilt route above.

Fishing

Sandyknowes fly-fishery at Bridge of Earn, T01738-813033, a few miles southeast of Perth. Located between the rivers Earn and Tay, there are facilities for the novice, right up to the most experienced angler with great fishing in a beautiful landscape. The season runs from Mar-Dec and currently costs £10 per day. Details of all the Perthshire fisheries are available from the Tourist Information Centre.

Skiing

Glenshee ski centre is at the crest of the Cairnwell Pass (2,199 ft), the highest main road pass in Britain, on the border of Perthshire and Aberdeenshire. It is the most extensive skiing area in Scotland, with 38 pistes, as well as Nordic skiing. Ski rental is around £13 per day (£12 for snowboards) and lessons are £18 for four hours. A one-day lift pass costs £18, or £72 for five days, including tuition and hire.

For more information, call Ski Glenshee (T01339-741320, www.ski.scotland.net). For the latest snow and weather conditions, call the Ski Hotline (T0900-1-654656). The only public transport is a daily postbus service (Mon-Sat only) from Blairgowrie to Spittal of Glenshee, or to the ski resort from Braemar and Ballater.

Sports centres

Perth Leisure Pool, T01738-492410, open daily 1000-2200, west of the town centre on the Glasgow Rd, claims to have the best leisure swimming pool in Scotland. Next door is **Dewar's Rinks**, T01738-624188, where the visitor can curl, ice skate or bowl. Bell's Sports Centre, on Hay Street, T01738-622301, open daily 0900-2200, covers virtually every sport and leisure activity imaginable.

Watersports

Croft-Na-Caber, near the Crannog Centre, T01887-830588, Scotland's best watersports and activities centre, where you can try water-skiing, windsurfing, sailing, rafting, jet biking, river sledging, fishing, parascending, clay-pigeon shooting, walking and Nordic skiing. You can hire bikes from the **Loch Tay Boating Centre**, also in Kenmore, T01887-830291, open Apr-Oct, where you can hire speedboats, fishing boats and canoes.

Transport

Perth and around *p770, map p771*

Bus Scottish Citylink buses (T08705-505050) run frequently to **Glasgow** (1 hr 25 mins), **Edinburgh** (1½ hrs), **Dundee**

For an explanation of the sleeping and eating price codes used in this guide, see the inside front cover. Other relevant information is provided in the Essentials chapter, page 36.

(35 mins), **Aberdeen** (2½ hrs) and **Inverness** (2½ hrs). Stagecoach (T629339) run local buses to **Dunkeld**, **Pitlochry**, **Aberfeldy** and **Crieff**; and Strathtay Scottish (T01382-228054) buses serve **Blairgowrie**, **Alyth** and **Dundee**.
Car hire Arnold Clark, St Leonard's Bank, T01738-442202.
Train There's an hourly train service (Mon-Sat; 2-hourly on Sun) to **Glasgow Queen St** (1 hr); and frequent trains to **Edinburgh** (1 hr 20 mins). There are also hourly trains to **Stirling** (30 mins), **Dundee** (25 mins) and **Aberdeen** (1 hr 40 mins), and several daily to **Inverness** via **Pitlochry** (30 mins) and **Aviemore**.

Dunkeld and Birnam *p772*
Citylink **buses** between Perth and Inverness stop at the train station by **Birnam** several times daily in either direction. **Stagecoach** buses from Perth to Pitlochry and Aberfeldy stop in **Dunkeld**, and **Strathtay Scottish** buses between Blairgowrie and Aberfeldy also stop in the village (twice daily Mon-Sat). There are several **trains** daily, T08457-484950, to and from **Perth** and **Inverness**.

Pitlochry *p773*
Taxi Elizabeth Yule Transport, T01796-472290.

Around Pitlochry *p773*
Not all **trains** stop at Blair Atholl. **Elizabeth Yule Transport** (see Pitlochry Transport above) runs a service between Pitlochry and **Blair Atholl**, via Killiecrankie, a few times daily, except Sun.

Stirling and around

→*Colour map 5*

Standing between Edinburgh and Glasgow, yet only a short distance from some of the country's most beautiful scenery, the ancient town of Stirling is synonymous with the country's two greatest historical heroes, Robert the Bruce and William Wallace. It was once said that whoever controlled Stirling held the key to Scotland. Consequently the town and its surrounds have witnessed many crucial struggles between the Scots and the English. As you'd expect with such a strategically important town, Stirling has a long and fascinating history and is packed with major historical sights. It was here that the Scots under William Wallace defeated the English at the Battle of Stirling Bridge in 1297. A more famous battle was fought just a few miles away, at Bannockburn in 1314, when Robert the Bruce's small army routed Edward II's much larger English force. Being so close to both Edinburgh and Glasgow, the sights of Stirling can be visited in a day from either city, but it's also a very pleasant place to stay. It may lack the cosmopolitan feel of Edinburgh but has a lively buzz of its own during the busy summer months and there is a wide range of accommodation and other tourist facilities. ▸▸ *For Sleeping, Eating and other listings, see pages 784-785.*

Ins and outs

Getting there Stirling is easily reached from Edinburgh, Glasgow, Perth and most other main towns and cities by regular **bus** and **train** services. The **train station** is on Station Rd, near the town centre, and the **bus station** is close by, on Goosecroft Rd, behind the Thistle Shopping Centre. ▸▸ *For further details, see Transport, page 785.*

Getting around Most of the important sights, except Bannockburn and the Wallace Monument, are within easy walking distance of each other. There's an open-topped 'hop on, hop off' Heritage Bus Tour which runs from Jun to Sep and includes the castle and Wallace Monument. There are tours every 30 mins from 1000 till 1700. A day ticket costs £6.50. Check details at the TIC. There are regular buses to Doune from Stirling, via Blair Drummond.

Stirling

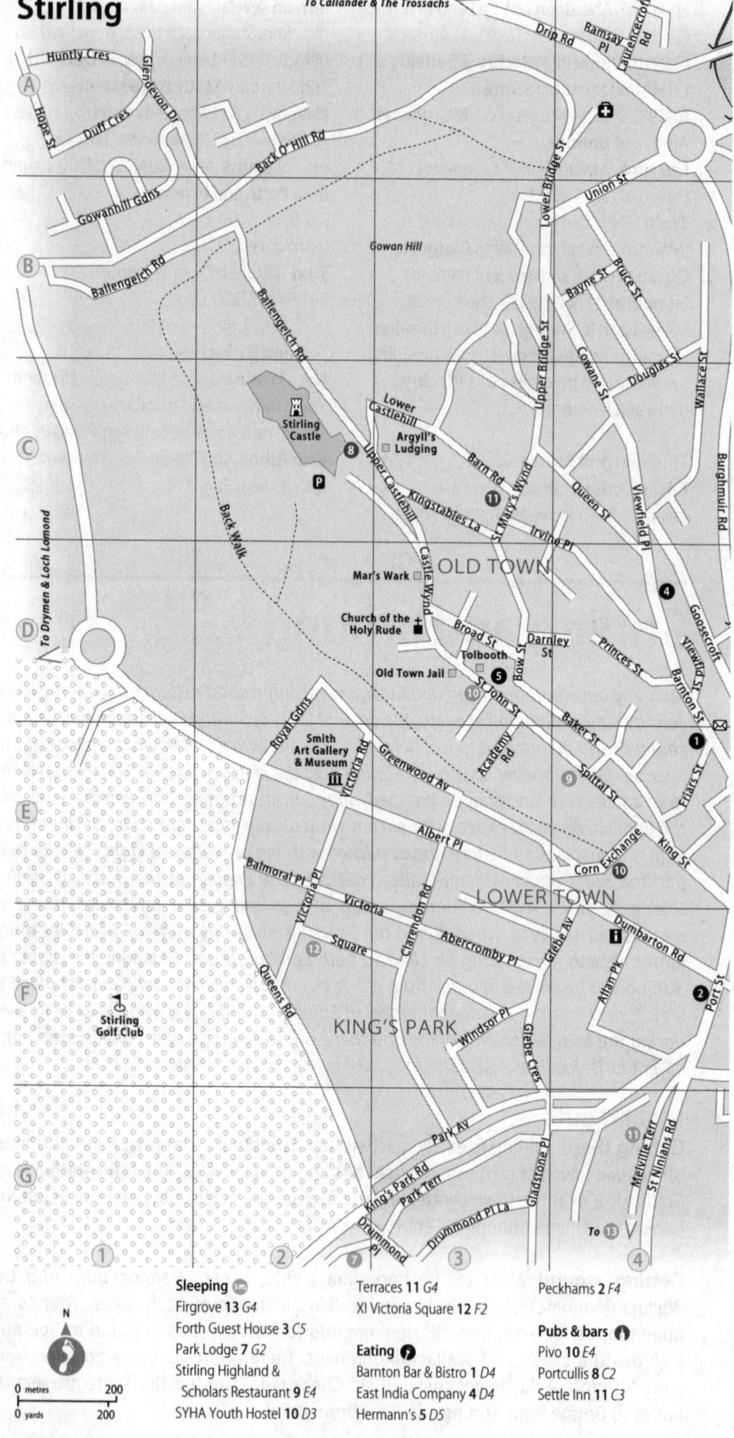
To Callander & The Trossachs
Huntly Cres
Glendevon Dr
Hope St
Duff Cres
Drip Rd
Ramsay Pl
Laurencecroft Rd
Back O' Hill Rd
Lower Bridge St
Union St
Gowanhill Gdns
Gowan Hill
Ballengeich Rd
Bayne St
Bruce St
Upper Bridge St
Cowane St
Douglas St
Wallace St
Lower Castlehill
Stirling Castle
Argyll's Ludging
Upper Castlehill
Barn Rd
Burghmuir Rd
Kingstables La
St Mary's Wynd
Queen St
Viewfield Pl
Back Walk
Irvine Pl
To Drymen & Loch Lomond
Castle Wynd
OLD TOWN
Mar's Wark
Church of the Holy Rude
Broad St
Bow St
Darnley St
Princes St
Goosecroft
Viewfld St
Tolbooth
Old Town Jail
St John St
Barnton St
Baker St
Royal Gdns
Smith Art Gallery & Museum
Victoria Rd
Greenwood Av
Academy Rd
Spittal St
Friars St
Albert Pl
Corn Exchange
King St
Balmoral Pl
Victoria Pl
Victoria Square
Clarendon Rd
LOWER TOWN
Glebe Av
Dumbarton Rd
Abercromby Pl
Allan Pk
Port St
Queens Rd
Stirling Golf Club
KING'S PARK
Windsor Pl
Glebe Cres
Park Av
Melville Terr
St Ninians Rd
King's Park Rd
Park Terr
Gladstone Pl
Drummond Pl
Drummond Pl La
To 13
N
0 metres 200
0 yards 200
Sleeping
Firgrove 13 G4
Forth Guest House 3 C5
Park Lodge 7 G2
Stirling Highland & Scholars Restaurant 9 E4
SYHA Youth Hostel 10 D3
Terraces 11 G4
XI Victoria Square 12 F2
Eating
Barnton Bar & Bistro 1 D4
East India Company 4 D4
Hermann's 5 D5
Peckhams 2 F4
Pubs & bars
Pivo 10 E4
Portcullis 8 C2
Settle Inn 11 C3

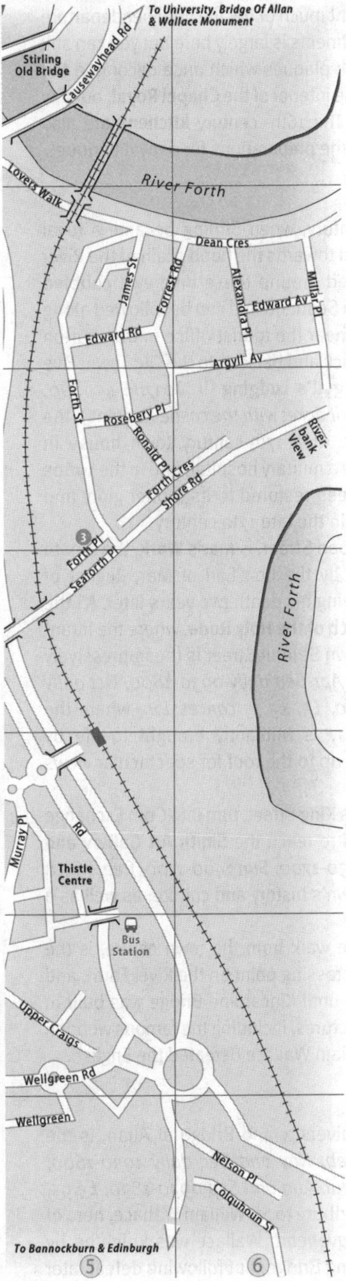

Information Stirling TIC ⓘ *41 Dumbarton Rd, T01786-475019, daily Jun-Sep Mon-Sat Oct-May.* It is the main office for Loch Lomond, Stirling and the Trossachs and stocks a wide range of books, guides, maps and leaflets. It also has information on the **guided walks** of the town, including the popular **ghost walks** which take place Tue-Sat at 1930 and 2130. **Dunblane TIC** ⓘ *Stirling Rd, T01786-824428, May-Sep.* **Linlithgow TIC**, in the Burgh Halls at The Cross, T01506-844600, Easter-Sep daily 1000-1700.

Sights

Stirling Castle

ⓘ *T01786-450000 (HS). Apr-Oct daily 0930-1800 (last entry 1715); Nov-Mar till 1700 (last entry 1615). £8, £6 concession (includes admission to Argyll's Ludging).*

The obvious place to begin a tour is the immensely impressive castle which stands 250 ft above the flat plain atop the plug of an extinct volcano. From the west there's a sheer drop down the side of the rocky crag, making the castle seem a daunting prospect to would-be attackers, and now presenting visitors with fantastic views of the surrounding area. There's been a fortress here since the Iron Age, though the current building dates mostly from the 15th and 16th centuries, when it was the favourite residence of the Stuart kings.

On the esplanade is a **visitor centre** which shows an introductory film giving a potted history of the castle. From here you proceed to the **Upper Square**, where you can see the magnificent **Great Hall**, built by James IV and which was recently restored to its original condition. He also built the royal residence known as the **King's Old Building**, which now houses the **museum** of the Argyll and Sutherland Highlanders, which traces the history of this famous regiment from its inception in 1794 to the present day. James V, whose wives were both French, brought masons from France to create the spectacular **Palace** (1540-42), the finest Renaissance building in Scotland. This was where the young Mary, Queen of Scots spent much of her life until her departure for France, in 1548. The interior of the royal apartments is largely bare but you can still see the **Stirling Heads**, 56 elegantly carved oak plaques which once decorated the ceiling of one of the rooms. Also impressive is the interior of the **Chapel Royal**, built by James VI in 1594 for the baptism of his son. The 16th- century **kitchens** are also interesting and have been restored to recreate the preparations for a royal banquet.

Other sights

The Old Town grew from around the 12th century, when Stirling became a royal burgh, and spread from the castle down the hill towards the flood-plain of the River Forth. Most of the historic sights are clustered around these medieval cobbled streets. The **town walls** are the best surviving in Scotland and can be followed along a path known as the **Back Walk**, which starts near the tourist office in Dumbarton Road and runs around the base of the Castle Rock and back up to the Old Town. Five minutes' walk downhill from the castle is **Argyll's Ludging** ⓘ *T01786-450000, same opening hours as the castle, £3.30, or joint ticket with the castle* (lodging), the finest and most complete surviving example of a 17th-century town house in Scotland. In the 18th century the house became a military hospital, and in the 1960s was used as a youth hostel. It has recently been restored to its former glory and rooms are furnished as they would have been in the late 17th century.

Further down Castle Wynd, at the top of Broad Street, is **Mar's Wark**, the ornate façade of a dilapidated town house, started by the first Earl of Mar, Regent of Scotland, in 1569 but left to fall into ruin following his death two years later. A little further down Castle Wynd is the medieval **Church of the Holy Rude**, where the infant James VI was crowned in 1567. A short way down St John Street is the impressively refurbished **Old Town Jail** ⓘ *T01786-450050, Apr-Sep daily 0930-1800, Oct daily till 1700, Nov-Feb daily till 1600, Mar till 1700, £5, £3.75 concession*, where the rigours of life behind bars in times gone by is brilliantly brought to life by enthusiastic actors. A glass lift then takes you up to the roof for spectacular views across the town and Forth Valley.

At the bottom of Spittal Street, where it joins King Street, turn into Corn Exchange Road and then head west up Dumbarton Road to reach the **Smith Art Gallery and Museum** ⓘ *T01786-471917, all year Tue-Sat 1030-1700, Sun 1400-1700, free*, which houses some interesting displays about the town's history and culture, as well as a fine collection of paintings.

At the north end of the town, a 20-minute walk from the town centre, is the 15th-century **Old Bridge**, which was the lowest crossing point on the River Forth, and one of the most important bridges in Scotland until Kincardine Bridge was built in 1936. The bridge was built to replace earlier structures, including the famous wooden bridge, scene of the battle in 1297 in which William Wallace defeated the English.

Around Stirling

Two miles northeast of the town, near the University and Bridge of Allan, is the **Wallace Monument** ⓘ *T01786-472140, Jan, Feb, Nov and Dec daily 1030-1600, Mar-May and Oct 1000-1700, Jun 1000-1800; Jul, Aug and Sep 0930-1830, £3.95, £2.75 children*, an impressive Victorian Gothic tribute to Sir William Wallace, hero of the successful but hugely inaccurate film, *Braveheart*. Wallace was knighted by Robert the Bruce for his famous victory at Stirling Bridge, but following defeat later at Falkirk he went off to Europe in search of support for the Scottish cause. During his absence he was betrayed by the Scots nobles and on his return found guilty of treason and cruelly hanged, drawn and quartered in London. Inside the monument are various exhibits including a Hall of Scottish Heroes and Wallace's mighty two-handed sword (5 ft 4 in long – about the same height as the actor who played him in the film). There are fantastic views from the top of the 220-ft tower. There's a shuttle bus which runs from the foot of the hill up to the tower every 15 minutes. An open-topped **tour bus** runs to the monument from Stirling Castle every half hour (see Ins and outs above).

A mile east of Stirling are the ruins of **Cambuskenneth Abbey** (open all year, free), founded in 1147 by David I for Augustinian canons, and once one of the richest abbeys in the country. Robert the Bruce held his parliament here in 1326, and King James III (1451-88) and his wife, Queen Margaret of Denmark, are buried in the grounds. The only substantial surviving feature is the 14th-century belfry. The abbey can be reached from Stirling on foot, via a footbridge over the River Forth, and from the Wallace Monument which is just a mile to the north.

A few miles south of Stirling is **Bannockburn** ⓘ *T01786-812664 (NTS), Site open all year, Heritage Centre open Apr-Oct daily 1000-1730, Oct-Mar 1030-1600, £3.50, £2.60 child/concession, to get there, take buses Nos 51 and 52 from Stirling (every 30 mins)*, the site of Scotland's greatest victory over the English, when Robert the Bruce defeated Edward II's army, on 24 June 1314. It was the **Battle of Bannockburn** which united the Scots and led to the declaration of independence at Arbroath in 1320 (the 'Declaration of Arbroath'). There's not an awful lot to see, but the **Bannockburn Heritage Centre** puts flesh on the bones and brings to life the full scale of the battle. Outside is an equestrian statue of Bruce, on the spot where he is said to have commended his forces, and the site of the bore stone, where Bruce planted his standard after victory. What's left of the original bore stone is on display in the visitor centre, safe from souvenir hunters.

Four miles north of Stirling is **Dunblane cathedral** ⓘ *Apr-Sep Mon-Sat 0930-1830, Sun 0930-1800, Oct-Mar Mon-Sat 0930-1630, Sun 1400-1630 (HS), free*, dating mainly from the 13th century, though the lower part of the tower is Norman. The cathedral was restored to its former glory in the late 19th century. Close by on the square, housed in the 17th-century Dean's house, is the tiny cathedral **museum** ⓘ *May-Oct Mon-Sat 1000-1230 and 1400-1630, free*, with a display on local history. Nearby is **Leighton Library** ⓘ *May-Oct Mon-Fri 1000-1230 and 1400-1630*, the oldest private library in Scotland, now open to the public.

Seven miles northwest of Stirling is the well-preserved 14th-century **Doune Castle** ⓘ *T01786-841742, Apr-Sep daily 0930-1830, Oct-Mar Mon, Wed and Sat 0930-1630, Thu 0930-1230, Fri and Sun 1400-1630, £2.50, £1.90 concession*, overlooking the River Teith. Built for the Regent Albany, it passed into the hands of the Earls of Moray (who still live there) following the execution of the Albany family by James I. Its most striking feature is the combination of tower, gatehouse and domestic quarters, which includes the Lord's Hall with its carved oak screen and musicians' gallery but is better known for its role in *Monty Python and the Holy Grail*.

A few miles south of Doune, off the A84 to Stirling, is the **Blair Drummond Safari Park** ⓘ *T01786-841203, Mar to early Oct daily 1000-1730, £8.50, £4.50 children*, Scotland's only wildlife park, with lions, tigers, elephants, monkeys, rhinos, giraffes, zebras and various other exotic animals. There's a safari bus for those without their own transport. There are also sea lion shows and numerous other kids' activities.

Falkirk and Linlithgow

Near Falkirk is the amazing **Falkirk Wheel** ⓘ *Apr-Oct daily 0930-1700, Nov-Mar 1000-1500, boat trips cost £8, concessions £6, children £4, family £21*, the world's first and only rotating boat lift. This huge steel structure, which resembles two gigantic ring-pulls, transfers craft from the Forth and Clyde Canal to the Union Canal and you can book a 45-minute boat trip to experience it for yourself. Halfway between Falkirk and Edinburgh is the pleasant little West Lothian town of Linlithgow, home of the magnificent Renaissance **Linlithgow Palace** ⓘ *T01506-842896 (HS), Apr-Sep daily 0930-1830; Oct-Mar Mon-Sat 0930-1630, Sun 1400-1630, £3, £2.30 concession*, one of the most impressive historic buildings in Scotland. It's off the beaten track and relatively little-visited but well worth the detour, for this is a real gem. The 15th-century ruin is set on the edge of Linlithgow Loch and is associated with many of Scotland's main historical players, including James V (1512) and Mary, Queen of Scots (1542), who were both born here. James V was also married here, to Mary of Guise, and Bonnie Prince Charlie popped in for a visit during the 1745 rebellion. One year later the palace was badly damaged by fire during its occupation by General Hawley's troops, prior to their defeat by Jacobite forces under Prince Charles at the Battle of Falkirk. The ruin still conveys a real sense of the sheer scale of the lavish lifestyle of the court, from the ornate fountain in the inner courtyard to the magnificent Great Hall with its massive kitchens.

Sleeping

Stirling *p779, map p780*

A **Stirling Highland Hotel**, Spittal St, T01786-272727, F272829. 78 rooms. Converted school refurbished to high standards with full facilities, including a pool and saunas. Their *Scholars Restaurant* is recommended.

B **Park Lodge Hotel**, 32 Park Terr, T01786-474862, F449748. 10 rooms. Luxurious Georgian/Victorian town house beautifully situated close to town centre, overlooking the park and castle, with a very fine restaurant.

B-C **Terraces Hotel**, 4 Melville Terr, T01786-472268, set off the main road.

C **X1 Victoria Square**, 11 Victoria Sq, T01786-475545. Extremely comfortable with great views of the castle.

D **Firgrove**, 13 Clifford Rd, T01786-475805, is a large, comfortable, Victorian house.

E **Forth Guest House**, 23 Forth Pl, T01786-471020. A short walk north of the train station. Recommended.

F **SYHA youth hostel**, in a converted church on St John St at the top of the town, T01786-473442, open all year.

There's a **campsite** at **Witches Craig Caravan Park**, at Blairlogie, 3 miles east of Stirling on the A91, T01786-474947, Apr-Oct.

Around Stirling *p782*

A **Hilton Dunblane Hydro**, T825403. Overlooking the town, set in 44 acres of woodland, luxurious and exclusive.

L **Cromlix House**, 4 miles north of Dunblane, near Kinbuck on the B8033, T822125. One of Scotland's best country-house hotels, with its own loch and chapel. It's worth coming here for dinner or Sun lunch.

Eating

Stirling *p779, map p780*

£££ **Scholars Restaurant** at the Stirling Highland Hotel (see Sleeping) has an excellent reputation for modern Scottish cuisine.

£££-££ **Hermann's**, 32 St John St, T01786-450632. At the Tolbooth on the road up to the castle, is an upmarket choice. It offers excellent Scottish/Austrian cuisine.

££ **Peckhams**, 52 Port St, T01786-463222. Mon-Fri 1000-2200, Sat and Sun 0930-2300. Deli out front and booth seating at rear. Good quality modern Scottish cuisine, also snacks and sandwiches.

£ **East India Company**, 7 Viewfield Pl, T01786-471330. The best curry in town.

£ **Barnton Bar & Bistro**, opposite the post office on Barnton St, T01786-461698. A favourite with students. Open till 2400 (0100 at weekends) and serves great breakfasts.

Falkirk and Linlithgow *p783*

£££ **Champany Inn**, 2 miles northeast of town, at the junction of the A904 and A803, T01506-834532. Seriously good dining, their steaks are legendary.

££ **Boozy Rouge at the Sheriffmuir Inn**, on the wild moors of Sheriffmuir south of Dunblane, T01786-823285. The inn dates from the early 18th century and serves fine food and ales, and is a wonderful place in the summer.

££ **Four Marys**, 65 High St, T01506-842171. Renowned in these parts for their bar meals and real ales. Food served daily 1200-1430, 1730-2030, 1230-2030 Sun. Booking essential.

For an explanation of the sleeping and eating price codes used in this guide, see the inside front cover. Other relevant information is provided in the Essentials chapter, page 36.

Pubs, bars and clubs

Stirling *p779, map p780*
Pivo, Corn Exchange, T01786-451904, is a trendy Czech bar which also serves light meals. **Portcullis**, on Castle Wynd, below the castle, T01786-472268, one of the best in Stirling. **Settle Inn**, St Mary's Wynd. The oldest hostelry in town (1773) and very popular with Stirling's large student population.

Entertainment

Stirling *p779, map p780*
The Tolbooth just off Broad St, T01786-274000, is a mutli-purpose arts centre with a lively programme of events and a good café and restaurant.

Transport

Stirling *p779, map p780*
Scottish Citylink **buses** run at least every hour to and from **Dundee** (1½ hrs) and at least every 30 mins to **Perth** (50 mins) and **Glasgow** (1 hr). There are also regular buses to **Inverness** (3½ hrs) and **Aberdeen** (3½ hrs), but you'll probably need to change at Perth and Dundee respectively. Buses also run to **Edinburgh**, but as the journey takes 1½ hrs you might prefer to take the train. Local buses are run by **First Edinburgh**, T01324-613777. There are frequent services to **Dunblane, Doune** via Blair Drummond (30 mins), **Callander** (45 mins), **Dollar** (35 mins), **Falkirk** (30 mins) and **Linlithgow** (1 hr), and several daily to **Aberfoyle** (45 mins). There are ScotRail **trains**, every 30 mins (Mon-Sat; hourly on Sun) to **Edinburgh** (45 mins) and **Glasgow** (45 mins), and regular services to **Perth** (35 mins), **Dundee** (1 hr) and **Aberdeen** (2¼ hrs).

Around Stirling *p782*
There are regular **buses** to Dunblane from Stirling (see Stirling Transport), and also frequent **trains** to and from Stirling, Edinburgh and Glasgow. Regular **buses** from Stirling and Edinburgh stop at The Cross in Linlithgow. The **train station** is at the southern end of town. There are hourly **trains** to and from Edinburgh (20 mins), Glasgow Queen Street (30 mins) and Stirling (35 mins).

Directory

Car hire Arnold Clark, Kerse Rd, T01786-478686. **Cycle hire** Wildcat Bike Tours, Stirling Enterprise Park, Unit 102, John Player Building, T/F01786-464333. Stewart Wilson Cycles, Barnton St, T01786-465292.

The Trossachs and Loch Lomond

→*Colour map 5*

Strictly speaking, the Trossachs is the narrow wooded glen between Loch Katrine and Loch Achray, but the name is now used to describe a much larger area between Argyll and Perthshire, stretching north from the Campsies and west from Callander to the eastern shore of Loch Lomond. It's a very beautiful and diverse area of sparkling lochs, craggy mountains and deep, forested glens, and for this reason is often called the 'Highlands in miniature', best visited in the autumn when the hills are purple and the trees are a thousand luminous hues, from lustrous gold to flaming scarlet and blazing orange.

West of the Trossachs is Loch Lomond, Britain's largest inland waterway, measuring 22 miles long and at certain points up to five miles wide. Its once 'bonnie' banks are now one of the busiest parts of the Highlands, due to their proximity to Glasgow (only 20 miles south along the congested A82). During the summer the western shore in particular becomes a playground for day-trippers who tear up and down the loch in speedboats and on jet skis, obliterating any notion visitors may have of a little peace and quiet. The eastern shores are altogether less hectic and form part of the new Loch Lomond National Park, the first to be established in the country. ▸▸ *For Sleeping, Eating and other listings, see pages 788-789.*

Ins and outs

Getting there There are regular **buses** from Stirling to Aberfoyle and Callander, T0870-6082608. There are also daily services to Aberfoyle from Glasgow, via Balfron. There's a **Scottish Citylink** service once daily in summer between Edinburgh and Fort William which stops in Callander. There's a **postbus service**, T01752-494527, www.royalmail.com/postbus, from Aberfoyle to Inversnaid on Loch Lomond. A postbus leaves Callander daily, except Sun, at 0915 to Trossachs Pier and connects with **cruises** on Loch Katrine (see 'Aberfoyle to Callander' above). There's also a postbus between Callander and Aberfoyle, via Port of Menteith (Mon-Fri in the afternoon). ▸▸ *For further details, see Transport, page 789.*

Getting around The **Trossachs Trundler** is a **bus** which makes a circuit of the Trossachs, linking Stirling, Callander, Aberfoyle and Port of Menteith, and stopping off at various scenic places en route. It also connects with departures of the *SS Sir Walter Scott* on Loch Katrine. It runs from Jun-Sep (not Wed) and costs £8 for a day ticket. Contact the local TIC for details.

Information Aberfoyle Tourist Information Centre ⓘ *On the main street, T01877-382352, Apr-Jun, Sep and Oct daily 1000-1700; Jul and Aug 0930-1900, weekends only Nov-Mar (hours subject to change)..* **Callander Tourist Information Centre** ⓘ *Ancaster Sq, T01877-330342. Same opening times as visitor centre below,* shares the same building as the **Rob Roy and Trossachs Visitor Centre. Loch Lomond Shores** ⓘ *T01389-721500*, is a large visitor centre and orientation centre as you come into town, which operates as the gateway to the National Park. At the 100-acre site you can see a film celebrating the area in addition to shops, restaurants and the restored steamer 'Maid of the Loch'. Also opposite Balloch train station, T01389-753533, Apr-Oct daily. **Tarbet TIC** ⓘ *T01301-702260, Apr-Oct.*

Walking in the Trossachs

The Trossachs is superb walking country. The two most challenging peaks are **Ben Venue** and **Ben A'an** around Loch Katrine and Loch Achray, about 10 miles west of Callander. **Ben Venue** (2,385 ft) is the more difficult climb. It starts from behind the *Loch Achray Hotel* and is waymarked, but it's a strenuous climb which requires hill walking experience, proper clothing and all the usual safety precautions. Allow about five hours for the return trip. **Ben A'an** (1,520 ft) isn't a giant of a hill, but it's a steep climb from the start, from the car park of the former *Trossachs Hotel* (now a timeshare development) on the north bank of Loch Achray, and there's a bit of scrambling involved near the summit. It takes about 1½ hours to the top. The views from both hills are stupendous on clear days, but remember that the weather is as unpredictable in the Trossach mountains as anywhere else in the Highlands. A useful guide is Collins' *Walk Loch Lomond and the Trossachs*. OS Landranger maps 56 and 57.

Both these mountains lie within the **Queen Elizabeth Forest Park**. This vast and spectacular wilderness of 75,000 acres borders Loch Lomond to the west and incorporates Loch Ard, Loch Achray and Loch Lubnaig, as well as Ben Venue, Ben A'An and **Ben Ledi**, which overlooks Callander. The park is run by the Forestry Commission and is criss-crossed by a network of less difficult waymarked trails and paths which start from the Queen Elizabeth Park **Visitor Centre** ⓘ *T01877-382258, Mar-Oct daily 1000-1800; Oct-Dec 1100-1600 (parking £1)*, about half a mile north of Aberfoyle on the A821. Available at the centre are audio-visual displays on the park's flora and fauna and information on the numerous walks and cycle routes around the park. Full details of the park are available from the Forest Enterprise in Aberfoyle.

Aberfoyle

The sleepy village of Aberfoyle suddenly bursts into life in the summer with the arrival of hordes of tourists. It lies on the edge of the Queen Elizabeth Forest Park and, along with Callander to the east, is one of the main tourist centres for the Trossachs. It makes an ideal base for walking and cycling in the surrounding hills. There's plentiful accommodation, though you'll have to book during the busy summer season. Three miles east of Aberfoyle is the **Lake of Menteith**, the only lake in Scotland (as opposed to loch). On Inchmahome island in the middle of the lake are the beautiful and substantial ruins of **Inchmahome Priory** ⓘ *T01877-385294 (HS), Apr-Sep Mon-Sun 0930-1830, £3.30, £2.60 concession*, the 13th-century Augustinian priory where the four-year-old Mary, Queen of Scots was sent in 1547, safe from the clutches of Henry VIII. A **ferry** takes visitors over to the island from **Port of Menteith**.

Aberfoyle to Callander

The A821 route north from Aberfoyle, through the spectacular **Duke's Pass**, and then east past Loch Achray and Loch Vennachar, is one of the most beautiful routes in the country and not to be missed. There are a couple of worthwhile diversions along the way. About five miles north of Aberfoyle, a track branches to the right and runs through Achray Forest and along the shores of Loch Drunkie, before rejoining the A821 further north. A few miles further on, a road turns left to **Trossachs Pier** on the eastern shore of **Loch Katrine**. This is the departure point for **cruises** on the **SS Sir Walter Scott** ⓘ *T01877-376316, cruises depart Apr to end of Oct at 1100 to Stronachlachar, returning at 1200, and around the loch at 1345 and 1515*In the mornings (daily except Wednesday) it sails to the remote settlement of **Stronachlachar** on the far western shores of the loch and back. In the afternoons (daily) it only sails around the loch for an hour. There's a road and cycle path around the loch as far as Stronachlachar, and you could take the morning cruise there and then cycle back to the pier.

Callander and around

Callander sits at the eastern end of the Trossachs, 14 miles northwest of Stirling, its wide streets totally and unashamedly devoted to tourism and lined with tearooms, restaurants and craft shops. The town's overworked Tourist Information Centre shares the same building as the **Rob Roy and Trossachs Visitor Centre** ⓘ *Mar-May and Oct-Dec daily 1000-1700, Jun 0930-1800, Jul and Aug 0900-2000, Sep 1000-1800, Jan and Feb weekends only 1000-1600, £3.25,* which gives an entertaining account of the life of Rob Roy MacGregor.

Two miles north of Callander, on the A84 route to the Highlands, are the **Falls of Leny**, in the narrow and dramatic Pass of Leny. The falls are accessible from the car park by the roadside or via the **Callander to Strathyre Cycleway**, which follows the old train line to Oban, from Callander north along the west bank of **Loch Lubnaig**. This forms part of the **Glasgow to Killin Cycleway**, which runs from the centre of Glasgow, via Balloch, Aberfoyle, Callander, Balquhidder and Lochearnhead, to Killin. This is the best way to see the Trossachs.

The A84 heads north from Callander along the east bank of Loch Lubnaig, and beyond towards **Loch Earn.** A few miles further north, a side road branches left to the tiny village of **Balquhidder**, famous as the burial place of Rob Roy. His grave in the churchyard, where his wife and two of his sons are also buried, is thankfully understated.

Lochearnhead and Killin

A few miles north of the turning to Balquhidder, where the A84 meets the A85 from Crieff to Crianlarich, is Lochearnhead, at the western tip of Loch Earn. The loch is a highly popular **watersports centre** and at *Lochearnhead Watersports*, T01567-830330, you can try water-skiing, canoeing and kayaking. Lochearnhead is also a good base for **walking** in the surrounding hills. In the far northwestern corner of

 Stirling region, just to the west of Loch Tay, is Killin, a pleasant little village which makes a good base for walkers wishing to explore the wild mountains and glens of the ancient district of **Breadalbane** (pronounced Bread-*al*binn). Killin's picture-postcard setting, with the beautiful **Falls of Dochart** tumbling through the centre of the village, makes it a popular destination for tourists. The **Tourist Information Centre** overlooks the falls (March-October daily).

Loch Lomond

The **west bank** of the loch, from Balloch north to Tarbet, is one long, almost uninterrupted development of marinas, holiday homes, caravan parks and exclusive golf clubs. At the southern end of the loch is the resort town of **Balloch**, packed full of hotels, B&Bs, caravan parks and any number of operators offering **boat trips** around the loch's overcrowded waters. North of **Tarbet**, at the narrow northern end of the loch, things quieten down a great deal and the road to **Ardlui**, at its northern tip, is very beautiful and peaceful. The A82 continues north of Ardlui, past **Inverarnan**, to meet the A85 at **Crianlarich**.

The tranquil **east bank** of Loch Lomond is a great place for walking. The **West Highland Way** follows the east bank all the way from **Drymen**, through **Balmaha**, **Rowardennan** and **Inversnaid**. Beyond Rowardennan this is the only access to the loch's east bank, except for the road to Inversnaid from the Trossachs. From Rowardennan you can climb **Ben Lomond** (3,192 ft), the most southerly of the Munros. It's not too difficult and the views from the top (in good weather) are astounding. An easier climb is **Conic Hill**, on the Highland fault line and very close to Glasgow. The route starts from the Balmaha car park. It takes about 1½ hours to reach the top, from where the views of the loch are stunning.

Sleeping

Aberfoyle *p787*

A **Lake Hotel**, in Port of Menteith, on the lakeshore overlooking Inchmahome, T01877-385258, www.lake-of-menteith-hotel.com. The best place to stay in the area. It's stylish, comfortable, very romantic and boasts a fine restaurant (lunch mid-range; dinner expensive).

C-D **Creag-Ard House** in Milton, 2 miles west of Aberfoyle overlooking Loch Ard, T01877-382297. Lovely place with fishing and boat hire available.

Camping is available at **Cobeland Campsite**, T382392, open Apr-Oct, 2 miles south of Aberfoyle on the edge of the Queen Elizabeth Forest Park; and the excellent **Trossachs Holiday Park**, T382614, open Mar-Oct, set in 40 acres with mountain bike hire.

Callander and around *p787*

L **Roman Camp Country House Hotel**, T01877-330003, www.roman-camp-hotel.co.uk. An exquisite 16th-century hunting lodge set in extensive grounds by the river, away from the hoi polloi. Queen Victoria was quite taken with the place. Also serves superb Scottish cuisine (expensive).

A **Leny House**, a 5-star B&B in the parkland of the Leny Estate, T01877-331078, www.lenyestate.com. Open Apr-Oct.

B **Creagan House**, at the northern end of Loch Lubnaig, in Strathyre, T01877-384638, a family-run 17th-century farmhouse offering excellent food (mid-range to expensive) and comfortable accommodation, open Mar-Jan.

B **Monachyle Mhor Hotel**, T01877-384622, on the road to Inverlochlarig. It offers great views of the loch, peace and quiet and fabulous Scottish/French cuisine (£££).

C-D **Brook Linn Country House**, T01877-330103, open Easter-Oct, a fine Victorian house overlooking the town;

F **Trossachs Backpackers**, A couple of miles out of town, along the Invertrossachs Rd which turns off the A81, T01877-331200, trosstel@aol.com. Relaxed and peaceful independent hostel which also rents bikes.

Lochearnhead and Killin *p787*
C **Dall Lodge Country House Hotel**, Killin, T01567-820217, www.dallodgehotel.co.uk, open Mar-Oct. The best place to stay in the village, offers idiosyncratic style and very good food.

Loch Lomond *p788*
B **Rowardennan Hotel**, Rowardennan, T01360-870273, comfortable choice, serves bar meals.
D **Inversnaid Hotel**, On the northeast shore, and only accessible by road via the B829 from Aberfoyle, T01877-386223. Splendidly isolated.
F **Loch Lomond SYHA Youth Hostel**, Arden, T01389-850226, www.syha.org.uk Grand 19th-century turreted mansion complete with the obligatory ghost.
There's a good campsite at **Lomond Woods Holiday Park at Tullichewan** T01389-755000, on the Old Luss Rd, where you can hire mountain bikes.

Eating

Aberfoyle *p787*
££ **Braeval Old Mill**, T01877-382711, a few miles east on the A873 to Port of Menteith. The best place to eat, excellent and very popular.

Callander and around *p787*
£££ **Roman Camp Hotel** (see above). The best place to eat by far. Superb.
££ **Byre**, at Brig o' Turk, on the A821, T01877-376292. A cosy bar serving good ales and hearty food, ideally placed for walkers and cylists.

Loch Lomond *p788*
££ **Inverbeg Inn**, a few miles north of Luss, at Inverbeg, T01436-860678, does good food.

Pubs, bars and clubs

Loch Lomond *p788*
Drover's Inn, Inverarnan, T01301-704234. The famous Highland watering hole, with smoke-blackened walls, low ceilings, bare floors, open fires, a hall filled with stuffed animals, barman in kilt and a great selection of single malts. The perfect place for a wild night of drinking in the wilderness. It simply doesn't get any better than this.

Activities and tours

Boat trips
Sweeney's Cruises, Balloch, T01389-752376, offer a wide range of trips, starting at around £4-5 for an hour. A daily 2½-hour cruise from Balloch to Luss leaves at 1430 (£7).

Transport

Loch Lomond *p788*
Scottish Citylink **buses** run regularly from Glasgow to **Balloch** (45 mins), and on to **Luss** and **Tarbet** (1 hr 10 mins). Some buses go to **Ardlui** (1 hr 20 mins) and on to **Crianlarich**. There are 2 **rail** lines from Glasgow to **Loch Lomond**. One runs to Balloch every 30 mins (35 mins) the other is the West Highland line to Fort William and Mallaig, with a branch line to Oban. It reaches Loch Lomond at Tarbet and there's another station further north at Ardlui. There's a passenger **ferry** service across the loch between Inverbeg and Rowardennan, T01360-870273, 3 times daily (Apr-Sep).

Lochearnhead and Killin *p787*
There are **buses** to **Killin** from Stirling via Callander (1 hr 45 mins). There's a **postbus** from Callander once daily Mon-Fri (1 hr), which continues to **Crianlarich** and **Tyndrum**. There's also a postbus service from Aberfeldy (see p774).

Directory

Cycle hire Wheels, Invertrossachs Rd, Callander, T01887-331100. **Trossachs** Cycle Hire, at Loch Katrine, T01887-382614, for £6.50-10 per half day and £10-16 for a whole day.

For an explanation of the sleeping and eating price codes used in this guide, see the inside front cover. Other relevant information is provided in the Essentials chapter, page 36.

Fife

→Colour map 5

For such a small region, Fife is a very diverse place. The difference between the blighted industrial landscape of the southwest and the prosperous-looking rural northeast couldn't be more marked. Northeast Fife consists of St Andrews and the East Neuk and if you only have a few days in which to visit, then this is the area to see. St Andrews, in particular, is important and attractive enough to visit on its own. The ruins of its cathedral and castle bear witness to its former importance, while the Royal and Ancient Golf Club is the sport's spiritual home and stands on the world's most famous links course. It also has the oldest university in Scotland The East Neuk of Fife is a string of picture-postcard old fishing villages, Those with more time on their hands could also venture inland to explore Falkland, Cupar and the Howe of Fife. Here, you'll find Falkland Palace, one of Scotland's most remarkable historic buildings.

▸▸ *For Sleeping, Eating and other listings, see pages 795-796.*

Ins and outs

Getting around The **train** line north from Edinburgh follows the coast as far as Kirkaldy and then cuts inland towards Dundee, stopping at Cupar and Leuchars. From Leuchars a bus can be taken to St Andrews. It is possible to explore the peninsula using public transport, but it can be a slow and time-consuming business as buses to the more remote parts are few and far between. Trains from Edinburgh connect with Dunfermline. Trains run hourly from North Queensferry to and from Edinburgh and there are 2 buses every hour to Dunfermline. The nearest train station to Falkland Palace is 5 miles away at Markinch, on the Edinburgh to Dundee line. Cupar is on the Edinburgh to Dundee rail line and trains depart in each direction roughly every hour, or every 2 hrs on Sun.

Information Dunfermline TIC ⓘ *13/15 Maygate (next to the Abbot House). T01383-720999.* **St Andrews TIC** ⓘ *70 Market St, T01334-472021, daily Apr-Sep, Oct-Mar Mon-Sat.* **Anstruther TIC** ⓘ *next to the Fisheries museum, T01334-311073. Easter to mid-Sep.*

Southwest Fife and the Howe

The main attraction in Southwest Fife is Dunfermline, a town steeped in history. It was once the capital of Scotland, from the 11th century to the Union of Crowns in 1603, and its great abbey and royal palace still dominate the skyline. Until the late 19th century, Dunfermline was one of Scotland's most important linen producers and a major coal-mining centre. In stark contrast to the industrial landscape of Southwest Fife, the Howe of Fife (Howe means valley) is a low-lying area of patchwork fields, woodlands and farming communities which runs from the attractive market town of Cupar in the east to Falkland, at the foot of the Lomond Hills.

Dunfermline and around

Dunfermline **Abbey** stands on the site of the Benedictine Priory, built by Queen Margaret in the late 11th century. Her son, David I, raised the priory to the rank of abbey and began building the new abbey church in 1128, on the foundations of Margaret's church. Frequently sacked and burned over the centuries, today's building is a combination of different tastes and styles. Much of the present abbey was built long after King David's death but the superb Norman nave, with its massive pillars, is still there to be admired. Close to the east gable of the parish church are the foundations of the shrine of St Margaret where she and her husband are buried. But they were not the only royal persons to be buried in the abbey. Six Scottish kings also lie there, with the grave of Robert the Bruce beneath the pulpit.

The Abbey church stands adjacent to the ruined **monastery** building and the **Royal Palace** ⓘ *T01383-739026, Apr-Sep daily 0930-1830, Oct-Mar Mon-Wed & Sat 0930-1630, Thu 0930-1230, Sun 1400-1630, £2, £1.50 concession, £0.75 children*, built when Malcolm and Margaret married. It has fallen into ruins, but what little remains still hints at its undoubted magnificence. For centuries, it was a favourite residence of the Kings of Scotland. David II, James I and Charles I were all born here, the latter being the last monarch to be born in Scotland.

The **Andrew Carnegie Birthplace Museum** ⓘ *T01383-724302, Apr-Oct Mon-Sat 1100-1700, Sun 1400-1700. Groups in winter by appointment only, £2, £1 concession, children free* is the small cottage in Moodie Street where the famous steel magnate and great philanthropist was born.

Culross (pronounced 'kooros') is a beautifully restored village containing the finest surviving examples of Scottish vernacular architecture from the 16th and 17th centuries. Culross was then one of the largest ports in Scotland, and enjoyed a flourishing trade in coal and salt with other Forth ports and the Low Countries. Following the industrial revolution, however, the little town went into near-terminal decline until the National Trust rescued it from decay in 1932. To appreciate the town's unique sense of history fully, explore its narrow cobbled streets on foot. A good starting point is the **National Trust Visitor Centre**, in the **Town House** ⓘ *T01383-880359, www.nts.org.uk, Palace and Town House daily Apr, May, Sep and weekends in Oct 1230-1630, Easter weekend and Jun-Aug 1000-1700, combined ticket for the Palace, Town House and Study £9, £6.50 child/concession, £23 family.*, or Tolbooth, on the main road beside the palace, which dates from 1626. Here you can watch an excellent video charting the history of the town. The **Palace** was built between 1597 and 1611 by local merchant, Sir George Bruce, who made his fortune from coal and salt panning. It's not so much a palace as a grand house, but its crow-stepped gables and pan-tiled roofs give a delightful example of Scottish architecture from this period. Inside, the main features are the wonderful original painted ceilings and wood panelling.

At the foot of the Forth Rail Bridge is North Queensferry home to the popular **Deep Sea World** ⓘ *T01383-411880, www.deepseaworld.com, Apr-Oct daily 1000-1800; July/Aug 1000-1830, Nov-Mar daily 1100-1700, £6.50, £4.75 concession, £3.95 children, under 3 free.* , Scotland's award-winning national aquarium, which boasts the world's largest underwater viewing tunnel, through which you pass on a moving walkway, coming face-to-face with sharks, conger eels and all manner of strange sea creatures. There is also a display of species from the Amazon rainforest.

Falkland

Tucked away at the foot of the Lomond Hills, off the A912, the ancient and beautiful village of Falkland is the most royal of Fife's Royal Burghs and holds a unique place in Scottish history, as it is the site of **Falkland Palace** ⓘ *T01337-T857397, Apr-Oct Mon-Sat 1000-1730, Sun 1330-1730, £9, £6.50 child/concession, £23 family*, the favourite residence of the Stuart monarchs. The palace, which stands in the heart of the village, is one of the grandest buildings in the country and its variety of styles is part of its charm. Facing the street, the south front is a splendid example of Scottish Gothic with its buttresses, niches and statues of Christ and the saints. The magnificent courtyard frontage in the classical style, with pillars and medallions, strikes an altogether different mood and an air of gracious living. Scotland has few surviving buildings that were in the mainstream of Renaissance architecture, but this one is by far the best.

Cupar and around

The main centre in the Howe of Fife is Cupar, a thriving market town that was once the administrative centre of Fife. There's an air of relative well-being about the place, verified by an array of shops catering to the retail connoisseur. One of the main reasons for stopping off at Cupar is to visit **Hill of Tarvit** ⓘ *House and garden open Easter & May-Sep, weekends in Oct, £5, £3.75 child/concession; garden and gounds only £2/£1*, two miles south of the town and one mile from Ceres (see below). This Edwardian mansion house was beautifully remodelled by Robert Lorimer in 1906. Among the fine collection of treasures inside are Flemish tapestries, Chinese porcelain, Dutch paintings and 18th-century French, Chippendale and vernacular furniture. The gardens are laid out in the French style, with box hedges and yew trees, and there is a woodland walk to a hilltop toposcope with a lovely view of the house.

St Andrews and the East Neuk

This well-groomed seaside resort on the northeastern coast of Fife is the 'Home of Golf' and a mecca for aficionados of the sport the world over. Here is the headquarters of the game's governing body, the Royal and Ancient Golf Club, and the world's most famous golf course, the Old Course. But it's not all Pringle sweaters and five irons. St Andrews has an air of calm dignity tinged with an inherent sense of history, as you'd expect from a place that was once the ecclesiastical capital of Scotland and the country's oldest seat of learning. To the southeast is the East Neuk. Here, on Fife's easternmost stretch of coastline are some of the kingdom's greatest attractions. From Largo Bay to Fife Ness lies a string of picturesque villages, each with its own distinctive character and charm. These were once thriving seaports trading with the Low Countries. The Dutch influence lives on

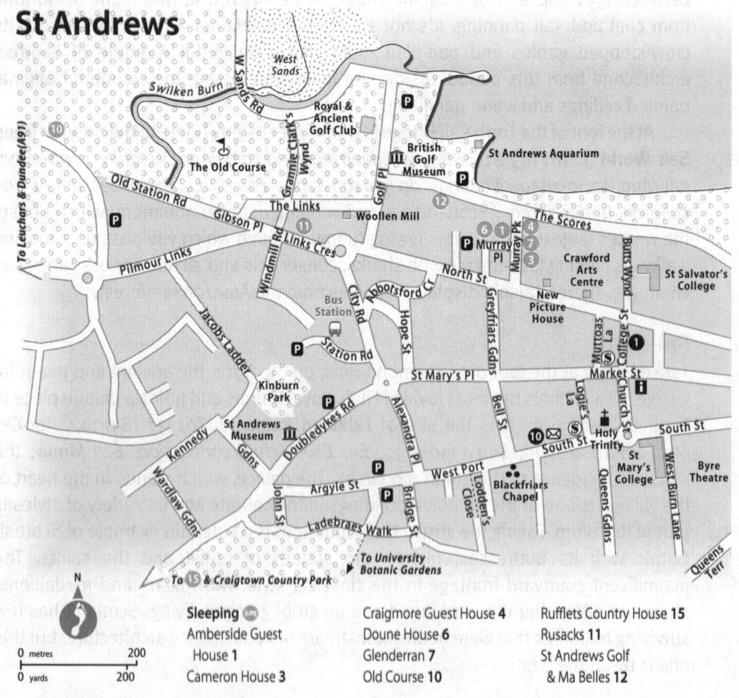

Sleeping
Amberside Guest House 1
Cameron House 3
Craigmore Guest House 4
Doune House 6
Glenderran 7
Old Course 10
Rufflets Country House 15
Rusacks 11
St Andrews Golf & Ma Belles 12

in their architectural styles. The red pan-tiled roofs and crow-stepped gables lend a particular continental feel to one of the most attractive corners of Scotland.

Ins and outs

Getting there St Andrews is not on the **train** line. The nearest station is 5 miles away at Leuchars, on the Edinurgh- Dundee-Aberdeen line. Regular **buses** make the 15-min journey from there to St Andrews. A **taxi** costs around £7. The bus station is on City Road, at the west end of town. There are frequent buses to Dundee (30 mins), the East Neuk villages and Cupar (20 mins). There is also a service to Stirling. Buses run from Edinburgh to St Andrews via Kirkcaldy. The No 95 **bus** runs every hour between Dundee and Leven, via St Andrews, Crail, Anstruther, Pittenweem, St Monans and Elie.

Sights

St Andrews' street plan has not changed since the Middle Ages. It basically consists of three main streets – North Street, Market Street and South Street – which still converge on the **Cathedral** ⓘ *T01334-472563, Apr-Sep daily 0930-1830, Oct-Mar Mon-Sat 0930-1630, Sun 1400-1630, joint ticket with castle £4, £1.25 child, £3 concession,* standing proudly, overlooking the harbour at the eastern end of the town. Founded in 1160, it was consecrated 160 years later, in 1318, by Robert the Bruce. Medieval pilgrims came in their thousands to pray at its many altars. This explains the exceptional width of North Street, which enabled the vast numbers to proceed to the cathedral. Though devastated over the years by fire and by religious reformers, the Cathedral ruins are still impressive, giving proof that this was by far the largest ecclesiastical building ever to be erected in Scotland. The Romanesque **St Rule's Tower** is where the holy relics of the Apostle were kept until the Cathedral was completed. It's a hard climb to the top of the tower, but the view on a clear day is worth the effort. The Cathedral visitor centre has a fine collection of early Christian sculptured stones from the church of St Mary of the Rock. Of particular interest is the unique eighth century Pictish sarcophagus.

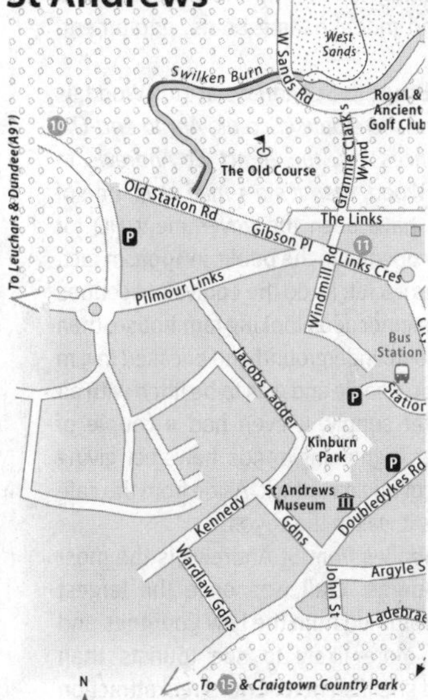

Poised on a rocky headland overhanging the sea stands the ruin of **St Andrews Castle** ⓘ *T01334-477196, opening times as for the Cathedral, joint ticket with cathedral (see above).* It was built at the end of the 12th century as the place and stronghold of the Bishops of St Andrews and has witnessed many violent incidents in the blood-stained history of the Scottish Church. A fascinating exhibition in the visitor centre brings the history of the castle to life.

As well as an impressive history, St Andrews has other attractions. There are two fine sandy **beaches**, the **East and West Sands**, that enclose the town like golden bookends. The latter provided the setting for the opening sequence in the film *Chariots of Fire*. If you've got children, then the huge **St Andrews Aquarium** ⓘ *T01334-474786, www. Standrews aquarium, daily in summer 1000-1800; phone for winter opening hours, £4.50, £3.50 child, £3.85 concession, £17 family,* is a must. Situated on The Scores, at the

St Andrews

West Sands
Swilken Burn
W Sands Rd
Royal & Ancient Golf Club
Grannie Clark's Wynd
The Old Course
Old Station Rd
The Links
Gibson Pl
Links Cres
Windmill Rd
Pilmour Links
To Leuchars & Dundee (A91)
Jacobs Ladder
Bus Station
Station
Kinburn Park
St Andrews Museum
Doubledykes Rd
Kennedy Gdns
Wardlaw Gdns
Argyle S
John St
Ladebrae
To 15 & Craigtown Country Park
N
0 metres 200
0 yards 200

Sleeping
Amberside Guest House 1
Cameron House 3

 west end of town near the Golf Museum, this is where you can legally indulge in any number of piscean pleasures with an array of weird and wonderful sea creatures.

The history of golf, and the town's intimate association with it, are all to be discovered in the **British Golf Museum** ⓘ *T01334-460046, www.britishgolfmuseum.co.uk, Easter to mid-Oct daily 0930-1730, mid-Oct to Easter Thu-Mon 1100-1500, £3.75, £1.50 children, £2.75 concession, £9.50 family*, standing directly behind the Royal and Ancient Clubhouse on Bruce Embankment. It is the most exciting of its kind, and audio-visual displays and touch activated screens bring the game to life and trace its development through the centuries.

East Neuk

Westernmost of the East Neuk villages are **Elie and Earlsferry**, which are really two halves of the same place. This is one of Fife's most popular resorts, with a mile of lovely sandy beaches, and is very popular with sailors and windsurfers. Further along the coast is **St Monans** and three miles inland from **Pittenweem**, on the B9171, stands **Kellie Castle** ⓘ *Easter to end-Sep, and weekends in Oct, 1330-1730, garden and grounds open Apr-Sep daily 0930-2100; Oct-Mar till 1630, £5, £3.75 concession/child, £14 family*, one of the oldest and most magnificent of Scottish castles. This is 16th- and 17th-century domestic architecture at its best, though the oldest part of the castle dates from 1360. The interior is notable for its superb plasterwork ceilings, which were then the height of fashion.

Anstruther is the largest of the East Neuk villages. Today, it is best known as the home of the Scottish Fisheries Museum, but it was Scotland's main fishing port at the end of the 19th century, with almost 1,000 boats in its fleet. This proud heritage has been well preserved in **The Scottish Fisheries Museum** ⓘ *T01334-310628, Apr-Sep Mon-Sat 1000-1730, Sun 1100-1700; Oct-Mar Mon-Sat 1000-1630, Sun 1200-1630. £3.50, £2.50 concession/child*, which faces the harbour on the site of the pre-Reformation St Ayles chapel. The museum, established in 1969, gives a fascinating insight into the life and work of a fishing community and is well worth a visit. There's also a fine collection of actual and model fishing boats, equipment, maps and compasses, as well as an aquarium.

Three miles north of Anstruther, just off the B9131 to St Andrews at Troy Wood, is **Scotland's Secret Bunker** ⓘ *T01334-310301, www.secretbunker.co.uk, Apr to end-Oct daily 1000-1700. £6.95, £3.75 child, £5.45 concession, the direct St Andrews to Anstruther bus takes you to the turn-off for Troy Wood, then it's a 1-mile walk*, one of Fife's most fascinating attractions. This was to have been the government HQ for Scotland in the event of nuclear war and was only opened to the public in 1994. In fact, part of the complex is still operational and remains secret, as do the equivalent centres in England and Wales. The approach is through an innocuous-looking farmhouse, then visitors descend via a huge ramp to the bunker, 30 m underground and encased in 5 m of reinforced concrete. The bunker could house 300 people and was to be fitted with air filters, an electricity generator and its own water supply. It even had a couple of cinemas, which are now used to show a rather frightening 1950s newsreel giving instructions to civilians on what to do in the event of nuclear attack. Aside from the café and gift shop, the bunker has been left exactly as it was in the 1950s.

Three miles northeast of Anstruther and 10 miles from St Andrews is the most ancient and picturesque of all Fife's Royal Burghs. **Crail** was once the largest fishmarket in Europe and for centuries its ships returned from the Low Countries and Scandinavia laden with cargo. Today you're more likely to see tourists than fishermen, but you can still buy fresh lobster and shellfish here. Crail's real attraction is its beautiful **harbour**, surrounded by whitewashed cottages with pan-tiled roofs and crow-stepped gables. It is one of the most photographed locations in all of Scotland and a favourite with artists. To reach the old harbour you go down the steep, winding Shoregate. At the foot of the Shoregate is the 19th-century customs house.

Sleeping

Dunfermline and around *p790*

A **Garvock House Hotel**, St John's Dr, Transy, T01383-621067, F621168, www.garvock.co.uk. 12 rooms with bathroom, elegant country house in woodland setting, short break deals available. Excellent.

A-B **Davaar House Hotel**, 126 Grieve St, T01383-721886, F623633. 10 en suite rooms, within walking distance of the town centre and bus and rail stations, good restaurant.

Falkland *p791*

B-C **Covenanter Hotel**, is near the palace, T01337-857224, F857163, www.covenanterhotel.com. 6 comfortable en suite rooms, excellent food served in the restaurant (mid-range) and bistro (cheap) downstairs.

E **Falkland Backpackers**, Back Wynd, T01337-857710, falkland@backpackers.connectfree.co.uk. Open Apr-Dec.

Cupar and around *p792*

A **Fernie Castle Hotel**, near Letham, 5 miles north of Cupar, T01337-810381, F810422, www.ferniecastle.demon.co.uk. A beautifully restored 14th-century castle set in 17 acres of grounds with its own loch, 15 comfortable en suite rooms, lovely dining room and bar.

B-C **Eden House Hotel**, 2 Pitscottie Rd, T01334-652510, F652277, www.eden-group.com. Elegant Victorian town house with 11 en suite rooms and excellent restaurant, also arranges golfing packages.

St Andrews *p792, map p792.*

L **Old Course Hotel**, T01334-474371, F477668, www.oldcoursehotel.co.uk. Internationally renowned golf resort and spa overlooking the 17th hole, 125 en suite rooms, bar and restaurants.

L **Rufflets Country House Hotel**, Strathkinnes Low Rd, T01334-472594, F478703, www.rufflets.co.uk. Small country house set in 10 acres of grounds on the outskirts of town by the B939, with 25 en suite rooms and good restaurant.

L **The Parkland Hotel**, Kinburn Castle, Double Dykes Rd, T01334-473620, F460850, www.parklandstandrews.com. A 19th-century castle in the town centre, its restaurant is highly-praised.

L-A **St Andrews Golf Hotel**, T01334-472611, www.standrews-golf.co.uk. 22 comfortable en suite rooms, good restaurant with extensive wine list, specialize in golf breaks.

Most of the guesthouses are around Murray Pk and Murray Pl between The Scores and North Street. Among those recommended are:

C-D **Amberside Guest House**, 4 Murray Pk, T/F01334-474644, amberside@talk21.com;.

C-D **Cameron House**, 11 Murray Pk, T01334-472306, www.cameronhouse-sta.co.uk;

B-C **Craigmore Guest House**, 3 Murray Park, T01334-472142, F477963;

C-D **Doune House**, 5 Murray Pl, T/F01334-475195, dounehouse@aolc.om; and

C-D **Glenderran**, 9 Murray Pk, T01334-477951, F477908, glenderran@ telinco.com

East Neuk *p794*

A **Craw's Nest Hotel**, Bankwell Rd, T01334-310691, F312216, www.smoothhoud.co.uk/hotels/crawsnes.html. Very good hotel with restaurant and full range of facilties, 50 en suite rooms. Also serves very good food,

C-D **The Grange**, 45 Pittenweem Rd, T/F01334-310842, www.thegrangeanstruther.fsnet.co.uk. 7 en suite rooms. Superior guesthouse, very friendly.

Eating

Falkland *p791*

££ **Stag**, whitewashed 17th century pub in Mill Wynd. A nice cosy place for lunch or a drink.

£ **Kind Kyttock's Kitchen**, Cross Wynd. opposite the palace. Good home baking.

Cupar and around *p792*

£££ **Peat Inn** 3 miles southeast of Ceres on the B940, T01334-840206. Well worth a detour, for here, in the 18th-century building, you can sample some of the finest food in the entire country. The proprietors have a Michelin star to verify this and the French-influenced décor and ambience match the culinary excellence.

££ **Ostler's Close**, 25 Bonnygate, Cupar, T01334-655574. The best place to eat in town. Does a 3-course lunch for under £20.

St Andrews *p792, map p792.*

Most of upmarket hotels have excellent restaurants (see Sleeping).

£££ **The Grange Inn**, on the Crail Rd, near Kinkell Braes overlooking the East

Sands, T01334-472670, F462604. Excellent restaurant.

£££ **The Vine Leaf**, 131 South St, T01334-477497, has a deservedly high reputation which is matched by the prices.

£ **Brambles**, 5 College St beside the Market Sq. One of the nicest places for lunch, a light snack or coffee and cakes.

East Neuk *p794*

£££ **The Cellar**, 24 East Green, just behind the Fisheries Museum, Anstruther, T01334-310378. The seafood here is among the finest in the country and will set you back around £30 for a 3-course dinner.

££ **Ship Inn**, Elie, down by the harbour. For tasty bar meals and a good pint.

££ **Bouquet Garni**, High St, Elie, T01334-330374. Open for lunch and 1900-2100, closed Sun. No smoking. Highly acclaimed cooking in unassuming surroundings.

££ **Seafood** Restaurant, 16 West End, just off the A917, T01334-730327. For some excellent seafood. 1200-1500 (1230 on Sun) and 1800-2300 Sat. Closed Mon.

£ **Anstruther Fish Bar**, on Shore St, does a mean takeaway fish supper.

Entertainment

St Andrews *p792, map p792.*

Byre Theatre, on Abbey St, T01334-475000, www.byretheatre.com, stages an excellent range of productions throughout the year and began its life in a cowshed of the old Abbey St Dairy Farm, hence its name.

Activities and tours

Golf

As well as the legendary **Old Course**, there are no fewer than 5 other 18-hole courses in and around the town: **Duke's Course** (T474371); **Eden Course; Jubilee** ; **New** ; and **Strathtyrum**. For information and reserving tee-times on all except the Duke's, T01334-466666. Green fees range from £17 up to £80 for the Old Course (day ticket).

Watersports

Elie Waterpsorts by the harbour, Elie, T01334-330962, offer windsurfing, sailing, water-skiing and canoe hire and instruction and also hire out mountain bikes.

Festivals and events

St Andrews *p792, map p792.*

Lammas Fair is Scotland's oldest surviving medieval market, with showmen from all over Britain setting up stalls and booths in the three main streets. This bright, lively carnival is held in early **Aug**. The other main event in the town's calendar is the **Kate Kennedy Pageant**, usually held on the 3rd Sat in Apr.

Northeast Scotland

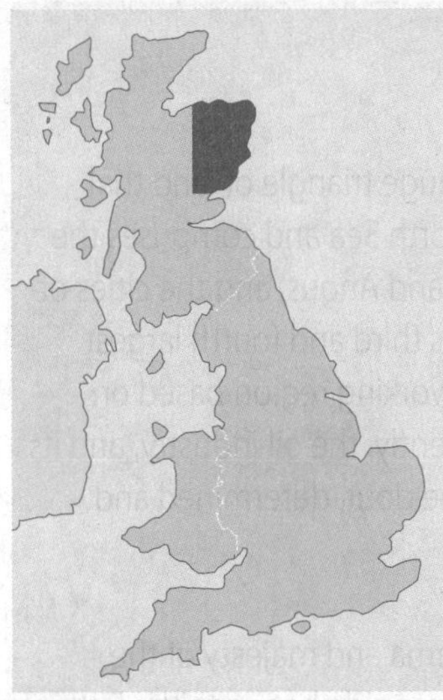

Introduction

The northeast of Scotland is the huge triangle of land that thrusts defiantly into the harsh North Sea and comprises the regions of Aberdeenshire, Moray and Angus, and the cities of Aberdeen and Dundee, Scotland's third and fourth largest cities respectively. This is a hard-working region based on agriculture, fishing and, more recently, the oil industry, and its people typify the stereotype of the dour, determined and thrifty Scot.

The region may lack the sheer drama and majesty of the northwest, but the coast and countryside between the Firth of Tay and the Moray Firth have their own, more subtle charms – and better weather. The Moray Firth, from the hardy fishing port of Fraserburgh west to the Findhorn community, has some of the country's most dramatic coastal scenery, with perfect little fishing villages clinging for dear life to storm-battered cliffs. There are also long stretches of apricot-coloured beaches, long hours of sunshine, and even dolphins frolicking in the waters offshore. Flowing into the Moray Firth is the River Spey, whose gentle, wooded valley is the centre of Scotland's malt whisky industry.

Another of the region's assets is its rich history. This is castle country and there are over 70 in Aberdeenshire and Moray alone. One of the most famous is Balmoral Castle, forever linked to the royal family since Queen Victoria came, saw and purchased in 1852. So strong is the connection that this area is better known as 'Royal Deeside' and visitors can indulge in a bit of royal spotting at the annual Braemar Gathering, the local Highland Games.

★ Don't miss...

1. Head down to the attractive little fishing village of **Auchmithie** and enjoy some superb seafood at the But'n'Ben restaurant, page 806.
2. Visit **Dufftown**, self-proclaimed 'Malt Whisky Capital of the World' and begin the tour of the region's many distilleries, page 817.
3. If you're not all castled-out, then crack on down to **Crathes**, the perfect fairytale castle, which, unbelievably, is almost overhshadowed by its gorgeous gardens, page 812.
4. If all that royal-spotting leaves you cold, then head for the **Lonach Highland Gathering**, held in August, and frequented by the likes of Billy Connolly and Judi Dench, page 816.

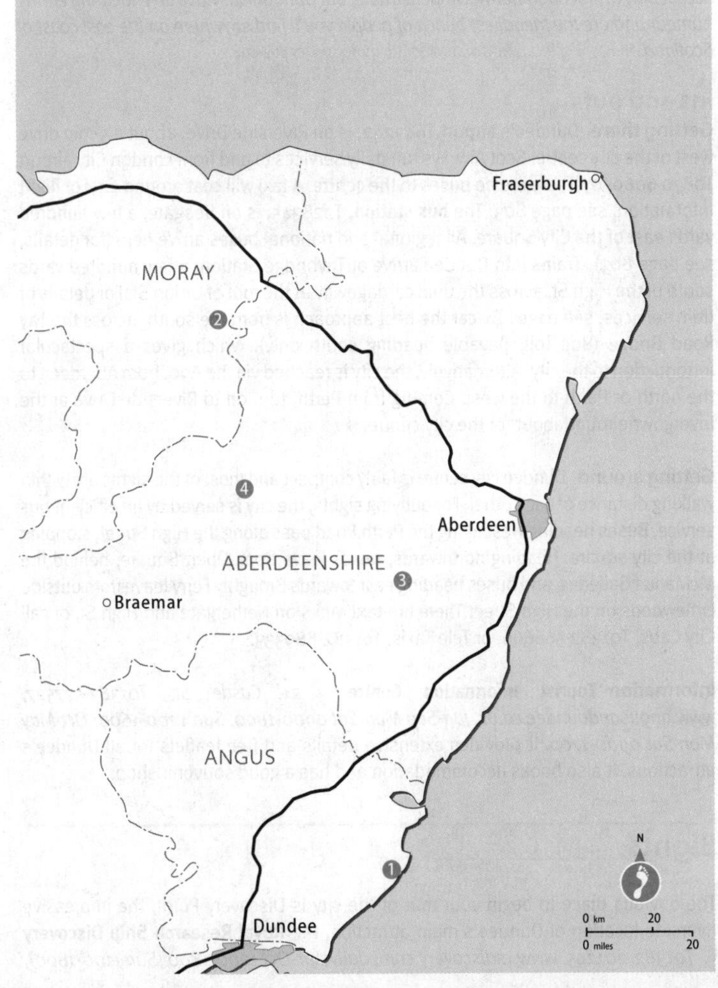

Dundee

→Colour map 5

Scotland's fourth largest city sits on two prominent hills, Balgay and the Law, overlooking the River Tay. Few cities in Britain can match Dundee's impressive setting, seen at its breathtaking best from across the Tay, in Fife. But, despite the common consensus that the views of the city are indeed spectacular, certain guide books have suggested that visitors keep their distance. Which just goes to show how out of touch they are, for Dundee has transformed itself into a vibrant, thriving city and an increasingly popular destination for tourists.

One of Dundee's big attractions is Captain Scott's ship, the Discovery, and such is the civic pride engendered by its return home that Dundee has become widely known through its slogan – City of Discovery. There are other, less publicized, attractions, such as the Law Hill, which commands fantastic views over the city and the Tay estuary, and the attractive seaside suburb of Broughty Ferry. Dundee also has a thriving arts scene and plenty of good shops, bars and restaurants. But the city's best kept secret is its people. The accent may at first be somewhat impenetrable, but Dundonians have an endearing earthy humour and are the friendliest bunch of people you'll find anywhere on the east coast of Scotland. ▸▸ *For Sleeping, Eating and other listings, see pages 802-803.*

Ins and outs

Getting there Dundee's **airport**,T643242, is on Riverside Drive, about a 5-min drive west of the city centre. Scot Airways run daily services to and from London City airport T0870 6060707.There are no buses to the centre. A taxi will cost around £4. For flight information, see page 803. The **bus station**, T228345, is on Seagate, a few hundred yards east of the City Square. All regional and national buses arrive here (for details, see page 803). **Trains** into Dundee arrive at Taybridge Station, a few hundred yards south of the High St, across the dual carriageway at the foot of Union St. For details of train services, see page . By **car** the best approach is from the south, across the Tay Road Bridge (80p toll; payable heading south only), which gives a spectacular introduction to the city. Alternatively, the city is reached via the A90, from Aberdeen to the north or Perth to the west. Coming from Perth, turn on to Riverside Drive at the Invergowrie roundabout for the city centre. ▸▸ *For further details, see Transport, page 803.*

Getting around Dundee city centre is fairly compact and most of the sights are within walking distance of each other. For outlying sights, the city is served by an efficient bus service. **Buses** heading west along the Perth Road pass along the High Street, stopping at the city square. Heading northwards, buses leave from Albert Square, behind the McManus Galleries, and buses heading east towards Broughty Ferry leave from outside Littlewoods on the High Street.There are **taxi** ranks on Nethergate and High St, or call City Cabs, T01382-566666, or Tele Taxis, T01382-889333.

Information Tourist Information Centre ⓘ *21 Castle St, T01382-527527, www.angusanddundee.co.uk, Jun-Sep Mon-Sat 0900-1800, Sun 1200-1600; Oct-May Mon-Sat 0900-1700.* It provides extensive details and free leaflets for all Dundee's attractions. It also books accommodation and has a good souvenir shop.

Sights

The obvious place to begin your tour of the city is Discovery Point, the impressive riverside location of Dundee's main attraction, the **Royal Research Ship Discovery** ⓘ *T01382-201245, www.rsdiscovery.com, daily Apr-Oct 1000-1800 (Sun 1100-1800),*

Nov-Mar till 1700, £6.25, £3.85 child, £4.45concession, £10.95/£8.15 for joint ticket with Verdant Works. She was the first specially designed scientific research ship and spent two winters in the Antarctic, where her wooden hull was able to withstand the enormous pressures of the pack ice. Famous as Captain Scott's ship, the Discovery and Scott parted company after his expedition in 1904. Another Dundee-built vessel, the Terra Nova, carried Scott to the South Pole in 1911 – the fateful expedition from which he never returned. After being purchased by the Maritime Trust, the Discovery was returned to Dundee in 1986 and moored at its present specially built quay with an excellent **visitor centre** at her side. The state-of-the-art centre presents an entertaining introduction, with audio-visual displays and an exhibition. On board the vessel you can see the cabins used by Scott and his crew, and hear some interesting anecdotes from the enthusiastic guides.

The pedestrianized Reform Street leads north from City Square to **Albert Square,** site of the **McManus Galleries** ⓘ *Mon-Sat 1030-1700 (1900 on Thurs) and 1230-1600 Sun, free,* housed in Gilbert Scott's impressive Victorian Gothic edifice. Inside are some very fine exhibits detailing the city's history from the Iron Age to the Tay Bridge Disaster. The latter event was chronicled by the inimitable William McGonagall, the 'World's Worst Poet', and here you can read his excruciatingly awful verse, along with an equally painful account of the famous 'Tay Whale', the skeleton of which is also on display. Upstairs is the superb **Albert Hall**, which contains various antique collections, and the **Victoria Gallery**, whose 19th- and 20th-century collections include some notable Scottish painters such as McTaggart. Also in Albert Square are the red sandstone offices of local publishing giant, DC Thomson, who have entertained generations of British kids with their *Beano* and *Dandy* comics. A five-minute walk west, along Meadowside and Ward Road, across the dual carriageway and up Guthrie Street, is the excellent **Verdant Works** ⓘ *T01382-225282, www.verdantworks.com, Apr-Oct Mon-Sat 1000-1800, Sun 1100-1800, Nov-Mar*

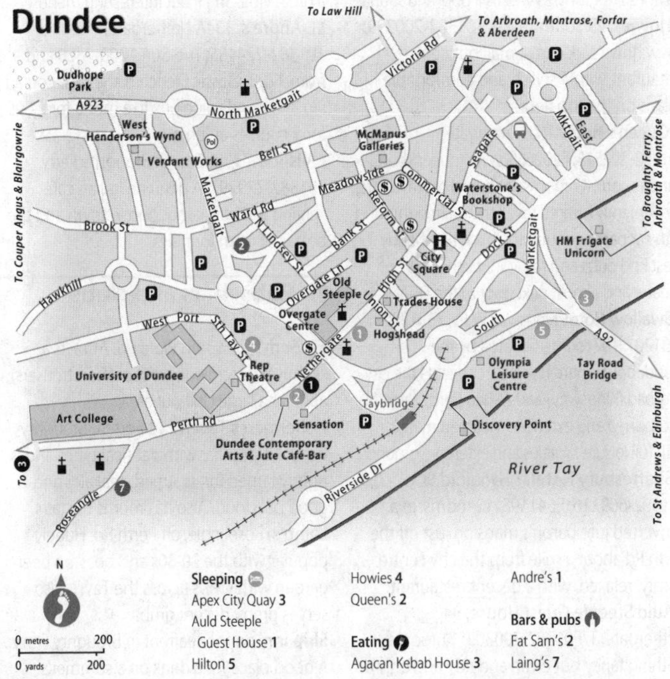

 Wed-Sat 1030-1630, Sun 1100-1630, £5.95, £3.95 child/concession, in West Henderson's Wynd. This former jute mill gives a rare insight into what life was like for mill workers, and details the history of the jute industry.

Four miles east of Dundee, is the attractive seaside resort of **Broughty Ferry**. 'The Ferry' was once a separate settlement, with fishermen's cottages lining the shore and the large villas of wealthy jute barons climbing the hills behind, but it has since been swallowed up by the city's eastern suburbs. There's a long sandy beach, which is now much cleaner than it used to be, and several good pubs and places to eat, as well as some good individual shops. The 15th-century **Broughty Castle** ⓘ *T01382-436916, Apr-Sep Mon-Sat 1000-1600, Sun 1230-1600, Oct-Mar closed Mon, free,* stands on the seafront, guarding the mouth of the Tay, and now houses an interesting **museum** of local history which includes a detailed description of the whaling industry.

Sleeping

A **Hilton Hotel**, Earl Grey Place, T01382-229271, www.hilton.com.uk. 54 double and 74 twin rooms. Reliable 4 star chain with car parking, a leisure club with a pool and a restaurant.

A **Apex City Quay Hotel**, West Victoria Dock Rd, T01382-202404, F 201401, www.apexhotels.co.uk. 153 rooms. Contemporary style comes to Dundee. This multi storey hotel has 4 star rooms with CD/DVD players, modem points as well as a restaurant and a brasserie. Yu Spa includes Japanese hot tubs, as well as a pool and sauna.

B **Howies**, 25 South Tay St, T01382-200399, www.howies.uk.com. Small but cool restaurant with 4 stylish and comfortable rooms on the top floor.

B **Queen's Hotel**, 160 Nethergate, T01382-322515, F202668, www.queenshotel-dundee.com. 47 rooms. Perennial old favourite, conveniently located for all the main sights and with car parking round the back, also handy for West End pubs and restaurants, the Rep Theatre and almost next door to the DCA.

B **Swallow Hotel**, Kingsway West, T631200, F631201. 107 rooms. Situated by the roundabout where Riverside Dr meets the city ringroad (Kingsway) and A90 to Perth, tastefully refurbished and extended Victorian mansion with full leisure facilities and extensive grounds.

C **Shaftesbury Hotel**, 1 Hyndford St, T01382-669216, F641598. 12 rooms. In a converted jute baron's mansion just off the Perth Rd about a mile from the city centre. Comfy, relaxed, with a decent restaurant.

C **Auld Steeple Guest House**, 94 Nethergate, T/F01382-200302. 11 rooms. Nothing fancy but clean and tidy and only a few mins' walk from the train station.

Eating

££ **Howies**, 25 South Tay St, T01382-200339. 1200-1430, 1730-2200. Contemporary restaurant. The set lunches are good value. Mains feature dishes like thyme baked pheasant or steak, and there's always a veggie choice. Cheaper meals in the basement bar.

££ **Agacan Kebab House**, 113 Perth Rd, T01382- 644227. Brightly decorated and cosy Turkish restaurant, open Tue-Sun.

££ **Jute Café-bar**, 152 Nethergate, in Dundee Contemporary Arts. Daily 1030-2400 (Sun till 2300). So stylish you could be in Glasgow, and a great vibe. Small but interesting menu.

££ **Andre's**, 134A Nethergate, T01382-224455. Tue-Sun 1200-1500 and from 1700. Classic French dishes like coq au vin and good value prix fixe menu for £7.95 for 3 courses at lunch.

£ **Visocchi's**, 40 Gray St,Broughty Ferry, T01382-779297. A genuine Italian café serving the best capuccino in town and the best ice cream for miles.

Pubs, bars and clubs

Fat Sam's, 31 South Ward Rd. Attracts a slightly older crowd (ie out of short trousers), and has a large chill-out area.

Fisherman's Tavern, 12 Fort St, Broughty Ferry. It's popular with nautical types and is rightly famed for its superb real ales and good pub food. Also has rooms upstairs.

Laing's, Roseangle, off Perth Rd. Hugely popular with the 20-30s and boasts a beer garden with views across the Tay. It also serves pretty decent grub.

Ship Inn, on the seafront in Broughty Ferry. A good place for a drink on a summer's evening, and a reputation for fine food.

Entertainment

Cinema and theatre

Dundee Contemporary Arts, 152 Nethergate, T01382-909900, www.dca.org.uk. Dundee's cultural hub, housed in a superb building, with two cinema screens showing current arthouse releases, also exhibition spaces, print studio, visual research centre and the **Jute Café-bar**. Dundee's excellent **Rep Theatre** is on Tay Square, off South Tay St, T01382-223530. It stages locally produced contemporary theatre and hosts various national touring companies. It is also a jazz venue and has a good café-restaurant in the foyer.

Transport

Air There are direct flights to Dundee from **London City Airport**, 4 times daily, with Scot Airways, T0870-6060707.
Bus National Express, runs 4 services daily to and from **London** (10 hrs direct). Scottish Citylink, operates an hourly service to and from **Edinburgh** (2 hrs) and **Glasgow** (2¼ hrs). Most Edinburgh and Glasgow buses stop en route in **Perth** (35 mins). There are also hourly buses to **Aberdeen** (2 hrs).
Train There are trains at least every hour, Mon-Sat, to and from **Glasgow** (1½ hrs) and **Edinburgh** (1½ hrs). Trains run less frequently on Sun. Trains run every 30 mins to and from **Aberdeen** (1¼ hrs), via **Arbroath**, **Montrose** and **Stonehaven**.

Directory

Car hire Arnold Clark, 14-22 Trades Lane, T01382-225382. Hertz 18 Marketgait, T01382-223711. **Cycle hire** Just Bikes, 57 Gray St, T01382-732100. Nicholson's, 2-4 Forfar Rd, T01382-461212. **Hospitals** Ninewells Hospital, T01382-660111 24-hr accident and emergency. **Internet** TIC (address above) £1/15 mins. Mailboxes etc, 17 Union St, T01382-228999. Inter Café in Debenhams, Overgate £1.50 for 30 mins. The library at the Wellgate Centre has free access. **Pharmacies** Boots, High St, Mon-Wed, Fri- Sat 0830-1745, Thu till 1900. Sun opening on rota basis; check press. **Post office**, 4 Meadowside, Mon-Fri 0900-1730, Sat 0900-1900.

Angus

→*Colour map 6*

The fishing and farming county of Angus was formerly part of the giant Tayside region but is now a separate authority with its own identity. Angus has much to recommend it to those who prefer to escape the summer hordes. The east coast, from Arbroath north to Montrose, is particularly attractive with its sheer red cliffs punctuated by sweeping bays of golden sand. In the north are the Angus Glens, stretching deep into the heart of the Grampian peaks and offering excellent walking opportunities. The heart of the county is the wide valley of Strathmore, with its string of neat market towns. This was part of the ancient Pictish Kingdom and there are still many interesting carved stones scattered around the area. ▸▸ *For Sleeping, Eating and other listings, see pages 806.*

Ins and outs

Getting around The towns along the main Dundee-Aberdeen routes are easy to get to by bus or train, but public transport to the more remote parts is limited. **Strathtay Scottish,** T01382-228054, runs hourly **buses** (Mon-Sat, less on Sun) to Kirriemuir from Dundee (1 hr 10 mins). There are also buses every hr to Forfar (25 mins) and twice a day (except Sun) to Glamis. There's a **postbus service,** T01463-256200, from Kirriemuir to Glen Prosen (once daily except Sun) and Glen Clova. (twice on weekdays, once Sat). Kirriemuir is the gateway to **Glens Isla, Prosen** and **Clova,** while the other two, **Glens Lethnot** and **Esk,** are reached via Brechin. There are regular **buses** to Brechin and Kirriemuir from Dundee, but getting around is not easy without own transport as there is only a limited service. For more information pick up Angus Council's *Public Transport Map & Guide*, available from tourist offices. ▸▸ *For further details, see Transport, page 806.*

 Information Angus is covered by the Angus & Dundee Tourist Board, which has offices in Arbroath, Brechin, Carnoustie, Forfar, Kirriemuir and Montrose.

Arbroath and around

The A92 coast road to Aberdeen heads to Arbroath, 17 miles northeast of Dundee. This is the home of that great Scottish delicacy, the **Arbroath smokie** – haddock smoked over oak chips – which you can buy in the tiny smokehouses around the harbour. The chief attraction is undoubtedly **Arbroath Abbey** ⓘ *T01241-878756, Apr-Sep daily 0930-1830; Oct-Mar Mon-Wed and Sat till 1630, Thu till 1230, Sun 1400-1630, £3.30, £2.50 concession*, on Abbey Street, near the top of the High Street not far from the tourist office. Founded by William the Lion in 1178 (who's buried here), it went on to become one of the wealthiest monasteries in the country. It is also one of the most important sites in Scottish history. It was here, on 6 April 1320, that the Declaration of Arbroath was issued, asking Rome to reverse its excommunication of Robert the Bruce and recognize him as King, thus asserting Scotland's independence from England. Pope John XXII finally agreed to the claim four years later.

Montrose and around

Fourteen miles north of Arbroath is the elegant town of Montrose, the most pleasant and interesting of the Angus towns, rich in history and with great beaches to the north and south. About four miles south of Montrose, reached by turning off the A92, is the great sweep of **Lunan Bay**, a stunningly beautiful, and usually deserted, sandy beach, once popular with smugglers. Like many beaches on the northeast coast, there are strong currents, so do not swim beyond your capabilities. There's a variety of **wildlife** around, including nesting puffins on the red sandstone cliffs. Overlooking the beach is the 12th-century ruin of **Red Castle**, which was originally a royal hunting lodge.

Three miles west of Montrose on the A935 is the **House of Dun** ⓘ *T01674-810264, Apr-30 Jun, Sep Fri-Tue 1200-1700, 1 Jul-31 Aug daily 1200-1700, garden and grounds all year daily 0930 to sunset, £7, concession £5.25, garden and grounds only £1, Strathtay bus No 30 to Brechin passes the entrance, ask to get off*, built in 1730 for David Erskine, Lord Dun. It is a very attractive Georgian building in the Palladian style, designed by William Adam, who was at the forefront of Scottish architecture between the Jacobite risings of 1715 and 1745, but otherwise somewhat eclipsed by his sons Robert and James. The courtyard has recently been restored, and **Angus Handloom Weavers**, Scotland's last handloom linen weavers, are based there. Fine linen is for sale by the yard, as well as linen goods. There's an attractive café and shop.

Five miles north of Brechin on the B966 is **Edzell**, an impossibly neat and picturesque planned village lying at the foot of Glen Esk. A mile west of the village is the red sandstone ruin of **Edzell Castle** ⓘ *T01356-648631, Apr-Sep 0930-1830, Oct-Mar Mon-Wed and Sat 0930-1630, Thu 0930-1200, Fri and Sun 1400-1630, £3, £2.30 concession, £1 child*, a 16th-century tower house which, over the course of its life, has been visited by Mary, Queen of Scots, James VI and, less happily, Cromwell's troops. But it is the magnificent **garden**, or 'Pleasance', which is the real attraction. Created by Sir David Lindsay in 1604, the superb heraldic and symbolic sculpted wall panels are rare examples of European Renaissance Art in Scotland.

Kirriemuir

Kirriemuir, or Kirrie as it's known locally, is the ideal spot for those wishing to explore the beautiful Angus Glens, or visit Glamis Castle. The town's claim to fame is as the birthplace of **JM Barrie** (1860-1937), creator of Peter Pan, the little boy who never grew up. Barrie was the son of a hand-loom weaver and ninth of 10 children. His classic tale of *Peter Pan and the Lost Boys*, written in 1904, is said to have been inspired by the memory of his older brother, who died while still young. **Barrie's birthplace** ⓘ *T01575-572646,1 Apr-30 Jun, Sep Fri-Tue 1200-1700, Jul and Aug daily 1200-1700, £5, concession £3.75, child £1*can be visited at 9 Brechin Road. The humble little weaver's cottage is now managed by the NTS, and the upper floor is furnished as it would have been when he lived there. The adjacent house features an exhibition of his literary and theatrical works. The outside wash-house is said to have been his first theatre and the model for the house built for Wendy by the Lost Boys in Never-Never Land. Barrie is also buried in Kirrie, at the nearby St Mary's Episcopal Church.

Glamis Castle

ⓘ *T01307-840393. Late Mar to end Oct daily 1030-1730 (Jul-Aug from 1000), last admission 1645. Guided tours last one hour and leave every 15 mins. £6.70, £5 concession,£3.50 child.There's a limited bus service from Dundee, Forfar and Kirriemuir with Strathtay Buses, T01382-228054.*

Five miles south of Kirrie is Glamis Castle (pronounced Glamz), the fabulous family home of the Earls of Strathmore and Kinghorne. Glamis is every inch the archetypal Scottish castle, and one of the most famous. This was the setting for Shakespeare's *Macbeth*, but its royal connection doesn't end there. It was the childhood home of the late Queen Elizabeth the Queen Mother, and the birthplace of the late Princess Margaret. The setting matches the impeccable pedigree. As you approach down the long, tree-lined drive, the castle suddenly appears in all its glory, the jumble of turrets, towers and conical roofs rising up against the backdrop of the Grampian Mountains like one of Walt Disney's fairy-tale fantasies. Most of the building you see dates from the 15th century, though the glamorous touches were added in the 17th century. Highlights of the tour include the 17th-century drawing room, with its impressive plasterwork ceilings, and the ghostly crypt, haunted by Lord Glamis and Crawford who was entombed within its walls as punishment for playing a few hands of gin rummy with the Devil on the Sabbath. The 17th-century chapel, with its biblical frescoes, is also haunted, this time by the 'grey lady', the ghost of the sixth Lady Glamis, who was burnt as a witch by James V. Duncan's Hall is reputedly where King Duncan was murdered by Macbeth, though, like much else in the play, this is very doubtful. You can also see the Royal Apartments, including the Queen Mother's bedroom, and the extensive grounds are also well worth exploring. There's a restaurant on site.

The Angus Glens

East of Perthshire, south of the Grampians and north of Dundee are the Angus Glens, a series of five glens running parallel to each other and all of them beautiful, peaceful and offering plenty of relatively painless hillwalking opportunities. Running parallel to Glen Shee, lovely **Glen Isla** is the furthest west of the Angus Glens and can also be reached from the little town of Alyth, east of Blairgowrie. Five miles north of Kirriemuir is the tiny village of Dykehead, at the foot of **Glen Clova**, where a side road branches northwest and runs into **Glen Prosen**. Both glens penetrate deep into the Grampian Mountains and are blessed with a rugged beauty, but Glen Prosen carries little of the cachet of its neighbour and is consequently a much more peaceful option for hillwalkers. The little road runs deep, into the glen but it's best explored on foot. A good walk is the relatively straightforward four-mile **Minister's Path**, which connects the two glens. It starts from behind the kirk in Glenprosen village and heads over the hilly moorland and down to the B955 just before Clova village. You can catch the **postbus** back to Kirriemuir from the *Clova Hotel* (see below). The Kirriemuir to Glen Prosen postbus runs once daily except Sun. Glen Clova leads north into **Glen Doll**, from where you can follow the old **drove roads** which lead to Ballater and Braemar in Deeside.

North from Edzell, the road runs 13 miles to the head of beautiful **Glen Esk**, the most easterly of the Angus Glens and, like the others, quiet and empty. About 13 miles north of Edzell, beyond Tarfside village, the public road ends at **Invermark Castle**. This is the start of one of the Mounth Roads, ancient rights of way leading from the Angus Glens across the mountains to Deeside. This route leads eventually to Ballater or **Glen Tanar**, near Aboyne. You can also hike from here to the summit of **Mount Keen** (3,081ft), Scotland's most easterly Munro, but – like the Mounth Road – this is a tough walk and you'll need full hill-walking equipment and a map (OS Landranger No 44). An easier walk is to the **Queen's Well**, three miles from the car park across the river from Invermark Castle. It's about three hours there and back.

Sleeping

Montrose and around *p804*

B **The Links Hotel**, Mid Links, T01674-671000, www.linkshotel.com. A short walk from the beach, comfortable town house hotel offering good Scottish/French cooking at mid-range prices.

D **Lunan Lodge**, T01241-830267, b&b@lunanlodge.sol.co.uk. An 18th-century country house in the village of Lunan overlooking lovely Lunan Bay.

B **Woodston**, on the coast road north to St Cyrus T01674-850226, info@woodstonfishingstation.co.uk. B&B in the old fishing station, evening meal available, great bird watching down on the sands.

Kirriemuir *p804*

C **Airlie Arms Hotel**, St Malcom's Wynd, T572847. A converted medieval monastery now a small, comfortable hotel, offers cheap bar meals and decent, moderately priced evening meals.

Those wishing to stay longer can rent a self-catering cottage next door to Barrie's birthplace, for £250-320 per week for up to 4 people. Contact the National Trust for Scotland head office (see p32).

The Angus Glens *p805*

B **Glenisla Hotel**, at Kirkton of Glenisla, on the B951, T01575-582223, glenislahotel@sol.co.uk, an impossibly cosy 17th-century inn with log fires, real ales, good grub and plenty of local characters. It's worth the trip just to spend a night here.

C **Clova Hotel**, Glen Clove, T01575-550222. A very friendly and popular climbers' retreat. As well as bar meals, the hotel lays on regular barbecues, ceilidhs and a multitude of various activities. There's also an eight-bed bunkhouse outside (F) which is open all year. It has a kitchen, but no shower. Four miles further north, near the end of the road, in Glen Doll, is a campsite, T01575-550233, by the bridge. It's open during the summer and has only basic facilities.

Eating

Arbroath and around *p804*

££ **But'n'Ben**, by the harbour in Auchmithie, near Arbroath, T01241-877223. Daily except Tue 1200-1500 for lunch, 1600-1730 for high tea and 1900-2200 for dinner.Their seafood is superb and great value.

Kirriemuir *p804*

££ **Lochside Lodge**, by the Loch of Lintrathen, 6 miles along the B951, then take the turning left for Bridge of Lintrathen, T01575-560340. The best restaurant in the area, this converted farmstead serves modern Scottish cooking and also rents rooms (C).

Festivals and events

Kirriemuir *p804*

Kirriemuir is well known for its **Folk Festival**, held on the first weekend in Sep each year.

Transport

The Angus Glens *p805*

There's a **postbus** service to **Glen Clova** from Kirriemuir twice a day Mon-Fri and once on Sat. The 0830 departure runs as far as the hostel and the 1500 departure (Mon-Fri only) stops at the Clova Hotel. The afternoon service leaves from the hotel at 1555.

Aberdeen

→Colour map 6

Scotland's third largest city, is a tough place. Tough because of the grey granite of its buildings and because of the nature of its people, who are industrious, thrifty, proud and uncompromising. First impressions are often determined by the weather: when it rains it's about as appealing as cold porridge, when the sky's blue and clear it has a salty grandeur. Sometimes leaden skies hang low over a uniform greyness, and a howling gale blows in from the North Sea, but when the clouds do part and the sun shines down, the tiny mica chips, which form a natural part of granite, sparkle and glisten like a display in a jeweller's window. Whatever the impression, it is a place that elicits a strong response. Lewis Grassic Gibbon, the northeast's most famous writer, wrote: "One detests Aberdeen with the detestation of a thwarted lover. It is the one haunting and exasperatingly lovable city in Scotland." ▸▸ For Sleeping, Eating and other listings, see pages 809-811.

Ins and outs

Getting there **Aberdeen airport** is 7 miles northwest of the city centre, at Dyce, off the A96 to Inverness. There are regular domestic flights to Scottish and UK destinations, including Orkney and Shetland, as well as international flights to several European destinations. For airport information, T01224-722331. There's car hire and currency exchange at the airport. Buses 27 run at peak times to and from the city centre (35 mins). For more information, T01224-650065. Alternatively, take a train to Dyce station and a bus or taxi from there. A taxi from the airport to Dyce railway station costs around £5, and £14 to the city centre.

Aberdeen is linked to Lerwick in Shetland and Kirkwall in Orkney by **Northlink ferries**, T08457-6000449, www.northlinkferries.co.uk. There are regular sailings from the passenger terminal in the harbour, a short walk east of the train and bus stations.

The **bus** terminal is next to the train station, on Guild St. **National Express** has daily buses from London and **Scottish Citylink** runs buses to all major Scottish towns. **Stagecoach Bluebird**, T01224-212266, are the main regional operator. The **train** station is on Guild St. There are regular services from London, and major Scottish towns and cities. ▸▸ For further details, see Transport, page 811.

Getting around Aberdeen city centre is compact and the best way to get around is on foot, though you may need to use local buses to reach some of the outlying sights. Almost all **buses** pass along Union St, the city's main thoroughfare. A good idea, if you're using public transport frequently, is to buy a prepaid First Bus travel card. These are available at the First Aberdeen Office, 47 Union St, T01224-650065.

Information **Tourist Information Centre** ⓘ *23 Union St, T01224-288828, www.aberdeen-grampian.com, Mon-Sat 0930-1730 (1900 mid June-mid Sep), Sun 1000-1600,*. As well as the usual accommodation booking service they have a wide selection of leaflets on walks in Aberdeen, and run bus tours.

Sights

Aberdeen's main artery is **Union Street**, one mile long and built on pillars (an amazing and expensive engineering feat). The street is a fascinating mix of Victorian Gothic and modern glass and concrete and is perpetually packed with buses, cars and pedestrians. The oldest part of the city is the 13th-century **Castlegate**, at the eastern end of Union Street, now dominated by the 17th-century **Mercat Cross**, which was the focus of Aberdeen's long history as a major market town and trading centre.

A little further west down Union Street is Broad Street off which, at 45 Guestrow, is Aberdeen's oldest surviving private house, the 16th-century **Provost Skene's House** ⓘ *T01224-641086, Mon-Sat 1000-1700, Sun 1300-1600, free*. Its distinctive style, with boldly pointed stone and little turrets, stands out from the adjacent modern buildings. The interior features a series of ornate tempera-painted ceilings dating from 1622, which somehow survived the orgy of vandalism in the wake of the Reformation. There are also furnished period rooms and an interesting display of memorabilia. There is a pocket watch given to him by the widowed queen, also a silver pipe and case from the same donor. Down in the cellar is a good little café.

Also off Broad Street is the imposing **Marischal College** (pronounced 'Marshall'), the second largest granite building in the world, after the Escorial in Madrid. This massive neo-Gothic sculpture is loved and loathed in equal measure, but cannot be ignored. It combined with King's College in Old Aberdeen in 1860 to form Aberdeen University. The **museum** ⓘ *T01224-274301, Mon-Fri 1000-1700, Sun 1400-1700, free*, entered through the main quadrangle and up the stairs, is open to visitors and worth visiting. It is divided into two exhibitions, the 'Encylopaedia of the Northeast', which depicts the region's distinctive culture, and 'Collecting the World', which features many wonderfully diverse items collected from around the globe.

The city's magnificent **Art Gallery** ⓘ *T01224-523700, Mon-Sat 1000-1700, Sun 1400-1700, free*, is a most elegant building of marble steps with a pillared gallery overlooking a central well. At the top of the stairs stands a showcase of lovely Meissen china. There are changing displays of costumes and applied arts. All the big names are here and there are also several works by **Joan Eardley**, who lived near Stonehaven.

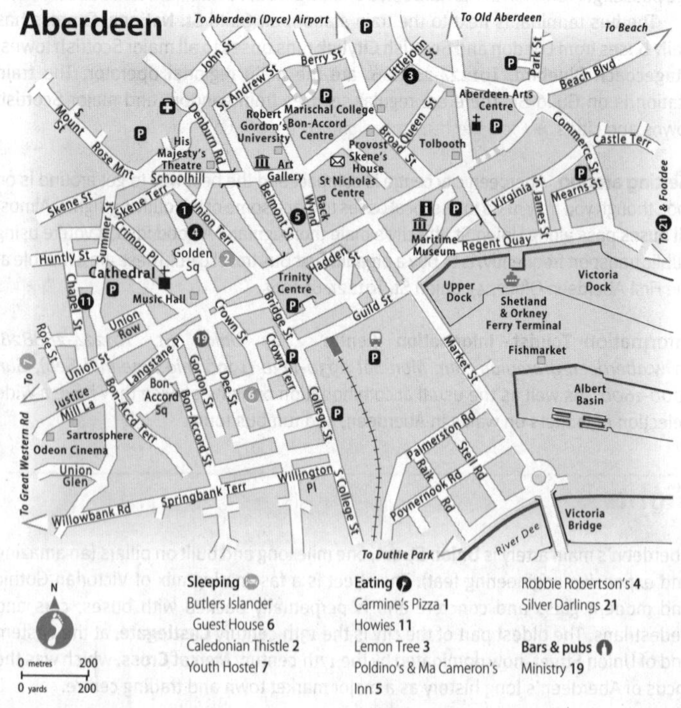

From the Castlegate, Shiprow, a steep cobbled street, leads down to the harbour and the gleaming glass and steel of the excellent **Maritime Museum** ⓘ *T01224-337700, Mon-Sat 1000-1700, Sun 1200-1500, free*, which traces Aberdeen's long seafaring history from earliest times up to the present day. The museum spills over into the adjoining Provost Ross' House dating from 1593, the oldest building in the city.

A 20-minute bus ride northwest of the city centre, on the banks of the Don, is the beautifully preserved suburb of Old Aberdeen, with its cobbled streets and peaceful atmosphere. An independent burgh until 1891, Old Aberdeen is clustered around **St Machar's Cathedral** ⓘ *T01224-485988, daily 0900-1700, free*, with its soaring twin spires. The cathedral was founded in the sixth century and is one of the oldest granite buildings in the city, dating from the 15th century. Next to it is the **Cruickshank Botanic Garden** ⓘ *Mon-Fri 0900-1700, free*, with beautiful floral displays.

Around Aberdeen

Five miles inland from Inverbervie, between the A92 and A90, is **Arbuthnott**, birthplace of the amazingly prolific author Lewis Grassic Gibbon (1901-35), and where he spent his formative years. From 1928 till his untimely death at the age of 34, he wrote an astonishing 17 books. *Sunset Song*, the first part of the *Scots Quair* trilogy, is his best-known work. It remains one of the true classics of Scottish literature and is an absolute must for anyone exploring this area. The **Grassic Gibbon Centre** ⓘ *T01224-361668, Mar-Oct daily 1000-1630. £2.50, £1705 child/concession*, at the east end of the village, traces his life and points out the places he wrote about. There is also a café and bookshop. Grassic Gibbon is also buried here, under his real name of James Leslie Mitchell, in a churchyard, about half a mile away at the other end of the village.

The solid and tidy old fishing port of **Stonehaven** lies 15 miles south of Aberdeen, where the coastal A92 joins the main A90 from Dundee. Not least of the town's attractions is its wonderful art deco outdoor, heated salt-water **swimming pool** ⓘ *1st Sat in Jun till end of Aug, 1100-1930 (there's also a midnight swim; ask for details at the TIC), day tickets £3.20*, one of only two in Scotland (the other is at Gourock). It is kept at a constant 82°F. The main reason for coming to Stonehaven is to visit the impressive and impregnable **Dunnottar Castle** ⓘ *T01569-762173, Easter-Oct Mon-Sat 0900-1800, Sun 1400-1700, Nov-Mar Fri-Mon 0930-sunset, £3.50, £1 child*, two miles south of town just off the A92. Dating from the 12th century, this ancient ruin was a stronghold for the Earls Marischal of Scotland. Standing 160 ft high, with the sea on three sides and a huge drop and 'curtain wall' on the fourth, it is not far short of an island. It is worth devoting considerable time to exploring one of the country's most outstanding castles, which is approached by a steep 400-yd walk from the car park. So dramatic is its setting, that it was used as the backdrop for Zeffirelli's film version of *Hamlet*, starring Mel Gibson.

Sleeping

Aberdeen has plenty of accommodation but its hotels are relatively expensive. The best value are the B&Bs andguesthouses, many of which can be found on Bon Accord St, Springbank Terrace and Crown St, both running south off Union St, and along Great Western Rd. Serviced apartments also offer very good value. Though full of transient oil workers and business people during the week, many hotels offer discounts at the weekend, when prices fall by up to 50%.

L-A **The Marcliffe at Pitfodels**, North Deeside Rd, T01224-861000, www.marcliffe.com. 40 rooms. This outstanding, luxurious country house hotel on the outskirts of town offers an unbeatable

For an explanation of the sleeping and eating price codes used in this guide, see the inside front cover. Other relevant information is provided in the Essentials chapter, page 36.

mix of baronial elegance and modern comforts, as well as exceptional hospitality and service, and superb cuisine.

A **Caledonian Thistle Hotel**, Union Terr, T01224-640233, F641627. 76 rooms. Superior city-centre hotel in a grand old Victorian building. Full facilities, friendly service and good restaurants.

A **Simpson's Hotel Bar/Brasserie**, 59 Queen's Rd, T01224-327777, reservations@simpsonshotel.com. 50 rooms. Very stylish, modern hotel with a Mediterranean look and feel. The attached restaurant has won many plaudits for its excellent Scottish/international cuisine.

A **Atholl Hotel**, 54 King's Gate, T323505, info@atholl-aberdeen.com. 35 rooms. 1 of many elegant granite mansions in the West End, this one has an excellent reputation for its reliability, service and good food.

B **Craiglynn Hotel**, 36 Fonthill Rd, T584050, www.craiglynn.co.uk. 8 rooms. Intimate and comfortable Victorian house close to the town centre, also has a good reputation for its food.

B **Mannofield Hotel**, 447 Great Western Rd, T01224-315888, www.hotels-rus.co.uk. 9 rooms. Small, friendly and elegant hotel about a mile west of Union St.

C **Butler's Islander Guest House**, 122 Crown St, T01224-212411, www.butlersguesthouse.com. Clean, comfortable accommodation and free internet access.

F **Aberdeen Youth Hostel**, 8 Queen's Rd, T01224-646988, a mile west of the bus (take 14 or 15 bus) and train stations . Open all year till 0200 and has 116 beds.

Campus accommodation is available at the **University of Aberdeen** Contact: Conference Office, Regent Walk, Old Aberdeen, T01224-272664, www.abdn.ac.uk/catering. **Robert Gordon's University**, T01224-262134, www.scotland2000.com/rgu also has self-catering flats throughout the city. For more details check with the TIC.

Eating

£££ **Courtyard on the Lane**, Alford La, T01224-213795, just off the west end of Union St. Highly rated bistro serving imaginative Scottish/European menu, with a more formal restaurant upstairs. Open Tue-Sat.

£££ **Robbie Robertson's**, 8 Golden Sq, T01224-624324, is the city's newest restaurant and already highly acclaimed. With only 7 tables (it's upstairs above Shiso) there's an intimate, stylish atmosphere while food is modern Mediterranean with an Asian twist. Open every evening from 1900.

£££ **Silver Darlings Restaurant**, Pocra Quay, North Pier, Footdee, at the southern end of the Beach Esplanade, T01224-576229. Highly recommended as serving the best seafood in town, also a great location overlooking the harbour entrance, best to book in advance. Open Mon-Fri 1200-1400, Mon-Sat 1900-2130.

££ **Howies**, 50 Chapel St, T01224-639500, cosy, contemporary interior and offers modern Scottish/French food. Set 3 course dinners for £17.95 Open daily 1200-1430, 1800-2230.

££ **Poldino's**, 7 Little Belmont St, T01224-647777. One of the city's most established Italian restaurants, so it's always busy. Mon-Sat 1200-1430, 1800-2245.

£ **Ashvale**, 46 Great Western Rd, T01224-596981. The northeast's most famous, and best, fish and chips, quite simply unmissable. This is the original branch and it's huge, with seating for 300; also takeaway. Open daily till late.

£ **Carmine's Pizza**, 32 Union Terr, T01224-624145. Best pizza in town and excellent-value 3-course lunches. Open Mon-Sat 1200-1730.

£ **The Lemon Tree**, 5 West North St, T01224-642230. Café inside the excellent arts centre (see also Entertainment). Relaxed and laid-back place for a light vegetarian lunch, or coffee and cakes. Open Wed-Sun 1200-1500.

Pubs, bars and clubs

There are lots of trendy bars in Belmont St, off Union St, the most happening area in the city. **The Prince of Wales**, 7 St Nicholas La, just off Union St, T01224-640597. The best pub in the city, with a great selection of real ales. Also does cheap bar food and gets very crowded. Traditional fiddle music on Sun evenings. **Ma Cameron's Inn**, Little Belmont St. The city's oldest pub, though the old bit now constitutes only a small section, serves food at lunch and early evening.

Aberdeen also has numerous nightclubs to choose from, most of which close at 0200. Pick of the bunch is:

Ministry, 16 Dee St, off Union St, T01224-211661. The faithful congregate in this converted church for a heavenly mix of cool sounds and atmosphere. Popular with students and oldies. Often has big-name guest DJs and open 7 days.

Entertainment

Aberdeen Arts Centre, 33 King St, T635208. Stages a variety of productions and exhibitions, and also shows arthouse movies.
The Lemon Tree, 5 West North St, T642230. The hub of the city's arts scene, with a wide and varied programme of events, including live jazz and folk, comedy and contemporary drama. Also has a café/bar-restaurant (see 'Eating').

Transport

Bus

Scottish Citylink runs direct buses to **Dundee** (2 hrs), **Perth** (2½ hrs), **Edinburgh** (4 hrs), **Stirling** (3½ hrs) and **Glasgow** (4½ hrs). Stagecoach Bluebird Buses, T212266, is the major local bus operator. Service No 10 goes every hour to **Inverness** via **Huntly** and **Elgin**. Service No 201 goes every 30 mins (hourly on Sun) to **Banchory**, every hour (Mon-Sat; less frequently on Sun) to **Ballatar** and several times daily to **Braemar**. There are also buses to **Stonehaven** (Service No 107), **Alford** (Service No 220), **Peterhead** (No 263), **Fraserburgh** (Nos 267/268) and **Ellon** (Nos 290/291).

Ferry

Northlinkferries, T0845 6000 449, have daily evening departures (Mon-Fri) to **Lerwick** on Shetland. They also sail to Kirkwall on Orkney. See also under **Orkney & Shetland** (page 908).

Train

There are services to **Edinburgh** (2½ hrs), **Glasgow** (2¾ hrs), **Dundee** (1¼ hrs), **Perth** (1¾ hrs), **Stirling** (2¼ hrs) and **Inverness** (2¼ hrs). Stonehaven is on the Aberdeen-Dundee rail line and there are regular trains in either direction.

Directory

Car hire Arnold Clark, Girdleness Rd, T01224-249159. and Lang Stracht, T01224-663723. Thrifty, 76 Huntly St, T01224-621033. **Cycle hire** Aberdeen Cycle Centre, 188 King St, T01224-644542. Alpine Bikes, 64 Holburn St, T01224-211455. From £12 per day. Open daily. **Hospitals** Aberdeen Royal Infirmary, T01224-681818, is on Foresthill, northeast of the town centre. It has a 24-hr A&E. **Internet** Facilities at the Central Library, also at the TIC, Union St and Costa Coffee, near John Lewis on George St. **Post office** In the St Nicholas Centre, T01224-633065. **Pharmacies** Boots, 161 Union St, T01224-211592. Mon-Sat 0800-1800.

Deeside

→ *Colour map 6*

The River Dee rises in the Cairngorms and flows down through the surrounding hills, eastwards to the sea at Aberdeen. The valley of the Dee is known as Deeside, or rather Royal Deeside, for its connections with the royal family, who have holidayed here, at Balmoral, since Queen Victoria first arrived in 1848. Originally, Queen Victoria and Prince Albert were looking for an estate further west, but were advised that the Deeside climate would be better for Albert's delicate constitution. The queen fell in love with this area and its people, and following Albert's death she sought out the company of northerners, preferring their down-to-earth honesty to the two-faced toadies she endured at court.

Today, Deeside's royal associations have made it the tourist honeypot of the northeast, but the royal presence has also saved it from mass development. There's an air of understated affluence and refinement in the villages strung out along the A93 that runs along the north bank of the Dee and, as well as the obvious attraction of Balmoral, there are many other examples of castles. Deeside is also a great area for outdoor activities, such as hiking, canoeing and skiing. ▸▸ *For Sleeping, Eating and other listings, see pages 813-814.*

Ins and outs

Getting there & around All the main tourist attractions on Deeside can be reached by **bus** from Aberdeen. **Bluebird Northern**, T01224-212266. If you wish to explore Deeside along a less popular route (though even in the summer, crowds are never great) take the B976 along the south bank of the River Dee.

Information For details of the **Castle Trail**, **Victorian Heritage Trail** and **Deeside Tourist Route**, contact the TIC in Aberdeen, or in any of the towns along the way. Banchory **Tourist Information Centre** ⓘ *in the local museum, on Bridge St, behind the High St, Apr-late Oct*. **Ballater Tourist Information Centre**, Old Royal Station, T01339-755306, ballater@agtb.org, daily Jan-end May 1000-1700, end May-end Sep 0900-1800, end Sep-end Dec 1000-1700. **Braemar Tourist Information Centre** ⓘ *Balmoral Mews, on Mar Rd, T01339-741600, braemar@agtb.org, daily all year, 1000-1800 end May-end Sep, closes earlier and for lunch rest of year, Sun afternoons only end Sept-end May.*

Aberdeen to Banchory

Fifteen miles west of Aberdeen, where the A93 meets the A957 from Stonehaven, is **Crathes Castle**, ⓘ *T01330-844525,1 Apr-30 Sep daily 1030-1730, 1-31 Oct daily 1030-1630 (last admission to castle 45 mins before closing), grounds and garden all year daily 0900-dusk, gardens only £4.50, concession £3, castle and grounds combined £7, concession £5*, a perfect 'fairytale' castle built over 40 years in the mid-16th century. The turreted tower-house is still furnished with many period pieces and wall hangings, and is notable for its superb painted ceilings. There are narrow spiral staircases leading to tiny rooms, one of which is said to be inhabited by the obligatory ghost. The castle is well worth exploring but is almost overshadowed by the exceptional gardens, which shouldn't be missed. There are no fewer than eight of them, so take your time. There's also a visitor centre, restaurant and shop. Banchory makes a very pleasant base for exploring the area, with the River Dee burbling through, but there's not a great deal to do here, apart from salmon fishing, which is popular in these parts. You can watch salmon leaping spectacularly at the **Bridge of Feugh**, to the south of town.

Ballater and Balmoral

The neat little town of Ballater is proud of its royal connections. Ever since Queen Victoria first arrived by train from Aberdeen in 1848, the royal family have been spending their holidays here in their summer residence, Balmoral. The town makes the ideal base for **hiking** (see below) as well as a number of other outdoor activities. Many of the walks set off from **Loch Muick** (pronounced 'Mick'), nine miles southwest of Ballater, at the head of Glen Muick. (see Walks in Deeside below). There's a visitor centre and car park at Spittal of Glenmuick. From here a track leads along the west shore of the loch to the lodge where Queen Victoria met John Brown.

Eight miles west of Ballater is the area's main attraction, **Balmoral Castle**. ⓘ *Apr to end Jul, daily 1000-1700, £5, concession £4, children £1, T01339-742334, buses run to Braemar from Aberdeen*. The 16th-century tower house, formerly owned by the local Gordon family, was bought for Queen Victoria by Prince Albert in 1852 and converted into today's baronial mansion. It has been the royal family's summer retreat ever since. Only the ballroom and the grounds are open to the likes of you and me, and only for three months of the year. **Pony trekking** and **pony cart rides** are available around the estate grounds and are favourite ways of enjoying the wonderful scenery. Opposite the castle gates is **Crathie Church**, which is used by the family when they're in residence. There's a small souvenir shop next to the main gates and a visitor centre which gives a lot of information on the castle and its owners.

Braemar

Nine miles west of Balmoral, is Braemar, the final town on Deeside, lying at the foot of the awesome, brooding **Cairngorm** massif, which dominates the Eastern Highlands. Even at the height of summer you can see a dab of snow still lying in a hollow in the surrounding mountains, and Braemar is an excellent base for **hiking** (see below), and winter skiing at Glenshee. It's an attractive little place, much loved by Queen Victoria and much visited during its annual Braemar Gathering (or games), see Festivals and events for details.

Just north of the village, and well signposted, is **Braemar Castle** ⓘ *T01339-741219, Mid-Apr to end Oct Sat-Thu 1000-1800, £3.50, concession £3, children £1*, dating from 1628. This impressive fortress was used by Hanoverian troops after the Jacobite Rising of 1745. It is L-shaped, with a star-shaped defensive wall and a central round tower with a spiral stair. There are barrel-vaulted ceilings and an underground prison. The world's largest cairngorm (a semi-precious stone, a variety of quartz, which is yellow, grey or brown in colour) weighing 52 lbs is on display in the morning room. There's also a piece of tartan worn by Prince Charles Edward, Bonnie Prince Charlie.

A very scenic side trip from Braemar is to the **Linn of Dee**, six miles west of the village, at the end of the road. Here, the river thunders through a narrow gorge to spectacular effect. There are numerous walks from here along the river, or for the more adventurous, the famous **Lairig Ghru**, which runs through the Cairngroms to Aviemore.

Walks in Deeside

Ballater and Braemar are ideal bases for walking in the surrounding Grampian Mountains, and if you feel like 'bagging a Munro' (ie climbing a mountain over 3,000 ft), there are some close at hand. All of this area is included in the new **Cairngorms National Park**, which opened in 2003. This is the largest national park in Britain, covering a vast 4,500 sq km, from Aboyne in the east to Dalwhinnie in the west, and from Blair Atholl north to Grantown-on-Spey. OS Landranger maps 43 and 44 cover the routes below.

The best walk in the area is to the summit of **Lochnagar** (3,786 ft), made famous by Prince Charles in the book he wrote for his brothers when young, *The Old Man of Lochnagar*. The noble and mysterious mountain dominates the Royal Forest of Balmoral and takes its name from a small loch at its foot (it's also known as the White Mounth). This fine granite mass is approached from the car park by the Rangers' **visitor centre** at Spittal of Glen Muick. For information on their free guided walks, T01339-755377. The path to the top is well trodden and well marked, though steep as you near the summit. It's 10 miles there and back, so allow a full day for the climb. You'll need to be properly equipped and take a map. An easier walk is to Cambus o' May, on the river, about four miles east of Ballater. It's a great spot for a picnic, or to swim in the river, or to enjoy a stroll along the riverbank.

Sleeping

Aberdeen to Banchory *p812*

A **Raemoir House Hotel**, 3 miles north of Banchory on the A980, T01330-824884, www.raemoir.com. A very wonderful country mansion set in 3,500 acres of woods and parkland, 20 rooms.

A **Banchory Lodge Hotel**, T01330-822625, a sporting lodge-type hotel superbly situated on the banks of the river near the town centre. It's also a great place to stop and have a bite to eat for lunch. The river runs past the lawn and you can watch the salmon leap as you perhaps enjoy the fruits of their labour.

A **Tor-na-Coille Hotel**, T01330-822242, www.tornacoille.com, outside town on the Inchmarlo Rd. This tastefully furnished Victorian country house hotel is set in lovely grounds and boasts a considerable reputation for its modern Scottish cooking (£££-££).

D **June Little**, 73 High St, T01330-824666. Excellent B&B.

There's also a campsite, **Silver Ladies Caravan Park**, T01330-822800, at Strachan, just outside Banchory.

Ballater *p812*

A **Darroch Learg Hotel**, T01339-755443, darroch.learg @exoams.wk.com, half a mile from town, off the A93 heading west to Braemar. 18 rooms, open Feb-Dec. Friendly country house hotel with fine views and a reputation for superb food (expensive), good value.

A **Hilton Craigendarroch**, on the Braemar Rd, T01339-755858, www.hilton.com. 45 rooms. Victorian country house converted into a modern resort hotel with full leisure and sports facilities, 2 good restaurants.

A **Balgonie Country House Hotel,** T/F01339-755482, on the western outskirts of town, off the A93. 9 rooms, open Feb-Dec. Friendly and comfortable country house hotel, excellent food (£££).

B **Deeside Hotel**, set back from the A93 heading out of town towards Braemar. T01339-755420, www.deesidehotel.co.uk. Friendly, good value and good food (££).

B **Inverdeen House**, 11 Bridge Sq, T01339-755759, www.inverdeen.com. French, German and Polish spoken, great breakfasts, no smoking.

Braemar *p813*

E **Rucksacks,** 15 Mar Rd, T741517, a cheap and friendly bunkhouse that's popular with hikers and also rents out mountain bikes.

Eating

Aberdeen to Banchory *p812*

£££ **The Green Inn**, on the green in Banchory, T/F01330-755701. Best in town, it boasts a well-deserved reputation as one of the very best restaurants in the region, classic Scottish cooking with an imaginative and health-conscious twist, expensive; also has 3 rooms upstairs (C full board).

££ **The Milton Restaurant**, opposite Crathes Castle gates, T01330-844566, serving excellent, moderately priced food daily till 2100 (lunch only on Sun and Mon).

Festivals and events

The **Braemar Gathering** attracts tens of thousands of visitors each year, amongst them members of the royal family. The games are held on the first Sat in Sep. Booking is essential and tickets can be bought in advance from the Booking Secretary, BRHS, Coilacreich, Ballater, AB35 5UH, T01339-755377, info@braemargathering.org

Activities and tours

Adventure Scotland, Banchory, T01330-850332, dlatham@netcomuk.co.uk, offers a wide range of adventure activities, including white-water rafting, mountain biking, skiing and hiking, also guides and equipment for canoeing, climbing, mountain biking and skiing.

The Don Valley

→Colour map 6

North of Royal Deeside is the lesser-known valley of the Don, Aberdeen's second river. This relatively little-visited corner of the northeast is an historian's and archaeologist's dream, as it's littered with medieval castles, Pictish stone circles and Iron-Age hillforts. A quarter of all Britain's stone circles can be found here (if you look hard enough). Local tourist offices have free leaflets on the region's archaeological sites, with background information and details of how to find them. The main sites are included in the tourist board's 'Stone Circle Trail'. There's also a well-signposted 'Castle Trail', which includes the area's main castles. One of these castles, Corgarff, stands at the southern end of the notorious Lecht Road, which runs from Cock Bridge to Tomintoul. This area, known as The Lecht, is one of Scotland's main ski centres. ▸▸ *For Sleeping and other listings, see page 816.*

Ins and outs

Getting there There are regular **trains** and **buses** to Inverurie, from Aberdeen and Inverness. **Bluebird Northern**, T01224-212266, No 220 runs regularly every day from Aberdeen to Alford (1¼ hrs).

Getting around Travelling around the Don Valley without your own transport is not easy. Bus No 219 runs from Alford to Strathdon (Mon-Sat), but services beyond Strathdon are virtually non-existent.

Information There are **Tourist Information Centres** in Inverurie, Alford and Tomintoul.

Inverurie and around

The solid farming town of Inverurie is 17 miles northwest of Aberdeen on the A96 to Inverness. It makes a useful base for visiting the numerous castles and ancient relics dotted around the area. About six miles southwest of Inverurie, off the B993 (turn first left after the village of Kemnay), is the magnificent **Castle Fraser** ⓘ *T01330-833463 (NTS), castle Apr-end June and 1-30 Sep Fri-Tue 1200-1730, 1 Jul-31 Aug daily 1100-1730, garden andgrounds all year daily 0800 till dusk, castle, garden and grounds £7, concession £5.25*, built in 1575 by the 6th Earl of Mar and similar in style to Crathes and Craigievar. The interior was remodelled in 1838 and many of the furnishings date from that period. There's a walled garden, tearoom and trails through the estate.

Thirteen miles north of Inverurie is **Fyvie Castle** ⓘ *T01651-891266 (NTS), Apr-end Jun and 1-30 Sep Fri-Tue1200-1700, 1 Jun-31 Aug 1100-1700, grounds open all year daily 0930-dusk, £7, £5.25 concession/children*, off the A947 between Oldmeldrum and Turriff. This grandest of Scottish baronial piles is a major feature on the 'Castle Trail' and shouldn't be missed if you're in the vicinity. The castle's five towers are each named after one of the five families who have had the pleasure of living here over the centuries. The last lot only moved out in 1980 so it has a rare lived-in feel to it. The oldest part of the castle dates from the 13th century and, apart from the great wheel-stair and the 17th-century morning room, the extravagantly opulent interior is largely from the Edwardian era. There's a superb collection of portraits including works by the likes of Raeburn, Batoni, Gainsborough and Hoppner, as well as 17th-century tapestries and collections of arms and armour. The landscaped grounds and Fyvie Loch are also worth exploring, and even the tearoom is great.

Alford and around

The main tourist centre on Donside is the little country town of Alford (pronounced 'Ah-ford'), 25 miles west of Aberdeen. Six miles south of Alford is one of the northeast's most gorgeous castles, the classic tower house of **Craigievar** ⓘ *T01339-883280, mid-Apr-30 Sep Fri-Tue 1200-1730, grounds all year daily 0930-dusk, £9, £5.25 concession*, with its impressive turrets, balustrades and cupolas. The castle remains much as it was when it was built in 1626 by wealthy local merchant, William Forbes. Unfortunately, though, its popularity led to its deterioration and the NTS now restricts entry to only a small number of visitors at a time to prevent further damage. The castle stands in well-tended grounds.

Six miles west of Alford, the A944 meets the A97 which heads north towards the town of Huntly, on Speyside (see page 817). A few miles south of the junction stand the extensive and impressive ruins of Kildrummy Castle ⓘ *T01975-571331, Apr-Sep daily 0930-1830, £2.20, £1.60 concession, £0.75 child*, Scotland's most complete 13th-century castle. Amongst the most infamous events in the castle's long and bloody history was the treacherous betrayal of Robert the Bruce's family to the English during the Wars of Independence. It was the seat of the Earls of Mar and used as an HQ for the Jacobite rebellion of 1715, after which the sixth Earl of Mar ('Bobbing John') fled to exile in France and the castle fell into ruin.

Strathdon and around

The tiny village of Strathdon, 10 miles southwest of Kildrummy, is famous for its **Highland Games**, known as the *Lonach Highland Gathering*, held on the third Saturday in August, and a healthy blast of authenticity in comparison to the rather more glitzy affair at Braemar on Deeside (see page 813). Five miles west of Strathdon the A944 meets the A939 Ballater-Tomintoul road. A few miles beyond the junction is the austere **Corgarff Castle** ⓘ *T01975-651460, Apr-Sep daily 0930-1830, Oct-Mar Sat 0930-1630, Sun 1400-1630, £3, £2.30 concession, £1 child*, a 16th-century tower house, later turned into a garrison post, with an eventful and gruesome history. Here Margaret Forbes and her family were burned alive by the Gordons in 1571 during the bitter feud between the two families. In the wake of the ill-fated 1745 rebellion the government remodelled the castle, building a star-shaped defensive wall, and garrisoned 60 men to maintain order and communications in this part of the Highlands. Corgarff continued in use into the 19th century when English Redcoats were stationed here in order to prevent whisky smuggling.

Sleeping

Inverurie and around *p815*

A-B **Pittodrie House Hotel**, near Chapel of Garioch, T01467-681444, www.mac donald.hotels.co.uk. 27 rooms. The best place to stay around Inverurie is this magnificent baronial mansion originally belonged to the Earls of Mar, and the 2,000-acre estate was granted to them by Robert the Bruce for their loyalty at the Battle of Bannockburn. The opulent surroundings are matched by the superb cuisine.

B **Thainstone House Hotel**, to the south of Inverurie off the A96, T01467-621643, is a luxurious country mansion offering excellent cuisine and leisure facilities.

Alford and around *p815*

L **Kildrummy Castle Hotel**, T01975-571288, www.kildrummycastelhotel.co.uk. Across the other side of the river from the castle ruins this spectacularly sited a baronial country mansion is one of the very best hotels in the northeast. It also has an excellent restaurant.

Strathdon and around *p816*

B **Glenavon Hotel**, Tomintoul, T01807-580218. The best place for a drink, and popular with après-skiers, tired walkers and locals.

E **Jenny's Bothy**, T01975-651449. Open all year. Just before Corgarff Castle an old military road leads for about a mile to this basic but wonderfully remote bunkhouse.

Activities and tours

Skiing

Alford is close to **The Lecht** ski centre which offers dry-slope skiing throughout the year and its snowmaking facilities mean that the winter season can be extended beyond Jan and Feb. The Lecht's gentler slopes make it ideal for beginners and intermediates and the emphasis is on family skiing. There's a snowboard fun park with half pipe, log slide, gap jump and table top. However, there are also more difficult runs for the more experienced skier, and extensive off piste skiing. A day ticket costs £15 for adults, and £8 for children; a half-day ticket costs £12. There's a ski school and equipment hire at the base station, T01975-651440, thelecht@sol.co.uk. For latest snow and weather conditions call the base station, or the Ski Hotline, T09001-654657.

For an explanation of the sleeping and eating price codes used in this guide, see the inside front cover. Other relevant information is provided in the Essentials chapter, page 36.

Speyside

→ *Colour map 6*

The River Spey is Scotland's second longest river, rising in the hills above Loch Laggan and making its way northeast to where it debouches at Spey Bay, on the Moray coast. Speyside is one of Scotland's loveliest valleys and is synonymous with two of Scotland's greatest products, salmon and whisky. The upper part, Strathspey, is equally famous for its hiking, skiing and watersports. It is covered in the Highlands chapter (see page 876). This section covers the lower part of the valley and comprises the famous Malt Whisky Trail. There are more malt whisky distilleries in this small area than in any other part of the country, including some famous brands such as Glenlivet and Glenfiddich. However, it's not all whisky in these parts: there's also some fine walking along the Speyside Way, www.speysideway.org, which runs from Spey Bay south to Tomintoul. ▸▸ *For Sleeping, Eating and other listings, see page 819.*

Ins and outs

Getting there **Bluebird Buses**, T01224-212266, run a daily service from Elgin (No 336). A service (Nos 360 & 361) connects Dufftown with Keith and Aberlour (Mon-Fri).

Information There are **Tourist Information Centres** in Dufftown and Huntly.

Dufftown

A good place to start your whisky tour is Dufftown, founded in 1817 by James Duff, the fourth Earl of Fife, and the self-proclaimed 'Malt Whisky Capital of the World', with no fewer than seven working distilleries. Just outside of town, on the A941 to Craigellachie, is the **Glenfiddich Distillery**, the town's most famous distillery and one of the best known of all malt whiskies (see box, page 818). Four miles north of Dufftown, at the junction of the A941 and A95, is the little village of **Craigellachie**, site of the **Speyside Cooperage** (see below).

About eight miles southwest of Craigiellachie, on the A95 to Grantown-on- Spey, is beautiful **Ballindalloch Castle**, a mile west of the village of Marypark. The castle is one of the loveliest in the northeast and has been lived in continuously by its original family, the Macpherson-Grants, since 1546. It houses a fine collection of Spanish paintings and the extensive grounds are home to the famous Aberdeen-Angus herd of cattle, bred here since 1860. ⓘ *T01807-500206 Easter-Sep Sun-Fri 1030-1700. £5 entry, £4.00 conc, child £2.00.* Also in Ballindalloch is the **Glenfarclas Distillery**. ⓘ *T01807-500257, www.glenfarclas.co.uk. Tours Apr-Sep Mon-Fri 1000-1700; Jun-Sep also Sat 1000-1700; Oct-Mar Mon-Fri 1000-1600. £3.50, under 18s free.* A restored old train powered by a diesel engine runs from Dufftown to Drummuir (5 miles) and on to Keith (10 miles) on Saturday and Sunday, T821181, at 1330 and 1500. Adult ticket £6.

Huntly

Ten miles east of Dufftown is the pleasant and prosperous-looking little town of Huntly. Close to the Whisky Trail and on the main Aberdeen to Inverness train route, it makes a convenient base from which to explore this area. The town also boasts a lovely little castle all of its own. The 16th-century **Huntly Castle** ⓘ *T793191 , Apr-Sep daily 0930-1830; Oct-Mar Mon-Wed and Sat 0930-1630, Thu 0930-1200, Fri and Sun 1400-1630, £3.00, £2.30 concession , children £1,* stands in a beautiful setting on the banks of the River Deveron, on the northern edge of town. It was built by the powerful Gordon family and is notable for its fine heraldic sculpture and inscribed stone friezes, particularly over the main door.

The Malt Whisky Trail

Speyside is Scotland's most prolific whisky-producing region and the **Malt Whisky Trail** is a well-signposted 70-mile tour around seven of the most famous distilleries, plus the Speyside Cooperage. Most of the distilleries offer guided tours, and most (with the exception of Glenfiddich) charge an entry fee, which can then be discounted, in full or in part, from the cost of a bottle of whisky in the distillery shop. Tours also include a free dram. Those listed below are the most interesting. For more information, visit www.maltwhiskytrail.com

The **Spirit of Speyside Whisky Festival** is a celebration of "the water of life" with various whisky-related events taking place throughout the region (3-6 May 2002). For details consult www.spiritofspeyside.com

Strathisla, in Keith, is the oldest working distillery in the Highlands (1786) and perhaps the most atmospheric, in a beautiful setting on the River Isla. This is a relatively rare malt, which is also used in the better-known Chivas Regal blend. *T01542-783044. Open Feb to end Nov Mon-Sat 0930-1600, Sun 1230-1600. £4 (includes £2 discount voucher).*

Speyside Cooperage is near iellachie Craig, four miles north of Dufftown. Here you can watch the oak casks for whisky being made. *T01340-871108. Open Jun-Sep Mon-Sat 0930-1630; Oct-May Mon-Fri 0930-1630. £2.25.*

Dallas Dhu is a bit off the beaten track, a mile south of Forres off the A940. It no longer produces whisky but it's a beautifully preserved Victorian distillery which you can explore on your own. *T01309-676548. Open daily Apr-Sep 0930-1830; Oct-Mar Mon-Wed and Sat 0930-1630, Thu 0930-1200, Fri and Sun 1400-1630. £3, £1.90 concession.*

Cardhu is seven miles west of Craigiellachie, at Knockando on the B9102. This lovely little distillery is now owned by United Distillers, and their fine malt is one of many used in the famous Johnny Walker blend. *T01340-872555. Open Mar-Nov Mon-Fri 0930-1630, Sun 1100-1600; Jul-Sep also Sat 0930-1630 and Sun 1100-1600; Dec-Feb Mon-Fri 1000-1600. £3 (includes £2 discount voucher).*

Glen Grant is in Rothes, on the A941 to Elgin. This distillery tour has the added attraction of a Victorian garden and orchard, woodland walks by the burn and the rebuilt 'Dram Pavilion'. *T01542-783318. Open mid-Mar to end Oct Mon-Sat 1000-1600, Sun 1130-1600; Jun-Sep Mon-Sat 1000-1700, Sun 1130-1700. £3 (includes £2 discount voucher).*

Glenfiddich is just north of Dufftown, on the A941. Probably the best known of all the malts and the most professionally run operation. It's the only distillery where you can see the whisky being bottled on the premises, and the only major distillery that's free (including the obligatory dram). *T01340-820373. Open all Apr to mid-Oct Mon-Sat 0930-1630 and Sun 1200-1630; mid-Oct to Mar Mon-Fri only. Free.*

Glenlivet is 10 miles north of Tomintoul on the B9008. This was an illicit whisky until it was licensed in 1824. The distillery was later founded in 1858 and this malt has gone on to become one of the world's favourites. It was then taken over in 1978 by Seagram's. *T01542-783220. Open mid-Mar to end Oct Mon-Sat 1000-1600, Sun 1230-1600; Jul-Aug till 1800. £3 (includes £2 discount voucher).*

Sleeping

Dufftown *p817*

A **Craigellachie Hotel**, T01340-881204, www.craigellachie.com. The best place to stay.

A **Minmore House Hotel**, 10 miles southwest of Dufftown, in the village of Glenlivet, T01807-590378, www.minmorehouse hotel.com, open May-end Jan. Right beside the distillery and is the former home of the owner.

B **Highlander Inn**, on Victoria St, T/F01340-881446. Popular and serves decent bar meals.

Huntly *p817*

A **The Castle Hotel**, T01466-792696, castlehot@enterprise.net. There's a decent selection of accommodation in and around Huntly but this is the most impressive place to stay is The former home of the Duke of Gordon, it's approached through the castle entrance and then over the river.

Eating

Dufftown *p817*

££ **La Faisandarie**, T01340-821273, has a good reputation, book first.

££ **A Taste of Speyside**, on Balvenie St, T01340-820860. Also good.

£ **The Fife Arms Hotel**, on the square, T01340-820220, does good bar meals.

Activities and tours

Skiing

Near the castle in Huntlyis the **Nordic Ski Centre**, T01466-794428, the only year-round cross-country ski centre in the UK. The centre also hires out ski equipment and mountain bikes.

The Northeast coast

→*Colour map 6*

The northeast coast holds some of Scotland's best coastal scenery, particularly the Moray Coast from Spey Bay to Fraserburgh. Here you'll find some picturesque little villages clinging to the cliffs like limpets, and miles of windswept, deserted sandy beaches. Portsoy, Pennan, Gardenstown and Crovie are all well worth visiting, and there are great beaches at Cullen, Lossiemouth, Rosehearty and Sunnyside. Other highlights in the region include the beautiful Duff House, the working abbey at Pluscarden, and Findhorn, famous worldwide for its alternative, spiritual community. ▸▸ *For Sleeping, Eating and other listings, see pages 821-822.*

Ins and outs

Getting around The two largest towns along the coast are the hard-working, no-nonsense fishing ports of Peterhead and Fraserburgh, both linked by a regular bus service from Aberdeen. Fochabers, Elgin and Forres are all on the main Aberdeen-Inverness **bus** route and served regularly, and **trains** between Aberdeen and Inverness stop at Elgin and Forres. Otherwise, public transport is somewhat limited and it can be difficult getting to the more out-of-the-way places without your own transport. ▸▸ *For further details, see Transport, page 822.*

Information There are **Tourist Information Centres** in Banff, Elgin and Forres.

North of Aberdeen

The A90 runs north to Peterhead. Fifteen miles north of Aberdeen is the turn-off to **Ellon,** and five miles west of Ellon, on the A920 to **Oldmeldrum,** are **Pitmedden Gardens** ⓘ *T01651-842352 (NTS), 1 May-30 Sep daily 1000-1730, £5, £4 concession, £1 child*. The centrepiece of the property, the Great Garden, was originally laid out in 1675 by Sir Alexander Seton, and the elaborate, orderly floral patterns have been lovingly recreated. Also on the 100-acre site is the **Museum of Farming Life,** where you can see how the estate workers lived. There's also a visitor centre, tearoom and a woodland walk. Four miles north of Pitmedden, reached via the B9005 from Ellon, is the elegant Palladian mansion of **Haddo House** ⓘ *T01651-851440 (NTS), Jun, Fri-Mon 1100-1630, Jul-end Aug daily 1100-1630, garden and country park open all year 0930-dusk, £7, £5.25 concession/child*, one of the most impressive of Scotland's country houses. Designed by William Adam for the 2nd Earl of Aberdeen in 1732, and later refurbished in the 1880s, the house beautifully marries graceful Georgian architecture with sumptuous late-Victorian interiors. Home of the Gordon family for over 400 years, Haddo is a wonderfully tasteful legacy of how the other half lived. The house sits in 177 acres of country park, where you can stroll around the woodland and lakes, home to abundant wildlife such as deer, red squirrels and pheasants. Haddo also hosts a varied programme of music, drama and arts events. For details of forthcoming productions, contact the Haddo Arts Trust, T01651-851770, or the National Trust.

Peterhead and Fraserburgh

Thirty miles north of Aberdeen is the harsh, uncompromising town of Peterhead, Europe's busiest white-fish port. Eighteen miles north of Peterhead, at the very northeastern tip of the northeast coast, is the hardy, windswept fishing town of Fraserburgh. At the northern tip of the town is **Kinnaird Head Castle and Lighthouse**, which now houses Scotland's **Lighthouse Museum** ⓘ *T01346-511022, Apr-Oct Mon-Sat 1000-1700, Sun 1200-1700, 1800 in summer, Nov-Mar till 1600*. It offers a truly fascinating illumination of the engineering skill and innovation involved in the design and workings of the lighthouse, with displays of the huge lenses and prisms, as well as a history of the Stevenson family (Robert Louis' father and grandfather) who designed many of Scotland's lighthouses. The highlight is the guided tour to the top of Kinnaird Head Lighthouse itself.

Banff and around

The road west from Pennan leads on to the busy fishing port of Macduff, separated only by a bridge from neighbouring Banff, whose town centre still retains its faded Georgian elegance. The great attraction in the area is **Duff House** ⓘ *T818181, 01261-Apr-Oct daily 1100-1700, Nov-Mar Thu-Sun 1100-1600, £4, £3 child/concession*, on the Banff side of the River Deveron, a short walk upstream from the bridge. This magnificent Georgian mansion was designed by William Adam in 1735 for local entrepreneur William Duff, who later became Earl of Fife. The house was supposed to act as the capital of Duff's huge estate, but the whole project collapsed after a major disagreement between architect and patron and ended with a lawsuit in 1747. The wings were never built but Duff House remains one of the finest Georgian baroque houses in Britain. After a variety of uses and a period of dereliction, the house has been meticulously restored and reopened as an important outpost of the **National Gallery of Scotland**. The extensive collection on display includes works by Scottish artists Ramsay and Raeburn, as well as an El Greco.

West of Banff are two of the most attractive towns on the Moray coast, Portsoy and Cullen. Portsoy is particularly lovely, with its 17th-century harbour, restored merchants' houses and narrow streets. The famous Portsoy marble, used in the building of Versailles, was quarried nearby. Five miles north of Fochabers, at the mouth of the River Spey, is **Spey Bay**, site of the **Moray Firth Wildlife Centre** ⓘ *T01261-820339, mfwc@dial.pipex.com, Mar-Dec daily 1100-1630; Jul-Aug 1030-1900, £1.50, £0.75 concession*, which has an exhibition on the Moray Firth dolphins, as well as other local wildlife, including grey and common seals, otters and ospreys. The centre also houses a research unit studying the resident bottlenose dolphins.

Elgin

Nine miles west of Fochabers and 38 miles east of Inverness, is the busy market town of Elgin, which dates back to the 13th century. Elgin has retained much of its medieval streetplan, making it one of the loveliest towns in the country. The main tourist attraction is **Elgin Cathedral** ⓘ *T01343-547171.Apr-Sep daily 0930-1830, Oct-Mar Mon-Wed and Sat 0930-1630, Thu 0930-1200, Sun 1400-1630, £3, £2.30,* on North College Street, round the corner from the tourist office. Though partially ruined, the scattered remains still bear testament to what was once a majestic and beautiful cathedral. Founded in 1224, the cathedral was considered the finest in Scotland until 1390 when it was burned to the ground by the big, bad 'Wolf of Badenoch', the name given to Alexander Stewart, the illegitimate son of Robert II, following his excommunication by the bishop. And if that weren't bad enough, it was rebuilt, only to suffer further damage during the orgy of vandalism that followed the Reformation. There are still some 13th-century features remaining amongst the ruins, particularly the Pictish cross-slab and the octagonal chapterhouse.

Six miles southwest of Elgin, set in a sheltered valley, is the giant hulk of **Pluscarden Abbey** ⓘ *T01343-890257, www.pluscardenabbey.org, daily 0445-2045, free.* The abbey was founded in 1230, but in 1390 became another victim of the incredibly vengeful Wolf of Badenoch (see above). It recovered, but then fell into disrepair after the Reformation, until 1948 when it was rebuilt by an order of Benedictine monks, who still inhabit the abbey, making it the only medieval monastery in Britain that still houses a monastic community. Today it is a residential retreat for men and women and is open all year round. It has 26 single rooms and two doubles. Maximum stay stay is two weeks and charges are by donation. There are also guided tours.

Forres and Findhorn

Twelve miles west of Elgin is the solid little town of Forres. On Inverene Road is **Benromach Distillery** ⓘ *T01309-675968, www.benromach.com, Oct-Mar Mon-Fri 1000-1600, Apr-Sep Mon-Sat 0930-1700, also Sun Jun-Aug 1200-1600, £2.50.* On the eastern edge of town is the 20-ft high **Sueno's Stone**, one of the most remarkable and important Pictish carved stones in Scotland. About six miles south of Forres is one of the northeast's best-kept secrets, the very beautiful **Randolph's Leap**, a spectacular gorge on the River Findhorn which is the perfect place for a picnic, or a swim in the river. To get there, head south on the A940 and just beyond **Logie Steading** take the right fork (the B9007) for a half a mile. It's on the right side of the road as you head south.

A few miles northeast of Forres is **Kinloss**, site of a major RAF base. The B9011 heads north from Kinloss and past the RAF base; on the right is a sign to the 'Findhorn Bay Caravan Park'. In the shadow of the RAF base in a landscape of gorse and pine-clad dunes, the caravan park is the original site and nucleus of the **Findhorn Foundation**, a world-renowned spiritual community. You can join the community as a short-term guest, eating and working on-site and staying at local recommended B&Bs, and there's a full programme of courses and residential workshops on spiritual growth and healing etc. For more information, T690311. The on-site shop/deli by the car park sells books, new-age paraphernalia and organic food (open Monday-Friday till 1800; weekends till 1700). There's also a very good vegetarian café. The caravan park is open to the public and you can camp beside the Foundation, T690203, caravan@findhorn.org

Sleeping

Banff and around *p820*

A **Banff Springs Hotel**, T01261-812881, is on the western outskirts of town on the A98 to Elgin. It's a friendly, modern hotel with a good restaurant (££).

Elgin *p820*

A **Mansion House Hotel**, The Haugh (north of the High St, overlooking the river), T01343-548811. 23 rooms. Full leisure facilities and a good restaurant in an elegant and comfortable town house.

A **Mansfield House Hotel**, on Mayne Rd (1 block south of the High St), T01343-540883. 35 rooms. Centrally located, elegant town house. Its restaurant is very popular with locals and reputed to be the best in town (£££).

B-C **The Pines Guesthouse**, T01343-552495, www.thepinesguesthouse.com, on East Rd, a short walk from the town centre.

B-C The Old Church of Urquhart, T01343-843063, www.oldkirk.co.uk, a converted church in the tiny village of Urquhart, 5 miles east of Elgin, off the A96 to Aberdeen.

Forres and Findhorn *p821*

A **Knockomie Hotel**, T01309-673146, overlooking the town on the A940 south to Grantown. Best of the hotels. Excellent

B **Ramnee Hotel**, T01309-672410, on Victoria Rd. Has a highly acclaimed restaurant.

Eating

Elgin *p820*

The best place to eat in town is the **Mansfield House Hotel** (see above).

Gordon and McPhail, 50-60 South St, is an excellent deli, with a lip-smacking variety of fine foods and a huge range of malt whiskies.

A good pub is the 17th-century **Thunderton House**, in Thunderton Pl, off the High St.

Forres and Findhorn *p821*

Kimberley Inn, Findhorn, T01309-690492. A good place to eat. Serves seafood and real ales in a colourful pub atmosphere.

Transport

Banff and around *p820*

Bluebird buses, T01224-212266, run services from Banff to **Fraserburgh** (Mon-Sat) via Gardenstown and Pennan, and from Macduff to **Huntly/Keith** (Mon-Sat). Bus No 305 leaves hourly (Mon-Sat; less frequent on Sun) to **Aberdeen**, and to **Elgin** via Portsoy, Cullen and Buckie

Forres and Findhorn *p821*

Forres is on the main Aberdeen to Inverness bus route and rail line, and there are regular **buses** and **trains** in either direction. Bluebird Buses Nos 310 and 311 run from Elgin to **Forres**, via Kinloss and Findhorn several times daily (Mon-Sat).

The Highlands

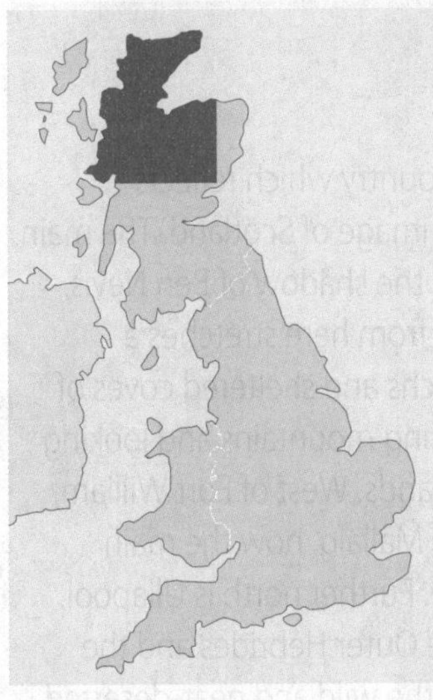

Introduction

The Highlands is the part of the country which reflects perfectly most people's romantic image of Scotland. The main town is Fort William, which lies in the shadow of Ben Nevis, Britain's highest mountain. North from here stretches a dramatic shoreline of deep sea lochs and sheltered coves of pure white sand backed by towering mountains and looking across to numerous Hebridean islands. West of Fort William, via the lyrical 'Road to the Isles', is Mallaig, now the main departure point for ferries to Skye. Further north is Ullapool, one of the main ferry ports for the Outer Hebrides and the ideal base from which to explore the wild and near-deserted far northwest.

Inverness became a city in 2000. It is the largest settlement in the region and 'capital of the Highlands'. It lies at the northeastern end of the Great Glen, which cuts diagonally across the southern Highlands to Fort William, linking deep and mysterious Loch Ness with the west coast and giving access to Glencoe, one of the most beautifully evocative Highland glens and a major climbing and skiing centre. Inverness is also ideally situated for exploring the northeast coast, with its charming old fishing ports, and the storm-lashed north coast, running west from John O'Groats to Cape Wrath, as wild and remote a place as you could ever wish for.

★ Don't miss...

1. Go for a drive up glorious **Glen Affric**, one of the very loveliest of Highland glens, page 831.
2. Choose the **West Highland choo-choo**, one of the world's great train journeys, page 852.
3. Take a trip from **Shiel Bridge** to the splendidly isolated village of **Glenelg**, page 855.
4. Travel the stunning route to **Applecross** and enjoy some wonderful seafood in the cosy **Applecross Inn**, page 858.
5. Go for a walk along the beach at **Sandwood Bay** and watch the sun set with a good malt and someone special, page 866.

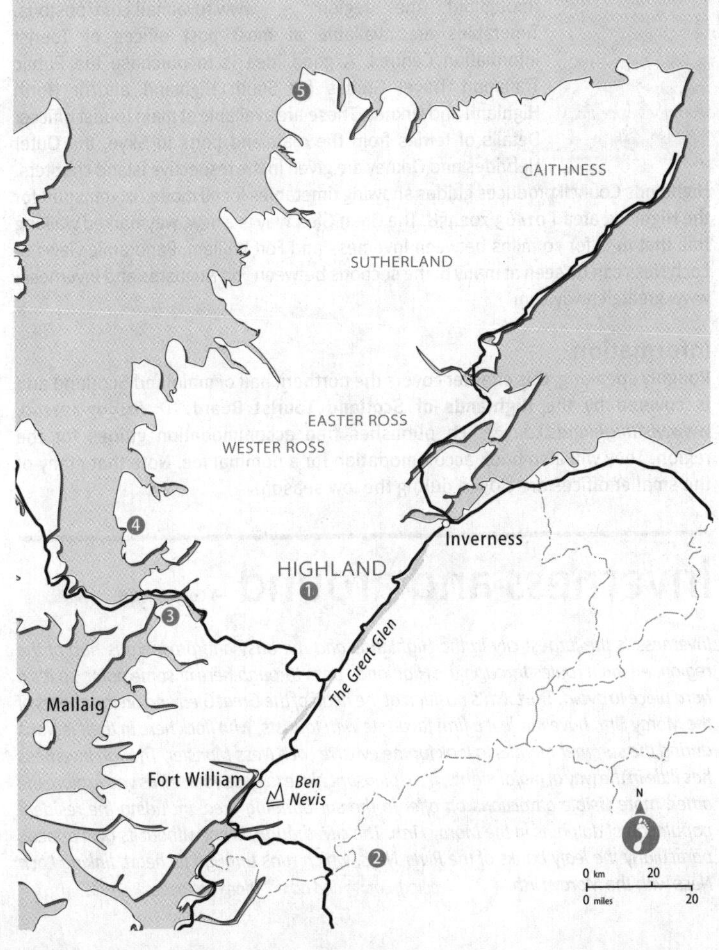

Ins and outs

Getting there

Inverness is linked to the south by the fast A9 from Edinburgh and Perth, to Aberdeen by the A96 and to Fort William by the A82, and is well served by buses. Wick, Thurso, Ullapool and Kyle of Lochalsh can all be reached by bus from Inverness. The rail line from Edinburgh closely follows the A9 to Inverness, and there are connections north to Wick and Thurso, west to Kyle of Lochalsh and east to Aberdeen. There are also daily flights to Inverness airport from London, Glasgow and Edinburgh. **Fort William** is easily reached from Glasgow by buses and trains, which continue to Mallaig for the ferry to Skye.

Getting around

Getting around in the Highlands is a lot easier with your own transport, especially in the more remote parts, but it's not difficult to reach the main tourist centres by bus or train. Getting off the beaten track can be a little more complicated, but with forward planning is achievable. Much of the time you'll need to rely on the local postbus service, which runs between the various remote post offices throughout the region – www.royalmail.com/postbus. Timetables are available at most post offices or Tourist Information Centres. A good idea is to purchase the Public Transport Travel Guides for South Highland and/or North Highland and Orkney. These are available at main tourist offices. Details of ferries from the mainland ports to Skye, the Outer Hebrides and Orkney are given in the respective island chapters. Highlands Council produces guides showing timetables for all modes of transport for the Highland area T 01463 702458. The Great Glen Way is a new, waymarked walking trail that runs for 70 miles between Inverness and Fort William. Panoramic views of Loch Ness can be seen at many of the sections between Fort Augustus and Inverness: www.greatglenway.com

By far the most scenic route to the Highlands is the spectacular West Highland Railway, one of the world's great rail journeys, particularly the section from Fort William to Mallaig.

Information

Roughly speaking, this chapter covers the northern half of mainland Scotland and is covered by the **Highlands of Scotland Tourist Board**, ⓘ *T01997-421160, www.visithighlands.com* which publishes free accommodation guides for the region. They will also book accommodation for a nominal fee. Note that many of the smaller offices are closed during the low season.

Inverness and around

→ Colour map 6

Inverness is the largest city in the Highlands and the busy and prosperous hub of the region. All main routes through the Highlands pass through here at some point, so it's a hard place to avoid. The town's position at the head of the Great Glen and on the shores of the Moray Firth have made it a firm favourite with tourists, who flock here in their legions during the summer months to look for the evasive Loch Ness Monster. Though Inverness has little in the way of major sights, it's a pleasant place to base yourself as you explore the other, more visible attractions on offer in the surrounding area, including the resident population of dolphins in the Moray Firth. The city, though, is not without its own appeal, particularly the leafy banks of the River Ness, which runs through its heart, linking Loch Ness with the Moray Firth. ▸▸ For Sleeping, Eating and other listings, see pages 832-835.

Ins and outs

Getting there There are daily **flights** to and from London Gatwick, Glasgow and Edinburgh with **British Airways** (continuing to Kirkwall and Sumburgh), and daily flights to and from London Luton and London Gatwick with **easyJet**. There are also flights to and from Birmingham and Manchester (Monday-Friday) with Eastern Airways, and to and from Stornoway Monday-Saturday with **British Airways Express**. **Snowflake airlines** are also due to start twice weekly services to Stockholm.The airport is 7 miles east of the town, at Dalcross (T01667-464000, www.hial.co.uk). A twice-daily airport bus to and from the town centre connects with London and Stornoway flights. It takes 20 mins and costs £2.50. A taxi to/from the airport costs £10-13. The **bus station** is nearby, just off Academy St (T01463-233371). Left luggage costs £2-3 per item, open Monday-Saturday 0830-1800, Sunday 1000-1800.

The **train station** is at the east end of Academy Street (T01463-239026). There are regular services to Aviemore, Perth, Glasgow, Edinburgh and Kyle of Lochalsh (for Skye). Left luggage lockers at the train station cost £2-4 per 24 hrs. » *For further details, see Transport, page 834.*

Getting around Inverness town centre is compact and easy to explore on foot, and most of the hotels and guesthouses are within a 15-min walk of the TIC. Loch Ness is not within walkable distance, so you'll need your own transport, or alternatively book a tour. » *See Activities and Tours, page 834.*

Information The **TIC**, ⓘ *Castle Wynd, near Ness Bridge, 5-mins walk from the train station, T01463-234353, Easter-Nov daily, Nov-Easter Mon-Sat* It stocks a wide range of literature on the area, can book accommodation and transport and gives out free maps of the town and environs.

Sights

The city is dominated by its red sandstone castle. Built in 1834, this Victorian edifice is very much the new kid on the block in terms of Scottish castles. The original castle dates from the 12th century. The present castle houses the Sheriff Court and also stages the **Castle Garrison Encounter** ⓘ *T01463-243363, Mar-Nov Mon-Sat (Sun only in Jul/Aug) 1030-1730, £4, concession/child £3*, where you can sign up as a mid-18th-century soldier. New recruits (that's you) pass through the Quartermaster's Store and are introduced to the Sergeant of the Guard, before being accosted by a female camp follower and finally led out through the garrison shop. Below the castle is **Inverness Museum and Art Gallery** ⓘ *Mon-Sat 0900-1700, free*, on Castle Wynd beside the Tourist Information Centre. The museum gives a decent overview of the history of the town and the region, while the gallery hosts some special exhibitions that have included paintings by the Scottish colourist JD Fergusson.

On the corner of Bridge Street and Church Street, is the **Tolbooth Steeple** which dates from 1791 and which had to be repaired after an earth tremor in 1816. Church Street also boasts the town's oldest building, **Abertarff House** (built around 1592), which is now a contemporary art and jewellery gallery (T01463-250999). Almost opposite is the much-restored **Dunbar's Hospital**, built in 1688 as an almshouse for the town's poor. At the end of Church Street, where it meets Friar's Lane, is the **Old High Church** ⓘ *Fri 1245-1315 (mid Jun-mid Sept Fri 1200-1400 with guided tour at 1230)*, founded in the 12th century and rebuilt in 1772, though the 14th-century vaulted tower remains intact. In the adjoining graveyard prisoners taken at Culloden were executed, and you can still see the bullet marks left by the firing squads on some of the gravestones.

At the corner of Huntly Street and Ness Bridge, is the **Kiltmaker Centre** ⓘ *T01463-222781, www.hector-russell.com, Mid-May-end Sep Mon-Sat 0900-2100, Sun 1000-1700, Oct-mid-May Mon-Sat 0900-1700, £2, concession £1,* where you can learn everything you ever wanted to know about tartan (including what Scotsmen wear under their kilts). You can also see kilts being made in the factory and, in the shop downstairs, be measured up for one of your own.

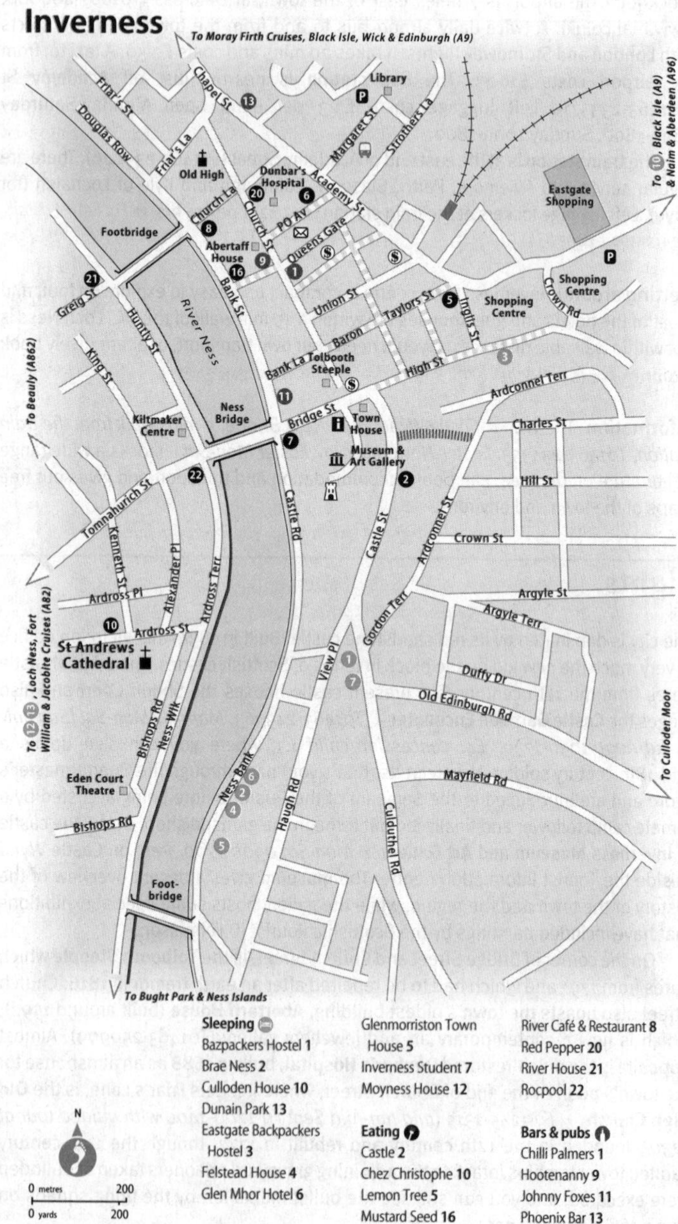

Nearby, directly opposite the castle, is the neo-Gothic **St Andrews Cathedral** which dates from 1869, and is worth a peek if you're passing by. Continuing south along Ness Bank, past the **Eden Court Theatre** (see Entertainment), you reach **Bught Park** (see 'Sleeping'), which overlooks the **Ness Islands**, joined by footbridge to both banks. The islands are attractively laid out as a park and are a favourite with local anglers. This also happens to be a lovely place for a peaceful evening stroll.

Around Inverness

East of Inverness along the **Moray Firth** stretches a long coastline of cliff-top walks, fine beaches, attractive old towns and many historic sites and castles. The Moray Firth is perhaps best known for its large resident population of **bottlenose dolphins**, the largest dolphins in the world. Over 100 of these beautiful and intelligent mammals live in the estuary, the most northerly breeding ground in Europe, and there's a very good chance of seeing them, particularly between June and August. The Moray Firth dolphins have become a major tourist attraction and several companies run dolphin-spotting boat trips. You can also see them from the shore. Two of the best places are **Chanonry Point**, on the southern shore of the Black Isle (see page 871), and **Fort George**, on the opposite shore (see below). The **Kessock Bridge**, which crosses the Moray Firth to the Black Isle, is another good dolphin-spotting location and also has a **visitor centre**, where you can can listen in to their underwater conversations.

Culloden

ⓘ *Site open daily all year. Visitor Centre and shop open Feb-31 Mar and 1 Nov to 31 Dec daily 1100-1600; 1 Apr-30 Jun, 1 Sept-31 Oct daily 0900-1800, Jul and Aug daily 0900-1900. Visitor centre, including audio-visual presentation, and Old Leanach cottage. £5, concession £3.75, children £1. Wheelchair access, bookshop, restaurant.To get there by public transport, Highland Country Bus No 7 leaves from Inverness – pick it up at the Post Office Mon-Sat (last bus back about 1830). The City Sightseeing tour bus leaves from Bridge Street, May to September from 1030, last bus returns at 1745.*

The eerie and windswept Culloden Moor, five miles to the east of Inverness on the B9006, was the site of the last major battle fought on the British mainland. The Jacobite cause was finally lost here, on 16 April 1746, when the army of Prince Charles Edward Stuart was crushed by the superior Government forces, led by the Duke of Cumberland, whose savagery earned him the nickname 'Butcher'. Contrary to popular myth this was not a battle between the Scots and the English, more a civil war: there were English Jacobites while many Scots fought for the Government. Now owned by the National Trust for Scotland, Culloden is a melancholy place and by far the most painfully evocative of Scotland's battlefields, particularly on a bleak and windy winter's day.

The battlefield has been restored to its original state (minus the dead bodies). The Visitor Centre is the obvious starting point and gives a graphic audio-visual description of the gruesome episode. From the Visitor Centre paths lead across the field to the clan graves, marked by simple headstones which bear the names of the clans who fought. Next to the Visitor Centre, the restored cottage of Old Leanach – which was used by the Jacobites as a headquarters, and where 30 Highlanders were burnt alive – is arranged as it would have been at the time of the battle. A memorial cairn, erected in 1881, is the scene each April of a commemorative service organized by the Gaelic Society of Inverness.

Fort George

ⓘ *Apr-Oct daily 0930-1830; Oct-Mar Mon-Sat 0930-1630, Sun 1400-1630. £5.50, concession £4, children £1.50. Wheelchair access, café. Fort George is 11 miles northeast of Inverness and 6 miles west of Nairn Highland Bus and Coach No 11 from the Post Office in Inverness, several daily except Sun; also buses from Nairn.*

Standing proudly on a sandy spit that juts out into the Moray Firth is Fort George, Europe's finest surviving example of 18th-century military architecture. Begun in 1748, it was the last in a chain of three such fortifications built in the Highlands – the other two being Fort Augustus and Fort William – as a base for George II's army to prevent any potential threats to Hanoverian rule. It was completed in 1769, by which time the Highlands were more or less peaceful, but was kept in use as a military barracks. Today it remains virtually unchanged, and there are even armed sentries at the main gate. You can walk along the ramparts to get an idea of the sheer scale of the place and also enjoy the sweeping views across the Moray Firth. You may even be lucky enough to see a school of dolphins. Within the fort are the barracks, a chapel, workshops and the Regimental Museum of the Queen's Own Highlanders, which features the fascinating Seafield Collection of arms and military equipment, most of which dates from the Napoleonic Wars.

Cawdor Castle

ⓘ *T01667-404401, May to mid-Oct daily 1000-1730. £6.50. Take the Highland Country Buses No 12 from Inverness Post Office. It runs several times daily (except Sun), the last bus returns around 1800. There are also regular buses from Nairn.*

Though best known for its legendary association with Shakespeare's *Macbeth*, Cawdor Castle post-dates the grisly historical events on which the great Bard based his famous tragedy. The oldest part of the castle, the central tower, dates from 1372, and the rest of it is mostly 16th or 17th century. But despite the literary disappointment, the castle is still one of the most appealing in Scotland. It has been in the hands of the Cawdor family for over six centuries and each summer they clear off, leaving their romantic home and its glorious gardens open for the enjoyment of ordinary folks like us. There's also a nine-hole golf course.

According to family legend, an early Thane of Cawdor, wanting a new castle, had a dream in which he was told to load a donkey with gold, let it wander around for a day and watch where it lay down, for this would be the best spot for his new castle. He duly followed these instructions and the donkey lay down under a thorn tree, the remains of which can still be seen in the middle of a vaulted chamber in the 14th-century tower.

Brodie Castle

ⓘ *T01309-641371. Castle open Apr, Jul, Aug daily 1200-1600; May, Jun, Sep, Sun-Thu 1200-1600. Grounds open all year daily 0930-sunset. Castle: £5, concession £3.75, children £1; grounds only £1. The castle is 8 miles east of Nairn, just off the main A96 to Forres. Bluebird buses run to Brodie from Inverness, via Culloden and Nairn; 45 mins*

Here is one of Scotland's finest castles. The oldest part of the castle, the Z-plan tower house, is 16th-century, with additions dating from the 17th and 19th centuries, giving it the look of a Victorian country house. The interior of the house is the epitome of good taste, with some fabulous ceilings, and you can look round several rooms, including the huge Victorian kitchen. The collections of furniture and porcelain are wonderful but most notable are the outstanding paintings, which include Edwin Landseer and Scottish Colourists. The grounds, too, are a delight, especially in spring when the daffodils are in bloom. There's also a tearoom.

Beauly

West of Inverness, the Moray Firth becomes the Beauly Firth, a relatively quiet little corner despite its proximity to Inverness, as most traffic heading north crosses the Kessock Bridge on the main A9. The sleepy little market town of Beauly is 10 miles west of Inverness, where the Beauly river flows into the Firth. It's a lovely wee place – hence its name. According to local legend, when Mary, Queen of Scots stayed here, at the priory, in 1564, she was so taken with the place that she cried "Ah, quel beau lieu!" (What a beautiful place!). At the north end of the marketplace is the ruin of **Beauly Priory,** ⓘ *Jun-30 Sep daily 0930-1830, £1.20, concession £0.90, children £0.50*, founded in 1230 for the Valliscaulian order, but like so much else of Scotland's ecclesiastical heritage, destroyed during the Reformation. The River Beauly is one of Scotland's best salmon-fishing rivers, and five miles south of Beauly at **Aigas** (Monday-Friday 1000-1500) is a fish lift, where you can watch salmon bypass the dam with the aid of technology.

Glen Strathfarrar and Glen Affric

Southwest of Beauly are glens Affric and Strathfarrar. **Glen Strathfarrar**, the lesser known of the two, is unspoiled and considered by some to be the more beautiful. To get there, take the A831 nine miles south from Beauly to **Struy** and follow the signs. Access to the glen is restricted by the owners, Scottish Natural Heritage, to 12 cars at a time and you have to leave by 1900. The glen is also closed from mid-August to October. But once you're in there is a tremendous feeling of peace, and there's good climbing, fishing and walking. The little ungraded road runs for 14 miles all the way to the impressive Monar Dam at the head of the glen. Glen Strathfarrar can also be reached from Drumnadrochit, via Cannich (see below).

The A831 continues south from Struy through **Strathglass** to the village of **Cannich**, gateway to glorious **Glen Affric**, a dramatic and beautiful gorge, with the River Affric rushing through it, and surrounded by Caledonian pine and birch forest (this is one of the few places where you can still see the native Scots pine). There are few, if any, more stunning sights in the Scottish Highlands and it's perfect for walking, or even just to drive through and stop for a picnic on a nice, sunny day.

Glen Affric reaches west into the very heart of the Highlands and is great for a spot of Munro-bagging. Beyond Loch Affric the serious walking starts. From Affric Lodge, nine miles west of Cannich, begins a 20-mile trail west to Morvich, near **Shiel Bridge**, on the west coast near Kyle of Lochalsh (see page 856). This strenuous walk is for experienced hikers only, and takes around 10 hours. You can stop off halfway at one of the most remote **youth hostels** in Scotland, *Glen Affric Youth Hostel*, at Allt Beithe (no phone; open mid-March till end October).

There are also many shorter, easier walks around Glen Affric. There are some short, circular marked trails at the end of the road which runs west from Cannich almost to Loch Affric, and also from the car park at the impressive **Dog Falls**, 4½ miles from Cannich and a great place to stop for a picnic and swim. Cycling in the forests around Cannich is good too – you can hire bikes at *Cannich Caravan and Camping Park*.

Glen Affric can also be reached from **Drumnadrochit** (see page 836) by heading west on the A831 through **Glen Urquhart** to Cannich. Just before Cannich, on the road from Drumnadrochit, a single track road leads left (south), past the Caravan and Camping Park, to the tiny village of **Tomich**. From here, it's a three-mile hike up a woodland trail to a car park. A few hundred yards down through the trees takes you to the lovely **Plodda Falls**. An old iron bridge affords a spectacular view of the waterfall as it plunges 150 yards into the foaming waters below.

Sleeping

You shouldn't have much trouble finding somewhere to stay in Inverness, though in Jul and Aug it's advisable to book ahead. This can be done through the tourist information centre, or (less cheaply) in the train station at the Thomas Cook booth, but you'll be charged a booking fee. There are several good quality hotels in and around town and plenty of B&Bs. The best places to look are along both banks of the river south of the Ness Bridge, Old Edinburgh Rd, and Ardconnel St, all to the east of the castle, and on the west bank, around Bruce Gardens, Ardross St, Kenneth St and Fairfield Rd. There are also several budget hostels in and around the centre, and a couple of large campsites.

Inverness *p826, map p828*

L **Culloden House Hotel**, Milton of Culloden, about 3 miles east of town near the A9. T01463-790461, F01463-792181. www.cullodenhouse.co.uk. 28 rooms. Superb Georgian mansion with 1st-class facilities, service and restaurant.

A **Dunain Park Hotel**, about 3 miles southwest of the town centre, just off the A82 Fort William Rd. T01463-230512, F01463-224532, www.dunainparkhotel.co.uk. 11 rooms. An elegant Georgian mansion house with its own grounds, lovely and peaceful with an excellent restaurant (see below) and its own indoor pool.

A **Glenmoriston Town House Hotel**, 20 Ness Bank. T01463-223777, F01463-712378. 15 rooms. Recently refurbished and now one of the classiest places in town, with a superb Italian restaurant (see below).

B **Glenruidh House Hotel**, Old Edinburgh Rd South, 2 miles from the town centre (phone for directions). T01463-226499, F01463-710745, www.cozzee-nessie-bed.co.uk. 5 rooms. No smoking. Comfortable and peaceful hotel in secluded setting, with friendly service and excellent food.

B **Moyness House Hotel**, 6 Bruce Gardens, T/F01463-233836, www.moyness.co.uk. Fine Victorian villa in a quiet area near the theatre, with very clean and comfortable en-suite rooms and nice touches like Body Shop products in the bathrooms. Non smoking.

B **Brae Ness Hotel**, 17 Ness Bank. T01463-712266, F01463-231732. www.braenesshotel.co.uk. 10 rooms. No smoking. Family-run Georgian hotel overlooking the river and Eden Court, with a licensed restaurant for residents.

B **Felstead House**, 18 Ness Bank. T/F01463-231634, felsteadgh@aol.com. 8 rooms, 5 with en suite. Family-run Georgian guesthouse, large and comfortable rooms, good breakfast and overall good value.

E **Bazpackers Hostel**, 4 Culduthel Rd (at the top of Castle St), T01463-717663. 48 beds in dorms of 4-8, twin and double rooms available, cooking facilities and garden for barbecues, also has laundrette, good atmosphere.

E **Eastgate Backpackers Hostel**, 38 Eastgate T/F01463-718756, www.hostelsaccommodation.com. 40 beds, free tea and coffee, and continental breakfast for £1.50.

E **Inverness Student Hotel**, 8 Culduthel Rd, next door to **Bazpackers**, T01463-236556. 9 dorms with 54 beds, some dorms have good views. Friendly and laid-back atmosphere with all the usual facilities.

Around Inverness *p829*

B **Lovat Arms Hotel**, Beauly, T01463-782313, lovat.arms@cali.co.uk. the best place to stay in the village. A relaxed and comfortable place with an excellent restaurant and great bar food, lots of tartan and the occasional ceilidh. Offers cheap meals in the bar or an expensive 4-course dinner in the restaurant.

B-C **Kerrow House**, in Cannich village, T01463-415243, F01463-415425, stephen@kerrow-house.demon.co.uk.

E **SYHA Cannich Youth Hostel**, T01463-415244, open mid-Mar to end Oct.

E **Glen Affric Backpackers**, T/F01463-415263, which is open all year.

A **The Tomich Hotel**, Tomich, T01456-415399, F01456-415469. The price includes dinner, and it's a comfortable place with good food and free use of the nearby indoor heated pool; also great for fishing holidays.

E **Cougie Lodge**, near Tomich, T01456-415459, which is open Apr-Sep and will pick you up from Tomich or Cannich if you phone ahead.

Eating

Inverness *p826, map p828*
£££ **Chez Christophe**, 16 Ardross St, T01463-717126. High quality French cuisine a few minutes from the city centre.
£££ **Dunain Park Hotel** (address as above). Award-winning Scots-French cuisine in elegant surroundings, and a superb list of malts. Take a stroll in the lovely gardens afterwards.
£££ **Glen Mhor Hotel**, 9-12 Ness Bank, T01463-234308. *Riverview* restaurant at the front is good, especially for seafood.
£££ **La Riviera**, at the *Glenmoriston Town House Hotel* (see above). Excellent Italian food. T01463-223777.
£££ **River House Restaurant**, 1 Grieg St, T01463-222033. Tue-Sat 1200-1400, 1830-late. Green tartan outside is a clue to the fact that this restaurant serves good quality Scottish produce. Dishes might include sea bass, or Highland game stew. 3 courses for £27.95.
££ **Rocpool**, 1 Ness Walk, T01463-717274. 1200-1430, 1800-2200. Very popular contemporary restaurant with wooden floors and crisp white tablecloths. Serves dishes like fillet of beef or lemon and herb risotto.
££ **The Mustard Seed**, 16 Fraser St, T01463-220220. Daily 1200-1500, 1800-2200. Lovely contemporary restaurant, with cheery yellow walls and sculptural flowers as well as an imaginative menu. Lunch choices like spinach and gorgonzola polenta, dinner might include salmon or guinea fowl.
££ **The River Café and Restaurant**, 10 Bank St, T01463-714884. Mon 1000-2030, Tue-Sat 1000-2130, Sun 1200-2030. Offers high teas and traditional dishes like haggis.
£ **Castle Restaurant**, 41 Castle St. Clean, no nonsense cafe serving huge portions of stodgy, filling grub at low prices, convenient for backpacker's hostels, open till 2100.
£ **The Lemon Tree**, 18 Inglis St. Located in the pedestrianized town centre, family-run café offering good home baking and basic but filling meals.
£ **The Red Pepper**, Bow Court, 74 Church St, T01463-237111. Mon 1000-2030, Tue-Sat 1000-2130, Sun 1200-2030. Bustling little café/takeaway offering fresh paninis, sandwiches, soups and salads.

Pubs, bars and clubs

Phoenix 108 Academy St. One of the best pubs in town and always lively.
Gellions, on Bridge St, has varied live music throughout the week.
Johnny Foxes, at 26 Bank St, features Irish folk music every night in summer as well as boasting an unusual pub menu.
Chilli Palmers, on the corner of Queensgate and Church St, is a trendy new bar offering decent food and a DJ at weekends. A great bet for atmosphere and all things Scottish is **Hootananny**, 67 Church St a bar which has live music every night, anyone is welcome to get involved with the Mon and Tues sessions. They have ceilidhs 1500-1700 on Sats and Gallic speaking meetings 1930-2030 on Mon.
Sofa Bar (due to open at time of writing) is above Hootenanny and aims to please a younger crowd with live bands and DJs.

Entertainment

Theatre and cinema

Eden Court Theatre is on Bishops Rd, overlooking the River Ness. It offers a varied programme of theatre, dance and all kinds of music. There's also a bar and self-service restaurant with good food and views over the river. The attached cinema shows a programme of art-house and newly released movies, for information: T01463-234234. Prices vary depending on the performance.
Warner Village is on the A96 Nairn Rd, about 2 miles from the town centre. Cinema tickets cost from £4. 7 screens.

Festivals

There are numerous events held in and around Inverness throughout the year. These range from a humble pub ceilidh and a food festival and to a full-blown Highland Games. For details contact the Tourist Information Centre or visit their website. The best of the local folk festivals are held over the **Easter weekend** (T01738-623274), and the **Highland Festival** takes place over several days at the end of **Jun** (T01463-711112, www.highland festival.demon.co.uk). **Inverness Music Festival** takes place Feb/Mar, T01463-716616, and there's an **Inverness Tattoo** in **Jul** held in the Northern meeting Park.

Shopping

Inverness *p826, map p828*
Inverness is a good place to buy a **kilt**, or practically anything else in tartan. To find your own clan tartan, head for the Scottish Kiltmaker Visitor Centre (see Sights above). Other places which sell highland dress and traditional gifts are Chisholm's Highland Dress, 47-51 Castle St, T01463-234599, 0900-1730 and 1900-2130 in Jul and Aug; and Hector Russell, 4-9 Huntly St, T01463-222781, and James Pringle Weavers, Holm Mills, Dores Rd, T01463-223311.

Activities and tours

The Highland Riding Centre is at Borlum Farm, Drumnadrochit, T01456 450892, www.borlum.com. The Aquadome Leisure Centre is at Bught Park, T01463-667500. Mon-Fri 0730-2200, Sat-Sun 0730-2100. Competition-sized pool, flumes, wave machine and kiddies' pool, also health suites, gym and other indoor sports facilities. The Inverness Tennis and Squash Club is at Bishop's Rd, T01463-230751. There's also an Ice Centre at Bught Park, T01463-235711, www.inverness-ice-centre.org.uk

Transport

Bus

There are regular daily buses to **Glasgow** and **Edinburgh** via Aviemore, Pitlochry and Perth with Scottish Citylink (T0990-505050). There are regular daily Citylink buses to **Ullapool**, connecting with the ferry to **Stornoway**; also to **Fort William** and **Oban**. There are daily Citylink buses to **Kyle of Lochalsh**, **Portree** and **Uig** (connecting with ferries to **Tarbert** and **Lochmaddy**). There are regular Citylink buses to **Fort Augustus** via Drumnadrochit and Urquhart Castle (also with Highland Bus & Coach, T01463-233371), and to **Scrabster**, for the ferry to **Stromness**, via Wick and Thurso; also with Morrison's Coaches, T01847-821241. There are Inverness Traction buses, T01463-239292, every hour to **Beauly**, and on to **Muir of Ord**, from Inverness and from Dingwall. There's also a Ross's Minibus service from Beauly 3 days a week, T01463-761250.

Highland Bus & Coach, T01463-233371, runs buses 3 days a week Mon-Fri from Inverness to **Cannich** and **Tomich**, via Drumnadrochit. There are also buses from Inverness to Cannich and Tomich, via Beauly (2 on Tue and Fri, and 1 on Sat).

Ferry

For details of connections to Stornoway (Lewis) see page, or contact the *CalMac* office in Inverness, T01463-717681. For Scrabster to Stromness, run by Northlink Ferries, T01856 851144, www.northlinkferries.co.uk, see page908.

Taxi

Rank Radio Taxis, T01463-221111/220222; Tartan Taxis, T01463-233033. For a Taxi Tour of the area T01463-220222

Train

There are direct trains to/from **Aberdeen**, **Edinburgh** via Aviemore, and **Glasgow**. There are several daily services to/from **London King's Cross**, via Perth and Edinburgh, and a Caledonian Sleeper service from London Euston to Inverness and Fort William, ScotRail, T08457 550033, www.scotrail.co.uk.There is also a regular service to **Wick** and **Thurso**, via Tain, Lairg and Helmsdale. The journey from Inverness to **Kyle of Lochalsh** (for Skye) is one of the most scenic in Britain. There are 3 trains daily (none on Sun).

Directory

Banks All the major banks can be found in the town centre. **Car hire** Avis is at the airport (T01667-462787); Budget is on Railway Terr behind the train station (T01463-713333); Europcar has an office at 16 Telford St (T0870 050 0289), and at the airport (T0870 870 0120); Sharps Reliable Wrecks, Railway Station, Academy St, T01463-236694 and at the airport T01463-461212, www.sharpsreliable wrecks.co.uk. Thrifty is at 33 Harbour Rd (T01463-224466). Expect to pay from around £30 per day. **Cultural centres** Inverness library is opposite the bus station. It has an excellent genealogical research unit. Consultations with the resident genealogist cost £12 per hr; T01463-236463, for an appointment. The library also houses the Highland archives, where you can research the history and culture of the region. Mon-Fri 1100-1300 and 1400-1700; Oct-May 1400-1700 only. **Cycle hire** Barney's Bicycle Hire & Shop, 35 Castle St, T01463-232249. 0900-2100 in season. Mountain bike hire from £12.00 per day. Highland Cycles, Telford St, T01463-234789. Mon-Sat 0900-1730 all year, range of bikes available from £11.00 per day. Also bikes for hire from Bazpacker's Hostel (see Sleeping). **Hospitals** Raigmore Hospital is on the southeastern outskirts of town near the A9 (T01463-704000) for accidents and emergencies. **Internet** available from the TIC, the Launderette on Young St, The Mail Box on Station Sq and at the library .The Gate café bar, opposite the post office, has internet facilities and serves drinks and snacks from 1000-2100. **Pharmacies** Boots is in the Eastgate Shopping Centre; open daily 0900-1730, Thu till 1900. **Post office** The main branch is at 14-16 Queensgate, T01463-234111. Mon-Thu 0900-1730, Fri 0930-1730, Sat 0900-1320.

Loch Ness to Fort Augustus

→Colour map 6

One of Scotland's biggest attractions is the narrow gash of Loch Ness, Britain's deepest body of fresh water, stretching 23 miles from Fort Augustus in the south almost to Inverness in the north. The loch is scenic in its own right, with rugged hills rising steeply from its wooded shores, but visitors don't come here for the views. They come every year, in their hundreds of thousands, to stare across the dark, cold waters in search of its legendary inhabitant, the Loch Ness Monster. A huge tourist trade has grown up around 'Nessie', as the monster is affectionately known, and every summer the main A82 which runs along its western shore is jam packed with bus-loads of eager monster-hunters, binoculars trained on the loch surface, desperate for one glimpse of the elusive beast.

The best way to see the loch is on a cruise from Inverness (details from the tourist office). There are also boat trips from Drumnadrochit and Fort Augustus (see below). Most of the tourist traffic uses the congested A82, which offers few decent views of the loch. By far the best views of the loch are from the quiet and picturesque B862/852 which runs along its eastern shore, from Fort Augustus up to Inverness. It's possible to make a complete circuit of the loch, which is best done in an anti-clockwise direction heading south from Inverness on the A82, but you'll need your own transport (or take a tour), as there are no buses between Fort Augustus and Foyers. ▸▸ *For Sleeping, Eating and other listings, see pages 837-838.*

Ins and outs

Getting around Citylink **buses** between Inverness and Fort William stop at Drumnadrochit several times daily in either direction. Additional services run between Inverness and Urquhart Castle during the summer months. There are also buses from Inverness to Cannich and Tomich, via Drumnadrochit. Fort Augustus is a convenient stopover between Fort William and Inverness, and there are several **buses** daily in either direction. It takes 1 hr to both towns. There is an additional service between Fort Augustus and Invergarry (see below) once a day Mon-Sat. The route from Fort Agustus to Dores, on the east bank of the loch, is only possible if you have your own transport. There are buses south from Inverness, but they only run as far as Foyers (3 times Mon-Fri, twice on Sat). Alternatively, it can be done by **bike**, as a full-day circular trip from Fort Augustus or from Inverness.

Information **Fort Augustus TIC** is in the car park next to the petrol station ⓘ *T01456-366367, Apr-Jun Mon-Sat 1000-1700; Jul-Aug 0900-2000; Sep-Oct 0900-1800.*

The Great Monster Hunt

In a country full of myths and legends, the Loch Ness Monster is the greatest of them all. As elusive as a straight answer from a politician, Nessie has single-handedly sold more tins of tartan-wrapped shortbread to foreign visitors than Edinburgh Castle.

Tales of Nessie go way back to the sixth century, when St Columba is said to have calmed the beast after she had attacked one of his monks. But the monster craze only really took off with the completion of the A82 road along the loch's western shore in 1933. Since then there have been numerous sightings, some backed up with photographic evidence, though the most impressive of these – the famous black-and-white movie footage of Nessie's humps moving through the water, and the classic photograph of her head and neck – have been exposed as fakes.

In recent decades determined monster hunters have enlisted the help of new technology, such as sonar surveys, but have failed to come up with conclusive evidence. Enter Cyber Nessie, the latest attempt to end the years of rumours, hoaxes and speculation. Nessie's very own website – www.lochness.scotland.net/camera.htm – is a 24-hour real-time video watch of Loch Ness, and has already produced a couple of claimed sightings. But nothing could compare with the excitement of seeing the monster in the flesh.

Inverness to Fort Augustus

'Nessiemania' reaches its zenith in the village of Drumnadrochit, 15 miles south of Inverness. The monster hype is almost overpowering, with two rival Monster Exhibitions and the souvenir shops selling tartan tack. There's a TIC in the Car Park T01456-459086. Of the two Monster Exhibitions, the **Original Loch Ness Visitor Centre** ⓘ *T01456-450342, Apr to end of Oct daily 1000-1800 (Jul-Aug till 2100), £3.50, students £3, children and OAPs £2.75,* is the least worthwhile. It's a glorified gift shop with an amateurish audiovisual show. Those genuinely interested in the history of the search for 'Nessie' should visit the **Loch Ness 2000 Exhibition** ⓘ *T01456-450573, Easter-end May 0930-1700; Jun and Sep 0900-1800; Jul-Aug 0900-2000; Oct 0930- 1730; Nov-Mar 1000-1530, £5.95, students/seniors £4.50, children £3.50.* Though it's more expensive, it gives a detailed description of the many eye-witness accounts over the years and also explains the recent research projects carried out in the loch.

A few miles south of Drumnadrochit are the ruins of **Castle Urquhart** ⓘ *T01456-450551, Apr-Sep daily 0930-1830; Oct-Mar daily 0930-1630, £6, concession £4.50, children £1.20.* The castle bears the scars of centuries of fighting but its setting, perched on a rocky cliff on the loch's edge, is magnificent. Dating from the 14th century, the castle was a strategic base, guarding the Great Glen during the long Wars of Independence. It was taken by Edward I, held by Robert the Bruce against Edward II, and was then almost constantly under siege before being destroyed in 1692 to prevent it from falling into Jacobite hands. Most of the existing buildings date from the 16th century, including the five-storey tower, the best-preserved part of the complex, from where you get great views of the loch and surrounding hills. There's also a visitor centre.

Between Drumnadrochit and Fort Augustus is the tiny village of Invermoriston, probably the nicest spot on the entire Inverness to Fort Augustus stretch of the A82. Here, the A887 heads west through **Glen Moriston** to meet the A87, which runs from **Invergarry** (see below) all the way through the rugged and dramatic **Glen Shiel** to the awesome mountains of **Kintail** on the west coast near **Kyle of Lochalsh**. *Citylink* buses between Inverness and Kyle of Lochalsh stop at Invermoriston.

Fort Augustus

At the more scenic southern end of Loch Ness stands the village of Fort Augustus, originally set up as a garrison after the Jacobite rebellion of 1715, and headquarters of General Wade's campaign to pacify the Highlands. Today Fort Augustus is a busy little place, full of tourists and boats using the flight of five locks to enter or leave Loch Ness on their journey along the **Caledonian Canal**. On the shores of Loch Ness is **Fort Augustus Abbey**, a Benedictine Monastery founded in 1876 on the site of the original fort. The abbey closed in 1998. By the canal locks is **The Clansman Centre,** ⓘ *T01320-366444, Apr, May, Jun and Sep daily 1100-1700; Jul-Aug 1000-1800, £3, concession £2.50*, a lively presentation of 17th-century Highland family life in an old turf house.

Fort Augustus to Dores

A worthwhile detour from Fort Augustus is to take the B862/852 up the **east shore of Loch Ness** on a mostly single-track road that skirts the loch for much of its length to the village of Dores. It's a much quieter and more scenic route than the busy A82.

The road winds its way up into rugged hills before returning to the lochside at **Foyers**. Three miles further north, at **Inverfarigaig**, is the spooky and sinister **Boleskine House**, once home of Alastair Crowley, who is said to have practised devil worship here. In the 1970s the house was bought by Jimmy Page of Led Zeppelin, but sold some years later after the tragic death of his daughter. Those of a nervous disposition may wish to pass on quickly and continue to the little village of **Dores**, at the northeastern end of the loch, where you can enjoy a good pint of ale and some decent grub at the *Dores Inn*. You can then continue to Inverness, or return via the beautiful hill road that leads up to **Loch Mhor** and back to Fort Augustus via the **Stratherrick** valley. From **Errogie**, at the northern end of Loch Mhor, there's a dramatic section of road that winds down to the loch through a series of tight, twisting bends, reminiscent of an Alpine pass, and great for cyclists. There are also some interesting marked woodland trails around Errogie.

Sleeping

Loch Ness to Fort Augustus *p835*

A **Polmaily House Hotel**, 3 miles from Drumnadrochit on the A831 to Cannich, in Glen Urquhart, T01320-450343, polmailyhousehotel@btinternet.com. 10 rooms. A comfortable, child-friendly country house far enough away from the madding crowd to offer peace and quiet, many walks nearby, also tennis courts, horse riding and covered pool, and a good restaurant.

D **Drumbuie Farm**, Drumnadrochit, T01320-450634. a modern farmhouse on the right as you enter the village from Inverness, with its own herd of Highland cattle.

E **Loch Ness Backpackers Lodge**, at Coiltie Farmhouse in East Lewiston, T01320-450807, immediately south of Drumnadrochit, on the left. It's open all year, has excellent facilities, and arranges boat trips and local walks.

E **SYHA Loch Ness Youth Hostel**, A few miles north of Invermoriston, on the main A82 overlooking Loch Ness, T01320-351274, open mid-Mar to end Oct.

F **Loch Ness Caravan & Camping Park** 1½ miles south of Invermoriston, and 6 miles north of Fort Augustus, T01320-351207, right on the shores of the loch with great views and excellent facilities (open Easter-Oct).

Fort Augustus *p837*

C **Lovat Arms Hotel**, T01320-366206. 23 rooms. A beautiful old mansion house standing above the village.

D **Kettle House** on Golf Course Rd, T01320-366408. Open Feb-Nov. Friendly.

E **Morag's Lodge**, T01320-366289. Offers backpacker accommodation between Mar and Oct.

Eating

Fort Augustus *p837*

££ **Loch Inn**, by the canal, is the best place for a drink, and also serves decent pub grub.

£ **Bothy Bite**, T366710, by the canal bridge, serves cheap meals from 1200-2100.

Activities and tours

Boat trips
Loch Ness Cruises operate from the Original Loch Ness Visitor Centre in Drumnadrochit from Apr to Oct and run daily from 0930-1800. They last one hour and cost £9 per adult and £5 per child. *Cruise Loch Ness* setoff from the canal in the centre of Fort Augustus. Apr-Oct hourly from 1000. The trip lasts 50 mins and costs £6 per adult. Also boat and bike hire. T01223-208939.

Pony trekking
Fort Augustus Riding Centre, Pier House, T01320-366418.

Fort Augustus to Fort William

→Colour map 6

South of Fort Augustus, the A82 leaves behind Loch Ness and runs along the west shore ofLoch Oich and then the east shore of Loch Lochy, till it reaches Spean Bridge. Here the A82 continues south to Fort William, while the A86 branches east through Glen Spean to join the A9 Perth to Inverness road finally at Kingussie. All along this route are many opportunities to get off the beaten track and explore huge chunks of real wilderness, deserted since the Clearances and soaked in the blood of history. ▸▸ *For Sleeping, Eating and other listings, see pages 839-840.*

Ins and outs

Getting there There are regular **buses** to and from Fort William and Inverness. Spean Bridge is also on the Fort William-Glasgow **rail** line (see page 845). Invergarry is on the Fort William to **Inverness** bus route (see Fort Augustus above). It is also on the main **Fort William** to Kyle of Lochalsh (and **Skye**) Citylink route, and a couple of buses pass through daily in both directions. There's a **postbus** from Invergarry post office on Mon, Wed and Fri, which runs to Kingie, which is halfway to Kinloch Hourn. A 4-seater post car runs all the way to Kinloch Hourn from Invergarry on Tue, Wed, Thu and Sat. A scenic return would be the **ferry** from Kinloch Hourn to **Arnisdale** (summer only; daily by arrangement) and then head to **Glenelg**, from where you can take a ferry across to **Kylerhea** on Skye (see page 884). There are **buses** from Fort William to Roy Bridge (3 times daily Mon-Fri; 1 on Sat). Roy Bridge is also on the Fort William-Glasgow **rail** line.

Information Spean Bridge TIC is just off the road behind the post office. ⓘ *Easter-Oct. T01320-712576, F01320-712675.*

Glen Garry and around

The old village of Invergarry stands where the A82 turns west to meet the A87. There's not much to see or do in the village, but the surrounding area merits some exploring, particularly the route west through Glen Garry, and there are several places to stay. The A87 leads west from Invergarry through Glen Shiel to **Shiel Bridge**, on the way to Kyle of Lochalsh on the west coast (see page 855). About seven miles along the A87, past the turning for Kinloch Hourn (see below), is the Glen Garry viewpoint, from where you get one of the most stunning, and famous, of all Highland views. From this angle Loch Garry looks uncannily like a map of Scotland, so get out the camera for that classic holiday snap.

A mile or so before the Glen Garry viewpoint, where the A87 begins to leave the shores of Loch Garry, is the turning left for the road through Glen Garry, described as the longest and most beautiful cul-de-sac in Britain. The little single-track road turns and twists for 22 glorious miles along the shores of **Loch Garry** and **Loch Quoich** all the way to **Kinloch Hourn**, at the head of Loch Hourn, a sea loch on the west coast.

Glen Garry is virtually deserted but was once home to some 5,000 people who were driven out during the infamous Highland Clearances in the 19th century. The road passes the hamlet of **Tomdoun**, once the junction of the main road to Skye, until the post-war hydroelectric schemes changed the landscape. Experienced hillwalkers can still follow the old route to Skye, through Glen Kingie, along Loch Hourn and then across the wild **Knoydart peninsula** till they reach the tiny settlement of **Inverie**. From here a little ferry runs twice a day on Monday-Wednesday and Friday to **Mallaig**.

Beyond Tomdoun the road passes a dam, built in the 1950s. The road then reaches its highest point, at 1,200 ft, before descending to **Kinloch Hourn**, once a fishing village but now remote and isolated. Incredible as it may seem, you can actually stay here.

Spean Bridge and around

The main A82 runs down the east shore of Loch Lochy to the village of Spean Bridge, at the head of Glen Spean, beneath the towering Lochaber mountains. The village gets its name from Thomas Telford's bridge across the River Spean. Two miles west are the remains of the old 'Highbridge', built in 1736 by General Wade, and the site of the first clash between Government troops and the Jacobites, three days before Prince Charles raised his standard at Glenfinnan.

Spean Bridge is only eight miles north of Fort William so gets busy in the summer, but it still makes a more peaceful and attractive alternative base for exploring this astoundingly beautiful part of the Highlands. Spean Bridge is also the starting point for the excellent **Grey Corries ridge walk** (OS Landranger Map No 41).

From Spean Bridge the A86 runs east through Glen Spean to meet the A9 Perth to Inverness road which leads to **Aviemore**, Scotland's main ski centre (see page 876). The road passes through **Roy Bridge**, which is the turn-off for **Glen Roy**, noted for its amazing 'parallel roads'. These are not in fact roads, but three gravel ledges etched on to the mountains at different heights. The 'roads' marked the shorelines of a glacial lake formed during the last ice age.

The road continues east towards Loch Laggan. After a couple of miles it passes **Cille Choirille**, an ancient church built by a 15th-century Cameron chief as penance for a life of violence. The church fell into disrepair but was restored and reopened in 1932 and now attracts people of all creeds as it's said to inspire peace and spiritual healing. Further east, at the eastern end of Loch Laggan, is the massive **Laggan Dam**, built in 1933 to provide water for the aluminium smelter at Fort William. The road runs along the north shore of the loch, past the **Creag Meagaidh National Nature Reserve**, where you can see herds of red deer right by the reserve car park. A track leads from here up to **Lochan a' Choire** (about four hours).

Sleeping

Glen Garry and around *p838*

A **Glengarry Castle Hotel**, Invergarry, T01809-501254, castle@glengarry.net. Set in 60 acres of woodland running down to Loch Oich. 26 rooms, open Mar-Nov. The hotel has been in the MacCallum family for over 40 years and is still one of the best in the Highlands.

A **Skiary**, Kinloch Hourn, T01809-511214, open May-Sep, phone ahead to arrange for a boat to meet you. This is perhaps the most remote guesthouse in the Highlands. It is accessible only by boat or foot and has no mains electricity. There are 3 rooms and prices are for full board, and include the boat trip both ways. The food is wonderful and the setting is simply magnificent.

E **SYHA Loch Lochy Youth Hostel**, south of Invergarry, at South Laggan, T01809-501239, open mid-Mar to end-Oct.

Spean Bridge and around *p839*

A **Old Pines Restaurant with Rooms**, T01397-712324, www.lochaber. com/oldpines. 8 rooms, just past the Commando Memorial on the B8004; price includes dinner. This Scandinavian-style chalet is a great place to stay, especially if you have kids in tow, and is renowned for its exceptional, award-winning Scottish cuisine. Food is available to non-residents (the 5-course dinner is expensive but lunch is much cheaper).

A **Corriegour Lodge Hotel**, 9 miles north of Spean Bridge on the A82, T01397-712685. 9 rooms, open Feb-Dec. Lovely Victorian hunting lodge on the shores of Loch Lochy, with fine views and an excellent restaurant (non-residents dinner only; expensive).

C **Invergloy House**, further south, on the shores of Loch Lochy, T01397-712681. A very good B&B.

D **Smiddy House**, In the village itself, T01397-712335, F01397-712043. A comfortable guesthouse with a bistro attached, serving good, cheap meals.

F **Grey Corrie Lodge**, in Roy Bridge, T712236, F712241, is handy for shops and transport, serves cheap bar meals and also has laundry facilities. Five miles east, at Tulloch train station, is

F **Station Lodge**, T/F732333, which also serves meals (including vegetarian).

Eating

Spean Bridge and around *p839*

£££ Old Station Restaurant, T01397-712535, in a converted railway station. Has a very good reputation, lunch by prior arrangement only, open Apr-Oct, Tue-Sun 1800-2100. Also recommended is

£££-££ The Coach House Restaurant, T01397-712680, crann_tara@bigfoot.com. Late Apr to late Oct, daily 1200-1500 and 1800-2100. About 3 miles north of town on the right-hand side, at Glenfintaig. It's a popular place and small, so you'll have to book ahead for lunch (cheap) or dinner (mid-range to expensive).

Activities and tours

Bus tours

Glengarry Mini Tours, T01809-501297, run various minibus day tours in the Great Glen, Glen Coe and Glen Nevis.

Fishing

Fishing Scotland, T/F01397-712812, www.fishing-scotland.co.uk, runs fishing courses and trips on the surrounding lochs. Loch Arkaig in particular is renowned for its trout fishing.

Hiking and climbing

Nevis Guides, Bohuntin, Roy Bridge, T01397-712356.

Watersports

Great Glen Water Park, on the east shore of Loch Oich, near North Laggan, is the T01809-501381, an outdoor activities centre offering numerous adventure sports, including white-water rafting, canoeing, mountain biking, rock climbing, sailing, windsurfing, hill walking and water skiing. There are also self-catering lodges for rent.

Fort William and around

→*Colour map 6*

Fort William is the gateway to the Western Highlands and one of the country's main tourist centres. It stands at the head of Loch Linnhe, with the snow-topped mass of Ben Nevis towering behind. You could be forgiven for assuming that it's quite an attractive place, but you'd be wrong. Despite its magnificent setting, Fort William has all the charm of a motorway service station. A dual carriageway runs along the lochside, over a litter-strewn pedestrian underpass and past dismal 1960s concrete boxes masquerading as hotels.

Most of the good things about Fort William are outside the town. The surrounding mountains and glens are amongst the most stunning in the Highlands and attract hikers and climbers, namely Ben Nevis – Britain's highest peak at 4,406 ft – and also the very beautiful Glen Nevis. There's also skiing and snowboarding at nearby Aonach Mhor, one of Scotland's top ski areas, see page844, and some good mountain biking around the Leanachan Forest, see page 844. ▸▸ *For Sleeping, Eating and other listings, see pages 843-845.*

Ins and outs

Getting there Fort William is easily reached by **bus,** from Inverness, Glasgow and Oban, and by **train,** direct from Glasgow via the amazing and beautiful West Highland Railway. The train and bus stations are next to each other at the north end of the High St, on the other side of the dual carriageway. If you're driving, parking can be a problem. There's a big **car park** beside the loch at the south end of town, and another behind the tourist office. You can also walk to Fort William, from just north of Glasgow, along the 95 mile-long **West Highland Way** (see page 846). ▸▸ *For further details, see Transport page 845.*

Getting around The town is strung out for several miles along the banks of Loch Linnhe. The centre is compact and easy to get around on foot. Many of the **guesthouses** and **B&Bs**, and a few youth hostels, are in **Corpach**, 1½ miles to the north, but there are frequent buses from the town centre. There are also buses to the youth hostel in **Glen Nevis**. For information on these and on **taxis** and **car hire** see under Transport, page 845.

Information The busy **TIC** is on Cameron Sq, just off the High St, ⓘ *T01397-703781, F01397-705184, open daily Apr-Sep, Nov-Mar Mon-Sat.* They stock a good range of books, maps and leaflets covering local walks. They will also help arrange transport to more remote Highland parts.

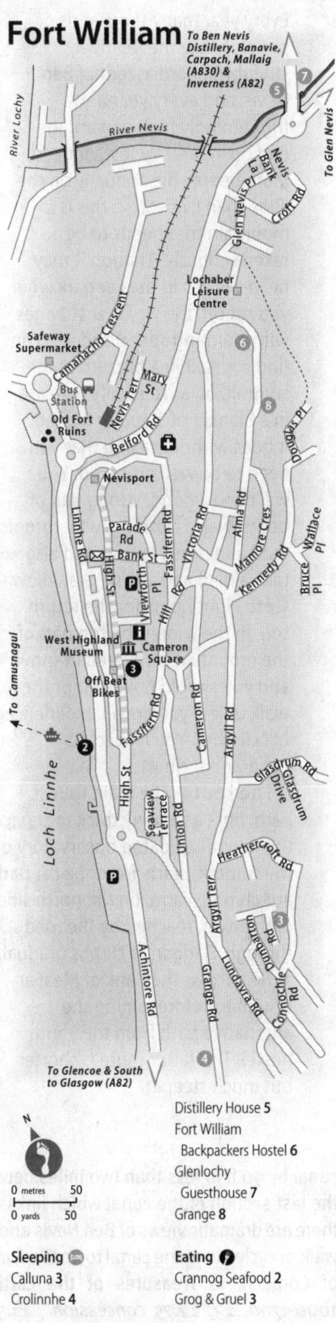

Sights

There's little of real interest in the town, though the **West Highland Museum**, on Cameron Square by the tourist office, is a worthwhile exception, ⓘ *Jun-Sep Mon-Sat 1000-1700; Oct-May 1000-1600; Jul-Aug also Sun 1400-1700, £2, £1.50 concession, £0.50 child, T01397-702169.* It contains excellent exhibits of Jacobite memorabilia and displays on Highland clans and tartans, wildlife and local history. The **Ben Nevis Distillery** ⓘ *T01397-700200, Mon-Fri 0900-1700 (Jul-Aug also Sat 1000-1600), tours £2 per person,* is at Lochy Bridge, at the junction of the A82 to Inverness and the A830 to Mallaig, about a mile north of the town centre. To get there take a Caol or Corpach bus.

Three miles from the town centre along the A830 to Mallaig, in the suburb of Banavie, is **Neptune's Staircase**, a series of eight linked locks on the Caledonian Canal. The locks lower the

Walking up Ben Nevis

Every year many thousands of people make the relatively straightforward ascent of Ben Nevis, and every year a frighteningly high percentage end up injured, or lost, or dead. More people die annually on the 'Ben' than Everest, so this is a mountain that needs to be taken seriously. Though it may be in the 70s in the car park when you set off, the weather changes with alarming speed and you can find yourself in a blizzard at the summit, or, as is usually the case, in a blanket of cloud or hill fog. It goes without saying that you need to be well prepared. You will need a good, strong pair of boots, warm clothing, waterproofs, food and drink. You should also take a map and a compass. Allow six to eight hours for the return trip. In the winter the top part of the mountain is covered in snow and you should not attempt the walk unless you are an experienced hill climber. You'll need OS Landranger No 41.

The route The main tourist path, built as a pony track to service the now-dilapidated observatory on the summit, starts from the car park at Achintee Farm, on the north side of the river, reached by the road through Claggan. It climbs gradually at first across the flank of Meal an t-Suidhe, before joining the alternative path from the youth hostel. This latter route is shorter but much steeper.

The trail continues to climb steadily as it begins to follow the Red Burn, until it reaches a junction, with Lochan Meal an t-Suidhe down to the left. Here, an alternative route down from the summit heads left under the north face of the mountain (see below).This is the halfway point of the main route. The path crosses the Red Burn and then climbs by a series of long and seemingly never-ending zig-zags up to a plateau. The path splits in two, but both paths take you up to the summit, marked by a cairn and emergency shelter, on the ruins of the old observatory. Note that on the upper sloping plateau the path can 'disappear' in mist and snow, and some cairns and beacons have been removed by vandals masquerading as purists. If conditions deteriorate, a compass is a life-saver. There is a shelter on the summit and at least two others on the mountain.

To return simply retrace your steps all the way. If the weather is settled enough and you have time, you can follow the alternative route below the north face. This leads right round the mountain to the Charles Inglis Clark mountain hut, then heads down into the Allt a' Mhuilinn glen which leads all the way down to the distillery on the A82, a mile north of the town centre. Note that this route adds an extra three or four miles to the descent and should only be attempted by fit and experienced hillwalkers.

canal by 90 ft in less than two miles between Loch Lochy and Loch Eil and comprise the last section of the canal which links the North Sea with the Irish Sea. From here there are dramatic views of Ben Nevis and its neighbours behind Fort William. You can walk or cycle along the canal towpath. Further along the A830 to Mallaig, in the village of Corpach, is **Treasures of the Earth**, ⓘ *May-Sep daily 0930-1900; Oct-Apr 1000-1700, £3, £2.75 concession , £1.50 child, T01397-772283*, an exhibition of crystals, gemstones and fossils displayed in a huge simulated cave.

Glen Nevis

Only 10 minutes' drive from Fort William is one of Scotland's great glens, the classic Glen Nevis. The sparkling Water of Nevis tumbles through a wooded gorge, closed in by steep, bracken-covered slopes, with the massive hulk of Ben Nevis watching over. The whole scene is both rugged and sylvan, and the nearest you'll get to a Himalayan valley in the Scottish Highlands.

There are many walks in and around the glen, not least of which is the trek up to the summit of Britain's highest mountain. Aside from the walks described below, there are several easy, marked forest walks which start from the car park at Achriabhach. There are buses into Glen Nevis, as far as the youth hostel, from Fort William bus station (see 'Transport' above).

Sleeping

Many of the B&Bs are in **Corpach** and **Banavie** to the north of town. As a main tourist centre, Fort William gets very busy in the high season and you'll need to book ahead at this time. The tourist office will book a room for you, for a small fee, or you can ask for their free *Fort William & Lochaber Visitor Guide* and phone around yourself.

Achintore Rd, which runs south along the loch, is packed with B&Bs and hotels, many of which are large and characterless. Running parallel is Grange Rd, which is lined with B&B accommodation. Two of the best are A **Crolinnhe**, T01397-702709, open Mar-Nov; and A **The Grange**, T01397-705516, open Mar-Nov.

Fort William *p840, map 841*

L **Inverlochy Castle Hotel**, 3 miles north of town on the A82 to Inverness, T01397-702177, www.inverlochy.co.uk 16 rooms. One of the best hotels in the country, and everything you'd expect to find in a real castle: unsurpassed elegance, impeccable service and superb food (see Eating below), all set in 500 acres of beautiful grounds.

A **The Moorings Hotel**, 3 miles out of town in Banavie, on the road to Corpach and Mallaig, T01397-772797, F01397-772441. 21 rooms. Overlooks 'Neptune's Staircase'; well situated and comfortable with an excellent restaurant.

B **Glenloy Lodge Hotel**, about 6 miles from town on the B8004 north from Banavie, T/F01397-712700. 9 rooms. Open mid-Dec to late Oct. Friendly and comfortable little hotel tucked away in a quiet, secluded location, and with a good restaurant.

B-C **Glenlochy Guesthouse**, Nevis Bridge, North Rd, T01397-702909, is recommended.

C **Distillery House**, across the road from the *Glenlochy Guesthouse* (opposite the road into Glen Nevis), T01397-700103, F01397-702980. 6 rooms. Comfortable, upmarket guesthouse.

E **Fort William Backpackers** is on Alma Rd, 500 yds from the train station, T01397-700711.

E **Calluna**, T01397-700451, www.guide.u.net.com, is at Heathercroft, about a 15-min walk from the tourist office (see map). It's run by experienced mountain guide, Alan Kimber.

E **Scottish International Backpackers** is at Farr Cottage Activity Centre, T01397-772315, www.fort-william.co.uk/farrcottage, which also organizes hill walking trips and rents out mountain bikes.

Glen Nevis *p843*

D **Achintee Farm Guesthouse**, T01397-702240, mcy@btinternet.com, by the start of the path to Ben Nevis. For details of how to get there, see Transport below.

E **SYHA Youth Hostel**, 3 miles out of town in Glen Nevis, near the start of the path up Ben Nevis, T01397-702336, gets very busy in summer. A better bet is the independent E **Ben Nevis Bunkhouse**, at Achintee Farm, across the river from the visitor centre (see above). Two miles up the Glen Nevis Rd is **Glen Nevis Caravan & Camping Park**, T01397-702191, open mid-Mar to late Oct, which has excellent facilities. Five miles from town on the road to Mallaig, is **Linnhe Caravan & Chalet Park**, T01397-772376, open Christmas to late Oct, also with full facilities.

Eating

Fort William *p840, map 841*

£££ Inverlochy Castle (see above). It's expensive but the food is superb and the surroundings are the last word in grandeur. Open daily 1230-1345, 1900-2115.

££ Crannog Seafood Restaurant, on the Town Pier, T01397-705589, crannogallan@msn.com Housed in an old smokehouse, the seafood is as fresh as you can get and the surroundings are unpretentious. It gets very busy and service can be slow, so book ahead and take your time (lunch cheap to mid-range; dinner mid-range).

££ An Crann, 4 miles from town, take the A830 to Mallaig, then turn right to Banavie on the B8004, T01397-772077. This converted barn is a local favourite and offers good Scottish cooking in a friendly atmosphere. Lunch 1230-1500, dinner 1700-2100, closed Sun. Open late Mar to mid-Oct.

£ The Grog & Gruel, 66 High St, T01397-705078, is a pub-cum-restaurant offering good-value pizza, pasta and Tex Mex, and a wide range of superb cask ales. Open till 2400/0100.

Glen Nevis *p843*

££ Glen Nevis Restaurant, near the SYHA hostel, T01397-705459, serves a cheap to mid-range 2-course lunch and mid-range 3-course dinner. Open 1200-2200, Apr-Oct.

Café Beag, T01397-703601, nearby, is a cosy place with log fire. Good vegetarian food.

Activities and tours

Canoeing

There are several rivers around Fort William, ranging in difficulty from Grade 1 to 6. Canoe courses are run by **Snowgoose Mountain Centre**, which is attached to **The Smiddy Bunkhouse** (see 'Sleeping' above). The **Nevis Canoe Club**, T01397-705388, are useful.

Fishing

Torlundy Trout Fishery, at Torlundy Farm in Tomacharich, 3 miles north off the A82, T01397-703015, has 3 lakes filled with rainbow trout and hires out rods. Pony trekking from £15/hr, book in advance.

Hiking and climbing

Fort William is a mecca for hikers and climbers. For information on the climb up Ben Nevis and walks around Glen Nevis, see page 843. If you want to hire a guide, try **Lochaber Walks**, 22 Zetland Av, T01397-703828; **Fort William Mountain Guides**, T01397-700451; **Alba Walking Holidays**, T01397-704964; and **Snowgoose Mountain Centre** (see 'Sleeping' above). Fort William has 2 excellent outdoor activity equipment shops: **Nevisport**, T01397-704921, is on the High St, and has a huge selection of books, maps and guides, a bureau de change and bar-restaurant. At the other end of the High St is **West Coast Outdoor Sports**, T01397-705777. There's an indoor climbing wall at the **Lochaber Leisure Centre** (see below).

Mountain biking

The Leanachan Forest, below Aonach Mhor, is 4 miles north of Fort William. Access is via the road to the Aonach Mhor ski development. The forest covers a huge area with 25 miles of mountain bike trails, ranging from easy to demanding. There is also the **Great Glen Cycle Route**, which is mainly off-road and runs all the way from Fort William to Inverness. For the hire, sale or repair of bikes, and good advice on local cycle routes, visit **Off Beat Bikes**, 117 High St, and at the Nevis Range Ski Centre, T01397-704008, www.offbeatbikes.co.uk, open only Jul-Aug.

Skiing

Nevis Range Ski Centre, 4 miles northeast of Fort William at Torlundy, is situated on the mountain of Aonach Mhor (4,006 ft). It's Scotland's highest skiing and snowboarding area and has the longest ski season, running from Christmas to May. It also boasts the country's only cable-car system, built in 1989. The 1½ mile gondola ride is a popular attraction not only with skiers and snowboarders in the winter but also during the summer off-season period, when it's used by hill walkers to gain easy access to the mountains. For most tourists, though, it's an easy way to climb to over 2,000 ft and enjoy the wonderful views from the terrace of the self-service restaurant at the top. There are ski and snowboarding schools and also a dry slope for summer skiing in July and August (open

Sun-Thu 1100-1230, £18 including gondola). The gondola is open all year, except early Nov to the week before Christmas, 1000-1700 (Jul-Aug 0930-1800, Thu-Fri till 2100), T01397-705825, www.ski.scotland.net

Transport

Bus

Local There are buses every 10-20 mins to and from **Caol** and Corpach, and every hour on Sun and in the evening. There is an hourly service to **Glen Nevis**, Mon-Sat from 0800-2300, Jun to Sep only (less frequent on Sun). There are 4 buses daily to **Aonach Mhor** during the ski season.

Bus

Long distance There are several daily Citylink buses to **Inverness** (1 hr, £7.40); to **Oban** (1¾ hrs, £6.90) via **Glencoe** (30 mins); and to **Uig** (3½ hrs, £17), via **Portree** and **Kyle of Lochalsh** (1 hr 50 mins). Citylink buses also go several times daily to **Glasgow** (3¼ hrs, £11.80), via Glencoe and Tyndrum, and to **Edinburgh** (4 hrs, £16.50), via **Stirling** (3 hrs, £12.90). There is a bus to **Mallaig** (1½ hrs, £4) daily except Sun with **Shiel Buses**, T01967-431272. **Highland Country Buses**, T702373, run several times a day to **Kinlochleven** (50 mins) via Glencoe. There is a postbus service (Mon-Sat) to **Glen Etive**.

Ferry

There is a passenger-only ferry service to **Camusnagaul**, on the opposite bank of Loch Linnhe, from the Town Pier. It sails several times daily (Mon-Sat) and takes 10 mins. For times etc contact Highland Council, T01463-702695, or ask at the tourist office.

Train

There are 2-3 trains daily from Glasgow to **Fort William** (3¾ hrs) via Crianlarich. They continue to Mallaig (a further 1 hr 20 mins) where they connect with ferries to Armadale on Skye. There are no direct trains to Oban; you need to change at Crianlarich. There is a sleeper service from London Euston (see Essentials chapter), but you'll miss the views.

Directory

Car hire Easydrive, at Lochy Bridge, T01397-701616; **Volkswagen Rental**, at Nevis Garage, Argour Rd, Caol, T01397-702432; **Budget**, at North Rd, T01397-702500, or **Practical Car & Van Hire**, at Slipway Autos, Corpach, T01397-772404. Prices start from around £35 per day.

Internet The library on the High St offers free **internet** access. Otherwise there's Thing King, on High St, £1.50/15 mins

Fort William to Glen Coe

→*Colour map 6*

Few places, if any, can compare to the truly awesome scenery of Glen Coe. No one could fail to be moved by its haunting beauty, with imposing mountains, their tops often wreathed in cloud, rising steeply on either side from the valley floor. The brooding atmosphere of the landscape is only enhanced by the glen's tragic history. Once you've heard of the Glen Coe Massacre it sends a shiver down the spine every time you pass this way. ▸▸ *For Sleeping, Eating and other listings, see pages 847-848.*

Ins and outs

Getting there Highland Country Buses, T01397-702373, runs 6 times a day (Mon-Sat) between Fort William and Kinlochleven (50 mins). **Highland Country Buses** run several times daily from **Fort William** to Glencoe village (30 mins). **Citylink** buses to **Glasgow** (2 ½ hrs) and **Fort William.** The daily *postbus* from **Fort William** to the **Kingshouse Hotel** and **Glen Etive** stops at the Glencoe crossroads.

Information Ballachulish Tourist Information Centre is in the car park off the main road, ⓘ T801855-11296, Apr-Oct daily.

Kinlochleven and Ballachulish

The B863 turns east off the A82 at North Ballachulish and heads to Kinlochleven, at the head of Loch Leven. It can also be reached on the same road from Glencoe village, seven miles west. It's an unlikely place to find a huge aluminium factory, but it kept the village alive for many years. Now, though, it's threatened with closure and there's talk of Kinlochleven being developed as a major mountaineering centre. You can find out all about the long and often tragic history of aluminium-working in Lochaber at **The Aluminium Story**, in the Kinlochleven Visitor Centre and Library on Linnhe Road, ⓘ *Apr-Oct Tue-Fri 1030-1800, Sat-Sun 1100-1500, free, T01855-831663.*

The West Highland Way passes through the village and many walkers spend the night here before setting out on the last stretch before Fort William. There are also several good walks in the surrounding hills and glens. A fairly easy but rewarding half-day walk is to follow the **West Highland Way** south from the village to the top of the **Devil's Staircase**, where it meets the A82 at the eastern end of Glen Coe. The route starts from the British Aluminium Visitor Centre, runs around the side of the aluminium factory, then crosses a wooden bridge and climbs gradually on a dirt jeep-track up to Penstock House, at 1,000 ft. At the top, near the house, the track forks to the right and continues on a rough footpath to the **Devil's Staircase**. The path is marked with the West Highland Way thistle sign, so it's easy to follow uphill to the top of the pass (1,804 ft), from where you get great views of Loch Eilde Mór and the Mamores to the north. The path then descends down the staircase to Glen Coe, with breathtaking Buachaille Etive Mór in front of you all the way. You'll have to return to Kinlochleven by the same route, or you could carry on to the *Kingshouse Hotel* (see below). The return trip from Kinlochleven should take four to five hours, or you can start out from Glencoe (see below). OS Landranger No 41 covers the route.

Glen Coe

Scotland's most famous glen is also one of the most accessible, with the A82 Glasgow to Fort William road running through it. Much of the area is owned by the National Trust for Scotland and virtually uninhabited, leaving huge tracts of glen and mountain which provide outstanding climbing and walking. There's also skiing at the Glencoe Ski Centre (see below), and canoeing on the River Coe and River Etive. There's a small **National Trust for Scotland Visitor Centre** , ⓘ *Early Apr to mid-May and early Sep to end Oct daily 1000-1700; mid-May to end Aug 0930-1730, 50p, T01855-811307*, at the western end of the glen, about three miles south of Glencoe village. It shows a short video on the Glencoe Massacre and has a gift shop selling the usual stuff

At the western entrance to the glen, on the shores of Loch Leven, is Glencoe village, 16 miles south of Fort William just off the A82. There are several places to stay in and around the village, as well as a general store, post office and the thatched **Glencoe Folk Museum**, ⓘ*Late May to Sep 1000-1730, £1.50*, which has collections of costumes, military memorabilia, and domestic and farm tools and equipment.

Climbing and hiking in Glen Coe → *OS Landranger No 41*

Glen Coe offers some of Britain's most challenging climbing and hiking, with some notoriously treacherous routes and unpredictable weather conditions that claim lives every year. The routes described below are some of the least strenuous, but you'll still need a map, good boots, warm clothing, food and water, and you should take the usual precautions.

One of the most popular walks is the relatively straightforward hike up to the **Lost Valley**, a secret glen where the ill-fated MacDonalds hid the cattle they'd stolen. Allow around three hours for the return trip. Start from the car park by the large boulder, opposite the distinctive **Three Sisters**. Head down to the valley floor and follow the gravel path which leads down to a wooden bridge across the River Coe. Cross the bridge and follow the path up and over the stile. From here there's a choice of two routes. The less obvious route heads right and offers an easier climb into the valley. This eventually meets the lower, well-worn track, which involves a bit of scrambling but is more exciting as it follows the rushing waters of the **Allt Coire Gabhail**. The upper and lower paths meet a few miles further up and here you cross the river by some stepping stones. Proceed up the steep scree slope till you reach the rim of the Lost Valley, where many of the MacDonalds fled on the night of the infamous massacre. Once in the valley there are great views of **Bidean nam Bian**, **Gearr Aonach** and **Beinn Fhada** and you can continue for a further 20-30 minutes to the head of the valley. From here it's possible to climb Bidean, but you'll need to be fit, experienced and well equipped.

Glen Coe also offers one of the world's classic ridge walks, the **Aonach Eagach**. It's not for the inexperienced or faint-hearted as there are some fairly exposed pinnacles. The ridge runs almost the entire length of the glen, starting at **Am Bodach** and ending at **Sgor nam Fiannaidh**. Don't make the mistake of descending from the last summit straight down to the Clachaig Inn. This is not the correct route.

Another difficult route is to the summit of **Buachaille Etive Mór**, one of the most photographed mountains in Scotland and one you'll probably recognize immediately the first time you see it from the A82 on the way to or from Glencoe. The mountain is best viewed from the *Kingshouse Hotel* and the route starts from Altnafeadh, a couple of miles west of the hotel. This is also the start or finish point for the fairly easy half-day walk over the **Devil's Staircase**, which is part of the **West Highland Way** (for a description of the route, see page 846).

Glen Etive runs southwest from the hotel. It's a very beautiful and little-visited place, and great for wild camping. There's a postbus service once a day from Fort William.

Finally, there are some short, pleasant walks around **Glencoe Lochan**, an artificial loch created in the mid-19th century by Lord Strathcona for his homesick Canadian wife. Take the left turning off the minor road to the youth hostel just beyond the bridge over the River Coe. There's a choice of three walks of between 40 minutes and an hour, all detailed at the car park.

Sleeping

Kinlochleven and Ballachulish *p846*

L **The Isles of Glencoe Hotel**, T01855-811602, reservations@mysteryworld.co.uk. 39 rooms. A modern hotel and leisure complex next to Highland Mysteryworld. Excellent location on the shores of the loch, and facilities include heated pool, sauna and gym. The restaurant serves a mid-range to cheap 3-course lunch and expensive to mid-range 3-course dinner.

L **Ballachulish Hotel**, in South Ballachulish by the bridge, T01855-821582, reservations @mysteryworld.co.uk. 54 rooms. Grand old hotel, handily placed for Glen Coe, Fort William or Oban; restaurant serves meals all day (3-course lunch mid-range to cheap; 3-course dinner expensive).

L **Ballachulish House**, T01855-811266, F01855-811498, open Mar-Oct. 7 rooms. 200 yd beyond the *Ballachulish Hotel* on the A828 to Oban. This comfortable and elegant hotel/guesthouse is steeped in history and said to be the most haunted house in Scotland. The seat of the Stewarts of Ballachulish since the 16th century, this was where the final order for the Glencoe Massacre was signed (see below). Hospitality is second-to-none and the food is superb; even if you're not staying you can enjoy the experience of dining here , but book. There's also a wide selection of cheaper B&Bs and guesthouses in the village, including D **Fern Villa**, T01855-811393.

Glencoe *p846*

C **Clachaig Inn**, 3 miles south of the village, on the old road which leads from the village to the NTS visitor centre, T01855-811252, inn@glencoe-scotland.co.uk. 19 rooms. Good-value accommodation and one of the great Highland pubs. It's a favourite haunt of climbers and there's a lively atmosphere as well as some fine real ales and decent cheap food. There are also 3 chalets which can be rented on a weekly basis (phone for details), and mountain bike hire (see below).

On the same road, about 2 miles from the village, is the excellent

E **SYHA Youth Hostel**, T01855-811219. It's open all year and is very popular with climbers, so you should book ahead. Nearby are the

E **Leacantium Farm Bunkhouses**, T01855-811256, which offer cheap, basic accommodation in 2 bunkhouses and an alpine barn. The same people also run the **Red Squirrel Campsite** further along the road, which charges £3.50 per person per night.

C **Kingshouse Hotel**, T01855-851259, at the east end of the glen, almost opposite the turn-off to the Glencoe Ski Centre. 22 rooms. This is Scotland's oldest established inn and such a landmark that it even appears on maps, marked as 'hotel'. It's on the West Highland Way and is popular with hikers, climbers and skiers.

Activities and tours

Climbing

Mountain guides includes Hadrian Mountaineering, 19b Carnoch, T/F01855-811472, www.glencoe-mountain-sport.co.uk. Glencoe Guides, T01855-811402. Dave Hanna, Ardarroch, Ballachulish, T01855-811620.

Outdoor activities

Alfresco Adventure, T01855-821248, just to the east of North Ballachulish on the B863 to Kinlochleven, offers boat hire and various outdoor activities such as mountain biking and canoeing.

Skiing

Glencoe Ski Centre, just over a mile from the Kingshouse Hotel, on the other side of the A82, on Meall A'Bhuiridh (3,636 ft). This is Scotland's oldest ski centre, established in 1956, and remains one of the best, with the longest single descent. The chair lift operates daily 0930-1700. A full day pass, including lifts, costs £17 (children £9.50). There's also a combined five-day pass for Glencoe and Nevis Range. T01855-851226, www.ski.scotland.net

Directory

Cycle hire Glencoe Mountain Bike Centre at the Clachaig Inn (see above); £12 for a full day, £8 for a half day.

Ardgour, Ardnamurchan and Morvern

→*Colour map 6*

West of Fort William is one of the most remote parts of the Highland region, stretching south from **Loch Ailort** *to the* **Morvern Peninsula**, *and west to the wild and beautiful* **Ardnamurchan Peninsula**. *This lonely, southwestern corner features a dramatic landscape of rugged mountains, desolate moorland and near-deserted glens, fringed by a coastline of sparkling white beaches and clear turquoise seas with wonderful views across to the isles of Mull and Skye. This is one of the least-populated areas in Britain, mainly due to the legacy of the Highland Clearances in the mid-19th century, when whole communities were evicted by landlords in favour of more profitable sheep.*

With so few people around, this is an area noted for its wildlife, with a huge variety of birds and animals. If you have both the time and the energy, it's worth exploring on foot. There's are footpaths throughout the area, particularly around Ardnamurchan. ▸▸ *For Sleeping and other listings, see page 850.*

Ins and outs

Getting there This is an area of few roads. Once you leave the A830 Fort William to Mallaig road, **buses** are few and far between, so it's not easy to get around quickly without your own transport. *Shiel Buses*, T01967-431272, run most of the bus services. There's a bus once a day on Tue, Thu and Sat from Fort William to Lochaline (2 hrs), via the **Corran Ferry.** There's a bus once a day (Mon-Sat) from Fort William to Acharacle (1 hr 30 mins), via Lochailort. There's also a bus (Mon-Fri) to Acharacle from Mallaig (1 hr 30 mins). There's a bus once a day (Mon-Sat) from Fort William to Kilchoan (2 hrs 25 mins), via Strontian (1 hr), Salen and Glenborrodale.

Getting around For details of the **ferry** from Lochaline to Fishnish on Mull and from Kilchoan to Tobermory, see page 753. If you're travelling by **car**, access is via the A861, leaving the A830 before Glenfinnan or at Lochailort. You can also make the 5-min ferry crossing to Ardgour from the Corran Ferry, about 8 miles south of Fort William on the A82, see page 849. Those intending to get around in foot should have OS Map numbers 40, 47 and 49, which cover the area.

Information There are **Tourist Information Centres** in **Strontian** (T402131) and **Kilchoan** (T510222), both open Easter-Oct.

Ardgour and Morvern

The name Ardgour means 'height of the goats', and you can still see feral goats in this huge, sparsely populated wilderness bordered by Loch Shiel, Loch Eil, Loch Linnhe and Loch Sunart. Access is via the A861 south from Kinlocheil, or on the Corran Ferry to the tiny lochside villages of **Corran** and **Clovulin**. The attractive little village of Strontian, on the shores of Loch Sunart, is the largest settlement in these parts and has a couple of shops, a post office and TIC.

Just east of Strontian the A884 leads south through the bleak, desolate landscape of Morvern to the tiny remote community of **Lochaline** on the Sound of Mull, departure point for the *CalMac* ferry to **Fishnish**. About three miles before Lochaline is the turning left for the track which leads down the side of Loch Aline to the 14th-century ruins of **Ardtornish Castle**. First you'll come to **Kinlochaline Castle** (keys available at the cottage) and **Ardtornish House.** This house stands on the site of the original house, which was visited on several occasions by Florence Nightingale, who was a family member of the original owners. The author John Buchan spent many summers here in the 1930s.

Ardnamurchan Peninsula

The main places of interest in this area are to be found on the rugged Ardnamurchan peninsula, the end of which is the most westerly point on the British mainland. The winding A861 runs west from Strontian along the north shore of Loch Sunart to **Salen,** where the single-track B8007 branches west and runs all the way out to the tip of the peninsula. The A861 meanwhile turns north to **Acharacle.**

The first settlement you reach heading west out to Ardnamurchan Point is **Glenborrodale**. Before you reach the tiny hamlet look out on the left for the castellated late-Victorian towers of Glenborrodale Castle, once the property of a certain Jesse Boot, who founded a chain of chemist shops which you may have heard of. Just west of Glenborrodale is the excellent **Glenmore Natural History Centre** ⓘ *Apr-Oct 1030-1730 (Sun 1200-1730), £2.50, concession £2, children £1.50, T01972-500254*, local photographer Michael McGregor's interactive exhibition which features some of his most stunning photographs of local wildlife. The centre is designed to interact with the environment and there's live video action of the surrounding wildlife, including pine martens, birds and even fish in the nearby river. It's a great place for kids, and adults too. There's also a café serving snacks, and a bookshop.

A mile to the east is the **RSPB Reserve** where you can see golden eagles, otters and seals. You can take a two-hour wildlife trip to the **seal colonies** – or further afield to Tobermory on Mull or Staffa and the Treshnish Islands – with **Ardnamurchan Charters** ⓘ *T01972-500208, or T01967-431263*.

A few miles west of the centre, the B8007 turns away from the coast. Here you'll see the bay of **Camas nan Geall**. Between Glenborrodale and Kilchoan, a road runs to the north coast of the peninsula and the beautiful beaches at **Fascadale**, **Kilmory** and **Ockle**. The straggling crofting village of Kilchoan is the main settlement on Ardnamurchan. Shortly after passing the sign for the village, you can turn left to the scenic ruin of **Mingary Castle**, built around the 13th century. A car and passenger **ferry** leaves Kilchoan for Tobermory on Mull (see page 753).

Beyond Kilchoan the road leads to the **lighthouse** at mainland Britain's most westerly point, with views across to the small isles of Rùm, Eigg, Muck and Canna, with the Cuillins of Skye rising behind Rùm. The former lighthouse was designed the father of Robert Louis Stevenson, and built in 1849. The buildings have been converted into the **Ardnamurchan Visitor Centre** ⓘ *1 Apr-31 Oct daily from 1000-1800 (1700 in Oct), £2.50, concession/children £1.50, T01972-510210.* where you can learn about the history and workings of lighthouses. There's also accommodation, a café and gift shop.

A mile northwest of Kilchoan a road branches to the right to the long, white beach at **Sanna Bay**. It's worth making the trip here to walk on the beach, but this is also a good place to spot whales and dolphins. On the road to Sanna Bay is the tiny settlement of **Achnaha**, which is famed for its rare natural rock formation which is the crater of an extinct volcano. You'll need your own transport to reach Ardnamurchan Point and Sanna Bay as there are no buses beyond Kilchoan (see 'Getting around' page 849).

North of Salen on the A861 is the scattered crofting township of Acharacle, at the western end of Loch Shiel surrounded by rolling hills. A couple of miles to the west a road leads to beautiful **Kentra Bay**. Cross the wooden bridge, follow the footpath round the side of Kentra Bay and then follow the signs for Gortenfearn, where you'll find the famous **'singing sands'**. Not only is the beach music to the ears as you walk its length, but the view across to Skye and the small isles is a feast for the eyes.

Three miles north of Acharacle is **Loch Moidart**. Here, perched on a rocky promontory in the middle of the loch, is the 13th-century ruin of **Castle Tioram** (pronounced 'Cheerum'). This was the seat of the MacDonalds of Clanranald, until it was destroyed by their chief in 1715 to prevent it from falling into Hanoverian hands while he was away fighting for the Jacobites. There are plans to restore the castle, but you can visit it (free) via the sandy causeway that connects it to the mainland at low tide.

Sleeping

Ardgour and Morvern *p849*

L-A **Kilcamb Lodge Hotel**, Strontian, T01967-402257, F402041, open Mar-Nov, stands in its own grounds on the lochside and serves superb food.

Ardnamurchan Peninsula *p849*

A **Far View Cottage**, Kilchoan, T01972-510357, www.ardnamurchan.com/farview. Mar-Nov. Superior and friendly B&B with great views and excellent food.

A **Meall Mo Chridhe**, Kilchoan, T/F01972-510328. Open Apr-Oct. Great sea views and fine cooking. Full board also available (A). Dinner available for non-residents (expensive), but booking essential.

B **Loch Shiel House Hotel**, Acharacle, T01972-431224, F431200. 10 rooms. Comfortable and decent bar meals (cheap lunch; mid-range to cheap dinner). Contact them for details of cruises on Loch Shiel. A couple of good B&Bs in Acharacle are B **Belmont House**, T01972-431266; and C-D **Ardshealach House**, T01972-431301; open Apr-Sep. About 5 miles east of the village, on a side road off the A861 north to Lochailort and Mallaig, is the very beautiful C **Dalilea House**, T01972-431253; open Apr-Oct.

Activities and tours

Outdoor activities

From Dalilea Pier you can cross to The **Achnanellan Centre**, T01967-431265, an outdoor activities centre on the south shore of Loch Shiel at the foot of Beinn Resipol (2,772 ft). They hire out mountain bikes, canoes, sail boats and camping equipment, as well as providing cheap, basic bunkhouse accommodation (F).

The Road to the Isles

→ *Colour map 6*

The 46-mile stretch of the A830 from Fort William to Mallaig is known as 'The Road to the Isles'. It's a very beautiful journey, particularly by train, through a landscape that resonates with historical significance. This is Bonnie Prince Charlie country, where the ill-fated Jacobite Rising not only began, but also ended, with the Prince's flight to France. ▸▸ *For Sleeping and Eating see page 854.*

Ins and outs

Getting there Shiel Buses, T01967-431272, run 2 **buses** daily Mon-Sat from Mallaig to **Fort William** (1½ hrs, £4.50) from Jul-Sep, and on Mon, Thu and Fri the rest of the year. CalMac, T01687-462403, **ferries** run throughout the year to **Armadale** on Skye (see page 884) to **Lochboisdale** and **Castlebay** (see page 898), and to the **Small Isles** (see page 851). **Bruce Watt Sea Cruises,** T01687-462320, have trips to the remote village of **Inverie**, on the Knoydart Peninsula (see below), and **Tarbet** on Loch Nevis (see above). They sail on Mon, Wed and Fri throughout the year, departing at 1015 (to Inverie only) and 1415, and returning at 1155 and 1745. They also sail on Sat during Jun-Aug to Inverie, departing at 1030 and returning at 1215. The best way to arrive in Mallaig is by **train.** There are several services daily (1 on Sun) to and from **Fort William,** with connections to **Glasgow.** There's also a steam train which runs in the summer months (see page 852).

Getting around The only way to reach the Knoydart Peninsula in is by boat or on foot. A 2-day **hiking** route starts from Kinloch Hourn, reached by bus from Invergarry (see page 839). The trail winds its way around the coast to Barrisdale and on to Inverie. Another route into Knoydart starts from the west end of Loch Arkaig and runs through Glen Dessarry. Both are tough hikes and only for fit, experienced and well-equipped hill walkers. An easier way in is by **boat**. (see above). There's also a ferry service from **Arnisdale,** on the north shore of Loch Hourn, to Barrisdale. To arrange a crossing, contact Len Morrison, Croftfoot, Arnisdale, T01599-522352. It's a small open boat which takes 5 passengers, and all sailings are subject to weather.

Information **Mallaig Tourist Information Centre** is by the harbour, ⓘ *T01687-462170. Apr-Oct Mon-Sat 0900-2000, Sun 1000-1700; Nov-Mar Mon, Tue, Fri 1100-1500.*

Sights

Glenfinnan

The Jacobite Rebellion started on 19 August 1745 at Glenfinnan, 19 miles west of Fort William at the head of Loch Shiel. Less than a month earlier, Prince Charles Edward Stuart had landed on the Scottish mainland for the first time, to claim the British throne for his father, James, son of the exiled King James VII of Scotland and II of England.

There's a powerful sense of history here. A commemorative **tower** stands proudly at the head of the loch, erected in 1815 by Alexander MacDonald of Glenaladale in memory of the clansmen who fought and died for the Prince. You can climb to the top of the tower (mind your head, though) for even better views down the loch. The Glenfinnan Games are held here in mid-August.

On the other side of the road is the **National Trust for Scotland visitor centre,** ⓘ *1 Apr-18 May and 1 Sep-31 Oct daily 1000-1700; 19 May-31 Aug 0930-1800, adult £1.50, concession £1, T01397-722250,* which has displays and an audio programme of the Prince's campaign, from Glenfinnan to its grim conclusion at Culloden. There's also a café.

Riding the rails

Running from Glasgow to Mallaig via Fort William, the West Highland Railway is only 164 miles long but is widely acknowledged as one of the most scenic railway journeys in the world. The great thing about this journey is its variety, taking you from the distinctive red tenements of Glasgow and the former shipbuilding areas of the River Clyde, to the windy wilderness of Rannoch Moor and the chilly splendour of the hills. It's about an hour after leaving Glasgow that you get your first taste of highland scenery when the train hugs the eastern bank of sinewy Loch Long. Then it's on past the 'bonnie banks' of Loch Lomond, Britain's largest body of inland water. It's impossible not to pass this serene loch without thinking of the famous ballad about two Jacobite soldiers captured after the '45 rebellion. The soldier taking 'the low road' is due to be executed, his companion taking the 'high road' is due to be released.

After Ardlui, at the top of Loch Lomond, the countryside gets more rugged. Wherever you look you see something of interest: a waterfall gushing down a hillside, a buzzard surfing on the breeze – perhaps a herd of Highland Cattle wallowing in a river. The West Highland Way, the long distance footpath from Glasgow to Fort William, is close to the line now and at stations such as Crianlarich, Upper Tyndrum and Bridge of Orchy you can often spot footsore walkers with muddy boots – who get on the train looking slightly guilty and collapse on their seats with sighs of relief.

The landscape gets wilder and bleaker as the railway crosses the lonely, peaty wastes of Rannoch Moor and on to Corrour, which featured in the film version of Irvine Welsh's cult book Trainspotting. Then you descend to the lusher country around Tulloch, before pulling in to Fort William. This is a popular visitor centre as it's close to Ben Nevis, Britain's highest mountain, and beautiful Glen Nevis, which has featured in films such as Braveheart and Rob Roy. Now comes the most spectacular part of the journey, for the West Highland Line leaves the best 'till last. Leaving Fort William, the train crosses Thomas Telford's Caledonian Canal – where you can see an impressive series of eight locks known as 'Neptune's Staircase' – hugs the shore of Loch Eil, then crosses the magnificent Glenfinnan Viaduct, a masterpiece in concrete. You soon get superb views of the evocative Glenfinnan Monument that commemorates the start of the 1745 rebellion, before pulling in to Glenfinnan Station. The train now takes you through a landscape of craggy hills and glacial lochs etched with birch and pine trees. You pass Loch nan Uamh, from where Bonnie Prince Charlie fled for France after his defeat at Culloden, then draw in to Arisaig, the birthplace of the man who inspired RL Stevenson's Long John Silver. Next is beautiful Loch Morar, Britain's deepest inland loch and home – so legend has it – to a mysterious monster. Soon you get views across the water to the islands of Eigg and Rhum, before finally pulling in to the port of Mallaig.

Arisaig was the birthplace of Long John Silver, who worked on the construction of one of the many lighthouses designed by Stevenson's father. Silver so impressed the young writer that he immortalized him in his classic novel Treasure Island.

A mile away, in Glenfinnan village, is the **Station Museum**, ⓘ *Apr-Oct daily 0930-1630, £0.50, T01397-722295*, which is housed in the railway station on the magnificent Fort-William to Mallaig railway line. It has displays of memorabilia from the line's 100-year history. . You can also sleep and eat here (see below). The 1,000-ft span of the **Glenfinnan viaduct**, between the visitor centre and the village, is one of the most spectacular sections of the famous **West Highland Railway** (see page 852) and was recently made famous by its appearance in *Harry Potter and the Chamber of Secrets*.

You can take a cruise down Loch Shiel, from Glenfinnan to Acharacle (see above) at its southern end. Contact *Loch Shiel Cruises* at the *Glenfinnan House Hotel* (see below). There are sailings most days from April to October.

Arisaig and Morar

At the western end of the Morar Peninsula is the little village of Arisaig, scattered round a sandy bay. There are some nice beaches around, and the road west from the village out to the **Rhue Peninsula** is great for seal spotting. You can also take a **cruise** from Arisaig to the islands of **Rùm, Eigg and Muck.** ⓘ *There are sailings daily Mon-Fri, and also Sat-Sun during the summer months. For details contact Murdo Grant, T450224.*

Between Arisaig and Morar is a string of glorious beaches of white sand backed by beautiful machair, washed by turquoise seas and enjoying magnificent views across to Rùm and the Cuillins of Skye. This is one of the most stunning stretches of coastline in Britain, despite the presence of too many ugly holiday bungalows and caravan sites. Eight miles north of Arisaig is **Morar,** where the famous beach scenes from the movie *Local Hero* were filmed – with not a caravan in sight.

This coastline gets very busy in summer but, like so much of the Highlands, it's easy to get away from it all. A single-track road leads up behind the village of Morar to dark, mysterious **Loch Morar**, the deepest inland loch in the country and home of Morag, Scotland's other, lesser-known monster. You could always try to elicit further information from the locals over a wee dram in the bar of the *Morar Hotel.*

Mallaig

The end of the road is Mallaig, a busy fishing port and main departure point for the ferry to Skye. It's not a particularly appealing place, but it's always busy with people waiting for the ferry or the train to Fort William. The train and bus stations and *CalMac* ferry office are all within a few yards of each other.

If you have some time to kill you could visit **Mallaig Marine World,** ⓘ *Jun-Sep Mon-Sat 0900-2100, Sun 1000-1800; Oct-May Mon-Sat 1200-1730, £2.75, children £1.35, T01687-462292*, an aquarium with indigenous marine creatures as well as displays on the history of the local fishing industry.Beside the train station is the **Mallaig Heritage Centre,** ⓘ *May-Sep Mon-Sat 0930-1700, Sun 1300-1700, £1.80, children £1*, with interesting descriptions of the local Clearances, the railway line and the fishing industry.

Knoydart Peninsula

The Knoydart Peninsula, the most remote and unspoilt region in Britain and one of Europe's last great wildernesses, literally lies between Heaven and Hell, for it is bordered to the north by **Loch Hourn** ('Loch of Hell') and to the south by **Loch Nevis** ('Loch of Heaven'). It can only be reached on foot or by boat and consequently attracts walkers, who can wander for days around a network of trails without seeing another soul. The peninsula's only settlement of any size is tiny **Inverie**, with just 60 inhabitants. It's the only village in Scotland which can't be reached by road, but still has a post office, a shop, a few places to stay and Britain's most remote pub.

Sleeping

Glenfinnan *p851*

A **The Prince's House**, on the main road, half a mile past the monument on the right, heading west, T01397-722246, princeshouse@glenfinnan.co.uk. 9 rooms, open Mar-Nov. Comfortable old coaching inn which offers good food (mid-range).

A-B **Glenfinnan House Hotel**, T/F01397-722235. 17 rooms, open Apr-Oct. Historic house with lots of charm, which is more than can be said for the staff. Dinner served from 1930 (expensive to mid-range for 4 courses). You can also walk in the vast grounds or fish on the loch.

E **Glenfinnan Sleeping Car**, at the train station, T01397-722400. Bunkhouse accommodation for 10 people, also mountain bike hire. You can eat here, too, in the **Glenfinnan Dining Car** (cheap 2-course lunch; mid-range 3-course dinner).

Arisaig and Morar *p853*

A **Arisaig Hotel**, T01687-450210, arisaighotel@dial.pipex.com. They serve moderately priced food 1200-1400 and 1800-2100. A good restaurant is **The Old Library Lodge**, T01687-450651, open Apr-Oct, which also has rooms (**A**).

Mallaig *p853*

B **Marine Hotel**, T01687-462217, Marinehotel@btinternet. Next to the train station and much nicer inside than it appears. Their restaurant also serves the best food in town (mid-range). Follow the road round the harbour to East Bay, where you'll find the excellent-value

D-E **Western Isles Guesthouse**, T/F01687-462320, open Jan-Nov, which serves dinner to guests. Nearby is

D **Glencairn**, T01687-462412, open Apr-Sep.

E **Sheena's Backapackers Lodge**, T01687-462764, a friendly, easy-going independent hostel, with dorm beds, double rooms and kitchen facilities.

Knoydart *p853*

A **Doune Stone Lodge**, 3 or 4 miles up the peninsula's only road, T01687-462667. Highly recommended and standing in splendid isolation. The minimum stay is 3 nights as guests are picked up from Mallaig by boat.

B **Pier House**, Inverie, T01687-462347, offers good, old-fashioned hospitality and wonderful local seafood (mid-range prices).

E **Torrie Shieling**, T01687-462669. It's a bit more expensive than most other hostels, but is very comfortable, and popular with hikers. They also have their own transport for trips around the peninsula and will collect guests from Mallaig by arrangement.

Eating

Knoydart *p853*

££ **The Old Forge**, T01687-462267, the most remote pub on mainland Britain. You can enjoy some tasty local seafood and a pint of real ale in front of an open fire. There's even the occasional impromptu ceilidh.

The Great Glen to Kyle of Lochalsh

→ *Colour map 6*

The A87 is one of the main Highland tourist routes, connecting the Great Glen with the west coast and the Isle of Skye. It runs west from Invergarry between Fort Augustus and Fort William, through Glen Moriston and Glen Shiel to Shiel Bridge, at the head of Loch Duich, and on to Kyle. At Shiel Bridge a road branches off to Glenelg, from where you can sail across to Skye. It's a beautiful journey and by far the best way to reach the island. ▸▸ *For Sleeping, Eating and other listings, see pages 856-857.*

Ins and outs

Getting there **Scottish Citylink** buses run to Kyle of Lochalsh from **Inverness, Glasgow** via **Fort William** and **Edinburgh** via Fort William. These buses continue to **Portree** (a further hour) and **Uig**, for ferries to Tarbert on Harris and Lochmaddy on North Uist. There's also a regular shuttle service across the bridge to **Kyleakin** (every 30 mins). The train journey from Inverness to Kyle, though not as spectacular as the West Highland line, is very scenic. It runs 3-4 times Mon-Sat (2 ½ hrs) and once or twice on Sun from May to Sep. There's also an observation car and dining car in the summer.

Getting around **Citylink** buses between Fort William, Inverness and Skye pass through Glen Shiel several times daily in each direction. There's a *postbus* service between Kyle and Glenelg (see below) and **Highland Country Buses** run from *Ratagan Youth Hostel* to Kyle (30 mins) and on to Plockton (50 mins), on schooldays only, departing at 0755 and returning at 1640. There's a *postbus* service from **Kyle of Lochalsh** to **Arnisdale** and **Corran** via Glenelg at 0945 Mon-Sat. It takes 3 ¾ hrs. The return bus from Corran departs at 0725.

Information **Kyle of Lochalsh Tourist Information Centre** ⓘ *Seafront car park, T534276. Apr, May and mid-Sep to late Oct Mon-Sat 0930-1730; Jun to mid-Jul and late Aug to mid-Sep Mon-Sat 0930-1900; mid-Jul to late Aug Mon-Sat 0930-2100, Sun 1230-1630.*

Glen Shiel

The journey from Invergarry to **Shiel Bridge** is worth it for the views alone. Glen Shiel is a spectacular sight, with 3,000 ft-high peaks soaring up on either side. This is one of the most popular hiking areas in Scotland, with the magnificent and much-photographed **Five Sisters of Kintail** on the north side of the glen, and the equally beautiful **South Glen Shiel Ridge** on the other.

Glenelg

One of the most beautiful journeys in Scotland is the road from Shiel Bridge to the picturesque little village of Glenelg on the Sound of Sleat, only a short distance opposite Kylerhea on Skye. he unclassified single-track road turns off the A87 and climbs steeply and dramatically through a series of sharp switchbacks to the top of the **Mam Ratagan Pass** (1,115 ft). From here the view back across Loch Duich to the Five Sisters of Kintail is simply amazing, and the all-time classic calendar shot.

The road then drops down through Glen More to Glenelg, the main settlement on the peninsula. This is Gavin Maxwell country and featured in *Ring of Bright Water*, but he disguised the identity of this beautiful, unspoiled stretch of coastline, calling it Camusfearna, and today it remains a quiet backwater.

You can see the famous otters at **Sandaig**, on the road running from Glenelg, where Gavin Maxwell lived. The site of his cottage is now marked with a cairn. As well as otters, you can see numerous seabirds, seals and porpoises in the Sound of Sleat, and around the peninsula you may be lucky enough to catch a glimpse of wildcats, pine martens, golden eagles and the recently reintroduced sea eagles.

The village consists of a row of whitewashed cottages surrounded by the ruins of the 18th-century Bernera Barracks. Just before the village the road forks. The right turning leads to the **Glenelg-Kylerhea ferry**, which makes the five-minute crossing to Skye. The tiny six-car ferry runs from April to October and is the most scenic and romantic route to the misty isle. For more details, see the Skye chapter (page 884).

A road runs south from Glenelg to Arnisdale. About a mile and a half along this road, a branch left leads to the **Glenelg Brochs** – Dun Telve and Dun Dun Troddan – two of the best-preserved Iron-Age buildings in the country. Dun Telve stands to a height of over 30 ft and the internal passages are almost intact.

The road south from Glenelg continues past Sandaig Bay and runs along the north shore of unearthly Loch Hourn, with great views across the mountains of Knoydart. The road ends at the little fishing hamlet of **Arnsidale**, from where you can take a boat across the loch to Barrisdale on the Knoydart peninsula. For details, see page 853.

Eilean Donan Castle

ⓘ *Apr-Oct daily 0900-1700. £3.95, concession £3.20, groups £2.95. T01599-555202. Citylink buses between Fort William and Inverness and Skye stop by the castle.*

One of Scotland's most photographed sights is the stunningly located Eilean Donan, 10 miles west of Shiel Bridge on the A87. It stands on a tiny islet at the confluence of Loch Duich and Loch Alsh, joined to the shore by a narrow stone bridge and backed by high mountains. This great calendar favourite has also featured in several movies, including *Highlander*, which starred Sean Connery.

The original castle dates from 1230 when Alexander III had it built to protect the area from marauding Vikings. It was destroyed by King George in 1719 during its occupation by Spanish Jacobite forces sent to help the 'Old Pretender', James Stuart. It then lay in ruins, until one of the Macraes had it rebuilt between 1912 and 1932. Inside, the Banqueting Hall with its Pipers' Gallery is most impressive, and there's an exhibition of military regalia and interesting displays of the castle's history. The views from the battlements are also worthwhile.

Kyle of Lochalsh

Before the coming of the controversial Skye Bridge a mile to the north (see page 884), the little town of Kyle, as it is known, was the main ferry crossing to Skye and consequently a place which attracted a busy tourist trade. Now, though, the tourist traffic bypasses Kyle, which is probably the most sensible thing to do as it's not the most attractive of places. There are a couple of banks with ATMs, two small supermarkets and a post office in the village.

Plockton

If there were a poll taken of visitors' favourite Highland villages then you can bet your bottom dollar that Plockton would come top with most folk. If you look for a definition of picturesque in your dictionary, it'll say "see Plockton". Well, maybe not – but it should.

Plockton's neat little painted cottages are ranged around the curve of a wooded bay, with flowering gardens and palm trees. Yachts bob up and down in the harbour and there are views across the island-studded waters of Loch Carron to the hills beyond. Even on the telly Plockton's charms proved irresistible, and millions of viewers tuned in each week to watch the TV series *Hamish Macbeth*, which featured Robert Carlyle as the local bobby.

There are lots of good walks around the village. One of the best ways to appreciate it is to head up to Frithard Hill, from where there are great views of the bay. Another good walk is along the beach, starting from the High School playing fields at the top of the village.

Sleeping

Shiel Bridge *p855*

B **Cluanie Inn**, About 9 miles east of Shiel Bridge, T0320-340238. One of the Highlands' classic hotels, this is a firm favourite with hikers and climbers and it's easy to see why. After a hard day's ridge walking, what could be better than jumping into the jacuzzi, then having a hot dinner and a good pint beside a log fire. You can also camp nearby, but why deny yourself the pleasure if you can afford it? A less salubrious option is the E **Ratagan Youth Hostel**, T01599-511243, just outside Shiel Bridge. It's also popular with hikers, and is open all year except Jan. You can camp at **Morvich Caravan Club Site**, T01599-511354, open late Mar to late Oct; or at Shiel Bridge, T01599-511211.

Glenelg *p855*

D **Glenelg Inn**, T01599-522273. It's worth stopping in Glenelg, if you've got the time, to experience a night in this cosy place. Even if you can't spend the night, at least spend an hour or two enjoying the atmosphere, good ale and fine seafood. It's one of those places that almost makes you glad it's raining.

Eilean Donan Castle *p856*
There are several places to stay in the nearby village of **Dornie**.
C **Dornie Hotel**, T01599-555205, is a good option and serves very good food (mid-range). Just across the bridge is
C **Loch Duich Hotel**, T01599-555213. It offers comfortable accommodation, meals and live music in the bar on a Sun evening. There are several good B&Bs, including
D **Tigh Tasgaidh**, T01599-555242; and
E **Fasgadale**, T01599-588238.
E **Silver Fir Bunkhouse**, Carndubh, T01599-555264. A cheaper place to stay at this 6-bed accomodation.
A **Conchra House Hotel**, Killilan, at the head of Loch Long, T01599-555233, conchra@aol.com. 6 rooms. This historic 18th-century hunting lodge is peaceful, has lovely views and boasts a reputation for good food.

Kyle of Lochalsh *p856*
C **Old Schoolhouse**, 3 miles north, at Erbusaig, T01599-534369, a very comfortable B&B with a highly rated restaurant.

Plockton *p856*
B **The Haven Hotel**, T01599-544223, on Innes St. 15 rooms, open Feb-Dec. The best place to stay, and eat. Good value and the food in the restaurant is quite superb (5-course dinner; expensive).
C **Plockton Hotel**, Harbour St, T01599-544274. Wonderful and busy, serves good food (mid-range) and has a great little beer garden at the front where you can sit and enjoy a drink on a balmy summer evening.
D **Craig Highland Farm**, a few miles out of Plockton, on the road to Achmore, T01599-544205. Offers B&B accommodation and self-catering cottages from £235 per week. The farm is also a conservation centre, where you can see and feed rare and ancient breeds of domestic animals.

Eating

Kyle of Lochalsh *p856*
£££-££ Seagreen Restaurant & Bookshop, just outside the village, on the road to Plockton, T01599-534388. Bistro-cum-bookshop and gallery serving wholefood and local seafood throughout the day.
£££-££ The Seafood Restaurant, at the railway station, T534813, which has a good reputation for seafood, open Easter-Oct 1000-1500 and 1830-2100. Another option is **Lochalsh Hotel**, which does very good bar lunches.

Plockton *p856*
££-£ Off the Rails, T01599-544423, at the railway station. It's open from 0830 for breakfast, snacks, lunch and evening meals.

Activities and tours

Boat trips
The *Seaprobe Atlantis* sails from Kyle of Lochalsh. It is fitted with underwater windows allowing you to watch 'the world beneath the waves'. Check sailing times at the pier. If you prefer, you could take a **seafood cruise** – a 2½-hour wildlife-spotting and seafood-eating boat trip. Contact Neil MacRae, T01599-577230. From Plockton, **Leisure Marine**, T01599-544306, runs one-hour seal- and otter-watching cruises in the summer for £3.50 per person. They also hire out boats. Similar trips are run by **Sea Trek Marine**, T01599-544346.

Wester Ross →*Colour map 6*

From Loch Carron north to Ullapool, is the region of Wester Ross, an area of dramatic mountain massifs, fjord-like sea lochs and remote coastal villages. Here lies some of Europe's most spectacular scenery, from the isolated peninsula of Applecross to the mighty peaks of Torridon, which offer some of Scotland's best climbing and hillwalking. There are also gentler attractions such as the magnificent gardens at Inverewe and the beautiful pink sands of Gruinard Bay. ▸▸ *For Sleeping, Eating and other listings, see pages 861-864.*

Ins and outs

Getting there Ullapool is the mainland terminal for **ferries** to **Stornoway** (Lewis). **Scottish Citylink buses**, T08705-505050, to and from **Inverness** (twice daily Mon-Sat, 1 hr 20 mins) connect with the ferry to and from **Stornoway**. For further details of ferries, see page 884), or contact the local **CalMac** office on Shore St, opposite the pier, T01854-612358. There are also buses to places further north, and south along the coast. Buses stop at the pier near the ferry dock. There are **buses** to Gairloch from **Inverness** 3 times a week. ▸▸ *For further details, see Transport, page 863.*

Information **Ullapool Tourist Information Centre** ⓘ *6 Argyle St, T01854-61213, Easter-Jun and Sep-Nov Mon-Sat 0900-1800, Sun 1300-1800; Jul and Aug Mon-Sat 0900-1900, Sun 1300-1800; Nov-Easter Mon-Fri 1300-1630*. It is well run and provides an accommodation booking service as well as information on local walks and trips, and has a good stock of books and maps. **Gairloch Tourist Information Centre,** ⓘ *T01854-712130, at the car park in Auchtercairn, where the road branches off to Strath. Jan-Mar, Nov and Dec Mon-Thu 0900-1230 and 1300-1700, Fri 0900-1230 and 1300-1630; Apr and May, Sep and Oct Mon-Sat 0900-1730, Sun 1300-1800; Jun-Aug Mon-Fri 0900-1800, Sat 1000-1800, Sun 1300-1800*. They will book accommodation for you and sell a wide range of books and maps.

Lochcarron to Applecross

West of Lochcarron at Loch Kishorn, a side road leaves the A896 and heads to Applecross. There are many scenic routes in the Highlands but this one beats them all. The **Bealach na Ba** ('Pass of the Cattle') is the highest road in Scotland and is often closed during the winter snows. It climbs relentlessly and dramatically through a series of tortuous switchbacks – both spectacular and terrifying in equal measure. The high plateau, at 2,053 ft, is cold and desolate, but from here you have the most stunning views: from Ardnamurchan Peninsula to Loch Torridon, taking in Eigg, Rùm, the Cuillins of Skye, the Old Man of Storr and the Quirang.

The narrow, single-track road then begins its gradual descent to the isolated little village of Applecross, site of one Scotland's first Christian monasteries, founded in 673 AD. The village consists of a row of whitewashed fishermen's cottages looking across to the island of **Raasay** and backed by wooded slopes. It's a beautifully tranquil place where you can explore beaches and rock pools or enjoy a stroll along sylvan lanes.

Torridon to Loch Maree

Torridon is perhaps the most striking skyline in the Scottish Highlands. The multi-peaked mountains of **Beinn Alligin**, **Liathach** (pronounced '*Lee*-ahakh') and **Beinn Eighe** ('Ben-*eay*') form a massive fortress of turrets, spires and pinnacles that provides an awesome backdrop to Loch Torridon, as well as the most exhilarating walking and climbing on the Scottish mainland (see below).

The coast road from Applecross meets the A896 from Lochcarron at the lovely little village of **Shieldaig** on the southern shore of **Loch Torridon**. There's a shop, a post office, a campsite, a couple of B&Bs. Several miles east, a side road turns off the A896 by **Torridon** village and winds its way along the northern shore of the loch, then climbs through dramatic scenery before dropping to the beautiful little village of **Diabaig** (pronounced 'Jee-a-beg'), 10 miles from Torridon village. It's a worthwhile side trip, as the views across to the Applecross peninsula and Raasay are fantastic. There's also a great seven-mile coastal walk from Diabaig to Redpoint.

Much of the Torridon massif is in the care of the National Trust for Scotland, and just before Torridon village is the **NTS countryside centre**, T01443-791221, where you can get information and advice on walks in the area, as well as books and maps. About 400 yards past the centre is the **Deer Museum**, which has a small display describing the management of red deer in the Highlands as well as some live specimens outside.

Torridon offers some of the most spectacular walking on the Scottish mainland but also presents some of the most serious challenges. You need to be fit, experienced and well prepared and also be aware of the notoriously unpredictable weather. For those who are not experienced hill walkers, there's a Ranger Service for visitors. During July and August the ranger, Seamus McNally, T01443-791221, takes guided walks up into the mountains three times a week.

On the north side of the Torridon mountains is beautiful Loch Maree, dotted with islands and bordered by the mass of **Slioch** (3,215 ft) to the north and ancient Caledonian pine forest to the south. Beinn Eighe (which means 'File Peak' in Gaelic) is Britain's oldest National Nature Reserve, set up in 1951 to protect the ancient Caledonian pine forest west of Kinlochewe. It has since been designated an International Biosphere Reserve and extended to cover 30 square miles. The reserve is the home of a great variety of rare Highland wildlife, including pine martens, wildcats, buzzards, Scottish crossbills and golden eagles. There's also a wide range of flora which can best be appreciated on the excellent mountain trail described below which climbs from the ancient pine woods through alpine vegetation to the tundra-like upper slopes. About half a mile northwest of Kinlochewe on the A832, is the **Beinn Eighe Visitor Centre**, which has information on the flora and fauna in the reserve and sells pamphlets on the various trails. Note that camping is restricted to the official campsite at Taagan Farm.

Gairloch and around

Gairloch consists of a string of tiny crofting townships scattered around the northeastern shore of the loch of the same name. The waters around Gairloch are home to a wide variety of marine mammals such as seals, otters, porpoises, dolphins, minke whales and even killer whales.

The beach by the golf course at Gairloch is nice, but the beach at **Big Sand**, a few miles northwest of Strath, is better, and quieter. Further north is Melvaig, from where you can walk to **Rubha Reidh Lighthouse**. Around the headland from the lighthouse is the beautiful, secluded beach at **Camas Mor**. This is a good place for spotting sea birds, and there's a great walk from here on a marked footpath to **Midtown**, four miles northwest of Poolewe. You'll have to walk or hitch from here as there's no public transport to Poolewe.

The narrow B8056 runs west for nine miles to **Red Point** from the junction three miles south of Gairloch, at Kerrysdale. This is a lovely little side trip and well worth it, especially on a clear evening to enjoy the magnificent sunsets at Red Point beach. The beach itself is extremely beautiful, backed by steep dunes and looking across to the Trotternish peninsula on Skye. Red Point is the start or finish point for the excellent coastal walk to or from **Diabaig**. On the road to Red Point is the picturesque little hamlet of **Badachro**, tucked away in a wooded, sheltered bay with fishing boats moored in its natural harbour. It's worth stopping off here on the way back from Red Point for a wee dram at the *Badachro Inn*. There are lots of other good walks in the area, including to **Flowerdale Falls** and the **Fairy Lochs** and the **USAAF Liberator**. The TIC (see previous page) has a selection of walking guides and OS maps.

Five miles east of Gairloch on the other side of the peninsula, by the the neat little village of Poolewe, is **Inverewe Garden**, ⓘ *Garden open 15 Mar-31 Oct daily 0930-2100; 1 Nov-14 Mar daily 0930-1700, visitor centre open 15 Mar to 31 Oct 0930-1730, guided garden walks 15 Apr to 15 Sep Mon-Thu at 1330, £5, concession £4, children £1, T01443-781200,* where you'll find an astonishing collection of exotic subtropical plants growing on the same latitude as Siberia, thanks to the mild climate created by the North Atlantic Drift. This wonderful 50-acre oasis of colour is a mecca for garden lovers, but even those who flinch at the mere sight of a lawn-mower will be bowled over by the sheer scale and diversity of plants and flowers on view. The garden is well worth visiting in any weather and at any time of the year, but especially from the end of April through the summer when the rhododendrons are in bloom. You should allow at least a couple of hours to do it justice. The garden is about a mile north of Poolewe on the main A832. There's a visitor centre and gift shop and a good restaurant, which serves snacks and hot meals.

North of Poolewe the A832 passes **Aultbea** on its way to **Laide**, where it then skirts the shores of Gruinard Bay, with its lovely coves of pink sand. From Laide Post Office a side road branches north to **Mellon Udrigle** and **Opinan**, both with great beaches. Gruinard Bay is a very beautiful part of the northwest coast but will always be synonymous with **Gruinard Island**, standing ominously in the middle of the bay. The island was used as a testing ground for biological warfare during the Second World War and was contaminated with anthrax spores. The Ministry of Defence finally agreed to decontaminate it in 1990 and it has now been declared 'safe'.

The road heads inland then runs along the southern shore of **Little Loch Broom** to **Dundonnell**, from where there are spectacular views of awesome **An Teallach** (3,483 ft), a mountain of almost mythical status amongst Scottish climbers and spoken of in hushed, reverential tones. The A832 coastal road from Gairloch and Poolewe meets the A835 Ullapool-Inverness main road at **Braemore junction**, 12 miles south of Ullapool. Before heading on to Ullapool it's worth stopping at the very impressive Falls of Measach, just by the junction. The falls plunge 150 ft into the spectacular **Corrieshalloch Gorge** (or 'ugly/fearsome gorge' in Gaelic) and can be crossed by a distinctly wobbly suspension bridge (not for vertigo sufferers). The falls can be reached from the A835, but the most dramatic approach is from the A832 Gairloch road.

Ullapool

The attractive little fishing port of Ullapool, on the shores of Loch Broom, is the largest settlement in Wester Ross. It is an important fishing centre as well as being the major tourist centre in the northwest of Scotland and one of the main ferry terminals for the Outer Hebrides. At the height of the busy summer season the town is swamped by visitors passing through on their way to or from Stornoway on Lewis, heading north into the wilds, or south to Inverness. It has excellent tourist amenities and services and relatively good transport links, making it the ideal base for those exploring the northwest coast and a good place to be if the weather is bad.

Ullapool's attractions are very much of the outdoor variety and include the **Falls of Measach**, **Achiltibuie** and **Stac Pollaidh**. There are also many good local walks and cruises to the **Summer Isles** (see 'Tours' below). The only real 'sight' as such is the **Ullapool Museum and Visitor Centre,** ⓘ *Apr-Oct Mon-Sat 0930-1730; Jul and Aug also 1930-2130; Nov-Mar 1200-1600, £2, concession £1.50, children free, T01854-612987*, in a converted church in West Argyle Street. It has some interesting displays on local history, including the story of those who set sail from here in 1773 on board *The Hector*, the first ship to carry emigrants from the Highlands to Nova Scotia in Canada. Between Ullapool and Knockan Crag is the turn-off west (left) to the distinctive craggy peak of **Stac Pollaidh**. A new path has been recently established by the John Muir Trust, which takes you on a circular walk around the peak from the car park. Take the right-hand path and go round at the same level, or climb up the rear to the top, go around the summit and descend by the same path. You'll need a head for heights to reach the summit as much of the route is exposed, but the stunning views are worth it. Be careful not to stray from the path; it's been put there because of the damage inflicted by tens of thousands of pairs of boots each year, resulting in serious erosion on the south face. It's a fairly easy 2½ hour walk. OS Landranger No 15.

Sleeping

Lochcarron to Applecross p858

D **Applecross Inn**, Applecross, T01443-744262. There are, sadly, too few authentic Highland hostelries where you could quite happily while away a few hours, or even an entire afternoon, but if you have to be holed up somewhere to escape the rotten weather, then this place is as good as any and better than most. The welcome is warm, the craic is good and the seafood is so fresh you can almost see it swimming past as you order (try a half pint of prawns for a fiver or scallops for £7.50). Bar food served 1200-2100, children welcome till 2030, ceilidhs on Fri evening. The rooms upstairs are nothing fancy, but comfortable, with sea views.

Torridon and around p858

L **Loch Torridon Hotel**, about a mile south of the turn-off to Torridon village, T01443-791242, www.lochtorridonhotel.com. 22 rooms. This elegant former hunting lodge sits on the lochside surrounded by majestic mountains and offers the ultimate in style and comfort. It also boasts one of the finest restaurants in the area (expensive).
A **The Old Mill Highland Lodge**, at Talladale, halfway between Kinlochewe and Gairloch, T01443-760271. Open mid-Dec to mid-Oct. A converted mill set in its own gardens. It's friendly and comfortable, offers great food (price includes dinner) and great views.
A-B **Loch Maree Hotel**, T01443-760288, lochmaree@easynet.co.uk. This beautifully located hotel is being returned to its former glory. It also offers superb cuisine (**A** including dinner).
D **Upper Diabaig Farm**, in Upper Diabaig, T01443-790227. Open Apr-Sep. Excellent B&B.
E **SYHA hostel**, in Torridon village, T01443-791284, open 29 Jan-31 Oct, with an adjacent campsite.

Gairloch and around p859

There are numerous cheaper B&Bs scattered throughout the area. Most of the owners will provide maps and information on local walks.
A-B **Myrtle Bank Hotel**, T01443-712004, myrtlebank@email.msn.com 12 rooms. Modern hotel in the centre of Gairloch overlooking the loch, very good food and service in the restaurant.
E **Bains House**, on the main street in Strath, near the shops, T01443-712472, which is friendly and great value.
E **Rubha Reidh Lighthouse**, 13 miles north of Gairloch, at the end of the road, T/F01443-771263, ruareidh@netcomuk.co.uk, which offers comfortable B&B (**E** including dinner) and hostel accommodation. It's best to book ahead in the high season. They also have a tearoom serving home baking, snacks and light lunches; open Easter-Oct Sun, Tue and Thu 1100-1700. Self-catering is also available for private rooms or the hostel. There are buses from Gairloch as far as Melvaig (see below), then it's a 3-mile hike along the road to the lighthouse.
E **Auchtercairn Hostel**, open Mar-Nov, is at Gairloch Sands Apartments, just before the turn-off to Strath, T01443-712131.
E **Carn Dearg Youth Hostel**, 3 miles beyond Gairloch, on the road to Melvaig, T01443-712219, open 15 May-3 Oct.
Gairloch Caravan & Camping Park, T01443-712373, is at Strath, with full facilities and close to all amenities. **Sands Holiday Centre**, T01443-712152, open Easter-Oct, is at Big Sand, about a mile beyond Strath.
L **Pool House Hotel**, in Poolewe, on the Cove road by the lochside, T01443-781272, poolhouse@inverewe.co.uk, open Mar- Dec. It enjoys great views and serves good food.
C **Old Smiddy Guest House**, in the village of Laide, T01443-731425, oldsmiddy@aol.com. Apr-Oct. Its excellent restaurant is also open to non-residents, but it's best to book well in advance (expensive).

Ullapool p860

There is no shortage of places to stay in Ullapool, ranging from one of the very finest hotels in the UK to numerous guesthouses and B&Bs, a couple of good youth hostels and a campsite.
A **The Ceilidh Place**, 14 West Argyle Pl, T01854-612103, reservations@ceilidh.demon.co.uk. 23 rooms. This former boat-shed has grown over the years to become one of the most refreshingly different hotels in the country, with comfortable bedrooms, cosy lounge, bookshop, restaurant, bar and coffee shop. They also host a varied programme of arts events such as live music, plays, poetry

readings, exhibitions and ceilidhs (see below); a great place to relax and soak up some local culture. Across the road is their clubhouse, with basic but comfortable dorms (**D-E**).

B-C Harbour Lights Hotel, Garve Rd (on the left, heading into Ullapool on the A835), T01854-612222, harbour@vacations-scotland.co.uk. 22 rooms, open 1 Mar-31 Oct. Modern hotel offering good service and very good food available all day (mid-range).

C Ferry Boat Inn, Shore St, T01854-612366, www.ferryboat-inn.com. On the lochside, decent accommodation and food and the best pub in town.

B-C Morefield Hotel, North Rd, T01854-612161. Open May-Oct. On the edge of town heading north, in the middle of a housing estate, motel-style accommodation and a superb seafood restaurant.

C Point Cottage Guest House, 22 West Shore St, T01854-612494, www.pointcottage.co.uk. Lovely old fishing cottage at the quieter end of the loch-front.

D Brae Guest House, Shore St, T01854-612421. 8 rooms, open May-Oct. Comfortable guesthouse on the loch-front.

D Eilean Donan Hotel, 14 Market St, T01854-612524. Friendly and central.

D Strathmore House, Strathmore, Morefield (1 mile north of town), T01854-612423, murdo@strathmore.fsnet.co.uk. Open Apr-Oct. Friendly, comfortable and good value.

E SYHA youth hostel on Shore St, T01854-612254, open Feb-Dec, where you can pick up some good information on local walks, alsobike hire, internet and laundry facilities.

E West House, on West Argyle St, T01854-613126, open all year. It has the full range of facilities, including free internet for guests, hires out mountain bikes and runs local bus tours.

The only campsite is at **Broomfield Holiday Park**, T01854-6120020, on Shore St at the west end of the village, with great views across to the Summer Isles and a laundrette on site. It's open Easter-Sep.

Eating

Gairloch and around *p859*

£££ Myrtle Bank Hotel (see above) serves very good, expensive, meals, and its bar lunches are good value.

££ The Old Inn, near the harbour in Gairloch, T01443-712006. The best place for a good pint of real ale and some pub grub. The best place to eat in Poolewe is probably the licensed restaurant at Inverewe Garden which is open daily 1000-1700 (see below). If you need to grab a quick snack, or fancy a coffee, try the **Bridge Cottage Café**, which is on the left at the turn-off to Cove.

Ullapool *p860*

££ Mariner's Restaurant is part of the *Morefield Hotel* (see above). The setting may be a little incongruous but there's nothing wrong with the food. The seafood is sensational, which is why people travel from miles around and it's always busy. Excellent value.

££ The Ceilidh Place (see above) is one of those places that tourists seem to hang around for hours or even days. It exudes a laid-back, cultured ambience. The self-service coffee shop does cheap wholefood all day during the summer, while the restaurant serves more expensive full meals, with an emphasis on vegetarian and seafood at night. There's even outdoor seating. Open 1100-2300. Also live music and various other events (see below).

You can also get cheap pub food at lunchtime and early evening in the **Ferry Boat Inn**, the **Seaforth Inn** and the **Arch Inn** (see below).

Entertainment

Ullapool *p860*

Ullapool's favourite pub has to be the **Ferry Boat Inn** (or 'FBI' as it's known locally), on Shore St. It has a Thu night live music session year round and during the summer you can sit outside on the sea wall and watch the sun go down as you drain your glass.

The Ceilidh Place, where you can enjoy a quiet drink in the cosy **Parlour Bar** or take advantage of their varied programme of events. There's live music nightly (except Sun) throughout the summer and on a Mon in winter, also ceilidhs and poetry readings. The clubhouse opposite stages plays.

Shopping

Ullapool *p860*

The town is well supplied with shops. **Boots** the chemist is on Shore St by the pier, and there's a **Safeway** supermarket next to the car park north of Seafield Rd. A good outdoor equipment shop is **Mountain Man Supplies**, opposite the museum on West Argyle St. The best **bookshop** in the northwest is the one at The Ceilidh Place (see above). The **Captain's Cabin**, on the corner of Quay St and Shore St, also sells books, as well as crafts and souvenirs. An excellent **jewellers** is the **Knockan Studio**, opposite the TIC on Argyle St, T01854-613365, open Mar-Oct, Mon-Sat 0900-1800. For **pottery**, look no further than **Highland Stoneware**, T01854-612980, on Mill St heading north towards Morefield. You can wander round the studios before browsing in their gift shop, which is pricey but you may have luck in their bargain baskets. They also have a factory in Lochinver. Open Mon-Fri 0900-1800 (Easter-Oct also Sat 0900-1700).

Activities and tours

Boat trips

You can take a wildlife-spotting cruise with *Sail Gairloch*, Gairloch, T01443-712636. The cruise lasts 2 hrs and leaves daily from Gairloch Pier (subject to weather conditions). It can be booked at the Gairloch Marine Life Centre by the pier. During the summer the **MV Summer Queen** runs 4-hr cruises to the Summer Isles, with a 45-min landing on Tanera Mór. These leave Mon-Sat at 1000 from the pier. There are also 2-hr wildlife cruises around Loch Broom, Annat Bay and Isle Martin, which leave daily at 1415 and also on Sun at 1100. Cruises can be booked at the booth by the pier or by calling, T01443-612472.

Walking

Walking tours can be arranged daily with **Northwest Frontiers**, T01854-612628, with the experienced Andy Cunningham, and **Celtic Horizons**, T01854-612429, both in Ullapool.

Transport

It's possible to reach **Applecross** by public transport, but only just. A **postbus** service leaves Strathcarron train station daily (except Sun) at 0955, arriving in Shieldaig at 1040. Another **postbus** then leaves Shieldaig at 1130 and arrives in Applecross at 1300, via the beautiful and winding coast road. No buses run over the Bealach na Ba. A **postbus** leaves Applecross at 0915 and arrives in Shieldaig at 1010. It continues to **Torridon** (see below) and arrives at 1030. Another **postbus** leaves Shieldaig at 1045 and arrives at **Strathcarron** train station at 1130. There are train connections from Strathcarron to Inverness and Kyle (for times T08457-484950).

Lochcarron to Applecross *p858*

The **postbus** from Applecross to Shieldaig continues to **Torridon** village (see above). There's a postbus from Strathcarron station at 0955 which arrives in **Shieldaig** at 1040. **Duncan Maclennan** buses (T01520-755239) have a service which leaves Strathcarron at 1230 and arrives in Torridon at 1330 (daily except Sun). There's also a daily (Mon-Sat) **postbus** service from Diabaig to **Kinlochewe** and **Achnasheen**, via Torridon, at 0955. There are also **Duncan Maclennan** buses between Torridon and Shieldaig and Strathcarron.

Torridon and around *p858*

Kinlochewe is 9 miles west of Achnasheen rail station which is on the Inverness-Kyle line. There's a daily (except Sun) **postbus** service. There's also a **postbus** (Mon-Sat) from Kinlochewe to **Torridon** and **Diabaig**, and a bus to Torridon and **Shieldaig**, T01520-755239. Buses between Gairloch and Inverness (see below) stop in Kinlochewe.

Gairloch and around *p859*

There's a bus from Inverness to **Gairloch** 3 times a week (Mon, Wed and Sat) at 1705 with **Westerbus**, T712255. The return bus is at 0805. **Westerbus** also have services to **Kinlochewe** (Mon-Sat at 0730) and to **Mellon Charles/Laide**, via Poolewe (Mon-Sat). There's a Melvaig-Gairloch-Red Point **postbus** service Mon-Sat which leaves Gairloch at 0820 heading north to **Melvaig** and leaves Gairloch heading south to **Red Point** at 1035. On Fri only there's a subsidized taxi service between Gairloch and Melvaig 1030-1230 (to book T712559/712497). There are daily buses to **Laide** from Gairloch with **Westerbus**, T01443-712255. Some of them continue to **Mellon Udrigle**. There are buses between

Laide and Inverness 3 times a week (Tue, Thu and Fri), leaving at 0805 and returning at 1705. There are also buses on other days between Gairloch and Inverness which stop at Laide (see above under Gairloch).

Ullapool *p860*
Scottish Citylink buses run 2-3 times daily (except Sun) between Ullapool and Inverness, connecting with the ferry to **Stornoway**. There are also buses daily (except Sun) to and from Inverness with **Rapson's Coaches**, T01463-710555, and **Spa Coaches**, T01997-421311. There's a service to **Lochinver** (1-2 times daily except Sun, 1 hr) with **Spa Coaches** and **Rapson's of Brora**, T01408-621245, and to **Achilitibuie** (twice daily Mon-Thu, once on Sat, 1 hr) with **Spa Coaches**. There's also a daily bus to and from **Gairloch**, which continues to Inverness, during the summer only.

North of Ullapool

→*Colour map 6*

North of Ullapool you enter a different world. The landscape becomes ever more dramatic and unreal – a huge emptiness of bleak moorland punctuated by isolated peaks and shimmering lochs. A narrow and tortuously twisting road winds its way up the coast, past deserted beaches of sparkling white sand washed by turquoise sea. There's not much tourist traffic this far north and once you get off the main road and on to the backroads, you can enjoy the wonderful sensation of having all this astonishingly beautiful scenery to yourself.

The region north of Ullapool is called Assynt, and is heaven for hill walkers and climbers. Though most are not Munros, and not particularly difficult by Scottish standards, they attract some of the worst weather imaginable, even in summer. Remember to check locally regarding access during the deer-stalking season which runs from mid-August to mid-October. Amongst the most spectacular of Assynt's distinctive 'island peaks' are Suilven (2,398 ft), Ben More Assynt (3,275 ft), Quinag (2,650 ft) and Canisp (2,775 ft). Much of this region is protected in the Inverpolly and Inchnadamph National Nature Reserves, home to an extremely rich and diverse wildlife. ▸▸ *For Sleeping, Eating and other listings, see pages 866-867.*

Ins and outs

Information Lochinver Tourist office is in the **Assynt Visitor Centre** has displays on the local geology, history and wildlife and there's also a ranger service with guided walks throughout the summer. ⓘ *The centre is open Apr-Oct Mon-Fri 1000-1700 and Sun 1000-1600. T01571-844330.* ▸▸ *For further details, see Transport, page 867.*

Ullapool to Achiltibuie

About 12 miles north of Ullapool on the main A835 is the exceptional SNH visitor centre at **Knockan Crag**. It's an interactive display of the geology, flora and fauna of the area and is open all year round 24 hours a day, T01854-666234. From the visitor centre there's a marked trail which leads up to the Crag, and the views from the clifftop are excellent, across to Inverpolly's 'island' peaks of **Cul Mór, Cul Beag** and **Stac Pollaidh**. The unclassified single-track road winds its way west past Stac Pollaidh to the turn-off for Achiltibuie. This old crofting village, with whitewashed cottages set back from the sea views across to the beautiful **Summer Isles**, is home to one of the northwest's main tourist attractions. The **Hydroponicum**, ⓘ *Easter to end of Sep daily 1000-1800, guided tours every hour on the hour, £4.75, concession £3.50, children £2.75, T01854-622202, www.race.co.uk/hydroponicum*, or 'Garden of the Future', is a gigantic greenhouse which is pioneering the system of hydroponics to grow plants from all over the world. Hydroponics uses water instead of soil to carry nutrients to the plants and can be carried out anywhere. Here you can see an incredible variety of subtropical trees, orchids, flowers, vegetables, herbs and fruits. A guided tour takes you through the different climatic zones, and you can taste their produce, including the famous strawberries, in the *Lilypond Café*, which serves meals and snacks.

Another worthwhile attraction is the **Achiltibuie Smokehouse**, ⓘ *May-Sep Mon-Sat 0930-1700, free, T01854-622353*, five miles to the north, at Altandhu. Here you can watch the salmon, herring, trout and other fish being cured before buying some afterwards.

Lochinver and around

The road from Achiltibuie north to Lochinver is known locally as the 'wee mad road', and you'd be mad to miss this thrilling route which twists and winds its way through some the northwest's most stunning scenery. The village of Lochinver is a working fishing port and the last sizeable village before Thurso. It has a good tourist office, lots of accommodation, a bank with ATM, post office and petrol station.

The area east of Lochinver is a remote wilderness of mountains and moorland dotted with lochs and lochans. As well as being a favourite haunt of hardy climbers and walkers, Assynt is a paradise for anglers. Most of the lochs are teeming with brown trout, and fishing permits are readily available throughout the area from the TIC in Lochinver or at local hotels, guesthouses and B&Bs. There's also salmon fishing on the River Kirkaig, available through the *Inver Lodge Hotel* (see page 866), and on Loch Assynt through the *Inchnadamph Hotel* (see page 867).

The A837 Lochinver-Lairg road meets the A894 to Durness 10 miles east of Lochinver at **Skiag Bridge** by Loch Assynt. To the east of the road lies the **Inchnadamph National Nature Reserve**, dominated by the massive peaks of **Ben More Assynt** and **Conival**, which should only be attempted by experienced hill walkers. A few miles south of the village of **Inchnadamph**, at the fish farm, is a steep, but well-marked footpath up to the **Bone Caves**. This is one of Scotland's oldest historical sites, where the bones of humans and animals such as lynx and bear were found together with sawn-off deer antlers dating from over 8,000 years ago.

Lochinver to Kylesku: the coast road

The quickest way north from Lochinver is the A837 east to the junction with the A894 which heads to Kylesku. But by far the most scenic route is the B869 coast road that passes moorland, lochs and beautiful sandy bays. It's best travelled from north to south, giving you the most fantastic views of Suilven. Untypically, most of the land in this part of Assynt is owned by local crofters who, under the aegis of the *Assynt Crofters' Trust*, bought 21,000 acres of the North Assynt Estate, thus setting a precedent for change in the history of land ownership in the Highlands.

The trust now owns the fishing rights to the area and sells permits through local post offices and the tourist office in Lochinver. It has also undertaken a number of conservation projects, including one at **Achmelvich**, a few miles north of Lochinver, at the end of a side road which branches off the coast road. It's worth a detour to see one of the loveliest beaches on the west coast, with sparkling white sand and clear turquoise sea straight out of a Caribbean tourist brochure.

The road runs east from Drumbeg, under the shadow of towering **Quinag** (2,654 ft), to meet the A894 heading north to **Kylesku**, site of the sweeping modern road bridge over Loch a'Cháirn Bháin. From Kylesku you can visit Britain's highest waterfall, the 650-ft high **Eas a'Chùal Aluinn**, near the head of Loch Glencoul. **Cruises** leave from the old ferry jetty below the *Kylesku Hotel* to the falls on board the *MV Statesman*, T01571-844446. You can also see porpoises, seals and minke whales en route. You may be able to get closer to the falls by getting off the boat and walking to the bottom, then getting on the next boat. ⓘ *The 2-hr round trip runs Apr-Sep daily at 1100 and 1400 (Jul and Aug also at 1600), and costs £9, children £3*. There's also a trail to the top of the falls. It starts at the south end of Loch na Gainmhich, about three miles north of Skiag Bridge. Skirting the loch, follow the track in a southeasterly direction up to the head of the **Bealach a Bhuirich** (the Roaring Pass). Continue until you meet a stream, with several small lochans on your right. Follow this stream until it plunges over the **Cliffs of Dubh** (the Dark Cliffs). You can get a better view of the falls by walking to the right about 100 yards and descending a heather slope for a short distance. Allow about three to four hours for the round trip.

Scourie and Handa Island

Ten miles north of Kylesku is the little crofting community of Scourie, sitting above a sandy bay. Anyone remotely interested in wildlife is strongly advised to make a stop here to visit Handa Island, a sea bird reserve run by the Scottish Wildlife Trust, and one of the best places in the country for bird life. The island is now deserted, except for the warden, but once supported a thriving community of crofters, until the potato famine of 1846 forced them to leave, most emigrating to Canada's Cape Breton. Now it's home to huge colonies of shags, fulmars, razorbills, guillemots and puffins. The best time to visit is during the summer breeding season, from late May to August. There's a footpath right round the island, which is detailed in the free SWT leaflet available at the warden's office when you arrive. You should allow three to four hours. ⓘ *Apr-Sep Mon-Sat 0930-1700*. There's a ferry service to the island from Tarbet Beach, 3 miles northwest off the A894, about 3 miles north of Scourie. It sails continuously, depending on demand. The 15-min crossing costs £7.50 return. T01971-502077.

Kinlochbervie and around

The road north from Scourie passes **Laxford Bridge**, where it meets the A838 running southeast to **Lairg**. The A838 also runs north to Durness, on the north coast (see below). At **Rhiconich**, the B801 branches northwest to Kinlochbervie. This is one of the west coast's major fishing ports, and huge container lorries thunder along the narrow single-track roads carrying frozen fish and seafood to all corners of Europe. A few miles beyond Kinlochbervie is **Oldshoremore**, a tiny crofters' village scattered around a stunning white beach, and a great place to swim. The less hardy can instead explore the hidden rocky coves nearby.

At the end of the road is **Blairmore**, from where a footpath leads to **Sandwood Bay**, the most stunning and beautiful beach on the west coast. It's a long walk, but because of its isolation you'll probably have this mile-long stretch of white sand all to yourself. The beach is flanked at one end by a spectacular rock pinnacle and is said to be haunted by the ghost of an ancient shipwrecked mariner. Allow three hours for the walk there and back, plus time at the beach. You could take a tent and watch the sunset. Sandwood Bay can also be reached from **Cape Wrath**, a day's hike to the north (see page 868).

Sleeping

Ullapool to Achiltibuie *p864*

L **Summer Isles Hotel**, near the Hydroponicum is the T01854-622282, summerislesyhotel@aol.com. Open Easter-Oct. which enjoys magnificent views across to the Summer Isles. It also boasts an excellent restaurant (expensive). Even if you're not staying or eating here, it's worth stopping to have a drink on the terrace and watch the sun set over the islands.

Lochinver and around *p865*

L **Inver Lodge Hotel**, Iolaire Rd, T01571-844496, inverlodge@compuserve.com. 20 rooms, open Apr-Oct. A modern luxury hotel standing above the village with great views and excellent restaurant (lunch mid-range; dinner expensive).

L **The Albannach Hotel**, at Baddidaroch, T01571-844407, F844285. This wonderful 18th-century house overlooking Loch Inver is one of the very best places to stay in the northwest, and the food offered in the award-winning restaurant is sublime. The price includes dinner. Non-residents are also welcome but booking is essential.

C-B **Inchnadamph Hotel**, T01571-822202, inchnadamphhotel@assynt99.freeserve.co.uk. An old-fashioned Highland hotel on the shores of Loch Assynt, catering for the hunting and fishing fraternity (see above).
E **Inchnadamph Lodge**, T01571-822218, assynt@presence.co.uk, or *Assynt Field Centre*, which offers basic hostel accommodation in bunk rooms, as well as twin, double and family rooms. Continental breakfast is included. It's open all year, but phone ahead between Nov and Mar. It's ideally situated for climbing Ben More Assynt and guides are available.

Lochinver to Kylesku *p865*

A **Kylesku Hotel**, Kylesku, T01571-502231, kylesku.hotel@excite.co.uk, before you leave on the boat trip, pop in here for some great-value pub seafood, or for B&B, open Mar-Oct.
A **Eddrachilles Hotel**, a few miles south of Scourie, in Badcall Bay, T01971-502080, eddrachilles@ compuserve.com. 11 rooms, open Mar-Oct, this is one of the most magnificently situated hotels in the country. The 200 year-old building stands in 300 acres of grounds, the food on offer is superb, though the atmosphere is a little stuffy.

Scourie *p866*

A **Scourie Hotel**, Scourie, T01971-502396, www.scourie-hotel.co.uk, open 1 Apr-mid-Oct. Another excellent place to eat, this 17th-century former coaching inn popular with anglers (lunch mid-range; dinner expensive).
B **Scourie Lodge**, Scourie, T01971-502248, open Mar-Oct. Best B&B around, also does good evening meals.

Kinlochbervie and around *p866*

C **Old School Hotel**, halfway between Kinlochbervie and the A838 at Rhiconich, T/F01971-521383, www.host.co.uk. They serve great food here at mid-range prices, daily 1200-1400 and 1800-2000.

Eating

Scourie and Handa Island *p866*

££ **Seafood Restaurant**, just above the jetty at Tarbet. If you're up this way, don't miss a visit to this wonderful restaurant which serves seafood caught by owner Julian Pearce. It's a great place and you can even stay here, in the self-catering caravan next door, which sleeps up to six.

Activities and tours

Boat trips

The Summer Isles lying offshore can be visited from Achiltibuie pier on board the Hectoria. Cruises leave Mon-Sat at 1030 and 1415 and last 3½ hrs, with 1 hr ashore on the islands. To book, contact I Macleod at Achiltibuie Post Office, T01971-622200, or at home, T01971-622315. Cruises cost £12 per person (half price for children). There are also deep-sea angling trips (1800-2100) which cost £6 per person and £15 per rod.

An excellent wildlife boat trip leaves from Fanagmore, a mile from Tarbet on the other side of the peninsula, with **Laxford Cruises**, T01971-502251. They sail around beautiful Loch Laxford, where you can see lots of birds from nearby Handa Island, as well as seals, porpoises and otters. Trips leave Easter till the end of Sep daily except Sun at 1000, 1200 and 1400 (also at 1600 in Jul and Aug). The trips last 1 hr 45 mins and cost £10 for adults, £5 for children. For bookings contact Julian Pearce, who also runs the Seafood Restaurant.

Transport

Ullapool to Achiltibuie *p864*

There are 2 buses daily (Mon-Thu) to **Ullapool** with Spa Coaches, T01997-421311, leaving Achiltibuie Post Office at 0800 and 1300. The early bus starts in Reiff (at 0740) and the other one leaves from Badenscallie. The journey takes an hour. There's also a bus on Sat, leaving at 0750.

Scourie and Handa Island *p866*

There's a postbus service to **Scourie** from Durness and Lairg once a day, Mon-Sat. It leaves Durness at 0820 and arrives at 0935 and continues to **Lairg**. It returns at 1245 and arrives at 1420. There's also a **postbus** service between Scourie and **Elphin**, with connections to **Lochinver**.

Kinlochbervie and around *p866*

A postbus leaves Kinlochbervie harbour at 0900 and goes to **Scourie** (35 mins) and on to **Lairg** (1 hr 50 mins) from where there are connections to **Inverness**. The same postbus returns from Lairg at 1245, arrives in Kinlochbervie at 1448, then continues to **Durness** (35 mins).

The North Coast

→ Colour map 6

Scotland's rugged north coast attracts few visitors, but those who do venture this far find that's there's plenty to write home about. This is some of Britain's most spectacular and undisturbed coastline, from the wild and remote Cape Wrath in the far northwest, to John O'Groats, that perennial favourite of sponsored walkers, in the far northeast. In between lie over 100 miles of storm-lashed cliffs, sheer rocky headlands and deserted sandy coves, all waiting to be explored. It's also a great place for birdwatching, with vast colonies of seabirds, and there's a good chance of seeing seals, porpoises and minke whales in the more sheltered estuaries. ⏩ *For Sleeping, Eating and other listings, see pages 870-871.*

Ins and outs

Getting there There are daily buses to Thurso from Inverness which connect with buses to Edinburgh. There are regular daily buses to and from **Wick airport** (see page 871). Ferries to **Stromness** in Orkney leave from **Scrabster**, 2 miles north of Thurso (see page 908), and a bus service runs between **Thurso** train station and Scrabster ferry pier. The train station is at the south end of Princes St, 500 yd from the TIC (see below). There are daily trains from Inverness. ⏩ *For further details, see Transport, page 870.*

Information Durness Tourist Information Centre ⓘ *T01971-511259, Apr-Oct Mon-Sat, Jul and Aug also Sun*, arranges guided walks and has a small visitor centre with displays on local history, flora and fauna and geology. There's a small Tourist Information Centre in **Bettyhill**, T01641-521342, *open Easter-Sep Mon-Sat*. **Thurso** Tourist Information Centre Riverside Rd, T01847-892371. *Apr-Oct Mon-Sat 0900-1800, Jul and Aug also Sun 1000-1800*. They have a leaflet on local surfing beaches. **John O'Groats Tourist Information Centre** ⓘ *T01955-611373, open Apr-Oct Mon-Sat 0900-1700.*

Durness and Cape Wrath

Durness is not only the most northwesterly village on the British mainland, but also one of the most attractively located, surrounded by sheltered coves of sparkling white sand and machair-covered limestone cliffs. A mile east of the village is the vast 200 ft-long **Smoo Cave**. A path from near the youth hostel leads down to the cave entrance which is hidden away at the end of a steep, narrow inlet. Plunging through the roof of the cathedral-like cavern is an 80-ft waterfall which can be seen from the entrance, but the more adventurous can take a boat trip into the floodlit interior.

A few miles east of the Smoo Cave are a couple of excellent beaches, at **Sangobeg** and **Rispond**, where the road leaves the coast and heads south along the west shore of stunning **Loch Eriboll**, Britain's deepest sea loch, which was used by the Royal Navy during the Second World War as a base for protecting Russian convoys.

There are several excellent trips around Durness, but the most spectacular is to Cape Wrath, Britain's most northwesterly point. It's a wild place and the name seems entirely appropriate, though it actually derives from the Norse word hwarf, meaning 'turning place'. Viking ships used it as a navigation point during their raids on the Scottish west coast. Now a lighthouse stands on the cape, above the 1,000 ft-high **Clo Mor Cliffs**, the highest on the mainland, and breeding ground for huge colonies of seabirds. You can walk south from here to Sandwood Bay (see page 866). It's an exhilarating but long coastal walk, and will take around eight hours. It's safer doing this walk from north to south as the area around the headland is a military firing range and access may be restricted, which could leave you stranded.

Durness to Thurso

The road east from Durness runs around Loch Eriboll on its way to the lovely little village of Tongue. A causeway runs across the beautiful **Kyle of Tongue**, but a much more scenic route is the single-track road around its southern side, with great views of **Ben Hope** (3,041 ft) looming to the southwest. The village of Tongue is overlooked by the 14th-century ruins of **Varick Castle**, and there's a great beach at **Coldbackie**, two miles northeast.

The A836 runs south from Tongue, through **Altnaharra**, to **Lairg**. It also continues east to the crofting community of **Bettyhill**, named after the Countess of Sutherland who ruthlessly evicted her tenants from their homes in Strathnaver to make way for more profitable sheep. The whole sorry saga is told in the interesting **Strathnaver Museum**, ⓘ *Apr-Oct Mon-Sat 1000-1300 and 1400-1700, £1.90, concession £1.20, children £0.50, T01641-521418*, housed in an old church in the village. There are also Pictish stones in the churchyard behind the museum.There are a couple of great beaches around Bettyhill, at **Farr Bay** and at **Torrisdale Bay**, which is the more impressive of the two and forms part of the **Invernaver Nature Reserve**.

East from Bettyhill the hills of Sutherland begin to give way to the fields of Caithness. South from Melvich the A897 heads to Helmsdale through the **Flow Country**, a vast expanse of bleak bog of major ecological importance. About 15 miles south of Melvich, at **Forsinard**, is an **RSPB Visitor Centre**, ⓘ *Easter-Oct daily 0900-1800, guided walks through the nature reserve leave from the visitor centre, T01641-571225*.The peatlands here are a breeding ground for black- and red-throated divers, golden plovers and merlins as well as other species. Otters and roe deer can also be spotted.

Thurso and around

Thurso is the most northerly town on the British mainland and by far the largest settlement on the north coast. The town increased in size to accommodate the workforce of the new nuclear power plant at nearby Dounreay, but the plant's demise has threatened the local economy. Today Thurso is a fairly nondescript place, mostly visited by people catching the ferry to Stromness in Orkney. Thurso is also known to keen surfers who come here for the unbeatable surf. To the east of town, at **Dunnet Bay**, is a three-mile-long beach with an excellent reef break and there's another good reef break, at **Brims Ness** to the west. Further west, at **Strathy Bay** (see above) you'll find rollers that can match anything in Hawaii (though the water's a lot colder).

About 10 miles northeast of Thurso is Dunnet Head, the most northerly point on the British mainland, reached by turning off the Thurso-John O'Groats road at Dunnett, at the east end of **Dunnett Bay**, a three-mile-long sandy beach that's popular with surfers who come to tackle the gigantic waves of the **Pentland Firth**, the wild and treacherous strait between the mainland and Orkney. It's a much nicer place than John O'Groats, with marvellous views across to Orkney and along the entire north coast (on a clear day). There's a Victorian lighthouse out at the point, and the dramatic seacliffs are teeming with seabirds. There's also a great little café, the *Dunnett Head Tearoom*, T01847-851774, a few miles from the lighthouse, which serves cheap snacks and meals (open April-October daily 1500-2000).

The dreary tourist trap that is John O'Groats is boring at best and pretty miserable most of the time. It gets its name from the Dutchman Jan de Groot, who was commissioned by King James IV to run a ferry service to Orkney in 1496. Ferries still operate from here to Burwick in Orkney (see Transport below). Two miles east of John O'Groats is **Duncansby Head**, which is far more rewarding. South of the headland a path leads to the spectacular **Duncansby Stacks**, a series of dramatic rock formations. The 200-ft cliffs are home to countless seabirds and you can see the narrow, sheer-sided inlets known locally as *geos*.

Sleeping

Durness and Cape Wrath *p868*

B **Cape Wrath Hotel**, T01971-511212, jack@capewrathhotel.co.uk, is just off the A838 on the road to the ferry at Keoldale. It overlooks the loch and is popular with fishermen and passing tourists who stop here to enjoy the great food and superb views.

A-B **Port-Na-Con Guest House**, T01971-511367, portnacon70@hotmail.com, is on the west shore of Loch Eriboll, 7 miles from Durness. It's popular with anglers and divers so you'll need to book ahead to take advantage of such comfort amidst all this great scenery. The food in the adjoining restaurant is superb and also great value, especially the seafood. Non-residents are welcome but should book.

Durness to Thurso *p869*

A-B **Tongue Hotel**, Tongue, T01971-611206, is a former hunting lodge of the Duke of Sutherland. It overlooks the Kyle of Tongue and does good food.

C **Ben Loyal Hotel**, T01971-611216, Thebenloyalhotel@byinternet.com. Recommended for the food.

D **Rhian Cottage**, T01971-611257, jenny.anderson@ tesco.net. Excellent value accommodation.

E **SYHA Youth Hostel**, T01971-611301, open mid-Mar to late Oct, beautifully situated at the east end of the causeway; and a couple of campsites: one is at Talmine, T01971-601225, 5 miles north of Tongue by the beach; and the **Kincraig Camping and Caravan Site**, T01971-611218, just to the south of the village.

Thurso and around *p869*

A **Forss Country House Hotel**, 4 miles out of town at Bridge of Forss T01847-861201, jamie@forsshouse.freeserve.co.uk. This small family-run hotel is set in 20 acres of lovely woodland and has an excellent restaurant, The Bower Inn, open to non-residents (mid-range to expensive). Thurso has 3 independent hostels:

E **Sandra's Backpackers**, 24-26 Princes St, T01847-894575;

E **Thurso Hostel**, Ormlie Lodge, Ormlie Rd, T/F01847-896888; and

E **Thurso Youth Club**, Old Mill, Millbank, T01847-892964, open 1 Jul-30 Aug. The nearest campsite is **Thurso Camping Site**, T01847-607771, north of town on the road to Scrabster.

Activities and tours

From John O'Groats there are **Orkney Islands Day Tours**, which leave daily 1 May-30 Sep at 0900, and return at 1945. A shorter day tour departs daily from 1 Jun-2 Sep 1030, and returns at 1800. There's also a wildlife cruise 20 Jun-31 Aug, which departs at 1430. Contact: **John O'Groats Ferries**, Ferry Office, John O'Groats, T01955-611353, www.jogferry.co.uk. Tours also leave from Inverness.

Transport

Durness and Cape Wrath *p868*

Bus

A daily bus runs to and from **Thurso**, via Tongue and Bettyhill (Jun-Aug, Mon-Sat) with **Highland Country Buses**, T01847-893123, leaving Thurso at 1130 and Durness at 1500. There's also a daily bus service (May to early Oct) to and from **Inverness** via Ullapool and Lochinver, with **Bluebird/Inverness Traction**, T01463-239292. There's a **postbus** service to **Lairg** via Tongue and Altnaharra, Mon-Sat at 1115; also via Kinlochbervie and Scourie Mon-Sat at 0820. To get to **Cape Wrath**, first take the ferry across the Kyle of Durness from Keoldale, 3 miles south of Durness, T511376. It runs May-Sep hourly 0930-1630. The ferry connects with a minibus, T01971-511287, for the 11 miles to the cape (40 mins).

Thurso and around *p869*

Bus

Buses arrive at Sir George's St Port Office and depart from Sir George's St Church. **Citylink** buses run to and from **Inverness** (3 ½ hrs) 4 times daily, T0870-5505050, continuing to **Scrabster** to connect with the ferries to and from **Stromness** in Orkney. **Citylink** buses to Inverness connect with buses to **Edinburgh**. **Highland Country Buses**, T01847-893123, run local services to **Bettyhill** (3 times daily Mon-Thu, twice on Sat; 1 hr 10 mins) and to **Reay** (4 times daily Mon-Thu, 3 times on Sat). There are regular daily buses to and from **Wick** via Halkirk or Castletown. **Highland Country Buses** also run the service between Thurso train station and Scrabster ferry pier. **Harrold Coaches**, T01955-631295, run a service to and from **John O'Groats** (4 times daily Mon-Thu, twice on Sat; 1 hr). There's also a postbus service to **Wick airport**, leaving Riverside Rd at 0920 and arriving at 1000.

Ferry

Ferries to Stromness in Orkney leave from Scrabster, 2 miles north of Thurso. For details, see page 908). Ferries to Burwick (Orkney) sail twice daily from May to September (45 mins). A connecting bus takes passengers on to Kirkwall (40 mins).

Train

Three trains leave daily from Inverness (3 ½ hrs), 2 of them connecting with the ferries from Scrabster to Stromness in Orkney. Trains continue to Wick (30 mins) and return trains to Inverness leave from Wick.

The East Coast

→ *Colour map 6*

The east coast of the Highlands, from Inverness north to Wick, doesn't have the same draw as the west coast and attracts far fewer visitors, but it has its own, gentler appeal, and there are many lovely little seaside towns to explore. The sea lochs and estuaries of the inner Moray Firth are fringed with fields and woods, a fertile lowland landscape dotted with farms and crofts. Fast-flowing rivers drop from the hills through deep, wooded straths. The bulk of Ben Wyvis dominates the horizon northwest of Dingwall. ▸▸ *For Sleeping, Eating and other listings, see pages 875-876.*

Ins and outs

Getting there Wick has an **airport**, a few miles north of town, with daily direct flights to and from **Kirkwall** (Orkney), **Sumburgh** (Shetland), **Aberdeen** and **Newcastle.** There are regular daily **buses** to Cromarty from **Inverness** and a bus service twice a week to and from **Dingwall.** There are buses to Wick from **Inverness** and **Thurso,** and trains to **Inverness.** Tain is on the **Inverness-Thurso** rail line and there are **trains** daily in each direction. There are also daily **buses** to and from Inverness and Thurso. There are **buses** to Dornoch from **Inverness.** ▸▸ *For further details, see Transport, page 875.*

Information On the north side of the Kessock Bridge is the **North Kessock Tourist Information Centre,** ⓘ *T01463-731505; open daily Easter-Oct.* Next door is the **Dolphin and Seal Visitor Centre,** which gives details of accredited dolphin cruises. **Lairg Tourist Information Centre,** ⓘ *T402160, open Mon-Sat 0900-1700 and Sun 1300-1700.* **Dornoch Tourist Information Centre,** ⓘ *T810400*, is on the main square. *Open Mon-Sat 0900-1300 and 1400-1700.* The **Tourist Information Centre** ⓘ *Whitechapel Rd (just off the High St), T602596, open all year Mon-Fri 0900-1700, Sun 0900-1300.*

The Black Isle

Across the Kessock Bridge from Inverness is the Black Isle, which is neither an island nor black. Its main attractions are the picturesque town of **Cromarty** *and* **Chanonry Point**, *on the southern side near Rosemarkie, which is one of the best* **dolphin-spotting** *sites in Europe.*

One of the many sacred wells (and caves) in the area is the unmissable **Clootie Well,** on the verge of the main road between Tore and Munlochy Bay Nature Reserve. It was once blessed by St Curitan (see below under Rosemarkie) and is thought to cure sick children. Thousands of rags still flutter from the surrounding trees, though well-worshippers are in danger of being mown down by traffic. Despite the presence of traffic, it's an eerie place. Go at night, if you dare.

Further east on this road, Chanonry Point is a great place for seeing **dolphins**. They come close to shore at high tide and there's a good chance of seeing them leaping above the waves. A few miles from the village of Fortrose, on the north side of Chanonry Point, is the tiny village of **Rosemarkie** where **Groam Museum**, ⓘ *Easter-Sep Mon-Sat 1000-1700, Sun 1400-1630; Oct-Apr Sat and Sun 1400-1600, £1.50, concession £1, children £0.50, T01381-620961*, houses a superb collection of Pictish sculptured stones found locally, imaginatively displayed alongside contemporary artwork inspired by them. A year-round programme of events and lectures is devoted to the study of Pictish culture.

Cromarty Firth

On the northeastern tip of the Black Isle Peninsula, at the mouth of the Cromarty Firth, is the gorgeous village of Cromarty, one of the east coast's major attractions. Its neat white-harled houses interspersed with merchants' residences are almost unchanged since the 18th century when it was a sea port thriving on trade as far afield as Russia and the Baltic. Although restored and much inhabited, Cromarty now has the atmosphere of a backwater, but an attractive one at that, where you feel as if you're stepping back in time, in stark contrast to the oil rigs moored on the opposite shore in **Nigg Bay** (see below). For an insight into the history of the area, visit the 18th-century **Cromarty Courthouse**, in Church Street, which houses the town's museum. ⓘ *Apr-Oct daily 1000-1700; Nov, Dec and Mar daily 1200-1600, £3, concession/children £2; includes loan of headset for recorded tour of the town's other historic buildings, T01381-600418*. Next to the courthouse is the thatch-roofed **Hugh Miller's Cottage,** ⓘ *1 May-30 Sep daily 1100-1300 and 1400-1700 (Sun afternoon only), £2.50, concession £1.70, family ticket £7, T01381-600245*, birthplace of the local geologist and author.

One of Cromarty's main attractions is its **dolphins**. They can be seen from the shore, or with a **boat trip**, but make sure you go with an accredited operator, such as *Dolphin Ecosse*, T01381-600323. Full-day or half-day trips leave from the harbour and you can see porpoises and seals as well as dolphins, and perhaps even killer whales further out. To the west, the mudflats of **Udale Bay** are an RSPB reserve and a haven for wading birds and wintering duck and geese, which can be viewed from a hide. In the winter other birds such as pinkfooted geese and whooper swans use the bay as a roost.

Dingwall, at the head of the Cromarty Firth, has two major claims to fame. Not only is it believed to be the birthplace of Macbeth, it was also the home for many years of **Neil Gunn** (1891-1973), perhaps the Highlands' greatest literary figure. It's a fairly dull, though functional town, with good shops and banks (with ATMs) lining its long main street.

Tain

Squeezed between the Cromarty Firth to the south and the Dornoch Firth to the north is the **Tain Peninsula**, whose largest town is Tain, a place with a 1950's time-warp feel. It has an impressive historical portfolio. Its backstreets are an intriguing jigsaw of imposing merchants' houses, steep vennels, secret gardens and dormer windows. Tain was the birthplace of the 11th-century missionary **St Duthac**. Pilgrims flocked here in the Middle Ages to his shrine, and a ruin near the links is thought to be the original **chapel**. His head and heart, encapsulated in gold and silver reliquaries, were later kept in the still extant medieval **Collegiate church** until their disappearance during the Reformation. The Collegiate church is on Castle Brae, just off the High Street, and inside is a 17th-century panel painted with the badges of the trade guilds, a reminder of the town's busy international trade. Another reminder is the imposing 16th-century **Tolbooth** in the High Street. One of Tain's main attractions is the **Glenmorangie whisky distillery**, ⓘ *All year Mon-Thu 0900-1700; Jun-Aug also Sat 1000-1600 and Sun 1200-1600, tours from 1030-1530, £2, T01862-892477*, just off the A9 to the north of town, where you can see how the world-famous whisky is made and try a sample.

The Dornoch Firth

Fairies were said to cross the Dornoch Firth on cockle shells and were once seen building a bridge of fairy gold, perhaps a forerunner of the Dornoch Bridge which carries the A9 across the Firth just north of Tain. A more pleasant and interesting route is to follow the A836 along the south shore. Ten miles from Ardgay, at the end of lovely **Strathcarron**, is the isolated **Croick church**, one of the most poignant reminders of the infamous Clearances. Here in 1845, 90 local folk took refuge in the churchyard after they had been evicted from their homes in Glencalvie by the Duke of Sutherland to make way for flocks of sheep. A reporter from *The Times* described the 'wretched spectacle' as men, women and children were carted off, many never to return. The report is there to read. Far more evocative and harrowing, though, are the names and messages the people scratched in spidery copperplate in the window panes.

After the Dornoch Ferry disaster of 1809, a bridge was built over the Kyle at **Bonar Bridge**, from where the A949 runs eastwards to join the main A9 just before Dornoch, while the A836 continues north to Lairg (see below). A few miles north of **Invershin** are the **Falls of Shin**, an excellent place to watch salmon battling upstream on their way to their spawning grounds (best seen June to September). A visitor centre and café/restaurant/shop has information about six easy walks in the immediate area; all are under an hour long. Eleven miles north of Bonar Bridge is the uninspiring village of Lairg, the region's main transport hub.

Dornoch

Dornoch is another architectural gem with its deep, golden sandstone houses and leafy cathedral square. Bishop Gilbert of Moravia (Moray) built the cathedral circa 1245. His family's success in gaining a foothold in Northeast Scotland against the Norsemen was rewarded with the Earldom of Sutherland. It was trouble with the Jarls which prompted Gilbert to move his power base here from Caithness, mindful that his predecessor had been boiled in butter by the locals.

The 13th-century **cathedral** ⓘ *Mon-Fri 0730-2000, you can climb the cathedral tower during Jul and Aug*, was badly damaged in 1570, then subjected to an ill-conceived 'restoration' by the Countess of Sutherland in 1835. Among the few surviving features is a series of gargoyles, including a green man, and the effigy of an unknown knight.Opposite the cathedral is the 16th-century **Bishop's Palace**, now a hotel (see below).

Nowadays Dornoch is famous for its links **golf course**, rated as one of the world's finests and relatively easy to get on. It overlooks miles of dunes and pristine sandy beach. A stone near the links marks the spot where the last **witch** in Scotland was burned in 1722. North of Dornoch is **Loch Fleet**, a river estuary with a ferocious tide race at its mouth and an SNH reserve protecting rare birds and plants. The rotting skeletons of the fishing fleet abandoned in the First World War lie in the sand on the south shore west of the car park. Nearby **Skibo Castle** is where Madge and Mr Ritchie tied the knot, in relative secrecy. It is an exclusive club, but details of accommodation are available from the Dornoch tourist office. There are several walks in the forestry plantations in the area.

Dornoch to Wick

Golspie lives in the dark shadow of the Sutherlands. On **Beinn a'Bhraggaidh** (1,293 ft), to the southwest, is a huge, 100 ft-high **monument** to the Duke of Sutherland. Those who make it up to the monument and who know something of the Duke's many despicable acts may find the inscription risible, as it describes him as "a judicious, kind and liberal landlord". There's no reference to the fact that he forcibly evicted 15,000 tenants from his estate. Not surprisingly, locals would like to see this eyesore removed from the landscape, broken into tiny pieces and then scattered far and wide. Unfortunately, they have thus far been unsuccessful.

The aptly named **Dunrobin Castle**, one mile north of the village, is the ancient seat of the Dukes of Sutherland, who once owned more land than anyone else in the British Empire. Much enlarged and aggrandized in the 19th century with fairy-tale turrets, the enormous 189-room castle, the largest house in the Highlands, is stuffed full of fine furniture, paintings, tapestries and *objets d'art* and bears witness to their obscene wealth. The castle overlooks beautiful gardens laid out with box hedges, ornamental trees and fountains. The **museum,** ⓘ *1 Apr-31 May and 1-15 Oct Mon-Sat 1030-1630, Sun 1200-1630; 1 Jun-30 Sep Mon-Sat 1030-1730, Sun 1200-1730, £6, students £5, OAPs & children £4.50, T01862-633177,* is an animal-lover's nightmare and almost a caricature of the aristocracy, with a spectacular Victorian taxidermy collection. There are also local antiquities, some from ancient brochs, and Pictish stonecarvings

North of Brora is the former herring port of Helmsdale, most notable for its excellent **Timespan Heritage Centre,** ⓘ *Easter-Oct Mon-Sat 0930-1700, Sun 1400-1700, £3.50, concession £2.80, children £1.75, T01862-821327,* which brings the history of the Highlands to life through a series of high-tech displays, sound effects and an audiovisual programmeNorth from Helmsdale the A9 climbs spectacularly up the **Ord of Caithness** and over the pass enters a desolate, treeless landscape; an area devastated during the Clearances. At **Berriedale** a farm track leads west to the **Wag**, from where you can climb **Morven** (2,313 ft), the highest hill in Caithness, with amazing views across the whole county.

The A9 coast road then drops down into **Dunbeath**, a pleasant little village and birthplace of one of Scotland's foremost writers, **Neil Gunn** (1891-1973). His finest works, such as *The Silver Darlings* and *Highland River*, reflect his experiences of growing up in the northeast and are fascinating accounts of life here during the days of the herring boom, though the sleepy harbour of today is barely recognizable as the erstwhile bustling fishing port. The villages of Dunbeath, and **Latherton** to the north, are included on the *Neil Gunn Trail*, as is the beautiful walk up the glen, described in the leaflet available at the **Dunbeath Heritage Centre,** ⓘ *Apr-Sep daily 1100-1700, £1.50, concession £0.50, children free, T01862-731233.* Here, you can learn all about the life and works of the famous novelist as well as the history of Caithness.

Wick

A century ago Wick was Europe's busiest herring port, its harbour jam-packed with fishing boats and larger ships exporting tons of salted fish to Russia, Scandinavia and the West Indian slave plantations. The fishing industry has long since gone, and the demise of the nearby nuclear power station at Douneray has only added to the sense of a place that's past its best. However, there are some interesting archaeological sites in Caithness, as well as the dramatic landscapes, and Wick makes a useful base for exploring the area. In **Pulteneytown**, on Bank Row, is the superb **Wick Heritage Centre,** ⓘ *May-Sep Mon-Sat 1000-1700, £2, children £0.50, T01955-605393.*The highlight of the centre is its massive photographic collection dating from the late 19th century.

One of the most fascinating archaeological sites in the north are the well-preserved **Grey Cairns of Camster**. These chambered cairns, dating from the third and fourth millenia BC, are burial mounds of stone raised around carefully structured circular chambers with narrow entrance passages.To get there, head a mile east of **Lybster** on the A9, then turn left on to the minor road leading north to Watten. The cairns are five miles along this road, on the left-hand side. They comprise two enormous prehistoric burial chambers dating from 2500 BC. They are amazingly complete, with corbelled ceilings, and can be entered on hands and knees through narrow passageways.

Sleeping

Cromarty Firth *p872*

B **Royal Hotel**, on Marine Terr, T01381-600217, royalcrom@cali.co.uk. The best place to stay in town, it has a good restaurant, and cheaper meals are available in the bar.

Tain *p872*

L **Mansfield House Hotel**, Scotsburn Rd, T01862-892052, www.mansfield-house.co.uk. 19th-century baronial splendour and superb cuisine. Restaurant also open to non-residents (mid-range to expensive). There's the excellent value
B **Morangie House Hotel**, on Morangie Rd, T01862-892281. It's popular locally for its food (mid-range) and is open for lunch and dinner.

Dornoch Firth *p873*

There are several B&Bs in Lairg but the most interesting place to stay is 9 miles east at Rogart train station, where you can get cheap hostel accommodation at the
E **Rogart Railway Carriages**, T01408-641343, rogmail@globalnet.co.uk. Two rail carriages have been converted to sleep 16 people and there's a 10% discount for bike or train users.
E **Carbisdale Castle** Youth Hostel, overlooking the Kyle, at Culrain, is the 19th-century former home of the exiled King of Norway, which now houses the largest and most sumptuous youth hostel in Scotland, and possibly anywhere else, T01549-421232. It's open 26 February-31 October (except the first two weeks in May). Trains between Inverness and Thurso stop at Ardgay and Culrain. The youth hostel is half a mile up a steep hill from the station. Buses between Inverness and Lairg (see below) stop in Ardgay and Bonar Bridge.

Dornoch *p873*

A-C **Dornoch Castle Hotel**, T01862-810216, www.dornochcastle.com, open Apr-Oct. Formerly the Bishop's Palace, this 16th-century building is full of character and boasts excellent food (expensive).

Wick *p874*

A **Portland Arms Hotel**, about 15 miles south, in Lybster, T01593-721208, www.portlandarms. co.uk A 19th-century coaching inn, full of character and offering great food (mid-range to expensive). The best of the guesthouses and B&Bs are
D **Wellington Guest House**, 41-43 High St, T01955-603287, open Mar-Oct; and
D **The Clachan**, on South Rd, T605384. Also good value is
D **Greenvoe**, George St, near the town centre, T603942.

Eating

Dornoch *p873*

Apart from the hotels a good place to dine is **£££ The Two Quails**, on Castle St, where you can enjoy an expensive but top-class dinner cooked by a chef trained at the Ritz. Luigi's, next door, has excellent coffee and a range of exotic ice creams.

Wick *p874*

The best places to eat are also out of town. These include **The Bower Inn**, and the **£££ Old Smiddy Inn**, in Thrumster, 5 miles south of Wick, T01955-651256, open daily 1200-2100.

Transport

Cromarty Firth *p872*

A 2-car ferry crosses to **Nigg** every half hour from Apr to Oct, 0900-1800. **Highland Bus & Coach**, T01463-233371, runs a **bus** service from **Inverness** to **Fortrose** and **Cromarty** (4-7 times daily Mon-Sat). There is also a bus service to and from Dingwall on Wed and Thu. Dingwall is on the rail line between Inverness and Kyle of Lochalsh and Thurso. There are several **trains** daily in each direction (30 mins to Inverness). There are hourly buses between Inverness and **Invergordon**, via Dingwall. There are also hourly buses between Inverness and **Dingwall** via Muir of Ord. There are buses between Dingwall and **Rosemarkie** (twice a day Mon-Thu), and between Dingwall and **Cromarty** (Wed and Thu).

Tain *p872*

Tain is on the Inverness-Thurso rail line and there are 3 **trains** daily in each direction. **Citylink buses** between Inverness and Thurso pass through Tain 4 times a day.

Dornoch Firth *p873*

Trains between Inverness and Thurso stop at **Lairg** and **Rogart** stations 3 times daily. **Inverness Traction** buses, T01463-239292, run from here to **Ullapool**, with connections to Lochinver and Durness, from May to early Oct (Mon-Sat). Lairg is also the central point for several postbus routes, T01463-256228.

Wick *p874*

Air

Wick has an airport (T01955-602215), a few miles north of town, with daily direct flights to and from **Kirkwall** (Orkney), **Sumburgh** (Shetland), **Aberdeen** and **Edinburgh** with and British Airways Express, T08457-733377. Also direct flights to/from Newcastle with Eastern Airways, T01955-603914.

There's a postbus service to **Wick** airport Mon-Sat at 1015.

Bus

Scottish Citylink, T08705-505050, buses between Inverness and Thurso stop en route in **Wick** (3 daily). There are also regular local buses to **Thurso**, via Halkirk or Castletown, and buses to **Helmsdale** (2-6 times daily Mon-Sat, 1-4 on Sun) and **John O'Groats** (5 daily Mon-Sat, 4 on Sun).

Train

The train and bus stations are next to each other behind the hospital. Trains leave for **Inverness** (3 daily Mon-Sat, 2 on Sun; 3¾ hrs) via **Thurso**, **Helmsdale**, **Golspie**, **Lairg** and **Dingwall**.

Strathspey and the Cairngorms

→ *Colour map 6*

One of Scotland's busiest tourist areas is Strathspey, the broad valley of the River Spey, Scotland's second longest river, which rises high in the hills above Loch Laggan and flows northeast to its mouth on the Moray Firth. The lower reaches are famous for salmon fishing and whisky and are covered in the Speyside section of this guide (see page 817), while the upper reaches attract outdoor sports enthusiasts in droves. Hemmed in between the mighty Monadhliath mountains to the north and the magnificent Cairngorms, Britain's second highest range, to the south. The Cairngorms National Park extends from Grantown on Spey to the heads of the Angus Glens and is the largest in Britain. It is an area which offers excellent hiking, watersports, mountain biking and above all, winter skiing. Much of this area is better known to many as Monarch of the Glen country, as it is where the TV series is filmed. The fictional Glenbogle is actually Ardverikie, near Loch Laggan, but many places like Aviemore, Grantown-on-Spey, Newtonmore and Kingussie have featured in the series. » *For Sleeping, Eating and other listings, see pages 878-880.*

Ins and outs

Getting there There are **buses** to Aviemore from Inverness Perth and Edinburgh and direct **trains** to and from Glasgow, Edinburgh and Inverness. » *For further details, see Transport, page 880.*

Information Aviemore TIC, ⓘ *Grampian Rd, about 400 yd south of the train station, T01479-810363, Apr-Oct Mon-Fri 0900-1800, Sat 1000-1700, Sun 1000-1600; Nov-Mar Mon-Fri 0900-1700, Sat 1000-1700.* They will book accommodation as well as provide free maps and leaflets on local attractions and change foreign currency.

Aviemore and around

The main focus of the area is the tourist resort of Aviemore, a name synonymous with winter sports. In the 1960s Aviemore was transformed from a sleepy Highland village into the jumble of concrete buildings, tacky gift shops and sprawling coach parks that it is today. However Aviemore is working hard at turning itself around and was recently described as 'most improved' resort. It is certainly more pleasant than it used to be and the range of accommodation is improving.The town is also the most important tourist centre in the area and has a wide range of facilities.

Aviemore is surrounded by towering peaks, lochs, rivers and forests of native Caledonian pine which are home to rare wildlife such as pine martens, wildcats, red squirrels, ospreys and capercaillie, and Britain's only herd of wild reindeer. Most of upper Strathspey is privately owned by the Glen More Forest Park and Rothiemurchus Estate which has been in the possession of the Grant family since the 16th century, but both owners allow free access to their lands and provide generous outdoor facilities.

Around Aviemore

There's nothing of real interest in Aviemore. The real enjoyment lies in the surrounding mountains and forests, though there are a few interesting places close at hand. A great place for kids is the **Cairngorm Reindeer Centre** ⓘ *Guided walks to see the herd and feed them leave daily at 1100 and also at 1430 during the summer, £6, children £3, T01479-861228,* in Glen More Forest Park, on the road from Coylumbridge, seven miles from Aviemore.

Eight miles northeast of Aviemore is the tiny village of Boat of Garten which suddenly shot to fame when a pair of **ospreys**, which had disappeared from these shores, reappeared on nearby **Loch Garten**, two miles east of the village. Now these beautiful birds of prey have established themselves here and elsewhere and there are thought be well over 100 pairs throughout the Highlands. The **Abernethy Forest RSPB Reserve** on the shore of Loch Garten is best visited during the nesting season, between late April and August, when the RSPB opens an **observation centre**. ⓘ T 01479-821409, *daily in season 1000-1800, £2.50 for non-members.* This is the only place in the world to see Scottish crossbills. You can also see ospreys at the Rothiemurchus trout loch at Inverdruie, and maybe even on Loch Morlich and Loch Insh. The reserve is also home to several other rare species such as capercaillie, whooper swans and red squirrels. Caperwatch takes place from Apr-mid May 0530-0800.

There's a website dedicated to 'Monarch Country' where devotees can log on to check out behind the scenes stories and locations: www.monarchcountry.com.

The quiet village of **Kingussie** (pronounced King-yoosie) lies 12 miles southwest of Aviemore and makes a pleasant alternative as a place to stay. The main attraction here is the excellent **Highland Folk Museum**, ⓘ*T01479-661307, May-Aug Mon-Fri 0930-1730, Sat and Sun 1300-1700; Apr, Sep and Oct guided tours only Mon-Fri 1030-1630, adult £4, concession and children £2.40,* which contains a fascinating collection of traditional highland artefacts, as well as a farming museum, an old smokehouse, a water mill and traditional Hebridean 'blackhouse'. During the summer there are also demonstrations of spinning, woodcarving and peat-fire baking.

Another worthwhile attraction is **Ruthven Barracks**, standing on a hillock across the river. This former barracks was built by the English Redcoats as part of their campaign to tame the Highlands after the first Jacobite rising in 1715. It was destroyed by the Jacobites in the wake of defeat at Culloden to prevent it from falling into enemy hands, and it was from here that Bonnie Prince Charlie sent his final order which signalled the end of his doomed cause. Access is free and the ruins are particularly attractive at night when floodlit. At nearby **Kincraig** village, between Kingussie and Aviemore, is the **Highland Wildlife Park**, ⓘ *T01479-651270, Apr, May, Sep and Oct daily 1000-1800; Jun-Aug till 1900; Nov-Mar 1000-1600, park tours adult £7.50, concession £6.00, children £5.00,* which has a captive collection of rare native animals.

Sleeping

Aviemore *p876*

A **Corrour House Hotel**, at Inverdruie, 2 miles southeast of Aviemore, T01479-810220, www.corrourhouse.co.uk, open Dec-Oct. This Victorian country house oozes charm, enjoys wonderful views and offers superb cuisine.

B **Rowan Tree Restaurant & Guest House**, at Loch Alvie, 1½ miles south of Aviemore on the B9152, T01479-810207, enquiries@rowantreehotel.com, open Jan-Dec. This is one of the oldest hotels in the area and offers excellent food (lunch cheap; dinner moderate).

B **Lynwilg House**, 1 mile south of Aviemore, at Lynwilg, T01479-811685, marge@lynwilg.co.uk, a charming, friendly guesthouse with a reputation for good food.

E **SYHA hostel**, T01479-810345, on Grampian Rd near tourist office, open all year.

E **Aviemore Independent Bunkhouse and Backpackers Hostel**, T01479-811137, on Dalfaber Rd. There are several good campsites, including the **Rothiemurchus Camping & Caravan Park**, T01479-812800, at Coylumbridge; and a **Forest Enterprise** site at Glenmore, T01479-861271.

Around Aviemore *p877*

B **Heathbank – The Victorian House**, T01479-831234, Boat of Garten, www.heathbankhotel.co.uk, is a must for Art Nouveau lovers and offers goodfood. There are several places to stay in Carrbridge: top of the range is the stylish A **Dalrachney Lodge Hotel**, T01479-841252, www.dalrachney.co.uk, Boat of Garten, a former hunting lodge with good restaurant.

C **Cairn Hotel**, T01479-841212, Boat of Garten, cairn.carrbridge@lineone.net More down to earth, but nonetheless comfortable, this hotel serves good-value bar meals.

B **The Osprey Hotel**, Ruthven Rd, Kingussie, T01479-661510, www.ospreyhotel.co.uk, a comfortable little hotel with a very good restaurant (expensive).

B **Scot House Hotel**, Newtonmore Rd, T01479-661351, www.scothouse.com, is another good choice and also offers great food. There are several decent hostels in the area:

E **The Laird's Bothy**, T01479-661334, is on the High St next to the *Tipsy Laird* pub;

E **Bothan Airigh Bunkhouse**, T01479-661051, is at Insh, a few miles east of Ruthven Barracks on the B970;

E **Kirkbeag Hostel**, T01479-651298, is in Kincraig, between Kingussie and Aviemore; and at Balachroick House in Glen Feshie, near Kincraig, is

E **Glen Feshie Hostel**, T01479-651323.

In Newtonmore, a few miles west of Kingussie on the A86, is

E **Newtonmore Independent Hostel**, T01479-673360, newtonmore@HighlandHostel.co.uk; and at Laggan Bridge, 8 miles further west on the A86, is the

E **Pottery Bunkhouse**, T01528-544231, attached to the *Caoldair Pottery*.

Eating

Aviemore *p876*

Apart from the hotels and guesthouses listed above, the best place to eat in Aviemore is

££ **Old Bridge Inn**, T01479-811137, on Dalfaber Rd. This lovely old pub serves excellent-value food and hosts ceilidhs and Highland dinner dances in the summer months.

Around Aviemore *p877*

The Cross, T01479-661166, on Tweed Mill Brae, a private drive leading off Ardbroilach Rd. The outstanding place to eat in this area. This restaurant with rooms (A for dinner, B&B) is expensive but well worth it. Open Tue-Sat, Feb just before Christmas.

Activities and tours

Skiing

Cairngorm is Scotland's longest-established ski resort and, though it cannot compare to anything in the Alps or North America, it remains Scotland's largest ski area, with 28 runs and over 20 miles of pistes. The season normally runs from Jan until the snow disappears, which can be as late as Apr. For latest snow conditions call the **Ski Hotline** T0900-1654655. The Cairngorm Ski Area is about nine miles southeast of Aviemore, above Loch Morlich in Glen More Forest Park, and reached by a frequent bus service. You can rent skis and other equipment from the Day Lodge at the foot of the ski area (T01479-861261), where you can also buy a lift pass (£21 per day). Ski hire (skis, poles and boots) costs £13 per day, and snowboard hire is £16. The **Cairngorm Mountain Railway** T 01479 861261, www.CairnGorm Mountain.com is a funicular railway that runs to the top of Cairn Gorm from May-Oct, from 1000 to 1630, on demand in winter, £8 adult. For more information on the National Park T 01479 873535, www.cairngorms.co.uk.

If there's enough snow, the area around **Loch Morlich** and **Rothiemurchus Estate** provides good cross-country skiing, though in recent years snowfall has been below average. The tourist office provides a free *Cairngorm Piste Map & Ride Guide* leaflet and a *Ski Scotland* brochure, which lists ski schools and rental facilities.

Walking

Walks around Strathspey are covered by OS Landranger map No 36 & OS Outdoor Leisure Map No 3 .

The **Cairngorms** provide some of Scotland's most challenging walking, with no fewer than 49 Munros and half of Britain's eight mountains over 4,000 ft (Ben MacDrui, Braeriach, Cairn Toul and Cairn Gorm). These mountains come into their own in winter, providing experienced climbers with a wide range of classic ice climbs. They should not be taken lightly. They require a high degree of fitness, experience and preparation (see page for safety precautions).

The summit of Cairn Gorm (4,084 ft) is readily accessible as you take the mountain railway up to the Ptarmigan Restaurant. However the Railway cannot be used to access the high mountain plateau beyond the ski area and mountain walkers may not use the railway for their return journey. There are 50 miles of footpaths through this area, including some lovely walks through the forests. There are also ranger-led guided walks. You can find out more at the **Rothiemurchus Estate Visitor Centre**, T01479-810858, which is a mile from Aviemore along the Ski Road. It' s open daily 0900-1700 and can provide a free *Visitor Guide and Footpath Map*.

Another good area for walking is around **Glen More Forest Park**. The visitor centre, T01479-861220, near Loch Morlich has a *Glen More Forest Guide Map* which details local walks. The best known of the long-distance trails is the Lairig Ghru, a 25-mile hike from Aviemore over the Lairig Ghru Pass to Braemar. The trail is well marked but can take at least eight hours and is very tough in parts, so you'll need to be properly equipped and prepared.

Watersports

In summer, the main activities are watersports, and there are two centres which offer sailing, canoeing and windsurfing tuition and equipment hire.

The **Loch Morlich Watersports Centre** (T01479-861221, lochmorlichw-s@ sol.co.uk; open Apr-Oct) is 5 miles east of Aviemore. The **Loch Insh Watersports Centre**, T01479-651272, user@lochinsh.dial.netmedia.co.uk, Apr-Oct, offers the same, plus fishing, mountain bike hire and instruction on a dry ski slope.

Fishing

Fishing is a major pursuit in the area. You can fish for trout and salmon on the River Spey, and the Rothiemurchus Estate has trout fishing on its stocked loch at Inverdruie, where you can hire rods. Fishing permits cost around £10-15 per day for the stocked lochs and £20-30 per day for the River Spey. They are sold at local shops such as **Speyside Sports** in Aviemore, and at **Monster Activities** which also hires out rods and tackle. **Alvie Estate**, T01540-651255, near Kingussie also hires rods.

Mountain biking

Rothiemurchus and Glen More estates are great areas for mountain biking, with lots of excellent forest trails. The Rothiemurchus Visitor Centre (see above) at Inverdruie has route maps and you can also hire bikes. Bike hire and good advice on routes is also available at **Bothy Bikes**, Unit 7, Grampian Rd, Aviemore, T01479-810111, open daily 0900-1800. **Aviemore Mountain Bikes**, T01479-811007, at 45a Grampian Rd, organises guided bike tours.

Horse riding

Horse riding and pony trekking are on offer at various places throughout Strathspey. There's **Alvie Stables**, at Alvie near Kincraig, T01540-651409, mobile T0831-495397;

Carrbridge Trekking Centre, Station Rd, Carrbridge, T01479-841602; and **Strathspey Highland Pony Centre**, Rowanlea, Faebuie, Grantown-on-Spey, T01479-873073.

Transport

Aviemore *p876*

There are **Scottish Citylink** buses, T0990-505050, between Aviemore and **Inverness** (45 mins), **Kingussie** (20 mins), **Pitlochry** (1¼ hrs), Perth (2 hrs), **Glasgow** (3½ hrs) and **Edinburgh** (3½ hrs). For **Aberdeen**, change at Inverness.

There are direct trains to and from Glasgow and Edinburgh (3 hrs) and Inverness (40 mins). The **Strathspey Steam Railway**, T01479-810725, www.strathspeyrailway.co.uk runs between Aviemore, Boat of Garten and Broomhill. The station is just to the east of the main train station.

Skye and the Outer Hebrides

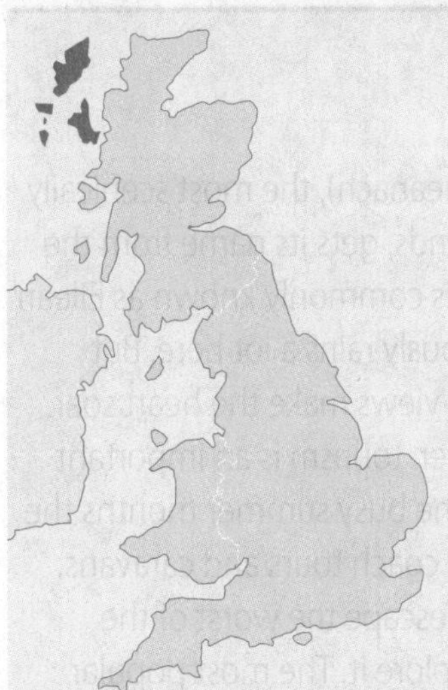

Introduction

The Isle of Skye (An t-Eilean Sgitheanach), the most scenically spectacular of all the Scottish islands, gets its name from the Norse word for cloud (skuy) and is commonly known as Eilean a Cheo (the Misty Isle), so it obviously rains a lot here. But when the rain and mist clear, the views make the heart soar. Despite the unpredictable weather, tourism is an important part of the island's economy. In the busy summer months the main roads become choked with coach tours and caravans, but the island is large enough to escape the worst of the crowds if you take the time to explore it. The most popular destination is the Cuillins, with the greatest concentration of peaks in Britain. They provide Scotland's best climbing and have become a mecca for all serious and experienced walkers. Equally spectacular are the bizarre rock formations of the Trotternish Peninsula in the north.

The Outer Hebrides – or Long Island as they are also known – consist of a narrow 130-mile long chain of islands, lying 40 miles off the northwest coast of the Scottish mainland. The main population centre is Stornoway on Lewis, the only major town in the islands. The rest of the population is scattered throughout the islands in much smaller villages, mostly strung out along the coast. These storm-battered islands are remote in every sense. Unlike Skye, tourism is of far less importance to the local economy. In many ways, the islands are the last bastion of the old Highland life and visiting them is not only like being in a different country, but also being in a different time. There are also miles of superb beaches, wild mountain scenery, numerous archaeological treasures and long hours of summer daylight in which to appreciate it all.

★ Don't miss...

1. Visit the standing stones at **Callanais**, preferably at night when there's a spooky atmosphere, page 892.
2. Take a stroll along the wonderful **Uig sands**, the loveliest beach on Lewis, page 893.
3. Hire a car and drive along the amazing **Golden Road**, on the east coast of Harris, page 896.
4. Fly to the island of **Barra**, where the planes land on the beach, page 902.
5. Take a trip to **St Kilda**, home to some of the largest seabird colonies in Europe, page 904.

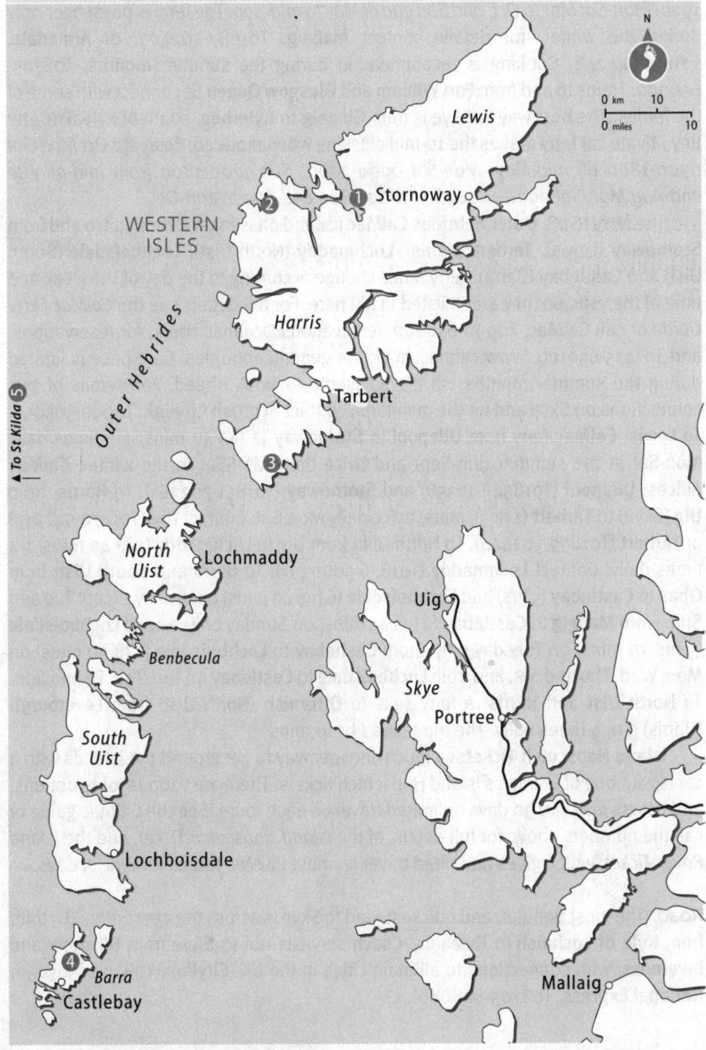

Ins and outs

Getting there

Air British Airways, T08457-733377, flies daily except Sunday from **Glasgow** to **Stornoway** on **Lewis** (1 hr), **Barra** (1 hr 5 mins) and **Benbecula** on **North Uist** (1 hr). There are also flights from **Edinburgh** to **Stornoway** (1hr 10 mins), **Inverness** to **Stornoway** (40 mins) daily except Sun, and to **Benbecula** (2 hrs 40 mins) Monday-Friday. Note that weather conditions are so changeable that flights are prone to delay and can be very bumpy. Flights to **Barra** have an added complication in that they land on the beach, meaning that the runway disappears twice a day under the incoming tide.

Ferry The ferry to **Skye** goes from **Mallaig** to **Armadale**, on the southern Sleat Peninsula. The car and passenger ferry makes the 30-min crossing 7 times daily each way (first one leaves Mallaig at 0840, Armadale at 0925; the last one at 1845 and 1920) *Mon-Sat Mar to Oct, and Sun end of May to mid-Sep*. The ferry is passenger-only during the winter; for details contact **Mallaig**, T01687-462403, or **Armadale**, T01471-844248. Booking is recommended during the summer months, T08705-650000. Trains to and from **Fort William** and **Glasgow Queen St** connect with some of the ferries. The best way to Skye is from **Glenelg** to **Kylerhea**, south of Kyleakin. The tiny private car ferry makes the 10-min crossing when required, *Easter to Oct Mon-Sat 0900-1800 till mid-May; Mon-Sat 0900-2000, Sun 1000-1800 from mid-May to end-Aug Mon-Sat 0900-1800, Sun 1000-1800 end-Aug to end-Oct.*

The **ferry** to the **Outer Hebrides CalMac** car and passenger ferries sail to and from **Stornoway** (Lewis), **Tarbert** (Harris), **Lochmaddy** (North Uist), **Lochboisdale** (South Uist) and **Castlebay** (Barra). Ferry times change according to the day of the week and time of the year, so they aren't listed in full here. For full details see the *CalMac Ferry Guide* or call **CalMac**, T0990-650000, reservations@calmac.co.uk, for reservations, and T01475-650100, www.calmac.co.uk, for general enquiries. Car space is limited during the summer months, so it's advisable to book ahead. For details of bus connections on Skye and on the mainland, contact **Scottish Citylink**, T0990-505050. To **Lewis**: **CalMac** ferry from **Ullapool** to **Stornoway** (2 hrs 40 mins) 2-3 times daily Mon-Sat in the summer (Jun-Sep) and twice daily Mon-Sat in the winter. **CalMac** offices: **Ullapool** (T01854-612358) and **Stornoway** (T01851-702361). To **Harris**: from **Uig** (Skye) to **Tarbert** (1 hr 35 mins) twice daily Mon-Sat. Contact **Uig** (T01470-542219) or **Tarbert** (T01859-502444). To North Uist: from Uig to Lochmaddy (1 hr 40 mins) 1-2 times daily. Contact **Lochmaddy** (T01876-5000337). To **Barra** and **South Uist**: from **Oban** to **Castlebay** (5 hrs) and **Lochboisdale** (6 hrs 40 mins) once daily except Tue and Sun. From **Mallaig** to **Castlebay** (3 hrs 45 mins) on Sunday only, and to **Lochboisdale** (3 hrs 30 mins) on Tuesday only. From **Castlebay** to **Lochboisdale** (1 hr 50 mins) on Mon, Wed, Thu and Sat, and from **Lochboisdale** to **Castlebay** on Tue, Thu, Fri and Sun. To **North Uist** and **Harris**: a ferry sails to **Otternish** (North Uist) from **Leverburgh** (Harris) 3 or 4 times daily. The trip takes 1 hr 10 mins

Island Hopscotch Tickets: a much cheaper way to get around the islands with a car is with one of CalMac's Island Hopscotch tickets. There are various route options, and tickets give you 30 days unlimited travel on each route. See the CalMac guide or call the numbers above for full details of the *Island Hopscotch Ticket*, and the *Island Rover Ticket*, which gives unlimited travel on most CalMac routes for 8 or 15 days.

Road The most popular, and quickest road to Skye is across the new bridge (£5 toll), from **Kyle of Lochalsh** to **Kyleakin**. **Coach** services run to **Skye** from **Glasgow** and **Inverness**, with connections to all main cities in the UK (**Citylink**, T08705-5505050; **National Express**, T08705-808080).

Getting around

Loganair (operating as **British Airways**) fly between **Barra, Benbecula** and **Stornoway** Mon-Fri. For full details, T08457-733377. There are **CalMac ferries** between **Harris** and **North Uist**, and **South Uist** and **Barra**. Passenger ferries run regularly between **Ludag** in South Uist to both **Eoligarry** in Barra and to the island of **Eriskay**, T01878-720238/265.

Skye It is possible to get around by **public transport** midweek, with postbuses supplementing the normal services, but, as everywhere in the Highlands and Islands, buses are few and far between at weekends, especially Sunday, and during the winter months. Buses run between **Portree, Broadford, Uig** (for ferries to the Western Isles), **Kyleakin**, **Armadale** (for ferries to Mallaig), **Dunvegan** and **Carbost**, and a more limited service runs from **Broadford** to **Elgol** and **Portree** to **Glen Brittle.**

Outer Hebrides Bus services run regularly to most main towns and villages on the islands. You should invest in a copy of the *Highlands & Islands Travel Guide* (£1) which is available from the local Tourist Information Centres. Drivers should note that petrol stations are few and far between, expensive and closed on Sunday. **Lewis** and **Harris** are actually one island. The more southerly islands of **North Uist**, **Benbecula** and **South Uist**, joined together by bridges and causeways. Toll-free road bridges connect the island of **Scalpay** with **Harris** and **Great Bernera** with **Lewis**, and a causeway connects **Berneray** with **North Uist**. A causeway connecting **Eriskay** to **South Uist** opened in August 2001. » *For further details, see Transport, pages 891, 894 and 897.*

Information

There are tourist information centres in **Stornoway** and **Tarbert** which are open all year round, and also in **Lochmaddy, Lochboisdale** and **Castlebay** which are open early April to mid October. The **Western Isles Tourist Board** produces an accommodation brochure as well as the essential **Western Isles Official Tourist Map** (Estate Publications; £3.95), which gives place names in English and Gaelic. They also have their own website ⓘ www.witb.co.uk, which provides lots of information on the islands, including up and coming events. Information about the islands can also be obtained at www.hebrides.com Skye is covered by the **Highlands of Scotland Tourist Board** and there are offices in **Portree** (open all year), **Broadford, Uig** and **Dunvegan.**

Isle of Skye

→ *Colour map 7*

Skye, the largest of the Hebridean islands, at almost 50 miles long and between 7 and 25 miles wide, is also the most visited, and has been since Victorian times when climbers returned home extolling its beauty. Skye today is one of Britain's top climbing destinations but manages to lure less active souls with its mix of clan history and phenomenally beautiful scenery. » *For Sleeping, Eating and other listings, see pages 889-891.*

Ins and outs

Information In **Portree** ⓘ *just off Bridge St, T01478-612137*. In **Uig** ⓘ *inside the CalMac office at the ferry pier, T01470-542404*. In **Broadford** ⓘ *by the Esso petrol station, T01471-822361.*

Portree

Portree is the island's capital and main settlement. It's a fairly attractive little fishing port, built around a natural harbour, with a row of brightly painted houses along the shorefront and the rest of the town rising steeply up to the central Somerled Square.

 The Aros Experience ⓘ *T01478-613649, aros@ demon.co.uk, daily 0900-2100 (off season 0900-1800), £3, concession £2, children £1 on Viewfield Road, half a mile from the town centre on the road to Broadford*, is an exhibition and audio-visual display of the island's history and cultural heritage.

Trotternish Peninsula

North from Portree is the 30-mile long Trotternish Peninsula, sticking out like a giant thumb. The interior of the peninsula is a basaltic lava wilderness full of bizarre rock formations. A 20-mile long escarpment of sheer cliffs and towering pinnacles dominates the landscape. At **Kilmuir**, in the far north of the peninsula, is **The Skye Museum of Island Life** ⓘ *Easter to Oct Mon-Sat 0930-1700. £2, children £1.* The group of thatched houses give a fascinating insight into the way of life of a crofting community at the end of the last century, and is the most authentic of several such museums on Skye. Behind the museum, at the end of the road, is **Flora MacDonald's Monument**, which marks the grave of Skye's most famous daughter, with her husband buried alongside.

At the northwest tip of the peninsula, 15 minutes' drive from Uig, is **Duntulm Castle**, a fairy-tale ruin dramatically perched on a steep cliff. This 15th-century structure, built on the site of an ancient Norse stronghold, became the chief Skye residence of the powerful MacDonalds and was the most imposing castle in the Hebrides.

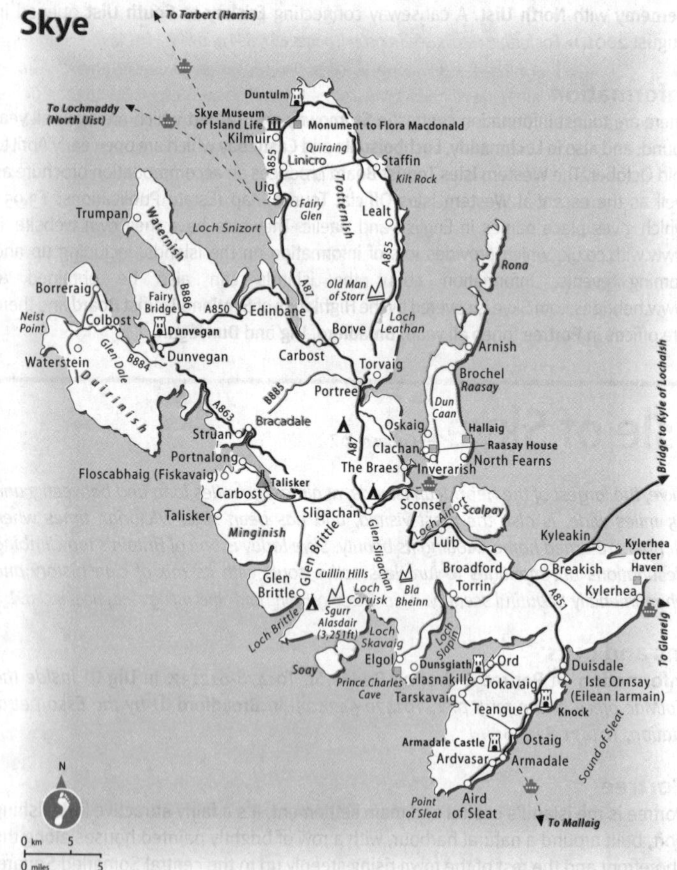

Beyond Duntulm the A855 heads across the tip of the peninsula to the east coast, where the famous bizarre rock scenery is found. At the north end of **Staffin Bay**, a minor road cuts across the peninsula to Uig. This road is the access point for the **Quiraing**, the famous jumble of strangely shaped hills and rocks that is one of the island's classic walks. Even if you don't attempt the walk, the road over the back of the Trotternish ridge from Uig makes a worthwhile detour. A few miles further south, and 7 miles north of Portree, is a car park which is the starting point for another of Skye's famous walks: up to the **Old Man of Storr**, the distinctive pinnacle of rock which has detached itself from the cliffs of the Storr behind.

Dunvegan Castle

ⓘ *T01470-521206, Mid-Mar-Oct daily 1000-1730. Castle: £6, £5.50 concession, £3 children . Seal-spotting cruise: £4, children £2.50. Boat trip: £4, children £2.50, a bus leaves Portree at 1000, arrives at the castle at 1048 and returns at 1252 (Mar-Oct only).*

This is the home of the chiefs of the Clan Macleod who have lived here for over seven centuries, making it the oldest inhabited castle in Britain. The present structure dates from the 15th and 16th centuries and, though the Victorian restoration has left it looking more like a baronial house, a look inside reveals its true age. Among the many relics on display is Rory Mor's horn, a huge drinking vessel which the chief's heir must drain 'without setting down or falling down', when filled with claret (about 1½ bottles). There's also a lock of Bonnie Prince Charlie's hair, clipped from his head by Flora MacDonald as a keepsake, but pride of place goes to the **Fairy Flag**. The flag has been dated to between the fourth and seventh centuries and is made of Middle Eastern silk. It is said to have been given to the clan chief by a fairy, and has the power to ensure victory in battle for the clan on three occasions. It has been used twice so far. The lovely castle gardens lead down to the lochside jetty, from where you can take a seal-spotting cruise or a boat trip around the loch. There's also a busy restaurant and gift shop by the castle gates.

The Cuillins and Minginish → *OS Landranger No 32, OS Outdoor Leisure No 8*

The district of Minginish is the wildest and least-populated part of the island, but for many it is the greatest attraction, for this is where the Cuillins are to be found. This hugely impressive mountain range, often shrouded in rain or cloud, is the spiritual heartland of the island, and when it's clear their heart-aching grandeur can be appreciated from every other peninsula on Skye.Though officially called the Cuillin 'Hills', these are the most untamed mountains in Britain. The magnificent scenery and vast range of walks and scrambles have attracted climbers and walkers for centuries, but have also claimed many lives. It cannot be stressed too strongly that the Cuillins are the most dangerous mountains in Britain and only for experienced climbers (for more on safety.

There are three routes into the Cuillins: from the *Sligachan Hotel* (see below); from Glen Brittle (see below); and from Elgol (see below). The eastern part of the range is known as the **Red Cuillins**. Their smoother, conical granite peaks contrast sharply with the older, darker gabbro of the jagged-edged **Black Cuillins** to the west. The latter are particularly suitable for rock climbing and best approached from Glen Brittle, while the former are accessed from the *Sligachan Hotel*. There are 20 'Munros' (mountains over 3,000 ft in height) in the Cuillins, with the highest being Sgurr Alasdair, at 3,251 ft. Though the sheer majesty of the mountains can only be appreciated at close quarters by the climber, there are impressive views from Elgol, from the road into Glen Brittle and, more distantly, from the west coast of Sleat.

According to local legend, Duntulm castle was abandoned around 1732 when a nursemaid accidentally let the baby heir fall from a window on to the cliffs below.

Glen Sligachan is one of the most popular routes into the Cuillin range and the main access point for the more forgiving Red Cuillins, the walk to **Loch Coruisk**, or the ascent of **Marsco**. Another main access is Glen Brittle. From here there are numerous paths leading up to the corries of the Black Cuillins.

A recommended trip for whisky drinkers, or if it's raining, is to the **Talisker Distillery** ⓘ *Apr-Jun Mon-Fri 0900-1630; Jul-Sep Mon-Sat 0900-1630; Oct Mon-Fri 0900-1630; Nov-Mar Mon-Fri 1400-1630, tours £3.50 (includes discount voucher). T01478-614308, large groups need to book in advance.* at **Carbost** on the shores of Loch Harport, on the B8009 (not in the village of Talisker itself, which is on the west coast). This is Skye's only whisky distillery and produces a very smoky, peaty single malt. The informative tours last around 20-30 minutes and begin with a complimentary dram.

Broadford and around

Eight miles west of Kyleakin is Broadford (An t-Ath Leathann), Skye's second largest village, which basically consists of a mile-long main street strung out along a wide bay. About four miles out of Kyleakin a road turns left off the A87 and heads southeast to Kylerhea (pronounced Kile-ray). The bridge may be the most convenient route to Skye, but the best way to cross is on the small car and passenger ferry that makes the 10-minute crossing to Kylerhea from Glenelg (see page 884). Near Kylerhea is the Forestry Commission **Otter Haven** ⓘ *T01320-366322, daily 0900 till 1 hr before dusk, free* An hour-long nature trail takes you to an observation hide where you can look out for these elusive creatures.

One of the most rewarding drives on Skye is the 14-mile single-track road from Broadford to Elgol (Ealaghol), a tiny settlement near the tip of the Strathaird Peninsula, from where you can enjoy the classic view of the Cuillins from across Loch Scavaig and of the islands of Soay, Rùm and Canna. There's also the added attraction of a dramatic boat trip (see page 890) to the mouth of **Loch Coruisk**, in the heart of the Black Cuillin. The glacial sea loch, romanticized by Walter Scott and painted by Turner, is over two miles long but only a few hundred yards wide, closed in by the sheer cliffs on either side and overshadowed by the towering mountains of black basalt and gabbro.

Sleat Peninsula

East of Broadford is the turn-off to the peninsula of Sleat (pronouned 'slate'), a part of the island so uncharacteristically green and fertile that it's known as 'The Garden of Skye'. Sleat is another entry point to the island. Ferries cross from Mallaig on the mainland to Armadale on the southeastern shore of the peninsula. While the rest of the island is the preserve of the Macleods, Sleat is MacDonald country. The MacDonalds of Sleat are one of the major surviving branches of Clan Donald, and have the right to use the title Lord MacDonald (but not Lord of the Isles, which is now used by the heir to the throne).

Just before the ferry pier at Armadale is **Armadale Castle** ⓘ *T01471-844305, Apr to end-Oct daily 0930-1730, £3.95, concession/children £2.85, office@cland.demon.co.uk,* which was built in 1815 as the main residence of the MacDonalds of Sleat. Most of the castle is now a roofless ruin but the servants' quarters contain an excellent exhibition and accompanying video explaining the history of the Lordship of the Isles. The Clan Donald Lords of the Isles took over from their Norse predecessors in ruling the Hebrides until their power was broken in 1493. The former stables at the entrance comprise offices, a restaurant and bookshop, while the estate manager's house has been converted to accommodate an extensive library and archives. The castle is surrounded by 40 acres of handsome gardens and woodland, and there are ranger-led walks along nature trails with fine views across to the mainland.

Just beyond Armadale Castle is the tiny village of **Armadale** which is strung out along the wooded shoreline and merges into the neighbouring village of **Ardvasar** (pronounced Ard-vaa-sar), which has a post office, general store. Armadale's *raison d'être* is the ferry pier and there's not a huge amount to keep you occupied.

Isle of Raasay

The beautiful island of Raasay lies only a few miles off the east coast of Skye yet remains well and truly off the tourist trail. Its hilly terrain and superb cliff scenery offer numerous walking opportunities and the views from the highest point, **Dun Caan** (1,456 ft), with the Cuillins on one side and Torridon on the other, are, quite simply, beyond compare.

Raasay was for much of its history the property of the Macleods of Lewis, whose chief residence was the ruined **Brochel Castle**, before moving to **Clachan**, where **Raasay House** is now located (see below). The original Raasay House was torched by government troops after Culloden, along with all the island's houses and its boats, as punishment for the Macleods giving refuge to Bonnie Prince Charlie. After the Macleods sold the island in 1843, the Clearances began in earnest and Raasay suffered a long period of emigration, depopulation and poverty. It is not surprising, then, that the island's most famous son, the great poet **Sorley Maclean**, writes so passionately about this lost society. Born in Oskaig in 1911, he writes in his native Gaelic as well as in English, and is highly regarded internationally.

Sleeping

Portree *p885*

A **Bosville Hotel**, Bosville Terr, T01478-612846, www.macleodhotels.co.uk/bosville 18 rooms. Comfortable and stylish accommodation with friendly service. Boasts 2 award-winning restaurants (see 'Eating' below).

A **Viewfield House Hotel**, on the road into Portree from the south, T01478-612217, www.skye.co.uk/viewfield 9 rooms. Open mid-Apr to mid-Oct. Grand old country house full of antiques, set in 20 acres of woodland garden. Log fire adds to the welcoming atmosphere; great value.

D **Portree Independent Hostel**, Old Post Office, The Green, T01478-613737. 60 beds. Right in the centre of town, with laundrette (£3 per wash) and email facilities (£3 per hr).

Trotternish Peninsula *p886*

A **Duntulm Castle Hotel**, near the castle, T01470-552213, www.duntulmcastle.co.uk Open Mar-Nov. Friendly and homely with great views across the Minch to the Outer Hebrides. Idyllic and good value. Restaurant is open to non-residents.

A **Flodigarry Country House Hotel**, a few miles north of Staffin and 20 miles north of Portree, T01470-552203, F552301. Beautifully located at the foot of the mighty Quiraing and with stunning views across Staffin Bay, this is one of the great country house hotels, with a relaxing old-world atmosphere and excellent restaurant. Flora MacDonald's actual cottage is in the grounds and has been tastefully refurbished, giving the chance to stay in a place steeped in the island's history. The lively bar is a good place to enjoy a laugh and a jig.

A **Uig Hotel**, on the right of the road into the Uig from Portree, beside a white church and opposite Frazer's Folly, T01470-542205, F542308 17 rooms, open year round. Classy accommodation with great views across the bay, good food and a friendly island welcome. Offers clay pigeon shooting and fly fishing.

B **Glenview Inn and Restaurant**, at Culnacnoc, just north of the Lealt Falls, T01470-562248, F562211. 5 rooms. Cosy and relaxed accommodation with a very fine restaurant.

D **Dun Flodigarry Backpackers Hostel**, T/F01470-552212. 66 beds. Open Mar-Oct. Laundry facilities, breakfast available and only 100 yds from the bar of the *Flodigarry Country House Hotel*.

Dunvegan *p887*

A **Harlosh House Hotel**, just beyond Roskhill, turn south off the A863, T/F01470-521367, harlosh.house@virgin.net. 6 rooms. Easter to mid-Oct. Cosy, comfortable, great views and a reputation for superb food (evenings only).

B **Roskhill House**, 3 miles south of Dunvegan Castle on the A863, T01470-521317, stay@roskhill. demon.co.uk Recommended guesthouse. 5 cosy rooms, peaceful setting, great food.

The Cuillins and Minginish *p887*

A **Sligachan Hotel**, 7 miles south of Portree, where the A87 Kyleakin-Portree road meets the A863 to Dunvegan, T01471-8650204, F650207. The legendary rallying point for climbers who come to Skye for the Cuillins. The hotel's

Seamus bar stocks an impressive selection of malts and also serves the island's real ales as well as meals. The campsite opposite is the most popular place to stay in the area.

A **Talisker House**, in the village of Talisker, T01478-640245, jon_and_ros.wathen@virgin.net 4 rooms. This excellent guesthouse makes an ideal retreat from the summer hordes, and serves fine food.

D **Croft Bunkhouse & Bothies**, north of Carbost, near Portnalong, T/F01478-640254, pete@skyehostel.free-online.co.uk Sleeps 26. Also room for camping, transport from Sligachan or Portree, rents mountain bikes, pub and shop nearby.

Broadford and around *p888*

B **Lime Stone Cottage**, 4 Lime Park, T01471-822142, kathielimepark@btinternet.com. Full of rustic charm.

D **Skye Backpackers Hostel**, Kyleakin, T/F01471-534510, open all year.

D **Dun Caan Hostel**, near the old ferry quay in Kyleakin, T01471-534087, open all year and also hires bikes.

Sleat peninsula *p888*

L **Kinloch Lodge**, T01471-833214, www.kinloch-lodge.com, at the head of Loch na Dal. Mar-Nov. Lord and Lady MacDonald's family home has 10 en suite rooms and is also an award-winning restaurant, offering the rare chance to enjoy superb food in the grandest of settings. The track that leads to the 19th-century Sporting Lodge turns off the A851 about 8 miles south of Broadford. Lady Claire MacDonald is one of the best known cooks in Scotland and author of several cookbooks, and if you do decide to treat yourself make sure you leave enough room for their exquisite puddings. The 5-course fixed menu is in our expensive range, but well worth it.

L **Hotel Eilean Iarmain**, at Isle Ornsay, T01471-833332, F833275, www.eileanarmain.co.uk. 12 rooms. Award-winning Victorian hotel full of charm and old-world character, with wonderful views. It is utterly lovely and romantic and an absolute must if you're in the area and can afford it. Award-winning restaurant features local shellfish landed only yards away (open to non-residents). A cheaper option is to eat in the cosy **bar** next door, which serves pub grub of an impossibly high standard in a more informal atmosphere. The hotel also offers winter shooting on the local estate, and you can enjoy a tasting of the local whisky.

A **Ardvasar Hotel**, T01471-844223, www.ardvasar.com, a traditional whitewashed coaching in with 9 rooms, an excellent restaurant and the liveliest pub in the vicinity.

D **Sleat Independent Hostel**, at Kilmore, T01471-844440, F844272. Newly refurbished with all facilities, 24 beds, open all year, and free transport to and from Armadale Pier.

D **SYHA Hostel**, just before the turn-off to the ferry pier, T01471-844260. 42 beds. Open mid-Mar to end Oct, rents bikes.

Eating

Portree *p885*

£££ **Chandlery Seafood Restaurant**, next door to the *Bosville Hotel* (see under 'Sleeping' for details). Superb French/Scottish cuisine using local produce.

£££ **Lower Deck Seafood Restaurant**, on the harbour front at the foot of Quay Brae, T01478-613611. Freshest of seafood and a contender with the **Chandlery** for the best food in town. Open Apr-Oct daily 1100-2200. For a budget treat try the excellent fish and chips from their takeaway next door.

££ **Ben Tianavaig**, 5 Bosville Terr, T01478-612152. Vgetarian bistro. Seating is limited so you'll need to book. Open lunchtimes at weekends, and Tue-Sun 1800-2130.

Dunvegan *p887*

£££ **The Three Chimneys**, next to the Colbost Croft Museum, T01470-511258, www.threechimneys.co.uk, considered by many to be the best restaurant in the north of Scotland and, judging by the numerous awards they've won, that judgement can't be far wrong. Local seafood, meat, veg and dairy produce and a great wine list. Open daily 1230-1400 (except Sun) and 1830-2130; expensive. They also have accommodation a few yards away at

A **The House Over-By** (6 rooms).

Activities and tours

Boat trips

The **Bella Jane**, sails into Loch Coruisk from Rigol, to book T0800- 7313089 (freephone). Return boat trips take 3 hrs, including about 1½ hrs ashore, and cost £13.50, £6.50 child. You should be able to see seals and porpoises en route. There's also a one-way trip for walkers/ climbers who wish to make the return journey on foot or explore the Cuillins. There are also trips on the **Nicola**, T866236. Trips to Rùm or Canna cost £20-35.

Outdoor activities

Raasay Outdoor Centre, half a mile beyond Inverarish, which is a 15-min walk from the ferry dock on Raasay, T01478-660266. Housed in the huge Georgian mansion that was Raasay House, which runs many and various adventure courses, from climbing to windsurfing, as well as offering basic accommodation from Mar to mid-Oct, and a **campsite**.

Transport

Bus

There are 4 buses daily (Mar-Oct) Mon-Fri (2 on Sat) around the **Trotternish Peninsula**, in each direction, via **Uig**. There are daily buses (4 Mon-Sat, 3 on Sun) to **Kyleakin**, and 3 buses daily Mon-Sat to **Armadale** via **Broadford**. There are 2 daily buses to **Carbost** (for the Talisker Distillery) and **Fiskavaig** Mon-Fri (1 on Sat), and 2 daily buses to **Glenbrittle** (in the summer only). There are 3 buses daily Mon-Fri to **Glendale** via **Dunvegan** (1 on Sat), and 3 buses to **Waternish** via **Dunvegan** (Mon-Sat). There's a Scottish Citylink service from Inverness (3 Mon-Sat, 2 on Sun, 3 hrs) and also from **Glasgow** via **Fort William** to **Kyleakin**, **Portree** and **Uig** 3-4 times daily (3 hrs from **Fort William** to **Portree**). Winter services are limited with only a few buses in each direction each day.

Ferry

The **CalMac** car and passenger ferry runs from **Sconser** to **Raasay** daily Mon-Sat every hour from 0830 till 1800 (2130 in Jul/Aug). Last return is at 1700 (2100 in Jul/Aug). It takes 15 mins.

Directory

Portree *p885*

Internet Portree Independent Hostel (see 'Sleeping' above), at the post office and at Portree Backpacker's Hostel on Dunvegan Rd.

Leodhas (Lewis)

→*Colour map 7*

Lewis constitutes the northern two thirds of the most northerly island in the Outer Hebrides (which includes Harris to the south). It is by far the most populous of the Outer Hebridean islands and, with over 20,000 inhabitants, makes up two thirds of the total population. The majority of the rest of the population live in the long line of crofting townships strung out along the west coast between Port Nis (Ness) and Càrlabhagh (Carloway). The west coast is also where you'll find the island's most interesting sites. The interior of the northern half is flat peat bog, hence the island's name which means 'marshy' in Gaelic. Further south, where Lewis becomes Harris, the scenery is more dramatic as the relentlessly flat landscape gives way to rocky hills, providing the backdrop to the sea-lochs that cut deep into the coast and the beautiful beaches around Uig. ▸▸ *For Sleeping, Eating and other listings, see page 894.*

Ins and outs

Information Stornoway **Tourist Information Centre** ⓘ *26 Cromwell St, T01851-703088. Apr-May and Sep-Oct Mon-Fri 0900-1800, Sat 0900-1700; Jun-Aug Mon-Fri 0900-2000; Oct-Mar Mon-Fri 0900-1700.*

Steòrnabhagh (Stornoway)

The fishing port of Stornoway, the only town in the Outer Hebrides, is the islands' commercial capital and has the full range of banks, shops, hotels, guest- houses, pubs and restaurants, garages, car hire firms, sports facilities, an airport and ferry terminal, and for the visiting tourist it presents a rare opportunity to stock up on supplies.

Anyone remotely interested in Harris Tweed should visit the **Lewis Loom Centre** ⓘ *T01851-703117, Mon-Sat 1000-1700, £2,* housed in the Old Grainstore at the northern end of Cromwell Street, just off Bayhead. The 40-minute guided tour includes demonstrations of traditional methods of warping, dyeing and spinning, and a detailed lecture on the history of Harris Tweed. There's also a craft shop.

The West Coast

At **Barabhas (Barvas)** the road forks. The A857 bears right (north) and continues all the way to **Nis (Ness)** and the Butt of Lewis (see page 893), while A858 bears left (west). A few miles along this road is the turn-off for **Arnol**. At the end of the village is the **Blackhouse Museum** ⓘ *T01851-710395, Apr-Sep Mon-Sat 0930-1830; Oct-Mar Mon-Sat 0930-1630, Sun 1400-1630, £2.80, concession £2, children £1,* one of the best surviving examples of an original blackhouse in Scotland and well worth visiting. These traditional thatched houses were once common throughout the Highlands and Islands, and inhabited until the 1960s. They were well adapted to the harsh local climate. They had no windows or chimney and were built with local materials – stone, turf and thatch of oat, barley or marram grass, and with a peat fire burning continually in the central hearth – and attached to the living quarters was the cattle byre. This particular blackhouse was built in 1885 and lived in until 1964.

The landscape gradually becomes more undulating and scenically interesting as the road then passes through the village of **Càrlabhagh (Carloway)**, Lord Leverhume's proposed fishing port. Here, a branch road leads to the ruined and deserted 'blackhouse' village of **Gearrannan (Garenin)**. The village now boasts a Gatliff Trust hostel, heritage centre, café and holiday dwellings. Above the village a footpath can be followed through the lazybeds and above the sea cliffs to reveal a stunning view of **Dal More Bay**.

A little further on, standing a few hundred yards from the main road, is the **Dùn Chàrlabhaigh (Doune Carloway) Broch**, the best-preserved building of its type in the Outer Hebrides. The impressive 2,000 year-old drystone habitation is beautifully situated on a rocky outcrop, commanding great views across Loch Carloway to the sea beyond. There's also the **Doune Broch Visitor Centre** ⓘ *T01851-643338, Apr-Oct Mon-Sat 1000-1800, free,* by the car park, which tastefully complements the architectural style of the site, and which gives a good audio-visual description of how life must have been in one of these structures around 50 BC.

Calanais (Callanish)

ⓘ *Visitor Centre, T01851-621422, calanais.centre@btinternet.com Site open daily all year. Apr-Sep 1000-1900; Oct-Mar 1000-1600. Free. Visitor Centre closed Sun. Exhibition: adult £1.75, concession £1.25, children £0.75.*

Five miles south of Dun Chàrlabhaigh is the jewel in the islands' prehistoric crown, the **Calanais Standing Stones,** which are unique in Scotland and the equal of Stonehenge in historical value. The stones are in a beautiful setting overlooking Loch Roag and are very atmospheric, especially at sunset or at night, when no one's around. They are in the form of a Celtic cross, and in the centre is a circle of 13 stones with a central monolith over 12-ft tall, and a chambered burial cairn. The oldest part of this great ceremonial site – probably the stone circle – dates from around 3,000 BC (older than Stonehenge) and continued in use until about 800 BC. The full significance of the site is not yet known, though it is probably connected to the seasonal cycle, as many of the stones are aligned with the rising and setting moon. There are also a number of smaller and more isolated stone circles a few miles south of Calanais on the road to Gearraidh na h-Aibhne (Garynahine). Next to the stones is the Calanais Visitor Centre, which features 'The Story of the Stones' exhibition, a restaurant and gift shop.

The Uig Peninsula

From Gearraidh na h-Aibhne the main A858 runs back to Stornoway, while the B8011 forks west to the remote Uig peninsula in the southwest of the island. Four miles down this road is a turning to the right onto the B8059, which leads to the island of **Bearnaraigh (Great Bernera)**, now connected to the mainland of Lewis by a single-track road bridge. The main settlement on the island is **Breacleit (Breaclete)**. The rest of the island is fairly interesting with tiny fishing villages, and one or two brochs and some standing stones. The nicest part, though, is on the north coast, near the tiny hamlet of **Bostadh (Bosta)**, where a lovely little sandy bay looks out to the nearby island of **Bearnaraigh Beag (Little Bernera)**.

Beyond Ardroil the road continues to **Mangersta** where at Aird Fenish is some of the most spectacular and photogenic coastal scenery in the Outer Hebrides. The cliffs plunge dramatically beyond the road to the inaccessible beach below with a series of crumbling sea stacks battered by the fearsome waves and seabirds riding the updraughts adding to the sense of natural beauty, energy and power.

At **Timsgearraidh (Timsgarry)** are the **Traigh Chapadail (Uig sands)** at the village of **Eadar Dha Fhadhail (Adroil)**. This is the loveliest of all the beaches on Lewis, with miles of sand dunes and machair, but it is famous for an entirely different reason. It was here in 1831 that a crofter dug up the 'Lewis Chessmen', 78 pieces carved from walrus ivory and belonging to at least eight incomplete chess sets from 12th-century Scandinavia. Some are now in the Museum of Scotland in Edinburgh, but most can be found in the British Museum in London.

North to Nis (Ness)

The A857 leaves Stornoway and runs northwest through barren, treeless and relentlessly bleak moorland to **Barabhas (Barvas)**. The landscape is scarred by deep gashes caused by peat digging, and the unfamiliar smell you detect in your nostrils is peat burning – a strange mixture of burning grass, whisky and coffee. Peat is the main source of domestic fuel used on the islands, and outside most houses you'll see large stacks of peat, or '*cruachs*'.

Just beyond Barabhas is a turning right to **Baile an Trùiseil (Ballantrushel)**, site of the huge **Clach an Trùiseil**, a 20-ft monolith (the largest in Europe). This is the first of a number of prehistoric sights between here and **Siadar (Shader)** which may be of interest to the keen archaeologist, but otherwise there's little of note on the road north to Nis. The road ends at the fishing village of **Port Nis (Port of Ness)**. It's a lovely spot, with a picturesque little harbour and golden sweep of beach enclosed by steep cliffs. Each September the locals head out to the island of **Sula Sgeir**, 30 miles to the north, for the annual cull of young gannets (or *gugas*), which are considered something of a delicacy by the people of Lewis. A few minutes to the northwest, the Butt of Lewis lighthouse forms the most northerly tip of the Outer Hebrides.

Just before Port Nis, is Lìonal, where the B8015 turns off right and leads to the start of the 10-mile **coastal trail** that works it way round to **Tòlstadh (Tolsta North)** and the beautiful beaches of Traigh Mhor and Garry. Another minor road heads northwest to the tiny hamlet of **Eòropaidh (Eoropie)** (pronounced 'Yor-erpee'). By the road junction that leads to Rubha Robhanais is the ancient **Teampull Mholuaidh (St Moluag's Church)**, thought to date from the 12th century and restored to its present state in 1912. It is now used on certain Sundays by Stornoway's Episcopal Church. From Eòropaidh a narrow road runs to the lighthouse at **Rubha Robhanais (Butt of Lewis)**, which marks the nothernmost tip of the Outer Hebrides. It's a great place for spotting seabirds or whales and dolphins, but also very wild and windy. Half a mile back down the road a path leads down to the tiny beach of **Port Sto**, which is more sheltered.

Sleeping

As well as the usual guesthouses and B&Bs, there are several official **youth hostels**. Some are difficult to get to without your own transport, but you can hitchhike. They are run by the **SYHA** or the **Gatliff Hebridean Hostels Trust**. They are basic and adequate, but take a sleeping bag and food. Most don't have phones, so you can't book in advance, and try not to arrive or leave on Sun. The Gatliff Trust has 4 hostels on the islands. Contact them at 71-77 Cromwell St, Stornoway, or visit their website, www.gatliff. ic24.net.

Stornoway *p891*
There are many B&Bs in and around the centre, most of which offer a 'room only' rate for those requiring an early start to catch the first ferry. Several are along Matheson Rd, close to the centre and ferry terminal.
A **Royal Hotel**, Cromwell St, T01851-702109, F702142. 24 rooms. Good value, and good food in its restaurant and bistro.
A **Park Guest House**, 30 James St, T01851-702485, F703482. 10 rooms. Only 500 yds from the ferry terminal, and the best of the guesthouses. It also has an excellent restaurant.

Callanish *p892*
C **Debbie Nash**, 19 Tolsta Chaolais, T01851-621321. A few miles north of the stones, in Tolastadh a' Chaolais (Tolsta Chalois). Recommended vegetarian B&B.

Uig Peninsula *p893*
A **Baile Na Cille Guest House**, in Timsgarry, T01851-672242, F672241, RandJGollin @com puserve.com. Open Apr-Sep, offers dinner for residents and non-residents alike.

North to Ness *p893*
C **Galson Farm Guest House**, halfway between Barabhas and Port Nis, T01851-850492. Friendly and beautifully restored 18th-century house.

Eating

Stornoway *p891*
£££-££ Park Guest House (see Sleeping above). Probably the best restaurant in town, it offers top-class modern Scottish cooking using local fish, lamb and venison. It also caters for vegetarians and is open Tue-Sat.

Callanish *p892*
££ Tigh Mealros, a few miles south of Calanais Visitor Centre, at Gearraidh na h-Aibhne, T01851-621333. They serve good local grub in a cosy, relaxed atmosphere, with scallops a speciality (closes at 2100).

Activities and tours

Tour companies
MacDonald's Coaches, at the Ferry Terminal, T01851-706267. Coach tours. **Hebridean Exploration**, 19 Westview Tce, Stornoway, T01851-705655 (T0374-292746 mobile). **Elena C**, 5a Knock, Point, T01851-870537, F706384. Wildlife trips from Stornoway harbour.

Transport

Buses leave from Stornoway to all parts of the island, but not on Sun. To **Port Niss (Ness)** via Barabhas (Barvas) 4-6 times per day; to **Arnol, Siabost (Shawbost), Càrlabhagh (Carloway), Calanais (Callanish)**, and back to Stornoway ('West Side Circular') 4-6 times per day; to **Bearnaraigh (Great Bernera)** via Gearraidh na h-Aibhne (Garynahine) 4 per day; to **Uig District** 3-4 per day; to **Ranais (Ranish)** 6-8 times per day. For full details, T01851-840269. There are buses from Stornoway to **Tarbert** and on to **Leverburgh** (for the ferry to North Uist) 4-5 times per day (T01859-502441).

Directory

Stornoway *p891*
Banks The Bank of Scotland is directly opposite the tourist office and has an ATM. The other major banks are also in the centre of town and also have ATMs. **Car and bike rental** is available at good rates from Lewis Car Rentals, 52 Bayhead St, T01851-703760, F705860. You can rent bikes at Alex Dan's Cycle Centre, 67 Kenneth St, T01851-704025, F701712. **Internet** Captions, 27 Church St, T01851-702238, F706782, bayble@ captions. co.uk, www.captions. co.uk. Open Mon-Sat till late in the summer months. Internet facilities also available at the public library on Cromwell St. **Post office** on Francis St.

Na Hearadh (Harris)

→ Colour map 7

Harris is not an island, but together with Lewis forms the largest of the Outer Hebrides, with Harris taking up the southern third. The two parts are divided by the long sea lochs of Loch Seaforth in the east and Loch Resort in the west, though this division is rarely shown on maps. Though joined, the two are very different in terms of geography. Harris is largely mountain and rock whereas Lewis is flat moorland.

Harris itself is almost split in two by the sea at An Tairbeart (Tarbert), the largest town and ferry terminal. To the north are the highest peaks in the Outer Hebrides, surrounded by some of the finest unspoilt wilderness in the whole country, while to the south are miles of wonderful sandy beaches and, on the east coast, an almost indescribably strange lunar landscape straight out of a science fiction film. ▸▸ *For Sleeping, Eating and other listings, see page 897.*

Ins and outs

Information Tarbert **tourist information centre** ⓘ *T01859-502011. Apr-Oct Mon-Sat 0900-1700. It also opens in the winter (check times) and when the ferry arrives,* is close to the ferry terminal.

An Tairbeart (Tarbert) and Ceann a Tuath na Hearadh (North Harris)

Tarbert, the largest settlement on Harris, lies in a sheltered bay on the narrow isthmus that joins North and South Harris. It's a tiny place and there's not much to do, but as it's the main ferry port for Harris it has more facilities than anywhere else, such as shops, a bank, post office and tourist information centre.

North Harris is the most mountainous part of the Outer Hebrides and its wild, rugged peaks are ideal for hill walking. The A859 south from Lewis gets progressively more scenic as it skirts **Loch Siophort (Seaforth)** and the mountains rise before you like a giant barrier. The road then climbs past **Bogha Glas (Bowglass)** and **Aird a Mhulaidh (Ardvourlie)** with **Clisham** (2,619 ft), the highest peak in the Outer Hebrides, and **Sgaoth Aird** (1,829 ft) towering overhead on either side.

The A859 continues west across the crest of the craggy hills then drops down to the turn-off for the single-track B887 which winds its way all the way out to Huisinis (Hushinish) between the impressive mountains of the Forest of Harris on one side and the northern shore of West Loch Tarbert on the other, with views across to the Sound of Taransay and the beaches of South Harris. Immediately beyond the turn-off you pass through **Bun Abhainn Eadarra (Bunavoneadar),** which was a thriving whaling station until 1930 and one of Lord Leverhulme's many schemes for the island. The old whaling station is worth a visit even though the site has not been developed as a tourist attraction.

At **Amhuinnsuidhe Castle** (pronounced 'Avan-soo-ee') you'll see a beautiful waterfall spilling straight into the sea. The road then runs right past the front door of the castle before passing through an archway and continuing to the tiny crofting township of **Huisinis (Hushinish),** beautifully situated in a sandy bay. This is where the road ends; next stop the USA! Follow the track to the right across the machair where a footpath above the jetty and rocky beach can be followed to the old fishing lodge at **Cravadale** and Loch Cravadale beyond. Make a detour to the golden sands and turquoise waters of **Traigh Mheilein** overlooking the rocky island of **Scarp.**

Ceann a Deas na Hearadh (South Harris)

An absolute must while you're in the Outer Hebrides is the 45-mile circular route around South Harris. If you only do one thing while you're here, then make sure this is it, for the change in scenery from the west coast to the east is utterly fascinating. One thing you're sure to puzzle over as you travel round is the fact that most people live on the harsh and inhospitable east coast, known as **Na Baigh (Bays)**, while the beautiful west coast with its miles of glorious golden sands is scarcely populated. This is not through choice. The fertile west coast housed most of the population until the end of the 18th century when they were cleared to make way for sheep farms. Some emigrated to Cape Breton, while others chose instead to stay in Harris and moved to the east side.

The main road from Tarbert runs south, skirting East Loch Tarbert, then cuts inland and heads west through a dramatic lunar landscape of rocks dotted with tiny lochans. It then begins to descend towards the sea and you can see the vast expanse of **Losgaintir (Luskentyre)** beach directly ahead. A single-track road turns off to the right and runs out to the tiny settlement of Losgaintir. The road cuts through the rich machair as it follows the magnificent stretch of bleached white sand that fills the entire bay, washed by turquoise sea and backed by steep dunes. All this set against the backdrop of the mountains to the north.

The road follows the coast, passing through the tiny settlements of **Seilebost**, **Horgabost** and **Burgh (Borve)**. A few miles further on is another beautiful stretch of white sands at **Sgarasta Bheag (Scaristabeg)**. Beyond Sgarasta Bheag, the village of **Taobh Tuath** (Northton) provides access to the scenic promontory of **Toe Head**, almost cut off from the rest of Harris by the huge expanse of the golden sands of Sgarasta. At the MacGillivary Machair Centre you can learn about the ecology of the local machair which forms such a distinctive and attractive element of the landscape of the west coast of the Hebrides. A ruined chapel of 16th-century origin is situated on the machair below **Chaipaval** (365m), whose heathery slopes can be climbed for one of the best views out to sea towards St Kilda some 40 miles distant.

Ant-Ob (Leverburgh) and Ròghadal (Rodel)

The road then runs along the south shore till it reaches the sprawling village of **An t-Ob (Leverburgh)**, site of Lord Leverhulme's ambitious plan to turn a sleepy crofting township into a major fishing port. A few of the original buildings can be seen near the pier, which is the departure point for **CalMac**'s **car ferry** to Otternish on North Uist (for details, see Ins and outs.

Three miles east of Leverburgh, at the southeastern tip of Harris, is Ròghadal (Rodel), dominated by the 12th-century **St Clement's Church**, something of an unusual sight in such a remote spot and one of the most impressive religious building in the Hebrides (only the Benedictine abbey on Iona is larger). The church stands on a site which goes back 1,500 years and was built by Alastair Crotach (Hunchback) Macleod of Harris in the 1520s. Though impressive from the outside, particularly the huge tower, the real interest lies inside, with a collection of remarkable carved wall tombs. There are three tombs, the most notable of which is that of the founder, Alastair Crotach. The one in the south wall of the choir is also worth a close look.

Na Baigh (Bays)

Running north from Ròghadal up the east coast of South Harris is the **Golden Road**, so named by the locals because the of the huge expense of building it. This twisting single-track road runs through a striking moonscape. It seems inconceivable that anyone could survive in such an environment, but the road passes through a string of townships created in the 19th century by the people evicted from the west coast (see page 895). People here have spent years eking a meagre living from the thin soil by building 'lazy beds' (thin strips of piled-up earth between the rocks) for planting potatoes. Weaving and fishing also provide much-needed income.

At **Lingreabhagh (Lingarabay)** the road skirts the foot of **Roinebhal**, the proposed site of one of the largest superquarries in Europe, which would demolish virtually the entire mountain over many decades. Local people and environmentalists are up in arms at the prospect of losing fishing grounds, not to mention a unique and natural asset.

Sleeping

Tarbert and North Harris *p895*

A **Ardvourlie Castle Guest House**, Just off the A859 near Ardvourlie, T01859-502307, F502348. 4 rooms. Apr-Oct. This hunting lodge on the shores of Loch Seaforth oozes charm and elegance. They also serve excellent food.

A **Harris Hotel**, on the main road from Stornoway on the left before the turning for the ferry, T01859-502154, F502281. An old established favourite, and the only place serving food on a Sun (see below). The bar next door also serves meals.

A **Leachin House**, 1 mile out of Tarbert on the Stornoway road, T/F01859-502157. Luxurious Victorian home with great views and superb home cooking (for residents only). Only 2 rooms so book ahead.

B **Allan Cottage Guest House**, on the left after the turning into the village, T01859-502146. Open Apr-Sep. Close to the ferry, very comfortable rooms and exceptional food. Book ahead.

C **Macleod Motel**, right beside the ferry pier, T01859-502364. Very handy for the early-morning ferry, also has room-only rate.

South Harris *p895*

A **Scarista House**, overlooking the beach in a wonderful setting, T01851-550238, tnpmartin@ukgateway.net 5 rooms, open May-Sep. To add to the peace and quiet, there's no TV, only an extensive library and drawing room with open fires. The food on offer is amongst the best on the islands, particularly the seafood. Even if you're not staying, you should treat yourself to dinner here. Expensive but well worth it. There are also self-catering cottages in the grounds. The golf course over the road is so scenic the views may put you off your swing.

D **Am Bothan Bunkhouse**, T01851-520251, also to the ferry in Leverburgh, has full facilities, space for tents and is open all year.

Eating

Eating options are limited. Most guesthouses and B&Bs will provide dinner on request, but check in advance if they do so on a Sun.

££ **Harris Hotel** (see Sleeping) serves food every day till around 2030. They do a 3-course fixed menu or basic and cheap bar meals, as does the bar next door Mon-Sat.

Transport

Ferry details are given in the Ins and outs section on p884. There's a **bus** service 4-5 times per day from Stornoway to **Tarbert** (1 hr 15 mins), which continues to **Leverburgh** (for the ferry to North Uist) via the west coast of South Harris. There's also a service 3-4 times per day from Tarbert to **Leverburgh** via the east coast (45 mins), along the so-called 'Golden Road'. There are also services to **Huisinis** (2-4 per day on schooldays, 45 mins), to **Reinigeadal** (2 per day on schooldays) and to **Scalpaigh** (2-5 per day, 10 mins). Bus timetables are available at the tourist office (see above).

Uibhist a Tuath (North Uist)

→ *Colour map 7*

North Uist is the largest of the southern chain of the Outer Hebrides, about 13 miles from north to south and 18 miles east to west at its widest point. At first sight it comes as something of a disappointment after the dramatic landscapes of Harris. In fact, it's barely a landscape at all, as over a third of the island's surface is covered by water. The east coast around Lochmaddy, the main settlement, is so peppered with lochs it resembles a giant sieve. But heading west from Lochmaddy the island's attractions become apparent, particularly the magnificent beaches on the north and west coast. Also on the west coast, the Balranald Nature Reserve is the ideal place for bird watching. You're also likely to see otters. There are numerous prehistoric sites scattered across the island, and with all that water around there's obviously plenty of good fishing to be had. ▸▸ *For Sleeping, see page 898.*

Ins and outs

Getting there There are three **car ferry** services to North Uist. One is to Otternish from Leverburgh on South Harris, the others are to Lochmaddy, from Uig on Skye, and from Tarbert on Harris. North Uist is joined to the islands of Benbecula and South Uist to the south by causeway and bridge. There are several **buses** daily (Mon-Sat) from Otternish to Lochmaddy and on to Lochboisdale on South Uist.

Getting around There are 4-6 **buses** per day (not Sun) from Otternish to Lochmaddy. These buses continue to Baile a Mhanaich (Balivanich) on Benbecula, where there is an airport (see page 899), and Lochboisdale and Ludag on South Uist (see page 900). There are 4-7 buses per day from Lochmaddy to Otternish. These continue via the new causeway to the island of Bearnaraigh (Berneray) just off the north coast in the sound of Harris. There are 3 buses per day from Lochmaddy to Clachan na Luib (Clachan-a-Luib) which run in an anti-clockwise direction around the north and west coasts. Two buses per day connect Clachan-a-Luib with Baile Sear (Baleshare) and also with Saighdinis (Sidinish). There are also Royal Mail post buses linking the main settlements. Local bus timetables are available at the tourist office in Lochmaddy (see below).

Information Lochmaddy **tourist information centre** is near the ferry pier ⓘ *T01876-500321. Mid-Apr to mid-Oct Mon-Sat 0900-1700, and for the arrival of the evening ferry.* They provide transport timetables.

Loch nam Madadh (Lochmaddy)

Lochmaddy, the island's main village and ferry port, is a tiny place, so small you're almost through it before you realize. Though it's on the east coast and not close to the beaches, it is the best base for exploring the island as it boasts most facilities. It has a bank (next to the tourist office), a hotel and pub, a tourist office, a few shops, post office, hospital (T01876-500325) and petrol station. If you have time the **Taigh Chearsabhagh Museum and Arts Centre** (T/F01876-500293, www.taigh-chearsabhagh.com) is worth visiting and has a café.

Around the island

The real charms of North Uist are its fabulous beaches on the north and west coasts. Heading anti-clockwise from Lochmaddy, the A865 runs northwest, passing the turning for Otternish and **Bearnaraigh** (see above), which is now connected to North Uist by a causeway. It continues west through the township of **Sollas (Solas)**, where there are a couple of B&Bs, and then past the beautiful sands of **Bhalaigh (Vallay) Strand.** Near the northwestern tip of the island is **Scolpaig Tower**, standing on an islet in Loch Scolpaig, a 'folly' built for famine relief in the 19th century. Three miles south of here is the turning to **Balranald RSPB Reserve**, an area of rocky coast, sandy beaches and dunes, machair and lochs. The reserve is ideal for bird watching, especially waders. A two-hour guided walk along the headland allows you to see Manx shearwaters, gannets, skuas and storm petrels, and during the summer you can listen out for the distinctive rasping call of the corncrake, one of the rarest birds in Britain. There's a basic visitor centre, which is open April-September.

Sleeping

A **Lochmaddy Hotel**, T01876-500332, F500210. Right by the ferry terminal. Open all year. Their restaurant serves great seafood, and the lively bar serves snacks. This is also the place to ask about fishing, as they rent out boats and sells permits for trout and salmon fishing.

C **Burnside Croft**, on Berneray, T01876-540235, splashmackilloop@burnsidecroft.fsnet.co.uk You can share the Prince Charles's crofting experience with Donald (Splash) MacKillop, who also offers cycle hire and stories round the fire for evening entertainment.

D **Lochmaddy Uist Outdoor Centre**, half a mile from the ferry pier, T01876-500480. Open all year and offers a wide range of outdoor activities including kayaking, windsurfing and rock climbing.

E **Gatliff Trust Hostel** (12 beds, no phone, open all year) in two restored blackhouses overlooking a lovely sandy beach and old Viking pier about a mile up the east coast from the old ferry pier.

Beinn na Faoghla (Benbecula)

→Colour map 7

Tiny Benbecula may be suffering from delusions of stature. Its Gaelic name means 'mountain of the fords', but the highest point is a mere 407 ft, with the rest of the island as flat as a pancake. It lies between Protestant North Uist and Catholic South Uist, and most visitors use it solely as a means of getting from one to the other via the A865 which cuts straight through the middle. »» *For Sleeping, Eating and other listings, see pages 916-918.*

Ins and outs

Benbecula's **airport** is at Balivanich (see below) and there are direct flights to Glasgow, Barra and Stornoway (see page 884). The island is connected by causeways to both North and South Uist, and **buses** travelling to and from Lochmaddy and Lochboisdale pass through the villages of Balivanich, Lionacleit (Liniclate) and Creag Ghoraidh (Creagorry). There are also regular island buses which run between these settlements.

Baile a Mhanaich (Balivanich)

Like North Uist, the east of the island is so pitted with lochs that most people live on the west coast. A large percentage of the population are Royal Artillery personnel and their families stationed at **Baile a Mhanaich (Balivanich)**, a sprawling army base of utilitarian buildings in the northwest of the island. The influx of so many English-speakers has had a less than positive impact on Gaelic culture, and the military facilities have blighted much of the island's natural beauty, but Benbecula has benefited economically from the army's presence. There are worries, however, that the base may be run down or closed, which would have a devastating effect on the local economy.

South to Lionacleit (Liniclate)

South of Balivanich the B892 runs around the west coast before joining the main A865 at the southern end of the island. It runs past **Culla Bay**, overlooked by **Baille nan Cailleach (Nunton)**. It was from here in 1746 that Bonnie Prince Charlie set off with Flora MacDonald over the sea to Skye, disguised as her maid. To the south is **Poll-na-Crann**, better known as 'stinky bay' because of the piles of seaweed deposited there by fierce Atlantic storms. From the mid-18th century this kelp was used extensively in making glass, and provided a source of income for many communities. By 1820 the so-called kelp boom was over, though it is still gathered today and used for fertilizer. he B892 ends at **Lionacleit (Liniclate)**, where the new community school serves the Uists and Benbecula.

Sleeping

A **Dark Island Hotel**, in Lionacleit, where you'll find most of the accommodation, T01870-603030, F602347. A lot nicer inside than its name may suggest, and has a good restaurant.

D **Tigh-na-Cille Bunkhouse**, in Balivanich, T01870-602522, open all year and sleeps 10 in 2 dorms and 2 twin rooms.

Eating

£££-££ **Stepping Stone Restaurant** in Balivanich, T01870-603377, F603121. By far the best place to eat on the island. Offers good wholesome from 1000 till 2100. Snacks, sandwiches, takeaways and home baking are all available, as well as 3- or 5-course meals.

Directory

Car hire Maclennan Self Drive, Balivanich, T01870-602191. Ask Car Hire, Lionacleit, T01870-602818.

Uibhist a Deas (South Uist)

→ *Colour map 7*

South Uist is the largest of the southern chain of Outer Hebridean islands and the most scenically attractive. Like its southern neighbour, Barra, South Uist is Roman Catholic and generally more relaxed about Sunday openings.Its 20 miles of west coast is one long sandy beach, backed by dunes with a mile or two of beautiful, flowering machair behind. To the east of the main A865 that runs the length of the island rises a central mountainous spine of rock and peat dotted with numerous lochs. Its two highest peaks, Beinn Mhor (2,034 ft) and Hecla (1,988 ft), tower over the rocky cliffs of an inaccessible eastern coastline indented by sea lochs. ►► *For Sleeping, see page 901.*

Ins and outs

Getting there The island's main **ferry port** is Loch Baghasdail (Lochboisdale), which is reached from Oban and Mallaig via Castlebay on Barra (it arrives late at night). There are also inter-island ferries from Ludag, at the southern tip of South Uist: a private **passenger-only** ferry sails to Barra. There are passenger ferry sailings on Sun to and from Barra and a car ferry to Castlebay and Oban, but no ferry arrival from Oban, Mallaig or Castlebay and no bus services. The ferry to Eriskay was replaced by a causeway in Aug 2001.

Getting around A **causeway** connects South Uist to Benbecula by road and regular **buses** (4-6 per day Mon-Sat) run between Lochboisdale and Lochmaddy on North Uist, stopping en route at Dalabrog (Daliburgh), Tobha Mòr (Howmore) and Lionacleit and Balinavich on Benbecula. There is also a regular bus service between Lochboisdale and Ludag (for ferries to Barra). Eriskay is reached by a frequent car ferry from Ludag (Monday-Saturday only; for times, T01878-720261), which lands at the ferry jetty at **Haun**. Construction of a new causeway was completed in August 2001 linking Eriskay to South Uist.

Information Lochboisdale **tourist information** ⓘ *Pier Road, T01878-700286, open early Apr to mid-Oct.*

Around the island

At the north of the island a causeway leads across **Loch Bi** (pronounced 'Bee') to the distinctive modern statue of Our Lady of the Isles, standing by the main road on the lower slopes of **Rueval** hill. Further up the hill is the Royal Artillery control centre, known by the locals as 'Space City', due to its forest of aerials and 'golf balls', which tracks the missiles fired from a range on the northwestern corner of the island out into the Atlantic.

Just to the south of here is **Loch Druidibeag Nature Reserve,** on the site of the large freshwater loch, one of the largest breeding grounds in the British Isles for greylag geese and also a favourite haunt for mute swans (there's a warden nearby at Groigearraidh

(Grogarry) Lodge). From here the main road runs down the spine of the island, and all along the way little tracks branch off to the west, leading down to lovely beaches. Not far south of Loch Druidibeag is the turning to the tiny village of **Tobha Mòr (Howmore)**, where you can see a collection of old traditional thatched 'blackhouses' beside the seemingly endless stretch of golden sand. One of the houses has been converted into a Gatliff Trust Youth Hostel which overlooks the ruins of an ancient church and graveyard. The warden lives at Ben More House, at the junction with the main road. From the hostel it's a five-minute walk across the machair to the sandy beach which stretches almost the entire length of South Uist.

From Tobha Mòr, there are superb walks through the lonely hills of **Beinn Mhor** (620 m), **Beinn Corodale** (527 m) and **Hecla** (606 m) to the picturesque and dramatic valleys of Glen Hellisdale, Glen Corodale and Glen Usinish on the east coast. In 1746 Bonnie Prince Charlie is reputed to have taken refuge in a cave above **Corodale Bay** for three weeks following his defeat and escape from Culloden. Near **Bornais (Bornish)** another minor road can be followed east of the A865 to **Loch Eynort** that penetrates far inland from the Minch. An old stalkers path can be followed along the north shore of the loch towards the sea, with views of numerous seals and the occasional otter and the steep upper slopes of Beinn Mhor towering above to the north. A few miles south, at **Gearraidh Bhailteas (Milton)**, a cairn marks the birthplace of that famous Hebridean lass, **Flora MacDonald**. The A865 continues south for a few miles to the village of **Dalabrog (Daliburgh)**, then heads east to the island's main ferry port, **Lochboisdale**. South Uists's largest settlement is set on a rocky promontory in a beautiful island-dotted sea loch. The imposing entrance is guarded by Calvay island with its 13th-century castle ruin. Lochboisdale is a tiny place, with little in the way of tourist sights, though it does have a hotel, bank and post office. About 10 miles south of Lochboisdale, on the southern coast of the island, is **Ludag jetty**, the departure point for the small private passenger ferry to **Eòlaigearraidh (Eoligarry)** on Barra.

Eirisgeidh (Eriskay)

The tiny island of Eriskay, with a population of less than 200, gives its name to the native breed of pony, said to have been ridden by King Robert the Bruce at the Battle of Bannockburn in 1314. In the late 1970s it nearly became extinct, but one surviving stallion saved the breed and numbers are growing. A series of paths take you around the island in about three hours. Most people come to Eriskay to pay a visit to **Coilleag a' Phrionnsa (Prince's beach)**, the sandy beach on the west coast. This is where Bonnie Prince Charlie first stepped on to Scottish soil on July 23, 1745, at the start of the ill-fated Jacobite Rebellion. The rare pink convolvulus which grows there today is said to have been planted by the Prince himself from seeds brought from France. A small memorial cairn situated in the dunes behind the beach was erected by the local school to commemorate the occasion.

Sleeping

You should book accommodation in advance, as the ferry arrives in Lochboisdale late in the evening.

A **Lochboisdale Hotel**, T01878-700332, F700367. This fishing hotel is right by the ferry terminal, and the best place to stay and the only place to have a drink or a meal.

There is a **B&B** on **Eriskay** (T01878-720232), and a self-catering flat (T01878-720274), or you can **wild camp** – though there are few amenities, other than a shop, pub and post office.

For an explanation of the sleeping and eating price codes used in this guide, see the inside front cover. Other relevant information is provided in the Essentials chapter, page 36.

Bharraigh (Barra)

→ Colour map 7

It may be tempting to overlook the little island of Barra, only about eight miles long by five miles wide, but this would be a great mistake, as it's one of the most beautiful of all the islands in the Outer Hebrides. Here you'll find the best of the islands in miniature – beaches, machair, peat-covered hills, tiny crofting communities and Neolithic remains – and a couple of days spent on Barra gives a real taster of Hebridean life. Gaelic culture is also strong here but, with its Catholic tradition, Barra is a bit more laid-back than many of the other islands in the Outer Hebrides and doesn't follow the others' strict Sabbatarianism. ▸▸ *For Sleeping, Eating and other listings, see pages 903-904.*

Ins and outs

Getting there The best way to arrive is by **air** at Tràigh Mhòr ('Cockle Strand'), the famous airstrip on the beach at the north end of the island. This is the only airport in the UK where flight schedules are shown as 'subject to tides'. Barra is reached by **car ferry** from Oban and Mallaig on the mainland, and also by car ferry from Lochboisdale on South Uist, and by passenger-only ferry from Ludag on South Uist (for more details, see page 884).

Getting around There is a regular bus/postbus service (5-8 times per day Monday-Saturday) that runs from Castlebay to the ferry port of Eòlaigearraidh, via the **aiport**. There are also buses (3-4 per day Monday-Saturday) from Castlebay to Bhatarsaigh (Vatersay). You can also hire a car or a bicycle to tour the island at your leisure (see below).

Information As the main ferry port, Castlebay provides the full range of services: hotels, B&Bs, shops, a bank (but no ATM) and post office.The **tourist information centre** ⓘ *T01871-810223, Apr to mid-Oct Mon-Sat 0900-1700; also open for the arrival of the evening ferry*, is on the main street near the ferry terminal. It has information on local walks and will book accommodation.

Bàgh a' Chaisteil (Castlebay)

The main settlement is Castlebay, on the southern side of the island, overlooked by **Sheabhal** (383 m), on top of which is a statue of the Blessed Virgin and Child. Castlebay's most notable feature is the 15th-century **Kisimul Castle** ⓘ *T01871-810313, the castle can be visited by boat from the pier, weather permitting, Apr-Sep daily 0930-1830; Oct Mon-Wed 0930-1630, Thu 0930-1230, Sat 0930-1630, Sun 1400-1630, £3, concession £2.30, children £1,* built on an island in the middle of the harbour. This was the home of the Chief of the MacNeils. It was then sold to Colonel Gordon of Cluny, along with South Uist and Benbecula, and the people of Barra suffered the same cruel fate, 600 of them being shipped to Canada to starve. A hundred years later the castle and much of the island was bought back for the MacNeils by American architect, Robert Lister MacNeil, who became the 45th Clan Chief and restored the castle to its present state. It is now in the care of Historic Scotland. For more on the island's history, visit the **Barra Heritage Centre.** ⓘ *T01871-810403, Apr-Sep Mon-Fri 1100-1700, £1.*

Around Bharraigh

The A888 follows a circular route of 14 miles around the island, making an ideal day's bike tour from Castlebay. Heading west, it passes the turning for the causeway to **Vatersay** (see below), then runs northwest between two hills (**Sheabhal** to the east and **Beinn Tangabhal** to the west) to the west coast, where you'll find the nicest beaches. One of these is at **Halaman Bay**, near the village of **Tangasdal (Tangasdale)**, overlooked by the **Isle of Barra Hotel** (see below). At the turning for **Borgh (Borve)** there are standing stones.

Next is the turning for the small settlement of **Baile Na Creige (Craigston)**, where you'll find the **Thatched Cottage Museum**, an original 'blackhouse' and the chambered burial cairn of **Dun Bharpa**. ⓘ *Museum open Easter-Oct Mon-Fri 1100-1700, £1.* From Dun Bharpa there are pleasant walks into the surrounding hills, with the summit of **Sheabhal** offering tremendous views from the highest point on the island.

North of the turning, near **Allathsdal (Allasdale)**, is another lovely beach, and just beyond are the remains of **Dun Cuier**, an Iron-Age fort. Make a short detour at Greian, and follow the headland to the rugged cliffs at Greian Head.

The A888 then heads east to **Bagh a Tuath (Northbay)**, where a branch left leads to the village of Eòlaigearraidh (Eoligarry), near the northern tip, surrounded by sandy bays washed by Atlantic rollers. A private passenger ferry leaves from here to Ludag on South Uist. The road to Eoligarry passes the island's airport at Tràigh Mhòr, the 'cockle strand', which once provided 100 to 200 cartloads of delicious cockles each day. Now the cockleshells are gathered and used for harling, the roughcast wall covering used on many Scottish houses. By the beach is the house that was once the home of Compton MacKenzie, author of *Whisky Galore!* (see page 901). He lies buried at **Cille Bhara**, to the west of the village of Eòlaigearraidh, along with members of the MacNeil clan. This was one of the most important religious complexes in the Outer Hebrides, built in the 12th century, and consists of a church and two chapels. One of these, St Mary's, has been re-roofed and houses several carved medieval tombstones and a copy of a runic stone. The original is in the Museum of Scotland in Edinburgh.

Bhatarsaigh (Vatersay) and Mingulay

A worthwhile trip from Castlebay is to the island of Vatersay, now linked to Barra by a causeway built in an effort to stabilise the island community (the present population is around 70). The island boasts two lovely shell-sand beaches backed by beautiful machair, only a few hundred yards apart on either side of the narrow isthmus that leads to the main settlement of Vatersay. On the west beach, Bagh Siar, is the **Annie Jane Monument**, which commemorates the terrible tragedy in 1853, when the emigrant ship *Annie Jane* was wrecked off the coast of Vatersay, with the loss of 333 lives, many of them islanders.

On a clear day from Vatersay you can enjoy the view of the smaller islands to the south – Sandray, Pabbay and **Mingulay**. The latter was inhabited until 1912, and can still be visited from Barra. It has recently been acquired by the National Trust for Scotland.

Sleeping

It's a good idea to book in advance if arriving on the evening ferry from Oban or Mallaig.

A **Isle of Barra Hotel** a few miles west of Castlebay, T01871-810383, F810385, BarraHotel@aol.com 30 rooms, open Apr-Oct. Modern, purpose-built, overlooking a lovely beach with fantastic sea views.

B **Castlebay Hotel**, by the ferry terminal, T01871-810223, F810445. 14 rooms. Friendly, good food, good value and a great bar.

B **Craigard Hotel**, T01871-810200, is a family-run hotel with hearty home cooking.

Although there are also no official campsites on Barra, there are endless opportunities for **wild camping** across the island, with the most popular spots to be found on the machair at **Traigh Mhor** (north Barra), **Borve Point** (west Barra) and **Ledaig** (Castlebay). Generally no permission is required from the landowner, but ensure all waste and litter is removed when you leave the site.

Activities and tours

Boat trips

Day trips to **Mingulay** can be arranged with Mr John Allan MacNeil in Castlebay, T01871-810449 (approximately £15 per person), who sails to the island in settled weather when sufficient people can be found to fill the boat. It is one of the most rewarding excursions in the Outer Hebrides, particularly during the puffin season from Jun to early Aug. The trip normally includes a 2-hr sail from Barra past the neighbouring islands of Sandray and Pabbay, a circumnavigation of Mingulay to view the spectacularly high western sea cliffs, and a landing on the east coast for a three-hour exploration of the beach of Mingulay Bay, the deserted village and surrounding hills and coast. There are also fine views to the lighthouse on Barra Head, the most southerly outpost of the Outer Hebrides island chain. Similar boat trips can also be organised by Mr George McLeod at the Castlebay Hotel, T01871-810223 or ask at the tourist office in Castlebay.

Directory

Car hire is available from £20 per day at Barra Car Hire, T01871-810243, and MacMillan Self Drive, T01871-890366. **Bicycles** can be hired at Barra Cycle Hire, T01871-810284. **Taxi services** and **island tours** with Hatcher's Taxis, T01871-810486; and Nellie's Taxi, T01871-810302.

St Kilda

Over 40 miles west of the Outer Hebrides lie the spectacular and isolated islands of St Kilda, Scotland's first UNESCO World Heritage Site. St Kilda captures the imagination of most visitors to the Outer Hebrides, whether they actually get there or just dream about romantic voyages to mysterious lands across perilous seas.

In 1957 the islands become the property of the National Trust for Scotland, who in turn leased them to the Nature Conservancy (the forerunner of Scottish Natural Heritage) as a National Nature Reserve. St Kilda is the most important seabird breeding station in northwest Europe. The islands are home to the largest colony of gannets in the world, the largest colony of fulmars in Britain, and one the largest colonies of puffins in Scotland. These huge numbers of seabirds were vital to the islanders' survival. Their eggs provided food in the summer, and gannets and fulmers were caught each season to be plucked, dried and stored for the winter. Their feathers and oil were kept for export to generate income, whilst their bones were shaped into useful tools and their skins into shoes.

Ins and outs

Getting there The biggest problem apart from accessibility is cost. **Island Cruising** in Uig, on Lewis (T01851- 672381, F672212) arranges boat trips to St Kilda from April to October starting from about £300 (4-day all-inclusive). The tour comprises the journey to and from St Kilda and a landing on Hirta with a visit to the museum, the old village and a wider exploration of the island including a climb up to the highest sea cliffs in the British Isles at Conachair (430 m).

The **National Trust for Scotland** also organises two-week long voluntary Work Parties throughout the summer every year to undertake restoration, maintenance and archaeology projects around the old village on Hirta. The groups are very popular, and each volunteer must complete an application form, so apply early. The fortnight costs between £450 and £500 and this covers transport from Oban to St Kilda and all food and lodging costs while on the island. For details contact National Trust for Scotland in Oban ⓘ *T01631-570000, F570011, stkilda@nts.org.uk*

Hirta

The largest of the islands, **Hirta**, was the remotest community in Britain, if not Europe, until 1930, when the remaining 36 Gaelic-speaking inhabitants were evacuated at their own request, in one of the most poignant episodes of Scottish history. Today Hirta is partly occupied by the army as a radar-tracking station for the rocket range on South Uist and managed by **Scottish Natural Heritage** ⓘ *135 Stilligarry, South Uist, HS8 5RS, T01870-620238*. For details of tours, ask at one of the main tourist information centres in the Outer Hebrides.

Orkney and Shetland

Introduction

To some these two archipelagos will never be anything more than distant and overlooked specks of land peppering the wild north Atlantic, above an already remote north coast of mainland Scotland. It is true – they are remote and they have maintained a social and political, as well as geographical, distance from the rest of Scotland which goes a long way to explaining the relatively few visitors each year.

Orkney was under Norse rule until the mid-13th century, and Shetland was only 'given' (as part of a princess' dowry) to Scotland in 1469. Somehow, seeing them as a part of Scotland can be very misleading and each must be seen within the context of its own unique cultural background and unusual geography.

It is these two qualities that make the islands worth visiting and the ones that the tourist boards are keen to plug. Both Orkney and Shetland are littered with outstanding archaeological evidence, not just of Norse occupation, such as at Jarlshof at the very southern tip of Shetland, but also of life back in 3000 BC at Skara Brae and the Knap of Howar in the Orkneys. They are also the best places in Britain to see wildlife as yet untamed by the 21st century. Here you can sail alongside porpoises and seals, and watch a million migratory seabirds nest and bring up their young during the summer months. And, thanks to fast and frequent transport links, it doesn't take an Arctic expedition to get here.

★ Don't miss...

1. Visit the amazing archaeological wonders of **Maes Howe** and **Skara Brae**, page 910.
2. Take the spectacular clifftop walk to meet the **Old Man of Hoy**, page 913.
3. Fly from **Westray** to **Papa Westray**, which takes all of two minutes, page 915.
4. Brave the white-knuckle boat trip to **Fair Isle**, one of the best places on earth for birdwatching, page 922.
5. Explore the dramatic coastal scenery of **Hermaness National Nature Reserve** from where you can look out to Muckle Flugga, site of the most northerly lighthouse in the British Isles, page 924.

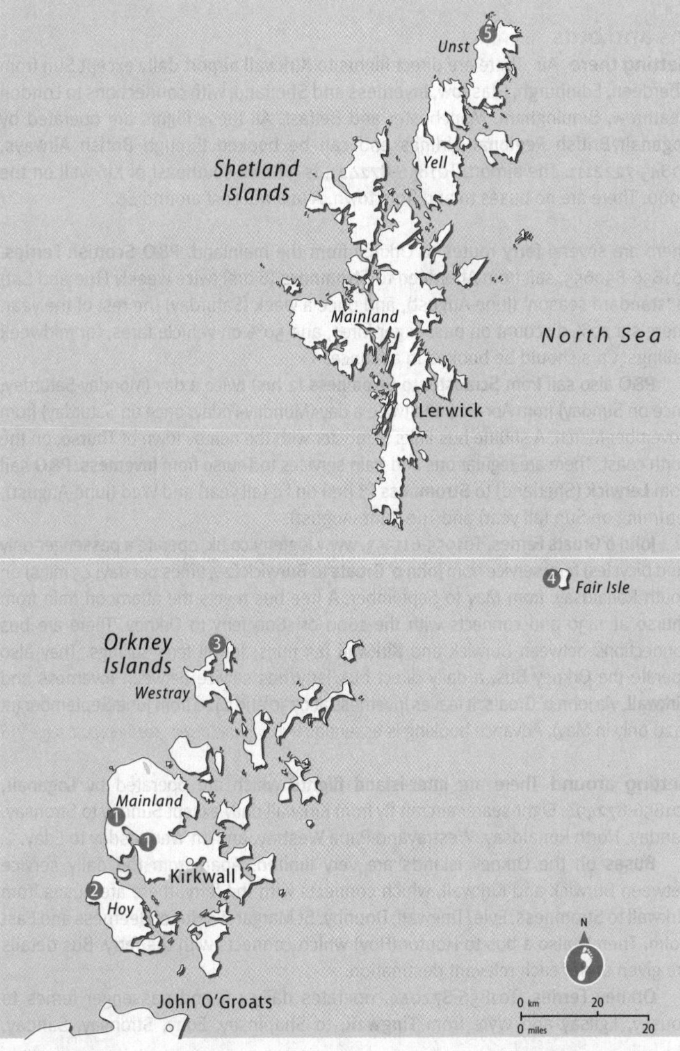

Orkney

→ Colour map 8

Orkney may only be a short step away from John O' Groats, but to the fiercely independent Orcadians, 'Mainland' means the largest of the Orkney islands and not the Scottish mainland.

Mainland is also the site of the two main towns and ferry terminals: the capital Kirkwall and the beautiful old fishing port of Stromness. Here, you'll also find many of Orkney's most precious archaeological treasures: the Stones of Stenness*;* Maes Howe*; the* Broch of Gurness*; and the remarkable Neolithic village of* Skara Brae. *Aside from Mainland, there are a dozen smaller islands to explore, including* Hoy, *with its wild, spectacular coastal scenery. The even more remote northerly islands offer miles of deserted beaches, and nothing but the calls of myriad birds to shatter the all-pervading peace and quiet.* ›› *For Sleeping, Eating and other listings, see pages 916-918.*

Ins and outs

Getting there Air There are direct flights to **Kirkwall airport** daily except Sun from Aberdeen, Edinburgh, Glasgow, Inverness and Shetland, with connections to London Heathrow, Birmingham, Manchester and Belfast. All these flights are operated by **Loganair/British Regional Airlines** and can be booked through **British Airways,** T0845-7222111. The airport, T01856-872421, is 3 miles southeast of Kirkwall on the A960. There are no buses to and from town. A taxi will cost around £6.

There are several **ferry** routes to Orkney from the mainland. **P&O Scottish Ferries,** T01856-850655, sail from Aberdeen to **Stromness** (8 hrs) twice weekly (Tue and Sat) in 'standard season' (June-August), and once a week (Saturday) the rest of the year. There's a 20% discount on passenger fares, and 50% on vehicle fares, for midweek sailings. Cars should be booked in advance.

P&O also sail from **Scrabster** to **Stromness** (2 hrs) twice a day (Monday-Saturday; once on Sunday) from Apr-Oct, and twice a day (Monday-Friday; once on Saturday) from November-March. A shuttle bus links Scrabster with the nearby town of **Thurso**, on the north coast. There are regular bus and train services to Thurso from **Inverness. P&O** sail from **Lerwick** (Shetland) to **Stromness** (8 hrs) on Fri (all year) and Wed (June-August), returning on Sun (all year) and Tue (June-August).

John o'Groats Ferries, T01955-611353, www.jogferry.co.uk, operate a passenger-only (and bicycles) ferry service from **John o' Groats** to **Burwick** (2-4 times per day; 45 mins) on South Ronaldsay, from May to September. A free bus meets the afternoon train from **Thurso** at 1430 and connects with the 1600 or 1800 ferry to Orkney. There are bus connections between Burwick and **Kirkwall** (45 mins) for all ferry sailings. They also operate the **Orkney Bus**, a daily direct bus/ferry/bus service between **Inverness** and **Kirkwall**, via John o' Groats. It leaves Inverness at 0730 and 1420 from June-September (at 1420 only in May). Advance booking is essential. ›› *For further details, see Transport, page 918*

Getting around There are **inter-island flights** which are operated by **Loganair,** T01856-872494. Eight-seater aircraft fly from Kirkwall daily except Sunday to Stronsay, Sanday, North Ronaldsay, Westrayand Papa Westray, and on Wednesday to Eday.

Buses on the Orkney islands are very limited. Apart from the daily service between Burwick and Kirkwall, which connects with the ferry, there are buses from Kirkwall to Stromness, Evie/Tingwall, Dounby, St Margaret's Hope, Deerness and East Holm. There's also a bus to Houton(Hoy) which connects with the ferry. Bus details are given under each relevant destination.

Orkney Ferries, T01856-872044, operates daily car and passenger ferries to Rousay, Egilsay and Wyre from **Tingwall**; to Shapinsay, Eday, Stronsay, Sanday,

Westray and Papa Westray from **Kirkwall**; to Graemsay and Hoy from **Stromness**; and to Hoy and Flotta from **Houton**. There's a ferry on Fri to North Ronaldsay from **Kirkwall**. Contact **Orkney Ferries** or the tourist board for the latest schedules. Those travelling by car should book all ferry journeys in advance. Ferry details are given under the relevant destination.

Only the main population centres on **Mainland** are served by public transport, and having a **car** is essential to visit many of the most interesting sights. Bringing a car to Orkney is expensive, but there are several **car hire** firms on the Mainland and on the other islands.

Orkney is relatively flat and most of its roads are quiet, which makes it ideal for touring by **bike**, though the wind can make it difficult if it's blowing in the wrong direction. Bicycles can be hired in Kirkwall, Stromness and on many of the other islands. Details are given in the relevant section.

Information The **Orkney Tourist Board** ⓘ *www. visitorkney.com*, has tourist offices in Kirkwall and Stromness. They will book accommodation for you, or provide a list of what's available, though many B&Bs are not included in the tourist board scheme. They can also provide information on various sights, walks and the islands' wildlife. Those wishing to leave Mainland and visit the smaller islands should pick up a free copy of the tourist board's excellent information and travel guide, *The Islands of Orkney*.

Kirkwall

The town's outstanding sight is the huge and impressive red sandstone **St Magnus Cathedral** ⓘ *Apr-Sep Mon-Sat 0900-1800, Sun 1400-1800; Oct-Mar Mon-Sat 0900-1300 and 1400-1700, Sun service at 1115*, built by masons who had worked on Durham Cathedral in the north of England. It was founded in 1137 by Rognvald Kolson, Earl of Orkney, in memory of his uncle, Magnus Erlendson, who was slain by his cousin, Haakon Paulson, on Egilsay in 1115. Magnus was buried at Birsay and it is said that heavenly light was seen over his grave. It soon became a shrine, attracting pilgrims from as far afield as Norway. Magnus was canonized in 1133, and four years later his nephew commissioned construction of the cathedral. The building wasn't completed until the 14th century, and major additions were made during the intervening centuries. The most recent addition was a new west window for the nave, to celebrate the cathedral's 850th anniversary in 1987. The bones of St Magnus now lie in the north choir pillar, while those of St Rognvald lie in the south one. There's also a memorial to John Rae, the 19th-century Arctic explorer who is buried in the graveyard, as well as a monument to the 833 men of the HMS Royal Oak who died when it was torpedoed in Scapa Flow in 1939.

Looming impressively nearby are the ruins of the **Bishop's Palace**, built in the 12th century as the first Kirkwall residence of the Bishop of Orkney. Here King Haakon of Norway died in 1263 after his defeat at the Battle of Largs. The palace was repaired and extended in the mid-16th century by Bishop Reid, and most of what you see dates from that period. There's a good view of the town from the top of the '*Moosie Too'r*'. The adjacent **Earl's Palace** ⓘ *Apr-Sep daily 0930-1830, £2.20, concession £1.60, children £0.75, joint ticket for all Orkney monuments also available*, was built around 1600 by the notorious Patrick Stewart, Earl of Orkney, using forced labour. Still very much intact, it is one of Scotland's most elegant Renaissance buildings and was occupied by the tyrannical Stewart only for a very short time, until he was imprisoned and later executed. Opposite St Magnus Cathedral is **Tankerness House and Gardens**, a 16th-century former manse which has been restored and now houses the **Orkney Museum** ⓘ *T01856-873191, Oct-Mar Mon-Sat 1030-1230, 1330-1700; Apr-Sep 1030-1700; May-Sep also Sun 1400-1700, free*, which features various archaeological artefacts from Neolithic times to the Vikings.

A mile south of the town centre on the road to South Ronaldsay is the 200-year-old **Highland Park Distillery** ⓘ *T01856-874619, Tours every half hour Apr-Oct Mon-Fri 1000-1700 (last tour at 1600); Jul and Aug also Sat and Sun 1200-1700; Nov, Dec and Mar Mon-Fri at 1400 and 1530 only, £3, concession £2, children £1.50,* the most northerly of Scotland's whisky distilleries. There are tours of the distill- ery, one of the few that still has its own floor maltings, and a wee dram of this particularly fine single malt at the end.

Evie and the Broch of Gurness

Nine miles northwest of Kirkwall is the tiny village of Evie. A track leads from the village towards the coast, past a sandy beach, to the **Broch of Gurness.** ⓘ *T01856-751414 (HS), Apr-Sep daily 0930-1830, £3, concession £2.30, children £1.* Standing on an exposed headland on the north coast, with warm, gentle views across towards the island of Rousay, this is the best-preserved broch on Orkney, thought to date from around 100 BC. It is surrounded by an Iron-Age village whose houses are well-preserved, with the original hearths, beds, cupboards and even a toilet still in evidence.

Birsay and Marwick Head

At the far northwestern corner of the Mainland is the parish of Birsay, which was a favourite residence of the Earls of Orkney in Viking times as well as the first seat of the Bishop, before the building of St Magnus Cathedral in Kirkwall. Earl Thorfinn the Mighty lived here (1014-64) and built Orkney's first cathedral, **Christchurch**, for the new Bishop. In the centre of the village are the ruins of the **Earl's Palace** ⓘ *Open at all times, free,* built by the infamous Earl Robert Stewart in the late 16th century, and once described as "a sumptuous and stately dwelling". Not much remains today, but enough to give some idea of the sheer scale of the place.

At the southern end of Birsay Bay are the wild and spectacular 300 ft-high cliffs of Marwick Head, topped by the distinctive **Kitchener Memorial**, erected after the First World War to commemorate Lord Kitchener and the crew of the *HMS Hampshire*, which was sunk by a German mine off the coast in 1916 with the loss of all but 12 of her crew. Marwick Head is also an **RSPB Reserve**, and during the nesting season in early summer is home to many thousands of guillemots, razorbills, kittiwakes and fulmars, as well as a few puffins.

Skara Brae and Skaill House

ⓘ *T01856-841815. Apr-Sep daily 0930-1830. £5, concession £3.75, children £1.30. Oct-Mar (Skara Brae only) Mon-Sat 0930-1630 and Sun 1400-1630. £4, concession £3, children £1.20. Joint ticket for all Orkney Historic Scotland monuments also available.*

South of Birsay, eight miles north of Stromness, in the magnificent setting of the dazzling white sands of the Bay of Skaill, is Skara Brae, the best-preserved Stone-Age village in northern Europe. First revealed in 1850 after a violent storm blew away the dunes, the site dates from around 5,000 years ago and was occupied for about 600 years.

The houses contain stone furniture, fireplaces, drains, beds, dressers and even have damp-proof coursing in the foundations. The whole complex presents a unique picture of the lifestyle of its inhabitants, and there's also a replica 'house' that you can enter, and wander around in through the gloom, empathizing with that 3000 BC lifestyle.

The modern visitor centre has a useful introductory video and exhibition which is worth seeing before you look round the site (it's also worth buying their guidebook). After leaving the visitor centre, you walk down a 'path of time', which takes you back through landmark achievements of the last seven millennia, gradually building up the suspense and putting the achievements of Skara Brae in perspective – they may only be rudimentary buildings that once had turf for their rooves, but they were built 2000 years before the pyramids of Egypt, and in one of the world's most northerly outposts.

During the summer a ticket to Skara Brae includes admission to nearby **Skaill House**, an early 17th-century mansion which contains a few old artefacts, including Captain Cook's dinner service from the *Resolution*, but is a bit of a let-down after what you will have just witnessed, not 300 yards away at Skara Brae.

Standing Stones of Stenness and Ring of Brodgar

Northeast of Stromness on the road to Kirkwall is the tiny village of **Stenness**, near some of Orkney's most interesting prehistoric sites. The Standing Stones of Stenness comprise the four remaining stones from an original circle of 12 stones, dating from 3000 BC. The largest of the stones stands over 15 ft high.

About a mile northwest of Stenness is another stone circle, the Ring of Brodgar. This is a particularly impressive henge monument. It is over 100yds in diameter and 27 of the original 60 stones are still standing, some of them up to 15 ft high. Given the importance of these sites, it is particularly refreshing to realize when you get there that you can walk about amongst the stones in the still calm of a summer evening, with only a few oyster catchers for company, but both do get busy with coach parties during the day.

Maes Howe

ⓘ *T01856-761606. Tickets to Maes Howe from Tormiston Mill, on the other side of the road, where there's a an exhibition, introductory video and café. Apr-Sep daily 0930-1830; Oct-Mar Mon-Sat 0930-1630 and Sun 1400-1630, £3, concession £2.30, children £1. Joint ticket for all Orkney Historic Scotland monuments also available.*

Less than a mile northeast of the Stones of Stenness is Maes Howe, the finest Neolithic burial chamber in Europe. It was built around 2750 BC, making it contemporary with the Standing Stones and Skara Brae, and is amazingly well preserved. A huge mound covers a stone-built entrance passage which leads into a central chamber – over 12 ft square and the same in height – with three smaller cells built into the walls of the tomb. A fascinating feature of the site is that the winter solstice sun sets directly over the Barnhouse Stone, half a mile away, and shines down the entrance passage of Maes Howe and on to the back wall of one of the cells.

When it was opened in 1861, no human remains or artefacts were found, giving no clues as to its usage. However, in the 12th century Vikings returning from the Crusades broke into the tomb searching for treasure. They found nothing but left behind one of the largest collections of runic graffiti anywhere in the world, as well as carvings of a dragon, serpent and walrus. A guide gives you an excellent overview of the chamber's mysterious architectural attributes, but the fact remains that the history of this extraordinary place is still largely unsolved – something that obviously adds to the site's attraction.

Orphir

On the southern shores of West Mainland, overlooking Scapa Flow, is the scattered community of Orphir, which has a few sights worth visiting, especially if you're heading across to Hoy from the ferry terminal at **Houton**, a little further west.The main point of interest in Orphir is the **Orkneyinga Saga Centre** ⓘ *All year daily 0900-1700, free*, where a small exhibition and video introduces the saga, written circa 1200, possibly by an Icelander, which tells the history of the Viking Earls of Orkney from around 900 AD to 1200 AD, when the islands became a part of Scotland rather than Norway. As you would expect, there's plenty of gore and Machiavellian goings-on, including an assassination attempt that went disastrously wrong, when a poisoned shirt meant for Earl Harold was unwittingly and fatally worn by his brother Paul instead.

Behind the centre is **The Earl's Bu**, looking out across Orphir Bay south to Cava Island. These are the 12th-century foundations of the home of the Norse Earls of Orkney written about in the saga. Inside the cemetery gates is a section of the church built by Haakon and modelled on the rotunda of the Church of the Holy Sepulchre in Jerusalem.

Stromness

Ferries from Scrabster arrive in Stromness, one of the classic Scottish fishing villages. It consists largely of one narrow, winding main street, paved with flagstones, which hugs the shoreline. Running off the street are numerous little lanes and alleyways, many with fascinating names such as **Khyber Pass**, and full of interesting buildings which reflect the town's proud maritime heritage. The **Stromness Museum** ⓘ *52 Albert St, T01856-850025, May-Sep daily 1000-1700; Oct-Apr Mon-Sat 1030-1230 and 1330-1700, £2.50, children £0.50*, has exhibitions on natural and maritime history, and contains artefacts from Scapa Flow and the days of the Hudson Bay company. Opposite the museum is the house where **George Mackay Brown** (1921-96), Orkney's most famous poet and story-writer, spent the last two decades of his life. On a jetty to the south of the new harbour is the excellent **Pier Arts Centre** ⓘ *Tue-Sat 1030-1230 and 1330-1700; Jul and Aug also Sun 1400-1700, free,* housing a permanent collection of works of the St Ives school, including Barbara Hepworth, Ben Nicholson and Patrick Heron, amongst others, in a lovely gallery. The **Tourist Information Centre** is at the new ferry terminal ⓘ *T01856-850716, Apr-Oct Mon-Sat 0800-1800, Sun 0900-1600; Nov-Mar Mon-Fri 0900-1700.* Its exhibition, *This Place Called Orkney,* is a useful introduction to the islands, and its free *Stromness Heritage Guide* takes you round all the buildings of interest in the town.

East Mainland

The East Mainland is mainly agricultural land though, and it contains little of the amazing archaeological wealth of its western counterpart, there are some attractive fishing villages, fine coastal walks and many poignant reminders of Orkney's important wartime role. There is not much to see inland on the road running southeast from Kirkwall past the airport, but head on towards the Deerness Peninsula and you will be richly rewarded by a truly serene, gentle beauty. There are sandy bays, which make for very pleasant short walks and picnics (if you can find a sheltered spot), jutting cliffs and a great variety of birdlife.

The Churchill Barriers

East Mainland is linked to a string of islands to the south by four causeways, known as the Churchill Barriers, built on the orders of Prime Minister Winston Churchill during the Second World War as anti-submarine barriers to protect the British Navy which was based in Scapa Flow at the time. His decision was prompted by the sinking of the battleship *HMS Royal Oak* in October 1939 by a German U-boat which had slipped between the old blockships, deliberately sunk during the First World War to protect Scapa Flow, and the shore. After the war, a road was built on top of the causeways, linking the islands of Lamb Holm, Glimps Holm, Burray and South Ronaldsay to Mainland.

On the island of Lamb Holm camps were built to accommodate the men working on the construction of the barriers, many of whom were Italian Prisoners of War. The camps have long since gone, but the Italians left behind the remarkable **Italian Chapel** ⓘ *Open all year during daylight hours, free*, fittingly known as 'The Miracle of Camp 60'. It is difficult to believe that such a beautiful building could have been made using two Nissen huts, concrete and bits of scrap metal, and the chapel's enduring popularity with visitors is a tribute to the considerable artistic skill of the men involved. One of them, Domenico Chiochetti, returned in 1960 to restore the interior paintwork.

South Ronaldsay

The main settlement on South Ronaldsay is the picturesque little village of **St Margaret's Hope** on the north coast. The village smithy has been turned into the **Smiddy Museum**, with lots of old blacksmith's tools to try out. ⓘ *Open May and Sep daily 1400-1600, Jun-Aug 1200-1600, Oct Sun 1400-1600, free.* The museum also features a small exhibition on the annual **Boys' Ploughing Match**, a hugely popular event held each year in August. Boys from the village (and now girls as well) dress up as horses and parade in the village square (prizes are given for the best costume). Afterwards the boys and their fathers, or grandfathers, head for the **Sand of Wright,** a few miles west, and have a ploughing match with miniature ploughs, which are usually family heirlooms. The categories are: best ploughed ring, best *feering* or guiding furrow, neatest ends and best kept plough. This sheltered beach is well worth a visit anyway, ploughing or no ploughing. The views stretch in a spectacular 180 degree panorama, south across the Pentland Firth to Caithness on mainland Scotland, west to South Walls and Cantick Head on Hoy, and northwest to Flotta and the west Mainland.

At the southeastern corner of South Ronaldsay is the recently-excavated **Tomb of the Eagles** ⓘ *Apr-Oct daily 1000-2000, Nov-Mar 1000-1200, £2.50*, one of the most interesting archaeological sights on Orkney. The 5,000-year-old chambered cairn was discovered by local farmer and amateur archaeologist, Ronald Simison, whose family now runs the privately owned site and museum. The interior contents of the tomb were practically intact and there were up to 340 people buried here, along with carcasses and talons of sea eagles, hence the name. Various objects were also found outside the tomb, including stone tools and polished stone axes.

Hoy

To the southwest of the Mainland is Hoy, the second largest of the Orkney islands. The name is derived from the Norse *Ha-ey*, meaning High Island, which is appropriate as much of the island is more reminiscent of the Scottish Highlands than Orkney, with only the southern end being typically low and fertile.

Orkney's highest point, **Ward Hill** (1,571 ft) is in the north of the island, and the north and west coasts are bounded by spectacular cliffs. At **St John's Head** the sheer cliffs rise out of the sea to a height of 1,150 ft, the highest vertical cliffs in Britain. The island is most famous for its **Old Man of Hoy,** a great rock stack rising to 450 ft. This northern part of Hoy forms the **North Hoy RSPB Reserve** which has a variety of habitats ranging from woodland to tundra-like hill-tops and sea cliffs. The reserve is home to a huge variety of birds including great skuas and Arctic skuas, Manx shearwaters and puffins. On the hills there are red grouse, curlews, golden plovers and dunlins, as well as peregrine falcons, merlins, kestrels and even golden eagles. Mountain hares are quite common and, if you are very lucky, you can also see otters along the Scapa Flow coastline.

On the southeast coast of the island is Lyness, site of a large naval base during both world wars when the British fleet was based in Scapa Flow. Many of the old dilapidated buildings have gone, but the harbour area is still scarred with the scattered remains of concrete structures. Lyness has a large **Naval Cemetery,** last resting place of those who died at Jutland, of Germans killed during the scuttle and of the crew of *HMS Royal Oak*. The old pump house opposite the new ferry terminal is now the **Scapa Flow Visitor Centre** ⓘ *T01856-791300, Mid-May to mid-Sep Mon-Sat 0900-1630, Sun 1030-1545, Jul and Aug Mon-Sat 0900-1630, Sun 0945-1800, mid-Sep to mid-May Mon-Fri 0900-1630, £2*, a naval museum with photographs, wartime artefacts, a section devoted to the scuttling of the German Fleet, and an audio-visual feature on the history of Scapa Flow.

Rousay

Rousay is a hilly island about five miles in diameter and known as the 'Egypt of the North' due to the large number of archaeological sites. It also has the important **Trumland RSPB Reserve,** home to merlins, hen harriers, peregrine falcons, short-eared owls and red-throated divers, and its three lochs offer good trout fishing. A road runs right around the island, and makes a 13-mile bike ride, but most of the sights are within walking distance of the ferry pier on the southeast side of the island, where most of the 200 inhabitants live. A short distance west of the pier by the road is

 Tavershoe Tuick, an unusual two-storey burial cairn, discovered in the late 19th century. A mile further west, to the north of the road, is **Blackhammer**, a Neolithic burial cairn. Further west, and a steep climb up from the road, is **Knowe of Yarso**, another stalled cairn, which contained the remains of at least 21 people. The tomb dates from around 2900 BC.

Most of the island's archaeological sights are to be found along the **Westness Walk**, a mile-long walk which starts from Westness Farm, about four miles west of the ferry pier, and ends at the remarkable Midhowe Cairn. The walk is described in detail in a leaflet available from the tourist offices on Mainland. **Midhowe Cairn** is the largest and longest thus far excavated on Orkney – over 100 ft long and 40 ft wide – and, like the others, dates from around 3000 BC. Housed in a large building to protect it, the 'Great Ship of Death', as it is known, contained the remains of 25 people in crouched position on or under the eastern shelves of the chamber, which is divided into 12 sections. Standing nearby, with fine views across to Eynehallow island, is **Midhowe Broch**, one of the best-preserved brochs on Orkney, occupied from around 200 BC to 200AD. The outer walls are about 60 ft in diameter and up to 14 ft high in places.

Egilsay and Wyre

These two small islands lie to the east of Rousay and have a couple of interesting sights of their own. Egilsay's claim to fame is the murder here of St Magnus in 1115, and a **cenotaph** marks the spot where he was slain. The island is dominated by the 12th-century **St Magnus church**, built on the site of an earlier church, possibly as a shrine to St Magnus. It is the only surviving example on Orkney of a round-towered Viking church. Much of Egilsay has been bought by the RSPB as a reserve to preserve the habitat of the very rare **corncrake**, whose distinctive rasping call may be heard.

Tiny Wyre features strongly in the Viking saga as the domain of Kolbein Hruga, and the remains of his 12th-century stronghold, **Cubbie Roo's Castl**e, and nearby **St Mary's chapel** can be still be seen. Kolbein's home, or *Bu*, was on the site of the nearby Bu Farm, where the poet Edwin Muir (1887-1959) spent part of his childhood. The far westerly point of the island, known as the Taing, is a favourite haunt of seals, and a great place to enjoy a summer sunset.

Shapinsay

Less than 30 minutes by ferry from Kirkwall is the fertile, low-lying island of Shapinsay. The main attraction is **Balfour Castle** ⓘ *T01856-872856, tour leaves from Kirkwall on Wed and Sun May-Sep, on the 1415 ferry. Tours must be arranged in advance at the tourist office in Kirkwall. They cost around £15 per person which includes ferry ticket, guided tour of the castle and gardens (at 1500) and complimentary tea and cakes in the servants' quarters. You can take an earlier ferry if you wish to explore the island*, an imposing baronial pile which is in fact a Victorian extension to a much older house called 'Cliffdale'. The house, and the rest of the island, was bought by successive generations of the Balfour family who had made their fortune in India. Today the castle is the home of the Zawadski family and can only be visited as part of an inclusive half-day tour.

Eday

The long, thin and sparsely populated island of Eday lies at the centre of the North Isles group. The island has numerous chambered cairns and these, along with the other attractions, are concentrated in the northern part. They are all covered in the signposted five-mile **Eday Heritage Walk**, which starts from the *Community Enterprises Shop* and leads up to the Cliffs of Red Head at the northern tip. The walk takes about three hours to complete, and it's worth picking up the *Eday Heritage Walk* leaflet.

Sanday

Sanday is the largest of the North Isles, 12 miles long and flat as a pancake except for the cliffs at Spurness. It is well-named, as its most notable feature is its sweeping bays of sparkling white sand backed by machair, and turquoise seas. There are numerous burial mounds all over the island, the most impressive being **Quoyness Chambered Cairn**, a 5,000 year-old tomb similar to Maes Howe. The 13 ft-high structure contains a large main chamber with six smaller cells opening through low entrances. Most of the burial tombs remain unexcavated, such as those at **Tofts Ness** at the far northeastern tip, where there are over 500 cairns, making it potentially one of the most important prehistoric sites in Britain. At **Scar**, in Burness, a spectacular Viking find was made recently, and at **Pool** a major excavation has uncovered the remains of at least 14 Stone-Age houses.

Stronsay

The peaceful, low-lying island of Stronsay has some fine sandy beaches and cliffs which attract large colonies of grey seals and nesting seabirds. There are few real sights on this largely agricultural island, but the coastline has some pleasant walks. One of the best is to the **Vat of Kirbister** in the southeast, a spectacular '*gloup*' or blow-hole spanned by the finest natural arch in Orkney. To the south of here, at **Burgh Head**, you'll find nesting puffins and the remains of a ruined broch, and at the southeastern tip, at **Lamb Head**, is a large colony of grey seals, lots of seabirds and several archaeological sites.

Westray and Papa Westray

Westray is the second largest of the North Isles, with a varied landscape of farmland, hilly moorland, sandy beaches and dramatic cliffs. The main settlement is **Pierowall**, in the north of the island, though the main ferry terminal is at **Rapness**, on the south coast. About a mile west of the village is Westray's most notable ruin, the impressive **Notland Castle** ⓘ *T01856-841815 (HS), Jun-Sep daily 0930-1830, £1.50, concession £1.10, children £0.50*a fine example of a 16th-century fortified Z-plan tower-house.

There are some great coastal **walks** on the island, particularly to the spectacular sea cliffs at **Noup Head**, at the far northwestern tip, which are an **RSPB Reserve** and second only to St Kilda in terms of breeding seabirds, with huge colonies of guillemots, razorbills, kittiwakes and fulmars, as well as puffins.

Tiny Papa Westray, known locally as 'Papay', can be reached on the world's shortest scheduled flight – all of two minutes – from Westray, but there are other reasons to visit this little island, one of the most remote of the Orkney group. Papay is home to Europe's oldest house, the **Knap of Howar**, which was built around 5,500 years ago and is still standing (they knew how to build 'em in those days). It's on the west coast, just south of the airport. Half a mile north is **St Boniface Kirk**, one of the oldest Christian sites in the north of Scotland, founded in the 8th century, though most of the recently restored building dates from the 12th century. Papay is famous for its birds, and **North Hill**, on the north of the island, is an important **RSPB Reserve**. The cliffs are home to many thousands of breeding seabirds, and at Fowl Craig on the east coast you can see nesting puffins. The interior is home to the largest arctic tern colony in Europe, as well as many arctic skuas. If you wish to explore you have to contact the warden at Rose Cottage, T01857-644240, who runs regular guided walks.

It's worth taking a boat trip to the even tinier, deserted **Holm of Papay** ⓘ *Contact Jim Davidson, T01857-644259, for boat trips between May and Sep*, off the east coast. This is the site of several Neolithic burial cairns, including one of the largest **chambered cairns** on Orkney. You enter the tomb down a ladder into the main chamber which is nearly 70 ft long, with a dozen side-cells.

North Ronaldsay

Remote and storm-battered, North Ronaldsay is the most northerly of the Orkney islands and a place where old Orcadian traditions remain. This small, flat island, only three miles long, has few real attractions, except to keen ornithologists who flock here to catch a glimpse of its rare migrants. From late March to early June and mid-August to early November there are huge numbers of migratory birds. The **Bird Observatory**, in the southwest corner of the island by the ferry pier, gives information on which species have been sighted, as well as providing accommodation. There are also colonies of grey seals and cormorants at **Seal Skerry**, on the northeast tip of the island.

Sleeping

Kirkwall *p909*

A **Ayre Hotel**, on the harbour front, T01856-873001, www.ayrehotel.co.uk. The top hotel in Kirkwall, very comfortable.

A-C **Albert Hotel**, on Mounthoolie Lane in the centre of town, T01856-876000, enquiries@alberthotel.co.uk. Also has a restaurant and a couple of lively bars (see below).

B **Foveran Hotel**, 2 miles from town on the A964 Orphir road at St Ola, T01856-872389, www.foveranhotel.com, overlooking Scapa Flow. It is friendly and comfortable, and also offers very good food, including vegetarian.

D SYHA Youth Hostel, T01856-872243, open Apr-Sep. On Old Scapa Rd, about 15 mins' walk from the centre.

West Mainland

A **Merkister Hotel**, on the shores of Loch Harray, near Stenness, T01856-771366, merkisterhotel@ecos.co, has a very good restaurant and a popular bar.

B-C **Barony Hotel**, T01856-721327, baronyhotel@btinternet.com. Open May- Sep, on the north shore of Boardhouse Loch. It specializes in fishing holidays and is about the only place offering food in these parts.

B-C **Mill of Eyreland**, T01856-850136, www.orknet.co.uk/mill, lovely converted mill 3 miles from Stromness.

C **Woodwick House**, Evie, T01856-751330. Comfortable country house hotel offering food and occasional cultural events.

C-D **Primrose Cottage**, T/F01856-721384, i.clouston@talk21.com, a comfortable B&B overlooking Marwick Bay.

Stromness *p912*

B-C **Stromness Hotel**, T01856-850298, www.stromnesshotel.com.The best hotel in town, recently refurbished and offering good-value meals.

C **Ferry Inn**, near the ferry terminal, on John St, T01856-850280, www.ferryinn.com/ serves food and has a lively bar.

C **Thira**, a few miles behind Stromness, at Innertown, T01856-851181. Comfortable, friendly and non-smoking modern bungalow with spectacular views of Hoy. Also serves an excellent cooked breakfast, and will provide a fantastic dinner made from the finest local ingredients on request.

D **Brown's Hostel**, 45 Victoria St, T01856-850661. This popular independent hostel has no curfew and is open all year round.

South Ronaldsay *p912*

B **Creel Restaurant & Rooms**, Front Rd, St Margaret's Hope, T01856-831311, www.thecreel.co.uk. It offers comfortable rooms and superb food using fresh, locally grown ingredients. Dinner only.

Hoy *p913*

C **Stoneyquoy**, south of Lyness, T/F01856-791234, www.visithoy.com The owner, Louise Budge, also runs guided tours of the island for £40 for up to 4 people, including lunch.

D **Hoy Youth Hostel**, is about a mile from Moaness Pier. It's open from May-Sep.

D **Rackwick Youth Hostel** in Rackwick Glen (open mid-Mar to mid-Sep). To book ahead for both hostels, contact Orkney Council, T01856-873535, ext 2404.

Rousay *p913*

B-C **Taversoe Hotel**, near Knowe of Yarso, about 2 miles west of the pier, T01856-821325, which offers excellent-value meals. The seafood is particularly recommended (closed Mon to non-residents).

Shapinsay *p914*

A **Balfour Castle**, T01856-711282, www.balfourcastle.co.uk, Enjoy all that Victorian splendour. The price includes

dinner. The castle has a private chapel and a boat is available for bird watching and fishing trips for residents.
B **Girnigoe**, T01856-711256, near the northern end of Veantro Bay. Comfortable B&B and offers evening meals.

Eday *p914*
C **Mrs Poppelwell's**, at Blett, Carrick Bay, opposite the Calf of Eday, T01857-622248. She also provides evening meal and packed lunch, and has a self-catering cottage for up to 3.

Sanday *p915*
C **Kettletoft Hotel**, in Kettletoft T/F01857-600217, also serves meals and has a lively bar.
C-D **Quivals**, T01857-600467, run by Tina and Bernie Flett. Tina also runs the ferry bus service and Bernie runs a car and bike hire service. Bernie also runs full-day tours of the island, on Wed and Fri, from mid-May to early Sep, departing from **Kirkwall** pier at 1010 and returning at 1940 (around £30 per person, minimum of 4 people).

Stronsay *p915*
D **Stronsay Fish Mart Hostel**, T01857-616360. Open all year, is well-equipped and comfortable andh does cheap meals.
D **Stronsay Bird Reserve**, T01857-616363, on Mill Bay to the south of Whitehall, where you can also camp overlooking the wide sandy bay.
E **Torness Camping Barn**, on the shore of Holland Bay near Lea-shun Loch, T01857-616314. Very basic and very cheap They also organize nature walks to the nearby seal-hide. Phone for pick-up from the ferry.

Westray and Papay Westray *p915*
A-B **Cleaton House Hotel**, T01857-677508, www.orknet.co.uk/ cleaton A converted Victorian manse about 2 miles southeast of Pierowall. It serves excellent meals in the restaurant and in the bar.
C **Pierowall Hotel**, in Pierowall, T01857-677208, www.orknet.co.uk/pierwall, which is less stylish, but comfortable and friendly. It also serves good-value bar meals.
B-C **Beltane House Guest House**, Papay Westray, T01857-644267, a row of converted farm workers' cottages to the east of Holland House. It offers dinner (££). It's run by the island community co-operative.
D **Papa Westray Hostel**, T01857-644267. Open all year, housed in the same complex at Beltane. The co-operative also runs a shop and restaurant. They have a minibus which takes ferry passengers from the pier to anywhere on the island.

North Ronaldsay *p916*
C **North Ronaldsay Bird Observatory**, T01857-633200, alison@ nrbo.prestel.co.uk It offers wind-and solar-powered full-board accommodation in private rooms or dorms.
B-C **Garso House**, about 3 miles from the ferry pier, T01857-633244, christine.muir@virgin.net. Full-board accommodation. They also have a self-catering cottage (up to 5 people) and can arrange car hire, taxis or minibus tours. The **Burrian Inn and Restaurant** is the island's pub, and also serves food. Camping is possible on the island, contact, T01857-633222.

Eating

Stromness *p912*
££ **Hamnavoe Restaurant**, 35 Graham Pl, T01856-850606. Specializes in local seafood and offers good vegetarian dishes. Mar-Oct Tue-Sun from 1900. Also the **Stromness Hotel and Ferry Inn** see Sleeping.

Activities and tours

Boat trips
For boat trips to **Papa Westray** contact Tom Rendall, T01856-677216. **Discover Orkney**, T/F01856-872865, run day tours on a Sun to **Westray** from Kirkwall, leaving at 0940 and returning at 2015, and costing around £30 per person including ferry. They also run a day tour on a Mon to **Papa Westray**.

Bus tours
On Rousay you can take one of the very informative minibus tours run by **Rousay Traveller**, T01856-821234. These run from Jun-early Sep Tue-Fri, meeting the 1040 ferry from Tingwall and lasting 6 hrs. There are guided minibus tours of Westray with Alex Costie of **Island Explorer**, T01857-677355, which connect with the ferry at Rapness.

Diving
The Diving Cellar, 4 Victoria St, Stromness, T01856-850055. Offers diving packages, equipment rental and boat charters. Open Mon-Fri 1100-1400 and 1700-1900, Sat 1300-1700.
Scapa Scuba, 13 Ness Rd, Stromness, T/F01856-851218. Diving course, guided dives, night dives and boat charters.

Transport

Hoy *p913*
A passenger **ferry** sails between **Stromness** and **Moaness Pier** in the north (30 mins) 3 times a day Mon-Fri and twice on Fri evenings, twice daily Sat and Sun. There's a reduced winter service (mid-Sep to mid-May). There's also a **car and passenger** service between **Houton** and **Lyness** and **Longhope** (45 mins) up to 6 times daily (Mon-Sat). There's a limited Sun service from mid-May to mid-Sep.
Transport on Hoy is very limited. North Hoy Transport, T01856-791315, runs a **minibus** service between **Moaness Pier** and **Rackwick**, which meets the 1000 ferry from Stromness. Call the same number for a taxi.

Rousay, Egilsay and Wyre *p913*
A **car ferry** sails from **Tingwall** (20 mins) to Rousay 6 times a day (Mon-Sat; 5 times on Sun). Most call in at **Egilsay** and **Wyre**, but some are on demand only and should be booked in advance, T01856-751360. A **bus** connects **Tingwall** and **Kirkwall**.

Shapinsay *p914*
The **car ferry** makes 6 sailings daily (including Sun in summer) from **Kirkwall** (25 mins).

Eday *p914*
There are **flights** from **Kirkwall** to Eday with **Loganair**, T01856-872494, on Wed only. There are **ferries** from **Kirkwall** (1¾ hrs to 2 hrs) twice daily via **Sanday** or **Stronsay**. Orkney Ferries, T01856-872044, also run the *Eday Heritage Tour* every Sun from mid-Jun to mid-Sep. It leaves **Kirkwall** at 0920 and return at 1955 and costs around £30 per person, which includes ferries, guided walks or minibus tour, entry to Carrick House and lunch. Book with **Orkney Ferries** or at the tourist office in Kirkwall.

Sanday *p915*
There are Loganair **flights** to Sanday from **Kirkwall** twice daily Mon-Fri and once Sat. **Ferry** service twice daily from **Kirkwall** (1½hrs).

Stronsay *p915*
There are Loganair **flights** to Stronsay from **Kirkwall**, twice daily Mon-Fri. A **ferry** service runs from Kirkwall (1 hr 30 mins) twice daily Mon-Sat (once on Sun), and once daily Mon-Sat from Eday (35 mins).

Westray and Papa Westray *p915*
Flights to **Westray** with Loganair depart **Kirkwall** twice daily Mon-Fri and once on Sat. There's a **car ferry** service from **Kirkwall to Rapness**, on the south coast of the island (1 hr 30 mins). It sails twice daily in summer (mid-May to mid-Sep) and once daily in winter. There's also a passenger ferry from **Pierowall** to **Papa Westray** (see below). The famous **flight** from **Westray** leaves twice daily Mon-Sat. There is also a direct flight to **Papay** from **Kirkwall** daily Mon-Sat, except Fri. There's a **passenger ferry** from **Pierowall** on Westray 3-6 times daily (25 mins). The **car ferry** from **Kirkwall** to **Westray** continues to **Papa Westray** on Tue and Fri (2 ¼ hrs).

North Ronaldsay *p916*
There are Loganair **flights** from **Kirkwall** twice daily Mon-Sat, T01856-872494. There's a car and passenger **ferry** which sails from **Kirkwall** (2 hrs 40 mins) once a week (usually Fri) and also on some Sun between May and Sep. Contact **Orkney Ferries** for details, T01856-872044.

For an explanation of the sleeping and eating price codes used in this guide, see the inside front cover. Other relevant information is provided in the Essentials chapter, page 36.

Shetland

→ Colour map 8

Shetland is so far removed from the rest of Scotland it can only be shown as an inset on maps. In fact, it is easier and quicker to get there from Norway than it is from London. This seems entirely appropriate, for Shetland is historically and culturally closer to Scandinavia than Britain. Many of its place-names are of Norse origin, and people here still celebrate ancient Viking festivals, such as Up Helly-Aa.

Modern-day visitors tend to come by plane rather than longboat, and usually bring binoculars, for Shetland is a birdwatchers' paradise. It is home to countless bird species, many of them seeking refuge from the madding crowds. And, let's face it, there's no better place than here to get away from it all. ▸▸ *For Sleeping, Eating and other listings, see pages 925-926.*

Ins and outs

Getting there Shetland has good **air** connections with the rest of the UK. There are regular flights to and from several mainland airports which are operated by **British Airways'** franchise partners **Loganair** and **British Regional Airlines**, T08457-733377. Shetland's main airport is at **Sumburgh**, 25 miles south of Lerwick, T01950-460654.

There are direct daily flights from **Aberdeen** (4 Mon-Fri; 2 on Sat and Sun), which has frequent services to all other major British airports. There are also direct flights from **Glasgow** (daily), **Edinburgh** (daily except Sunday), **London Heathrow** (daily), **Inverness** (Monday-Friday), **Orkney** (daily except Sunday), **Wick** (Monday-Saturday) and **Belfast** (daily except Saturday). There are also international flights to and from **Bergen** and **Oslo** (Norway) on Thursday and Sunday.

P&O Scottish Ferries, T01224-572615, www.poscottishferries.co.uk, operate car ferries to Lerwick from **Aberdeen** and **Stromness** (Orkney). There are sailings from **Aberdeen** once a day Mon-Fri; the journey takes 14 hrs. For details of ferries from Stromness, see page 908. Children aged 4-14 travel for half price and under 4s go free. Ferries from Aberdeen arrive at the main Holmsgarth terminal, which is about a mile north of the old harbour. There's a regular **bus** service between **Lerwick** and **Sumburgh airport** (50 mins) run by **John Leask & Son**, T01595-693162. Taxis (around £25) and car hire are also available. All island bus services start and end at the **Viking bus station**, which is on Commercial Road, a short distance north of the town centre. The town is small and everything is within easy walking distance.

Getting around There is a regular scheduled inter-island **flight** service from **Tingwall Airport** near Lerwick, with **Loganair**, T01595-840246, to the islands of **Foula**, **Fair Isle**, **Papa Stour** and **Out Skerries**.

A frequent **ferry** service links the larger islands with the Shetland Mainland. There are regular daily car ferries between **Lerwick** and **Bressay** (5 mins), **East Mainland** and **Whalsay** (30 mins), **North Mainland** and **Yell** (20 mins), **Yell** and **Unst** (10 mins), and **Yell** and **Fetlar** (25 mins). Fares on all these routes are £1.20 per passenger and £2.90 per car. There's a less frequent car ferry service between **East Mainland** and **Skerries** (Monday, Friday, Saturday and Sunday; 1 hr 30 mins), and **Lerwick** and **Skerries** (Tuesday and Thursday; 2 hrs 30 mins). Bookings are essential. There's also a passenger/cargo ferry service between **West Mainland** and **Papa Stour** (Monday, Wednesday, Friday, Saturday and Sunday; 40 mins), **West Mainland** and **Foula** (Tuesday, Saturday and alternate Thursday; 2 hrs), **Scalloway** and **Foula** (alternate Thursday; 3 hrs), **South Mainland** and **Fair Isle** (Tuesday, Saturday and alternate Thursday; 2 hrs 30 mins), and **Lerwick** and **Fair Isle** (alternate Thursday; 4 ½ hrs).

An extensive public **bus** service links Lerwick with all towns, villages and tourist sights. There are several bus operators. For detailed information on all bus services,

T01595-694100 (Monday-Saturday 0900-1715). A *Shetland Transport Timetable*, published by Shetland Islands Council, contains details of all air, sea and bus services throughout the islands. It is available from the tourist office in Lerwick.

Information The main **Tourist Information Centre** ⓘ *Market Cross, on Commercial Street, T01595-693434, www.shetland-tourism.co.uk*, can book accommodation and are a good source of information, books and maps . They also change foreign currency.

Lerwick

Lerwick is the capital and administrative centre of Shetland and the only sizeable town. Though the islands have been inhabited for many centuries, Lerwick only dates from the 17th century, when it began to grow as a trading port for Dutch herring fishermen, thanks to its superb natural sheltered harbour, the Bressay Sound. The town spread along the waterfront, where merchants built their *lodberries*, which were houses and warehouses with their own piers so that they could trade directly with visiting ships. By the late 19th century Lerwick had become the main herring port in northern Europe.

Lerwick has continued to grow and is now home to a third of Shetland's population. The discovery of **oil** in the North Sea in the early 1970s led to the building of the **Sullom Voe Oil Terminal**, and the effect on Lerwick has been dramatic. It is now the main transit point to the North Sea oil rigs and there have been major extensions to the harbour area, bringing increased shipping and prosperity to the town.

In town is the **Up Helly-Aa Exhibition** ⓘ *In the Galley Shed off St Sunniva St, Mid-May to mid-Sep Tue 1400-1600 and 1700-1900, Fri 1700-1900, Sat 1400-1600, £2.50, concession £1.* It gives a taste of the famous Viking fire festival (see Festivals and events). A mile west of town are the substantial remains of **Clickimin Broch**, a fortified site occupied from 700 BC to around the fifth or sixth century AD. A path leads to the site from opposite the *Safeway* supermarket on the A970. About a mile north of the ferry terminal is the **Böd of Gremista,** ⓘ *Jun to mid-Sep Wed and Sun 1000-1300 and 1400-1700, free,* a restored 18th-century fishing *böd* (booth) which was the birthplace of Arthur Anderson (1791-1868), co-founder of the Peninsular and Oriental Steam Navigation Company, now *P&O*. One of the rooms features an exhibition on Anderson's life and involvement with *P&O*.

Bressay and Noss

Lying to the east of Lerwick across the Bressay Sound is the island of Bressay (pronounced 'bressah'). Bressay is only seven miles long by three miles wide, and makes an ideal day trip for **cyclists**. Another good way to get around is on foot, and there's a fine walk to the top of **Ward Hill** (742 ft), the highest point, from where you get great views of the island and as far afield as Foula and Out Skerries. There are also some good coastal walks, particularly along the cliffs from Noss Sound south to **Bard Head**, **The Ord** and **Bressay Lighthouse**, where you can see large colonies of seabirds. Serious birdwatchers should head for **Noss**, a tiny, uninhabited island off the east coast of Bressay, which is a **National Nature Reserve** with over 100,000 pairs of breeding seabirds. A walk around the perimeter of the island takes at least three hours but is highly recommended. At the east side is the **Noup of Noss**, where the 600-ft cliffs are packed full of nesting gannets. The reserve is managed by Scottish Natural Heritage who have a small **visitor centre** at Gungstie.

Central Mainland

The Central Mainland is Shetland's slim waist, and only a few miles of land separates the east and west coast. Six miles from Lerwick on the west coast is **Scalloway,** once the capital of Shetland and now a fishing port and fish-processing centre. In 1942, during the Second World War, Scalloway became the headquarters of the **Shetland Bus** operations.

This was the name given to the Norwegian fishing boats which sailed to Shetland during the night from German-occupied Norway, bringing refugees to safety and returning with ammunition and resistance fighters. An interesting exhibition on the 'Shetland Bus' can be seen at **Scalloway Museum** on Main Street. ⓘ *May to Sep Tue-Thu 1400-1630, Sat 1000-1230 and 1400-1630.* The harbour is dominated by the ruins of **Scalloway Castle**, built in 1600 by the notorious Earl Patrick Stewart. Inside, an interpretative display explains its history. Next to the castle is the **Shetland Woollen Company**, T01595-880243, where you can buy the famous Shetland wool and Fair Isle sweaters.

North of Scalloway, the B9074 runs through the Tingwall Valley, and the **Loch of Tingwall**. At the northern end of the loch is a promontory called **Law Ting Holm**, which was the site of the *Althing*, or parliament, during the period of Norse rule. Overlooking the loch is **Tingwall Kirk**, built in the late 18th century on the site of the earlier church of St Magnus which dated back to the early period of Norse Christianity. In the graveyard is the old burial vault with several interesting old grave slabs.

The A971 continues northwest towards Weisdale. At the head of **Weisdale Voe** the B9075 branches north to **Weisdale Mill**, which now houses the **Bonhoga Gallery** ⓘ *Wed-Sat 1030-1630, Sun 1200-1630, T01595-830400,* a purpose-built art gallery featuring varied exhibitions of local, national and international works. Weisdale Mill was part of the Kergord estate, known until 1945 as Flemington, and was built from the stones of evacuated crofthouses. Over 300 crofters were forcibly evicted in the mid-19th century during the 'Clearances', when lairds expanded their more profitable sheep-farming activities. In 1940 the mill was requisitioned as the intelligence and administrative HQ for the 'Shetland Bus' operations (see Scalloway above). The Kergord estate today is the largest area of woodland in Shetland, and attracts a variety of migratory birds.

The Westside → *OS Landranger maps Nos 3 & 4*

The western Mainland of Shetland, stretching west from Weisdale to Sandness, is known as The Westside. This part of Shetland is notable for its varied landscape of spectacular sea cliffs, rolling green hills, bleak moorland, peaty freshwater lochs and numerous long sea lochs, or *voes*. This is excellent **walking** country, with many fine coastal routes, especially around **Culswick** and **Dale of Walls**. It is also great for **birdwatching** and **trout fishing**, and there are many opportunities for spotting **whales, dolphins** and **otters**.

The pretty little village of **Walls** (pronounced 'waas') is set around a sheltered natural harbour and is a popular spot with visiting yachts. It also attracts many visitors during its Agricultural Show in August, the biggest such event on Shetland.

Foula

Walls is the departure point for **ferries** to the remote island of Foula, whose name derives from the Norse *fugl ey*, meaning 'bird island'. Lying 15 miles west of the Shetland Mainland, tiny Foula is the second most remote inhabited island after Fair Isle. It supports a population of around 40 people, who are greatly out-numbered by the many thousands of seabirds, including a small colony of gannets and the rare Leach's petrel. There are also about 2,500 pairs of great skuas, the largest colony in the UK. The island is dominated by its sheer cliffs, which reach their most awe-inspiring peak at **The Kame** (1,220 ft), the second highest sea cliffs in Britain after St Kilda.

Papa Stour

A ferry sails from **West Burrafirth** on the Westside, near Sandness, to the little island of Papa Stour, only a mile offshore. The island, which has a population of around 30, is mostly made up of volcanic rock which has been eroded to form an amazing coastline of stacks, arches and caves, most spectacular of which is **Kirstan's Hole**. The island is home to large colonies of auks, terns and skuas, and also has a fascinating history of its own. Pick up the island trails leaflet from the tourist office in Lerwick.

South Mainland

From Lerwick a long, narrow finger of land points south. The main road runs down the east coast for 25 miles till it ends at **Sumburgh Head**, near Shetland's main airport. This southern part of the Shetland Mainland holds the islands' two most important archaeological sights and main tourist attractions.

Fifteen miles south of Lerwick, the scattered crofting communities of **Sandwick** look across to the **Isle of Mousa**, free, site of the best-preserved broch in Scotland. This fortified tower was built around 2,000 years ago and still stands close to its original height of 45 ft. It's a very impressive structure when you see it from the inside and has chambers, galleries, an internal staircase and a parapet. The broch features in a Viking saga of the 12th century when the mother of Harald, Earl of Orkney, took refuge there with her lover. The Earl, who did not approve of the liaison, laid siege to the broch, but it proved impregnable and he gave up. Mousa island is also home to many seabirds and waders, most notably the Storm Petrel, which is best seen at dusk as they return to their nests amongst the beach rocks. You can also see seals on the white-sand beach at West Voe. If you have time, it's a good idea to walk right around the coast, starting from the landing stage at West Ham and first heading south to the broch. A **passenger ferry** sails to the island from **Leebitton harbour** in Sandwick, ⓘ *daily from mid-Apr to mid-Sep, weather permitting, at 0930, 1230 and 1400, allowing visitors 2½ hours to see the island.*

On the west coast, near Bigton village, a signposted track leads to the spectacular sandy causeway (known as a tombolo) which leads to **St Ninian's Isle**. The tombolo is the best example of its kind in Britain, and you can walk across to the island which is best known for the hoard of Pictish treasure which was discovered in 1958 in the ruins of the 12th-century church. The 28 silver objects included bowls, a spoon and brooches, probably dating from around 800 AD, and are now on display in the Royal Scottish Museum in Edinburgh, though you can see replicas in the Shetland Museum in Lerwick.

The west coast south of Bigton is beautiful with long, sandy beaches interspersed with dramatic cliff scenery. On the other side of the road from the long, sheltered beach at **Scousburgh Sands** is the **Loch of Spiggie RSPB Reserve**. The loch is an important winter wildfowl refuge, particularly for Whooper Swans, and during the summer you can see various ducks, waders, gulls, terns and skuas. There's a hide on the northern shore with an information board. Nearby is the *Spiggie Hotel*, T01950-460409, which offers bar meals, afternoon tea or dinner. A few miles south of the loch is the village of **Quendale,** overlooking a wide, sandy bay. Here you'll find the beautifully restored and fully working 19th-century **Quendale Mill**, the last of Shetland's watermills. ⓘ *May-Sep daily 1000-1700, £1.50.*

At the southern tip of Mainland is the village of Sumburgh, site of Shetland's main **airport** for external passenger flights and for helicopters and planes servicing the North Sea oil industry. South of the airport is Shetland's prime archaeological site, **Jarlshof**, ⓘ *T01950-460112 (HS), Apr-Sep daily 0930-1830, £3.30, concession £2.20, children £1,* a hugely impressive place which spans 4,000 years of occupation, from Neolithic times through Norse settlement to the 16th century. The original Stone-Age dwellings are topped by a medieval broch, Pictish wheelhouses, Viking longhouses and, towering over the whole complex, the ruins of a 16th-century mansion. This remarkable site was only discovered at the end of the 19th century when a violent storm ripped off the top layer of turf. A helpful guidebook available from the visitor centre helps to bring the place to life.

Fair Isle

Fair Isle is the most isolated of Britain's inhabited islands. Only three miles long by 1½ miles wide, the island has a population of around 70 and is best known for its intricately patterned knitwear, which is still produced by a co-operative, Fair Isle Crafts. Co-operative could be said to sum up the friendly islanders, whose lifestyle is based on mutual help and community effort.

Fair Isle is a paradise for **birdwatchers**, and keen ornithologists form the majority of the island's visitors. It stands in the flight path of many thousands of migrating birds, and over 340 species have been recorded here at the **Fair Isle Bird Observatory**, which also offers accommodation and where visitors are welcome to take part. As well as the almost obscenely rich birdlife there are around 240 species of flowering plants, making the island an especially beautiful haven for naturalists. Fair Isle's coastline, especially in the north and west, also boasts some outstanding cliff scenery.

The bird observatory was the brainchild of George Waterston, an ornithologist who first visited in 1935 and then bought the island in 1948 to begin his task of building the observatory. The island was given to the National Trust for Scotland in 1954 and declared a National Scenic Area. It was recently designated a place of outstanding natural beauty and cultural heritage by the Council of Europe. The **George Waterston Memorial Centre** ⓘ *May to mid-Sep Mon and Fri 1400-1600, Wed 1030-1200, donations welcome,* has exhibits and photographs detailing the island's natural history, as well as the history of crofting, fishing, archaeology and knitwear.

North Mainland

The main road north from Lerwick branches at **Voe**, a peaceful and colourful little village nestling in a bay at the head of the Olna Firth. One branch leads to the Yell car and passenger ferry terminal at **Toft**, past the turn-off to the massive **Sullom Voe Oil Terminal**, the largest oil and liquefied gas terminal in Europe. The other road heads northwest to Brae, where there is a good selection of accommodation and decent facilities.

Mavis Grind, the narrow isthmus where it's claimed you can throw a stone from the Atlantic to the North Sea, leads into Northmavine, the northwest peninsula of North Mainland. This is excellent **walking** country, and it's a good idea to abandon the car and explore it on foot. **Hillswick Ness**, to the south of **Hillswick** village, is a nice walk, but further west, around the coastline of **Eshaness**, is the most spectacular cliff scenery and amazing natural features, all with unusual and evocative names. North of the lighthouse are the **Holes of Scraada**, **Grind o' da Navir** and the **Villians of Hamnavoe**, which are not the local gangs but eroded lava cliffs with blowholes, arches and caves. East of Eshaness are the **Heads of Grocken** and **The Drongs**, a series of exposed sea stacks, which offer superb diving. Further north, overlooking the deep sea inlet of **Ronies Voe**, is the dramatic red granite bulk of **Ronies Hill** (1,477 ft), with a well-preserved burial cairn at the summit. The coastal scenery to the north and west of here is even more breathtaking, but very remote and exposed. You should be well equipped before setting out.

Whalsay and Out Skerries

South of Voe, the B9071 branches east to **Laxo**, the ferry terminal for the island of **Whalsay**, one of Shetland's most prosperous small islands owing to its thriving fishing industry, which helps support a population of around 1,000. The fleet is based at **Symbister**, the island's main settlement. In the seas around Whalsay you can see porpoises, dolphins, minke whales and orcas, hence its Viking name which means 'island of whales'. One of Scotland's great poets, Hugh McDiarmid (Christopher Grieve), spent most of the 1930s in Whalsay, where he wrote much of his finest poetry, until he was called for war work in 1942, never to return. His former home, at Sodom near Symbister, is now a camping böd. It's open April-September and has no electricity.

The **Out Skerries** is a small group of rocky islands about five miles from Whalsay and 10 miles east of Shetland Mainland. It's made up of three main islands: the larger islands of **Housay** and **Bruray**, which are connected by a road bridge; and the uninhabited island of **Grunay**. The Skerries boast some spectacular and rugged sea cliffs which are home to many rare migrant seabirds in spring and autumn.

Yell, Fetlar and Unst

Yell, the second largest of the Shetland islands, was described rather damningly by Shetland-born writer Eric Linklater as 'dull and dark'. And it's true that the interior is consistently desolate peat moorland. But the coastline is greener and more pleasant and provides an ideal habitat for the island's large **otter** population. Yell is also home to a rich variety of birds, and offers some good coastal and hill walks, especially around the rugged coastline of **The Herra**, a peninsula about half way up the west coast.

Fetlar is the smallest of the North Isles but the most fertile, and known as 'the garden of Shetland'. Indeed, the name derives from Norse meaning 'fat land', as there is good grazing and croftland and a rich variety of plant and bird life. The whole island is good for birdwatching, but the prime place is the 1,700 acres of **North Fetlar RSPB Reserve** around Vord Hill (522 ft) in the north of the island. This area has restricted access during the summer months, and visitors should contact the warden at Bealance, T733246. The warden will also let you know if and when you can see the one or two female Snowy Owls which sometime visit.

The north cliffs of the reserve are home to large colonies of breeding seabirds, including auks, gulls and shags, and you can also see common and grey seals on the beaches in late autumn. Fetlar is home to one of Britain's rarest birds, the **red-necked phalarope**, which breeds in the loch near **Funzie** (pronounced 'finnie') in the east of the island. You can watch them from the RSPB hide in the nearby marshes. Red-throated divers and whimbrel also breed here. The island is also good for **walking,** and a leaflet describing some of the walks is available from the tourist office in Lerwick.

Unst is the most northerly inhabited island in Britain, and scenically one of the most varied of the Shetland islands, with spectacular cliffs, sea stacks, sheltered inlets, sandy beaches, heather-clad hills, fertile farmland, freshwater lochs and even a sub-arctic desert. Such a variety of habitats supports over 400 plant species and a rich variety of wildlife. Unst is a major breeding site for gannets, puffins, guillemots, razorbills, kittiwakes, shags, Arctic and great skuas and whimbrels, amongst others, and in the surrounding waters you can see seals, porpoises, otters and even killer whales.

In the east of the island, north of **Baltasound**, is the **Keen of Hamar National Nature Reserve,** 74 acres of serpentine rock which breaks into tiny fragments known as 'debris', giving the landscape a strange, lunar-like appearance. This bleak 'desert' is actually home to some of the rarest plants in Britain. Baltasound is the island's main settlement, with an airport, hotel, pub, post office, leisure centre with pool and Britain's most northerly brewery, the **Valhalla Brewery** which can be visited by appointment, T711348.

To the north of here is the village of **Haroldswick**, home of Britain's most northerly post office, where your postcards are sent with a special stamp to inform everyone of this fact. The road ends at Skaw, where there's a lovely beach and Britain's most northerly house. The road northwest from Haroldswick leads to the head of **Burra Firth**, a sea inlet flanked by high cliffs, and site of Britain's most northerly golf course.

To the west of Burra Firth is the remote **Hermaness National Nature Reserve,** 2,422 acres of dramatic coastal scenery and wild moorland which is home to over 100,000 nesting seabirds including gannets, and the largest number of puffins and great skuas (or 'bonxies') in Shetland. There's an excellent **visitor centre** in the former lighthouse keeper's shore station, where you can pick up a leaflet which shows the marked route into the reserve, and see the artistic efforts of many of Unst's children. Whilst in the reserve, make sure you keep to the marked paths to avoid being attacked by bonxies: they are highly protective and rest assured that they will attack if they think that their territory is being threatened. ⓘ *0830-1800. T711278 daily late Apr to mid-Sep.*
The views from Hermaness are wonderful, out to the offshore stacks and skerries including **Muckle Flugga**, and then to the wide open north Atlantic ocean. Muckle Flugga is the site of the most northerly lighthouse in Britain, built in 1857-58 by Thomas Stevenson, father of Robert Louis Stevenson. The writer visited the island in 1869, and the illustrated map in his novel *Treasure Island* bears a striking similarity to the outline

of Unst. Beyond the lighthouse is **Out Stack**, which marks the most northerly point on the British Isles. With nothing between you and the North Pole but water, this is the place to sit and contemplate what it feels like to be at the end of the world.

Sleeping

Lerwick *p920*
Shetland's best accommodation is outside Lerwick, whose hotels are mostly geared towards the oil industry. During the peak months of Jul and Aug and the Folk Festival in Apr, it's a good idea to book in advance.

A **Kveldsro House Hotel**, Greenfield Pl, T01595-692195, www.kghotels.co.uk. The most luxurious hotel in town. Pronounced 'kel-ro', it overlooks the harbour and has an upmarket restaurant as well as cheaper bar food.

A **Lerwick Hotel**, 15 South Rd, 10 mins from the centre, T01595-692166, reception@lerwickhotel.co.uk, has a reputation for fine cuisine.

B **The Old Manse**, 9 Commercial St, T01595-696301. Pleasant guesthouse.

Central Mainland *p920*
A **Herrislea House Hotel**, near the airport, by the crossroads, T01595-840208, www.herrislea-house.shetland.co.uk, offers good home cooking daily till 2100, and live music in its *Starboard Tack* bar.

D **Hildasay Guest House**, in Scalloway, in the upper part of the village is T01595-880822, which has disabled facilities and arranges fishing trips.

The Westside *p921*
A **Burrastow House**, 2 miles southwest of Walls, T01595-809307, burr.hs.hotel@zetnet.co.uk, a restored 18th-century house overlooking Vaila Sound. It's full of character and has a reputation for serving superb cuisine (some say the best on the islands, so you'll need to book ahead).

There's a camping böd in Walls, at **Voe House**, a restored 18th-century house overlooking the village. Open Apr-Sep. Book through Lerwick tourist office.

Foula *p921*
C **Leraback**, T01595-753226, includes dinner in the price. There is also self-catering accommodation available on the island, £90-150 per week for a cottage sleeping 4-6 people. Contact Mr R Holbourn, T01595-753232.

Fair Isle *p922*
A **Fair Isle Lodge and Bird Observatory**, T01595-760258, www.fairislebirdobs.co.uk, offers full-board accommodation in private rooms or in a dormitory (**D**).

North Mainland *p923*
A **Busta House Hotel**, T01806-522506, www.mes.co.uk/busta A luxurious and wonderfully atmospheric 16th-century country house overlooking Busta Voe about 1½ miles from Brae village. The superb restaurant (mid-range to expensive) is the finest on Shetland, with a selection of malts to match, and there are also meals in the bar.

E **Sail Loft** , by the pier in Voe. This former fishing store is now Shetland's largest camping böd, open Apr-Sep.

E **Johnny Notion's Camping Böd**, In Hamnavoe, reached by a side road which branches north from the road between Hillswick and Eshaness. Book through Lerwick tourist office. Birthplace of John Williamson, known as 'Johnny Notion', an 18th-century craftsman who developed an effective innoculation against smallpox. It's open Apr-Sep and has no electricity.

Yell, Fetlar and Unst *p924*
B **The Glebe**, T01957-733242, a lovely old house overlooking Papil Water. You can also camp at **Gerth's Campsite**, T01957-733227, which overlooks the beach at Tresta and has good facilities.

B **Buness House**, on Unst, T01957-711315, buness@zetnet.co.uk, a lovely old 17th-century Haa in Baltasound. Staying here is a bizarre and rather surreal experience, given that you are on the most northerly island in Britain. The house is crammed full of Indian Raj relics, and the stuffed eagle, tiger and leopard skins hanging in the hallway are a wildlife close-up almost as impressive, though considerably more unsettling and un-'PC', as the Hermaness Nature Reserve in the north of the island that the family own. The food is excellent and the accommodation comfortable.

Eating

Despite a ready supply of fresh local produce, Shetland is a gastronomic desert. The best places to eat are the hotels and guesthouses that are recommended in the Sleeping section.

Festivals and events

Jan Up Helly-Aa Viking fire festival held annually in Lerwick on the last Tue in Jan, when a torch-lit procession through the town by hundreds of people dressed in Viking costumes (*guizers*) is followed by a replica Viking longship built especially for the event. At the end of the procession the ship is set ablaze when the guizers throw their flaming torches on to it.
Apr Folk music has a strong following in Shetland and the islands play host to 2 of Scotland's top folk events. In mid-Apr the islands are alive with the sound of music as musicians from around the globe come to play at the Shetland Folk Festival.
Oct Later, in mid-Oct, is the Shetland Accordion and Fiddle Festival. For details of both events, contact the Folk Festival office, 5 Burns Lane, Lerwick, T01595-694757.

To find out what's going on, buy a copy of the *Shetland Times* on Fri, or check out their website, www.shetland-times.co.uk Also check the tourist board's Events phoneline, T01595-694200.

Directory

Lerwick *p920*
Car hire Bolts Car Hire, Toll Clock Shopping Centre, 26 North Rd, T01595-693636. John Leask & Son, Esplanade, T01595-693162. Star Rent-a-Car, 22 Commercial Rd, T01595-692075. Also have offices at Sumburgh Airport. **Cycle hire** Grantfield Garage, North Rd, T01595-692709, Mon-Sat 0800-1300 and 1400-1700. **Embassies and** consulates Denmark, Iceland, Netherlands and Sweden at Hay & Company, 66 Commercial Rd, T01595-692533; Finland, France, Germany and Norway at Shearer Shipping Services, Garthspool, T01595-692556. **Post office** Commercial St (open Mon-Fri 0900-1700, Sat 0900-1200), also in Toll Clock Shopping Centre, 26 North Rd. **Taxi** There are several taxi companies in Lerwick:
6050 Cabs, T01595-696050;
Sheilds Taxis, T01595-695276;
Abbys Taxis, T01595-696666.

Background

History

First settlement

The human colonization of Europe took place during the Ice Age, when Britain was still linked to mainland Europe. Human remains, from *homo erectus* (800,000 years ago) to our more immediate ancestors, *homo sapiens* (40,000 years ago), have been found in Boxgrove on the south coast and Swanscombe, Kent, now the bastion of middle-class respectability, but then the home of hirsute creatures wielding clubs. The remains of exotic wildlife, such as elephants, hippopotami, giant beavers and sharks have all been uncovered in the more hospitable lowlands of southeast England. The Neolithic age witnessed bands of hunters wandering the country in search of food, and it wasn't until some 6000 years ago, long after the seas had finally swallowed up Britain's link to mainland Europe, that Stone Age hunters began to settle. Clearings were formed, crops grown, homes built and stone tombs erected to house the dead. Wayland's Smithy, just off the Ridgeway to the west of Wantage, is one of the most impressive of a clutch of Neolithic and early Bronze Age settlements to be found scattered around the Marlborough Downs; West Kennet, Wiltshire, is one of the largest.

Bronze Age folk lived in thatched roundhouses and by 2000-1500 BC had been joined by **Beaker folk**, so named from their distinctive pottery found in their barrows and tumuli in Wiltshire), and grain-cultivating Megalithic people, arriving by sea via Spain and Portugal, who were tempted to settle by a then prevailing near-Mediterranean climate. The Beaker folk brought new and relatively sophisticated knowledge of bronze metalwork. They also transported huge bluestones to Stonehenge (from Pembrokeshire in South Wales) which formed the second stage of the building of the megalithic structure. Stonehenge was built over three stages from the early Bronze Age in around 2500 BC through to 1500 BC in the late Bronze Age. The purpose of the monuments is still disputed (although its links with the summer solstice are surely more than coincidence), but they are undoubtedly the work of a society of spiritual and some technological sophistication. The pottery and other artefacts of the Beaker people have been found in burial mounds or cairns, such as **Maeshowe** on Orkney Mainland (see page 911), from around this time and suggest a complex social structure and perhaps, more importantly, a belief in the afterlife, as do the prehistoric settlements and monuments in Caithness, Orkney, Shetland and the Outer Hebrides, notably at **Skara Brae** (page 910), **Stenness**, and the **Ring of Brodgar** on Orkney Mainland, and **Callanish** on Lewis (see page 892).

The Iron Age

The Celts originally came from the area around the Rhine in Europe. A tall, fair people with sophisticated social structures, they began to arrive around 800BC, easily achieving supremacy over the existing (primitive) residents. They settled in farmsteads and villages, caring for livestock and working the patchworks of fields that they established. They were noted for their love of war and imposed their ways on the existing tribes of Britain very quickly. They used **iron**, rather than other metals; were artistically skilled, and had distinctive religious beliefs – with their religious leaders, the **Druids**, enjoying huge power. Caesar wrote of Celtic society that there were 'only two classes of men who are of any account...the common people are treated almost as slaves ...the two privileged classes are the Druids and the Knights'. They also brought with them a new **language** which had two distinct strands: **Goidelic** (the basis of the Celtic languages in the Isle of Man, Scotland and Ireland) and **Brythonic** – the basis of Cornish and Welsh.

Aside from the farmsteads, large hill-forts dotted the countryside: Danebury in Hampshire and Maiden Castle in Dorset, the capital of the large Durotriges tribe, are notable examples which survive to this day. Such forts, sometimes built with up to eight lines of defence against attack, were arranged in 'streets' and housed workshops, granaries and shrines as well as extensive accommodation. In Scotland, the **brochs**, or towers, the remains of many of which can still be seen dotted along the west coast and in the islands, date from this time. The Celts flourished until the arrival of the Romans, who first came to Britain in 55BC, and finally conquered much of it in 43AD.

The Romans

Tales of the extent of England's natural resources, and the ferocity of its warriors, would have reached Roman ears long before they began to invade her shores. At first these sorties were tentative. Under **Julius Caesar** (in 55 and 54BC), the Romans landed briefly, struck deals with one or two local chiefs and returned to Gaul. In 43AD, however, Emperor Claudius determined to annex the island for himself, partly for its metal deposits, and partly to finally rout the remaining Belgae who had retreated to England after their recent defeats in Gaul. Therefore the 40,000 Romans who arrived at Richborough in Kent ensured that any resistance from the beleaguered Belgae was cursory. For the most part the local Kings were open to negotiation and where that failed, to a combination of threats and rewards. However Caractacus, the King of the Catuvellauni, resisted for nine years, and was pardoned such was the Romans' admiration for his courage and tenacity. Later, **Boudicca**, Queen of the Iceni and to this day a potent symbol of British courage and tenacity, led an army against the Romans in East Anglia. She managed to lay waste to the Roman strongholds of Colchester and London, before finally taking her own life by means of poison when all seemed lost. However, while her fortitude and success was a dent to the image of Roman invincibility, she had not always been a die-hard rebel. Her husband the King had been happy to co-operate with the Roman invaders and it was only when a newly arrived Governor tried to make slaves of the Iceni people, in the process killing the King and having her daughters raped before her eyes, that Boudicca turned rebel.

Despite the occasional hiccup, and the occasional dagger-happy governor, **Britannia**, as the Romans named the island, became a largely peaceful place. What had worked elsewhere across their dominions also seemed to work here, as the Empire began to reproduce its tried and tested systems. Towns emerged, bigger, grander and altogether more sophisticated than those devised by the Celts; road networks spread across the country; water systems were created, and trade with the rest of the Empire flourished. As the decades passed, a **Romano-British society** began to be established. Towns such as Bath, with its fabulous spa (still in existence today), Chichester, Colchester, St Albans and London grew to be major Roman towns. Local bigwigs adopted the Roman tradition of building villas in the countryside – Fishbourne Palace in Sussex, Woodchester in Gloucestershire and Rockbourne in Hampshire, all of which retain some of their fine mosaics, attest to this. The Romans built roads throughout Wales, linking important forts at **Caernarvon** (Segontium) and **Carmarthen** (Moriduum), and settled down for a long occupation. Their language and ways of living – and later their new Christian religion – started to influence local Celtic culture. Even today the Welsh language shows Latin influences with words like 'pont' for bridge, ffenestre (window), and cwmwl (cloud). Towards the end of the Roman occupation several forts were built along England's south and east coasts, as raids on its cities by German pirates became frequent. The remains of one such fort are still visible in Richborough, Kent.

North of the border, indigenous Iron-Age tribes inhabited most of the country and were identified by the Romans as **Picts** – possibly meaning 'painted, or tattooed, people'. They thwarted Roman imperial ambition in Alba, the land north of the Forth and Clyde, in around AD 80, and a string of Roman military outposts along the Highland line remain from this abandoned campaign. Defensive walls built by Emperors **Hadrian** (built circa AD 123 from the Solway Firth to the Tyne) and **Antoninus** (from the Clyde to the Forth circa AD 143) against the Picts inadvertently set a precedent for the eventual polarization of Scotland and England, beginning around the ninth century, out of the mass of tribal kingdoms. An endlessly disputed border led to centuries of retaliatory raids and devastation on either side.

Picts south of the Antonine wall became semi-Romanized and were known as **Britons**, kin to the Welsh. Their kingdom of Strathclyde, with a stronghold on Dumbarton Rock near Glasgow, once extended into Lancashire and retained a separate identity into the 11th century. Meanwhile an Irish tribe, **the Scots**, who claimed descent from an Egyptian Pharaoh's daughter, had been settling in Pictish territory in Argyll from around the fourth century. Once in Argyll, the sons of the Scots' leader, Erc, established a kingdom called **Dalriada**, sharing it between themselves under a high king at **Dunadd**. When their fellow countryman, **Columba**, arrived in the sixth century on **Iona**, they were aided in their cause by his diplomatic skills at the hostile Pictish court of King Brude, in Inverness. In the ninth century the Scots under **Kenneth MacAlpin** took over the Picts. Although their written records were destroyed, or falsified by the conquering Scots, they left a rich legacy of unique sculptured stones denoting a civilized and artistic culture. When Kenneth set up at **Scone**, and Alba became Scotland, the seven kingdoms of Pictland in the north and east survived as great earldoms.

The Dark Ages

It was only when the Roman Empire began experiencing trouble closer to home near Rome, and the legions were called away, that the Roman presence in Britain began to diminish. As the Romans left, so the Germanic migrants such as the Saxons and the Angles became more frequent intruders, and when Rome was finally sacked in 410AD, and the last two legions had left, Britain welcomed a new arrival.

The newcomers were a motley crew: predominantly **Saxons** from the mouth of the Rhine, **Angles** from Germany and **Jutes** from Denmark. These tribes settled across much of England, with the names of a number of modern English counties bearing this out. The South Saxons settled in Sussex, the east Saxons in Essex, and the West Saxons in Wessex (a name no longer used on maps, but recently revived by the Prince Edward, Earl of Wessex). The new immigrants did not, however, manage to spread to the western extremities of the island. A small proportion of Romano-British society had fled to Devon and Cornwall and remained loyal to the banner of Ambrosius Aurelianus, an aristocrat of Roman descent. There Ambrosius and his followers built an earthen barrier from Wiltshire to Berkshire which succeeded in keeping out the Saxon hordes. Ambrosius' successor, according to legend, was Arthur, he of the Round Table and the castle of Camelot. The true genesis of Arthur and the **Arthurian legend** is still something of a mystery. The Welsh have claimed him for their own (with some justification), the 12th century Frenchman Chretien de Troyes is credited with the Round Table and Camelot story but actual historical records throw little light on the matter. There is some evidence of a courageous and noble warrior in the southwest of England who fought 12 (victorious) battles against the Saxons. In further support of this, Cornwall, in the southwest tip of Britain, remained a Celtic stronghold, relatively untroubled by the Saxon invaders until well into the ninth century. Some say that Arthur was born at Tintagel, a Cornish coastal settlement and a rare but fine relic of an early sixth-century royal centre. Whatever the true facts of Arthur's life and death, his legend lives on.

Anglo-Saxon England continued to take shape through the sixth and seventh centuries. The towns tended to be abandoned in favour of a more rural life, and although some urban centres did emerge (Southampton and Ipswich, for example), even London saw the population shift to outside its city walls. Gradually, three kingdoms began to emerge across England – Northumbria in the north (which dominated the seventh century), Mercia in what we now call the Midlands (dominant in the eighth), and Wessex in the south (supreme in the ninth century).

Early Christianity

In 597, another crucial event in England's history took place: St Augustine was consecrated Bishop of the English and given permission to build a cathedral at Canterbury. Christianity was not new to England (the three previous centuries had known

Celtic Christianity) but at the Synod of Whitby in 664, it was decided to follow the Church of Rome, and move away from the Christianity advocated by Celtic missionaries such as St Aidan, the founder of the monastery on Lindisfarne. Such a decision was to define English Christianity for the next nine hundred years or so, until Henry VIII's rejection of papal authority in the sixteenth century. The seventh and eighth century not only saw the shaping of the spiritual heart of the country, but also the emergence of a fine literary tradition, including the illuminated **Lindisfarne gospels** (the monastery was Romanised by St Cuthbert after the Synod), the poems of Caedmon and the *Ecclesiastical History of the English People* by a monk from Jarrow, the Venerable Bede.

Well before this time, around AD 397, **Ninian** founded a Christian Mission in Whithorn, in Galloway, in southern Scotland, along eastern Mediterranean monastic lines vastly different from the Roman model. From here he and countless missionaries such as Kentigern, Moluag and Comgan went north to convert the Picts, as far as St Ninian's Isle in Shetland. In AD 563 Columba arrived on **Iona** (see page 756), where he went on to found the Celtic Church, or the Church of the Culdees, with centres throughout Scotland, which differed in many ways from the Church of Rome. Iona became known as the 'Cradle of Christianity in Scotland', but the arrival of the Vikings inhibited sea travel and the monks were driven from Iona. About this time, the Scots took over the Pictish nation and the Columban church moved to **Dunkeld**, with Columba's relics transported in the *breacbannoch*, or Monymusk reliquary. This was carried at Bannockburn and is now in the Museum of Scotland in Edinburgh. **St Andrews** later became the principal seat of the church, although Iona retained special status. Communities of Culdees (one of which was at St Andrews) survived into the 13th century, outwith the Columban and later Roman church. These were thought to be adherents of Ninian's church, preserving elements of pre-Christian druid religion.

Christianity, which had only taken a tenuous hold through the Romans, returned to Wales during the fifth and sixth centuries, with the arrival of missionaries from Ireland. **Illtud** introduced the idea of Celtic monasticism and established a religious school at **Llantwit Major** in south Wales.

Around the same time Irish settlers (who spoke the Goidelic tongue) began moving into western parts of Wales, but were expelled, from the north at least, by Cunedda, leader of the Brythonic speaking Votadini (Gododdin) tribe. Well organised, they established themselves in north Wales, eventually spreading as far south as the Teifi. They set up the royal house of Gwynedd and, more significantly, consolidated the Brythonic language in Wales. By the sixth century a distinctive Welsh language was evolving – Latin was used for formal affairs like legal matters, but everyday speech was Welsh. The earliest known example of written Welsh is on an eighth-century stone.

The teutonic Angles and Saxons had efficiently established themselves in the south and east and in the sixth and seventh centuries began to move north and west.

The Vikings

As Anglo-Saxon influence was spreading, Britain was visited by one of the age's most advanced and belligerent forces, the **Danish** and **Norwegian Vikings**. This 'great heathen host', colonisers of Iceland and Greenland, and early discoverers of America, brought with them skilled metalwork, advanced and adventurous seafaring skills, exotic goods such as amber and furs and lyrical tales told in their poetry sagas. They also brought with them death and destruction. In time, the Vikings destroyed the Saxon kingdoms in the north and east, and the raids turned to invasion and settlement.

The rampaging Vikings were threatening to overthrow even the Saxon kingdoms of the south and west until the arrival of **Alfred, King of Wessex**, in 878. This Saxon king is best known for burning the cakes of an old lady in Somerset, but his achievements are of much more lasting importance. Not only did he co-ordinate resistance to the Vikings, and force them to confine their interests to the northeast of

 England (a region then known as Danelaw), but he also built over the ruins of Roman London to re-establish the city as the hub of country. He constructed a fleet, which helped divert later Danish invaders towards Normandy for easier game. He repaired pillaged churches, brought over foreign scholars, founded schools for the nobility, translated Bede and began the compilation of the Anglo-Saxon Chronicle, a forerunner to the Domesday Book of 1086.

The Welsh coast was also subject to raids from Vikings. The tribes in the west, who saw themselves as **Cymry** (compatriots), became isolated. And Wales – which had been given an obvious border in the late 700s when King Offa built the great earthwork **Offa's Dyke**, to delineate his Mercian territory- began to develop a distinct identity. In 856 **Rhodri Mawr** (the Great) beat off the Vikings and created a largely unified Wales – although as the practice of primogeniture (first born inherits) did not apply in Wales, inheritance squabbles meant it was never such a stable unit as England. More Viking raids in the mid ninth-century served only to increase links with England for defensive reasons, but Rhodri's grandson **Hywel Dda** (the Good) effectively became king of most of Wales. He was the first Welsh ruler known to issue his own coins – and is also recognised as the codifier of **Welsh Law**. But the country once again descended into anarchy after his death – only coming together under the rule of **Gruffydd ap Llywelyn** – who even managed to grab some lands off Edward the Confessor – before being killed by his own people at the behest of Harold, Edward's successor.

Scotland did not escape the Viking invasion. The late eighth century saw the first of many coastal raids of unimaginable savagery. By the late ninth century Norsemen had colonized **Orkney**, and from Birsay Palace Earl Sigurd wielded power as far south as Moray. A renegade bunch of mixed Norse and Gaelic ancestry, the **Gall-Gaels**, appeared in the Hebrides and Galloway. Some of these, like chieftain Ketil Flatnose's family, became early settlers of Iceland.

Once surrounded by aggressive Norse colonies, now also in Dublin and York, the newly formed 'Scotland' survived through a combination of fighting spirit and a network of shifting alliances with the various Norse powers. Some of these alliances were enduring. In the ninth century 'Torf' Einar, credited with introducing peat cutting, founded a dynasty from which sprang the Earls of Angus.

After the Dublin colony collapsed in 1014, a Viking kingdom of 'Man and the Sudreys' (Hebrides) filled the vacuum, and the isles continued to be ravaged by warring Norsemen. By around 1100 Norwegian king Magnus Barelegs' empire included the entire northern and western seaboard. Against this backdrop, pursuing his own interests, appears **Somerled,** Hebridean hero of Norse-Gaelic blood, progenitor of Clan Donald and the powerful Lordship of the Isles. In 1153 he supported a rebellion against the Scottish crown. Later, in the early 13th century, he built a series of castles around the coast, such as Sween, Tioram, Mingary and Dunstaffnage, which foiled the intermittent attempts made by the Scottish crown to assert control.

The last of the great Norse kings, Hakon, was defeated by the Scots in 1263 at Largs, with the aid of bad winter weather. Orkney and Shetland were only returned to Scotland in the 15th century. A Norse dialect was spoken there into the 18th century, and vestiges of Norwegian law still survive, as does the Viking St Magnus Cathedral in Kirkwall.

By the time of his death in 900, Alfred had been proclaimed king of all England not under Danelaw. Alfred's epithet, 'the Great' was only accorded him several hundred years later, when historians saw the significance of his reign to the formation of an English state. However, when the fledgling state envisioned by this act was finally realised is open to debate. Certainly the early Anglo-Saxon settlers have long been seen as the fathers of the English nation, but when this nation came into being is unclear. Some might argue that it preceded Alfred, when at the dawn of the ninth century, Egbert, King of Wessex, subdued the Celts in Devon and Cornwall, defeated the Mercians in battle, and so nominally became the first King of England (even though subsequent Viking invasions disrupted the hegemony). Others trace it back to 886 when Alfred captured London and made peace with the Danes, as the treaty made mention of "all the English race". Or was it one of Alfred's grandsons? Athelstan introduced a single currency and by 937 had succeeded in commanding respect as a single king from a land populated by Norsemen, Danes and Saxons from Northumbria, Wessex and Mercia. His successor, Edmund, was accepted by both the Saxon and Danish settlers and proclaimed the first King of the English. Certainly after Edmund's reign, even though the country now called England was ruled by Kings from many countries in Europe, and there were several disputed successions, it was never again divided between competing monarchs.

The ensuing decades saw England's population grow, and the English and the Danes learning, for the most part, to co-exist in relative harmony. The English shires and counties began to take shape, and local justice was implemented by a royal appointee. Ethelred the Unready, so called because of his clear unsuitability to rule anything, anywhere, lost his throne to the Viking Cnut when his ill-judged tax regime tested even the heartiest of Saxon loyalists. Even under King Cnut, when England was part of a Danish Empire that also incorporated Norway, the country thrived in relative peace. King Cnut changed little, and employed Anglo- Saxons, such as Earl Godwine (father to Harold II, who lost an eye, his life and his throne at the Battle of Hastings), as advisers. Cities such as Winchester, Ipswich and Southampton grew as important centres, and London continued to prosper. York, or Jorvik, became the second largest city, a thriving Viking settlement busy with textile production, glassworks and metallurgy, and conducted trade with Ireland and Scandinavia.

The Norman Conquest

Cnut's sons allowed the Danish Empire to collapse, so in 1042 Edward the Confessor (son of Ethelred the Unready) became king of an independent England. A religious recluse, Edward's greatest achievement was to build a palace on Thorney island in London with a church, the West Minster, nearby. Both are still in existence today and are better known as the Palace of Westminster and Westminster Abbey. Edward died childless in 1066 and the succession was initially won by Harold Godwinson, Earl of Wessex. However King Harold's accession was not undisputed. While Harold was up at Stamford Bridge near York defeating his brother Tostig and another claimant to the throne, the Norwegian King Harald Hadrada, he received word of another invasion, this time from France in the form of William the Bastard of Normandy. The English king marched his exhausted battle-weary army swiftly south to meet the Normans, who had landed at Pevensey Bay. The historic Battle of Hastings ensued, fought on a field near the coastal town of Battle, on 14th October 1066. It famously saw not only Harold killed, shot through the eye by an arrow, but also the death of about half of England's noblemen and came to be known by the Normans as 'senlac', or 'the lake of blood'.

So William the Bastard became William the Conqueror. A domineering, temperamental and tremendously strong man, he ruled England with uncompromising efficiency. Any resistance to William, mainly centring round York and Ely, was dealt with swiftly and without mercy. The few remaining Eglish nobles were deprived of their lands, which William then bestowed on his followers. The feudal system was formalized and strengthened, a sheriff represented the king in every shire and, to ensure that every penny was eked out of his subjects, a thorough survey was conducted of all the manors in England. This survey, which came to be known as the Domesday Book, has left historians with a remarkable picture of 11th-century England. It tells us that in 1086, half the cultivated land was owned by only 170 barons, of which fewer than five were English, and that the church owned over one third of the country. By 1087, William had established a new England, one whose Norman legacy remains to this day.

Having secured England as his own, William set about fortifying his position. Some 90 castles were built during his reign and it was under William that the wooden motte and bailey castle was replaced by stone buildings. The most notable is the White Tower, part of the Tower of London, but others such Corfe in Dorset, Arundel in

Sussex, Hedingham (Essex) and Warwick Castle in the Midlands are among those that still stand in some form of ruin or repair. These strongholds became the administrative centres and often the focal point of a town. They served to oversee and defend a baron's lands, acted as a home for the local magnate, as a store for winter fuel and food and accommodation for the local servants and horses.

William also reorganized the church, placing his own supporters in key posts and making his own choice, Lanfranc, Archbishop of Canterbury. Norman churches and cathedrals were built in the new Romanesque style. The status of the church grew, as it formed both the spiritual and often secular hub of the community. Saints days dotted the calendar, and religious relics drew worshippers on pilgrimages. The church also served as a centre for education in the country. Every cathedral provided a school, and around the beginning of the 13th century both **Oxford** and **Cambridge Universities** emerged from the schools set up. Benedictine, Carthusian, Franciscan and Cistercian orders built and maintained monasteries and nunneries, farming the land around while promoting a holiness and level of education not always in evidence among the parish priests.

The first Norman castle in Wales was built in 1067 at **Chepstow** and the Normans gradually encroached on Welsh lands. By the end of the 11th-century they had reached Pembroke in the south and other parts of Wales. Norman barons, the **Marcher Lords**, were installed in castles along the border so as to get control of as much land as possible. Welsh kings paid **homage** to the Normans, securing peace until William's death.

William's son, William Rufus, made some incursions into Wales and the Marcher lords gradually helped to secure much of the country – although the north west region of Gwynedd remained independent. There was much infighting and under **Owain Gwynedd**, operating from his power base at Aberffraw on Anglesey, Gwynedd began expanding its influence, sucking in weaker Welsh territories. **Llywelyn ap Iorwerth** (known as 'the Great') further extended Gwynedd and even managed to capture some Norman castles, until King John retaliated. Matters were complicated still more when Llywelyn – who wanted to achieve feudal overlordship over all Wales- consolidated his powerful position by marrying King John's daughter. He paid homage to the king – and accepted him as his heir should his marriage not produce a son. Further struggles ensued, with Llywelyn gaining Welsh support for his demands for land and a degree of autonomy. He united with the barons who made King John sign the Magna Carta (see below) and in essence ruled most of Wales. After he died the infighting started again and the Normans pushed back into Wales – until Llywelyn's grandson **Llywelyn ap Gruffyd** ('the Last') took control, managing to regain lost lands. In 1267 Henry 111 acknowledged his influence with the Treaty of Montgomery, in which Llywelyn recognised the English crown – and in turn was recognised as **'Prince of Wales'**. Llywelyn consolidated his lands, but then Edward 1 succeeded to the English throne and set out to gain control of the whole of Britain.

Medieval England

The politics of medieval England followed the predictable course of family feuds leading to dynastic struggles and civil wars; expansionist ambitions triumphantly achieved and then rudely interrupted or tragically lost; and an eclectic mix of wise and successful policies or glamorous disasters and ignominious defeats. When William the Conqueror's second son, Henry I, died childless in 1135 there was civil war between two of William's grandchildren, Stephen and Matilda. It was Stephen who ultimately triumphed to become king in 1135.

During the course of the 12th century a sense of political autonomy was slowly but steadily growing among the body of royal advisers and it was these figures who would eventually emerge as a parliament. Matters came to a head under King John whose insensitive, bullish threats against the barons led to what is considered to be one of the greatest watersheds in English constitutional history. The **Magna Carta**, foisted on the king by aggrieved barons and signed at Runnymede in Berkshire in 1215, attempted to outline what the monarch was and was not allowed to do. In short, it established the principle that the monarch was not above the common law but subject to it. Later that century, in 1264 when the commoner Simon de Montfort won the Battle of Lewes, England flirted with republicanism as a parliament of knights and noblemen presumed to discuss the fate of the country's King and Prince (Henry III and Edward I to be).

This was also an era of almost continuous conflict with France. The Angevin dynasty, as Henry II and his Plantagenet successors came to be known, hailed from Anjou in France. With the lands from his marriage to Eleanor of Aquitaine, Henry II controlled more of France than his supposed feudal overlord, the King of France, as well as most of England and Wales. For the next three hundred or so years, England and France were involved in battles over the empire, culminating in the **100 Years' War** (1337-1453) and the attempts by Edward III and his successors to realize their claim to the French throne. The later medieval period was taken up with the **Wars of the Roses**, a 30-year war between the house of Lancaster, whose emblem was a red rose, and the house of York, whose emblem was a white rose. It was only in 1485, after the infamous reign of Richard III (York) made famous in the Shakespeare play of the same name, that the war was resolved by the quiet determination of Tudor King Henry VII.

Medieval Wales

Llywelyn gradually began to lose Welsh support – he wanted to marry Simon de Monfort's daughter, and his brother Dafydd united against him with the ruler of Powys. Edward 1 seized his chance and the resulting struggle became known as the **First War of Welsh Independence** (1267-77). The result was the **Treaty Of Aberconwy** (1277), in which Llywelyn lost most of his lands but was allowed to keep the title Prince of Wales. To keep the troublesome Welsh in order, Edward built castles at Flint, Aberystwth, Builth Wells and Rhuddlan. A **Second War of Welsh Independence** was fought from 1282-83, when Llywelyn's brother Dafydd rose against Edward – who brutally crushed the Welsh. Llywelyn was captured and killed at Cilmeri, near Builth Wells in 1282 – some think due to treachery by his own people. Edward 1 strengthened his grip on Wales by starting to build more castles at Conwy, Caernarfon, Harlech and Beaumaris. In 1283 Dafydd was killed and the power of the Welsh princes ended.

In 1284 Edward signed the **Statute of Rhuddlan**, which established how Wales was to be governed: it was to be largely controlled by Norman lords and divided into new administrative units. English law took over for criminal matters, although Welsh law was retained for civil cases. Many of the powerful Welsh worked under this system happily enough and a rebellion in 1294 led by **Madog ap Llywelyn** was quickly crushed. In 1301 Edward revived the title of Prince of Wales, conferring it on his son Edward 11, who had been born at Caernarvon.

The 14th-century saw Britain plagued by famine and the Black Death, and Welsh anger and discontentment at their subjugation increased. The country was ripe for revolt – all they needed was a leader. In 1400 **Owain Glyndwr** (1354-c1416) declared himself Prince of Wales and attacked ruling barons. He quickly gathered support and took castles such as Conwy, Harlech and Aberystwyth. Rebellion spread throughout Wales and Glyndwr briefly established parliaments at Machynlleth and Dolgellau. He established alliances with powerful figures such as the Earl of Northumberland, and planned an independent Welsh state, garnering support from the Scots and the French. However his support began to wane and after various defeats, with the Crown retaking Harlech and Aberystwyth castles he seemed to fade away. No one is sure how or when he died although it is thought to be 1416.

Medieval Scotland

Macbeth, the last truly Celtic king, was also one of the most able early kings. He was the first to establish and implement a fair legal system and, a firm supporter of the Celtic church, he went on pilgrimage to Rome where an Irish monk observed him liberally scattering money to the poor. The popular image of Macbeth as portrayed by Shakespeare is, in fact, a false one. He vilified Macbeth in order to please his king, James VI, who claimed descent from Duncan, Macbeth's rival for the throne. But it was Duncan who was the nasty piece of work, and he was slain not at Glamis, as in the famous play, but on the battlefield, while invading Macbeth's territory.

Macbeth's usurper, the uncouth **Malcolm III**, Canmore (meaning 'big head'), was an illegitimate son of Duncan and a miller's daughter. In 1067 Malcolm married Margaret, a Saxon princess born in Hungary and sister of Edgar Atheling, the English heir to the throne, who had fled north with his family to escape William the Conqueror and the Norman conquest (see above). Margaret was a devout Catholic and was largely responsible for introducing the religious ideas of the Roman Catholic Church into Scotland, for which she was canonized in 1251.

Malcolm's belligerent instincts were not curbed by the influence of the saintly Margaret, however, and one of his many raids into Northumberland provoked a visit from William the Conqueror. The result was that Malcolm was forced to swear allegiance to William, an oath he didn't take too seriously, as he continued to raid England at whim, but one which would lead to a greater degree of southern interference in Scottish constitutional matters.

The Normans began to exert their influence over Scotland in many other ways. They were granted land as far as the Highland fringes, establishing a feudal system based on loyalty to the crown. The traditional patriarchal tribal culture was eroded, causing constant rebellions in the North and Galloway. The Norman successor to the Scottish throne, **David I**, like many of his Norman friends, had English estates, acquired through his wife. This wealth built the great Border abbeys and established the Roman church more fully. New parishes and dioceses revolutionized administration, and burghs were founded to develop international trade, attracting **Flemish** settlers. Society in medieval Scotland became more typically European than England or even France.

One of the depressingly familiar themes running through Scottish history has been the unwillingness of the Scots nobility to resist English ambitions towards Scotland. This has always been their Achilles heel and, in 1290, it provoked a crisis of succession, when the new child queen, Margaret, Maid of Norway, died en route from Norway. Following her death, no fewer than 13 rival contestants materialized. Two main factions emerged: the Balliols and Comyns against the Bruces. But instead of reverting to the traditional method of tanistry, or 'natural selection', the pusillanimous Scots nobles appealed to Edward I of England to adjudicate.

Edward eventually chose John Balliol, and he was crowned king at Scone in June 1292. Balliol was anxious to prove to his fellow Scots that he was not as weak as they claimed him to be. He negotiated an agreement with the French, the beginning of the Auld Alliance. He then invaded Cumberland in 1296, but in retaliation Edward attacked Berwick and slaughtered its inhabitants. Balliol abdicated and went into exile. Edward then destroyed the great Seal of Scotland and moved the Stone of Destiny, the crowning throne for all Scottish kings, to Westminster Abbey, where it lay under the Coronation Chair for 700 years. Scotland was left in disarray.

However, resistance found a leader in **William Wallace**, son of a Renfrew laird. He began a revolt against the English in 1297 and built up a substantial army. By September of that year he had secured a small but strategic victory against English forces at **Stirling Bridge**. This galvanized support, and he was quickly declared 'Guardian of the Realm'. Following his defeat at Falkirk he was betrayed to Edward by one of the Scots noblemen, captured and taken south to be executed (disembowelled, then hung, drawn and quartered) in Smithfield, London, in 1305.

This stirred **Robert the** Bruce to take up the cause of independence. Once he had killed his treacherous rival, 'Red' Comyn, Bruce was crowned king with full ceremony at Scone before the inevitable blow of Papal excommunication fell. But it was not only that Rome refused to recognize Bruce as king. Edward I, the self-proclaimed 'Hammer of the Scots', was not best pleased, and for the next seven years Bruce was a virtual outlaw fighting a guerrilla campaign against Edward from hiding in the west.

During this time the indomitable Edward died, and Bruce felt bold and confident enough to raid the northern counties of England as far south as Appleby and Richmond. Of his castles captured by the English, only Stirling remained to be wrested from Edward's successor, Edward II. So the scene was set for the most significant battle in Scottish history, at **Bannockburn**, near Stirling, in 1314, where Bruce confronted Edward II's vastly superior army. His incredible victory has ensured him a place in the heart of every patriotic Scot. Bannockburn brought the Scots a rare victory over their southern enemy, and led to the signing of the **Declaration of Arbroath**, manifesto of Scotland's independence, in 1320. There followed a temporary peace with England, and Bruce was finally recognized as king by the Pope, before he died in 1329.

Reformation and renaissance

In the wake of the Wars of the Roses came one of the strongest dynasties of the early modern period. The Tudors were of Welsh origin, but in the language of the Roses, Henry Tudor, who plucked the crown from the thorn hedge at Bosworth Field in 1485, was a Lancastrian. And a particularly wise one at that, for one of his first acts was to marry Elizabeth of York, and so unite the two houses. Henry VII's reign, however, was largely uneventful, certainly compared to those of his successors, and marked only by the peace and security he brought to England, both militarily and financially. So when his son Henry VIII succeeded to the throne, he had at his disposal a broadly united England and full coffers with which to posture abroad, a bountiful wealth of which he took full advantage.

Under Henry VIII's powerful administrator, Thomas Cromwell, Wales was brought far more under English control with the **Acts of Union** in 1536 and 1542. Although the Welsh were given legal equality, the legal system was unified with English common law taking the place of Welsh. The country was reorganised into shires, primogeniture became the method of inheritance and English became the language of the courts.

One of the defining features of the Tudor dynasty was the religious rollercoaster that England endured through the 16th century. Desperate for a male heir and clearly besotted with his pregnant mistress Anne Boleyn, in 1532 Henry VIII was determined to divorce the ageing Catherine of Aragon and marry her. The Pope, however, would not annul Henry's marriage to Catherine, so in 1534 Henry engineered the **Break with Rome**, rejecting papal authority and declaring himself head of the church in England. And so was born the Anglican church, the Church of England. Nevertheless, although this followed hard on the heels of the emergence of the Lutheran (Protestant) church in Germany, England could not be said to have fully embraced the Protestant cause, but more to have developed a form of English Catholicism. Indeed Henry's motives were as much economic and political as spiritual. For with the break came the opportunity to claim all the monasteries as his own. The **Dissolution of the Monasteries**, was a boost to the royal coffers, allowing Henry to exploit the wealth of the church. Monasteries and abbeys were torn down and their lands sold off.

After Henry VIII's death in 1547, England wavered in its religious direction. The child king Edward VI (he was nine when he came to the throne, 16 when he died) and his 'protectors' Somerset and Northumberland, departed from the Catholic way, introducing two new Prayer Books whose sympathies undoubtedly lay with the Protestant side. Edward soon died, however, and Mary I, daughter of Catherine of Aragon and a devout Catholic herself, set about restoring the 'true faith' to England, encouraged by her long absent husband, Philip II of Spain. Her methods were simple and direct, causing the death of over 400 heretics in five years. Her attacks on the heretics earned her the epithet 'Bloody Mary'; yet another piece of Protestant propaganda from the later 16th century.

When Mary I died in 1558, the country's religious direction hung in the balance. Elizabeth I adopted a wise course. Although she didn't pursue her Protestant religious convictions with the aggressive zeal displayed by her elder sister, she observed enough of a Protestant line to prompt the Pope to excommunicate her in 1570. Elizabeth maintained that she did not want to make 'windows into men's souls', and it was only when a Catholic rebellion threatened, as with the Rising of the Northern Earls in 1569 or the Armada in 1588, that she was punitive of her Catholic subjects. By 1603, when James I (James VI of Scotland) came to the throne, it could safely be said the monarch sat firmly at the head of a Protestant Church of England.

Under Elizabeth I, who wanted to ensure that Wales became Protestant rather than Catholic, an Act of Parliament was passed which laid down that the Bible be translated in Welsh within four years. This **Welsh Bible** should then be used in parishes where Welsh was the main language. The Welsh New Testament appeared in 1567, followed by the complete Bible in 1588. It was this that effectively saved the Welsh language – which was otherwise under threat from its use in court. In 1547 the first Welsh book was published and in 1571 Jesus College, Oxford was founded for Welsh scholars.

The Reformation came relatively late to Scotland and the motives were as much political as religious, though, of course, in 16th-century terms the two were inextricably linked. A pro-English Protestant faction had grown over decades, opposing the French Catholic Regent, Mary of Guise, and in 1560 a rebel parliament banned Catholic Mass, thus shattering for good the Auld Alliance with France, first formalized in 1295.

The casualties of the Reformation were countless, and included religious buildings, works of art and even whole libraries. It amounted to a complete obliteration of the past over which even today amnesia prevails, though, unlike in England, there were very few martyrs. So began 100 years of bitter struggle to establish the reformed church. Cue the Protestant exile, **John Knox**, a Calvinist rabble-rouser of dubious character and little diplomacy who was prone to blasting his trumpet off against the 'monstrous regiment of women,' namely Mary, Queen of Scots. There is no more tragic and romantic figure in Scottish history than Mary, Queen of Scots. Raised in France for safekeeping as a Catholic, her brief reign was dogged by bad luck, bad judgement and bad timing. She arrived back in Scotland in 1561, a young widow, at the height of Reformation turmoil in which both France and Catholicism were inimical. Something of a loose cannon, she was embroiled in a power struggle not helped by her disastrous choice of husbands. Implicated in the celebrated murder of the first one, her cousin, Henry Lord Darnley, she then swiftly married one of the chief suspects, the Earl of Bothwell, incurring the fury of everyone else. Imprisoned after the Battle of Carberry on the island fortress of Loch Leven, she escaped only to throw herself on the mercy of her cousin Queen Elizabeth I, who, mindful that in Catholic eyes Mary had the better claim to the English throne, locked her up at Fotheringhay for 19 years before deciding to do away with her altogether.

Revolution and Restoration

After Elizabeth's death, Mary Queen of Scots' son became James VI of Scotland. **Jacobean Scotland** was vibrant and vigorously European. Religious extremists were checked by James VI and unprecedented peace allowed Renaissance culture to blossom. In 1603 James VI ascended to the English throne as James I, with the Union of Crowns. At this time the Scottish Parliament had so little power that James VI/I was able to write from his palace in London: "Here I sit and govern Scotland with my pen. I write and it is done." In contrast, the English parliament had begun to assume some genuine power. James restored some control to royal expenditure after the expensive wars of Elizabeth's reign, and earned himself the ambiguous title of 'the wisest fool in Christendom', but his son Charles I, who succeeded in 1625, quickly proved that he had little desire to consult parliament in either Scotland or England.

Ever since Elizabeth's reign parliament had made growing demands of their monarchs. After all, they were the principal collectors and payers of tax, and yet they had no say in the disastrous and costly foreign policies pursued by their kings. In addition, the members of the House of Commons wished for more say in the choice of advisers made by the king – again with a view to avoiding costly policies that would ultimately hurt their pockets. Charles, however, was impervious to their demands, considering them to be both impertinent (he believed in the Divine Right of Kings, whereby he was answerable only to God) and unjustified. In 1629 he dismissed parliament, and resorted to a series of outdated laws to raise the funds he needed. When financial desperation forced him to recall parliament in 1640, he was met with a barrage of demands. And when he broke into the House of Commons to arrest some of its members, the Speaker nailed his colours to the Parliamentary mast: "I have neither eyes to see nor ears to hear except that which this house commands me". This sounded the death knell for the monarch's authority over parliament, and Civil War seemed inevitable.

The **English Civil War** of the 1640s was a revolutionary period in Britain. Families were split in two, some supporting the Parliamentarians (the Roundheads, so called because their hair was closer cropped than the longhaired Cavaliers, or 'swaggerers'), and others remaining loyal to the King (the Cavaliers), with brother fighting brother, and families never speaking again. The battles themselves, saw the emergence of the first truly organised and trained army, the **New Model Army**, under the leadership of Oliver Cromwell. When the crown finally fell, along with Charles I's head in 1641, it was Oliver Cromwell who succeeded as Lord Protector. During the Civil War Wales was largely on the side of the king, until Parliamentarian forces finally gained the upper hand. The Scots, too, wanted to keep the monarchy and proclaimed his son, Charles II as their king, despite falling under Cromwell's military 'Protectorate'. Cromwell acted swiftly to bring the country under his control. In 1651 he forbade the Scots from holding their own parliament – forcing them to send representatives to Westminster instead.

Cromwell's rule was not particularly distinguished. His puritanical streak ensured that some traditional religious practices were outlawed and entertainment was frowned upon – the celebration of Christmas was 'banned', many alehouses were closed, actors were "whipped till their bodies be bloody" and bear-baiting was banned not, some say, because it was cruel to bears, but because humans enjoyed it. Radicalism and non-conformism, however, flourished, although without the approval of the Protectorate. The Levellers, a quasi-political sect of Puritans, demanded universal suffrage and religious tolerance and were a foretaste of later radical thinkers. They were imprisoned in and finally shot down outside St John the Baptist church in Burford, Oxfordshire and they are still celebrated today by socialist radicals. The Diggers believed that the land belonged to everyone, and so began farming where they chose. To his credit, Cromwell did allow the Jews to return to England – they had officially been expelled in 1290. All sorts of other non-conformist groups emerged, all broadly under the Puritan banner – Millenarians, Baptists, Muggletonians, Independents, Seekers, Calvinists, Presbyterians and Fifth Monarchists. Of more lasting consequence was Cromwell's attempted suppression of Ireland, and particularly his laying waste to Drogheda and Wexford, attacks that left thousands dead. Of all the British or English injustices against the Irish, the Cromwellian abuses still serve as one of the most potent rallying cries.

It is indicative of the ambivalence with which many of the English, including some Parliamentarians, viewed the Protectorate that it was a cause for celebration when Charles I' son was invited to take the throne in 1660. Cromwell's head was exhumed and placed upon the top of Westminster Hall, there to remain for a further 25 years.

The first years of Charles II's reign were not uneventful. In 1664 the bubonic plague once again spread throughout the country. Outbreaks of plague were not uncommon, but only the Black Death of the 14th century matched the ferocity of this visitation. Aided by hot weather and the narrow, dirty streets, whole towns and villages were wiped out, and cities such as London lost almost half its population over the next 18 months. Hard on the heels of the **Great Plague** was the **Great Fire of London** in 1666, a fire that began in a bakery in the city, but that ended up destroying much of the capital. One lesson had been learnt, however – out went the timber-framed houses that had burnt so readily, and architects favoured brick or stone buildings. Furthermore, one of the greatest English architects of all time left his mark on the city. In the weeks that followed, as the embers died on the city's streets, **Sir Christopher Wren** could be seen pacing and measuring any number of his magnificent churches. Greatest of all was St Paul's Cathedral, a Protestant church to match the grandeur of the Catholic St Peter's in Rome. It dominated the London skyline in the 18th century (it wasn't completed until 1710) in a manner unimaginable today.

As both an astronomer as well as an architect, Wren was invited to join the Royal Society, a club founded by Charles II whereby a number of intellectuals were brought together to discuss the 'Advancement of Natural Science'. The diarists Samuel Pepys and John Evelyn, physicist Robert Boyle, philosopher John Locke and Sir Isaac Newton were among its members. England's first scientific journal was produced, and with the help of Newton's advanced telescope and Robert Hooke's extensive use of the microscope, scientific understanding grew. Meanwhile Charles was also a great patron of the arts. Theatres reopened, palaces were refurbished and parks laid out. After the austerity of Cromwell's Protectorate, some semblance of vitality was returning to English society.

Cromwell had made adultery a capital offence, a law that would challenge the population of any society, but would certainly have seen the early demise of Charles II. Charles had several illegitimate sons, but none by his wife Catherine of Braganza, so when he died his brother James assumed the throne. James VII/II, was a Roman Catholic, and in 1687 he tried to introduce more tolerant policies towards Catholics. His actions were seen as a threat to the privileged position held by the Church of England, and also displeased Presbyterians in Scotland. At first the feeling was that this state of affairs wouldn't last: James was ageing, and as both his daughters were Protestants, the Protestant succession seemed safe. However, when his heir James Francis Edward was born and brought up as a Catholic, a crisis was precipitated, James was ousted from the throne, and fled in 1689. His Protestant daughter, **Mary**, and her husband **William of Orange**, were invited to take the throne of England. Despite some resistance in Scotland, and a battle at the Boyne in Ireland in 1690 still celebrated in Northern Ireland today, the Glorious Revolution was largely bloodless. William and Mary had to sign a Bill of Rights confirming the rights and authority of Parliament (parliament had to be called every year, not on the monarch's whim), and although the Crown retained significant powers, parliament ensured that it would play an ever-present role in government.

Union of Parliaments

While a number of Scots began to feel that greater co-operation with England could be economically advantageous, at around the same time a further constitutional crisis was brewing. William of Orange had no children and was to be succeeded by James VII/II's daughter, Anne, who was Protestant. However, Anne had no surviving children and English politicians began to search for an heir. They decided on the Hanoverians, who were descended from the daughter of James VI/I. In 1701 the English parliament passed the **Act of Settlement**, ruling that on Anne's death the throne should pass to the House of Hanover. In 1702 William died and the throne passed to Anne.

The assumption was that the Scots would follow England's lead and accept the Hanoverian succession. But the nation was still smarting over the disastrous attempts to establish a permanent colony at Darién, on the Panama Isthmus in Central America. Scotland had lost a vast proportion of her wealth and pride was dented. Relations between the two countries were strained and the difficulties over having two separate governments would not go away. In 1703 the Scottish parliament passed the **Act of Security** which declared that on Anne's death Scotland would take a different successor to England, unless some settlement could be agreed upon that restored 'the honour and sovereignty of this Crown and Kingdom'. They wanted to guarantee the power of the Scottish parliament; the freedom of Scottish religion; and freedom of trade. In addition Parliament ordered people to arm themselves and prepare to fight.

Although Anne signed the Act of Security, Scotland's triumph was shortlived. England passed the **Alien Act**, which declared that all Scots except those resident in

England should be treated as aliens, and Scottish trade with England was to be blocked. The Act was to remain in force until Scotland agreed to make moves towards parliamentary union, or accepted Hanoverian succession.

There were obvious economic advantages to closer ties with England, and Scotland was in a vulnerable position. Not only had the Darién venture weakened the economy, the country was also suffering from several years of harvest failure which had led to famine. Although public opinion was against union with England, it counted for little. It certainly appealed to many in parliament. The Church of Scotland, initially suspicious of Union, withdrew its objections when it was assured that Presbyterianism would be safeguarded. The English were assured that union would end the threat of invasion from Scotland; the Scots assured of great economic benefits.

The people were not swayed. There were violent demonstrations in the streets, and riots in Glasgow, Dumfries and Edinburgh. But public opinion was not of consequence. Although some members, notably Andrew Fletcher of Saltoun, were opposed to union, the treaty was comfortably passed by the Scottish Parliament on 16th January 1707. It had to be signed in secret in Edinburgh to protect politicians from the mob.

In April the act was passed in the English Parliament, and on 1st May 1707 the Union came into effect. The Kingdoms of Scotland and England were united into Great Britain, though Scotland preserved its separate legal system, educational system and church. Despite the vigorous opposition, threats and bribery assured that a bankrupt and exhausted Scotland was, in popular mythology, sold to England for £398,085 – part compensation for Darién, part wages for the Commissioners who closed the deal.

Jacobite rebellion and the Clearances

The Act of Settlement was not forgotten, and dwindling trade and increased taxation fuelled dissatisfaction with the Union. A lively underground resistance, aided by long-standing French connections, revolved around the Jacobite court in exile at St Germain. Sympathy also came from English quarters. Four attempts ensued to reinstate a Stewart monarchy, supported erratically by France, and culminating at **Culloden** in 1746.

Charles Edward Stuart, the 'Young Pretender', better known as 'Bonnie Prince Charlie', was the grandson of James II. Born in Italy, Prince Charles first setting foot on Scottish soil aged 23, with seven companions (the Seven Men of Moidart). His forceful personality persuaded reluctant clan chiefs to join him in raising the Standard for his father at Glenfinnan in 1745. Inadequately prepared government troops enabled his swift progress to Edinburgh, where he held court at Holyrood, dazzling the populace with a grand ball. Edinburgh was charmed but embarrassed. With sights set on the English throne, he reached Derby. Encouraging reports about panic in London were offset by news of advancing government troops which prompted retreat. The pursuing redcoats were outwitted as far as Inverness, and the ensuing bloodbath at **Culloden**, though Charles' only defeat, was decisive. Fleeing to the Hebrides, he was given shelter by **Flora MacDonald** and then spent a summer as a fugitive. Despite a £30,000 reward for his capture, he escaped on a frigate. Too late by a fortnight, 40,000 *louis d'ors* then arrived from France, enough to revive the whole campaign.

After defeat at Culloden, savage reprisals were led by the 'Butcher' Cumberland. Rebels were beheaded or hanged, estates confiscated, and the pipes and Highland dress proscribed until 1782. Clansmen were enlisted into Highland regiments and 1,150 were exiled, swelling the ranks of emigrants to the colonies. Gaelic culture was effectively expunged and Scotland as a whole suffered disgrace.

Enlightenment

Over the next 100 years Britain emerged as the greatest power in the world. Her dominance of the seas was emphasised by the threefold increase in her trading fleet over the course of the century while her **colonial possessions** extended to several West Indian Islands, bases in India such as Bombay and Calcutta, and in time control of Canada was wrested from the French. Trade flourished, as the colonies absorbed some 40% of British produce, and she grew fat on the wealth created by the slave trade. Bristol and Liverpool were particular beneficiaries of this as the ports bulged with goods exchanged for slaves in the West Indies or Americas. While the 13 colonies were lost to American Independence in 1782, in 1770 Captain Cook raised the Union Jack at Botany Bay to claim Australia. The country's population also grew almost two-fold by 1800, by which time London could claim to be the largest city in the world.

This was also the age of enlightenment. Grand piles were erected by those who benefited from the new found wealth. **Blenheim Palace** was built as a royal reward to the Duke of Marlborough, and was so colossal as to prompt Alexander Pope to write "tis a house but not a dwelling". Other houses such as Castle Howard, Chiswick House or Stourhead all reflected the English interest in the Baroque and Palladian styles, influences brought to this country by the growing popularity among the wealthy for doing the 'Grand Tour' of Europe. British artists earned reputations abroad. Portraits by Joshua Reynolds and Thomas Gainsborough captured the aspirations of the wealthy, as did the equine portraits by George Stubbs, and in music celebrated works by George Frederick Handel and welcomed residences from Haydn and Mozart. The century saw the publication of Pope's *Rape of the Lock*, Defoe's *Robinson Crusoe*, Johnson's *Dictionary* and the first edition of the *Encyclopaedia Britannica*. Furthermore, although Britain was firmly immersed in the **slave trade**, in 1772 it was determined that a slave became free on entering Britain. This was consistent with the country's tradition for political debate and protest – whether economic theories as proposed by Adam Smith or political philosophies explored by Thomas Paine, Edmund Burke, David Hume and Mary Wollstonecraft. In the early 19th century Jeremy Bentham and anti-establishment radicals William Cobbett and Robert Owen were among those who articulated the discontent over the lack of parliamentary and labour reform.

The period saw the emergence of an urban society. In Tudor and Stuart times Britain had remained a largely rural economy, but with the scientific revolution came industrial innovations that boosted the economy. While the **Industrial Revolution** as we now know it was yet to fully take off, the country's manufacturing and industrial base grew decade by decade, burgeoned by new inventions and better communications. Textile production was aided by inventions such as John Kay's flying shuttle and James Hargreaves's spinning jenny, and James Watt's steam engine provided a more efficient source of power. Stephenson's Rocket speeded communications, while the rivers and new canals linked the major ports of England – Hull, Bristol, Liverpool and London. Improved (private) roads called turnpikes allowed for goods and people to travel around the country with greater efficiency and speed: carriages, and later the canal network, improved communications enormously. Journeys that at the beginning of the century took three days, say from London to York, could by 1800 be completed in 24 hours.

Home industry was slowly replaced by factories and workshops, as villages became towns and towns became cities billowing unhealthy smoke. Towns such as Birmingham, Sheffield, Leeds, Derby and Manchester became the home to small steel-making and metalworking industries. In agriculture new machinery revolutionised farming techniques, and increased yield. The smaller landowners were bought out by the large landowners, so rendering more labourers without the security of their own patch of land. Many agricultural labourers, therefore, moved to the towns in search of work, further inflating the growing urban population.

The peak of **worker exploitation** and misery was yet to come, but such were the conditions by the end of the 18th century that protests and uprisings were not unheard of. The Luddites broke machines in factories across Nottingham, Leicester, Lancashire, Cheshire and Yorkshire as a protest against the replacement of workers with new technology, and by 1829 such protests had spread throughout the country. Added to this were concerns over low wages, but the employers and authorities response was unsympathetic: hundreds were sent to prison and hundreds more transported to the

Australian colonies. In 1834 some farm labourers in the village of Tolpuddle in Dorset were transported for trying to organise a union, a court ruling that earned them martyr status in labour history, such that they are celebrated to this day.

Industry and Empire

The accession of **Victoria** to the throne in 1837 signalled the beginning of a golden age for Britain, one in which her wealth and influence grew further still and her pre-eminence throughout the world was assured. **The Empire** expanded into Africa and established a firmer and more lucrative grip on Asia, such that by 1900 it spread so far and wide across the globe that the 'sun never set on the British Empire'. In fact, despite the abolition of slavery in the colonies in 1833 (£20 million had to be paid to compensate the slave owners), her trading outlets were as healthy as ever. The Great Exhibition of 1851, laid out in a sparkling Crystal Palace in Hyde Park in London, displayed the triumph and achievements of 'the workshop of the world'.

Inventions transformed life across the country with the railway, the telephone, the automobile and the postal service allowing for the quicker and freer movement of people and information. Double-decker buses were introduced in the 1850s, the electric tram in the '80s, and the underground in London in the 1860's. The iron and steel industry benefited from new inventions that revolutionized production, fuelled by the coal mines of the north of England, central Scotland and south Wales. Many feats of engineering and architecture still exist today, such as the **Clifton Suspension Bridge** near Bristol and the **Forth Rail Bridge** in Scotland, **St Pancras station** in London, seaside piers, countless school buildings, and much of the railway network.

As the industrial revolution took hold, **cotton mills** spread across Lancashire in England and Lanarkshire in Scotland, and **woollen mills** in Yorkshire. Towns such as Manchester underwent a rapid transformation, tripling in population in the space of 30 years. The Prime Minister, Benjamin Disraeli described it as a "modern Athens" as it grew and adapted as a textile centre. But there was the less glamorous side too. Smoke hung over the city, slum areas developed, such as 'Little Ireland', and the rivers were open sewers. The middle-classes moved out to the surrounding villages, and the town began to swelter in its own smoke-riddled population boom. The second great Victorian city, Glasgow, was meanwhile thriving on trade with America. Its population mushroomed, absorbing many from the Highlands, as well as thousands of Irish refugees from the potato famine of the 1840's.

As the growth of Manchester and Glasgow illustrated, all these symbols of wealth and power hid a harsher side to Victorian Britain. This was an age of **extreme poverty** for some and overcrowding and disease became chronic. Open drains emptied into the rivers which in turn fed the water-pumps. Children (who made up 25% of the nation's labour force) worked 14-hour days down the mines, up the chimneys or in the cotton mills, and the factory owners paid their workers in tokens to ensure that the workers had to spend their earnings in the factory owner's shop. Industrial injuries were commonplace, not least because the exhausted workers often fell asleep at their machines and physical abuse by the foremen was standard practice. Being sent to the workhouse was a common fate for orphans or those who needed support rather than further punishment. With such poor standards of public health, it is unsurprising that cholera epidemics swept the country. There were several people and organizations that fought for the dispossessed. The **Earl of Shaftesbury** argued for factory reform and the protection of women and children in the mines; **William Booth**, a Methodist minister, set up the Salvation Army to provide shelter for the destitute; **Dr Barnardo** founded homes for children; **Elizabeth Fry** campaigned for prison Reform and the American philanthropist **George Peabody** gave money to build 'model dwellings'.

Indeed, as the century wore on the workers, whether urban or rural, began to flex their collective muscles. Following the limited concessions of the **1832 Reform Act,** a group of radicals known as the Chartists produced the **People's Charter** demanding the right to vote for all men, secret ballots and the end to restrictions on who could become an MP. Parliament refused to listen, but by the end of the century almost all the demands had been introduced. Nevertheless the movement served as a precursor of the trade union movement, which grew in strength and authority, such that towards the end of the century strikes were successfully forcing changes upon the employers. On Clydeside, skilled labour built steel ships for world markets as well as for the Royal Navy. Business boomed during the **First World War**, when political activity among skilled workers inspired by the Bolshevik revolution, led by Marxist and Scottish Nationalist John Maclean, gave rise to the myth of 'Red Clydeside'.

In 1900 the union movement spawned its own political party in Westminster, The Labour Party. With the dawn of a new political era came the death of another. When Victoria died in 1901 Britain was no longer the leading power in the world. Both America and Germany had industrialised, and were overtaking Britain as foremost manufacturers. The Empire was proving increasingly difficult to control, with war in South Africa reflecting an increasing restlessness among the Empire's subjects.

Two World Wars

The first half of the 20th century, of course, was dominated by two wars, both against Germany. Britain itself remained largely untouched by the **Great War**, save for the devastation it caused to families as their young went off to the killing fields of northern France. As if to add insult to injury, a flu epidemic in 1919 killed more people than did the war itself. The call-up of the nation's young men also allowed the nation's women to demonstrate their worth, as they kept the nations industrial and agricultural output afloat. This strengthened the **suffragette movement**'s demands for universal suffrage (it was finally achieved in 1928).

Some distraction from the war was to be found in **Ireland**, where Britain still ruled the roost, with support from the loyalist Protestant community, and tremendous resentment from the nationalist majority. The nationalists were particularly frustrated by the British delay on home rule on account of the Great War, and had life faith that it would be achieved anyway, and so rose up against the British. The **Easter Rising** of 1916, led by Patrick Pearse, was fiercely suppressed by the British, and the sixteen leaders executed. Such repression backfired – while in the short term the 'Irish Question' was manageable, it created martyrs and pushed many nationalists to support the more extreme policies of Sinn Fein, and ultimately the Irish Republican Army (IRA). In 1921 the island was divided into the Unionists in the Protestant north (which remained within the United Kingdom) and the Republicans in the Cathoic south (now Eire), a situation that still remains to this day. The IRA's terrorist acts, and others perpetrated by unionist paramilitaries, have plagued both Northern Ireland and mainland Britain since the 1970s, and involved attacks on politicians, the military and civilians. It is only now, following the **Good Friday Agreement** of 1998, that there is some hope for a peaceful solution.

Following the war, Ramsay Macdonald, albeit briefly, led the first Labour Government, and in 1926 a **General Strike** across the country demonstrated the power of the unions. However, the strike only lasted a week, and the miners were left to continue their strike alone. The **Jarrow Crusade** some 10 years later is equally famous in the history of the trade union movement, but also achieved little. The 200 or so shipbuilders who marched 300 miles south from the northeastern town on the River Tyne to London earned much support and praise along the way, and represented a brave and courageous stand on behalf of the unemployed, but gained little for them or their region.

Following the **Wall Street Crash** in 1929 and **Depression** in America, Europe had also suffered from the slump in world trade, and unemployment remained very high in some areas (it had been 75% in Jarrow). Not everyone, of course, was affected by the depression, and for those in work the 1930s was a good time, as prices fell and the standard of living rose. While the old industries of the north – coal mines, textile mills, shipyards and iron and steel foundries all saw a fall in trade, the southeast enjoyed growing job opportunities for the young in the so-called 'new industries' of car manufacturing, electrical and chemical goods. The number of motor cars in the country doubled from 1 million in 1930 to 2 million in 1939, although the towns and cities were still busy with horse and carts and electric trams. The cinemas were popular venues for films and as the source of news, and even though 1936 saw the first public broadcast by the BBC (the first in the world), it wasn't until after the war that television began to threaten the popularity of the cinema. Meanwhile in the same year **King Edward VIII** abdicated in order to marry the American divorcee **Wallace Simpson** causing a constitutional crisis that was only resolved when his brother took the throne as George VI.

With the outbreak of the **Second World War** in 1939, Britain once again faced the prospect of invasion. Hitler failed to invade with an army, but first his bombers and later his V1 and V2 rockets devastated many of the country's cities. **The Blitz** of 1940-41 was largely centred on London, but not exclusively so. Cities such as Coventry, Liverpool, Manchester and Glasgow suffered tremendous damage, with hundreds killed and wounded on any given night. Families were torn apart not only by death and conscription, but also by evacuation, whereby children were despatched to the country or abroad to live with families that they had never met before in surroundings they had never experienced. Many would subsequently lose one or both parents in the course of the war, and never return to their urban past. In the cities Anderson shelters were erected in the gardens and Morrison shelters doubled as tables in the kitchens. Air raids became less frequent when Hitler turned his attention towards Russia, but austerity measures such as rationing still ensured a grim existence at home. Furthermore, when the unmanned rockets (the 'doodlebug') began landing on the cities in 1944 people once again looked skyward in fear and trepidation. When the war finally ended in 1945 street parties sprung up throughout the towns and cities, although the constraints of rationing continued for many years to come.

Post-War Britain

However, some hope of relief was provided by one of the most influential series of reforms in the country's history – the formation of the **Welfare State**. The Labour Government swept into power on a landslide, (the Conservative Churchill was revered as a wartime leader, but the British electorate was not going to get sentimental), promising to tackle the five great 'evils' facing the country – squalor, disease, want, idleness and ignorance. Not only were a number of industries such as steel, coal, gas, electricity and the railways nationalised, but education and health received huge boosts from central government. The school leaving age was raised to 15, and health care, from hospitals to opticians and dentistry were paid for by the government out of the taxes collected. In addition, a pension scheme was established for the older generation.

The war had also destroyed millions of homes across the country, causing an unprecedented housing shortage. The problem was initially tackled by 'prefab' houses, almost a 'kit' that could be erected with relative speed and ease to provide emergency housing. During the course of the 1950's, however, a number of new towns emerged such as Corby, Harlow, Peterlee, Swindon and Milton Keynes, while modern housing estates were built on the outskirts of existing towns. When rationing finally ended in 1954, the British economy picked up, with machines taking over many of the jobs previously done by manual labourers, and all sorts of new domestic goods changing life at home – television, fridges, and telephones became increasingly commonplace. Meanwhile American rock 'n' roll was absorbing the country's youth, with teddy boys, their hair slicked back and wearing winkle picker shoes would listen to Elvis Presley or Buddy Holly, or home-grown talent such as Tommy Steel or Cliff Richard. By 1959 Prime Minister Harold Macmillan was confident enough to tell the people "You've never had it so good".

The 1950s and '60s saw a new wave of **immigration**, this time in the aftermath of Empire. In 1947 India had become the first British colony to win Independence – in the next two decades Britain lost most of its overseas possessions. At the same time, immigration from Commonwealth countries grew, especially from the Caribbean and South Asia. Labour shortages in Britain meant government incentives to draw workers to Britain, and although immigration numbers reached 30,000 a year in the 1960s (most settling in the poorer areas of the inner cities), and racial tensions could sometimes lead to riots, emigration still outpaced immigration.

Meanwhile, in the 1960's England become the **fashion centre** for the western world'. Bands such as the Who, the Rolling Stones and the Small Faces earned huge followings, but it was the Beatles that took the world by storm. From a basement club in Liverpool emerged four Liverpudlians who were to revolutionise popular music and challenge America's dominance of the **music scene**. Pirate radio stations blossomed, many of them broadcasting from the Channel. Alongside the youth revolution, and partly contributing to it, was the production in 1961 of the contraceptive pill. This gave women far greater autonomy, and so helped to create the **sexual revolution**, a more liberal view of sexual morality that horrified the older generation, but was enthusiastically embraced by the 'love and peace' generation of hippies. Carnaby Street and the King's Road in London became the fashion focus of the country and beyond, the mini-skirt a fashion classic, and the model Twiggy a cultural icon. The growth in youth politics and influence, and the increase in teenage population was also reflected in the opening of new universities.

Welsh Nationalism

In Wales, the cause of Welsh Nationalism has always been closely linked to the survival of the **language**. Events such as the Chartist movement, which had been strong in Wales, led many in authority to express concern at the radicalism of the working classes and the issue of language, which was still being spoken in non-conformist schools, was linked to political unrest. In 1846 a Welshman, representing an English constituency, set up an inquiry into Welsh education, focusing on the 'means afforded to the labouring classes of acquiring a knowledge of English'. English Anglicans were sent round the schools and came back with a report published in 1847.It declared that standards in education were terrible, sadly they put much of this down to the use of Welsh. Their report was branded *Brad y Llyfrau Gleision* – the **'Treachery of the Blue Books'**.

In 1872 the system of education was expanded with the opening of the University College of Wales at **Aberystwyth**. A campaign began to grow for greater autonomy for Wales and there was a revival of interest in Welsh culture – as evidenced by the reintroduction of the eisteddfod into Welsh life – the first being the National Eisteddfod of 1858. In 1885 the Welsh Language Society was started, which succeeded in ensuring that Welsh was taught in schools, and a political movement for a separate Wales was formed in 1886 as part of the Liberal party.

The political scene in Wales became increasingly radical and in1900 Merthyr Tydfil elected a Scot, **Keir Hardie** as their MP – Britain's first Labour MP. WW1 saw a Welshman, **David Lloyd George** become Prime Minister. The Labour Party continued to grow in importance in Wales, but there was dissatisfaction at their failure to introduce Home Rule for Wales – and the lack of safeguards for the language.

Plaid Genedlaethol Cymru (The Welsh National Party) formed in Pwllheli in 1925 by a group of intellectuals led by Saunders Lewis, focused on the defence of the Welsh language. Cymdeithas yr Iaith was established in 1962 as one of the first single issue pressure groups. Using a non-violent means of civil disobedience, it led a campaign towards the Welsh Language Act 1967, which made the existence of Welsh language a more accepted part of life in the principality. It is predominately due to Cymdeithas yr Iaith that you will see bilingual road signs, as this was brought about in the 1960s when they launched a large-scale campaign against monolingual road-signs.

The activities of Cymdeithas yr Iaith coincided with the granting to Wales of a significant degree of administrative autonomy by the appointment of a Minister of State for Wales in 1964 and the establishment of the Welsh Office.

Demands for home rule led, in 1979, to a **referendum.** The result, however, was a huge disappointment for the nationalists with 80% of people voting against a Welsh assembly. But interest in the Welsh language did increase (the 1967 Welsh Language Act had already allowed the use of Welsh in court) and in 1982 a Welsh language TV channel, **S4C**, started up. Nationalist protests began to be directed at English 'incomers' – particularly at those buying second homes in Wales. The Sons of Glyndwr started setting fire to English owned holiday homes – giving rise to the joke 'Come home to a real fire – buy a Welsh cottage'.

After the Thatcher government was finally defeated and Labour took power again, another referendum was held in 1997. This time there was a tiny majority in favour and elections to the **National Assembly for Wales** took place in May 1999. Unlike the Scottish Parliament it has no tax raising powers. After much wrangling work on a new building to house the assembly began in summer 2003 – it is sited in Cardiff Bay.

Scottish Nationalism

In a Liberal tradition dedicated to reform, the issue of Home Rule reared its head repeatedly after the 1880s. The stirrings of nationalism were heard after the First World War and voiced by writers such as Lewis Spence, Hugh MacDiarmid, Grassic Gibbon and Neil Gunn. These sentiments took political shape as the **Scottish National Party** (SNP) in 1934. Support grew through the 1950s and 1960s, and in 1967 the SNP was revealed as a potent force when Winifred Ewing won the Hamilton by-election.

Nationalist fervour reached its height in the 1970s, roused by expectations that revenue from the **oil and gas** recently discovered in the North Sea would reverse economic decline. These hopes were dashed by oil revenues disappearing into the British Treasury at Westminster. In 1974, 11 SNP MPs were elected to Westminster – and, although many felt that this was a protest vote, Labour felt concerned. In 1979 it held a referendum on the establishment of a Scottish Assembly. Turnout was low and support was lukewarm, so no assembly was established.

Labour were soon ousted from office and the Thatcher government swept to power in 1979, bringing with them a disdain for Scotland that was to have far reaching consequences. The new Conservative government also introduced policies that did not sit easily with most Scots. When the unpopular Poll Tax, which notoriously taxed 'dukes the same as dustmen', was introduced in Scotland a year earlier than in the rest of Britain, the country felt that it was increasingly being governed by politicians who cared little for its people. Years of Tory rule served only to widen the gap between Scotland and Westminster, and it was almost inevitable that some form of devolution would follow.

Twenty years on, the Scots voted emphatically in favour of devolution, and the **Scottish Parliament** reconvened after 292 years on 12 May, 1999. The early years of the Parliament have not been without controversy, and its relationship with Westminster has at times proved frosty. The most pressing issue is the so-called 'West Lothian Question', the anomaly that allows Scottish MPs at Westminster to vote on issues solely affecting England, while English MPs cannot vote on solely Scottish issues. MSPs, for example, recently voted to fund all care for all elderly people in Scotland. Yet this went against the policy of the Labour government, leading to the possible scenario of Scottish Labour MPs at Westminster voting against such funding for the elderly in England. As one commentator said: "The English have been the silent and uninvited guests at the devolutionary feast". In addition, Scotland still benefits from higher spending per head than any other part of Britain – a situation which is almost certain to change.

The new parliamentary building has attracted controversy as its estimated £50 mn construction costs have spiralled to around £400 mn. Further controversy followed the tragic and sudden death of Donald Dewar, the first First Minister, when his successor Henry McLeish resigned in the face of allegations of financial shenanigans. His own successor, Jack McConnel, immediately had to contend with the tidal wave of tabloid sex scandal. Despite this, Scotland's Parliament is finding its feet – and there's no chance that an arrogant monarch will control it again. Whether devolution is a step on the road to full independence remains to be seen.

New Britain

The 1970's and early 1980's were partly defined by the number of strikes, and the power of the Trade unions. Conservative Prime Minister Edward Heath's government was brought down by a miner's strike, but not before he ensured Britain joined the European Union, some 16 years after its inception in 1957. When **Margaret Thatcher** became the country's first female Prime Minister in 1979, she set about a rigorous economic policy designed to, among other things, take on the unions and restore Britain's 'self-confidence and her self-respect', or as she more alarmingly had it, 'put the Great back into Britain'. The result was harsh for many. Britain's manufacturing base was severely hit, both in the north and the south, but while new technology and service industries reappeared in the south, the north struggled to fill the employment gap.

A **north-south divide** was becoming more accentuated, and an 'underclass' of unemployed and homeless were beginning to fill the cities' shop doorways and underpasses. The high **unemployment** led to inner city riots in Brixton, London, Toxteth, Liverpool and St Paul's, Bristol, all areas where black and Asian youths felt discriminated against by both employers and police. Meanwhile the City of London, the square mile of the capital that still broadly follows the lines of its Roman walls, became the financial capital of Europe, if not the world – in the 1980s there were more foreign banks located here than anywhere else in the world. Thatcher's period in office only came to an end when she was brought down by her own party, concerned by her increasingly isolated and intransigent position over Europe, and her obstinacy over a local tax, the **Poll Tax**. Indeed, while the Conservative Party retained power for another seven years until 1997, their constant squabbling over Europe and some high profile sexual and financial misdemeanours among their members meant that the moderniser Tony Blair led a Labour government to electoral victory in 1997 after 18 years in opposition.

Britain today

The issue of how completely to embrace the **European union** and the **single currency** still plagues all the major parties, while the Channel Tunnel ensures the free movement of people and goods between Britain and the Continent. Britain therefore maintains an uneasy relationship with its neighbours across the channel, most recently demonstrated by the difference of opinion over how far to go in order to disarm Iraq. Whichever side you take on this particular issue, it is symbolic of the history of British foreign relations – fractious mistrust of France, and friendly bonhomie with America (despite the late 18th century blip). And while almost all political parties have emphasised the need for Britain to be at the 'heart of Europe', it quite clearly cannot fully embrace the idea. It is an island geographically detached from the continent, with an island mentality.

More recently the constitutional changes pushed through by the Labour government, giving Wales its own Assembly and Scotland its own Parliament, have changed once again the political map of Britain. It will be interesting to see what **devolution** means for the English.

Whatever makes up this 'nation of shopkeepers' as Napoleon called the British, it is once again experiencing massive changes. There are countless languages in common usage throughout the country, and some parts of cities have fewer whites than blacks or Asians. It all sounds very familiar – the assimilation of immigrants and their language and culture, which in time creates a **new Britain**. Indeed, what with the talk of a single European currency, increasing independence for the home nations, and an urban traffic system barely faster than the horse, Britannia seems to be returning to its Roman past.

Footnotes

Index

Footnotes

D

E

F

L

M

Footnotes Index

S

Y

Maps

Credits

Footprint credits

Text editor: Davina Rungasamy
Map editor: Sarah Sorensen
Picture editor: Claire Benison

Publisher: Patrick Dawson
Editorial: Sophie Blacksell, Sarah Thorowgood, Claire Boobbyer, Felicity Laughton, Caroline Lascom, Laura Dixon
Cartography: Robert Lunn, Claire Benison, Kevin Feeney
Series development: Rachel Fielding
Design: Mytton Williams and Rosemary Dawson (brand)
Advertising: Debbie Wylde
Finance and administration: Sharon Hughes, Elizabeth Taylor

Photography credits

Front cover: Alamy – sheepfolds, Gunnerside, Yorkshire.
Back cover: Alamy, David Crausby – buckets and spades.
Inside colour section:
Britain on View, British Museum Press Office, Ben Winston, National Trust, English Heritage, Chris Parry.

Print

Manufactured in Italy by LegoPrint
Pulp from sustainable forests

Footprint feedback

We try as hard as we can to make each Footprint guide as up to date as possible but, of course, things always change. If you want to let us know about your experiences – good, bad or ugly – then don't delay, go to **www.footprintbooks.com** and send in your comments.

Publishing information

Footprint Britain
1st edition

ISBN 1 903471 89 3
CIP DATA: A catalogue record for this book is available from the British Library

Published by Footprint
6 Riverside Court
Lower Bristol Road
Bath BA2 3DZ, UK
T +44 (0)1225 469141
F +44 (0)1225 469461
discover@footprintbooks.com
www.footprintbooks.com

Distributed in the USA by
Publishers Group West

Neither the black and white nor colour maps are intended to have any political significance.

Every effort has been made to ensure that the facts in this guidebook are accurate. However, travellers should still obtain advice from consulates, airlines etc about travel and visa requirements before travelling. The authors and publishers cannot accept responsibility for any loss, injury or inconvenience however caused.

Acknowledgements

Charlie Godfrey-Faussett would like to thank the various contributors: Alex Studholme, Christi Daugherty, Laura Dixon, Max Carlish, Andrew White, Ben Joliffe and Chris Moore. Also the many people who have helped with the England chapters, especially Steve Watson, Siam Chowkwanyun, Jason Gathorne-Hardy, Rowland Trafford-Roberts, Rupert John Gale, Keith Coventry, Lizzie Taylor, Jessica Greenman, Peter Oswald, John Ford, Clare de Jong, Hugh Simpson, Alice Lucas-Tooth, Matthew Brett, Tim Clark, Nicky Mist, Jessica Purcell, James Christopher, Nick Barton, Fi Godfrey-Faussett, Caro Taverne, Arthur Tewungwa, David Butler, and most of all Addie Godfrey-Faussett.

Alan Murphy would like to thank those who contributed to the Scotland chapters, especially Rebecca Ford, Laura Dixon, Norma Rowlerson, Nigel Easton, John Murphy, Jane Hamilton, John Binney, Suzy Kennard. Thanks go to the staff of the many local and regional tourist offices for their invaluable advice and assistance, to the staff at Caledonian McBrayne, the National Trust for Scotland and Historic Scotland, and especially Philippa for her support.

Rebecca Ford would like to thank Rachael Norris, Glenda Lloyd Davies and all at the Welsh Tourist Board, Laurence Main, Nerys Lloyd-Pierce, Martin Husband, Debbie Roberts, the Ramblers Association and CADW.

Authors

Charlie Godfrey-Faussett has lived in London north and south of the river for the best part of the last 17 years. In that time he has produced plays, worked in television and written for the screen. The author of the Footprint guides to England and London, he has also reviewed theatre and contributed to guides for Time Out as well as a variety of national newspapers and magazines.

A graduate of St Andrews University, **Rebecca Ford** worked in public relations and advertising for several years before becoming a full-time travel writer and photographer. Her travels now take her all over the world, although she specializes in writing about the British Isles and Italy. She is also co-author of the Footprint Glasgow guide and has contributed to Footprint Scotland.

Alan Murphy has worked as a journalist on various publications across the globe – from Dundee to La Paz. During his spell in Bolivia he began updating information for the famous South American Handbook and hasn't looked back since. Following on from writing the early editions of Footprint's Bolivia, Peru, Ecuador and Venezuela guides, he then came home to his native Scotland to write and research a new guide to Scotland. He now lives with his wife, Philippa, and children, Rosa and Ruben, in deepest darkest Somerset, where he writes Footprint guides to Scotland, Scotland Highlands and Islands, Edinburgh and Glasgow.

Complete title listing

Footprint publishes travel guides to over 150 destinations worldwide. Each guide is packed with practical, concise and colourful information for everybody from first-time travellers to travel aficionados. The list is growing fast and current titles are noted below.
Available from all good bookshops and online

www.footprintbooks.com

(P) denotes pocket guide

Latin America and Caribbean
Argentina
Barbados (P)
Bolivia
Brazil
Caribbean Islands
Central America & Mexico
Chile
Colombia
Costa Rica
Cuba
Cusco & the Inca Trail
Dominican Republic
Ecuador & Galápagos
Guatemala
Havana (P)
Mexico
Nicaragua
Peru
Rio de Janeiro
South American Handbook
Venezuela

North America
Vancouver (P)
New York (P)
Western Canada

Africa
Cape Town (P)
East Africa
Libya
Marrakech & the High Atlas
Marrakech (P)
Morocco
Namibia
South Africa
Tunisia
Uganda

Middle East
Egypt
Israel
Jordan
Syria & Lebanon

Australasia

Australia
East Coast Australia
New Zealand
Sydney (P)
West Coast Australia

Asia

Bali
Bangkok & the Beaches
Cambodia
Goa
Hong Kong (P)
India
Indian Himalaya
Indonesia
Laos
Malaysia
Nepal
Pakistan
Rajasthan & Gujarat
Singapore
South India
Sri Lanka
Sumatra
Thailand
Tibet
Vietnam

Europe

Andalucía
Barcelona
Barcelona (P)
Berlin (P)
Bilbao (P)
Bologna (P)
Britain
Copenhagen (P)
Croatia
Dublin
Dublin (P)
Edinburgh
Edinburgh (P)
England
Glasgow
Glasgow (P)
Ireland
Lisbon (P)
London
London (P)
Madrid (P)
Naples (P)
Northern Spain
Paris (P)
Reykjavík (P)
Scotland
Scotland Highlands & Islands
Seville (P)
Spain
Tallinn (P)
Turin (P)
Turkey
Valencia (P)
Verona (P)

Also available
Traveller's Handbook (WEXAS)
Traveller's Healthbook (WEXAS)
Traveller's Internet Guide (WEXAS)

Map symbols

Administration

- Capital city
- Other city/town
- International border
- Regional border
- Disputed border

Roads and travel

- Motorway
- Main road
- Minor road
- 4WD track
- Footpath
- Railway with station
- Airport
- Bus station
- Metro station
- Cable car
- Funicular
- Ferry

Water features

- River, canal
- Lake, ocean
- Seasonal marshland
- Beach, sand bank
- Waterfall

Topographical features

- Contours (approx)
- Mountain
- Volcano
- Mountain pass
- Escarpment
- Gorge
- Glacier
- Salt flat
- Rocks

Cities and towns

- Main through route
- Main street
- Minor street
- Pedestrianized street
- Tunnel
- One way street
- Steps
- Bridge
- Fortified wall
- Park, garden, stadium
- Sleeping
- Eating
- Bars & clubs
- Entertainment
- Building
- Sight
- Cathedral, church
- Chinese temple
- Hindu temple
- Meru
- Mosque
- Stupa
- Synagogue
- Tourist office
- Museum
- Post office
- Police
- Bank
- Internet
- Telephone
- Market
- Hospital
- Parking
- Petrol
- Golf
- Detail map
- Related map

Other symbols

- Archaeological site
- National park, wildlife reserve
- Viewing point
- Campsite
- Refuge, lodge
- Castle
- Diving
- Deciduous/coniferous/palm trees
- Hide
- Vineyard
- Distillery
- Shipwreck
- Historic battlefield

Britain

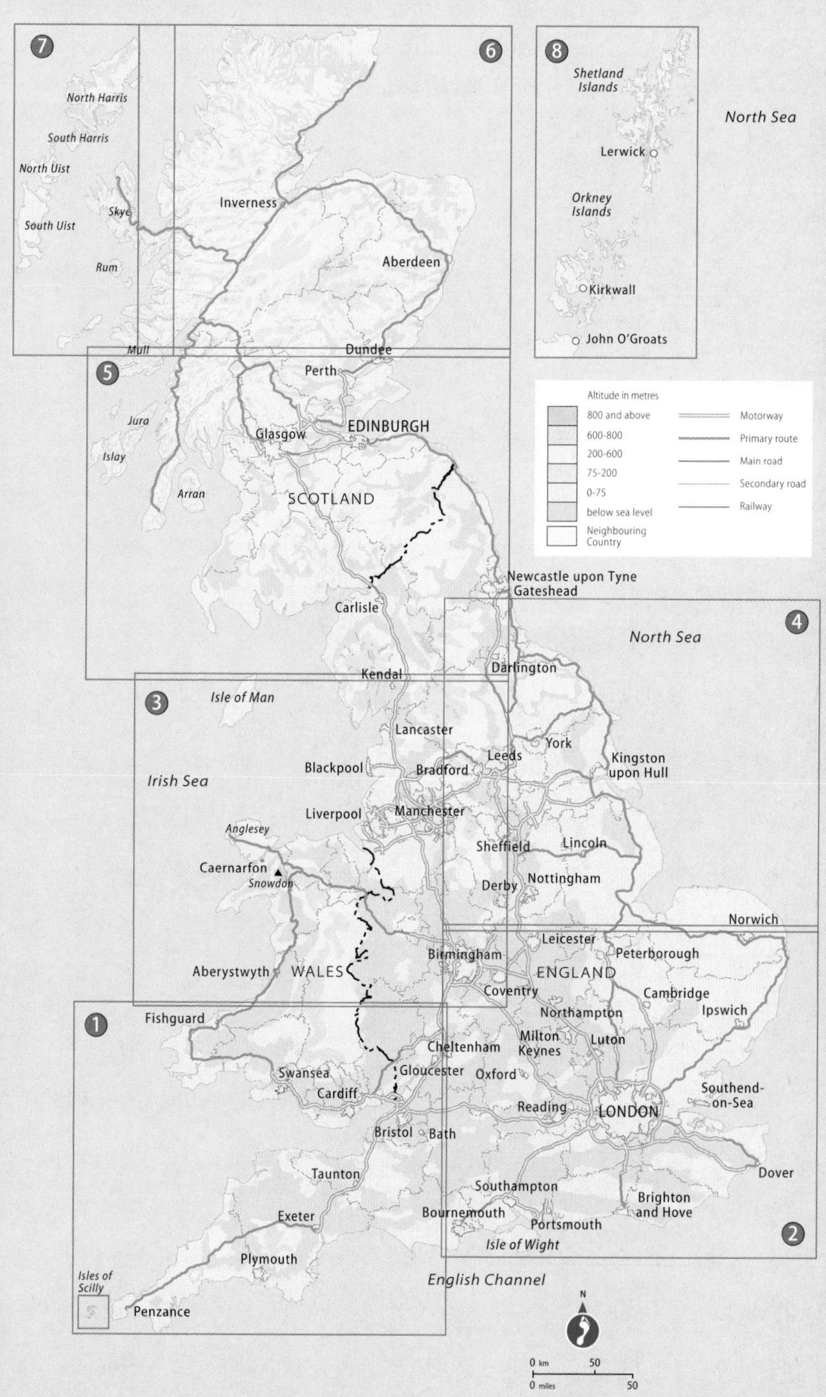

7
6
8
North Harris
South Harris
North Uist
Skye
South Uist
Rum
Inverness
Aberdeen
Shetland Islands
North Sea
Lerwick
Orkney Islands
Kirkwall
John O'Groats
Mull
Dundee
5
Perth
Jura
Islay
Glasgow
EDINBURGH
Arran
SCOTLAND
Altitude in metres
800 and above
600-800
200-600
75-200
0-75
below sea level
Neighbouring Country
Motorway
Primary route
Main road
Secondary road
Railway
Newcastle upon Tyne
Gateshead
Carlisle
4
North Sea
Kendal
Darlington
3
Isle of Man
Lancaster
York
Leeds
Kingston upon Hull
Blackpool
Bradford
Irish Sea
Liverpool
Manchester
Anglesey
Sheffield
Lincoln
Caernarfon
Snowdon
Derby
Nottingham
Norwich
Leicester
Peterborough
Birmingham
Aberystwyth
WALES
ENGLAND
Coventry
Cambridge
1
Fishguard
Northampton
Ipswich
Milton Keynes
Luton
Cheltenham
Swansea
Gloucester
Oxford
Cardiff
Southend-on-Sea
Reading
LONDON
Bristol
Bath
Taunton
Dover
Southampton
Brighton and Hove
Bournemouth
Exeter
Portsmouth
2
Isle of Wight
Plymouth
Isles of Scilly
English Channel
Penzance
N
0 km
50
0 miles
50

Map 1

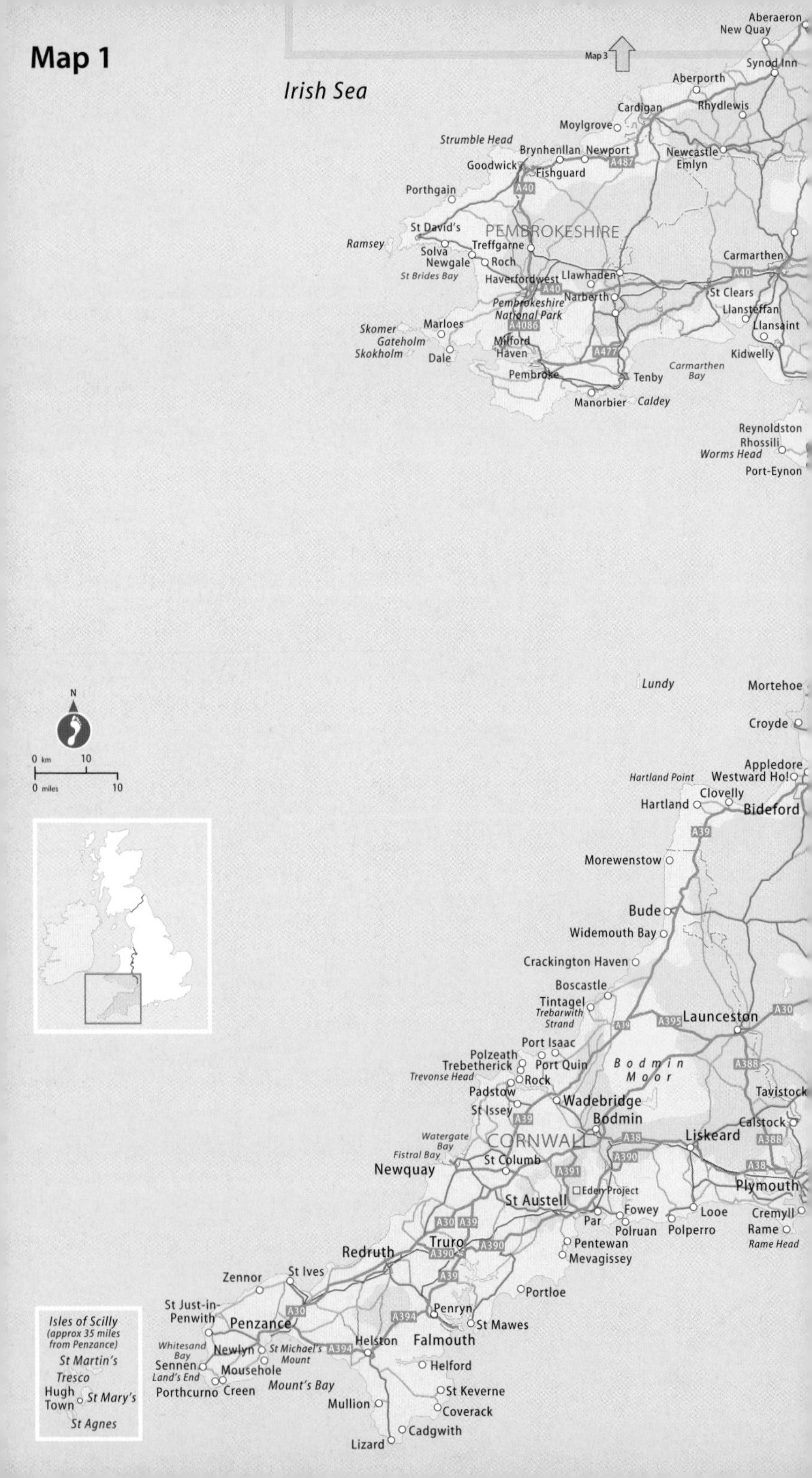

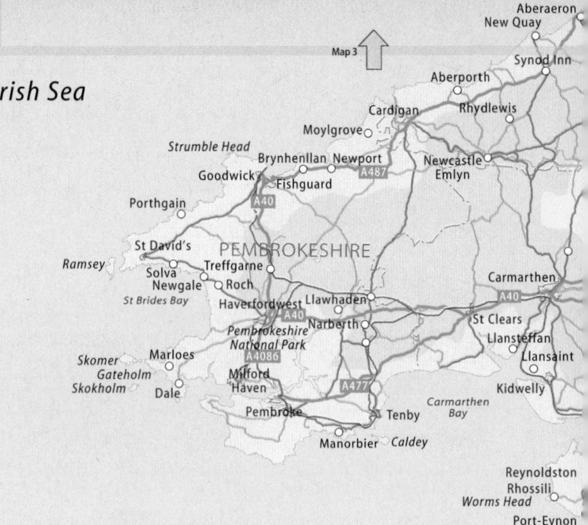

Irish Sea
Map 3
Aberaeron
New Quay
Synod Inn
Aberporth
Cardigan
Rhydlewis
Moylgrove
Strumble Head
Brynhenllan
Newport
Newcastle Emlyn
Goodwick
Fishguard
Porthgain
St David's
PEMBROKESHIRE
Ramsey
Solva
Treffgarne
Newgale
Roch
Carmarthen
St Brides Bay
Haverfordwest
Llawhaden
Pembrokeshire National Park
Narberth
St Clears
Llansteffan
Llansaint
Skomer
Marloes
Gateholm
Skokholm
Dale
Milford Haven
Kidwelly
Carmarthen Bay
Pembroke
Tenby
Manorbier
Caldey
Reynoldston
Rhossili
Worms Head
Port-Eynon
Lundy
Mortehoe
Croyde
N
0 km 10
0 miles 10
Appledore
Hartland Point
Westward Ho!
Clovelly
Hartland
Bideford
Morewenstow
Bude
Widemouth Bay
Crackington Haven
Boscastle
Tintagel
Trebarwith Strand
Launceston
Port Isaac
Polzeath
Trebetherick
Port Quin
Bodmin Moor
Trevonse Head
Rock
Padstow
Tavistock
Wadebridge
St Issey
Bodmin
Calstock
Watergate Bay
CORNWALL
Liskeard
Fistral Bay
Newquay
St Columb
Eden Project
Plymouth
St Austell
Fowey
Looe
Cremyll
Par
Polruan
Polperro
Rame
Rame Head
Redruth
Truro
Pentewan
Mevagissey
Zennor
St Ives
Portloe
St Just-in-Penwith
Penryn
Penzance
St Mawes
Whitesand Bay
Newlyn
St Michael's Mount
Helston
Falmouth
Sennen
Land's End
Mousehole
Helford
Porthcurno
Creen
Mount's Bay
St Keverne
Mullion
Coverack
Cadgwith
Lizard
Isles of Scilly (approx 35 miles from Penzance)
St Martin's
Tresco
Hugh Town
St Mary's
St Agnes
A40
A487
A4086
A477
A39
A395
A30
A388
A38
A390
A391
A394

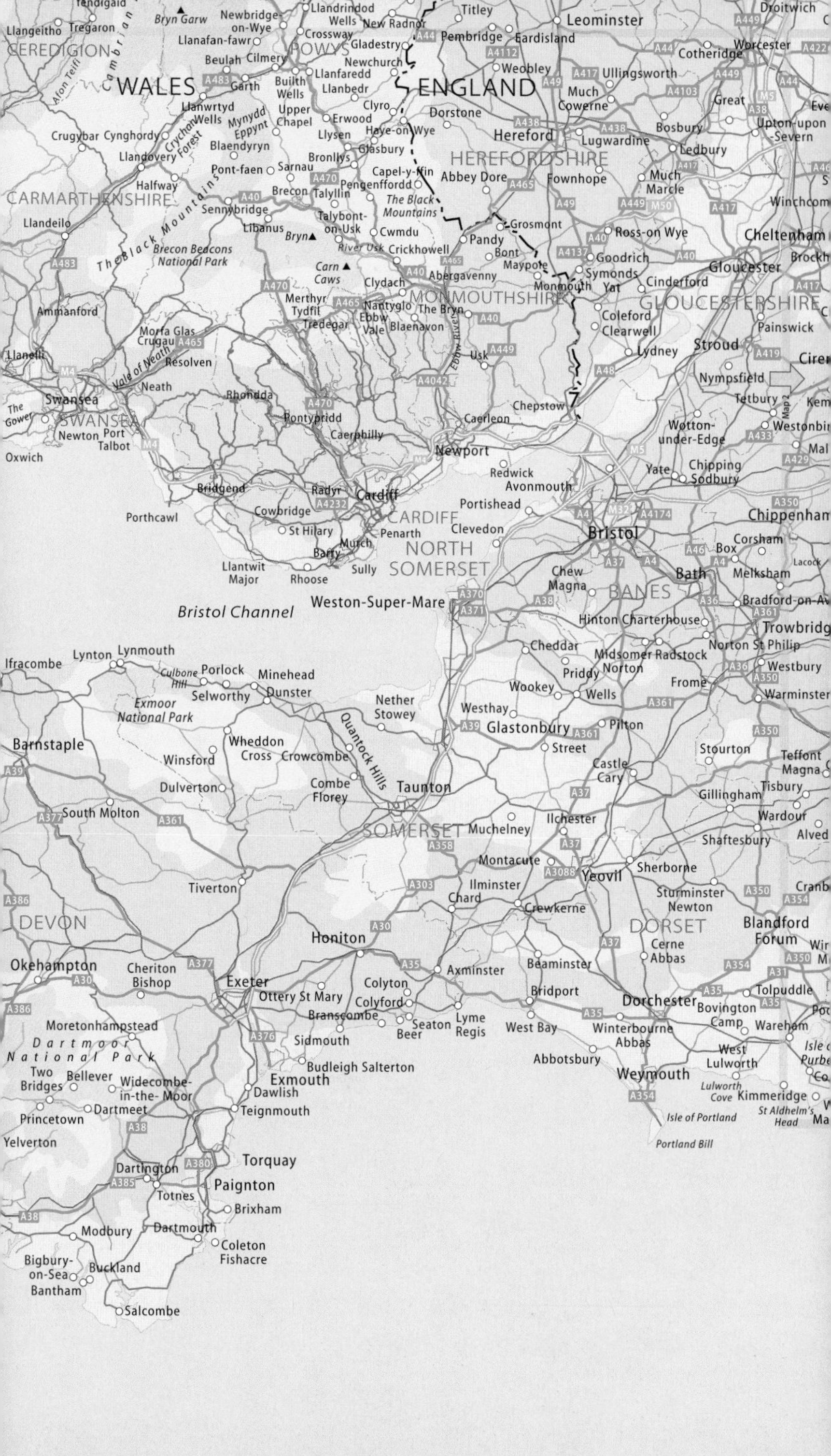

WALES
ENGLAND
CEREDIGION
POWYS
CARMARTHENSHIRE
HEREFORDSHIRE
MONMOUTHSHIRE
GLOUCESTERSHIRE
SWANSEA
CARDIFF
NORTH SOMERSET
BANES
SOMERSET
DEVON
DORSET
Pontrhyd-fendigaid
Tregaron
Llangeitho
Afon Teifi
Cambrian Mountains
Bryn Garw
Llanwrthwl
Newbridge-on-Wye
Llanafan-fawr
Beulah
Cilmery
Garth
Builth Wells
Llanwrtyd Wells
Crychan Forest
Mynydd Eppynt
Upper Chapel
Erwood
Llanfaredd
Llanbedr
Crugybar
Cynghordy
Llandovery
Blaendyryn
Pont-faen
Sarnau
Halfway
Sennybridge
Brecon
Talyllin
Libanus
Bryn
Llandeilo
The Black Mountains
Brecon Beacons National Park
Penybont
Llandrindod Wells
Crossway
Kinnerton
Presteigne
New Radnor
Gladestry
Newchurch
Clyro
Llysen
Hay-on-Wye
Glasbury
Bronllys
Capel-y-ffin
Pengenffordd
The Black Mountains
Talybont-on-Usk
Cwmdu
River Usk
Crickhowell
Carn Caws
Clydach
Abergavenny
Merthyr Tydfil
Tredegar
Nantyglo
Ebbw Vale
Blaenavon
The Bryn
Ebbw River
Usk
Titley
Pembridge
Eardisland
Leominster
Weobley
Dorstone
Hereford
Lugwardine
Abbey Dore
Fownhope
Pandy
Grosmont
Bont
Maypole
Monmouth
Symonds Yat
Goodrich
Ross-on Wye
Much Cowerne
Ullingsworth
Much Marcle
Bosbury
Ledbury
Cotheridge
Worcester
Droitwich
Great
Upton-upon-Severn
Winchcombe
Cheltenham
Gloucester
Cinderford
Coleford
Clearwell
Lydney
Stroud
Painswick
Nympsfield
Tetbury
Wotton-under-Edge
Westonbirt
Chepstow
Caerleon
Newport
Ammanford
Llanelli
Morfa Glas
Crugau
Vale of Neath
Resolven
Neath
Swansea
The Gower
Newton
Port Talbot
Oxwich
Rhondda
Pontypridd
Caerphilly
Bridgend
Radyr
Cardiff
Cowbridge
St Hilary
Penarth
Murch
Barry
Sully
Rhoose
Llantwit Major
Porthcawl
Redwick
Avonmouth
Portishead
Clevedon
Bristol
Yate
Chipping Sodbury
Chippenham
Corsham
Box
Melksham
Lacock
Bath
Bradford-on-Avon
Trowbridge
Chew Magna
Weston-Super-Mare
Bristol Channel
Hinton Charterhouse
Norton St Philip
Westbury
Warminster
Midsomer Norton
Radstock
Frome
Cheddar
Priddy
Wookey
Wells
Westhay
Glastonbury
Pilton
Street
Castle Cary
Stourton
Teffont Magna
Tisbury
Gillingham
Wardour
Shaftesbury
Alved
Ilchester
Muchelney
Montacute
Yeovil
Sherborne
Sturminster Newton
Blandford Forum
Ilminster
Chard
Crewkerne
Cerne Abbas
Beaminster
Bridport
West Bay
Dorchester
Winterbourne Abbas
Abbotsbury
Bovington Camp
Tolpuddle
Wareham
Weymouth
West Lulworth
Lulworth Cove
Kimmeridge
St Aldhelm's Head
Isle of Portland
Portland Bill
Isle of Purbeck
Lynton
Lynmouth
Ifracombe
Culbone Hill
Porlock
Minehead
Selworthy
Dunster
Exmoor National Park
Nether Stowey
Quantock Hills
Barnstaple
Winsford
Wheddon Cross
Crowcombe
Dulverton
Combe Florey
Taunton
South Molton
Tiverton
Honiton
Okehampton
Cheriton Bishop
Exeter
Ottery St Mary
Colyton
Colyford
Axminster
Branscombe
Seaton
Beer
Lyme Regis
Sidmouth
Budleigh Salterton
Exmouth
Dawlish
Teignmouth
Moretonhampstead
Dartmoor National Park
Two Bridges
Bellever
Widecombe-in-the-Moor
Dartmeet
Princetown
Yelverton
Torquay
Paignton
Dartington
Totnes
Brixham
Dartmouth
Modbury
Coleton Fishacre
Bigbury-on-Sea
Buckland
Bantham
Salcombe
Map 2

Map 2
Stafford
Burton upon Trent
Melbourne
Melton Mowbray
Spalding
Bourne
LEICESTERSHIRE
Ashby-de-la-Zouch
Lichfield
Empingham
Stamford
Rutland Water
Normanton
Brownhills
Tamworth
Leicester
Walsall
Sutton Coldfield
Peterborough
Map 3
Nuneaton
Rockingham
Market Harborough
Corby
Dudley
Birmingham
Ramsey
Birmingham International Airport
Coventry
Kettering
Rugby
Spaldwick
Packwood
Kenilworth
Cottlesbrooke
Bromsgrove
Buddesley Clinton
NORTHAMPTONSHIRE
Huntingdon
Royal Leamington Spa
Redditch
Warwick
Althorp
Northampton
Droitwich
Ufton
Eltisley
Coughton
WARWICKSHIRE
Thurleigh
Bishop's Itchington
Stratford-on-Avon
Bedford
Farnborough
Sandy
Edgehill
Cockayne Hatley
Evesham
Sulgrave
Elstow
Vale of Evesham
Shipston-on-Stour
Chipping Camden
Upton-upon-Severn
BEDFORDSHIRE
Banbury
Broadway
Paxford
Milton Keynes
Addebury
Aynho
Stanton
Stanway
Deddington
Woburn
Letchworth
Winchcombe
Stow-on-the-Wold
Great Tew
Steeple Ashton
HERTFORDSHIRE
Leighton Buzzard
Luton
Upper Slaughter
Chipping Norton
Stevenage
Cheltenham
Lower Slaughter
Bleddington
BUCKINGHAMSHIRE
Dunstable
Brockhampton
Woodstock
Cotswold Hills
Bourton-on-the-Water
Islip
Aylesbury
Whipsnade
Welwyn Garden City
Northleach
Great Barrington
Kidlington
Aldbury
Tring
Hemel Hempstead
Chedworth
Burford
Eynsham
Wendover
St Albans
Painswick
Sapperton
Aldsworth
Witney
Oxford
Stanton Harcourt
Great Missenden
Amersham
Potters Bar
Bibury
OXFORDSHIRE
Cirencester
Kelmscott
Buckland
Wootton
Stadhampton
West Wycombe
Chalfont St Giles
Watford
Kemble
Lechlade on Thames
Buscot
Chiltern Hills
Chenies
Abingdon
Chalgrove
Barnet
Faringdon
Sutton Courtenay
High Wycombe
Rickmansworth
Westonbirt
Ashton Keynes
Uffington
Didcot
Fingest
Beaconsfield
GREATER LONDON
Malmesbury
Wantage
Ardington
Wallingford
Marlow
Uxbridge
Swindon
Henley-on-Thames
Hurley
Cookham
LONDON
Moulsford
Maidenhead
Slough
Westminster
Streatley
Lower Basildon
Lambourn
Mapledurham
Bray
Eton
Chippenham
Aldbourne
Windsor
River Thames
Reading
Richmond
Ramsbury
Avebury
Axford
Yattendon
Hungerford
Bracknell
Lacock
Newbury
Marlborough
Wootton Rivers
Highclere
Burghclere
Woking
Devizes
Pewsey
Camberley
Kingsclere
East Clandon
Trowbridge
WILTSHIRE
Fleet
Guildford
Basingstoke
SURREY
Aldershot
Westbury
Whitchurch
Dorking
Reigate
Andover
Redhill
Farnham
Warminster
Godalming
Stonehenge
Holmbury St Mary
Middle Wallop
Gatwick Airport
HAMPSHIRE
Alton
New Arlesford
Crawley
Teffont Magna
Compton Chamberlayne
Selborne
Salisbury
Stockbridge
Tisbury
Winchester
Horsham
Fovant
Wardour
Nunton
West Meon
Warnford
Petworth
Alvediston
Whitsbury
Romsey
Breamore
Droxford
WEST SUSSEX
Map 1
Fordingbridge
Amberley
Ditchling
Cranborne
Southampton
Bishop's Waltham
North Gorley
Lyndhurst
Steyning
Havant
Chichester
Blandford Forum
Ringwood
New Forest
Worthing
Brighton and Hove
Fawley
Fareham
Beaulieu
Wimborne Minster
Burley
Portsmouth
Shoreham-by-Sea
Bucklers Hard
Sway
Gosport
Boldre
Southsea
Bognor Regis
Tolpuddle
New Milton
Lymington
Fishbourne
Ryde
Christchurch
Poole
Keyhaven
Newtown
Seaview
Wareham
Bournemouth
Milford-on-Sea
Carisbrooke
Bembridge
Yarmouth
Isle of Purbeck
Studland
Totland
Isle of Wight
Brading
Sandown
Shorwell
Brighstone
Corfe Castle
Shanklin
ISLE OF WIGHT
Swanage
Godshill
English Channel
Kimmeridge
Worth Matravers
St Aldhelm's Head
Chale
Ventnor

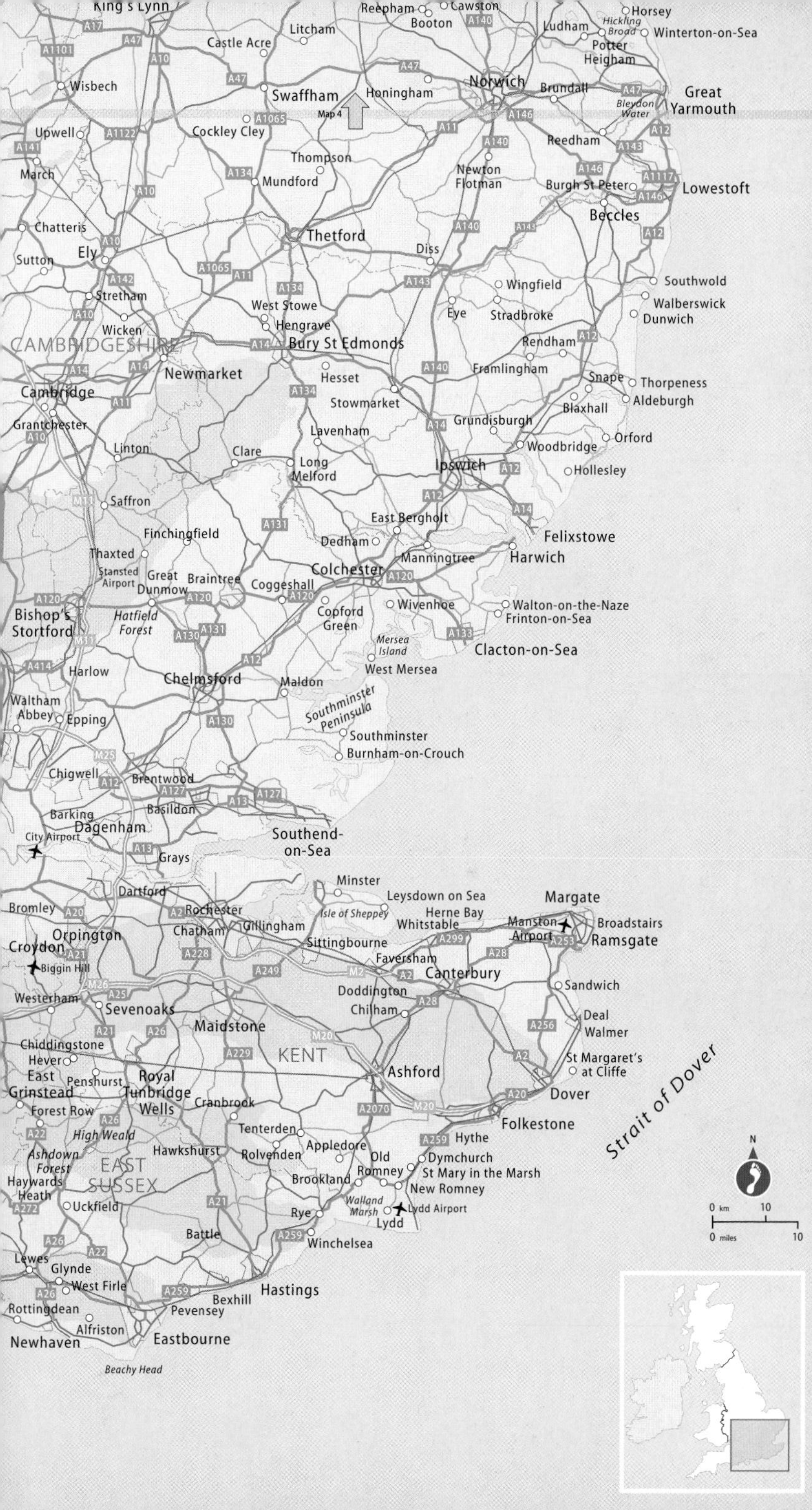

King's Lynn
Reepham
Cawston
Booton
Horsey
Hickling Broad
Winterton-on-Sea
Ludham
Potter Heigham
Litcham
Castle Acre
Wisbech
Swaffham
Honingham
Norwich
Brundall
Great Yarmouth
Bleydon Water
Map 4
Cockley Cley
Upwell
Reedham
March
Thompson
Mundford
Newton Flotman
Burgh St Peter
Lowestoft
Beccles
Chatteris
Thetford
Ely
Sutton
Diss
Southwold
Wingfield
Stretham
West Stowe
Walberswick
Dunwich
Eye
Stradbroke
Hengrave
Wicken
CAMBRIDGESHIRE
Bury St Edmonds
Rendham
Newmarket
Hesset
Framlingham
Snape
Thorpeness
Cambridge
Stowmarket
Aldeburgh
Blaxhall
Grantchester
Grundisburgh
Lavenham
Orford
Woodbridge
Linton
Clare
Long Melford
Ipswich
Hollesley
Saffron
East Bergholt
Finchingfield
Felixstowe
Dedham
Manningtree
Harwich
Thaxted
Stansted Airport
Great Dunmow
Braintree
Colchester
Coggeshall
Copford Green
Wivenhoe
Walton-on-the-Naze
Frinton-on-Sea
Bishop's Stortford
Hatfield Forest
Mersea Island
Clacton-on-Sea
West Mersea
Harlow
Chelmsford
Maldon
Waltham Abbey
Epping
Southminster Peninsula
Southminster
Burnham-on-Crouch
Chigwell
Brentwood
Basildon
Barking
Dagenham
City Airport
Southend-on-Sea
Grays
Minster
Dartford
Leysdown on Sea
Margate
Herne Bay
Bromley
Rochester
Isle of Sheppey
Whitstable
Manston Airport
Broadstairs
Ramsgate
Chatham
Gillingham
Orpington
Croydon
Sittingbourne
Faversham
Biggin Hill
Canterbury
Sandwich
Doddington
Westerham
Sevenoaks
Chilham
Deal
Maidstone
Walmer
Chiddingstone
Hever
KENT
St Margaret's at Cliffe
East Grinstead
Penshurst
Royal Tunbridge Wells
Ashford
Strait of Dover
Dover
Cranbrook
Forest Row
Folkestone
Tenterden
High Weald
Hythe
Appledore
Ashdown Forest
Hawkshurst
Rolvenden
Old Romney
Dymchurch
EAST SUSSEX
St Mary in the Marsh
Haywards Heath
Brookland
New Romney
Uckfield
Walland Marsh
Lydd Airport
Rye
Lydd
Battle
Winchelsea
Lewes
Glynde
West Firle
Hastings
Bexhill
Rottingdean
Pevensey
Alfriston
Newhaven
Eastbourne
Beachy Head
N
0 km 10
0 miles 10

Map 3

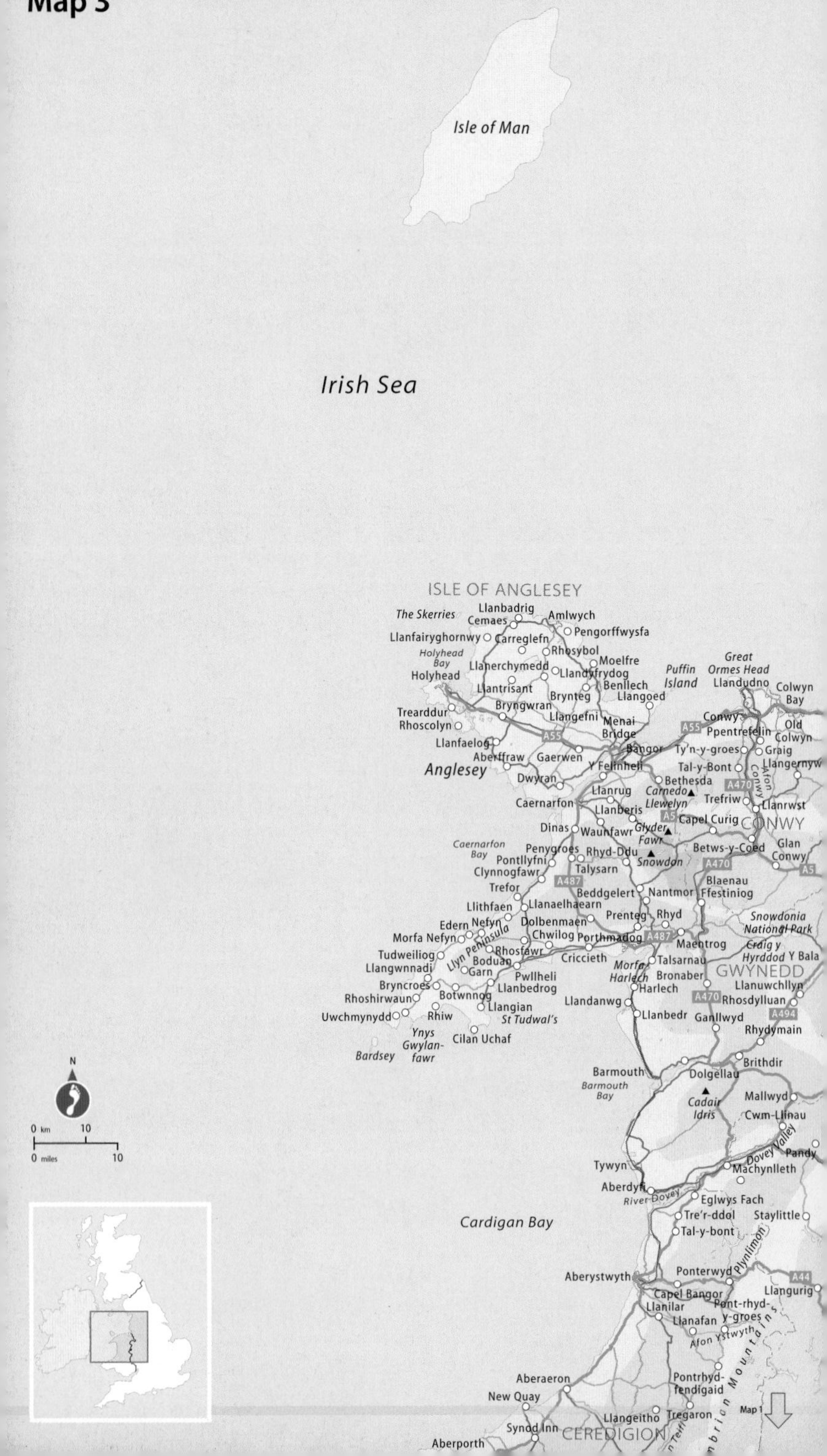

Isle of Man

Irish Sea

ISLE OF ANGLESEY
The Skerries
Llanbadrig
Cemaes
Amlwych
Pengorffwysfa
Llanfairyghornwy
Carreglefn
Holyhead Bay
Rhosybol
Moelfre
Great Ormes Head
Holyhead
Llanerchymedd
Llandyfrydog
Puffin Island
Llandudno
Colwyn Bay
Llantrisant
Benllech
Brynteg
Llangoed
Trearddur
Bryngwran
Conwy
Rhoscolyn
Llangefni
Menai Bridge
A55
Pentrefelin
Old Colwyn
Llanfaelog
A55
Graig
Aberffraw
Gaerwen
Bangor
Ty'n-y-groes
Llangernyw
Anglesey
Y Felinheli
Tal-y-Bont
Dwyran
Bethesda
A470
Afon Conwy
Llanrug
Carnedd Llewelyn
Trefriw
Caernarfon
Llanberis
Llanrwst
A5
Capel Curig
CONWY
Dinas
Waunfawr
Glyder Fawr
Caernarfon Bay
Penygroes
Rhyd-Ddu
Betws-y-Coed
Glan Conwy
Pontllyfni
Snowdon
Talysarn
A470
A5
Clynnogfawr
A487
Blaenau Ffestiniog
Trefor
Beddgelert
Nantmor
Llithfaen
Llanaelhaearn
Snowdonia National Park
Edern
Nefyn
Dolbenmaen
Prenteg
Rhyd
Morfa Nefyn
Llyn Peninsula
Chwilog
Porthmadog
A487
Maentrog
Craig y Hyrddod
Y Bala
Tudweiliog
Rhosfawr
Boduan
Criccieth
Morfa Harlech
Talsarnau
Llangwnnadi
Garn
Bronaber
GWYNEDD
Bryncroes
Pwllheli
Harlech
Llanuwchllyn
Llanbedrog
Botwnnog
A470
Rhosdylluan
Rhoshirwaun
Llangian
Llandanwg
Uwchmynydd
Rhiw
St Tudwal's
Llanbedr
Ganllwyd
A494
Ynys Gwylan-fawr
Cilan Uchaf
Rhydymain
Bardsey
Brithdir
Barmouth
Dolgellau
Barmouth Bay
Cadair Idris
Mallwyd
Cwm-Llinau
Dovey Valley
Pandy
Tywyn
Machynlleth
Aberdyfi
River Dovey
Eglwys Fach
Cardigan Bay
Tre'r-ddol
Staylittle
Tal-y-bont
Plynlimon
Aberystwyth
Ponterwyd
A44
Capel Bangor
Llangurig
Llanilar
Pont-rhyd-y-groes
Llanafan
Afon Ystwyth
Cambrian Mountains
Aberaeron
Pontrhyd-fendigaid
New Quay
Map 1
Llangeitho
Tregaron
Synod Inn
CEREDIGION
Afon Teifi
Aberporth

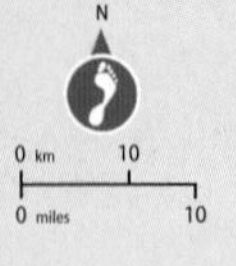

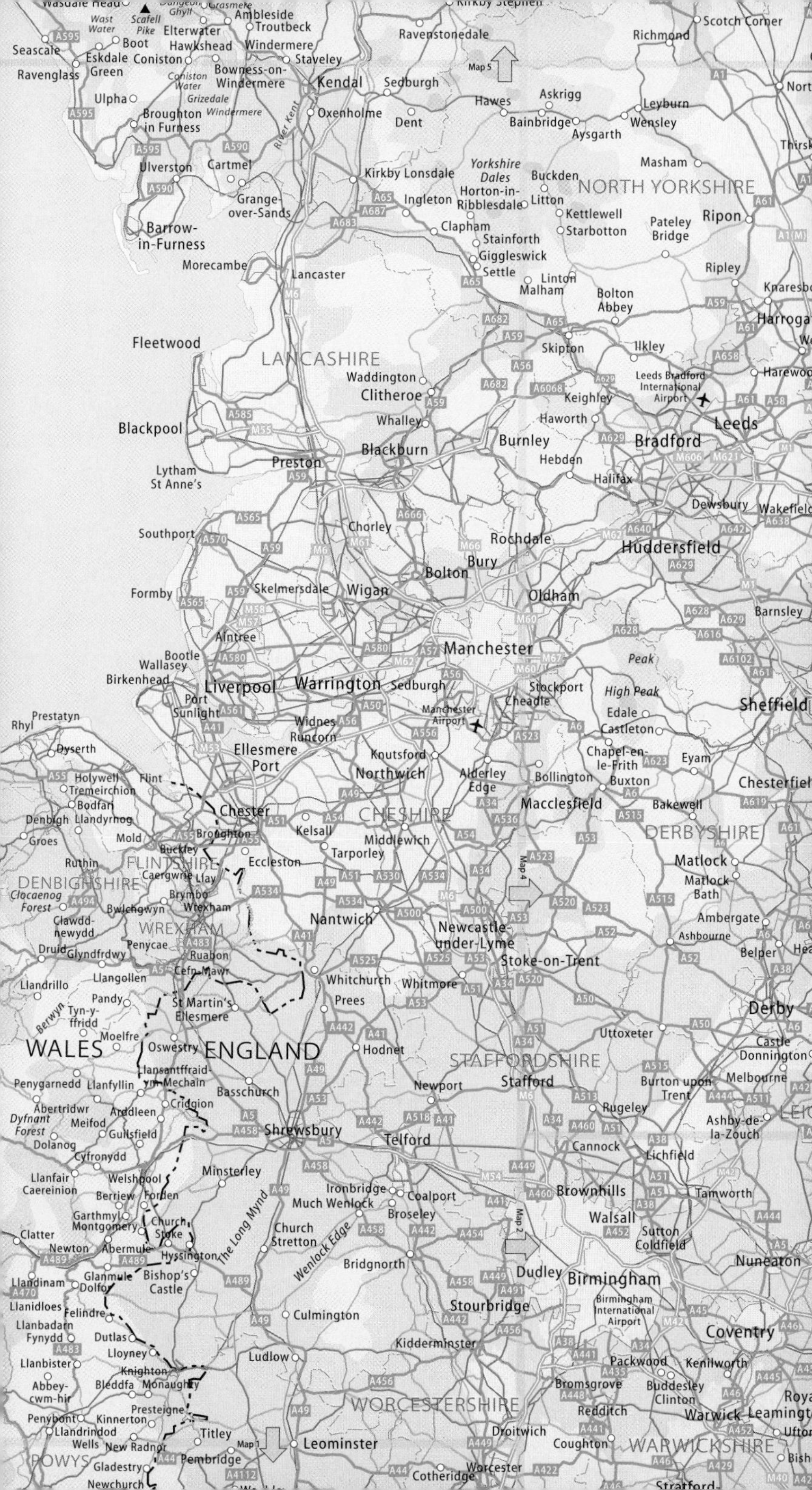

Scafell Pike
Wast Water
Grasmere
Ambleside
Troutbeck
Elterwater
Hawkshead
Windermere
Staveley
Seascale
Boot
Eskdale Green
Coniston
Ravenglass
Coniston Water
Bowness-on-Windermere
Grizedale
Ulpha
Broughton in Furness
Windermere
Kendal
Oxenholme
River Kent
Ulverston
Cartmel
Grange-over-Sands
Barrow-in-Furness
Morecambe
Lancaster
Fleetwood
Blackpool
Lytham St Anne's
Preston
Southport
Formby
Bootle
Wallasey
Birkenhead
Aintree
Liverpool
Port Sunlight
Prestatyn
Rhyl
Dyserth
Holywell
Flint
Tremeirchion
Bodfari
Denbigh
Llandyrnog
Groes
Mold
Ruthin
FLINTSHIRE
DENBIGHSHIRE
Clocaenog Forest
Bwlchgwyn
Clawdd-newydd
WREXHAM
Druid
Glyndfrdwy
Penycae
Llandrillo
Llangollen
Berwyn
Pandy
Tyn-y-ffridd
Moelfre
WALES
ENGLAND
Oswestry
Penygarnedd
Llanfyllin
Llansantffraid-ym-Mechain
Abertridwr
Ardleen
Dyfnant Forest
Meifod
Guilsfield
Dolanog
Cyfronydd
Llanfair Caereinion
Welshpool
Berriew
Forden
Garthmyl
Montgomery
Church Stoke
Clatter
Newton
Abermule
Hyssington
Llandinam
Glanmule
Dolfor
Bishop's Castle
Llanidloes
Felindre
Llanbadarn Fynydd
Dutlas
Lloyney
Llanbister
Knighton
Abbey-cwm-hir
Bleddfa
Monaughty
Presteigne
Penybont
Kinnerton
Llandrindod Wells
New Radnor
Titley
POWYS
Gladestry
Newchurch
Pembridge
Kirkby Stephen
Ravenstonedale
Map 5
Sedburgh
Dent
Kirkby Lonsdale
Ingleton
Clapham
Hawes
Askrigg
Bainbridge
Aysgarth
Scotch Corner
Richmond
Leyburn
Wensley
Masham
Thirsk
Yorkshire Dales
Horton-in-Ribblesdale
Buckden
Litton
Kettlewell
Starbotton
NORTH YORKSHIRE
Pateley Bridge
Ripon
Stainforth
Giggleswick
Settle
Linton
Malham
Ripley
Bolton Abbey
Knaresbo
Harroga
Skipton
Ilkley
Harewoo
Leeds Bradford International Airport
LANCASHIRE
Waddington
Clitheroe
Keighley
Haworth
Whalley
Leeds
Bradford
Burnley
Blackburn
Hebden
Halifax
Dewsbury
Wakefield
Chorley
Rochdale
Huddersfield
Bury
Bolton
Skelmersdale
Wigan
Oldham
Barnsley
Manchester
Peak
Warrington
Sedburgh
Stockport
High Peak
Cheadle
Sheffield
Widnes
Runcorn
Manchester Airport
Edale
Castleton
Ellesmere Port
Knutsford
Chapel-en-le-Frith
Eyam
Northwich
Alderley Edge
Bollington
Buxton
Chesterfield
Chester
Macclesfield
Bakewell
CHESHIRE
Kelsall
Broughton
Middlewich
DERBYSHIRE
Buckley
Tarporley
Eccleston
Caergwrle
Llay
Brymbo
Wrexham
Matlock
Matlock Bath
Map 4
Nantwich
Newcastle-under-Lyme
Ambergate
Ashbourne
Belper
Ruabon
Cefn-Mawr
Stoke-on-Trent
Whitchurch
Whitmore
St Martin's
Ellesmere
Prees
Derby
Uttoxeter
Castle Donnington
Hodnet
STAFFORDSHIRE
Melbourne
Newport
Stafford
Burton upon Trent
Basschurch
Criggion
Rugeley
Ashby-de-la-Zouch
Shrewsbury
Telford
Cannock
Lichfield
Minsterley
Ironbridge
Coalport
Brownhills
Tamworth
Much Wenlock
Broseley
Walsall
The Long Mynd
Church Stretton
Wenlock Edge
Sutton Coldfield
Map 2
Bridgnorth
Nuneaton
Dudley
Birmingham
Birmingham International Airport
Stourbridge
Culmington
Coventry
Kidderminster
Packwood
Kenilworth
Ludlow
Bromsgrove
Buddesley Clinton
WORCESTERSHIRE
Redditch
Warwick
Royal Leamington
Droitwich
Map 1
Leominster
Coughton
WARWICKSHIRE
Worcester
Cotheridge
Stratford
A595
A590
A65
A687
A683
M6
A682
A59
A56
A6068
A629
A658
A61
A58
A585
M55
A666
M61
M66
M62
A640
A642
A638
A565
A570
M58
M57
A580
M62
A57
A56
M60
M67
A628
A616
A6102
A561
A50
A56
A556
A41
M53
A55
A51
A54
A49
A523
A6
A623
A34
A536
A515
A619
A53
A494
A483
A534
A530
A51
A500
A520
A52
A525
A442
A5
A458
A518
A449
M54
A460
A38
A444
A452
A454
A456
A491
A442
A435
A441
A445
A46
A448
A4112
A44
A422
A429
A45
A489
A470
A1
A1(M)
M1
M42
M40

Map 4
Consett
Chester-le-Street
Durham
Easington
Bishop Auckland
DURHAM
Hartlepool
Barnard Castle
Bowes
Stockton-on-Tees
Middlesbrough
Staithes
Kettleness
Goldsborough
Whitby
Darlington
Stephen
Robin Hood's Bay
Scotch Corner
Richmond
North York Moors
Osmotherley
Rosedale Abbey
Goathland
Askrigg
Leyburn
Northallerton
Lastingham
Levisham
Bainbridge
Wensley
Hutton le Hole
Lockton
Scarborough
Aysgarth
Rievlaux
Thornton-le-Dale
Thirsk
Helmsey
Pickering
Masham
Filey
Buckden
NORTH YORKSHIRE
Litton
Flamborough Head
Kettlewell
Pateley Bridge
Ripon
Bempton
Starbotton
Flamborough
Kirkham
Bridlington
Ripley
The Wolds
Linton
Knaresborough
YORK
Malham
Bolton Abbey
Harrogate
Skipton
Ilkley
Wetherby
York
EAST RIDING OF YORKSHIRE
Hornsea
Hornsea Mere
Harewood
Leeds Bradford International Airport
Keighley
Beverley
Haworth
Leeds
Burnley
Bradford
Selby
Hull
Hebden
Halifax
Barton-upon-Humber
Patrington
Goole
Dewsbury
Wakefield
Pontefract
NORTH LINCOLNSHIRE
Rochdale
Huddersfield
Crowle
Scunthorpe
Grimsby
Oldham
Doncaster
Brigg
Barnsley
Haxey
Waddingham
Nettleton
Peak
Tealby
Gainsborough
Stockport
High Peak
Cheadle
Glentham
Market Rasen
Louth
Edale
Sheffield
Chapel-en-le-Frith
Castleton
Eyam
Bollington
Buxton
Chesterfield
Lincoln
Bardney
Horncastle
Macclesfield
Bakewell
DERBYSHIRE
NOTTINGHAMSHIRE
Potterhanworth
LINCOLNSHIRE
Sherwood Forest
Matlock
Matlock Bath
Navenby
Coningsby
Biddulph
Newark-on-Trent
North Kyme
Ambergate
Ashbourne
South Kyme
Stoke-on-Trent
Belper
Heanor
Sleaford
Boston
Nottingham
Donnington
Derby
Belvoir
Grantham
Billborough
Uttoxeter
Castle Donnington
East Midlands Airport
Kroxton Kerrial
Corby Glen
Spalding
Stafford
Burton upon Trent
Melbourne
Melton Mowbray
Bourne
Rugeley
LEICESTERSHIRE
Ashby-de-la-Zouch
Map 2
Map 3
Map 5
Cannock
Lichfield
Empingham
Stamford
Rutland Water
Normanton
Brownhills
Tamworth
Leicester
Peterborough

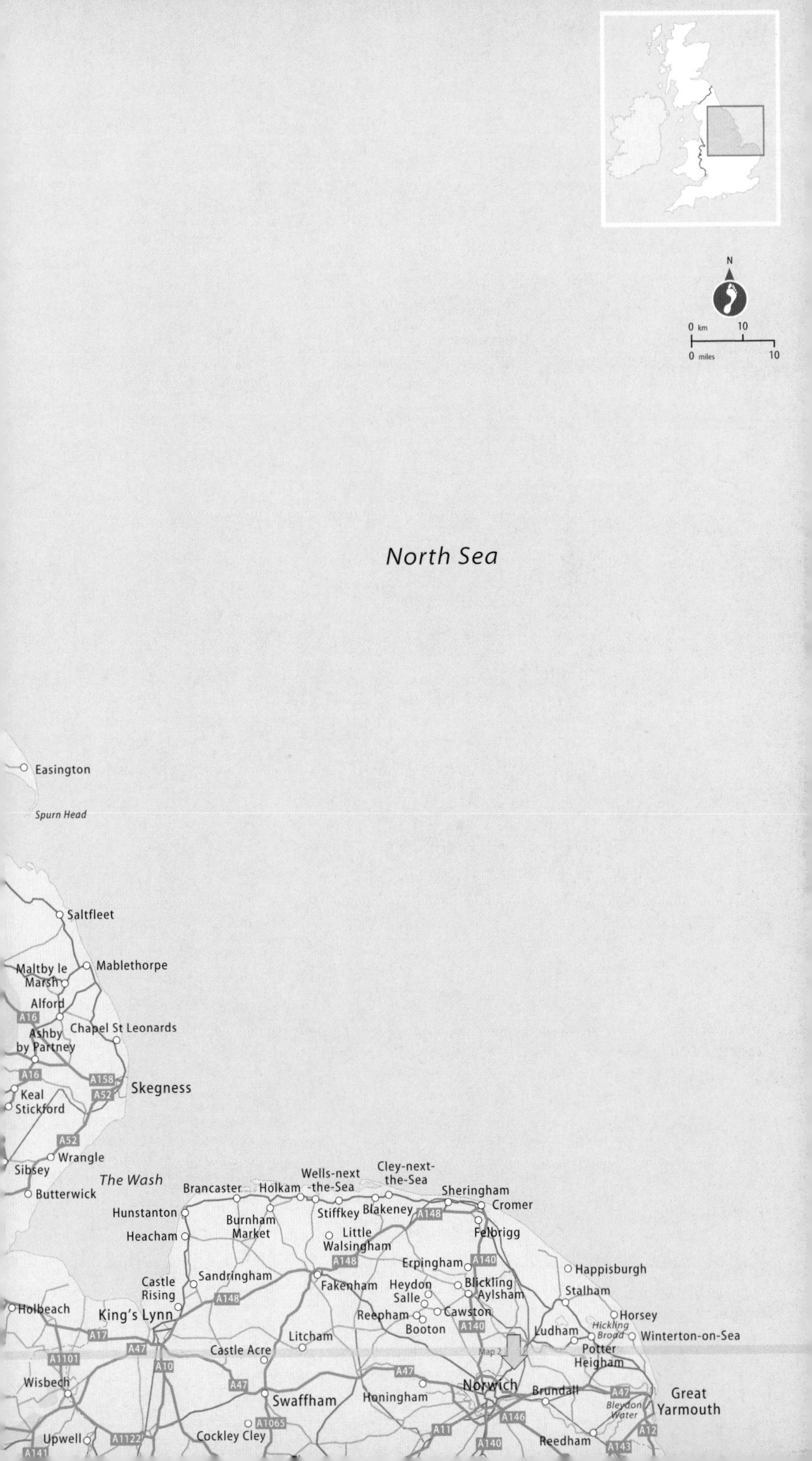

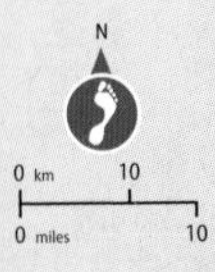

North Sea

Easington
Spurn Head
Saltfleet
Maltby le Marsh
Mablethorpe
Alford
A16
Ashby by Partney
Chapel St Leonards
A16
A158
A52
Skegness
Keal
Stickford
A52
Wrangle
Sibsey
The Wash
Butterwick
Brancaster
Holkam
Wells-next -the-Sea
Cley-next- the-Sea
Sheringham
Cromer
Hunstanton
Stiffkey
Blakeney
A148
Burnham Market
Felbrigg
Heacham
Little Walsingham
A148
Erpingham
A140
Happisburgh
Castle Rising
Sandringham
Fakenham
Heydon
Salle
Blickling
Aylsham
Stalham
A148
Holbeach
King's Lynn
Reepham
Booton
Cawston
Horsey
A140
Hickling Broad
Ludham
Winterton-on-Sea
A17
Litcham
Potter Heigham
A47
Castle Acre
Map 2
A1101
A10
A47
Wisbech
A47
Norwich
Brundall
A47
Great Yarmouth
Swaffham
Honingham
Bleydon Water
A1065
A146
Upwell
A1122
Cockley Cley
A11
A140
Reedham
A143
A12
A141

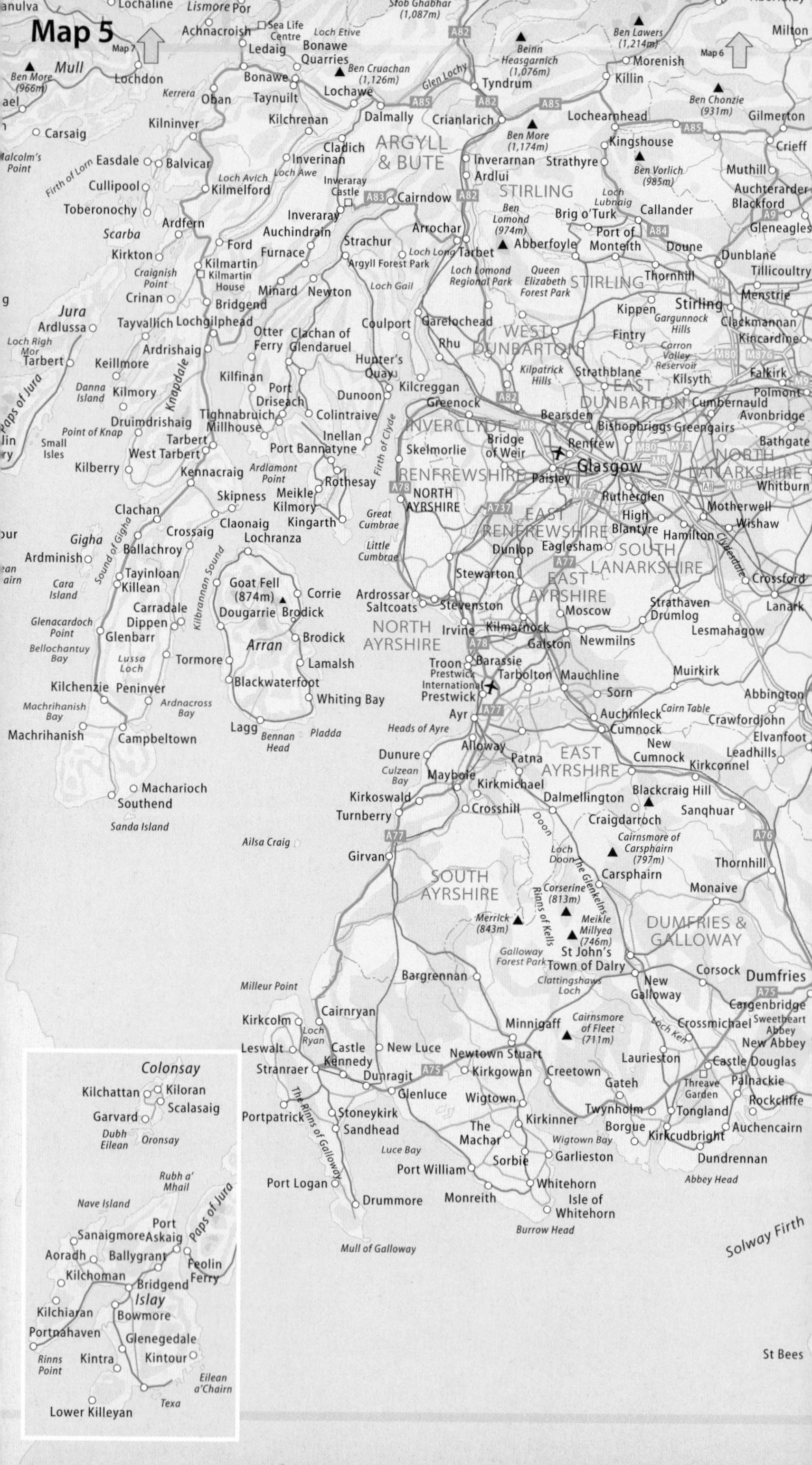

Map 5
Map 7
Map 6
Lochaline
Lismore
Achnacroish
Sea Life Centre
Loch Etive
Stob Ghabhar (1,087m)
A82
Fortingall
Aberfeldy
Ben Lawers (1,214m)
Milton
Mull
Ben More (966m)
Ledaig
Bonawe Quarries
Ben Cruachan (1,126m)
Beinn Heasgarnich (1,076m)
Morenish
Killin
Lochdon
Bonawe
Taynuilt
Lochawe
Glen Lochy
Tyndrum
Ben Chonzie (931m)
Kerrera
Oban
A85
Kilninver
Kilchrenan
Dalmally
Crianlarich
Ben More (1,174m)
Lochearnhead
Gilmerton
Carsaig
Kingshouse
Crieff
ARGYLL & BUTE
Cladich
Inverinan
Inverarnan
Strathyre
Ben Vorlich (985m)
Malcolm's Point
Easdale
Balvicar
Loch Avich
Loch Awe
Ardlui
Muthill
Firth of Lorn
Cullipool
Kilmelford
Inveraray Castle
A83
Cairndow
STIRLING
Loch Lubnaig
Auchterarder
Blackford
Toberonochy
Inveraray
Arrochar
Ben Lomond (974m)
Brig o'Turk
Callander
A9
Gleneagles
Ardfern
Auchindrain
Port of Menteith
A84
Scarba
Ford
Strachur
Loch Long
Tarbet
Abberfoyle
Doune
Dunblane
Kirkton
Kilmartin
Furnace
Argyll Forest Park
Craignish Point
Kilmartin House
Loch Lomond Regional Park
Queen Elizabeth Forest Park
STIRLING
Thornhill
Tillicoultry
Minard
Newton
Loch Gail
M9
Menstrie
Crinan
Bridgend
Jura
Kippen
Stirling
Gargunnock Hills
Ardlussa
Tayvallich
Lochgilphead
Coulport
Garelochead
Clackmannan
Otter Ferry
Clachan of Glendaruel
Fintry
Kincardine
Loch Righ Mor
Ardrishaig
WEST DUNBARTON
Carron Valley Reservoir
M80
M876
Tarbert
Keillmore
Knapdale
Rhu
Hunter's Quay
Falkirk
Kilfinan
Kilpatrick Hills
Strathblane
EAST DUNBARTON
Kilsyth
Polmont
Paps of Jura
Danna Island
Kilmory
Port Driseach
Kilcreggan
Dunoon
Cumbernauld
Greenock
Druimdrishaig
Tighnabruich
Millhouse
Colintraive
INVERCLYDE
Bearsden
Avonbridge
Point of Knap
Inellan
Bishopbriggs
Greengairs
Small Isles
Tarbert
West Tarbert
Port Bannatyne
Firth of Clyde
Skelmorlie
Bridge of Weir
Renfrew
Bathgate
Kilberry
Kennacraig
Ardlamont Point
RENFREWSHIRE
Glasgow
NORTH LANARKSHIRE
Rothesay
Paisley
Whitburn
Skipness
Meikle Kilmory
A78
NORTH AYRSHIRE
M77
Rutherglen
Motherwell
Clachan
Claonaig
Kingarth
Great Cumbrae
A737
EAST RENFREWSHIRE
High Blantyre
Hamilton
Wishaw
Gigha
Crossaig
Lochranza
Eaglesham
SOUTH LANARKSHIRE
Clydesdale
Ardminish
Ballachroy
Little Cumbrae
Dunlop
Sound of Gigha
Kilbrannan Sound
Tayinloan
Goat Fell (874m)
Stewarton
A77
EAST AYRSHIRE
Crossford
Cara Island
Killean
Corrie
Ardrossan
Saltcoats
Stevenston
Strathaven
Lanark
Carradale
Dougarrie
Brodick
Moscow
Drumlog
Glenacardoch Point
Dippen
NORTH AYRSHIRE
Irvine
Kilmarnock
Newmilns
Lesmahagow
Glenbarr
Brodick
Arran
A78
Galston
Bellochantuy Bay
Lussa Loch
Tormore
Lamalsh
Troon
Barassie
Prestwick International
Tarbolton
Mauchline
Muirkirk
Kilchenzie
Peninver
Blackwaterfoot
Prestwick
Sorn
Whiting Bay
Abbington
Machrihanish Bay
Ardnacross Bay
Ayr
Auchinleck
Cairn Table
Crawfordjohn
Machrihanish
Campbeltown
Lagg
Bennan Head
Pladda
Heads of Ayre
Cumnock
Alloway
New Cumnock
Elvanfoot
Dunure
Patna
EAST AYRSHIRE
Leadhills
Culzean Bay
Maybole
Kirkconnel
Kirkmichael
Blackcraig Hill
Machariocch
Kirkoswald
Dalmellington
Southend
Crosshill
Sanquhar
Turnberry
Doon
Craigdarroch
Sanda Island
Ailsa Craig
A77
Cairnsmore of Carsphairn (797m)
A76
Loch Doon
Girvan
Thornhill
SOUTH AYRSHIRE
The Glenkens
Carsphairn
Corserine (813m)
Monaive
Merrick (843m)
Rinns of Kells
Meikle Millyea (746m)
DUMFRIES & GALLOWAY
Galloway Forest Park
St John's Town of Dalry
Bargrennan
Corsock
Dumfries
Clattingshaws Loch
New Galloway
A75
Milleur Point
Cargenbridge
Cairnryan
Kirkcolm
Loch Ryan
Minnigaff
Cairnsmore of Fleet (711m)
Loch Ken
Crossmichael
Sweetheart Abbey
New Abbey
Leswalt
Castle Kennedy
New Luce
Newtown Stuart
Laurieston
Stranraer
A75
Dunragit
Kirkgowan
Creetown
Castle Douglas
Colonsay
Gateh
Threave Garden
Palnackie
Kilchattan
Kiloran
Glenluce
Wigtown
The Rinns of Galloway
Rockcliffe
Scalasaig
Portpatrick
Stoneykirk
Kirkinner
Twynholm
Tongland
Garvard
The Machar
Borgue
Kirkcudbright
Auchencairn
Dubh Eilean
Oronsay
Sandhead
Wigtown Bay
Luce Bay
Sorbie
Garlieston
Port William
Dundrennan
Rubh a' Mhail
Port Logan
Whitehorn
Abbey Head
Nave Island
Drummore
Monreith
Isle of Whitehorn
Port Askaig
Paps of Jura
Sanaigmore
Burrow Head
Solway Firth
Aoradh
Ballygrant
Feolin Ferry
Mull of Galloway
Kilchoman
Bridgend
Islay
Kilchiaran
Bowmore
Portnahaven
Glenegedale
Kintra
Kintour
St Bees
Rinns Point
Eilean a'Chairn
Texa
Lower Killeyan

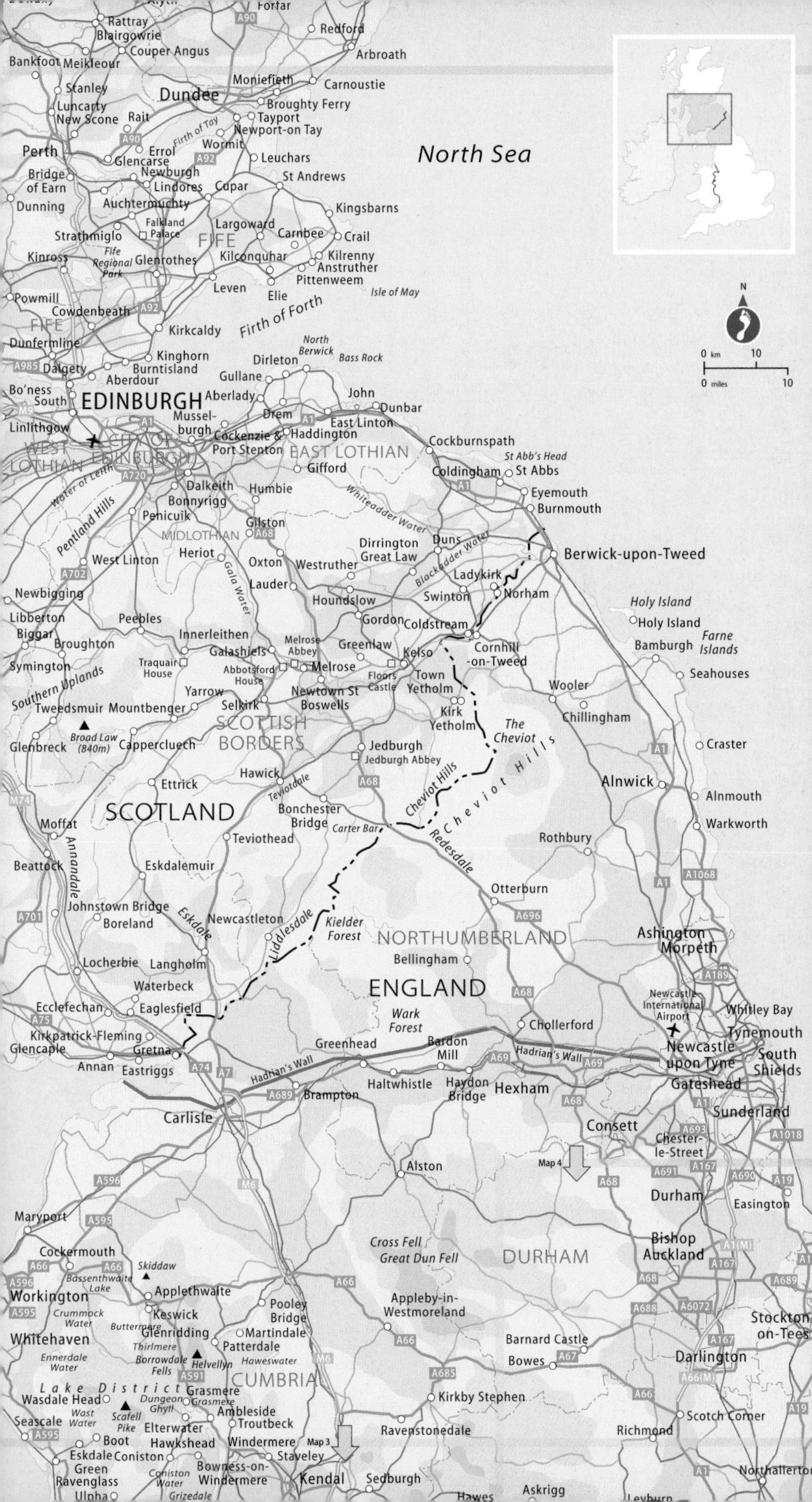

Forfar
Rattray
Blairgowrie
Redford
Couper Angus
Arbroath
Bankfoot
Meikleour
Monifieth
Carnoustie
Stanley
Dundee
Broughty Ferry
Luncarty
New Scone
Rait
Tayport
Newport-on Tay
Firth of Tay
Errol
Wormit
Perth
Glencarse
Leuchars
North Sea
Bridge of Earn
Newburgh
St Andrews
Lindores
Cupar
Dunning
Auchtermuchty
Kingsbarns
Falkland Palace
Largoward
Strathmiglo
FIFE
Carnbee
Crail
Fife Regional Park
Kinross
Glenrothes
Kilconquhar
Kilrenny
Anstruther
Pittenweem
Leven
Elie
Isle of May
Powmill
Cowdenbeath
Firth of Forth
Kirkcaldy
Dunfermline
North Berwick
Dirleton
Bass Rock
Kinghorn
Dalgety
Burntisland
Gullane
Aberdour
John
Bo'ness
South
EDINBURGH
Aberlady
Dunbar
Drem
East Linton
Linlithgow
Mussel-burgh
Cockenzie & Port Stenton
Haddington
WEST LOTHIAN
CITY OF EDINBURGH
EAST LOTHIAN
Cockburnspath
St Abb's Head
Water of Leith
Gifford
Coldingham
St Abbs
Dalkeith
Humbie
Eyemouth
Bonnyrigg
Whiteadder Water
Burnmouth
Pentland Hills
Penicuik
Gilston
MIDLOTHIAN
Dirrington Great Law
Duns
Berwick-upon-Tweed
Heriot
West Linton
Oxton
Westruther
Blackadder Water
Ladykirk
Gala Water
Lauder
Newbigging
Swinton
Norham
Houndslow
Holy Island
Libberton
Peebles
Gordon
Coldstream
Holy Island
Biggar
Innerleithen
Melrose Abbey
Farne Islands
Broughton
Galashiels
Greenlaw
Cornhill-on-Tweed
Bamburgh
Symington
Traquair House
Abbotsford House
Melrose
Kelso
Seahouses
Southern Uplands
Yarrow
Floors Castle
Town Yetholm
Selkirk
Newtown St Boswells
Wooler
Tweedsmuir
Mountbenger
Kirk Yetholm
Chillingham
SCOTTISH BORDERS
The Cheviot
Broad Law (840m)
Glenbreck
Cappercluech
Jedburgh
Craster
Jedburgh Abbey
Ettrick
Hawick
Cheviot Hills
Alnwick
Teviotdale
Alnmouth
Bonchester Bridge
SCOTLAND
Moffat
Carter Bar
Warkworth
Teviothead
Redesdale
Rothbury
Annandale
Eskdalemuir
Beattock
Otterburn
Johnstown Bridge
Eskdale
Newcastleton
Kielder Forest
Boreland
NORTHUMBERLAND
Ashington
Morpeth
Liddlesdale
Bellingham
Locherbie
Langholm
ENGLAND
Waterbeck
Newcastle International Airport
Whitley Bay
Ecclefechan
Eaglesfield
Wark Forest
Chollerford
Tynemouth
Kirkpatrick-Fleming
Bardon Mill
Newcastle upon Tyne
Glencaple
Greenhead
Hadrian's Wall
South Shields
Gretna
Annan
Eastriggs
Haltwhistle
Haydon Bridge
Hexham
Gateshead
Brampton
Carlisle
Sunderland
Consett
Chester-le-Street
Map 4
Alston
Durham
Easington
Maryport
Cross Fell
Great Dun Fell
Bishop Auckland
DURHAM
Cockermouth
Skiddaw
Bassenthwaite Lake
Workington
Applethwaite
Pooley Bridge
Appleby-in-Westmoreland
Crummock Water
Keswick
Stockton-on-Tees
Buttermere
Whitehaven
Glenridding
Martindale
Barnard Castle
Thirlmere
Patterdale
Ennerdale Water
Borrowdale Fells
Helvellyn
Haweswater
Bowes
Darlington
CUMBRIA
Lake District
Grasmere
Kirkby Stephen
Wasdale Head
Dungeon Ghyll
Wast Water
Scafell Pike
Ambleside
Seascale
Troutbeck
Scotch Corner
Elterwater
Ravenstonedale
Richmond
Boot
Hawkshead
Windermere
Map 3
Eskdale Green
Coniston
Staveley
Coniston Water
Bowness-on-Windermere
Northallerton
Ravenglass
Kendal
Sedburgh
Askrigg
Ulpha
Grizedale
Hawes
Leyburn
A90
A92
A985
M9
A1
A720
A68
A702
M74
A701
A75
A74
A7
A689
A69
A696
A1068
A189
A693
A1018
A691
A167
A690
A19
A596
M6
A595
A66
A1(M)
A689
A688
A6072
A685
A67
A591
A66(M)
0 km 10
0 miles 10
N

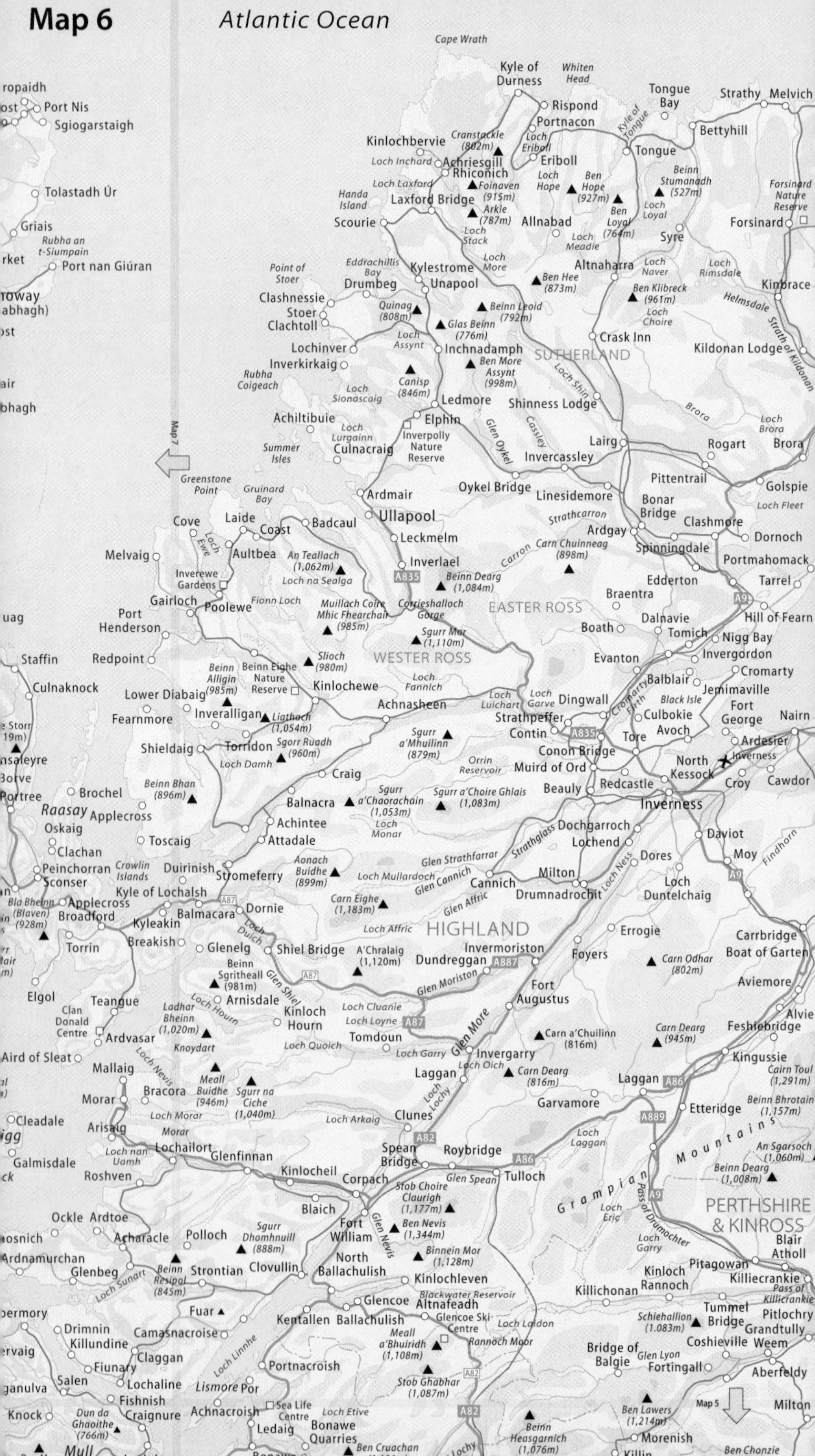

Map 6
Atlantic Ocean
Cape Wrath
Kyle of Durness
Whiten Head
Rispond
Portnacon
Tongue Bay
Strathy
Melvich
Port Nis
Sgiogarstaigh
Kinlochbervie
Cranstackle (802m)
Loch Eriboll
Eriboll
Kyle of Tongue
Tongue
Bettyhill
Loch Inchard
Achriesgill
Rhiconich
Loch Laxford
Foinaven (915m)
Loch Hope
Ben Hope (927m)
Beinn Stumanadh (527m)
Forsinard Nature Reserve
Tolastadh Úr
Handa Island
Laxford Bridge
Arkle (787m)
Ben Loyal (764m)
Loch Loyal
Forsinard
Scourie
Allnabad
Griais
Loch Stack
Loch Meadie
Syre
Rubha an t-Siumpain
Loch More
rket
Port nan Giúran
Eddrachillis Bay
Kylestrome
Altnaharra
Loch Naver
Loch Rimsdale
Point of Stoer
Unapool
Ben Hee (873m)
Drumbeg
Ben Klibreck (961m)
Kinbrace
Clashnessie
Quinag (808m)
Beinn Leoid (792m)
Helmsdale
Stoer
Loch Choire
Clachtoll
Glas Beinn (776m)
Strath of Kildonan
Loch Assynt
Lochinver
Inchnadamph
Crask Inn
Kildonan Lodge
Ben More Assynt (998m)
SUTHERLAND
Inverkirkaig
Rubha Coigeach
Canisp (846m)
Loch Shin
Loch Sionascaig
Ledmore
Shinness Lodge
bhagh
Brora
Achiltibuie
Loch Lurgainn
Elphin
Loch Brora
Inverpolly Nature Reserve
Glen Oykel
Cassley
Summer Isles
Culnacraig
Lairg
Rogart
Brora
Map 7
Invercassley
Greenstone Point
Gruinard Bay
Pittentrail
Golspie
Oykel Bridge
Ardmair
Linesidemore
Bonar Bridge
Loch Fleet
Cove
Laide
Ullapool
Strathcarron
Clashmore
Loch Ewe
Coast
Badcaul
Ardgay
Dornoch
Leckmelm
Carn Chuinneag (898m)
Spinningdale
Melvaig
Aultbea
An Teallach (1,062m)
Carron
Portmahomack
Inverlael
Inverewe Gardens
A835
Beinn Dearg (1,084m)
Edderton
Tarrel
Loch na Sealga
Braentra
A9
Gairloch
Fionn Loch
Muillach Coire Mhic Fhearchair (985m)
Corrieshalloch Gorge
EASTER ROSS
Hill of Fearn
Poolewe
Port Henderson
Dalnavie
Boath
Tomich
Nigg Bay
Sgurr Mor (1,110m)
Invergordon
Staffin
Redpoint
Slioch (980m)
WESTER ROSS
Evanton
Cromarty
Beinn Alligin (985m)
Beinn Eighe Nature Reserve
Loch Fannich
Balblair
Culnaknock
Kinlochewe
Cromarty Firth
Jemimaville
Lower Diabaig
Loch Luichart
Loch Garve
Dingwall
Black Isle
Fort George
Achnasheen
Culbokie
Nairn
Fearnmore
Inveralligan
Liathach (1,054m)
Strathpeffer
Contin
A835
Tore
Avoch
Ardesier
Sgurr a'Mhuilinn (879m)
Shieldaig
Torridon
Sgorr Ruadh (960m)
Conon Bridge
Inverness
North Kessock
Loch Damh
Orrin Reservoir
Muird of Ord
Cawdor
Craig
Croy
Redcastle
Beauly
Brochel
Beinn Bhan (896m)
Sgurr a'Chaorachain (1,053m)
Sgurr a'Choire Ghlais (1,083m)
Inverness
Portree
Raasay
Applecross
Balnacra
Achintee
Loch Monar
Dochgarroch
Oskaig
Attadale
Strathglass
Daviot
Toscaig
Lochend
Clachan
Glen Strathfarrar
Dores
Moy
Crowlin Islands
Aonach Buidhe (899m)
Findhorn
Peinchorran
Duirinish
Loch Mullardoch
Milton
Loch Ness
Sconser
Stromeferry
Glen Cannich
Cannich
Loch Duntelchaig
A9
Kyle of Lochalsh
Drumnadrochit
Bla Bheinn (Blaven) (928m)
Applecross
A87
Dornie
Carn Eighe (1,183m)
Glen Affric
Broadford
Balmacara
Kyleakin
Loch Affric
HIGHLAND
Errogie
Loch Duich
Carrbridge
Breakish
Invermoriston
Torrin
Glenelg
Shiel Bridge
A'Chralaig (1,120m)
Dundreggan
A887
Foyers
Boat of Garten
Carn Odhar (802m)
Beinn Sgritheall (981m)
Glen Shiel
A87
Glen Moriston
Fort Augustus
Aviemore
Elgol
Arnisdale
Teangue
Loch Hourn
Kinloch Hourn
Loch Cluanie
Alvie
Clan Donald Centre
Ladhar Bheinn (1,020m)
Loch Loyne
A87
Carn a'Chuilinn (816m)
Carn Dearg (945m)
Feshiebridge
Ardvasar
Tomdoun
Glen More
Loch Quoich
Aird of Sleat
Loch Garry
Invergarry
Kingussie
Knoydart
Loch Nevis
Loch Oich
Carn Dearg (816m)
Cairn Toul (1,291m)
Mallaig
Laggan
Laggan
A86
Meall Buidhe (946m)
Sgurr na Ciche (1,040m)
Loch Lochy
Beinn Bhrotain (1,157m)
Bracora
Morar
Garvamore
Etteridge
Loch Morar
Cleadale
Clunes
A889
Arisaig
Loch Arkaig
Morar
A82
Loch Laggan
An Sgarsoch (1,060m)
Loch nan Uamh
Lochailort
Glenfinnan
Spean Bridge
Roybridge
Mountains
Galmisdale
A86
Beinn Dearg (1,008m)
Kinlocheil
Glen Spean
Tulloch
Roshven
Corpach
Stob Choire Claurigh (1,177m)
A9
Blaich
Grampian
PERTHSHIRE & KINROSS
Ockle
Ardtoe
Fort William
Loch Ericht
Pass of Drumochter
Ben Nevis (1,344m)
Sgurr Dhomhnuill (888m)
Glen Nevis
Loch Garry
Blair Atholl
Acharacle
Polloch
North Ballachulish
Binnein Mor (1,128m)
Ardnamurchan
Glenbeg
Beinn Resipol (845m)
Strontian
Clovullin
Pitagowan
Loch Sunart
Kinlochleven
Kinloch Rannoch
Killiecrankie
Killichonan
Pass of Killicrankie
Glencoe
Blackwater Reservoir
Altnafeadh
Fuar
Tummel Bridge
Pitlochry
Kentallen
Ballachulish
Glencoe Ski Centre
Loch Laidon
Schiehallion (1,083m)
Grandtully
Drimnin
Camasnacroise
Meall a'Bhuiridh (1,108m)
Rannoch Moor
Coshieville
Weem
Killundine
Loch Linnhe
Bridge of Balgie
Glen Lyon
Claggan
Fortingall
Portnacroish
Fiunary
Aberfeldy
Salen
Lochaline
Stob Ghabhar (1,087m)
A82
Lismore
Por
Fishnish
Map 5
Knock
Dun da Ghaoithe (766m)
Craignure
Achnacroish
Sea Life Centre
Loch Etive
A82
Ben Lawers (1,214m)
Milton
Ledaig
Bonawe Quarries
Beinn Heasgarnich (1,076m)
Morenish
Mull
Ben More
Lochdon
Bonawe
Ben Cruachan (1,126m)
Glen Lochy
Tyndrum
Killin
Ben Chonzie (931m)

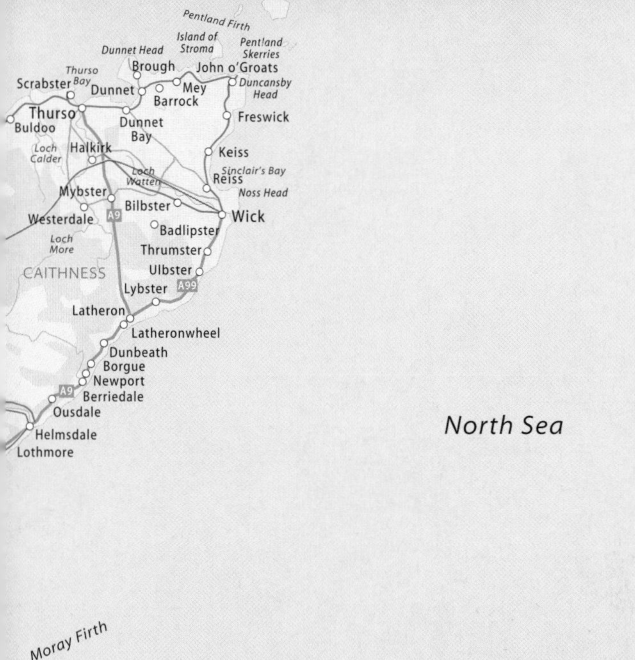

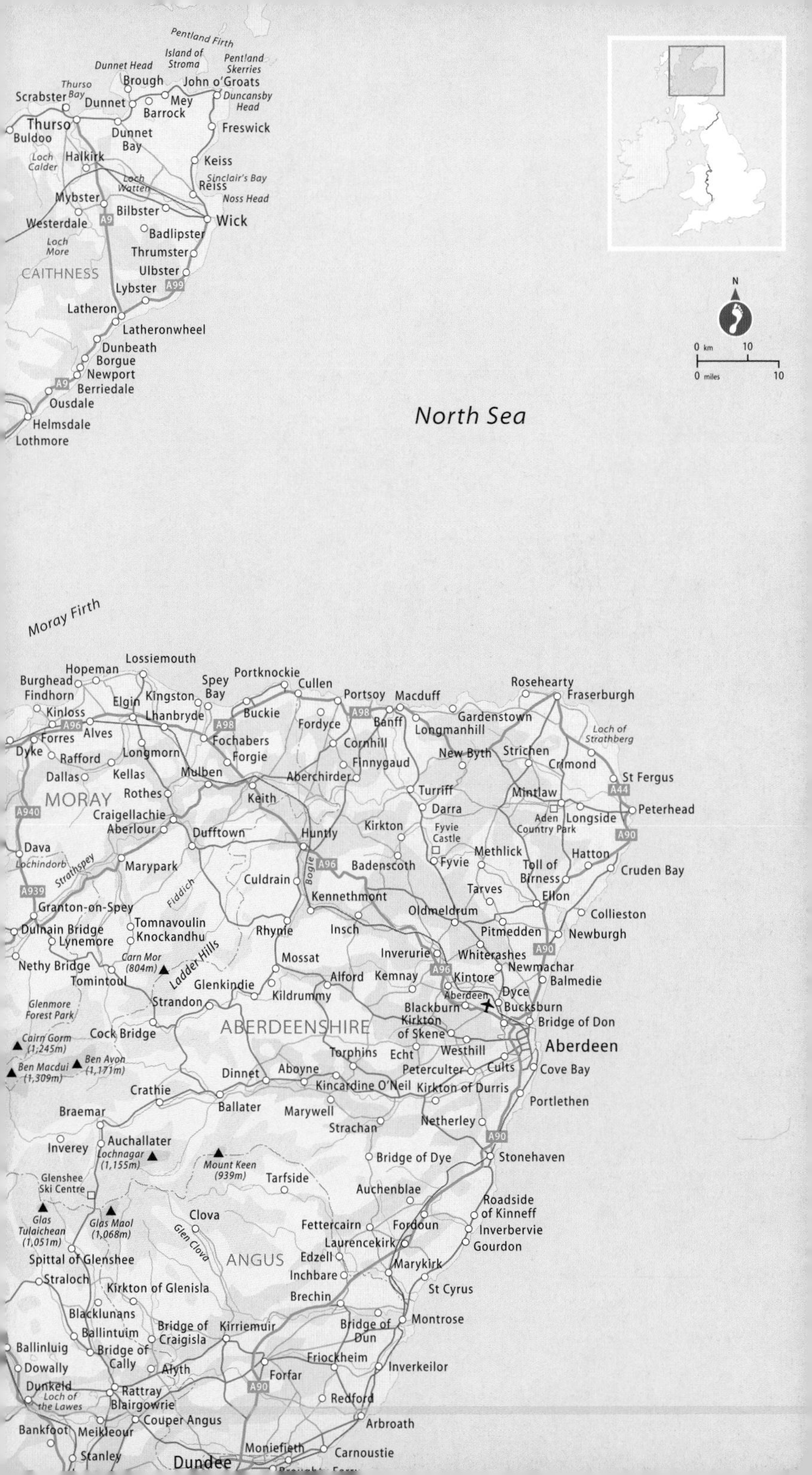

Pentland Firth
Island of Stroma
Pentland Skerries
Dunnet Head
Brough
John o'Groats
Thurso Bay
Scrabster
Dunnet
Mey
Barrock
Duncansby Head
Thurso
Buldoo
Dunnet Bay
Freswick
Loch Calder
Halkirk
Keiss
Loch Watten
Sinclair's Bay
Reiss
Noss Head
Mybster
Bilbster
Wick
Westerdale
A9
Badlipster
Loch More
Thrumster
CAITHNESS
Ulbster
Lybster
A99
Latheron
Latheronwheel
Dunbeath
Borgue
Newport
A9
Berriedale
Ousdale
Helmsdale
Lothmore
N
0 km 10
0 miles 10
North Sea
Moray Firth
Lossiemouth
Hopeman
Portknockie
Burghead
Spey Bay
Cullen
Findhorn
Kingston
Portsoy
Macduff
Rosehearty
Fraserburgh
Elgin
Kinloss
Lhanbryde
Buckie
A98
Banff
Gardenstown
A96
Alves
A98
Fordyce
Longmanhill
Loch of Strathberg
Forres
Fochabers
Cornhill
Dyke
Rafford
Longmorn
Forgie
Finnygaud
New Byth
Strichen
Crimond
Dallas
Kellas
Mulben
Aberchirder
St Fergus
MORAY
Rothes
Keith
Turriff
Mintlaw
A44
A940
Craigellachie
Darra
Aden Country Park
Longside
Peterhead
Aberlour
Dufftown
Huntly
Kirkton
Fyvie Castle
A90
Dava
Lochindorb
Strathspey
Marypark
Bogie
A96
Badenscoth
Fyvie
Methlick
Hatton
Toll of Birness
Cruden Bay
Fiddich
Culdrain
Tarves
A939
Kennethmont
Ellon
Granton-on-Spey
Oldmeldrum
Collieston
Dulnain Bridge
Tomnavoulin
Rhynie
Insch
Pitmedden
Newburgh
Lynemore
Knockandhu
Ladder Hills
A90
Inverurie
Whiterashes
Nethy Bridge
Carn Mor (804m)
Mossat
A96
Newmachar
Tomintoul
Alford
Kemnay
Kintore
Balmedie
Glenkindie
Kildrummy
Aberdeen
Dyce
Glenmore Forest Park
Strandon
Blackburn
Bucksburn
ABERDEENSHIRE
Kirkton of Skene
Bridge of Don
Cairn Gorm (1,245m)
Cock Bridge
Aberdeen
Ben Avon (1,171m)
Torphins
Echt
Westhill
Ben Macdui (1,309m)
Dinnet
Aboyne
Peterculter
Cults
Cove Bay
Kincardine O'Neil
Kirkton of Durris
Crathie
Ballater
Portlethen
Braemar
Marywell
Strachan
Netherley
A90
Auchallater
Inverey
Lochnagar (1,155m)
Mount Keen (939m)
Bridge of Dye
Stonehaven
Glenshee Ski Centre
Tarfside
Auchenblae
Roadside of Kinneff
Glas Tulaichean (1,051m)
Glas Maol (1,068m)
Clova
Glen Clova
Fettercairn
Fordoun
Inverbervie
Laurencekirk
Gourdon
Spittal of Glenshee
ANGUS
Edzell
Inchbare
Marykirk
Straloch
Kirkton of Glenisla
St Cyrus
Brechin
Blacklunans
Montrose
Ballintuim
Bridge of Craigisla
Kirriemuir
Bridge of Dun
Ballinluig
Bridge of Cally
Friockheim
Dowally
Alyth
Forfar
Inverkeilor
Dunkeld
Rattray
A90
Loch of the Lawes
Blairgowrie
Redford
Coupar Angus
Arbroath
Bankfoot
Meikleour
Stanley
Monifieth
Carnoustie
Dundee

Map 7

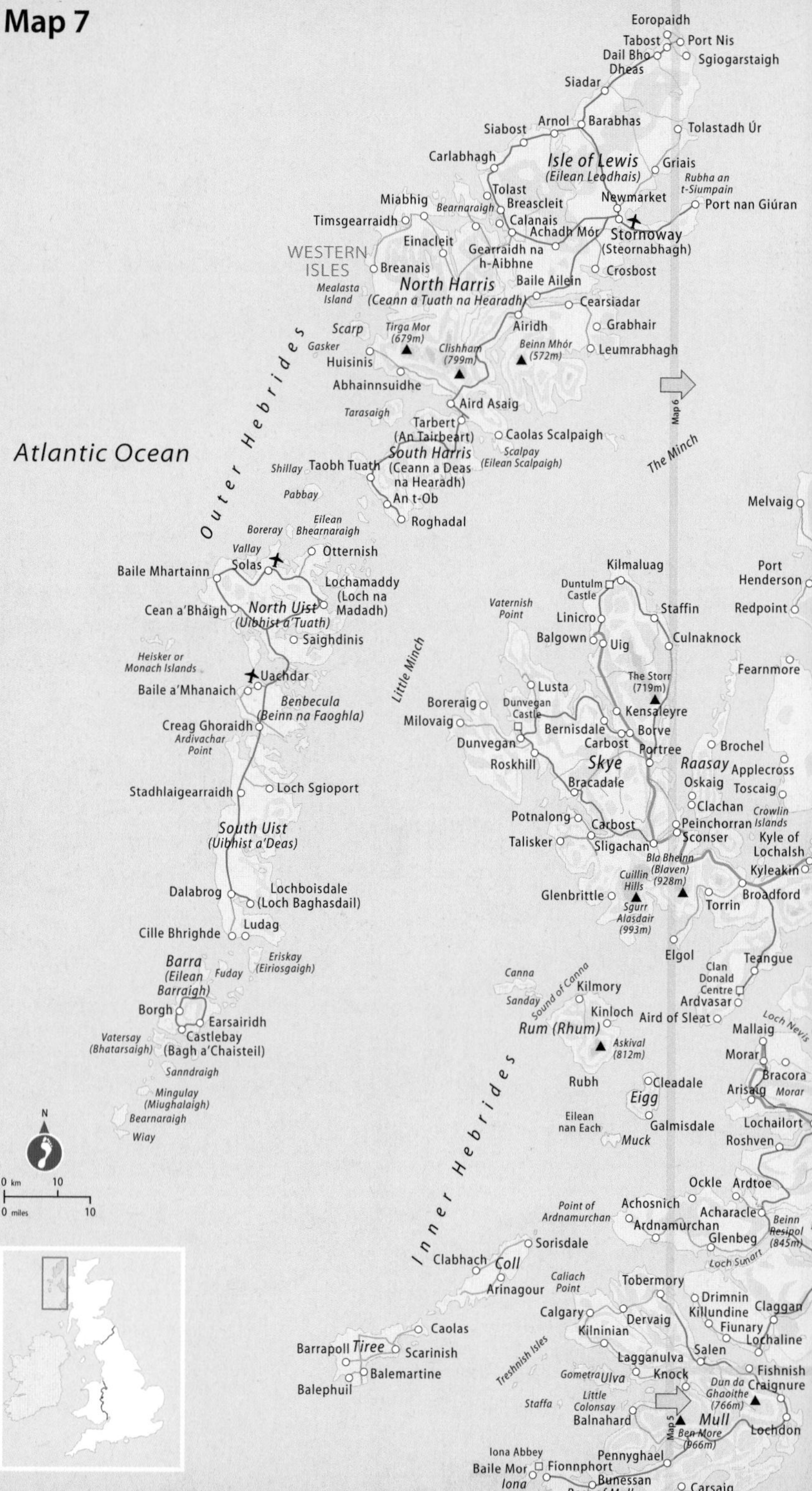

Eoropaidh
Tabost
Port Nis
Dail Bho Dheas
Sgiogarstaigh
Siadar
Arnol
Barabhas
Siabost
Tolastadh Úr
Carlabhagh
Isle of Lewis
(Eilean Leodhais)
Griais
Rubha an t-Siumpain
Tolast
Newmarket
Miabhig
Bearnaraigh
Breascleit
Port nan Giúran
Timsgearraidh
Calanais
Achadh Mór
Stornoway
(Steornabhagh)
Einacleit
Gearraidh na h-Aibhne
WESTERN ISLES
Breanais
Crosbost
Mealasta Island
North Harris
(Ceann a Tuath na Hearadh)
Baile Ailein
Cearsiadar
Scarp
Tirga Mor (679m)
Airidh
Grabhair
Gasker
Clishham (799m)
Beinn Mhór (572m)
Leumrabhagh
Huisinis
Abhainnsuidhe
Map 6
Aird Asaig
Tarasaigh
Tarbert
(An Tairbeart)
Caolas Scalpaigh
Atlantic Ocean
Outer Hebrides
South Harris
(Ceann a Deas na Hearadh)
Scalpay
(Eilean Scalpaigh)
The Minch
Shillay
Taobh Tuath
Pabbay
An t-Ob
Melvaig
Roghadal
Eilean Bhearnaraigh
Boreray
Vallay
Otternish
Solas
Kilmaluag
Port Henderson
Baile Mhartainn
Lochamaddy
(Loch na Madadh)
Duntulm Castle
North Uist
(Uibhist a'Tuath)
Cean a'Bháigh
Vaternish Point
Staffin
Redpoint
Linicro
Saighdinis
Balgown
Uig
Culnaknock
Heisker or Monach Islands
Little Minch
Fearnmore
Uachdar
The Storr (719m)
Lusta
Baile a'Mhanaich
Benbecula
(Beinn na Faoghla)
Boreraig
Dunvegan Castle
Kensaleyre
Milovaig
Bernisdale
Borve
Creag Ghoraidh
Ardivachar Point
Dunvegan
Carbost
Portree
Brochel
Roskhill
Skye
Raasay
Applecross
Stadhlaigearraidh
Loch Sgioport
Bracadale
Oskaig
Toscaig
Clachan
Potnalong
Carbost
Peinchorran
Crowlin Islands
South Uist
(Uibhist a'Deas)
Talisker
Sligachan
Sconser
Kyle of Lochalsh
Bla Bheinn
(Blaven)
(928m)
Cuillin Hills
Kyleakin
Dalabrog
Lochboisdale
(Loch Baghasdail)
Glenbrittle
Sgurr Alasdair (993m)
Torrin
Broadford
Ludag
Cille Bhrighde
Elgol
Eriskay
(Eiriosgaigh)
Teangue
Barra
(Eilean Barraigh)
Fuday
Canna
Clan Donald Centre
Sound of Canna
Kilmory
Sanday
Ardvasar
Borgh
Kinloch
Aird of Sleat
Earsairidh
Rum (Rhum)
Loch Nevis
Vatersay
(Bhatarsaigh)
Castlebay
(Bagh a'Chaisteil)
Mallaig
Askival (812m)
Morar
Sanndraigh
Bracora
Rubh
Cleadale
Mingulay
(Miughalaigh)
Arisaig
Morar
Bearnaraigh
Eigg
Wiay
Eilean nan Each
Galmisdale
Lochailort
Muck
Roshven
N
Inner Hebrides
0 km 10
0 miles 10
Ockle
Ardtoe
Point of Ardnamurchan
Achosnich
Acharacle
Ardnamurchan
Beinn Resipol (845m)
Glenbeg
Sorisdale
Loch Sunart
Clabhach
Coll
Caliach Point
Tobermory
Arinagour
Drimnin
Killundine
Claggan
Calgary
Dervaig
Fiunary
Kilninian
Lochaline
Caolas
Treshnish Isles
Salen
Barrapoll
Tiree
Scarinish
Lagganulva
Fishnish
Balemartine
Gometra
Ulva
Knock
Dun da Ghaoithe (766m)
Craignure
Balephuil
Staffa
Little Colonsay
Balnahard
Mull
Map 5
Ben More (966m)
Lochdon
Iona Abbey
Pennyghael
Baile Mor
Fionnphort
Bunessan
Iona
Ross of Mull
Carsaig